FIRST CORINTHIANS

VOLUME 32

THE ANCHOR YALE BIBLE is a fresh approach to the world's greatest classic. Its object is to make the Bible accessible to the modern reader; its method is to arrive at the meaning of biblical literature through exact translation and extended exposition, and to reconstruct the ancient setting of the biblical story, as well as the circumstances of its transcription and the characteristics of its transcribers.

THE ANCHOR YALE BIBLE is a project of international and interfaith scope: Protestant, Catholic, and Jewish scholars from many countries contribute individual volumes. The project is not sponsored by any ecclesiastical organization and is not intended to reflect any particular theological doctrine. Prepared under our joint supervision, THE ANCHOR YALE BIBLE is an effort to make available all the significant historical and linguistic knowledge which bears on the interpretation of the biblical record.

THE ANCHOR YALE BIBLE is aimed at the general reader with no special formal training in biblical studies; yet it is written with the most exacting standards of scholarship, reflecting the highest technical accomplishment.

This project marks the beginning of a new era of cooperation among scholars in biblical research, thus forming a common body of knowledge to be shared by all.

William Foxwell Albright
David Noel Freedman
GENERAL EDITORS

THE ANCHOR YALE BIBLE

FIRST CORINTHIANS

◆

A New Translation with Introduction and Commentary

JOSEPH A. FITZMYER, S.J.

THE ANCHOR YALE BIBLE

Yale University Press New Haven and London

Printed in the United States of America.

Library of Congress Control Number: 2007939224
ISBN 978-0-300-14044-6 (cloth : alk. paper)

A catalogue record for this book is available from the British Library.

The paper in this book meets the guidelines for permanence and
durability of the Committee on Production Guidelines for Book
Longevity of the Council on Library Resources.

10 9 8 7 6 5 4 3 2 1

*To My Confrères of the Jesuit Community
at Georgetown University*

CONTENTS

◆

COMMENTARY AND NOTES

Contents

PREFACE

◆

The First Letter to the Corinthians is not Paul's most important writing. That description belongs to his letter to the Romans, on which I have already commented in this series of the Anchor Bible. First Corinthians, however, is the letter in the Pauline corpus that reveals the Apostle at his best, for it shows him coping realistically with problems that have arisen in the Christian community that he founded in that important city in the eastern Mediterranean world of his time. It is only part of his correspondence with Corinthian Christians, because he also wrote Second Corinthians, which likewise reveals aspects of his ministry. That letter, however, is much more personal, and it may even be a composite of missives that he sent to the church of Corinth. First Corinthians is less personal and more topically oriented, as Paul comments on scandals that have been reported to him in that Christian community, answers queries sent to him by Corinthian Christians or reacts to problems that he has heard about in moral and liturgical matters, and instructs them about the resurrection of the dead and its relation to the Christian kerygma and gospel.

The multiple topics that Paul addresses in this letter that he sends to Corinthian Christians have produced in recent decades a cascade of commentaries, monographs, and articles dealing with all their details. The excellent commentary on First Corinthians by the German New Testament scholar, Wolfgang Schrage, is a *tour de force*, but its four stout volumes, published in the course of a decade (1991–2001), are an accomplishment that few scholars will ever emulate. By contrast, the aim of this modest commentary on First Corinthians is to discuss the topics with which Paul deals in a less comprehensive way in imitation of many other recent commentators of varying language and background.

My intention has been to write a commentary of classic proportions like that on the Letter to the Romans for the modern reader of the twenty-first century. It is hoped that it will explain Paul's thoughts in a not-too-technical form for general readers. I have at times introduced into the discussion Greek words in transcription, where necessary, in order to clarify the issue at hand, but an English translation is always provided, so that the reader may understand how I understand the Greek terms. When the translation given in the lemma of the Notes may be a bit free, I have invariably included a literal rendition of Paul's Greek words so that the reader will know just what is at issue, for neither an overly literal translation nor one based on dynamic equivalence passes muster.

Earlier commentators on First Corinthians are mentioned by their last names, but I have simplified the mode of giving the titles of their commentaries: *1 Cor*, with a page number (following the commentator's name). That refers to any commentary in any modern language no matter how it is entitled. The exact title of such commentaries is given in the GENERAL BIBLIOGRAPHY. In that bibliography, commentators are broken down into groups according to time: patristic period (Greek and Latin writers, listed chronologically); medieval period (Greek and Latin writers, listed chronologically); fifteenth — to eighteenth-century commentators (listed chronologically according to the year of their death); nineteenth — to twenty-first-century commentators (ordered alphabetically). In the specific bibliographies at the end of pericopes authors are listed in alphabetical order. When a new or unfamiliar name appears in COMMENTS or NOTES, the reader should consult first the specific bibliography at the end of the pericope; if the information is not found there, then the GENERAL BIBLIOGRAPHY should be consulted, where not only commentaries are listed, but also monographs on First Corinthians as well as some periodical articles on general topics treated in more than one pericope. The index of modern authors offers guidance to the needed information. References to OT books cite the chapter and verse numbers according to the Hebrew or Aramaic text of the MT, not that of some English Bibles. This is to be noted especially in the case of the Psalter, where psalms are always referred to according to the numbering of the Hebrew text, even when the discussion may involve the Greek translation of the LXX. In case of doubt, one can usually consult the NAB, which uses the Hebrew-text numbering.

In the INTRODUCTION to the commentary the reader will find discussion of the usual questions about the letter's addressees, the authorship of the letter, its occasion and purpose, unity and integrity, structure and outline, text and language. In addition, there is a synthetic sketch of Paul's teaching in this letter, along with a bibliography. During the course of the commentary, reference will be made at times to this synthesis in order to avoid repetitious treatment of topics that appear at different places in the letter.

As in my other commentaries in this series, I present a fresh translation of the Greek text of each pericope, followed by a COMMENT on it as a whole, and then by NOTES on lemmata derived from its individual verses. COMMENT is the term used throughout for the introductory discussion of the pericope, and the NOTES are reserved for the detailed treatment of problematic words and phrases in the lemma. At times the discussion of problems in the NOTES may become technical, and the general reader will have to bear with this aspect of the discussion or learn to pass over them. The overall thrust of the letter and its parts will be treated in the COMMENTS. The division of the Pauline text into pericopes follows the outline of the letter given in Section V of the INTRODUCTION. References, sometimes in parentheses, without the mention of a biblical book's title mean a chapter and verse in First Corinthians; "1 Cor" will be added only to avoid ambiguity in a particular context. Translations of biblical passages other than First Corinthians are usually my own, except on occasion when another standard version is needed in the discussion.

Finally, I must express my thanks to many persons who have aided me in recent years while I have been working on this commentary. In particular, the graduate students at the Biblical Institute in Rome and at the Catholic University of America, with whom I discussed many of the problem of this Pauline text; J. Leon Hooper, S.J., the director of the Woodstock Theological Center Library, housed at Georgetown University, and his staff; Henry Bertels, S.J., who was then the librarian at Pontificio Istituto Biblico, Rome—all of whom helped with many bibliographical items. Finally, my gratitude is owed to David Noel Freedman, the editor of the Anchor Bible series, for his suggestive criticism and helpful advice; to Andrew Corbin, the editor at Doubleday, and his staff for their cooperation in bringing the manuscript to book form; and to Leslie Phillips for her careful copy-editing.

Joseph A. Fitzmyer, S.J., Professor Emeritus, Biblical Studies
The Catholic University of America
Resident at the Jesuit Community, Georgetown University
Washington, DC 20057-1200
(fitzmyja@georgetown.edu)

ABBREVIATIONS

◆

PRINCIPAL ABBREVIATIONS

AB	Anchor Bible
ABD	Freedman, D. N. (ed.), *The Anchor Bible Dictionary* (6 vols.; New York: Doubleday, 1992)
ABQ	*American Baptist Quarterly*
ABR	*Australian Biblical Review*
ABRL	Anchor Bible Reference Library
Acts	J. A. Fitzmyer, *The Acts of the Apostles* (AB 31; New York: Doubleday, 1998)
AER	*American Ecclesiastical Review*
AfrTJ	*African Theological Journal*
AGJU	Arbeiten zur Geschichte des antiken Judentums und des Urchristentums
AGSU	Arbeiten zur Geschichte des Spätjudentums und Urchristentums
AI	R. de Vaux, *Ancient Israel: Its Life and Institutions* (New York: McGraw-Hill, 1961)
AION	*Annali dell'Istituto Orientale di Napoli*
AJA	*American Journal of Archaeology*
AJT	*Asia Journal of Theology*
AmBenR	*American Benedictine Review*
AnBib	Analecta biblica
AnGreg	Analecta gregoriana
AnnStorEseg	*Annali della storia esegetica*
ANRW	H. Temporini and W. Haase (eds.), *Aufstieg und Niedergang der römischen Welt*, (Berlin: de Gruyter, 1972–)
ANTF	Arbeiten zur neutestamentlichen Textforschung
Anton	*Antonianum*
AOT	H. F. D. Sparks (ed.), *The Apocryphal Old Testament* (Oxford: Clarendon, 1984)
AP	A. Cowley, *Aramaic Papyri of the Fifth Century B.C.* (Oxford: Clarendon, 1923)
AsSeign	*Assemblées du Seigneur*
AsTJ	*Asbury Theological Journal*
ATANT	Abhandlungen zur Theologie des Alten und Neuen Testaments
ATJ	*Ashland Theological Journal*
ATR	*Anglican Theological Review*

ATRSup	Supplement to ATR
Aug	*Augustinianum*
AUSS	*Andrews University Seminary Studies*
BA	*Biblical Archaeologist*
BAC	Biblioteca de autores cristianos
BARev	*Biblical Archaeology Review*
BB	Bonner Bibel
BBR	*Bulletin for Biblical Research*
BCH	*Bulletin de correspondance hellénique*
BDAG	W. Bauer, F. W. Danker, W. F. Arndt, and F. W. Gingrich, *A Greek-English Lexicon of the New Testament and Other Early Christian Literature* (3d ed.; Chicago: University of Chicago Press, 2000)
BDB	F. Brown, S. R. Driver, and C. A. Briggs, *Hebrew and English Lexicon* (rev. ed.; Peabody, MA: Hendrickson, 1979)
BDF	F. Blass and A. Debrunner, *A Greek Grammar of the New Testament and Other Early Christian Literature* (tr. R. W. Funk; Chicago: University of Chicago, 1961)
BDR	F. Blass and A. Debrunner, *Grammatik des neutestamentlichen Griechisch* (14th ed.; rev. F. Rehkopf; Göttingen: Vandenhoeck & Ruprecht, 1976)
BeO	*Bibbia e Oriente*
BETL	Bibliotheca ephemeridum theologicarum lovaniensium
BFCT	Beiträge zur Förderung christlicher Theologie
BGBE	Beiträge zur Geschichte der biblischen Exegese
BGNTE	Beiträge zur Geschichte der neutestamentlichen Exegese
BHT	Beiträge zur historischen Theologie
Bib	*Biblica*
BiBh	*Bible Bhashyam*
BibInt	*Biblical Interpretation*
BibS(F)	Biblische Studien (Freiburg)
Bijdr	*Bijdragen*
BJRL	*Bulletin of the John Rylands (University) Library (of Manchester)*
BK	*Bibel und Kirche*
BLE	*Bulletin de Littérature Ecclésiastique*
BLeb	*Bibel und Leben*
BLit	*Bibel und Liturgie*
BLT	*Brethren Life and Thought*
BMAP	E. G. Kraeling, *The Brooklyn Museum Aramaic Papyri* (New Haven: Yale University Press, 1953)
BN	*Biblische Notizen*
BR	*Biblical Research*
BRev	*Bible Review*
BSac	*Bibliotheca sacra*
BT	*The Bible Translator*
BTB	*Biblical Theology Bulletin*
BTZ	*Berliner theologische Zeitschrift*
BU	Biblische Untersuchungen
BurH	*Buried History*
BVC	*Bible et vie chrétienne*

BWANT	Beiträge zur Wissenschaft vom Alten und Neuen Testament
BZ	*Biblische Zeitschrift*
BzHT	Beiträge zur historischen Theologie
BZNW	Beihefte zur ZNW
CB	*Cultura bíblica*
CBET	Contributions to Biblical Exegesis and Theology
CBQ	*Catholic Biblical Quarterly*
CCLat	Corpus Christianorum, series latina
CdT	*Cuadernos de Teología*
CIG	*Corpus inscriptionum graecarum*
CIL	*Corpus inscriptionum latinarum*
CJ	*Classical Journal*
CJT	*Canadian Journal of Theology*
CNT	Commentaire du Nouveau Testament
ColT	*Collectanea theologica*
ConcJ	*Concordia Journal*
ConNeot	*Coniectanea neotestamentica*
CP	*Classical Philology*
CQ	*Classical Quarterly*
CQR	*Church Quarterly Review*
CR	*Clergy Review*
CRINT	Compendia rerum iudaicarum ad Novum Testamentum
CS	*Chicago Studies*
CSEL	Corpus scriptorum ecclesiasticorum latinorum
CSR	*Christian Scholars Review*
CTJ	*Calvin Theological Journal*
CTM	*Concordia Theological Monthly*
CTQ	*Concordia Theological Quarterly*
CTR	*Criswell Theological Review*
CurTM	*Currents in Theology and Mission*
CV	*Communio viatorum*
DACL	*Dictionnaire d'archéologie chrétienne et de liturgie*
DBM	*Deltion biblikon meleton*
DBSup	*Dictionnaire de la Bible, Supplément*
DH	H. Denzinger and P. Hünermann, *Enchiridion symbolorum definitionum et declarationum de rebus fidei et morum* (37th ed.; Freiburg im B.: Herder, 1991)
DJD	Discoveries in the Judaean Desert
DRev	*Downside Review*
EBib	Études bibliques
ED	*Euntes docete*
EDNT	H. Balz and G. Schneider (eds.), *Exegetical Dictionary of the New Testament* (3 vols.; Grand Rapids: Eerdmans, 1990–93)
ÉgT	*Église et théologie*
EKKNT	Evangelisch-katholischer Kommentar zum Neuen Testament
EpRev	*Epworth Review*
ErbA	*Erbe und Auftrag*
ErIsr	Eretz Israel
ERT	*Evangelical Review of Theology*

ESBNT	J. A. Fitzmyer, *Essays on the Semitic Background of the New Testament* (London: Chapman, 1971; repr. Missoula: Scholars, 1974; repr. as part of *SBNT*)
EstBíb	*Estudios bíblicos*
EstEcl	*Estudios eclesiásticos*
EstTrin	*Estudios trinitarios*
ETL	*Ephemerides theologicae lovanienses*
ÉTR	*Études théologiques et religieuses*
EV	*Esprit et vie*
EvJ	*Evangelical Journal*
EvQ	*Evangelical Quarterly*
EvT	*Evangelische Theologie*
Expos	*Expositor*
ExpTim	*Expository Times*
FilolNT	*Filología neotestamentaria*
FM	*Faith & Mission*
FQ	*Friends Quarterly*
FRLANT	Forschungen zur Religion und Literatur des Alten und Neuen Testaments
FzB	Forschungen zur Bibel
GAGNT	M. Zerwick, *A Grammatical Analysis of the Greek New Testament* (2 vols.; Rome: Biblical Institute, 1974, 1979)
GCS	Die griechischen christlichen Schriftsteller der ersten (drei) Jahrhunderte
GGA	*Göttingische gelehrte Anzeigen*
GGBB	D. B. Wallace, *Greek Grammar beyond the Basics: An Exegetical Syntax of the New Testament* (Grand Rapids, MI: Zondervan, 1996)
GL	*Geist und Leben*
GNS	Good News Studies
Goodspeed	E. J. Goodspeed, *The New Testament: An American Translation* (Chicago: University of Chicago Press, 1951)
GOTR	*Greek Orthodox Theological Review*
Greg	*Gregorianum*
GTA	Göttinger theologische Arbeiten
GTJ	*Grace Theological Journal*
GTS	Gregorian Theological Series (Tesi Gregoriana, serie teologica)
GTT	*Gereformeerd theologisch tijdschrift*
HBT	*Horizons in Biblical Theology*
HeyJ	*Heythrop Journal*
HJPAJC	E. Schürer, *The History of the Jewish People in the Age of Jesus Christ (175 B.C.–A.D. 135)* (3 vols.; rev. G. Vermes et al.; Edinburgh: Clark, 1973–87)
HNT	Handbuch zum Neuen Testament
HNTC	Harper's New Testament Commentaries
HTR	*Harvard Theological Review*
HUCA	*Hebrew Union College Annual*
HUT	Hermeneutische Untersuchungen zur Theologie
IB	G. A. Buttrick (ed.), *Interpreter's Bible* (12 vols.; Nashville, TN: Abingdon, 1951–57)

IBNTG	C. F. D. Moule, *An Idiom Book of New Testament Greek* (Cambridge: Cambridge University Press, 1953)
IBS	*Irish Biblical Studies*
ICC	International Critical Commentary
IDB	G. A. Buttrick (ed.), *The Interpreter's Dictionary of the Bible* (4 vols.; Nashville: Abingdon, 1962)
Int	*Interpretation*
ITM	H. L. Strack and G. Stemberger, *Introduction to the Talmud and Midrash* (Edinburgh: Clark, 1991)
ITQ	*Irish Theological Quarterly*
JAAR(Sup)	*Journal of the American Academy of Religion* (and Supplement to)
JAC	*Jahrbuch für Antike und Christentum*
JATS	*Journal of the Adventist Theological Society*
JBC	R. E. Brown, et al. (eds.), *The Jerome Biblical Commentary* (Englewood Cliffs, NJ: Prentice-Hall, 1968)
JBL	*Journal of Biblical Literature*
JBR	*Journal of Bible and Religion*
JES	*Journal of Ecumenical Studies*
JETS	*Journal of the Evangelical Theological Society*
JHC	*Journal of Higher Criticism*
JITC	*Journal of the Interdenominational Theological Center*
JJS	*Journal of Jewish Studies*
JLA	*Jewish Law Annual*
JOTT	*Journal of Translation and Textlinguistics*
JPT	*Journal of Pentecostal Theology*
JQR	*Jewish Quarterly Review*
JR	*Journal of Religion*
JRA	*Journal of Roman Archaeology*
JRASup	Supplement to *JRA*
JRE	*Journal of Religious Ethics*
JSNT	*Journal for the Study of the New Testament*
JSNTSup	Supplement to *JSNT*
JSSR	*Journal for the Scientific Study of Religion*
JTS	*Journal of Theological Studies*
JTSA	*Journal of Theology for Southern Africa*
KD	*Kerygma und Dogma*
KlT	Kleine Texte
LAB	Pseudo-Philo, *Liber antiquitatum biblicarum*
LAE	A. Deissmann, *Light from the Ancient East* (2d ed.; London: Hodder & Stoughton, 1927)
LB	*Linguistica biblica*
LCL	Loeb Classical Library
LD	Lectio divina
LJ	*Liturgisches Jahrbuch*
LS	*Louvain Studies*
LSJ	H. G. Liddell and R. Scott, *A Greek-English Lexicon* (ed. H. S. Jones with the assistance of R. McKenzie; 2 vols.; Oxford: Clarendon, 1925–40; repr. in one vol., 1966; with a Revised Supplement, 1996)
LTJ	*Lutheran Theological Journal*

LTQ	*Lutheran Theological Quarterly*
Luke	J. A. Fitzmyer, *The Gospel according to Luke* (AB 28, 28A; Garden City, NY: Doubleday, 1981, 1985)
LumVie	*Lumière et vie*
LumVit	*Lumen vitae*
MeyerK	Meyer Kommentar (= Kritisch-exegetischer Kommentar über das Neue Testament)
MilS	*Milltown Studies*
MM	J. H. Moulton and G. Milligan, *The Vocabulary of the Greek Testament* (London: Hodder & Stoughton, 1930)
MNTC	Moffatt New Testament Commentary
MTS	Marburger theologische Studien
MTZ	*Münchener theologische Zeitschrift*
NAWG	*Nachrichten (von) der Akademie der Wissenschaften in Göttingen*
NBf	*New Blackfriars*
NCE	B. L. Marthaler, *New Catholic Encyclopedia* (15 vols.; 2d ed.; Detroit: Gale-Thomson, 2003)
NedTT	*Nederlands theologisch tijdschrift*
NETR	*Near East School of Theology Theological Review*
New Docs	G. H. R. Horsley, et al. (eds.), *New Documents Illustrating Early Christianity* (9 vols.; North Ryde, N.S.W.: Ancient History Documentary Research Center, Macquarrie University; Grand Rapids: Eerdmans, 1981–2002)
NHL	J. M. Robinson (ed.), *Nag Hammadi Library in English* (4th ed.; Leiden: Brill, 1996)
NICNT	New International Commentary on the New Testament
NIGTC	New International Greek Testament Commentary
NJBC	R. E. Brown, et al. (eds.), *The New Jerome Biblical Commentary* (Englewood Cliffs, NJ: Prentice-Hall, 1990)
NKZ	*Neue kirchliche Zeitschrift*
Notes	*Notes on Translation*
NovT	*Novum Testamentum*
NovTSup	Supplement to *NovT*
NPNF	Nicene and Post-Nicene Fathers
NRT	*La nouvelle revue théologique*
NTAbh	Neutestamentliche Abhandlungen
NTApocr	W. Schneemelcher, *New Testament Apocrypha* (2 vols.; rev. ed.; Louisville: Westminster/John Knox, 1991–92)
NTD	Das Neue Testament deutsch
NTOA	Novum Testamentum et orbis antiquus
NTR	*New Theology Review*
NTS	*New Testament Studies*
NTTS	New Testament Tools and Studies
OCD	N. G. L. Hammond and H. H. Scullard (eds.), *The Oxford Classical Dictionary* (2d ed.; Oxford: Clarendon, 1970)
ODCC	F. L. Cross and E. A. Livingstone (eds.), *The Oxford Dictionary of the Christian Church* (New York: Oxford University Press, 1997)
OTP	J. H. Charlesworth (ed.), *The Old Testament Pseudepigrapha* (2 vols.; Garden City, NY: Doubleday, 1983–85)

PAHT	J. A. Fitzmyer, *Paul and His Theology: A Brief Sketch* (2d ed.; Englewood Cliffs, NJ: Prentice-Hall, 1989)
P&P	*Priests & People*
PG	Migne, J. (ed.), Patrologia graeca
Philemon	J. A. Fitzmyer, *The Letter to Philemon* (AB 34C; New York: Doubleday, 2000)
PIBA	*Proceedings of the Irish Biblical Association*
PKGK	K. Staab, *Pauluskommentare aus der griechischen Kirche: Aus Katenenhandschriften gesammelt und herausgegeben* (NTAbh 15; Münster in W.: Aschendorff, 1933).
PL	Migne, J. (ed.), Patrologia latina
PRSt	*Perspectives in Religious Studies*
PSB	*Princeton Seminary Bulletin*
PTMS	Pittsburgh Theological Monograph Series
PW	*Paulys Real-Encyclopädie der classischen Altertumswissenschaft*, ed. G. Wissowa (Stuttgart: Metzler; Munich: Druckenmüller, 1893–1978)
PWSup	Supplement to PW
QD	Quaestiones disputatae
QR	*Quarterly Review*
RAC	T. Klausner (ed.), *Reallexikon für Antike und Christentum* (Stuttgart: Hiersmann, 1950–)
R&T	*Religion & Theology*
RB	*Revue biblique*
RBR	*Ricerche bibliche e religiose*
RCB	*Revista de cultura bíblica*
RechBib	Recherches bibliques
RefR	*Reformed Review*
REG	*Revue des études grecques*
ResQ	*Restoration Quarterly*
RevBén	*Revue bénédictine*
RevExp	*Review and Expositor*
RevistB	*Revista Bíblica*
RevQ	*Revue de Qumran*
RevScRel	*Revue des sciences religieuses*
RGG	K. Galling (ed.), *Die Religion in Geschichte und Gegenwart* (3d ed.; Tübingen: Mohr [Siebeck], 1957–65)
RHE	*Revue d'histoire ecclésiastique*
RHPR	*Revue d'histoire et de philosophie religieuses*
RivB	*Rivista biblica*
RNT	Regensburger Neues Testament
Romans	J. A. Fitzmyer, *Romans* (AB 33; New York: Doubleday, 1993)
RRef	*Revue reformée*
RSPT	*Revue des scienes philosophiques et théologiques*
RSR	*Recherches de science religieuse*
RTL	*Revue théologique de Louvain*
RTP	*Revue de théologie et de philosophie*
RTR	*Reformed Theological Review*
Salm	*Salmanticensis*
SANT	Studien zum Alten und Neuen Testament

SBB	Stuttgarter biblische Beiträge
SBEC	Studies in Bible and Early Christianity
SBFLA	*Studii biblici franciscani liber annuus*
SBL	Society of Biblical Literature
SBLDS	Dissertation Series of the SBL
SBLMS	SBL Monograph Series
SBLSCS	Septuagint and Cognate Studies of the SBL
SBLSP	*Seminar Papers of the SBL*
SBM	Stuttgarter biblische Monographien
SBNT	J. A. Fitzmyer, *The Semitic Background of the New Testament: Combined Edition of ESBNT and WA* (Grand Rapids: Eerdmans; Livonia, MI: Dove Booksellers, 1997)
SBS	Stuttgarter biblische Studien
SBT	Studies in Biblical Theology
SC	Sources chrétiennes
ScCatt	*Scuola cattolica*
SCE	*Studies in Christian Ethics*
ScEc	*Sciences ecclésiastiques*
ScEs	*Science et esprit*
ScrB	*Scripture Bulletin*
ScrC	*Scripture in Church*
SE I, II, IV, VI	*Studia evangelica I, II, IV, VI* (= TU 73, 87, 102, 112)
SEA	*Svensk Exegetisk Årsbok*
SJLA	Studies in Judaism in Late Antiquity
SJOT	*Scandinavian Journal of the Old Testament*
SJT	*Scottish Journal of Theology*
SNT	Studien zum Neuen Testament
SNTSMS	Studiorum Novi Testamenti Societas, Monograph Series
SNTU	*Studien zum Neuen Testament und seiner Umwelt*
SPCIC	*Studiorum paulinorum congressus internationalis catholicus 1961* (AnBib 17–18)
SR	*Studies in Religion/Sciences Religieuses*
ST	*Studia theologica*
StC	*Studia catholica*
STDJ	Studies on the Texts of the Desert of Judah
StPat	*Studia patavina*
Str-B	H. Strack and P. Billerbeck, *Kommentar zum Neuen Testament aus Talmud und Midrasch* (6 vols.; Munich: Beck, 1926–63)
StudBibLit	*Studies in Biblical Literature*
StZ	*Stimmen der Zeit*
SUNT	Studien zur Umwelt des Neuen Testament
SVTP	Studia in Veteris Testamenti Pseudepigrapha
SwJT	*Southwestern Journal of Theology*
TAG	J. A. Fitzmyer, *To Advance the Gospel: New Testament Studies* (2d ed.; Grand Rapids: Eerdmans; Livonia, MI: Dove Booksellers, 1998)
TANZ	Texte und Arbeiten zum neutestamentlichen Zeitalter
TBei	*Theologische Beiträge*
TBl	*Theologische Blätter*
TBT	*The Bible Today*

TCGNT	B. M. Metzger, *A Textual Commentary on the Greek New Testament* (2d ed.; Stuttgart: Deutsche Bibelgesellschaft, 1994)
TD	*Theology Digest*
TDNT	G. Kittel and G. Friedrich (eds.), *Theological Dictionary of the New Testament* (10 vols.; Grand Rapids: Eerdmans, 1964–76)
Tgeg	*Theologie der Gegenwart*
TGl	*Theologie und Glaube*
THKNT	Theologischer Handkommentar zum Neuen Testament
ThViat	*Theologia viatorum*
TLNT	C. Spicq, *Theological Lexicon of the New Testament* (3 vols.; Peabody, MA: Hendrickson, 1994)
TLZ	*Theologische Literaturzeitung*
TNT	R. Bultmann, *Theology of the New Testament* (2 vols.; London: SCM, 1952–55)
TorJT	*Toronto Journal of Theology*
TPQ	*Theologisch-praktische Quartalschrift*
TQ	*Theologische Quartalschrift*
TRev	*Theologische Revue*
TrinJ	*Trinity Journal*
TS	*Theological Studies*
TSK	*Theologische Studien und Kritiken*
TTE	*The Theological Educator*
TTod	*Theology Today*
TTZ	*Trierer theologische Zeitschrift*
TU	Texte und Untersuchungen
TV	*Teología y vida*
TvT	*Tijdschrift voor theologie*
TynBul	*Tyndale Bulletin*
TZ	*Theologische Zeitschrift*
UBS	United Bible Societies
USQR	*Union Seminary Quarterly Review*
VC	*Vigiliae christianae*
VDom	*Verbum Domini*
VR	*Vox reformata*
VS	Verbum salutis
WA	J. A. Fitzmyer, *A Wandering Aramean: Collected Aramaic Essays* (SBLMS 25; Missoula, MT: Scholars, 1979; repr. as part of *SBNT*)
WAusg	Luther, M., *Werke* (Weimar Ausgabe)
WD	*Wort und Dienst*
WLQ	*Wisconsin Lutheran Quarterly*
WMANT	Wissenschaftliche Monographien zum Alten und Neuen Testament
WTJ	*Westminster Theological Journal*
WUNT	Wissenschafliche Untersuchungen zum Neuen Testament
WW	*Word and World*
ZAH	*Zeitschrift für Althebraistik*
ZBG	Zerwick, M., *Biblical Greek* (Scripta Pontificii Instituti Biblici 114; Rome: Biblical Institute, 1963)
ZBKNT	Zürcher Bibelkommentare, Neues Testament
ZEE	*Zeitschrift für evangelische Ethik*

ZeitNT	*Zeitschrift für Neues Testament*
ZfdT	*Zeitschrift für dialektische Theologie*
ZKG	*Zeitschrift für Kirchengeschichte*
ZKT	*Zeitschrift für katholische Theologie*
ZNW	*Zeitschrift für die neutestamentliche Wissenschaft und die Kunde der älteren Kirche*
ZPE	*Zeitschrift für Papyrologie und Epigraphik*
ZTK	*Zeitschrift für Theologie und Kirche*
ZWT	*Zeitschrift für wissenschaftliche Theologie*

GRAMMATICAL ABBREVIATIONS

abs.	abstract	mid.	middle
absol.	absolute	neut.	neuter
acc.	accusative	nom.	nominative
act.	active	obj.	object(ive)
adj.	adjective, adjectival	opt.	optative
adv.	adverb(ial)	pass.	passive
aor.	aorist	perf.	perfect
bis	twice	pers.	person(al)
cog.	cognate	plur.	plural
conj.	conjunction, conjunctive	poss.	possessive
dat.	dative	prep.	preposition(al)
fem.	feminine	pres.	present
fut.	future	pron.	pronoun, pronominal
dem.	demonstrative	ptc.	participle
gen.	genitive	rel.	relative
imperf.	imperfect	sing.	singular
impv.	imperative, imperatival	subj.	subject, subjective
indef.	indefinite	subjunct.	subjunctive
indic.	indicative	subst.	substantive
infin.	infinitive	ter	thrice
masc.	masculine	voc.	vocative

DEAD SEA SCROLLS AND RELATED TEXTS

CD	Cairo (Genizah text of the) Damascus (Document)
Mur	Wadi Murabbaʿat text
p	*Pesher* (commentary)
Q	Qumran
1Q, 2Q, etc.	Numbered caves of Qumran, yielding written materials, followed by abbreviation of biblical or nonbiblical writing
1QapGen	*Genesis Apocryphon* of Qumran Cave 1
1QH[a]	First copy of *Hôdāyôt* (*Thanksgiving Psalms*) of Cave 1
1QM	*Milḥamah* (*War Scroll*) of Cave 1
1QpHab	*Pesher on Habakkuk* of Cave 1
1QS	*Serek hayyaḥad* (*Rule of the Community, Manual of Discipline*) of Cave 1
1QSa	Appendix A of 1QS (*Rule of the Congregation*)
4QD[b]	Second copy of the *War Scroll* of Cave 4
4QEnoch[b]	Second copy of *Enoch* of Cave 4

4QpIsa[a]	First copy of a *Pesher on Isaiah* of Cave 4
11QTemple[a]	First copy of *Temple Scroll* of Cave 11

Qumran texts published in DJD have numbers (e.g., 1Q2 [= 1QExod],
4Q161 [= 4QpIsa[a]]); also some texts not in DJD (e.g., 11Q19 [= 11QTemple[a]]).

OTHER ABBREVIATIONS

1 Clem.	Clement of Rome, *Ep. to Corinthians*
Ag. Ap.	Josephus, *Against Apion*
Ant.	Josephus, *Antiquities of the Jews*
Apoc.	Apocalypse
app. crit.	apparatus criticus
b.	*Babylonian Talmud* (tractate named)
ET	English version, versification
ep.	epistle, *epistola*
ESV	English Standard Version (of the Bible)
HE	Eusebius, *Historia Ecclesiastica*
JB	Jerusalem Bible
J. W.	Josephus, *Jewish War*
KJV	King James Version (or Authorized Version of 1611)
LXX	Septuagint
m.	*Mishnah* (tractate named)
MS(S)	manuscript(s)
MT	Masoretic Text (of Hebrew OT)
N-A	E. Nestle and B. and K. Aland, *Novum Testamentum graece* (27th ed.; Stuttgart: Deutsche Bibelgesellschaft, 1993)
NAB	New American Bible
NEB	New English Bible
NIV	New International Version
NJB	New Jerusalem Bible
NKJV	New King James Version
NRSV	New Revised Standard Version
n.s.	new series (any language)
NT	New Testament
or.	oration, *oratio*
OT	Old Testament
OxyP	Oxyrhynchus Papyrus
P.	Papyrus
QL	Qumran Literature
REB	Revised English Bible
RSV	Revised Standard Version
SBJ	*Sainte Bible (de Jérusalem)*
tg.	targum
tos.	*Tosephta* (tractate named)
v. l.	*varia lectio*, variant reading
Vg	Vulgate
VL	Vetus Latina, Old Latin

FIRST LETTER TO THE CORINTHIANS: TRANSLATION

◆

1   1:1 Paul, called by the will of God to be an apostle of Christ Jesus, and our brother Sosthenes, 2 to the church of God that is in Corinth, to those sanctified in Christ Jesus, called to be holy, together with all those who in every place call upon the name of our Lord Jesus Christ, their Lord and ours. 3 Grace and peace to you from God our Father and the Lord Jesus Christ!

2   4 I constantly give thanks to my God on your behalf for the grace of God granted to you in Christ Jesus. 5 For in him you have been enriched in every way, in all discourse and all knowledge, 6 as the testimony about Christ has grown strong among you. 7 Consequently, you do not lack any spiritual gift, as you eagerly await the revelation of our Lord Jesus Christ. 8 He will also keep you strong to the end, blameless on the Day of our Lord Jesus [Christ]. 9 Trustworthy is God, through whom you have been called into companionship with his Son, Jesus Christ our Lord.

3   10 I appeal to you, brothers, in the name of our Lord Jesus Christ, that all of you may agree in what you say and that there be no dissensions among you, but that you may be united in the same mind and same purpose. 11 For it has been reported to me about you, my brothers, by some of Chloe's people that there are rivalries among you. 12 What I mean is this: One of you says, "I side with Paul!"; another, "I side with Apollos!"; or "I side with Cephas!"; or "I side with Christ!" 13 Is Christ divided? Was Paul crucified for you? Or were you baptized in the name of Paul? 14 I give thanks [to God] that I baptized none of you, save Crispus and Gaius, 15 so that no one can say that you were baptized in my name. 16 I did baptize the household of Stephanas too; otherwise I do not know whether I baptized anyone else. 17 For Christ did not send me to baptize, but to preach the gospel, and not with eloquent wisdom, lest the cross of Christ be emptied of its meaning.

4   18 For the message of the cross is folly to those who are perishing, but to us who are being saved it is the power of God. 19 For it stands written, *"I will destroy the wisdom of the wise, and the learning of the learned I will confound."*[a] 20 Where is the sage? Where is the scribe? Where is the inquirer of this age? Has not God made the wisdom of the world foolish? 21 For since, in God's wisdom, the world did not come to know God through its own wisdom, God was pleased to save those who believe through the folly of the proclamation. 22 Whereas Jews demand signs and Greeks seek wisdom, 23 we proclaim Christ crucified, a stumbling block to Jews and folly to Gentiles, 24 but for those who are called, both Jews and Greeks, Christ is the power of God and the wisdom of God. 25 For God's foolishness is wiser than human wisdom, and God's weakness is stronger than human strength. 26 Look now at your own calling, brothers. For not many of you were wise by human standards; not many were powerful; not many were of noble birth. 27 But God chose what is foolish in the world in order to shame the wise, and what is

---

[a] Isa 29:14.

weak in the world to shame the strong. 28 God chose what is lowly and despised in the world, things that do not exist, to nullify the things that do, 29 so that no human being might boast in God's sight. 30 It is because of him that you are in Christ Jesus, who became for us wisdom from God, uprightness and sanctification and redemption, 31 so that, as it stands written, *"Let the one who would boast, boast of the Lord."* [b]

5   2:1 When I came to you, brothers, announcing to you God's mystery, I did not come with sublimity of word or wisdom. 2 For I resolved to know nothing while I was with you except Jesus Christ and him crucified. 3 I was among you in weakness, fear, and much trembling; 4 and my message and my proclamation were not adorned with persuasive [words of] wisdom, but with a demonstration of the Spirit and of power, 5 so that your faith might not be based on human wisdom, but on God's power. 6 Yet to those who are mature we do utter wisdom, not a wisdom of this age or of the rulers of this age who are doomed to destruction. 7 We speak rather of God's wisdom, hidden in a mystery, which God predetermined for our glory before time began. 8 None of the rulers of this age understood it; for, if they had, they would not have crucified the Lord of glory. 9 But, as it stands written,

> *What eye has not seen and ear has not heard,*
> *and what has not surged in a human heart,*
> *what God has prepared for those who love him—* [c]

10 and this God has revealed to us through the Spirit. For the Spirit scrutinizes everything, even the profound things of God. 11 For among human beings, who understands what is truly human, except the human spirit that is within? Similarly, no one comprehends what pertains to God except the Spirit of God. 12 Now we have not received the spirit of the world, but rather the spirit coming from God so that we may understand the gifts bestowed on us by God. 13 We also speak about them not with words taught by human wisdom, but with words taught by the Spirit, interpreting spiritual realities in spiritual terms. 14 The animated human being does not accept what comes from God's Spirit; for to such a one that is folly, and he is unable to understand it, because it is spiritually discerned. 15 The spiritual human being, however, discerns all things, but is himself subject to no one's scrutiny. 16 *"For who has known the mind of the Lord so as to instruct him?"* [d] But we have the mind of Christ.

3:1 Brothers, I could not speak to you as spiritual people, but only as worldly, mere infants in Christ. 2 I fed you milk, not solid food, because you were not yet able (to take it). Even now, you are still unable. 3 For you are still worldly. Wherever jealousy and strife exist among you, are you not worldly and behaving in a secular human way? 4 Whenever someone says, "I side with Paul," and another says, "I side with Apollos," are you not merely human?

---

[b] Jer 9:22-23.
[c] ? Isa 64:3; 52:15; Apocryphon of Elijah.
[d] Isa 40:13.

6   ⁵What after all is Apollos, and what is Paul? Only servants through whom you came to believe, just as the Lord assigned to each. ⁶I planted, Apollos watered, but God caused the growth. ⁷Consequently, neither the one who plants nor the one who waters amounts to anything, but only God who causes the growth. ⁸The one who plants and the one who waters have one purpose, but each will be recompensed according to his labor. ⁹For we are God's fellow-workers; you are God's field, God's building. ¹⁰According to the grace of God granted me, I laid a foundation as an expert builder, and someone else is building upon it. But each one should see to it how he builds on it. ¹¹For no one can lay a foundation other than the one already laid, which is Jesus Christ. ¹²If someone builds on the foundation with gold, silver, precious stones, wood, hay, or straw, ¹³the work of each builder will become obvious, because the Day will bring it to light. It will be revealed by fire. Fire [itself] will test the quality of each one's work. ¹⁴If the work that someone has built survives, he will be recompensed. ¹⁵If someone's work is burned up, he will be deprived of recompense, but he himself will be saved, but only as through fire. ¹⁶Do you not realize that you are the temple of God and that the Spirit of God dwells in you? ¹⁷If anyone destroys God's temple, God will destroy him. For the temple of God, which you are, is sacred.

7   ¹⁸Let no one deceive himself. If someone among you thinks that he is wise in this age, let him become a fool, in order to become wise. ¹⁹For the wisdom of this world is folly in God's sight. As it stands written, *"He catches the wise in their craftiness."ᵉ* ²⁰And again, *"The Lord knows the thoughts of the wise, that they are futile."ᶠ* ²¹Consequently, no one should boast about human beings. For all things belong to you, ²²whether it be Paul or Apollos or Cephas, or the world, or life or death, or the present or the future—all belongs to you, ²³and you belong to Christ, and Christ to God.

8   ⁴:¹One should think of us in this way: as servants of Christ and stewards of God's mysteries. ²In this case, moreover, it is required of stewards that they be found trustworthy. ³But for me it matters little that I be judged by you or by any human court. I do not even judge myself. ⁴I am not conscious of anything against me, but in this I do not stand vindicated; the one who judges me is the Lord. ⁵So do not judge anything before the proper time, before the Lord comes who will bring to light what is hidden in darkness and will expose the motives of our hearts. At that time, the commendation of each one will come from God.

⁶Now, brothers, I have transferred this to myself and Apollos for your sake, that you may learn from us not (to go) beyond what is written, that none of you will become arrogant, siding with one over against another. ⁷For who concedes you any distinction? What do you have that you did not receive? If then you did really receive it, why are you boasting as though you did not? ⁸You have already been sated! You have become rich already! Without us, you have become kings! Would that you had become kings so that we too might be kings with you! ⁹For it seems

---

ᵉ Job 5:12–13.
ᶠ Ps 94:11.

to me that God has depicted us, the apostles, as last of all, as people sentenced to death, because we have become a spectacle to the world, both to angels and human beings. [10]We are fools for Christ, but you are wise in Christ; we are weak, but you are strong; you are honored, but we are despised. [11]Up to this very hour we go hungry and thirsty; we are in rags; we are mistreated; we are homeless. [12]We toil, working with our own hands. When reviled, we bless; when persecuted, we put up with it. [13]When slandered, we answer kindly. We have become, and are even now, like the rubbish of the world, the scum of the earth.

[14]I am writing this not to make you ashamed, but to admonish you as my beloved children. [15]Even if you have ten thousand guides in Christ, you do not have many fathers, for in Christ Jesus I became your father through the gospel. [16]Therefore, I urge you, be imitators of me. [17]For this reason I am sending to you Timothy, who is my dear and faithful child in the Lord; he will remind you about my ways in Christ [Jesus], just as I teach them everywhere in every church. [18]Some have become arrogant pretending that I am not coming to you. [19]I shall come to you very soon, if the Lord wills, and I shall ascertain not the talk of these arrogant people, but their power. [20]For the kingdom of God is not a matter of talk, but of power. [21]What do you prefer? Shall I come to you with a stick or with love and a gentle spirit?

9   [5:1]It is widely reported that there is sexual immorality in your midst, and of such a kind found not even among pagans: a man living with his father's wife. [2]And you have become arrogant! Should you not rather have grieved, so that the one who has done this should be removed from your midst? [3]I, for my part, though absent in body but present in spirit, have already passed judgment on the one who has committed this deed, just as if I were present. [4]When you are gathered together in the name of [our] Lord Jesus and (with) my spirit, [5]hand this man over with the power of our Lord Jesus to Satan for the destruction of the flesh so that the Spirit may be saved on the Day of the Lord.

[6]Your boasting is not a good thing. Do you not know that a little leaven ferments the whole batch of dough? [7]Clear out the old leaven so that you may become a new batch, as you really are unleavened. For Christ, our passover lamb, has been sacrificed. [8]Let us, then, celebrate the feast, not with old leaven, or with the leaven of wickedness and evil, but with the unleavened bread of sincerity and truth.

[9]I wrote to you in my letter not to associate with sexually immoral people, [10]not at all meaning the immoral people of this world, or the greedy and swindling, or idolaters, since then you would have to leave this world. [11]But now I am writing to you not to associate with anyone who bears the name of brother, if he is sexually immoral or greedy or an idolater, slanderer, drunkard, or swindler; do not even eat with such a one. [12]For what have I to do with judging outsiders? Is it not those within, you are to judge? [13]God will judge those outside. *"Drive out the evil one from among you."*[g]

---

[g] Deut 17:7; 19:19; 22:21, 24; 24:7.

10   *6:1* Does any one of you, who has a case against another, dare to take it to court before evildoers instead of before God's dedicated people? *2* Or do you not realize that God's people are going to judge the world? And if the world is to be judged by you, are you unqualified for petty courts? *3* Do you not realize that we are to judge angels — not to mention affairs of everyday life? *4* If, then, you have courts for everyday affairs, do you seat as judges those who have no standing in the church? *5* I say this to your shame. Can it be that there is no one among you wise enough to settle a case between brothers? *6* Yet does a brother goes to court against a brother, and this before unbelievers? *7* In fact [then], it is already a disaster on your part that you have lawsuits against one another. Why not rather put up with injustice? Why not rather be cheated? *8* But you yourselves do wrong and cheat, and this to your brothers. *9* Or do you not realize that evildoers will not inherit the kingdom of God? Do not be deceived! Neither fornicators nor idolaters, neither adulterers nor catamites, neither sodomites *10* nor thieves, neither the greedy nor drunkards, neither slanderers nor swindlers will inherit the kingdom of God. *11* This is what some of you were; but now you have been washed, you have been sanctified, you have been justified in the name of the Lord Jesus Christ and by the Spirit of our God.

11   *12* "For me all things are permissible," but not all are beneficial. "For me all things are permissible," but I will not be dominated by anything. *13* "Food for the stomach, and the stomach for food, and God will do away with both the one and the other." Yet the body is not meant for fornication, but for the Lord; and the Lord for the body. *14* But God has raised up the Lord, and he will raise us up too by his power. *15* Do you not realize that your bodies are members of Christ? Shall I then take Christ's members and make them members of a prostitute? Of course not! *16* [Or] do you not realize that anyone who joins himself to a prostitute becomes one body with her? For it says, *"The two will become one flesh."* [h] *17* But whoever is joined to the Lord becomes one spirit (with him). *18* Flee from fornication! "Every sin that one commits is outside the body." But the fornicator sins against his own body. *19* Or do you not realize that your body is the temple of the Holy Spirit, which is within you and which you have from God, and that you are not your own? *20* For you have been bought at a price. So glorify God with your body.

12   *7:1* Now for the matters about which you wrote: It is good for a man not to touch a woman. *2* Yet because of instances of fornication, each man should have his own wife, and each woman her own husband. *3* The husband should fulfill his conjugal duty to his wife, and likewise the wife to her husband. *4* The wife does not have authority over her own body, but rather her husband does; likewise a husband does not have authority over his own body, but rather his wife does. *5* Do not deprive one another, except perhaps by mutual consent for a time, to be free for prayer; but then be together again, so that Satan may not tempt you because of your lack of self-control. *6* I say this as a concession, not as a command. *7* I wish that all were as I myself am, but each one has a particular gift from God, one of one

---

[h] Gen 2:24.

kind and one of another. [8] Now to the unmarried and to widows I say: it is good for them to remain as I am, [9] but if they are not exercising self-control, they should marry; for it is better to marry than to burn.

13   [10] To the married, however, I give this command, not I but the Lord: that a wife should not be separated from her husband; [11] but if indeed she is separated, she must either remain unmarried or be reconciled to her husband; and that a husband should not divorce his wife.

14   [12] To the rest I say, I and not the Lord: if any brother has a wife who is an unbeliever and she agrees to live with him, he should not divorce her; [13] and if any woman has a husband who is not a believer and he agrees to live with her, she should not divorce her husband. [14] For the unbelieving husband has been made holy through his wife, and the unbelieving wife has been made holy through the brother. Otherwise your children would be unclean, but as it is they are holy. [15] If the unbelieving partner separates, however, let him do so. The brother or sister is not bound in such cases. But God has called you in peace. [16] For all you know, wife, you might save your husband; or for all you know, husband, you might save your wife.

15   [17] Nevertheless, each one should lead the life that the Lord has assigned, as God has called each of you. So I order in all the churches. [18] Was anyone called when he was circumcised? He should not try to undo his circumcision. Was anyone called when he was uncircumcised? He should not be circumcised. [19] Circumcision means nothing, and uncircumcision means nothing; but obeying God's commandments is what counts [20] Each one should remain in the state in which he was called. [21] Were you a slave when you were called? Do not worry about it, but if indeed you can gain your freedom, take advantage rather of it. [22] For the one who was a slave when called by the Lord is the Lord's freedman; so too the one who was free when called is Christ's slave. [23] You were bought at a price; do not become slaves to human beings. [24] Brothers, each one should remain before God in the state in which he was called.

16   [25] Now concerning virgins, I do not have a command from the Lord, but I give my opinion as one who by the Lord's mercy is trustworthy. [26] I think, therefore, that, in view of the impending crisis, it is good for a person to remain as he is. [27] Are you bound to a wife? Do not seek release. Are you without a wife? Do not look for one. [28] But if indeed you do marry, you would not sin; and if a virgin marries, she would not sin. Yet such people will face troubles in earthly life, and I would spare you that. [29] What I mean, brothers, is that time is running out. From now on let even those who have wives live as though they had none; [30] those who mourn as though they did not; those who are happy as though they were not; those who buy as though they had no possessions; [31] and those who deal with the world as though they had no use of it. For the shape of this world is passing away. [32] I want you to be free of concern. The unmarried man is concerned about the Lord's affairs, how he may please the Lord. [33] But a married man is concerned about the affairs of this world, how he may please his wife; [34] and he is divided. An unmarried woman or virgin is concerned about the Lord's affairs, that she may be holy in both body and spirit; but the married woman is concerned about the affairs of this world, how she may please her husband. ³⁵I am saying this for your own good, not to lay a restriction on you, but for the sake of good order and devotion to the Lord without distraction.

17   ³⁶If someone thinks that he is behaving improperly toward his virgin, and if she (or he) is at a critical stage, and so it has to be, let him do as he wishes. He is committing no sin; let them get married. ³⁷But the one who stands firm in his mind, who is under no compulsion and has control of his own will, and has made up his mind to keep his virgin (unmarried) will be doing well. ³⁸So then both the one who marries his virgin does well, and the one who does not marry her will do better.

18   ³⁹A wife is bound to her husband as long as he lives; but if her husband dies, she is free to be married to whomever she wishes, but only in the Lord. ⁴⁰In my judgment, she is more blessed if she remains as she is—and I think that I too have God's Spirit.

19   ⁸:¹Now for meat sacrificed to idols: we realize that "we all possess knowledge." Knowledge puffs up, but love builds up. ²If anyone imagines that he knows something, he does not yet know it as he ought to. ³But if anyone loves God, that one is known by him. ⁴So about the eating of meat sacrificed to idols: we know that "an idol is nothing at all in this world" and that "there is no God but one." ⁵For even if there are so-called gods either in heaven or on earth—indeed, there are many "gods" and many "lords"—

⁶yet for us there is one God, the Father,
from whom come all things and toward whom we tend;
and there is one Lord, Jesus Christ,
through whom all things come and through whom we are destined.

⁷But all do not possess this knowledge. Some because of their habitual association up to this time with idols eat such meat as sacrificed to idols, and their conscience, being weak, is defiled. ⁸Yet food will not bring us before God. We are neither worse off if we do not eat, nor better off if we do. ⁹Only see to it that this very right of yours does not become a stumbling block for the weak. ¹⁰For if someone sees you, with your knowledge, reclining at table in an idol's temple, will not his conscience, weak as it is, be emboldened to eat meat sacrificed to idols? ¹¹So because of your knowledge this weak person, a brother for whom Christ died, is brought to destruction. ¹²When you sin in this way against your brothers and strike at their conscience, weak as it is, you are sinning against Christ. ¹³Therefore, if food causes my brother to fall, I shall never eat meat again, so that I may not cause my brother to fall.

20   ⁹:¹Am I not free? Am I not an apostle? Have I not seen Jesus our Lord? Are you not the product of my work in the Lord? ²If to others I am not an apostle, surely I am to you. For you are the seal of my apostolate in the Lord. ³This is the defense I make before those who would pass judgment on me. ⁴Do we not have the right to eat and drink? ⁵Do we not have the right to bring along a Christian wife, as do the rest of the apostles, and the Lord's brothers, and Cephas? ⁶Or is it only I and Barnabas who do not have the right not to work? ⁷Who serves as a soldier at his own expense? Who plants a vineyard and does not eat of its fruit? Who shepherds a flock and does not drink of its milk? ⁸Am I saying this merely from a human point of view, or does not the law also say the same thing? ⁹For it stands written in the law of Moses, "*You shall not muzzle the ox while it is thresh-ing.*"ⁱ Is God concerned about oxen? ¹⁰Or does he really speak for our sake? For it was written for our sake, because the plowman ought to plow in hope, and the thresher (thresh) in hope of receiving a share. ¹¹If we have sown spiritual seed among you, is it too much that we should reap a material harvest from you? ¹²If others share this rightful claim on you, should not we all the more so? Yet we have not used this right. Rather, we put up with everything so as not to put an obstacle in the way of the gospel of Christ. ¹³Do you not realize that those who are engaged in temple service eat [what] belongs to the temple, and those who minister at the altar share in what is offered on the altar? ¹⁴In the same way the Lord too has or-dered those who preach the gospel to get their living from the gospel. ¹⁵I, how-ever, have used none of these things. Nor do I write this that it may be done so in my case. I would rather die than have someone deprive me of my boast. ¹⁶If I preach the gospel, there is no reason for me to boast. For compulsion lies upon me! Woe to me if I do not preach it! ¹⁷If I do so willingly, I have a recompense; but if I do so unwillingly, I have been entrusted with a stewardship. ¹⁸What then is my recompense? That, when I preach, I may offer the gospel free of charge so as not to make full use of my right in preaching the gospel. ¹⁹For though I am free and belong to no one, I have made myself a slave to all so that I may win over as many as possible. ²⁰To Jews I became like a Jew to win over Jews; to those under the law I became like one under the law—though I myself am not under the law—that I might win over those under the law. ²¹To those without the law I became like one without the law—though I am not without God's law, being under the law of Christ—that I might win over those without the law. ²²To the weak I became weak, that I might win over the weak. I have become all things to all people that I might save at least some. ²³I do it all for the sake of the gospel, so that I may have a share in it. ²⁴Do you not realize that all runners in the stadium run in the race, but only one wins the prize? Run, then, so as to win. ²⁵Every athlete exercises self-control in every way; they do it to win a perishable crown, but we an imperishable one. ²⁶I at least do not run aimlessly; I do not box as if I were beating the air. ²⁷Rather, I pommel my body and subjugate it, lest in preaching to others I myself might be disqualified.

21   ¹⁰:¹I do not want you to be unaware, brothers, that all our ancestors were under the cloud and that all passed through the sea. ²All of them were baptized into Moses in the cloud and in the sea. ³All ate the same spiritual food, ⁴and all drank the same spiritual drink, for they used to drink of a spiritual rock that fol-lowed them, and the rock was Christ. ⁵Nevertheless, God was not pleased with

---

ⁱ Deut 25:4.

most of them, for they were laid low in the wilderness. [6] Now in view of these things they have become archetypes for us, so that we may not crave for evil as they did. [7] Do not become idolaters as some of them did, as it stands written: *"The people sat down to eat and drink, and they got up to revel."*[i] [8] We should not indulge in fornication, as some of them did; and twenty-three thousand of them fell in a single day. [9] We should not put Christ to the test, as some of them did, and were destroyed by serpents. [10] Do not grumble, as some of them did, and were destroyed by the Destroyer. [11] These things were happening to them prefiguratively and were written down as a warning for us, upon whom the ends of the ages have met. [12] Consequently, whoever thinks that he is standing firm should see to it that he does not fall. [13] No trial has overtaken you but what is human. God is trustworthy, and he will not allow you to be tried beyond what you can bear; but with the trial he will provide also a way out, so that you may be able to endure it. [14] Therefore, my dear friends, flee from idolatry. [15] I am speaking as to wise people; judge for yourselves what I am saying. [16] Is not the cup of blessing that we bless a participation in the blood of Christ? Is not the bread that we break a participation in the body of Christ? [17] Because there is one loaf, we, though many, are one body, for we all partake of the one loaf. [18] Consider the people of Israel. Are not those who eat the sacrifices participants in the altar? [19] What then am I saying? That meat sacrificed to idols is something? Or that an idol is something? [20] Rather, what they sacrifice [they sacrifice] to demons and not to God, and I do not want you to become partners of the demons. [21] You cannot drink the cup of the Lord and the cup of demons as well; you cannot partake of the table of the Lord and the table of demons. [22] Or are we stirring the Lord to jealousy? Are we stronger than he?

22   [23] "All things are permissible," but not all are beneficial. "All things are permissible," but not all edify. [24] No one should seek his own advantage, but that of his neighbor. [25] Eat whatever is sold in the meat market, without raising a question in conscience. [26] *"For the earth and its fullness are the Lord's."*[k] [27] If some unbeliever invites you (to dinner) and you want to go, eat whatever is put before you without raising a question in conscience. [28] But if someone says to you, "This is sacrificial meat," do not eat it for the sake of the one who informed you and for the sake of conscience— [29] I mean, not your conscience, but the other's. For why should my freedom be determined by someone else's conscience? [30] If I partake with thanks (to God), why am I reviled for what I give thanks? [31] So whether you eat or drink or whatever you do, do all for the glory of God. [32] Avoid giving offense, whether to Jews or Greeks or the church of God, [33] even as I try to please everyone in every way, not seeking my own good but that of the many that they may be saved. [11:1] Be imitators of me, as I am of Christ.

23   [11:2] I praise you because you have been mindful of me in everything and are holding to the traditions, just as I passed them on to you. [3] But I want you to re-

---

[i] Exod 32:6.
[k] Ps 24:1.

alize that Christ is the head of every man, man is the head of woman, and God is the head of Christ. [4] Every man who prays or prophesies with covered head brings disgrace upon his head; [5] and every woman who prays or prophesies with uncovered head brings disgrace upon her head, for that is one and the same thing as her shaved head. [6] For if a woman does not cover her head, she should have her hair cut off; but if it is disgraceful for a woman to have her hair cut off or to be shaved, then she should cover her head. [7] A man ought not cover his head, since he is the image and glory of God; but a woman is the glory of man. [8] For man did not come from woman; but woman from man. [9] Nor was man created for woman, but woman for man. [10] For this reason a woman ought to have authority over her head, because of the angels. [11] In the Lord, however, neither is woman independent of man, nor man of woman. [12] For just as woman came from man, so man is born of woman; but everything comes from God. [13] Judge for yourselves: Is it proper for a woman to pray to God with uncovered head? [14] Does not nature itself teach you that if a man wears his hair long, it is degrading for him; [15] but if a woman wears her hair long, it is her glory? For her hair has been given [to her] for a covering. [16] If anyone is inclined to be argumentative (about this), we have no such custom, nor do the churches of God.

24   [17] In giving the following instructions, I do not praise (you), because you hold your meetings not to your advantage, but to your disadvantage. [18] First of all, I hear that, when you meet as a church, there are divisions among you, and in part I believe it. [19] No doubt there have to be factions among you, so that the tried and true among you may be recognized. [20] Although you hold your meetings in one place, it is not to eat the Lord's supper. [21] For as you eat, each one goes ahead with his own meal, and one goes hungry, while another gets drunk. [22] Do you not have houses to eat and drink in? Are you not showing contempt for the church of God and making those who have nothing feel ashamed? What am I to say to you? Should I praise you? In this I offer no praise. [23] For I received from the Lord what I passed on to you, that the Lord Jesus, on the night he was handed over, took bread, [24] and having given thanks, broke it, and said, "This is my body, which is for you. Do this in remembrance of me." [25] In the same way, the cup too, after the supper, saying, "This cup is the new covenant in my blood. Do this, whenever you drink it, in remembrance of me." [26] For as often as you eat this bread and drink the cup, you proclaim the Lord's death until he comes. [27] Consequently, whoever eats the bread or drinks the cup of the Lord unworthily will have to answer for the body and blood of the Lord. [28] One should take stock of himself and so eat of the bread and drink of the cup. [29] For anyone who eats and drinks without acknowledging the body eats and drinks judgment upon himself. [30] For this reason many among you are weak and infirm, and a number are dying. [31] But if we were to evaluate ourselves correctly, we would not be subject to judgment. [32] Since we are being judged by [the] Lord, we are being chastened, that we may not be condemned along with the world. [33] Consequently, my brothers, when you meet together to eat, await the arrival of one another. [34] If anyone gets hungry, he should eat at home, that you may not meet together only to be condemned. As for the other matters I shall give directives when I come.

25   12:1 Now, brothers, I do not want you to be uninformed about spiritual gifts. 2 You realize that, when you were pagans, you were attracted and carried away again and again to dumb idols. 3 Therefore, I make known to you that no one who is speaking by the Spirit of God says, "Accursed is Jesus"; and no one can say, "Jesus is Lord," save by the Holy Spirit.

26   4 There are different sorts of gifts, but the same Spirit; 5 there are different sorts of service, but the same Lord; 6 there are different sorts of work, but the same God, who produces all of them in everyone. 7 To each individual is given the manifestation of the Spirit for some good. 8 To one is given through the Spirit the utterance of wisdom; to another, the utterance of knowledge through the same Spirit; 9 to another, faith by the same Spirit, and to another, gifts of healing by that one Spirit; 10 to another, the working of mighty deeds; to another, prophecy; to another, discernment of spirits; to another, kinds of tongues; to another, the interpretation of tongues. 11 But one and the same Spirit produces all these, bestowing them individually on each one as it wills.

27   12 For as the body is a unit and has many members, and all the members of the body, though many, form one body, so too it is with Christ. 13 For by one Spirit we were all baptized, in fact, into one body, whether Jews or Greeks, slaves or free, and we were all given one Spirit to drink. 14 Indeed, the body does not consist of one member, but of many. 15 If the foot says, "Because I am not a hand, I do not belong to the body," it would not for that reason belong any less to the body. 16 And if the ear says, "Because I am not an eye, I do not belong to the body," it would not for that reason belong any less to the body. 17 If the whole body were an eye, where would hearing be? If the whole body were hearing, where would the sense of smell be? 18 Now as it is, God has arranged the members in the body, each one of them, just as he wanted them. 19 If they were all one member, where would the body be? 20 As it is, there are many members, but one body. 21 So the eye cannot say to the hand, "I have no need of you"; or again, the head to the feet, "I have no need of you." 22 Rather, the members of the body that seem to be weaker are all the more necessary; 23 and those parts of the body that we consider less honorable we surround with greater honor; and our unpresentable parts are treated with greater propriety, 24 whereas our presentable parts have no need of this. Indeed, God has so blended the body, giving greater honor to a part that lacks it, 25 so that there may be no discord in the body, but that the members have the same concern for each other. 26 If, indeed, one member suffers, all suffer with it; if [one] member is honored, all the members rejoice with it. 27 Now you are the body of Christ, and individually members of it; 28 and in the church God has appointed some to be, first of all, apostles; second, prophets; third, teachers; then, workers of mighty deeds, then those with gifts of healing, assistants, administrators, speakers of kinds of tongues. 29 Are all apostles? Are all prophets? Are all teachers? Do all work mighty deeds? 30 Do all have gifts of healing? Do all speak in tongues? Do all interpret? 31 But are you striving for the greater gifts? Now I shall show you a still more excellent way.

28   13:1 If I speak with human and angelic tongues, but do not have love, I am only resounding brass or a clanging cymbal. 2 If I have the gift of prophecy and

comprehend all mysteries and all knowledge, and if I have all the faith to move mountains, but do not have love, I am nothing. [3] If I dole out all I own and hand over my body in order to boast, but do not have love, I gain nothing. [4] Love is patient; love is kind. [Love] is not jealous; it does not brag; it is not arrogant. [5] It is not rude; it does not seek its own interest; it does not become irritated; it does not reckon with wrongs. [6] It does not delight in wrongdoing, but rejoices with the truth. [7] It puts up with all things, believes all things, hopes for all things, endures all things. [8] Love never fails. If there are prophecies, they will be brought to naught; if tongues, they will come to an end; if knowledge, it will be brought to naught. [9] For we know in part, and we prophesy in part, [10] but when what is perfect comes, the partial will be brought to naught. [11] When I was a child, I spoke as a child, I thought as a child, I reasoned as a child. When I became a man, I did away with childish things. [12] For at present we see by reflection, as in a mirror, but then face to face; at present I know only in part, but then I shall know fully, even as I have been fully known. [13] And now faith, hope, love remain, these three; but the greatest of these is love.

29   [14:1] Pursue love, and strive earnestly for spiritual gifts, especially that you may prophesy. [2] For one who speaks in a tongue speaks not to human beings, but to God, since no one comprehends, and he utters mysteries in spirit. [3] The one who prophesies, however, speaks to human beings for their edification, encouragement, and consolation. [4] The one who speaks in a tongue edifies himself, but the one who prophesies edifies the church. [5] I should like everyone of you to speak in tongues, but even more so to prophesy. One who prophesies is greater than one who speaks in tongues, unless he interprets, so that the church may be edified. [6] Now, brothers, if I come to you speaking in tongues, what good will I be to you, if I do not speak to you with some revelation or knowledge or prophecy or instruction? [7] Similarly, if inanimate things that make sounds, such as a flute or a harp, do not emit their tones distinctly, how will what is being played with flute or harp be recognized? [8] In fact, if a trumpet gives an unclear sound, who will get ready for battle? [9] So with you too. Unless you utter intelligible speech with your tongue, how will the utterance be comprehended? For you will be speaking into the breeze. [10] For there are perhaps many different kinds of languages in the world, and none without meaning. [11] If then I do not understand the meaning of a utterance, I shall be a foreigner to the one who speaks, and the speaker a foreigner to me. [12] So too with you. Since you strive earnestly for spirits, seek to abound in them for the edification of the church. [13] For this reason, the one who speaks in a tongue should pray that he may interpret (what he says). [14] [For] if I pray in a tongue, my spirit is praying, but my mind is unproductive. [15] So what is to be done? I shall pray with my spirit, but I shall also pray with my mind; I shall sing with my spirit, but I shall also sing with my mind. [16] Otherwise, if you bless [with] your spirit, how shall one who holds the place of an outsider say "Amen" to your thanksgiving, when he does not know what you are saying? [17] You are giving thanks well enough, but the other person is not edified. [18] I thank God that I speak in tongues more than all of you! [19] But in church I prefer to speak five words with my mind, so as to instruct others, than ten thousand words in a tongue. [20] Brothers, stop being childish in your thinking; rather be infants in regard to wickedness, but in thinking be mature. [21] It stands written in the law:

> "By people speaking strange tongues and by lips of foreigners
>> will I speak to this people,
> but even so they will not listen to me,"[l] says the Lord.

[22] Consequently, tongues are meant to be a sign not for believers, but for unbelievers; prophecy, however, is not for unbelievers, but for believers. [23] If then the whole church meets in one place and everyone speaks in tongues and outsiders or unbelievers come in, will they not say that you are out of your mind? [24] But if everyone prophesies and some unbeliever or outsider comes in, he will be convinced by all and called to account by all: [25] the secrets of his heart will be laid bare, and so, falling down, he will worship God and declare, "God is truly in your midst."[m]

30   [26] So what is to be done, brothers? When you come to a meeting, everyone has a psalm, an instruction, a revelation, a tongue, or an interpretation. All these things should be for edification. [27] If someone speaks in a tongue, it should be two, or at most three, but each in turn, and someone should give an interpretation. [28] But if there is no interpreter, the speaker should keep silent in church and speak only to himself and to God. [29] Two or three prophets should speak, and the rest should evaluate (what is said). [30] If something is revealed to another person sitting there, the first speaker should become silent. [31] For you are all able to prophesy one by one, in order that all may learn and all be encouraged. [32] Indeed, spirits of prophets are subject to the control of prophets. [33] For God is not a God of disorder, but of peace, as in all the churches of the saints.

31   [34] "Women should remain silent in the churches. For they are not allowed to speak, but should be subordinate, even as the law says. [35] If they want to learn something, they should ask their own husbands at home. For it is disgraceful for a woman to speak in church." [36] What, did the word of God originate with you? Or are you the only ones it has reached?

32   [37] If anyone considers himself a prophet or a spiritual person, he should know well that what I am writing to you is a commandment of the Lord. [38] If anyone disregards it, he is disregarded. [39] Consequently, [my] brothers, strive earnestly to prophesy, and do not forbid speaking in tongues. [40] But all things should be done properly and in due order.

33   [15:1] I make known to you, brothers, the gospel that I preached to you, which you received, and on which you have taken your stand; [2] by it you are also being saved, if you hold fast to the word I preached to you. Otherwise you have believed in vain. [3] For I passed on to you as of prime importance what I also received: that Christ died for our sins according to the Scriptures; [4] that he was buried; that

---

[l] Isa 28:11–12.

[m] Isa 45:14.

he was raised on the third day according to the Scriptures; [5] and that he appeared to Cephas. Then to the Twelve; [6] thereafter he appeared at one time to more than five hundred brothers, most of whom are still alive, though some have fallen asleep. [7] Thereafter he appeared to James, and then to all the apostles. [8] Last of all, as to one untimely born, he appeared to me. [9] For I am the least of the apostles, and not fit to be called an apostle, because I persecuted the church of God. [10] But by the grace of God I am what I am, and his grace in me has not been without effect; rather, I worked harder than all of them—not I, but the grace of God [that is] with me. [11] So whether it was I or they, in this way we preach, and in this way you came to believe.

34   [12] If, then, Christ is preached as raised from the dead, how can some of you say that there is no resurrection of the dead? [13] If there is no resurrection of the dead, then neither has Christ been raised. [14] If Christ has not been raised, then our preaching has [also] been useless, and useless has been your faith. [15] Then we have been found to be false witnesses about God, because we testified of God that he raised Christ, when he did not raise him, if indeed the dead are not raised. [16] For if the dead are not raised, neither has Christ been raised. [17] Yet if Christ has not been raised, your faith is worthless, and you are still in your sins; [18] and those who have fallen asleep have perished in Christ. [19] If only for this life we have hoped in Christ, then we are of all human beings the most to be pitied.

35   [20] Now, then, Christ has been raised from the dead as the firstfruits of those who have fallen asleep. [21] For since death came through a human being, so the resurrection of the dead comes also through a human being. [22] For just as in Adam all die, so too in Christ all will be brought to life; [23] but each one in turn: Christ the firstfruits, then at his coming, those who belong to Christ. [24] Then will come the end, when he hands over the kingdom to God the Father, after having destroyed every dominion, authority, and power. [25] For he must reign until *he has put* all *enemies under his feet.*[n] [26] The last enemy to be destroyed is death; [27] *for he has put all things in subjection under his feet.*[o] When it says that "all things" have been subjected, it clearly means, apart from him who subjected all things to him. [28] When all things are subjected to him, then the Son himself will [also] be made subject to him who subjected all things to him, so that God may be all in all.

36   [29] Otherwise what will people do who undergo baptism on behalf of the dead? If the dead are not raised at all, why then are people baptized on their behalf? [30] As for us, why do we endanger ourselves at every hour? [31] Day after day I face death—as surely as is the boast over you, [brothers], that I have in Christ Jesus our Lord. [32] If, humanly speaking, I fought with wild beasts at Ephesus, what did I gain? If the dead are not raised, *"Let us eat and drink. for tomorrow we die."*[p] [33] Do not be led astray. " Bad company corrupts good habits." [34] Become sober as you ought, and sin no more. For some have no knowledge of God, and I say this to your shame.

---

[n] Ps 110:1.

[o] Ps 8:7.

[p] Isa 22:13.

37   35 But someone will say, "How are the dead raised? With what kind of a body will they come?" 36 Fool! What you sow is not brought to life unless it dies. 37 And what you sow is not the body that will come to be, but a bare kernel, perhaps of wheat or of something else. 38 God gives it a body as he has chosen, and to each kind of seed its own body. 39 For all flesh is not the same; there is one kind for human beings, another for animals, another for birds, and another for fish. 40 There are both heavenly bodies and earthly bodies; the splendor of the heavenly bodies is one thing; that of the earthly is another. 41 There is one splendor for the sun, another for the moon, and still another for the stars. For star differs from star in splendor.

38   42 So too it is at the resurrection of the dead. What is sown is perishable; what is raised is imperishable. 43 It is sown in dishonor; it is raised in splendor. It is sown in weakness; it is raised in power. 44 An animated body is sown, a spiritual body is raised. If there is an animated body, there is also a spiritual body. 45 Thus it also stands written: *The* first *man,* Adam, *became a living being;* q the last Adam, a life-giving Spirit. 46 But the spiritual was not first; rather, the animated was, and thereafter the spiritual. 47 The first man was from the earth, earthly; the second man, from heaven. 48 As was the earthly one, so too are all the earthly; and as is the heavenly one, so too are all the heavenly. 49 Just as we have borne the image of the earthly one, so too shall we bear the image of the heavenly one.

39   50 Now, what I mean, brothers, is that flesh and blood cannot inherit the kingdom of God; nor does the perishable inherit imperishability. 51 Look, I am telling you a mystery: we shall not all fall asleep, but we shall all be changed, 52 in an instant, in the twinkling of an eye, at the last trumpet. For the trumpet will sound, and the dead will be raised imperishable, and we shall all be changed. 53 For what is perishable must don imperishability; and what is mortal, immortality. 54 When what is perishable dons imperishability and what is mortal dons immortality, then the saying that stands written will come true:

"*Death has been swallowed up in victory.*r
55 *Where, O death, is your victory?*
Where, O death, is your sting?"s

56 The sting of death is sin, and the power of sin is the law. 57 But thanks be to God! He grants us the victory through our Lord Jesus Christ. 58 Consequently, my dear brothers, be steadfast, unshaken, devoting yourselves at all times to the work of the Lord, knowing that in the Lord your toil is not in vain.

40   16:1 Now for the collection for God's dedicated people: As I ordered the churches of Galatia, so you too should do. 2 On the first day of every week, each one of you should lay something aside and store it up, in keeping with your income, so that there will be no collections at the time when I come. 3 When I

q Gen 2:7.
r Isa 25:8.
s Hos 13:14.

arrive, I shall send those whom you accredit with letters to carry your gift to Jerusalem. ⁴If it will be fitting for me to go too, they will go along with me.

41   ⁵I shall come to you, after I pass through Macedonia; for I shall be going through Macedonia. ⁶Perhaps I shall stay or even spend the winter with you so that you may send me on my way, wherever I shall be going. ⁷For I do not want to see you now only in passing. I hope to spend some time with you, if the Lord permits. ⁸But I shall stay on in Ephesus until Pentecost. ⁹A great door for effective work has opened to me, but there are many opponents.

42   ¹⁰If Timothy comes, see that he has nothing to fear in your company; for he is doing the work of the Lord, just as I am. ¹¹No one, then, should disdain him. Send him on his way in peace, so that he may come to me, for I am awaiting him with the brothers. ¹²As for our brother Apollos, I strongly urged him to come to you with the brothers; but it was not at all his will to come now. He will come when he has the opportunity.

43   ¹³Be on your guard. Stand fast in the faith; be courageous; be strong. ¹⁴Let all your deeds be done in love. ¹⁵You know that the household of Stephanas is the firstfruits of Achaia, and that they have devoted themselves to the service of God's dedicated people—so I urge you, brothers, ¹⁶be submissive to such people and to every fellow worker and laborer (among them). ¹⁷I was happy at the arrival of Stephanas, Fortunatus, and Achaicus, because they have made up for what was lacking from you. ¹⁸They have refreshed my spirit as well as yours. So give recognition to such people.

44   ¹⁹The churches of Asia send you greetings. Aquila and Prisca, together with the church at their house, send you many greetings in the Lord. ²⁰All the brothers greet you. Greet one another with a holy kiss. ²¹I, Paul, write this greeting in my own hand. ²²If anyone does not love the Lord, let him be accursed! *Marana tha!* ²³The grace of our Lord Jesus be with you! ²⁴My love be with all of you in Christ Jesus!

INTRODUCTION

◆

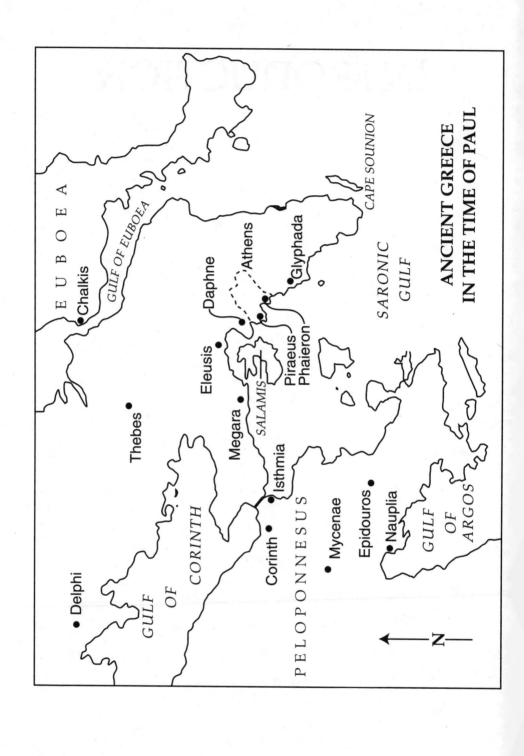

ANCIENT GREECE
IN THE TIME OF PAUL

I. CORINTH: THE CITY AND ITS HISTORY

◆

The ancient city of Corinth lay just a short distance south of the narrow isthmus that joins the Peloponnesus to the central part of Greece. Its location thus enabled it to achieve an importance in ancient Greece that few other cities could have rivaled. Anyone traveling from Macedonia, Attica, or Athens to Arcadia, Argos, Achaia, or Sparta, would have had to travel across the isthmus of 5,950 meters and pass Corinth en route. Its strategic location also enabled it to dominate two important harbors, one on each side of the isthmus. Eight and a half kilometers to the east was Cenchreae (*Kenchreai*) on the Saronic Gulf, which gave access to ships traveling from Asia and the Aegean Sea (Apuleius, *Metamorphoses* 10.35); and two kilometers to the north was Lechaeum (*Lechaion*) on the Gulf of Corinth, which gave access to the Adriatic Sea and Italy. This ideal situation of Corinth was noted by the ancient geographer Strabo (*Geogr.* 8.6.20) and was known to Latin writers, who spoke of *bimaris Corinthus*, "Corinth on two seas" (Horace, *Carm.* 1.7.2; Ovid, *Heroides* 12.27). Consequently, after classical Athens, Corinth was the second most important city in ancient Greece, but in the first century A.D. it would have been more important than Athens. Along with Rome, Alexandria, and Antioch on the Orontes (Syria), it would have been one of the four most important cities of the Mediterranean world.

Many springs in the area and the nearby rivers, Nemea and Longopotamus, made the coastal area about Corinth quite fertile and rich. The city of Corinth was built to the north of the base of a peak called Acrocorinth, which was 575 meters high, and from at least the fourth century B.C. it served as the citadel of Corinth. On the summit of Acrocorinth was a Temple of Aphrodite Hoplismene (with a statue of her bearing arms), the patroness of Corinth. Behind the temple was a spring, apparently fed by the same water as the Peirene fountain in the agora (forum) of Corinth (Pausanias, *Descr. Graec.* 2.3).

Both Acrocorinth and the city were enclosed within a walled area, more or less trapezoidal in shape, which was over four square kilometers in area. The circumference of the walls was over 10,000 meters. Two other parallel walls connected the enclosed city with the port of Lechaeum. Not all of that enclosed area was built up and populated, so there was considerable open space for parks and springs. Corinthia, the territory controled by the city-state, stretched well beyond the narrow isthmus and included to the north the promontory along the Halcyon Bay and to the south the area roughly up to Mount Onium.

The area of Corinthia had been settled already in Neolithic times, and early Helladic settlements were extensive there. The origins of the city of Corinth, however, are shrouded in legends. Apparently it was called at one time Ephyrē, and Sisyphus, son of Aeolus, whom Homer called "the most crafty of men" (*Iliad* 6.152–54), was said to be the king of Ephyrē.

The historical period of Corinth is divided into two eras. The earlier era begins with the Dorian invasion of the Peloponnesus in the tenth century B.C., when Temenos, one of the Heraclidae, conquered Argos. Around 850 B.C., the Dorian oligarchy of the Bacchiadae ruled in Corinth, named after Bacchis, king of Corinth. In this early period, about 733, the city spread its influence by establishing colonies at Corcyra (modern Korfu), off the coast of Epirus, at Syracuse in Sicily, and elsewhere. About 725, a renowned style of Greek pottery was developed that came to be known as Proto-Corinthian and Corinthian ware, which was widely used in the eastern Mediterranean world. Corinth was famous also for a fleet of triremes, which the historian Thucydides later praised (*Hist.* 1.13.2–4). Homer sang of "wealthy Corinth" (*Iliad* 2.570), and that was echoed by Strabo centuries later (*Geogr.* 8.6.20).

About 657, Cypselus overthrew the Bacchiadian oligarchy and set himself up as *tyrannos* of Corinth, under whom the city again thrived in prosperity, power, and colonization. Cypselus reigned until 625, when he was succeeded by his son Periander (625–585), who continued his father's policies. In the sixth century, Periander built the *diolkos* across the isthmus at its narrowest point, i.e., from Schoenus on the Saronic Gulf, not far from Cenchreae, to the opposite bank, a distance of 5950 meters (Strabo, *Geogr.* 8.2.1; 8.6.22). *Diolkos* means "hauling across," and it was the name given to a stone-paved road with channels constructed in it, which guided the wheels of a movable platform used to transfer small boats and their cargo across the isthmus from one gulf to the other. This was intended to be a shortcut for shipping freight from Asia to Italy, which would spare small craft from coping with the wind-swept and dangerous route around Cape Maleae and the other capes at the southern tip of the Peloponnesus. (The *diolkos* was a substitute for a canal, which many administrators of Corinth and elsewhere had hoped to construct throughout the centuries, e.g., Demetrius I Poliorcetes of Macedon [end of the fourth century B.C.]; Julius Caesar, Caligula, and Nero [in the first century B.C. and A.D.]. Only in 1881–93 was the Corinthian Canal finally cut through the isthmus by French engineers to connect the two gulfs.)

When Periander died, the rule passed to his nephew Psammetichus (Cypselus II), who was assassinated within a short time. Then a constitutional government was set up with eight *probouloi* (executive magistrates) and a council of 80 men to rule instead. In the early sixth century, the Isthmian Games were started, and they continued to be sponsored by the city of Corinth for centuries. In the sixth and fifth centuries, Corinth often sided with other Peloponnesian city-states and battled against other cities throughout Greece, especially Sparta, Athens, and Thebes. In the fifth century, in particular, it countered the influence of Athens, which sought to spread its dominion over Megara and other towns about the Corinthian Gulf. This led eventually to the Peloponnesian War (431–404 B.C.).

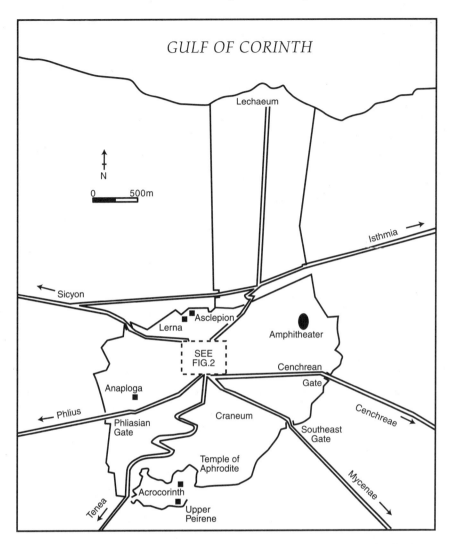

FIGURE 1. City plan of Corinth (Redrawn from Murphy-O'Connor 1983a: 20, fig. 4.)

Corinth suffered greatly during the war, but in the end the Athenian fleet was defeated at Aegospotami in the Hellespont, after which Athens capitulated (404). Eventually, in 395 Corinth joined forces with Argos, Athens, and Boeotia to curb the spread of Sparta's domination, which led to the so-called Corinthian War. As a result of the war Corinth lost its independence and was united with Argos (395–386).

By this time the influence of Macedonia in northern Greece was spreading, and in 338 the battle of Chaeronea took place, when Philip II of Macedon conquered the Greek city-states and strove to unite Greece into one kingdom. That was also the beginning of the Hellenic League, which was proclaimed at Corinth by Philip, as he started his crusade against Persian interference in the land. In 280, the Achaean League was refounded, and it lasted until 146. In 243, a leading statesman of the League was Aratus of Sicyon, a neighboring city-state; he freed Acrocorinth and Corinth from Macedonian domination and its degrading influence; he adopted an explicit anti-Macedonian policy, which Corinth eventually also espoused.

Roman contact with Greek city-states began about 228 B.C., and Roman interference in the Peloponnesus became strong in 197, after the Second Macedonian War (200–197), when Roman officials sought to reorganize boundaries and alter civic governments. A few years later Corinth became the chief city-state of the Achaean League, which was then seeking to offset Roman interference. In 147, a Roman delegation arrived in Corinth, demanding the dissolution of the League. The result was the Achaean War. Then under the leadership of the Roman general, Lucius Mummius, Corinth was defeated in battle in 146; the city was sacked, burned, and razed to the ground. All the male citizens were killed, and the women and children sold into slavery (Pausanias, *Descr. Graec.* 1.20.4; Cicero, *Verr.* 2.55). "The Sicyonians obtained most of the Corinthian territory" (Strabo, *Geogr.* 8.6.23). Mummius, however, shipped most of the art treasures of Corinth to Rome (Cicero, *De Officiis* 3.11.46; Vitruvius, *De archit.* 5.5.8), and he was awarded the title "Achaicus," so that he is known in history as Lucius Mummius Achaicus (Pliny, *Nat. Hist.* 35.8.24; Arafat, *Pausanias' Greece,* 89–97). City-states such as Corinth, Euboea, Phokis, came under Roman domination, rule, and taxation. So ended the early era of Corinth.

Ancient writers report that for more than a century the site of Corinth was desolate and largely deserted. The *chōra,* or site where the city had been, became *ager publicus* (Roman public property). Sometime between 79–77 B.C., the future Roman orator and statesman, M. Tullius Cicero (106–43), while still a student in Greece, visited the site of Corinth and wrote of it: *Corinthi vestigium vix relictum est,* "hardly a trace of Corinth has been left" (*De lege agraria* 2.32 §87 [composed in 63]). Among Cicero's letters there is also one sent to him by S. Sulpicius Rufus, who speaks of Piraeus and Corinth as towns once most florishing, but now lying prostrate and demolished before one's very eyes (*oppida quodam tempore florentissima, nunc prostrata et diruta ante oculos iacent* [Ad *Fam.* 4.5.4]). See also Velleius Paterculus, *Hist. Romae* 1.13.1. However, elsewhere Cicero admits that as a youth he was in Peloponnesus and saw "Corinthians" living there, as he had seen Argives and Sicyonians (*Tusc. Disp.* 3.22.53 [composed in 45 B.C.]). For some natives continued to dwell in Corinth as squatters, as material archaeological evidence shows. Williams ("Corinth 1977," 21) reports: "Some evidence has been accumulating over the years of excavation, however, that reinforces the statement made by Cicero that persons did live among the ruins of the city in the interim period." He mentions stamped amphoras, coins from before the Roman refounding of Corinth, continuity of cult places, pottery, and glassware. So it appears that the destruction of ancient Corinth may have been far less extensive than is normally thought. Similarly, Wiseman reports, "The destruction of Corinth was far less extensive than scholars have preferred to believe. . . . At the South

Stoa the monuments along the terrace were carried away, but the buiding itself was standing 'fairly intact' when the colony was established in 44 B.C." ("Corinth and Rome I," 494). See further Broneer, *South Stoa*, 100–155; Oster, "Use, Misuse," 54–55.

At any rate, the second era of ancient Corinth began in 44 B.C., when Julius Caesar, a short time before he was assassinated, issued a decree refounding Corinth as a Roman colony, *Colonia Laus Iulia Corinthiensis*, "Corinthian Colony, to the honor of Julius" (Dio Cassius, *Rom. Hist.* 43.50.3–5; cf. Pausanias, *Descr, Graec.* 2.1.2; 3.11.4; Broneer, "Colonia"). This second period is usually called Roman Corinth, which differed considerably from the older Greek city and its glorious past. As a Roman colony, its culture and laws were those of Rome; the Roman town was laid out in a grid of parallel streets according to Roman town-planning, with fine public buildings. The new town's forum was built about three feet higher than the old Greek agora and was expanded to the south. Some edifices of the pre-146 Corinth were rebuilt. The south stoa of the old city was reused, as was the archaic temple (of Apollo?), but they were rebuilt in italic architectural style. Temple E (see fig. 2, no. 19), dedicated to the imperial cult, at the west end of the forum, was built totally in Roman design and dominated the forum.

Some of the intrigues of J. Caesar, Brutus, Octavian, and M. Antony ensued on Grecian territory, especially the battle of Actium (31 B.C.) off the coast of Epirus. In time, Roman Corinth became the capital of the province of Achaia and the seat of the Roman governor, the center for assizes and the collection of taxes. Under Augustus, about 27 B.C., Achaia (roughly the equivalent of modern Greece, save for Thessaly, Macedonia, and Crete) was made a senatorial province. The strategic location of the capital, with Acrocorinth as a point of defense, and its character of a crossroad between East and West made it necessary for the Roman occupiers to rebuild the city. This they did, stressing discontinuity with the past (old Greek Corinth). *Romanitas* and a prolonged *pax Romana* reigned until Byzantine times.

About 7 B.C., Roman Corinth recovered the administration of the Isthmian Games, which ranked in importance just after the Olympics; they were held every other year. To these were added the Caesarean Games and the Imperial Contests, which were held every four years in honor of the emperor Tiberius. Because of later administrative difficulties, Tiberius attached Achaia to the imperial province of Moesia (A.D. 15 [Tacitus, *Ann.* 1.76]), but eventually, in A.D. 44, the emperor Claudius restored Achaia to the full status of a senatorial province. So Corinth continued to be the seat of the proconsul governing the Roman province of Achaia in the time when Paul first visited and evangelized the city.

After Paul's time, noteworthy events in Corinth included the fifteen-month visit of Nero to Greece in the years 66–67, when he granted the province of Achaia autonomy, *libertas*, and *immunitas* (which proved to be shortlived [Pausanias, *Descr, Graec.* 7.17.3–4]) and started the building of a canal across the isthmus, where the *diolkos* had been; but that project did not continue long. In the year 77, an earthquake struck the area and destroyed much of Roman Corinth, which was subsequently rebuilt. Under the Flavian emperors, the Latin name of the colony was sometimes given as *Colonia Iulia Flavia Augusta Corinthiensis*,

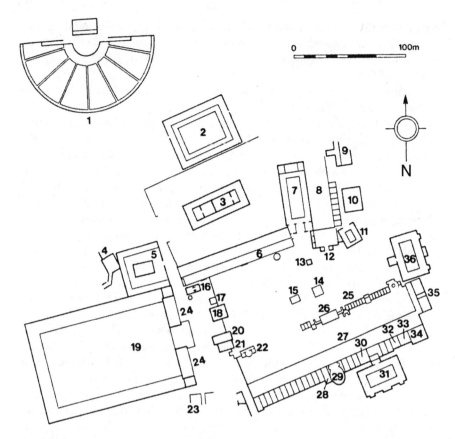

FIGURE 2. Plan of Corinth—central area, ca. 50 C.E. 1, theater; 2, N market; 3, archaic temple, 6th century B.C.; 4, Fountain of Glauke, 6th century B.C.; 5, temple C (unidentified); 6, NW stoa; 7, N basilica; 8, Lechaeum Road; 9, bath (of Eurycles?); 10, Peribolos of Apollo; 11, Fountain of Peirene; 12, Propylaea; 13, Tripod; 14, statue of Athena; 15, altar (unidentified); 16, temple D *(Tychē)*; 17, Babbius monument; 18, Fountain of Poseidon (Neptune); 19, temple of the imperial cult; 20, temple G (Pantheon?); 21, temple F (Aphrodite); 22, unidentified building (temple or civic structure); 23, "Cellar Building" (public restaurant or tavern); 24, W shops; 25, central shops; 26, *bēma*; 27, S stoa; 28, room XX (Sarapis shrine); 29, *Bouleutērion*; 30, "Fountain House"; 31, S basilica; 32, room C *(Agonotheteion)*; 33, room B; 34, room A; 35, SE building (Tabularium and library?); 36, Julian Basilica. (Redrawn from Furnish, II Corinthians AB, 11, fig 2.)

"Julian, Flavian, Augustan, Corinthian Colony." So it appears at times on coins of the Flavian period, especially in the 80s. The earthquake and the rebuilding of Corinth must be kept in mind when one reads Pausanias's description of the Corinth that he knew. In the second century, Corinth retained its importance, as is evident from a remark of Apuleius (A.D. 123–?), calling it *caput totius Achaiae provinciae*, "head of the entire province of Achaia" (*Metamorphoses* 10.18).

Much can be learned about the shape of Roman Corinth, because details of its history and geography have been recorded by Strabo (64 B.C–A.D. 21) in his *Geographia* 1.3.11; 10.5.4.; 17.3.25; and esp. 8.6.20–23; and also by second-century Pausanias (fl. ca. A.D. 150) in his *Descriptio Graeciae* 2.1.1–2.5.5 (also 5.1.2; 7.16.7–10). Strabo visited Roman Corinth in 29 B.C. and completed his geographical work about 7 B.C., but revised it about A.D. 18, a few years before his death. Hence much of what Strabo records about ancient Corinth would be true of the Roman city that Paul knew. Pausanias, however, seems to have visited rebuilt Corinth sometime after A.D. 165; consequently, his elaborate description of Corinth sometimes includes things that would not have been seen when the apostle Paul was there. Yet his account, when read with care and in comparison with Strabo, is still valuable for our knowledge of first-century Corinth.

The texts of Strabo and Pausanias, along with many details about Roman Corinth found in other ancient Greek and Latin authors can be found in the very useful book of Murphy-O'Connor, *St. Paul's Corinth: Texts and Archaeology*. It not only supplies a translation of the ancient texts, but summarizes the work of the archaeologists who have labored for over a century (since 1896) excavating the site of ancient Corinth (see *Corinth: Results of Excavations Conducted by the American School of Classical Studies at Athens* [18 vols.; Princeton, 1929–1997]). Fundamental to the study of ancient Corinth are two works by Wiseman, "Corinth and Rome I: 228 B.C.–A.D. 267" and *The Land of the Ancient Corinthians*, on both of which Murphy-O'Connor heavily depends, as he himself admits. See also Furnish, "Corinth in Paul's Time," for good illustrations.

When one looks at a plan of Roman Corinth in Paul's day (fig. 2), one studies it from the perspective of Acrocorinth, therefore looking toward the north. From the forum, which more or less corresponded to the agora of ancient Corinth, the Lechaeum Road (8) led to the northern city-wall. Near to the wall and to the west of the road were the Asclepieion and the Lerna Fountain. Access to that road from the forum was gained by a massive gate, called Propylaea (12). To the right of that gate was the Peirene Fountain (11). Leading north from the gate was a ramp to the Lechaeum Road, which was flanked on the left by the North Basilica (7) and on the right by the colonnaded *Peribolos* (Basilica) of Apollo (10). To the west of that basilica and perpendicular to its southern end ran the Northwest Stoa (6), to the north of which was the Archaic Temple (3), dedicated to Apollo [?]. Farther north and beyond the courtyard of that temple was the North Market (2). The western edge of the temple's courtyard was flanked by a road that turned and led westward to the city-state of Sicyon. Across the road was a colonnaded courtyard in the center of which was the Temple C (of Hera Acraea?[5]), and on the western edge of the courtyard was situated the ancient Glauke Fountain (4). To the south of Temple C was the large colonnaded court of Temple E, the Temple of Octavia (19), the main entrance to which, flanked by shops, opened also onto the road to Sicyon.

In the forum proper, one found to the west a small Temple of Tyche (16), the Monument of Babbius (17), and Temple G (of Apollo?[20]) and Temple F of Aphrodite (21). Within the forum, almost due east of the Temple of Aphrodite, was a line of structures: a stone platform, the *Bēma* or judicial tribunal (26), shops (25), a structure dedicated (it seems) to Artemis of Ephesus, and more shops. To the east of these structures were the Julian Basilica (36) and the *Tabularium* or Records Office (35). The south border of the forum was marked by the South Stoa (27), onto which a number of structures opened. Chief among them was the City Council Chamber (29), and nearby a shrine to Sarapis (probably 28). To the south of it was the South Basilica (31). The forum itself was the most important part of Roman Corinth, and in the center of it was a great statue of Athena (14).

When leaving the forum of Roman Corinth to the south, just behind the South Basilica, one met the juncture of four roads: one led to the east and the Cenchrean Gate, which gave access to the road going to Corinth's other port, Cenchreae; the second road headed toward the Southeast Gate and to Mycenae; the third road headed south, skirted the Acrocorinth on its west side, and led to Tenea; and the fourth road led southwest to the Phliasian Gate and the town of Phlius (figure 1).

BIBLIOGRAPHY

Alcock, S. E., *Graecia Capta: The Landscapes of Roman Greece* (Cambridge: Cambridge University Press, 1993).

Arafat, K. W., *Pausanias' Greece: Ancient Artists and Roman Rulers* (Cambridge: Cambridge University Press, 1996) 90–97.

Broneer, O., "The Apostle Paul and the Isthmian Games," *BA* 25 (1962) 2–31.

——, "Colonia Laus Iulia Corinthiensis," *Hesperia* 10 (1941) 388–90.

——, "Corinth: Center of St. Paul's Missionary Work in Greece," *BA* 14 (1951) 78–96.

——, *Isthmia I: The Temple of Poseidon* (Princeton: American School of Classical Studies at Athens, 1971); *Isthmia II: Topography and Architecture* (1973).

——, "The Isthmian Victory Crown," *AJA* 66 (1962) 259–63.

——, "Paul and the Pagan Cults at Isthmia," *HTR* 64 (1971) 169–87.

——, *The South Stoa and Its Roman Successors* (Corinth: Results of Excavations . . . , Vol. 1, part 4; Princeton: American School of Classical Studies at Athens, 1954) 100–155.

Callaway, J. A., "Corinth," *RevExp* 57 (1960) 381–88.

Engels, D., *Roman Corinth: An Alternative Model for the Classical City* (Chicago: University of Chicago Press, 1990).

Feger, R., "Cicero und die Zerstörung Korinths," *Hermes* 80 (1952) 436–56.

Finegan, J., "Corinth," *IDB*, 1:682–84.

Freeman, S. E., *The Excavation of a Roman Temple at Corinth* (Baltimore: Johns Hopkins University Press, 1941).

Furnish, V. P., "Corinth in Paul's Time," *BARev* 14/3 (1988) 14–27.

Gill, D. W. J., "Corinth: A Roman Colony in Achaea," *BZ* 37 (1993) 259–64.

Jacobson, D. M., and M. P. Weitzman, "What Was Corinthian Bronze?" *AJA* 96 (1992) 237–47.

Larsen, J. A. O., "Roman Greece," *An Economic Survey of Ancient Rome* (6 vols.; ed. T. Frank; Baltimore: Johns Hopkins University, 1938), 4:259–498.

Lenschau, T., "Korinthos," *PWSup* 4 (1924) 991–1036.

Meyer, E., "Korinthos," *Der kleine Pauly* (5 vols.; ed. K. Ziegler and W. Sontheimer; Stuttgart: Druckenmüller, 1964–75); 3 (1969) 301–5.

Murphy-O'Connor, J., "Corinth," *ABD*, 1. 1134–39.

——, "The Corinth That St. Paul Saw," *BA* 47 (1984) 147–58.

——, "Corinthian Bronze," *RB* 90 (1983) 80–93.

——, *St. Paul's Corinth: Texts and Archaeology* (GNS 6; 3d ed.; Collegeville, MN: Liturgical Press, 2002).

Oster, R. E., "Use, Misuse and Neglect of Archaeological Evidence in Some Modern Works on 1 Corinthians (1 Cor 7, 1–5; 8, 10; 11, 2–16; 12, 14–26)," *ZNW* 83 (1992) 52–73.

Robinson, H. S., "Excavations at Ancient Corinth, 1956–63," *Klio* 46 (1965) 289–305.

Romano, D. G., "Post-146 B.C. Land Use in Corinth, and Planning of the Roman Colony of B.C.," *The Corinthia in the Roman Period* (ed. T. E. Gregory; Ann Arbor: Journal of Roman Archaeology, 1993) 9–30 and fig. 3.

Rothaus, R. M., *Corinth: The First City of Greece: An Urban History of Late Antique Cult and Religion* (Religions in the Graeco-Roman World 139; Leiden: Brill, 2000).

Salmon, J. B., *Wealthy Corinth: A History of the City to 338 BC* (Oxford: Clarendon, 1984).

Scranton, R., et al., *Kenchreai: Eastern Port of Corinth: I. Topography and Architecture* (Leiden: Brill, 1978).

——, *Monuments in the Lower Agora and North of the Archaic Temple* (Corinth: Results of Excavations . . . , Vol. 1, part 3; Princeton: American School of Classical Studies at Athens, 1951).

Waele, F. J. de, *Corinthe et Saint Paul: Les antiquités de la Grèce* (Les Hauts Lieux de l'histoire 15; Paris: Guillot, 1961).

——, "Korinthos," *PWSup* 6 (1935) 182–99.

——, "The Roman Market North of the Temple at Corinth," *AJA* 34 (1930) 432–54.

Walbank, M. E. H., "The Foundation and Planning of Early Roman Corinth," *JRA* 10 (1997) 95–130.

——, "What's in a Name? Corinth under the Flavians," *ZPE* 139 (2002) 251–64.

Weinberg, S. S., *The Southeast Building, the Twin Basilicas, the Mosaic House* (Corinth: Results of Excavations . . . , Vol. 1, part 5; Princeton: American School of Classical Studies at Athens, 1960).

Williams, C. K., II, "Corinth 1977, Forum Southwest," *Hesperia* 47 (1978) 1–39.

——, "The Refounding of Corinth: Some Roman Religious Attitudes," *Roman Architecture in the Greek World* (ed. S. Macready and F. H. Thompson; London: Society of Antiquaries, 1987) 26–37.

——, and J. E. Fisher, "Corinth, 1970: Forum Area," *Hesperia* 40 (1971) 1–51.

Willis, W., "Corinthusne deletus est?" *BZ* 35 (1991) 233–41.

Wiseman, J., "Corinth and Rome I: 228 B.C.–A.D. 267," *ANRW* II/7.1 (1979) 438–548.

——, *The Land of the Ancient Corinthians* (Studies in Mediterranean Archaeology 50; Göteborg: Åström, 1978).

II. THE PEOPLE OF CORINTH

◆

The people who inhabited old Corinth called themselves *Hellēnes*. They were actually descendants of Myceneans and Dorians. By the fifth century B.C., the Corinthians were speaking a dialect of Greek, Doric, along with most of the people in the Peloponnesus, except for Arcadia and Elis. Their culture was that of the great classical period, and Cicero in the first century could reminisce about Corinth as *totius Graeciae lumen*, "the light of all Greece" (*Pro lege Manilia* 5.11).

Pausanias says of Corinth restored in 44 B.C., "none of the old Corinthians dwells in Corinth; the inhabitants are those sent out by the Romans" (*Descr. Graec.* 2.1.2; cf. 2.3.7). Latin became the official language for the rest of the first century B.C. and A.D.; this is shown by official inscriptions found in Roman Corinth: of the 104 texts which are prior to the reign of Hadrian (A.D. 117–38), 101 are in Latin and only three in Greek (Kent, *Inscriptions*, 8/3, 19). This was to be expected because the colonial administration had seen to the introduction of Roman people, laws, culture, customs, taxation, and religion; in other words *Romanitas*. Coins used in Corinth were inscribed in Latin as late as A.D. 69, and pottery was made up to the middle of the first century A.D. by potters with Latin names inscribed in the Latin alphabet. Latin-speaking Corinthians referred to themselves as *Corinthienses* in order to distinguish themselves from the people of old Corinth, whom they called *Corinthii* (see Winter, *After Paul*, 12–14).

It would be a mistake, however, to think that Greek was not used also in the colony. After all, in the mid-50s A.D. Paul wrote at least two letters in Greek to Corinthian Christians, and many educated Romans spoke Greek. Moreover, Plutarch (A.D. 46/47–120), who would have been a young boy when Paul visited Corinth, knows of it as a city where Greek was spoken (*De Herodoti malignitate* 39 §870F). Part of the reason for the reemergence of the Greek language in Roman Corinth in the second century was owed to the hellenizing influence of the Roman emperor Hadrian, who was much enamoured of classical Greek culture, and to the rise of the Second Sophistic (see Alcock, *Graecia Capta*, 16–17; also Pliny, *Ep.* 8.24.1–4).

Paul's first letter to the Corinthians seems at times to be coping with secular thinking among the members of the Christian community there, thinking that is at times akin to Epicurean teaching, Stoic tenets, and the rhetoric of the Sophists. That elements of such popular Greek philosophy and secular education were affecting the Christians of Corinth, along with the Roman culture that predominated, is to be expected, because of the heritage of Greek culture and philosophy that would have been there (see Tomlin, "Christians and Epicureans"; Deming, *Paul on Marriage and Celibacy,* 5–10; Winter, *Philo and Paul among the Sophists,* 109–40).

Although Roman Corinth would not have had a landed aristocracy, its population became rich, prosperous, and independent. In addition to many Roman colonists, the population would have also included resident aliens (*metoikoi*), who would have been attracted to this strategically located metropolis, *bimaris Corinthus.* Such aliens would have brought with them their own customs, cultures, and religions. This influx of aliens would account for some of the traits that relate Roman Corinth not only to Egypt, but also to Syria, Asia Minor, and the rest of the eastern Mediterranean world (see Alcock, *Graecia Capta,* 156, 161–62).

Among such inhabitants of Roman Corinth would have been Jews from Judea, although they are not mentioned by the ancient Greek writers who have described Corinth for us. A Greek inscription, discovered in 1898, was inscribed on a white marble lintel-slab, said to have been found on the east side of the Lechaeum Road about 100 meters from the Propylaea and the entrance to the forum. It is preserved only in part, but clearly reads [*syn*]*agōgē ebr*[*aiōn*], "synagogue of Hebrews" (see Wiseman, "Corinth and Rome I," pl. V, §8; Powell, "Greek Inscriptions," 60–61 [§40]). This inscription has often been taken as a confirmation of Jewish presence in Corinth and even of the Jewish synagogue mentioned in Acts 18:4 (Barrett, *1 Cor,* 2; Conzelmann, *1 Cor,* 12). The inscription was not found *in situ,* however, and it is impossible to date the crudely written Greek characters; so no one knows how old it really is; it probably comes from more than a century or two later than Paul (see de Waele, "Uit de geschiedenis," 165, 170). The presence of Jews in the nearby city-state of Sicyon is implied in 1 Macc 15:23, and Philo speaks of the Jewish diaspora in Greece as found in "Thessaly, Boeotia, Macedonia, Aetolia, Attica, Argos, Corinth, and most of the best areas of the Peloponnesus" (*Leg. ad Gaium* 36 §281). So a Jewish community in Corinth would have been part of that diaspora. Moreover, Acts 18:4 tells of Paul "arguing in the synagogue" of Corinth every sabbath.

Christians recognize Jerusalem, the chief city of Roman-occupied Judea, as the matrix of their religion. Having come to life there, Christianity spread through the evangelistic activity of apostles and disciples to the great urban centers of the eastern Mediterranean world. Thus, "within a decade of the crucifixion of Jesus, the village culture of Palestine had been left behind, and the Greco-Roman city became the dominant environment of the Christian movement" (Meeks, *First Urban Christians,* 11). The result was that "the mission of the Pauline circle was conceived from start to finish as an urban movement" (ibid., 10). It is not surprising that Paul spent a considerable amount of time in the metropolis of Corinth, laboring among Greeks, Roman colonists, Jews, and resident aliens of that important city, dominated by Roman culture and law, which thrived because of its privileged status of being refounded by a Roman ruler.

There Paul encountered "the household of Stephanas," whom he calls "the firstfruits of Achaia" (1 Cor 16:15), and whose household he admits having baptized along with "Crispus and Gaius" (1:14, 16). To judge from their names, Stephanas may have been a Greek, but Crispus and Gaius seem to have been Greek-speaking Romans, for their names are Latin. Another Corinthian Christian with a Greek name is mentioned in Rom 16:23, "Erastus, the treasurer of this city," probably the same person as the one mentioned in Acts 19:22 and 2 Tim 4:20, and undoubtedly the same as the aedile who paved a square in first-century Roman Corinth, according to a Latin inscription still partly in situ in the square near the eastern parados of the theater: ERASTVS PRO AEDILIT[AT]E S P STRAVIT, "Erastus, in return for (his) aedileship, laid the pavement at his own expense (s. p. = *sua pecunia*). See Kent, *Inscriptions*, 8/3, 17–31, 99–100 (pl. 21, no. 232 [dated to time of Nero]). Although Cadbury ("Erastus"), Roos ("De titulo"), and Lane Fox (*Pagans*, 293) have been reluctant to identify the Erastus of the Corinthian inscription with the Erastus of Paul's letter, Broneer, Furnish, Kent, and Murphy-O'Connor see no difficulty in accepting the likelihood of the identity. A second Corinthian inscription mentioning an Erastus has also been found (see Clarke, "Another"), but it scarcely refers to the same person, since it is dated to the second century A.D.

It is not easy to determine the social status of inhabitants of Roman Corinth. The evidence for any landed aristocracy is almost nil. According to Strabo, many freedmen (*liberti, apeleutheroi*) were settled there (*Geogr.* 8.6.23; cf. Pausanias, *Descr. Graec.* 2.3.1). Plutarch knows also of veteran soldiers who were brought there (*Vita Caesaris* 57.5). The freedmen would have been emancipated slaves; hence members of a social class just above slaves. Among them were the poor, who begged for food (Appian, *Libyca* 8.20.136). The strategic location of the city, however, would have attracted many people to a thriving Corinth, and a good number of the inhabitants would have become well-to-do merchants who flourished on the prosperity of the Roman colony. A Greek poet of the first century B.C., named Crinagoras, composed a hardly flattering epigram when he wrote about the populace of Roman Corinth: "O city to be pitied, what inhabitants you have found! Alas for the fate of mighty Greece! It were better for you, O Corinth, to lie lower than the ground and more abandoned than the sands of Libya, than to be given over wholly to good-for-nothing slaves, and so distress the bones of the ancient Bacchiadae!" (*Anthologia Graeca* 9.294). As a philhellene, he compared the colonial settlers with the earlier Greek inhabitants of ancient Corinth and did not care for the Romanized population of his day (see Oster, "When Men Wore Veils," 490–91).

However, many of the settlers, along with some slaves, would have become the artisans and craftsmen in the city, who would have profited eventually from the traffic and wealth of the metropolis. Many shops have been uncovered in the excavations of the forum and along the roads leading to it and in the different markets surrounding the forum. The North Market (fig. 2, 2) was constructed not long before Paul arrived in Corinth. Paul himself calls attention to the social status of Corinthian Christians, when he says, "Not many of you were wise by human standards; not many were powerful; not many were of noble birth" (1 Cor 1:26). His mode of formulation, however, implies that there were indeed some Christians of each class mentioned: a few wise, a few powerful, a few of noble birth. Still later, as he insists on the unique character of the community as the body of Christ, he recalls that they have all been "baptized into one body, whether Jews or Greeks, slaves or free" (12:13). The last two phrases probably describe the majority of the Corinthian Christian population. The Isthmian Games, held every other year, and the other games of Roman Corinth would also have attracted many visitors, some of whom may have become resident aliens. Gill ("In Search of the Social Élite") has amassed a considerable amount of evidence, however, to show that in the Corinth of Paul's day there were many persons who would have been among the socially élite, and some of these would have been among the converts to Christianity.

Diverse, then, would have been not only the sociological and economic character of Roman Corinth, but also the religious character of its cosmopolitan population. Many of its inhabitants would have venerated a number of gods, to judge from the temples excavated in and near the forum. These were not only traditional Greek deities, but also foreign gods. Both Strabo (*Geogr.* 8.6.20) and Pausanias (*Descr. Graec.* 2.5.1) tell of the Temple of Aphrodite, the chief goddess of the city, on the summit of ancient Acrocorinth. Nearby, on the slope leading up to the citadel, were smaller temples dedicated to Demeter and Korē, which have been excavated (see Bookidis-Fisher, "Sanctuary"). In the forum itself, north of the North Stoa, was an Archaic Temple dating from the sixth century (fig. 2, 3), which the Romans restored. It was dedicated to either Apollo or Athena (uncertain, see Wiseman, "Corinth and Rome I," 530). Behind it, across the road leading to Sicyon, was a smaller Temple, possibly of Hera Acraea (fig. 2, 5). Along the western side of the forum were temples dedicated to Tychē (Fortune), Apollo, and Aphrodite. In the center of the forum stood a statue of Athena (fig. 2, 14), but near the *bēma* was a shrine of Artemis of Ephesus (recall Acts 19:24–28). In nearby Isthmia, Poseidon was venerated in a Doric Temple, and in the port of Cenchreae, archaeological evidence reveals the cult of Aphrodite, Poseidon, Asclepius, and Egyptian Isis. Pausanias (*Descr. Graec.* 2.4.6) mentions that as one goes up the road to Acrocorinth one passes two precincts dedicated to Isis (Isis Pelagia and Isis Aegyptia) and two to Sarapis. The cult of Isis is noted at Cenchreae by Apuleius (*Metamorphoses* 11.3–5) and Pausanias (*Descr. Graec.* 2.2.3), and inscriptions from Roman Corinth mention Isis and Sarapis (Smith, "Egyptian Cults"). Hence, the cult in Roman Corinth was not confined to Greek deities only, but included foreign gods such as the Egyptian Isis and Sarapis, and also Artemis of the Ephesians. Greek gods, such as Poseidon, Zeus, and Aphrodite, were venerated under Latin titles as Neptune, Jupiter, and Venus (see Engels, *Roman Corinth*, 93–105).

Moreover, shortly after Paul had been in Corinth the imperial cult or worship of the Roman emperor was established there ca. A.D. 54, having been initiated by the province and approved by the emperor and the Roman Senate. It was a mode of emphasizing loyalty to the emperor and was promoted by the Achaean League (Spawforth, "The Achaean Federal Imperial Cult"); it was celebrated every year in Corinth. Although Tiberius wanted nothing to do with divine honors, the cult of him is attested on inscriptions, and the rest of the Julio-Claudian emperors and others from Augustus on were so honored. The Temple of Octavia (fig. 2, 19), dedicated to the deified sister of Augustus, dominated the forum and older Greek temples, because it was constructed on a raised area and was the site of the imperial cult in Roman Corinth.

A question is often raised about some of the Corinthians: Were any of them known to be Gnostics in Paul's day? This question is raised because some (mainly German) commentators have maintained that Paul's letters to the Corinthians were intended to counter Gnostic thinking among Corinthian Christians (see Fascher, "Die Korintherbriefe"; Grassi, "Underground Christians"). Part of the reason for raising this question is Paul's use of gnōsis, sophia, pneumatikos, and psychikos in chaps. 1–4 of this letter, which are often considered to be patent allusions to such Gnostic teaching that he is seeking to correct. What Paul says about knowledge and wisdom, however, differs considerably from the knowledge the Gnostics once claimed to have about an innate spark of the divine, differing from body and soul, which enabled them to escape from the degrading and demonic elements of this visible world and to come to "know" the unknown god who provides redemption for those who through this knowledge are related to him. Schmithals's book, Gnosticism in Corinth, and that of Wilckens, Weisheit und Torheit, are leading examples of such an interpretation.

The Gnostic heresy, however, had not yet raised its head in Paul's day. That had to await the coming of Valentinus or Basilides of Alexandria and their followers in the mid-second century. The matrix of that varied and complex second-century phenomenon, however, is to be sought much more in Greek philosophical thinking, especially as it developed in religious circles of Egypt, than it is confronted in Paul and other Christian writers of the third quarter of the first Christian century. That some OT ideas and some Pauline terms or ideas fed into later Gnosticism is certainly admissible, but there is simply no evidence of Gnostic sophia-myths in Corinth in Paul's day, not to mention alleged full-blown Gnosticism in pre-Christian times. Eventually in the second century, Gnosticism tainted Christian teaching and met with the reaction of Tertullian, Irenaeus of Lyons, and Clement of Alexandria. Hence to label the error that Paul is combating in this letter as "Gnostic" is simply petitio principii and an anachronism. Normally, I shall refrain from commenting further on this issue in the course of the commentary, but a few cases will have to be discussed (see Wilson, "How Gnostic Were the Corinthians?"; Prümm, "Zur neutestamentlichen Gnosis-Problematik"; Yamauchi, Pre-Christian Gnosticism, 39–43, 172, 184–86; Sevrin, "La gnose à Corinthe," 129–30; Arai, "Die Gegner des Paulus"; Williams, Rethinking "Gnosticism").

An often-quoted statement of Strabo about the Corinthians and their cult of Aphrodite needs some explanation, since he wrote in the time of Roman Corinth. Strabo wrote:

> The Temple of Aphrodite became so wealthy that it acquired more than a thousand temple-slaves (hierodoulous), courtesans (hetairas) whom both men and women dedicated to the goddess. Consequently, because of these women the

city became crowded with people and grew rich. For ship-captains carelessly squandered their money there; hence the saying, "Not for every man is the trip to Corinth!" Moreover, a certain courtesan is remembered as having said to a woman who reproached her that she did not like to work or come into contact with wool, "Yet, such as I am, I have already in a short time brought down three masts" [i.e., debauched three ship-captains]. (*Geogr.* 8.6.20)

Moreover, at the end of the fifth century, the playwright Aristophanes (450–385 B.C.) coined the verb *korinthiazomai*, "act like a Corinthian," i.e., be a fornicator, harlot (*Fragm.* 354), and Plato (429–347 B.C.) used the phrase, *korinthia korē*, "a Corinthian maid," to mean a harlot (*Resp.* 3.404d). The saying that Strabo quoted eventually found its way into a Latin proverb, *Non cuivis homini contingit adire Corinthum*, "It's not the lot of every man to go to Corinth" (Horace, *Ep.* 1.17.36). So grew the reputation of ancient Corinth! (That Latin saying, however, was meant actually in a different sense: life is full of ups and downs [*sedit qui timuit ne non succederet*, "he who was afraid that he might not win sat still"].)

Strabo, however, must have been referring, not to the Roman Corinth that he knew, but to old Corinth, the days prior to 146. For "excavations have not revealed any temple of Aphrodite of any period capable of accommodating the numbers mentioned" by Strabo (Murphy-O'Connor, *St. Paul's Corinth*, 56; cf. Conzelmann, "Korinth und die Mädchen"). Indeed, it has been questioned whether Aphrodite's temple was ever a place of sacred prostitution (Saffrey, "Aphrodite à Corinthe"). So Strabo's story about Corinth has to be taken with a grain of salt, at least as far as Roman Corinth is concerned . As in any metropolis, Corinth may have had its red-light district, but it was probably no worse than other seaport towns, where money was wantonly spent.

BIBLIOGRAPHY

Adams, J. N., " '*Romanitas*' and the Latin Language," *CQ* 53 (2003) 184–205.
Arai, S., "Die Gegner des Paulus im I. Korintherbrief und das Problem der Gnosis," *NTS* 19 (1972–73) 430–37.
Barrett, C. K., "Christianity at Corinth," *BJRL* 46 (1963–64) 269–97.
Beatrice, P. F., "Gli avversari di Paolo e il problema della Gnosi a Corinto," *Cristianesimo nella storia* 6/1 (1985) 1–25.
Bookidis, N., and J. E. Fisher, "Sanctuary of Demeter and Kore on Acrocorinth," *Hesperia* 43 (1974) 267–307.
Cadbury, H. J., "Erastus of Corinth," *JBL* 50 (1931) 42–58.
Clarke, A. D., "Another Corinthian Erastus Inscription," *TynBul* 42 (1991) 146–51.
Conzelmann, H., "Korinth und die Mädchen der Aphrodite: Zur Religionsgeschichte der Stadt Korinth," *NAWG* 8 (1967) 247–61.
Duff, A. M., *Freedmen in the Early Roman Empire* (New York: Barnes & Noble, 1958).
Fascher, E., "Die Korintherbriefe und die Gnosis," in *Gnosis und Neues Testament: Studien aus Religionswissenschaft und Theologie* (ed. K.-W. Tröger; Gütersloh: Mohn, 1973) 281–91.

Gill, D. W. J., "In Search of the Social Elite in the Corinthian Church," *TynBul* 44 (1993) 323–37.

Grassi, J. A., "Underground Christians in the Earliest Church," *AER* 167 (1973) 11–19.

Harding, M., "Church and Gentile Cults at Corinth," *GTJ* 10 (1989) 203–23.

Johnson, S. E., "Paul in the Wicked City of Corinth," *LTQ* 17 (1982) 59–67.

Jongkind, D., "Corinth in the First Century AD: The Search for Another Class," *TynBul* 52 (2001) 139–48.

Kent, J. H., *The Inscriptions 1926–1950* (Corinth: Results of Excavations . . . , Vol. 8, part 3; Princeton: American School of Classical Studies at Athens, 1966).

Lane Fox, R., *Pagans and Christians* (Harmondsworth, UK: Penguin, 1988) 293.

Levinskaya, I., *The Book of Acts in Its Diaspora Setting* (The Book of Acts in Its First Century Setting 5; Carlisle: Paternoster; Grand Rapids: Eerdmans, 1996) 162–66.

McGraw, L., "The City of Corinth," *SwJT* 32/1 (1989) 5–10.

McRay, J., "Inscriptions at Corinth," *Archaeology in the Biblical World* 2 (1994) 5–7.

Meritt, B. D., *Greek Inscriptions 1896–1927* (Corinth: Results of Excavations . . . , Vol. 8, part 1; Cambridge: Harvard University Press, 1931).

Oster, R. "When Men Wore Veils to Worship: The Historical Context of 1 Corinthians 11.4," *NTS* 34 (1988) 481–505.

Powell, B., "Greek Inscriptions from Corinth," *AJA* 2/7 (1903) 26–71.

Prümm, K., "Zur neutestamentlichen Gnosis-Problematik: Gnostischer Hintergrund und Lehreinschlag in den beiden Eingangskapiteln von 1 Kor?" *ZKT* 87 (1965) 399–442; (1966) 1–50.

Rees, W., "Corinth in St. Paul's Time," *Scripture* 2 (1947) 71–76, 105–11.

Roos, A. G., "De titulo quodam latino Corinthi huper reperto," *Mnemosyne* 58 (1930) 160–65.

Saffrey, H. D., "Aphrodite à Corinthe: Réflexions sur une idée reçue," *RB* 92 (1985) 359–74.

Sevrin, J.-M., "La gnose à Corinthe: Questions de méthode et observations sur 1 Co 1:17–3:3," *The Corinthian Correspondence* (BETL 125; ed. R. Bieringer; Louvain: Leuven University/Peeters, 1996) 121–29.

Smith, D. E., "The Egyptian Cults at Corinth," *HTR* 70 (1977) 201–31.

Spawforth, A. J. S., "The Achaean Federal Cult I: Pseudo-Julian, Letters 198," *TynBul* 46 (1995) 151–68.

Tomlin, G., "Christians and Epicureans in 1 Corinthians," *JSNT* 68 (1997) 51–72.

Waele, F. J. M. de, "Uit de geschiedenis van Korinthos in de dagen van Paulus," *StC* 4 (1927–28) 145–70.

West, A. B., *Latin Inscriptions 1896–1927* (Corinth: Results of Excavations . . . Vol. 8, part 2; Cambridge: Harvard University Press, 1931).

Williams, M. A., *Rethinking "Gnosticism": An Argument for Dismantling a Dubious Category* (Princeton: Princeton University Press, 1996).

Wilson, R. M., "Gnosis at Corinth," *Paul and Paulinism: Essays in Honour of C. K. Barrett* (ed. M. D. Hooker and S. G. Wilson; London: SPCK, 1982) 102–14.

———, "How Gnostic Were the Corinthians?" *NTS* 19 (1972–73) 65–74.

Winter, B. W., "The Achaean Federal Imperial Cult II: The Corinthian Church," *TynBul* 46 (1995) 169–78.

———, *Philo and Paul among the Sophists: Alexandrian and Corinthian Responses to a Julio-Claudian Movement* (2d ed.; Grand Rapids: Eerdmans, 2002).

Yamauchi, E. M., *Pre-Christian Gnosticism: A Survey of the Proposed Evidences* (Grand Rapids: Eerdmans, 1973).

III. PAUL'S RELATION TO CORINTH AND ITS CHURCH

♦

From the two letters to the Corinthians in the NT we know that Paul evangelized Corinth. In 1 Cor 2:3 Paul himself speaks of coming to Corinth for the first time "in weakness, fear, and much trembling."

In Acts 16:8, Luke tells of a night vision that Paul had at Troas, about "a man of Macedonia beckoning him and saying, 'Come over to Macedonia and help us!' " Paul understands that as a call to begin the evangelization of Europe. He responds to the call and makes his way to Philippi, then to Thessalonica, Beroea, Athens, and finally to Corinth. All of this happens on Paul's so-called second missionary journey (15:36–18:22), roughly A.D. 50–52. The Lucan story of that journey tells how Paul came from Athens and arrived in Corinth (18:1). That was Paul's first contact with Corinthians, and it occurred not long after "Claudius had ordered all Jews to leave Rome" (18:2), some of whom undoubtedly made their way to Roman Corinth. Paul then, in effect, became the founder of the church in Corinth, only a short time after he had founded the church in Thessalonica, to which he has also written correspondence that is still available to us. How different is 1 Thessalonians from 1 Corinthians; for a comparison of the different ways in which these churches developed, see Barclay, "Thessalonica and Corinth."

The expulsion of Jews from Rome by Claudius helps us to date Paul's arrival in Corinth. Suetonius, a Roman biographer who wrote *Lives of the Caesars*, recounts the same incident: *Iudaeos impulsore Chresto assidue tumultuantis Roma expulit*, "He [Claudius] expelled Jews from Rome, who were constantly making disturbances at the instigation of Chrestus" (*Claudii vita* 25.4). That remark might seem to mean that someone called "Chrestus" was inciting Roman Jews to an uprising. The Greek adjective, *chrēstos*, "good, worthwhile," was often used as a name for a slave. So it might seem that a slave (or some "extremist" [Benko, "The Edict," 417]) named *Chrēstos* was the cause of those disturbances in Rome. The Greek name, however, would have been pronounced *Christos* (by itacism) in Suetonius's day. As a result, the reason given by Suetonius for the disturbances, *impulsore Chresto*, undoubtedly refers to a controversy in Rome that arose between Jews and Jewish Christians feuding over "the Christ," i.e., whether Jesus of Nazareth was indeed the "messiah" or not. Not understanding the Greek name *Christos*, "anointed (one)," the equivalent of Hebrew *māšîăḥ*, "messiah," Suetonius seems to have confused it with the more commonly used name, *Chrēstos*, which he wrote in Latin as *Chrestus*. So his report is interpreted often today by many modern historians of ancient Rome (Momigliano, *Claudius*, 31–34; Scramuzza, *Emperor Claudius*, 151; Piganiol, *Histoire de Rome*, 258). Centuries ago, Tertullian commented on the confusion between the hated name *Christianus* and its mispronunciation as *Chrestianus* (*Apologeticum* 3.5; CCLat 1.92; cf. Lactantius, *Institutiones divinae* 4.7.5; SC 377.70).

A fifth-century Christian writer, Paulus Orosius (*Historiae adversum paganos* 7.6.15–16; CSEL 5.451), quoted Suetonius's text and dated the expulsion of the Jews to Claudius's ninth regnal year (25 Jan. 49–24 Jan. 50):

> Josephus refers to the expulsion of Jews by Claudius in his ninth year, but Suetonius means more to me when he says, 'Claudius expelled from Rome the Jews constantly making disturbances at the instigation of Christus.' It cannot be determined whether he ordered only the Jews agitating against Christ to be restrained and suppressed, or whether he also wanted to expel Christians as being people of a related faith.

Although Orosius quotes Suetonius accurately, he claims that Josephus recorded the same expulsion. The Jewish historian, however, never wrote a word about it; or, if he did, it is no longer extant. For this reason and because of the way Orosius speaks about "Christians being people of related faith," his testimony about the date of the expulsion, is considered untrustworthy by some modern scholars, who maintain that his information is erroneous. In fact, no one knows where Orosius got the information about the ninth year; but it remains not unlikely, and a number of interpreters rightly accept it (Smallwood, *Jews under Roman Rule*, 211–16; Jewett, *Chronology*, 36–38; Schürer, *HJPAJC*, 3:77–78; Benko, "The Edict," 417). Unfortunately, some of the arguments used to support Orosius's dating have been specious, and Murphy-O'Connor (*St. Paul's Corinth*, 132–34) has done well to expose them, e.g., the use of the so-called Nazareth inscription, which is irrelevant.

Murphy-O'Connor and some others, however, have sought to interpret Suetonius's testimony as referring to a decision made by Claudius, not in his ninth regnal year (A.D. 49–50), but in his first regnal year (A.D. 41). The latter decision is reported by Dio Cassius (*Roman History* 60.6.6), who writes that the emperor, noting the growing number of Jews in Rome and realizing that it would be difficult to expel them from the city without causing a tumult, "did not drive them out," but ordered them "not to hold meetings." In other words, both Suetonius and Dio Cassius are said by Murphy-O'Connor and others to be referring to the same Claudian decision, and the two reports would be only two different views of what Claudius did. Murphy-O'Connor argues that Suetonius's statement means that "Claudius expelled only the trouble-makers among the Jews" (*St. Paul's Corinth*, 156). Following Lüdemann, he also maintains that Dio Cassius was consciously correcting the obvious meaning of Suetonius's text. Being unaware of any such punishment as expulsion, he substituted a lesser penalty, because Suetonius's words would not refer to "the entire Jewish population" of Rome, but "in all probability it would have been directed only against a single synagogue" (*ibid.*; note how that "probability" becomes a certainty on p. 139).

In all probability, such an interpretation of Suetonius is erroneous. Murphy-O'Connor also argues:

> If neither Suetonius nor Dio Cassius can be taken at face value, we cannot conclude that they are referring to two distinct events. It is preferable, according to the rules of normal literary criticism, to see them as partial accounts, confused and inaccurate, of the same episode. The historical kernel underlying both accounts can be reconstructed as follows. As a result of a disturbance concerning Christ in a Roman synagogue, Claudius expelled the missionaries who were not Roman citizens, and temporarily withdrew from that Jewish community the right of assembly. (Lüdemann 1984, 188, quoted in *St. Paul's Corinth*, 156)

Lüdemann (*Early Christianity*, 11) even says that "most scholars all over the world are agreed" about the date of A.D. 41. That, however, is an exaggeration. Such a reconstruction is wholly gratuitous. Even Murphy-O'Connor once granted that his mode of reconciling Suetonius and Dio Cassius was "admittedly tenuous" (*St. Paul's Corinth* [1st ed., 1983], 136), but now maintains that it "is confirmed by Philo" (3d ed., 2002, 156). With all due respect, it is not supported by the quotation from Philo (*Leg. ad Gaium* 23 §§156–57), as Murphy-O'Connor claims. That passage speaks about Augustus, and not about Claudius. Nor is the reconstruction supported by what is known about Claudius's benign attitude toward the Jews at the beginning of his reign, as recorded by Josephus (*Ant.* 19.5.3 §§287–91). That attitude may have been true at the beginning of his reign, but it says nothing about what would have prompted Claudius's expulsion of Jews reported by Suetonius.

According to the rules of normal literary criticism, one must conclude that Suetonius and Dio Cassius were writing about two different incidents in Claudius's reign. Dio Cassius says explicitly that Claudius did *not* expel Jews at that time (*Roman History* 60.6.6), which would be in his first regnal year. Moreover, Dio Cassius makes no mention of *Chrēstos*, which is a major obstacle to the identification of the two events. Yet, as both Suetonius and Luke affirm, without indicating the date, Claudius expelled Jews (which could be A.D. 49–50). (Admittedly, one has to allow for Lucan hyperbole, when he says "all the Jews," whereas Suetonius writes merely *Iudaeos*, "Jews" or "the Jews.") Unfortunately, Dio Cassius's history for the year 49–50 exists only in a Byzantine epitome, and the lack of a reference to such an expulsion in his writing for that year may be owing to the summary nature of the extant epitome (see Hemer, *Book of Acts*, 168; Tajra, *Trial*, 53; Hengel, *Acts and the History*, 108; Slingerland, *JQR* 79, 305–22). *Pace* Slingerland (*JQR* 83), the year 49 still remains the best explanation, because despite problems in Orosius's testimony the Lucan witness is not wholly "unreliable."

The mention of Claudius's expulsion yields, then, a date about 49–50 for the arrival from Italy of Aquila, a Jewish native of Pontus in Asia Minor, with his wife Priscilla (Acts 18:2). It is difficult to say whether they were Jews or Jewish Christians at the time of their arrival. They appear later in the Lucan account (Acts 18:18, 22, 26), and in 1 Cor 16:19; Rom 16:3–5a (cf. 2 Tim 4:19), from which we learn that they were Jewish Christians. (Luke uses the diminutive form *Priskilla* of the wife's name, whereas Paul calls her *Priska*.)

A short time later, perhaps at the beginning of the year 51, Paul arrived in Corinth and not only lodged with Aquila and Priscilla, but engaged in the same kind of work with them (Acts 18:3). Luke says that they were *skēnopoioi*, a term whose meaning is debated. Literally, it means "tent makers," i.e., weavers of tent fabric; but patristic writers often interpreted it to mean *skyotomoi*, "leather workers," considering tents to have been made of hides. In Roman times, tents were often made of *cilicium*, "(goat's) haircloth;" the name even suggests its provenience in Cilicia, the name of the province in which Paul's native city, Tarsus, was found. Hence the debate about the nature of Paul's handicraft. Acts 20:34; 1 Cor 4:12; 1 Thess 2:9 also suggest that his work was technical and carried out in a metropolitan area.

Luke describes Paul's evangelical activity in Corinth thus: "Every sabbath Paul would lead discussions in the synagogue and tried to convince both Jews and Greeks, . . . bearing witness to Jews that Jesus was the Messiah" (Acts 18:4–6). While thus engaged in Corinth, Paul was joined in his evangelical activity by Silas and Timothy, who had come from Macedonia. Early during his sojourn in Corinth, probably shortly after his arrival, Paul wrote 1 Thessalonians (see 1 Thess 3:1, 6). He eventually changed his residence and lodged with Titius Justus, who lived next door to a synagogue. Luke likewise recounts that "many were the Corinthians who also listened (to Paul), came to believe, and were baptized," chief among whom was "Crispus, the leader of the synagogue" (Acts 18:8; cf. 1 Cor 1:14). Paul's efforts, however, were not always successful, even though on this first visit to Corinth he was active there for "a year and six months, teaching the word of God among them" (18:11).

Toward the end of that sojourn in Corinth, as Luke records it, "while Gallio was proconsul of Achaia, the Jews rose up in a body against Paul and brought him to court, charging, 'This fellow is influencing people to worship God in ways that are against the law'" (Acts 18:12–13). This refers to Lucius Junius Gallio Annaeus, the governor of Achaia. Luke's text speaks of the *bēma*, "dais, platform," which was often used in the sense of a judicial bench or seat of judgment (18:12). Its place has been discovered in the rostrum of the excavated forum (fig. 2, 26); it would have been the "court" before which Paul was haled. Gallio dismissed the case against Paul as having no pertinence in Roman law: "If it were a crime or some serious evil trick, I would tolerate the complaint of you Jews, but since this is a dispute about words and titles and your own law, you must see to it yourselves. I refuse to judge such matters" (18:14–15).

This incident in the life of Paul, which is not mentioned in any of his letters, is generally judged as the "one link between the apostle's career and general history that is accepted by all scholars" (Murphy-O'Connor, *St. Paul's Corinth*, 161)—even by those who tend to distrust the historical value of much of the Lucan narrative. The reason for this judgment is that Gallio's proconsulship is mentioned in a Greek inscription that had been set up in a temple of Apollo at Delphi. Four fragments of it were discovered and published by Emile Bourguet in 1905, and three others discovered by him in 1910 were published by A. Brassac in 1913. Two further fragments were eventually found, and the full publication of all nine fragments (by A. Plassart) occurred only in 1970.

The inscription is a copy of a letter sent by Claudius to the city of Delphi about its depopulation problems. The main part of the inscription runs as follows:

1 *Tiber[ios Klaudios Kais]ar S[ebast]os G[ermanikos, dēmarchikēs exou]*
2 *sias [to IB', autokratōr t]o KZ, p[atēr p]atridos . . . chairein].*
3 *Pal[ai men t]ēi p[olei tē] tōn Delph[ōn ēn o]u mo[non eunous all'*
  epimelēs ty]
4 *chēs aei d' etērē[sa t]ēn thrēskei[an t]ou Apo[llōnos tou Pythiou. epei de]*
5 *nyn legetai kai [pol]eitōn erē[mo]s einai, hō[s moi arti apēngeile L. Iou]*
6 *nios Galliōn ph[ilos] mou ka[i anthy]patos, [boulomenos tous Delphous]*
7 *eti hexein ton pr[oteron kosmon entel]ē e[tellomai hymein kai ex al]*
8 *lōn poleōn kal[ein eu gegonotas eis Delphous hōs neous katoikous kai]*
9 *autois epitre[pein ekgonois te ta] pres[beia panta echein ta tōn Del]*
10 *phōn hōs pole[itais ep' isē kai homoia, e]i men gar tines . . . hōs polei]*
11 *tai metōkis[anto eis toutous tou]s topous, kr[. . .]*

[1]Tiber[ius Claudius Caes]ar A[ugust]us G[ermanicus, invested with tribunician po]wer [2][for the 12th time, acclaimed *imperator* for t]he 26th time, F[ather of the Fa]ther[land . . . sends greetings to . . .]. [3]For a l[ong time I have been not onl]y [well disposed toward t]he ci[ty] of Delph[i, but also solicitous for its [4]pros]perity, and I have always sup[ported th]e cul[t of Pythian] Apol[lo. But] [5]now [since] it is said to be desti[tu]te of [citi]zens, as [L. Jun][6]ius Gallio, my fri[end] an[d procon]sul, [recently reported to me, and being desirous that Delphi] [7]should continue to retain [inta]ct its for[mer rank, I] or[der you (pl.) to in]vite [well-born people also from [8]ot]her cities [to Delphi as new inhabitants and to] [9]all[ow] them [and their children to have all the] privi[leges of Del]phi [10]as being citi[zens on equal and like (basis). For i[f] so[me . . .] [11]were to trans[fer as citi]zens [to those regions . . . *(The rest of the document is broken and inconsequential; the text follows the reading of J. H. Oliver.)*

From the text of this inscription, one sees that Gallio was proconsul of Achaia during the twelfth regnal year of Claudius (A.D. 41–54) and after the twenty-sixth acclamation of him as *imperator*. The emperor was invested with *potestas tribunicia*, "tribunician power," each year, and that investment marked his regnal years. The emperor's name and the twelfth year of his tribunician power have in large part been reconstructed in this inscription, but the reconstruction is certain, being based on other known inscriptions of Claudius (see Charlesworth, *Documents*, 11–14). Claudius's twelfth regnal year began on 25 January A.D. 52.

Acclamation as *imperator*, "Victor," was sporadic and depended on military victories in which the emperor was engaged or at least indirectly involved. To date an event by such acclamations, one has to learn when a given acclamation occurred. From other inscriptions it is known that the twenty-second to the twenty-fifth acclamations took place in Claudius's eleventh regnal year (25 Jan. 51–24 Jan. 52) and that the twenty-seventh acclamation occurred in his twelfth regnal year before 1 August A.D. 52. Theoretically, then, the twenty-sixth acclamation could have occurred during the winter of 51 or in the spring or early summer of 52. The matter is settled by a Greek inscription often neglected in the discussions of Pauline chronology and the Delphi inscription: an inscription from Kys in Caria (published 1887). It combines the twenty-sixth acclamation with the twelfth regnal year: *dēmarchikēs exousias to dōdekaton, hypaton to penpton, autokratora to eikoston kai hekton,* "(invested with) tribunician power for the twelfth time, consul for the fifth, *imperato*r for the twenty-sixth time" (see G. Cousin and G. Deschamps, "Emplacements," 306–8; cf. *CIL* 6.1256; 8.14727; Frontinus, *De Aquis* 1.13). So the combination of the twenty-sixth acclamation of Claudius as *imperator* and his twelfth regnal year points to a time between 25 January 52 and 1 August 52. Claudius would have written the letter, in which he mentions Gallio, to the people of Delphi in this period.

Because Achaia was a senatorial province of praetorian rank, it was governed by a proconsul (Gk. *anthypatos*, Acts 18:12; 13:7; Josephus, *Ant.* 14.10.21 §244). Such a provincial governor normally ruled for a year and was expected to assume his task by 1 June (Dio Cassius, *Roman History* 57.14.5) and to leave for the province by 1 April, or mid-April at the latest (*ibid.*, 60.11.6; 60.17.3). Claudius's letter mentions that Gallio had reported to him about conditions in Delphi on his arrival. This would mean that Gallio was already in Achaia by late spring or early summer of 52 and had written to Claudius about the situation that he found there.

The problem has always been to determine whether Gallio's proconsular year stretched from a time in 51–52 or 52–53. In other words, was Paul haled before Gallio at the end of his proconsular year or at the beginning of it? Deissmann (*Paul*, 272), Finegan (*Handbook*, §501), and Hemer (*Book of Acts*, 168) have espoused the former view and have influenced many others. However, Gallio had a younger brother, the Latin writer Seneca, who recorded that Gallio developed a fever in Achaia and "took ship immediately," insisting that the disease was not of the body, but of the place" (*Ep.* 104.2). So it seems that Gallio cut short his proconsular stay in Achaia and hurried home to Italy. Having arrived in Achaia in the spring of 52 and reported to Claudius about conditions there, he must have spent the summer of 52 in Achaia, but departed from the province not later than the end of October, before *mare clausum* (the closed sea), when ship travel on the Mediterranean was impossible because of winter storms (see Acts 27:9). This means, then, that Paul would have been haled before Gallio at the beginning of his proconsular year, some time in the late spring, summer, or early autumn of 52.

Not all interpreters reckon the year of Gallio's proconsulship in this way, often neglecting the Carian inscription, and preferring to use 51–52 instead. The suggestion of Lüdemann (*Paul*, 163–64) that Claudius's letter was actually sent to Gallio's successor and that Gallio's term should be reckoned as falling "in the years 51/52 C.E." is far-fetched and based on mere speculation.

According to Acts 18:18, "Paul stayed on in Corinth for a considerable time" after the Gallio incident. Eventually he sailed for Syria with Priscilla and Aquila and landed at Ephesus, went to Jerusalem to greet the church there (18:22), and then to Antioch. After some time spent there, he started out on his third missionary journey (18:23, roughly A.D. 54–58).

During the third missionary journey (described in Acts 18:23–20:38), Paul was based in Ephesus, the capital of the Roman province of Asia. There he spent "three years" (Acts 20:31), preaching the word of the Lord to Jews and Greeks for "two years" in the hall of Tyrannus (Acts 19:10). The three years would mean roughly 54–57, and during this time he wrote his letters to the Galatians (ca. A.D. 54), to the Philippians, and possibly to Philemon (A.D. 56–57).

During this time in Ephesus, reports came to Paul about the situation in the Corinthian community—dissensions, doubts, scandals, and resentment of Paul himself. To cope with this situation, Paul wrote at least five different letters to the Corinthian Christians, two of which survive, 1 Corinthians and 2 Corinthians (the latter in its present form undoubtedly being a composite made up of some of these writings). The order of such correspondence would be aCor, 1 Cor, a painful visit, bCor, 2 Cor; then the apocryphal correspondence.

One letter (aCor), about which we know only from 1 Cor 5:9, preceded 1 Corinthians: "I wrote to you in my letter not to associate with sexually immoral people." It apparently counseled the Corinthian Christians against other problems too and also urged them to take up a collection in Corinth for the poor of Jerusalem. This letter raised questions, about which the Corinthians seem to have sent a subsequent inquiry, to which Paul replies in 1 Cor 7:1; see also 16:1. This earlier letter (aCor) is now lost, but some interpreters have thought that 2 Cor 6:14–7:1 was part of it (J. Weiss, Héring). That view, however, is not likely, because *pornoi*, "sexually immoral," does not appear in those verses of 2 Corinthians, which otherwise have a contrast of negative and positive elements that might have included such an issue.

Having sent off that letter (aCor), Paul sent Timothy to Corinth by way of Macedonia (1 Cor 4:17; 16:10; cf. Acts 19:22), apparently hoping that Timothy would be able to bring some order to the Corinthian community and ameliorate his relations with it. Meanwhile, more reports about Corinth (from Chloe's people, 1 Cor 1:11; cf. 11:18) reached Paul in Ephesus, and messengers sent to him (Stephanas, Fortunatus, and Achaicus, 16:17–18) from Corinth arrived with questions of the community, and perhaps bearing the letter mentioned in 7:1 (a reply to aCor[?]). In order to comment on the reports and answer questions sent to him, Paul composed a second letter, what we call First Corinthians (1 Cor). It was written from Ephesus sometime before Pentecost (1 Cor 16:8), probably early in the year 57 (but the end of 56 is also possible). This letter was apparently not well received, and Paul's relations with the Corinthian community only worsened.

That situation called for a hasty second visit to Corinth, which Paul mentions in 2 Cor 2:1 ("a painful visit"); 12:14, 21; 13:1–2. It apparently did little good. So Paul, on his return to Ephesus, wrote a third letter (bCor), composed "with many tears" (2 Cor 2:3–4, 9; 7:8, 12; 10:9). This letter is not extant, unless we are to believe, as some have proposed (T. W. Manson), that it forms part of 2 Corinthians (= 2 Cor 10:1–13:10). It seems to have been carried to Corinth by Titus, who went there in an attempt to smooth out relations with the Corinthian Christians.

Eventually, Paul left Ephesus in the late summer of A.D. 57 and traveled to

Troas (2 Cor 2:12). Not finding Titus there, as he had hoped, he went on to Macedonia (2:13). Somewhere in Macedonia, possibly at Philippi, he met the returning Titus and learned from him that a reconciliation with the Corinthians had been effected. From Macedonia Paul wrote his fourth letter to the Corinthians, which is part of what we call 2 Corinthians (2 Cor 1:1–9:15) in the autumn of A.D. 57. For a slightly different reconstruction of this sequence of letters and visits, see Gilchrist, "Paul and the Corinthians."

Paul does not seem to have proceeded directly to Achaia, but went rather from Macedonia into Illyricum, which he mentions in Rom 15:19 as the farthest limit of his evangelization of the eastern Mediterranean world from Jerusalem.

In time Paul arrived in Corinth on his third visit, probably in the winter of A.D. 57–58, "where he stayed for three months" (Acts 20:3), during which time he wrote his Letter to the Romans (in either Corinth or its port, Cenchreae). Certain elements in 1 Corinthians show that this letter is temporally related to the Letter to the Romans. Following Conzelmann (1 Cor, 5), one can compare 1 Cor 1:18–20 with Rom 1:16–21; 1 Cor 8–10 with Rom 14:1–15:6; 1 Cor 12 with Rom 12:3–8; 1 Cor 15:19, 44–49 with Rom 5:12–14. These elements are treated in 1 Corinthians in a more practical way, whereas the treatment in Romans is more theoretical and thematic. (See also Richards ["Romans and I Corinthians"] who seeks to invert the chronological order of the two letters and establish the priority of Romans, which is hardly likely.)

In the spring of A.D. 58, Paul traveled back to Jerusalem with the collection taken up in the churches of Galatia, Macedonia, and Achaia for the poor among God's dedicated people there (1 Cor 16:3–4). That was the last stage of his evangelization of the eastern Mediterranean world, and his thoughts and plans turned thereafter to Rome and Spain in the west.

That, however, may not have been the end of Paul's dealings with Corinth and its Christian community, because two further ancient writings tell us of further correspondence between him and the Christians of that city. These writings are not part of the NT canon but are among the apocryphal writings related to it. Moreover, it is not easy to say how authentic they are or how trustworthy the information contained in them really is.

One is a letter sent by Stephanas (probably the same individual as in 1 Cor 1:16; 16:15, 17) and four presbyters of the Corinthian church to Paul with questions about further problems that have arisen since his last visit there, and the other is usually called "Third Corinthians," which gives Paul's reply to the letter from Stephanas and the presbyters of Corinth and its problems. The two writings are often considered part of the Acts of Paul, an ancient writing that Tertullian (A.D. 160–225) considered to be a forgery foisted on Paul by "a presbyter in Asia" (De Baptismo 17.5; CCLat 1.291–92). The two writings have also been transmitted to us independently of the Acts of Paul; they seem to have been originally separate compositions only subsequently made part of the Acts of Paul.

The apocryphal correspondence of the Corinthians and Paul has been transmitted in various ancient writings: (a) as part of the NT in eleven MSS of the Armenian Bible; (b) in five independent Latin MSS; (c) in Ephrem's Syriac commentary on Paul's epistles; (d) in a Coptic translation of the *Acts of Paul* (Papyrus Heidelberg 1); and (e) in the Greek Papyrus Bodmer X (of the third century A.D.). For details, see Klijn, "Apocryphal Correspondence," 2–4; Schneemelcher, *NTApocr*, 2:217, 254–56; V. Hovhanessian, *Third Corinthians*.

The letter sent to Paul by Stephanas and the four presbyters of the Corinthian church informs him about the problems caused by two men, Simon and Cleobius, who have come to Corinth and have been spreading troublesome teaching about various topics: (a) one should not pay attention to the [OT] prophets; (b) God is not almighty; (c) there is no resurrection of the flesh; (d) creation of mankind is not (the work) of God; (e) the Lord Jesus did not come in the flesh and was not born of Mary; (f) the world is not (the work) of God, but of angels. Hence Paul must come to Corinth, so that the church may remain without scandal and the folly of these two men may be laid bare.

In *3 Corinthians*, the imprisoned Paul recognizes such teaching as the work of "the Evil One" and assures the Corinthians that the Lord Jesus Christ will come soon. He then recalls how he preached to them what he had received from those who were apostles before him: that the Lord was born of Mary of the line of David, when God sent his Spirit into her; that the Lord came into this world to redeem all flesh by his own flesh; that he might raise human mortals from the dead by being himself the type [of the resurrection]; that since humanity had been created by the Father, it was sought out when it went astray that it might be made alive again in adoptive sonship; that the God of all things, the Almighty One, the maker of heaven and earth, first sent prophets to the Jews that they might be drawn away from their sins, for he had determined to save the house of Israel and had apportioned to it some of the Spirit of Christ.

So Paul sought to offset the false teachings of Simon and Cleobius among the Corinthians. For the rest of *3 Corinthians*, see *NTApocr*, 2:255–56. The next correspondence with the Corinthian church comes from Clement of Rome among the writings of the Apostolic Fathers, *First Epistle of Clement to the Corinthians*, written ca. A.D. 75–110. At times it refers to Paul's first canonical letter (e.g., 47.1–4).

BIBLIOGRAPHY

Barclay, J. M. G., "Thessalonica and Corinth: Social Contrasts in Pauline Christianity," *JSNT* 47 (1992) 49–74.

Benko, S., "The Edict of Claudius of A.D. 49 and the Instigator Chrestus," *TZ* 25 (1969) 406–18.

Boese, H., "Über eine bisher unbekannte Handschrift des Briefwechsels zwischen Paulus und den Korinthern," *ZNW* 44 (1952–53) 66–76.

Borse, U., "Tränenbrief und 1. Korintherbrief," *SNTU* A9 (1984) 175–202.

Bourguet, E., *De rebus delphicis imperatoriae aetatis capita duo* (Montpellier: C. Coulet et Fils, 1905).

Brassac, A. "Une inscription de Delphes et la chronologie de saint Paul," *RB* 10 (1913) 36–53, 207–17.

Bratke, E., "Ein zweiter lateinischen Text des apokryphen Briefwechsel zwischen dem Apostel Paulus und den Korinthern," *TLZ* 17 (1892) 585–88.

Bruyne, D. de, "Un nouveau manuscrit de la troisième lettre de Saint Paul aux Corinthiens," *RevBén* 25 (1908) 431–34; see also *RevBén* 45 (1933) 189–95.

Burgos Nuñez, M. de, "La correspondencia de Pablo con las comunidades de Corinto," *Communio* 26 (1993) 33–67.

Carrière, A., and S. Berger, "La correspondance apocryphe de Saint Paul et des Corinthiens: Ancienne version latine du texte arménien," *RTP* 24 (1891) 333–51.

Charlesworth, M. P., *Documents Illustrating the Reigns of Claudius and Nero* (Cambridge: Cambridge University, 1951).

Cousin, G., and G. Deschamps, "Emplacements et ruines de la ville de KYC en Carie," *BCH* 11 (1887) 305–11.

D'Anna, A., "La pseudepigrafa *Corrispondenza tra Paolo e i Corinzi*: Il suo contesto e la sua funzione nella costruzione di un'identità dottrinale cristiana," *AnnStorEseg* 20/1 (2003) 111–37.

Deissmann, A., *Paul: A Study in Social and Religious History* (New York: Harper, 1957).

Elliger, W., *Paulus in Griechenland: Philippi, Thessaloniki, Athen, Korinth* (SBS 92–93; Stuttgart: Katholisches Bibelwerk, 1978) 200–51.

Finegan, J., *Handbook of Biblical Chronology* (Princeton: Princeton University, 1964).

Gilchrist, J. M., "Paul and the Corinthians—The Sequence of Letters and Visits," *JSNT* 34 (1988) 47–69.

Harnack, A., *Die apokryphen Briefe des Paulus an die Laodicener und Korinther* (KlT 12; Bonn: Marcus und Weber, 1905; 2d ed., 1931) 6–23.

Hemer, C. J., *The Book of Acts in the Setting of Hellenistic History* (Winona Lake, IN: Eisenbrauns, 1990).

Hengel, M., *Acts and the History of Earliest Christianity* (London: SCM, 1979; Philadelphia, PA: Fortress, 1980).

Hovhanessian, V., *Third Corinthians: Reclaiming Paul for Christian Orthodoxy* (StudBibLit 18; Frankfurt am M./New York: Peter Lang, 2000).

Howard, G., "The Beginnings of Christianity in Rome: A Note on Suetonius, Life of Claudius xxv. 4," *ResQ* 24 (1981) 175–77.

Jewett, R., *A Chronology of Paul's Life* (Philadelphia: Fortress, 1979).

Klijn, A. F. J., "The Apocryphal Correspondence between Paul and the Corinthians," *VC* 17 (1963) 2–23.

Lüdemann, G., *Early Christianity according to the Traditions in Acts: A Commentary* (London: SCM; Minneapolis: Fortress, 1989).

———, *Paul, Apostle to the Gentiles: Studies in Chronology* (Philadelphia: Fortress, 1984).

Manson, T. W., "St. Paul in Ephesus: (3) The Corinthian Correspondence," *BJRL* 26 (1941–42) 101–20.

Momigliano, A., *Claudius: The Emperor and His Achievement* (New York: Barnes & Noble, 1961).

Murphy-O'Connor, J., "Paul and Gallio," *JBL* 112 (1993) 315–17.

Oliver, J. H., "The Epistle of Claudius Which Mentions the Proconsul Junius Gallio," *Hesperia* 40 (1970) 239–40.

Peterlin, D., "The Corinthian Church between Paul's and Clement's Time," *AsTJ* 53 (1998) 49–57.

Piganiol, A., *Histoire de Rome* (Clio; Paris: Presses Universitaires de France, 1949).

Plassart, A., "L'Inscription de Delphes mentionnant le proconsul Gallion (Act 18:12–17)," *REG* 80 (1967) 372–78.

——, *Les inscriptions du temple du iv siècle* (Ecole Française d'Athènes, Fouilles de Delphes III/4; Paris: Boccard, 1970) 26–32 §286.

Richards, J. R., "Romans and I Corinthians: Their Chronological Relationship and Comparative Dates," *NTS* 13 (1966–67) 14–30.

Scramuzza, V. M., *The Emperor Claudius* (Cambridge: Harvard University Press, 1940).

Slingerland, D., "Acts 18:1–18, the Gallio Inscription, and Absolute Pauline Chronology," *JBL* 110 (1991) 439–49.

——, "Suetonius *Claudius* 25.4, Acts 18, and Paulus Orosius' *Historiarum adversum paganos libri VII*: Dating the Claudian Expulsion(s) of Roman Jews," *JQR* 83 (1992–93) 127–44.

——, "Suetonius *Claudius* 25.4 and the Account in Cassius Dio," *JQR* 79 (1988–89) 305–22.

Smallwood, E. M., *The Jews under Roman Rule* (SJLA 20; Leiden: Brill, 1976).

Tajra, H. W., *The Trial of St. Paul* (WUNT 2/35; Tübingen: Mohr [Siebeck], 1989).

Testuz, M., "La correspondance apocryphe de Saint Paul et des Corinthiens," *Littérature et théologie pauliniennes* (RechBib 5; ed. A. Descamps; Bruges: Desclée de Brouwer, 1960) 217–23.

——, *Papyrus Bodmer X–XII, X: Correspondance apocryphe des Corinthiens et de l'apôtre Paul . . .* (Cologny-Geneva: Bibliotheca Bodmeriana, 1959) 30–45.

Winter, B. W., "Gallio's Ruling on the Legal Status of Early Christianity (Acts 18:14–15)," *TynBul* 50 (1999) 213–24.

IV. THE FIRST LETTER
TO THE CORINTHIANS

◆

The letter that is commonly called "First Corinthians" was written from Ephesus toward the end of Paul's three-year ministry there, either toward the end of A.D. 56 or, more likely, at the beginning of A.D. 57, before Pentecost (see 1 Cor 16:8, 19). (For an explanation of how this letter fits into the chronology of Paul's life and ministry that is being presupposed here, see *PAHT*, §P38–45.)

Echoes of 1 Corinthians are found elsewhere in the Pauline corpus, especially in the Deutero-Pauline and Pastoral letters: Col 2:5 seems to echo 1 Cor 5:3 (absent in body, but not in spirit); Eph 3:8 and 1 Cor 15:9–10 (God's grace given to the least of the saints); 1 Tim 1:20 and 1 Cor 5:5 (delivering someone to Satan); 1 Tim 2:11–12 and 1 Cor 14:34–35 (women silent in church).

Clement of Rome (fl. ca. A.D. 96), in a letter addressed to Corinthian Christians, not only quoted or alluded to passages in Paul's 1 Corinthians (*1 Clem.* 37.5; 49.5), but also ascribed this letter to "the blessed Paul, the Apostle" (47.1), alluding there to 1 Cor 1:10–12. He apparently knew of only this letter of Paul to the Corinthians.

Similar allusions to 1 Corinthians occur in the writings of Ignatius of Antioch (ca. 35–107) in *Eph.* 12.2 (echo of 1 Cor 1:2); 16.1 (1 Cor 6:9–10); 18.1 (1 Cor 1:18–23); *Rom.* 5.1 (1 Cor 4:4b); *Phld.* 3.3 (1 Cor 6:9–10); 4.1; *Trall.* 12.3 (1 Cor 9:27). Also in Polycarp, *Phil.* 11.2 (1 Cor 6:2); Pastor Hermae, *Mand.* 4.4.1–2 (1 Cor 7:39–40). Marcion (died ca. 160) admitted 1 Corinthians into his *Apostolus* (see Tertullian, *Adv. Marcionem* 3.5.4; CCLat 1.513 [alluding to 1 Cor 9:9]; cf. 3.5.6–10); and Irenaeus, bishop of Lyons (A.D. 140–200), often quoted it as a Pauline writing, as he argued against the Gnostics of his day (*Adv. Haer.* 5.6.1 [SC 153.72–74]; 5.11.1 [SC 153.136]). So for centuries thereafter the Pauline authorship of this letter has been acknowledged, and it is not seriously questioned today.

Some interpreters have regarded 1 Corinthians as a composite letter, made up of several Pauline writings. This view has been proposed because of the difference of topics treated in this long letter, its abrupt transitions, its mention of an earlier letter in 5:9, and certain tensions in the argumentation. For instance, Paul criticizes factions in chaps. 1–4, but then reckons with the inevitability of them (11:18–19). Paul promises to come quickly to Corinth in 4:19, after which further diverse topics are then discussed at some length; and in 16:5 he mentions a long journey through Macedonia that he has to make in coming to them. Moreover, in

5:1–13 and 6:12–20 he discusses various problems related to *porneia*, which is interrupted in 6:1–11 by the problem of petty lawsuits. Again, in 10:1–22 he forbids the partaking of cultic meals, whereas in 8:1–13 and 10:23–11:1 he prohibits the eating of food offered to idols only because of weak members of the Corinthian community. In 11:2–16 he discusses the head-covering of women in public prayer, but silence is demanded of them in 14:34–35. Paul speaks of reports (from Chloe's people, 1:11), things that he has "heard" (5:1; 11:18), the letter that he has received (7:1), and various new topics introduced by *peri de* (8:1; 12:1).

Because of such features in 1 Corinthians, some interpreters have concluded that Paul wrote distinct letters on the various topics, which were eventually gathered into the one letter called today "First Corinthians." Such a view (*Teilungshypothese*) was first proposed by Hagge in 1876; and ever since, others have tried to analyze the letter on this basis. Their analysis has resulted in theories about its composition from two letters (J. Weiss 1910, Héring 1949, Dinkler 1960); three letters (J. Weiss 1914, Schmithals 1956, Sellin 1987); four letters (Schenk 1969, Senft 1979); six letters (Jewett 1978); and nine letters (Schmithals 1973). Some of these proposals involve 2 Corinthians (or parts of it). Such an analysis of 1 Corinthians has yielded no certainty, and the very multiplicity and diversity of the theories about the composition are the best evidence of its improbability. The pros and cons of the *Teilungshypothese* have been well discussed by Merklein ("Die Einheitlichkeit"), who opts for its integrity.

Many other interpreters have insisted on 1 Corinthians as a unified letter: Barrett, Belleville, Bruce, Collins, Conzelmann, Fee, Garland, Hurd, Kümmel, Marxsen, Mitchell, Murphy-O'Connor. This would not necessarily mean that Paul wrote it all at one time, in a single draft, because he may have composed it in stages as he reacted to reports brought to him about the Corinthian community (1:11), the letter sent to him (7:1), or questions asked of him by messengers (16:16–17). This is the reasonable explanation given by de Boer, who argues plausibly that Paul had written chaps. 1–4 as an answer to the reports from Chloe's people, and then added chaps. 5–16 after the arrival of Stephanas and the others (16:17) together with the letter mentioned in 7:1. He thinks, then, that 1 Corinthians is "in a qualified sense a composite of two letters, *a composite of Paul's own making*" ("Composition," 230–31 [his emphasis]). Moreover, as Murphy-O'Connor, following Fee, has remarked, "all the so-called internal contradictions in 1 Corinthians can be resolved by a more exacting exegesis" (*Paul, a Critical Life*, 254).

An opposite extreme position has been adopted by Goulder who insists on "the unity of the Corinthian correspondence," meaning that in both 1 and 2 Corinthians Paul is arguing against "a single opposition behind both letters," viz., "Jewish Christian enthusiasts who spoke of themselves as 'of Cephas,' and whom I shall call 'Petrines' " ("Unity," 221). His arguments, presented under seven headings, however, are derived largely from 1 Corinthians, and the evidence from 2 Corinthians to support most of them is tenuous and far from convincing.

Some commentators, even some who admit that 1 Corinthians is a unified writing, think, however, that a few passages have been interpolated, viz., 1:2c;

14:33b–36; and chap. 13. In 1:2c, one finds the phrase, "together with all those who in every place call upon the name of our Lord Jesus Christ, their Lord and ours." This is considered a catholicizing interpolation because it ill-suits this letter, which otherwise is pointed so concretely at the Corinthians that it could not have been intended for all Christians (so J. Weiss, Dinkler, Schmithals [*Gnosticism*, 89 n. 13]). Yet, as it has often been noted, Paul may be borrowing here a liturgical formula that merely fills out the greeting he is sending to the Corinthians.

Again, when Paul says that "women should remain silent in the churches, . . ." in 14:34–36, those words are seen as problematic when they are compared with 11:5, "every woman who prays or prophesies . . . ," or with 11:13, "Is it proper for a woman to pray to God with uncovered head?" Moreover, 14:33 leads smoothly into 14:37, so that the intervening verses seem to be difficult to explain in such a context. Hence, it is argued that vv. 34–36 have been interpolated and were not really written by Paul. However, those verses are found in all the Greek MSS of 1 Corinthians, even in the few Western MSS that transpose vv. 34–35 to follow v. 40 (D, F, G, 88*). Although no one has yet been able to explain convincingly why vv. 34–35 appear where they do, the explanation that they have been interpolated is highly improbable.

As for chap. 13, the so-called hymn to love, which is said to disturb the sequence of chaps. 12 and 14, there is little reason to regard it as an interpolation, given the mention of wisdom, knowledge, and faith in 13:2, which alludes to 12:8–9. See further the COMMENT on chap. 13.

In sum, then, one has to consider that such passages as these, with their abrupt transitions and tensions, may owe more to their being dictated by Paul to a scribal secretary, possibly at various times, than we realize today. In 16:21, Paul says that he writes the closing greeting in his "own hand," which seems to imply that he has been dictating the letter to a scribe.

The thesis of Hurd in *The Origin of I Corinthians* is another matter. Although he insists on the unity and integrity of 1 Corinthians (see "Good News"), he explains it as a product of Paul's developing relations with the Corinthians. The first stage was constituted by what Paul had preached to the Corinthians early in his ministry. On sexual morality, he would have taught them that it was good for a man not to touch a woman, thus encouraging intramarital asceticism, "spiritual" marriage, and celibacy (remaining unmarried on principle). On life in the world, he would have advocated that all things were permissible, that an idol was nothing, and that one could eat meat from public markets. On worship, he would have tolerated unveiled women in liturgical gatherings and would have spoken in tongues more than others. On eschatology, he would have believed that the end was near at hand, that all would soon enter the kingdom, and that the Lord's Supper would preserve all until then. The second stage developed when he wrote a letter that preceded 1 Corinthians, mentioned in 5:9, in which he sought to enforce the so-called Apostolic Decree (Acts 15:20, 29), with its prohibition of *porneia* and *eidōlothyta*. Now he would have commended marriage as a remedy for fornication, rejected all association with *pornoi*, forbidden the eating of idol-meat (and blood?), sought to keep the liturgy free from pagan contamination (unveiled women, speaking in tongues), taught the resurrection of the dead at the Parousia, and recommended a collection for the poor of Jerusalem. The third stage was the reply that Corinthian Christians sent him, both by a letter (1 Cor 7:1) and messengers (1 Cor 1:11; 16:15, 17), in effect, asking him where he stood: do we marry or not? do we eat idol meat? do we veil women in liturgical gatherings? how do the dead rise again? The fourth stage was the writing of 1 Corinthians, in which Paul synthesizes and adjusts his teaching on various points (marriage in chap. 7, idols in 8:1–11:1, liturgy in chap. 11, spiritual gifts in chaps. 12–14, resurrection in chap. 15, and the collection in chap. 16).

Although this analysis of the origin of 1 Corinthians is ingenious, it encounters certain major difficulties. First, nowhere in 1 Corinthians or in any other Pauline letter is any mention of, or allusion to, the so-called Apostolic Decree ever found. Second, even in the Lucan story Paul learns about that Jerusalem decision when he returns to the city at the end of his third missionary journey (Acts 21:25), when he goes up to greet James and the presbyters of that church (21:18). Third, in Gal 2:1–10, where Paul refers to the decision made at the Jerusalem "Council," he maintains that Gentile Christians do not have to be circumcised or have to observe the Mosaic law (as it is recorded in the narrative of Acts 15:1–12). Nothing is said in Galatians about the four topics treated in the Jerusalem Decree (Acts 15:20, 29). Indeed, how would the Antioch Incident (Gal 2:11–14) have occurred, if that decree were a decision of the Jerusalem "Council"? Nevertheless, Gal 2:10 does know about the advice "to remember the poor" (= the collection). Fourth, it is well recognized today by many commentators on Acts that chap. 15 is composite, with a record of two decisions made at Jerusalem: the "Council" decision not to impose circumcision and obligation to observe the Mosaic law on Gentile converts (15:3–12), and the decision made by James and the presbyters about the four topics that are to be observed by Gentile Christians living with Jewish Christians in local churches of Antioch, Syria, and Cilicia (15:13–29), usually misnamed "Apostolic Decree." Finally, many topics in 1 Corinthians have nothing to do with that Decree (e.g., women with head-coverings, resurrection of the dead). See further *Acts*, 544–54; Barclay, "Thessalonica and Corinth," 67 n. 32; Freeborn, "Development of Doctrine." So one has to reckon with the problems of 1 Corinthians without any reference to the so-called Apostolic Decree of Acts 15.

As for the occasion of the writing of 1 Corinthians, it is customary to consider the following five points:

1. Paul speaks in 1:10–12 about reports of "dissensions" (*schismata*) and "rivalries" (*erides*) brought to him by "some of Chloe's people."
2. Paul mentions "the matters about which" the Corinthians have written to him (7:1); although the letter is no longer extant, it is answered, beginning in chap. 7.
3. Paul mentions how glad he has been "at the arrival of Stephanas, Fortunatus, and Achaicus" (16:15–17), who by their presence have reminded him of the Corinthian community and "refreshed" his spirit. They may have brought reports about problems and scandals other than those brought to him by Chloe's people and the letter; see 3:4–5; 5:1; 6:1–11; 8:1; 11:18–19;

12:1. Some questions of the letter Paul introduces with *peri de*, each of which de la Serna ("Los orígenes") takes as a new topic mentioned in the letter, but Mitchell disputes this interpretation of the preposition.

4. Paul also knows somehow of the Corinthians' desire to have Apollos visit them again. He writes now to assure them that he has urged Apollos to come there "when he has the opportunity" (16:12).

5. Although Paul says in 4:21 that he will come to them "very soon," he eventually realizes that it may not be immediately, because he has to wait until Timothy, whom he is sending to them, comes back to him (16:10–11). These reasons are different in character, but taken together they reveal the occasion of Paul's writing this letter to Corinthian Christians.

The purpose of the letter is clearly to bring order and unity into the Corinthian community, about whose unhappy condition Paul has heard from the numerous reports mentioned above. He writes to the community as a whole as its founder (3:10): to stress the need for unity among them and to restore proper order (14:40). He castigates them for their arrogant attitude of freedom and tolerance of sexual immorality and petty litigation; and seeks to dispel all doubts about marriage, celibacy, and the eating of food offered to idols; and counsels them about wisdom, spiritual gifts, speaking in tongues, and about the place of Christian love in their lives. He wants to teach them to think rightly about the gifts of the Spirit, the Lord's Supper, their common meals, and the most important issue of all, the resurrection of the dead.

These matters are diverse, but Paul's intention in treating them is, above all, to reassert his apostolic authority (1:1) and to restore respect for the Christian gospel, which he, as the founder of the community, has already preached to them (15:1), as Fee (*1 Cor*, 6) has rightly recognized. Paul's initial preaching of that gospel in Roman Corinth resulted in his making a considerable number of converts there. When other preachers came, such as Apollos and perhaps Cephas, the original Corinthian Christians heard the same gospel preached in other forms, which seems to have distracted them gradually from the nucleus of the gospel message. So Paul is concerned to recall them to that fundamental message of the cross and of the risen Christ, and of the role of his Spirit in their lives.

Paul clearly is not engaging in a polemic against outsiders in this letter; he sees his adversaries as "some of you" (4:18; 15:12). He is not seeking to counter the influence of Judaizers, as some commentators have tried to maintain (T. W. Manson, Schoeps). That may have been the purpose of the letter to the Galatians, but there is no such attitude evident in this letter. Moreover (*pace* Schmithals, Jewett, Kümmel, Wilckens), Paul is not building up a "front against a Gnostic perversion of the Christian message" (Kümmel, *Introduction*, 274).

Moreover, Paul during the course of his discussion of the diverse problems is not addressing now one group, and now another. He is addressing the Corinthian community as a whole; and the second plural dominates throughout the letter. He recognizes, especially in chaps. 1–4, that there are diverse groups within the community, but his aim is to recall such groups to unity, and so he addresses them all equally and at the same time. They may be ethnic groups, socially stratified groups, people of diverse status (men, women, slaves, free, rich, poor); see Klauck, "Gemeindestrukturen." Those in the Corinthian community who have been reacting against him (4:18–19) have, in effect, not only been undermining his authority, but have been watering down the gospel that he has been preaching. Their secular Roman and Hellenistic background may be making them consider themselves to be "wise," but Paul seeks to counter that "wisdom of the world" with his "message of the cross" (1:18–20). The purpose of the letter is summed up in one verse: "We proclaim Christ crucified, a stumbling block to Jews and folly to Gentiles." (1:23).

BIBLIOGRAPHY

Belleville, L. L., "Continuity or Discontinuity: A Fresh Look at 1 Corinthians in the Light of First Century Epistolary Forms and Conventions," *EvQ* 59 (1987) 15–37.

Blevins, J. L., "Introduction to 1 Corinthians," *RevExp* 80 (1983) 315–24.

Boer, M. C. de, "The Composition of 1 Corinthians," *NTS* 40 (1994) 229–45.

Brown, R. E., *An Introduction to the New Testament* (ABRL; New York: Doubleday, 1997) 511–40.

Freeborn, J. C. K., "The Development of Doctrine at Corinth," *SE IV* (TU 102; Berlin: Akademie, 1968) 404–10.

Goulder, M., "The Unity of the Corinthian Correspondence," *JHC* 5 (1998) 220–37.

Hagge, H., "Die beiden überlieferten Sendschreiben des Apostels Paulus an die Gemeinde zu Korinth," *Jahrbücher für protestantische Theologie* 2 (1876) 481–531.

Hurd, J. C., Jr., "Good News and the Integrity of 1 Corinthians," *Gospel in Paul: Studies in Corinthians, Galatians and Romans for Richard N. Longenecker* (JSNTSup 108; ed. L. A. Jervis and P. Richardson; Sheffield: Sheffield Academic, 1994) 38–62.

Jewett, R., "The Redaction of I Corinthians and the Trajectory of the Pauline School," *JAAR* 46 (1978) 571 (Abstract of 44/4, Supp. B).

Klauck, H.-J., "Gemeindestrukturen im ersten Korintherbrief," *BK* 40 (1985) 9–15.

Kümmel, W. G., *Introduction to the New Testament: Revised Edition* (Nashville: Abingdon, 1975) 269–79.

Marxsen, W., *Introduction to the New Testament* (Philadelphia: Fortress, 1968).

Merklein, H., "Die Einheitlichkeit des ersten Korintherbriefes," *ZNW* 75 (1984) 153–83.

Mitchell, M. M., "Concerning *peri de* in 1 Corinthians," *NovT* 31 (1989) 229–56.

Morgan-Wynne, J., "Introduction to I Corinthians," *SwJT* 26/1 (1983) 4–15.

Murphy-O'Connor, J., *Paul, a Critical Life* (Oxford/New York: Oxford University, 1996).

Schenk, W., "Der 1. Korintherbrief als Briefsammlung," *ZNW* 60 (1969) 219–43.

Schmithals, W, "Die Korintherbriefe als Briefsammlung," *ZNW* 64 (1973) 263–88.

Sellin, G., "1 Korinther 5–6 und der 'Vorbrief' nach Korinth: Indizen für eine Mehrschichtigkeit von Kommunikationsakten im ersten Korintherbrief," *NTS* 37 (1991) 535–58.

Serna, E. de la, "Los orígenes de 1 Corintios," *Bib* 72 (1991) 192–216.

Stewart-Sykes, A., "Ancient Editors and Copyists and Modern Partition Theories: The Case of the Corinthian Correspondence," *JSNT* 61 (1996) 53–64.

Wikenhauser, A., and J. Schmid, *Einleitung in das Neue Testament* (6th ed.; Freiburg im B.: Herder, 1973) 420–32.

V. THE FORM OF
FIRST CORINTHIANS

◆

First Corinthians has to be understood as a "letter," and not as an "epistle," in the sense in which Deissmann proposed his often-used distinction. "A letter is something non-literary, a means of communication between persons who are separated from each other. Confidential and personal in nature, it is intended only for the person or persons to whom it is addressed, and not at all for the public or any kind of publicity" (*LAE*, 218). Its tone, style, and form can be intimate, free, or familiar as conversation itself. An epistle, however, is "an artistic literary form, just like the dialogue, the oration, or the drama. It has nothing in common with the letter except its form: apart from that one might venture the paradox that the epistle is the opposite of a real letter. The contents of an epistle are intended for publicity—they aim at interesting 'the public' " (ibid., 220; cf. *Bible Studies*, 9–10).

Although the Pauline writings form a corpus today, which have often been given the title "epistles," it is far from certain that they were originally intended as such by their author; this title for Romans and 1 Corinthians has often been queried, and especially for the latter. Moreover, Deissmann's distinction has in recent times been considered too rigid (see Doty, *Letters*, 4–8; Rahn, *Morphologie*, 157–59; Fitzmyer, *Romans*, 68–69). In the case of 1 Corinthians, though as a whole it is a letter, it has passages that transcend the immediate preoccupying problems for which it has been written, e.g., the so-called hymn to love (13:1–13), and the instruction about the kerygma, gospel, and resurrection of the dead (15:1–58). Such passages would relate it more to the form of an epistle, but, important as they are, they do not overshadow the multiple other topics of *ad hoc* character that make this missive a letter.

Moreover, 1 Corinthians is a substitute for Paul's personal presence at the church in Roman Corinth, even though he envisages a future visit to it. Like many other ancient Greek letters in Hellenistic times, the letter expresses Paul's *parousia* ("presence" [see Koskenniemi, *Studien*, 38–42]), even though he himself is physically absent. Indeed, in 5:3 Paul will call attention explicitly to this difference. In expressing his epistolary presence in this way, Paul is engaging in "the other half of a dialogue," as the ancient grammarian Artemon, quoted by Demetrius, once described such letter-writing (*On Style* 223). The letter is, then, an authoritative means by which Paul communicates with the Christian community that he has founded, giving his apostolic reactions to multiple reports and information about the situation in that church. Paul is writing as an individual, despite the mention of a co-sender, "brother Sosthenes" (1:1). He addresses members of the Corinthian church and writes more as an apostle and its founder.

It is not easy to specify the literary form of 1 Corinthians because of the length of the letter and multiplicity of topics discussed in it. Lührmann believes that it belongs to the ancient category of a friendship-letter because of its rhetorical buildup and despite its tensions. Because of 1:4 and the use of *parakalō*, "I appeal" (1:10; 4:16), the whole letter can be seen as *Paraklese*, "exhortation." There is certainly much exhortation coming from a friend, but that fails to account for some of the stern advice that occurs at times in it.

Betz and Mitchell have analyzed 1 Corinthians rather as a "deliberative letter," making use of well-known elements of ancient rhetoric to set forth its structure: Prescript (1:1–3); *Exordium* (Thanksgiving, 1:4–9); *Narratio* (Statement of Facts, 1:10–17, with the *prothesis* [proposition] in 1:10); *Probatio* (Proof, 1:18–15:57 [in four subsections: 1:18–4:21; 5:1–11:1; 11:2–14:40; 15:1–57]); *Peroratio* (Conclusion and Epistolary Ending, 15:58–16:24). Thus "the argument of the entire letter . . . calls on the Corinthians to end their factions and be reconciled with one another" ("Corinthians," 1143). That is indeed the burden of chaps. 1–4, but it is an oversimplification of the argument of "the entire letter," and sections in the *probatio*, with their multiple and diverse topics, scarcely function as a proof of the alleged *narratio*. In an effort to show the rhetoric of the letter, a procrustean bed has been made. As the outline of 1 Corinthians given below makes clear, certain details in it relate this writing to the ancient Greek letter-form: its opening prescript, thanksgiving, concluding exhortation, greetings, and farewell. In between, the structure is free, or what K. Barth called "the haphazard character of the series of subjects dealt with in 1 Cor. i–xiv," for the topics discussed do not have a perceptible logical order—or even a rhetorical order, despite the contention of Collins (*1 Cor*, 29–30), who also has outlined the letter according to six rhetorical demonstrations, which stress the alleged oratorical aspect, but leave the reader in the dark about their content. That Paul makes use at times of rhetoric in his argumentation no one will deny (see Smit, "Epideictic Rhetoric"). That this letter as a whole, however, follows a deliberate rhetorical pattern is highly questionable. The order of topics is dictated almost certainly by the sequence of topics that have come to Paul's attention in the reports about the scandals in the Corinthian community and by the questions sent to him in its letter (7:1).

In taking up each topic, Paul is concerned to relate it to the Christian faith of the Corinthians, especially to the way that faith should be working itself out in love, i.e., in their charitable dealings with one another in the Christian *ekklēsia*, "church," of which they are all part. This is why he so often and so variedly recalls their fundamental status "in Christ (Jesus)" (e.g., 1:30; 3:1, 23; 4:10, 17; 6:11, 15; 12:27). In spite of this unstructured order of topics, Paul's teaching and exhortation are perceived quite clearly. In trying to determine the kind of letter that Paul is writing, one should recall 4:14, where Paul says, "I am writing this not to make you ashamed, but to admonish you as my beloved children" (*all' hōs tekna mou agapēta nouthetō[n]*). In using the verb *noutheteō*, Paul is putting his letter in the

ancient letter-type known as *typos nouthetikos,* an admonition intended to instill
proper action in the person(s) so counseled (see Collins, "Hellenistic Letter,"
47–48).

Yet what is striking about this admonitory letter is the absence of a clear-cut
hortatory section, separate from the doctrinal section, such as one finds in Rom
12:1–15:13 or Gal 5:1–6:10. In 1 Corinthians the teaching and the exhortation
are rather intermingled in the discussion of each topic. The imperative follows directly from the indicative, "become what you are," as Bultmann once put it (*TNT,*
1:332–33). "You are a Christian!" "Act like a Christian!"

One should note how frequently Paul quotes or alludes to sayings of Corinthians, about which he has learned from the oral reports or the letter sent to him,
in order to criticize them. Thus 6:12a, 13a; 8:1, 4, 5; 10:23; 15:12b; possibly 1:12;
7:1b; 8:8; 11:2 (see NOTES on these verses); and probably 14:34–35; cf. Omanson,
"Acknowledging." Such quotations or allusions reveal the source of the topic
under discussion, and undoubtedly its order in the discussion. In each case, "the
more Paul's position is attacked, the more firmly must he ground his statements"
(Conzelmann, *1 Cor,* 7).

1 Corinthians is unique in the Pauline corpus of the NT in the amount of allusions to the sayings of Jesus of Nazareth. The two most prominent are the prohibition of divorce passed on in 7:10–11 and the words of institution at the Last
Supper preserved in 11:23–25. Allusions to other sayings have been noted elsewhere (4:12; 9:14; 13:2), and interpreters have sought to relate some of these sayings to the source "Q" of the Synoptic Gospels (Robinson, "Basic Shifts," 82–86;
Balch, "Backgrounds," 352–58; Kuhn, "Der irdische Jesus," 311–16); but that attempt has not been wholly convincing (see Tuckett, "1 Corinthians and Q").

The structure of 1 Corinthians is relatively easy to analyze in its major parts, but
the subdivisions of those parts are analyzed in widely different ways by individual
interpreters. *Quot homines, tot sententiae,* as the Roman poet Terence once put it,
"As numerous are humans, so are opinions." As in other Pauline letters, one can
easily discern in 1 Corinthians its opening address or epistolary prescript (1:1–3),
its thanksgiving (1:4–9), its epistolary conclusion (16:13–24). In between, the
body of the letter has three major parts: a section in which Paul reacts to oral reports about scandals that have been plaguing the Corinthian church (1:10–6:20);
a second section in which he replies to queries sent to him in a letter or comments
on other reports about moral and liturgical problems (7:1–14:40); and a third section in which Paul instructs the Corinthians about the kerygma, the gospel, and
the resurrection of the dead (15:1–58).

The outline that follows will enable the reader who uses this commentary to see
the contents of 1 Corinthians as a whole in its five major sections (indicated by
capital roman numerals). The numbers on the left (1–44) indicate the pericopes
as they will be annotated in the commentary proper.

BIBLIOGRAPHY

Balch, D. L., "Backgrounds of I Cor. vii: Sayings of the Lord in Q; Moses as an Ascetic *theios anēr* in II Cor. iii," *NTS* 18 (1971–72) 351–64.

Betz, H. D., and M. M. Mitchell, "Corinthians, First Epistle to the," *ABD* 1:1139–48.

Collins, R. F., "Reflections on 1 Corinthians as a Hellenistic Letter," *The Corinthian Correspondence* (BETL 125; ed. R. Bieringer), 39–61.

Deissmann, G. A., *Bible Studies* (Edinburgh: Clark, 1909).

Doty, W. G., *Letters in Primitive Christianity* (Philadelphia: Fortress, 1973).

Koskenniemi, H., *Studien zur Idee und Phraseologie des griechischen Briefes bis 400 n. Chr.*

(Annales Academiae Scientiarum Fennicae B/102.2; Helsinki: Suomalaisen Tiede-akatemia, 1956).

Kuhn, H.-W., "Der irdische Jesus bei Paulus als traditionsgeschichtliches und theo-logisches Problem," *ZTK* 67 (1970) 295–320.

Lührmann, D., "Freundschaftsbrief trotz Spannungen: Zu Gattung und Aufbau des Ersten Korintherbriefs," *Studien zum Text und zur Ethik des Neuen Testaments: Festschrift . . . Heinrich Greeven* (BZNW 47; ed. W. Schrage; Berlin: de Gruyter, 1986) 298–314.

Moody, D., "The First Epistle of Paul to the Corinthians (A.D. 55)," *RevExp* 57 (1960) 450–53.

Omanson, R. L., "Acknowledging Paul's Quotations," *BT* 43 (1992) 201–13.

Rahn, H., *Morphologie der antiken Literatur: Eine Einführung* (Darmstadt: Wissen-schaftliche Buchgesellschaft, 1969).

Robinson, J. M., "Basic Shifts in German Theology," *Int* 16 (1962) 76–97.

——, and H. Koester, *Trajectories through Early Christianity* (Philadelphia: Fortress, 1971) 40–43.

Tuckett, C. M., "1 Corinthians and Q," *JBL* 102 (1983) 607–19.

VI. THE GREEK TEXT OF FIRST CORINTHIANS

◆

The Greek text of 1 Corinthians on which this translation and commentary have been based is that of E. Nestle and B. and K. Aland, *Novum Testamentum graece* (27th ed.; Stuttgart: Deutsche Bibelgesellschaft, 1993; hereafter N-A[27]). It is dominated by the Hesychian or Alexandrian text-tradition in the transmission of the Greek writings of the NT and represents the best available form of the text of 1 Corinthians. It is impossible in a commentary such as this to set forth in detail the reasons for preferring this form of the Greek text. A few details must be mentioned, however, so that the reader will know on what the decision has been made to follow this Greek form of 1 Corinthians, even though one may not comprehend all the intricacies of this abstruse, but necessary, aspect of NT scholarship.

The oldest copies of the Greek text of 1 Corinthians are found on papyrus manuscripts, either in the form of a codex or leaves of a codex. They are the following seven papyrus MSS:

Papyrus	Date	Name	Contents
1. P[11]	6th cent.	Ross. Nac. Bibl., Gr. 258A (St. Petersburg)	1:17–22; 2:9–12, 14; 3:1–3, 5–6; 4:3–5:5, 7–8; 6:5–9, 11–18; 7:3–6, 10–14
2. P[14]	6th cent.	St. Catherine Monastery, P. Sinai II, Harris 14 (Mt. Sinai)	1:25–27; 2:6–8; 3:8–10, 20
3. P[15]	3d cent.	Egyptian Museum, JE 47423; P. Oxy. 1008 (Cairo)	7:18–8:14
4. P[34]	7th cent.	Österr. Nat. Bibl. Pap. G. 39784 (Vienna)	16:4–7, 10
5. P[46]	ca. 200	Chester Beatty Libr., P. Chester Beatty II (Dublin); Univ. of Michigan, Inv. 6238 (Ann Arbor)	1:1–9:2; 9:4–14:14; 14:16–15:15; 15:17–16:22

Papyrus	Date	Name	Contents
6. P⁶¹	ca. 700	Pierpont Morgan Libr., P. Colt 5 (New York)	1:1–2, 4–6; 5:1–3, 5–6, 9–13
7. P⁶⁸	7th cent.(?)	Ross. Nac. Bibl., Gr. 258B (St. Petersburg)	4:12–17; 4:19–5:3

The most important parchment MSS of 1 Corinthians are those written in uncials or majuscules and dating from the third to the ninth centuries. These are the following 23 codices or leaves of codices:

Parchment Manuscript	Gregory Numbering	Date	Name	Contents
1. ℵ	01	4th cent.	Sinaiticus, Brit. Libr. Add. 43725 (London)	All of 1 Corinthians
2. A	02	5th cent.	Alexandrinus, Brit. Libr., Royal I D. VIII (London)	All
3. B	03	4th cent.	Vaticanus, Vatican Libr. Gr. 1209 (Rome)	All
4. C	04	5th cent.	Ephraemi Rescriptus, Bibl. Nat., Gr. 9 (Paris)	All, exc. 1:1–2; 7:18–9:6; 13:8–15:40
5. Dᴾ	06	6th cent.	Claromontanus, Bibl. Nat., Gr. 107, 107AB (Paris)	All, exc. 14:13–22
6. F	010	9th cent.	Augiensis, Trinity Coll. Libr., BXVII.1 (Cambridge, UK)	All, exc. 3:8–15; 6:7–14
7. Gᴾ	012	9th cent.	Boernerianus, Sächische Landesbibl. A 145B (Dresden)	All, exc. 3:8–15; 6:7–14
8. H	015	6th cent.	Great Lavra s. n. (Mt. Athos); Centr. Naučn. Bibl. F. 301 (Kiev)	10:22–29; 11:9–16
9. I	016	5th cent.	Freer Gallery of Art, 06.275 (Washington)	10:29; 11:9–10, 18–19, 26–27; 12:3–4, 14, 27–28; 14:12–13, 22, 32–33; 15:3, 15, 27–28, 38–39, 49–50; 16:1–2, 12–13
10. K	018	9th cent.	Hist. Mus. V. 93, S. 97 (Moscow)	All, exc. 1:1–6, 13; 8:8–11

Parchment Manuscript	Gregory Numbering	Date	Name	Contents
11. L	020	9th cent.	Bibl. Angelica 39 (Rome)	All
12. P	025	9th cent.	Ross. Nac. Bibl., Gr. 225 (St. Petersburg)	All, exc. 7:15–17; 12:23–13:5; 14:23–39
13. Ψ	044	8th/9th cent.	Lavra, B' 52 (Mt. Athos)	All
14.	048	5th cent.	Vatican Libr., Gr. 2061 (Rome)	2:1–3:11, 22; 4:4–6; 5:5–11; 6:3–11; 12:23–15:17, 20–27
15.	088	5th/6th cent.	Ross. Nac. Bibl., Gr. 6, II, fol. 5–6 (St. Petersburg)	15:53–16:9
16.	0185	4th cent.	Österr. Nat. Bibl., Pap. G. 39787 (Vienna)	2:5–6, 9, 13; 3:2–3
17.	0199	6th/7th cent.	Brit. Libr., Pap. 2077B (London)	11:17–19, 22–24
18.	0201	5th cent.	Brit. Libr., Pap. 2240 (London)	12:2–3, 6–13; 14:20–29
19.	0222	6th cent.	Österr. Nat. Bibl., Pap. G. 29299 (Vienna)	9:5–7, 10, 12–13
20.	0270	4th/5th cent.	Univ. Bibl. GX 200 (Amsterdam)	15:10–15, 19–25
21.	0278	9th cent.	St. Catherine Mon., N.E.MΓ 2 (Mt. Sinai)	7:37–40; 8:1–6
22.	0285 cum 081	6th cent.	St. Catherine Mon., N.E.MΓ 70 (Mt. Sinai); Ross. Nac. Bibl., Gr. 9 (St. Petersburg)	4:2–7; 12:16, 18, 21–30; 14:26–33
23.	0289	7th/8th cent.	St. Catherine Mon., N.E.MΓ 99 (Mt. Sinai)	2:11–4:12; 13:13–14:1, 3–11, 13–19

There are also many parchment MSS written in minuscules that have the Greek text of Corinthians, which cannot be recorded here. The two most important of them are (in the Gregory numbering) the 9th century MS 33 (Athos, Lavra B' 64, called "the Queen of the Minuscules") and the 10th century MS 1739 (Paris, Bibl. Nat., Gr. 14).

It is remarkable how uniformly the Greek text of 1 Corinthians as a whole has been transmitted in the various text-traditions. It is found in the usual threefold text-traditions of the Pauline corpus: (a) the Alexandrian or Hesychian, which is represented mainly by P^{46} (sometimes called a Free Text), P^{11}, ℵ, B, C, and minuscules 33, 1739; (b) the Western, in D, F, G, and VL and various patristic writers; and (c) the Byzantine or *Koine*, e.g., in L, 049.

BIBLIOGRAPHY

Aland, K., *Kurzgefasste Liste der griechischen Handschriften des Neuen Testaments*, Vol. 1: *Gesamtübersicht* (ANTF 1; Berlin/New York: de Gruyter, 1963) 29–33, 37–57.

——, "Die Entstehung des Corpus Paulinum," *Neutestamentliche Entwürfe* (Theologische Bücherei 63; Munich: Kaiser, 1979) 302–50.

——, *Studien zur Überlieferung des Neuen Testaments und seines Textes* (ANTF 2; Berlin/New York: de Gruyter, 1967) 91–154.

——, and B. Aland, *The Text of the New Testament: An Introduction to the Critical Editions and to the Theory and Practice of Modern Textual Criticism* (Leiden: Brill; Grand Rapids: Eerdmans, 1987).

——, A. Beduhn-Mertz, and G. Mink (eds.), *Text und Textwert der griechischen Handschriften des Neuen Testaments*, Vol. 2: *Die paulinischen Briefe: 1. Allgemeines, Römerbrief und Ergänzungsliste* (Berlin/New York: de Gruyter, 1991).

Benoit, P., "Le Codex paulinien Chester Beatty," *RB* 46 (1937) 58–82.

Comfort, P. W., and D. P. Barrett, *The Complete Text of the Earliest New Testament Manuscripts* Grand Rapids: Baker Books, 1999) 83–88, 240–72.

Hoskier, H. C., "A Study of the Chester-Beatty Codex of the Pauline Epistles," *JTS* 38 (1937) 148–63.

Junack, K., *Das Neue Testament auf Papyrus: II. Die paulinischen Briefe, Teil 1: Röm., 1. Kor., 2. Kor.* (ANTF 12; Berlin/New York: de Gruyter, 1989) 152–327.

Kenyon, F. C., *The Chester Beatty Biblical Papyri . . . , Fasciculus III Supplement Pauline Epistles* (London: E. Walker Ltd., 1937), pls. 38 v.–60 v.

Kim, Y. K., "Palaeographical Dating of P^{46} in the Later First Century," *Bib* 69 (1988) 248–57.

Metzger, B. M., *The Text of the New Testament: Its Transmission, Corruption, and Restoration* (3d ed.; New York/London: Oxford University Press, 1992).

——, *A Textual Commentary on the Greek New Testament* (2d ed.; Stuttgart: Deutsche Bibelgesellschaft, 1994) 478–504.

Sanders, H. A., *A Third-Century Papyrus Codex of the Epistles of Paul* (University of Michigan Studies, Humanistic Series 38; Ann Arbor: University of Michigan Press 1935) 74–75.

Vogels, H. J., "Der Codex Claromontanus der paulinischen Briefe," *Amicitiae corolla: A Volume of Essays Presented to James Rendel Harris . . .* (ed. H. G. Wood; London: University of London Press, 1933) 274–99.

Zuntz, G., *The Text of the Epistles: A Disquisition upon the Corpus Paulinum* (Schweich Lectures 1946; London: Oxford University Press, 1953).

VII. LANGUAGE AND STYLE

◆

Although Latin was spoken in Roman Corinth since 44 B.C., Greek was the language of the indigenous people, some of whom continued to live there, and of others who came to Corinth, as it began to thrive anew. Greek was also widely used in the eastern Mediterranean world under Roman domination, and even by the Romans themselves who dwelt there. It had become the lingua franca of that area, even in Asia Minor, Syria, and Palestine, taking the place of Aramaic, which had functioned as such since about the eighth or seventh century B.C. Greek supplanted Aramaic mainly as a result of the conquests of Alexander the Great (356–323) and the subsequent hellenization of that whole region. The Attic dialect that dominated the Golden Age of Greek literature (fifth–fourth centuries B.C.) was supplanted by a pan-Hellenic form of Greek known as *Koinē* ("common" [language]). It served as the lingua franca in the Hellenistic period after Alexander and perdured until the Byzantine era.

The Greek that Paul writes in 1 Corinthians is a good example of such *Koinē*. Although it is not as good as the Greek of Luke-Acts or of the Epistle to the Hebrews, it is still a good example of literary *Koinē*, and at times (e.g., in 1 Corinthians 13) is a very good instance of it. Paul's Greek is normally correct, even though it is punctuated at times by anacoluthon (syntactical inconsistency, e.g., 2:9; 7:37 [see BDF §468.3]; 9:15 [BDF §393.2]; 11:14 [BDF §466.1], 18 [BDF §447.4]; 12:28 [BDF §442.9]) or zeugma (use of a word to modify or govern two words in different senses, e.g., 3:2; 14:34 [created by copyists of some MSS; cf. BDF §479.2]). Both of these features may be owing to Paul's practice of dictating his letters to a scribe. This practice would account also for the ubiquitous conjunction *gar*, "for," found at the beginning of many sentences (e.g., 1:11, 17, 18, 19, 21, 26; 2:8, 10, 11, 14, 16); indeed, it is so common (106 occurrences in 1 Corinthians) that it becomes tiresome, and one cannot always translate it properly (BDF §452).

Paul's use of the Greek language reveals not only his good Hellenistic education and knowledge of the popular Greek philosophical thinking and rhetoric of the day, but also his Jewish training and background. Norden once claimed that Paul's style was "as a whole, unhellenic" (*Die antike Kunstprosa*, 499), as he alluded to Paul's Semitic background; but that was certainly an exaggeration, because his Greek prose is not saturated with Aramaisms or Semitisms, as are the

Gospels and Acts. It is noteworthy that, when M. Black published his book about Aramaic interference in NT Greek, he limited his discussion to the Gospels and Acts. Moreover, van Unnik's attempt to discover Aramaisms in Pauline writings really did not succeed. ("Aramaisms").

Paul's Greek, even in 1 Corinthians, is affected by that of the LXX, from which he draws his quotations of the OT (e.g., 1:19, 31; 2:9, 16; 3:19, 20; 5:13; 6:16; 9:9; 10:7, 26; 14:21, 25; 15:25, 27, 32, 45, 54, 55). His Septuagintisms can be seen in the following features, some of which also can be found at times in earlier classical Greek, but the frequency of these features in his writings leads one to think of Septuagintal influence.

1. The use of the article before a noun and again before its modifier: *ho logos ho tou staurou*, "the message of the cross" (1:18); *ho anēr ho apistos . . . hē gynē hē apistē*, "the unbelieving husband . . . the unbelieving wife" (7:14); *ho logos ho gegrammenos*, "the saying that stands written" (15:54); *to pneuma to ek theou*, "the Spirit from God" (2:12); *tas hodous mou tas en Christou [Iēsou]*, "my ways in Christ [Jesus]" (4:17); see also 2:11–12; 15:10 bis. This feature is known also from classical Greek: *to strateuma to tōn Athēnaiōn*, "the army of the Athenians" (Thucydides, *Hist.* 8.50). In the LXX, see Gen 9:24 (*ho huios autou ho neōteros*).

2. The use of the article with a substantivized neut. adj. instead of an abstract noun: *to mōron tou theou*, "God's foolishness" (1:25); *to hymōn autōn symphoron*, "your own good" (7:35); *to euschēmon kai euparedron*, "good order and devotion" (7:35); similarly 7:5. This usage is said not to appear in Greek papyrus texts, but does show up in Hellenistic writers like Josephus and Strabo, and rarely in classical Greek: *to koinon*, "the comonwealth" (Aristophanes, *Eccles.* 208).

3. The position of the verb at the head of a sentence or clause: *edēlōthē gar moi peri hymōn*, "for it has been reported to me about you" (1:11); *ou gar apesteilen me Christos baptizein*, "for Christ did not send me to baptize" (1:17); *tolma tis hymōn pragma echōn pros ton heteron krinesthai epi tōn adikōn kai ouchi tōn hagiōn*, "does anyone of you who has a case against another dare to take it to court before the ungodly instead of before God's dedicated people?" (6:1); *hēgiastai gar ho anēr ho apistos en tē gynaiki kai hēgiastai hē gynē hē apistos en tō adelphō*, "for the unbelieving husband has been made holy through his wife, and the unbelieving wife has been made holy through the brother" (7:14). Compare the LXX usage: *kai eplasen ho theos ton anthrōpon choun apo tēs gēs*, "and God formed man as dust from the earth" (Gen 2:7); *kai ephyteusen kyrios ho theos paradeison en Eden*, "and the Lord God planted a garden in Eden" (Gen 2:8). See BDF §472.

4. The use of *eis to* with the infin. to express purpose or result: *oikodomēthēsetai eis to ta eidōlothyta esthiein*, "be emboldened to eat meat sacrificed to idols" (8:10); *eis to mē katachrēsasthai tē exousia mou en tō euangeliō*, "so as not to make full use of my right in preaching the gospel" (9:18); *tauta de typoi hēmōn egenēthēsan eis to mē einai hēmas epithymētas kakōn*, "now in view of these things have become archetypes for us so that we may not crave for evil" (10:6); similarly 11:22, 33. See BDF §§402.2, 406.3. This feature is found at times in earlier Greek, e.g., *megiston agathon to peitharchein phainetai eis to kataprattein tagatha*, "obedience appears to be the greatest advantage for accomplishing ex-

cellent objects" (Xenophon, *Cyropaedia* 8.1.3; cf. Smyth, *Greek Grammar*, §2034); *to thysiastērion to chrysoun eis to thymian*, "the golden altar for burning incense" (LXX Exod 40:5); *tois de neois hypodeigma gennaion kataleloipōs eis to prothymōs kai gennaiōs hyper tōn semnōn kai hagiōn nomōn apeuthanatizein*, "having left for the youth a noble example to die willingly and nobly for the revered and holy laws" (2 Macc 6:28; see Beckwith, "Articular Infinitive," 162–66).

5. The use of *en tō* with the infin. in a temporal sense: *en tō phagein*, "as you eat" (lit., "in eating," 11:21). See BDF §404.1. This feature too is found in earlier Greek: *en tō phronein gar mēden hēdistos bios*, "for life is sweetest in being conscious of nothing" (Sophocles, *Ajax* 553).

When it comes to matters of Greek style or literary subforms, one has to note the use in this letter of a number of rhetorical devices, such as:

1. *Anaphora*, i.e., emphatic repetition: "not many of you . . . , not many . . . , not many . . ." (1:26); similarly 9:20; 12:4, 5, 6; 13:7; 14:15, 31; 15:10, 13–14.
2. *Antithesis*: "to those who are perishing, but to us who are being saved" (1:18); similarly, 1:22, 23, 25; 2:5, 13; 4:10, 19, 20, 21; 5:3, 8; 7:38; 9:25; 11:17; 13:11, 12; 14:2, 4, 20; 15:21, 22, 42, 44, 49, 51.
3. *Asyndeton*: "in an instant, in the twinkling of an eye, at the last trumpet" (15:52); similarly, 4:12–13; 12:28; 13:4–5, 13a; 14:26; 15:23.
4. *Chiasmus*, i.e., inversion of the order of syntactical elements in the second of two juxtaposed and syntactically parallel phrases or clauses: *ho gar en kyriō klētheis doulos, apeleutheros kyriou*, "for the one who was a slave when called by the Lord is the Lord's freedman" (7:22); similarly, 1:24–25; 4:10, 13; 6:13; 7:22; 13:2, 4; 14:22. See BDF §477.2; but also Jeremias, "Chiasmus."
5. *Homoioteleuton*, i.e., similar ending of words or phrases: *ean eipē ho pous . . . , ean eipē to ous*, "if the foot says . . . , if the ear says . . ." (12:15–16); similarly 3:15.
6. *Paronomasia*, i.e., play on similar-sounding words: *dei gar to phtharton touto endysasthai aphtharsian kai to thnēton touto endysasthai athanasian*, "for what is perishable must don imperishability, and what is mortal immortality" (15:53); similarly, 12:23, 26; 15:42–43, 54.
7. *Polysyndeton*, i.e., multiple conjunctions: "in weakness and in fear and in much trembling" (2:3); similarly, 4:11–12; 6:9; 15:29–30.
8. *Rhetorical Questions*: Paul's use of rhetorical questions is important in this letter, because they are often used to drive home a point in his admonitory argument, and sometimes they express his exasperation at the situation to which he refers. Thus 1:13; 9:1, 4–8, 9b–12; 10:16, 18b, 19, 22; 11:22; 12:29; 14:6–8, 23, 36; 15:29, 30, 32, 35. See BDF §496; Wuellner, "Paul as Pastor."
9. *Enthymeme*, i.e., a truncated syllogism in which one of the propositions or premises is understood but not stated: "If the world is to be judged by you,

are you unqualified for petty courts" (6:2); similarly 6:1, 3,:15; see Holloway, "Enthymeme."

10. *Diatribē*, i.e., a dialogical form of argumentation developed by certain teachers such as Bion the Borysthenite (ca. 325–255 B.C.), Teles (fl. ca. 235 B.C.), Dio Chrysostom of Prusa (A.D. 40–112[?]), Musonius Rufus (ca. A.D. 30–102), and Epictetus of Hierapolis (A.D. 55–135) and used in the Cynic and Stoic schools of philosophy. It was a pedagogical discourse conducted in lively debate and familiar conversational style with an interlocutor, real or imaginary, which was peppered with apostrophes, proverbs, rhetorical questions, paradoxes, parodies, antitheses, and fictitious speech. This subform was used by Paul in the Letter to the Romans (1:18–2:11; 8:1–39; 11:1–24; cf. Stowers, *The Diatribe*). Elements of this style can be found in 1 Cor 4:6–15; 6:12–13; 7:16, 18–22; 9:1–18; 15:29–34, 35–49. The use of *mē genoito*, "of course not!" (6:15) is an example of this style, according to Malherbe; it occurs only once in this letter, but frequently in other Pauline writings (e.g., Rom 3:4, 6, 31; 6:2; Gal 2:17; 3:21). See Schmeller, *Paulus und die "Diatribe"*.

One has to note also the so-called hymn to love in 1 Corinthians 13, a composition that excels in its Greek rhetorical phraseology, even if its character as a "hymn" is seriously questioned today.

Note, too, Paul's use of supplication—a gentle urging expressed by using *parakalō*, "I appeal" (1:10; 4:16; 15:15–16)—a usage that appears much more frequently in other Pauline letters and is characteristic of official and private letters in the Hellenistic age (see Bjerklund, *Parakalō*; Turner, "Style," 83).

BIBLIOGRAPHY

Beckwith, I. T., "The Articular Infinitive with *eis*," *JBL* 15 (1896) 155–67.

Bjerkelund, C. J., *Parakalō: Form, Funktion und Sinn der parakalō-Sätze in den paulinischen Briefen* (Bibliotheca theologica norvegica 1; Oslo: Universitetsforlaget, 1967).

Black, M., *An Aramaic Approach to the Gospels and Acts* (3d ed; Oxford: Clarendon, 1967).

Boyer, J. L., "Noun Clauses in the Greek New Testament: A Statistical Study," *GTJ* 10 (1989) 225–39.

Bultmann, R., *Der Stil der paulinischen Predigt und die kynisch-stoische Diatribe* (FRLANT 13; Göttingen: Vandenhoeck & Ruprecht, 1910; repr. with preface by H. Hübner, 1984).

Cignelli, L. and G. C. Bottini, "L'articolo nel greco biblico," *SBFLA* 41 (1991) 159–99.

Duncan, T. S., "The Style and Language of Saint Paul in His First Letter to the Corinthians," *BSac* 83 (1926) 129–43.

Eschlimann, J.-A., "La rédaction des épîtres pauliniennes d'après une comparaison avec les lettres profanes de son temps," *RB* 53 (1946) 185–96.

Harmsen, E., "Ueber *eis to* mit dem artikulierten Infinitiv in den Briefen an die Römer und Corinther," *ZWT* 17 (1974) 245–60.

Holloway, P. A., "The Enthymeme as an Element of Style in Paul," *JBL* 120 (2001) 329–39.

Jeremias, J., "Chiasmus in den Paulusbriefen," *ZNW* 49 (1958) 145–56; repr. in *Abba* (Göttingen: Vandenhoeck & Ruprecht, 1966) 276–90.

Konopásek, J., "Les 'questions rhétoriques' dans le Nouveau Testament," *RHPR* 12 (1932) 47–66, 141–61.

Lund, N. W., *Chiasmus in the New Testament: A Study in Formgeschichte* (Chapel Hill: University of North Carolina Press, 1942) 145–96 (but see Jeremias, "Chiasmus," 145).

Malherbe, A. J., "*Mē genoito* in the Diatribe and Paul," *HTR* 73 (1980) 231–40.

Moulton, J. H. and W. F. Howard, *A Grammar of New Testament Greek* (4 vols.; Edinburgh: Clark, 1949–76).

Norden, E., *Die antike Kunstprosa vom VI. Jahrhundert v. Chr. bis in die Zeit der Renaissance* (2 vols.; Leipzig: Teubner, 1989; repr. Darmstadt: Wissenschaftliche Buchgesellschaft, 1958; Stuttgart: Teubner, 1983).

Schmeller, T., *Paulus und die "Diatribe": Eine vergleichende Stilinterpretation* (NTAbh n.s. 19; Münster in W.: Aschendorff, 1987).

Smyth, H. W., *Greek Grammar* (Cambridge: Harvard University Press, 1956).

Stowers, S. K., *The Diatribe and Paul's Letter to the Romans* (SBLDS 57; Chico, CA: Scholars Press, 1981).

Thomson, I. H., *Chiasmus in the Pauline Letters* (JSNTSup 111; Sheffield: Sheffield Academic Press, 1995) No examples from 1 Corinthians.

Thrall, M. E., *Greek Particles in the New Testament: Linguistic and Exegetical Studies* (NTTS 3; Leiden: Brill, 1962).

Turner, N., "The Style of Paul," in J. H. Moulton and W. F. Howard, *A Grammar of New Testament Greek* (4 vols.; Edinburgh: Clark, 1949–76), 4:80–100.

Unnik, W. C. van, "Aramaisms in Paul," *Sparsa collecta: The Collected Essays of W. C. van Unnik, Part I: Evangelia Paulina Acta* (NovTSup 29; Leiden: Brill, 1973) 129–43.

Williams, D. J., *Paul's Metaphors: Their Context and Character* (Peabody, MA: Hendrickson, 1999).

Wuellner, W., "Paul as Pastor: The Function of Rhetorical Questions in First Corinthians," *L'Apôtre Paul: Personnalité, style et conception du ministère* (BETL 73; ed. A. Vanhoye; Louvain: Leuven University/Peeters, 1986) 49–77.

Zedda, S., "L'uso di *gar* in alcuni testi di San Paolo," *SPCIC*, 2:445–51.

VIII. PAULINE TEACHING IN FIRST CORINTHIANS

◆

By "Pauline teaching" is meant an attempt to synthesize the reflections on the gospel that the apostle preached to ancient Corinthians as he tried to cope with various problems that had arisen in the Christian community in Roman Corinth since the time of his first evangelization of that town. Such reflections are scattered throughout the letter, because Paul writes as an apostle with a practical, missionary outlook. He has not written a systematic treatise on the topics that he has addressed. In his presentation of the teaching of this letter, Furnish wisely speaks of "Paul's theological reflection" on the gospel, which entails his exposition of Scripture (various OT passages quoted or alluded to), church traditions, and his own apostolic vocation and experience (*Theology*, 1, 18–25). This means that one is reading a synthetic organization of Paul's reflections that strives to paint a comprehensive picture of his teaching as a whole and prescinds from the concrete ways in which Paul himself has formulated matters.

The teaching found in Paul's first letter to the Corinthians is not as sublime or exalted as that in the letter to the Romans, and yet it is important. In fact, it contains significant topics that the letter to the Romans does not treat at all, or perhaps only fleetingly, e.g., ecclesiology, eucharist, eschatology. In 1 Corinthians, however, one finds little on justification or other effects of the Christ-event, which are treated at some length in the letter to the Romans. The main reason for the difference is the diversity of problems that Paul has to handle in this *ad hoc* letter, which is so diverse from the essay-letter that Romans is. If Romans is the most important letter in the Pauline corpus, 1 Corinthians is the second most important. For this reason it is necessary to concentrate on the theological teaching of 1 Corinthians in and for itself, with only minor comparisons with other Pauline writings, when they seem to be called for. Although 1 Corinthians is related to 2 Corinthians and at times shares with it some common topics, because of their common destination, it is necessary to treat the topics as they appear in the first letter.

Elsewhere I have discussed the key to Pauline theology and regard it as a Christological soteriology (*PAHT* §PT28). That formulation of the key is derived from a short passage in 1 Corinthians, which I believe sums up best the heart of the Apostle's theological teaching: "God was pleased to save those who believe through the folly of the proclamation (*kērygma*). Whereas Jews demand signs and

Greeks seek wisdom, we proclaim Christ crucified (*kēryssomen Christon es-taurōmenon*), a stumbling block to Jews and folly to Gentiles, but for those who are called, both Jews and Greeks, Christ is the power of God and the wisdom of God" (1 Cor 1:21–24). That proclamation is echoed in Rom 1:16, when Paul speaks of "the gospel" (*euangelion*) as "God's power (unleashed) for the salvation of everyone who believes, for the Jew first but also for the Greek." This is "the message of the cross" (1 Cor 1:18), and it puts Christ himself at the center of soteriology, God's new mode of salvation, and all else in Pauline teaching has to be understood in relation to it. That is why the sketch of Pauline teaching in this letter also has to take as its starting point that message of the cross, "we proclaim Christ crucified."

In that message, "Christ crucified" is the object of both *kērygma* and *euangelion* for Paul, because it encapsulates the content of all his preaching and teaching. Because of the *ad hoc* character of 1 Corinthians, which has already been emphasized in earlier introductory remarks, the succession of unrelated problems that Paul handles in this letter in response to reports about the Corinthian church (1:11), questions sent to him by Corinthian Christians (7:1), and other information about their conduct that he has acquired, his reactions and answers are always related to this basic *kērygma* and *euangelion*. For although Paul manifests himself as a conscious letter writer (16:21), he writes much more as the apostolic founder of the Corinthian church (1:1; 9:1–2; cf. 3:10; 4:15). He is concerned about its unity and solidarity and makes authoritative decisions concerning them in light of the gospel that he preaches. So this sketch of Pauline teaching begins with an analysis of his proclamation and gospel.

Kērygma, "proclamation," and its cognate verb *kēryssō*, "proclaim, preach," are used by Paul not only in his discussion of wisdom and rival preachers (chaps. 1–4), but elsewhere as well. In the passage quoted above as the key of Pauline theology, the noun appears for the first time (1:21) along with the verb (1:23). In 2:4, Paul admits that his "proclamation" was not adorned "with persuasive [words of] wisdom," when he first evangelized Corinth. Then in stressing his apostolic freedom and his restraint in making use of it, he invokes his disciplined example in "preaching to others" (9:27). Striking is the way he relates his preaching to the faith of Corinthian Christians so evangelized: "So whether it was I or they [i.e., other evangelists], in this way we preach (*kēryssomen*), and in this way you came to believe" (15:11). To which he adds immediately the essential object of that proclamation: "Christ is preached as raised from the dead" (15:12a). He continues, "If Christ has not been raised, then our preaching (*to kērygma hēmōn*) has been useless, and useless has been your faith" (15:14).

It is this important use of *kērygma* and *kēryssō*, especially in chap. 15, that has made commentators regard 15:3b–5a as a fragment of pre-Pauline proclamation of the early church that he passes on. Even though neither the noun nor the verb is found there, those verses (with the fourfold "that") are rightly understood as a nugget of early Christian *kērygma*.

Moreover, the beginning of chap. 15, where that proclamatory nugget appears, is clearly introduced as "the gospel that I preached to you" (*to euangelion ho euēngelisamēn hymin*, 15:1). Here both the noun *euangelion* and the verb *euan-*

gelizomai are connected with the primitive *kērygma*. The verb is repeated in the following verse, "the word that I preached to you" (15:2), lit. with what formulation of words (*tíni logō*) I preached. The object of such preaching is not only "Christ crucified" (1:23), but now also Christ as "raised on the third day according to the Scriptures" (15:4b) or "Christ raised from the dead" (15:12). For Paul insists that his mission stems from the risen Christ and involves the gospel, "Christ did not send me to baptize, but to preach the gospel" (*euangelizesthai*, 1:17). In the long discussion of his apostolic freedom and his restraint to exploit it in chap. 9, Paul often refers to "the gospel" (9:12, 14 bis, 18 bis, 23; 4:15 [see NOTE there]) and employs the verb (9:16 bis, 18), stressing that he has always served the gospel and has wanted to put no obstacle in the way of Christ's gospel (9:12). Even if the Lord wanted preachers of it to get their living from it (9:14), Paul boasts that he offers it free of charge (9:18) and does not exploit his right to do so. Hence his proclamation and gospel have as their content Jesus Christ and what he did for humanity in his crucifixion and resurrection. This leads to our first major topic of Pauline teaching, Christology.

A. Christology, Teaching about Christ Jesus

In writing 1 Corinthians, Paul assumes that his addressees have already heard from him the basic proclamation about Jesus Christ to which he alludes in this letter, because he has been the founding evangelist of that community. If Paul had ever met Jesus of Nazareth personally, he gives no hint of such an encounter in this letter, even if he does echo some of Jesus' sayings: on, e.g., divorce (7:10–11), gospel-preachers getting their living from it (9:14), the institution of the eucharist (11:23–25), and an unidentified commandment of the Lord (14:37).

Paul's Christology in 1 Corinthians can be synthesized under the following headings: the names and titles used of Jesus, the role ascribed to him, and the effects of the Christ-event.

Names and Title Use of Jesus of Nazareth

Jesus. The name "Jesus" alone is found only in the curse-formula, "Accursed is Jesus" (12:3a), as *Iēsous*. Paul does not seem to be aware of its heaven-given origin, even though it was a male name commonly used at that time in Palestinian Judaism. It is a grecized form of the Hebrew name *Yēšûăʿ*, "Jeshua" (RSV, Ezra 2:2; cf. LXX), a postexilic contracted form of *Yĕhôšûăʿ*, "Joshua" (Josh 1:1), which means "Yahweh, help!" (= *Yhw* + impv. *šwʿ*). Paul never plays on the meaning of the name, undoubtedly because Jesus of Nazareth had already become for him "Christ our Lord."

In 12:3, where the curse-formula appears, its counterpart, the confession-formula, joins "Jesus" with the title *Kyrios*, "Jesus is Lord" (12:3b). That combination, "the/our Lord Jesus," occurs a few times elsewhere in the letter (5:4 bis, 5; 9:1 [inverted]; 11:23; 16:23), more often in the formula, "the/our Lord Jesus Christ"

(1:2, 3, 7, 8, 10; 6:11; 8:6; 15:57), and once in inverted form, "Jesus Christ our Lord" (1:9). In the latter, one finds the combination also of "Jesus" and "Christ," as also in 2:2; 3:11.

Christ. In this letter, Paul makes no reference to the basic meaning of *Christos*, "anointed" (= Hebrew *māšîăḥ*; cf. Rom 9:5), and in the instances given in the preceding paragraph he has already used it as Jesus' second name, having so inherited it from the early tradition before him. On occasion, Paul will use only the second name, "Christ," the name that became common after Jesus' death and resurrection as the result of Easter-faith among his disciples, as they acknowledged him as God's Messiah in a new sense (1:6, 12, 13, 17 bis, 23, 24; 2:16; 3:1, 23 bis; 4:1, 10 bis, 15; 5:7; 6:15 bis; 7:22; 8:11, 12; 9:12, 21; 10:4, 9, 16 bis; 11:1, 3 bis; 12:12, 27; 15:3, 12, 13, 14, 15, 16, 17, 18, 19, 20, 22, 23 bis). Its most important form in this letter is "Christ crucified" (1:23; 2:2), the name that counteracts "human wisdom" (1:25) and "the wisdom of the world" (1:20). Sometimes Paul inverts the two names, "Christ Jesus" (1:1, 2, 4, 30; 4:15, 17; 15:31 [with "our Lord" added]; 16:24). Only he among NT writers uses the inverted form; instances where it is found in Acts (3:20; 5:42; 17:3; 18:5, 28; 24:24) are all variant readings, secondarily introduced by copyists familiar with Pauline usage.

Lord. Although *Kyrios* is a name for God in some OT passages that Paul quotes (3:20 [= Ps 94:11]; 10:26 [= Ps 24:1]), he uses it of Jesus, retaining its titular sense. For Paul it is the title par excellence for the risen Christ: "Jesus is Lord" (12:3b), thus repeating its kerygmatic and confessional usage from among those who were apostles before him. As Paul acknowledges in Rom 10:9b, it denotes that "God raised him from the dead," or is the title proper to his exalted status (Phil 2:11b). It thus expresses the risen Christ's lordship over all who accept him in faith. Noteworthy in this letter is the way Paul emphasizes the uniqueness of that lordship, when he asserts that "for us . . . there is one Lord (*heis kyrios*), Jesus Christ, through whom all things come and through whom we are destined" (8:6), thus playing down the other "many 'lords' " acknowledged in the contemporary world. He alone is "the Lord of glory" (2:8).

Paul often uses "(the) Lord" alone for the risen Christ in this letter (1:31; 4:4, 5, 17; 6:13, 14, 17; 7:10, 12, 22 bis, 25 bis, 32 bis, 34, 35, 39; 9:1, 2, 5; 10:9, 21 bis, 22; 11:11, 23, 26, 27, 32; 12:5; 14:37; 15:58; 16:10, 19, 22). *Kyrios* is also combined with other titles (see above). Only in this letter does Paul preserve an ancient prayer formula related to this title, *maranatha*, which is a transliteration of Aramaic *mārānā' thā'*, "our Lord, come!" (16:22 [see NOTE there]).

In so using *Kyrios*, Paul acknowledges along with the rest of the early church that the risen Christ is on a par with Yahweh of the OT. This is evident in Phil 2:10–11, where the same adoration is accorded him as *Kyrios*, as Isa 45:22–23 accords to God. By the time Paul writes, Palestinian Jews have come to call God "the Lord" (contrary to Bultmann's contention that "the unmodified expression 'the Lord' is unthinkable in Jewish usage" [*TNT*, 1:51]). For in the OT, Hebrew *'ādôn* usually denotes a human "master, lord" (Gen 45:8–9), *'ădōnî*, "my master"

(Exod 21:5), and *'ădōnāy* (lit., "my lords") was sometimes a surrogate for "Lord" (= God), but unmodified *'ādôn* was on occasion applied to Yahweh (Ps 114:7). Moreover, QL reveals that Palestinian Jews in the last pre-Christian century referred indeed to Yahweh as "(the) Lord": 4Q403 1 i 28, *bārûk [ha]'ādôn mele[k hak]kôl*, "Blest be the Lord, King of the universe"; 11QPsᵃ 28:7–8, possibly to be read as *maʿăśê ʿādôn*, "the works of the Lord." Or in Aramaic, one said *mārêh*, "Lord," or *māryā'*, "the Lord" (11QtgJob 24:6–7; 4QEnochᵇ 1 iv 5). Even the Jewish historian Josephus in the first Christian century used Greek *kyrios* of God *(Ant.* 20.4.2 §90; 134.3.1 §68). See Fitzmyer, "Semitic Background."

The Son. Although Paul refers to Jesus Christ as *ho huios* only twice in this letter, one instance is unique in that it expresses his relationship to God the Father as *autos ho huios,* "the Son himself," without a possessive pronoun or other modifier (15:28); it thus resembles the absolute formulation in Mark 13:32. Otherwise it is found only in 1:9, where Paul speaks of Christians called by God "into companionship with his Son, Jesus Christ our Lord." Strikingly, the formal title, "Son of God," is absent from 1 Corinthians, and there is little that otherwise stresses this special relationship to God, which is found elsewhere in the NT.

Adam of the Eschaton. In 15:45, Paul speaks of Jesus Christ as "the last Adam," who has become "a life-giving Spirit," as of his resurrection from the dead. This is affirmed in contrast to "the first man, Adam," who became "a living being," as a result of God's creative action in the Genesis account (2:7). As Adam was the head of humanity, so now the risen Christ is the head of a new humanity given life through the Spirit. Therefore Christ is the Adam of the eschaton. For "Christ has been raised from the dead as the firstfruits of those who have fallen asleep" (15:20), and "just as in Adam all die, so too in Christ all will be brought to life" (15:22). Here in 1 Corinthians the contrast of Adam and Christ is worked out in terms of death, whereas in Romans, although death is mentioned, the stress of the contrast falls on sin (5:12). The contrast is also expressed differently in that "all" are said to die "in Adam," by a sort of incorporation of humanity in him (1 Cor 15:22), whereas all humanity's sinfulness is partly ascribed to Adam as a consequence of his sin, but not through incorporation (Rom 5:12; see *Romans,* 405–23). Implied in Paul's assertions about Christ as the Last Adam is the idea that "Christ had first to share fully in the conditions and limitations of the life of Adam. He had borne fully the image of the man of dust before he became the man of heaven" (Caird, "Everything," 390). See 15:46–47. *Pace* Gaffin (" 'Life-Giving Spirit' "), this is one of the places in Pauline letters where the Apostle does not clearly distinguish the risen Christ from the Spirit (see also Rom 1:4; 8:9–11; 2 Cor 3:17), as he does in clearly triadic texts on other occasions (2 Cor 1:21–22; 13:13; 1 Cor 2:7–16; 12:4–6); see further *PAHT* §PT60–61.

The Role Ascribed to Jesus Christ in 1 Corinthians

The last two titles, "Son" and "Last Adam," already tell us something about how Paul understands the role of Jesus Christ in this letter. Implicit in the title "Son" may be his preexistence, to which Paul may allude in 10:4, where he identifies as "Christ" the "spiritual rock that followed" the Israelites wandering in the wilderness, from which they drank. According to many commentators, the last line of the acclamation in 8:6 likewise alludes to Christ's preexistence, when it says that he is the one Lord, "through whom all things come," i.e., come into being—a reference to his role in creation.

As far as the earthly life of Jesus is concerned, Paul makes only a few fleetings references to it in this letter. He knows of "the Lord's brothers" (9:5), his "apostles" (9:5; 15:5–7), Jesus' Last Supper and some of its elements: "on the night he was handed over" (11:23), his cross (1:17–18), his crucifixion (1:23), and his death and burial (15:3).

Implied in the use of the title *Kyrios* is Paul's affirmation of Christ's resurrection from the dead, to which he also devotes an explicit paragraph in chap. 15, as the basis of his teaching about the general resurrection of the dead (15:12–23), in addition to other passing references to it, e.g., "God has raised up the Lord, and he will raise us up too by his power" (6:14).

In quoting the primitive Christian *kērygma* in 15:3, Paul echoes the fundamental proclamation that "Christ died for our sins according to the Scriptures." That is simply a formulaic repetition of what he called earlier "the message of the cross" (1:18), i.e., the vicarious character of his giving up his life "for you" (11:23), but it is also a summary of Christ's role in this letter. The message, however, does not stop there, because that primitive kerygma also asserts "that he was raised on the third day according to the Scriptures" (15:4b). Although Paul separates the mention of the crucifixion and death of Jesus Christ (1:18–23) from the mention of his resurrection (15:12, 20), that is merely for the sake of his argument, for he clearly understands the role of Christ as that of Christ crucified and raised, as the quoted kerygma itself has proclaimed (15:3b–4b). In his critique of the preacher-rivalries and their undue emphasis on human wisdom, Paul finds it proper to emphasize Christ crucified, because that "message of the cross" is precisely the folly that God uses to confound "the wisdom of the world" (1:20). Then in time Paul will make use of the resurrection of Christ to show how victory over death has been achieved through the risen Christ so that those who belong to Christ and "have fallen asleep" will be "brought to life" (15:20–24). See Lampe, "Theological Wisdom," 119–28.

Paul goes still further in describing the role of the risen Christ in this letter, for he depicts him not only appearing to Cephas, James, and others (15:5–7) and to himself (9:1c; 15:8), but also "reigning until he has put all enemies under his feet" (15:25 [alluding to Ps 110:1]). His "last enemy to be destroyed is death" (15:26), as Christ is portrayed as the victor over death, who thus guarantees the resurrection of the dead, of all those who belong to Christ, but have fallen asleep.

A very distinctive role is set forth, however, in this letter, when Paul describes "Christ Jesus who became for us wisdom from God" (1:29), because that is Paul's answer in the first part of the letter to the world that "did not come to know God through its own wisdom" (1:21), to Jews who "demand signs and Greeks (who) seek wisdom" (1:22): "Christ (is) the power of God and the wisdom of God"

(1:24). As Furnish recognizes, "when we have come to terms with what Paul is saying about knowing God and belonging to Christ, we shall be very close to the theological center of 1 Corinthians, and with that, very close to the heart of his gospel as it finds expression here" (*Theology*, 29).

The one norm by which Paul judges almost every problem in the Corinthian church is its relationship to Christ Jesus, who is for him not only the content of the gospel that he preaches or the motivation of his exhortations, but also the norm of conduct for all individual Christians and of the activity of the community as a whole. Indeed, he even uses *Christos* in a collective sense as a surrogate for their corporate existence, asking in 1:13, "Is Christ divided?" See also 12:12.

> When he speaks of Christ, he has the whole Christ before his eyes. For he envisages the risen Christ (15:1ff.) as well as the exalted Lord (8:6), the One who is to come (7:29ff.) as well as the One present to the community (10:16ff.). The risen and exalted One is not to be separated from the earthly Jesus. He refers his own followers and those wisdom-seekers to the crucified One (1:17–18; 2:2). The community must sever itself from the incestuous man, "for Christ, our passover lamb, has been sacrificed (5:7). Paul reminds both the married and those who disrupt the celebration of the Lord's Supper about sayings of the Lord (7:10; 11:23–25), and through his death on the cross Jesus has redeemed both masters and slaves (7:22–23); for he died for the weak brother (8:11). As the confession, "Jesus is Lord," and the words of the Last Supper reveal, the earthly Jesus and the exalted Kyrios belong together. (Friedrich, "Christus, Einheit und Norm," 258)

Noteworthy in this letter is the number of references to the parousia of Christ. It first appears in the thanksgiving section, when Paul acknowledges that Corinthian Christians lack no spiritual gift as they "eagerly await the revelation of our Lord Jesus Christ" (1:7) and will be kept "blameless on the Day of our Lord Jesus [Christ]" (1:8). That revelation (*apokalypsis*) and Day (*hēmera*) are eventually related to "his coming" (*hē parousia autou*, 15:23). That seems also to be the reference intended in the testing of evangelization, which "the Day will bring to light" (3:13). Paul urges that Corinthian Christians "not judge anything before the proper time, before the Lord comes who will bring to light what is hidden in darkness and will expose the motives of our hearts. At that time, the commendation of each one will come from God" (4:5; cf. 11:26b). Unfortunately, these references to the parousia of Christ are hardly clear in details, apart from the implication of some kind of judgment of human conduct and attitude (5:13a). Likewise unclear is whether "the impending crisis" (7:25) is a covert reference to that parousia, before which "time is running out" (7:29) and "the shape of this world is passing away" (7:31), in light of which Paul recommends celibacy, etc. The lack of clarity is owing to the futurity of the Day, of which Paul has had no experience, and so he resorts to apocalyptic assertions about it.

Because of the emphasis that is put on ecclesiology in 1 Corinthians, it is not surprising to find Paul affirming that Jesus Christ is the unique "foundation" of the church, the one that has already been laid (*themelion . . . ton keimenon*, 3:11), which no one else can lay. See Furnish, *Theology*, 124–27.

The Effects of the Christ-Event

In describing what Christ has achieved for humanity, Paul in 1 Corinthians makes use of images drawn from his Jewish and Hellenistic background and applies them to the soteriological work of Christ. That work is difficult to describe, and that is why Paul does not always speak of it figuratively with the same image. In Pauline theology one can find at least ten different images that he uses, but they do not all occur in this letter (see *PAHT* §PT67–80), or with the same frequency as in the letter to the Romans.

Three of them are listed together in 6:11, "now you have been washed, you have been sanctified, you have been justified in the name of the Lord Jesus Christ and by the Spirit of our God." The "washing" refers to baptism, the initiatory rite by which sinners are cleansed from sin and introduced into "a new way of life" (Rom 6:4).

Sanctification as an effect is mentioned also in 1:2, where it is explained as those "called to be holy," and again in 1:30 (where it is listed in the abstract as *hagiasmos* along with two other effects). It expresses the dedication of Christians to the awesome service of God. The figure is derived by Paul from the OT, where things and persons were often said to be "holy," i.e., marked off from the profane or secular for cultic service of God or His Temple (e.g., Exod 3:5; 19:14; 26:33; Lev 19:2; Isa 48:2).

Justification is likewise a figure drawn from Paul's Jewish background, to express the right judicial relationship of human beings with God as they stand before His tribunal acquitted or vindicated (as in Exod 23:7; 1 Kgs 8:32; Job 31:35–37; cf. Ps 7:9–12; 119:1–8). Its effect is called "uprightness" or "righteousness" and is mentioned in 1:30 (along with sanctification and redemption). The three effects are attributed by Paul to "the Lord Jesus Christ," who through his life, ministry, passion, death, resurrection, and heavenly intercession graciously brings them about for sinful people (see further *Romans*, 116–19, 123, 139). This effect, so important in Pauline theology in general and especially in the letters to the Galatians and Romans, is thus alluded to only in two verses, 1:30; 6:11. In the former, it is related to "Christ Jesus" as "wisdom from God," and in the latter to "the name of our Lord Jesus Christ" and "the Spirit of our God." Nowhere in this letter is justification by grace through faith linked to the gospel that Paul preaches, which shows that for all its importance in Pauline theology, it is not the sole way of summing up what Paul means by "gospel."

In 1:30, Paul also singles out *apolytrōsis*, "redemption," as another abstract effect of the Christ-event. It has often been explained as a term related to the emancipation of war prisoners or the sacral manumission of slaves in the Greco-Roman world (see *Ep. Arist.* 12.35; Josephus, *Ant.* 12.2.3 §27; Deissmann, *LAE*, 320–23); more than a thousand Delphic inscriptions record that "Pythian Apollo purchased so-and-so for freedom." From 7:20–22 it is clear that Paul was aware of the social institution of emancipation in the Greco-Roman world, but his terminology is notably different from that in Delphic inscriptions, and so the pertinence of such an institution to Pauline "redemption" has been seriously questioned. Since his verb *apolytroō* is found for the "redeeming" of a slave in LXX Exod 21:8 and the noun *apolytrōsis* occurs in LXX Dan 4:34 (however, in a different sense), and the simple forms *lytron*, "ransom," and *lytroō*, "redeem," occur often in the LXX, it seems better to explain the Pauline notion of redemption from this background (Exod 6:6; 15:13–16; 21:30; 30:12). Behind the OT usage lies the idea of Yahweh as Israel's *gōʾēl*, "redeemer," the kinsman who had the duty of buying back an enslaved Israelite (Isa 41:14; 43:14; 44:6). So Yahweh is described because of His ransom of Israel from Egyptian bondage (Deut 7:6–8; 9:26; 13:6; Ps 74:2; 111:9). Later on, the idea acquired an eschatological nuance (Hos 13:14; Isa 59:29; see further *Romans*, 122–23; *EDNT*, 1:138–40). Paul now teaches that through Christ Jesus such "redemption" is extended to Christians by God Himself (1:30).

Although Paul does not use the abstract *sōtēria*, "salvation," in this letter, he often speaks of Christians who are "being saved" (*hoi sōzomenoi*, 1:18; cf. 15:2), of God "saving" those who believe (1:21), or of himself helping others to be saved (9:22; 10:33). In 1 Corinthians this effect is not ascribed directly to Christ, but it would have to be reckoned as an implicit effect of the Christ-event, because of the way it is used elsewhere in Paul's writings (see *PAHT*, §PT71). Indeed, it is not easy to say what is meant by "being saved" in this letter, since none of the few passages where the verb occurs even hints at an explanation. Hence one has to be wary of much of the discussion about so-called Corinthian spiritual enthusiasts who "believed themselves to have reached the goal of salvation already" (Käsemann, "On the Subject," 125). Such discussion is tied up with one way of explaining the denial of the resurrection of the dead among Corinthian Christians (see COMMENT on 15:12–19; cf. Doughty, "Presence and Future of Salvation").

A most distinctive effect of the Christ-event in this letter, however, is the victory over death that comes through the risen Christ in the resurrection of the dead (15: 54–57). This effect is the one up to which all the others have been leading, for it explains the goal of washing, sanctification, justification, redemption, salvation. See de Boer, *The Defeat of Death*, 93–140.

The name of Jesus Christ is involved in a number of minor ways in this letter, which indirectly say something more about his role. For instance, in his name Paul sends his greeting of "grace and peace" to the Corinthians (1:3); he regards himself as "an apostle of Christ Jesus" (1:1). He speaks of "Christ our passover lamb" as "sacrificed" (5:7), and in the eucharist—Christians participate in "the body of Christ" and "the blood of Christ" (10:16). He quotes the slogan of those who say, "I side with Christ" (1:12) and asks whether Christ is "divided" (1:13), as the other slogans might imply. Paul considers himself as having become the father of the Corinthian Christians "in Christ Jesus" and "through the gospel" (4:15). Nevertheless, the most important affirmation is that "you belong to Christ" (3:23), for that is the heart of the Christian vocation, and that leads to our next consideration, because "Christ belongs to God" (3:23).

B. Theology Proper, Teaching about God

(Ho) Theos occurs in 1 Corinthians as the designation of God, the God of the OT, the God of Israel, the God to whom Christ "belongs" (3:23), and whom Paul worships (1:4) and thanks for the graces given to him (1:14; 3:10; 14:18; 15:10 bis, 56). By His will, Paul has been "called to be an apostle of Christ Jesus" (1:1). The name *theos* occurs almost twice as frequently as *Christos* in the letter (105 times vs. 62 times; and 43 of them are concentrated in 1:18–4:21); e.g., *theos* is found three times in 1:21 alone, and again in 3:9. On occasion, Paul makes it clear that *theos* is the designation for God the Father (1:3; 8:6; 15:24) and even calls Him "the head of Christ" (11:3). That is also the reason why Paul ends his discussion in 3:23 with "all belongs to you, and you belong to Christ, and Christ to God," which is, in effect, Paul's corrective answer to the slogan of 1:12d, "I side with Christ," if that were really representative of some group rivalry in the Corinthian church. See further Richardson, *Paul's Language*, 107–16. *(Ho) kyrios* is also used alone for God in the following passages: 2:16; 3:5, 20; 4:19; 7:17; 14:21; 16:7.

Having asserted that "an idol is nothing at all in this world," Paul continues with "there is no God but one" (8:4), because "there is one God, the Father, from whom come all things and toward whom we tend" (8:6a, b). Thus he affirms that God is not only the efficient cause of all that exists (cf. 11:12), but also the final cause toward which all human life is destined (cf. 15:28). This is the unique and essential teaching about the creator God in this letter.

In contrast to the important divine attributes that Paul mentions in Romans (God's love, uprightness or righteousness, wrath, and power; see *Romans*, 105–8), the attributes that Paul singles out in 1 Corinthians are God's trustworthiness, power, and wisdom: *pistos ho theos*, "trustworthy is God" (1:9; 10:13); *dynamis theou*, "God's power" (1:18; 2:5; cf. 6:14); *sophia theou*, "God's wisdom" (1:21; 2:7). Then he goes on to identify Christ as "the power of God and the wisdom of God" (1:24). These personifications are unique to this letter.

The first feature ascribed to God in this letter is the divine reaction to human wisdom, as Paul queries, "Has not God made the wisdom of the world foolish?" (1:20). His answer is given in different formulations: "the wisdom of this world is folly in God's sight" (3:19); "God's folly is wiser than human wisdom" (1:25); "God chose what is foolish in the world in order to shame the wise" (1:27; cf. 1:28–29). The reason for this divine reaction: "in God's wisdom, the world did not come to know God through its own wisdom" (1:21a), and so God was pleased to make salvation available "through the folly of the proclamation" (*kērygma*, 1:21b), which is none other than "the message of the cross" (1:18). This fundamental teaching, to which Paul devotes much of chaps. 1–4, is his answer to the folly of preacher rivalries and their divisive effect on the Christian community of Roman Corinth.

Moreover, that proclamation is the wisdom of God, "God's mystery" (2:1), which none of the rulers of this age have understood (2:8), for that wisdom has been "hidden in a mystery, which God predetermined for our glory before time began" (2:7). So Paul speaks in this letter of what has often been called God's plan of salvation for humanity: "what God has prepared for those who love him" (2:9).

Now, however, that mystery "God has revealed to us through the Spirit" (2:10; cf. 2:12–14), and Paul has been announcing it without the trappings of human wisdom and eloquence (2:1), for he and other evangelists have become "the stewards of God's mysteries" (4:1). In these passages Paul is using *mystērion* not in the sense of something opaque and hard to understand, but rather as a secret hidden in God for ages and now revealed in Christ.

A second important feature of God in this letter is the divine indwelling in the Christian community: "Do you not realize that you (plural) are the temple of God and that the Spirit of God dwells in you" (3:16); "for the temple of God, which you are, is sacred" (3:17c). God dwelling in the midst of Israel was an OT motif (e.g., Exod 25:8; 29:45; Num 35:34), which Paul adopts and applies anew to the Christian community. Differently from Rom 8:9–11, where Paul restricts the indwelling to the Spirit, it is said of *theos* first and then of the Spirit. Moreover, in 6:19 he will speak of the individual human body as "the temple of the Holy Spirit, which is within you and which you have from God," but that is an indwelling that differs from the corporate indwelling.

A third very important feature about God in this letter is the way Paul ascribes the raising of Christ from the dead and the coming resurrection of the dead: "God raised up the Lord, and he will raise us up too by his power" (6:14); "we testified of God that he raised Christ" (15:15b); "Christ has been raised from the dead as the firstfruits of those who have fallen asleep" (15:20), expressed with a divine passive verb.

A fourth feature is "the kingdom of God" (see NOTE on 4:20), which "flesh and blood cannot inherit" (15:50); this is affirmed in the context of attaining the resurrection of the dead. In other words, no merely human power can reach that goal. A fortiori, it will not be inherited by "evildoers" (6:9), i.e., any of the unrighteous people listed in 6:9–10. "The kingdom" also denotes the regal status that the risen Christ enjoys and that at "the end" will hand over to "God the Father" (15:24), "for he must reign until he has put all enemies under his feet" (15:25).

Finally, God is mentioned in a number of isolated ways of lesser significance: as the one "who causes the growth" (3:7) of what has been planted and watered; who gives the body its shape (15:38; cf. 12:18, 24); who "will do away with" both food and stomach (6:13); who "grants victory" (over death) (15:56); who "has appointed in the church some . . . to be apostles, prophets," etc. (12:28); who "is not a God of disorder, but of peace" (14:33) and "has called you in peace" (7:15); who "will judge those outside" the Christian community (5:13); and from whom "commendation of each one will come" (4:5) at the time of the Lord's coming. Paul also mentions "the grace of God" that has been granted to Corinthian Christians (1:4) and to himself (3:10; 15:10bis).

C. Pneumatology, Teaching about God's Spirit

No account of Pauline teaching in 1 Corinthians about God would be complete without a consideration of the relation of *pneuma*, "Spirit," to *theos*, as some of the passages already quoted in section B show, because the activity of God's Spirit is prominent in chaps. 2–6 and in chap. 12. These are important passages about the Spirit in this letter, but none so important as the treatment of the Spirit in the letter to the Romans (see *Romans*, 124–26).

When Paul speaks of God's Spirit, he does not understand *pneuma* as in the Greco-Roman world of his day, as the power of thaumaturgy and ecstasy. Rather, he takes over an aspect of OT teaching about *rûaḥ*, which was often considered as a manifestation of God's presence. In the OT, "Spirit" expresses God's presence to His people, agents, or world in a creative, prophetic, quickening, or renovating mode (Gen 1:2; Num 24:2; 1 Sam 19:20, 23; 2 Chr 15:1; 24:20; Pss 51:12; 139:7; Isa 11:2; 61:1; Ezek 2:2; 11:5). That manifestation of God's presence is continued here too, as Paul adapts it to his understanding of the risen Christ. Above, note was taken of the "last Adam," who became "a life-giving Spirit" (15:45), which reveals something of the relation of "Spirit" to the risen Christ, for Paul does not always clearly distinguish them (see Rom 1:4; cf. *Romans*, 235–37).

The main role of the Spirit in 1 Corinthians is described in its external "manifestation" or in the bestowal of *pneumatika*, "spiritual gifts" (12:1) for the good of the Christian church. Although Paul distinguishes the *pneumatika* into different sorts, *charismata*, "gifts," *diakoniai*, "services," and *energēmata*, "works," and ascribes the source of them respectively as the "same Spirit," "same Lord," and "same God" (12:4–6), eventually they are also said to be "the manifestation of the Spirit for some good" (12:7), i.e., for the good of the community as a whole.

> To one is given through the Spirit the utterance of wisdom; to another, the utterance of knowledge through the same Spirit; to another, faith by the same Spirit, and to another gifts of healing by that one Spirit; to another, the working of mighty deeds; to another, prophecy; to another, discernment of spirits; to another, kinds of tongues; to another, the interpretation of tongues. But one and the same Spirit produces all these, bestowing them individually on each one as it wills. (12:8–11)

Although Paul acknowledges the diversity of *pneumatika* that Corinthian Christians enjoy, he wants them to reflect on the purpose of them for the good of the unique community that they make up, despite the diversity. Hence he stresses, "by one Spirit we were all baptized, in fact, into one body, whether Jews or Greeks, slaves or free, and we were all given one Spirit to drink" (12:13). Moreover, the individual baptized believer can acknowledge the lordship of the risen Christ only through the Spirit of God: "No one can say, 'Jesus is Lord,' save by the Holy Spirit" (12:3c). Yet, as all have been baptized into one body, they constitute "the temple of God," because "the Spirit of God dwells in" them (3:16), as already noted. Hence, "you have been washed, you have been sanctified, you have been justified in the name of the Lord Jesus Christ and by the Spirit of our God" (6:11). See further Martin, *The Spirit and the Congregation*.

To a "demonstration" of this Spirit, Paul also ascribes his own message or proclamation (2:4), which was not delivered "with persuasive [words of] wisdom," so that the faith of Corinthian Christians did not result from "human wisdom," but from "God's power." For Paul speaks "with words taught by the Spirit, interpreting spiritual realities in spiritual terms" (2:13). Consequently, since "no one comprehends what pertains to God except the Spirit of God" (2:11), through it we receive not "the spirit of the world, but rather the spirit coming from God so that we may understand the gifts bestowed on us by God" (2:12). All the good things that God has prepared for those who love Him are "revealed to us through the Spirit" (2:10). Finally, at the end of his lengthy chapter on marriage and celibacy, Paul concludes his own recommendations by saying, "I think that I too have the Spirit of God" (7:40); in other words, his recommendations having divine approbation.

D. Ecclesiology, Teaching about the Church

As important as the Pauline teaching in 1 Corinthians is about Christ, God, and the Spirit, this letter excels in what it teaches about the Apostle's understanding of the Christian community. In his letter to the Romans, Paul has very little to say about *ekklēsia*, "church," which occurs there only in chap. 16 and then only in the sense of a local church or a house church. He does not even address the letter to "the church at Rome," and when he speaks of Christians becoming "one body in Christ" (Rom 12:4), he never even hints that it could be called "the church." By contrast, his teaching about the church and its unity in 1 Corinthians is remarkably detailed. For this reason, Schlier has rightly emphasized it as the letter's *Hauptanliegen* (chief concern).

In the initial prescript of this letter, Paul addresses "the church of God that is in Corinth" (1:2). The phrase *hē ekklēsia tou theou* has been found in earlier Pauline letters, denoting the primitive local Christian community in Judea (1 Thess 2:14 [plur.]; Gal 1:13; cf. 2 Thess 1:4 [plur.]), and it seems to carry the nuance of the mother-church. In this sense, it appears again in 1 Cor 11:16 (plur.); and possibly in 15:9. According to Cerfaux (*The Church*, 112–14), this use of the titular phrase does not denote the "universal church" as embodied at Corinth, but is rather a Pauline way of flattering a particular church with which he has had some difficult relations, now that they are beginning to be smoothed out (see 2 Cor 1:1). Paul would be according the Corinthian community the title that he has previously used of the mother-church(es) of Judea (see 1 Cor 10:32; 11:22). In this extension of the titular usage, however, one detects a broadening of Paul's understanding of *ekklēsia*, which initially was used of a local or particular Christian community (e.g., Gal 1:2 [plur.]), but which was beginning to denote the community as transcending local boundaries, hence the universal church.

In any case, *ekklēsia* as a name for the Christian community was almost certainly in use among Greek-speaking Christians before Paul, but it is impossible to tell how early it came to be used among them and how it gradually supplanted other more primitive names, such as *adelphoi*, "brothers" (Acts 1:15), *mathētai*, "disciples" (Acts 6:1), *koinōnia*, "communal form of life" (Acts 2:42), *hē hodos*, "the Way" (Acts 9:2; 19:9, 23; 22:4; 24:14, 22 [cf. *Acts*, 423–24]), or even *Chris-*

tianoi, "Christians" (Acts 11:26 [cf. *Acts,* 477–78]). The etymology of the name
(from *ekkaleō,* "call out") does not really help to explain its usage.

In ancient Greek literature, the noun *ekklēsia* meant "gathering, meeting, or
assembly" often in a civic, political, or military sense. Acts 19:32, 40 shows that
ekklēsia can designate a disorderly gathering of a mob, which the town-clerk of
Ephesus contrasted with a "statutory assembly" (19:39). Indeed, the Greek noun
normally denoted the gathering or meeting itself, and not the body of people so
assembled. Normally, when the gathering dispersed, the *ekklēsia* ceased to exist.
In ancient Athens, there was a body called *boulē,* "council," even when it was not
in session, and its meeting would have been an *ekklēsia.* Hence the Christian use
of the word to designate a group or body of Christian believers would not have developed from the simple Hellenistic usage of *ekklēsia* (see further Campbell,
"Origin and Meaning").

In the LXX, however, the noun *ekklēsia* often designates the Hebrews wandering as a group in the desert (e.g., Deut 4:10 ["day of the gathering at Horeb"]; 9:10;
18:16; 31:30), or the gathering of returned exiles (Ezra 10:8), or the cultic gathering of Israel (2 Chr 6:3). There it often translates Hebrew *qāhāl,* "gathering, assembly," which was also rendered at times by Greek *synagōgē,* "congregation,"
the term that more often translated Hebrew *ʿēdāh,* "the (Israelite) congregation."
For instance, when Korah and 250 leaders of the congregation (*něśîʾê ʿēdāh;* LXX:
archēgoi synagōgēs) gathered together (*wayyiqqāhălû*) against Moses and Aaron
and accused them of exalting themselves above "the assembly of the Lord" (*qěhal
Yahweh*), the LXX renders that last phrase as *tēn synagōgēn kyriou* (Num 16:3).
When, however, David assembled all Israel in Jerusalem to transmit to the leaders
of the people the plans for the building of the Jerusalem Temple by his son
Solomon, he instructed the people, "Now, then, in the sight of all Israel, the assembly of the Lord (*qěhal Yahwēh;* LXX: *ekklēsia kyriou*), observe and seek out all
the commandments of the Lord your God" (1 Chr 28:8). See also Deut 23:2–4, 9
for a list of those not fit to enter "the assembly of the Lord" (*qěhal Yahwēh;* LXX:
ekklēsia kyriou). Here the "assembly of the Lord" begins to denote the religious
community of Israel. See also Sir 50:13, 20 ("whole congregation [*ekklēsia*] of Israel"); 31:11. *Qāhāl* occurs occasionally also in QL as a name for the Essene community, and one finds there the exact Hebrew counterpart of the Pauline phrase
(e.g., 1QM 4:10 [*qěhal ʾēl,* "assembly of God"]; 1QSa 1:25; 2:4; CD 7:17; 11:22;
12:6). This Qumran usage shows its aptness for describing a group of persons
holding the same religious convictions.

From such a use of *ekklēsia* by Greek-speaking Jews, there eventually developed the common word "church" for the Christian community, at first for the
local or particular community (1 Cor 14:23, 33, 34; 16:19 bis), and eventually for
the universal church that transcended local boundaries (Acts 9:31). Certain instances in 1 Corinthians (e.g., 6:4; 10:32; 11:22; 12:28; 14:19, 28, 35) contributed
to the latter understanding of it, for it is the gathering of God's people who have
been "called to be holy" (1:2).

In this letter, Paul speaks as one aware of his apostolic foundation of the Corinthian church: "I planted" (3:6); "I laid a foundation as an expert builder" (3:10); "I

write this not to make you ashamed, but to admonish you as my beloved children. Even if you have ten thousand guides in Christ, you do not have many fathers, for in Christ Jesus I became your father through the gospel" (4:14–15). He also recalls how he first came to announce "God's mystery" to the Corinthians, "not with sublimity of word or wisdom" (2:10). For the details, see INTRODUCTION pp. 37, 39–40.

The body of 1 Corinthians is devoted to multiple and diverse problems that have arisen in the young Corinthian church, especially since Paul left Corinth after the initial evangelization of it. In his treatment of these problems, however, Paul is most concerned about two aspects of the Corinthian church, its unity or solidarity, and the building up of the community that constitutes it.

In this letter, Paul insists that for Christians there is "one God, the Father" and "one Lord, Jesus Christ" (8:6), yet he never brings himself to speak of *mia ekklēsia*, "one church." The descriptive metaphors that he applies to the Corinthian community, however, such as *theou geōrgion, theou oikodomē*, "God's field, God's building" (3:9), imply oneness, as does also *naos theou*, "God's temple" (3:16). That is why Paul criticizes Corinthian Christians for their tolerance of *schismata*, "dissensions, divisions" (1:10; 11:18), *erides*, "rivalries" (1:11), *zēlos kai eris*, "jealousy and strife" (3:3), and *haireseis*, "factions" (11:19) among them; and he takes careful note of their individuality, when he recalls that *hekastos hymōn legei*, "each one of you says . . ." (1:12). This dissension and individuality, however, emerge not only because of Corinthians expressing their allegiance to certain preachers (chaps. 1–4), but also because of the selfish way some of them are celebrating the Lord's Supper. Apropos of the latter, Paul writes, "I hear that, when you meet as a church (*synerchomenōn hymōn en ekklēsiā*), there are divisions among you, and in part I believe it" (11:18).

In such an ecclesial context, Paul recalls what Christ did at the Last Supper, as he passes on a tradition about the institution of the Eucharist: "that the Lord Jesus, on the night he was betrayed, took bread, and having given thanks, broke it, and said, 'This is my body, which is for you. Do this in remembrance of me.' In the same way, the cup too, after the supper, saying, 'This cup is the new covenant in my blood. Do this, whenever you drink it, in remembrance of me' " (11:23–25). Thus, the Lord's giving of himself "for you" in this context is particularly significant, especially when the words quoted are recalled together with the idea of "Christ as the sacrificed passover lamb" (5:7) and with what Paul has taught earlier about "the cup of blessing" as "a participation in the blood of Christ" and the bread that is broken as "a participation in the body of Christ" (10:16). Thus when Paul uses *koinōnia* for "participation" in this passage, he is stressing the ecclesial aspect of that eucharistic meal. For Paul uses the phrase, "the body of Christ," not only in the eucharistic sense (10:16), but for the first time in his writings in the ecclesial sense. In 12:27, having asserted that "you are the body of Christ, and individually members of it," thus expressing the ecclesial sense very clearly, he continues, "and in the church God has appointed some to be, first of all, apostles, second, prophets . . ." (12:28). Here it is clear the "the body of Christ" now means "the church." (This identification becomes a major affirmation in the Deutero-Pauline writings: Col 1:18, 24; Eph 1:22–23.)

For this reason Paul urges the Corinthians to "be united in the same mind and purpose" (*ēte de katērtismenoi en tō autō noï kai en tē autē gnōmē*, 1:10). Such advice is supported by the rhetorical question that Paul poses later in the same passage, "Is Christ divided?" (1:13), where he uses a collective sense of *Christos* to denote the Christian community, called by God "into companionship (*koinōnian*) with his Son, Jesus Christ our Lord" (1:9). To counteract the divisive conduct of some at the celebration of the Lord's Supper, Paul asks, "Are you not showing contempt for the church of God and making those who have nothing feel ashamed?" (11:22). So he handles the problems that tend to undermine the unity of the Corinthian community or church. See further Mitchell, "*Reconciliation.*"

Other scandals that Paul treats in the letter are not equally divisive, but they are of a sort that fails to "build up" the Christian community, and in these matters he displays again his apostolic concern for *oikodomē*, "upbuilding, edification" of the church. Even though *oikodomē* is used metaphorically of the Christian community considered as "God's building" (3:9), Paul also uses the same word for the "building up" or the "edification" of the community, i.e., for its common improvement, especially in the discussion of the two *pneumatika* handled in chap. 14. There he finds that the gift of prophecy contributes to the "edification" of human beings or of "the church," whereas the one who speaks in tongues "edifies himself" (14:3–5). Paul's remedy: "Since you strive earnestly for spirits, seek to abound in them for the edification of the church" (14:12); "all these things should be for edification" (14:26d), because "to each individual is given the manifestation of the Spirit for some good" (12:7), i.e., for the common good of all. Even when Paul discusses the problem of eating idol meat and a repeated Corinthian slogan is quoted, "All things are permissible," he retorts, "but not all edify" (10:23), i.e., build up community life. To another Corinthian slogan, "We all possess knowledge" (8:1), Paul answers, "Knowledge puffs up, but love builds up" (8:1). So whether it be in favor of his preferred "prophecy" or of love, Paul shows his concern in these matters for the building up of the Christian church. In chap. 13, Paul will explain how love can do that, but he does not explicitly name "the church" in that context. Similarly, in giving instructions about women praying with uncovered heads, Paul is concerned about good order and the building up of the community, as he ends his discussion by saying, "We have no such custom, nor do the churches of God" (11:16). Toward the end of his discussion of speaking in tongues and prophesying, Paul concludes, "For God is not a God of disorder, but of peace, as in all the churches of the saints" (14:33). See further Schlier, "Über das Hauptanliegen"; Ward, "Theological Issues," 427–33.

Even when Paul's main concern in this letter is the treatment of the multiple problems facing the Christian community of Roman Corinth, he seeks to relate this community to other churches evangelized by him elsewhere. Hence, "I am sending to you Timothy," who "will remind you about my ways in Christ [Jesus], just as I teach them everywhere in every church" (4:17). Similarly, when he counsels Corinthian Christians to "lead the life that the Lord has assigned, as God has called each of you," he adds immediately, "So I teach in all the churches" (7:17).

Again, "if anyone is inclined to be argumentative (about this), we have no such custom, nor do the churches of God" (11:16). Finally, at the end of the letter, when he writes about the collection to be taken up, he says, "As I ordered the churches of Galatia, so you too should do" (16:1). See Furnish, *Theology*, 130–31.

In all these churches, Paul is concerned about those whom he calls *hoi hagioi*, "the holy ones, saints," which I have often translated as "God's dedicated people" (see 1:2; 6:1, 2; 14:33; 16:1, 15), i.e., "those sanctified in Christ Jesus" (1:2b). It is also the Apostle's generic term for members of the Christian church, i.e., "all those who call upon the name of our Lord Jesus Christ, their Lord and ours" (1:2c). Their "sanctification" (1:30), as an effect of the Christ-event, is thus a characteristic of the Corinthian community or church, "for the temple of God, which you are, is sacred" (3:17).

E. Anthropology, Teaching about Human Beings

In some of the passages from 1 Corinthians already cited, details are found that reveal Paul's understanding of humanity itself. In this matter, however, one finds more of a difference from his understanding of human nature in the letter to the Romans. There the great issues of life and death, uprightness and sin, law and grace are dealt with in some depth, whereas in 1 Corinthians one meets such issues only in one verse, "the sting of death is sin, and the power of sin is the law" (15:56). That is a statement that Paul never explains in this letter, where the context deals with the victory over death that has come with Christ. So one has to rely on other Pauline writings for the explanation of it (see NOTE there). Rather in 1 Corinthians, Paul is preoccupied with a multitude of minor issues, some of which are sinful, seriously so or less so, and others almost indifferent, even if they are the cause of division or disorder on a scale that concerns the corporate good of the community much more than that of individuals. This letter has no discussion like that of the famous *Egō* of Romans 7, and its relation to law.

Nevertheless, in this letter Paul does use a number of terms that appear also in other of his writings, including Romans, that give us some idea of his understanding of human beings and their problems, corporate and individual. The physical makeup of a human being includes "body," "soul," "flesh," "spirit," "mind," "heart," and "conscience," some of which tolerate the same description as that given in *Romans*, 126–28, but others do not.

Body. In 1 Cor 9:27;13:3, *sōma* may designate the visible, tangible, biological aspect of a human being, so that it has the nuance of "self," as Bultmann once maintained (*TNT*, 1:194), as I once accepted for the letter to the Romans. Now, however, in the majority of the instances of the word in 1 Corinthians, it denotes what was commonly understood in Greek philosophical writings that distinguish the "body" and the "soul" (*sōma kai psychē*): 5:3; 6:13 bis, 15, 18 bis, 19, 20; 7:4 bis; 12:12 ter, 14, 15 bis, 16 bis, 17 bis, 18, 19, 20, 22, 23, 24, 25; 15:44a, c. Even in chap. 15 (vv. 35, 37, 44b), *sōma* is used of the resurrection-body, and applied analogously to other objects (vv. 38 bis, 40 bis). "An animated body is sown, a spiritual body is raised. If there is an animated body, there is also a spiritual body" (15:44). The often-quoted interpretation of *sōma* given by Bultmann simply does not work in most of these instances, as Gundry (*Soma in Biblical Theology*) has made clear. There are, moreover, a few instances of the metaphorical use of "body": for instance, "we, though many, are one body, for we all partake of the one loaf" (10:17); see also 6:16; 12:13, 27.

Soul. The noun *psychē* occurs only in 15:45 ("the first man, Adam, became a living being"), where LXX Gen 2:7 is quoted, and where its basic meaning as the vital principle of biological life is important to Paul's argument. From it he derives the adjective form *psychikos*, "animated," in 2:14; 15:44 bis, 46 (in the last three instances modifying "body").

Flesh. Apart from two idiomatic expressions, *kata sarka* ("according to the flesh," meaning "by a human standard," 1:26; 10:18) and *sarx kai haima* ("flesh and blood," meaning "frail human nature," powerless to inherit the kingdom of God, 15:50), the noun *sarx* denotes a "human being" (1:29), or that which can be punished in a human being (5:5) or troubled (7:28), i.e., the substance that makes up a body (15:39 [four occurrences]), where it is almost the equivalent of *sōma*. Only in 5:5 does one find it in contrast to "spirit," and the meaning of the latter is controverted (see NOTE there). There is no instance in this letter of the notorious spirit vs. flesh contrast (well known from Rom 8:4–9, 13). Related to the noun is the adj. *sarkinos*, "fleshy, worldly" (3:1) or *sarkikos*, "fleshy" (3:3 bis; 9:11). See NOTE on 1:26.

Spirit. Besides the numerous instances cited above, where the noun denotes the Holy Spirit or the risen Christ (once, 15:45) as a "life-giving Spirit," *pneuma* occurs frequently in 1 Corinthians as that faculty or organ of a human being that is the affective and willing self; it expresses what is especially open to or apt to receive God's Spirit: 2:11a, 12 bis; 4:21; 5:3, 4; 6:17; 7:34; 12:10; 14:2, 12, 14, 15 bis, 16, 32; 16:18. Related to it is the adj. *pneumatikos*, "spiritual" (2:23 bis, 15; 3:1; 9:11; 10:2, 4 bis; 12:1; 14:1, 37; 15:44 bis, 46 bis) and the adv. *pneumatikōs* (2:13, 14).

Mind. The noun *nous* denotes the faculty in a human being that knows, plans, judges, and criticizes; it expresses intelligence and reflects on God's created world as a human being's highest capacity (1:10; 2:16 bis;14:14,15 bis, 19). In chap. 14, it stands in contrast and is considered superior to "the spirit" (involved in tongue speaking).

Heart. The noun *kardia* is taken over by Paul from LXX usage, where it translates Hebrew *lēb* or *lēbāb*, "inner person, heart, mind" (Ps 104:15; 1 Sam 16:7); it is a literary variant, denoting practically the same thing as *nous* (2:9; 4:5; 7:37 bis; 14:25).

Conscience. Also related to *nous* is the noun *syneidēsis*, "conscience" (Latin *conscientia*), which expresses the ability of the intelligent human being to judge one's actions in retrospect as right or wrong or in prospect as a guide for proper action (8:7 [see NOTE there], 10, 12; 10:25, 27, 28, 29 bis. Paul refers to it only in his discussion of the eating of idol meat.

Humanity. Apart from such notions about the physical makeup of human beings, Paul reckons in this letter with people of different cultural, ethnic, and religious backgrounds, distinguishing them as Jews (*Ioudaioi*, 1:22, 23, 24; 9:20 ter; 10:32; 12:13) or "people of Israel" (10:18), Greeks (*Hellēnes*, 1:22, 24; 10:32; 12:13), and Gentiles or pagans (*ethnē*, 1:23; 5:1; 10:20; 12:2). The noun *barbaros* occurs only in the generic sense of "foreigner" (14:11 bis). Such distinctions are made as Paul discusses the quest of human wisdom among them in chaps. 1–4, or their eating or avoidance of idol meat in chap. 10. "Though I am free and belong to no one, I have made myself a slave to all so that I may win over as many as possible" (9:19), i.e., to the gospel. "I have become all things to all people that I might save at least some" (9:22b).

Paul testifies to the "faith" (*pistis*) of Corinthian Christians. It is based not "on human wisdom, but on God's power" (2:5), which is the only way he hints in this letter at its grace-character: "No one can say 'Jesus is Lord,' save by the Holy Spirit" (12:3b). It is for him the response to "the gospel that I preached to you, which you received . . . ; by it you are also being saved, if you hold fast to the word I preached to you. Otherwise you have believed in vain" (15:1–2). "So whether it was I or they, in this way we [i.e., Paul, Apollos, Cephas] preach, and in this way you came to believe" (15:11; cf. 3:5). Hence, Paul urges Corinthian Christians to "stand fast in the faith" (16:13), i.e., in their loyalty to the preached gospel, through the proclamation of which those who believe are saved (1:21).

This saving faith, however, differs from the *pistis* mentioned in 12:9; 13:2, which is rather one of the *pneumatika*, the "faith to move mountains," a manifestation of the Spirit. In this letter, there is no mention of the justifying faith of the letters to the Romans or Galatians or any explanation of the relation of faith to love, such as one finds in Gal 5:6, "faith working itself out through love" (on which see *Romans*, 137–38). The latter omission is striking in view of the elaborate rhetorical treatment of *agapē*, "love," in chap. 13, which ends, "Now faith, hope, and love remain, these three; but the greatest of these is love."

Linked to the human experience of union with Christ through faith is baptism, the initiatory rite that incorporates human beings into Christ and the church, which already existed in pre-Pauline Christianity. Apart from the several rather negative statements about baptism conferred by Paul himself in 1:13–17, there is only one meaningful reference to the rite in this letter: "By one Spirit we were, in fact, all baptized into one body, whether Jews or Greeks, slaves or free, and we were all given one Spirit to drink" (12:13). From the immediately preceding verse one learns that all Christians, like the members of a body, many though they are, "form one body," and so too "it is with Christ" (*Christos* now used in a collective sense). Hence Paul adds in 12:27, "you are the body of Christ." Thus baptism is the rite of Christian unification, incorporating the many members of the church into the one body of Christ. Alluding to this experience as a prime analog, Paul even says that "all our ancestors . . . were baptized into Moses in the cloud" (10:1–2), thus explaining the unique relationship of ancient Israelites to Moses as somehow similar to the incorporation of Christians into Christ. The details of that incorporation, however, have to await Paul's writing of the letter to the Romans (see *Romans*, 139–40), where his fuller teaching on baptism is proposed. Paul's reference to those "who undergo baptism on behalf of the dead" remains enigmatic (see NOTE on 15:29).

Paul is, moreover, aware of the varied cultural, social, and economic backgrounds of the Corinthians whom he is addressing. The variety of terms that he uses to express their differences give some inkling of the numerous problems with which he has to cope in the Corinthian Christian community: some are "slaves" (7:21–23); some "wise" or "sages" (*sophoi*, 1:20, 26, 27; 3:18; *phronimoi*, 4:10; 10:15); some "scribes" or philosophical "inquirers" (1:20); some "powerful" and "of noble birth" (1:26); some "weak" (1:27; 8:11; 9:22; 11:30); some "strong" (1:25, 27; 4:10); some "spiritual" (3:1; 14:32); some "worldly" (3:1, 3); some "sexually immoral" (5:9–11; 6:9); some "married" (7:10, 33, 34), "unmarried" (7:8, 32, 34), "virgins" (7:25, 28, 34, 36–38); or "widows" (7:8, 39); some "evildoers" (6:1, 9); some "speakers in tongues" (12:29; 14:2, 4); some "prophets" (12:28–30; 14:2, 4).

Yet with due allowance for such diversity of cultural and social backgrounds, Paul emphasizes two human qualities, freedom and love. For a Christian, "called by the Lord" is basically the "Lord's freedman" (7:22), having been "bought at a price" and being a "slave" to no "human beings" (7:23). Such liberty includes freedom of conscience: "Why should my freedom be determined by someone else's conscience?" (10:29). That, however, is not the whole story, because the love that "builds up" (8:1c) the community demands that the very right one has because of such freedom must not "become a stumbling block for the weak" (8:9). This relationship of freedom and love is exemplified fully by what Paul writes about himself in chap. 9 about his apostolic right and his reluctance to exploit that right, when occasion demands consideration of others. So he concludes, "If food causes my brother to fall, I shall never eat meat again, so that I may not cause my brother to fall" (8:13). See Friedrich, "Freiheit und Liebe."

Another unique teaching in this letter is the way Paul speaks about virginity or celibacy as a mode of Christian life. Although some commentators describe his discussion of this topic as "the superiority of virginity" (Furnish, *Theology*, 137), that is hardly the way to sum up what he says about it in chap. 7. Even though he says, "I wish that all were as I myself am," he quickly adds, "but each one has a particular gift from God (*idion charisma ek theou*), one of one kind and one of another" (7:7). He uses the adj. *kalos*, "good," to describe his own status (7:8; cf. 7:26), but that is the same description that he used when beginning his discussion of reasons for monogamous marriage (7:1). The only comparative expressions used in chap. 7 (vv. 9b, 40) have nothing to do with a comparison of marriage and virginity. Once one has noted that aspect of Paul's discussion in chap. 7, one can proceed to examine the reasons for the celibate way of Christian life that he advocates. He finds two reasons for it: one is derived from his conviction that "the shape of this world is passing away" (7:31; cf. 7:26–27, 29a), i.e., an eschatological consideration; the other is the single-minded service that the celibate person can devote to "the Lord's affairs" (7:32), i.e., how one "may please the Lord" without distraction from "the affairs of this world," how one may please the spouse (7:33). That emphasis on a virginal mode of Christian life is found only in this letter, and it is an important Pauline view, which should not always be encumbered with the way later patristic writers (e.g., Tertullian, Jerome) interpreted it.

When Paul is critical of the conduct of Corinthian Christians, he reminds them of the arrogance that governs their behavior and their tendency to boast. Such attitudes are manifest in their predilection for preachers, and his counsel is, therefore, "no one should boast about human beings. For all things belong to you, whether it be Paul or Apollos or Cephas . . ." (3:21–22). Again, "now, brothers, I have transferred this to myself and Apollos for your sake, . . . that none of you will become arrogant, siding with one over against another. For who concedes you any distinction? What do you have that you did not receive? If then you did really receive it, why are you boasting as though you did not?" (4:6–7). This same "arrogance" and "boasting" are what Paul finds to be at fault in the Corinthian toleration of incest in their midst (5:2, 6), and the claim of some of them to possess knowledge that enables them to eat idol meat (8:1, "knowledge puffs up"), which can, however, "become a stumbling block for the weak" (8:9). So he urges them, "whoever thinks that he is standing firm should see to it that he does not fall" (10:12), and "no one should seek his own advantage, but that of his neighbor" (10:24). Finally, he finds this arrogance even in their attitude toward himself: "Some have become arrogant in pretending that I am not coming to you" (4:18; cf. 4:19). How serious does Paul consider this attitude among Corinthian Christians? It is not easy to say. It is noteworthy that the few instances in the letter in which the noun or verb "sin" occurs have nothing to do with Paul's comments on such arrogance or boasting.

The noun *hamartia*, "sin," occurs only in chap. 15 of 1 Corinthians: first, in the kerygmatic fragment, "Christ died for our sins" (15:3). Then, "if Christ has not been raised, . . . you are still in your sins" (15:17); and "the sting of death is sin, and the power of sin is the law" (15:56), already cited above. The verb *hamartanō* apears there too in a hortatory injunction, "Sin no more!" (15:34). Otherwise, one finds it only in chaps. 6–8. In 6:18, Paul exhorts the Corinthian Christians: "Flee from fornication!" Then having quoted what is most likely a Corinthian saying, "every sin that one commits is outside the body," Paul retorts, "But the fornicator sins against his own body." In chap. 7, Paul assures the Corinthians that to marry would not be a sin (v. 28 bis, 36d), and in chap. 8, Paul regards those Corinthians who possess knowledge about idol meat and fail to consider the weak consciences of fellow Christians a sinful situation: "When you sin in this way against your brothers and strike at their conscience, weak as it is, you are sinning against

Christ" (8:12). Neither the noun nor the verb "sin" occurs in the passage about incest (5:1–5) or in the lists of those who will not "inherit the kingdom of God" (6:9–10; cf. 5:9–13). Again, despite the few instances in which Paul allows us to understand some of the things he considers sinful, one has to look to other Pauline writings to discern what he thinks sin really is in human life.

In two passages of this letter, however, Paul does express himself strongly as he lists those whom he considers "evildoers" (*adikoi*, 6:1, 9). In 5:9–11, he classes them as "sexually immoral, . . . greedy, swindlers, idolaters, slanderers, drunkards," and in 6:9–10, as "fornicators, idolaters, adulterers, catamites, sodomites, thieves, greedy, drunkards, slanderers, and swindlers." Such people "will not inherit the kingdom of God" (6:9), and that is why he advises, "Drive out the evil one from among you" (5:13, quoting Deut 17:7).

Those two passages, however, express Paul's reaction to evildoing in its extreme forms, and there are many other passages in which he counsels wisely the conduct of men and women in their sexual relationships. If in 6:13, he warns against fornication, stressing that "the body is not meant for fornication, but for the Lord, and the Lord for the body," he eventually makes it clear that "because of instances of fornication, each man should have his own wife, and each woman her own husband" (7:2). This is a clear affirmation of the goodness and propriety of monogamous marriage, in which sexual relationships are fully approved, even if he does concede that spouses might want to abstain from such relationship for a good reason at times (7:3–6). It is wrong to read 7:1–6 as if Paul were merely tolerating marriage or reckoning with it as something inferior to the celibacy that he prefers. He clearly recognizes the good in marriage, as he does also in celibacy, affirming that "each one has a particular gift from God, one of one kind and one of another" (7:7bc), thus acknowledging the divine call to both marriage and celibacy.

A different, yet important aspect of Paul's exhortation in this letter is the way he proposes himself as a model, sometimes implicitly, sometimes explicitly. "When I came to you, brothers, announcing to you God's mystery, I did not come with sublimity or word or wisdom . . . , so that your faith might not be based on human wisdom, but on God's power" (2:1–5). "Therefore, I urge you, be imitators of me" (4:16), a counsel that he later repeats, while adding, "as I am of Christ" (11:1). He sends Timothy to the Corinthian Christians to "remind" them "about my ways in Christ [Jesus]" (4:17). Even though Paul is absent "in body, but present in spirit," he has "already passed judgment on the one who has committed this deed" (of incest), and he bids them do the same (5:2–5). The unmarried Paul exclaims, "I wish that all were as I myself am, but each one has a particular gift from God, one of one kind and one of another" (7:7; cf. 7:8, 40). In the matter of eating idol meat, he admits, "If food causes my brother to fall, I shall never eat meat again, so that I may not cause my brother to fall" (8:13), implying that they should do the same. This is especially true of the whole of chap. 9, where he asserts his apostolic freedom and rights, but willingly forgoes the exploitation of them. He even praises Corinthian Christians for being mindful of him and holding to the traditions that he has passed on to them (11:2)

F. Eschatology

Pauline eschatological teaching in this letter is especially pronounced. Mention has already been made in section A above of the references to Christ's parousia. They are scattered through various chapters, beginning in the letter's thanksgiving section (1:7–8), and reveal how pervasively Paul's thinking has been normed by this consideration, that "God has raised up the Lord, and he will raise us up too by his power" (6:14). His reflections on this topic, however, surface also in 7:29–31, where Paul introduces the passing character of "this world" in his discussion of virginity or celibacy, and they especially come to a peak in his treatment of the resurrection of the dead in chap. 15, where he is astonished that there are "some" among the Corinthian Christians who are questioning such a belief.

Paul's reflections, however, do not amount to a full treatise on eschatology, for the discussion even in chap. 15 remains *ad hoc*, treating the denial of the resurrection of the dead. Although some interpreters consider Paul's argument in this chapter to be wholly apocalyptic (e.g., Beker, *Paul the Apostle*, 135), it is better to analyze the flow of the argument differently. For in vv. 1–11, his argument is kerygmatic, i.e., based on the preaching of the early church about Christ's resurrection. Then, in vv. 12–19 and 29–34, it becomes *argumentum ad hominem*, i.e., a logical, quasi-philosophical discussion. In vv. 20–28, the discussion is at first typological (vv. 21–23), and then it becomes apocalyptic (vv. 24–28), and his apocalyptic argument is continued later in vv. 42–58, whereas that in vv. 35–41 is analogical, i.e., as he argues from three different analogies (seeds, bodies, splendors).

Now Paul once again speaks of Christ's "coming" (*parousia*, 15:23), when all "those who belong to Christ" will be "brought to life" (15:22–23). Then he continues, "Then will come the end," where *to telos* (15:24), the meaning of which is quite debated (see NOTE there), probably is only another way of expressing the parousia, when Christ will hand over "the kingdom to God the Father." In all of this discussion, Paul is most concerned to repeat the primitive kerygma, that Christ "has been raised," which he fills out as he asserts not only that he "has been raised from the dead" (15:12, 20), but also "as the firstfruits of those who have fallen asleep" (15:20). Hence the guarantee of the resurrection of the dead is the resurrection of Christ itself, as proclaimed in the primitive kerygma. This will be the final victory over death that comes "through our Lord Jesus Christ" (15:57).

Paul indulges in an apocalyptic description of the "mystery" of that victory, maintaining that "we shall all be changed" (15:51) and that "what is mortal dons immortality" (15:54); for the merely animated body is raised as "a spiritual body" (15:44 [see NOTE there]). Some of this eschatological teaching recalls what Paul wrote in 1 Thess 4:13–17, where he likewise indulged in an apocalyptic description of the destiny that awaits the Christian who will "always be with the Lord" (4:17; cf. Phil 1:23, where the same destiny is taught, but without apocalyptic trappings). Underlying this Pauline conviction is the idea that the resurrection of Christ itself is the guarantee of the general resurrection of the Christian dead. This eschatological teaching, then, is a christological development of a belief that began to emerge in Palestinian Judaism in the last two pre-Christian centuries (e.g., Dan 12:2; *1 Enoch* 62:15; 1QS 4:7–8; see Furnish, *Theology*, 128–30).

The way that Paul has written 1 Corinthians, in which his hortatory counsel is mingled so closely with his doctrinal instruction, makes the theology that this letter contains important for Christian life even in the twenty-first century. Certain aspects of his teaching may indeed be time-conditioned and tied to his own day (e.g., the question of eating idol meat, or the problem of certain *pneumatika*, such as speaking in tongues), but invariably in such passages Paul enunciates a principle of conduct or behavior that is easily applied to Christian life today, so that the modern reader of chaps. 8, 10, 12, 14 can often find therein counsels for present-day Christian behavior. As Furnish has put it, ". . . because 1 Corinthians is . . . in its own way a profoundly *theological* letter, it undoubtedly does have a significance for Christian thought that transcends the particularities of its own time and place" (*Theology*, 143).

BIBLIOGRAPHY

Ahern, B. M., "The Christian's Union with the Body of Christ in Cor, Gal, and Rom," *CBQ* 23 (1961) 199–209.

Becker, J., *Paul Apostle to the Gentiles* (Louisville: Westminster/John Knox, 1993) 187–239.

Beker, J. C., *Paul the Apostle: The Triumph of God in Life and Thought* (Philadelphia: Fortress, 1980).

Blank, J., "Gemeinsam glauben in Korinth," *Diakonia* 14 (1983) 16–24.

Boer, M. C. de, *The Defeat of Death: Apocalyptic Eschatology in 1 Corinthians 15 and Romans 5* (JSNTSup 22; Sheffield: Sheffield Academic Press, 1988).

Brister, C. W., "The Ministry in I Corinthians," *SwJT* 26/1 (1983) 18–31.

Caird, G. B., "Everything to Everyone: The Theology of the Corinthian Epistles," *Int* 13 (1959) 387–99.

Campbell, J. Y., "The Origin and Meaning of the Christian Use of the Word *ekklēsia*," *JTS* 49 (1948) 130–42.

Cerfaux, L., *The Church in the Theology of St. Paul* (New York: Herder and Herder, 1959).

Doughty, D. J., "The Presence and Future of Salvation in Corinth," *ZNW* 66 (1975) 61–90.

Dunn, J. D. G., *The Theology of Paul the Apostle* (Grand Rapids: Eerdmans, 1998).

Fee, G. D., "Toward a Theology of 1 Corinthians," *Pauline Theology Volume II* (see Hay below) 37–58.

Fitzmyer, J. A., "The Semitic Background of the New Testament *Kyrios*-Title," *WA*, 115–42; *SBNT* 115–42.

Friedrich, G., "Christus, Einheit und Norm der Christen: Das Grundmotiv des 1. Korintherbriefs," *KD* 9 (1963) 235–58.

——, "Freiheit und Liebe im ersten Korintherbrief," *TZ* 26 (1970) 81–98.

Furnish, V. P., "Belonging to Christ: A Paradigm for Ethics in First Corinthians," *Int* 44 (1990) 145–57.

——, "Theology in 1 Corinthians," *Pauline Theology Volume II* (see Hay below), 59–89.

——, *The Theology of the First Letter to the Corinthians* (New Testament Theology; Cambridge: Cambridge University Press, 1999).

Gaffin, R. B., Jr., " 'Life-Giving Spirit': Probing the Center of Paul's Pneumatology," *JETS* 41 (1998) 573–89.

Hall, D. R., "Pauline Church Discipline," *TynBul* 20 (1969) 3–26.

Hasler, V., "Das Evangelium des Paulus in Korinth: Erwägungen zur Hermeneutik," *NTS* 30 (1984) 109–29.

Hay, D. M. (ed.), *Pauline Theology Volume II: 1 and 2 Corinthians* (Minneapolis: Fortress, 1993).

Hays, R. B., "The Conversion of Imagination: Scripture and Eschatology in 1 Corinthians," *NTS* 45 (1999) 391–412.

——, "Ecclesiology and Ethics in 1 Corinthians," *Ex auditu* 10 (1994) 31–43.

Käsemann, E., "On the Subject of Primitive Christian Apocalyptic," *New Testament Questions of Today* (ed. E. Käsemann; Philadelphia: Fortress, 1969), 108–37.

Lambrecht, J., "Christ the Universal Savior according to 1 and 2 Corinthians," *Pauline Studies* (BETL 115; Louvain: Leuven University/Peeters, 1994), 161–73.

Lampe, P., "Theological Wisdom and the 'Word about the Cross,' " *Int* 44 (1990) 117–31.

Lemcio, E. E., "Images of the Church in 1 Corinthians and 1 Timothy: An Exercise in Canonical Hermeneutics," *AsTJ* 56 (2001) 45–59.

Martin, R. P., *The Spirit and the Congregation: Studies in 1 Corinthians 12–15* (Grand Rapids: Eerdmans, 1984).

Mearns, C. L., "Early Eschatological Development in Paul: The Evidence of 1 Corinthians," *JSNT* 22 (1984) 19–35.

Mitchell, M. M., "*Reconciliation: Biblical Reflections:* III. Paul's 1 Corinthians on Reconciliation in the Church: Promise and Pitfalls," *NTR* 10/2 (1997) 39–48.

Pujana, J., "El Espíritu Santo en la vida cristiana según la primera carta a los Corintios," *EstTrin* 17 (1983) 215–54.

Richardson, N., *Paul's Language about God* (JSNTSup 99; Shefield: Sheffield Academic Press, 1994).

Schlier, H., "Über das Hauptanliegen des 1. Briefes an die Korinther," *Die Zeit der Kirche: Exegetische Aufsätze und Vorträge* (Freiburg im B.: Herder, 1972) 147–59.

Sellin, G., "Hauptprobleme des Ersten Korintherbriefes," *ANRW* II/25.4 (ed. H. Temporini and W. Haase; Berlin: de Gruyter, 1987) 2940–3044.

——, *Der Streit um die Auferstehung der Toten: Eine religionsgeschichtliche und exegetische Untersuchung von 1. Korinther 15* (FRLANT 138; Göttingen: Vandenhoeck & Ruprecht, 1986).

Söding, T., "Kreuzestheologie und Rechtfertigungslehre: Zur Verbindung von Christologie und Soteriologie im Ersten Korintherbrief und im Galaterbrief," *Catholica* 46 (1992) 31–60.

Tomlin, G., "The Theology of the Cross: Subversive Theology for a Postmodern World," *Themelios* 23/1 (1997) 59–73.

Van Linden, P., "Paul's Christology in First Corinthians," *TBT* 18 (1980) 379–86.

Ward, W. E., "Theological Issues Raised in First Corinthians," *RevExp* 57 (1960) 422–37.

Williams, H. H. D., "Living as Christ Crucified: The Cross as a Foundation for Christian Ethics in 1 Corinthians," *EvQ* 75 (2003) 117–31.

GENERAL
BIBLIOGRAPHY

◆

Introductory Surveys

Langevin, P.-E., *Bibliographie Biblique, Biblical Bibliography, Biblische Bibliographie, Bibliografia Biblica, Bibliografía Bíblica* (3 vols.; Quebec: Presses
de l'Université Laval, 1972, 1978, 1985), 1:427–37; 2:859–77; 3:1021–36.

Metzger, B. M., *Index to Periodical Literature on the Apostle Paul* (NTTS 1;
Leiden: Brill, 1960) 60–75.

Mills, W. E., *1 Corinthians* (Bibliographies for Biblical Research, NT Series 7;
Lewiston, NY: Mellen Biblical Press, 1996).

Commentaries

I. Patristic Period

GENERAL ITEMS

*Biblia patristica: Index des citations et allusions bibliques dans la littérature patris-
tique* (6 vols.; ed. J. Allenbach et al.; Paris: Editions du Centre National de la
Recherche Scientifique, 1975, 1977, 1980, 1987, 1991, 1995).

Bray, G., *1–2 Corinthians* (Ancient Christian Commentary on Scripture, NT 7;
Downers Grove, IL: Inter-Varsity Press, 1999) 1–190.

Cramer, J. A. (1793–1848), *Catenae graecorum patrum in Novum Testamentum*
(8 vols.; Oxford: Typographeum academicum, 1840–44; repr. Hildesheim:
Olms, 1967).

Devreese, R., "Chaînes exégétiques grecques, Saint Paul," *DBSup* 1:1209–24.

Kovacs, J. L., *1 Corinthians Interpreted by Early Christian Commentators* (The
Church's Bible; Grand Rapids: Eerdmans, 2005).

Staab, K., *Pauluskommentare aus der griechischen Kirche: Aus Katenenhand-
schriften gesammelt und herausgegeben* (NTAbh 15; Münster in W.: Aschendorff, 1933).

SPECIFIC ITEMS: GREEK WRITERS

Origen (185–ca. 254), "Fragmenta," Cramer, *Catenae*, 5, 1844. Cf. C. Jenkins,
"Origen on I Corinthians," *JTS* 9 (1907–8) 231–47, 353–72, 500–514; 10
(1908–9) 29–51; D. D. Hannah, *The Text of I Corinthians in the Writings of
Origen* (SBL NT in the Greek Fathers 4; Atlanta: Scholars, 1997).

Didymus the Blind of Alexandria (313–398), "Fragmenta (1 Cor 15–16)," *PKGK*,
6–14.

John Chrysostom (347–407), *Homiliae in Epistolam I ad Corinthios*, PG
61.7–382. Cf. *Homilies on the Epistles of Paul to the Corinthians* (NPNF
1/12; ed. P. Schaff; Peabody, MA: Hendrickson, 1994) 1–269.

Theodore of Mopsuestia (350–428), "Fragmenta," *PKGK*, 172–96.

Theodoret of Cyrrhus (393–460), *Interpretatio primae epistolae ad Corinthios*,
PG 82.225–376.

Severian of Gabala (fl. ca. 400), "Fragmenta," *PKGK*, 225–77.

Cyril of Alexandria (d. 444), *Explanatio in epistolam I ad Corinthios*, PG 74.855–916. Cf. P. E. Pusey, *Sancti patris nostri Cyrilli archiepiscopi Alexandrini in d. Joannis evangelium* . . . (3 vols.; Oxford: Clarendon, 1868–72), 3:249–319.

Gennadius of Constantinople (d. 471), "Fragmenta," *PKGK*, 418–19.

SPECIFIC ITEMS: LATIN WRITERS

Tertullian (160–225), *Adversus Marcionem* 5.5.1–5.10.15 (CCLat 1.675–95).

Ambrosiaster (4th cent.), *Ambrosiastri qui dicitur commentarius in epistulas paulinas: Pars secunda in epistulas ad Corinthios* (CSEL 81/2; ed. H. J. Vogels; Vienna: Hoelder-Pichler-Tempsky, 1968) 1–194. Cf. *Commentarius in epistolam b. Pauli ad Corinthios primam*, PL 17.193–290.

Pelagius (ca. 354–ca. 420), *In primam epistolam ad Corinthios*, PL 30:745–806. Cf. A. Souter, *Pelagius's Exposition of Thirteen Epistles of St Paul: II. Text and Apparatus Criticus* (Texts and Studies 9/1–3; Cambridge: Cambridge University Press, 1926) 127-230; *III. Pseudo-Jerome Interpolations* (1931) 27–43.

II. Medieval Period

GREEK WRITERS

Photius of Constantinople (810–895), "Fragmenta," *PKGK*, 544–83; cf. PG 101–4.

Arethas of Caesarea (860–940), "Fragmenta," *PKGK*, 659–70.

Oecumenius of Tricca (10th cent.), *Commentarius in epistolam I ad Corinthios*, PG 118.635–906.

Theophylact of Okhrid (Bulgaria) (1050/60-1125?), *Epistolae primae divi Pauli ad Corinthios expositio*, PG 124.559–794.

LATIN WRITERS

Hatto of Vercelli (924–961), *Epistola prima ad Corinthios*, PL 134.287–412.

Hervaeus Burgidolensis (Hervé de Bourg-Dieu) (1080–1150), *In epistolam I ad Corinthios expositio*, PL 181.813–1002.

Petrus Lombardus (1100–1160), *In epistolam I ad Corinthios*, PL 191.1533–1696. Cf. *Collectanea in omnes d. Pauli apostoli epistolas* . . . (Esslingen: Conrad Fyner, 1473; Paris: I. Badius Ascensius, 1535); A. Landgraf, "Ein neuer Fund zur Kommentierung des Paulinenkommentares des Petrus Lombardus," *Bib* 25 (1944) 50–61.

Gilbert de la Porrée (d. 1154), *In primam epistolam ad Corinthios*, reworked by some unknown writer. Cf. A. M. Landgraf (ed.), *Commentarius Porretanus in Primam Epistolam ad Corinthios* (Studi e Testi 117; Vatican City: Biblioteca Apostolica Vaticana, 1945).

Thomas Aquinas (1225–1274), *In omnes d. Pauli apostoli epistolas commentaria* (3 vols.; Liège: Dessain, 1857–58), 1.291–549; "Epistola I ad Corinthios," in *Sancti Thomae Aquinatis . . . opera omnia* (25 vols.; Parma: P. Fiaccadori, 1852–73; repr. New York: Musurgia, 1948–50), 13.157–298.

III. Fifteenth- to Eighteenth-Century Writers

Erasmus, Desiderius (1459–1536), *Epistola Pauli ad Corinthios prima*, in *Opera omnia* (ed. J. Leclerc; Leiden, 1705; repr. Hildesheim: Olms, 1962), 6.661–748. Cf. *Erasmus' Annotations on the New Testament: Acts— Romans—I and II Corinthians: Facsimile of the Final Latin Text with All Earlier Variants* (Studies in the History of Christian Thought 42; ed. A. Reeve and M. A. Screech; Leiden: Brill, 1990).

Colet, John (1466–1519), *An Exposition of St. Paul's First Epistle to the Corinthians Now First Published, with a Translation, Introduction, and Notes* (tr. J. H. Lupton; London, 1874; repr. Ridgewood, NJ: Gregg, 1965). Cf. B. O'Kelly and C. A. L. Jarrott (eds.), *John Colet's Commentary on First Corinthians: A New Edition of the Latin Text, with Translation, Annotations, and Introduction* (Binghamton, NY: Medieval & Renaissance Texts & Studies, 1985).

Luther, Martin (1483–1546), "Commentary on 1 Corinthians 7," "Commentary on 1 Corinthians 15," in *Luther's Works* 28 (ed. H. C. Oswald; St. Louis: Concordia, 1973) 1–56, 57–213. Cf. WAusg. 12.95–142; 36.478–696.

Melanchthon, P. (1497–1560), "Annotationes in epistulas Pauli ad Corinthios," *Melanchthons Werke in Auswahl* (Gütersloh: Mohn, 1963), 4.15–84. Cf. *Annotations on the First Epistle to the Corinthians* (tr. J. P. Donnelly; Milwaukee: Marquette University Press, 1995).

Calvin, Jean (1509–1564), *The First Epistle of Paul to the Corinthians* (Calvin's NT Commentaries 9; Grand Rapids: Eerdmans, 1960). Cf. O. Weber, *Auslegung des Römerbriefes und der beiden Korintherbriefe* (Auslegung der heiligen Schrift 16; Neukirchen-Vluyn: Erziehungsverein, 1960).

Estius, Gulielmus (1542–1613), *In omnes d. Pauli epistolas, item in catholicas commentarii* . . . (3 vols.; ed. J. Holzammer; 2d ed.; Mainz: Kirchheim, 1858–59), 1:360–792.

Cornelius a Lapide (Cornelis Cornelissen van den Steen, 1567–1637), *Commentaria in omnes d. Pauli epistolas* (Antwerp: M. Nutius and J. Meursius, 1614).

Locke, John (1632–1704), *A Paraphrase and Notes on the Epistles of St Paul to the Galatians, 1 and 2 Corinthians, Romans, Ephesians* (2 vols.; ed. A. W. Wainwright; Oxford: Clarendon, 1987) 161–259, 413–60, 685.

Bengel, J. A. (1687–1752), *Gnomon Novi Testamenti* (Tübingen: L. F. Fues, 1742; 3d ed., 1855; also London: D. Nutt, 1855). Cf. *Gnomon of the New Testament: A New Translation* (tr. C. T. Lewis and M. R. Vincent; 2 vols.; Philadelphia: Perkinpine & Higgins, 1862); repr. as *New Testament Word Studies* (Grand Rapids: Kregel, 1971), 2:165–273.

Wettstein, J. J. (1693–1754), *Hē Kainē Diathēkē: Novum Testamentum graece* . . . (2 vols.; Amsterdam: Dommer, 1751–52), 2:101–76.

IV. Nineteenth- to Twenty-First-Century Writers

Allo, E.-B., *Saint Paul: Première épître aux Corinthiens* (EBib; Paris: Gabalda, 1934; 2d ed., 1956).

Bachmann, P., *Der erste Brief des Paulus an die Korinther* (3d ed.; Leipzig: Deichert, 1921; 4th ed.; rev. E. Stauffer, 1936).

Baljon, J. M. S., *De tekst der brieven van Paulus aan de Romeinen, de Corinthiërs en de Galatiërs als voorwerp van de conjecturaalkrititiek beschouwd* (Utrecht: J. van Boekhoven, 1884).

Balz, H. R., *Christus in Korinth: Eine Einführung in den ersten Korintherbrief* (Kleine Kasseler Bibelhilfe; Kassel: Oncken, 1970).

Barclay, W., *The Letters to the Corinthians* (Daily Study Bible; 2d ed.; Philadelphia: Westminster, 1956) 1–169.

Barnes, A., *Notes on the New Testament Explanatory and Practical: I. Corinthians* (Grand Rapids: Baker, 1949).

Barrett, C. K., *A Commentary on the First Epistle to the Corinthians* (HNTC; New York: Harper & Row; London: Black, 1968; repr. Peabody, MA: Hendrickson, 1993).

Barton, B. B., et al., *1 and 2 Corinthians* (Life Application Bible Commentary; Wheaton, IL: Tyndale House, 1999).

Bassler, J. M., "1 Corinthians," *The Women's Bible Commentary* (ed. C. A. Newsom and S. H. Ringe; London: SPCK; Louisville: Westminster/John Knox, 1992) 321–29.

Baudraz, F., *Les épîtres aux Corinthiens: Commentaire* (Collection de commentaires bibliques; Geneva: Labor et Fides; Paris: Librairie Protestante, 1965) 19–135.

Beardslee, W. A., *First Corinthians: A Commentary for Today* (St. Louis: Chalice, 1994).

Beet, J. A., *Commentary on St. Paul's Epistles to the Corinthians* (New York: Whittaker, 1883) 1–316.

Billroth, G., *A Commentary on the Epistles of Paul to the Corinthians* (Biblical Cabinet; 2 vols.; Edinburgh: Clark, 1837–38), 1:1–289; 2:1–135.

Bisping, A., *Erklärung des ersten Briefes an die Korinther* (Exegetisches Handbuch zum Neuen Testament 5/2; 3d ed.; Münster in W.: Aschendorff, 1883).

Blomberg, C., *1 Corinthians* (NIV Application Commentary; Grand Rapids: Zondervan, 1994).

Boer, C. den, *De eerste brief van Paulus aan de Korinthiërs* (3 vols.; Kampen: Kok Voorhoeve, 1992–93).

Boor, W. de, *Der erste Brief des Paulus an die Korinther* (Wuppertaler Studienbibel; Wuppertal: Brockhaus, 1968; 2d ed., 1976).

Branick, V. P., *First Corinthians: Building Up the Church* (Hyde Park, NY: New City Press, 2001).

Bratcher, R. G., *A Translator's Guide to Paul's First Letter to the Corinthians* (Helps for Translators; London/New York: United Bible Societies, 1982).

Brown, E. F., *The First Epistle of Paul the Apostle to the Corinthians with Introduction and Notes* (Indian Church Commentaries; London: SPCK, 1923).

Brown, R. B., "1 Corinthians," *Broadman Bible Commentary* (12 vols.; Nashville: Broadman) 10 (1970) 287–397.

Bruce, F. F., *1 and 2 Corinthians* (New Century Bible Commentary; London: Marshall, Morgan & Scott, 1971; repr. Grand Rapids: Eerdmans, 1981) 17–162.

Butler, P. T., *Studies in First Corinthians* (Bible Study Textbook Series; Joplin, MO: College Press, 1985).

Callan, C. J., *The Epistles of St. Paul: Vol. 1. Romans, First and Second Corinthians, Galatians* (London: B. Herder; New York: Wagner, 1922) 246–445.

Cantinat, J., *The Epistles of St. Paul Explained* (Staten Island: Alba House, 1967) 45–71.

Caudill, R. P., *First Corinthians: A Translation with Notes* (Nashville: Broadman, 1983).

Chafin, K. L., *1, 2 Corinthians* (Communicators Commentary 7; Waco: Word, 1985) 15–195.

Clark, G. H., *First Corinthians: A Contemporary Commentary* (Trinity Paper 29; 2d ed.; Jefferson, MD: Trinity Foundation, 1991).

Collins, R. F., *First Corinthians* (Sacra Pagina 7; Collegeville, MN: Liturgical Press, 1999).

Conzelmann, H., *1 Corinthians: A Commentary on the First Epistle to the Corinthians* (Hermeneia; Philadelphia: Fortress, 1975).

Cornely, R., *Commentarius in s. Pauli apostoli epistolas: II. Prior epistola ad Corinthios* (Cursus Sacrae Scripturae; Paris: Lethielleux, 1890; 2d ed., 1909).

Craig, C. T., and J. Short, "The First Epistle to the Corinthians," *IB* 10 (1953) 1–262.

Deluz, G., *A Companion to I Corinthians* (London: Darton, Longman & Todd, 1963).

Dods, M., *The First Epistle to the Corinthians* (Expositor's Bible; London: Hodder and Stoughton, 1889).

Dumortier, F., *Croyants en terres païennes: Première épître aux Corinthiens* (Paris: Editions Ouvrières, 1982).

Dunn, J. D. G., *1 Corinthians* (NT Guides: Sheffield: Sheffield Academic, 1995).

Edwards, T. C., *A Commentary on the First Epistle to the Corinthians* (3d ed.; New York: Armstrong, 1896; London: Hodder and Stoughton, 1897; 4th ed., 1903).

Ellicott, C. J., *St. Paul's First Epistle to the Corinthians: With a Critical and Grammatical Commentary* (London: Longmans, Green, 1887).

Ellingworth, P., and H. Hatton, *A Handbook on Paul's First Letter to the Corinthians* (UBS Translators Handbook; New York: UBS, 1985; 2d ed., 1994).

Erdman, C. R., *The First Epistle of Paul to the Corinthians: An Exposition* (Philadelphia: Westminster, 1928).

Evans, E., *The Epistles of Paul the Apostle to the Corinthians in the Revised Version with Introduction and Commentary* (Clarendon Bible; Oxford: Clarendon, 1930) 9–152.

Fascher, E., *Der erste Brief des Paulus an die Korinther: Erster Teil, Einführung und Auslegung der Kapitel 1–7* (THKNT 7/1; Berlin: Evangelische Ver-lagsanstalt, 1975; *Zweiter Teil, Kapitel 8–16* by C. Wolff; 3d ed., 1984). See C. Wolff below.

Fee, G. D., *The First Epistle to the Corinthians* (NICNT; Grand Rapids: Eerd-mans, 1987).

Findlay, G. G., *St Paul's First Epistle to the Corinthians* (EGT; London, 1900; repr. Grand Rapids, MI: Eerdmans, 1979).

Fisher, F. L., *Commentary on 1 and 2 Corinthians* (World Bible Commentary Series; Waco: Word Books, 1975).

Fisk, B. N., *First Corinthians* (Interpretation Bible Studies; Louisville: Geneva, 2000).

Garland, D. E., *1 Corinthians* (Baker Exegetical Commentary on the New Testa-ment; Grand Rapids: Baker Academic, 2003).

Gavigan, J., et al., *St Paul's Epistles to the Corinthians* (Navarre Bible; Blackrock, Ireland: Four Courts, 1991) 24–159.

Getty, M. A., "1 Corinthians," *The Collegeville Bible Commentary* . . . (ed. D. Bergant and R. J. Karris; Collegeville, MN: Liturgical, 1989) 1100–33.

Getty-Sullivan, M. A., *First Corinthians, Second Corinthians* (Collegeville Bible Commentary 7; Collegeville, MN: Liturgical, 1983) 7–82.

Giavini, G., *Vita, peccati e speranze di una chiesa: Introduzione e note alla prima lettera di s. Paolo alla chiesa di Corinto* (Milan: Ancora, 1978).

Godet, F. L., *Commentary on St. Paul's First Epistle to the Corinthians* (2 vols.; Edinburgh: Clark, 1886–87; repr. Grand Rapids: Zondervan, 1971).

Goudge, H. L., *The First Epistle to the Corinthians, with Introduction and Notes* (Westminster Commentaries 43/1; 5th ed.; London: Methuen, 1926).

Grasso, S., *Prima Lettera ai Corinzi* (Rome: Città Nova Editrice, 2002).

Gromacki, R. G., *Called to Be Saints: An Exposition of 1 Corinthians* (Grand Rapids: Baker, 1977).

Grosheide, F. W., *Commentary on the First Epistle to the Corinthians: The English Text with Introduction, Exposition and Notes* (NICNT; London: Marshall, Morgan & Scott, 1954; Grand Rapids: Eerdmans, 1953).

Gutjahr, F. S., *Die zwei Briefe an die Korinther erklärt* (2 vols.; Graz: Styria, 1907; 2d ed., 1922) part 1.

Gutzke, M. G., *Plain Talk on First and Second Corinthians* (Grand Rapids: Zondervan, 1978) 11–155.

Hamar, P. A., *The Book of First Corinthians* (Radiant Commentary on the New Testament; Springfield, MO: Gospel, 1980).

Hargreaves, J., *A Guide to 1 Corinthians* (London: SPCK, 1978).

Harner, P. B., *First Epistle of St. Paul to the Corinthians* (Bryn Mawr Commen-taries; Bryn Mawr, PA: Bryn Mawr College, Dept. of Greek, 1983).

Harris, W. B., *The First Epistle of St Paul to the Corinthians* (Madras [Tamizhgam], India: Serampore Christian Literature Society, 1958).

Harrisville, R. A., *I Corinthians* (Augsburg Commentary on the New Testament; Minneapolis: Augsburg, 1987).

Hays, R. B., *First Corinthians* (Interpretation; Louisville: John Knox, 1997).

Heinrici, C. F. G., *Der erste Brief an die Korinther* (MeyerK 5; 8th ed.; Göttingen: Vandenhoeck & Ruprecht, 1896).

———, *Das erste Sendschreiben des Apostels Paulus an die Korinther* (Berlin: Hertz, 1880).

Héring, J., *The First Epistle of Saint Paul to the Corinthians* (London: Epworth, 1962).

Hodge, C., *An Exposition of the First Epistle to the Corinthians* (Grand Rapids: Eerdmans, 1965).

Hofmann, J. C. K., *Der erste Brief Pauli an die Korinther* (Die Heilige Schrift Neuen Testaments 2/2; 2d ed.; Nördlingen: Beck'sche Buchhandlung, 1874).

Holladay, C., *The First Letter of Paul to the Corinthians* (Living Word Commentary; Austin: Sweet, 1979).

Holtzmann, O., *Das Neue Testament nach dem Stuttgarter griechischen Text übersetzt und erklärt: II. Die Paulusbriefe* . . . (3 vols.; Giessen: Töpelmann, 1925–26).

Horsley, R. A., *1 Corinthians* (Abingdon New Testament Commentaries; Nashville: Abingdon, 1998).

Horton, S. M., *I and II Corinthians* (Springfield, MO: Logion, 1999).

Huby, J., *Saint Paul: Première épître aux Corinthiens* (VS 13; Paris: Beauchesne, 1946).

Hughes, R. B., *First Corinthians* (Everyman's Bible Commentary; Chicago: Moody, 1985).

Ironside, H. A., *1 Corinthians* (rev. ed.; Neptune, NJ: Loizeaux, 2001).

Jacono, V., *Le epistole di S. Paolo ai Romani, ai Corinti e ai Galati* (Sacra Bibbia; Turin: Marietti, 1951) 253–409.

Jensen, I. L., *Corinthians* (Chicago: Moody Bible Institute, 1972).

Kilgallen, J. J., *First Corinthians: An Introduction and Study Guide* (New York: Paulist, 1987).

Kistemaker, S. J., *Exposition of the First Epistle to the Corinthians* (New Testament Commentary; Grand Rapids: Baker, 1993).

Klauck, H.-J., *1. Korintherbrief* (Neue Echter-Bibel, NT 7; Würzburg: Echter-V., 1984).

Kling, C. F., *The First Epistle of Paul to the Corinthians* (rev. D. W. Poor; New York: Scribner, 1868).

Kremer, J., *Der erste Brief an die Korinther übersetzt und erklärt* (RNT; Regensburg: Pustet, 1997).

Kugelman, R., "The First Letter to the Corinthians," *JBC* art. 51, 2:254–75.

Kürzinger, J., *Die Briefe des Apostels Paulus: Die Briefe an die Korinther und Galater* (Echter-Bibel, NT 2; Würzburg: Echter-V., 1954) 3–41.

Kuss, O., *Die Briefe an die Römer, Korinther und Galater übersetzt und erklärt* (RNT 6; Regensburg: Pustet, 1940) 118–96.

Lambrecht, J., "1 Corinthians," *The International Bible Commentary: A Catholic and Ecumenical Commentary for the Twenty-First Century* (ed. W. R. Farmer et al.; Collegeville, MN: Liturgical, 1998) 1601–32.

Lamparter, H., *Der 1. Korintherbrief* (Christus heute 12; Stuttgart: Kreuz-V., 1955).

Lang, F., *Die Briefe an die Korinther* (NTD 7; Göttingen: Vandenhoeck & Ruprecht, 1986).

Lattey, C., *Readings in First Corinthians: Church Beginnings in Greece* (London/ St. Louis: B. Herder, 1928).

Leal, J., "Primera carta a los Corintios," *La Sagrada Escritura* (BAC 211/1; Madrid: Editorial Católica, 1962) 329–480.

Lemonnyer, A., *Epîtres de Saint Paul: Traduction et commentaire* (2 vols.; Paris: Bloud & Cie., 1907–8), 1: 89–176.

Lenski, R. C. H., *The Interpretation of St. Paul's First and Second Epistles to the Corinthians* (Columbus, OH: Lutheran Book Concern, 1935).

Lias, J. J., *The First Epistle to the Corinthians* (Cambridge Greek Testament for Schools and Colleges; Cambridge: Cambridge University Press, 1886, repr. 1905).

Lietzmann, H., *An die Korinther I/II* (HNT 9; 5th ed.; rev. W. G. Kümmel; Tübingen: Mohr [Siebeck], 1969) 1–96.

Lightfoot, J., *Horae hebraicae et talmudicae* (Oxford: Oxford University Press, 1859; repr. as *A Commentary on the New Testament from the Talmud and Hebraica* (4 vols.; Grand Rapids: Baker, 1979), 4:165–314.

Lightfoot, J. B., *Notes on the Epistles of St Paul from Unpublished Commentaries* (2d ed.; London: Macmillan, 1904; repr. Grand Rapids: Zondervan, 1957) 137–235.

Lindemann, A., *Der erste Korintherbrief* (HNT 9/1; Tübingen: Mohr Siebeck, 2000).

Lockwood, G. J., *1 Corinthians* (Concordia Commentary; Saint Louis: Concordia, 2000).

MacArthur, J., *1 Corinthians* (Chicago: Moody, 1984).

McFadyen, J. E., *The Epistles to the Corinthians and Galatians* (Interpreter's Commentary on the New Testament 6; New York: Barnes, 1909) 1–116.

MacRory, J., *The Epistles of St Paul to the Corinthians with Introductions and Commentary* (Dublin: Gill & Son; St. Louis: B. Herder, 1915) i–xxvi, 1–267.

Maillot, A., *L'Eglise au présent: Commentaire de la première épître de St. Paul aux Corinthiens* (Tournon: Réveil, 1978).

Maly, K., *Der erste Brief an die Korinther* (Die Welt der Bibel, Kleinkommentare zur Heiligen Schrift 13; Düsseldorf: Patmos, 1971).

Mare, W. H., *1 Corinthians* (Expositor's Bible Commentary 10; Grand Rapids: Zondervan, 1976) 173–297.

Martin, A., *First Corinthians* (Neptune, NJ: Loizeaux Bros., 1990).

Martin, R. P., *1, 2 Corinthians, Galatians* (London: Scripture Union; Philadelphia: Holman, 1968).

Massie, J., *Corinthians* (New York: Frowde; Edinburgh: Jack, n.d.) 1–259.

Maunoury, A.-F., *Commentaire sur les deux épîtres de Saint Paul aux Corinthiens* (Paris: Bloud et Barral, 1879) 1–345.

Merklein, H., *Der erste Brief an die Korinther* (Ökumenischer Taschenbuchkommentar zum Neuen Testament 7/1–2; Gütersloh: Mohn; Würzburg: Echter-V., 1992, 2000)

——, and M. Gielen, *Der erste Brief and die Korinther, Kapital 11,2 – 16,24* (Ökumenischer Taschenbuchkommentar zum Neuen Testament 7/3; Gütersloh; Gütersloher Verlagshaus, 2005).

Meyer, H. A. W., *Critical and Exegetical Commentary on the New Testament: Handbook to the Epistles to the Corinthians* (2 vols.; Edinburgh: Clark, 1877–79; repr. 1883–84).

Meyer, W., *Der erste Korintherbrief* (Prophezei; Zurich: Zwingli-V., 1947).

Micklem, N., *A First Century Letter, Being an Exposition of Paul's First Epistle to the Corinthians* (London: Students Christian Mission, 1920).

Moffatt, J., *The First Epistle of Paul to the Corinthians* (MNTC 7/1; London: Hodder and Stoughton; New York: Harper and Bros., 1938; 8th ed., 1954).

Morris, L., *The First Epistle of Paul to the Corinthians: An Introduction and Commentary* (Tyndale New Testament Commentaries; Leicester, UK: Inter-Varsity; Grand Rapids: Eerdmans, 1958; 2d ed. 1985).

Murphy-O'Connor, J., *1 Corinthians* (New Testament Message 10; Wilmington: Michael Glazier, 1979; repr. Collegeville, MN: Liturgical Press, 1991).

——, *1 Corinthians* (Doubleday Bible Commentary; New York: Doubleday, 1998).

——, "The First Letter to the Corinthians," *NJBC* (1990) art. 49, 798–815.

Noack, B., *Kommentarhæfte til Første Korinterbrev* (Copenhagen: Gad, 1967).

Olshausen, H., *Biblical Commentary on St Paul's First and Second Epistles to the Corinthians* (Edinburgh: Clark, 1855) 1–268.

O'Rourke, J. J., "1 Corinthians," *A New Catholic Commentary on Holy Scripture* (ed. R. C. Fuller et al.; London: Nelson, 1969) 1143–60 (§§867–86).

Orr, W. F., and J. A. Walther, *I Corinthians: A New Translation: Introduction with a Study of the Life of Paul, Notes, and Commentary* (AB 32; Garden City, NY: Doubleday, 1976).

Ortkemper, F.-J., *1. Korintherbrief* (Stuttgarter kleiner Kommentar, NT 7; Stuttgart: Katholisches Bibelwerk, 1993).

Oster, R., *1 Corinthians* (College Press NIV Commentary; Joplin, MO: College Press, 1995).

Osty, E., *Les Épîtres de Saint Paul aux Corinthiens* (SBJ; 3d ed.; Paris: Cerf, 1959) 7–70.

Parry, R. St J., *The First Epistle of Paul the Apostle to the Corinthians* (Cambridge Bible for Schools and Colleges; Cambridge; Cambridge University Press, 1916).

Patterson, P., *The Troubled, Triumphant Church: An Exposition of First Corinthians* (Nashville: Nelson, 1983).

Picirilli, R. E., *1, 2 Corinthians* (Randall House Bible Commentary; Nashville: Randall House Publications, 1987), 1–250.

Price, J. L., "The First Letter of Paul to the Corinthians," *Interpreter's One-Volume Commentary on the Bible* (ed. C. M. Laymon; Nashville: Abingdon, 1971) 795–812.

Prior, D., *The Message of 1 Corinthians: Life in the Local Church* (The Bible Speaks Today; Leicester, UK/Downers Grove, IL: Inter-Varsity Press, 1985).

Proctor, W. C. G., "The Epistles to the Corinthians," *The New Bible Commentary* (ed. F. Davidson et al.; Grand Rapids: Eerdmans, 1953) 967–89.

Ramsay, W. M., "Historical Commentary on the Epistles to the Corinthians," *Expos* 6/1 (1900) 19–31, 91–111, 203–17, 273–89, 380–87; 6/2 (1900) 287–302, 368–81, 429–44; 6/3 (1901) 93–110, 220–40, 343–60.

———, *Historical Commentary on First Corinthians* (ed. M. Wilson; Grand Rapids: Kregel, 1996).

Rendell, K. G., *Expository Outlines from 1 and 2 Corinthians* (London: Pickering and Inglis, 1969).

Robertson, A., and A. Plummer, *A Critical and Exegetical Commentary on the First Epistle of St Paul to the Corinthians* (ICC; New York: Scribner's Sons, 1911; 2d ed. 1914; repr. 1975).

Robertson, E. H., *Corinthians 1 and 2* (J. B. Phillips' Commentaries 7; New York: Macmillan, 1973) 11–101.

Rückert, L. I., *Die Briefe Pauli an die Korinther: Erster Teil, Der erste Brief* (2 vols.; Leipzig: Köhler, 1836–37).

Ruef, J. S., *Paul's First Letter to Corinth* (Pelican New Testament Commentaries; Baltimore: Penguin Books, 1971; repr. Philadelphia: Westminster, 1977).

Sacchi, A., *Una comunità si interroga: Prima lettera di Paolo ai Corinzi* (Milan: Paoline, 1998).

Sampley, J., "The First Letter to the Corinthians," *The New Interpreter's Bible*, Vol. 10 (Nashville: Abingdon, 2002) 771–1003.

Schlatter, A., "Der frühere Brief an die Korinther," *Erläuterungen zum Neuen Testament* (3 vols.; Stuttgart: Calwer, 1928), 2:1–217.

———, *Die Korintherbriefe ausgelegt für Bibelleser* (Stuttgart: Calwer, 1950; repr. 1962).

———, *Paulus der Bote Jesu: Eine Deutung seiner Briefe an die Korinther* (2d ed.; Stuttgart: Calwer, 1956; 3d ed., 1962).

Schmidt, J., *Letter to Corinth* (Philadelphia: Muhlenberg, 1947).

Schmiedel, P. W., *Die Briefe an die Thessalonicher und an die Korinther* (Hand-Commentar zum Neuen Testament 2; 2d ed.; Freiburg/Leipzig: Mohr [Siebeck], 1893) 47–209.

Schmitz, O., *Urchristliche Gemeindenöte: Eine Einführung in den ersten Korintherbrief* (Die urchristliche Botschaft 7; Berlin: Im Furche-V., 1939).

Schnedermann, G., *Die Briefe an die . . . Korinther . . .* (Kurzgefasster Kommentar zu den heiligen Schriften des Alten und Neuen Testamentes, NT 3; Munich: Beck, 1894) 127–287.

Schoch, M., *Information über Freiheit und Liebe: Der erste Korintherbrief des Paulus ausgelegt* (Zurich/Stuttgart: Gotthelf-V., 1969).

Schrage, W., *Der erste Brief an die Korinther* (EKKNT 7/1–4; Zurich: Benziger; Neukirchen-Vluyn: Neukirchener-V.; 1991–2001).

Schüssler Fiorenza, E., "1 Corinthians," *Harper's Bible Commentary* (ed. J. L. Mays; San Francisco: Harper & Row, 1988) 1168–89.

Senft, C., *La première épître de Saint Paul aux Corinthiens* (CNT 2/7; Neuchâtel: Delachaux et Niestlé, 1979; 2d ed., Geneva: Labor et Fides, 1990).

Sickenberger, J., *Die Briefe des heiligen Paulus an die Korinther und Römer* (BB 6; 4th ed.; Bonn: Hanstein, 1932) 1–88.

Simon, W. G. H., *The First Epistle to the Corinthians: Introduction and Commentary* (Torch Bible Commentaries; London: SCM, 1959).

Snyder, G. F., *First Corinthians: A Faith Community Commentary* (Macon: Mercer University Press, 1992).

Soards, M. L., "First Corinthians," *Mercer Commentary on the Bible* (ed. W. E. Mills and R. F. Wilson; Macon: Mercer University Press, 1995) 1163–89.

———, *1 Corinthians* (New International Biblical Commentary, NT 7; Peabody, MA: Hendrickson, 1999).

Somerville, R., *La première épître de Paul aux Corinthiens: Tome I* (Commentaire évangélique de la Bible 22; Vaux-sur-Seine: ÉDIFAC, 2001).

Spicq, C., "Épîtres aux Corinthiens," *La Sainte Bible* (ed. L. Pirot et A. Clamer; Paris: Letouzey et Ané, 1948), 11/2:161–297.

Stam, C. R., *Commentary on the First Epistle of Paul to the Corinthians* (Chicago: Berean Bible Society, 1988).

Stanley, A. P., *The Epistles of St. Paul to the Corinthians: With Critical Notes and Dissertations* (5th ed.; London: John Murray, 1882) 1–341.

Strobel, A., *Der erste Brief an die Korinther* (ZBKNT 6/1; Zurich: Theologischer-V., 1989).

Surgy, P. de and M. Carrez, *Les épîtres de Paul: Vol. 1, Corinthiens: Commentaire pastoral* (Paris: Bayard/Centurion, 1996).

Talbert, C. H., *Reading Corinthians: A Literary and Theological Commentary on 1 and 2 Corinthians* (New York: Crossroad, 1987) 1–107.

Thiselton, A. C., *The First Epistle to the Corinthians: A Commentary on the Greek Text* (NIGTC; Grand Rapids: Eerdmans; Carlisle, UK: Paternoster, 2000).

Thrall, M. E., *The First and Second Letters of Paul to the Corinthians* (Cambridge Bible Commentary: New English Bible; Cambridge: Cambridge University Press, 1965) 1–118.

Toussaint, C., *Épîtres de S. Paul: Leçons d'exégèse* (2 vols.; Paris: Beauchesne, 1910–13), 1:224–425.

Vaughan, C., and T. D. Lea, *1 Corinthians* (Bible Study Commentary; Grand Rapids: Zondervan, 1983).

Walter, E., *The First Epistle to the Corinthians* (New Testament for Spiritual Reading 13; London: Sheed and Ward; New York: Herder and Herder, 1971).

Watson, N., *The First Epistle to the Corinthians* (Epworth Commentaries; London: Epworth, 1992).

Weiss, B., *A Commentary on the New Testament* (4 vols.; New York/London: Funk & Wagnalls, 1906), 3:147–276.

Weiss, J., *Der erste Korintherbrief* (MeyerK 5; 9th ed.; Göttingen: Vandenhoeck & Ruprecht, 1910; repr. 1977).

Wendland, H.-D., *Die Briefe an die Korinther übersetzt und erklärt* (NTD 7; 13th ed.; Göttingen: Vandenhoeck & Ruprecht, 1972) 1–163.

Wette, W. M. L. de, *Kurze Erklärung der Briefe an die Corinther* (Kurzgefasstes exegetisches Handbuch zum Neuen Testament 2/2; Leipzig: Weidmann, 1841; 3d ed., 1855).

Williams, C. S. C., "I and II Corinthians," *Peake's Commentary on the Bible* (ed. M. Black and H. H. Rowley; London: Nelson, 1962) 954–66.

Willis, M., *A Commentary on Paul's First Epistle to the Corinthians* (Fairmount, IN: Cogdill Foundation, 1979).

Willoughby, W. R., *First Corinthians: Fostering Spirituality* (Deeper Life Pulpit Commentary; Camp Hill, PA: Christian Publications, 1996).

Wilson, G. B., *I Corinthians: A Digest of Reformed Comment* (London: Banner of Truth Trust, 1971).

Witherington, B., III, *Conflict and Community in Corinth: A Socio-Rhetorical Commentary on 1 and 2 Corinthians* (Grand Rapids: Eerdmans; Carlisle, UK: Paternoster, 1995) 69–324.

Wolff, C., *Der erste Brief des Paulus an die Korinther* (THKNT 7; Leipzig: Evangelische Verlagsanstalt, 1996; 2d ed., 2000).

V. Monographs

Applebury, T. R., *Studies in First Corinthians* (Bible Study Textbook; Joplin, MO: College Press, 1963).

Arrington, F. L., *Paul's Aeon Theology in 1 Corinthians* (Washington, DC: University Press of America, 1978).

Aune, D. E., *Prophecy in Early Christianity and the Ancient Mediterranean World* (Grand Rapids: Eerdmans, 1984).

Baird, W., *The Corinthian Church—A Biblical Approach to Urban Culture* (Nashville: Abingdon, 1964).

Balthasar, H. U. von, *Paul Struggles with His Congregation: The Pastoral Message of the Letters to the Corinthians* (San Francisco: Ignatius, 1992).

Barth, K., *The Resurrection of the Dead* (London: Hodder and Stoughton; New York: Fleming H. Revell, 1933; repr. New York: Arno, 1977).

Batelaan, L., *De kerk van Korinthe en wij: De actualiteit van Paulus' eerste brief aan Korinthiërs (1 Kor. 8–11:1)* (Franeker: Wever, 1971).

Baumann, R., *Mitte und Norm des Christlichen: Eine Auslegung von 1 Korinther 1:1–3:14* (NTAbh n.s. 5; Münster in W.: Aschendorff, 1968).

Baumgarten, J., *Paulus und die Apokalyptik: Die Auslegung apokalyptischer Überlieferungen in den echten Paulusbriefen* (WMANT 44; Neukirchen-Vluyn: Neukirchener-V., 1975).

Berquist, M. J., *Studies in First Corinthians* (Nashville: Convention, 1960).

Bétoulières, J., and V. Guénel (eds.), *Le corps et le Corps du Christ dans la première épître aux Corinthiens: Congrès de l'ACFEB, Tarbes (1981)* (LD 114; Paris: Cerf, 1983).

Bieringer, R., (ed.), *The Corinthian Correspondence* (BETL 125; Louvain: Leuven University/Peeters, 1996).

Birge, M. K., *The Language of Belonging: A Rhetorical Analysis of Kinship Language in First Corinthians* (CBET 31; Louvain: Peeters, 2002).

Boldrey, R., and J. Boldrey, *Chauvinist or Feminist? Paul's View of Women* (Grand Rapids: Baker, 1976).

Bornkamm, G., *Early Christian Experience* (London: SCM; New York: Harper & Row, 1969).

Bouttier, M., *En Christ: Étude d'exégèse et de théologie pauliniennes* (Études d'histoire et de philosophie religieuses; Paris: Presses Universitaires de France, 1962).

Boyer, J. L., *For a World Like Ours: Studies in I Corinthians* (Grand Rapids: Baker, 1971).

Braun, H., *Qumran und das Neue Testament* (2 vols; Tübingen: Mohr [Siebeck], 1966).

Bristow, J. T., *What Paul Really Said about Women* (San Francisco: Harper & Row, 1988).

Brown, A. R., *The Cross and Human Transformation: Paul's Apocalyptic Word in 1 Corinthians* (Minneapolis: Augsburg Fortress, 1995).

Brown, R. E., *An Introduction to the New Testament* (ABRL; New York: Doubleday, 1997).

Bultmann, R., *Theology of the New Testament* (2 vols.; London: SCM, 1952).

Byrne, B., *Paul and the Christian Woman* (Collegeville, MN: Liturgical, 1989).

Campbell, R. C., *The Gospel of Paul* (Valley Forge: Judson, 1973).

Carson, D. A., *The Cross and Christian Ministry: An Exposition of Passages from 1 Corinthians* (Grand Rapids: Baker, 1993).

Chester, S. J., *Conversion at Corinth* (Edinburgh: Clark, 2003).

Chow, J. K., *Patronage and Power: A Study of Social Networks in Corinth* (JSNTSup 75; Sheffield: JSOT, 1992).

Clarke, A. D., *Secular and Christian Leadership in Corinth: A Socio-Historical and Exegetical Study of 1 Corinthians 1–6* (AGJU 18; Leiden: Brill, 1993).

Cousar, C. B., *A Theology of the Cross: The Death of Jesus in the Pauline Letters* (Overtures to Biblical Theology 24; Minneapolis: Fortress, 1990).

Davies, R. E., *Studies in I Corinthians* (London: Epworth, 1962).

Davies, W. D., *Paul and Rabbinic Judaism: Some Rabbinic Elements in Pauline Theology* (London: SPCK, 1965).

Dean, R. J., *First Corinthians for Today* (Nashville: Broadman, 1972).

Doohan, H., *Corinthian Correspondence: Ministering in the Best and Worst of Times* (San Jose: Resource Publications, 1996).

Dowling, R., and S. Dray, *1 Corinthians: Free to Grow* (Baker Bible Guides; Grand Rapids: Baker, 1996).

Dungan, D. L., *The Sayings of Jesus in the Churches of Paul: The Use of the Synoptic Tradition in the Regulation of Early Church Life* (Philadelphia: Fortress, 1971).

Dupont, J., *Gnosis: La connaissance religieuse dans les épîtres de Saint Paul* (Universitas Catholica Lovaniensis, Dissertationes 2/40; Louvain: Nauwelaerts, 1949).

Eckstein, H.-J., *Der Begriff Syneidesis bei Paulus: Eine neutestamentlich-

exegetische Untersuchung zum 'Gewissensbegriff (WUNT 2/10; Tübingen: Mohr [Siebeck], 1983).

Engberg-Pedersen, T., (ed.), *Paul in His Hellenistic Context* (Minneapolis: Fortress, 1995).

Eriksson, A., *Traditions as Rhetorical Proof: Pauline Argumentation in 1 Corinthians* (ConNeot 29; Stockholm: Almqvist & Wiksell, 1998).

Evans, C. A., and J. A. Sanders (eds.), *Paul and the Scriptures of Israel* (JSNTSup 83; Sheffield: JSOT, 1993).

Fee, G. D., *God's Empowering Presence: The Holy Spirit in the Letters of Paul* (Peabody, MA: Hendrickson, 1994).

Feuillet, A., *Le Christ Sagesse de Dieu d'après les épîtres pauliniennes* (EBib; Paris: Gabalda, 1966).

Fitzgerald, J. T., *Cracks in an Earthen Vessel: An Examination of the Catalogues of Hardships in the Corinthian Correspondence* (SBLDS 99; Atlanta: Scholars, 1988).

Fjärstedt, B., *Synoptic Tradition in 1 Corinthians: Themes and Clusters of Theme Words in 1 Corinthians 1–4 and 9* (Uppsala: Teologiska Institutionen, 1974).

Fröhlich, U., (ed.), *Epistula ad Corinthios 1: 1. Lieferung, Einleitung* (Vetus Latina: Die Reste der altlateinischen Bibel 22; Freiburg im B.: Herder), 1.3 (1995), 1.2 (1996), 1.3 (1998).

Gerhardsson, B., *Memory and Manuscript: Oral Tradition and Written Transmission in Rabbinic Judaism and Early Christianity* (Acta seminarii neotestamentici upsaliensis 22; Uppsala: Almqvist & Wiksells, 1961; repr. together with *Tradition and Transmission in Early Christianity* (Grand Rapids: Eerdmans; Livonia, MI: Dove Booksellers, 1998).

Gillièron, B., *Pour l'amour de Corinthe: L'Apôtre Paul dicte ses souvenirs* (Poliez-le-Grand: Editions du Moulin, 1999).

Glen, J. S., *Pastoral Problems in First Corinthians* (London: Epworth; Philadelphia: Westminster, 1964).

Gooch, P. W., *Partial Knowledge: Philosophical Studies in Paul* (Notre Dame: University of Notre Dame Press, 1987).

Grant, R. M., *Paul in the Roman World: The Conflict at Corinth* (Louisville: Westminster/John Knox, 2001).

Green, M., *To Corinth with Love: Paul's Message to the Troubled Church at Corinth—and Its Relevance to Christians Today* (Waco: Word Books, 1988).

Grudem, W., *Evangelical Feminism & Biblical Truth* (Sisters, OR: Multnomah, 2000).

Gundry, R. H., *Sōma in Biblical Theology with Emphasis on Pauline Anthropology* (SNTSMS 29; Cambridge: Cambridge University Press, 1976; repr. Grand Rapids: Academic Books, 1987).

Hainz, J., *Ekklesia: Strukturen paulinischer Gemeinde-Theologie und Gemeinde-Ordnung* (BU 9; Regensburg: Pustet, 1972).

———, *Koinonia: "Kirche" als Gemeinschaft bei Paulus* (BU 16; Regensburg: Pustet, 1982).

Hanson, A. T., *The Paradox of the Cross in the Thought of St Paul* (JSNTSup 17; Sheffield: JSOT, 1987).

Heim, K., *Die Gemeinde des Auferstandenen: Tübinger Vorlesungen über der ersten Korintherbrief* (TVG Monographien und Studienbücher 239; 2d ed.; Giessen/Basel: Brunnen, 1987)

Heitmüller, W., *"Im Namen Jesu": Eine sprach- und religionsgeschichtliche Untersuchung zum Neuen Testament, speziell zur altchristlichen Taufe* (FRLANT I/2; Göttingen: Vandenhoeck & Ruprecht, 1903)

Hengel, M., *Crucifixion: In the Ancient World and the Folly of the Message of the Cross* (London: SCM; Philadelphia: Fortress, 1977).

Hofius, O., *Paulusstudien I* (WUNT 51; Tübingen: Mohr [Siebeck], 1989); *II* (WUNT 143, 2002).

Hooker, M. D., *Pauline Pieces* (London: Epworth, 1979); published in U.S.A. as *A Preface to Paul* (New York: Oxford University Press, 1980).

Hoppe, R., *Der Triumph des Kreuzes: Studien zum Verhältnis des Kolosserbriefs zur paulinischen Kreuzestheologie* (SBB 28; Stuttgart: Katholisches Bibelwerk, 1994).

Horrell, D. G., *The Social Ethos of the Corinthian Correspondence: Interests and Ideology from 1 Corinthians to 1 Clement* (Studies of the New Testament and Its World; Edinburgh: Clark, 1996).

Horsley, R. A., *Paul and Empire: Religion and Power in Roman Imperial Society* (Harrisburg: Trinity Press International, 1997) 242–52.

Hübner, H., *Vetus Testamentum in Novo: Band 2, Corpus Paulinum* (Göttingen: Vandenhoeck & Ruprecht, 1997) 221–305.

Hunt, A. R., *The Inspired Body: Paul, the Corinthians, and Divine Inspiration* (Macon: Mercer University Press, 1996).

Hurd, J. C., *The Origin of I Corinthians* (London: SPCK; New York: Seabury, 1965; new ed., Macon: Mercer University Press, 1983).

Jeremias, J., *The Eucharistic Words of Jesus* (London: SCM; Philadelphia: Fortress, 1966).

Jervell, J., *Imago Dei: Gen 1,26f. im Spätjudentum, in der Gnosis und in den paulinischen Briefen* (FRLANT 76; Göttingen: Vandenhoeck & Ruprecht, 1960).

Jervis, L. A., and P. Richardson (eds.), *Gospel in Paul: Studies on Corinthians, Galatians and Romans for Richard N. Longenecker* (JSNTSup 108; Sheffield: Sheffield Academic, 1994).

Jewett, R., *Paul's Anthropologiocal Terms: A Study of Their Use in Conflict Settings* (AGJU 10; Leiden: Brill, 1971) 23–40.

Käsemann, E., *Essays on New Testament Themes* (SBT 41; London: SCM 1964).

——, ed., *New Testament Questions of Today* (Philadelphia: Fortress, 1969).

Keener, C. S., *Paul, Women and Wives: Marriage and Women's Ministry in the Letters of Paul* (Peabody, MA: Hendrickson, 1992).

Klauck, H.-J., *Herrenmahl und hellenistischer Kult: Eine religionsgeschichtliche Untersuchung zum ersten Korintherbrief* (NTAbh n.s. 15; Münster in W.: Aschendorff, 1982).

Klein, G., *Die Zwölf Apostel: Ursprung und Gehalt einer Idee* (FRLANT 79; Göttingen: Vandenhoeck & Ruprecht, 1961).

Knox, J., *Chapters in a Life of Paul* (New York: Abingdon-Cokesbury, 1950; London: Black, 1954).

Kramer, W., *Christ, Lord, Son of God* (SBT 50; London: SCM, 1966).

Lambrecht, J., *Collected Studies on Pauline Literature and on the Book of Revelation* (AnBib 147; Rome: Biblical Institute, 2001).

———, *Pauline Studies* (BETL 115; Louvain: Leuven University/Peeters, 1994).

Lamp, J. S., *First Corinthians 1–4 in Light of Jewish Wisdom Traditions: Christ, Wisdom and Spirituality* (SBEC 42; Lewiston, NY: Mellen, 2000).

Lanci, J. R., *A New Temple for Corinth: Rhetorical and Archaeological Approaches to Pauline Imagery* (Studies in Biblical Literature 1; New York: P. Lang, 1997).

Laurin, R. L., *First Corinthians: Where Life Matures* (Grand Rapids: Kregel, 1987).

Liftin, D., *St. Paul's Theology of Proclamation: 1 Corinthians 1–4 and Greco-Roman Rhetoric* (SNTSMS 79; Cambridge: Cambridge University Press, 1994).

Longenecker, R. N., *Biblical Exegesis in the Apostolic Period* (Grand Rapids: Eerdmans, 1973).

Lorenzi, L. de (ed.), *Charisma und Agape (1 Ko 12–14)* (Monographische Reihe von Benedictina 7; Rome: St. Paul's Abbey, 1983).

———, *Freedom and Love: The Guide for Christian Life (1 Co 8–10; Rm 14–15)* (Monographic Series of Benedictina 6; Rome: St. Paul's Abbey, 1981).

———, *Paolo a una chiesa divisa (1 Co 1–4)* (Série monografica di Benedictina 5; Rome: St. Paul's Abbey, 1980).

———, *Paul de Tarse: Apôtre de notre temps* (Série monographique de Benedictina 1; Rome: St. Paul's Abbey, 1979).

———, *Résurrection du Christ et des chrétiens (1 Co 15)* (Série monographique de Benedictina 8; Rome: St. Paul's Abbey, 1985).

MacArthur, J., *Guidelines for Singleness and Marriage* (Chicago: Moody, 1986).

Maleparampil, J., *The "Trinitarian" Formula in St. Paul: An Exegetical Investigation into the Meaning and Function of Those Pauline Sayings Which Compositely Make Mention of God, Christ and the Holy Spirit* (European University Studies 23/546; Frankfurt am M./New York: P. Lang, 1995).

Maly, K., *Mündige Gemeinde: Untersuchungen zur pastoralen Führung des Apostels Paulus im 1. Korintherbrief* (SBM 2; Stuttgart: Katholisches Bibelwerk, 1967).

Manson, T. W., *Studies in the Gospels and Epistles* (ed. M. Black; Manchester: Manchester University Press, 1962).

Marshall, P., *Enmity in Corinth: Social Conventions in Paul's Relations with the Corinthians* (WUNT 2/23; Tübingen: Mohr [Siebeck], 1987; 2d ed., 1991).

Martin, R. P., *1, 2 Corinthians* (Word Biblical Themes; Dallas: Word, 1988).

Meeks, W. A., *The First Urban Christians: The Social World of the Apostle Paul* (New Haven: Yale University Press, 1983).

Meyer, B. F., (ed.), *One Loaf, One Cup: Ecumenical Studies of 1 Cor 11 and Other Eucharistic Texts: The Cambridge Conference on the Eucharist, August 1988* (Louvain: Peeters; Macon: Mercer University Press, 1993).

Meyer, M. W., *The Ancient Mysteries: A Source-Book* (San Francisco: Harper & Row, 1987).

Mitchell, M. M., *Paul and the Rhetoric of Reconciliation: An Exegetical Investigation of the Language and Composition of 1 Corinthians* (HUT 28; Tübingen: Mohr Siebeck; Louisville: Westminster/John Knox, 1991).

Morton, A. Q., *A Critical Concordance to I and II Corinthians* (Computer Bible 19; Wooster, OH: Biblical Research Associates, 1979).

Mühlberger, S., *Mitarbeiter Gottes: Ein Arbeitsheft zum 1. Korintherbrief* (Gespräch zur Bibel 4; Klosterneuburg: Österreichisches Katholisches Bibelwerk, 1978).

Müller, E., *Anstoss und Gericht: Eine Studie zum jüdischen Hintergrund des paulinischen Skandalon-Begriffs* (SANT 19; Munich: Kösel, 1969).

Murphy, D. J., *The Apostle of Corinth* (Melbourne: Campion, 1966).

Murphy-O'Connor, J., *Paul: A Critical Life* (Oxford/New York: Oxford University Press, 1997).

——, Paul the Letter-Writer: His World, His Options, His Skills (GNS 41; Collegeville, MN: Liturgical Press, 1995).

Neugebauer, F., *In Christus, En Christō: Eine Untersuchung zum paulinischen Glaubensverständnis* (Göttingen: Vandenhoeck & Ruprecht, 1961).

Ollrog, W.-H., *Paulus und seine Mitarbeiter: Untersuchungen zu Theorie und Praxis der paulinischen Mission* (WMANT 50; Neukirchen-Vluyn: Neukirchener-V., 1979).

Oropeza, B. J., *Paul and Apostasy: Eschatology, Perseverance, and Falling Away in the Corinthian Congregation* (WUNT 2/115; Tübingen: Mohr Siebeck, 2000)

Ortkemper, F.-J., *Das Kreuz in der Verkündigung des Apostels Paulus: Dargestellt an den Texten der paulinischen Hauptbriefe* (SBS 24; Stuttgart: Katholisches Bibelwerk, 1967).

Panikulam, G., *Koinōnia in the New Testament: A Dynamic Expression of Christian Life* (AnBib 85; Rome: Biblical Institute, 1979).

Pappas, B., *The Christian Life in the Early Church and Today according to St. Paul's First Epistle to the Corinthians* (Westchester, IL: Amnos Publications, 1989).

Pesch, R., *Paulus ringt um die Lebensform der Kirche: Vier Briefe an die Gemeinde Gottes in Korinth: Paulus—neu gesehen* (Herderbücherei 1291; Freiburg im B.: Herder, 1986).

Peterson, B. K., *Eloquence and the Proclamation of the Gospel in Corinth* (SBLDS 163; Atlanta: Scholars, 1998).

Pfammatter, J., *Die Kirche als Bau: Eine exegetisch-theologische Studie zur Ekklesiologie der Paulusbriefe* (AnGreg 110; Rome: Università Gregoriana, 1960).

Pickett, R., *The Cross in Corinth: The Social Significance of the Death of Jesus* (JSNTSup 143; Sheffield: Sheffield Academic, 1997).

Plank, K. A., *Paul and the Irony of Affliction* (SBL Semeia Studies; Atlanta: Scholars, 1987).

Pöttner, M., *Realität als Kommunikation: Ansätze zur Beschreibung der Grammatik des paulinischen Sprechens in 1 Kor 1,4–4,21 im Blick auf literarische Problematik und Situationsbezug des 1. Korintherbriefes* (Theologie 2; Münster: Lit, 1995).

Prat, F., *The Theology of Saint Paul* (2 vols.; Westminster, MD: Newman, 1956), 1:85–144.

Preisker, H., *Christentum und Ehe in den ersten drei Jahrhunderten: Eine Studie zur Kulturgeschichte der alten Welt* (Neue Studien zur Geschichte der Theologie und der Kirche 23; Berlin: Trowitsch & Sohn, 1927).

Quast, K., *Reading the Corinthian Correspondence: An Introduction* (New York: Paulist, 1994) 17–99.

Ramsaran, R. A., *Liberating Words: Paul's Use of Rhetorical Maxims in 1 Corinthians 1–10* (Valley Forge: Trinity Press International, 1996).

Reitzenstein, R., *Hellenistic Mystery-Religions: Their Basic Ideas and Significance* (PTMS 15; Pittsburgh: Pickwick, 1978).

Richards, W. L., *1 Corinthians: The Essentials and Nonessentials of Christian Living* (Abundant Life Bible Amplifier; Nampa, ID: Pacific Press, 1997).

Robertson, F. W., *Expository Lectures on St. Paul's Epistles to the Corinthians . . .* (London: Smith, Elder, 1859) 1–314.

Robinson, J. A. T., *The Body: A Study in Pauline Theology* (2d ed.; Philadelphia: Westminster, 1977).

Rohr, I., *Paulus und die Gemeinde von Korinth auf Grund der beiden Korintherbriefe* (BibS[F] 4; Freiburg im B.: Herder, 1899).

Rosner, B. S., *Paul, Scripture and Ethics: A Study of 1 Corinthians 5–7* (AGJU 22; Leiden: Brill, 1994; repr. Grand Rapids: Baker Books, 1999).

Sand, A., *Der Begriff "Fleisch" in den paulinischen Hauptbriefen* (BU 2; Regensburg: Pustet, 1967).

Schäfer, K., *Gemeinde als "Bruderschaft": Ein Beitrag zum Kirchenverständnis des Paulus* (Europäische Hochschulschriften 23/333; Frankfurt am M./New York: P. Lang, 1989).

Schenk, W. et al., *Gemeinde im Lernprozess: Die Korintherbriefe* (Bibelauslegung für die Praxis 22; Stuttgart: Katholisches Bibelwerk, 1979) 9–101.

Schlatter, A., *Die korinthische Theologie* (BFCT 18/2; Gütersloh: Bertelsmann, 1914).

Schmithals, W., *Gnosticism in Corinth: An Investigation of the Letters to the Corinthians* (Nashville: Abingdon, 1971).

——, *The Office of the Apostle in the Early Church* (Nashville: Abingdon, 1969).

——, *Paul & the Gnostics* (Nashville: Abingdon, 1972).

Schreiber, A., *Die Gemeinde in Korinth: Versuch einer gruppendynamischen Betrachtung der Entwicklung der Gemeinde von Korinth auf der Basis des ersten Korintherbriefes* (NTAbh n.s. 12; Münster in W.: Aschendorff, 1977).

Schüssler, Fiorenza, E., *In Memory of Her* (New York: Crossroad, 1984)

Schütz, J. H., *Paul and the Anatomy of Apostolic Authority* (SNTSMS 26; Cambridge: Cambridge University Press, 1975) 187–203.

South, J. T., *Disciplinary Practices in Pauline Texts* (Lewiston, NY: Mellen, 1992).

Spittler, R. P., *The Corinthian Correspondence* (Springfield: Gospel, 1976).

Stanley, C. D., *Paul and the Language of Scripture: Citation Technique in the Pauline Epistles and Contemporary Literature* (SNTSMS 69; Cambridge: Cambridge University Press, 1992) 185–215.

Stedman, R. C., *Expository Studies in 1 Corinthians: The Deep Things of God* (Waco: Word Books, 1981).

Theis, J., *Paulus als Weisheitslehrer: Der Gekreuzigte und die Weisheit Gottes in 1 Kor 1–4* (BU 22; Regensburg: Pustet, 1991).

Theissen, G., *The Social Setting of Pauline Christianity: Essays on Corinth* (Philadelphia: Fortress, 1982).

Thrall, M. E., *Greek Particles in the New Testament: Linguistic and Exegetical Studies* (NTTS 3; Leiden: Brill, 1962).

Tomson, P. J., *Paul and the Jewish Law: Halakha in the Letters of the Apostle to the Gentiles* (CRINT 3/1; Assen: Van Gorcum; Minneapolis: Fortress, 1990).

Trail, R., *An Exegetical Summary of 1 Corinthians 10–16* (Dallas: SIL International, 2001).

Trobisch, D., *Paul's Letter Collection: Tracing the Origins* (Minneapolis: Fortress, 1994).

Vanhoye, A., (ed.), *L'Apôtre Paul: Personnalité, style et conception du ministère* (BETL 73; Louvain: Leuven University/Peeters, 1986).

Weder, H., *Das Kreuz Jesu bei Paulus: Ein Versuch, über den Geschichtsbezug des christlichen Glaubens nachzudenken* (FRLANT 125; Göttingen: Vandenhoeck & Ruprecht, 1981).

Welborn, L. L., *Politics and Rhetoric in the Corinthian Epistles* (Macon: Mercer University Press, 1997).

Wilckens, U., *Weisheit und Torheit: Eine exegetisch-religionsgeschichtliche Untersuchung zu 1. Kor. 1 und 2* (BzHT 26; Tübingen: Mohr [Siebeck], 1959).

Wingard, R. W., *Paul and the Corinthians: The Life and Letters of Paul* (Nashville: Abingdon, 1999).

Winter, B. W., *After Paul Left Corinth: The Influence of Secular Ethics and Social Change* (Grand Rapids: Eerdmans, 2001).

Wire, A. C., *The Corinthian Women Prophets: A Reconstruction through Paul's Rhetoric* (Minneapolis: Fortress, 1990).

Yinger, K. L., *Paul, Judaism and Judgment according to Deeds* (SNTSMS 105; Cambridge: Cambridge University Press, 1999).

VI. Articles on General Topics

Barclay, J. M. G., "Thessalonica and Corinth: Social Contrasts in Pauline Christianity," *JSNT* 47 (1992) 49–74.

Barefoot, H. E., "Discipline in the Corinthian Letters," *RevExp* 57 (1960) 438–49.

Barton, S. C., "Christian Community in the Light of 1 Corinthians," *SCE* 10 (1997) 1–15.

Batey, R., "Paul's Interactions with the Corinthians," *JBL* 84 (1965) 139–46.

Betz, H. D., and M. M. Mitchell, "Corinthians, First Epistle to the," *ABD*, 1:1139–48.

Blomberg, C. L., "Applying 1 Corinthians in the Early Twenty-first Century," *SwJT* 45 (2002) 19–38.

Bowe, B. E., "Paul and First Corinthians," *TBT* 35 (1997) 268–74.

Braun, H., "Exegetische Randglossen zum 1 Kor," *ThViat* 8 (1948–49) 26–50.

Brown, R., "The Nature of the Corinthian Correspondence," *RevExp* 57 (1960) 389–97.

Byars, R. P., "Sectarian Division and the Wisdom of the Cross: Preaching from First Corinthians," *QR* 9/4 (1989) 65–96.

Caird, G. B., "The Corinthian Letters," *Int* 13 (1959) 387–99.

Casey, M., "Paul's Response to Corinthian Enthusiasm," *TBT* 88 (1977) 1075–81.

Castelli, E. A., "Interpretations of Power in 1 Corinthians," *Semeia* 54 (1991) 197–222.

Cleary, P., "The Epistles to the Corinthians," *CBQ* 12 (1950) 10–33.

Corry, N., "Questions of Authority, Status and Power," *Scriptura* 70 (1999) 181–94.

Craddock, F. B., "Preaching to Corinthians," *Int* 44 (1990) 158–68.

Cullmann, O., "Parousieverzögerung und Urchristentum: Der gegenwärtige Stand der Diskussion," *TLZ* 83 (1958) 1–12.

Dinkler, E., "Korintherbriefe," *RGG* 4:17–23.

Durken, D., "The Corinthian Connection," *TBT* 35 (1997) 295–99.

Ellingworth, P., "Translating 1 Corinthians," *BT* 31 (1980) 234–38; *CV* 23 (1980) 29–34.

Engberg-Pedersen, T., "The Gospel and Social Practice according to 1 Corinthians," *NTS* 33 (1987) 557–84.

Feuillet, A., "Paul: 2. Corinthiens (Les épîtres aux)," *DBSup*, 7:170–95, esp. 171–83.

Gächter, P., "Zum Pneumabegriff des hl. Paulus," *ZKT* 53 (1929) 345–408.

Genest, O., "L'Interprétation de la mort de Jésus en situation discursive: Un cas-type: L'articulation des figures de cette mort en 1–2 Corinthiens," *NTS* 34 (1988) 506–35.

Gilmour, S. M., "Corinthians, First Letter to the," *IDB*, 1:684–92.

Graham, R. W., "Paul's Pastorate in Corinth: A Keyhole View of His Ministry," *LTQ* 17 (1982) 45–58.

Harrison, J., "St Paul's Letters to the Corinthians," *ExpTim* 77 (1965–66) 285–86.

Hemphill, K., "Preaching from First Corinthians," *SwJT* 45 (2002) 39–52.

Hogan, L. L., "Wrestling with the World: Paul's First Letter to the Corinthians," *QR* 19 (1999) 303–22.

Jewett, R., "Paul's Dialogue with the Corinthians . . . and Us," *QR* 13 (1993) 89–112.

———, "The Redaction of I Corinthians and the Trajectory of the Pauline School," *JAARSup* 44 (1978) 389–444.

Kijne, J. J., "*We, Us* and *Our* in I and II Corinthians," *NovT* 8 (1966) 170–79.

Klauck, H.-J., "Gemeindestrukturen im ersten Korintherbrief," *BK* 40 (1985) 9–15.

Koenig, J., "Christ and the Hierarchies in First Corinthians," *ATRSup* 11 (1990) 99–113.

Krentz, E., "Preaching to an Alien Culture: Resources in the Corinthian Letters," *WW* 16 (1996) 465–72.

Lea, T. D., "An Introduction to 1 Corinthians," *TTE* 14/1 (1983) 22–34.

Melconian, V. D., "First Corinthians," *Int* 7 (1953) 62–77.

Moore, R., "The Letters to Corinth," *FQ* 25 (1988) 125–33.

Morgan-Wynne, J., "Introduction to 1 Corinthians," *SwJT* 26 (1983) 4–15.

Morton, A. Q., "Dislocations in 1 and 2 Corinthians," *ExpTim* 78 (1966–67) 119.

Mounce, R. H., "Continuity of the Primitive Tradition: Some Pre-Pauline Elements in I Corinthians," *Int* 13 (1959) 417–24.

Murphy-O'Connor, J., "Interpolations in 1 Corinthians," *CBQ* 48 (1986) 81–94.

Nichols, D. R., "The Problem of Two-Level Christianity at Corinth," *Pneuma* 11 (1989) 99–111.

Oepke, A., "Irrwege in den neueren Paulusforschung," *TLZ* 77 (1952) 449–58.

Omanson, R. L., "Acknowledging Paul's Quotations," *BT* 43 (1992) 201–13.

Padgett, A., "Feminism in First Corinthians: A Dialogue with Elisabeth Schüssler Fiorenza," *EvQ* 58 (1984) 121–32.

Perkins, D. W., "Superspirituality in Corinth," *TTE* 14/1 (1983) 41–52.

Peterlin, D., "The Corinthian Church between Paul and Clement's Time," *AsTJ* 53 (1998) 49–57.

Pfitzner, V. C., "Proclaiming the Name: Cultic, Narrative and Eucharistic Proclamation in First Corinthians," *LTJ* 25 (1991) 15–25.

Pietrantonio, R., "Para leer la correspondencia corintia," *CdT* 19 (2000) 59–86.

Prümm, K., "Die pastorale Einheit des 1 Kor," *ZKT* 64 (1940) 202–14.

Reinmuth, E., "Narratio und Argumentatio—Zur Auslegung der Jesus-Christus-Geschichte im ersten Korintherbrief: Ein Beitrag zur mimetischen Kompetenz des Paulus," *ZTK* 92 (1995) 13–27.

Richardson, P., and P. W. Gooch, "Accommodation Ethics," *TynBul* 29 (1978) 89–142.

Robbins, J. K., "The Second Thoughts of a Captive Intellect: Pastoral Reflections on Paul's Letters to the Corinthians," *WW* 16 (1996) 401–12.

Sanders, J. T., "Paul between Jews and Gentiles in Corinth," *JSNT* 65 (1997) 67–83.

Schüssler Fiorenza, E., "Rhetorical Situation and Historical Reconstruction in 1 Corinthians," *NTS* 33 (1987) 386–403.

Sciotti, G., "Problemi introdottivi e significati più rilevanti," *RBR* 8 (1973) 9–27.

Sellin, G. "Hauptprobleme des Ersten Korintherbriefes," *ANRW* II/25.4 (1987) 2940–3044.

Summers, R., "First Corinthians: An Exposition," *RevExp* 57 (1960) 398–421.

Swartz, S. M., "Praising or Prophesying: What Were the Corinthians Doing?" *Notes* 6/2 (1992) 25–36.

Terry, R. B., "Patterns of Discourse Structure in 1 Corinthians," *JOTT* 7 (1996) 1–32.

Theissen, G., "Soziale Schichtung in der korinthischen Gemeinde: Ein Beitrag zur Soziologie des hellenistischen Urchristentums," ZNW 65 (1974) 232–72.

Thiselton, A. C., "Realized Eschatology at Corinth," NTS 24 (1977–78) 510–26.

Tomson, P. J., "La première épître aux Corinthiens comme document de la tradition apostolique de Halakha," *The Corinthian Correspondence* (BETL 125; ed. R. Bieringer) 459–70.

Vos, J. S., "Theologische und historisch-kritische Exegese des Neuen Testaments: Bemerkungen zu K. Barths Auslegung des ersten Korintherbriefes," *ZfdT* 13 (1997) 12–31.

Ward, W. E., "Theological Issues Raised in First Corinthians," *RevExp* 57 (1960) 422–37.

Weder, H., "Un nouveau commentaire de la première épître aux Corinthiens," *RTP* 31 (1981) 167–71.

Wenham, D., "Whatever Went Wrong in Corinth?" *ExpTim* 108 (1977) 137–41.

Winter, B. W., "Secular and Christian Responses to Corinthian Famines," *TynBul* 40 (1989) 86–106.

Young, F., "Mission in the Corinthian Correspondence," *EpRev* 16 (1989) 76–81.

COMMENTARY
AND NOTES

◆

I. INTRODUCTION (1:1–9)

◆

1   ADDRESS AND GREETING
(1:1–3)

[1:1] Paul, called by the will of God to be an apostle of Christ Jesus, and our brother Sosthenes, [2] to the church of God that is in Corinth, to those sanctified in Christ Jesus, called to be holy, together with all those who in every place call upon the name of our Lord Jesus Christ, their Lord and ours. [3] Grace and peace to you from God our Father and the Lord Jesus Christ!

COMMENT

In addressing the Christians of Roman Corinth, Paul was fully aware that he not only had been involved in founding the church there (3:10), but also that his relations with that church had been affected by much of what had happened there recently since he left Corinth in A.D. 52. As he begins this letter to them, he summons the Corinthian Christians to recall not only his own God-given role and relation to them, but the goal of their own vocation as well as that of all who, like them, reverence the Lord Jesus Christ.

Paul does not send this letter as an individual as he has done in some other instances, e.g., when writing to the Galatians or to the Romans. He mentions Sosthenes as a co-sender, even if he himself is the one who is actually dictating the message that this letter will bring to the Christians of Roman Corinth. Sosthenes is mentioned because he is known to them, and Paul is making use of Sosthenes' acquaintance and reputation among them as a way to influence them in the matters about which he is going to address them.

This epistolary prescript is not as lengthy as that in Rom 1:1–7, but it too forms one sentence in the Greek text, even if it is customary to break it up into shorter sentences in modern translations. Moreover, it follows the customary form of an ancient *praescriptio* or opening formula of many ancient Greek letters: X (nom.) to Y (dat.), and a stereotyped infin. *chairein*, meaning lit. "to rejoice," but = "greetings" (as in Acts 15:23; 23:26; Jas 1:1). Note also the similar formula in the Aramaic letter of King Artaxerxes to Ezra in Ezra 7:12; cf. Dan 3:31. Paul never uses the simple secular greeting *chairein*; rather he substitutes for it his own characteristic combination, *charis hymin kai eirēnē*, "grace and peace (be) to you." The elements of the customary formula are found in vv. 1 and 3; the rest is the Pauline expansion of the formula (see further *NJBC*, art. 45 §§6–8; *Romans*, 227–28; cf. Lieu, " 'Grace to You' "; Doty, *Letters*, 22).

In addition to the mention of Sosthenes as the co-sender of the letter, Paul expands the opening formula by a single identification of himself, "called by the will of God to be an apostle of Christ Jesus." He thus attributes his role as *apostolos* (recall Rom 1:1) to God's will. This is an idea that he explains more in Gal 1:15, maintaining that he has been set apart for this role even before he was born. Paul also looks on himself as one sent forth by Christ Jesus, and to this notion he will return in 9:1. He now addresses Corinthian Christians in an ad hoc apostolic letter, which is best seen as an admonitory discourse set forth in epistolary form (see further Berger, "Apostelbrief"; INTRODUCTION pp. 55–56).

Paul further expands the opening formula by recalling to the Christians of Roman Corinth that they have been "sanctified in Christ Jesus" and are "called to be holy." In saying that, Paul not only mentions one of the effects of the Christ-event, "sanctification," but associates these Gentile Christians with the holiness of the people of God in the OT heritage (Lev 19:2: "You shall be holy, for I the Lord your God am holy"). In the Greek world in which they lived, persons and things were often said to be *hagios*, "holy," i.e., dedicated to the gods (Herodotus, *Hist.* 2.41.44; Aristophanes, *Birds* 522). Paul's notion of holiness, however, is derived more from his Jewish background, where the adj. *qādôš* characterized things (e.g., the ground [Exod 3:5]; Jerusalem [Isa 48:2]; its Temple [Isa 64:10]); or people (Israelites [Exod 19:14]; priests [1 Macc 2:54]; or prophets [Wis 11:1]). The term did not express so much an inner state of ethical piety as the dedication of people or things to the awesome service of God. It was above all a cultic term that set them off from the secular or profane for such service. Paul sees such holiness or sanctification rooted in what Christ Jesus has done for humanity: he is our "sanctification" (1 Cor 1:30).

Paul also expands the opening formula by associating Christians of Roman Corinth with "all those who in every place call upon the name of the Lord Jesus Christ, their Lord and ours." Calling on the name of the Lord is a well-known OT notion (see NOTE on 1:2), but Paul modifies it by identifying "the Lord" as Jesus Christ. In this he is simply echoing the most primitive Christian proclamation, "Jesus is Lord" (Phil 2:11; Rom 10:9), which he will repeat in 1 Cor 12:3. He thus acknowledges Christ as the risen *Kyrios*.

So Paul begins an important letter addressed to "the church of God" in Corinth. His authoritative words as a called apostle of Christ Jesus speak also to the church of God today, reminding individual Christians that they too are "called to be holy." His words have become part of the written Word of God, and what he will seek to persuade the Christians of Roman Corinth about in the rest of the letter, he addresses also to all Christians of the twenty-first century. As he expanded his greeting to hail "all those who in every place call upon the name of our Lord

Jesus Christ," so he invites the modern reader to reflect on what he is about to call
to the attention of the Corinthian Christians.

NOTES

1:1. *Paul.* The Apostle identifies himself as *Paulos*, the only name that he uses in
all his uncontested letters or that is used of him in the Deutero-Paulines, Pastorals, and 2 Pet 3:15. *Paulos* is the Greek form of a well-known Roman name,
Paul(l)us, a cognomen used by the *gens Aemilia*, the Sergii, Vettenii, and others
(see F. Münzer, "Paullus," PW 18.4.2362–63). It is the only thing in Paul's letters
that supports the Lucan identification of him as a Roman citizen (Acts 16:37;
22:25–29; 23:27). Paul himself mentions neither his Roman citizenship nor his
birth in Tarsus of Cilicia, inhabitants of which enjoyed Roman citizenship.
Ramsay (*The Cities*, 205) traces Roman citizenship in Tarsus to Pompey's con-
quest of Cilicia in 64 B.C.

Luke alone records Paul's other name, Saul (in the grecized form *Saulos* [Acts
7:58; 8:1, etc.] or in the transliterated Hebrew form *Saoul* [Acts 9:4, 17; 22:7, 13;
26:14]). The two names occur together in Acts 13:9, *Saulos de, ho kai Paulos*,
"Saul, also called Paul." This reflects the custom of Jews bearing two names, one
Semitic, the other Greco-Roman. Paul was his *(cog)nomen*, and Saul was the Semitic *signum* or *supernomen* (see *PAHT* §P3; cf. Dessau, "Der Name"; Harrer,
"Saul Who also Is Called Paul"). His Semitic name associated him with the ancient King Saul, son of Kish, of the tribe of Benjamin (1 Sam 9:1–2), the tribe to
which Paul himself belonged (Phil 3:5).

Paul will name himself again in 1:13 bis; 3:5, 22; 16:21; and in 1:12; 3:4 he will
quote the Corinthian slogan that names him. Cf. 1 Thess 2:18; Gal 5:2; 2 Cor
10:1; Phlm 9, 19.

called by the will of God to be an apostle of Christ Jesus. Lit. "called (as) an apostle." Paul attributes his call to be *apostolos* to God's will, as in 2 Cor 1:1; Gal 1:15;
and as he does with other events in his life (see Rom 1:10; 15:32; 2 Cor 8:5; Gal
1:4). His call stems not from the earthly Jesus, as was true of the Twelve, but from
"Jesus Christ and God the Father, who raised him from the dead" (Gal 1:1). Paul
insists on this status of being "called" by God because it indicates his official position in the Christian community and forms the basis of his authority. As "an apostle of Christ Jesus," he emphasizes that the risen Lord has appeared to him (9:1)
and commissioned him to evangelize, and in this capacity he writes this letter to
the Christians of Roman Corinth. He does not have this status because of personal
qualities; nor has he assumed it by a personal decision. He has been called by
God, as were prophets of old (Jer 1:5; Isa 6:8–9; Amos 7:14–15). Paul described
that call in Gal 1:15–16. The verbal adj. *klētos*, "called," is omitted here in some
MSS (P[61], A, D, 81), perhaps because of homoeoteleuton, and "Christ Jesus" is inverted in some (ℵ, A, L, P).

Apostolos, derived from the vb. *apostellein*, "send," means "someone/some-
thing sent." In extrabiblical Greek, it is not normaly used in a religious sense,
where it denotes rather a naval "expedition" (Lysias, *Or.* 19.21; Demosthenes, *Or.*

3.5; 18.80, 107), or "a colony to be sent out" (Dionysius of Halicarnassus, *Antiq. Rom.* 9.59.2), or "a trade vessel" (Plato, *Ep.* 346a), or "an envoy, messenger" (Herodotus, *Hist.* 1.21; 5.38). In the last sense, it also occurs in the NT (Phil 2:25; John 13:16). *Apostolos* is found only once in the LXX (1 Kgs 14:6), translating the pass. ptc. *šālûaḥ*, "sent," used of Ahaziah dispatched by God as a stern messenger to the wife of Jeroboam. Consequently, the religious sense of *apostolos* is not easily explained from such an extrabiblical or LXX background. It has been related rather to a Palestinian Jewish institution, in which Jerusalem authorities sent out rabbis as *šělûḥîm* (Hebrew) or *šělîḥîn* (Aramaic), "commissioned emissaries," empowered to act in their name to settle financial, calendaric, or doctrinal questions among Jews living outside Jerusalem. Vogelstein ("Development of the Apostolate") has even traced this notion back to the Book of Chronicles; cf. Rengstorf, *TDNT* 1:407–20, esp. 414–17. Although this Palestinian origin of the Christian apostolate has been questioned at times (e.g., Klein, *Die zwölf Apostel*, 22–32; Schmithals, *Office of Apostle*, 98–110), it still remains the best explanation. It is rooted in the use of *šělîāḥ* in Ezra 7:14 and builds on such OT data about God sending messengers to his people on religious matters, and specifically on passages such as 2 Chr 17:7–9, where Jehoshaphat "sends" princes, Levites, and priests to teach the people in all the cities of Judah. Here the Hebrew text uses *šlḥ*, and the LXX *apostellein*. Between the Palestinian Jewish institution of *šělûḥîm* and the Christian apostolate intervened the action of the risen Christ commissioning followers to bear witness or preach in his name (Luke 24:47–48; Acts 1:8; cf. Matt 28:19–20; John 20:21). From this commission developed the specifically Christian sense of *apostolos*, which was not translated into Latin as *nuntius*, "messenger," but merely transliterated as *apostolus* and preserved in many modern languages as "apostle." So it has become a specifically Christian word.

In writing "Christ Jesus," Paul is employing *Christos* in its nontitular sense. He is aware of its titular meaning, because in Rom 9:5 he adds it, "the Messiah," to the seven prerogatives of Israel that he has listed in 9:4. In the vast majority of the instances when he uses *Christos*, however, it is Jesus' second name, "Jesus Christ" (e.g., Rom 1:4, 6, 8), a double name that he has inherited from the early Christian tradition before him. In a distinctive way, Paul often reverses the order of the names, "Christ Jesus," as here (see also 1:2, 4, 30; 15:31; Rom 6:3, 11; 8:1, 39; 15:5, 16, 17; 16:3; 2 Cor 1:1; Gal 2:4, 16; 3:14, 26). Only he among NT writers uses this form (the inverted names in Acts 3:20; 5:42; 17:3; 18:5, 28; 24:24 are variant readings introduced by copyists familiar with the Pauline usage).

and our brother Sosthenes. Lit. "Sosthenes the brother." Paul names *Sōsthenēs* as the cosender of this letter, not as the coauthor, as Ellis ("Coworkers," 188) and Lindemann (*1 Cor*, 26) rightly recognize. Paul clearly regards him as a fellow worker in Ephesus, but even more as one who is known to the Christians of Corinth. He appears nowhere else in Paul's letters. The plur. verbs in 1:18–31 and 2:6–16, followed by an emphatic *kagō*, "I myself," cannot be taken as a sign that Sosthenes was actually involved in the writing of this letter along with Paul, *pace* Murphy-O'Connor ("Co-authorship"), Soards (*1 Cor*, 18); see further Verhoef, "The Senders," 418–21.

Adelphos, meaning "fellow-Christian," imitates the Jewish use of Hebrew or Aramaic *'aḥ,* "brother," for a fellow Jew (see Lev 19:17; 2 Macc 1:1; Josephus, *J.W.* 2.8.3 §122), and that broad meaning of *adelphos* will occur frequently in this letter (e.g., 1:10, 11, 26; 2:1; 3:1; 4:6; 5:11; 6:5, 6, 8; 7:12, 14, 15, 24, 29; 8:9, 12, 13; 10:1; 11:33; 12:1; 14:6, 20, 26, 39; 15:1, 6, 31, 50, 53). (*Christianos* [Acts 11:26] had not yet come into common usage.) For the broad metaphorical use of *adelphos* for officials, friends, business partners, members of guilds and mystery cults in Greek documentary texts, see Arzt-Grabner, " 'Brothers' and 'Sisters' "; Harland, "Familial Dimensions."

A Sosthenes is mentioned in Acts 18:17 as a "leader of the synagogue" (*archisy-nagōgos*) in Roman Corinth, on whom Paul's Jewish opponents pounced and whom they beat "in full view of the court" (*bēma*), when the Roman proconsul of Achaia, Lucius Junius Gallio, refused to hear the case brought by them against Paul. See *Acts,* 630. This Sosthenes may be the same person whom Paul now mentions, as has been suggested often since John Chrysostom (*In Acta Apost. hom.* 39; PG 60.278) and Theodoret (*Interpr. Ep. 1 ad Cor.* 1:1; PG 82.229), but there is no certainty about it despite the fact that he was a prominent person in Corinth and connected with Paul's missionary work there. (In fact, Chrysostom even identified him with Crispus [1 Cor 1:14], because the latter is called *archisy-nagōgos* in Acts 18:8 and is said to have become a Christian along with his house-hold; see Myrou, "Sosthenes.") If this Sosthenes were the same person, then he must have been converted subsequently to Christianity, for Paul now calls him "brother," i.e., fellow Christian. The identification of the two has been accepted by Bengel, Godet, Moffatt, Barrett. However, "Sosthenes," although not a very common Greek name, has been found in inscriptions; so the persons could be dif-ferent. Lietzmann regarded the identification as fantasy (*1 Cor,* 4), and it has been rejected by Ramsay. Eusebius (*HE* 1.12.1) regarded Sosthenes as one of the Sev-enty disciples of Jesus (Luke 10:1). It is sometimes maintained that Sosthenes was Paul's "secretary"; so Prior (*Paul the Letter-Writer,* 42; Fee, *1 Cor,* 31, 837).

2. *to the church of God that is in Corinth.* Lit. "the one being in Corinth." This last participial phrase follows "to those sanctified in Christ Jesus" in the important MSS (P⁴⁶, B, D*, F, G), but it creates a difficult combination of words, which "ap-parently arose through the accidental omission of one or more phrases and their subsequent reintroduction at a wrong position" (Metzger, *TCGNT,* 478). "The transposition is stylistically intolerable. *Tē ousē* . . . cannot be separated from *ekklēsiā* (cf. 1 Thess 2:14)" (Conzelmann, *1 Cor,* 21).

The phrase *hē ekklēsia tou theou* turns up in earlier Pauline letters as a designa-tion for the local primitive Christian community in Judea (Gal 1:13; 1 Thess 2:14 [plur.]; cf. 2 Thess 1:4 [plur.]), where it seems to have the sense of mother-church, as again in 1 Cor 11:16 (plur.); possibly 15:9. See INTRODUCTION pp. 81–82. In addressing this letter to the Corinthian "church," Paul was fully aware of its social stratification, which he does not try to change, but in spite of its diversity he seeks to strengthen its unity and solidarity (see Spilly, "Church in Corinth").

Korinthos was a city in Greece near the isthmus of Corinth, which funneled traffic from northern and central Greece to the southern Peloponnesus, and lay about 60 km W of Athens. It was situated between two ports: Cenchreae (Rom 16:1; Acts 18:18), eight-and-a-half km to the E on the Saronic Gulf, serving trade with Asia, and Lechaeum, two km to the NW on the Gulf of Corinth, serving trade with Italy. See further INTRODUCTION, pp. 21–28. For the Lucan account of Paul's first evangelization of Corinth, see Acts 18:1–17 (cf. *Acts*, 617–31).

   to those sanctified in Christ Jesus. I.e., made holy in God's sight by what Christ Jesus has done for humanity in his life, passion, death, resurrection, and exaltation. The ptc. *hēgiasmenois* is in the dat. plural, but stands in apposition to the singular *tē ekklēsiā*, "the church of God that is in Corinth," to which the letter is being sent. Christ has set Christians apart from the Roman colony in which they were living for the cultic service of God. To this dedicated status God "has called" these Christians (1 Thess 4:7), making them such through his "Holy Spirit" (Rom 15:16). This dedicated service echoes the role of ancient Israel, called to be "holy" (Exod 19:5–6; Lev 19:2; 22:32; Deut 7:6), precisely as God's people; cf. 1QM 3:5; 12:7. This status explains the following phrase too. Paul mentions Christ (with varying titles) nine times over in the course of this opening formula and the following thanksgiving. This repetition may be deliberate in order to stress the importance of Christ in light of the preacher factions and rivalries. This letter is being sent to "that church of God that is in Corinth," which is clearly addressed as singular, even though it is made up of individuals whose plurality is noted (by the plur. ptc.). Thus Paul is laying the groundwork for the argument of unity that he will develop, as Mitchell (*Paul*, 193) rightly stresses.

   called to be holy. Lit. "called saints," i.e., dedicated people. Thus *hagioi* becomes a common designation for Christians in Paul's letters (e.g., Rom 1:7; Phil 1:1). He recognizes that God's call has not come to him alone, but includes the addressees to whom he writes, even though the call is now more generic than his own.

   together with all those who in every place call upon the name of our Lord Jesus Christ. This clause is not easily interpreted. It is scarcely to be taken with "Paul, . . . and our brother Sosthenes," which is too far removed from *syn pasin.* . . . It is best understood as modifying "the church of God that is in Corinth." Ever since the time of J. Weiss, however, commentators have queried whether this clause (to the end of the verse) is actually a generalizing post-Pauline interpolation, because the greeting strangely associates with the Corinthians, to whom the letter is addressed, "all" other Christians "in every place." Similarly Fascher, Schmithals. Is it meant to express a secondary set of addressees? Hardly, because Paul does not use *kai,* "and" (to all those), but rather *syn,* "(together) with" or "in company with," so that he merely is associating his addressees with other Christians and reminding them of their solidarity with the others. It could be part of a liturgical formula that Paul simply adds to achieve this effect (Allo, *1 Cor,* 2–3; Fee, *1 Cor,* 33–34). Thus Paul is saying that the status of Christians of Roman Corinth is not isolated, because by reason of their sanctification they share in this effect of the Christ-event with all others who acknowledge the lordship of Jesus Christ no matter where they are or how they are living in conditions of distance from one another.

"To call upon the name of the Lord" is a well-known OT expression for the recognition, praise, and worship of Yahweh as the God of Israel (e.g., by patriarchs, Gen 4:26; 12:8; 13:4; by others, 2 Kgs 5:11; Ps 79:6; 99:6). Paul adapts it for the risen Christ, whom he acknowledges as the risen *Kyrios*. The expression thus becomes a designation for all Christians, as in Rom 10:12–13, because it binds together all those who invoke and acknowledge the name of Christ as Lord to whom they turn; they are *Christianoi* (so called in Acts 11:26), because they belong to him and acknowledge his lordship. Cf. 2 Tim 2:22; Acts 9:14, 21. Here it takes on an ecclesial connotation, being addressed to the church of God in Corinth. *Pace* Guerra, it is not a role restricted to directors of the Christian community. Paul will use "the name of our Lord Jesus Christ" again in 1:10 (with prep. *dia*); 5:4; 6:11 (with prep. *en*); cf. Rom 10:13 (where Joel 3:5 [2:32 ET] is quoted). See further Cullmann, "All Who"; Langevin, "Ceux qui"; Steyn, "Reflections."

their Lord and ours. Lit. "theirs and ours," with no noun expressed. Since these words follow in the Greek text immediately on the prepositional phrase, "in every place" (where they gather), they could be taken with that phrase; but that would be a rather banal assertion; and so it is better to understand the words with "Lord." Wickert ("Einheit und Eintracht") notes that Paul is stressing his own solidarity with the Christians of Corinth ("our Lord") and all others ("their Lord"), because of the exhortation to unity and companionship, to which he will soon summon the Corinthians in 1:10.

Not only does Paul use *kyrios* of the risen Christ and acknowledge that "Jesus is Lord" (1 Cor 12:3), but he repeats the primitive kerygma of those who were apostles before him and who carried the good news from Jerusalem to the Mediterranean world, for that title had become for him the confessional affirmation of all Christians, who recognized that "God raised him from the dead" (Rom 10:9b). In using *Kyrios*, Paul acknowedges along with the rest of early Christians that the risen Christ is on a par with Yahweh of the OT; see INTRODUCTION pp. 72–73. Thus Paul acknowledges that the risen Christ has become an ever-abiding influence in his life, and in that of all Christians.

3. *Grace and peace to you from God our Father and the Lord Jesus Christ!* For the ellipsis of the verb "to be," either (impv.) *estō* or (opt.) *eiē*, see BDF §128.5. The same greeting is found in Rom 1:7; 2 Cor 1:2; Gal 1:3 (expanded); Phil 1:2; Phlm 3; cf. Eph 1:2; 2 Thess 1:2. Note the modification in the Pastorals (Titus 1:4; 1 Tim 1:2; 2 Tim 1:2).

Pace Barrett (*1 Cor*, 34), Paul's "combination" does not occur in 2 Macc 1:1 (which rather has *chairein . . . eirēnēn agathēn*), or in *Syr. Apoc. Baruch* 78:2 (which rather has "mercy and peace"). Lohmeyer regards the Pauline greeting as a pre-Pauline liturgical salutation used at the beginning of a cultic service ("Probleme"), but that it is hardly correct, as Friedrich rightly noted ("Lohmeyers These"), defending the Pauline origin of the formula.

The Pauline substitution of *charis kai eirēnē* (v. 3) for the conventional Greek greeting has often been explained as the combination of Greek *chairein*, for which Paul substitutes *charis*, "grace," and the Greek equivalent of Hebrew *šālôm* or Aramaic *šĕlām*, "peace" (Ezra 4:17 [LXX: *eirēnēn*]; 5:7 [LXX: *eirēnē pasa*];

5/6Hev 4:1; 10:2; cf. Fitzmyer, "Aramaic Epistolography," 34; an interesting variant of this formula, in which X similarly sends a letter to Y, can be found in Dan 3:31; 6:26).

An explanation of this type is found as early as Tertullian, *Adv. Marcionem* 5.5.1; CCLat 1.675. It may be so formed, but the combination "grace and peace" may also be an echo of elements of the priestly blessing uttered by sons of Aaron over the Israelites (Num 6:24–26): "May the Lord bless you and keep you; may the Lord make his face shine upon you, and may he be *gracious* to you; may the Lord lift up his countenance on you and give you *peace*." If Paul's greeting does echo this blessing, then "grace" would represent God's merciful bounty or covenantal favor (*hēn*) revealed in Christ Jesus, and "peace" would connote the fullness of prosperity and well-being characteristic of God's goodness to Israel of old. For all of this Paul prays: may grace come to the Christians of Corinth from God our Father and the Lord Jesus Christ as the sum of evangelical blessings and may they share in this divinely bestowed peace (see Eastman, *Significance of Grace*, 33–69). Lieu has rightly shown that the Pauline greeting, with its Semitic influence, "was a Pauline innovation" and that "the weight of the evidence does point to Pauline priority," for he "deliberately chose not to use the conventional Greek greeting with which to open his letters. Instead he used a form that would probably have something of a 'Scriptural' feel about it, but which would do more than this" ("Grace to You and Peace," 170).

For Paul *theos* is clearly the Father, and "our Father" is a phrase derived from LXX Isa 63:16; 64:7. In Rom 15:6 he is hailed as "the Father of our Lord Jesus Christ," and in Rom 8:15 Paul explains in what sense he is regarded as Father for Christians: "you received a Spirit of sonship, one in which we cry, 'Abba, Father.' " The source of the blessing is now double, coming not only from God our Father, but also from Jesus Christ as Lord (see Delling, "Zusammengesetzte Gottes- und Christusbezeichnungen"; Buscemi, "Dio Padre").

The lordship of Jesus Christ is thus affirmed. Jesus of Nazareth is given a second name, Christ, which originally was a title acknowledging his messianic status (recall Rom 9:5).

BIBLIOGRAPHY

Arzt-Grabner, P., " 'Brothers' and 'Sisters' in Documentary Papyri and in Early Christianity," *RivB* 50 (2002) 185–204.

Berger, K., "Apostelbrief und apostolische Rede / Zum Formular frühchristlicher Briefe," *ZNW* 65 (1974) 190–231.

Bünker, M., *Briefformular und rhetorische Disposition im 1. Korintherbrief* (GTA 28; Göttingen: Vandenhoeck & Ruprecht, 1983).

Buscemi, M., "Dio Padre in S. Paolo," *Anton* 76 (2001) 247–69.

Cullmann, O., "All Who Call on the Name of Our Lord Jesus Christ," *JES* 1 (1964) 1–21.

Delling, G., "Zusammengesetzte Gottes- und Christusbezeichnungen in den Paulusbriefen," *Kirche—Theologie—Frommigkeit: Festgabe für Gottfried Holtz* . . . (Berlin: Evangelische Verlagsanstalt, 1965) 65–71.

Dessau, H., "Der Name des Apostels Paulus," *Hermes* 45 (1910) 347–68.

Doty, W. G., *Letters in Primitive Christianity* (Philadelphia: Fortress, 1973).

Eastman, B., *The Significance of Grace in the Letters of Paul* (StudBibLit 11; Bern/New York: P. Lang, 1999).

Fitzmyer, J. A., "Aramaic Epistolography," *Studies in Ancient Letter Writing* (Semeia 22; ed. J. L. White; Chico, CA: Society of Biblical Literature, 1982) 25–57.

Friedrich, G., "Lohmeyers These über das paulinische Briefpräskript kritisch beleuchtet," *TLZ* 81 (1956) 343–46.

Guerra, M., "Los 'epikaloumenoi' de 1 Cor 1, 2, directores y sacerdotes de la comunidad cristiana en Corinto," *Scripta theologica* 17/1 (1985) 11–72.

———, "1 Cor 1,1–3: Los ministros en la comunidad de Corinto: Análisis filológico y traducción del protócolo de la Primera Carta a los Corintios," *Scripta theologica* 9 (1977) 761–96.

Harland, P. A., "Familial Dimensions of Group Identity: 'Brothers' (*adelphoi*) in Associations of the Greek East," *JBL* 124 (2005) 481–513.

Harrei, G. A., "Saul Who also Is Called Paul," *HTR* 33 (1940) 19–34.

Klein, G., *Die zwölf Apostel: Ursprung und Gehalt einer Idee* (Göttingen: Vandenhocck & Ruprecht, 1961).

Langevin, P.-E., " 'Ceux qui invoquent le nom du Seigneur' (1 Co 1, 2)," *ScEc* 19 (1967) 373–407; 20 (1968) 113–26; 21 (1969) 71–122.

Lieu, J. M., " 'Grace to You and Peace': The Apostolic Greeting," *BJRL* 68 (1985–86) 161–78.

Lohmeyer, E., "Probleme paulinischer Theologie: I. Briefliche Grussüberschriften," *ZNW* 26 (1927) 158–73.

Murphy-O'Connor, J., "Co-authorship in the Corinthian Correspondence," *RB* 100 (1993) 562–79.

Myrou, A., "Sosthenes: The Former Crispus(?)," *GOTR* 44 (1999) 207–12.

Prior, M., *Paul the Letter-Writer and the Second Letter to Timothy* (JSNTSup 23; Sheffield: Sheffield Academic, 1989).

Schmithals, W., *The Office of Apostle in the Early Church* (Nashville: Abingdon, 1969).

Spilly, A. P., "The Church in Corinth," *CS* 24 (1985) 307–21.

Steyn, G. J., "Reflections on *to onoma tou kyriou* in 1 Corinthians," *The Corinthian Correspondence* (BETL 125; ed. R. Bieringer) 479–90.

Verhoef, E., "The Senders of the Letters to the Corinthians and the Use of 'I' and 'We,' " *The Corinthian Correspondence* (BETL 125; ed. R. Bieringer) 417–25.

Vogelstein, H., "The Development of the Apostolate in Judaism and Its Transformation in Christianity," *HUCA* 2 (1925) 99–123.

Wickert, U., "Einheit und Eintracht der Kirche in Präskript des ersten Korintherbriefes," *ZNW* 50 (1959) 73–82.

2   THANKSGIVING (1:4–9)

[1:4] I constantly give thanks to my God on your behalf for the grace of God granted to you in Christ Jesus. [5] For in him you have been enriched in every way, in all discourse and all knowledge, [6] as the testimony about Christ has grown strong among you. [7] Consequently, you do not lack any spiritual gift, as you eagerly await the revelation of our Lord Jesus Christ. [8] He will also keep you strong to the end, blameless on the day of our Lord Jesus [Christ]. [9] Trustworthy is God, through whom you have been called into companionship with his Son, Jesus Christ our Lord.

COMMENT

Paul adds to his opening greeting sent to the Christians of Roman Corinth an expression of thanks. This Thanksgiving follows the pattern that one finds in other Pauline letters (1 Thess 1:2–5; Phil 1:3–8 [or 3–11]; Rom 1:8–9; Phlm 4–7); in 2 Cor 1:3–11 Paul substitutes a blessing, which is more appropriate to that letter of reconciliation. Here one finds only a thanksgiving without a petitionary prayer. In Gal 1:6–9 there is no thanksgiving at all, because Paul there expresses his annoyed surprise that Galatians were turning to another gospel. Compare also the Deutero-Pauline 2 Thess 1:3–10; Col 1:3–8; and esp. Eph 1:15–23, where a thanksgiving follows a blessing and is joined to a prayer of intercession. See also 2 Macc 1:11.

In thus introducing the Thanksgiving, Paul is following the custom of Greek letter writing of his day, in which a thanksgiving often had to do with the addressee's good health (see 3 John 2; cf. *NJBC* art. 45 §8). Pauline Thanksgivings are constructed carefully and rhetorically and often incorporate elements that annonce main themes of the body of the letter (e.g., *logos*, "discourse," *gnōsis*, "knowledge," *martyrion*, "testimony," *apokalypsis*, "revelation," *hēmera tou kyriou*, "day of the Lord," and *koinōnia*, "sharing, companionship"). In light of what he is going to say about these topics in the letter itself, the mention of them now forms a sort of *captatio benevolentiae* (striving for good attention). Paul, however, does not thank God for the faith or love of the Corinthian Christians, as he does in other letters (1 Thess 1:3; Rom 1:8); the absence of that in this Thanksgiving is, in part, due to the issues that he will discuss in the letter. Again, there is in it no mention of the gospel, which appears so frequently in the Thanksgiving of other letters (Rom 1:9; Phil 1:5, 7; 1 Thess 1:5). Nor does a petitionary prayer play any part in it (O'Brien, *Introductory Thanksgivings*, 107).

In this prayer, Paul thanks God the Father for the rich grace and spiritual gifts that have come to Corinthian Christians through Christ Jesus, who is mentioned in every verse of this prayer with differing formulaic titles. Paul prays to "my God," meaning the God of the OT whom he still worships even as a Christian apostle. He expresses his thanks because he recognizes the divine favors that have been shown to the Corinthian commnity in and through Christ Jesus. Paul also introduces into his Thanksgiving an eschatological perspective, as he speaks of the Corinthians awaiting "the revelation of our Lord Jesus Christ" (1:7). He also assures the Corinthians that God will sustain them and keep them blameless until that "day of our Lord Jesus Christ" (1:8). Moreover, he recalls God's trustworthiness, in that they have already been called to "companionship with his son, Jesus Christ our Lord" (1:9). Finally, Paul reflects that these graces have come as a way of ratifying the testimony about Christ that he once bore to them. Thus, Paul's prayer not only thanks God, but also encourages his Corinthian addressees about their relationship to God and his son, Jesus Christ, the risen Lord. Strangely enough, there is no mention of the Holy Spirit in the Thanksgiving, even though the Spirit will play an important role later in the discussion of the gifts received.

Paul introduces into the Thanksgiving-prayer itself an element that will be important in the first four chapters of the epistle: the Corinthians have in every way been enriched "in all discourse and knowledge." This enrichment he attributes to "testimony about Christ," which he recognizes has already "grown strong" among his addressees.

Paul's Thanksgiving invites Christian readers of this letter to realize how they too have been enriched in every way by the grace of God granted them in Christ Jesus. The conviction of faith that they enjoy is itself a spiritual gift that should enlighten all their knowledge and discourse. Such rich graces received within the Christian community should not blind them to the awaited revelation of the Lord. For God who cannot but be faithful will keep them strong and blameless until then, since he has called them into companionship with His Son, as Paul has tried to assure the Corinthian addressees of his letter.

NOTES

1:4. *I constantly give thanks to my God on your behalf.* Paul speaks in the first singular, showing that Sosthenes is not a coauthor of the letter. To express his own incessant prayer for the Christians of Roman Corinth, Paul uses the verb *eucharistein*, as in 1 Thess 1:2; 2:13; Phil 1:3; Rom 1:8; Phlm 4; cf. 2 Thess 1:3; Col 1:3; Eph 5:20; 2 Macc 1:11 and also the adv. *pantote*, "at all times"(as in Rom 1:10; 2 Cor 2:14; Phil 1:4). See *EDNT* 2:88 for the background of the thanksgiving formula; also J. M. Robinson, "Hodajot-Formel." Paul is praying for the Corinthian Christians not only as he writes this letter, but also on many other occasions. Cf. Rom 1:9.

The phrase "my God" is also found in Phil 1:3; 4:19; 2 Cor 12:21; Rom 1:8; Phlm 4. The meaning of the phrase is given in Rom 1:9, "God whom I worship with my spirit in the evangelization of his Son" (see *Romans*, 244). Actually, it is an OT phrase, being found in Pss 3:8; 5:3; 7:2, where the LXX reads *ho theos mou*. The reading *theō mou* is well attested in many good Greek MSS, but *mou* is omitted in **ℵ***, B.

for the grace of God granted to you in Christ Jesus. The grace of which Paul speaks has its origin in God and has been accorded the Christians of Roman Corinth in Christ Jesus, who is the channel through which new life has come to them, enabling them to serve one another and the church as a whole. The combination of *charis* and the vb. *didōmi* is also found in Rom 12:3, 6; 15:15; 1 Cor 3:10; 2 Cor 8:1; Gal 2:9, and often in the context of the evangelization of Gentiles. The next verse explains what specifically the "grace" is.

One meets here the first instance of *en Christō Iēsou*, "in Christ Jesus," a formula that occurs very frequently in Pauline writings. The prep. *en* with the object "Christ" or "the Lord" or "him" occurs about 165 times, and commentators have debated its various uses and meanings: spatial, mystical, dynamic, instrumental, or eschatological. With the object "Christ," it often has the instrumental sense, especially when it refers to the historical activity of Jesus (2 Cor 5:19) or to an effect of that activity (Gal 2:17; Rom 3:24). That seems to be the sense intended here (see Büchsel, " 'In Christus,' " 145; cf. Neugebauer, *In Christus*, 86).

5. *For in him you have been enriched in every way.* Paul repeats the idea of the last phrase of v. 4, stressing that divine favor has been accorded abundantly to Corinthian Christians, and that they have not been enriched by their own endeavors. Paul uses *ploutizein*, "enrich, make wealthy," also in 2 Cor 6:10; 8:9; 9:11.

in all discourse and all knowledge. The combination of *logos* and *gnōsis* is found again in 2 Cor 8:7, along with other qualities. The combination may be derived from LXX of Prov 22:21, "I therefore teach you true discourse and knowledge good to hear." Here the pair concretizes the form in which God's grace has been made manifest among Corinthian Christians, in the way they speak eloquently of their faith-experience and in the knowledge and insight they have of its benefits. Compare 12:8, where *logos sophias* and *logos gnōseōs* appear together as gifts of the Spirit. This may sound a bit ironic, because Paul will have to criticize the Corinthians in this letter (1:18–25; 2:1–5) because of some of their pretensions to wisdom and the rivalries that have arisen as a consequence. Note the threefold emphatic use of *pas*, "every, all," in the verse.

6. *as the testimony about Christ has grown strong among you.* Lit. "the testimony of Christ has been made strong" (*ebebaiōthē*). Paul means that his evangelization of Corinth and that of others have been validated and confirmed by gifts that the Corinthians have received. He has borne witness to Christ among them by the preaching of the gospel, upon which the Corinthian community has been founded; and it has consequently been enriched by the divine favors shown them. *Christou* is best understood as an objective genitive (so Collins, *1 Cor*, 63; Fee, *1 Cor*, 40; O'Brien, *Introductory Thanksgivings*, 120), but Kremer (*1 Cor*, 25) thinks that the gen. could be taken as subj.; so too Soards: " 'the testimony of Christ' is another way of referring to *the gospel*" (*1 Cor*, 25). The pass. verb *ebebaiōthē* is to be taken as divine ("made strong by God" [through the spiritual gifts to be mentioned in v. 7]), as Lindemann (*1 Cor*, 31) understands it. In a few MSS (B*, F, G, 81, 1175) the gen. is rather *theou*, "(testimony) about God," perhaps influenced by 2:1.

7. *Consequently, you do not lack any spiritual gift.* Lit. "you are not lacking in any. . . ." The clause is introduced by *hōste*, which has to be understood in a consecutive, not a final sense, *pace* Allo (*1 Cor*, 4). What is meant by *charisma* will become clear in chap. 12. Paul is content now to use the word merely in a generic way, as the gift of Christian existence. This verse repeats v. 5, but in a negative formulation.

as you eagerly await the revelation of our Lord Jesus Christ. Paul introduces an eschatological perspective into his prayer of thanks. What he calls here *apokalypsis kyriou*, he calls *hē parousia tou kyriou hēmōn Iēsou*, "the coming of our Lord Jesus," in 1 Thess 3:13, even though he does not otherwise use *apokalypsis*, "revelation," in the parousiac sense. In 1 Cor 4:5, he will clearly speak of this revelation: "before the Lord comes"; and in 15:23 of "his coming" (*en tē parousiā autou*). Compare, however, the Deutero-Pauline letter, 2 Thess 1:7, and 1 Pet 1:7, 13; 4:13 for the same sense of *apokalypsis*. The awaited presence of the Lord is expressed as "the day of our Lord Jesus [Christ]" in v. 8 (cf. 5:5; 2 Cor 1:4; Phil 1:6), and differently in 7:29.

Kyrios occurs elsewhere in Pauline passages when he alludes to the parousia (see 4:4–5; 11:26; Phil 3:20; 4:5). Recall too the prayer with which Paul will end this letter, *marana tha,* "Our Lord, come!" (16:22). That Paul is using a common early Christian mode of referring to the coming of the Lord Jesus is evident from Luke 17:30. This verse then contributes to the eschatological teaching of this letter.

8. *He will also keep you strong to the end.* The eschatological perspective is continued, but the rel. clause, introduced by *hos kai,* at first sight might seem to have as its antecedent the immediately preceding "Lord Jesus Christ" (v. 7). It is rather "God" (v. 4) who is meant, as the rest of the verse makes clear, and as many commentators have understood it (J. Weiss, Conzelmann, Fee, Kremer, Senft); cf. 2 Cor 1:21. Barrett, Robertson-Plummer, Lindemann, Soards, however, take the antecedent to be Christ, as did Origen and Chrysostom.

Von der Osten-Sacken ("Gottes Treue") thinks that Paul in vv.8–9 has reversed the order of a traditional formula, *pistos ho . . . , hos kai . . . ,* "God is trustworthy, by whom you were called into companionship with his Son (. . .), who will also keep you strong (. . .) blameless (. . .), as you await the revealing of our Lord."

As he continues his eschatological perspective, Paul uses the fut. verb *bebaiōsei,* the same verb that appears in v. 6, where it is employed in the passive of the "testimony" about Christ that has been borne to the Corinthians in his preaching (see MacRae, "A Note."). Now he asserts that God will sustain them until the parousia of the Lord. He will not permit what has been begun to come to naught or be undone. The best Greek MSS read *heōs telous,* "up to the end," but MSS D, F, G, read rather *achri,* "until"; and P[46] reads *teleious* instead of the prepositional phrase, "will keep you perfect," which may be a copyist's correction leading up to the characterization in the following phrase.

blameless on the day of our Lord Jesus [Christ]. This ending of the verse echoes that of v. 7. Mss P[46] and B omit "Christ," possibly because the full name occurs in vv. 7 and 9 (Metzger, *TCGNT,* 479), or possibly because of homoeoteleuton. Paul is certain that the Christians of Corinth will appear blameless at the time of Christ's parousia (cf. Phil 1:6, 10; 2:16). This is a strange admission to make in view of the topics that Paul is going to discuss in the letter and some of the criticism that he is going to level against the Corinthians, but it is undoubtedly his mode of *captatio benevolentiae.*

Paul adapts an often-used OT expression, *yôm Yhwh,* LXX *(hē) hēmera (tou) kyriou* (Amos 5:18, 20; Joel 2:31; Isa 2:12; 13:6, 9; Zeph 1:17–18), which denoted the time of Yhwh's coming to judge his people. Paul not only understands *kyriou* in the Christological sense, but also alludes to the expected judgment of Christians by the risen Christ. The phrase appears again in 5:5, and is alluded to in 15:23, 50–58 (now anticipated here in the Thanksgiving); see also 2 Cor 1:14;

5:10. In 3:13 it becomes simply "the Day." Mss of the western tradition (D, F, G) substitute *parousiā* for *hēmerā* (see 1 Thess 5:23).

9. *Trustworthy is God*. Paul ends his prayer of Thanksgiving with the praise of God's fidelity. The epithet *pistos* is used of God again in 10:13; 2 Cor 1:18; 1 Thess 5:24; cf. 2 Tim 2:13; Heb 10:23. It imitates Deut 7:9 *hā'ēl hanne'ĕmān*, "the faithful God"; cf. Deut 32:4; Isa 49:7. The Christian's conviction of eschatological salvation is based on such trust in God, whose fidelity is assured, and Paul seeks to instill this assurance in Corinthian Christians.

through whom you have been called into companionship with his Son, Jesus Christ our Lord. The prep. *dia* denotes the source, not the mediation, of assurance that comes from God (BDR §223.3). Soards (*1 Cor*, 30), however, strangely understands *di' hou*, "through whom," to refer "to the Lord Jesus Christ through whom God acts in relation to humanity." That might be a good Pauline idea, but that is not what the text says. The rel. pronoun in the prep. phrase *di' hou* has God as its antecedent, and the relation to Christ is expressed by *eis koinōnian*. Rather than *di' hou*, mss D, F, G, read rather *hyph' hou*, "by whom," followed by the RSV.

The verb "you have been called" echoes the call of v. 2 above, and also that of the OT idea of a divine call (Isa 41:9; 42:6; 48:12). In this case, the call envisages a goal or purpose, expressed by the prep. *eis*, as in 1 Thess 2:12 (see Klein, "Paul's Use," 60–61).

"Companionship" or "fellowship" is only one of a variety of meanings that *koinōnia* has in Pauline writings; in 10:16 it will denote rather the "participation" of Christians in the "table of the Lord." By it Paul now emphasizes rather the union of Christians with Christ in the church as a result of their call by God to be a holy people associated with his Son through faith and baptism (1:2; 6:11; see Reumann, "Koinonia in Scripture," 45; Hainz, *Koinonia*, 15–17; Panikulam, *Koinōnia*, 8–16). The companionship is above all with God's Son, through whom God has been achieving the salvation of His people in a new way (recall Gal 4:4–6; Rom 8:29), but it also connotes the companionship of Christians one with another, resulting from all that Paul has said in vv. 4–8, and not just from the eschatological perspective of vv.7–8. With this thought Paul ends his Thanksgiving.

BIBLIOGRAPHY

Büchsel, F., " 'In Christus' bei Paulus," ZNW 42 (1949) 141–58.

Klein, W. W., "Paul's Use of *kalein*: A Proposal," *JETS* 27 (1984) 53–64.

MacRae, G. W., "A Note on 1 Corinthians 1:4–9," *Harry M. Orlinsky Volume* (Eretz Israel 16; ed. B. A. Levine and A. Malamat; Jerusalem: Israel Exploration Society, 1982) 171*–75*.

O'Brien, P. T., *Introductory Thanksgivings in the Letters of Paul* (NovTSup 49; Leiden: Brill, 1977) 107–37.

———, "Thanksgiving and the Gospel in Paul," *NTS* 21 (1974–75) 144–55.

Osten-Sacken, P. von der, "Gottes Treue bis zur Parusie: Formgeschichtliche Beobachtungen zu 1 Kor 1,7b–9," ZNW 68 (1977) 176–99.

Reumann, J., "Koinonia in Scripture: Survey of Biblical Texts," *On the Way to Fuller Koinonia* (Faith and Order Paper 166; ed. T. F. Best and G. Gassmann; Geneva: WCC Publications, 1994) 37–69.

Robinson, J. M., "Die Hodajot-Formel in Gebet und Hymnus des Frühchristentums," *Apophoreta: Festschrift für Ernst Haenchen* . . . (BZNW 30; Berlin: Töpelmann, 1964) 194–235.

Schubert, P., *Form and Function of the Pauline Thanksgivings* (BZNW 20; Berlin: Töpelmann, 1939) 30–31, 44, 51.

II. SCANDALS REPORTED ORALLY TO PAUL ABOUT THE CORINTHIAN CHURCH (1:10–6:20)

◆

A. SCANDAL OF PREACHER-FACTIONS: ITS FACT AND ROOTS (1:10–4:21)

3   a. *Dissensions in the Corinthian Church (1:10–17)*

1:10 I appeal to you, brothers, in the name of our Lord Jesus Christ, that all of you may agree in what you say and that there be no dissensions among you, but that you may be united in the same mind and the same purpose. 11 For it has been reported to me about you, my brothers, by some of Chloe's people that there are rivalries among you. 12 What I mean is this: One of you says, "I side with Paul!"; another, "I side with Apollos!"; or "I side with Cephas!"; or "I side with Christ!" 13 Is Christ divided? Was Paul crucified for you? Or were you baptized in the name of Paul? 14 I give thanks [to God] that I baptized none of you, save Crispus and Gaius, 15 so that no one can say that you were baptized in my name. 16 I did baptize the household of Stephanas too; otherwise I do not know whether I baptized anyone else. 17 For Christ did not send me to baptize, but to preach the gospel, and not with eloquent wisdom, lest the cross of Christ be emptied of its meaning.

COMMENT

Paul now opens the body of his letter to the Christians of Roman Corinth with a plea that they come to agreement and unity among them. He begins by telling them what he has heard about them: how dissensions among them have caused division and rivalry in their community, which he does not consider proper. Paul makes it clear that he is commenting on reports that have come to him "by some of Chloe's people" (v. 11). Chloe seems to have been a prominent Christian woman, someone known to Paul from his earlier dealings with the Corinthian church and apparently known to the rest of the Christians there, for Paul mentions her by name.

The dissensions and quarrels stem mainly from Corinthians who have been arguing about different Christian preachers who have evangelized them or somehow influenced their lives. As a result, these Christians seem to be divided into rival groups expressing allegiance to such preachers, either to Paul himself, or Apollos, or Cephas, and even to Christ. Perhaps, however, some Christians are annoyed at such rivalries, often called factions, and such allegiance to human preachers; and they are vaunting allegiance only to Christ. It is hard to tell whether there are three or four groups that Paul is mentioning. The parallelism of the four clauses, "I side with . . . ," may mean that there are actually four rival factions; and it should be noted that Paul writes, *egō men eimi Paulou*, and then joins the following three with the correlative *de*, which seems to indicate that there was a Christ-Party, parallel to the Apollos-Party and the Cephas-Party. In 3:4–5, however, Paul mentions only two preachers (Apollos and himself), and in 3:22 he names three (Paul, Apollos, and Cephas). From these different passages arises the problem of determining how many are the groups with which Paul is coping. Even though Munck, in his reaction to the radical thesis of Baur (that Paul was opposed in Corinth by a Judaizing faction headed by Cephas), maintained that there were neither factions nor Judaizers in the Corinthian church, but only much quarrelling and the cult of personalities, one has to reckon with factions, at least three of them, in the Corinthian Christian community of Paul's day. That is the surface issue with which Paul is dealing in chaps. 1–4 of this letter. This is commonly held today.

As Paul begins his argument in this first section of the letter, he deals with three main themes, which do not follow any particular sequence, but which are interwoven and thus make the argument somewhat difficult to follow: the factions in the Corinthian community (1:10–17; 3:4–5, 21; 4:6); the fascination of that community with a certain mode of wisdom-preaching (1:18–2:16; 3:18–20; 4:10); and how one is to estimate Christian ministry (1:17; 2:1–5; 3:1–4:13).

It is important, however, to understand how the section of 1 Corinthians that begins here (1:10–4:21) functions in the letter as a whole. In analyzing it, I am following basically the analysis of Dahl ("Paul and the Church at Corinth"). He agrees with Baur in regarding this part of the letter as the first apologetic section, in which Paul seeks to gives a justification for his apostolic authority and ministry. It is a section that is framed by exhortations (1:10 and 4:16), both using the verb *parakalō*, "I appeal to you." Many statements and clues are given in this section that reveal the situation in the Corinthian church with which Paul was coping, as he sought to assert his authority. Chapters 5 and 6, which follow this apologetic section, are also related to problems treated in it, but they are also transitional to the topics that will be dealt with in chapters 7–15, beginning with the questions raised in the letter of 7:1.

The surface problem of this first section is the scandal of preacher-factions in the Corinthian church, but underlying that scandal is Paul's attempt to reestablish his authority and proper relation with the Corinthian community in view of the opposition to him that has grown up there. The dissension and quarrels at Corinth were manifestations of that opposition, and they have been reported orally to Paul by "some of Chloe's people" (1:11), who have come on a visit to

Ephesus. Such reports tell of "dissensions," "rivalries" (*erides*, 1:11; 3:3), and arrogance (4:18), based on the belief that Paul would never come back to Corinth (see 4:19). This situation arose after Paul had left Corinth, when the Corinthian Christians decided to send a delegation (Stephanas, Fortunatus, and Achaicus [16:17]) along with a letter to Paul (7:1), asking him to help them understand what they should do and think about various problems that have arisen since his departure. Because many believed that Paul would not return and did not really care about them, opposition to him seems to have broken out in the form of the factions. Quarreling Corinthians were opposing the delegates as much as they were opposing Paul and were annoyed that the delegation had been sent. As Dahl imaginatively sums up the opposition,

> Why write to Paul? He has left us and is not likely to come back. He lacks eloquence and wisdom. He supported himself by his own work; either he does not have the full rights of an apostle, or he did not esteem us to be worthy of supporting him. Why not write to Apollos, who is a wise teacher? I am his man! Or, if we turn to anybody, why not write to Cephas, who is the foremost of he twelve. I am for Cephas! But why ask anyone for counsel? Should we not rather say: I belong myself to Christ? As spiritual men we ought to be wise enough to decide for ourselves. (325)

The opposition to Paul also came from the fact that he had baptized so few of the Corinthians (1:14–16), and he felt that he had been "roughly handled" (4:11).

Before Paul could answer the questions in the letter, he had to overcome the false appraisals and reestablish his apostolic authority as the founder and spiritual father of the whole church at Corinth. For this reason he does not champion any group, but writes as the Apostle of Christ to the church as a whole.

Paul begins with a plea and resolutely calls on the Christians of Corinth, "that all of you may agree in what you say"; and "that there be no dissensions among you, but that you may be united in the same mind and the same purpose" (v. 10). Paul does not defend those who side with him, for he is concerned about the general situation, realizing how the Corinthian Christians have misunderstood the relative value of the community's teachers; they have also misunderstood themselves and have exaggerated the knowledge they have. He feels that Christ himself is suffering division (v. 13): the lack of unity in the community implies a misunderstanding of Christ among them. He fears that such a situation might even empty the very cross of Christ of its meaning (v. 17). Implied in his argumentation is the conviction that Christ died for all human beings, and not only for those who pledge allegiance to one of his preachers. His answer to this problem will be expressed in 3:5, 22–23, and esp. in 4:6, "that none of you will become arrogant, siding with one over against another."

In the course of his remarks about this divisive situation, Paul tells us something about how he understands his own apostolate and the mission to which he has been called by God and the risen Christ. He is convinced that he has been sent, not to baptize, but "to preach the gospel" (v. 17). What he says here about his commission finds an echo later on in 15:9–11 and in Rom 10:8–10.

That there would be groups with differing opinions in the Corinthian church is not surprising and could be taken for granted, but the way Paul writes about them makes it clear that the differences were serious and of no little concern to him. The nature of the rival groups, often called factions, has been a matter of much discussion, even though it is difficult to distinguish them or ascertain their differences with any certainty. John Chrysostom (*In Ep. I ad Cor. hom.* 3.1; PG 61.24) thought that there really were not four parties and that Paul, for reasons of tact, mentioned four names "by way of hyperbole" instead of the real "dividers of the church." Indeed, commentators who hold that there were four or three parties are hard pressed to provide real evidence of them or how they differed one from the other (see Hurd, *Origin*, 117; Munck, "Church without Factions," 135). Be that as it may, Paul's argument is not directed against any one group, but at the church of Roman Corinth as a whole; so Strüder would speak of preferences, not parties in 1:12.

Baur reduced the four factions to two, Paul and Apollos vs. Cephas and Christ, as Paulinists vs. Petrine Judaizers. Reitzenstein considered them to be like the *thiasoi*, "guilds," of the Greek mystery religions, in which the confrères grouped about a certain master who had initiated them into the mystery (*Hellenistic Mystery Religions*, 426). Schmithals reduces them to "one opponent" as the Gnostic Christ-Party (*Gnosticism in Corinth*, 114). Such explanations of the factions are problematic because there is no evidence in the letter that Paul is coping with Judaizers (as he was in the Epistle to the Galatians) or with Gnostics (who have not appeared on the scene in the first century). As for the guilds of the mystery religions, there is no evidence that they were competitive and contentious.

Other explanations have been given: The factions have been interpreted as those who align themselves with the preachers who baptized them (as v. 13 might suggest [Barrett]), or perhaps with those belonging to differing social levels in Corinth (as v. 26 might suggest [Theissen]), or with differing political parties (Welborn), or with preachers of differing eloquence or rhetorical training (an explanation derived from the emphasis in chap. 1 on *sophia* and *logos*, "wisdom" and "discourse"): new Christians, having been affected by the secular educational mores of Roman Corinth, were acting like the disciples of the Sophists in the Roman empire. Such Sophists were wandering teachers of rhetoric who had come of Corinth and vied with each other to attract followers who would be loyal to them in their competitive rivalry. Having lived in such an environment before their conversion to Christianity, Corinthian Christians would still be influenced by such practices and so came to express their allegiance to either Paul, or Apollos, or Cephas (Winter, *After Paul Left Corinth*, 31–43). It does not seem best to follow Chrysostom and regard the names of the first three in v. 12 as creations of Paul merely to illustrate the dissensions. The opposition to Paul comes from the Christian community as a whole because of such dissensions that have arisen since he left Corinth, which show that they have not comprehended "the gospel" that he was sent to preach, the gospel about Christ crucified (1:17–18; 2:2).

Some commentators take v. 17 as the first verse of the following passage (so George), but that verse is introduced by *gar*, "for," and gives the reason why Paul has said what he has been saying in vv. 10–16. So it is best taken as the concluding verse of this passage. Lindemann (*1 Cor*, 33–34) considers this first passage to extend to v. 25, but even he admits a caesura between v. 17 and v. 18.

As a whole, this passage reveals how concerned Paul was about the unity and solidarity of the early Christian community in Roman Corinth. His appeal "in the name of our Lord Jesus Christ" to those whom he does not hesitate to call "brothers" becomes a challenge to Christians of all ages, who also have to consider the dangers of liberal or conservative thinking within the communities in which they live. The source of the dissension in Roman Corinth was nominally siding with various preachers, but the underlying favoritism is the perennial problem of arrogance that can afflict the Christian community anywhere and at any time. "Is Christ divided?" Paul asks, in an effort to counteract the divisiveness. As he wants the Corinthian Christians to consider well the consequences of their rivalries, he also calls on all Christians to reflect on the consequences of such favoritism in order to make sure that the message of the cross of Christ is not emptied of its significance in any way. For Christ was crucified for all, not just for a favored few.

NOTES

10. *I appeal to you, brothers, in the name of our Lord Jesus Christ.* As often, Paul uses *parakaleō*, a verb denoting an urgent appeal (see 4:16 [which corresponds to the problem in the first section of this letter]; 16:12, 15; Rom 12:1; 15:30; 16:17; 2 Cor 2:8; 10:1; Phil 4:2; 1 Thess 4:10; Phlm 10; cf. Bjerkelund, *Parakalô*, 14, 18, 142, 146). Paul appeals as an authorized apostle (1:1; Rom 1:5), as "the apostle of the Gentiles" (Rom 11:13), and does not hesitate to urge or implore the Christians of Roman Corinth. He makes use of a standard literary form called "petition," along with a divine-authority phrase (see Mullins, "Petition," 53; White, "Introductory Formulae," 93–94). That is formulated "in the name of our Lord Jesus Christ" (recall 1:2 and its NOTE). Paul does not appeal in his own name, but in Christ's name, because the divided Christians of Roman Corinth have forgotten that Christ is among them as the source of their unity. Cf. 2 Thess 3:6. In exhorting them to unity, he addresses them as *adelphoi*, "brothers," i.e., fellow Christians, whether male or female, using the same term as for Sosthenes in v. 1 above (see NOTE there). Because they are *adelphoi*, Paul believes that he must address them, even if some of the things he is going to say may not be what they want to hear.

that all of you may agree in what you say. Lit. "that all may say the same thing." This appeal for unity is phrased positively and generically at first, but as one reads further, it not only concerns the essential unity expected of a Christian community, but acquires a negative formulation. Paul is not forbidding the expression of different opinions in general, but is urging agreement in conduct that will guarantee common unity (= community). He uses an idiom well known in classical Greek; see Thucydides, *Hist.* 5.31.6: "The Boeotians and Megarians, holding the same opinion (*to auto legontes*), kept silent" (cf. 4.20.4).

that there be no dissensions among you. Paul adds a negative appeal, introduced by *hina mē*, as in vv. 15, 17, as he likens the situation in the Corinthian community to the conflicts between city-states in the Greco-Roman world, using the noun *schisma* derived from the verb *schizō* that historians employ for such conflicts (*eschizonto*, Herodotus, *Hist.* 7.219.2; 4.119.1; Diodorus Siculus, *Bibl. Hist.* 12.66.2; see Welborn, "On the Discord," 86). Most Greek MSS read the plur. *schismata*, "divisions, dissensions, schisms," but P⁴⁶, 33 have the sing. *schisma*. Such dissension has resulted from allegiance to the different preachers to be named and the struggles for domination that they engendered. Paul will speak again of *schismata* in a different, but perhaps related, sense in 11:18 (dissensions at the celebration of the Lord's Supper) and 12:25 (cf. John 7:43; 9:16; 10:19, where the word denotes dissension among people). Clement of Rome repeats the Pauline terminology and adds to it: *ereis kai thymoi kai dichostasiai kai schismata kai polemos*, "strife and passion and cleavage and dissension and war" (*1Clem.* 46.5). One cannot say that the term necessarily connotes "parties" or "factions" with fixed membership, ideology, or structure (Mitchell, *Paul*, 71; Mcinertz, "*Schisma*," 115). Nor does the term yet have the connotation it will acquire in later centuries, as in canon law, "schism."

that you may be united in the same mind and the same purpose. Or "conviction." This clause reformulates the first clause of this verse. The agreement that Paul recommends concerns not only what they say, but also how they think and plan, when it comes to what is really needed for Christian unity. Bultmann (*TDNT*, 1:717) rightly notes that it is very difficult to differentiate *nous*, "mind" and *gnōmē*, "disposition." The former stresses more the notion of thinking and observing, whereas the latter that of judging and planning. See Phlm 14 (cf. *Philemon*, 111).

11. *For it has been reported to me about you, my brothers.* Mss P⁴⁶, C*, 104 omit "my." This statement supplies the reason why interpreters label this section of the letter as oral reports.

by some of Chloe's people. Lit. "by those of Chloe." She is otherwise unknown, but was probably a resident of Corinth with friends in Ephesus, where Paul now is; most likely a Christian woman. If she were rather a resident of Ephesus, she must have been known at least to Christians of Corinth, because Paul's use of her name would imply that. Who her "people" are is not clear; possibly members of her household, slaves or former slaves (so Meeks, *First Urban*, 59, 63), or business partners. Because Paul mentions her, that does not mean that she was one of "the outstanding women leaders" of the Corinthian church, *pace* Schüssler Fiorenza (*In Memory*, 219). Nothing in the text suggests that she was the overseer of a house church or that she sent them to Paul with a message or report; they seem to have been in Ephesus for some other reason and simply told Paul of the situation. In any case, there is no evidence that these people belonged to any of the groups mentioned. Hitchcock ("Who Are") claims that Paul would not have mentioned a Corinthian lady by name in connection with a report that reflected discredit on Corinthian Christians; so, because *Chloē* is a well-known epithet of the goddess Demeter (e.g., Aristophanes, *Lysistrata* 835; Pausanias, *Descr. Graec.* 1.22.3; and various Greek inscriptions), he understands *hoi Chloēs* to denote "some votaries (*mystai*) of Demeter with whom Paul was acquainted." There was a temple of Demeter on the slopes of Acrocorinth. This explanation is ingenious, but far-fetched. As a Thracian woman's name, "Chloe" is known elsewhere in antiquity (Horace, *Carmina* 1.23.1; 3.9.6, 9; the "Daphnis and Chloe," of Longus, 1.6.3).

that there are rivalries among you. Now Paul calls the Corinthian dissension *eris*, "strife, discord, quarrel, wrangling," a literary variant for *schisma* (1:10), used again in 3:3 (*zēlos kai eris*); it was often used of political disputes and quarrels (Plutarch, *Caesar* 33; Aristophanes, *Thesm.* 788; Thucydides, *Hist.* 6.31). Although the Corinthian community may appear outwardly united, not all are acting in the same way or thinking and saying the same thing.

12. *What I mean is this.* Lit. "this I say" (*legō de touto*). Paul begins the statement with *legō*, a verb that he uses elsewhere (7:6, 35; 15:51; 2 Cor 6:13; 11:16) when he wants to address the Corinthian community with emphasis.

One of you says, "I side with Paul." Lit. "Each one of you says, 'I am of Paul.'" So Paul explains what he meant in v. 11. In good Greek style, Paul puts himself first in the lineup of rival preachers to be named. It is not a question of theological differences or personal quarrels, but of the secular mind-set of individual Christians in the Corinthian community. When Paul speaks of "each one," he rhetorically expresses the individuality and divisive character of the situation in Corinth. "I side with Paul" sounds like a Corinthian slogan, but it could also be merely Paul's way of formulating such allegiance. It imitates the twice-repeated phrase, *tou theou eimi* of LXX Isa 44:5, and it is hardly the noted revelation formula (John 8:58). It is a mere genitive of relationship (BDF §162.7), as in Acts 27:23; and at best a possible "declaration of party allegiance" (Conzelmann, *1 Cor*, 33). Paul is thought of as the head of such a group, because he was the church founder (3:6, 10), the leader who first preached the gospel in Corinth (15:1–11). Mitchell notes, however, that no comparable party slogans have yet been discovered in ancient political texts. So they seem to be rather Paul's own creation, a caricature that employs the language "most commonly used of parent-child relationships and master-slave relationships" (*Paul*, 85). "While the Corinthians themselves may not have expressed their allegiance in this fashion, Paul interprets their factional activity as indicative, not of political sophistication, but of childishness and renunciation of their precious freedom through their alignment behind various missionaries" (ibid., 86).

another, "I side with Apollos." Lit. "but I of Apollos." *Apollōs* was a Christian preacher from Alexandria who worked in Ephesus and Corinth; he is mentioned again in 3:4–6, 22; 4:6; 16:12; see also Titus 3:13; *1 Clem.* 47.3 (which refers to this Pauline passage). He would have arrived in Corinth only after Paul had departed, and the two of them would never have worked there together. Apollos was undoubtedly responsible for the conversion of further Corinthians to Christianity, who may not have known Paul. The group that is said here to use his name probably emerged after Apollos had also departed from Corinth. Paul knows that some Corinthian Christians had a high regard for Apollos and may think that they even preferred to have Apollos among them rather than himself (see 16:12). Despite that awareness, however, Paul remains in contact with Apollos and considers him a colleague, not a rival, even if he does not speak of him as much as he does about himself, because Paul is concerned not only to mend the disunity of the Corinthian community, but also to establish his own apostolic authority there. Yet in 16:12, Paul will speak of Apollos as an equal and will scarcely seek to undercut his ministry, *pace* Ker, "Paul and Apollos."

In Acts 18:24–28, Luke describes Apollos as "a Jew, a native of Alexandria, an eloquent speaker (*anēr logios*), learned in the Scriptures" (*dynatos ōn en tais graphais*, lit. "capable in the [OT] writings"), who has just arrived in Ephesus. Although he had been instructed in the Way of the Lord, he knew only the baptism of John. So Priscilla and Aquila schooled him "more accurately" about the Way so that he could proceed to "Achaia" to work there. In Acts 19:1 he is said to be already in Corinth, when Paul arrives in Ephesus (see *Acts*, 638–40). What Apollos's particular preaching or teaching was is not easy to say. Schwarz ("Wo's Weisheit ist") thinks that his followers identified Christ with preexistent Wisdom (Sirach 24; Wisdom of Solomon).

This Pauline passage implies that Apollos was well known in Corinth and has been an eloquent preacher there. Because of the Lucan description of Apollos as *anēr logios*, one tends to identify him with the *sophia*, "wisdom," that Paul criticizes in 1:18–31. His mode of interpreting Scripture may have been similar to the allegorical method of Philo of Alexandria and of the Alexandrian Church Fathers, but one cannot extrapolate from either Philo or the patristic writers to say for sure what his preaching was like. A fortiori, it had nothing to do with Gnostic teaching (see Sellin, "Das 'Geheimnis' "; Ollrog, *Paulus und seine Mitarbeiter*, 37–41).

or "I side with Cephas." Lit. "but I (am) of Cephas." *Kēphas* is the name that Paul normally uses for the apostle Simon Peter (3:22; 9:5; 15:5; Gal 1:18; 2:9, 11, 14), but *Petros* appears in Gal 2:7–8.

"Cephas" recalls the name-change attributed to Jesus in the Gospels (John 1:42; Matt 16:17–18: "Blessed are you, Simon bar Jonah! . . . I tell you, you are Peter (*Petros*), and on this rock (*petra*) I will build my church."). On the basis of John 1:42, the early church interpreted *Kēphas* as *Petros*. The wordplay in Matt 16:18 has often been explained by referring to the Hebrew common noun, *kēph*, "rock" (Jer 4:29; Job 30:6); or Aramaic *kēphāʾ* (the form reflected in the Greek *Kēphas*). The common noun appears in Qumran Aramaic texts: 11QtgJob 32:1; 33:9 ("on the crag it [the black eagle] dwells, and it nests"); 4QEnoch^e 4 iii 19 ("and the sheep climbed to the summit of a certain high crag" [= *1 Enoch* 89:29]); 4QEnoch^c 4:3 (= *1 Enoch* 89:32). In all these instances, *kēphāʾ* means "rock" or "crag," part of a mountainous or hilly region. The word has also turned up in a pre-Christian Aramaic text as a personal name, the patronymic of a witness in a legal document from Elephantine (*BMAP* 8:10), dated to 416 B.C.: *šhd ʿqb br kpʾ*, "Witness: 'Aqab son of Kepha' " (see Fitzmyer, "Aramaic Kēphāʾ," *TAG*, 112–24, esp.113–18). *Pace* U. Luz, *kēphāʾ* would not have been heard by Aramaic-speaking people only as "stone" or "round stone" (*Matthew 8–20* [Hermeneia; Minneapolis: Fortress, 2001] 358–59); it meant "a crag" or a "rock," at least big enough for an eagle to build its nest on it or for a sheep to climb on; and so it is an apt basis for the building of a structure and for the figurative use of it in Jesus' saying.

Allegiance to Cephas creates a problem, however, because it is difficult to trace

Peter's movements on the basis of NT evidence. When would Cephas have been in Corinth? Because both Paul and Apollos have preached in Corinth, this passage implies that Cephas had been there too and even evangelized the town. When would he have been there? Scholars such as Lietzmann, Lake, E. Meyer et al., who admit that Peter made his way to Rome, think that he arrived there from Corinth. Moreover, Eusebius later wrote to this effect: "That they [Peter and Paul] were martyred together at the same time, Dionysius, a bishop of the Corinthians, thus asserts in a passage of his correspondence with Roman [Christians], 'By so great an instruction you too have linked together the planting of Romans and Corinthians that took place under Peter and Paul. For both of them planted our Corinth and taught us in the same way; and likewise they taught together in Italy and were martyred at the same time' " (*HE* 2.25.8). This testimony, however, is often dismissed as a "worthless deduction from 1 Corinthians" (Barrett, "Cephas and Corinth," 6). However, Barrett (ibid.) sought to make a strong case for Peter having evangelized Corinth as well as Paul (see also Manson, "St. Paul in Ephesus," 194; Dockx, "Essai," 230; Lietzmann, *1 Cor*, 7, 167; Vielhauer, "Paul and the Cephas Party," 132–33 [Vielhauer exaggerates when he speaks of Paul opposing Petrine primacy; that issue simply does not emerge in this letter]).

Such a Petrine evangelization of Corinth, however, is usually thought to conflict with what Paul says in 3:6 ("I planted, Apollos watered, but God caused the growth"), 3:10 ("I laid a foundation as an expert builder"), 4:15b ("In Christ Jesus I became your father through the gospel"), and 2 Cor 10:14. If Peter had been there before Paul, would the latter have undertaken the evangelization of Corinth, in light of his claim in Rom 15:20, "It has been my ambition to preach the good news where Christ has not been named, lest I build on the foundation of someone else"? It is practically impossible to say when Peter might have come to Corinth after Paul had founded the church there. So no matter how one handles these testimonies, one has to reckon in this letter with the presence of some mode of apostolic preaching that differs from that of Paul and Apollos, which is being associated with Cephas.

Certain other details in this letter are said to point to Peter's presence in Corinth: e.g., the mention of Cephas and his wife, or Cephas's relation to the rest of the apostles (9:5); God's fellow workers (3:1–9); even 5:9–13 (claimed to echo the Antioch controversy of Gal 2:11–14); and 6:1–6 have been so interpreted (Barrett, "Cephas and Corinth," 6–7). Yet none of these passages enables one to conclude with certainty that Peter was there before Paul wrote this letter (see Goguel, "L'Apôtre Pierre, 469–70, 488–89; Kremer, *1 Cor*, 32; Lindemann, *1 Cor*, 39–40; Romaniuk, "Le problème").

Another explanation of the Cephas-group has been that the phrase may mean no more than that some Jewish Christian devotees of Peter, to whom he may have preached elsewhere, have migrated to Corinth and become rivals to the others (Bachmann). Or they may have learned about Cephas from what Paul told them about him (Dahl, "Paul and the Church," 323 n. 1). In any case, Paul is not arguing against Peter, as he once did in Gal 2:11, 14. Nor is he arguing only against Peter's people; he is against all rival groups, no matter to whom their allegiance is.

Moreover, there is no evidence in the letter that the Cephas-group has been contesting the apostolic role of Paul, as Lietzmann once maintained apropos of 9:1–2; or that it was making concessions to Judaizers, as Fitch contends ("Paul, Apollos," 20).

or "I side with Christ." The strict parallelism of this last statement with the three that precede suggests that there was a fourth group in Corinth that so identified itself. The wording (esp. the *men . . . de* construction) and the logic of this verse would argue for that interpretation. They have been said to be Jewish Christians, who would not align themselves with Paul, the "apostle of the Gentiles" (Rom 11:13), or who regarded Jesus as "the promised Messiah" and dissociated "themselves from the more developed Christology of Paul" (Fitch, "Paul and Apollos," 21).

Was there actually such a group? The identification of those who might use this phrase as a slogan is more problematic than the other three. Would Paul be putting Christ on the same level as himself, Apollos, and Cephas? It is also problematic, because in 3:22 Paul mentions only himself, Apollos, and Cephas and declares that Corinthian Christians belong to Christ. Hence interpreters ever since the time of John Chrysostom have concluded that only three rival groups are mentioned. This is suggested also by *1 Clem.* 47:3, "In truth, he [Paul] spiritually charged you about himself, and Cephas, and Apollos, because even then you had made yourselves partisans."

Hence, "I side with Christ" may have been added in irony by Paul (or possibly by some Corinthian Christians) to the three preceding groups to reduce them to absurdity, as if to say, "You acknowledge human preachers, but I acknowledge only Christ." Such an understanding of the fourth statement accords well with the following v. 13, where Paul asks whether they were not dividing Christ. Cf. 2 Cor 10:7, where Paul may be giving yet another answer to this problem: "If anyone is confident that he belongs to Christ, let him remind himself that as he sides with Christ, so do we too." The phrase, however, may represent what all Christians should be saying, as in 1 Cor 3:23: "You belong to Christ, and Christ to God."

13. *Is Christ divided?* Lit. "has Christ been broken in pieces?" Possibly one should translate, "Christ is divided!" since the Greek sentence could be taken as either a question or a declaration (i.e., a judgment accusing the Corinthian community). In view of the two following rhetorical questions, however, it is better to take it as a question; moreover, MSS P⁴⁶, 326, 1962, etc. add *mē* before the verb, making it a question expecting the answer "no." The verb *merizō* is used in a similar sense by Polybius, *Hist.* 8.21.9, for political strife; also Appian, *Bell. Civ.* 1.1; a different sense is found in 1 Cor 7:17.

In any case, the three questions make it likely that Paul is speaking only of three groups, which he considers to be divisive of Christ. He is not accusing the Corinthians of rejecting Christ in favor of one of his disciples (Paul, Cephas, or Apollos), but he finds the church in Corinth divided indeed by such strife. That situation affects its relation to Christ himself, who died for all without distinction, in whose name all have been baptized, and into whose *koinōnia* they have all been called (1:9). Christ is one and cannot be divided; so his church should not be divided either. There is no need to introduce here the notion of the church as body of Christ; that will appear in due course, in 12:27–28. Rather *Christos* may have here the collective sense, as in 12:12 (see NOTE there).

Was Paul crucified for you? Lit. "Paul was not crucified for you, was he?" The sentence is introduced by *mē*, expecting the answer "no." Paul singles himself out, even if he could have mentioned either Cephas or Apollos instead, to stress the absurdity of the factious groups, as he molds his question on the confessional formula (15:3). It is rather the vicarious death of Christ on the cross that has brought salvation to humanity (see Rom 4:25). With this verse Paul is beginning to formulate his answer to the opposition to him encountered in Corinth and his relation to the Corinthian church; his answer will continue in various ways until it reaches its climax in 4:14–21.

Or were you baptized in the name of Paul? Again the answer is "no," as in the two preceding questions. Paul is parodying an early Christian formula, *baptizesthai eis to onoma tou*, "be baptized in the name of . . . ," which he himself does not otherwise use. It is found in Matt 28:19; Acts 8:16; 19:5; with *en* in Acts 10:48; with *epi* in Acts 2:38; cf. Rom 6:3–4; 1 Cor 12:13 (for related assertions). The formula has been explained by Heitmüller ("*Im Namen Jesu*") as derived from Hellenistic texts that record the transfer of money from one account to another; hence the one baptized is recorded in the financial ledger to the account of Christ. This meaning, however, has been contested by Bietenhard (*TDNT*, 5:275–76 and nn. 214, 219), who claims that the formula has been shown to have rather a Semitic origin (= Hebrew *lĕšēm*) "in Rabb. usage"; but when one scrutinizes the evidence for this usage (5:267–68), it is all derived from late sources such as the sixth-century Babylonian Talmud, even though *lĕšēm* itself is often used in the OT (in various senses). There does not seem to be any evidence for the precise sense of it used here (of ritual washings) that would be prior to or contemporary with Paul or the early Christian usage. Similarly Hartman, *EDNT*, 2:522.

14. *I give thanks [to God] that I baptized none of you, save Crispus and Gaius.* Despite the fact that Paul was largely responsible for the evangelization of Corinth, he admits (with irony) that he baptized only a few Corinthians. He understands his mission to be other than the administration of baptism. "To God" is bracketed because it is missing in the important MSS ℵ*, B, 6, 1739 and Coptic versions; in some MSS (A, 33, 81, 326) one finds *tō theō mou*, "my God," a copyist's addition undoubtedly derived from 1:4. The same rhetorical expression is found in 14:18, something like our colloquialism, "Thank God!" Paul realizes the absurdity of the Corinthian situation and reacts accordingly, even as he reacts with irony in 14:18.

Krispos was the "leader of the synagogue" in Corinth (Acts 18:8), who "put his faith in the Lord" (see NOTE on Sosthenes, 1:1). This is the same individual, whom Paul now says he baptized. *Gaïos* of Corinth is the same as Gaius, whom Paul calls his "host" and the host of "the whole church" in Rom 16:23, i.e., the church of Corinth that probably met in his house.

By "baptism" Paul means the new washing by which people become followers of Jesus Christ. It is presented as linked to the Christian experience of union with

Christ through faith. This initiatory rite, which incorporates human beings into Christ and the church, already existed in the pre-Pauline Christian tradition, but it is Paul who has developed its significance (esp. in his Letter to the Romans). Through baptism the Christian is identified with the death, burial, and resurrection of Christ, the main phases of his salvific activity (Rom 6:4–5). Identified with Christ in death, Christians die to the law and to sin (Rom 6:6, 10; 7:4); they are said to have "grown into union with him" (Rom 6:5), so that they now share his risen life and have been baptized into one body (1 Cor 12:13).

15. *so that no one can say that you were baptized in my name.* Paul repeats the idea expressed in the third question of v. 13 in a different way. The conj. *hina* expresses result (ZBG §352; BDF §391.5). Paul thus insists that no matter what relationship the Paul-group of Corinth might be claiming to him, it does not stem from him as their baptizer. Some interpreters have argued that this was the nature of the rival groups, that Corinthians who had been baptized by a certain preacher developed a bond of allegiance to him. Now Paul would be countering that claim.

16. *I did baptize the household of Stephanas too.* Paul corrects the sweeping statement made in v. 14, as he recalls what he did for Stephanas and his *oikos,* "house" (probably household, but "house church" is not impossible). *Stephanas* and his *oikia* are mentioned again in 16:15, where they are called "the first fruits of Achaia" and are said to "have devoted themselves to the service of God's dedicated people." His name is Greek, and so he may not have been one of the colonists, but either an indigenous citizen or an immigrant (so Meeks, *First Urban,* 58). Since Stephanas has come to Ephesus with other delegates (16:17), his presence may have sparked the correction recorded here. He seems to have been a fairly important person in Roman Corinth, possibly sent by the church there to Paul. .

otherwise I do not know whether I baptized anyone else. All told, then, Paul admits that he baptized at Corinth Crispus, Gaius, and the household of Stephanas. At least he cannot recall others.

17. *For Christ did not send me to baptize.* This startling statement is not meant to undermine the value of baptism or liturgical actions. It reveals only how Paul understands his own authorized mission: cultic or liturgical ministry was not as important to him as that of preaching the gospel. Others can baptize, but he must preach, because he was called by God to preach his son "among the Gentiles" (Gal 1:16); now he ascribes his call and sending to Christ himself (*Christos* without an article, hence Jesus' second name).

but to preach the gospel. I.e., to proclaim the good news (*euangelizesthai*) of salvation that comes through Christ Jesus. What Paul says here he will develop further in Rom 1:15; 15:20, and esp. 10:8–10: " '*The word is near to you, on your lips and in your heart'* [quotation of Deut 30:14] (that is, the word of faith that we preach): if you profess with your lips that 'Jesus is Lord,' and believe in your heart that God raised him from the dead, you will be saved. Such faith of the heart leads to uprightness; such profession of the lips to salvation." Cf. Gal 1:8–10, 16, 23. For Paul's idea of *euangelion,* "gospel," see INTRODUCTION pp. 70–71; *PAHT*

§PT31–36. Implied here is that Paul's preaching does not depend on speculative thinking or on rhetorical artifice. It is certainly more than "a ministry of public speaking," *pace* Litfin (*St. Paul's Theology of Proclamation*, 152). There is in this passage, however, not the slightest hint that Paul's reluctance to baptize had anything to do with his reaction to people claiming to speak in tongues, as Ford would have us believe: " 'induced tongues' associated with baptism may have led him to refrain from administering" baptism ("Paul's Reluctance," 520).

and not with eloquent wisdom, lest the cross of Christ be emptied of its meaning. Lit. "not with the wisdom of word/speech (*en sophiā logou*) lest there be emptied the cross of Christ." Noteworthy is the emphatic position that the phrase *ho stauros tou Christou* occupies at the end of the verse, as J. Weiss recognized (*1 Cor*, 23 n. 1). In this part of this verse, Paul introduces a theme that will be developed in the coming passages of his letter, "eloquent wisdom," i.e., human wisdom or the wisdom of this world (1:18–2:5).

Wisdom (*sophia*) usually means accumulated philosophic, scientific, and experiential learning that includes an ability to discern essential relationships of people and things. It connotes competence in and a profound understanding of domains of human endeavor (philosophy, literature, art, science). It was highly prized and an important characteristic of the Greco-Roman culture in Paul's day, but he feels it necessary to pit himself as a preacher of the gospel over against the rhetorical eloquence of trained orators, whom he regards as merely human sages. His reason? "Lest the cross of Christ be emptied of its meaning," i.e., be dissipated in a cloud of learned rhetoric and words. The cross has been introduced in v. 13, where Paul alludes to the crucifixion of Jesus, and in the following v. 18 he will speak of "the message of the cross" (*ho logos ho tou staurou*), which is the heart of his gospel and which stands over against *sophia logou*, which may even be a phrase bandied about in Roman Corinth. Needless to say, Paul is not an anti-intellectual and is not inveighing against the use of philosophy or other polished modes of communication in his endeavor to preach the gospel, but he is concerned that such preaching modes not obscure the mystery of the cross. "The evidence of Paul's own testimony strongly suggests that the apostle deliberately chose not to make use of ancient rhetoric in his preaching of the Gospel and his written correspondence with various churches" (Weima, "What Does Aristotle," 467). I hesitate to go along with Goulder's sense of "wisdom" in this letter, which he sees as a way of life in accord with the Torah and halakhic regulations ("*Sophia*").

BIBLIOGRAPHY (See also Bibliography on 1:10–4:21)

Barrett, C. K., "Cephas and Corinth," *Abraham unser Vater: Juden und Christen im Gespräch über die Bibel: Festschrift für Otto Michel* . . . (AGSU 5; ed. O. Betz et al.; Leiden: Brill, 1963) 1–12; repr. *Essays on Paul* (Philadelphia: Westminster, 1982) 28–39.

Baur, F. C., "Die Christuspartei in der korinthischen Gemeinde, der Gegensatz des petrinischen und paulinischen Christenthums in der ältesten Kirche, der Apostel Petrus in Rom," *Ferdinand Christian Baur, Ausgewählte Werke in Einzelgaben* (ed. K. Scholder; 5 vols.; Stuttgart-Bad Cannstatt: Frommann, 1963), 1:1–146.

Bjerkelund, C. J., *Parakalô: Form, Funktion und Sinn der parakalô-Sätze in den paulinischen Briefen* (Bibliotheca theologica norvegica 1; Oslo: Universitetsforlaget, 1967).

Carter, T. L., " 'Big Men' in Corinth," *JSNT* 66 (1997) 45–71.

Dockx, S., "Essai de chronologie pétrienne," *RSR* 62 (1974) 221–41.

Fitch, W. O., "Paul, Apollos, Cephas, Christ: Studies in Texts: 1 Corinthians 1:12," *Theology* 74 (1971) 18–24.

Fitzmyer, J. A., "Aramaic Kepha' and Peter's Name in the New Testament," *TAG*, 112–24.

Ford, J. M., "Paul's Reluctance to Baptise," *NBf* 55 (1974) 517–20.

Goguel, M., "L'Apôtre Pierre a-t-il joué un rôle personnel dans les crises de Grèce et de Galatie?" *RHPR* 14 (1934) 461–500.

Goulder, M., "*Sophia* in 1 Corinthians," *NTS* 37 (1991) 516–34.

Hartman, L., "Baptism," *ABD*, 1:583–94.

Hitchcock, F. R. M., "Who Are 'the People of Chloe' in I Cor. i 11," *JTS* 25 (1923–24) 163–67.

Ker, D. P., "Paul and Apollos—Colleagues or Rivals?" *JSNT* 77 (2000) 75–97.

Lake, K., "The Chronology of Acts," *The Beginnings of Christianity* (cd. F. J. Foakes Jackson and K. Lake; 5 vols.; Grand Rapids: Baker Book House, 1979) 5:445–74.

Lütgert, W., *Freiheitspredigt und Schwarmgeister in Korinth: Ein Beitrag zur Charakteristik der Christuspartei* (BFCT 12/3; Gütersloh: Bertelsmann, 1908).

Manson, T. W., "St. Paul in Ephesus: The Corinthian Correspondence," *BJRL* 26 (1941–42) 101–20, 327–41; repr. *Studies in the Gospels and Epistles* (Manchester, UK: Manchester University Press; Philadelphia: Westminster, 1962) 190–224.

Meinertz, M., "*Schisma* und *hairesis* im Neuen Testament," *BZ* 1 (1957) 114–18.

Pherigo, L. P., "Rival Leadership in Corinth," *JBR* 19 (1951) 197–99.

Romaniuk, K., "Le problème de l'activité missionnaire de saint Pierre à Corinthe," *ColT* 46/fasc. spec. (1976) 123–25.

Sanders, J. T., "The Transition from Opening Epistolary Thanksgiving to Body in the Letters of the Pauline Corpus," *JBL* 81 (1962) 348–62.

Schwarz, E., "Wo's Weisheit ist, ein Tor zu sein: Zur Argumentation von 1Kor 1–4," *WD* 20 (1989) 219–35.

Strüder, C. W., "Preferences not Parties: The Background of 1 Cor 1,12," *ETL* 79 (2003) 431–55.

Vielhauer, P., "Paul and the Cephas Party in Corinth," *JHC* 1 (1994) 129–42.

Weima, J. A. D., "What Does Aristotle Have to Do with Paul? An Evaluation of Rhetorical Criticism," *CTJ* 32 (1997) 458–68.

Welborn, L. L., "On the Discord in Corinth: 1 Corinthians 1–4 and Ancient Politics," *JBL* 106 (1987) 85–111.

White, J. L., "Introductory Formulae in the Body of the Pauline Letter," *JBL* 90 (1971) 91–97.

BIBLIOGRAPHY ON 1:10–4:21

Baumann, R., *Mitte und Norm des Christlichen: Eine Auslegung von 1 Korinther 1,1–3,14* (NTAbh n.s. 5; Münster in W.: Aschendorff, 1968).

Betz, O., "Der gekreuzigte Christus, unsere Weisheit und Gerechtigkeit (Der alttestamentliche Hintergrund von 1.Korinther 1–2)," *Tradition and Interpretation in the New Testament: Essays in Honor of E. Earle Ellis . . .* (ed. G. F. Hawthorne and O. Betz; Grand Rapids: Eerdmans, 1987) 195–215.

Borghi, E., "Il tema *sophia* in 1 Cor 1–4," *RivB* 40 (1992) 421–58.

Branick, V. P., "Source and Redaction Analysis of 1 Corinthians 1–3," *JBL* 101 (1982) 251–69.

Dahl, N. A., "Paul and the Church at Corinth according to 1 Corinthians 1:10–4:21," *Christian History and Interpretation: Studies Presented to John Knox* (ed. W. R. Farmer et al.; Cambridge: Cambridge University Press, 1967) 313–35.

Fiore, B., " 'Covert Allusion' in 1 Corinthians 1–4," *CBQ* 47 (1985) 85–102.

George, A., "Sagesse du monde et sagesse de Dieu (d'après la 1re aux Corinthiens)," *BVC* 38 (1961) 16–24.

Getty, M. A., "The Paradox of the Cross," *TBT* 32 (1994) 207–12.

Harvey, A. E., "The Opposition to Paul," *SE IV* (TU 102; Berlin: Akademie-V., 1968) 319–32.

Hillmer, M. R., "Knowledge, New Age, Gnosticism and First Corinthians," *McMaster Journal of Theology* 3 (1992) 18–38.

Hyldahl, N., "The Corinthian 'Parties' and the Corinthian Crisis," *ST* 45 (1991) 19–32.

Joseph, M. J., " 'Jesus Christ and Him Crucified' (A Study of 1 Corinthians Chapters 1 and 2)," *BiBh* 14 (1988) 176–84.

Klauck, H.-J., "Gemeindestrukturen im ersten Korintherbrief," *BK* 40 (1985) 9–15.

Kottackal, J., "The Folly of the Cross," *BiBh* 6 (1980) 97–103.

Le Gal, F., "L'Évangile de la folie sainte," *RSR* 89 (2001) 419–42.

Litfin, D., *St. Paul's Theology of Proclamation: 1 Corinthians 1–4 and Greco-Roman Rhetoric* (Cambridge: Cambridge University Press, 1994).

Munck, J., "The Church without Factions: Studies in I Corinthians 1–4," *Paul and the Salvation of Mankind* (London: SCM, 1959) 135–67.

Pogoloff, S. M., *Logos and Sophia: The Rhetorical Situation of 1 Corinthians* (SBLDS 134; Atlanta: Scholars, 1992).

Polhill, J. B., "The Wisdom of God and Factionalism: 1 Corinthians 1–4," *RevExp* 80 (1983) 325–39.

Reese, J. M., "Paul Proclaims the Wisdom of the Cross: Scandal and Foolishness," *BTB* 9 (1979) 147–53.

Rosaeg, N. A., "Paul's Rhetorical Arsenal and 1 Corinthians 1–4," *Jian Dao* 3 (1995) 51–75.

Schlier, H., "Kerygma und Sophia," *EvT* 10 (1950–51) 451–507; repr. *Die Zeit der Kirche* (Freiburg im B.: Herder, 1956) 147–59, 206–32.

Sellin, G., "Das 'Geheimnis' der Weisheit und das Rätsel der 'Christuspartei' (zu 1 Kor 1–4)," *ZNW* 73 (1982) 69–96.

Serna, E. de la, "La cruz y el crucificado en 1 Cor.," *RevistB* 49 (1987) 209–13.

———, "La iniciativa divina en 1 Cor.," *RevistB* 51 (1989) 39–44.

Smit, J. F. M., "Epideictic Rhetoric in Paul's First Letter to the Corinthians 1–4," *Bib* 84 (2003) 184–201.

———, " 'What Is Apollos? What Is Paul?' In Search for the Coherence of First Corinthians 1:10–4:21," *NovT* 44 (2002) 231–51.

Söding, T., "Kreuzestheologie und Rechtfertigungslehre: Zur Verbindung von Christologie und Soteriologie im Ersten Korintherbrief und im Galaterbrief," *Catholica* 46 (1992) 31–60.

Trevijano Etcheverría, R., "El contraste de sabidurías (1 Cor 1, 17–4, 20)," *Salm* 34 (1987) 277–98.

Vos, J. S., "Die Argumentation des Paulus in 1 Kor 1,10–3,4," *The Corinthian Correspondence* (BETL 125; ed. R. Bieringer), 87–119.

Voss, F., *Das Wort vom Kreuz und die menschliche Vernunft: Eine Untersuchung zur Sote-*

riologie des 1. Korintherbriefes (FRLANT 199; Göttingen: Vandenhoeck & Ruprecht, 2002) 53–61.

Watson, F., "Christ, Community, and the Critique of Ideology: A Theological Reading of 1 Corinthians 1.18–31," *NedTT* 46 (1992) 132–49.

Welborn, L. L., "*Mōros genesthō*: Paul's Appropriation of the Role of the Fool in 1 Corinthians 1–4," *BibInt* 10 (2002) 420–35.

Wilckens, U., "Kreuz und Weisheit," *KD* 3 (1957) 77–108.

Williams, H. H. D., *The Wisdom of the Wise: The Presence and Function of Scripture within 1 Cor. 1:18–3:23* (AGJU 49; Leiden: Brill, 2001).

Wuellner, W., "Haggadic Homily Genre in I Corinthians 1–3," *JBL* 89 (1970) 199–204.

4   b. *False and Correct Ideas of Wisdom (1:18–31)*

[1:18] For the message of the cross is folly to those who are perishing, but to us who are being saved it is the power of God. [19] For it stands written, *"I will destroy the wisdom of the wise, and the learning of the learned I will confound."* [20] Where is the sage? Where is the scribe? Where is the inquirer of this age? Has not God made the wisdom of the world foolish? [21] For since, in God's wisdom, the world did not come to know God through its own wisdom, God was pleased to save those who have faith through the folly of the proclamation. [22] Whereas Jews demand signs and Greeks seek wisdom, [23] we proclaim Christ crucified, a stumbling block to Jews and folly to Gentiles, [24] but for those who are called, both Jews and Greeks, Christ is the power of God and the wisdom of God. [25] For God's foolishness is wiser than human wisdom, and God's weakness is stronger than human strength. [26] Look now at your own calling, brothers. For not many of you were wise by human standards; not many were powerful; not many were of noble birth. [27] But God chose what is foolish in the world in order to shame the wise, and what is weak in the world to shame the strong. [28] God chose what is lowly and despised in the world, things that do not exist, to nullify the things that do, [29] so that no human being might boast in God's sight. [30] It is because of him that you are in Christ Jesus, who became for us wisdom from God, uprightness and sanctification and redemption, [31] so that, as it stands written, *"Let the one who would boast, boast of the Lord."*

COMMENT

Paul continues his treatment of the scandal of preacher-factions with a further consideration. Because some Corinthian Christians seem to have preferred the eloquence of Apollos (*anēr logios*, Acts 18:24) and Paul maintained that he himself had not been preaching "with eloquent wisdom" (1:17), he now feels the need to say more about human wisdom and its relation to the Christian gospel. So he contrasts these ideas and the effects that they have on human beings, whether Jews or Greeks.

Noteworthy are the eight assertions that he makes concerning the gospel in this pericope. For Paul it is (1) "the message of the cross" (18a); (2) "the power of God" (18b); (3) "the folly of proclamation" (21b); (4) "Christ crucified" (23a); (5) "a stumbling block to Jews and folly to Gentiles" (23b); (6) "Christ the power of God and the wisdom of God" (24); (7) "what is foolish in the world" (27); (8) "wisdom from God, uprightness and sanctification and redemption" (30).

Over against such a characterization of the gospel stand the five ways he regards human wisdom or the wisdom of this world: (1) "the wisdom of the wise," a phrase derived from Isa 29:14 (19); (2) unable "to know God" (21); (3) wisdom "of human beings" (25); (4) "the things that exist" (*ta onta*, 28); and (5) boasting (29).

The paragraph has two parts: vv. 18–25 and vv. 26–31. In 1:18–25 Paul develops the contrast by four comparisons and a quotation from the OT. In v. 18, the contrast is double, comparing the folly of the message of the cross and God's power in it and comparing those who are perishing with those who are saved by it. In vv. 20–21, the contrast is again double, as Paul compares the sage, the scribe, and the debater of this age with God, and the wisdom of this world with the folly of Christian proclamation. In vv. 22–23, the Jewish demand for signs and the Greek search for wisdom are contrasted with Christ crucified. In v. 25, God's foolishness and weakness are contrasted with human wisdom and strength. In v. 24, Paul concludes as he states his fundamental thesis: "For those who are called, both Jews and Greeks, Christ is the power of God and the wisdom of God."

In vv. 26–31 Paul applies what he has been propounding to Corinthian Christians to their initial call to faith: many of them were not wise, or powerful, or of noble birth. Yet God chose the foolish and the weak, the lowly and the despised, "even things that are not, to nullify the things that are" (v. 28). Paul again concludes by insisting that because of God Corinthian Christians are "in Christ Jesus, who became for us wisdom from God, uprightness and sanctification and redemption" (v. 30). Thus Paul emphasizes such diverse effects of the Christ-event. He further maintains that no human being, then, can boast in God's sight, because the condition and status of Corinthian Christians come from God alone, and Paul ends by summarizing Jer 9:22–23.

Although Paul is inveighing against human eloquence, he employs many stylistic devices: rhetorical questions (v. 20), various kinds of parallelism (standard, antithetical) (v. 18, 22), anaphora (the threefold "where?" v. 20), and developed contrasts. Whether one can speak of the passage as poetry, as does Bailey ("Recovering the Poetic Structure") is highly questionable; his attempt to lay our verses in parallel lines is scarcely successful.

Interpreters have sometimes found little coherence between Paul's reaction to the factional strife expressed in 1:10–17 and the topic of wisdom treated in 1:18–31; 2:6–16; and 3:18–23. The latter three passages are even said to have been a carefully composed homily on wisdom, "very probably written for another group" rather than the Christians of Corinth, for whom it has only general relevance and little specific pertinence. So Branick, "Source and Redaction," 267,

269. However, it may be at first a bit difficult to see a connection between the factional strife of 1:10–17 and what Paul develops in this paragraph, where he speaks of God's negative judgment on human wisdom, or even in 2:6–16; but in 3:5–23 he joins the two topics and relates the general discussion of wisdom to the specific topic of factional strife (see further Lampe, "Theological Wisdom"; Borghi, "Il tema *sophia*").

A prime teaching of Pauline theology comes to expression in this passage, the theology of the cross or of Christ crucified. It is a teaching that he has inherited from the early Christians before him, as the primitive *kērygma* quoted in 15:3 makes clear: "Christ died for our sins according to the Scriptures." That is the basis of what he teaches in this paragraph about those who are saved. The salvific character of the crucifixion of the historical Jesus is the background and basis of Paul's thinking. He understands Jesus to have died as a representative of sinful human beings and to have sacrificed himself as the Passover lamb as a mean to expiate human sin, as 1 Cor 5:7; Rom 8:3; and 2 Cor 5:21 make clear (see Dunn, "Paul's Understanding"). All of this is seen also as a manifestation of God's wisdom and power. That is why he even calls Jesus Christ "the wisdom of God" (v. 24) or the "wisdom from God" (v. 30); for Paul nothing is true wisdom but Christ crucified.

Although some interpreters have tried to single out the particular rival faction (e.g., the Apollos-group) against which Paul is making his diverse statements about wisdom in this paragraph, it is really an idle endeavor, because his statements are generic. He obviously intended them for all the different groups.

In v. 23 (also 2:7), Paul uses "we" in contrast to the "I" of vv. 14, 16, 17 and 2:1–4. From this difference, Murphy-O'Connor ("Co-authorship") concludes that the "we" includes Sosthenes as the co-author, who is thus addressing the Corinthian Christians too. This conclusion, however, is unlikely, because the "us" in v. 18 clearly refers to more than Paul and Sosthenes, his co-sender, who are rather identifying themselves with all the "saved." When Paul says, "We proclaim Christ crucified" (v. 23), that statement is not limited to the preaching of Sosthenes and himself, as 15:11 makes clear, "So whether it was I or they, in this way we preach, and in this way you came to believe." By using the first plural, Paul is identifying himself with all other Christian preachers, as well as with all Christian believers, as v. 30 makes clear (so too Lindemann, *1 Cor*, 44).

Similarly far-fetched is the alleged connection of this paragraph with the cry of jubilation uttered by Jesus in Matt 11:25–27; Luke 10:21–22 (a "Q" passage), as if that dominical logion might have been the subject of controversy in the Corinthian community. There may be a few verbal similarities, but nothing really establishes the connection, *pace* Henaut, "Matthew 11:27." Likewise overdrawn is the view of Horsley ("Spiritual Marriage with Sophia") that the Corinthian *pneumatikoi* also thought in terms of a spiritual marriage with Sophia [whom he claims to be a 'divine figure'] and that this is related to their asceticism [i.e., sexual asceticism as expressed in chap. 7, like Philo's *Therapeutae*].

Paul continues to reflect on the risks of human wisdom when it is exalted disproportionately to the detriment of the meaning of Christ and his cross. Wisdom, eloquence, and rhetoric may have their place in human life, but there is a further consideration for Christians, whether they come from a Jewish or a Gentile background, viz., the gospel or the message of the cross. Paul insists that all Christians must draw strength for human life and its endeavors from "Christ crucified," who is "wisdom from God," the only one in whom we can find our uprightness, sanctification, and redemption.

NOTES

1:18. *For the message of the cross is folly to those who are perishing.* This statement, introduced by *gar*, "for," explains the last part of v. 17. *Ho logos ho tou staurou*, "the word of the cross," which is the heart and norm of all that is Christian, stands in contrast to *sophia logou*, "eloquent wisdom." It also summarizes the gospel that Paul preaches, as 1:23; 2:2 make clear, "Jesus Christ and him crucified," because it proclaims God's power and wisdom. By anaphora, "the message of the cross" also picks up on "the cross of Christ" of v. 17; cf. Gal 3:1. Some MSS (P[46], B, F*, G*, 630, 1739) omit the second *ho* before the attributive gen. (see BDF §271).

"The message of the cross" is the answer that Paul is giving to those whom he will call *pneumatikoi* in 2:15, whose opinion he respects, whether they be Jews or Greeks (1:22). His discussion in this paragraph is also an answer to the implicit question that they pose by their queries and seeking: A mature Christian can be a mature wisdom-seeking Greek. That wisdom, however, has to come from "the message of the cross," God's wisdom (so Betz, "The Gospel").

The Greek word *stauros* means "an upright, pointed stake," but it came to be used of the T-shaped instrument of execution to which criminals were nailed in the Roman world; hence the translation, "cross." Crucifixion had been derived from the Persians (see Herodotus, *Hist.* 1.128.2; 3.125.3; 3.132.2). For the use of it in Roman-occupied ancient Palestine, see Fitzmyer, "Crucifixion." The Roman orator Cicero called crucifixion *crudelissimum taeterrimumque supplicium*, "a most cruel and disgusting punishment" (*In C. Verrem* 2.5.65); and "unworthy of a Roman citizen" (*Pro Rabirio* 5.16; cf. Hengel, *Crucifixion*, 22–24; *TDNT*, 7:573–74). For Gospel passages that speak of the "cross" as the mode of Jesus' execution and death, see Mark 15:21, 30, 32; Matt 27:32, 40, 42; Luke 23:26; John 19:17, 25, 31.

Paul's gospel proves indeed to be "folly" to most of his contemporaries because of the contemporary conventional wisdom about crucifixion in the Roman world. Justin Martyr recalls how people in his day reacted to Christian "madness" (*mania*): "They say that our madness consists in this that we put a crucified man in second place after the unchangeable and eternal God, the Creator of the world" (*Apology I*, 13.4). Pliny the Younger called Christianity a madness (*amentia*) and a perverse and outlandish superstition (*superstitio prava et immodica*, *Ep.*10.96.4, 8). Similarly Tacitus, "a pernicious superstition" (*exitiabilis superstitio*, *Annales* 15.44.3); Suetonius, "a new and mischievous superstition" (*superstitio nova ac malefica*, *Nero* 16.2). So the crucifixion of Jesus differentiates "the message of the cross" from all the myths of the ancient world (see Hengel, *Crucifixion*, 1–10).

"Those who are perishing" occurs elsewhere (2 Cor 2:15; 4:3; cf. 2 Thess 2:10) and denotes those who have not accepted the Christian gospel, and hence can eventually be "lost" in the sight of God. It stands in contrast to those "who are being saved" in the next clause. There is no implication that those perishing or being saved are the object of a divine predestinarian decree or call (1:24), but the contrast of folly and wisdom implies judgment of eschatological nature. Compare Bar 3:28.

but to us who are being saved it is the power of God. The same contrast is found in 2 Cor 2:15. Salvation is one of the effects of the Christ-event in Pauline theology. Although Paul looks at this effect as already achieved in the Christ-event, he recognizes that it will be accomplished only in the future, because it is an eschatological blessing (1 Thess 2:16; 5:8–9; 1 Cor 3:15; 5:5; Rom 5:9–10; 8:24 ["In hope we have been saved"]). See *PAHT* §PT71; cf. Luke 13:23; Acts 2:47; for the contrast of perishing and salvation, see Phil 1:28. In some MSS (F, G, 6) and some patristic citations, the pron. *hēmin*, "to us," is omitted.

The gospel or the message of the cross is the power of God, because in that message the crucified Jesus is proclaimed as the one who brings God's power to deliver human beings from the evil of sin and moral destruction. Thus the cross of Christ is not emptied of its meaning (1:17). Cf. 2 Cor 4:3–5. The anarthrous phrase *dynamis theou*, "power of God," denotes not only an attribute of God, but also designates what God has done for those whom he calls (1:24), as in Rom 1:16. This will be echoed in 2:4–5, which is a résumé of what Paul affirms in 1:17–18. See Lambrecht, "The Power of God."

19. *For it stands written.* Lit. "for it has been written," i.e., in Scripture. So Paul often explicitly introduces an OT quotation (sometimes with *kathōs*, "as"): 1:31; 2:9; 3:19; 2 Cor 8:15; 9:9; Rom 1:17; 2:24; 3:4, 10; 4:17; 8:36; 9:13, 33; 10:15; 11:8, 26; 12:19; 14:11; 15:3, 9, 21. In 1 Cor 14:21, Paul writes, *en tō nomō gegraptai*, "it stands written in the law." *Kathōs gegraptai* occurs in Dan 9:13 (Theodotion), translating Hebrew *ka'ăšer kātûb*, and in 2 Kgs 14:6, translating *kakkātûb*. The former of these Hebrew introductory formulas is often found in QL (1QS 5:17; 8:14; CD 7:19; 4QFlor 1–2 i 12; 4Q178 3:2; see Fitzmyer, *ESBNT*, 3–58, esp. 8–9).

"I will destroy the wisdom of the wise, and the learning of the learned I will confound." Paul cites LXX Isa 29:14, which has the same wording save for the final word, *krypsō*, "I will hide," instead of Paul's *athetēsō*, "I will thwart, confound," perhaps adopted from LXX Ps 33:10. The MT of Isaiah reads rather, "The wisdom of its wise men will perish; the discernment of its discerning people will be hidden." Paul quotes Scripture, convinced that the warning that God expressed of old is still valid even for Christians (see 9:10; Rom 4:23). God will not only "hide" such wisdom, as the LXX puts it, but He will confound or thwart it. Compare also Isa 5:21. This introductory quotation will find its counterpart in 3:19–20, where Paul says that "the wisdom of this world is foolishness in God's sight," and he there quotes Job 5:13 and Ps 94:11, to bolster his argument further. See also Stanley, *Paul and the Language of Scripture*, 185–86.

God will sit in judgment and bring to naught both *sophia*, "wisdom," and *synesis*, "intelligence, learning," so highly esteemed among those who now consider the message of the cross to be foolishness. The two nouns often occur together in

Greek writings (LXX Deut 4:6; Aristotle, *Nich. Ethics* 1.13.20; Diodorus Siculus, *Bibl. Hist.* 9.3.3). See Malan, "The Use."

20. *Where is the sage? Where is the scribe? Where is the inquirer of this age?* Paul's three verbless rhetorical questions imitate, or perhaps allude to, Isa 19:12, *pou eisin nyn hoi sophoi sou?*, "Where now are your wise men?" In Isaiah, it was a rhetorical device to stress the uselessness of the Egyptian princes of Zoan, counsellors of the Pharaoh. See also Isa 33:18, where one finds a similar use of the triple *pou*, "where?"; and one being, *pou eisin hoi grammateis*, "Where are the scribes?" Cf. Bar 3:9–4:4, esp. 3:14–16, which has a similar question in what has often been regarded as a homily based on Jer 8:13–9:24, a text used in Jewish liturgy for the Day of Atonement (Peterson, "1 Korinther 1,18f."). The last phrase, "of this age," is to be understood with all three individuals, not just the "inquirer." It will turn up again in 2:6 bis, 8; 3:18; its counterpart, "the age to come," occurs in Eph 2:7. Verses 20–25 are the first stage of Paul's argument, as he contrasts the proclamation of the cross as God's power and wisdom with the wisdom of this world.

Since patristic times, the *sophos* has been understood as the wise man among Greeks (or Egyptians), the *grammateus*, "scribe," as the learned man among Jews (an expert interpreter of the Mosaic Law [Matt 2:4; Mark 12:38; Acts 23:9]), and *suzētētēs* has often been taken to be a pejorative term, "disputant, debater." Lautenschlager ("Abschied vom Disputierer"), however, has shown that the real meaning of *syzētētēs* is not pejorative, but rather a technical term for a seeker after truth. It was so used in the Greek philosophical and patristic tradition and often meant a Greek philosopher. In the Greek philosophical tradition, the verb *suzētein* commonly means "join in examining" (Plato, *Cratylus* 384c; *Meno* 80d, 90b); and the noun *syzētētēs* denotes the "(philosophical) searcher, student" (*Resp.* 10.618c). Cf. Acts 28:29 (a verse preserved only in the Western Text: *pollēn echontes en heautois syzētēsin*, "seriously arguing among themselves"). Latin versions of the NT (VL, Vg) and Latin patristic writers (Tertullian, Ambrose) translate the noun not with *disputator*, but with *conquisitor*, "inquirer."

The three rhetorical questions emphasize with irony the futility of such learning in view of "the message of the cross," which makes known "the power of God," who is implementing the threat announced in v. 19.

Welborn thinks that Paul has actually appropriated the role of a "fool" from the popular theater and mime, so that "folly" would be best understood as a designation of an attitude and behavior of a particular social type, the lower class buffoon, who would then stand in contrast with the eloquent and sophisticated Apollos ("*Mōros genesthō*"). Perhaps.

Has not God made the wisdom of the world foolish? So the sentence is read in MSS P⁴⁶, ℵ*, A, B, C*, D, 33, etc., but many other good MSS add *toutou*, "this (world)," as at the end of the preceding sentence (Metzger, *TCGNT*, 479–80). In using the verb *mōrainō*, "make foolish," Paul may be alluding to LXX Isa 19:11, where its fut. pass. is employed for the "counsel" of Egyptian sages, which "will be made foolish." The same idea is formulated a bit differently in Rom 1:22, "Pretending to be wise, they became fools," or "they were made foolish." Cf. Jer 10:14,

"Every human being has become a fool without knowledge"; also Wis 11:15. For Paul, this has happened because God's power is having an effect; it has turned "the wisdom of the world" into folly. *Kosmos* appears as a synonym for "this age" (v. 20c) and has to be understood as the "world" with all in it that is hostile to and alienated from God (BDAG, 562b); it is a subj. gen., the world that supports such wisdom. Cf. Ps.-Philo (*LAB* 40.4), "I [the Lord] have tied up the tongue of the wise ones of my people in this generation. . . ." (see Reinmuth, "LAB 40,4").

"The wisdom of the world" will be called "human wisdom" (*sophia anthrōpōn*) in 2:5. What is meant by it? The answer has to be based on Paul's discussion here in the first section of the letter, even though "the utterance of wisdom" is mentioned among the spiritual gifts (12:8), which are misunderstood. That is found, however, in an entirely different context, where gifts of the Spirit are the problem. Now it is human wisdom, and there is no hint that this "human wisdom" involves a mistaken eschatological perspective, some sort of realized eschatology, which is not the issue in these early chapters. Rather, it denotes the mindset of some Corinthian Christians who were denying the soteriological significance of Christ's cross or crucifixion (Wilckens, *Weisheit*, 20, 214).

21. *For since, in God's wisdom, the world did not come to know God through wisdom.* I.e., through its own wisdom, or by way of wisdom (*dia* being used as a modal prep.). This clause is not easily rendered because of the prep. phrase after the causal conj. *epeidē*, "since." Apart from that phrase, the rest of the clause is readily understood, being a statement that Paul will develop more at length in Rom 1:19–23, when he discusses the failure of the pagan world to come to a proper knowledge of God in spite of His having made evident for it what can be known about Him ever since the creation of the world. This clause, then, is the beginning of an explanation of God's attitude expressed in v. 20.

Problematic is the sense of the prep. in the phrase, *en tē sophiā tou theou*: how did the world fail to know God through its wisdom "in God's wisdom"? Interpreters have sought to understand the prep. *en* in four different ways: (1) causally: "owing to the wise dispensation of God" (J. B. Lightfoot, Schlatter, Schottroff), but this is a rare use of *en*; (2) modally, "by God's wisdom," i.e., as it has made itself manifest in creation, but human philosophy failed to recognize God (J. Weiss), but is *sophia* elsewhere used as a manifestation of wisdom; (3) temporally, "in (the time of) God's wisdom" (Lietzmann), i.e., while the world was under the influence of a revelation of God's wisdom, but that adds a nuance not expressed in the text; (4) locally, "in (the works of) God's wisdom," as it is revealed in them, as understood in the Jewish tradition (Bornkamm, Schlier, Lindemann). The best of these ways is a modification of the first one, as Barrett has taken it, "by God's wisdom," meaning His wise plan, which then stands in contrast to the last prep. phrase in the sentence, *dia tēs sophias*, "through (its own) wisdom." In other words, "the wise God saw fit that the world of men should not come to know him through its own wisdom" (Wedderburn, *En tē sophiā*, 133–34). So "the wisdom of God" stands in contrast to "the wisdom of this world." The "world" would include Greeks (pagans) and Jews, as vv. 22–24 make clear. Paul seems to be prescinding from what he might otherwise say about Jews' knowledge of God.

No matter which one of these ways may be preferred, Paul is evidently discussing the matter in light of his Jewish wisdom tradition, as Schlier, Conzelmann, and others have noted, according to which real wisdom has disappeared among humans, and that which now comes from God is known only to "those who are called" (v. 24) or to "those who are being saved" (v. 18). The idiom *ginōskein en*, "to recognize something by," is found in Luke 24:35; John 13:35; 1 John 3:16; Sir 11:28.

God was pleased to save those who have faith through the folly of the proclamation. Lit. "those believing," i.e., those who respond with faith to the preaching of the Christian gospel about God's activity in Christ crucified, as Paul will explain in Rom 10:8c–10. "The folly of the proclamation" corresponds to "God's wisdom" in the preceding verse. It is called "folly," because of its content: the proclamation makes known "the message of the cross" (1:18). For the first time, Paul mentions *kērygma*, "proclamation," the technical term for what apostles and early Christian missionaries announced to their contemporaries, as they preached that "Jesus is Lord" (12:3; Rom 10:9). It will appear again in 2:4; 15:14. Paul, however, now calls that *kērygma* "folly" (*mōria*), echoing what he said in v. 18, as he quotes the reaction of skeptical humanity that cannot accept the idea that human salvation comes from a crucified man. Yet he insists that it is the sovereign God's good pleasure to make use of such folly to confound "the wisdom of the world" and to save those who are believers (*tous pisteuontas*). It is "God's resolve" (Conzelmann) to use what *is* indeed folly. "The folly of the proclamation" is nothing less than "the wisdom of God," the way God deals wisely with the world of humanity, not only revealing to it something about Himself, but thereby communicating the means of salvation. For an OT instance of salvation through faith or belief, see 1 Macc 2:59.

22. Whereas Jews demand signs and Greeks seek wisdom. Lit. "seeing that. . . ." Paul now passes from "the world" to its inhabitants, and as often he uses the pair, Jew(s) and Greek(s), as a division of humanity, when he speaks about its reaction to the Christ-event (Gal 3:28; 1 Cor 1:23–24; 10:32; 12:13; Rom 1:16; 2:9, 10; 3:9; 10:12). This is a Jewish way of speaking of humanity; in Rom 1:14 he uses the Greek way, Greeks and barbarians, when he wants to express his indebtedness to the non-Jewish world (see *Romans*, 250). In this case, although Paul distinguishes Jews and Greeks, he finds that they are alike in their psychological reaction to the Christ-event, in that both are demanding *proof*. "In this way they set themselves up as an authority that can pass judgment upon God. This is what makes their attitude 'worldly' " (Conzelmann, *1 Cor*, 47). Paul has used what H. D. Betz ("The Gospel") calls "ethnic clichés": "Jews demand signs" and "Greeks seek wisdom."

Jews want "signs," and such a demand is recorded as made of Jesus by scribes and Pharisees in Mark 8:11; Matt 12:38; Luke 11:16; cf. Matt 16:1–4; John 6:30. In the LXX, the phrase *terata kai sēmeia*, "portents and signs," often occurs (Exod 7:3; Deut 4:34; 28:46; 34:11; Ps 135:9; Isa 8:18) to describe the mighty acts of God on behalf of his people Israel. From this tradition came the practice of asking God for a sign (Isa 7:11), but Paul does not specify what signs such Jews were seeking.

In contrast, "Greeks" want "wisdom," in the sense of the philosophical advantage and power that those who have it can exert over those who do not. Herodotus (*Hist.* 4.77.1) knows the proverb, "All Greeks are busily engaged in the pursuit of all wisdom"; Aristotle (*Nic. Ethics* 6.7.2): "It is clear that wisdom is the most precise of the modes of understanding"; Aelius Aristides (1.330): "The Athenians are the leaders in all education and wisdom." Barrett rightly notes, however, "*Greeks* does not means Hellenes; this is shown by the synonymous use in the same sentence of *Gentiles*" (*1 Cor,* 55). It does not follow, however, that "the wisdom sought is that of gnosticism, religious thought without the practice of religion (in the cultic sense)" (ibid.). Nor is there any evidence of "Jewish gnosticism in Corinth" (ibid.) in Paul's day.

23. *we proclaim Christ crucified, a stumbling block to Jews and folly to Gentiles.* The "we" are Paul and those "who are being saved" (v. 18); they stand over against the Jews and Greeks. So Paul sums up the primitive Christian *kērygma* as "Christ crucified," which he will repeat in 2:2. It also explains "the message of the cross" (v. 18), because Christ crucified is the one who speaks in that message that the cross conveys. Recall too how Paul speaks of Jesus' demise as "even death on a cross" (Phil 2:8), and how he would not boast "save in the cross of our Lord Jesus Christ, through which the world has been crucified to me, and I to the world" (Gal 6:14). The consequence is that the believing Christian knows that he or she is "co-crucified with Christ; it is no longer I who live, but Christ who lives in me; and the life I now live in the flesh I live by faith in the Son of God, who loved me and gave himself for me" (Gal 2:20). For the Christian "always carries in the body the death of Jesus, so that the life of Jesus may also be manifested in our bodies" (2 Cor 4:10).

Paul writes *Christon estaurōmenon,* using the perf. pass. ptc. of *stauroō,* "fasten to a cross" (BDAG, 941), a verb that was used by Greek historians and others who mention crucifixion (Polybius, *Hist.* 1.86.4; Diodorus Siculus, *Bibl. Hist.* 16.61.2; Epictetus, *Diss.* 2.2.20; Josephus, *Ant.* 2.5.4 §77; 17.10.10 §295; cf. LXX Esth 1:9; 8:12r [= 16:18 ET]). Such an expression, however, has become and remains for Jews *skandalon,* "a stumbling block," i.e., "the stumbling block of the cross" (Gal 5:11). It is such because, as Paul puts it in Gal 3:13, Christ became a "curse" of the law, an allusion to Deut 21:23, which says that a "hanged man is accursed by God." In the Roman period of Palestine, that saying of Deuteronomy was understood to refer to crucifixion, as 4QpNah 3–4 i 4–9 and 11QTemplea 64:6–13 now make clear, when they are related to Josephus, *Ant.* 13.14.2 §380; *J.W.* 1.4.5 §§93–98. Hence the crucified Christ could be seen as accursed, and thus a stumbling block (see Fitzmyer, "Paul and the Dead Sea Scrolls," 607–9).

It is also "folly to Gentiles," because such wisdom seekers regard the *kērygma* as the opposite of the goal of their search. Above, in vv. 18–20, "folly" was contrasted with the "wisdom" of all unbelievers; now it is restricted, as it stands in contrast to the wisdom of "Gentiles." So the satirical Sophist, Lucian of Samosata (A.D. 120–180?), mocked Christians: *ton de aneskolopismenon ekeinon sophistēn auton proskynōsin kai kata tous ekeinou nomous biōsin,* "they worship that crucified sophist himself and live according to his laws" (*De morte Peregrini* 13). What lies behind such an attitude is the recognition that Jesus died the death that was known in the contemporary Roman world as *servile supplicium*, "the slave's punishment" (Valerius Maximus, *Factorum* 7.12; cf. Hengel, *Crucifixion*, 51–63).

In effect, both Jew and Greek become adversaries of the crucified Christ. "The cross always remains scandal and foolishness for Jew and Gentile, inasmuch as it exposes man's illusion that he can transcend himself and effect his own salvation, that he can all by himself maintain his own strength, his own wisdom, his own piety, and his own self-praise even toward God" (Käsemann, "Saving Significance," 40). There is more involved in this theology of Christ crucified, because Paul is going to use it to transcend all individualism and interpersonal disputes in order to make it the basis on which the Christians of Corinth should be building their unity, agreement, and community life itself (see Pickett, *The Cross in Corinth*, 37–68). Finney ("Christ Crucified") goes so far as to maintain that Paul is seeking to undermine the imperial cult (emperor worship) among the Corinthians, at least among those who became Christians.

Ethnesin, "Gentiles," is the reading in the vast majority of Greek MSS, but a few (C³, D², 6, 1739, 1881, etc.) read rather *Hellēsi*, "to Greeks," a copyist correction to make Paul's terminology consistent in 1:22–24.

This formulation, "Christ crucified," supplies the key to Pauline theology, because from it Paul develops all his other doctrinal and ethical teaching, for Christ crucified is for Paul the criterion and norm of all Christian thought and conduct (see *PAHT* §PT24–29; Romaniuk, "Nos autem").

24. *but for those who are called, both Jews and Greeks, Christ is the power of God and the wisdom of God.* The pron. *autois* is in emphatic position at the head of the verse. For them Christ crucified is neither a stumbling-block nor foolishness. "Those who are called" are those "who are being saved" of v. 18 and "those who have faith" of v. 21, i.e., Jewish and Gentile Christians, as this verse now makes clear. For Paul preaching to and converting Jews, see 9:20. All are "called," i.e., invited to faith by the preached gospel. For them, if truly believers, the person of the crucified Jesus Christ has become the manifestation of God's power and wisdom (1:18, 21). That God is powerful and wise needs no demonstration, but how he is such and how he manifests such qualities is now made clear in Christ Jesus himself. Paul, however, realizes that even some Christian factions of Corinth could be making themselves adversaries of the crucified Christ, and these he is warning by this consideration of Jews and Greeks.

This elliptical clause of v. 24, *Christon theou dynamin kai theou sophian*, stands in apposition to *Christon estauromenon*, "Christ crucified," of v. 23, which is also accusative and the object of "we proclaim," but P⁴⁶ casts the clause in the nominative: *Christos theou dynamis kai theou sophia*, and that would mean, "but for those who are called . . . Christ is the power of God. . . . " Noteworthy is the emphatic position of *theou*, which precedes both *dynamis* and *sophia*. The first attribute, "power of God," echoes v. 18, where it explains "the message of the cross." By linking "power" and "wisdom," Paul is showing that wisdom is not merely speculative, but is a manifestation of God's dynamic action. As attributes of God, "wisdom" and "power" are found together in LXX Job 12:13; Jer 10:12; Dan 2:20, 23 (see Mangan, "Christ the Power").

Whence does Paul derive the notion of Christ as "the wisdom of God"? According to Sir 24:23–25, "the law that Moses commanded" overflows "with wisdom"; cf. Sir 6:37; Bar 4:1. Paul has transformed this Hellenistic Jewish teaching about the *tôrāh* or law as "wisdom," which was perceived to be "a breath of the power of God, an unalloyed emanation of the radiance of the Almighty" (Wis 7:25), as he adopts that typology and applies it to Christ, who is for Christians an "instruction" in the form of "the wisdom of God." There is a difference, however, because Paul neither identifies Christ as a wisdom teacher, as he appears in the gospel tradition, nor as wisdom personified, as in the Jewish tradition (Wis 6:12–18; 9:4, 10); nor does he speak of the preexistent Christ as wisdom, as van Roon ("The Relation") rightly argues. He rather identifies "Christ crucified" as the wisdom of God, and also as the power of God "for the salvation of everyone who believes" (Rom 1:16). In doing so, he is preparing for a development on God's wisdom to be set forth in 1:30; 2:2; 2:6–3:4. However, van Roon goes too far when he relates Paul's idea of Christ as the wisdom of God to the Messiah and even to God's hidden wisdom. There is no evidence for these relationships in this letter (see further Klauck, "Christus, Gottes Kraft und Gottes Weisheit"; Davis, *Wisdom and Spirit*).

25. *For God's foolishness is wiser than human wisdom.* Lit. "than human beings." This verse formulates a maxim or epigram of timeless validity. Paul does not use his usual word for folly, *mōria*, but rather the neut. sing. of the adj. *mōros*, "foolish," as a noun, because he is trying to express "God's foolishness," as it is judged by unbelievers. What appears such to them is what is superior to their own so-called wisdom. This verse draws a temporary conclusion to Paul's discussion in vv. 18–24; in vv. 26–31 he will apply his teaching about worldly wisdom to the Corinthian scene.

and God's weakness is stronger than human strength. Lit. "than human beings." The parallelism with the first clause is evident; not so evident is the order a, b, b', a' in vv. 24–25: the power of God : the wisdom of God :: God's foolishness : God's weakness, as Lindemann (*1 Cor*, 48) has noted. What God has done in the crucifixion of Christ directly contradicts what human beings consider wisdom and might, but it accomplishes what human wisdom and might can never achieve. So Paul concludes this discussion about wisdom.

26. *Look now at your own calling, brothers.* Paul seeks to apply what he has been saying about divine and human wisdom to the situation of Corinthian Christians. Verses 26–31 thus form the second stage of his argument, as he shifts to the second plural and addresses the Christians of Roman Corinth. The "calling" of them echoes "those who are called" of vv. 9 and 24. In an *argumentum ad hominem*, Paul summons these Christians to consider their initial status at the time the gospel of Christ crucified actively accosted them and the divine act brought them to faith. In effect, they are the best proof that God does not make much of human wisdom or might. So they should not take the paradoxes expressed in vv. 22–25 as empty rhetoric. Paul addresses them as *adelphoi* in the sense of "fellow-Christians" (see NOTE on 1:1), who have been called by God. He will refer further to such a divine call in 7:15, 17–18, 20–22, 24.

For not many of you were wise by human standards; not many were powerful; not many were of noble birth. Lit. "according to the flesh," i.e., from a purely human viewpoint. Paul uses *kata sarka* in a transferred sense, as in 2 Cor 11:18; cf. Col 3:22; Eph 6:5. This is the first mention in this letter of *sarx*, "flesh," which Paul uses in various ways to designate: (1) the substance covering the bones of a human or animal body, as in 15:39 four times; 2 Cor 12:7; Gal 6:13; (2) the physical body, as in 5:5; 6:16 quoting Gen 2:24; 2 Cor 7:1; Gal 4:13–14; (3) a physical limitation of human existence, as in 7:28; 2 Cor 4:11; (4) flesh as prone to sin or dominated by sin, as in Rom 6:19; 7:18, 25; 8:3a, 4–9 (often opposite *pneuma*, "spirit," as in Rom 8:13; Gal 3:3; 5:16. (5) fleshy being (= human being), as in 1:29 (cf. LXX Isa 42:5); Gal 2:16; (6) a variant of 5, "flesh and blood," as in 15:50; Gal 1:16; (7) earthly, ancestral connection, as in 10:18; (8) outward side of life, as in this verse (1:26); 10:18; 2 Cor 5:16; 11:18; Phil 3:3–4; Phlm 16. Many of these nuances of *sarx* can be found in the use of *bāsār* in QL; see Frey, "Notion of Flesh"; "Flesh and Spirit."

There is no verb in the three parallel statements expressed with litotes; Paul writes merely *ou polloi sophoi, ou polloi dynatoi, ou polloi eugeneis*. For that reason, Bailey ("Recovering," 282) translates the statements with pres. tense copulas, claiming that that is required because the verb in v. 25 is pres.; but he neglects the first clause of v. 26, where Paul invites the Corinthian Christians to think about the time of their "calling" (*klēsis*).

The mention of the three groups undoubtedly refers to the social status of Corinthian Christians, diverse as it was. For few among them would have been philosophers or even members of the educated class; few would have been influential people or even politically adept; few were wellborn or of the upper class of Corinthian society. That also means, however, that some were such, so that it cannot be said that the early Christians of Roman Corinth were all lower-class proletarians or the poor. For one at least, Erastus of Rom 16:23, was undoubtedly a man of means. Sänger ("Die *dynatoi*") maintains that the "powerful" were actually the "rich," whose wealth enabled them to wield power in their society, as the term is used in Josephus, JW 1.17.2 §326; 2.17.3 §411. For Nordling (*Philemon*, 115), *"the vigorous Christianity revealed in the texts of the NT was quintessentially a slaves' religion"* (his emphasis), but Hengel (*Crucifixion*, 62) thinks differently: "early Christianity was not particularly a religion of slaves." Meggitt is certainly right in saying that Paul's meaning here is "more elusive than has traditionally been assumed," but he goes too far when he says that "the verse can no longer be taken as unambiguous evidence of the presence of the élite, or near élite, within a Pauline church" (*Paul, Poverty and Survival*, 105–6).

Wuellner ("The Sociological Implications") would understand the three clauses as questions: "Were not many of you wise by human standards, were not many powerful, were not many of noble birth?" To which the Corinthians would reply in the affirmative. Such an interpretation changes the traditional way of reading this verse, and it makes Paul admit that the Christians of Corinth were indeed of higher social standing than is usually thought. Is it really an improvement? O'Day ("Jeremiah 9:22–23") thinks that it is, because she says that Paul is speaking in irony. She also sees the Corinthian triad, the wise, powerful, and of noble birth, as derived from the triad of Jer 9:22, the sage, the mighty, and the rich man. It would be better to say that Paul is imitating the triad of Jeremiah, because of the difference in Greek wording (Paul has *dynatoi*, but Jeremiah *ischyros* [sing.]; Paul has *eugeneis*, but Jeremiah *plousios* [sing.]). Moreover, it is not correct to say that *hoti* at the head of the first clause is "interrogative" (ibid., 265), an error that she repeats from Wuellner's discussion. The object of *blepete* is *tēn klēsin*, and the conj. *hoti* denotes causality, "because," or more loosely, "for" (BDAG, 732). Even if one understands the clauses as statements, *ou . . . alla* still marks a contrast, which is what v. 27 supplies.

27. *But God chose what is foolish in the world to shame the wise, and what is weak in the world to shame the strong.* Lit. "the foolish things of the world . . . the weak things"; in both cases the plur. is neuter, and so Paul is not restricting his examples to persons. After the triple negation of v. 26, the conj. *alla* marks a strong difference. In this verse, Paul is commenting on 1:26bc and emphasizing the sovereignty of God in his purposeful decision to cope with the would-be wisdom and the power of human beings in Corinth, when he summoned some of them to Christian commitment: God deliberately chose what was foolish and weak. The wording *exelexato ho theos* (vv. 27–28) imitates that of LXX Bar 3:27.

28. *God chose what is lowly and despised in the world, things that do not exist, to nullify the things that do.* This verse comments on 1:26d, for *agenē*, "lowly born" (neut.), stands in contrast to *eugeneis*, "of noble birth" (masc.), and Paul expands this comment by adding *ta exouthenēmena*, lit. "the things that have been treated as nothing," which evokes the further comment, "things that do not exist"; cf. Dan 4:14 (Theodotion). The upshot is that God has reversed all modes of human judgment and would-be wise counsel; no one can claim to be something in God's sight (10:12). Theissen (*Social Setting*, 71) has shown that *oudenia*, "nothingness," was a *topos* employed in philosophical ridicule; Socrates called the truly wise "nothing" (Plato, *Phaedrus* 234E; *Theatetus* 176c); also that *to mēden onta*, "what is nothing," is an expression used in Euripides, *Trojan Women* 613–14, as a contrast to *to eugenes*, "wellborn, nobility." Hence these terms can also designate social standing. Cf. 4:10. Conzelmann (*1 Cor*, 50) translates *ta mē onta* as "things that are nothing," but that is already expressed in *exouthenēmena*; it would be better to say, "things that are nonentities." In Rom 4:17, Paul uses the same words in the sense of "things that exist not," which is preferable here too. *Kosmos*, "world," denotes human beings who oppose God, as also in 11:32.

29. *so that no human being might boast in God's sight.* Lit. "so that all flesh might not boast before God," or "before him," as some MSS have it ([ℵ²], C*, Ψ, 629, 1241). Paul uses *pasa sarx* in the OT sense of "all humanity" (see Isa 40:5; Joel 3:1). Boasting is excluded because of God's reaction to human self-reliance and pretense of wisdom. In vv. 27–28, Paul expressed God's immediate purpose, using the conj. *hina*, "in order to," three times; now he employs another final conj. *hopōs* to convey God's ultimate purpose in all His reactions to human wisdom. For Paul, boasting denotes the fundamental mindset of human beings in their relation to God, manifested especially in the pursuit of their own ability and wisdom. It is an attitude with which God in the OT already found fault: "lest Israel

vaunt itself against me and say, 'My hand has saved me' " (Judg 7:2). In 3:21 Paul will extend the object of such boasting even to individual "human beings," meaning the preacher-allegiance that has been so divisive in the Corinthian community. For Paul insists: humans cannot bring about their salvation by wisdom in any ordinary or natural sense through allegiance to human beings or by their accomplishments. In 4:7 he will insist further that one's standing before God is itself a gift: "What do you have that you did not receive?"

30. *It is because of him that you are in Christ Jesus*. The union that Corinthian Christians now enjoy with Christ comes only from God and his gracious call (1:9, 24), which is still challenging them through the proclamation of the gospel. Compare 2 Cor 5:18, where Paul will again assert that "all comes from God." To be "in Christ (Jesus)" is a Pauline way of expressing the essential Christian mode of existence (Rom 8:1, 39; 12:5; 16:7; 1 Cor 3:1; 2 Cor 5:17; Gal 2:4; 3:28; 5:6; Phil 1:1), because it is a mode of explaining the effects of the Christ-event that follow. In any case, he is now stressing that Corinthians owe that existence to God, and not to themselves, or any pursuit of wisdom, or any allegiance to a preacher.

who became for us wisdom from God, uprightness and sanctification and redemption. Or "who was made for us. . . ." In v. 24, Paul identified Christ as "the wisdom of God," but now as "wisdom from God," which is only a literary variant of the same idea. It is a way of introducing three effects of the Christ-event that are related to it, which are expressed in other Pauline writings: uprightness (or righteousness [see *Romans*, 258, for my preference in rendering *dikaiosynē*]), sanctification (*hagiasmos*), and redemption (*apolytrōsis*); see INTRODUCTION pp. 76–77; *PAHT* §PT68–70, 75, 77. Their relation to wisdom, however, is peculiar to this letter.

In his person, Jesus Christ brings God's wisdom to human beings willing to accept it in faith. This is no longer the wisdom of this world, but "wisdom from God." In Prov 8:22–31 and Wis 7:22b–8:1, wisdom is personified as a mediator between God and his created world and the human race. Paul adopts this notion of Jewish theology and applies is to the crucified Christ in order to emphasize that true wisdom is not found in rhetorical eloquence, but in a gift of God, viz. Christ Jesus himself. Similarly, the crucified Christ has become for Christians "uprightness" or "righteousness." In 2 Cor 5:21 Paul will maintain that "in him [Christ] we may become the uprightness of God" (*dikaiosynē theou*), an abstract way of expressing the status of uprightness that Christians possess through what Christ has done for them. That summary expression for justification is paralleled in this verse, but it is related in this paragraph to "the message of the cross," so that the gift of justification comes from the crucified Christ. Cf. Phil 3:9; Rom 3:23–24.

"Sanctification" is also an abstract way of expressing the dedication of Christians to God and his cultic service that is derived from the crucified Christ. In 6:11 Paul will again link justification and sanctification as effects of the Christ-event: "you have been washed, you have been sanctified, you have been justified." Cf. 1 Thess 4:7; Rom 15:16.

Likewise "redemption" denotes that Christians have been ransomed or bought back from bondage to sin to become God's people through the crucified Christ.

Cf. Rom 3:24; 8:23. All of this has come about through the gracious activity of God on behalf of humanity, as Lindemann rightly stresses (*1 Cor,* 51–52); similarly Schrage, *1 Cor,* 1:215–16; Garland, *1 Cor,* 79. The three qualities that Christians inherit from Christ supply the reason for what is to be said in the next verse.

Bender ("Bemerkungen"), however, claims that the prep. phrase *en Christō Iēsou* is always used in an instrumental sense in Pauline writings, and so it must be understood here, where it is followed by a parenthetical rel. clause, "who became for us wisdom from God," and then by the three real predicates of *hymeis este*: "Because of him [God] you are through Christ Jesus . . . uprightness and sanctification and redemption." He understands the three predicates in the same way as *dikaiosynē theou* in 2 Cor 5:21, as three abstract expressions of effects of the Christ-event. That, however, is somewhat far-fetched, even though the abstract expressions have some parallels elsewhere in Pauline letters, because it is not true that *en Christō Iēsou* is always used in an instrumental sense; see the instances given above in the NOTE on the first clause in this verse.

31. *so that, as it stands written, "Let the one who would boast, boast of the Lord."* Although this saying is introduced as a quotation of the OT (see NOTE on 1:19), it is actually a concise summary of Jer 9:22–23, which reads in the LXX version, "Let not the sage boast of his wisdom, let not the mighty boast of his might, and let not the rich man boast of his riches, but let the boaster boast of this, that he understands and knows that I am the Lord displaying mercy, justice, and uprightness on the earth." See also a differently worded form of this same saying in LXX 1 Sam 2:10. Thus Paul not only understands "the Lord" in the words from Jeremiah as the crucified Christ (as Collins, Fee rightly note), but he also echoes his Jewish tradition, for Philo also teaches it: "Let God alone be your boast and your supreme glory" (*De spec. leg.* 1.57 §311). As Jeremiah found fault with wisdom, power, and wealth, so too does Paul, because they impede what God does in Christ Jesus (see O'Day, "Jeremiah 9:22–23"). In any case, the summary allusion serves as an apt conclusion to the rhetorical discussion that Paul has engaged in on the value of human wisdom confronted by the message of the cross. In 4:7 Paul will return to this boasting and ask, "What do you have that you did not receive? Why are you boasting as if you did not (receive it)?" "So no one should boast about human beings" (3:21). Cf. 2 Cor 10:17. For Paul's dependence on the Book of Jeremiah, see Rusche, "Zum 'jeremianischen' Hintergrund."

BIBLIOGRAPHY (See also Bibliography on 1:10–4:21, pp. 149–51)

Bailey, K. E., "Recovering the Poetic Structure of I Cor. i 17–ii 2: A Study in Text and Commentary," *NovT* 17 (1975) 265–96.

Bender, W., "Bemerkungen zur Übersetzung von 1 Korinther 1,30," *ZNW* 71 (1980) 263–68.

Betz, H. D., "The Gospel and the Wisdom of the Barbarians: The Corinthians' Question behind Their Questions," *Bib* 85 (2004) 585–94.

Bohatec, J., "Inhalt und Reihenfolge der 'Schlagworte der Erlösungsreligion' in 1. Kor. 1, 26–31," *TZ* 4 (1948) 252–71.

Chevallier, M. A., "La prédication de la croix," *ETR* 45 (1970) 131–61, 233–46.

Cipriani, S., " 'Sapientia crucis' e sapienza 'umana' in Paolo," *RivB* 36 (1988) 343–61.

Clark, G. H., "Wisdom in First Corinthians," *JETS* 15 (1972) 197–205.

Conzelmann, H., "Paulus und die Weisheit," *NTS* 12 (1965–66) 231–44.

Cooper, J. M., "The Foolishness of God versus the Wisdom of Man," *TTE* 14/1 (1983) 35–40.

Davis, J. A., *Wisdom and Spirit: An Investigation of 1 Corinthians 1.18–3.20 against the Background of Jewish Sapiential Traditions in the Greco-Roman Period* (Lanham, MD: University Press of America, 1984).

Dunn, J. D. G., "In Search of Wisdom," *EpRev* 22 (1995) 48–53.

———, "Paul's Understanding of the Death of Jesus," *Reconciliation and Hope: New Testament Essays on Atonement and Eschatology Presented to L. L. Morris . . .* (ed. R. Banks; Grand Rapids: Eerdmans, 1974) 125–41.

Ellis, E. E., " 'Wisdom' and 'Knowledge' in I Corinthians," *TynBul* 25 (1974) 82–98.

———, " 'Christ Crucified,' " *Reconciliation and Hope . . .* (ed. R. Banks; Grand Rapids: Eerdmans, 1974), 69–75.

Finney, M. T., "Christ Crucified and the Inversion of Roman Imperial Ideology in 1 Corinthians," *BTB* 35 (2005) 20–33.

Fitzmyer, J. A., "Crucifixion in Ancient Palestine, Qumran Literature, and the New Testament," *CBQ* 40 (1978) 493–513; repr. *TAG*, 125–46.

———, "Paul and the Dead Sea Scrolls," *The Dead Sea Scrolls after Fifty Years: A Comprehensive Assessment* (ed. P. W. Flint and J. C. VanderKam; Leiden: Brill, 1999) 599–621.

Frey, J., "Flesh and Spirit in the Palestinian Jewish Sapiential Tradition and in the Qumran Texts: An Inquiry into the Background of Pauline Usage," *The Wisdom Texts from Qumran and the Development of Sapiential Thought* (BETL 159; ed. C. Hempel et al.; Louvain: Leuven University Press/Peeters, 2002) 367–404.

———, "The Notion of Flesh in 4QInstruction and the Background of Pauline Usage," *Sapiential, Liturgical and Poetic Texts from Qumran: Proceedings of the Third Meeting of the International Organization for Qumran Studies—Oslo 1998* (STDJ 35; ed. D. K. Falk et al.; Leiden: Brill, 2000) 197–226.

Gärtner, B. E., "The Pauline and Johannine Idea of 'to Know God' against the Hellenistic Background: The Greek Philosophical Principle 'Like by Like' in Paul and John," *NTS* 14 (1967–68) 209–31.

Heckel, T. K., "Der Gekreuzigte bei Paulus und im Markusevangelium," *BZ* 46 (2002) 190–204.

Henaut, B. W., "Matthew 11:27: The Thunderbolt in Corinth?" *TorJT* 3 (1987) 282–300.

Horsley, R. A., "Spiritual Marriage with Sophia," *VC* 33 (1979) 30–54.

———, "Wisdom of Word and Words of Wisdom in Corinth," *CBQ* 39 (1977) 224–39.

Hübner, H., "Der vergessene Baruch: Zur Baruch-Rezeption des Paulus in 1 Kor 1,18–31," *SNTU* 9 (1984) 161–73.

Käsemann, E., "The Saving Significance of the Death of Jesus in Paul," *Perspectives on Paul* (Philadelphia: Fortress, 1971) 32–59.

Keck, L. E., "God the Other Who Acts Otherwise: An Exegetical Essay on 1 Cor 1:26–31," *WW* 16 (1996) 437–43.

Klauck, H.-J., " 'Christus, Gottes Kraft und Gottes Weisheit' (1 Kor 1,24): Jüdische Weisheitsüberlieferungen im Neuen Testament," *Wissenschaft und Weisheit* 55 (1992) 3–22.

Lambrecht, J., "The Power of God: A Note on the Connection between 1 Cor 1,17 and 18," *Collected Studies* (AnBib 147), 35–42.

Lautenschlager, M., "Abschied vom Disputierer: Zur Bedeutung von *syzētētēs* in 1 Kor 1,20," *ZNW* 83 (1992) 276–85.

Lindemann, A., "Die Schrift als Tradition: Beobachtungen zu den biblischen Zitaten im Ersten Korintherbrief," *Schrift und Tradition: Festschrift für Josef Ernst* . . . (ed. K. Backhaus und F. G. Untergassmair; Paderborn: Schöningh, 1996) 199–225.

Malan, F. S., "The Use of the Old Testament in 1 Corinthians," *Neotestamentica* 14 (1981) 134–70.

Mangan, C., "Christ the Power and the Wisdom of God: The Semitic Background to 1 Cor 1:24," *PIBA* 4 (1980) 21–34.

Masson, C., "L'Évangile et la sagesse selon l'apôtre Paul: D'après I Corinthiens 1:17 à 3:23," *RTP* 7 (1957) 95–110.

Megitt, J. J., *Paul, Poverty and Survival* (Edinburgh: Clark, 1998).

Merklein, H., "Das paulinische Paradox des Kreuzes," *TTZ* 106 (1997) 81–98.

Montagnini, F., " 'Videte vocationem vestram' (1 Cor 1,26)," *RivB* 39 (1991) 217–21.

Müller, K., "1 Kor 1,18–25: Die eschatologisch-kritische Funktion der Verkündigung des Kreuzes," *BZ* 10 (1966) 246–72.

Nordling, J. G., *Philemon* (Concordia Commentary Series; St. Louis: Concordia, 2004).

O'Day, G. R., "Jeremiah 9:22–23 and 1 Corinthians 1:26–31: A Study in Intertextuality," *JBL* 109 (1990) 259–67.

Peterson, E., "1 Cor. 1,18f. und die Thematik des jüdischen Busstages," *Bib* 32 (1951) 97–103.

Reinmuth, E., "LAB 40,4 und die Krise der Weisheit im 1. Korintherbrief: Ein Beitrag zu den hermeneutischen Voraussetzungen der paulinischen Argumentation," *The Corinthian Correspondence* (BETL 125; ed. R. Bieringer), 471–78.

Romaniuk, C., " 'Nos autem praedicamus Christum et hunc crucifixum' (1 Cor 1,23)," *VDom* 47 (1969) 232–36.

Roon, A. van, "The Relation between Christ and the Wisdom of God according to Paul," *NovT* 16 (1974) 207–39.

Rusche, H., "Zum 'jeremianischen' Hintergrund der Korintherbriefe," *BZ* 31 (1987) 116–19.

Sänger, D., "Die *dynatoi* in 1 Kor 1,26," *ZNW* 76 (1985) 285–91.

Schottroff, L., " 'Nicht viele Mächtige': Annäherungen an eine Soziologie des Urchristentums," *BK* 40 (1985) 2–8.

Schreiner, K., "Zur biblischen Legitimation des Adels: Auslegungsgeschichtliche Studien zu 1. Kor. 1, 26–29," *ZKG* 85 (1974) 317–57.

Söding, T., " 'Was schwach ist in der Welt, hat Gott erwählt' (1 Kor 1,27): Kreuzestheologie und Gemeinde-Praxis nach dem Ersten Korintherbrief," *BL* 60 (1987) 58–65.

Wedderburn, A. J. M., "*En tē sophiā tou theou* – 1 Kor 1,21," *ZNW* 64 (1973) 132–34.

Wells, P., "Que s'est-il passé à la croix?" *RRef* 49/4 (1998) 45–58.

Wuellner, W. H., "The Sociological Implications of I Corinthians 1:26–28 Reconsidered," *SE VI* (TU 112; Berlin: Akademie-V., 1973) 666–72.

5   c. *Paul Preaches God's Wisdom*
          Revealed through the Spirit (2:1–3:4)

2:1 When I came to you, brothers, announcing to you God's mystery, I did not come with sublimity of words or wisdom. 2 For I resolved to know nothing while I was with you except Jesus Christ and him crucified. 3 I was among you in weakness, fear, and much trembling; 4 and my message and my proclamation were not adorned with persuasive [words of] wisdom, but with a demonstration of the Spirit and of power, 5 so that your faith might not be based on human wisdom, but on God's power. 6 Yet to those who are mature we do utter wisdom, not a wisdom of this age or of the rulers of this age who are doomed to destruction. 7 We speak rather of God's wisdom, hidden in a mystery, which God predetermined for our glory before time began. 8 None of the rulers of this age understood it; for, if they had, they would not have crucified the Lord of glory. 9 But, as it stands written,

> What eye has not seen and ear has not heard,
> and what has not surged in a human heart,
> what God has prepared for those who love him—

10 and this God has revealed to us through the Spirit. For the Spirit scrutinizes everything, even the profound things of God. 11 For among human beings, who understands what is truly human, except the human spirit that is within? Similarly, no one comprehends what pertains to God except the Spirit of God. 12 Now we have not received the spirit of the world, but rather the spirit coming from God so that we may understand the gifts bestowed on us by God. 13 We also speak about them not with words taught by human wisdom, but with words taught by the Spirit, interpreting spiritual realities in spiritual terms. 14 The animated human being does not accept what comes from God's Spirit; for to such a one that is folly, and he is unable to understand it, because it is spiritually discerned. 15 The spiritual human being, however, discerns all things, but is himself subject to no one's scrutiny. 16 *For who has known the mind of the Lord so as to instruct him?* But we have the mind of Christ.

3:1 Brothers, I could not speak to you as spiritual people, but only as worldly, mere infants in Christ. 2 I fed you milk, not solid food, because you were not yet able to take it. Even now, you are still unable. 3 For you are still worldly. Wherever jealousy and strife exist among you, are you not worldly and behaving in a secular human way? 4 Whenever someone says, "I side with Paul," and another says, "I side with Apollos," are you not merely human?

COMMENT

Paul now continues his treatment of the contrast of the gospel and the wisdom of the world that was begun in 1:18–31, as he unfolds his understanding of wisdom still further. In vv. 2–5, Paul develops what he has been saying in 1:18–25 and applied to Corinthian Christians in 1:26–31, now referring to himself and his ministry. He shows that his own preaching among the Corinthians has been done, not with the eloquent wisdom of noted Greek and Roman orators or sages (see NOTE on 1:17), but with the inspiration of God's Spirit. He did not come among them as one of the contemporary Sophists or as someone wise in the ways of the world; his message was the gospel about Christ alone, and him crucified (1:23a). From v. 6 on, Paul will explain more in detail what he means by "God's wisdom." As he addressed the Corinthian Christians as *adelphoi* in 1:26, he does so again in 2:1 and 3:1.

Verses 6–16 of chap. 2 are somewhat problematic, because for a number of commentators they seem to be a self-contained unit distinct from its context. The problem begins with the style of these verses. Whereas in 2:1–5 Paul has been writing in the 1st pers. sing., as he reminisces about his original evangelization of Corinth and continues to write so in 3:1–2, in 2:6–16 he writes rather in the 1st pers. plur. Moreover, 3:1–4 seems to such commentators to be a logical sequel to 2:1–5. Conzelmann even maintains that vv. 6–16 are a "contradiction" of Paul's "previous statements" (*1 Cor*, 57), a "direct polemic against the Corinthians" (ibid., 59), and that "the content . . . is in substance not Christian" (ibid.). Older commentators, such as Bousset and Bultmann, were convinced that Paul had accommodated his thinking about wisdom, esp. in vv. 6–16, to contemporary Hellenistic mystery-religions and the thought-world of Gnosticism; that conviction still persists in the interpretations of Käsemann, Wilckens, Conzelmann (*1 Cor*, 58–61) and Weder (*Das Kreuz Jesu*, 165–67). Others have judged that vv. 6–16 are actually an interpolation (Widmann, "Ein Einspruch"; Walker, "1 Corinthians 2.6–16"). For some who regard the verses as authentically Pauline, they are interpreted as midrashic (Ellis, *Prophecy*, 213–16), or as a Pauline interpretation of Jesus' words preserved in the "Q" saying of Matt 11:25–27; Luke 10:22–23 (Gaffin, "Some Epistemological Reflections").

Such interpretations of 2:6–16 are, however, equally problematic, because, as Lindemann (*1 Cor*, 60–61) rightly notes, they are neither interpolated (see Murphy-O'Connor, "Interpolations," 81–84), nor polemical in tone or style, nor ill-suited to the context. This is evident because, when the verses are rightly analyzed, they fall into three parts: (1) vv. 6–9, where Paul continues to proclaim "God's wisdom," as already in 1:21, 24; 2:2; (2) vv. 10–12, where Paul affirms that such wisdom, hidden until now in a mystery (cf. 2:1), is revealed through God's Spirit; and (3) vv. 13–16, where Paul asserts that what he proclaims is done with words taught by the Spirit, a further clarification of 2:4–5.

As for the use of the 1st pers. plur., one has to recall its use already in 1:23. By it, Paul is not speaking editorially or identifying himself with other apostolic preachers (*pace* Robertson-Plummer, *1 Cor*, 34–35), but he means simply "we Christians" (so Lindemann, *1 Cor*, 61; Collins, *1 Cor*, 120).

In these verses, Paul is not saying anything different from what he has already said in 1:24, 30, but they do make up an important paragraph in the letter as a whole, because Paul clarifies in them what he means by real "wisdom." When he uses the 1st pers. plur., he is summoning the individuals of the Corinthian community (and modern readers) to reflect on their understanding of their common calling and conduct, which should be properly oriented to God's saving wisdom.

In this entire section (2:1–3:4), Paul develops his explanation of the gospel that he proclaims under four headings: (1) It is "God's mystery" (2:1), or "God's wisdom, hidden in a mystery . . . predetermined for our glory before time began" (2:7); (2) "a demonstration of the Spirit and of power" (2:4); (3) "revealed to us through the Spirit" (2:10), through "the spirit coming from God" (2:12b); and (4) "with words taught by the Spirit" (2:13).

The wisdom of this world, however, is contrasted as a "sublimity of words" (2:1); "persuasive [words of] wisdom" (2:4); the "wisdom" of human beings (2:5), "of this age or the rulers of this age" (2:6); and "words taught by human wisdom" (2:13).

Paul insists that God has revealed his wisdom to Christians through the Holy Spirit. Such wisdom once imparted makes receptive Christians "mature" (*teleioi*, 2:6) and "spiritual" (*pneumatikoi*, 2:15), capable of comprehending spiritual realities. They are differentiated from the merely "animated" or worldly (*psychikoi*, 3:1), who are said even to be "infants" (*nepioi*, 3:1). What makes the difference between such individuals is "faith" (*pistis*), which is not a form of human wisdom, but proceeds from God's power (2:5). For "faith" is the human response to the gospel, as Paul teaches in Rom 10:7, 9, 17 (where it begins as a hearing and ends in personal commitment [Rom 1:5; 16:26]). It is a faith that works itself out through love (Gal 5:6), and that means that it must govern an individual's behavior or conduct. Hence Paul's message is indeed a form of real wisdom destined for all Christians of all ages, for it is "God's wisdom" (2:7), which is not comprehended by the rulers of this age; if they had grasped it, they would never have crucified "the Lord of glory" (2:8). A paradox indeed is involved, because the "folly" of the cross is "wisdom" for Christian believers. Such wisdom, coming from God's Spirit, makes human beings different from those who fail to open themselves to God's Spirit or consider all such realities as incomprehensible foolishness.

Finally, Paul admonishes Corinthian Christians, reminding them that they are in reality "mere infants in Christ" (3:1), immature and worldly, because of the rivalries they have allowed to develop among them. When they side with Apollos or himself, they are conducting themselves in a merely human way and revealing that they are not "spiritual" or guided by God's Spirit. Paul realizes that he has fed the Corinthians like a mother who feeds an infant milk (3:2); later on, Paul will contrast his dealing with them as a father (4:5).

This passage makes it clear that Paul understood the rivalries among the Christians of Roman Corinth to be not merely sociological (so Theissen) or even ethical differences (so Munck), but fundamentally symptomatic of theological error, as Grindheim ("Wisdom for the Perfect") has shown.

It is all too easy for Christians of any time to fail to grasp the implications of what Paul has been saying about the important place that "God's wisdom," made known through His Spirit, should be playing in their lives and dealings with one another.

NOTES

2:1. *When I came to you, brothers.* Lit. "and I, coming to you." Paul recalls his first arrival in Corinth, during what is often called his second missionary journey described in Acts 15:36–18:22. According to Acts 18:1–2, he came there from Athens and lodged with Aquila and Priscilla (ca. A.D. 50). See Gal 3:1–5; 4:13; Phil 1:5; 1 Thess 1:5 for other instances of Paul recalling his intial contact with Christians of other towns. Paul begins with *kagō*, "and I," which he will repeat in v. 3; it stands in contrast to *hymōn*, "you" (plur.) of 1:26, as he stresses his mode of presence among the Corinthian Christians. Again, *adelphoi* occurs in the sense of "fellow Christians" (see NOTE on 1:1).

announcing to you God's mystery. Or perhaps "the testimony of God," if one prefers to read *martyrion* with MSS ℵ², B, D, F, G, Ψ, 33, 1739, 1881, and the Koine text-tradition. That reading, however, seems to be dependent on 1:6, "the testimony about Christ." As there, the gen. would be objective. However, *mystērion*, "mystery," is found in MSS P⁴⁶ᵛⁱᵈ?, ℵ*, A, C, 88, 436; and it suits the context better (see 2:7 below; cf. Metzger, *TCGNT*, 480). It is preferred by Collins, Lindemann, Senft, but Fee maintains that "the reading *martyrion* is to be preferred on all counts" (*1 Cor*, 88); similarly Kistemaker, Robertson-Plummer, Soards; cf. Vg, *testimonium*. Yet the combination of *mystērion* and *sophia* is found also in Dan 2:30 (LXX and Theodotion), and it is comprehensible.

By "God's mystery" Paul means "the message of the cross" (1:18), preached by him in his own rhetorical form, with the Spirit's assistance. It stands in contrast to *sophia anthrōpōn*, "human wisdom" (2:5). In other words, when Paul first preached in Corinth, he announced this mystery, or truth hidden in God, to all who would listen. See v. 7 ("God's wisdom") and Söding, "Das Geheimnis."

Mystērion, "secret," was a term widely used in the Greco-Roman world of Paul's day in so-called Mystery Religions (Eleusinian, Dionysiac, Mithraic), which offered some form of salvation, new life, or fertility to their adepts. Those initiated into them had to swear to guard the esoteric cult-secrets (see Meyer, *Ancient Mysteries*, 17–45, 63–109, 197–221).

The word *mystērion* is also found in the LXX, not only in deuterocanonical writings (e.g., Wis 2:22; 6:22; 14:15, 23), but in the Greek translation of Daniel too (2:18, 19, 27–30, 47; esp. Theodotion Dan 2:30). There it renders Aramaic *rāz*, a Persian loanword for "secret," which usually connotes heavenly secrets revealed in a dream or vision. In this Semitic sense, although it may seem to mean something opaque or hard to understand, it more commonly denotes a truth, teaching, or decision made in God's heavenly court, hitherto hidden but now made known or revealed, as in Rom 16:25. See Brown, *The Semitic Background of the Term "Mystery"*, 40–50. In using this term, Paul is referring to the meaning that God has revealed in "the message of the cross," i.e., the love of God for human beings manifested in the crucified Jesus, who is the savior of humanity.

I did not come with sublimity of words or wisdom. I.e., not like the contemporary Sophists who excelled in human eloquence and gave samples of it in order to be accepted as sages in the city. He refused to provide such a display, and his frank admission echoes the phrase "eloquent wisdom" of 1:17, as he strives to develop his theme further. Paul wanted to be known not as a Sophist, but as a preacher of Christ crucified (see Winter, *Philo and Paul*, 155–59).

2. *For I resolved to know nothing while I was with you except Jesus Christ and him crucified.* Paul explains his behavior as indicated in v.1. What might have been considered consummate human wisdom was not a concern for Paul, as he evangelized the Corinthians. He realized that an ornate preaching style would not suit the object of his preaching, Christ crucified. He repeats what he has said already in 1:17, 23a, stressing the meaning of "the message of the cross," what it meant and what it still means for humanity. In 15:3, Paul will speak differently when he adds mention of the risen Christ, but, as in Gal 3:1, Paul now concentrates his preaching on Christ crucified. This is the heart of Pauline christology (see Popkes, "1Kor 2,2").

3. *I was among you in weakness, fear, and much trembling.* Lit. "and I, I was among you," repeating the *kagō* of v. 1. Paul was among them not only without the characteristics of a practised and eloquent orator, but as a person who lacked prestige. In 1:18, Paul compared the message of the cross with God's power, but now he speaks of himself as the weak and insignificant bearer of that message, echoing 1:27. According to the Lucan account, Paul arrived in Corinth after his discourse at the Areopagus failed to convince the Athenians who listened, an experience that unsettled him (Acts 17:16–32). In 2 Cor 10:10, Paul even quotes what people were saying of him, "His letters are grave and strong, but his bodily presence is weak, and his speech of no significance." He will speak again of his "weakness" in 1 Cor 4:10; 9:22; 2 Cor 11:30, but now he combines it with "fear and trembling," emotions that display his weakness (see Burchard, "Fussnoten," 169). The pair of words can be found also in 2 Cor 7:15; Phil 2:12; cf. Eph 6:5; often in the LXX (Exod 15:16; Deut 2:25; Judg 2:28; Ps 55:5; Isa 19:16; 4 Macc 4:10). It sums up the dread that people sense in God's presence or at the thought of His judgment. Paul uses the terms to describe his attitude as he undertook the evangelization of Corinth. They serve to recall for Corinthian Christians how unlike his preaching was to discourses of Sophists and how paradoxical was the success of his preaching among them.

4. *and my message and my proclamation were not adorned with persuasive [words of] wisdom.* This part of the verbless verse is badly transmitted. Mss ℵ c, A, C, P, Ψ, 81, 614, 1962, 2495 add *anthrōpinēs* either before or after *sophias*, "human wisdom." Moreover, the adj. *peithois* is found in no other passage in all of Greek literature, and the poorly attested variant *peithoi* (dat. of *peithō*, "persuasion") creates a syntactic problem. N-A[27] reads *en peithoi[s] sophias [logois]* (translated above), but *logois* is lacking in P[46], G, 35* (see Metzger, *TCGNT*, 481). Huby ("Comment") prefers the short reading, *ouk en peithoi sophias*, "n'était point dans une persuasion de sagesse" (not at all with an argument of wisdom).

Paul combines *logos*, "message," and *kērygma*, "proclamation," as a rhetorical pair to describe his own preaching, insignificant in eloquence, as lacking persuasive force. Cf. 2 Cor 11:6, where he again admits that he was "unskilled in speaking"(but "not in knowledge"). Thus Paul is rejecting explicitly the art of persuasion cultivated by the orators trained in Greco-Roman rhetorical tradition. *Peithō*, "persuasion," was the goal of such orators, and this is undoubtedly why he uses the prep. phrase in his rejection of their rhetorical mode. According to Quintilian, the renowned first-century teacher of oratory, rhetoric was *vis persuadendi*, "the power of persuading" (*Inst. orat.* 2.15.3–22). Compare Josephus's statement about Plato's eloquence (*Ag. Ap.* 2.31 §223: *dynamei logōn kai peithoi*, "with power of words and persuasion."

but with a demonstration of the Spirit and of power. This is rather what has made Paul's preaching effective and significant; it is the opposite of "persuasive words." He rejects the use of the studied art of persuasive speech for preaching the message of the cross. What he has achieved is derived from the Spirit and accompanied by its power, which is the antidote of his "weakness" (2:3). BDAG (109) understands the "power" to be "miracle-working power," perhaps to be understood as a gift of the Spirit (see 1:18, 24b; but also Gal 3:5; 1 Thess 1:5); however, the phrase may be hendiadys, and Rom 15:13 provides an interesting parallel: *en dynamei pneumatos hagiou*, "by the power of the Holy Spirit." Conzelmann (*1 Cor*, 55) maintains that *pneumatos* and *dynameōs* are to be understood as poss. gen., but that is hardly correct; they are rather obj. gens. *Apodeixis* is a technical term commonly used in Greek rhetoric for a "compelling or conclusive demonstration, evident proof" (Philo, *De Vita Mosis*, 1.16 §95). As Paul employs it, he means that God's Spirit and power provide such proof (see Hartman, "Some Remarks," 116–18; Lim, " 'Not in Persuasive Words,' " 147).

Pneuma, "spirit," appears now for the first time in this letter. It is often a problem to determine its sense, whether the human spirit or God's Spirit is meant. When it is used anthropologically, as in v. 11a, it denotes that aspect of a human being that is the affective and willing self. As such, it expresses what is especiallly suited in a human being to receive the Spirit of God, as in Rom 1:9; 8:16 (see *Romans*, 127); see also 1 Cor 5:3–5; 7:34; 14:14; 16:18; Gal 6:18; Phil 4:23; Phlm 25; Rom 8:16. In 2:12a Paul will also speak of "the spirit of the world," which is an extension of the anthropological sense.

Here, however, the preferred meaning is God's Spirit, as in 2:10 bis, 11b, 12b, 14a; 3:16; 6:11; 7:40; 12:3 bis, 4, 7, 8 bis, 9 bis, 11, 13 bis, as it is rendered in the KJV, NKJV, RSV, NRSV, EVS, NIV, NJB, but others use "a demonstration of spirit and power" (NAB) or "convincing spiritual power" (Goodspeed; cf. NEB, REB). The meaning of *pneuma* as "Spirit" is not normal in secular Greek of the Classical or Hellenistic periods of the language; a supramundane intelligent being would rather have been called *daimōn* or *daimonion* (see Paige, "Who Believes"). As such, the term now used by Paul comes from the LXX, where it often denotes the presence and controlling influence of God in a creative, prophetic, or renovating way (Gen 1:2; Ps 51:13; 139:7; Isa 11:2; 61:1; Ezek 2:2). It is not considered there to be a distinct being, or person, and normally it is not even personified (see further *PAHT* §PT61–64; Gächter, "Zum Pneumabegriff"; Kleinknecht et al., "*Pneuma, ktl*," *TDNT*, 6:332–455; Puech, "L'Esprit saint à Qumrân"; Rossano, "La parola"). Paul means that God's Spirit has provided him in his weakness with the power needed for him to preach Christ crucified effectively, as the next clause makes clear.

5. *so that your faith might not be based on human wisdom, but on God's power.* Lit. "on the wisdom of human beings." Because *pistis*, "faith," is the human reaction to the proclamation of the gospel (1:21) or the "preached word" (Rom 10:8), it clearly cannot rest on or be born of human wisdom and its achievements (see 1 Thess 1:5). Faith begins as a "hearing" (*akoē*, Rom 10:17) of the "word" about Christ and his salvific role, results in an assent of the mind acknowledging that "Jesus is Lord" (Rom 10:9), and ends in *hypakoē pisteōs* (Rom 1:5; 16:26), "a commitment of faith," i.e., a commitment of the whole person to the lordship of the risen Christ. Hence "human wisdom" has nothing to do with it. In order to believe, however, one depends on "God's power" (see 1:18; cf. Rom 1:16); so Paul hints at the grace-character of Christian faith: "no one can say, 'Jesus is Lord,' save by the Holy Spirit" (1 Cor 12:3b). Later Eph 2:8 will state it formally: "For by grace you have been saved through faith; and this does not come from you; it is the gift of God" (see further *PAHT* §PT109). Cf. 1 Pet 1:5.

So Paul reminisces about his first evangelization of Corinth, which was successful not because of human eloquence or wisdom, but because of God's power, which remedied Paul's weakness, as he sought to proclaim God's mystery, the message of Christ crucified.

6. *Yet to those who are mature we do utter wisdom.* Lit. "among the perfect" (*en tois teleiois*). Paul's 1st pers. plur. formulation echoes the use he made of it in 1:23 ("we proclaim"). The verb *laleō* is used frequently in this letter, often meaning merely "say, utter," but it can also connote "proclaim, announce," as in 14:3; 1 Thess 2:2, 4, 16; Phil 1:14. What Paul proclaims is the message to which he referred in vv. 4–5 above; and Paul is now insisting it too can be called *sophia*, "wisdom," but it is a wisdom that counteracts any so-called wisdom that some Corinthian Christians may have been vaunting, as they missed the real meaning of the gospel preached about Christ crucified (see Horsley, "Wisdom of Word").

The adj. *teleios* is substantivized and would denote Christians who have developed fully in their faith-lives, as 3:1–3, 18 will indicate. Per se, it denotes something that is "perfect," that pertains to the acme of quality. Some commentators have claimed that Paul has derived this term from Hellenistic mystery religions, where allegedly it was used to designate those "initiated" into mystic rites (Iamblichus, *De Myst.* 3.7; Philo, *De somniis* 2 §234 [Reitzenstein, *Hellenistic Mystery Religions*, 432]). This derivation has been contested, however (see Delling, *TDNT*, 8:69); others would relate it to Gnostic writings, where it is said to denote "a higher class of believers" (Wilckens, *Weisheit*, 52–60). *Teleios* contrasted with *nēpios*, "infant," is also found in Philo, *De Agricultura* 2 §9; *Legum allegoria* 1.30 §94. That Paul is using a term known in other religious movements of the time may be admitted, but it is difficult to see how such extrabiblical usage has shaped his use of it either here or elsewhere (14:20; Phil 3:15; cf. Col 1:28). However, in speaking of Corinthian Christians as *teleioi*, he could be speaking with no little irony, meaning that some may think of themselves as different from others, claiming to be more mature in their openness to God's Spirit or grace. In 3:1 Paul will speak of others as *nēpioi*, people considered to be less developed in their spiritual lives. It is, however, far from clear that Paul himself admits such a distinction or "two strata of Christians" (Willis, "The 'Mind of Christ,' " 113), because for him all Christians are "the elect," "the called," "the beloved." Hence "mature" has rather to be understood from the context, that those who hear the revealed word thereby become *teleioi*.

With *sophia* Paul no longer speaks of human wisdom. If he is borrowing perhaps the term from Corinthian Christians with whom he is finding fault, he is utilizing it to characterize instead "the message of the cross" (1:18), as is made clear in the following clause. Recall that in 1:24 he has already spoken of Christ as "the wisdom of God."

not a wisdom of this age or of the rulers of this age who are doomed to destruction. Or "of this world." The wisdom that Paul passes on does not come from or belong to the segment of human history in which Paul and the Corinthians live (see 1:20). The "wisdom of this age" is parallel to "the wisdom of this world" (3:19).

Paul uses the Greek equivalent of the Hebrew phrase *hā'ôlām hazzeh*, "the present age" (used frequently in later rabbinic literature, together with *hā'ôlām habbā'*, "the age to come"), but practically unattested in Jewish writings prior to A.D. 70 (*TDNT*, 1:206). Neither Philo nor Josephus nor QL makes such a distinction of aeons (see BDAG, 32). The counterpart of "a wisdom of this age" is an eschatological type of wisdom, which this age fails to comprehend; its *telos* escapes them.

The phrase, "the rulers of this age," which occurs again in 2:8, where it is said that they "crucified the Lord of glory," is problematic. It has been interpreted in three different ways: (1) As "spirits or demons" associated with Beelzebul, *archōn tōn daimoniōn*, "ruler of demons" (Matt 12:24); cf. 2 Cor 4:4; Col 2:15; Eph 1:21; 2:2. So Tertullian, Origen, and among modern commentators Adeyemi, Barrett, Bousset, Bultmann, Conzelmann, Héring, Kümmel, Lietzmann, Ling, Schrage, J. Weiss, Wilckens. (2) As "human political and social authorities" (e.g., Pilate, Herod, Caiaphas), because of the contrast between God's wisdom and human wisdom in the context of this paragraph. So Ballarini, Carr, Fee, Godet, Lightfoot, Lindemann, Miller, Munck, Pesce, Peterson, Robertson-Plummer, Schniewind, Strobel. (3) As "human rulers and the spiritual forces behind them," something like the angels of the nations (Deut 32:8; Sir 17:17; Dan 10:12–21). So Boyd, Caird, Collins, Cullmann, Garland, Macgregor, Thiselton.

The plur. *archontes* is used elsewhere in the NT only for human rulers, whereas the sing. *archōn* is found for a demon such as Beelzebul (Matt 9:34; 12:24; Mark 3:22; Luke 11:15; John 12:31; 14:30; 16:30). The plur. *archontes*, denoting human rulers, occurs often in a context having to do with the passion or death of Jesus: Luke 23:13, 35; 24:20; Acts 3:17; 4:8, 26 (quotation of Ps 2:1–2); 13:27. For other uses, see also Matt 20:25; Luke 14:1; John 7:26, 48; 12:42; Acts 4:5; 14:5; 16:19; Rom 13:3. Such ocurrences make it highly likely that the Pauline phrase here is to be understood in this way. This interpretation is further supported, first, by the use of "this age" in 1:20 and 3:19, where it refers to this world (*kosmos*) of human beings and, secondly, by the following ptc. *katargoumenōn*, which is more suited to those who trust their human wisdom than to spirits (see further Adeyemi, "The Rulers"; Carr, "The Rulers; Miller, "*Archontōn*").

The pres. ptc. *katargoumenōn*, lit. "being made powerless," has to be understood as in 1:28 and like the *proskaira* of 2 Cor 4:18, "transitory," for they are "doomed to perish" (BDAG, 525–26). Such rulers are part of the passing, unstable world (1 Cor 7:31).

7. *We speak rather of God's wisdom, hidden in a mystery.* I.e., the antithesis of the wisdom of this age, which has remained a mystery hidden until now (see NOTE on 2:1). Paul is thinking of himself as the one who by his preaching has been making known and revealing this divine secret as God's wisdom. He speaks of this mystery as a special wisdom (as in 1:21, 24), because he is seeking to correct Corinthian Christians, who apparently have been claiming to be wise. In reality, the mystery is "Jesus Christ and him crucified" (2:2), "the message of the cross" (1:18), not "a superior stage of Christian teaching, a kind of Christian theosophy ('*theou sophia*')," *pace* Héring, 1 *Cor*, 15. For Paul makes no real distinction between two kinds of teaching, and the OT background of this wisdom-teaching is found in Wis 6:22.

which God predetermined for our glory before time began. Lit. "before the ages." Paul thus traces the content of the hidden mystery (i.e., the new mode of salvation implemented through Jesus Christ) to a divine plan conceived aeons ago. Its purpose was to bring all believers to "glory," i.e., to a share in the risen life of Christ: "If we have died with Christ, we believe that we shall also come to live with him" (Rom 6:8).

Doxa, like Hebrew *kābôd* in the OT, denoted the radiant external manifestation of God's presence to His people (in the Tabernacle or Temple), an attribute allowed to no other being (Isa 42:8; see Weinfeld, *TDOT*, 7:22–38). In time, however, it came to be applied to objects of the cult and also to human beings, as expressive of the enhancing quality of a creature of God as well as the eschatological condition of human destiny. It was thought of as being communicated to them as they drew close to God (Rom 5:2; 8:18, 21; 9:23; 1 Thess 2:12; 2 Cor 3:18; 4:6; Phil 3:21). Estranged from that intimate presence of God, sinful humanity has been deprived of that enhancing quality for which it was destined (Rom 3:23). To that condition Paul now alludes as having been destined from of old.

8. *None of the rulers of this age understood it.* Lit. "which none . . . comprehended," another rel. clause parallel to v. 7b (see NOTE on 2:6). This clause continues the judgment of v. 6b and expresses negatively the consequence of "God's wisdom hidden in a mystery." To it the adversative clause introduced by *alla* (v. 9) stands in contrast.

for, if they had, they would not have crucified the Lord of glory. God's wisdom, hidden in mystery, was incomprehensible to rulers such as Pilate, Herod Antipas, or Caiaphas. It does not mean that the crucifixion of Jesus was the result of a misunderstanding, but rather that such rulers never comprehended what God was intending by it. Paul's contrary-to-fact condition highlights the problem of the crucifixion of Jesus. The rulers failed to realize that he would become thereby "the Lord of glory." In calling Jesus *Kyrios*, "Lord," Paul is using the title par excellence for the risen Christ (see NOTE on 1:2), retrojecting it into the end of the earthly ministry of Jesus. He is the "Lord of glory," because by his resurrection he has entered the glorious presence of the Father and so been glorified (see Rom 6:4; 2 Cor 3:18; 4:6; Phil 3:21). In applying "glory" to the risen Christ, Paul implicitly is putting him on the same level as Yahweh (see Ps 29:3, quoted in Acts 7:2).

The phrase "Lord of Glory" is found also in Jas 2:1; and in *1 Enoch* 63:2, where mighty kings of the earth fail in the same way to acknowledge God (see also *1 Enoch* 22:14; 25:3; 27:3, 5; 36:4; 40:3). Paul, however, now applies the title to the crucified Jesus of Nazareth (cf. Freeborn, "Lord of Glory").

9. *But, as it stands written.* See NOTE on 1:19. This clause introduces a quotation that is problematic, because it introduces a sentence made up of relative clauses that lack a main verb and its subject. Schrage, followed by Lindemann, Garland, thinks that these clauses are the object of *laloumen*, "we speak" (v. 7), which is highly unlikely. The introductory clause begins with the strong adversative conj., *alla*, "but," and it states positively a contrast to the negative statement in v. 8, "which none . . . understood." It can be said to be parallel to the conj. *alla*, "rather," in v. 7 and thus introduces an explanation of "God's wisdom," which Paul proclaims and reveals (v. 7), and all the relative clauses that follow in vv.7–9 logically have "God's wisdom" as their antecedent.

In this verse, the initial neut. rel. pron. *ha* of the quotation is not only the object of the verbs "seen" and "heard," but also the subject of "surged." One simply has to reckon with anacoluthon here (see Frid, "Enigmatic *alla*").

What eye has not seen and ear has not heard, / and what has not surged in a human heart, / what God has prepared for those who love him. So Paul states positively the knowledge that he and other Christians have in contrast to the ignorance of "the rulers of this age." The three clauses, in fact, purport to state the contents of the mystery of God's wisdom. Mss P[11vid], A, B, C[vid] read *hosa*, "how many (things)" instead of *ha* at the beginning of the last clause; that is a minor, inconsequential variant reading.

Although the words quoted are introduced with the common formula used when an OT passage is cited, no one has been able to identify the exact source of the words. The first clause echoes formulas found in Isa 64:3 (LXX: "From of old we have not heard, nor have our eyes seen any God but you and your deeds, which you do for those who await mercy") and 52:15 (LXX: "For they will see who have not been told about it, and those who have not heard will understand"). The second clause may echo either LXX Isa 65:16e ("it [distress of the past] will not surge in their hearts") or LXX Jer 3:16 ("it will not surge in the heart" [i.e., it will not come to mind]), or Jer 39:35; 51:21. The last clause may echo LXX Sir 1:10 ("he lavished her [wisdom] on those who love him"); cf. Rom 8:28, for a different way of expressing this idea). Cf. also Job 13:1–2; 19:26–27; 28:11, 17, 20, 22; Bar 3:16. Yet none of these OT passages corresponds exactly to the wording that Paul uses here.

Origen (*Comm. in Matt.* 27.9 §117 ad finem; GCS 38.250) maintained that the quotation "is found in no regular [i.e., canonical] book, but only in the apocryphon of Elijah the prophet" (*in secretis Eliae prophetae*); similarly Ambrosiaster, *Ad Corinthios Prima* 2.9; CSEL 81.26. Jerome, however, disagreed and maintained that Paul was not rendering *uerbum ex uerbo*, but simply quoting the substance of Isaiah (*In Esaiam* 17.64.4–5; CCLat 73A.734–35). See also Jerome, *Ep.* 57.9.5–7 (Ad Pammachium); CSEL 54.519–20 (cf. Verheyden, "Origen on the Origin," 496 n. 18).

An *Apocalypse of Elijah* is preserved in two Coptic recensions (with partial overlaps), dating from the fourth or fifth century, but they are clearly Christian compositions despite claims that are made sometimes about a Jewish core. This may be the writing to which Origen in the third century refers, but there is no evidence that it existed already in the time of Paul, and it contains no phrases that would correspond to what Paul writes here (see Wintermute, *OTP*, 1:728; Frankfurter, *Elijah in Upper Egypt*, 46–47; K. H. Kuhn, "The Apocalypse of Elijah," *AOT*, 759).

A similar saying in *Ascension of Isaiah* 11:34, a late second-century writing with Christian elements, most likely imitates Paul's formulation here; so too *1 Clem.* 34.8; *Gosp. Thomas* §17. Berger ("Zur Diskussion") has cited a number of parallels to the quotation in Jewish and early Christian literature: Ethiopic *Apocalypse of Ezra*, Syriac *Apocalypse of Daniel*, *Apocalypse of Ps.-Hippolytus*, *Apocalypse of Peter*, Arabic *Gospel of Ps.-John*, Ethiopic *Apocalypse of Mary*, and *Letter of Ps.-Titus*. These parallels are all later imitations of what Paul writes and cannot be regarded as the "origin" of Paul's quotation, *pace* Berger (see Ponsot, "D'Isaïe"). In the same way, it is highly unlikely that the Coptic *Testament of Jacob* 8.8, despite its almost identical wording, could be the source that Paul has used for 2:9, as von Nordheim ("Das Zitat") claims, because it contains all too many echoes of Pauline passages, such as 1 Cor 6:9; Rom 1:30; and other Christian writings (Rev 21:8; 22:15; *Did.* 2–5), as Hofius ("Das Zitat") and Sparks ("1 Kor 2,9") have shown. See further Prigent ("Ce que l'oeil") who thinks that the citation results from a freely quoted Isa 64:3, joined with words from Ps 31:20, as used in a Jewish synagogue liturgical tradition, such as is echoed in later rabbinic texts, like *Sifre, Deut* 3:26.

A few lines from the final hymn of the Essene *Manual of Discipline*, to which Feuillet ("L'Énigme," 58) has called attention are similar, but hardly the source of Paul's version:

> My eye has perceived the wisdom that is hidden from mankind, knowledge and prudent understanding (hidden) from the sons of man, a fountain of righteousness, a well of might, and a spring of glory (hidden) from the assembly of flesh. To those whom God has chosen, He has given them as an everlasting possession and has accorded them an inheritance in the lot of the saints. He has joined their assembly with the sons of heaven to become a council of the community and a foundation of a holy building for all ages to come. (1QS 11:6–9)

Noteworthy, however, is the parallel found in Pseudo-Philo (*LAB*, 26.13): *quod oculus non vidit nec auris audivit, et in cor hominis non ascendit, quousque tale aliquid fieret in seculum,* "What eye has not seen and ear has not heard and has not surged in a human heart." Paul has not derived his form of the composite quotation from Pseudo-Philo, since *LAB* comes from a slightly later date, and Pseudo-Philo is, practically speaking, unaware of Christianity and specifically of the Pauline letters. Hence perhaps both Paul and Pseudo-Philo have derived it from a common Jewish source known in the first Christian century (see Philonenko, "Quod oculus").

In any case, the words cited are intended to sum up the content of the hidden mystery, i.e., the wisdom of God: "what God has prepared for those who love him," viz., the eschatological blessings of salvation (see Rom 8:28), which no human being has ever imagined or desired. This eschatological interpretation of v. 9, proposed by Robertson-Plummer, Dupont, Merklein, Garland (?), is to be preferred rather than a mere reference to wisdom of the immediate context (so Huby, Héring, Wendland, Wilckens).

The quotation ends significantly with the blessings that God has prepared "for those who love him," a note that Paul will repeat in 8:3 and in Rom 8:28 (see *Romans* 521–22). It not only picks up an OT motif (Deut 6:5; 7:9; 10:12; Josh 22:5; 23:11; Ps 31:24; 97:10; Neh 1:5; Sir 1:10), but is made to suit Paul's theology, in which a Christian is one who loves God (see Bauer, ". . . *tois agapōsin*"; Wischmeyer, "*Theon agapan*"). The quotation introduces the all-important statement that Paul makes in the next verse.

10. *and this God has revealed to us through the Spirit.* Or "through his Spirit," if one were to follow the reading *autou* found in MSS ℵᶜ, D, F, G, L. *Hēmin de* is the reading given in MSS ℵ, A, C, D, G, P, Ψ, 33, etc., but MSS P⁴⁶, B, 88, 181, 326, 1739, etc. have rather *hēmin gar,* "for (this God has revealed) to us," a reading that is normally explained as a copyist's attempt at improvement (Metzger, *TCGNT,* 481). The verb *apekalypsen* actually has no object in the Greek text, probably because Paul is emphasizing the fact of revelation; something like "this" has to be understood, a reference to what precedes in v. 9, or possibly to "his wisdom." For God as revealer, see Matt 11:25; Dan 2:22. Verses 10–12 constitute the second part of this paragraph and thus present God's wisdom as revealed through the Spirit, which no human spirit can comprehend. This is one of the rare places in the NT in which the Spirit is said to be involved in "revelation," and it is not to be confused with the "inspiration" of Scripture, *pace* Kaiser ("Neglected Text"). That too is a divine gift, but quite different from revelation, and it is a notion derived from 2 Tim 3:16; 1 Pet 1:20–21, not from this passage.

The hidden mystery is made known by God Himself, but the mediation of the Spirit is emphasized. The Spirit makes known what God has prepared eschatologically for Christians, but it also aids the Christians' love of God. This activity of the Spirit resumes what was said in v. 4 about a "demonstration of the Spirit and power." *Hēmin,* "to us," is put at the beginning of the clause for emphasis; it designates not only the *teleioi,* "mature" Christians or the *pneumatikoi,* as Conzelmann (*1 Cor,* 65) would have it, but all Christians, who are the object of such revelation and who "love him" (2:9; so Lindemann, *1 Cor,* 68, following J. Weiss). It is Paul's way of stating the contrast between Christians who know and the rulers of this age who do not know (v. 8). Parallels in Jewish sapiential literature similarly extol wisdom: Wis 7:21–22, 25, "Whatever is hidden and whatever is manifest I have learned, for wisdom, the fashioner of all things, has taught me. There is in her a spirit that is intelligent, holy, unique, manifold, subtle, mobile, clear, unstained. . . . She is the breath of God's power." Similarly, 1QH^a 9(old 1):21: "These things I know from your knowledge, because you opened my ears to wondrous mysteries, even though I am a creature of clay." Paul, however, distinguishes wisdom from the Spirit, which he makes God's Spirit.

For the Spirit scrutinizes everything, even the profound things of God. Lit. "the depths of God." Paul attributes to the Spirit the power of searching and probing all things, even the inscrutable judgments and untraceable ways of God (Rom 11:33–34), which no human being can do. Cf. Job 11:7–8, which speaks of *haḥēqer 'ĕlôăh,* "the deep things of God," but the LXX renders it as *ichnos kyriou,* "trace of the Lord"; so the phrase that Paul uses, *ta bathē tou theou* is not found in the LXX as such. In the *Test. Job* (37.6c), a phrase closer to Paul's occurs: "Who can comprehend the depths of the Lord (*ta bathē tou kyriou*) and his wisdom, and does anyone dare to ascribe iniquity to the Lord?" Jdt 8:14, however, has a similar idea: "The depths of the human heart you cannot plumb, or understand the thoughts of the human mind. So how will you search out God, who has made all these things, and really know his mind or understand his thought?"

11. *For among human beings, who understands what is truly human, except the human spirit that is within?* Lit. "understands the things of a human being (*tou anthrōpou*), if not the spirit of the human being, which is within him?" In another similarly formulated sentence, Paul draws an analogy between the divine Spirit and the human spirit. In effect, he is making use of the Greek philosophical proverb, "Like is known only by like," *peri tou ta homoia tōn homoiōn einai gnōristika* (Diels fr. 68 [Demokritos] B 164), which Plato also quotes, *Laws* 4.716C: *hoti tō men homoiō to homoion oute metriō philon an eiē,* "would not like be dear to like for the moderate [= the good]?"; cf. Philo, *De Gigantibus* 2 §9; Homer, *Odys.* 17.218.

Paul's rhetorical question encapsulates the essence of being human, and the answer to it is no one. "The things of a human being" are what makes a human being what he or she is, and this is comprehended really only by the human self. By using *pneuma* of a human being, as in 16:18, he is saying the same thing as the "self" (BDAG, 833; see NOTE on 2:4). Paul writes with the presupposition that God has created the human spirit, as in Zech 12:1, which tells of God creating heavens and earth and "forming the human spirit within a being."

Similarly, no one comprehends what pertains to God except the Spirit of God. Lit. "the things of God," the parallel to "the things of man," in the preceding sentence, and the answer to the implied question is again no one. Paul uses the perf. *egnōken* not as a past tense, but as expressing the foregone conclusion about the knowledge of God's nature. The basis of this assertion is the Jewish conviction that no one has ever seen God (Exod 33:18–20; 19:21), which is echoed also by Christian writers (John 1:18; 5:37; 1 John 4:12, 20; 1 Tim 6:16).

12. *Now we have not received the spirit of the world.* Mss D, E, F, G add *toutou,*

"this world," probably under the influence of 3:19; 5:10a or of "this age" (2:6). After the digression in vv. 10–11, Paul returns to his main topic and applies the principle to the issue at hand, God's wisdom, as contrasted with the wisdom of the world. *Kosmos* is now used with a pejorative connotation of what is at odds with the realm of God. By "the spirit of the world," Paul means the ability to know what is peculiar or proper to that world, i.e., what makes it secular; it has nothing to do with the influence of evil spirits or demons, *pace* Ellis, J. Weiss (their way of understanding *to pneuma tou kosmou* as personal comes from the parallel sense of the phrase in the second half of the verse, *to pneuma to ek theou*, which they take to mean "God's Spirit," but which is incorrect). Here *to pneuma tou kosmou* simply denotes a spirit that comprehends what is actually of no consequence, because it echoes *hē sophia tou kosmou* (1:20), and *sophian tou aiōnos toutou* (2:6). For the expression, "receive the spirit," see Gal 3:2, 14; 2 Cor 11:4; Rom 8:15. The pron. *hēmeis* stands at the head of the sentence for emphasis, and it makes no distinction between kinds of believers. The formulation of the verse follows that of vv. 4b–5 above ("not . . . , but . . . , so that").

but rather the spirit coming from God so that we may understand the gifts bestowed on us by God. Lit. "the things graciously given to us." The phrase *to pneuma to ek theou* does not mean "the Spirit of God" or "Holy Spirit" (so RSV, MacRory, Cornely, Schrage [*1 Cor*, 1:260], Collins [*1 Cor*, 134]), but rather the human "spirit" that we have received from God, as in Zech 12:1 (quoted above), not because the former meaning "would contradict v. 11" (so Lindemann, *1 Cor*, 70, who otherwise rightly interprets the phrase), but because *pneuma* has to be understood as impersonal owing to its parallelism with "the spirit of the world" in the same verse (Martin, " 'Spirit,' " 393). "The spirit (coming) from God" makes Christians understand and appreciate what God has prepared for them who love him; so Paul explains the fuller meaning of the last part of the quotation in v. 9. Such a spirit confers true wisdom, the proper understanding of eschatological salvation now available through the crucified Christ, which is nothing less than a gracious gift from God himself. Cf. Rom 8:32; John 16:13–14. The purpose clause expresses the sovereign intention of God, as in 1:27, 29; Rom 4:16; 8:4.

13. *We also talk about them not with words taught by human wisdom.* Paul refers to the way he preaches about God's gifts, meaning that they are really indescribable, when judged by human standards. The verse begins with a neut. plur. rel. pron. *ha*, "which," the antecedent of which is *ta hypo tou theou charisthenta*, "the gifts bestowed by God." The sense of this verse, however, is linked to what Paul asserted in 2:6. Verses 13–16 make up the third part of this paragraph, in which the proclamation is described as uttered with words taught by the Spirit.

but with words taught by the Spirit, interpreting spiritual realities in spiritual terms. Or "by the holy Spirit," if one follows MS D and the Koine text-tradition. Instead of the dat. *pneumatikois*, MSS B and 33 read rather the adv. *pneumatikōs*, "spiritually," probably a copyist's change influenced by v. 14.

Two major problems are encountered here: the meaning of the dat. plur. *pneumatikois* and the meaning of the ptc. *synkrinontes*. Four modes of interpretation are current: (1) Understanding both *pneumatikois* and *pneumatika* as neut., "spiritual things," and the verb *synkrinō* as meaning "compare," as in 2 Cor 10:12: "comparing spiritual realities with spiritual realities" (so Reitzenstein, *Hellenistic Mystery Religions*, 336, who paraphrases, "comparing spiritual gifts and revelations [which we already possess] with spiritual gifts and revelations [which we are to receive] and judging them thereby"; similarly Lietzmann, *1 Cor*, 14; Schrage, *1 Cor*, 1:262; KJV). *But* since the ptc. *synkrinontes* modifies the subject of *laloumen*, it is not a question of receiving *pneumatika*, but of proclaiming them. (2) Understanding *pneumatika* as neut., *pneumatikois* as masc. and modifying *logois*, "words" (understood from earlier in the verse), and *synkrinontes* as "interpreting," i.e., with the meaning the verb often has in the LXX (Gen 40:8, 16, 22; 41:12; Judg 7:15; Dan 5:7): "interpreting spiritual realities in spiritual terms" (so Fee, *1 Cor*, 97, 115; Holladay; Conzelmann, *1 Cor*, 67 [but he says dat. is neut.!]; Barrett, *1 Cor*, 76; NIV). (3) Understanding *pneumatika* as neut., *pneumatikois* as a masc. subst., and *synkrinontes* as "interpreting": "interpreting spiritual realities for spiritual people" (or, "for those who possess the Spirit"; so RSV, NRSV; Collins, *1 Cor*, 40; Kremer, *1 Cor*, 61; Senft, Sickenberger, Heinrici, Bruce, Lindemann?). *But* this anticipates the antithesis of vv. 14–15. (4) Understanding *pneumatika* and *pneumatikois* as neut. and *synkrinontes* as meaning "combining, fitting together," a common meaning of the verb: "fitting spiritual things to spiritual expression" (so Kaiser, "Neglected Text," 317; Garland, *1 Cor*, 91, 100). Of these interpretations, #2 is preferred.

Here *pneuma* means God's "Spirit," for His Spirit enables Paul to interpret God's gifts properly for Christians: spiritual truths expressed in words inspired by God's Spirit. This is Paul's way of describing the influence of the Spirit in Christian life, with which one can compare the Johannine way of speaking about the Paraclete (John 16:13; cf. 1 John 5:20).

Paul uses now for the first time the adj. *pneumatikos*, "spiritual," which occurs also at 2:14 (as an adv.), 15; 3:1; 9:11; 10:3, 4 bis; 12:1; 14:1, 37; 15:44 bis, 46 bis. It modifies diverse things (food, drink, rock, body, and persons), which are always thought to be under the influence of God's Spirit in some way. Sometimes it is contrasted with *psychikos*, "animated" (2:14; 15:44 bis, 46); sometimes with *sarkinos* (*sarkikos*), "fleshy" (3:1, 3 bis; 9:11).

14. *The animated human being does not accept what comes from God's Spirit.* Lit. "the things of God's Spirit." In vv. 14–16, Paul analyses the human response to the revelation given through the Spirit: believing Christians welcome with faith the Spirit-effected revelation now made known by Paul's Spirit-guided preaching. He is echoing what he wrote in 1:18, applying it to people who are considered *psychikoi*. (If by *pneumatikois* Paul meant "for spiritual people" in v. 13 [alternate translation #3], then this verse, which mentions the opposite, *psychikos anthrōpos*, would be repeating what he has just asserted in different terms.)

The adj. *psychikos* is not easily translated. It means "animated," i.e., having an *anima* (= Greek *psychē*) and is intended to describe a human being whose activity is determined by the *psychē* in contrast to *pneumatikos*, one who is influenced by *pneuma*, "Spirit." RSV, NRSV, NEB render the first adj. as "unspiritual," which captures the contrast, but not the meaning; others use "natural" (NAB, ESV), or "worldly"; the Vg has *animalis homo*. Each has its drawbacks. The problem is that the adj. is formed from the noun *psychē*, "soul, life principle," the immaterial but vitalizing part of a living being, otherwise composed of skin, flesh, and bones. The whole being, animal or human, would be composed of *sōma kai psychē*, "body and soul" (Wis 9:15; Xenophon, *Memor.* 1.3.5; *Anab.* 3.2.20; Plato, *Alcib.* 1.130a), with *psychē* as the animating principle of natural life, a common way of speaking in Greek philosophy.

The contrast of *pneumatikoi* and *psychikoi* is formed from the distinction between *pneuma* and *psychē*, in which both terms are related to the vital principle of living things: *pneuma* means the affective and willing part of that principle, and *psychē* the lower, merely vitalizing part, whereas *nous*, "mind," would be its intellectual part (which Paul clearly distinguishes from *pneuma* in 14:14).

When applied to people, as here, the adj. *psychikoi* means that they are living only with *psychē* or *anima* and do not have the ability to be open to revelation or wisdom that comes from God's Spirit, whereas the *pneumatikoi* are those who do have the ability. As Paul uses the contrast to distinguish different Corinthian Christians, he is almost certainly borrowing the terminology from them; they seem to have been using the contrast to distinguish themselves one from another. Since this contrast appears only in this letter and nowhere else in the Pauline corpus, that seems to mean that Paul has borrowed it from Corinthian usage.

The contrast, however, really tells us nothing about the Gnostic character of the Corinthians with whom Paul is dealing, despite the claims of Reitzenstein *(Hellenistic Mystery Religions)*, Wilckens *(Weisheit)*, and others that it does. Gnostic literature uses "mind" (*nous*), but not "spirit" (*pneuma*) or "soul" (*psychē*), from which the adjectives could have been formed; and there is no evidence that Gnostics were already on the scene in Paul's day, despite the contention of Schmithals. The contrast of *pneumatikos* and *psychikos* is borrowed by patristic writers, especially in their refutation of the Gnostics of their day (e.g., Irenaeus, *Adv. Haereses* 1.6.1–2 [SC 264.92–9]; Clement of Alexandria, *Excerpta ex Theodoto* 54.1 [SC 23.170]; Origen, *Contra Celsum* 5.61.17 [SC 147.166]).

Dupont admitted that he could find no evidence for the provenience of the contrast of *pneumatikoi* and *psychikoi* in any pre-Pauline Greek sources (*Gnosis*, 17); he then explained it as derived from the reference to Adam in 15:45–47, where the contrast is found again, as well as the words *psychē* and *pneuma*, in an allusion to Gen 2:7. There God is described breathing into Adam's nostrils *pnoēn zōēs*, "a breath of life," so that he became *psychē zōsa*, "a living being" (ibid., 172–77). In this explanation of the provenience, Dupont has been followed by Pearson (The Pneumatikos-Psychikos Terminology), who regards it as derived from a Hellenistic Jewish interpretation of Gen 2:7, especially as used by Philo. The specific contrast, *pneumatikos-psychikos*, however, is not found in Philo's writings or in Wisdom of Solomon; and it is very difficult to see in these writings the same distinction being made between *pneuma*, *nous*, or *psychē*, even though Philo does distinguish two ways of speaking of *psychē*: *psychē holē*, "the whole soul" and *to hēgemonikon autēs meros, ho kyriōs eipein psychē psychēs esti*, "its principal part, which properly speaking is the soul's soul" (*Quis rer. div. heres* 11

184 COMMENTARY AND NOTES

§55). Using Lev 17:11, Philo identifies *holē psychē* with the blood, but *to hēgemonikon autēs meros* with the breath of life blown into the nostrils of created man. Using this distinction, Philo speaks of two kinds of human beings: those who live by reason (= by *theiō pneumati*, "divine inbreathing"), and those who live by blood (= *sarkos hēdonē*, "by the pleasure of the flesh," ibid., §57). Even though the distinction does not use the same adjectives that Paul has, one finds a similar division of humanity in this Philonic use of *psychē*. See also *De opif. mundi* 46 §135; Wis 15:11. So even though one does not yet find the exact provenience of the contrast that Paul is using, one can relate it to this sort of Hellenistic Jewish background. See Horsley, "Pneumatikos vs. Psychikos," 271–72.

In any case, the distinction between the adjs. *pneumatikos*, "spiritual," and *psychikos*, "animated, natural, worldly, unspiritual," as descriptive of two different types of Christians is clear. The former describes the human being who is open to God's Spirit and enlightened by it, whereas the latter is not. As Schweizer has put it, "*Psychikos* means neutrally the natural man who lives without the eschatological gift of the *pneuma* and who thus belongs to the world (v. 12) and not to God (v. 10)" (*TDNT*, 9:663). Paul asserts that such a natural person would "not accept what comes from God's Spirit." The philosophical principle lying behind Paul's estimate is that used above in v. 11, "Like is known only by like."

Kuhn ("The Wisdom Passage," 248–53) calls attention to Qumran texts that have some of the same elements of Paul's discussion: "wisdom," "Spirit of God," "mystery," and "revelation"; see 1QHᵃ 20(old 12):4–13 ‖ 4QHᵃ (4Q427) 3 ii 5–13; 1QS 11:5–9. Whereas Paul speaks of every believer as *pneumatikos*, having such wisdom from the Spirit, it is the Instructor (*maśkîl*) who is so endowed in the Qumran texts. Dependence on Paul's distinction is found in the third-century Gnostic text, *Hypostasis of the Archons* 11.87.17–20 (*NHL*, 163); cf. Winter, *Pneumatiker*, 175–80.

for to such a one that is folly, and he is unable to understand it, because it is spiritually discerned. Or, "that it is spiritually discerned," because the force of *hoti* is not clear, whether it should be understood as causal (BDF §456.1) or as factual (BDF §456.2). To receive something from God's Spirit would make no sense for the merely animated human being, who is incapable of grasping what can only be discerned in a spiritual way, i.e., guided by God's Spirit. "Folly" is now taken up again, as an echo of 1:18, 21, "folly to those who are perishing." In this context, that means that the *psychikoi* do not attain the knowledge required for salvation. Paul's argument does not proceed from an analysis of human nature as such, but rather from humanity's encounter with the revealed wisdom of God about what leads to salvation.

15. *The spiritual human being, however, discerns all things.* The *pneumatikos*, by contrast, judges rightly not only affairs of this world or age, but also "what comes from God's Spirit," and "the gifts bestowed on us by God" (v. 12). The reason is that such a person judges "spiritually," i.e., under the influence of God's renewing and enlightening Spirit. On the minor text-critical problems involving [*ta*] *panta*, "all things," see Metzger, *TCGNT*, 482.

but is himself subject to no one's scrutiny. Spiritual human beings are not subjected to the judgment of other human beings, because they transcend human limitations inasmuch as they are enlightened by God's Spirit. The sweeping nature of this assertion is startling. Paul means that the *pneumatikos* is subject to God's judgment (see Rom 2:6). Is he excluding judgment by other *pneumatikoi* or judgment by those who are only *psychikoi*? The basis of his assertion is given in 2 Cor 5:16–17: "From now on, then, we regard no one from a human point of view (*kata sarka*); even though we once regarded Christ from a human point of view, so we regard him no longer. Hence, if anyone is in Christ, he is a new creation (or: creature); the old has passed away; look, the new has come!" Paul is asserting the sovereignty of the conscience of the *pneumatikos* and personal judgment, but not the spiritual person as infallible or all-knowing.

16. *For who has known the mind of the Lord so as to instruct him?* In this case, Paul does not use an introductory formula, as he quotes Isa 40:13 in a shortened form.

The LXX reads:
tís egnō noun kyriou,	"Who has known the mind of the Lord;
kai tís autou symboulos egeneto,	who has been his counselor,
hos symbibā auton?,	who instructs him?"

The MT has:
mî tikkēn 'et rûăḥ Yhwh	"who has meted out the spirit of Yahweh,
wĕ'îš 'ăṣātô yôdî'ennû.	and instructs him as his counsellor?"

In the original context of Isaiah, the question refers to the deliverance of the Jewish people from Babylonian captivity by God's creative power, and they accordingly extol His great wisdom in providing for them. That question expects the answer, "No one." Paul accommodates the words of Isaiah to bring his discussion of God's wisdom to a fitting conclusion, because they support his contention that no ordinary human being can judge or scrutinize what comes from God and His Spirit. Paul also quotes part of the same verse of Isaiah in Rom 11:34, in his hymn of praise to God's wisdom and mercy; see also Wis 9:13; Jer 23:18; Jdt 8:14.

But we have the mind of Christ. Mss B, D*, F, G, 81 read *kyriou* instead of *Christou*. Although Howard defends the former as the more original reading ("The Tetragram," 80), the choice of the critical text (N-A²⁷) is *Christou*. That means that Paul now has changed the reading of the LXX (*kyriou*), which he retains in Rom 11:34, because *kyriou* could be ambiguous in this context. "We" means Paul and all Christians, as 3:1 will make clear. In using *nous*, "mind," he is adopting this word from the LXX form of Isa 40:13, and by it he means the intellectual part of *psychē*, by which a human being thinks and reasons what he or she will communicate. Hence for Paul the "mind" is the equivalent of "the spirit coming from God" (v. 12), but now it comes more immediately from Christ. Hence the mind of the Christian is influenced by Christ and is oriented toward him. In 14:14, Paul will make a clear distinction between *pneuma* and *nous*, which he does not do here (see Gaffin, "Some Epistemological Reflections").

The "mind of Christ" is best explained by reference to the hymn to Christ in Phil 2:5–11, which begins with the words, "Have this mind which you have in Christ Jesus." That hymn stresses Christ's "obedient self-emptying and sacrificial death" (Willis, "The 'Mind of Christ,' " 119). Such an ethical outlook formed by the message of the cross should be the guide of community life and conduct, as Paul will make clear in 3:1–4.

3:1. *Brothers, I could not speak to you as spiritual people, but only as worldly, mere infants in Christ.* Lit. "but only as fleshy," i.e., people whose mind-set is that of *sarx,* "flesh." Paul begins with *kagō* and speaks once more in the 1st pers. sing., as in 2:1–5, but uses a form of the verb *laleō,* as in 2:6, 13. Again, Paul addresses the Corinthians as *adelphoi,* "fellow Christians," as in 1:10, 11, 26; 2:1 (see NOTE on 1:1), even though he cannot identify them as *pneumatikoi,* "spiritual people," as he has defined that term in chap. 2. In his eyes, they are rather *sarkinoi,* "fleshy, composed of flesh," i.e., dominated by "worldly" ways. He has been discussing the wisdom that comes from God's Spirit, and he has not been trying to keep it to himself; but immature, worldly Corinthian Christians have not been able to understand it or cope with his communication.

Mss P⁴⁶, ℵ, A, B, C*, D*, 0289, 33, 1739 read *sarkinois,* "made of flesh," but MSS C³, D², F, G, Ψ, and the Koine text-tradition have *sarkikois,* "characteristic of flesh," which would be the form better suited to Paul's meaning. The two forms of the adj., however, are often used interchangeably by copyists; but those who copied MSS F and G attempted to retain the proper nuances of these words (see Parsons, "Sarkinos, Sarkikos"; BDF §113.2).

Paul often contrasts *pneuma* and *sarx,* "spirit" and "flesh" (5:5), especially in his other writings (2 Cor 7:1; Rom 8:4, 5, 6, 9, 13; Gal 3:3; 4:29; 5:17). In that contrast, *sarx* denotes all that keeps a human being tied to earthly, worldly, or selfish tendencies and makes him or her unresponsive to God's Spirit. "Those who live according to the flesh are concerned about things of the flesh" (Rom 8:5); "those who live by the flesh cannot please God" (Rom 8:8). The adjectival forms used here have the same sense. *Sarkinoi* may be a literary variant for *psychikoi* (2:14), but Schweizer (*TDNT,* 9:663) maintains that *psychikos* denotes "the neutrally natural man who lives without the eschatological gift of the *pneuma,*" whereas *sarkikos* is "the believer who is making no progress."

In addition, Paul calls his Corinthian addressees *nēpioi,* "infants," in their spiritual lives and in their relation to Christ, because they regard spiritual things from the viewpoint of a small child who is unable to comprehend their real meaning and worth. Such Corinthians may be "in Christ" (1:2, 4, 30), but they, having accepted the gospel and been converted, are behaving in childish, immature, worldly ways. Their conduct does not measure up to their conversion. "Paul chides his readers not for failure to advance their understanding (some were exceedingly proud of their knowledge), but for failing to allow what they had known and realised to be true to inform their on-going Christian life"; no little part of this is their failure to recognize Paul's apostolic authority (Francis, " 'As Babes in Christ,' " 57).

Paul has moved from the contrast between *pneumatikoi* and *psychikoi,* for

which he now substitutes *sarkinoi*, to a contrast between *nēpioi*, "infants, immature" and *teleioi*, "perfect, mature," a term that he already employed in 2:6 (see
Note there). This contrast basically makes the same distinction of human beings,
even though the terminology is different.

2. *I fed you milk, not solid food, because you were not yet able to take it.* Lit. "I
made you drink milk, not solid food," an elliptical expression called zeugma
(BDF §479.2). Paul continues the metaphoric comparison of the Corinthian
Christians with infants, by stressing that he was like a mother to them (see
Gaventa, "Our Mother"). Cf. the similar metaphor of the Qumran psalmist in
1QHª 15(old 7):20–21: "They [men of marvel] have opened their mouths like a
child at the breast of its mother."

What Paul had taught them was like baby food ("the message of the cross"), not
the food of mature adults, which he is now trying to pass on to them in this letter,
as he tries to instruct them about further spiritual implications of that message
concerning Christ crucified, "the wisdom of God," or Christ, who is not the wis
dom of this world. The real contrast, then, is not between "two quite different
diets which he has to offer, but between the true food of the Gospel with which he
has fed them (whether milk or meat) and the synthetic substitutes which the Corinthians have preferred" (Hooker, "Hard Sayings," 21). The same contrast of
milk and solid food is used by the author of the Epistle to the Hebrews in his exhortation addressed to backsliding Christians (5:12–14), and by Philo, *De agricultura* 2 §9, where he too speaks of milk as food for *nēpioi*, but wheat-bread for
teleioi, as does Paul in the next verse (see also *Legum alleg.* 1.30 §94; cf. Sterling,
"Wisdom," 367–76; Grundmann, "Die *nēpioi*"). The Corinthian Christians, fed
on such milk, may have criticized Paul, claiming that they were seeking, indeed,
the solid food of philosophical speculation, rhetorical eloquence, and advanced
knowledge. Then Paul would be refuting their contention, making the point that
they are still babes, as the next clause makes clear. His solid food is the wisdom of
God, which is foolishness to the world, and nothing other than "the message of
the cross," but now presented as "Christ crucified" (1:30), a wisdom turned upside
down, for it is not the wisdom the Corinthian Christians were seeking.

Even now, you are still unable. This is added by Paul, who will explain it in the
next verse. As in the preceding clause, the complementary infin. has to be supplied. The adv. *eti*, "still," is omitted in mss P⁴⁶, B, 0185. Paul does not exclude a
future possibility of their taking solid food.

3. *For you are still worldly.* Lit. "fleshy" (*sarkikoi*, in the best mss). They are still
affected by the customs and secular culture of pagan Roman Corinth. This condition would make Paul hesitate in his attempt to feed Corinthian Christians with
solid food. Why they are still worldly is explained in the next sentence, which
comments on their conduct.

*Wherever jealousy and strife exist among you, are you not worldly and behaving
in a secular human way?* Lit. "fleshy and walking as a (mere) human being," with
kata anthrōpon, a phrase known from classical Greek writings to express the status
of a member of the human race or an ordinary way of viewing or doing things
(Aeschylus, *Sept.* 425; Diodorus Siculus, *Bibl. Hist.* 16.11.2; Plato, *Phileb.* 370f);

see also 9:8; 15:32; Gal 3:15; Rom 3:5. They are still influenced by the secular social conventions of Roman Corinth. Some MSS (P⁴⁶, D, F, G, 33, and the Koine text-tradition) add a third cause, *kai dichostasiai*, "and dissensions," to the two causes.

So Paul characterizes the Corinthian situation caught up in its factious rivalries (1:10–11), which give rise to the "jealousy and strife" found among them: the Christian status of the members of the Corinthian church calls for more elevated and gracious conduct. Paul mentions the same pair, *zēlos kai eris*, "jealousy and strife," in an eschatological exhortation (Rom 13:13). and in a list of vices (2 Cor 12:20). Cf. Gal 5:20, where they are listed among the *erga tēs sarkos*, "works of the flesh." For this reason Oropeza speaks of vv. 3–4 as including one of Paul's various "vice lists" of this letter; see further 5:9–11; 6:9–10; 10:6–10; 13:4–7 ("Situational Immorality").

4. *Whenever someone says, "I side with Paul," and another says, "I side with Apollos," are you not being merely human?* Lit. "are you not human beings?" (*ouk* [or *ouchi*] *anthrōpoi este*). Are you not like the rest of Roman Corinth? Paul recalls what has been reported to him (1:10–12). Rival factions in the Corinthian church reveal that the addressees have been neglecting the nobility of their Christian calling to substitute for it allegiance to one preacher or another in a purely secular fashion. Mention of two groups is made only by way of example, not because of a difference in his relations with Apollos and Cephas, *pace* Barrett (*1 Cor*, 82).

BIBLIOGRAPHY (See also Bibliography on 1:10–4:21, pp. 149–50)

Adeyemi, M. E., "The Rulers of This Age in First Corinthians 2:6–8: An Exegetical Exposition," *DBM* 18/2 (1999) 38–45.

Allo, E.-B., "Sagesse et pneuma dans la première épître aux Corinthiens," *RB* 43 (1934) 321–46.

Ballarini, T., "Chi sono gli Arconti? Una ricerca su 1 Cor. 2,6.8," *Laurentianum* 21 (1980) 251–72, 404–27; 22 (1981) 59–71.

Bauer, J. B., " '. . . *tois agapōsin ton theon*': Rm 8,28 (I Cor 2,9, I Cor 8,3)," *ZNW* 50 (1959) 106–12.

Berger, K., "Zur Diskussion über die Herkunft von I Kor. ii. 9," *NTS* 24 (1977–78) 270–83.

Boyd, W. J. P., "1 Corinthians ii. 8," *ExpTim* 68 (1956–57) 158.

Brown, R. E., *The Semitic Background of the Term "Mystery" in the New Testament* (Facet Books, Biblical Series 21; Philadelphia: Fortress, 1968).

Bullmore, M. A., *St. Paul's Theology of Rhetorical Style: An Examination of I Corinthians 2.1–5 in Light of First Century Greco-Roman Rhetorical Culture* (San Francisco: International Scholars Publications, 1995).

Burchard, C., "Fussnoten zum neutestamentlichen Griechisch," *ZNW* 61 (1970) 157–71.

Carr, W., "The Rulers of This Age—I Corinthians ii. 6–8," *NTS* 23 (1976–77) 20–35.

Diels, H., *Die Fragmente der Vorsokratiker griechisch und deutsch* (3 vols.; 7th ed., W. Kranz; Berlin: Weidmannsche Verlagsbuchhandlung, 1954), 2:176.

Ellis, E. E., *Prophecy and Hermeneutic in Early Christianity* (Grand Rapids: Eerdmans, 1978).

Feuillet, A., "L'Énigme de *I Cor.*, ii, 9," *RB* 70 (1963) 52–74.

Francis, J., " 'As Babes in Christ' — Some Proposals Regarding 1 Corinthians 3.1–3," *JSNT* 7 (1980) 41–60.

Frankfurter, D., *Elijah in Upper Egypt: The Apocalypse of Elijah and Early Egyptian Christianity* (Studies in Antiquity & Christianity; Minneapolis: Fortress, 1993).

Freeborn, J., "Lord of Glory: A Study of James 2 and 1 Corinthians 2," *ExpTim* 111 (1999–2000) 185–89.

Frid, B., "The Enigmatic *alla* in 1 Corinthians 2. 9," *NTS* 31 (1985) 603–11.

Funk, R. W., "Word and World in I Corinthians 2:6–16," *Language, Hermeneutic, and Word of God: The Problem of Language in the New Testament and Contemporary Theology* (New York: Harper & Row, 1966) 275–305.

Gaffin, R. B., Jr., "Some Epistemological Reflections on 1 Corinthians 2:6–16," *WTJ* 57 (1995) 103–24.

Gaventa, B. R., "Mother's Milk and Ministry in 1 Corinthians 3," *Theology and Ethics in Paul and His Interpreters: Essays in Honor of Victor Paul Furnish* (ed. E. H. Lovering and J. L. Sumney; Nashville: Abingdon, 1996) 101–13.

———, "Our Mother St. Paul: Toward the Recovery of a Neglected Theme," *PSB* 17/1 (1996) 29–44.

Grindheim, S., "Wisdom for the Perfect: Paul's Challenge to the Corinthian Church (1 Corinthians 2:6–16)," *JBL* 121 (2002) 689–709.

Grundmann, W., "Die *nēpioi* in der urchristlichen Paränese," *NTS* 5 (1958–59) 188–205.

Hartman, L., "Some Remarks on 1 Cor. 2:1–5," *SEA* 39 (1974) 109–20.

Hofius, O., "Das Zitat 1 Kor 2,9 und das koptische Testament des Jakob," *ZNW* 66 (1975) 140–42.

Hooker, M. D., "Hard Sayings: I Corinthians 3:2," *Theology* 69 (1966) 19–22; repr. *From Adam to Christ: Essays on Paul* (Cambridge: Cambridge University Press, 1990) 103–5.

Horsley, R. A., "Pneumatikos vs. Psychikos: Distinctions of Spiritual Status among the Corinthians," *HTR* 69 (1976) 269–88.

———, "Wisdom of Word and Words of Wisdom in Corinth," *CBQ* 39 (1977) 224–39.

Howard, G., "The Tetragram and the New Testament," *JBL* 96 (1977) 63–83.

Huby, J., "Comment lire *I Corinthiens* ii, 4a" *RSR* 32 (1944) 245–47.

Kaiser, W. C., Jr., "A Neglected Text in Bibliology Discussion: 1 Corinthians 2:6–16," *WTJ* 43 (1980–81) 301–19.

Koperski, V., "Knowledge of Christ and Knowledge of God in the Corinthian Correspondence," *The Corinthian Correspondence* (BETL 125; ed. R. Bieringer), 377–96.

Kovacs, J. L., "The Archons, the Spirit and the Death of Christ: Do We Need the Hypothesis of Gnostic Opponents to Explain 1 Cor. 2.6–16?" *Apocalyptic and the New Testament: Essays in Honor of J. Louis Martyn* (JSNTSup 24; ed. J. Marcus and M. L. Soards; Sheffield: JSOT, 1989) 217–36.

Kuhn, H.-W., "The Wisdom Passage in 1 Corinthians 2:6–16 between Qumran and Proto-Gnosticism," *Sapiential, Liturgical and Poetical Texts from Qumran: Proceedings of the Third Meeting of the International Organization for Qumran Studies, Oslo 1988* (STDJ 35; ed. D. K. Falk et al.; Leiden: Brill, 2000) 240–53.

Lim, T. H., " 'Not in Persuasive Words of Wisdom, but in the Demonstration of the Spirit and Power' (I Cor. 2:4)," *NovT* 29 (1987) 137–49.

Ling, T., "A Note on 1 Corinthians ii. 8," *ExpTim* 68 (1956–57) 26.

Macgregor, G. H. C., "Principalities and Powers: The Cosmic Background of Paul's Thought," *NTS* 1 (1954–55) 17–28.

Martin, D. W., " 'Spirit' in the Second Chapter of First Corinthians," *CBQ* 5 (1943) 381–95.

Miller, G., "*Archontōn tou aiōnos toutou*—A New Look at 1 Corinthians 2:6–8," *JBL* 91 (1972) 522–28.

Miranda, A., "L'uomo spirituale' (*pneumatikos anthrōpos*) nella Prima ai Corinzi," *RivB* 43 (1995) 485–519.

Nordheim, E. von, "Das Zitat des Paulus in 1 Kor 2,9 und seine Beziehung zum koptischen Testament Jakobs," *ZNW* 65 (1974) 112–20.

Oropeza, B. J., "Situational Immorality: Paul's 'Vice Lists' at Corinth," *ExpTim* 110 (1998–99) 9–10.

Paige, T., "Who Believes in 'Spirit'? *Pneuma* in Pagan Usage and Implications for the Gentile Christian Mission," *HTR* 95 (2002) 417–36.

Parsons, M. C., "*Sarkinos, Sarkikos* in Codices F and G: A Text-Critical Note," *NTS* 34 (1988) 151–55.

Pearson, B. A., *The Pneumatikos-Psychikos Terminology in 1 Corinthians: A Study in the Theology of the Corinthian Opponents of Paul and Its Relation to Gnosticism* (SBLDS 12; Missoula: Scholars, 1973).

Pesce, M., *Paolo e gli arconti a Corinto: Storia della ricerca (1888–1975) ed esegesi di I Cor. 2,6.8* (Testi e ricerche di scienze religiose 13; Brescia: Paideia, 1977).

Philonenko, M., "Quod oculus non vidit, I Cor. 2, 9.," *TZ* 15 (1959) 51–52.

Ponsot, H., "D'Isaïe, lxiv, 3 à I Corinthiens, ii, 9," *RB* 90 (1983) 229–42.

Popkes, W., "1Kor 2,2 und die Anfänge der Christologie," *ZNW* 95 (2004) 64–83.

Prigent, P., "Ce que l'oeil n'a pas vu, I Cor. 2, 9.," *TZ* 14 (1958) 416–29.

Puech, E., "L'Esprit saint à Qumrân," *SBFLA* 49 (1999) 283–97.

Rossano, P., "La parola e lo Spirito: Riflessioni su 1 Tess 1,5 e 1 Cor 2,4–5," *Mélanges bibliques en hommage au R. P. Béda Rigaux* (ed. A. Descamps et A. de Halleux; Gembloux: Duculot, 1970) 437–44.

Scroggs, R., "Paul: *Sophos* and *Pneumatikos*," *NTS* 14 (1967–68) 33–55.

Söding, T., "Das Geheimnis Gottes im Kreuz Jesu (1 Kor): Die paulinische Christologie im Spannungsfeld von Mythos und Kerygma," *BZ* 38 (1994) 174–94.

Sparks, H. F. D., "1 Kor 2,9 a Quotation from the Coptic Testament of Jacob?" *ZNW* 67 (1976) 269–76.

Sterling, G. E., " 'Wisdom among the Perfect': Creation Traditions in Alexandrian Judaism and Corinthian Christianity," *NovT* 37 (1995) 355–84.

Stuhlmacher, P., "The Hermeneutical Significance of 1 Cor 2:6–16," *Tradition and Interpretation in the New Testament: Essays in Honor of E. Earle Ellis* . . . (ed. G. F. Hawthorne and O. Betz; Grand Rapids: Eerdmans; Tübingen: Mohr [Siebeck], 1987) 328–47.

Verheyden, J., "Origen on the Origin of 1 Cor 2,9," *The Corinthian Correspondence* (BETL 125; ed. R. Bieringer), 491–511.

Vos, J. S., "Die Argumentation des Paulus in 1 Kor 1,10–3,4," *The Corinthian Correspondence* (BETL 125; ed. R. Bieringer), 87–119.

Walker, W. O., "1 Corinthians 2.6–16: A Non-Pauline Interpolation?" *JSNT* 47 (1992) 75–94.

Widmann, M., "1 Kor 2,6–16: Ein Einspruch gegen Paulus," *ZNW* 70 (1979) 44–53.

Wilckens, U., "Zu 1 Kor 2,1–16," *Theologia Crucis—Signum Crucis: Festschrift für Erich Dinkler* . . . (ed. C. Andresen and G. Klein; Tübingen: Mohr [Siebeck], 1979) 501–37.

Willis, W., "The 'Mind of Christ' in 1 Corinthians 2,16," *Bib* 70 (1989) 110–22.

Winter, B. W., *Philo and Paul among the Sophists: Alexandrian and Corinthian Responses to a Julio-Claudian Movement* (2d ed.; Grand Rapids: Eerdmans, 2002).

Winter, M., *Pneumatiker und Psychiker in Korinth: Zum religionsgeschichtlichen Hintergrund von 1. Kor. 2,6–3,4* (MTS 12; Marburg: Elwert, 1975).

Wintermute, O. S., "Apocalypse of Elijah," *OTP*, 1:721–53.

Wischmeyer, O., "*Theon agapan* bei Paulus: Eine traditionsgeschichtliche Miszelle," *ZNW* 78 (1987) 141–44.

6   d. False Idea of the Role of Preachers Corrected (3:5–17)

[3:5] What after all is Apollos, and what is Paul? Only servants through whom you came to believe, just as the Lord assigned to each. [6] I planted, Apollos watered, but God caused the growth. [7] Consequently, neither the one who plants nor the one who waters amounts to anything, but only God who causes the growth. [8] The one who plants and the one who waters have one purpose, but each will be recompensed according to his labor. [9] For we are God's fellow-workers; you are God's field, God's building. [10] According to the grace of God granted me, I laid a foundation as an expert builder, and someone else is building upon it. But each one should see to it how he builds on it. [11] For no one can lay a foundation other than the one already laid, which is Jesus Christ. [12] If someone builds on the foundation with gold, silver, precious stones, wood, hay, or straw, [13] the work of each builder will become obvious, because the Day will bring it to light. It will be revealed by fire. Fire [itself] will test the quality of each one's work. [14] If the work that someone has built survives, he will be recompensed. [15] If someone's work is burned up, he will be deprived of recompense, but he himself will be saved, but only as through fire. [16] Do you not realize that you are the temple of God and that the Spirit of God dwells in you? [17] If anyone destroys God's temple, God will destroy him. For the temple of God, which you are, is sacred.

COMMENT

Paul continues his instruction about the contrast of the gospel and the wisdom of this world or the role of real wisdom in Christian life by explaining the role of preachers, because he realizes that Corinthian Christians have come to a false idea about their role (recall 3:4 from the end of the preceding pericope, "Whenever someone says, 'I side with Paul,' and another says, 'I side with Apollos,' are you not merely human?"). The problem comes from the fact that both Paul and Apollos, and perhaps Cephas too, have evangelized Corinth. If Corinthians became believers through such human evangelists, they should not think that they owe allegiance to those who were merely human instruments that God was employing in their coming to faith. In thus referring in 3:4 to the so-called slogans that first surfaced in 1:12, Paul is preparing for an *inclusio* that will appear in 3:22, where Paul will again use the genitives to turn such slogans on their head, when he will say, "all belongs to you," even Paul, Apollos, and Cephas (see further Byrne, "Ministry and Maturity").

Paul's argument runs thus: first, he asserts that he and Apollos are only servants (*diakonoi*, 3:5) and God's fellow workers (*synergoi*, 3:9), carrying out tasks to which the Lord God has assigned them. Each preacher has to see how he builds (3:10b), for all the construction is going to be tested (3:12–15). Paul puts all the emphasis on "God" in this pericope, mentioning Him in vv. 6, 7, 9, 10, 16, 17, 19, with a climax in v. 23. Second, to make his point clear, Paul continues to use figurative language or metaphors. He begins with an agricultural image, changes to an architectural image, and eventually to the kind and quality of the building material being used. Paul depicts himself as a planter (3:6–9a), then as an expert builder (3:10–15); in effect, he presents himself as the founder of the Corinthian church. Third, Paul offers the needed correction: God has caused the growth (3:6–7), and Jesus Christ is the only foundation of it all (3:11). Fourth, Corinthian Christians must realize that they are "God's field, God's building" (3:9), "the temple of God" (3:16a, 17b), and that "the Spirit of God dwells in them" (3:16b).

At first, the missionary Paul likens himself to a farmer who has planted seed by his evangelization, and Apollos to a fellow farmer who has watered the seeded ground. Each has his job to do, but neither of them makes the plants grow. The growth comes from God, who alone causes it. God may indeed reward such "fellow workers," but the field so seeded and watered belongs to God. That is why Paul ends his first comparison by telling the Corinthian community that it is "God's field," a field possessed by God.

Paul changes the metaphor and adds in the same sentence that they are "God's building," enabling him to introduce an architectural image, as he compares himself to a master builder who has laid a foundation by his evangelization. He does not name Apollos as a fellow builder in this comparison, as he did in the first one, but the unnamed person who builds on that foundation so laid might well be Cephas, otherwise unnamed. Paul, however, immediately corrects all that, insisting that the one foundation is none other than Jesus Christ, about whom he has been preaching (1:23; 2:2). Hence, Corinthian Christians must be aware that anyone who proceeds to build on such a foundation must choose carefully the materials with which the further construction is to be made. For in the long run, the work of any such builder will be scrutinized and judged for its adequacy and durability; it will be brought to light and tested by fire. If the construction withstands the fire, the builder will be duly recompensed. So the quality of evangelization is all important.

Although Branick considers vv. 10c–15 to be a "digression inserted here because of the key word *sophos* at 3:10b and is probably itself a composition written independently of both the homily on wisdom as well as the letter to the Corinthians" ("Source," 263), these verses make up an important element in Paul's argument about the diversity of the Corinthian Christian community and expand the thought of v. 8b, as Hollander ("The Testing," 89) and Kuck (*Judgment*, 171) rightly note. Although vv. 10–15 are vague, Paul expects his readers to apply what he is saying to all their teachers, and even to themselves as participants in the work of building.

The image of building enables Paul to push his instruction one step further, as he tells the Corinthians twice that as a community they are "the temple of God," because the Spirit of God dwells in them. Consequently, they are sacred (*hagioi*), i.e., dedicated to God's cultic service.

In this passage we meet with Paul's affirmation of judgment of "the work of each builder" that is to take place on "the Day" (i.e., the day of judgment), when "it is revealed by fire" (3:13). It is important, however, to realize that Paul is not discussing the deeds of individual Christians, as is often supposed, but the evangelistic work of Christian missionaries, especially those who have sought to erect a superstructure on the foundation that Paul has laid, or better, on the foundation "already laid, which is Jesus Christ" (v. 11; see Donfried, "Justification," 148–49).

What Paul writes in these verses of chap. 3 about esteem for human preachers of the gospel and proclaimers of God's wisdom now becomes a counsel that must guide all Christians in their attitude toward church leaders. Such authorities have been fitted out for their tasks in the Christian community by the gracious determination of God, and their effectiveness depends on the extent to which they cooperate with the grace of God, who alone causes the "growth" in the field in which they labor. Their competence comes only from God (2 Cor 3:5), and their different qualities depend on the gifts of His Spirit (1 Cor 12:28–30). They are, however, nothing more than "God's fellow-workers" (3:9). Even Paul unabashedly admitted that whatever foundation he laid, he did it only "according to the grace granted me" (3:10).

NOTES

3:5. *What after all is Apollos, and what is Paul?* Paul reverts to the report received from Chloe's people (1:11–12) about the rivalries grouped by names of the former evangelists of Roman Corinth. As in 3:4, he mentions only two of them, Apollos and himself. They were both well known as preachers in Corinth, but Paul seeks to correct the Corinthian Christians' understanding of their role. Note the rhetorical chiasmus in vv. 5–6: Apollos, Paul, I (Paul), Apollos. Paul does not ask, "Who is Apollos?" but "what is . . . ," in effect, imitating the question in Ps 8:5, "What is man . . . ," but MSS P⁴⁶ᵛⁱᵈ, ℵ², C, D, F, G, Ψ, 1881, and the Koine text-tradition read *tís*, "Who?"; but see v. 7, which shows that neut. *tí* is correctly read as the original reading. From these verses it is clear that Paul never blames Apollos for the rivalry and does not regard him as a rival; both are coworkers, servants, and stewards.

Only servants through whom you came to believe. Apollos and Paul are called *diakonoi*, not of the community itself, but of God (or Christ, as in 4:1); compare 2 Cor 6:4; 11:23.

Diakonos in the Greek language denotes an intermediary or agent in some activity, business, or transaction in which one gives assistance. So Josephus describes Rachel, who brings Jacob to Laban (*Ant.* 1.19.6 §298) and Elisha who follows Elijah (*Ant.* 8.13.7 §354). It was often used in Greek culture to denote agents of gods: Diogenes as *tou Dios diakonos*, "agent of Zeus" (Epictetus, *Diss.* 3.24.65; 3.22.63); *diakonos theōn* (Achilles Tatius 3.18.5). Similarly, Paul in 2 Cor 3:6 (*diakonous kainēs diathēkēs*, "agents of a new covenant"); 1 Thess 3:2 (as a variant for *synergos*); Rom 16:1. Here *diakonoi* denotes agents through whom Corinthians came to faith in God and Christ Jesus (cf. 2:5). Their work was *diakonia*, what Paul calls *diakonia tēs katallēgēs*, "a ministry of reconciliation" (2 Cor 5:18).

just as the Lord assigned to each. Lit. "and to each as the Lord gave," the dat. *hekastō* should really be a nom., *hekastos*, but its case is attracted to the indirect obj. of the verb *edōken* in the subordinate clause (BDF §475.1). Paul insists that he and Apollos were merely performing the task for which they had been called by the Lord and commissioned with a certain authority. He further develops this notion of his own commission in 15:10; 2 Cor 4:5. It may seem unclear whether *ho kyrios*, "the Lord," refers to the risen Christ or to God the Father, as in 4:19; 7:17; 2 Cor 8:21; but in view of the next verse, it is best understood as a title for God.

6. *I planted, Apollos watered, but God caused the growth.* So Paul describes the different but complementary tasks that the Lord desired the pair of them to perform as individuals in the Corinthian community. He sowed the seed (aor. tense), which Apollos later watered (aor.), but neither of them was responsible for the resulting gradual growth (imperf.), "a planting of the Lord" (Isa 61:3). That growth Paul ascribes clearly to God alone, which is consistent with his theology of grace. Cf. Rom 9:16; 2 Cor 9:10. This means that allegiance to a Paul-group or an Apollos-group in the Corinthian community is meaningless and only destructive of the unity it should have.

From this statement, one usually concludes that Paul was the founder of the Corinthian church. Paul's arrival in Corinth is recounted in Acts 18:1–4, where it is noted that there he discovered Aquila, a Jew from Pontus, who with his wife, Priscilla, had arrived a short time before from Italy. It is hard to say whether they were still Jews, whom Paul converted (about which neither he nor Luke ever say a word) or were already Jewish Christians, who had to leave Rome, when Claudius expelled Jews ca. A.D. 49–50 (see INTRODUCTION pp. 37–40; cf. *Acts*, 619–20). If they were already Christians, then there would have been at least two Christians in Corinth prior to Paul's evangelization of it, but he could still regard himself as the founder of the community there.

For the community as a "planting" in Jewish writings, see Isa 5:7; Jer 32:41; 1QS 8:5–8; CD 1:7; *Jub.* 1:16; 16:26; cf. Braun, *Qumran*, 1:190; Str-B 1:720–21.

7. *Consequently, neither the one who plants nor the one who waters amounts to anything, but only God who causes the growth.* In v. 6, Paul reflected on what Apollos and he had accomplished; now he concludes (in the pres. tense) from his agricultural metaphor, repeating in effect the statement of v. 6 and putting *theos* emphatically in the last place in the sentence, because God alone counts. God is the only "something" (*ti*) that matters. He and Apollos have no claim to allegiance among the Christians of Roman Corinth; they amount to nothing. Compare Paul's statement about others who were apostles before him in Gal 2:6. Paul is

stressing that he and Apollos, as well as all other teachers among Corinthian Christians, notwithstanding their unique contributions, are equal in God's sight; they are all part of His workforce, and each is recompensed according to the work that has been done, whatever that might be. For the phraseology, "neither . . . nor . . . , but . . . ," see 1 Thess 2:5–7; Gal 5:6; 6:15.

8. *The one who plants and the one who waters have one purpose.* Lit. "are one," an elliptical assertion, which may refer to the goal they both have in their activity, or it may refer to their status and responsibility: "are equal" (RSV), i.e., from a human point of view. Although they are "not . . . anything" (v. 7), the two are not opposed, but complement each other; the basis of this unity has been stated in v. 7: neither one amounts to anything, as they prepare together for the real (divine) activity.

but each will be recompensed according to his labor. Lit. "each will receive his own wages (*ton idion misthon*) according to his own labor." In other words, the remuneration for Apollos and Paul will come from God who has assigned them to their individual tasks, and not from the reputation or glory that they might enjoy among those who might side with them or show them allegiance in some way. Although Paul and Apollos have no merit by which they might claim recompense, they realize that in the end God will reward graciously those who serve Him in this special way. This part of v. 8 may sound like a parenthetic remark, but Paul is stating briefly what he will develop in 3:14–15, and again in 4:1–5, especially in an eschatological sense.

Paul uses *ton idion kopon,* "his own labor" (or "toil"), a term chosen to denote "the work done" (BDAG, 558) in evangelization. Paul is adopting an OT term: "where wisdom rewards the labor of holy ones" (Wis 10:17; see Ps 61:13; Prov 24:12; see further von Harnack, *"Kopos"*; Kuist, "Labors"; Pesch, "Der Sonderlohn").

9. *For we are God's fellow-workers.* The conj. *gar* links this verse to v. 8a, and the whole verse contrasts "we" (= Paul and Apollos) with "you" (= Corinthian Christians), and the emphasis in the verse falls on the triple use of *theos,* which stands emphatically in the first place in each clause and sums up the meaning of vv. 5–7. Since the gospel expresses God's power (1:18), its bearers are those who collaborate with God.

In the first clause, Paul regards both Apollos and himself as *synergoi theou,* a title that he used also of Timothy in 1 Thess 3:2. The phrase *synergoi theou* has been understood in two ways: (1) "God's fellow-workers," i.e., those who work together with God and are engaged in a common endeavor with God himself, who is the principal worker. It is so understood by KJV, RSV, NIV, NAB, Conzelmann, Godet, Kremer, J. B. Lightfoot, Lietzmann, Robertson-Plummer, Senft, Schrage, J. Weiss. This interpretation takes the Greek phrase for what it says, and means what is suggested by 2 Cor 6:1, "working together with Him, we entreat you. . . ." It may sound like synergism, but there is nothing wrong with that; and it is not rendering the Greek by a paraphrase, as in the next interpretation. (2) "Fellow workers in God's service," or "God's servants, working together" (NRSV), or "fellow workers who belong to God," i.e., Paul and his colleagues are those who work together and thus serve God by such shared labor. It is so understood by Barrett, Collins, Fee, Furnish ("Fellow Workers"), Garland, Grosheide, Hays, Lindemann, Merklein, Soards, Thiselton, Wolff. This interpretation claims that the phrase is not to be understood "synergistically 'God's fellow workers,' as the context clearly [?] shows, by emphasizing God's origination of the mission work, the responsibility of each worker's work, and the examination of the work of each before God (vv. 5–15)" (Ollrog, *EDNT*, 3:304). " 'God's coworkers' implies that Paul and Apollos are coworkers who work with one another and for God. They belong to God just as the field and the construction of v. 9b belong to God" (Collins, *1 Cor*, 147). Robertson-Plummer, however, rightly note that, if Paul had meant the second way of understanding the phrase, he would have expressed it as he did in Rom 16:3, where he speaks of Prisca and Aquila as *tous synergous mou en Christō Iēsou*, "my fellow-workers in Christ Jesus."

you are God's field, God's building. As he brings his agricultural metaphor to an end, Paul calls the Corinthian community *geōrgion*, "cultivated land, field." That explains why he has spoken of his own evangelical work in Corinth as a planting of seed, and of Apollos's work as a watering of it. The field so cultivated, however, belongs to God, not to Apollos or Paul. *Geōrgion* occurs a few times in the LXX meaning a real field; but in Sir 27:6 "the cultivation of a tree (*geōrgion xylou*) is shown by its fruit," and in *Test. Issachar* 5:3–6:2, the field takes on a symbolic meaning. Hence as "God's field," Corinthian Christians manifest God's activity among them, who are the spiritual fruit of His farming.

To this description, Paul adds another, as he mixes his metaphors: for the Corinthian community is also "God's building" (*oikodomē*). So Paul introduces an important second metaphorical argument, which he applies to the community also in 2 Cor 12:19, but which he will exploit in chap. 14.

For the Jewish background of the idea of the community as a plantation and a temple of God, see Jer 1:10d ("to build and to plant"); 18:9; 24:6; Ezek 17:5–8; 36:9–10; Deut 20:5–6; and esp. in QL, where Essenes speak of their community as "the temple of God." That was in part owing to their refusal to share in the Jerusalem Temple cult, which was not being conducted in their view with requisite propriety; hence their community was a substitute for the Temple of Jerusalem: "When these things come to be in Israel, the community council will be founded on fidelity to become an everlasting plantation, a holy house for Israel and a foundation for the holy of holies for Aaron, true witnesses for judgment and chosen by the will (of God) to make expiation for the land and render the wicked their retribution" (1QS 8:4–7; see also 9:3–6). Cf. Gärtner, *The Temple and the Community*, 16–46, 56–60. The notion is likewise used in Philo, *De mut. nom.* 37 §211 (see further Müller, *Gottes Pflanzung*).

10. *According to the grace of God granted me, I laid a foundation as an expert builder.* Besides being a planter, Paul presents himself as *sophos architektōn*, "a skilled master-builder," a phrase he borrows from LXX Isa 3:3 (which is, however, supposed to translate MT *ḥăkam ḥărāšîm*, "one skilled in magic"). His evangelization of Corinth resulted from a vocation to which God's special grace had called him. He is not referring to the grace that made him an apostle (*pace* Senft,

1 *Cor*, 59), but to that which made him the founder of the new church of Roman Corinth (Robertson-Plummer, *1 Cor*, 60). Paul's preaching has laid what he calls *themelion*, "a foundation," for what he achieved thereby was fundamental for the Corinthian church, but he does not call himself the foundation. It is, however, the basis of the authority that he now exercises over the community, and to it he will return in 9:1–2. Paul calls himself *architektōn*, "builder," a title found only here in the NT. For the idea of a "foundation of the community," see 1QS 7:17. Of what sort of building was Paul thinking? It is often thought that it was a "temple," which would link vv. 10–15 to vv. 16–17 (so Peterson), but it is in reality inconsequential.

Paul's awareness of God's grace in his life is often mentioned (15:10; Rom 12:3, 6; 15:15; Gal 2:9). Cf. 2 Pet 3:15. Some MSS (P[46], 81, 1505) omit "of God."

and someone else is building upon it. Paul recognizes this further activity, perhaps alluding to the work that Apollos did there after he had laid the foundation by beginning the evangelization of Roman Corinth (3:6), but Apollos is not mentioned in vv. 10–17. The "someone" (*tis*) may be neither a specific individual nor a specific group. As the master builder of this spiritual temple, which is the Corinthian community, Paul is exercising his authority over the other craftsmen who are working on it, whoever they may be. His activity is similar to that of head contractor mentioned in an Arcadian inscription from Tegea in Arcadia, engaged in the construction and repair of the temple of Athena Alea (see Shanor, "Paul as Master Builder").

According to T. W. Manson and Barrett, however, *allos*, "someone else," would be a covert reference to Cephas. The basis of such speculation is Matt 16:18, Jesus' saying to Peter, "on this rock I will build my church" (*oikodomēsō*, a verb related to *epoikodomei* used here). See Barrett, "Cephas and Corinth," 6–7; similarly Vielhauer ("Paul and the Cephas Party," 132–33), who even thinks that Paul has added this statement about the founding of the Corinthian church as a polemic against Petrine primacy. Yet there is not even a hint of this polemic in this letter, and Paul himself was reluctant to build upon someone else's foundation, as he says in Rom 15:20, in spite of the fact that at the beginning of that letter he announced to those Romans who had already become Christians his eagerness "to preach the gospel also to you who are in Rome" (1:13, 15).

But each one should see to it how he builds on it. Lit. "but let each one see to it." Paul introduces still another instruction; he has not only shifted the metaphor from planting to building, but now speaks about the quality of the superstructure and about the choice of materials with which it is to be constructed. This idea of building the house of God will become very important later in this letter, when Paul will use the word *oikdomē* no longer to mean "building," as v. 9, but in the sense of "edification" or the "building up" of the community as God's house (see 14:3, 5, 12, 26; even with the cog. verb *oikodomeō* in 14:4, 17; see further MacRae, "Building").

11. *For no one can lay a foundation other than the one already laid, which is Jesus Christ.* Before Paul explains in vv. 12–15 what he means about quality, he offers a needed correction to the metaphor of building, as he stresses something

basic. He returns to his fundamental conviction, that the entire structure of the Christian church is based on Jesus Christ, on his person, as in 2 Cor 11:4 (no "other Jesus"), and on his gospel, as in Gal 1:9 (no other gospel). Paul implies that he himself is not the "foundation" and makes this assertion as an answer to the variety of Corinthian groups and the preacher-allegiance that they advocate.

Paul adopts a technical expression used in architecture, *ho keimenos themelios*, found in a third-century B.C. Greek inscription from Lesbos (*Hermes* 90 [1915] 34; see Fridrichsen, "Neutestamentliche Wortforschung").

Paul's statement about Christ as the foundation stands in contrast to what is found in the Deutero-Pauline letter, Eph 2:20, where Christians are said to be members of God's household, "built on the foundation of apostles and prophets, Christ Jesus himself being the cornerstone." It is a different conception of the role of Christ in his church. Here Paul is insisting that the foundation he laid for the Corinthian community was nothing else than Jesus Christ himself and his gospel.

Paul seems to be inconsistent here, because in v. 10 he said that he had laid a foundation as an expert builder, but now he says that the foundation has already been laid ("Jesus Christ") and that no other foundation can be laid. The foundation laid in v. 10, however, was Paul's preaching, which made Jesus Christ known to the Corinthians, and so through his preaching Christ became known as the real fundament of the church. It was God who made Christ such; the ptc. *keimenos* has to be understood as a divine passive (ZBG §236). Paul wants to make sure that no one regards him as the foundation, and Conzelmann rightly notes that "the expression is paradoxical" (*1 Cor*, 75). Cf. 2 Cor 4:5, "What we preach is not ourselves, but Jesus Christ as Lord."

12. *If someone builds on the foundation with gold, silver, precious stones, wood, hay, or straw.* Paul returns to the metaphorical instruction of vv. 9–10. Some MSS (אֵ², C³, D, Ψ, 33, 1739, 1881) add *touton*, "this," to "foundation," but that is almost certainly a secondary reading (Metzger, *TCGNT*, 483). Again, *tis*, "someone," is neither a specific individual, nor a specific group. The materials mentioned for the superstructure are symbolic. Paul does not really think that a superstructure might be built from such materials, even if some of them might be used for adornments. He lists them from the most resistant to flames to the least resistant, meaning that the preaching of subsequent evangelists might be of fine quality (the gospel itself) or of very poor quality (stories and anecdotes of human wisdom), and that in time that difference would become apparent. It is not that Paul "had in mind imaginary buildings" (BDAG, 595) or "apocalyptic buildings" (Conzelmann, *1 Cor*, 76). The latter might suit Rev 21:18, but Paul's use of such materials is merely metaphorical. The possible materials are given in two sets of three. The first threesome, the fire-resistant gold, silver, and precious stones, is found also in 1 Chr 29:2; 2 Chr 32:27; Prov 8:10–11; Dan 11:38 (Theod.); 1QM 5:5–6; 12:2. The order of the materials mentioned differs in some MSS (see *apparatus criticus*). Busto Saiz ("¿Se salvará") regards v. 12 as a protasis of a condition, which is followed by parenthetical remarks in vv. 13–15a, and v. 15b as the real apodosis of the condition.

13. *the work of each builder will become obvious, because the Day will bring it to*

light. Lit. "will make (it) clear." The implied obj. of the verb *dēlōsei* is "the work" (*to ergon*), i.e., the superstructure, the quality of which will be made known. The term *hē hēmera*, "the day," is being used absolutely as the day of divine eschatological judgment, when the Lord will be revealed (1:7–8; 5:5), or as in 1 Thess 5:4, referring to "the day of the Lord" (5:2; cf. 1 Cor 5:5; 2 Cor 1:14; Phil 1:6,10; 2:16, which is usually a day of salvation or condemnation, whereas in Rom 2:5–6, 16 it is a day of judgment, as it is here). "Day of the Lord" is derived from OT usage in Mal 3:19; Isa 13:6, 9; Joel 1:15; 2:1, 11. The scrutiny of that Day will lay bare the quality of the superstructure, i.e., the further evangelization; and consequently the quality of the rivalries dependent on such evangelization. Although Paul seems to be using an apocalyptic description of judgment Day; his main emphasis falls on the note of disclosure. Compare 4:5. The implied exhortation that he is addressing to Corinthian Christians is that, since Jesus Christ is the foundation of the building, those who build on it with materials like gold, silver, and precious stones, will find their work tested by fire, and it will survive; but those who build with wood, hay, or straw will suffer loss of their superstructure, even if they themselves manage to find deliverance and rescue. One can also translate, "because the Day will make clear that it is revealed by fire," i.e., that (the work) is revealed (or possibly "reveals itself"). The object of *dēlōsei* is then the clause introduced by *hoti*.

The word *ergon* in this verse and vv. 14–15 has a special nuance, "building," as in 1 Macc 10:11; Aristophanes, *Birds* 1125; Polybius, *Hist.* 5.3.6; and in Greek inscriptions (Peterson, *"Ergon"*; BDAG, 391). Cf. 1 Cor 9:1; Rom 14:20.

it is revealed by fire. I.e., not the Day, despite the proximity of the noun in the preceding clause, *pace* Fee, Garland, Kistemaker, Kremer, Kuck, Lietzmann, Merklein, Robertson-Plummer, Schrage, J. Weiss, but "the work." The "Day" is not usually said to be revealed. Rather it is "the work of each (builder)," as Bachmann, Collins, Vielhauer, Hollander rightly understand it; compare Sir 11:27b. There is no tautology with v. 13d, as Kuck claims, because even he recognizes that v. 13d has "a different slant" (*Judgment*, 180). This is a generic statement about the action of that Day. Thus fire is recognized as a means of eschatological testing of the quality or purity of materials (cf. Rev 3:18). Judgment by fire is an OT motif (Isa 31:9; 43:2; 66:15–16; Zeph 1:18; Mal 3:2–3, 19; Isa 66:15–16; Joel 3:3; Sir 2:5; Zech 13:9). Gold or silver would stand the test, but the wood, straw, or hay would not. For the joint use of "fire" and "revelation," see 2 Thess 1:7–8 ("at the revelation of the Lord Jesus from heaven with his mighty angels in flaming fire"); 1 Pet 1:7 (see Proctor, "Fire in God's House").

Fire [itself] will test the quality of each one's work. I.e., the apostolic value of various preachers as they build the superstructure. The fire is understood as a testing agent, not a punitive agent. This clause spells out concretely what was implied in v. 13a. A close parallel to Paul's discussion has been found in the *Testament of Abraham* 13:18–20 (*AOT*, 412–13), which tells of an angel, Pyruel, who holds in his hand fire and probes the deeds of human beings with it. "If the fire burns up the deeds of anyone, immediately the angel of judgment takes him and carries him away into the place of sinners . . . ; but if the fire probes the deeds of anyone and does not destroy them, such a one is justified, and the angel of righteousness takes him and carries him up to be saved, in the lot of the righteous. Thus, most righteous Abraham, all things among all human beings will be tested and probed by fire and balance." Even the wording of phrases in vv. 3–15 finds parallels in the Greek text of the *Testament*, which causes a problem: Which is dependent on the other? James (*Testament of Abraham*, 55) claimed that the writing was composed by a second-century Jewish Christian, but Fishburne has contested that claim ("I Corinthians iii. 10–15"), maintaining that Paul depends on a genuinely Jewish writing. More likely, both Paul and the author of the *Testament* have composed independently, because despite the similarities of wording there are substantial differences (e.g., Abel as the judge of human beings after death [in the *Testament*]), as Hollander rightly notes ("The Testing," 99), who cites a more-or-less fixed tradition about fire as a means of testing human beings on the Last Day, also found in Pseudo-Philo, *LAB* 6:16–18; 39:3–4; *Pss. Sol.* 15:4–6; *Sib. Or.* 2:252–55. It is not, however, the fire of Gehenna, *pace* Robertson-Plummer (*1 Cor*, 65); nor is it correct to compare this testing of a "work" (or building) by fire (v. 13) with the judgment of all Christians before Christ's tribunal mentioned in 2 Cor 5:10. Cf. that passage rather with 2 Thess 1:7–8, where "fire" and "Day" again appear together; also 1 Thess 5:2–3. Evans ("How Are the Apostles") maintains that the work of apostolic missionaries will be revealed and tested during the eschatological time of persecution and tribulation that will precede the Lord's parousia.

The pron. *auto*, "itself," is missing in some MSS (P⁴⁶ᵛⁱᵈ, ℵ, D, L, Ψ, 104). The "work" has to be understood as the "building," or more precisely, the superstructure erected on the foundation, as the next verse makes clear; it continues Paul's metaphor for the Corinthian community in its corporate status, which is being compared to a house on fire. Paul is distinguishing two kinds of preachers, those who build with gold or silver (v. 14), i.e., the gospel, and those who build with wood, hay, and straw, i.e., stories and anecdotes of worldly wisdom, who thus allow their superstructure to be destroyed.

14. *If the work that someone has built survives, he will be recompensed.* Or "will survive," because *menei* can be taken either as present or future (depending on the accent, cf. BDF §372.2). If the superstructure remains as it was and withstands the fire, then there will be a good recompense for the builder. So Paul views the result of the testing fire in a positive conditional sentence; in v. 15a, he will set forth its counterpart in a negative clause. The "recompense" (*misthos*) is not salvation, because v. 15 makes it clear that if it is lost, one can still be delivered. Hence it must be something other than eternal salvation. The theme of such recompense resumes what was stated above in v. 8b.

15. *If someone's work is burned up, he will be deprived of recompense, but he himself will be saved, but only as through fire.* This verse is the negative counterpart of v. 14. The verb *zēmiōthēsetai* is problematic: it may mean "he will be punished" (BDAG, 428), but that seems to be in conflict with the next clause, "he himself will be saved." It has been translated as "he will suffer loss" (RSV), but that is already implied in the first clause. The verb has to be understood as a contrast to *misthon lēmpsetai*, "he will be recompensed" (3:14); so it must mean "will be de-

prived of recompense," i.e., the potential reward (so Barrett, *1 Cor*, 89: "will be mulcted of his pay").

The apodosis begins with *autos de*, "but he himself," which stands in contrast to the "recompense" (*misthos*). For Busto Sais ("¿Se Salvará"), this apodosis resumes the protasis of v. 12. In any case, Paul means that the Christian preacher who has done a poor job in using ill-suited building materials will not get an expected reward and will even lose what he sought to build, i.e., the superstructure. Yet he will find salvation, but only like a person who escapes from a burning house by going through a wall of fire (BDAG, 898). Paul is using "a proverbial saying to make the point that only with the skin of one's teeth, and not without great peril, will the one concerned attain to eternal salvation" (Lang, *TDNT*, 6:944). Escape from a burning house is "a symbol for the attainment of salvation," (BDAG, 983). One can agree with Conzelmann that Paul is using a particularly striking notion "of a punishment which does not cancel our eternal salvation," but whether Paul is envisaging "the wider context of the doctrine of justification" (*1 Cor*, 77) is an entirely different matter, one that has no pertinence here, as Kuck recognizes (*Judgment*, 185). Although this passage has nothing to do with "the good works of the individual Christian," it does refer to the "personal salvation" of the Christian preacher and "the validity and effectiveness" of his apostolic ministry, because "all apostolic work, good or bad, is known to God and will be judged by him on the last day" (*pace* Donfried, "Justification," 149). Paul is not using *sōthēsetai* merely in the sense of narrowly escaping from mundane flames, because the verb *sōzō* is always used by Paul in its full soteriological sense (see 1 Thess 2:16; 1 Cor 1:18, 21; 5:5; 7:16 bis; 9:22; 10:33; 15:2; 2 Cor 2:15; Rom 5:9, 10; 8:24; 9:27; 10:9, 13; 11:14, 26; so Barrett, *1 Cor*, 89). If he meant something less here, Paul would have used *ryomai*, as he does in Rom 15:31 (see Klinghardt, "Sünde und Gericht"; Kuck, *Judgment*, 183). Moreover, there is in the text no indication that Paul is thinking of two judgments on that "Day," one of preachers and the other of all other human beings.

From at least the time of Gregory the Great (who lived A.D. 540–604), this verse and all of vv. 11–15 have been cited in the teaching of the Western Church about the "purifying fire" of purgatory (*Dialogues* 4.41.5: *de igne futurae purgationis*, "about a fire of future purification"; SC 265.150). These verses are quoted explicitly in the letter, "Sub catholicae professione," of the First Council of Lyons, A.D. 1254 (DH 838); cf. Council of Florence, A.D. 1439–45 (DH 1304). That teaching, however, freely accommodates not only the metaphorical sense of these Pauline verses, but also other biblical passages, 2 Macc 12:39–45; Matt 12:32, 36, so that Cevetello rightly recognizes that it is "based on tradition, not Sacred Scripture" ("Purgatory," *NCE*, 11:825); and Gnilka has shown that the tradition is neither precise nor constant (*Ist 1. Kor. 3,10–15*).

Verses 14–15 do not speak of a purification or refining by fire, but rather of a testing of constancy and a subsequent deliverance achieved only with great difficulty. They thus give the addressees a criterion for judging preachers who have appeared on the scene in Corinth after Paul and caution them about overestimating their worth.

The later idea of a purifying fire apparently first surfaced with Origen's interpretation of this verse in terms of an eschatological fire that would consume the world (*tou kosmou ekpyrōsin*) as one of purification (*Contra Celsum* 5.15; SC 147.50: *to pyr katharsion*; *Hom. in Exodum* 6.4; SC 321.182: *igni resoluitur et purgatur*). It is found also in Augustine (*Enchiridion* 18.69; CCLat 46:87: *per ignem quendam purgatorium*; also *Enarr. in Ps.* 37 3; CCLat 38.384). See further Anrich, "Clemens und Origenes"; Bietenhard, "Kennt das Neue Testament"; Cipriani, "Insegna"; Michl, "Gerichtsfeuer."

A Jewish tradition, known from later rabbinic writings, attributed to the school of Shammai, is a belief in the existence of an intermediate Gehinnom, one of an atoning and purifying nature. It interpreted Zech 13:9 ("I will put this third [i.e., human beings, neither righteous nor godless, but those whose merit and guilt hung in the balance] into the fire and refine them as one refines silver, and test them as gold is tested. They will call on my name, and I will answer them") and 1 Sam 2:6 (Hannah's prayer, "The Lord kills and brings to life; he brings down to Sheol and raises up") and concluded to such an afterlife purification. See Str-B, 4/2:1036–49. However, Stauffer (*New Testament Theology*, 212 and n. 696) has claimed that this idea could already be found in "pre-Christian apocalyptic" writings, such as *Life of Adam and Eve* §47 [*sic*, but read §48.1–3]; *1 Enoch* 22:10. Cf. Bietenhard, "Kennt das Neue Testament?," 110–20, who has scrutinized radically the alleged pre-Christian Jewish evidence that Stauffer has set forth.

16. *Do you not realize that you are the temple of God and that the Spirit of God dwells in you?* Paul now changes his mode of argument, asking a question that implies that the Corinthian Christians should be familiar already with what he is about to ask. This is the first occurrence in this letter of a frequently-used expression, *ouk oidate hoti*, "Do you not realize that," as a means of introducing an important rhetorical question; see 5:6; 6:2, 3, 9, 15, 16, 19; 9:13, 24; also Rom 6:16. Cf. *thelō de hymas eidenai*, "I want you to realize," 1 Cor 11:3.

This double question, formulated in diatribe-like style, is the conclusion of Paul's metaphorical discussion of the evangelized community as a building. At the end of his first comparison of evangelization with planting and watering, he told the Corinthian Christian community that it was "God's field" (3:9); now he concludes his second comparison of evangelization with a building, telling them that it is "God's temple" (*naos theou*). The phrase, "God's temple," is an OT term found in Dan 5:3 (Theodotion) and Jdt 4:2 for the actual Temple in Jerusalem, but Paul uses it now in a metaphorical sense, which does not imply any antagonism for the Jerusalem Temple. The Christian congregation is no longer just a building belonging to God (3:9), but is God's very dwelling place, "the temple of God," the place where God's presence with Christians is to be found. It is called by this title also in 3:17; 2 Cor 6:16 (quoting Lev 26:11); cf. Eph 2:21. What Paul means by it is explained in the second part of the question: "The Spirit of God dwells in you," i.e., in their corporate being. On Spirit of God, see NOTE on 2:4. Paul speaks of the indwelling Spirit as the animating presence of God in the midst of the Christian community, making it in a special sense the place where God is present to Christians in their corporate being. Behind Paul's cultic imagery is the

OT idea of one place, Jerusalem, where Israel was to worship Yahweh (2 Kgs 23:4-25 [Josiah's reform]), because it was the symbol of the unity of Israel as one people of God; see also Wis 9:8, 17. Now the notion of God's temple again emphasizes the oneness of the Christian community, which can therefore tolerate no division or faction, no matter how widely it is spread out in area. The image is not limited to community leaders, but refers to all Christians (see MacRae, "Building").

In Rom 8:9, Paul asserts the same thing about the indwelling Spirit, but there it refers to Christians as individuals, which will appear again in 1 Cor 6:19. Here, however, the corporate idea of the indwelling is all-important, and it excludes any "individualistic, pietistic sense," as Draper has rightly noted ("Tip of an Ice-Berg," 57, 61). *Pace* Ford ("You Are God's 'Sukkah' "), Paul is not speaking about the *sukkāh*, "booth," or the feast of Tabernacles; he writes about *naos theou*, not *skēnē* (the word used in the LXX to translate *sukkāh*, Neh 8:14).

17. *If anyone destroys God's temple, God will destroy him.* This is a "sentence of holy law," as Käsemann has termed it ("Sentences," 66). Its legal style is obvious, as it serves as a parenetic warning, expressed in chiastic formulation. See Gen 9:6 for a parallel: "Whoever sheds the blood of a human being, by a human being shall his blood be shed." The future tense of the apodosis introduces the eschatological consideration, "divine action on the Last Day" (ibid., 67). Paul is warning everyone of the consequences that would flow from all activity that would damage the oneness of the community. In the present context, the "destruction of the temple" would mean the undermining of the Corinthian community by perverse or poor preaching and by rivalries. Such undermining would invoke the *ius talionis*, the tit-for-tat or appropriate reaction of God, because rivalries can destroy any political body (Mitchell, *Paul*, 103). Cf. Aeschylus, *Choephori* 312-13: *Anti de plēgēs phonias phonian plēgēn tinetō*, "For a murderous blow, let him pay a murderous blow." Again, the destruction of the spiritual temple of the Corinthian community is similar to the damage done to the physical temple of Athena Alea in the Arcadian inscription of Tegea mentioned above. Paul is concerned that none of the subcontractors damage the metaphorical temple, the foundation of which he himself has laid. Even though Paul speaks generically of "anyone" (*tis*), he is thinking specifically of preachers who have succeeded him in Corinth.

For the temple of God, which you are, is sacred. Paul predicates of the Corinthian community the adj. *hagios*, a description often used in the OT to convey the character of persons or objects set apart for or dedicated to the service of God in the Jerusalem Temple. In fact, *hagion* is sometimes predicated of the Temple (Ps 11:4; 65:5; 79:1) and *to hagion* is used as the name for "the temple" itself (LXX Num 3:38; Ezek 45:18). What was true of the sanctity of the Jerusalem Temple must be true also of the Corinthian community. Whoever violates the community, violates what pertains to God, which is sacrilege. The Corinthian community is also "sacred," because the Spirit of God dwells within it (3:16). As "the temple of God," its sacred character must be respected.

The relative clause is introduced not by a masc. sing. rel. pron., which one would expect, agreeing with the noun *naos*, but rather by the masc. plur. compound rel. pron. *hoitines*, which has been attracted to the plur. number of *este hymeis*, "which you are." Many though they are as individuals, they form one unit as the "temple of God."

BIBLIOGRAPHY (See also Bibliography on 1:10–4:21, pp. 149–51)

Anrich, G., "Clemens und Origenes als Begründer der Lehre vom Fegfeuer," *Theologische Abhandlungen: Eine Festgabe . . . für Heinrich Julius Holtzmann dargebracht* (ed. W. Nowack et al.; Tübingen/Leipzig: Mohr, 1902) 95–120.

Bietenhard, H., "Kennt das Neue Testament die Vorstellung vom Fegefeuer?" *TZ* 3 (1947) 101–22.

Busto Saiz, J. R., "¿Se salvará como atravesando fuego? 1 Cor 3,15b reconsiderado," *EstEcl* 68 (1993) 333–38.

Byrne, B., "Ministry and Maturity in 1 Corinthians 3," *ABR* 35 (1987) 83–87.

Cevetello, J. F. X., "Purgatory: In the Bible," *NCE* 11:824–25.

Cipriani, S., "Insegna *1 Cor.*, 3,10–15 la dottrina del Purgatorio?" *RivB* 7 (1959) 25–43.

Derrett, J. D. M., "Paul as Master-builder," *EvQ* 69 (1997) 129–37.

Dittberner, A., " 'Who Is Apollos and Who Is Paul?—I Cor. 3:5," *TBT* 71 (1974) 1549–52.

Donfried, K. P., "Justification and Last Judgment in Paul," *ZNW* 67 (1976) 90–110; in abridged form: *Int* 30 (1976) 140–52.

Draper, J. A., "The Tip of an Ice-Berg: The Temple of the Holy Spirit," *JTSA* 59 (1987) 57–65.

Evans, C. A., "How Are the Apostles Judged? A Note on 1 Corinthians 3:10–15," *JETS* 27 (1984) 149–50.

Fishburne, C. W., "I Corinthians iii. 10–15 and the Testament of Abraham," *NTS* 17 (1970–71) 109–15.

Ford, J. M., "You Are God's 'Sukkah' (I Cor. iii. 10–11)," *NTS* 21 (1974–75) 139–42.

Fridrichsen, A., "Neutestamentliche Wortforschung: Themelios, 1. Kor. 3,11," *TZ* 2 (1946) 316–17.

Furnish, V. P., " 'Fellow Workers in God's Service,' " *JBL* 80 (1961) 364–70.

Gärtner, B., *The Temple and the Community in Qumran and the New Testament: A Comparative Study in the Temple Symbolism of the Qumran Texts and the New Testament* (SNTSMS 1; Cambridge: Cambridge University, 1965).

Gnilka, J., *Ist I Kor 3,10–15 ein Schriftzeugnis für das Fegefeuer? Eine exegetisch-historische Untersuchung* (Düsseldorf: Zentral-Verlag für Dissertationen Triltsch, 1955).

Harnack, A. von, "*Kopos (kopian, hoi kopiōntes)* im frühchristlichen Sprachgebrauch," *ZNW* 27 (1928) 1–10.

Hogeterp, A. L. A., "Paul's Judaism Reconsidered: The Issue of Cultic Imagery in the Corinthian Correspondence," *ETL* 81 (2005) 89–108.

Hollander, H. W., "Revelation by Fire: 1 Corinthians 3.13," *BT* 44/2 (1993) 242–44.

——, "The Testing by Fire of the Builders' Works: 1 Corinthians 3.10–15," *NTS* 40 (1994) 89–104.

James, M. R., *The Testament of Abraham: The Greek Text Now First Edited with an Introduction and Notes* (Texts and Studies II/2; Cambridge: Cambridge University Press, 1892).

Käsemann, E., "Ministry and Community in the New Testament," *Essays*, 63–134.

——, "Sentences of Holy Law in the New Testament," *New Testament Questions*, 66–81.

Klinghardt, M., "Sünde und Gericht von Christen bei Paulus," *ZNW* 88 (1997) 56–80.

Kuck, D. W., *Judgment and Community Conflict: Paul's Use of Apocalyptic Judgment Language in 1 Corinthians 3:5–4:5* (NovTSup 66; Leiden: Brill, 1992).

———, "Paul and Pastoral Ambition: A Reflection on 1 Corinthians 3—4," *CurTM* 19 (1992) 174–83.

Kuist, H. T., "The Labors of the Christian Ministry," *Biblical Review* 16 (1931) 245–49.

Leithart, P. J., "Synagogue or Temple? Models for the Christian Worship," *WTJ* 64 (2002) 119–33.

MacRae, G. W., "Building the House of the Lord," *AER* 140 (1959) 361–76.

Michl, J., "Gerichtsfeuer und Purgatorium zu 1 Kor 3,12–15," *SPCIC*, 1:395–401.

Müller, C. G., *Gottes Pflanzung—Gottes Bau—Gottes Tempel: Die metaphorische Dimension paulinischer Gemeindetheologie in 1 Kor 3,5–17* (Fuldaer Studien 5; Frankfurt am M.: Knecht, 1995).

Pesch, W., "Der Sonderlohn für die Verkündiger des Evangeliums (1 Kor 3,8. 14f. und Parallelen)," *Neutestamentliche Aufsätze: Festschrift für Prof. Josef Schmid . . .* (ed. J. Blinzler et al.; Regensburg: Pustet, 1963) 199–206.

Peterson, E., "*Ergon* in der Bedeutung 'Bau' bei Paulus," *Bib* 22 (1941) 439–41.

Proctor, J., "Fire in God's House: Influence of Malachi 3 in the NT," *JETS* 36 (1993) 9–14.

Shanor, J., "Paul as Master Builder: Construction Terms in First Corinthians," *NTS* 34 (1988) 461–71.

Stauffer, E., *New Testament Theology* (London: SCM, 1955) 210–13.

Vadakkedom, J., " 'According to the Grace Given to Me' (1 Cor 3,10): St. Paul's Understanding of Grace," *BiBh* 28 (2002) 374–90.

Vielhauer, P., *Oikodome: Das Bild vom Bau in der christlichen Literatur vom Neuen Testament bis Clemens Alexandrinus* (ThB 65; ed. G. Klein; Karlsruh-Durlach: Tron, 1940).

7   e. *Admonition about Preachers and Wisdom (3:18–23)*

3:18 Let no one deceive himself. If someone among you thinks that he is wise in this age, let him become a fool, in order to become wise. 19 For the wisdom of this world is folly in God's sight. As it stands written, *"He catches the wise in their craftiness."* 20 And again, *"The Lord knows the thoughts of the wise, that they are futile."* 21 Consequently, no one should boast about human beings. For all things belong to you, 22 whether it be Paul or Apollos or Cephas, or the world, or life or death, or the present or the future—all belongs to you, 23 and you belong to Christ, and Christ to God.

COMMENT

The concluding verses of chap. 3 are uncomplicated and hortatory in character, especially vv. 18, 21. They exhort the Christians of Roman Corinth to think correctly about those who have been evangelizing them, as Paul returns to the "wisdom/folly theme" of 1:18–25. Allegiance to one preacher or another is not the mark of right-thinking Christians, especially if that allegiance causes rivalry and dissension among them. It may seem like "wisdom" in this world, but it is not rightly oriented in God's sight. Paul concludes that "the wisdom of this world is folly in God's sight," echoing what he said in 1:18–20. For this reason he seeks to discourage the Corinthians from boasting over human beings, or over anything of this world, as he alludes to 1:12–13. The right order of their existence is to see themselves in their proper relation to Christ and God.

This admonition amounts to a critique of boasting, because it is all too human and relies too much on human achievement, whereas real Christian ministry must be totally theocentric and serve the glory of God: *soli Deo gloria!* Note also the rhetorical *inclusio* in v. 22, referring to 3:4–5; and how the gen. of 1:12 and 3:4 are reversed in vv. 21 and 23.

The exhortation that Paul includes now addresses all Christians about the dangers of self-deception and trusting in one's own thinking and judging, which is misleading as a form of human wisdom. Paul will continue this mode of argumentation in 4:1–5.

NOTES

3:18. *Let no one deceive himself.* Paul begins his exhortation with a 3d pers. sing. negative impv., which is a warning about self-deceit, and this rebuke finds a parallel in 6:9; 15:33. Paul is addressing this warning to all members of the Corinthian community, and not just to those preaching to them. He considers such self-deception dangerous and disruptive of God's people, because it is not a deception that comes from without, as in Eph 5:6, whence probably comes the added phrase in ms D, *kenois logois,* "with empty words," i.e., meaningless claims. The added phrase is also found in LXX Exod 5:9; Deut 32:47 (sing.); as well as in Greek literature (Plato, *Laches* 196B; Josephus, *Ag.Ap.* 2.31 §225; *Ant.* 13.4.3 §89).

If someone among you thinks that he is wise in this age, let him become a fool, in order to become wise. Lit. "imagines that he is wise." Paul repeats what he said at the beginning of his discussion about wisdom among human beings in 1:20, where he spoke of "the wisdom of the world" made foolish by God. His repetition is a mere literary variant of the earlier formulation. Cf. 2:6–8. For Paul, self-deception is the mark of those who imagine that they are wise with the wisdom of this age; so he prefers that Christians be accounted fools, when it comes to the way people normally judge, seeing "the message of the cross" as sheer folly (1:18). Once Christians become foolish in this sense, they can become wise in God's sight. For there is no room in the sight of God for wisdom that amounts to self-assertion or self-deception; one must become foolish by acknowledging the folly of the cross. N-A[27] has rightly punctuated this verse, with a comma after *en tō aiōni toutō,* "in this age," and not after *en hymin,* "among you," but some commentators prefer the latter. Theoretically, *en tō aiōni toutō* could also be understood with the following words, "let him become a fool in this age, in order to. . . ." (so Schrage, *1 Cor,* 1:310, 312). That phrase, however, does not usually precede the word(s) that it modifies (Lindemann, *1 Cor,* 91; similarly Robertson-Plummer, *1 Cor,* 70).

In using the indef. *tis*, "someone," Paul is scarcely thinking of Apollos or Cephas. It refers to an unnamed Corinthian Christian. Recall the indef. use of *sophos* in 1:20.

19. *For the wisdom of this world is folly in God's sight.* Lit. "before God," as in Rom 2:13. Paul reformulates the paradox of 1:18, where he spoke of "the message of the cross" as "foolishness to those who are perishing." What was called there "the wisdom of this age" has now become "the wisdom of this world," as in 1:20.

As it stands written. See Note on 1:19.

He catches the wise in their craftiness. These words, *ho drassomenos tous sophous en tē panourgiā autōn*, seem to be a quotation of LXX Job 5:13, which describes God as *ho katalambanōn sophous en tē phronēsei*, "the one overtaking the wise in their intelligence." The preceding verse 5:12, however, speaks of the "plans of the crafty" (*panourgōn*), which immediately gives "intelligence" a pejorative connotation. Paul's form simplifies the citation, using the verb, *drassomai*, "grasp, grip," which does not appear elsewhere in his writings. It may come from a Greek translation of the Book of Job different from the LXX (see Cerfaux, "Vestiges"). In the Book of Job, the words form part of Eliphaz's first discourse, in which he argues that hope for mortals lies in God's greatness, when He confounds the crafty designs of human beings. Paul cites the words in order to upset the underhanded conduct of some Corinthian Christians and to turn human wisdom into its opposite. Cf. 1:20d, and recall the pertinence of 2:8.

20. *And again.* The words *kai palin* often introduce a second (or third) quotation of Scripture: Rom 15:10–12; Heb 1:5; 2:13; 4:5; 10:30; *1 Clem.* 10.4; 15.3–4. They are found also in secular Greek writers: Diodorus Siculus, *Bibl. hist.* 37.30.2 (quoting poetry); 1.96.6; Diogenes Laertius, *Vitae* 2.18; 3.16; Plutarch, *Moralia* 361a.

The Lord knows the thoughts of the wise, that they are futile. These words are taken from Ps 94:11, which in the LXX reads *tōn anthrōpōn*, "of human beings," a term that is also read in some MSS of this letter (33, 630, 1506). That, however, is clearly a copyist's harmonization of the Pauline text with the LXX. Paul has changed that word to *sophōn*, "the wise," which better suits his argument. In any case, the psalmist's words were contrasting the plans of human beings with those of God; but they correspond to Paul's judgment about human reasoning. Cf. Rom 1:21. *Kyrios* probably is to be understood as "God," as in the psalm, and not the risen Christ, because of v. 19.

21. *Consequently, no one should boast about human beings.* Lit. "let no one boast." This is Paul's hortatory answer to the problem of rival preachers in Roman Corinth. Christians should not be conceited in their wisdom or vaunt their allegiance to any preacher who is merely human. Boasting should not be the mark of any Christian, because it robs God of due glory. Recall 1:29–31, where Paul ended by summarizing Jer 9:22–23, "Let the one who would boast boast of the Lord." See Rom 3:27.

For all things belong to you. The following verse explains "all things," and the "you" has to be taken in the corporate sense of the entire Corinthian community. This conclusion turns the so-called slogans on their head: instead of saying, "I belong to Paul," or "I belong to Cephas," Paul asserts, "all things (including Paul, Apollos, and Cephas) belong to you."

Conzelmann (1 Cor, 80), Collins (1 Cor, 66), Lindemann (1 Cor, 93) maintain that Paul has borrowed "a Stoic maxim," that "all things belong to the wise man," i.e., he is lord over all that comes to him from without (see Diogenes Laertius, Vitae 6.37: panta ara esti tōn sophōn, "for all things belong to the sage"; 7.125.8; Seneca, De Beneficiis 7.2.5: omnia illius [i.e., sapientis] sunt, "all are his [i.e,, the sage's]"; Ep. Mor. 109.1: dicimus plenum omni bono esse sapientem, "we say that the sage is full of everything good"; Cicero, De finibus 3.22.75: recte eius [i.e., sapientis] omnia dicentur, "rightly all will be said to belong to him [i.e., the sage]"). If so, then Paul not only adopts the maxim, but makes it a principle for Christian faith and for the acceptance of "the message of the cross," which is otherwise folly in ordinary human eyes. For Paul, "all things" in this world belong to the Christian, who as such becomes rich and a king (4:8) and even judges the world (6:2); yet he understands the maxim also according to his Jewish background (see Gen 1:26–28; Ps 8:6–8), as Kremer rightly notes (1 Cor, 80).

22. whether it be Paul or Apollos or Cephas, or the world, or life or death, or the present or the future. Lit. "or things at hand or things coming to be," expressed by two ptcs., eite enestōta eite mellonta. Paul indulges in rhetoric in order to explain "all things" of v. 21; eight elements are detailed, each separated by eite, "whether . . . or," a threesome (the evangelists Paul, Apollos, Cephas, through whom Corinthians first became believers [3:5]), another threesome (world, life, death), and a twosome (present, future), with the principle repeated.

Paul mentions again the evangelists of Corinth, who first were named in 1:12 in the same order (see NOTE there). He implies that it is foolishness and self-deception to pledge allegiance to one or other such preacher. The addition of Cephas is striking, because the discussion from 3:1 on has been about Paul and Apollos. Barrett maintains that, "Peter was in fact a more dangerous potential cause of schism in Corinth than either Paul or Apollos" ("Cephas and Corinth," 5).

To the three evangelists, Paul adds mythical superhuman elements, spatial, vital, and temporal, almost personifying them: the kosmos, "the world" (actually the whole ordered universe, in which human beings live, as in 6:2), physical "life" (to which human beings cling), and "death" (which they dread); finally "the present" (with its earthly tensions and pressures) and "the future" (with its earthly anxieties). Cf. Rom 8:38–39; 14:8, where Paul spells out some of these same existential elements in greater detail. In Gal 1:4, Paul acknowledges that Christ Jesus gave himself for our sins in order to deliver us "from the present evil age," using the same perf. ptc. enestōtos, lit. "that is at hand." On death, see 15:26. Pace Senft, there is no advantage in understanding life, death, present, and future as a totality explaining kosmos, "world," because that leaves kosmos all alone.

all belongs to you. I.e., as Christians. This is the principle of v. 21b now repeated.

23. you belong to Christ, and Christ to God. Lit. "you (are) of Christ, and Christ (is) of God." Cf. Rom 14:8; Gal 3:29. Even though all things belong to Christians, they do not own themselves, because they belong to Christ and even bear the

name of Christ, i.e., *Christianoi* (see Acts 11:26d; cf. *Acts*, 477–78). The pertinence of the Corinthian community to Christ does not stop with him, because of
Christ's relation to God the Father as His Son. God has called Corinthian Christians "into companionship with his son, Jesus Christ our Lord" (1:9), and he it is
who has revealed and implemented his Father's designs for them, as Rom 8:31
makes clear. This relationship will be expressed in yet another way in 11:3; 15:28;
Phil 2:9–11 (see Thüsing, *Per Christum*, 10–20).

Related to this notion of belonging to Christ is the title that Paul sometimes
uses of himself, *doulos Christou Iēsou*, "slave of Christ Jesus" (Rom 1:1; Gal 1:10;
Phil 1:1), which stresses his total submission and commitment to Christ, who is
his *kyrios*, "master," but also his "Lord" (see *Romans*, 231). Such allegiance to the
crucified Christ and his lordship should replace allegiance to rival preachers, because now he is recognized as "the power of God and the wisdom of God" (1:24),
and this assertion fittingly concludes Paul's monitory exhortation.

BIBLIOGRAPHY (See also Bibliography on 1:10–4:21, pp. 149–51)

Cerfaux, L., "Vestiges d'un florilège dans I Cor., i,18–iii,23?" *RHE* 27 (1931) 521–34; repr.
    in *Recueil Lucien Cerfaux* (BETL 6–7; Gembloux: Duculot, 1954), 2:319–32.
Giavini, G., " 'Tutto è vostro, voi siete di Cristo!': I peccati del cristiano in I Corinti,"
    ScCatt 106 (1978) 266–89.
Thüsing, W., *Per Christum in Deum: Studien zum Verhältnis von Christozentrik und
    Theozentrik in den paulinischen Hauptbriefen* (NTAbh n.s. 1; 2d ed.; Münster in
    W.: Aschendorff, 1969).

8   f. *Think of Paul and Apollos as Lowly Servants of Christ (4:1–21)*

4:1 One should think of us in this way: as servants of Christ and stewards of God's
mysteries. 2 In this case, moreover, it is required of stewards that they be found
trustworthy. 3 But for me it matters little that I be judged by you or by any human
court. I do not even judge myself. 4 I am not conscious of anything against me, but
in this I do not stand vindicated; the one who judges me is the Lord. 5 So do not
judge anything before the proper time, before the Lord comes who will bring to
light what is hidden in darkness and will expose the motives of our hearts. At that
time, the commendation of each one will come from God. 6 Now, brothers, I have
transferred this to myself and Apollos for your sake, that you may learn from us not
(to go) beyond what is written, that none of you may become arrogant, siding with
one over against another. 7 For who concedes you any distinction? What do you
have that you did not receive? If then you did really receive it, why are you boasting as though you did not? 8 You have already been sated! You have become rich
already! Without us, you have become kings! Would that you had become kings
so that we too might be kings with you! 9 For it seems to me that God has depicted

us, the apostles, as last of all, as people sentenced to death, because we have become a spectacle to the world, both to angels and human beings. [10]We are fools for Christ, but you are wise in Christ; we are weak, but you are strong; you are honored, but we are despised. [11]Up to this very hour we go hungry and thirsty; we are in rags; we are mistreated; we are homeless. [12]We toil, working with our own hands. When reviled, we bless; when persecuted, we put up with it. [13]When slandered, we answer kindly. We have become, and are even now, like the rubbish of the world, the scum of the earth.

[14]I am writing this not to make you ashamed, but to admonish you as my beloved children. [15]Even if you have ten thousand guides in Christ, you do not have many fathers, for in Christ Jesus I became your father through the gospel. [16]Therefore, I urge you, be imitators of me. [17]For this reason I am sending to you Timothy, who is my dear and faithful child in the Lord; he will remind you about my ways in Christ [Jesus], just as I teach them everywhere in every church. [18]Some have become arrogant pretending that I am not coming to you. [19]I shall come to you very soon, if the Lord wills, and I shall ascertain not the talk of these arrogant people, but their power. [20]For the kingdom of God is not a matter of talk, but of power. [21]What do you prefer? Shall I come to you with a stick or with love and a gentle spirit?

COMMENT

Paul now concludes his discussion of wisdom and its bearing on allegiance to rival preachers in the Corinthian community by trying to instruct it further in the proper way to regard preachers like Apollos and himself who have labored in it. This concluding admonition is closely linked to 3:21–22, where Paul insisted that "all things belong to you," even Paul, Apollos, or Cephas, and even more closely to 3:1–17, because he will continue to contrast Apollos and himself with Corinthian Christians in order to explain their relationship in even more detail.

First, Paul describes anew his role and that of the other preachers. They are not only "servants" (3:5) or "God's fellow-workers" (3:9), but above all "servants of Christ and stewards of God's mysteries" (4:1). This leads Paul to recall the prime quality expected of such servants and stewards, viz., trustworthiness and fidelity. Since allegiance to one preacher implicitly involves judgment of other preachers, Paul makes it clear that he is not concerned about how human beings judge him. The only thing that matters is the Lord's eschatological judgment, which will follow, when the Lord comes (4:3–5). Then each will earn God's commendation. Moreover, they may be "apostles" (4:9), but they are at the end of the list, "last of all," and like "people sentenced to death." Furthermore, they have become "fools for Christ" (4:10), even "the rubbish of the world, the scum of the earth" (4:13). In spite of all this, Paul insists that he is a "father" to the Corinthian community, because he has begotten them "through the gospel" (4:15). So runs the description that Paul gives of himself in this pericope. In effect, he is formulating finally his relationship with the Corinthian church, with which his dealings have become somewhat stormy.

Second, Paul proceeds to contrast the new description of preachers with the Corinthian community. He insists that, though community members may be priding themselves over differing achievements, any distinctions they may have all come from what they have received. Consequently, there can be no arrogant boasting and no expression of allegiance to one preacher or another among them. Paul's rhetoric indulges in a lavish description of the gifts the Corinthians have received: they are sated, rich, and even "kings," but he and his fellow preachers are of the lowest rank. Corinthian Christians may have become wise, strong, and honored, but Paul and the preachers have become fools, weak, and despised. Verses 7–13 are full of irony, as Paul recalls his toil, deprivation, and suffering as a preacher among them.

Third, Paul insists that he is not writing all this to shame the Christians of Corinth, who are indeed his "beloved children" (4:14). Rather, his admonition is a commentary on all that he has been saying, and it seeks only to make them realize what really must shape the relationship between them and him. They must learn to "imitate" him (4:16) and his "ways in Christ Jesus" (4:17c).

Fourth, Paul concludes by telling the Christians of Corinth that they will learn more about this relationship from Timothy, whom he is sending to them (4:17a). He ends his concluding remarks by noting that some of them have been thinking that they could act arrogantly when he was not around. So Paul promises to come soon; but the question is whether they want him to come with a stick to curb such arrogance, or with love and a gentle spirit toward those who are his children.

Some commentators separate vv. 1–5 from the rest of chap. 4. For Robertson-Plummer, Garland, and a few others, 3:18–23 + 4:1–5 belong together. Schrage (*1 Cor*, 1:319) considers 4:1–5 to be a refutation (similarly Kremer, *1 Cor*, 82), but for Merklein (*1 Cor*, 1:289) 4:1–5 is a transitional paragraph that introduces a refutation in 4:6–13. Such attempts, however, isolate vv. 1–5 from the following vv. 6–21, or at least from vv. 6–16, and that is eventually futile. For in vv. 1–16, Paul sees no need to defend himself or to refute any opposite claims; he is rather trying to get the Christians of Corinth to think correctly about himself and other preachers such as Apollos. In doing so, he makes some passing remarks that may sound like self-defense (vv. 3–4), but they are really intended to get Corinthian Christians to understand the real role of Apollos and himself as "servants of Christ and stewards of God's mysteries." The stern tone that he adopts in vv. 19–21 reveals the seriousness of the admonition that he is addressing in this chapter.

This passage may well have been the end of the letter that Paul originally intended to write to the Corinthians, commenting on the reports that have come to him from "some of Chloe's people" (1:11). In it he has brought his discussion of wisdom and the rivalries of preacher-allegiance to a close. The next two chapters will deal with matters indirectly related to this first section, and after them eight further chapters will deal with entirely different affairs, some as answers to questions that Corinthian Christians have asked in a letter sent to Paul (7:1). The sequence of topics may be guided by the sequence of reports that have reached Paul, which caused him to expand what he had originally planned to write.

In 4:16, Paul again introduces his exhortation with *parakalō oun hymas*, which corresponds to that of 1:10, with which he opened the apologetic first section of the letter (see COMMENT there).

In this section of his letter, Paul insists that he and other preachers have no fear of human judgment or criticism, but want only to be found trustworthy in God's sight. This is an attitude that all Christians have to cultivate, for it will curb any tendency to arrogance and boasting. Moreover, it will lead most of them to an awareness that what they have or are is entirely a gift of God, whether they be rich, honored, or otherwise well-off. He may have become their father in Christ, having founded the church in Corinth, but he is aware that for many he is despised and considered at the bottom of the heap, even though this status has not been without divine sanction. So he has become a model for all, and he wants all who read his letter to realize that he has not written in order to shame his addressees. He wants all his readers to become imitators of him and to recall his "ways in Christ Jesus."

NOTES

4:1. *One should think of us in this way.* Lit. "let a human being so think of us," i.e., of Paul, Apollos, and Cephas, just mentioned in 3:22; but it could just as well apply to all evangelists. Paul wants Corinthian Christians to judge those who preach to them as objectively as possible, and not by the subjective standards of party allegiance. *Houtōs*, "in this way," refers not to what has been said at the end of chap. 3 (*pace* Lindemann, *1 Cor*, 95), but to what follows (BDAG, 742 §2).

as servants of Christ and stewards of God's mysteries. Although Paul repeats the idea expressed in 3:5, "servants through whom you came to believe," where he used the term *diakonoi*, now he uses *hypēretai Christou*, lit. "Christ's assistants," or "helpers." He thus insists on the role of preachers as secondary; they render service to Christ, who plays the principal role. *Hypēretēs* is used by Josephus along with *hiereus* for Temple ministers: *pas men hiereus pas d'hypēretēs tou theou*, "every priest and every minister of God" (*J.W.* 2.15.4 §321). Byron ("Slave of Christ") would translate it "willing servant."

They are also "stewards of God's mysteries." *Oikonomos* (from *oikos*, "house," and *nemō*, "distribute, manage, administer") was the title given to a "steward" or "manager," a slave or other person who administered with responsibility the property or estate of a householder (as in Luke 12:42; 16:1, 3, 8). It was widely used, however, as a term for a business agent, city treasurer (cf. Rom 16:23), or political administrator; and even as a title for a treasurer in private societies or guilds. It turns up in pre-Christian Greek texts also with a religious connotation, e.g., in the cult of Sarapis and in Hermes-Trismegistos (see *New Docs*, 4:160–61; *TLNT*, 2:568–75; Reumann, " 'Stewards of God,' " 345–48).

Paul applies the term to preachers of the Christian gospel. As such, they dispense the secret counsels of God announced in that gospel and the treasures of His teaching (see BDAG, 662); "the truths which the stewards are commissioned to teach" (Robertson-Plummer, *1 Cor*, 75). Cf. Titus 1:7; 1 Pet 4:10. On "mysteries," see NOTE on 2:1.

2. *In this case, moreover, it is required of stewards that they be found trustworthy.*

Lit. "that one be found trustworthy," i.e., that individuals be worthy of the trust that has been put in them; it is not merely a matter of wisdom or eloquence, but rather of fidelity. The verb *zēteitai* is a divine passive, "required" by God (ZBG §236). The Lucan Jesus also speaks of a trustworthy manager (Luke 12:42), and Sir 44:20 speaks of Abraham found to be *pistos*. The best MSS (P⁴⁶, ℵ, A, B, C, D*, F, G, P, Ψ, 33) read *hōde loipon*, "in this connection, moreover," but a few (D², 1739, 1881) have the neut. rel. pron. *ho de*, "which (is required)." For the introductory conj. *hōde*, see BDF §451.6; Thrall, *Greek Particles*, 26–27.

3. *But for me it matters very little that I be judged by you or by any human court.* Lit. "by a human day," where *hēmera* is being used in the sense of a day of judgment, fixed by some human judge. Although Lindemann (*1 Cor*, 97) says that this use of *hēmera* is not a technical term, but fashioned by Paul from *hē hēmera tou kyriou*, the use of *hēmera* in the sense of "judgment" is attested extrabiblically on a Greek amulet inscription; see Bonner who thinks that "the writer of the amulet was familiar with the passage in Paul's letter" ("Reminiscence," 165–68). In any case, this comment is Paul's reply to the Corinthian Christians who have fostered the rivalries, for allegiance to Apollos or Cephas implies that some of them have been passing judgment on Paul. Judgment by them or by any human being means little to Paul, because he knows that his faithfulness will be judged by the one who committed the task to him, and the spiritual human being is "subject to no one's scrutiny" (2:15). God can demand trustworthiness of him as a steward of His mysteries, but he fears no human judge.

I do not even judge myself. I.e., since I am a human being, my self-judgment is likewise of little value.

4. *I am not conscious of anything against me.* Paul uses a clause found in LXX Job 27:6, *ou gar synoida emautō atopa praxas*, "I am not conscious of having done outlandish things," as Job comments with irony on his lot in God's judgment. In using the words of Job, Paul is insisting on his clear conscience, as he does again in 2 Cor 7:2 ("wronged no one, destroyed no one, took advantage of no one"); Phil 3:6b ("as to uprightness under the law, blameless").

How Paul can say this has always been puzzling in light of what he says in Gal 1:13 about having persecuted "the church of God violently and sought to destroy it"; similarly 1 Cor 15:9. Cf. 1 Tim 1:13; Acts 8:3. However, one has to respect the context of the statement that Paul makes in this verse. He is speaking against the background of the rivalries and the implied critical judgments made of him by those who side with others. Certainly, in this regard he can stress that he is not aware of any failing, and his conscience is clear; he has not sought for allegiance to himself as a preacher.

but in this I do not stand vindicated. Lit. "I have not been justified," i.e., in God's sight. Paul's justification in this matter does not depend on human judgment. He is not using the verb *dikaioō* in the sense of "justification of the sinner" (*pace* Melanchthon, Maurer, *TDNT*, 7:916; Barrett, *1 Cor*, 102; Kistemaker [*1 Cor*, 131), because it is not a matter of *pistis*, "faith." His concern is rather integrity or honesty, and it is a verdict about workmanship or ministry, as noted by Merklein, *1 Cor*, 1:295; Robertson-Plummer, *1 Cor*, 77; Lindemann, *1 Cor*, 98.

the one who judges me is the Lord. As Paul rejects all human judgment of himself and his missionary role, he acknowledges that the Lord will judge him (the pres. tense has future connotation, as v. 5b makes clear). Here *kyrios* refers to the risen Christ at his parousia.

5. *So do not judge anything before the proper time.* Paul draws the conclusion that he wants his readers to understand. The prep. phrase uses *kairos*, "decisive time." What the *kairos* is the next clause reveals. Cf. the "Q" saying of Jesus in Luke 6:37; Matt 7:1.

before the Lord comes who will bring to light what is hidden in darkness and expose the motives of our hearts. Paul is thinking of the role of the risen Christ who at his parousia (1 Thess 4:16) will judge human actions, as he also emphasizes in 2 Cor 5:10: "We must all appear before the tribunal of Christ in order that each may receive good or evil, according to what he has done in the body." Similarly Rom 2:16. Paul will repeat his teaching about the disclosure of secrets of human hearts in 14:5. Cf. 3:13; and Luke 8:17.

At that time, the commendation of each one will come from God. In 3:8 Paul spoke of each preacher being recompensed according to his labor. There God's response is expressed as *misthos*, "pay, wages," but now the reward is praise (*epainos*) coming from God, through the judgment of Christ. Cf. 1 Thess 2:4; Rom 2:29; 13:3.

6. *Now, brothers, I have transferred this to myself and Apollos for your sake.* I.e., I have changed this teaching of mine into an exposition concerning Apollos and myself. In saying *tauta*, "these things," Paul is commenting on his own argument and referring to all his advice in 1:10–4:5 about Apollos and himself as servants of Christ and about how one should judge such preachers, not on just 3:5–4:5, as some commentators (e.g., Vos) prefer to understand the antecedent of this neut. pron. Again Paul addresses the Corinthian Christians as "brothers" (see NOTE on 1:1), as his argument moves closer to its end.

The verb *meteschēmatisa* is not easily explained. *Metaschēmatizō* means, "to change the form of" something (into something else), and it was so understood here by John Chrysostom (*In Ep. I ad Cor. Hom.* 12.1; PG 61.95–96); Theodoret (*Interpr. Ep. I ad Cor.* 4.6; PG 82.256); Theophylact (*Expos. in Ep. I ad Cor.* 1.12; PG 124.572). Among modern commentators, this meaning has been used by Meyer, and Robertson-Plummer (*1 Cor,* 80–81), who paraphrase, " 'I have transferred these warnings to myself and Apollos for the purpose of a covert allusion, and that for your sakes, that in our persons you may get instruction.' The *metaschēmatismos*, therefore, consists in putting forward the names of those not really responsible for the *staseis* instead of the names of others who were more to blame." The prep. *eis* indicates the end product of the transformation, and in this case it denotes people, Paul and Apollos. So Paul would be saying that he has been changing something or someone else into Apollos and himself. "In other words, when Paul describes the relationship between himself and Apollos, what he is really concerned about is certain unnamed teachers who were at work in the church at Corinth, and competing for allegiance of church members" (Hall, "A Disguise for the Wise," 144; similarly Schneider, *TDNT,* 7:958).

However, many modern commentators have been reluctant to use that normal meaning here or to adopt the sense of it found in 2 Cor 11:13–15 ("transform, disguise [oneself]") or Phil 3:21 ("change") for this passage and claim that it seems to have the sense of saying something with the help of a figure of speech. Hence the translation often employed, "I have applied," e.g., in RSV, NRSV, NAB, REB, Barrett, Collins, Fee, Kistemaker, Soards, Thiselton; others use similar translations, "exemplified" (Conzelmann). Since *schēma* was used in Greek rhetoric for a "figure of speech," some commentators have tried to render *metaschēmatizō* as "change the figure of speech" (Colson, "*Metaschēmatisa*"), but the word *schēma* is not used in the text, and that explanation introduces it gratuitously. Paul's purpose in making such a transfer or application is expressed in the rest of the verse (see further Pherigo, "Rival Leadership"; Vos, "Der *metaschēmatismos*").

that you may learn from us not (to go) beyond what is written. These words, along with the clause that follows, are even more obscure than *metaschēmatisa*, because two clauses are introduced by *hina*, both of which seem to express purpose. The first, translated in the lemma, is very problematic: *hina en hymin mathēte to mē hyper ha gegraptai*, which seems to say something like, "that you may learn in us the not beyond what has been written." (Note that in MSS D, F, G, and the Koine text-tradition one finds the sing. *ho* instead of the plur. *ha*, a minor insignificant variant.) However, the expression is elliptical, because *to* (neut. article) with *mē* (negative adv.) is a standard way of introducing an infin., but no infin. is found in any of the best MSS (P⁴⁶, ℵ*, A, B, D*, F, G, Ψ, 1739, 1881), whereas a few mms (2 ℵ, Cᵛⁱᵈ, D², 0285) add *phronein*, "think": "not to think beyond what has been written": "that ye might learn in us not (to think of men) above that which is written" (KJV).

Four different explanations have been given to the five words, *to mē hyper ha gegraptai.*

(1) They are considered an integral part of the verse and are understood either as (a) elliptical, as in the lemma above (so RSV, NAB); or (b) "what has been written" is taken to mean Scripture, either (i) generically, e.g., about preachers (e.g., Matt 7:1 or 23:12) or (ii) specifically, i.e., the passages already quoted in 1:19, 31; 2:16; 3:19–20 (Kremer, Lietzmann, J. B. Lightfoot, Robertson-Plummer, Schlatter, Schrage), or (iii) even more specifically to 1:31 alone (Wagner). For a critique of this mode of explanation, see Wallis, "Ein neuer Auslegungsversuch," 506–7.

Or (c) the words are understood to refer to the metaphors of planting and building used in 3:5–17: Paul would be warning false teachers not to add human wisdom to the gospel because they would be going "beyond the things that are written" (Hooker).

Or (d) the words would refer more generally to all that Paul himself has written in the preceding chapters as he set forth his views on Christian conduct (Erasmus, Luther). In this case, Paul would undoubtedly have written *ha proegrapsa*, as in Rom 15:4; Eph 3:3.

Or (e) the article *to* is said to introduce a Corinthian slogan or proverb, "Nothing beyond what has been written," such as was commonly used by philosophers or others addressing those who sought to arouse discord. in an effort to conciliate (NIV, NRSV, REB, Barrett, Fee, Lindemann, Ross, Soards, Tyler, Welborn).

Paul would mean that he and Apollos were living examples of playing within the rules. Similarly Wallis (507–8), who prefers, however, to take *to mē hýper* as a separate *Schlagwort*, followed by a comma, meaning simply, "Not too much!," "Don't exaggerate!"

(2) The words are considered utterly corrupt, and the text is simply left blank in the translation (Moffatt, *1 Cor*, 46: the meaning is "beyond recovery"); some declare the words unintelligible, but at least translate them somewhat as in the lemma (Conzelmann, *1 Cor*, 85–86; Weiss).

(3) The words are considered to be a marginal gloss that has been introduced secondarily into the text. A scribe perceived that the negative (*mē*) was missing from the first *hina* clause, and because the text without it would have read, "Now, brother, I have transferred this to myself and Apollos for your sake, that you may learn from us to become arrogant, siding with one against another," it would flatly contradict the point that Paul has been trying to make. So the scribe emended the text, writing *mē* above the *alpha* (the final letter) of *hina* and calling attention to it in a marginal note, which was subsequently added to the text. Baljon (*De tekst*, 49–51) was among the first to propose this explanation; it has been adopted by many others: Bousset, Héring, Howard, Legault, MacDonald, Murphy-O'Connor, Strugnell, C. S. C. Williams; cf. *IBNTG*, 64; BDR §230.4). (Although it is not noted in the usual *apparatus criticus*, the *mē* is absent in mss D and E.) Even though this explanation seems attractive, it involves anacoluthon in the first *hina* clause and makes the second *hina* clause the obj. of the verb *mathēte*, which is strange. Murphy-O'Connor, acknowledging these difficulties, nevertheless considers Strugnell's translation "undoubtedly correct" and raising "the hypothesis of a gloss to the level of certitude" ("Interpolations," 85); but Kilpatrick ("Conjectural Emendation," 352) remains "unconvinced by Strugnell's suggestion"; similarly Lindemann, *1 Cor*, 103.

(4) According to Hanges ("1 Corinthians 4:6"), *ha gegraptai*, "what is written," would refer to a public document of the Corinthian church modeled on cultic bylaws that would have been familiar to its members, in which Paul would have laid out guidelines and principles necessary for the church's peace and prosperity. A far-fetched explanation with allegedly pertinent evidence.

Interpretation #1e above seems the best, but no matter what explanation is preferred for these five highly controverted words, the first *hina* clause introduces the second one, in which Paul's purpose is clearly stated.

that none of you may become arrogant, siding with one over against another. Lit. "that no one of you be puffed up for one against another." This second purpose clause expresses Paul's main contention: he wants to promote concord and harmony and dissuade individual Corinthian Christians from their arrogance in forming rivalries and allegiances to one or another preacher. For preachers are only instruments that God employs. The general meaning of the verse is clear, even if its formulation is complicated. Cf. a similar counsel in Rom 12:3.

The verb *physioō* occurs again in 4:18–19; 5:2; 8:1; 13:4, but its form is strange here, an indicative introduced by *hina*, with which one normally expects the subjunctive or optative. Also strange is the verb in the 2d pers. plur. form *physiousthe*, when the subject is *mē heis*, "none" (sing.); the agreement is logical, not grammatical.

7. *For who concedes you any distinction?* I.e., sees any differing (or superior) quality in you (sing., an individual Christian of Roman Corinth), or in the factions that you are fomenting? The implied answer is "No one." The verb *diakrinei* is employed in the sense of "differentiate, conclude that there is a difference" (BDAG, 231). The question introduces a reason why such conceit is inadmissible. In irony, Paul formulates three rhetorical questions with catchword bonds and antitheses, as in diatribe-like style, which continues until v. 15.

What do you have that you did not receive? The implied answer is "Nothing." Paul is suggesting that any distinguishing characteristics of individual Corinthian Christians (or even of the groups) come from more than their own efforts or achievement. He is hinting at the role of God's grace in their lives, an idea that he expresses in Rom 12:3. He also turns on its head what he said in 3:21, "all things belong to you," which now becomes "nothing belongs to you," meaning that it is all a gift of God (or of Christ Jesus), and certainly not of Apollos or Paul. Cf. Paul's saying here with John 3:27.

If then you did really receive it, why are you boasting as though you did not? Lit. "as one not receiving." Once again Paul criticizes the notion of priding oneself on one's achievements so as to exclude it from a genuine concept of Christian life, as he did in 1:29–31; 3:21. Whatever superiority individual Corinthian Christians may have is not a product of their achievement; it is a gift of God. Hence the teachers, about whom the Corinthians are boasting, are only stewards of what they too have received from God. Recall the gift of God's Spirit in 2:12. The *Ep. Aristeas* has an interesting parallel: ". . . admonishing (your) descendants not to be struck by fame or riches, because it is God who gives these gifts, and not through themselves do they have preeminence over all" (196).

8. *You have already been sated!* I.e., you think you already have all the spiritual food you need (BDAG, 559); or, you are filled with self-assurance and sense no need of anything. Paul now shifts to the 2d pers. plur., addressing the Corinthian Christians as a community, as he indulges in bitter irony. Some commentators prefer to punctuate the first three statements of this verse as questions: "Are you already sated?" Thiselton ("Realized Eschatology"), however, interprets these statements as an indication that the Corinthian Christians were living on a new plane of life, being in the Spirit already and thus were believing in a realized eschatology. Similarly Schrage, *1 Cor,* 1:338; but see Ellis ("Christ Crucified," 73–74) for a telling criticism of such an interpretation.

You have become rich already! I.e., you have been plentifully supplied with wealth and even transcendent values. The aor. tense is ingressive (BDF §331). In an entirely different sense, Paul thanked God that the Corinthian community has already been enriched (1:5). Cf. Rev 3:17.

Without us, you have become kings! Lit. "you have come to rule (as kings)," i.e., attained the status of sovereignty. Paul may be using a motif well known in Greek philosophy that the sage in the world is as rich as a "king." See Horace, *Ep.* 1.1.16–7: *Sapiens uno minor est Iove, dives, liber, honoratus, pulcher, rex denique regum,* "The sage is second only to Jupiter, rich, free, noble, handsome, finally a king of kings." Similarly Philo, *De sobrietate* 11 §57, who also depicts the sage as God's "only son" (*monos huios*), "unique king" (*monos basileus*), and "sole free-man" (*monos eleutheros*), released from the tyranny of "vain opinion" (*kenē doxa*).

The Corinthian Christians in their wisdom may be persuaded that they have already a prominent part in God's kingdom, because they have been richly evangelized by noted preachers. Contrast this attitude with what Paul says about himself in Phil 3:12–14:

> Not that I have obtained this already or am already perfect; but I press forward to make it my own, because Christ Jesus has made me his own. Brothers, I do not consider that I have made it my own; but one thing I do, forgetting what lies behind and straining forward to what lies ahead, I press on toward the goal for the prize of the upward call of God in Christ Jesus.

The prep. phrase does not seem to mean "without our aid" or "without the assistance of such nonentities as Paul and Apollos" (Barrett, *1 Cor,* 108), but rather "without our company," as Robertson-Plummer (*1 Cor,* 84) understand it, i.e., in deliberately turning from us (preachers). The contrast is between the alleged status of Corinthian Christians and the actual condition of preachers like Paul.

Would that you had become kings so that we too might be kings with you! Lit. "did reign . . . might reign with you." To the three ironic statements, Paul adds an unattainable wish, introduced by an unaugmented second aor. *ophelon ge,* which is used as a particle introducing the wish (BDF §359.1). By it, Paul turns his three statements upside down and seeks to tell the Corinthian Christians that he refuses to consider them "kings." He says this even though they had indeed become such, Apollos and he would be sharing such a status in this world with them. Paul's wish prepares for what he will assert in the following verse.

9. *For it seems to me that God has depicted us, the apostles, as the last of all, as people sentenced to death.* Paul has already called himself an "apostle" (1:1), and will again do so (9:1); in 15:7 he speaks of "all the apostles," meaning there as here a restricted group of commissioned Christian emissaries (see NOTE on 1:1). If in 1:1 Paul mentions his apostolic status to enhance his authority as he addresses the Corinthian community, his use of the term here is paradoxical, because now in his view of God's designs such preachers have not been set up to govern, but they have become *eschatous,* "last (of all)" in rank, and *epithanatious,* "marked for death." Paul is really thinking of himself when he says "us," but he immediately adds mention of others with whom he shared apostolic authority and commission.

Paul sees himself as someone engaged by God in the service of Christ crucified and cast in a situation analogous to that of the crucified Christ, perhaps like a gladiator. Cf. Rom 8:36; 1 Cor 15:31.

because we have become a spectacle to the world, both to angels and to human beings. Or "to the world and angels and human beings," since *kosmos* may be used independently of the other two elements instead of taking them as the components of the world (*EDNT,* 1:14). Paul uses *theatron,* which can mean "a theater" (as in Acts 19:29, 31) or "a play, spectacle," what one sees in a theater. The latter sense of the term is found in Stoic philosophical writings about the philosopher's struggle with fate as a spectacle (*spectaculum*) for gods and men (Seneca, *De providentia* 2.9; *Ep.* 64.4–6). There is, however, a difference for Paul, because the term expresses the fate that has come about for him and other apostles whom people consider to be a wretched "spectacle," like gladiators fighting in an arena, when in reality they are viewing what God has ordained, who depicts the apostles as weak in the struggle of Christian missionaries in the world (*TDNT*, 3:43). Cf. Ps 69:12, for a Jewish mode of expressing the same idea.

For the first time, *angelos* appears; see further 6:3; 11:10; 13:1. In each case, the word does not denote merely a "messenger" or "envoy," but rather a transcendent being, connected in the Greco-Roman world with the nether realm, but depicted in Jewish literature as a messenger sent from God (see LXX Gen 16:10–11; 31:11; 32:2; Josephus, *J.W.* 5.9.4 §388; Philo, *Quod Deus immut. sit* 1 §1). The mention of "world" and "angels" gives a cosmic dimension to the spectacle that Paul and the other apostles have become.

10. *We are fools for Christ, but you are wise in Christ; we are weak, but you are strong; you are honored, but we are despised.* Paul uses three antithetical, verbless sentences, and the last two in chiastic order, as he contrasts ironically "we" and "you." Who are the "we"? The apostles of v. 9? Or is Paul using an editorial "we"? In v. 9, Paul used the 1st pers. sing. verb *dokō* and will use the 1st pers. sing. again in v. 14 (*graphō*). So the "we" here probably refers to himself and the other apostles or preachers (like Apollos and Cephas) who proclaim the foolishness of the crucified Christ (1:18, 23). In the eyes of the Corinthians and their contemporaries, they are fools (see 1:20–25, 27; 3:18), weak (1:25, 27), and despised. In formulating this triple description, Paul is echoing the three characteristics of 1:26, even though he changes the terms: *phronimoi*, "wise, thoughtful," instead of *sophoi*; *ischyroi*, "strong" instead of *dynatoi*, "capable" ; and *endoxoi*, "honored," instead of *eugeneis*, "noble." He is willing to tolerate this condition, since it is *dia Christon*, "because of Christ," i.e., Christ supplies the motivation for such tolerance. He states, in contrast, that Corinthian Christians are wise, strong, and honored, again in their own eyes and those of their contemporaries. Cf. 2 Cor 4:11–12.

It is a problem, however, to determine how they are such *en Christō*, "in Christ," because Paul has been maintaining that Corinthians, torn by rivalries, were really only wise with "the wisdom of the world" (1:20). Accordingly, he considered them to be "infants in Christ" (3:1), but now he is willing to admit that in some sense they are "wise in Christ," i.e., Christians who happen to be "wise." That, however, may be said with irony. Cf. 2 Cor 4:8–12; 6:4–10; 11:23–33; 13:9.

11. *Up to this very hour we go hungry and thirsty; we are in rags; we are mistreated; we are homeless.* In this and the two following verses, Paul abandons his irony and describes the actual adverse conditions of life as a missionary or evangelist. For passages in his writings that contain similar descriptions about his condition, see 2 Cor 4:8–10; 6:4–5; 11:23–27; 12:10. *Gymniteuō* means "be poorly clad"; *kolaphizō* means "hit with the fist, buffet," which is often used metaphori-

cally of mistreatment, as in 2 Cor 12:7; and *astateō* means "to be without a foothold," which often means "be unsteady," but now denotes rather "without fixed abode" (Oepke, *TDNT*, 1:503). Going "hungry and thirsty" stands in contrast to what Paul admitted of the Corinthian Christians, who were "sated" (4:8).

12. *We toil, working with our hands.* See 9:6, 14–15; also 2 Cor 11:7–11; 12:13; 1 Thess 2:9; 2 Thess 3:8, where Paul also tells of his own handiwork, and 1 Cor 3:8 of such work in general. Acts 18:3 depicts Paul as plying the same trade as Aquila and Priscilla, that of tent makers (*skēnopoioi*, the meaning of which is disputed [see *Acts*, 626; BDAG, 928–29]); cf. Acts 20:34. Working with one's hands was no disgrace in antiquity, and Paul will say more about it in 9:4–18. Cf. 1 Thess 2:9; 4:11; 2 Thess 3:8–12. The same two verbs, *kopiaō* and *ergazomai* are found together in the Greek version of 1 *Enoch* 103:11: *[eko]piasamen ergazomenoi*, "we toiled, working hard" (see von Harnack, "*Kopos (kopian)*").

When reviled, we bless; when persecuted, we put up with it. 13. *When slandered, we answer kindly.* Three antitheses record Paul's further reaction to some of the adverse criticisms that he has encountered. He does not return evil for evil and is still open to concern for others. In the first antithesis, there may be an echo of Jesus' words recorded in Luke 6:28a ("Bless those who curse you"), and in the second Paul is carrying out, in effect, the words of Jesus recorded in Matt 5:44 ("Pray for those who persecute you"). Cf. Ps 109:28; 1 Pet 2:23; 3:9; *Did.* 1.3 (see Neirynck, "The Sayings of Jesus," 156–58). Instead of *dysphēmoumenoi*, "reviled" (read by MSS P⁴⁶, ℵ*, A, C, P, 33, 81, 1175), some MSS have *blasphēmoumenoi*, "defamed" (P⁶⁸, ℵ², B, D, F, G, Ψ, 1739, and the Koine text-tradition), which has the same meaning. Cf. the list of adverse circumstances recorded in 1 *Enoch* 103:9–13.

13b. *We have become, and are even now, like the rubbish of the world, the scum of the earth.* Lit. "the dirt of the world, of all things the offscouring," formulated with chiasmus. So Paul records the impression that his missionary activity has been making among some of his contemporaries. The two terms, *perikatharmata*, "what is removed in a thorough cleansing," and *peripsēma*, "what is scraped all around," appear also in profane Greek texts as invectives or insults used against reprobate persons. However, because *perikatharma* occurs in Prov 21:18 and *peripsēma* in Tob 5:19 with the sense of "ransom," some interpreters have tried to use this meaning here: Paul, scorned and rejected by people, offers himself for them, being willing to become an expiatory victim or scapegoat, and so he assimilates himself to the crucified Redeemer (Spicq, *TLNT*, 3:94–95; Barrett, Héring). That, however, is far-fetched and goes beyond what suits the context (so Senft, 1 *Cor*, 89 n. 19). Hanson ("1 Corinthians"), however, thinks that Lam 3:45 lies behind the comparison. The Hebrew text does say, "You have made us offscouring and refuse among the peoples," whereas the LXX is quite different. If the suggestion were correct, one would have to suppose that Paul was using a different Greek translation that reflected better the Hebrew of the MT, or that he was translating the Hebrew.

In vv. 6–13, Paul has been trying to describe the tension between the way some Corinthian Christians have been thinking about him (and Apollos) and the reality of apostolic ministry or evangelization. With no little irony, he has been seeking to correct their way of evaluating those who have preached among them. He is stressing that the lowly status that he and other apostles have in the eyes of some is something that they endure because of Christ: "We are fools for Christ" (4:10).

14. *I am writing this not to make you ashamed, but to admonish you as my beloved children.* Since the argument that began at 1:10 has now come close to an end, Paul adopts a different style of addressing the Corinthian Christians and a different tone, as he seeks to conciliate them, while continuing to exhort them. His attitude is similar to that expressed in 4:6 above, and also 3:1–2. He contrasts the ptcs. *entrepōn*, "shaming," and *nouthetōn*, "admonishing," and calls the Corinthian Christians his "beloved children," as in 2 Cor 6:13. See also Gal 4:19; cf. Wis 11:10. Cf. his attitude in 6:5. The object *tauta*, "this," refers directly to 4:6–13, which precedes, and only indirectly to 1:10–3:23, as some would understand it. It is far from likely that "*graphō* in 1 Cor. 4.14 refers to the tearful letter" of 2 Cor 2:4, as well as to 1 Corinthians, *pace* Fellows ("Was Titus," 51); it refers to this letter alone.

15. *Even if you have ten thousand guides in Christ, you do not have many fathers.* Lit. "ten thousand child-leaders." Paul uses *paidagōgos*, from which English "pedagogue" is derived, but which etymologically has a different meaning, "child-leader." In the ancient Greek-speaking world, it denoted a man, usually an elderly slave (*oiketēs*) and often of foreign origin (or prisoner of war), who had to take a boy to school and supervise his conduct (seeing that he studied and did not play truant); he was not per se a teacher (*didaskalos*) but was one who had authority and to whom respect was owed. He usually had a great deal to do with the character training of those of whom he was in charge. His task often included shaming and admonishing (see Young, "Paidagogos"). *Paidagōgoi . . . en Christō* would have been those who have been leading Corinthians to Christian instruction, possibly even the same as those who are said in 3:10 to have been "building upon" the foundation that Paul had laid (so Schrage, *1 Cor*, 1:356).

Paul thus alludes to Apollos, Cephas, and other preachers at Corinth with rhetorical exaggeration, meaning that they may have functioned as boy leaders for the Corinthians who were thus led to Christ in countless ways, but they have only one who can claim to have begotten them in Christian faith. So Paul describes his own relationship "in Christ" to Corinthian Christians: their community was born through his evangelization, because he was their "father" in Christ, even though he has not used this title explicitly. Recall that in 3:2 Paul spoke as if he were their "mother," who fed them milk, because they were still "mere infants."

for in Christ Jesus I became your father through the gospel. Lit. "I have begotten you." Paul uses the same verb (*gennaō*) of the converted slave Onesimus, whom he calls "my child" in Phlm 10; cf. Gal 4:19. So he asserts a form of fatherhood vis-à-vis the Corinthian community, because he has founded it by his preaching of the gospel. This is also what he meant by "planting" (3:6) and laying "a foundation" (3:10); his position among the various preachers and tutors who have evangelized and instructed the Corinthians is, therefore, unique, and he does not hesitate to imply that he himself is their "father." Apparently he was unaware of the saying of Jesus about calling no one father on earth, recorded in Matt 23:9.

The paternity of which Paul speaks has been interpreted in three ways: 1. As a metaphor without any particular significance (so Theodoret of Cyrus, *In Ep. I ad Cor.* 4.15; PG 82.260; John Damascene, *In Ep. I ad Cor.* 4.15; PG 95.604; Büchsel, *TDNT*, 1:666). 2. Begotten through preaching (*kērygma*) as a preparation for baptism. Baptized Christians recognize Paul as father (so Oecumenius, *In Ep. I ad Cor.* 4.14–16; PG 118.693). 3. Begotten unto a new life through Paul's gospel. Christians enjoy a relation to him as children to a father, a honorific title (so John Chrysostom, *Hom. 13 in Ep. I ad Cor.* 2; PG 61.109–10; Conzelmann, *1 Cor*, 91: "no mere metaphor," but a "spiritual fatherhood"; not merely, however, in the manner of a mystagogue, reckoned as "father" by the initiands, as in Hellenistic mystery religions). The last mentioned is the preferred explanation, because Paul stresses that his spiritual fatherhood is "in Christ Jesus through the gospel" (see Saillard, "C'est moi"). Lindemann (*1 Cor*, 114) prefers to derive the title from the rabbinic usage of father for one who teaches the Torah (see Str-B, 3:340–41); but all the examples he uses are derived from texts centuries later than Paul. Lassen ("Use of the Father Image") has shown that Paul is following the idea of *pater* current in contemporary Roman society, where it was used as a title for generals, soldiers, and others who provided *salus* for the people (e.g., given to Romulus, Marius, Sulla). Julius Caesar was called *pater patriae*, "father of the country"; also Augustus.

For the first time in this letter, Paul uses *euangelion*, "gospel"; it will appear again in 9:12, 14, 18, 23; 15:1. By it he means the good news about God's salvific plan and activity manifested in the ministry, passion, death, and resurrection of Jesus Christ, which he proclaims: "God's gospel" (Rom 1:1). The term is derived from the LXX, where it occurs seven times in the sense of "good news" (2 Sam 18:20, 22, 25, 27; 2 Kgs 7:9) or "reward for good news" given to a herald (2 Sam 4:10; 18:22 [cf. Homer, *Odys.* 14.152–53, 166]). The cognate verb *euangelizomai* occurs in Isa 52:7; 60:6; 61:1 and is part of the OT background of the Christian usage. This verb has helped to give *euangelion* a religious connotation, which it did not have in pre-Christian times, and which makes of it a distinctively Christian word. This is why it was not translated later into Latin as *nuntius bonus*, but merely transliterated as *euangelium* (and then retained even in modern languages as *évangile, vangelo, evangelio, Evangelium*).

Paul sees the gospel as "apocalyptic," revealing God's salvific power and activity for His people in a new way (through Christ, Rom 1:17). It continues the promises made by God of old, "promised beforehand through the prophets in the holy Scriptures" (Rom 1:1). For Paul it is also a "force" (*dynamis*) unleashed by God in human history to bring about the salvation of all, Jew and Greek alike (Rom 1:16). It announces that "Jesus is Lord" (Rom 10:9; cf. 1 Cor 12:3) and proclaims him as risen (1 Cor 15:1, 3). See INTRODUCTION pp. 70–71; *PAHT* §PT31–36. In this instance, it is difficult to say whether *euangelium* denotes content ("the message of the cross") or the activity (evangelization), because it has both senses in Pauline writings.

16. *Therefore, I urge you, be imitators of me.* Paul will repeat this exhortation in 11:1, where he adds, "as I am of Christ," an addition that some inferior MSS (104, 614, 629) have added even here. Paul employs the verb *parakalō* again; see 1:10,

which is echoed now. He is giving paternal advice as he urges the Corinthians to regard him as a model for their Christian mode of life. He wants his "children" to imitate him, i.e., follow his way of living out the gospel, which is a humble way of life with much suffering, described in the foregoing vv. 11–13. Cf. 1 Thess 1:6–7; 2:14; Phil 3:17; 2 Thess 3:7–9; Eph 4:32–5:1. Normally Paul does not urge Christians to imitate Christ; the exception is 11:1, where it is only by indirection, because his own life is dedicated to service of the risen Lord (see Sanders, "Imitating"; Stanley, " 'Become Imitators,' " 303–5). In speaking of imitation, Paul is not merely using *mimētēs* in the sense of Greek *mimēsis*, "imitation," which played an important role in ancient Greek education, as Xenophon notes: *tōn allōn ergōn hoi didaskaloi tous mathētas mimētas heautōn apodeiknyousin*, "the teachers of other subjects instruct their students (to be) imitators of themselves" (*Memorabilia* 1.6.3). Elsewhere Paul has been accustomed to ask fellow Christians to pray for him in his sufferings (Phil 1:19; 2 Cor 1:10–11), but now he is concerned that those in Corinth will understand rightly his father-children relationship and imitate his service of the undivided Christ and the unity of what he will eventually call "the body of Christ" (12:27).

17. *For this reason I am sending to you Timothy, who is my dear and faithful child in the Lord.* Paul does not explain immediately what he means by imitation of himself, because he is sending Timothy who will explain it to the Corinthian Christians. In sending Timothy as an emissary, Paul is exercising his apostolic authority and power, because through Timothy he himself will be present to them. Timothy may also be carrying a letter from Paul, through which he would also be making himself present to them. This is what Funk has called Paul's "apostolic *parousia*." "Timothy will remind the Corinthians not only by words, but he will represent in his own personal conduct the ways he has learned from Paul (cf. Phil 2:19–22) and thus the patterns of behavior [that] can overcome the divisiveness in the church" (Sanders, "Imitating Paul," 363). He calls Timothy *mou teknon*, "my child," a term also used of the converted slave Onesimus in Phlm 10. Compare the way Mark is called "my son" in 1 Pet 5:13.

Epempsa (lit. "I sent") is an epistolary aor. denoting time contemporary with the writing and sending of the letter (BDF §334). Timothy has been sent already, and so he is not the bearer of this letter; he is already on his way to Corinth. Timothy will be mentioned again in 16:10 ("If Timothy comes"). That seems to mean that this letter may reach Corinth before Timothy arrives; he may have been sent by an indirect route through Macedonia (see Acts 19:21–22).

Timotheos ("One who honors God") is a Greek name, found in extrabiblical literature and the LXX (1 Macc 5:6, 11). How Timothy became a companion and fellow worker of Paul is recounted in Acts 16:1–4. There he is described as "a disciple (= a Christian), the son of a believing Jewish woman and a Greek father," who lived in the town of Lystra of Lycaonia. Since local Christians spoke highly of him, Paul wanted him to accompany him on his missionary journey. So Paul "took him and had him circumcised because of the Jews of those regions, for they all knew that his father was a Greek." Timothy sometimes appears as a co-sender of Pauline letters (1 Thess 1:1; 2 Cor 1:1; Phil 1:1; Phlm 1; cf. Col 1:1; 2 Thess

1:1); to him two of the Pastoral Letters are addressed (1 Tim 1:1; 2 Tim 1:1). He is mentioned at times in other Pauline writings (as having worked in Corinth, Rom 16:21; 2 Cor 1:19; Phil 2:19; 1 Thess 3:6), as he is here; cf. Acts 19:21–22. Although Paul calls him *mou teknon agapēton kai piston*, "my dear and faithful child in the Lord," which might suggest that Paul was involved in Timothy's becoming a Christian (so Conzelmann, *1 Cor*, 92 n. 19), that differs from the account in Acts 16:1 (quoted above). He came to Corinth earlier and was with Paul when 1 Thessalonians was written (see 1 Thess 3:2, 6). From this letter we now see that he must have been in Ephesus with Paul. Cf. the way Paul speaks of Timothy in Phil 2:19–22, where he hopes to send him to the Philippians and commends him, "as a child with a father, he served along with me in evangelization." Fellows ("Was Titus Timothy?") thinks that Timothy and Titus were the same person. That is hardly so.

he will remind you about my ways in Christ [Jesus], just as I teach them everywhere in every church. By *tas hodous mou* Paul means "my Christian directives (i.e., instructions, teachings)" (BDAG, 692). It is not that Corinthian Christians have forgotten all about what Paul taught them, but rather that Timothy will instruct them how to follow Paul in imitation (v. 16). MSS A, B, Ψ, 0150 read simply *Christō*, but others (P⁴⁶, ℵ, C, 33, 81, 1739) have *Christō Iēsou*; hence the square brackets.

The metaphorical use of *hodos*, "way," to denote a form of philosophical teaching is found in Greek literature (e.g., Lucian, *Herotimus* 46), but the LXX also provides instances of it as a way of speaking of God's commands (Deut 8:6; 5:33; Jer 7:23; Ps 25:4; 16:11). Moreover, it often translates Hebrew *derek*, which is used in the same way. In QL, *derek* is found in 1QS 8:14–15, where Isa 40:3 is quoted ("Prepare in the desert the way of ••••, make straight in the wilderness a path for our God"), and "the way" is interpreted as "the study of the law" (*midraš hattôrāh*; see further McCasland, "The Way"). On the final prep. phrase, "in every church," see 7:17c; 14:33; it means that in this regard Corinth is not a special case.

18. *Some have become arrogant pretending that I am not coming to you.* Lit. "have become puffed up, conceited," i.e., have swollen with self-importance. Paul seeks to correct the mistaken idea on which "some" Corinthians have been judging him and also the opposition among "some" of them, as he did already in 4:6. They seem to believe that he would not come back to them and do not care for his being among them, preferring even to have Apollos return (16:12). Cf. 2 Cor 10:14. How Paul has learned this is not said, but he is sure that the Christians of Corinth will know who the "some" are.

19. *I shall come to you very soon, if the Lord wills.* So he emphatically contradicts the assumption of some Corinthians that he did not care to return to their community, even if he does not say how quickly he will come (cf. Phil 2:24). At the end of this letter, Paul will reformulate this promise; see 16:5–9; cf. 11:34. He ends his promise with a paraphrase of a commonly-used saying, *tou theou thelontos*, "Deo volente" (Acts 18:21); see also 1 Cor 16:7; Heb 6:3; Jas 4:15; also in extrabiblical usage: Josephus, *Ant*.2.15.5 §333; 2.16.5 §347; 7.14.9 §373; Plato, *Alcibiades* 1.31 §135d. It is meant to eliminate arbitrary decisions of an individ-

ual. Paul's form (*ean ho kyrios thelēsē*) is similar to that in Sir 39:6, and *kyrios* in this expression undoubtedly refers to God, not the risen Christ.

and I shall ascertain not the talk of these arrogant people, but their power. In irony, Paul is implying that the Corinthians who are causing dissension rely too much on "talk" or eloquence, but he will assess what "power" they have and counter it with his own authority. See 2:1–4, for the proper understanding of his power, which he possesses in Christ despite his own weakness and sufferings (4:11–13). *Logos* now has a meaning different from that in 1:18; it is closer to that of 1:17; 2:1. The contrast of *logos*, "talk," and *dynamis*, "power," is also found in 1 Thess 1:5 (see Spencer, "The Power").

20. *For the kingdom of God is not a matter of talk, but of power.* This statement is added to provide the basis for the assessment Paul will undertake on his coming arrival in Corinth. It is formulated like an aphorism, as in Rom 14:17. *Hē basileia tou theou*, "the kingdom of God," will recur in 6:9–10; 15:50; cf. 15:24. The association of "the kingdom of God" with "power" is also found in Mark 9:1.

"Kingdom of God" is the prime kerygmatic topic of Jesus' preaching in the Synoptic Gospels, especially in Matthew, where it appears more frequently as the "kingdom of heaven" (55 times, but only 38 times in Luke, 14 times in Mark, [5 times in John]). Strangely enough, no explanation is ever given of its meaning either in the Synoptic tradition or by Paul. It is a phrase that echoes the OT idea of Yahweh as king (1 Sam 12:12; Isa 6:5; 33:22; 43:15; Jer 8:19; Mic 2:3; Ps 47:3, 8) or the kingship and royal authority that are ascribed to Him (Obad 21; Pss 103:19; 145:11–13) or His governance as king (Exod 15:18; Isa 24:23). The NT phrase finds its closest counterpart in postexilic writings (1 Chr 28:5, *malkût Yhwh*, LXX: *basileia kyriou*, "the Lord's kingship"; or 2 Chr 13:8, *mamleket Yhwh*, LXX: *basileia kyriou*, "the Lord's kingdom"). In the OT, the phrase can express an eschatological hope for a period when God's salvation would be realized, when his dominion over the minds, hearts, and lives of human beings would be implemented, and they would be drawn from subjection to danger, evil, and sin. It implies at times the divine guidance of human history, thwarted no longer by hostile opposition (Judg 21:25; Dan 7:22). In the NT, the OT understanding assumes a specific determination: the kingdom of God enters human history in Jesus' ministry, passion, death, and resurrection. Jesus proclaimed that kingdom and sought to establish it among people whom he accosted: "The kingdom of God is among you" (Luke 17:21). In the Pauline writings, the kingdom appears only a few times (1 Thess 2:12; 1 Cor 6:9–10; 15:50; Gal 5:21; Rom 14:17; cf. 1 Cor 15:24; Col 1:13; 4:11; Eph 5:5; 2 Thess 1:5), and it is scarcely the operative or dynamic element that it is in the Synoptics. It is used at times in catalogues of vices or statements reflecting early Christian catechetics (Gal 5:21; 1 Cor 6:9–10; 15:50). The phrase often has an eschatological or futurist connotation, but that is clearly lacking in this instance, as in Rom 14:17 (see Johnston, " 'Kingdom of God' Sayings").

As Paul uses the phrase here, it is meant to undercut the arrogance of those Corinthians who have been causing dissension with their would-be eloquence, their rivalries, and their allegiance to certain preachers. *Dynamis*, which is associated with the kingdom has been explained variously: "the power of working miracles"

(Chrysostom, *Hom. in Ep. I ad Cor.* 14.2; PG 61.116), a meaning that does not suit this context; the power of "winning men over to a Christian life" (Robertson-Plummer, *1 Cor*, 92); or "the power of the Gospel" (Ruef, *1 Cor*, 36–37; Lindemann, *1 Cor*, 117), which better suits this context and is supported by 1 Thess 1:5; Rom 1:16; or possibly the power displayed in Paul's sufferings in imitation of Christ as explained in the preceding context, vv. 11–13 (see Spencer, "The Power," 54–57).

21. *What do you prefer? Shall I come to you with a stick or with love and a gentle spirit?* Lit. "a spirit of gentleness," as in Gal 6:1; cf. 2 Tim 2:25. In conclusion, Paul leaves the choice to the Corinthian Christians, as in 2 Cor 12:20. Should he come with force or with fatherly affection? The "stick" is meant as the instrument of a superior or a disciplinarian (*paidagōgos*, v. 15a)—in effect, a sign of Paul's authoritative power that he is willing to use, if necessary, on his beloved, but unruly "children." The "gentle spirit" is meant as a sign of a father figure, used in v. 15b. Spicq ("Une réminiscence") finds in this verse a reminiscence of Job 37:13, although that text is hopelessly distorted in both the MT and the LXX. He sees there an antithesis between punishment and mercy. If that is all there is, it would be fine; but both the Hebrew and the Greek say much more, even if it can hardly be rendered in English in any intelligible way.

BIBLIOGRAPHY (See also Bibliography on 1:10–4:21, pp. 149–51)

Baird, W., " 'One against the Other': Intra-Church Conflict in 1 Corinthians," *The Conversation Continues: Studies in Paul and John in Honor of J. Louis Martyn* (ed. R. T. Fortna and B. R. Gaventa; Nashville: Abingdon, 1990) 116–36.

Boer, W. P. de, *The Imitation of Paul: An Exegetical Study* (Kampen, Netherlands: Kok, 1962).

Bonner, C., "A Reminiscence of Paul on a Coin Amulet," *HTR* 43 (1950) 165–68.

Brown, R., "Translating the Whole Concept of the Kingdom," *Notes* 14/2 (2000) 1–48.

Brun, L., "Noch einmal die Schriftnorm 1 Kor. 4,6," *TSK* 103 (1931) 453–56.

Byron, J., " 'Slave of Christ or Willing servant?': Paul's Self-description in 1 Corinthians 4:1–2 and 9:16–18," *Neotestamentica* 57 (2003) 179–93.

Castelli, E. A., "Interpretations of Power in 1 Corinthians," *Semeia* 54 (1991) 197–222.

Colson, F. H, "*Meteschēmatisa* 1 Cor. iv 6," *JTS* 17 (1916) 379–84.

Ellis, E. E., " 'Christ Crucified,' " *Reconciliation and Hope: New Testament Essays on Atonement and Eschatology Presented to L. L. Morris* . . . (ed. R. Banks; Grand Rapids: Eerdmans, 1974) 69–75.

Fellows, R. G., "Was Titus Timothy?" *JSNT* 81 (2001) 33–58.

Funk, R. W., "The Apostolic *Parousia*: Form and Significance," *Christian History and Interpretation: Studies Presented to John Knox* (ed. W. R. Farmer et al.; Cambridge: Cambridge University Press, 1967) 249–68.

Hall, D. R., "A Disguise for the Wise: *Metaschēmatismos* in 1 Corinthians 4.6," *NTS* 40 (1994) 143–49.

Hanges, J. C., "1 Corinthians 4:6 and the Possibility of Written Bylaws in the Corinthian Church," *JBL* 117 (1998) 275–98.

Hanson, A., "1 Corinthians 4[13b] and Lamentations 3[45]," *ExpTim* 93 (1981–82) 214–15.

Hooker, M. D., " 'Beyond the Things Which Are Written': An Examination of I Cor. iv.6," *NTS* 10 (1963–64) 127–32.

Howard, W. F., "1 Corithians iv. 6," *ExpTim* 33 (1921–22) 479–80.

Johnston, G., " 'Kingdom of God' Sayings in Paul's Letters," *From Jesus to Paul: Studies in Honour of Francis Wright Beare* (ed. P. Richardson and J. C. Hurd; Waterloo, Ont.: Wilfrid Laurier University Press, 1984) 143–56.

Kilpatrick, G. D., "Conjectural Emendation in the New Testament," *New Testament Textual Criticism: Its Significance for Exegesis: Essays in Honour of Bruce M. Metzger* (ed. E. J. Epp and G. D. Fee; Oxford: Clarendon, 1981) 349–60.

Lambrecht, J., "Paul as Example: A Study of 1 Corinthians 4,6–21," *Collected Studies* (AnBib 147) 43–62.

Lassen, E. M., "The Use of the Father Image in Imperial Propaganda and 1 Corinthians 4:14–21," *TynBul* 42 (1991) 127–36.

Legault, A., " 'Beyond the Things Which Are Written' (I Cor. iv. 6)," *NTS* 18 (1971–72) 227–31.

Linton, O., " 'Nicht über das hinaus, was geschrieben steht' (1 Kor. 4,6)," *TSK* 102 (1930) 425–37.

McCasland, S. V., " 'The Way,' " *JBL* 77 (1958) 222–30.

Matera, F. J., "Imitating Paul in Order to Follow Christ," *Living Light* 38/2 (2001) 35–43.

Neirynck, F., "The Sayings of Jesus in 1 Corinthians," *The Corinthian Correspondence* (BETL 125; ed. R. Bieringer) 141–76.

O'Neill, J. C., "Pedagogues in the Pauline Corpus (1 Corinthians 5,15; Galatians 3,24, 25)," *IBS* 23 (2001) 50–65.

Reumann, J., " 'Stewards of God'—Pre-Christian Religious Application of *oikonomos* in Greek," *JBL* 77 (1958) 339–49.

Rödiger, R., "*Boulomai* und *ethelō*: Eine semasiologische Untersuchung," *Glotta* 8 (1917) 1–24.

Ross, J. M., "Not Above What Is Written: A Note on 1 Cor 4[6]," *ExpTim* 82 (1970–71) 215–17.

Saillard, M., "C'est moi qui, par l'Evangile, vous ai enfantés dans le Christ Jésus (1 Co 4, 15)," *RSR* 56 (1968) 5–41.

Sanders, B., "Imitating Paul: 1 Cor 4:16," *HTR* 74 (1981) 353–63.

Schrage, W., "Das apostolische Amt des Paulus nach 1 Kor 4,14–17," *L'Apôtre Paul* (BETL 73; ed. A. Vanhoye), 103–19.

Spencer, W. D., "The Power in Paul's Teaching (1 Cor 4:9–20)," *JETS* 32 (1989) 51–61.

Spicq, C., "Une réminiscence de Job xxxvii,13 dans I Cor. iv, 21?" *RB* 60 (1953) 509–12.

Stanley, D. M., " 'Become Imitators of Me': The Pauline Conception of Apostolic Tradition," *Bib* 40 (1959) 859–77, esp. 871–73; repr. *The Apostolic Church in the New Testament* (Westminster, MD: Newman, 1965) 371–89. esp. 383–86.

———, "Imitation in Paul's Letters: Its Significance for His Relationship to Jesus and to His Own Christian Foundations," *From Jesus to Paul* (ed. P. Richardson and J. C. Hurd; Waterloo, Ont.: Wilfrid Laurier University Press, 1984), 127–41.

Still, E. C., "Divisions over Leaders and Food Offered to Idols: The Parallel Thematic Structures of 1 Corinthians 4:6–21 and 8:1–11:1," *TynBul* 55 (2004) 17–41.

Strugnell, J., "A Plea for Conjectural Emendation in the New Testament, with a Coda on 1 Cor 4:6," *CBQ* 36 (1974) 543–58, esp. 555–58.

Tyler, R. L., "First Corinthians 4:6 and Hellenistic Pedagogy," *CBQ* 60 (1998) 97–103.

———, "The History of the Interpretation of *to mē hyper ha gegraptai* in 1 Corinthians 4:6," *ResQ* 43 (2001) 243–52.

Vos, J. S., "Der *metaschēmatismos* in 1 Kor 4,6," ZNW 86 (1995) 154–72.

Wagner, J. R., " 'Not beyond the Things Which Are Written': A Call to Boast Only in the Lord (1 Cor 4.6)," NTS 44 (1998) 279–87.

Wallis, P., "Ein neuer Auslegungsversuch der Stelle I. Kor. 4,6," TLZ 75 (1950) 506–8.

Welborn, L. L., "A Conciliatory Principle in 1 Cor. 4:6," NovT 29 (1987) 320–46.

Young, N. H., "*Paidagogos*: The Social Setting of a Pauline Metaphor," NovT 29 (1987) 150–76.

9 B. SCANDAL OF INCEST AND ASSOCIATION WITH IMMORAL PEOPLE (5:1–13)

[5:1] It is widely reported that there is sexual immorality in your midst, and of such a kind found not even among pagans: a man living with his father's wife. [2] And you have become arrogant! Should you not rather have grieved, so that the one who has done this should be removed from your midst? [3] I, for my part, though absent in body but present in spirit, have already passed judgment on the one who has committed this deed, just as if I were present. [4] When you are gathered together in the name of [our] Lord Jesus and (with) my spirit, [5] hand this man over with the power of our Lord Jesus to Satan for the destruction of the flesh so that the Spirit may be saved on the Day of the Lord.

[6] Your boasting is not a good thing. Do you not realize that a little leaven ferments the whole batch of dough? [7] Clear out the old leaven so that you may become a new batch, as you really are unleavened. For Christ, our passover lamb, has been sacrificed. [8] Let us, then, celebrate the feast, not with old leaven, or with the leaven of wickedness and evil, but with the unleavened bread of sincerity and truth.

[9] I wrote to you in my letter not to associate with sexually immoral people, [10] not at all meaning the immoral people of this world, or the greedy and swindling, or idolaters, since then you would have to leave this world. [11] But now I am writing to you not to associate with anyone who bears the name of brother, if he is sexually immoral or greedy or an idolater, slanderer, drunkard, or swindler; do not even eat with such a one. [12] For what have I to do with judging outsiders? Is it not those within, you are to judge? [13] God will judge those outside. *"Drive out the evil one from among you."*

COMMENT

Paul has now finished his comments on the first problem about which he had heard from Chloe's people (1:11), the rivalries that were dividing the Corinthian community because of its mistaken ideas about human wisdom and allegiance to preachers, and because of arrogance, which is at the root of it all. He turns now to an unrelated problem concerning Christian behavior, about which he has heard (*akouetai*, 5:1), but one which stems from the same root cause. It is not clear, however, whether the scandal that he now takes up has been reported to him by the same people of 1:11; or whether it has been recounted by the delegates from the community mentioned in 16:17, Stephanas, Fortunatus, and Achaicus; or perhaps by those who brought the letter to be mentioned in 7:1, if they are different from the delegates.

In any case, Paul hinted in 4:18–21 at further problems that are born of arrogance, and he now takes up a scandal he has learned about and addresses it with even harsher terms than those he used in chaps. 1–4. The issue now is not so theoretical or abstract as that of wisdom and folly, but a matter of how Corinthians are leading their Christian lives and how they are conducting themselves as a community of God's holy people. In v. 9, Paul reminds them that he has already written in a previous letter (no longer extant), "not to associate with sexually immoral people." Having counseled the Corinthians once about such a topic, he is now scandalized to hear that a heinous disregard of such advice has come to his attention.

The scandal has been made by a specific case of "sexual immorality," viz., a man living with his father's wife. He is annoyed that the Corinthian Christian church has tolerated such a situation in its midst. Paul is not reacting so much against what the individual Corinthian Christian has done as against the image that the Corinthian community is projecting of itself. Are the Christians of Roman Corinth really aware of themselves as an assembly that meets in the Lord's name (5:4)? More fundamental, however, to the scandalous situation is that these Christians have become so smug in their mode of life. Paul calls it arrogance (5:2) and even "boasting" (5:6), which in his view is "not a good thing," as he once again utilizes terms that relate this problem to that discussed in chaps. 1–4. If they were not so confident about the way they have been conducting themselves, they would have reacted more properly to such a scandal. For what each believer does affects the whole community. Each as a Christian may be free, but each has obligations to the whole, because they are all insiders (5:12b).

Schmithals maintains that this situation has developed in the Corinthian community because "the evildoer belonged to that Gnostic *ecclesiola in ecclesia* from which the writers of the church's letter knew themselves to be dissociated from the first" (*Gnosticism in Corinth*, 237); he would identify those called "arrogant" (v. 2) with "the Gnostics with their haughty selfconsciousness" (ibid.). That is a highly questionable interpretation based on speculation.

In any case, Paul instructs the Corinthian Christians that, when they gather together "in the name of the Lord Jesus" (and he is with them in spirit), they are to "hand this man over to Satan" in order that the good name of the community may be restored. The Corinthian Christians are to function as a faith-community, in the local church as a whole, and not just their leaders. This is why Paul says that he is with them in spirit; it is not just the leaders who are to react (see Pfitzner, "Purified Community").

The specific case, however, is only one aspect, serious though it may be, of the condition in which the Corinthian community finds itself, because Paul realizes that it has been tolerating in its midst many other immoral persons. He cannot understand how they can allow this to be. So he counsels them "to clear out the old leaven" (5:7), which is nothing else but "wickedness and evil" (5:8). They are to "drive out the evil one" from among them (5:13). The basis for this advice is Paul's recommendation not to associate with a fellow Christian ("one who bears the name of brother"), who carries on in immoral ways that he considers unbecoming of a Christian (sexual immorality, greed, idolatry, slander, drunkenness, swindling). He insists that members of the community should not even eat with them (5:11).

The motivation for the remedy that Paul is applying to this situation in the Corinthian community is double: (a) eschatological: in view of judgment on the Day of the Lord (5:5); and (b) Christological: expressed in another metaphor, this time drawn from the baking of bread and the annual celebration of Passover. In the making of bread, a bit of leaven ferments the whole batch of dough. Immorality and other evil conduct have contaminated the community like "old leaven," because they have produced their evil effects in its corporate life. As Jews used to clear out of their houses on the eve of Passover all leavened products, so Corinthian Christians must now clear out of their midst the "old leaven," that they may celebrate the Christian Passover, and also that they may become "unleavened." The more remote motivation for this cleansing is Christ himself, who is called "our passover lamb," and who has been sacrificed (5:7). Hence Christians should celebrate their Passover not with "the leaven of wickedness and evil," but with "the unleavened bread of sincerity and truth" (5:8). That is Paul's fundamental answer to the boasting and over-confidence of the Corinthian Christian community.

Four further things should be noted in this pericope. First, Paul's concern about the image that the Corinthian church is projecting among "pagans" (5:1, *ethnesin*) and among "outsiders" (5:12–13a, *tous exō*). He is clearly speaking from his Jewish background in reacting to the problems that have been reported about the Corinthian community. Whereas only one verse describes what the wrongdoer has done (v. 1), the rest of the verses (2–13) treat of the community as a whole and the image that it is projecting to heathen citizens of Corinth.

Second, Paul is really concerned about the relationship between faith in the risen Christ and responsible moral conduct of Christians. The passage is, therefore, important for the study of Pauline ethics.

Third, the passage is developed with the rhetorical composition of deliberate persuasion, a hortatory argument that seeks to persuade the community to act corporately and urges it to adopt practical measures for its immediate future (see Puskas, *Letters of Paul*, 59–60; Smit, "That Someone"). The passage is also an example of what has been called the "judgment form" in Pauline writings (Roetzel). Such a form developed from preexilic prophetic pronouncements and has four parts: (a) introduction: "It is widely reported . . ." (5:1a); (b) offense: "a man living with his father's wife" (5:1c); (c) punishment: "the one who has done this should be removed from your midst . . ." (5:2c–5); (d) hortatory conclusion: "Clear out the old leaven so that you may become new dough" (5:7). The form is also found later in rabbinic writings (see Francis, "Baraita").

Fourth, the passage deals with what later came to be called "excommunication," for Paul recommends not only that "the one who has done this should be removed from your midst" (v. 2c; cf. v. 13b), but that Corinthian Christians should not associate with immoral fellow Christians (vv. 9–11).

The roots of such exclusion are found in the OT, where a person could be cut off from Israel or the assembly of God's people for violation of Passover regulations (Exod 12:15, 19), sacrificial rules and the eating of blood (Lev 17:4, 9–10, 14), defilement of the sanctuary (Num 19:20), or a marriage with a foreign woman (Ezra 10:2–3, 8). The reason for the exclusion was the corporate responsibility of Israel, if the wrongdoer were not cut off, as in the prayer of Moses and Aaron in Num 16:22, "O God, God of the spirits of all flesh, (if) one man sins, will you be enraged against the whole congregation?" That is why Paul ends his discussion with a modified quotation of Deut 17:7 (see Rosner, *"Ouchi mallon"*). Although Paul borrows an expression from LXX Lev 18:8 (*gynaikos patros*, "father's wife"), his argument against the wrong that has been done is not based on the Torah or any OT teaching; it is rather governed by what *ethne*, "pagans," think. Corinthian Christians should have "mourned," confessing their corporate sin of tolerating such an errant fellow Christian.

The Qumran Jewish community also developed its own elaborate system of exclusion for various faults: 1QS 6:24–7:18 (see Kuhn, "A Legal Issue," 497–99; Forkman, *Limits*, 39–86). For still later forms of exclusion in rabbinic Judaism, see *m. Kerithoth* 1:1 (among the 36 transgressions listed one is "connexion with his father's wife"); cf. Str-B, 4/1:309–18 for lists of further transgressions.

This exclusion, however, has to be related also to the punishment in Roman law, which punished an adulterous couple with *relegatio*, the sending of them off to separate islands or to an Egyptian oasis. To understand this passage properly, one has to recall that in the Corinth of Paul's day Roman law would have been in vogue, according to which adultery was a crime, and not a mere civil offense. In the provinces such a crime fell under the jurisdiction of a proconsul (*anthypatos*), who exercised *imperium*, "supreme administrative power," which included the making of war, interpreting and executing laws, and inflicting the death penalty. A criminal case of adultery would have entailed a formal accusation before the proconsul and was regulated specifically by the *lex Iulia de adulteriis coercendis*, which stemmed from the reign of Augustus in 18 B.C. (see Treggiari, *Roman Marriage*, 277–90). It decreed that a husband who knew of his wife's adultery had to divorce her, and he or her father had to prosecute her within 60 days. Her punishment would be the loss of half of her dowry, a third of her other property, and relegation to some island. The adulterous partner could be prosecuted too and lose half of his property and be relegated to a different island. The husband who failed to prosecute his adulterous wife was considered *leno*, "a panderer." A wife, however, could not prosecute her husband for his adultery with a married woman.

The case of incest that Paul mentions in this passage would have fallen under such Roman legislation, and this situation makes it all the more serious that the Christian community was not reacting properly to the evil that existed among them (see Winter, *After Paul Left*, 44–52; Robinson, *Criminal Law*, 55–57).

Even though this chapter may seem, at first sight, to have little relation to the topics to be discussed in chap. 6, there is a connection that has to be recognized, just as there are elements in this chapter that echo themes of chaps. 1–4. Verse 6 mentions the "boasting" of Corinthian Christians, an attitude that Paul has already addressed in 1:29, 31; 3:21; 4:7; and the verb *physioō*, which occurs in 4:6, 18, 19, appears again in 5:2. Similarly, the topic of chap. 5 will find echoes in chap. 6, esp. in vv. 9–11, 12–20, where *pornoi* and *porneia* again appear and thus unite these two chapters (see Bernard, "The Connexion"). Verses 1–11 in chap. 6 deal with judicial altercations, but 5:1–13 and 6:12–20 also have their criminal aspects. Moreover, Deming ("The Unity," 294–97), in trying to show the unity of chaps. 5 and 6, maintains that the Corinthian community actually was divided in its reaction to the offense of 5:1, and that those who wanted the offender punished took the man to court and lost the case, which only exacerbated the animosity in the community. To such a situation, Paul would be reacting, having learned about it. Hence there may be a subtle link between 5:1–2 and chap. 6, in that the case of incest might have led to a legal case such as Paul mentions in 6:1–11. However, the details in this explanation remain highly speculative, with little basis in the text itself, as Lindemann (*1 Cor*, 122) also recognizes. Moreover, the sexual offense mentioned in 5:1–13 would not have been a matter for "petty courts" (6:2b), because Roman law against incest and adultery was applicable in Roman Corinth of that time (see above). Another association of chaps. 5 and 6 can be seen in that 5:12–13 has different forms of the verb *krinō*, "judge," which appears again in 6:1–2. See further McDonough, "Competent to Judge."

In this chapter, which is a self-contained unit, there are five sections: (1) Paul's reproach about the scandal, vv. 1–2; (2) Paul's sentence of expulsion passed against the wrongdoer, vv. 3–5; (3) a generic exhortation about Christian life relative to its celebration of Passover, vv. 6–8; (4) further directives about associating with the immoral, vv. 9–11; and (5) return to the initial problem, vv. 12–13. Although the sections may seem at first disparate, Paul gives one and the same counsel throughout: "(he) should be removed from your midst" (v. 2); "clear out the old leaven" (v. 7); and "drive out the evil one from among you" (v. 13).

Paul's discussion at the end of this chapter, especially in vv. 9–12, is aimed at setting boundary limits for Corinthian Christianity. When he opposes idolatry and various forms of extramarital sexual activity, he is seeking to form the predominantly Gentile Christian community according to norms of his Jewish background (see the way Josephus sums up Judaism in *Ag.Ap.* 2.1.22–24 §§190–203: worship of the one God in the Jerusalem Temple and the Law's recognition of no sexual intercourse, except the natural union of husband and wife for the procreation of children). By way of contrast to what Paul is doing here, in his letter to the Galatians he was likewise setting boundaries for the Christians of Galatian communities in adopting Gentile practices in the face of Judaizing attempts: no circumcision, no obligation to observe the Mosaic law, especially its observance of the Sabbath and dietary regulations (see Sanders, "Paul between Jews and Gentiles").

NOTES

5:1. *It is widely reported that there is sexual immorality in your midst.* Lit. "it is heard everywhere," or possibly "it is actually heard," because the adv. *holōs* may be understood either in a extensive sense or an emphatic sense (BDAG, 704), although Lindemann (*1 Cor*, 122) claims that the former meaning of the adv. is not attested elsewhere. Yet Weiss (*1 Cor*, 124) has defended its use, and it appears in NAB, Conzelmann, Godet, Héring. In either case, it introduces a new topic that has nothing to do with the final verses of chap. 4. Paul addresses his moral exhortation not to the wrongdoer personally, but to the Christian community, in "whose midst" such sexually immoral conduct has been tolerated. *En hymin* means in the midst of the Christian community, and it finds its parallel expression in the following clause, *oude en tois ethnesin,* "not even among pagans" (Garland, *1 Cor*, 159).

The noun *porneia* occurs twice for the first time; it will appear again in 6:13, 18; 7:2; a person is called *pornos* in 5:9, 10, 11; 6:9; and the cog. verb *porneuō* is found in 6:18; 10:8. Strictly speaking, the abs. noun means "fornication, harlotry" (as in 6:9 [see NOTE there]), but the word was used widely in both biblical and extrabiblical Greek for many kinds of "unsanctioned sexual intercourse" (BDAG, 854), even apart from its OT metaphorical meaning of "idolatry" (*TDNT*, 6:580–90). In this verse, the first occurrence has a generic sense, "sexual immorality," but in the following clause it is used of a specific kind of it. In using the word twice, Paul gives the impression that the case to be mentioned was not even recognized as sexual immorality in the Corinthian community.

and of such a kind found not even among pagans: a man living with his father's wife. Lit. "and such immorality, which not even among the nations: that someone has the wife of the father." The word order is peculiar, *kai toiautē porneia hētis oude en tois ethnesin: hōste gynaika tina tou patros echein,* with a verbless rel. clause, followed by a result clause (*hōste* + infin.), in which the indef. pron. *tina* is placed within the phrase *gynaikos tou patros* (see BDF §473.1). MSS P⁶⁸, ℵ², Ψ, 1881 and the Koine text-tradition supply a verb at the end of the rel. clause, *onomazetai,* "(which) is (not even) named (among) . . . ," a scribal addition apparently borrowed from Eph 5:3, in an attempt to improve the grammar or increase the heinous character of the crime. *Ethnē* does not mean "Gentiles," as in 1:23 (opposite of Jews), but rather "pagans," as in 12:2; 10:20 (as variant reading). The expression *gynaika echein,* "have a wife," denotes a continuous state of union, not a casual adulterous act, as also in 7:2, 12, 13, 29; Gal 4:27 (quoting LXX Isa 54:1); John 4:17–18.

Generally, commentators refuse to understand *tina gynaika tou patros echein* directly of a son's marriage with his mother, because Paul would have written instead *heautou mētera,* "his own mother." Such a marital union not only was forbidden in Jewish law (Lev 18:7), but was equally unacceptable in the Greco-

Roman world (Iamblichus, *Vita Pythagorica*. 31.210; Aelian, *De natura anima-lium* 3.47).

It has usually been understood as a form of incest, viz., intercourse with a step-mother (so R. E. Brown [*Introduction*, 528], Collins, Conzelmann, Deming, Fee, Murphy-O'Connor, Yarbro Collins). Theoretically, this might mean that after the father's death his son has married the widowed second wife; so Lindemann (*1 Cor*, 123) has understood it. It is, however, much more likely that the son has entered into a continuous union with his father's second wife, who is separated from him, while he is still alive. Hence it would be a case of adulterous incest, which was a blatant violation of the *lex Iulia* in Roman law (Gaius, *Institutiones* 1.63: *Item eam [uxorem ducere non liquet] quae mihi quondam socrus aut nurus aut priuigna aut nouerca fuit*, "Likewise [it is not allowed to marry] her who was once to me a mother-in-law or daughter-in-law or stepdaughter or stepmother"). Cf. Treggiari, *Roman Marriage*, 37–39, 281; Robinson, *Criminal Law*, 54–55. Even though Barrett (*1 Cor*, 121) admits that the woman "was probably the of-fender's stepmother," he claims that the offence was neither adultery (Paul does not "call" it so), nor incest, but "fornication." Call it what one will, it seems to be not an isolated act of harlotry, but adulterous incest because of the ongoing state of the union (see above). Such a union is known in the Roman world from Mar-tial (A.D. 40–103), *Epigram.* 4.16.

However, De Vos has argued that the woman was not the Christian man's step-mother, but rather his father's *concubina*, which would have been an unusual but not an unknown or illegal relationship in the Roman world, of which the Corin-thian Christians were aware, but which Paul has judged to be *porneia*. That is an interesting explanation, but hardly convincing, because such a relationship could not be described by Paul as "found not even among pagans," as recognized by Lindemann (*1 Cor*, 124). Paul's assessment of the relationship makes use of a for-mulaic phrase borrowed from the LXX (see below), which denotes the relation-ship with what one normally calls a "stepmother."

The son was a Christian, because Paul so refers to him in vv. 2, 3, 5, using a masc. ptc. or pron., whereas the stepmother undoubtedly was not, and that is the reason why he says nothing about her. Paul seems to treat her as an "outsider" (5:12–13).

In any case, this sort of union was strictly forbidden in Jewish tradition: see Lev 18:8, "you shall not uncover the nakedness of your father's wife" (LXX: *gynaikos patros*, whence Paul derives his terminology); the LXX does not speak of it as *porneia*; also Lev 20:11; Deut 23:1; 27:20; cf. 11QTemple[a] (11Q19) 66:12. Philo (*De spec. legibus* 3.3 §§20–21) mentions that Jewish law does not permit the son of a first marriage to marry his stepmother (*mētruia*) because the names *mētēr*, "mother," and *mētruia* are closely akin; and a fortiori to marry his natural mother (*hē physei mētēr*). Similarly, *Sentences of Ps.-Phocylides* 179–80: "Touch not your stepmother (*mētruia*), your father's second wife." Cf. the later rabbinic condem-nation (*m. Sanhedrin* 7:4; *m. Kerithoth* 1:1; cf. Str-B, 3:347–50), where death by stoning is prescribed in such a case. That punishment is also mentioned in *Jub.* 33:10–13, which is a rewriting of the account of Reuben and Bilhah (his father's concubine [*pallakē*]) of Gen 35:22, but which is not the same case as that discussed by Paul. Josephus (*Ant.* 3.12.1 §274), however, calls intercourse with one's mother the "greatest evil" (*kakon megiston*) and says that union with one's stepmother (*patros gamētē*) is punishable by death.

When Paul says that such *porneia* is not found among pagans, he does not mean that no pagan has ever committed it, but his rhetorical exaggeration is coping with the recognition that even pagans did not tolerate it (Gaius, *Institutes* 1.63 [quoted above]; see also Apuleius, *Metamorph.* 10.2.3, which calls intercourse of a woman with her stepson *extremum flagitium*, "enormous outrage"). Paul knows that Gentiles developed certain moral standards, as he admits in Rom 2:14, and he was undoubtedly aware of the severe penalties of Roman law, which had no leniency for such conduct. That is the reason why pagans are used in his argument with the Christian community of Roman Corinth, and why no appeal is made to the Mosaic law.

Although Kruse ("The Offender and the Offence") would identify "the one who has caused pain" of 2 Cor 2:5–6 and 7:12 with the incestuous wrongdoer of this passage, there is no certainty regarding such an identification. More than likely Paul is referring there to an entirely different case of a wrongdoer who has caused pain to the Corinthian community. Kruse himself admits that his arguments "fall short of positive proof" (139).

2. *And you have become arrogant!* Lit. "become puffed up," which expresses the pride and self-confidence of some Corinthians, who were apparently considering themselves different or superior to such conduct. The incestuous union was not carried out secretly or out of weakness, but was known among many otherwise reputable members of the Corinthian community. They may have become a "new creation" in Christ (2 Cor 5:17; Gal 6:15) and claimed Christian freedom from the Mosaic law, but that would hardly mean license in behavior or even a boastful attitude tolerant of such a criminal act, with something like the attitude expressed in 6:12, "All things are permissible for me." On this aspect of the matter, Paul will comment further in v. 6. The same verb *physioō* appears in 4:6, where Paul spoke of the arrogance in siding with one preacher over against another. Its use provides an indirect link of this chapter to the preceding chapter(s).

Should you not rather have grieved? Lit. "have you not rather grieved/mourned?" Paul's rhetorical question sums up the matter: in shame, they should have mourned for themselves that a Christian man has done such a thing and that he is still among them; they have not sized up the situation properly in their Christian community. Paul maintains that the community should have purified itself of such a deleterious person. Some commentators, however, think that he means that the Corinthian Christians should be mourning over the impending loss of the wrongdoing fellow member (so Héring, Morris, Robertson-Plummer); that is possible, but more likely the reason for mourning should be shame at the tolerance of such evil among them and the realization that they as a community are corporately responsible.

so that the one who has done this should be removed from your midst? Part of the motivation for the removal of this wrongdoer from their midst is the notion that the Christian community is "the temple of God": "the temple of God, which you are, is sacred" (3:16–17). The holiness of such a temple calls for the removal of all that might defile it (cf. Deut 23:2–9; Ezek 20:38–40; see Rosner, "Temple and Holiness"). Mss P^{11vid}, $\aleph$, A, C, 33, 81, 104, 326, 1175 read *praxas*, whereas MSS P^{46}, P^{48}, B, D, F, G, Ψ, 1739, 1881 and the Koine text-tradition read *poiēsas*, which means practically the same thing, perhaps a bit less forcefully.

Paul's words *hina arthē* (or in some MSS *exarthē*) *ex hymōn*, lit. "that he should be taken from you," with *hina* used in a consecutive sense (BDF §379), owe their formulation to LXX Deut 17:7, which Paul will quote in v. 13, to sum up his discussion. Cf. the Hebrew of 1QS 6:25, *wybdylhw mtwk*, "he shall be excluded from the midst of"; 2:16, *wnkrt mtwk kwl bny 'wr*, "may he be cut off from the midst of all the sons of light." Thus Paul makes use of a traditional formula of exclusion for an ultimately good purpose, which he will express further in v. 5. One should guard against reading Paul's words as though they were execratory and nothing more (see Cambier, "La chair et l'esprit").

3. *I, for my part, though absent in body but present in spirit, have already passed judgment on the one who has committed this deed, just as if I were present.* Paul makes clear his own view of the matter, using *egō men gar* as an introductory phrase, which sets him apart from the Corinthian community, for it now has to react to this situation as a community. Paul states his individual apostolic opinion, as he considers himself present among them in spirit. He even repeats this idea of presence (*parōn de tō pneumati . . . hōs parōn*) in order to stress that by this letter, by "this written judgment," he is indeed with the Corinthian community in this crisis, even though he personally is not in Corinth (Cole, "1 Cor 5:4: ' . . . with my spirit' "). Cf. 2 Cor 10:11; 13:10 for similar expressions of spiritual presence. *Pace* Fee (*1 Cor*, 205) and Thiselton (*1 Cor*, 391), it is not a matter of God's Spirit being present with them; it is Paul's spirit, as the parallels in 2 Corinthians make clear. Moreover, he contrasts *sōma*, "body," with *pneuma*, "spirit," as a way of emphasizing his personal interest in the Corinthian community. His body is not in Corinth, but in Ephesus (16:8), yet he is with them "in spirit," i.e., psychologically. Cf. Col 2:5, where the same idea is expressed with *sarx*, "flesh," and *pneuma*. In contrast to the community's attitude in this situation, Paul personally has taken a different view of it; he himself has already made a formal and authoritative judgment against the culprit so that the community may be purified.

Verses 3–5 are closely related in the Greek text, but the syntax of them is quite complicated. Modern translations often break up the verses into shorter sentences, as has been done in the lemma above. One can read v. 3 as a self-standing unit, but then that reading encounters four problems: (1) With what is one to take the opening prep. phrase of v. 4, *en tō onomati tou kyriou [hēmōn] Iēsou*, "in the name of [our] Lord Jesus"? (2) On what is the infin. *paradounai*, "to hand over," of v. 5 dependent? (3) With what is one to take the final prep. phrase of v. 4, *syn tē dynamei tou kyriou hēmōn Iēsou*, "with the power of our Lord Jesus"? (4) Verse 4 strangely has no main verb and consists only of a gen. absol. and two prep. phrases, which introduce v. 5.

4. *When you are gathered together in the name of [our] Lord Jesus and (with) my*

spirit. The prep. phrase, "in the name of [our] Lord Jesus," stands at the head of v. 4, and it cannot modify the final clause of v. 3, "the one who has done this deed" (*katergasmenon*), since that would create nonsense, *pace* Murphy-O'Connor ("1 Corinthians v, 3–5"), who so takes it, understanding it as an expression of the "overweening confidence in their own rightness," born of the difference they experience because of baptism in the name of Jesus and a new freedom that Corinthians have found in Christ; so also NAB, Yarbro Collins ("Function," 253). Horsley (*1 Cor,* 79), Lindemann (*1 Cor,* 121, 125), Giblin ("Pauline Sexual Morality," 111 n. 11). However, would a Christian son having illicit intercourse with his stepmother invoke the name of Jesus to justify his actions? (Kistemaker, *1 Cor,* 160; similarly Garland, *1 Cor,* 166). The prep. phrase scarcely refers to the corporate confidence of the Corinthian Christians. Consequently, it has to be taken rather with the immediately following gen. absol. *synachthentōn hymōn kai tou emou pneumatos* (lit. "when you and my spirit are gathered together"), as in NJB, REB, ESV, NIV, NKJV; also J. Weiss, Lietzmann, Senft. Its meaning: with the sponsorship of the Lord Jesus.

Some commentators (Allo, Bachmann, Robertson-Plummer) prefer to take that prep. phrase with the infin. *paradounai* at the beginning of v. 5. That, however, is problematic, being too far removed, for it unduly complicates the syntax of these verses. Still others (Schlatter, RSV, NRSV) take it with *kekrika,* "have passed judgment in the name. . . ." (5:3), which is not impossible. See Heitmüller, *"Im Namen Jesu",* 73–74.

In any case, Paul is instructing the Corinthians that they should gather as a community and exercise their corporate obligation, taking united action against the man who has so sinned. They are to assemble in Jesus' name, as in Matt 18:20, and realize that his authority and sponsorship are with them, which is more important than the presence of Paul. "In the name of (the Lord) Jesus" occurs elsewhere in various forms (6:11; Col 3:17; 2 Thess 3:6; Acts 2:38; 16:18), but it does not always follow the verb that it is modifying, as Murphy-O'Connor contends ("1 Corinthians v, 3–5"); see Phil 2:10; Acts 3:6; 4:10. Paul is urging the Corinthian Christians to come to the same judgment that he has already made and to pass judgment with him. When he speaks of "my spirit," he is expressing at least his associative presence, but it may also be his epistolary presence, i.e., through this very letter (see above) they hear his apostolic voice.

5. *hand this man over with the power of our Lord Jesus to Satan.* Lit. "to hand over such a man as this. . . ." The infin. *paradounai* may be indirectly dependent on *kekrika* of v. 3, but it is separated from it by the gen. absol. and the prep. phrases that make up v. 4. Some commentators prefer to understand *dei,* "it is necessary," before *paradounai* at the beginning of v. 5 (SBJ; Murphy-O'Connor). Still others take the infin. as an imperative, as in the lemma above, which can be compared with Rom 12:15; Phil 3:16 (Collins, *1 Cor,* 212), even though BDF §389 and GGBB 608 limit the impv. infin. to those two NT passages only. In any case, Paul has already judged that such a person is to be handed over to Satan, and in v. 4 he is urging the Corinthian community to join him in so judging. The expression *ton toiouton,* "such a man," merely repeats "the one who has done this" (5:2);

cf. 2 Cor 2:6–7. The same sense of *paradidōmi* is predicated of God allowing his agent, Satan, to test Job (2:6, LXX: *paradidōmi soi auton,* "I hand him over to you"), which may well be the source of Paul's use of it here. This negative sense of the verb is found in the LXX (Judg 15:12; 16:23–24) and in Greek incantations on magical papyri of later date: *paradidōmi se eis to melan chaos en tais apōleiais,* "I am giving you over to dark chaos in utter destruction" (*P. Paris.* 574 1247 [3d cent. A.D.]). Cf. Spicq, *TLNT,* 3:19–20; *New Docs,* 4:165 §73; Yarbro Collins, "Function," 255–56.

The phrase, *syn tē dynamei tou kyriou hēmōn Iēsou,* "with power of the Lord Jesus," is also problematic, because it follows the gen. absol., *synachthentōn hymōn,* and precedes the infin., *paradounai,* "hand over," and commentators debate with which it should be taken. It makes sense with either, but extrabiblical parallels suggest that it is understood better with the infin.: *dēsō egō keinēn . . . syn th'Hēkatē chthōniā kai Erinysin,* "I shall bind her . . . with below-the-earth Hecate and the Erinyes" (*IG* 3.3.108; cf. Deissmann, *LAE,* 303).

Handing someone over to Satan is an expression found also in 1 Tim 1:20. It denotes the transfer of a wrongdoer from the salutary lordship of Jesus Christ to the realm and authority of inimical Satan; the wrongdoer is "severed from Christ" (Gal 5:4), and this is to be done "with the power" of the Lord himself. It thus connotes the exclusion of the person from the Christian community—what later came to be called excommunication. Although Paul will teach that Christ through his death and resurrection has "destroyed every dominion, authority, and power" (15:24), he now consigns this man to Satan's authority in order to exclude him from the influence of the risen Christ.

Hebrew *śāṭān,* "adversary," as a common noun, often denotes a human or heavenly figure sent to thwart a wrongdoer (Num 22:22, 32; 1 Kgs 11:14, 23; 1 Chr 21:1). In Job 1–2 and Zech 3:1–2 it is applied as a name to one of "the sons of Elohim," the accuser or prosecutor in God's heavenly tribunal. (There the LXX translates it as *diabolos,* "accuser," which becomes in time "devil.") In later Jewish literature, *śāṭān* becomes the name of a supramundane being who acts in opposition to God and seeks to frustrate divine influence and activity (Sir 21:27 [Vg 21:30]). So it occurs in QL in 11QPs^a 19:15 ("let Satan not rule over me, or any impure spirit"); otherwise it is used there as a common noun, "adversary." In that literature, however, Satan often bears other names such as Belial (*bĕlîyaʿal,* 1QS 1:18, 24; 2:5, 19; CD 4:13; 5:18); or *Maśṭēmāh* (4QPs-Juba [4Q225] 2 ii 6, 13, 14), a name developed from the same root (*śṭn*) as *śāṭān.* Note especially the parallel to this Pauline judgment in CD 8:1–2, "Thus will be the judgment against all those who enter His covenant, but who do not remain steadfast in them [the covenant rules]; they will be visited with destruction at the hand of Belial." See also 1QS 2:5–6, 15–17: "cut off from the midst of the sons of light" [i.e., excluded from the community]. From such a Jewish background, Paul has derived not only the name for the creature to whom he would consign the incestuous wrongdoer in this passage, but also the idea of exclusion itself; also 1QS 8:21–24. He otherwise mentions Satan in 1 Thess 2:18; 1 Cor 7:5; 2 Cor 2:11; 11:14; 12:7, Rom 16:20 (where Satan does not always appear as an enemy of God, but sometimes as His agent), but never in the letters to the Galatians, Philippians, or Phile-mon. Cf. 2 Thess 2:9; 1 Tim 1:20; 5:15. A concentration of references to Satan oc-curs in the Corinthian correspondence.

Pace Orr-Walther (*1 Cor*, 186), "Satan" does not refer "to the public prosecu-tor" or "Roman officials," who would punish the wrongdoer for the violation of Roman law. For what reason would Paul ever designate such officials as "Satan"? Similarly, it is eisegetical to say that Paul was thinking here of Azazel (Lev 16:7, 10) as a name "virtually synonymous with the name Satan" and of the scapegoat traditions of Judaism (Shillington, "Atonement Texture," 47). Where does one ever find such a virtual synonymous usage? It is likewise eisegetical to introduce into the discussion of Satan allusions to the social dynamics of witchcraft soci-eties, *pace* Johnson, "Satan Talk in Corinth." Nor is there any evidence that the Corinthian Christians, allegedly "ascetics," were condoning the incest because the offender was an important member of their community, *pace* Goulder ("Lib-ertines").

for the destruction of the flesh. The immediate goal of the action that the Corin-thian community is to take is to rid it of the evil that it has been tolerating. *Olethros,* "ruin, destruction," is found again 1 Thess 5:3; cf. 1 Tim 6:9 (where it is parallel to *apōleia*), but it is not said to be *olethros aiōnios,* "eternal destruction," as in 2 Thess 1:9. The problem is the meaning of *sarx,* "flesh," which is taken to be a synonym for *sōma,* "body" (as in 2 Cor 7:1, 5; Gal 4:13–14). Paul may be using here the contrast of "flesh" and "spirit" in the dualistic sense in which he does elsewhere (e.g., Rom 8:5–8; Gal 5:17), but the contrast of *sarx* and *pneuma* is stated absolutely (without a poss. "his" in either case) and with a certain openness. In using *sarx,* however, Paul seems to be speaking of bodily suffering, but scarcely of death (*pace* Barrett, *1 Cor*, 126; Conzelmann, *1 Cor*, 97; Senft, *1 Cor*, 74). The idea seems to be that Satan "must be given his due, but can claim no more; if he has the flesh he has no right to the spirit, even of a sinner" (Barrett, *1 Cor*, 127). The "destruction" is rather to be understood in a figurative, eschatological sense (as in 10:10–11; cf. LXX Jer 5:6; Ezek 6:14) as temporal torments and ruin result-ing from exclusion of the wrongdoer from God's new people, as vv. 2, 7, and 13 imply (see South, "A Critique," 553–55). Note also 11:30–32, which may express the principle of Paul's thinking here: "Since we are being judged by [the] Lord, we are being chastened that we may not be condemned along with the world."

so that the Spirit may be saved on the Day of the Lord. I.e., "God's Spirit present in the Corinthian congregation" (Donfried, "Justification," 150). Such an inter-pretation of *pneuma* runs counter to the common mode of understanding *pneuma* in this verse, which reads it as if Paul had written *autou pneuma,* "his spirit," i.e., the wrongdoer's spirit (so interpreted in the RSV, NRSV, NAB, NIV, ESV, REB, and by Merklein, Kremer, Robertson-Plummer [*1 Cor*, 100], Fee [*1 Cor*, 198, 211]; Schweizer [*TDNT*, 6:435]). However, Paul did not write *autou pneuma*; but just as *tēs sarkos* lacks a poss. pron., so too *pneuma.* It seems rather to mean "Spirit," i.e., God's Spirit, either as the Spirit given to the man, when he be-came a Christian (so Senft, *1 Cor*, 74); or as in 6:19, where Paul tells individual Christians that their bodies are the temple of the Holy Spirit, so that the man may still have it until judgment day; or as the Spirit present to the community, as in 3:16–17, where Paul tells Corinthian Christians that they are God's temple and that the Spirit of God dwells in them, so that it may not be lost to the community, but may continue to preserve the congregation for the day of judgment. The last alternative is the more likely, as it has been understood by Tertullian, *De Pudicitia* 13.24–25 (CCLat 2.1306), Ambrosiaster, *Ad I Cor.* 5.3.3 (CSEL 81.54), Donfried, Lindemann. In any case, this is the more remote goal of the handing over of the wrongdoer to Satan. Whatever is to happen to the wrongdoer, Paul is desirous that the community itself does not suffer; its Spirit is to be saved for the life of the community (Campbell, "Flesh and Spirit"). On "the Day of the Lord," see NOTE on 1:8.

In the long run, Paul is not so much concerned about the sin of the individual as he is about the smugness of community members in tolerating such a wrongdoer among them, which jeopardizes their status in God's sight and will not be in their interest on the Day of the Lord; hence his recommendation of the exclusion of all that is immoral. Cf. Gal 5:5, "For through the Spirit, by faith, we await the hope of righteousness," i.e., the congregation must see to it in faith that God's Spirit continues to dwell within it. So also Collins (*1 Cor*, 213); Yarbro Collins ("Function," 259); Lindemann (*1 Cor*, 127).

The added goal raises a further question about the role of Satan, who is not thought of as God's enemy, but is seen as an agent of God, as in Job 1–2, and specifically as an agent either for the salvation of the wrongdoer or for the good of the community. Recall 2 Cor 12:7, *angelos satana*, a thorn in the flesh, as "a messenger of Satan," to keep Paul from being too elated; cf. 1 Tim 1:20 (see Thornton, "Satan"). Some MSS (P⁶¹ᵛⁱᵈ, ℵ, Ψ, and the Koine text-tradition) add at the end "Jesus."

6. *Your boasting is not a good thing.* Lit. "not good (is the obj. of) your (2d plur.) boasting." At first sight, this statement follows strangely on the preceding five verses; but it is really fundamental to them, because Paul sees the underlying difficulty to be that the Christians of Roman Corinth have been too smug in their way of thinking and reacting to this scandalous situation that they have permitted to exist among them. Such "boasting" echoes 4:7 and is the result of the arrogance mentioned in 5:2.

Do you not realize that a little leaven ferments the whole batch of dough? Cf. the "Q" saying in Luke 13:20–21; Matt 13:33. Paul's rhetorical question quotes a common popular proverb, as also in Gal 5:9. The proverb suggests that it takes only one small instance of improper sexual conduct to contaminate the whole community; cf. the proverb cited in 15:33, "Bad company corrupts good habits." Philo (*De spec. leg.* 1.53 §293) mentions the "rising" effect of leaven and understands it as a symbol of arrogant conduct. The proverb is introduced by the expression, *ouk oidate hoti*, "Do you not realize," on which see NOTE on 3:16; Paul thus stresses a notion plainly admitted by everybody.

Zymē, though often, and wrongly, translated "yeast" (e.g., BDAG, 429), was actually old, sour dough that had been subjected to fermenting juices and stored away (see Luke 13:21) until it was to be used in new dough as a rising agent, to make the new bread light and palatable. Moreover, only a small amount of leaven was needed to impregnate the whole batch of new dough (*EDNT* 2:104–5). Such old dough, however, could easily be contaminated and could infect dangerously the whole batch of new dough into which it was introduced; hence the yearly Jewish practice of destroying all old leaven before the celebration of Passover. From that came the further connotation of "old leaven" (see Mitton, "New Wine").

7. *Clear out the old leaven so that you may become a new batch.* Now Paul alludes to the association of leaven with the celebration of the feast of Unleavened Bread and that of Passover. He writes *ekkatharate*, "clean out" (plur. impv.), which in this context means not only purification, but also connotes exclusion of that which contaminates, so that the community may become *neon phyrama*, "a new mixture," i.e., a new batch of dough. Paul uses "leaven" symbolically, as well as its Jewish association with Passover to make his point: Christians of Roman Corinth are to clear out from their midst that which has made it impossible for them to be celebrating the new Passover. One corrupt member in their midst is enough to make the whole community unworthy.

Passover was celebrated at sundown marking the beginning of 14 Nisan, the first month in the Babylonian/Jewish year. Then the Passover lamb, slain in the late afternoon hours of 13 Nisan, was roasted and eaten in a family circle at sundown (Lev 23:5–8). Everything leavened had to be "cleaned out" and removed from the dwelling (Exod 12:15) before the cultic slaying of the lamb (Deut 16:4; for further details, see the later regulations in *m. Pesaḥim* 1:1–4). The meal was not only eaten with unleavened bread and bitter herbs (Exod 12:8), but only that kind of bread might be eaten for seven days thereafter (Exod 12:17–20; 23:15; 34:18). This seven-day period was called technically "the feast of Unleavened Bread." In time, however, "Passover" became the name for all eight days (Deut 16:1–4; Ezek 45:21–25; Josephus, *Ant.* 6.9.3 §423; 20.5.3 §106); see Luke 22:1, 7, where the two are treated as one. The two feasts are mentioned together in 2 Chr 35:17.

as you are really unleavened. Paul mixes his metaphors as he tells the Corinthian Christians that they must recognize that they themselves are really "unleavened," i.e., already cleansed of the old leaven of their former selves, "in view of the fact that they have entered into a new Exodus through the death of a new Paschal Victim" (Howard, " 'Christ Our Passover' "). Therefore, they must now get rid of this corrupting element as well as of all arrogance.

For Christ, our passover lamb, has been sacrificed. Paul states his fundamental reason for their condition as *azymoi*, "unleavened," and for the instruction he has been giving. He derives his expression from the impv. of LXX Exod 12:21 (*thysate to pascha*, "slaughter the passover lamb"; cf. Deut 16:2, 6) and makes it a temporally past tense, thus supplying a reason why Christians are "unleavened." They have already passed through Passover (in Jesus' death). Paul regards Jesus Christ, who died on the cross (1:18) at Passover, as the passover lamb of a new dispensation. (For the motif of Christ as passover lamb, see also 1 Pet 1:19; John 19:36; Rev 5:6–12.) According to Jewish custom, one had to clean the dwelling of anything ˙ leavened in order to celebrate Passover; but Paul inverts the procedure, saying that Christ has already been sacrificed, and so unleavened Corinthian Christians must now clean out all corrupting material, like old leaven, from their midst. Through Christ they have entered a new Exodus experience; they have been released from bondage to the old order and now live in a new paschal situation (see Howard, " 'Christ Our Passover' ").

Paul writes *to pascha hēmōn*, "our passover lamb" or simply "our passover," because the noun *pascha* can denote either the feast or the animal. In the NT, the Greek form is *pascha*, but Josephus writes *phaska* (*Ant.* 5.1.4 §20; 17.9.3 §213). Both forms represent attempts to transliterate Aramaic *pashā'*. The Hebrew form is *pesah*, which is sometimes transliterated in the LXX as *phasek* (2 Chr 30:1, 2, 5) or *phasech* (2 Chr 35:1, 6, 7). The etymology of Hebrew *pesah* is uncertain, but it is popularly explained as the "passing over" (i.e., the sparing) of the Hebrew firstborn during the night of deliverance of the Hebrews from bondage, when Yahweh slew all other firstborn in the land of Egypt (Exod 12:13, 29).

Sometimes it is said that "the Paschal victim was not a sin-offering or regarded as a means of expiating or removing sins" (Gray, *Sacrifice in the Old Testament*, 397; cf. Lindemann, *1 Cor*, 129). However, Num 28:22 uses *lĕkappēr 'ălêkem*, "to make expiation on your behalf," as part of the passover offering by fire; and Ezek 45:22 speaks of the prince providing "a young bull for a sin offering" (*par hattā't*), as part of the passover sacrifice. These passages, then, show that the celebration of passover came indeed to connote the wiping away of sins. In any case, the Pauline understanding of the feast associates with Passover the expiating character of Jesus' death.

8. *Let us, then, celebrate the feast, not with old leaven, or with the leaven of wickedness and evil, but with the unleavened bread of sincerity and truth.* To the past indicative expressed in v. 7, Paul adds a hortatory subjunctive, introduced by *hōste* (BDF §391.2), in order to stress that, because Christians are to celebrate that classic feast in a new sense, they themselves (the "unleavened") must get rid of all the "old leaven," now explained in a moral sense by the synonymous pair, "wickedness and evil" (a phrase derived from LXX Sir 25:17, 19). In celebrating the new Passover, Christians must still consume "unleavened bread," now similarly explained by the pair, "sincerity and truth," i.e., sincerity of conduct and character (2 Cor 1:12; 2:17). These qualities must take the place of boasting and arrogance, which enabled them to tolerate the "wickedness and evil" among them, and so come to the knowledge of the truth.

Whether or not Corinthians were already celebrating the feast of Passover in a Christian sense is difficult to say; Jeremias thinks they were (*TDNT*, 5:901). So Paul may be using the image of a Christian Passover to make his hortatory point. Has Paul used this image because he was writing this letter near the time of Passover? Some commentators have raised the question, appealing to 16:8, where he speaks of staying in Ephesus until Pentecost. Perhaps, then, the image is derived from the time of the composition of the letter (Barrett, *1 Cor*, 129–30), an idea summarily dismissed by Garland (*1 Cor*, 180).

9. *I wrote to you in my letter not to associate with sexually immoral people.* That earlier letter is no longer extant (see INTRODUCTION, p. 43), and no paragraph in any other letter deals with that topic (not even 1 Cor 5:1–5). To it Corinthians

may have been replying in the letter Paul mentions in 7:1, as they asked how his advice was to be carried out. This gives him the occasion to make further comments (vv. 9–11) on what he meant and to show that he is aware of himself as a letter writer. The aorist *egrapsa* expresses past time; it is not an epistolary aorist.

Paul is not concerned about outsiders (v. 12), but about Christians in Roman Corinth who have been involved in social relations with people who are *pornoi*, "sexually immoral." The verb Paul uses, *synanamignymi*, "mix up together with, mingle," echoes similar OT expressions of association (LXX Hos 8:7; Ezek 20:18).

10. *not at all meaning the immoral people of this world, or the greedy and swindling, or idolaters.* The *pornoi* are only one class of wrongdoers in "this world," and Paul adds three other classes of them: *pleonektai*, "the greedy" (governed by a vice that Paul will condemn in Rom 1:29, as they are already in Sir 14:9); *harpages*, "the rapacious, robbers, swindlers" (who were to be excluded from Israel, Deut 24:7); and *eidōlolatrai*, "idolaters" (worshipers of pagan gods, criticized by Jews as well, Deut 17:5–7). The three classes of wrongdoers will reappear in v. 11, where others will be added, and in 6:9–10 (some are named in Eph 5:3, 5). Paul is not referring to all non-Christians who indulge in such practices, as the next clause makes clear. He is constructing an ethical list or catalogue of evil deeds (see further *PAHT* §PT142; Segalla, "Cataloghi dei peccati in S. Paolo"; Vögtle, *Die Tugend- und Lasterkataloge*, 31–32).

since then you would have to leave this world. I.e., the *kosmos*, as the habitation of humanity (BDAG, 562), where Christians live together with such wrongdoers. Although Paul recognizes that Corinthian Christians share this world with such people, he is scarcely advocating that Christians live in a ghetto, or retire to a desert retreat, as did some Essenes, who "withdrew from the dwelling of the men of perversity to walk in the desert (and) open there the path of HIM, as it stands written, 'In the desert, prepare the way of ●●●●, make straight in the wilderness a road for our God.' This is the study of the law" (1QS 8:13–14, quoting Isa 40:3).

11. *But now I am writing to you not to associate with anyone who bears the name of brother.* Lit. "if someone named a brother." Paul uses the epistolary aorist, *egrapsa* (BDF §334), "I wrote, have written," but its epistolary character is assured by the initial adv. *nyn*, "now," hence the present tense in English translations. Contrast the real aorist at the beginning of v. 9. The RSV, however, understands it as a real aorist, "But rather I wrote to you"; contrast the NRSV. Again, *adelphos*, "brother," means "Christian" (see NOTE on 1:1). Paul's advice is to avoid close association with any Christian who is one of the following six characters.

if he is sexually immoral or greedy or an idolater, slanderer, drunkard, or swindler. Four of these types are already mentioned in v. 10; two others are added, the fourth and fifth in this list: *loidoros*, "slanderer, reviler"; and *methysos*, "drunkard." They will be met again in 6:10, where a similar catalogue of evildoers is presented, which again relates this chapter to that one (see Zaas, "Catalogues"). This description gives one some idea of Pauline ethical teaching, for such modes of conduct are found incompatible with a Christian way of life, just as the Mosaic law proscribed association with certain types of wrongdoers (Deut 19:15–19; 21:20–21)

do not even eat with such a one. Not only is one not to share the Lord's Supper with such a wrongdoer, but one should not be found in social contact with him, or even dine with him. This expresses the extent of the exclusion to which Paul was referring in vv. 3–5, apparently because he has learned that Corinthian Christians were still eating with the man of v. 1. For an OT precedent, see Ps 101:5, "with him I have not eaten."

This Pauline injunction may seem to conflict with the practice of Jesus described in Mark 2:15–17 (his eating with "toll-collectors and sinners," to the scandal of scribes and Pharisees). Jesus' reason is explained: "I came not to summon the righteous, but sinners," i.e., those who could be converted to his cause. Paul's principle, however, is different: it concerns the purity of the Christian community, tainted unfortunately by the moral failure of one who was already a convert. Cf. his reaction to Peter's dining in Gal 2:11–14.

12. *For what have I to do with judging outsiders?* Paul uses two rhetorical questions in a highly compressed style of writing. This and the following question express the basic reasoning behind what he counseled in vv. 9–11. Since Paul does not want Christians to withdraw from the world in which they live and in which they have become followers of Jesus Christ, his characterization of people as *pornoi*, etc. was a judgment indeed, but its object was Christians who might indulge in such questionable practices. That is why he now insists that he was not judging non-Christians, not even the "wife" of v. 1. This first rhetorical question is verbless and introduced by *tí gar moi* (see BDF §§127.3; 299.3); his implied answer to it would be, "Nothing at all!" In Matt 7:1, Jesus says, "Do not judge, lest you be judged!"

Is it not those within, you are to judge? Lit. "are you not judges of those within?" i.e., within the Christian community. If one does engage in judging, the object should be those who are within the community. It matters little to Paul that some Corinthians have been judging him (4:3–5); they should be judging those who are wrongdoers in their midst, and they have not yet done so. So when Paul calls for judgment, he is not necessarily setting up a church court in Corinth, even though this passage is sometimes seen as the sociological beginning of church discipline (Harris, "The Beginnings"); that can be admitted, but one is still at a considerable distance from what came to be called canon law.

13. *God will judge those outside.* Or "God judges those outside," because the verb *krinei* can be taken as present (so the RSV) or as future (so the NAB), depending how it is accented. Paul leaves the judgment of non-Christians to God, who is their creator, for that is the divine prerogative. In 6:2a, however, Paul will add something different (in an eschatological sense).

This explains why he says nothing in this passage about the "father's wife," who has been dallying with the Christian son; she was apparently an "outsider." Cf. the view of God's judgment in Heb 13:4, "God will judge fornicators and adulterers."

Drive out the evil one from among you. Paul concludes this discussion of sexual immorality with a modified quotation of Deut 17:7, but without an introductory formula. In the LXX it reads: *exareis ton ponēron ex hymōn autōn,* "you (sing.) are to drive out the evil one from among you (plur.)," an injunction leveled against one who transgresses the covenant and becomes an idolater. Paul substitutes for the first word the plur. impv. *exarate.* The wrongdoer, who has not been called *pornos* in these verses, is now branded as *ponēros,* "evil one."

Such an injunction is found also in LXX Deut 19:19; 21:21; 22:21, 24; 24:7 (cf. 13:6), appended to cases of covenant transgression, false testimony, adultery, kidnapping, and theft. Thus, Paul uses the OT to bolster up his judgment already expressed in vv. 2c, 5a, 7a, 11a above, but not so bluntly as here. The Christian community is obliged to preserve its sanctity by excluding the wrongdoer from its midst, which is "the main point of the passage" (Rosner, "Function of Scripture," 515). The quoted Scripture is put in a rhetorically climactic position at the end to support the main theme of this chapter; according to McDonough ("Competent to Judge"), it is also the OT quotation that connects chaps. 5 and 6 of this letter.

Paul's final instruction is thus similar to the punishment of Roman law, which made use of *relegatio.* For the wrongdoer no longer belongs to the body of those who are being saved, but to those who are perishing (1:18). Tuckett ("Paul, Scripture and Ethics") queries whether first-century readers of Paul's letter would have recognized and taken account of the broken OT context of the citation used here or would have appreciated the allusion to such OT exclusion formulas. Zaas (" 'Cast out the Evil Man' "), however, affirms just that, noting especially the wordplay in *pornos* (vv. 9, 10, 11) and *ponēros* (v. 13).

BIBLIOGRAPHY

Bammel, E., "Rechtsfindung in Korinth," *ETL* 73 (1997) 107–13.

Benedict, J., "The Corinthian Problem of 1 Corinthians 5:1–8," *BLT* 32 (1987) 70–73.

Bernard, J. H., "The Connexion between the Fifth and Sixth Chapters of 1 Corinthians," *Expos* 7/3 (1907) 433–43.

Broek, L. van der, "Discipline and Community: Another Look at 1 Corinthians 5," *RefR* 48 (1994–95) 5–13.

Buchinger, H., "1 Kor 5,7 als Schlüssel der Paschatheologie des Origenes: Das Pascha der Juden, das Opfer Christi und das Pascha der Christen—eine Aporie?" *ZNW* 91 (2000) 238–64.

Callow, K., "Patterns of Thematic Development in 1 Corinthians 5:1–13," *Linguistics and New Testament Interpretation: Essays on Discourse Analysis* (ed. D. Black et al.; Nashville: Broadman, 1992) 194–206.

Cambier, J., "La chair et l'esprit en I Cor. v. 5," *NTS* 15 (1968–69) 221–32.

Campbell, B., "Flesh and Spirit in 1 Cor 5:5: An Exercise in Rhetorical Criticism of the NT," *JETS* 36 (1993) 331–42.

Cole, G. A., "1 Cor 5:4 '. . . with my spirit,' " *ExpTim* 98 (1986–87) 205.

Colella, P., "Cristo nostra Pasqua? *1 Cor 5,7*," *BeO* 28 (1986) 197–217.

Dahl, N. A., "Der Epheserbrief und der verlorene, erste Brief des Paulus and [sic] die Korinther," *Abraham unser Vater: Juden und Christen im Gespräch über die Bibel: Festschrift für Otto Michel* . . . (AGSU 5; Leiden: Brill, 1963) 65–77.

Deming, W., "The Unity of 1 Corinthians 5–6," *JBL* 115 (1996) 289–312.

Derrett, J. D. M., " 'Handing over to Satan': An Explanation of 1 Cor. 5:1–7," *Studies in the New Testament: Volume Four: Midrash, the Composition of Gospels, and Discipline* (Leiden: Brill, 1986) 167–86.

De Vos, C. S., "Stepmothers, Concubines and the Case of *porneia* in 1 Corinthians 5," *NTS* 44 (1998) 104–14.

Fascher, E., "Zu Tertullians Auslegung von 1 Kor 5,1–5 (de pudicitia c. 13–16)," *TLZ* 99 (1974) 9–12.

Forkman, G., *The Limits of the Religious Community: Expulsion from the Religious Community within the Qumran Sect, within Rabbinic Judaism, and within Primitive Christianity* (ConNeot 5; Lund: Gleerup, 1972).

Francis, F. O., "The Baraita of the Four Sons," *JAAR* 42 (1974) 280–97.

Giblin, C. H., "Pauline Sexual Morality," *ScrC* 53 (1984) 106–19.

Goulder, M. D., "Libertines? (1 Cor. 5–6)," *NovT* 41 (1999) 334–48.

Gray, G. B., *Sacrifice in the Old Testament: Its Theory and Practice* (Oxford: Clarendon, 1925; repr. New York: Ktav, 1971).

Harris, G., "The Beginnings of Church Discipline: 1 Corinthians 5," *NTS* 37 (1991) 1–21.

Horst, P. W. van der, *The Sentences of Pseudo-Phocylides: With Introduction and Commentary* (SVTP 4; Leiden: Brill, 1978).

Howard, J. K., " 'Christ Our Passover': A Study of the Passover-Exodus Theme in I Corinthians," *EvQ* 41 (1969) 97–108.

Johnson, L. A., "Satan Talk in Corinth: The Rhetoric of Conflict," *BTB* 29 (1999) 145–55.

Joy, N. G., "Is the Body Really to Be Destroyed? (1 Corinthians 5.5)," *BT* 39 (1988) 429–36.

Kruse, C. G., "The Offender and the Offence in 2 Corinthians 2:5 and 7:12," *EvQ* 60 (1988) 129–39.

Kuhn, H.-W., "A Legal Issue in 1 Corinthians 5 and in Qumran," *Legal Texts and Legal Issues: Proceedings of the Second Meeting of the International Organization for Qumran Studies, Cambridge 1995* (STDJ 23; ed. M. Bernstein et al.; Leiden: Brill, 1997) 489–99.

McDonough, S. M., "Competent to Judge: The Old Testament Connection between 1 Corinthians 5 and 6," *JTS* 56 (2005) 99–102.

McGinn, T. A. J., *Prostitution, Sexuality and the Law in Ancient Rome* (Oxford/New York: Oxford University Press, 1998) 140–215.

Minear, P. S., "Christ and the Congregation: 1 Corinthians 5–6," *RevExp* 80 (1983) 341–50.

Mitton, C. L., "New Wine in Old Wine Skins: IV. Leaven," *ExpTim* 84 (1972–73) 339–43.

Murphy-O'Connor, J., "I Corinthians v, 3–5," *RB* 84 (1977) 239–45.

Ostmeyer, K.-H., "Satan und Passa in 1. Korinther 5," *ZeitNT* 5/9 (2002) 38–45.

Pascuzzi, M., *Ethics, Ecclesiology and Church Discipline: A Rhetorical Analysis of 1 Corinthians 5* (Tesi Gregoriana, ser. teol. 32; Rome: Gregorian University, 1997).

Pfitzner, V. C., "Purified Community—Purified Sinner: Expulsion from the Community according to Matthew 18:15–18 and 1 Corinthians 5:1–5," *ABR* 30 (1982) 34–55.

Poste, E., *Gai Institutiones or Institutes of Roman Law by Gaius with a Translation and Commentary* (4th ed.; ed. E. A. Whittuck; Oxford: Clarendon, 1904).

Puskas, C. B., Jr., *The Letters of Paul: An Introduction* (Collegeville, MN: Liturgical, 1993).

Robinson, O. F., *The Criminal Law of Ancient Rome* (London: Duckworth, 1995).

Roetzel, C., "The Judgment Form in Paul's Letters," *JBL* 88 (1969) 305–12.

Rosner, B. S., " 'Drive out the Wicked Person': A Biblical Theology of Exclusion," *EvQ* 71 (1999) 25–36.

———, "The Function of Scripture in 1 Cor 5,13b and 6,16," *The Corinthian Correspondence* (BETL 125; ed. R. Bieringer), 513–18.

——, " '*Ouchi mallon epenthēsate*': Corporate Responsibility in 1 Corinthians 5," *NTS* 38 (1992) 470–73.

——, "Temple and Holiness in 1 Corinthians 5," *TynBul* 42 (1991) 137–45.

Segalla, G., "I cataloghi dei peccati in S. Paolo," *StPat* 15 (1968) 205–28.

Shillington, V. G., "Atonement Texture in 1 Corinthians 5.5," *JSNT* 71 (1998) 29–50.

Sisti, A., "La Pasqua del Cristiano (Note su 1 Cor. 5, 6–8)," *ED* 28 (1975) 395–411.

Smit, J. F. M., " 'That Someone Has the Wife of His Father': Paul's Argumentation in 1 Cor 5,1–13," *ETL* 80 (2004) 131–43.

South, J. T., "A Critique of the 'Curse/Death' Interpretation of 1 Corinthians 5.1–8," *NTS* 39 (1993) 539–61.

Thiselton, A. C., "The Meaning of *Sarx* in 1 Corinthians 5.5: A Fresh Approach in the Light of Logical and Semantic Factors," *SJT* 26 (1973) 204–28.

Thornton, T. C. G., "Satan—God's Agent for Punishing," *ExpTim* 83 (1971–72) 151–52.

Treggiari, S., *Roman Marriage: Iusti Conjuges from the Time of Cicero to the Time of Ulpian* (Oxford: Clarendon, 1991).

Trevijano Etcheverria, R., "A propósito del incestuoso (1 Cor 5–6)," *Salm* 38 (1991) 129–53.

Tuckett, C. M., "Paul, Scripture and Ethics: Some Reflections," *NTS* 46 (2000) 403–24.

Vögtle, A., *Die Tugend- und Lasterkataloge im Neuen Testament: Exegetisch, religions- und formgeschichtlich untersucht* (NTAbh 16/4–5; Münster in W.: Aschendorff, 1936).

Wenthe, D. O., "An Exegetical Study of I Corinthians 5:7b," *Springfielder* 38 (1974–75) 134–40.

Yarbro Collins, A., "The Function of 'Excommunication' in Paul," *HTR* 73 (1980) 251–63.

Zaas, P. S., " 'Cast Out the Evil Man from Your Midst' (1 Cor 5:13b)," *JBL* 103 (1984) 259–61.

——, "Catalogues and Context: 1 Corinthians 5 and 6," *NTS* 34 (1988) 622–29.

10   C. SCANDAL OF CHRISTIANS HALING ONE ANOTHER INTO PAGAN COURTS (6:1–11)

⁶:¹ Does any one of you, who has a case against another, dare to take it to court before evildoers instead of before God's dedicated people? ² Or do you not realize that God's people are going to judge the world? And if the world is to be judged by you, are you unqualified for petty courts? ³ Do you not realize that we are to judge angels—not to mention affairs of everyday life? ⁴ If, then, you have courts for everyday affairs, do you seat as judges those who have no standing in the church? ⁵ I say this to your shame. Can it be that there is no one among you wise enough to settle a case between brothers? ⁶ Yet does a brother go to court against a brother, and this before unbelievers? ⁷ In fact [then], it is already a disaster on your part that

you have lawsuits against one another. Why not rather put up with injustice? Why not rather be cheated? [8] Instead, you yourselves do wrong and cheat, and this to your brothers. [9] Or do you not realize that evildoers will not inherit the kingdom of God? Do not be deceived! Neither fornicators nor idolaters, neither adulterers nor catamites, neither sodomites [10] nor thieves, neither the greedy nor drunkards, neither slanderers nor swindlers will inherit the kingdom of God. [11] This is what some of you were; but now you have been washed, you have been sanctified, you have been justified in the name of the Lord Jesus Christ and by the Spirit of our God.

COMMENT

Having reacted to the scandal of incestuous behavior in the Corinthian community that has been reported to him, Paul now turns to another questionable practice in vogue among Christians in Corinth. He has not yet finished his discussion of sexual matters, because he will resume it in 6:12–20, and then deal further with them in chap. 7. Another practice among Corinthian Christians, however, affecting church order and discipline needs his attention, viz., that of haling fellow Christians into pagan courts over trifling matters. Although Paul does not say how he learned about this situation, he considers that such a practice seriously concerns how individual Christians should be conducting themselves with one another while living in this world. There may be some connection of this situation with the sexual case that precedes it, but that connection is not evident, apart from superficial links involving the use of the verb *krino* in 5:12–13 and 6:1–2, and in judgment, which in chap. 5 was corporate, but now is individual. Moreover, the situation does not involve an individual case, as vv. 4 and 8 reveal, *pace* Fee (*1 Cor*, 228–29). Paul does not find fault with secular civil courts, but his reaction to such a practice developing among Corinthian Christians, about which he has learned, is strong and expressed in two stages. In vv. 1–6, he tells them that they should be settling their disputes among themselves; but then in vv. 7–11, he reacts more firmly and tells them that they should not be having lawsuits at all. Some interpreters consider vv. 1–6 to be Jewish-Christian criticism, such as would come from the Cephas party (so Barrett, "Cephas and Corinth," 7), but that hardly explains why Paul recommends that *hagioi*, "God's dedicated people" should not try to settle their differences before judges who are *apistoi*, "unbelievers."

First, Paul recalls to the Corinthians that they are *hagioi*, and not "evildoers" (6:1, 9); they are *adelphoi*, not "unbelievers" (6:6). Second, as such, they have a role to play in this world. Eschatologically, they are destined "to judge the world," and even "to judge angels" (6:2b-3). This means, a fortiori, that they are qualified to handle "everyday affairs" and treat them in "petty courts" (6:2b-4); Paul's argument proceeds by enthymemes in vv. 1–3. Third, the scandal is that they have failed: "a brother goes to court against a brother, and this before unbelievers" (6:6); worse still, they "have lawsuits against one another" (6:7), do wrong, and cheat one another (6:8). Going to court against a fellow Christian is fundamentally wrong, and Christians who do such a thing have failed in the life to which they have been called. Fourth, instead of all this Paul recommends that they learn to put up with injustice and cheating, remembering that "evildoers will not inherit the kingdom of God" (6:9). Paul then lists ten different kinds of wrongdoers (6:9b–10): fornicators, idolaters, adulterers, catamites, sodomites, thieves, greedy people, drunkards, slanderers, and swindlers. His list includes the four examples of 5:10 and the six of 5:11, to which he now adds four more. Fifth, in any case, the list enables Paul to formulate his basic conviction about the vocation of a Christian: you have been washed, sanctified, and justified in the name of the Lord Jesus and by God's Spirit. Such a calling summons Corinthian Christians to a mode of life that cannot be marked by trivial lawsuits or other questionable conduct.

Paul's advice in 6:1–6 is the basis of the Christian church's development of an internal legal system parallel to that of civil society, with jurisdiction over its members in given cases. Paul's thinking may even have been colored by such OT passages as Exod 18:13–27 or Deut 1:9–17; 16:18–20, where Moses appointed judges for God's people, long before they became a nation or were regarded as a civil society (see Rosner, "Moses Appointing," 276).

At any rate, Paul himself does not pass the same severe judgment on this situation, as he did in the case of incest in 5:3–5. Instead, he asks, "Why not rather put up with injustice?" (6:7), as he will in another formulation, "Why then do you sit in judgment over your brother?" (Rom 14:10). Or again, "If your brother is indeed distressed because of what you eat, you are no longer conducting yourself in love" (Rom 14:15). The issue in Romans is different, indeed, but his solution is basically the same: a Christian's conduct should be governed by "love," which should enable the Christian to put up with even injustice and cheating. "Love does no wrong to a neighbor" (Rom 13:10).

In Rom 1:29–31, Paul presents a similar list of vices and evildoers, but there he does not relate them to "the kingdom of God." Here it sounds like an early Christian catechetical summary or a piece of traditional exhortation that Paul is quoting, using twice the expression "inherit the kingdom of God," as he has already in Gal 5:19–21.

Verses 9b–10 are generically formulated and belong to the literary form of a catalogue of vices, even if it mentions evil persons and not the vices as such. Elliott ("No Kingdom," 22) lists further examples of such catalogues. Although some commentators consider vv. 9b-10 (or even vv. 9–11) to be only loosely connected to Paul's argument (Orr-Walther, *1 Cor*, 198; Rosner, "The Origin"; Vischer, *Auslegungsgeschichte*), Zaas ("1 Corinthians 6.9ff") has rightly insisted on their close relation to the epistolary context in which they appear (see NOTE on 5:11). They may, however, be influenced in their formulation by the LXX of Dan 7:22 (with its mention of judgment, saints, and inheritance of the kingdom).

Most Christians today would agree with Paul's condemnation of such evildoers as idolaters, adulterers, thieves, greedy people, drunkards, slanderers, and swindlers (6:9–10), even though they might not be so severe in their judgment. Some, however, would express hesitation when it comes to the people he calls *pornoi*, *malakoi*, and *arsenokoitai*. These terms refer to offenders in certain types of sex and are problematic, above all, because of the way that they are often translated (see the NOTES below), but they are per se clear. They name three types of persons whose conduct is no better than the other seven in the list; none of such *adikoi* will inherit God's kingdom. Paul's condemnation of such persons is forthright, and it has to be reckoned with as a norm for all Christian behavior.

By *pornoi* Paul is not castigating the (sexually) "immoral" in a generic sense, but rather "fornicators," i.e., unmarried men and women who cohabit or have casual sexual intercourse, or male and female prostitutes. This specific meaning is clear, because it heads the list of other specific evildoers, is distinguished from "adulterers" and other sex offenders, and is the subject matter of his exhortation in 6:13, 15–18.

The words *malakoi* and *arsenokoitai* denote male persons who practice different kinds of sexual acts with other males. Although such persons fall under Paul's condemnation, along with other evildoers, they were often tolerated in ancient Greco-Roman society more than one realizes today (see Dover, *Greek Homosexuality*; Boswell, *Christianity, Social Tolerance*). Homosexual activity among males, especially ephebophiles, was common, especially because of the esteem held for the beauty of the youthful male body in Greek education, athletics, statuary, and vase painting (see Schrage, *1 Cor*, 1:431; Garland, *1 Cor*, 217–18). Although one commonly distinguishes today between homosexual orientation (an innate [?] erotic attraction toward a person of the same sex) and homosexual activity, that is a distinction that came into being only in modern times and was unknown in Paul's day. What he is writing about is homosexual acts of males (the terms are of masc. gender [for Paul's criticism of female homosexual activity, see Rom 1:26b–27a]). His condemnation of such acts stems from his Jewish background, where they were roundly denounced; see Gen 19:4–5, 11, 24–25; Lev 18:22; 20:13; Judg 19:22–26; Aristeas, *Letter to Philocrates*, 152; *Sibylline Oracles* 2.73; Philo, *De spec. leg.* 3.7 §§37–43 (*paiderastein*); *De Abrahamo* 26 §§135–36; *De vita cont.* 6 §52; 7 §§59–62; *Hypothetica* 7.1 (*paiderastēs*; cf. Ellis, "Philo's View"); Josephus, *Ag.Ap.* 2.24 §199 (*tēn* [*mixin*] *pros arrenas arrenōn*, "[intercourse] of males with males"); and later *m. Sanhedrin* 7:4 (stoning for *miškab zākār*, "sleeping with a male"). Indeed, in using the compound noun *arsenokoitēs*, Paul was certainly aware of the formulation of the condemnation in LXX Lev 20:13 ("a man lying with a male as with a woman" [RSV]); 18:22. He now uses two specific Greek words for the activity that he will also criticize in Rom 1:27b. Since he lists persons who engage in such activity among the evildoers who will not inherit the kingdom, he implies awareness of such persons among the Christians of Roman Corinth, where the mores of their former way of life could still have an influence in their conduct. Whatever the sense of vv. 9–10 proves to be, "it must be consistent with [the] integrating and unifying aim of the letter as a whole," as Elliott ("No Kingdom," 20) has rightly argued, because the behavior described there can pollute the sanctity of the community that Christians should be forming. Verse 11 concludes, "This is what some of you were; but now you have been washed, you have been sanctified, you have been justified. . . ."

Another aspect of this pericope must be considered, because Richardson ("Judgment"), following Bernard ("The Connexion"), argues that all of chaps. 5

and 6, including 6:1–11, has to do with sexual questions. The difficulty in this pericope is that Paul does not mention the reasons why Corinthian Christians have been haling others into pagan courts. Some commentators have suggested that he is referring to cheating in financial matters or unjust business practices as the background of the lawsuits. It is, however, possible that some of the terms used in this pericope are to be understood of sexual misconduct and that the lawsuits involved some sexual problem. The mention of *pornoi* and *moichoi* in v. 9 forms a link with the preceding context of 5:1, 9–11 and with the following one of 6:13, 15, 18. The lawsuit could, then, conceivably be one of adultery (possibly leading to divorce). Richardson thinks that it might be a case of males involved in some sexual fraud. The question, however, will always remain highly speculative (see also Shillington, "People of God").

NOTES

6:1. *Does any one of you, who has a case against another, dare to take it to court before evildoers instead of before God's dedicated people?* Lit. "before the unjust (*adikoi*) and not before the saints (*hagioi*)?" Paul begins his rhetorical question with *tolma*, "dares" or "presumes" to press charges, as he expresses his exasperation at the turn of events (*TDNT*, 8:185). His style now adopts a series of seven rhetorical questions (vv. 1, 2a, 2b, 3, 4, 5b, 6), as he challenges the Corinthians and seeks to make his point. *Tís hymōn* singles out an individual, as in 5:1, but the instance is not isolated, as the plur. verbs in vv. 4 and 8 show.

Although the noun *pragma* simply means "deed, occurrence, matter," it often developed specific nuances in Greek literature, depending on the context in which it was used. Here *pragma echōn pros tina* means, "having a case/lawsuit against someone," as in Xenophon, *Mem.* 2.9.1; Epictetus, *Diss.* 2.2.17; Josephus, *Ag.Ap.* 2.18 §177 (LSJ, 1457–58). It could be a lawsuit involving business (as in 1 Thess 4:6), or possibly involving adultery, because ever since the time of Augustus the *lex Iulia de adulteriis coercendis* considered adultery a crime that was to be tried in a special court (under a praetor; see *Digest* §48.5; Suetonius, *Div. Aug.* 34; Dio Cassius, *Rom. Hist.* 54.30.4; cf. *OCD*, 15; *TDNT*, 4:733).

Paul's use of *adikoi*, "evildoers," does not imply that the secular courts in Roman Corinth would have been benches where injustice was doled out routinely. The adj. simply describes non-Christians who are, from a Christian perspective, those who do not pursue justice or righteousness in the OT sense (Isa 51:1; Sir 27:8). Although this first occurrence of *adikoi* has a predominantly legal sense, Paul will use it again in 6:9 in a clearly moral sense, "evildoers"; and its verbal cog., *adikein*, "do wrong," appears in 6:7–8. Even Garland (*1 Cor*, 196), who insists on the moral sense of *adikoi* in this verse, has to admit that the term "may be a bit of rhetorical hyperbole" (following Winter). For "saints," as a designation for Christians, see NOTE on 1:2. For later rabbinic regulations against haling Jews before non-Jewish judges, see Str-B, 3:362–63. See Stein ("Wo trugen") for a misconceived attempt to explain the problem of this verse by appealing to such late Jewish legal procedures.

2. *Or do you not realize that God's people are going to judge the world?* Lit. "the saints." Paul continues his rhetorical questions. In 5:12–13, Paul, rejecting the idea of censorious criticism of members of the Corinthian community in the present age, wrote, "God will judge those outside." Now he asserts that God's dedicated people will share in the judgment of the world. This is meant as an eschatological destiny of Christians: Christ, the judge of the world, will associate with his prerogatives those who are united with him. This idea is based on the OT motif of judgment given over to the "holy ones" of the Most High (Dan 7:22; cf. Wis 3:8; 4:16). Similarly in QL, "Through his chosen ones God will pass judgment on all nations, and by their reproof will all evildoers of his people be pronounced guilty" (1QpHab 5:4–5; cf. 4QpIsa^a [4Q161] 8–10:20; *1 Enoch* 1:9; 38:6; 108:12–13). Paul adopts this Jewish notion and adapts it to his Christology and ecclesiology (see Hoskins, "Use"). Polycarp (*Phil.* 11.2) quotes this very idea from Paul's letter. *Kosmos* denotes the complex of personal beings, human (as in 1 Cor 1:20–21), but also angelic (as the next verse makes clear).

Paul does not mean that one day earthly courts will be filled with Christian judges (Robertson-Plummer, *1 Cor*, 111). The best reading here is the future *krinoûsin*, "will judge," but some accented MSS (B2, 81, 1175) have *krínousin*, "are judging" (pres. tense). On the rhetorical question, "Do you not realize?" see NOTE on 3:16; it will appear again five more times in this chapter (vv. 3, 9, 15, 16, 19).

And if the world is to be judged by you, are you unqualified for petty courts? I.e., are you unfit to handle cases dealing with the petty details of everyday life? With irony, Paul argues *a maiore ad minus*. Those who will be judges of the world in the eschaton are surely already fit to handle the minor problems of this life.

3. *Do you not realize that we are to judge angels — not to mention affairs of everyday life?* Lit. "everyday life-matters," i.e., matters of life in the present world. This rhetorical question shifts to the 1st pers. plur., as Paul repeats his question of v. 2 in a new form. The *angeloi* have to be understood comprehensively of good and bad angels, because Paul means not only human beings, but any higher order of God's creatures (*EDNT*, 1:14). So august is his sense of the calling of God's dedicated people. See 1 Cor 4:9; 11:10; 13:1 for other references to angels; also 2 Pet 2:4; Jude 6 (sinful angels); in 2 Cor 12:7 Paul knows of an angel of Satan. It is not easy to say where Paul has derived this idea of Christians judging angels. The closest one comes to it is found in *1 Enoch* 13–16, where Enoch is sent to judge the Watchers and other evil spirits (4QEnoch^c 1 vi 14–15); or 91.15, where the judgment of the Watchers is mentioned (4QEnoch^g 1 iv 22–23). Whatever the meaning may be, Paul is using the judgment of angels only as an illustrative example to contrast the eschatological destiny of Christians with their preoccupation with petty legal matters, such as *biōtika*, "things needed for ordinary human life."

4. *If, then, you have courts for everyday affairs, do you seat as judges those who have no standing in the church?* Lit. "those who have been counted as nothing." The verb in the apodosis of this present general condition is problematic. *Kathizete* is often understood as asking a question, "Do you seat?" (so RSV,

NKJV); but it may be a statement or an exclamation, "you seat" (so NJB, and some modern commentators); but it is hardly an impv., "seat!" (as it is understood by KJV, NIV; Kinman, "Appoint the Despised as Judges!"; Garland, *1 Cor*, 207). If one uses for the meaning of the ptc. *exouthēmenous*, "been counted as nothing," which is found in 1:28, it might refer to lowly Corinthian Christians who are to be set up as judges in the community, but that hardly suits this context. The series of rhetorical questions seems to call for the verb *kathizete* to be taken as a question in this case too. Paul would then be recalling to the Corinthian Christians that they are destined to judge at God's tribunal but already have courts for everyday problems; hence they should not appear in lawsuits before a proconsul or other Roman judge, no matter how competent he may be in Roman law and ordinary civil affairs; because such people are counted as nothing in the church, even if Christians have been involved in seating such judges on the *bēma* in the forum of Roman Corinth. Cf. LXX of Ps 53:6c, where the verb *exoudenoō* is used of God's treatment of Israel's enemies (see Lewis, "Law Courts in Corinth").

5. *I say this to your shame.* This statement refers to the five rhetorical questions just posed, even though the verb has no object in the Greek text. It is frankly uttered and differs considerably from what Paul said in 4:14, where he denied that he was so writing.

Can it be that there is no one among you wise enough to settle a case between brothers? Lit. ". . . who will be able to settle a case in the midst of his brother (sing.)." In a community where wisdom is so important (recall chaps. 1–2), Paul wants to know whether there is no Christian sage to handle such trivial legal issues that arise among fellow Christians. Again, *sophos* has a negative connotation.

This ironic rhetorical question is elliptical, and the verse may not be correctly transmitted. Some versions have the equivalent of an added phrase: "in the midst of a brother and his brother" (adding *kai tou adelphou* before *autou* [MSS f, g of VL; Vg^MSS, syr, boh]. This addition seems to be derived from v. 7, but it may be influenced by LXX Deut 1:16, *diakouete ana meson tōn adelphōn hymōn kai krinate dikaiōs*, "Hear the cases between your brothers and judge rightly" (see Rosner, "Moses Appointing Judges"; also Kloha, "1 Corinthians 6:5"). Mss D², L, and the Koine text-tradition read *sophos oude heis*, "Is there not even one sage?" *Adelphos* is used again in the sense of "fellow Christian" (see NOTE on 1:1).

6. *Yet does a brother go to court against a brother, and this before unbelievers?* Lit. "is a brother being judged with a brother, and this before unbelievers." Paul complains that the Corinthian community has failed in that some members think that they can get justice more easily from a pagan court than from a Christian one, from unbelievers rather than from believers. *Apistos*, "unbeliever," occurs for the first time; Paul uses it only in the Corinthian correspondence (7:12–15; 10:27; 14:22–24; 2 Cor 4:4; 6:14–15). This rhetorical question leads up to another Pauline statement of concern (v. 7).

7. *In fact [then], it is already a disaster on your part that you have lawsuits against one another.* Now Paul begins his second and more fundamental argument (vv. 7–11) against this Corinthian practice. From a Christian perspective, such Corinthians have already lost the case, in so bringing suit. That Christians

should have a court for everyday affairs is tolerated by Paul, but his real reaction is that there should be no lawsuits at all. He sees the disaster (*hēttēma*, "defeat," as in LXX Isa:18) to be a moral one in that Corinthian Christians are not giving up the right to arbitration, when fellow Christians are involved. In 6:1, Paul used *pragma echōn pros*, "have a case against," but now he writes *krimata echete meth' heauton*, "you have lawsuits against (lit. "with") one another." *Krima*, normally "judgment, decision," here has the nuance, "legal action taken against someone" (BDAG, 567), which is found in LXX Exod 18:22 (*pace* Conzelmann, *1 Cor*, 105; see Mitchell, *Paul*, 231–32).

Why not rather put up with injustice? Lit. "why not rather be wronged?" or "why not let yourselves be wronged" (BDF §314 [incorrectly labelled a "passive in the sense of 'to allow oneself to be . . .' "; *adikeisthe* and the majority of the examples cited are simply middle voice]). Paul asks two decisive questions, because he sees the matter of contest and appeal to a third party for arbitration as a failure and a lack of Christian love, which he will discuss in chap. 13. Cf. Jesus' sayings recorded later in Matt 5:39–42; Jesus' conduct described in 1 Pet 2:23; Paul's teaching in Rom 12:17–19.

Greek philosophers taught similarly. Plato (*Gorg.* 509c): "We say that to do wrong is the greater evil, to suffer wrong the lesser"; also 469bc. Cf. Epictetus, *Diss.* 4.5.10; Marcus Aurelius, *Medit.* 2.1; Philo, *De Josepho* 4 §20.

Why not rather be cheated? Or, "why not let yourselves be cheated?" The verb *apostereō* means "steal, rob, defraud," and often connotes theft of money or property of another (e.g., Mark 10:11, quoting prohibition of the Decalogue; Jas 5:4). In 1 Cor 7:5, it will be used of cheating in marital rights; cf. 1 Thess 4:3–6. Hence the suggestion that adultery, the third form of evildoing mentioned below in v. 9, might be a reason for a lawsuit in a secular court is plausible.

8. *Instead, you yourselves do wrong and cheat, and this to your brothers.* Paul goes a step further, turning from rhetorical questions to an accusatory statement. It is not simply that some Corinthian Christians were haling other Christians into pagan courts over wrongs done to them, but he even indicts them for doing the same wrongful things themselves. On what Paul bases this accusation is not indicated; was this also something reported to him? More than likely he is simply interpreting the litigious situation as wrong, as he tries to get to the root of the problem: Christians doing wrong to Christians. He is not aiming his remark at any specific group of Corinthians.

9. *Or do you not realize that evildoers will not inherit the kingdom of God?* Paul speaks again of *adikoi* (see NOTE on 6:1). *Pace* Garland (*1 Cor*, 211), such evildoers cannot be restricted to "those outside the church." Paul's last rhetorical question begins as did v. 2 above and includes the expression *theou basileian klēronomein*, "to inherit the kingdom of God," which recurs in 6:10; 15:50; Gal 5:21. It echoes Jesus' saying recorded in Matt 25:34, where it has a clearly eschatological nuance and is related to the question posed, *tí poiēsō hina zōēn aiōnion klēronomēsō*, "What am I to do to inherit eternal life?" (Matt 10:17; Luke 10:25; 18:18). The use of the verb *klēronomein* with "the kingdom of God" imitates the OT motif of inheriting the promised land (LXX Exod 23:30; Deut 1:38–39; Isa

49:8; Ps 25:13; 37:9, 11, 22; 1 Macc 2:56; cf. LXX Dan 7:22; see Rosner, "Origin and Meaning"). Christians are called to share in that inheritance, but they too can fail to attain it, if they do evil. On "kingdom of God," see NOTE on 4:20. For a "pastoral exposition" of this question of Paul that turns it upside down, see Tiede, "Will Idolaters," 154.

Do not be deceived! This introductory impv. is often found in exhortations; see 15:33; Gal 6:7; Jas 1:16. It also occurs in Stoic diatribes; see Epictetus, *Diss.* 4.6.23; 2.20.7; cf. *TDNT*, 6:244.

9b–10. *Neither fornicators nor idolaters, neither adulterers or catamites, neither sodomites nor thieves, neither the greedy nor drunkards, neither slanderers nor swindlers will inherit the kingdom of God.* Paul lists ten types of evildoers who will not come into possession of the kingdom of God or be part of it; the first seven are separated by *oute*, the last three simply by *ou(ch)*. This is Paul's second list of evildoers; see 5:10–11 (cf. Eph 5:5); in Gal 5:19, the list is a catalogue of vices. Whether Paul has constructed this list himself or borrowed it from Hellenistic Judaism, as some commentators maintain, is impossible to determine; he is using a well-known literary form in any case. Cf. the later rabbinic teaching about various sinners who will have no share in the world to come listed in *m. Sanhedrin* 10:1–4: the one who says that there is no resurrection of the dead, that the Law is not from heaven; Epicureans; three kings, and four commoners; etc.

fornicators. Often *pornoi* is translated here generically as "immoral" (RSV, Goodspeed), "impudiques" (SBJ) or "sexually immoral people" (NJB, NIV, ESV); but "fornicators" is the correct rendering, because it heads the list of other specific kinds of sexual immorality, and in 6:13, 15–18, Paul will treat of it (so NAB, NRSV, NEB, REB). Its meaning is explained in NOTES on 5:1; 6:13. Cf. 1 Tim 1:10; Polycarp, *Phil.* 5.3.

idolaters. See NOTE on 5:10. The association of idolatry with fornication or adultery is well known in the OT, where the latter terms are used metaphorically to designate idolatry or apostasy (Num 14:33; Hos 4:11; 6:10; Jer 2:20–23; 3:6–10; Wis 14:12, "The beginning of fornication is the invention of idols"). Cf. Eph 5:5; Rev 14:8; 17:1, 2, 4, 5, 15, 16; Philo, *De migr. Abr.* 12 §69.

adulterers. Paul employs the specific term *moichos*, "one who is unfaithful to a marital spouse." Though the form is masc., in this context it is used generically and would include adulteresses. Rom 7:3 has the specifically fem. noun, *moichalis.* Adultery is condemned by Paul again in Rom 13:9, where he repeats the prohibition of the Decalogue (Exod 20:14; Deut 5:18). In ancient Israel, adultery was the violation of the rights of a married man by either his wife if she had intercourse with another man or by the man who seduced the wife. It was severely punished in Jewish law (cf. Lev 20:10: death), as well as in Roman law (*Lex Iulia de adulteriis coercendis: relegatio,* and loss of part of dowry; cf. *OCD*, 10–11, 603).

catamites. The term *malakos* means "soft" (as used of garments in Luke 7:25), but it was often used in the ancient Greek world to denote someone who was "effeminate," or passive in same-sex relations: a catamite, a youth or boy kept for sodomy by another male; a "boy prostitute" (NAB). The word is so used in Dio Chrysostom, *Disc.* 66.25; Dionysius of Halicarnassus, *Rom. Antiq.* 7.2.4

(*Malakos . . . hoti thēlydrias egeneto pais ōn kai ta gynaixin harmottonta epaschen*, "[he was called] Malakos . . . because, when a boy, he was effeminate and allowed himself to be treated as a woman"); Diogenes Laertius, 7.173; cf. BDAG, 613; *Romans*, 287–88. The technical Greek name for such a person was *kinaidos* (Plato, *Gorgias* 494e), which was transliterated in Latin as *cinaedus*. Another Latin name was *catamitus*, which was actually a form of the name, Ganymedes. In Greek mythology, he was the son of a Trojan prince and was snatched up by gods to be the youthful cup bearer of Zeus.

Malakos is often mistranslated as "dépravés" (SBJ); "homosexuals" (NKJV); "self-indulgent" (NJB); "sensual" (Goodspeed); "masturbators" (Boswell). The NEB renders this and the following word together as "guilty . . . of sexual perversion"; similarly the RSV, "sexual perverts." Elliott's ("No Kingdom," 24, 27) attempt to translate it as "soft males," i.e., aristocratic wealthy fops given to the luxuries and refinements of life, or even males with soft physical features, or youths who made their bodies soft by shaving them and powdering them is no better; in the end such "softies" are said to submit sexually to older males, perhaps for pay (ibid., 28). So what is the difference? The word *malakos* is attested, indeed, in the Greek language in the sexual sense indicated in the preceding paragraph.

sodomites. The term *arsenokoitai* occurs again in a similar catalogue of evildoers in 1 Tim 1:10, but it is not found in the LXX or other Jewish Greek writings (*Test. Levi* 17.11 uses *paidophthoroi*). The compound noun is formed from *arsēn*, "male," and *koitē*, "bed" or "sexual relation" (this meaning is known from Rom 13:13; LXX Num 5:20), and reflects the use of the two words in LXX Lev 20:13 (*hos an koimēthē meta arsenos koitēn gynaikos, bdelygma epoiēsan amphoteroi*, "whoever sleeps with a male [as in] sexual relation with a woman, both of them have committed an abomination" [in MT: *'îš 'ăšer yiškab 'et zākār miškĕbê 'iššāh tôʿēbāh ʿāśû šnêhem*]); also Lev 18:22 (see Wright, "Homosexuals"). The meaning of the term is clear and denotes the active partner in same-sex (anal) intercourse with another male; hence it can be translated "sodomite" (as in LSJ, 246; NRSV, NJB, NKJV), even though this name originally denoted the violation of hospitality by the rape of male guests.

It too is often mistranslated: "sexual perverts" (RSV, REB), "practicing homosexuals" (NAB), "men who practice homosexuality" (NIV), "abusers of themselves with mankind" (KJV), "given to unnatural vice" (Goodspeed), "gens de moeurs infâmes" (people of unspeakable morality, SBJ), "active male prostitutes" (Boswell)—such versions paraphrase and fail to express what Paul's Greek does, especially the last-mentioned version, for which the Greeks used *pornokopoi*.

Arsenokoitēs should not be translated as "homosexual," because that is a modern term for male or female sexual orientation as well as activity, coined only in the nineteenth century to denote the affectional preference of a person for someone of the same sex and was unknown as a name for sexual intercourse between such persons in antiquity (see Petersen, "Can *arsenokoitai*"; Elliott, "No Kingdom," 18).

The term *arsenokoitēs* is rare in Greek literature, being an alternate form of *arrenokoitēs*: see *Anthologia Graeca* 9.686 (*barbaron ou tromeeis, ouk arrenas ar-*

renokoitas, "You do not have to be afraid of a barbarian or male sodomites"). Cf. Codex Parisinus 82 (*Catalogus codicum astrologorum graecorum VIII/4* [ed. P. Boudreaux and F. Cumont; Brussels: M. Lamertin, 1921] 196): *arrenokoitas*; *Oracula Sibyllina*, 2.73 (*mē arsenokoitein* [ed. Geffcken, GCS, 8.30; which in its Latin version is rendered as *ne corrumpe mares*, "do not corupt males"]). Also in *Acta Johannis* 36 (CCserApocr 1.189); *ho arsenokoitēs*. De Young ("The Source") suggests that Paul himself probably coined the word from LXX Lev 20:13.

Because of its relatively rare occurrence, some writers have contested the meaning of the term here in Paul's letter, and considerable debate has surrounded the understanding of this term, the meaning of which is per se clear and is in no way limited to pederasty. No Pauline text expresses even a qualified approval of such same-sex activity, no matter what Greek words are used by him (see Turner, "Biblical Texts"; D. F. Wright, "Homosexuality"). Even if it eventually proves correct that Paul has coined the word *arsenokoitai* from the LXX of Leviticus and that his strictures against homosexual practice were taken over from Hellenistic Judaism, it does no good to accuse Paul of subverting a web of human relations, as if that would make it possible to ignore his strictures in our ethics today, *pace* M. Davies ("New Testament Ethics and Ours"). Paul has simply repeated the attitude of his own Jewish tradition about homosexual activity, which has been said to have been "unique in the ancient world" (Wenham, "Old Testament Attitude," 360). That he has not gone beyond that tradition does not devalue his strictures (Wright, "Homosexuality," 300).

For the debate about the word and the issue, see Boswell, *Christianity*, 106–17, 335–53, 363–64; McNeill, *The Church*, 50–53; Scroggs, *The New Testament*, 106–8; Brawley, *Biblical Ethics*; Malick, "The Condemnation"; Petersen, "Can *arsenokoitai*"; D. F. Wright, "Homosexuals" and "Translating"; J. R.Wright, "Boswell"; Gagnon, *Bible and Homosexual Practice*; Hays, "Relations" (especially on Boswell's erroneous interpretation of Rom 1:26–27) ; Soards, *Scripture*; Williams, *Roman Homosexuality*; Garland, *1 Cor*, 211–13.

The term *arsenokoitai* is found later in a number of patristic writers who have derived it from this Pauline passage or, perhaps, from the LXX of Lev 18:22; 20:13: Polycarp, *Phil.* 5.3; Eusebius, *Dem. evang.* 1.6.67 (GCS 23.33); *Praepar. evang.* 6.10.25 (GCS 43/1.339); 13.20.7 (GCS 43/2.251–52); *Constitutio apostolica* 6.28 (PG 1.984). Cf. Origen, *Comm. in Rom.* 4.4 (PG 14.973), quoting 1 Tim 1:9–10 and Lev 18:22; in Latin, cf. Tertullian, *Adv. Marcionem* 1.29.4 (CCLat 1.473).

Because *malakoi* and *arsenokoitai* occur in a list of evildoers, where a number of the offenses are of lesser seriousness, it is not easy to grasp how seriously Paul regards these diverse sexual practices. His considered thinking about male and female homoerotic acts, however, is set forth still more clearly in Rom 1:26–27,

where he bases himself on God's creation of man and woman for each other, to cleave together as one. Accordingly he denounces as a graphic distortion of God's created order women who have exchanged natural intercourse for that against nature and men who have abandoned natural relations with women and burned with lust for one another. Overall, then, the evidence strongly favors the thesis that Paul was condemning not only sexual activity by pederasts but also by homosexuals—indeed any sexual activity outside of marriage between a man and a woman (R. E. Brown, *Introduction*, 530).

As Malick has put it, "Paul's prohibitions against homosexuality were indeed against all forms of sexual relationships between persons of the same sex" ("Condemnation," 479), and not "only 'abuses' in homosexual behavior" (ibid., 492).

10. *nor thieves.* Paul expands the list, which initially began with *pornoi* (5:9–10); several of those listed there are now repeated. Here Paul uses *kleptai*, whereas it was *harpages* in 5:10, which may be a more specific kind of thief. Cf. Rom 2:21; 13:9; 1 Pet 4:15.

neither the greedy. Or "covetous," i.e., those who seek to have more than their share in life; see NOTE on 5:10. Cf. Eph 5:5; *Ep. Barn.* 19.6; *Did.* 2.6.

nor drunkards, neither slanderers nor swindlers. See NOTE on 5:11.

will inherit the kingdom of God. See NOTE on 6:9 above.

11. *This is what some of you were.* Some Corinthian Christians before their conversion were undoubtedly to be found among the *adikoi* Paul has just enumerated.

but now you have been washed, you have been sanctified, you have been justified in the name of the Lord Jesus Christ and by the Spirit of our God. Three effects of the Christ-event are singled out: "washed," referring to baptism, the Christian rite by which the sinful status of the vices mentioned in vv. 9–10 is washed away (cf. Acts 22:16; Eph 5:26); "sanctified," or made holy (see NOTE on 1:2; cf. 2 Thess 2:12); "justified," or set in a right relationship with God, as in Rom 5:19 (saved by Christ from [God's] wrath; see *Romans*, 400). The three effects are simply mentioned with no chronological or logical order among them. Steyn ("Reflections," 488) notes that *apelousasthe* is aor. middle, lit. "you have washed yourselves" (BDAG, 117: in NT "only mid."), which distinguishes the human act of baptismal washing from the divine action of sanctification and justification expressed by the aor. passives, which are divine passives (BDF §342.1; ZBG §236).

in the name of the Lord Jesus Christ. See NOTES on 1:2; 5:4. This phrase has to be understood with each of the three preceding verbs. Cf. 1 John 2:12.

and by the Spirit of our God. The effects of baptismal washing, sanctification, and justification are thus related explicitly to the activity of the Holy Spirit; cf. 1 Tim 3:16. Noteworthy is the triadic ending of this section: God (the Father), Jesus Christ, Spirit of God.

BIBLIOGRAPHY

Awi, M. A., "¿Qué dice la Biblia sobre la homosexualidad?" *TV* 42 (2001) 377–98.

Bailey, K. E., "Paul's Theological Foundation for Human Sexuality: I Cor 6:9–20 in the Light of Rhetorical Criticism," *NETR* 3 (1980) 27–41.

Becker, J., "Zum Problem der Homosexualität in der Bibel," *ZEE* 31 (1987) 36–59.

Boswell, J., *Christianity, Social Tolerance, and Homosexuality: Gay People in Western Europe from the Beginning of the Christian Era to the Fourteenth Century* (Chicago: University of Chicago Press, 1980).

Brawley, R. J., (ed.), *Biblical Ethics and Homosexuality: Listening to Scripture* (Louisville: Westminster John Knox, 1996).

Davies, M., "New Testament Ethics and Ours: Homosexuality and Sexuality in Romans 1:26-27," *BibInt* 3 (1995) 315-31.

Derrett, J. D. M., "Judgement and 1 Corinthians 6," *NTS* 37 (1991) 22-36.

DeYoung, J. B., "The Source and Meaning of the Translation 'Homosexuals' in Biblical Studies," *ERT* 19 (1995) 54-63.

Dinkler, E., "Zum Problem der Ethik bei Paulus: Rechtsnahme und Rechtsversicht (1. Kor. 6,1-11)," *ZTK* 49 (1952) 167-200; repr. *Signum Crucis: Aufsätze zum Neuen Testament und zur christlichen Archäologie* (Tübingen: Mohr [Siebeck], 1967) 204-40.

Dover, K. J., *Greek Homosexuality* (Cambridge: Harvard University Press, 1989).

Elliott, J. H., "No Kingdom of God for Softies? or, What Was Paul Really Saying? 1 Corinthians 6:9-10 in Context," *BTB* 34 (2004) 17-40.

Ellis, J. E., "Philo's View of Homosexual Activity," *PRSt* 30 (2003) 313-23.

Gagnon, R. A. J., *The Bible and Homosexual Practice* (Nashville: Abingdon, 2002).

Haas, G., "Perspectives on Homosexuality: A Review Article," *JETS* 45 (2002) 497-512.

Hays, R. B., "Relations Natural and Unnatural: A Response to John Boswell's Exegesis of Romans 1," *JRE* 14 (1986) 184-215.

Hoskins, P. M., "The Use of Biblical and Extrabiblical Parallels in the Interpretation of First Corinthians 6:2-3," *CBQ* 63 (2001) 287-97.

Kinman, B., " 'Appoint the Despised as Judges!' (1 Corinthians 6:4)," *TynBul* 48 (1997) 345-54.

Kloha, J., "1 Corinthians 6:5: A Proposal," *NovT* 46 (2004) 132-42.

Lance, H. D., "The Bible and Homosexuality," *ABQ* 8 (1989) 140-51.

Lewis, L.A., Jr., "The Law Courts in Corinth: An Experiment in the Power of Baptism," *ATRSup* 11 (1990) 88-98.

Malick, D. E., "The Condemnation of Homosexuality in 1 Corinthians 6:9," *BSac* 150 (1993) 479-92.

McNeill, J. J., *The Church and the Homosexual* (4th ed.; Boston: Beacon, 1993).

Miller, E. L., "More Pauline References to Homosexuality," *EvQ* 77 (2005) 129-34.

Mitchell, A. C., "Rich and Poor in the Courts of Corinth: Litigiousness and Status in 1 Corinthians 6.1-11," *NTS* 39 (1993) 562-86.

Osten-Sacken, P. von der, "Paulinisches Evangelium und Homosexualität," *BTZ* 3 (1986) 28-49.

Petersen, W. L., "Can *arsenokoitai* Be Translated by 'Homosexuals'? (I Cor. 6.9; I Tim. 1.10)," *VC* 40 (1986) 187-91.

Pilch, J. J., "Adultery," *TBT* 41 (2003) 117-22.

Richardson, P., "Judgment in Sexual Matters in 1 Corinthians 6:1-11," *NovT* 25 (1983) 37-58.

Rosner, B. S., "Moses Apppointing Judges: An Antecedent to 1 Cor 6,1-6?" *ZNW* 82 (1991) 275-78.

———, "The Origin and Meaning of 1 Corinthians 6,9-11 in Context," *BZ* 40 (1996) 250-53.

Scroggs, R., *The New Testament and Homosexuality: Contextual Background for Contemporary Debate* (Philadelphia: Fortress, 1983).

Shillington, G., "People of God in the Courts of the World: A Study of 1 Corinthians 6:1–11," *Direction* 15/1 (1986) 40–50.

Soards, M. L., *Scripture and Homosexuality* (Louisville: Westminster John Knox, 1995).

Stein, A., "Wo trugen die korinthischen Christen ihre Rechtshändel aus?" *ZNW* 59 (1968) 86–90.

Steyn, G. J., "Reflections on *to onoma tou kyriou* in 1 Corinthians," *The Corinthian Correspondence* (BETL 125; ed. R. Bieringer) 479–90.

Strecker, G., "Homosexualität in biblischer Sicht," *KD* 28 (1982) 127–41.

Tiede, D. L., "Will Idolaters, Sodomizers, or the Greedy Inherit the Kingdom of God? A Pastoral Exposition of 1 Cor 6:9–10," *WW* 10 (1990) 147–55.

Turner, P. D. M., "Biblical Texts Relevant to Homosexual Orientation and Practice: Notes on Philology and Interpretation," *CSR* 26 (1997) 135–45.

Vischer, L., *Die Auslegungsgeschichte von I. Kor. 6,1–11: Rechtsverzicht und Schlichtung* (BGNTE 1; Tübingen: Mohr [Siebeck], 1955).

Wengst, K., "Paulus und die Homosexualität: Überlegungen zu Rom 1,26f.," *ZEE* 31 (1987) 72–81.

Wenham, G. J., "The Old Testament Attitude to Homosexuality," *ExpTim* 102 (1990–91) 359–63.

Williams, C. A., *Roman Homosexuality: Ideologies of Masculinity in Classical Antiquity* (Oxford: Oxford University Press, 1999).

Winter, B. W., "Civil Litigation in Secular Corinth and the Church: The Forensic Background to 1 Corinthians 6.1–8," *NTS* 37 (1991) 559–72.

Wright, D. F., "Homosexuality: The Relevance of the Bible," *EvQ* 61 (1989) 291–300.

——, "Homosexuals or Prostitutes? The Meaning of *arsenokoitai* (1 Cor. 6:9; 1 Tim. 1:10)," *VC* 38 (1984) 125–53.

——, "Translating *arsenokoitai* (1 Cor. 6:9; 1 Tim. 1:10)," *VC* 41 (1987) 396–98.

Wright, J. R., "Boswell on Homosexuality: A Case Undemonstrated," *ATRSup* 66 (1984) 79–94.

Zaas, P., "1 Corinthians 6.9ff: Was Homosexuality Condoned in the Corinthian Church?" *SBLSP* 52/2 (1979) 205–12.

11   D. SCANDAL OF PROSTITUTION (6:12–20)

6:12 "For me all things are permissible"; but not all are beneficial. "For me all things are permissible," but I will not be dominated by anything. [13] "Food for the stomach, and the stomach for food, and God will do away with both the one and the other." Yet the body is not meant for fornication, but for the Lord; and the Lord for the body. [14] But God has raised up the Lord, and he will raise us up too by his power. [15] Do you not realize that your bodies are members of Christ? Shall I then take Christ's members and make them members of a prostitute? Of course not! [16] [Or] do you not realize that anyone who joins himself to a prostitute becomes one body with her? For it says, *"The two will become one flesh."* [17] But whoever is joined to the Lord becomes one spirit (with him). [18] Flee from fornication! "Every sin that one commits is outside the body." But the fornicator sins against his own body. [19] Or do you not realize that your body is the temple of the Holy Spirit, which is within you and which you have from God, and that you are not your own? [20] For you have been bought at a price. So glorify God with your body.

COMMENT

Paul continues his discussion of sexual immorality (begun in 5:1–13), but now in the broader context of human freedom. His discussion begins with the quotation of a double slogan about human freedom, and with another about food to be eaten. These slogans may have been reported to him as mantras or maxims in use among Corinthian Christians, and their character expresses well the problem that Paul now takes up. He again engages in diatribe-like style throughout this passage, as he quotes the sayings, comments on the implications of them, and asks rhetorical questions, because such factors are basic to human and Christian conduct. He realizes that they touch the fundamental question of the purpose of human freedom, and even of the human body and food that one gladly eats. He wants the Corinthian Christians to reflect on the purpose of the human body and its sexuality, especially in light of human freedom, even though he does not present a thorough and formal treatise on either topic. His main message is stated succinctly in v. 18a: "Flee from fornication!" Thus Christian freedom can have nothing to do with harlotry, and this for five reasons: (1) the human body is "made for the Lord" (6:13), because human destiny is to be with the Lord; (2) the bodies of Christians are members of the risen Christ (6:14–15); (3) Christians are "joined to the Lord" and become "one spirit" with him (6:17); (4) the body of the Christian is actually the temple of the Holy Spirit, which is within and comes from God (6:19); and (5) Christians "have been bought at a price" (6:20); as a result, they must glorify God with their bodies. Although some interpreters see in this pericope no "indications of concrete abuses of this nature [i.e., of harlotry] in the Corinthian community" (Byrne, "Eschatologies," 290) and think that this pericope merely looks ahead to the treatment of marriage and celibacy in chap. 7, it is more likely that Paul is dealing with yet another abuse in the Christian community of Roman Corinth. He treats the abuse of harlotry in terms of a larger question, whether a Christian is free to do what he or she wants.

The passage has two sections: vv. 12–17 and vv. 18–20. The first section is marked by several parallel statements: v.12ab–12cd, vv.13abc–13def–14ab, v. 15abc, v. 16ab. An enthymeme is used in v. 15. The second section begins and ends with an impv. (v. 18a, v. 20b).

Freedom does not mean license to do what one wants without any regard for one's obligations. Not everything that is possible or permissible contributes to the good in life. So Paul seeks to inculcate detachment, lest Corinthian Christians be dominated by earthly or natural attractions. He is concerned that they reflect on why they have a body and its sexual instincts, and what the relation of both is to their life in Christ. As in 5:1–5, Paul deals with the matter of freedom or a libertine attitude towards a certain kind of sexual intercourse, especially in vv. 12–20, but even more generically in vv. 9–10. His stance is different here from what he will say in chap. 7, where other matters involving human sexuality will be discussed. It is, however, an obvious exaggeration to speak of "the glaring apparent contradiction, in contiguous passages 6:12–20/7:1–11," *pace* Goulder ("Libertines?").

Although Paul used *sōma*, "body," in passing in 5:3, this is the first place where the term occurs with some extended treatment (6:13, 15, 16, 18, 19, 20), and the interpretation of the word in these verses is complicated and somewhat debated. The term *sōma* is often understood in a holistic sense, meaning the whole human being or self under a certain aspect, especially when the person is the subject to which something happens or the object of one's own actions (so J. Weiss; Bultmann, *TNT*, 1:194–96; J. A. T. Robinson). That interpretation of *sōma* in these verses is controverted, and a number of other commentators take the term to mean the physical living body itself in the full Greek sense, as one of the components of the human complex along with *psychē*, "soul" (Gundry, *Sōma*; Murphy-O'Connor). That is the meaning of *sōma* in the LXX in the vast majority of its occurrences: physical human body (sometimes even the dead body). In only seven instances it seems to have a broader connotation, meaning person as a whole (Gen 47:12; 1 Chron 28:1; 1 Esdr 3:4; Tob 11:15; 13:7; Sir 51:2; Job 33:11; see Ziesler, "Sōma"). This physical sense is pressed still further by Käsemann (*Essays*, 129) and Byrne ("Sinning"), who stress that the physical body also provides the possibility of "personal self-communication," by which human beings are related to others and subject to the world in which they live; fornication or harlotry perverts the human faculty intended to be the instrument of intimate communication with another person.

Pace Rosner ("Temple Prostitution"), what gives rise to Paul's discussion in this paragraph is not temple prostitution, which, although it might be historically credible, has little to commend itself in the present context and lacks any real link with the kind of idolatry to be discussed in 1 Corinthians 10, where neither *porneia*, nor *pornos*, nor *pornē* is found, and *porneuō* is used with a different connotation. Rosner, however, rightly objects to the understanding of this paragraph in terms of sexual immorality in general or specifically of the incest of 5:1. Paul writes only about *pornē*, a common word for "prostitute" and never mentions either *hetaira*, "courtesan" (thought to be of higher class) or *hierodoulos*, "sacred prostitute," the two terms that Strabo (*Geogr.* 8.6.20) once used of the Temple of Aphrodite in pre-Roman Corinth.

In this final paragraph of chap. 6, Paul is enunciating a thesis against fornication and harlotry, which he regards as a sin against the human body, because that body has a special relationship to "the Lord," the risen Christ, and to "God," because from Him that body has become "the temple of the Holy Spirit." In this way Paul has enunciated a thesis about sexual ethics and a sexual asceticism, but here in chap. 6 it is discussed only in terms of fornication or harlotry. In chap. 7, when he begins to answer questions that Corinthian Christians have asked him in the letter mentioned there, he will continue to apply the thesis to other matters, to marriage and to celibacy. It is important that Paul's thesis be rightly understood and not subjected to any manipulation or toning down (see Nejsum, "The Apologetic Tendency").

NOTES

6:12. *"For me all things are permissible."* Some commentators (e.g., Robertson-Plummer, *1 Cor,* 121; Spicq) understand this saying as Paul's "own words," because they are used again in 10:23. Similarly, Dodd ("Paul's Paradigmatic 'I' "), for whom Paul is the author of v. 12 "in its entirety," because there are 32 instances where Paul clearly indicates that he is citing the words of others, whereas nothing similar is found here in this so-called slogan. Yet even though Paul may at times use the 1st pers. sing. in hortatory statements, or as in Rom 7:7–25, that is far from the situation envisaged in this verse, where the statement is rather proverbial. Dodd's explanation fails to cope with the following *all' ou(k),* which is found in each instance and which pits Paul's reaction over against the saying. Consequently, *panta moi exestin,* "for me all things are possible," is best taken as a slogan that sums up the attitude of freedom of certain Corinthian Christians in their attending moral problems (see Hurd, *Origin,* 68; and also many commentators). Paul disagrees with the slogan. He will repeat it again in the second half of this verse, and later in 10:23 (without "for me" [an insignificant difference]), and in each case, he reacts to it. This generic slogan is cited now as a justification for sexual licence, as some of the following verses reveal.

Some commentators ascribe the slogan to a "gnosticizing party in the church which was impatient of the restraints of conventional morality" (Bruce, *1 Cor,* 62); similarly Schmithals, *Gnosticism,* 230: "gnostically understood *eleutheria*"; Conzelmann, *1 Cor,* 108–9; Barrett, *1 Cor,* 144–45). This is highly questionable, as Lindemann (*1 Cor,* 145) notes. Evidence for Gnostics in Corinth at this time is nonexistent; hence it is better left merely as a Corinthian slogan, perhaps derived from Stoic ideas about freedom (*eleutheria*) and the "right of self-determined conduct" (*exousia autopragias,* Diogenes Laertius 7.121; Epictetus, *Diss.* 1.1.21). Such an idea is also known, however, to Philo, *Quod omn. prob. lib.* 9 §59: The one who acts rightly "will have the power to do anything and to live as he wishes, and having it would be free" (*hōst' exousian schēsei panta dran kai zēn hōs bouletai. hō de taut' exestin, eleutheros an eiē*). Hence it is difficult to say whether Paul is consciously reacting to a specific Stoic slogan; more than likely he knows that it is being bandied about in Roman Corinth, and that is sufficient reason for him to react to it (see further D'Agostino, "Un Paolo stoico?").

but not all are beneficial. I.e., do not contribute to my good or the good of the community. Paul's reaction echoes in fact an idea found in Sir 37:28, *ou gar panta pasin sympherei,* "not everything contributes to the good of everyone." Not everything builds up the community, a notion to which Paul will return in 7:35, also 10:23. Individualism or selfishness contributes nothing to the common good. In both Aristotelian and Stoic philosophy, *to sympheron,* "the beneficial," and *to agathon,* "the good," are so identified (see *TDNT,* 9:71).

"For me all things are permissible," but I will not be dominated by anything. Or

". . . by anyone," since *tinos* can be neut. or masc. As he repeats the slogan, Paul engages in a wordplay that cannot be reproduced in English. In the slogan, *exestin*, "it is permissible, right," is employed, but in Paul's second reaction to the slogan the fut. pass. of *exousiazō*, "have the right of control over" (someone/something), the verb is related to *exousia*, "right, power." With such a wordplay, Paul stresses that a real Christian will not be enslaved by anything. He is thus advocating detachment from all earthly things, which should characterize a follower of Christ. Cf. Gal 4:9b. It is difficult to determine whether "I" in Paul's reaction is to be emphasized (so Lindemann, *1 Cor*, 145) or it is merely reflecting the "me" of the slogan (so Robertson-Plummer, *1 Cor*, 122); either is possible.

13. *"Food for the stomach, and the stomach for food, and God will do away with both the one and the other."* Lit. "foods for the belly" (*koilia*, a noun with a wide connotation, sometimes meaning "womb, uterus" [Gal 1:15], "seat of desires" [LXX Job 15:35], but also "stomach," a part of the human body). Again, the chiastic two-part saying and its sequel is another Corinthian slogan that Paul is quoting, which is related somehow to the previous one cited twice. In a context that escapes us, the first-quoted generic slogan may have been utilized to curb restrictions on certain kinds of food and then developed into a more specific form that is now cited. Some interpreters understand the last clause as part of Paul's reaction to the slogan expressed in the first two clauses (so Miguens, "Christ's 'Members,' " 26), but the relationship expressed in the last part of v. 13 and v. 14 and especially the parallelism between v. 13a and v. 13b make it clear that God's reaction to food and stomach is matched by His reaction to the Lord's body and that of Christians. Whatever the relation is between the two slogans quoted, the relation in human life between food and sex is sufficient to have them joined here.

The antinomian who is being quoted regards fornication as fulfilling a human need, just as food and drink fulfill such a need. That God will do away with both stomach and food means that in good time (at the parousia) God will see to a change in the human constitution and the sensitive world in general so that neither the organs of digestion nor the foods usually consumed will be existent. "When the *sōma* ceases to be *psychikon* and becomes *pneumatikon* (xv. 44), neither *brōmata* nor the *koilia* will have any further function, and therefore 'God will bring to nought' both of them" (Robertson-Plummer, *1 Cor*, 123).

Paul, however, is not concerned about the purpose of food, and the last part of this verse reveals his real concern. He cites the slogan merely to build up his argument. What is implied in such a liberal slogan is that sexual intercourse is likewise for the human physical body, and the body for such intercourse. Hence his next statement, which is his reaction to the Corinthian slogan, as the parallelism of wording reveals; in it he will descend from the generic sense of sexual intercourse to the specific kind that he finds wrong.

Yet the body is not meant for fornication, but for the Lord; and the Lord for the body. The "stomach" (*koilia*) is indeed part of the body, but a human being is not all "body" (*sōma*). The physical body of a human being is indeed involved in and even intended for sexual intercourse, but not for *porneia*, because that mode of free intercourse is now seen to be contrary to the destiny of a human being. See

NOTE on *porneia* (5:1); although its generic sense of sexual prosmiscuity might seem to be meant here and is often so taken (e.g., RSV, Gundry), it soon becomes clear that the specific sense of "fornication" or "harlotry" is intended (vv. 15–16), i.e., casual coitus with a prostitute. What is affirmed in this verse shows that *sōma* cannot be understood in the Bultmannian sense of "self" or "der Mensch"; it has to be taken as the physical, living human body, and not as Bof ("Il *sōma*") would have it.

Pace Kempthorne ("Incest"), Malina ("Does *porneia*," 14), and Miguens ("Christ's 'Members,' " 43), the word *porneia* does not mean "incest" throughout chaps. 5 and 6; that meaning is restricted to 5:1–5. Here (in vv. 9, 13, 15, 16, 18) *porneia* means specifically either "harlotry, prostitution" (i.e., commercial sexual intercourse), as also in 10:8; Matt 21:31, 32; Luke 15:30; or simply "fornication," i.e., prebetrothal, premarital, or extramarital heterosexual intercourse, as in 1 Thess 4:3; LXX Tob 4:12 (see Jensen, "Does *porneia*," especially for the OT usage in the LXX; also O'Rourke, "Does the New Testament"). Paul makes no mention of marital infidelity here, and it is far from clear that one is to assume that some of the Corinthian men involved were married. If indeed some of them were so involved, that could be *moicheia*, "adultery," and Paul has distinguished already *pornoi* from *moichoi* in v. 9 above.

God, who is mentioned in the second Corinthian slogan, has other designs for the human body than its use in fornication. For the destiny of a human being is rather "the Lord," i.e., the risen Christ (see NOTE on 1:2), as Paul makes clear in the second part of the verse as well as in the next verse. He also states it plainly in 1 Thess 4:3–7, and especially in 4:17b (*houtōs pantote syn Kyriō esometha*, "so we shall always be with the Lord"); cf. Phil 1:23b. To make sure that he is understood, Paul not only asserts that the "body" is for the Lord, but he inverts the relationship: "the Lord (is) for the body," i.e., constitutes its destiny or goal, and consequently the body cannot be freely used in an arbitrary way.

Note the parallelism of formulation, as pointed out by Murphy-O'Connor ("Corinthian Slogans," 394): As the Corinthian slogan spoke of "food for the stomach, and the stomach for food," so Paul retorts, "the body . . . for the Lord, and the Lord for the body," making use of chiasmus. As the slogan used: *ho de theos kai tautēn kai tauta katargēsei*, "and God will do away with both the one and the other," so Paul retorts, *ho de theos kai ton kyrion ēgeiren kai hēmas exegerei*, "but God has raised up even the Lord and will raise us up too."

Gundry (*Sōma*, 59–60) rightly insists on the meaning of *sōma* here as the "physical body"; it does not mean the "human person" or the "inner man." "Paul's reference to the resurrection reinforces the physical connotation of *sōma*. Otherwise the Corinthians would not have entertained their objections to the doctrine, objections with which Paul must deal in ch. 15, to say nothing of the physicalness of resurrection in Paul's own Jewish, Pharisaical heritage." Surprising is the concluding clause of v. 13, "and the Lord for the body," because in Paul's view the relation of the Lord to a human being is not restricted to the spirit but involves even "the body."

14. *But God has raised up the Lord, and he will raise us up too by his power.* Paul

not only ascribes to the Father the resurrection of Jesus Christ, but associates the destiny of the Christian, determined by God, with that glorious status of the risen Christ. The "body" of the Christian is destined to share in that status, and not just the stomach. The "power" of which Paul speaks may refer to 1:18, but more probably it is "the power of his resurrection" (Phil 3:10), which must be traced back to the Father (see Fitzmyer, *TAG*, 202–17; cf. 1 Cor 15:15, 20; Rom 8:11; 2 Cor 4:14; 13:4). In the second clause, some MSS (P[46c2], B, 6, 1739) read rather the aor. *exēgeiren*, "raised" (us up [proleptically]); and others (P[11,46*], A, D*, P) have the pres. *exegeirei*, "raises," but the fut. *katargēsei*, "will do away with, will destroy" (v. 13) makes the parallel fut. *exegerei* the better reading here.

Because Paul writes "us" instead of "our *sōmata*," it does not mean that he is giving the noun *sōma* in this passage a meaning "which is most intimately connected with man and amounts to the same thing as 'self' " (Bultmann, *TNT*, 1:195; similarly J. Weiss, *1 Cor*, 161; J. A. T. Robinson, *The Body*, 29: "frequently . . . *sōma* is simply a periphrasis for the personal pronoun," as in 1 Cor 6:15, which is parallel to 1 Cor 12:27; also 31: "the body . . . stands throughout this passage for the 'personality' "); similarly Lindemann (*1 Cor*, 147). However, as Gundry rightly notes, Paul has used the noun *sōma* twice in v. 13 and will use it again in v. 15; so his use of the pers. pron. in this verse instead is merely a stylistic variant. This is clearly a better explanation than that of Schnelle("1 Kor 6:14"), who regards the whole verse as a post-Pauline gloss introduced because of the use of *kyrios*, "the Lord," in v. 13 and in light of the discussion coming in 15:12–19, 38, 42, 44, 48, 51–53; moreover, he claims that v. 14 would interrupt the otherwise cohesive argument of 6:12–20 to stress the salvific value of Christ's resurrection for Christians. The interruption is really only apparent (see Murphy-O'Connor, "Interpolations," 85–87).

15. *Do you not realize that your bodies are members of Christ?* As in vv. 2, 3, 9 above, Paul expostulates as he addresses the Corinthian Christians. This verse now explains why the body of a Christian "is for the Lord" (6:13). The physical *sōmata* of Christians are identified as "members" (*melē*) of Christ. This verse anticipates what will be explained further in 12:12–14, 27; and in Rom 12:4–5, where Christians themselves are said to be "members" of Christ or of his body; their bodies are united to him as his limbs etc., and their corporate existence in him makes him known in the world. The power of the risen Christ is now active in the bodies of Christians. In the present context, the emphasis is on the physical "bodies," because the topic being discussed involves such a body. *Sōma* does not have here a "more-than-physical meaning, . . . but . . . *melos* and *sōma* in ch. 12 have a figurative meaning when used ecclesiastically. . . . Verse 15a simply anticipates the figure of the Church as Christ's Body" (Gundry, *Sōma*, 61), but Lindemann (*1 Cor*, 148) contests this ecclesiastical aspect.

Shall I then take Christ's members and make them members of a prostitute? I.e., shall I take my body, the member that belongs to Christ, and indulge in bodily contact with a harlot? That would relate Christ to a harlot, and the even casual intercourse involved in harlotry would undo the Christian's commitment to Christ and the manifestation of him in the world. Paul asks this question of an imaginary interlocutor; it is a rhetorical question used in diatribe-like style, which also depends on his understanding of the verse of Genesis that he is going to quote in v. 16 about the mingling or contact of bodies in sexual intercourse.

The first Greek word is poorly transmitted; instead of the ptc. *aras*, "taking," found in the best MSS, some MSS (P, Ψ, 81) read the particle *ara*, which together with *oun* would mean, "Shall I consequently make Christ's members . . . ?"

Of course not! Lit. "May it not be (so)!" The Classical Greek optative mood is retained in a wish as a strong rejection of what has been suggested in the rhetorical question, as Paul moves to a new stage in his argument. On this exclamatory answer, which appears only here in 1 Corinthians, but often elsewhere in Pauline letters, see Malherbe, "*Mē genoito.*"

16. [*Or*] *do you not realize that anyone who joins himself to a prostitute becomes one body with her?* Lit. "anyone clinging to a prostitute is one body." For the formula *ouk oidate hoti*, see NOTE on 3:16. The formula introduces another rhetorical question that shows that the imaginary objection is a false conclusion of what Paul has been saying. Paul will cite Genesis to show that even casual copulation with a harlot has a lasting unitive effect and aligns the Christian against the Lord (v. 17). "To have extramarital sexual intercourse is to repudiate the relationship of belonging to the body of Christ" (Conzelmann, *1 Cor*, 111; similarly Rosner, "Function of Scripture," 526–27).

Paul uses the ptc. *kollōmenos*, the simple form of the compound Greek verb *proskollēthēsetai*, "will cling" (to his wife), which is in the full form of the Genesis verse to be quoted. *Pace* Miller ("Fresh Look"), there is no difference in the meaning, as the Greek form of Gen 2:24 quoted in Matt 19:5 shows (simple *kollēthēsetai*); both refer to intercourse or copulation, and the simple verb does not mean necessarily only "adhesion or loyalty" (see Sir 19:2, *ho kollōmenos pornais*, "one consorting with harlots"). Admittedly, a nonsexual metaphorical use of *(pros)kollasthai* is found also in LXX Deut 10:20; Ps 73:28; 2 Kgs 18:6, as well as Ruth 2:21, 23 (cited by Miller), but that is not its only meaning.

Porter ("How Should") argues that *kollōmenos* should be rendered, "the one who sells himself into bondage (i.e., obligates himself) to a prostitute," as in Luke 15:15 (where *ekollēthē* is used of the prodigal son). That, however, unduly introduces an economic nuance, which is not operative here. Mitchell more rightly recognizes that Paul's argument "centers on relations between insiders and outsiders. The insiders are *melē Christou*, but the prostitute clearly is not (6:15), and thus should not be mingled with. She is beyond the boundary and is indeed a threat to the health of the whole community" (*Paul*, 120).

For it says, "The two will become one flesh." Paul cites Gen 2:24 according to the LXX, *esontai hoi dyo eis sarka mian*, where "the two" has been added to the MT, which has only, "and they will become one flesh." In Genesis, the verse records the divine institution of human marriage and the full union of husband and wife, which casual and transitory copulation completely ignores; indeed, it even contradicts its very purpose. Even though the Genesis text speaks of "one flesh" (*sarx mia*), Paul applies the words to extramarital sexual intercourse, because, although he recognizes that the same union of flesh takes place, such intercourse not only militates against the divine institution of marriage, but also against the relationship of Christians to the body of Christ and their union with the risen Lord. Union with a prostitute is deleterious of the unique union that should be with Christ (see Baldanza, "L'uso"). Paul's application of Gen 2:24 to fornication is not a misuse of the OT, because it indirectly repeats the teaching of Genesis, while directly speaking against casual sexual intercourse, in that it expresses the mingling of human bodies that is indeed pertinent to his argument. Rosner rightly argues for Paul's correct use of Gen 2:24 to support his assertion at the beginning of this verse, because Paul appeals to that Genesis passage to remind the Corinthians that "sexual relations belong to marriage" ("Function of Scripture," 516). The quotation is introduced only by *phēsin*, "it says," which assumes that the readers will understand its subject to be something like *hē graphē*, "Scripture" (says); cf. *1 Clem.* 30:2; *2 Clem.* 7:6; *Ep. Barn.* 7:7.

In citing Gen 2:24, which uses *sarx*, "flesh," Paul is understanding it as a synonym for *sōma* (*sarx mia* = *hen sōma*). Cf. the fuller use of Gen 2:24 in Eph 5:31, and the different application of it to the problem of divorce in Matt 19:5; Mark 10:8–9.

17. *But whoever is joined to the Lord becomes one spirit (with him).* Lit. "is one spirit" (*hen pneuma*), in contrast to "one body" or "one flesh" of v. 16. One would have expected Paul to say "becomes one body" with the Lord, but instead he shifts because of his often-used contrast of "flesh" and "spirit." The union of Christians with the Lord is real, but on a different level; it has nothing to do with "flesh," for it is of a spiritual nature, being an intimate union with the risen Lord. As such, it precludes all free and casual use of the body (or flesh) in sexual intercourse. "Being joined to the Lord" means that a Christian cannot be "joined to a prostitute," even in a casual act. The quotation of Gen 2:24, which per se refers to the union of man and women in the marital act, now suggests that the spiritual union of the Christian with "the Lord" has a marital connotation (recall 6:13e: the body is "meant for the Lord"). Whoever thus joins himself to the Lord transcends human bodily existence and acquires a new identity, as one becomes "one spirit" with Christ (see Baldanza, "L'Uso").

18. *Flee from fornication!* This hortatory imperative is the main message of the pericope, resuming the last impv. of 5:13. The impv. *pheugete* may be an imitative allusion to Joseph's flight from Potiphar's wife in Gen 39:12 (so Godet, *1 Cor,* 1:311; Bruce, *1 Cor,* 65). *T. Reuben* 5.5 has the same advice, *pheugete oun tēn porneian,* the wording of which also depends on the Joseph story, as 4.8 reveals. For the double allusion, see Rosner, "A Possible Quotation." Even though Joseph's example was well known in ancient Judaism, Paul makes no explicit use of it.

"Every sin that one commits is outside the body." This sweeping rhetorical statement is uttered in the immediate context of a relationship with a prostitute. Again, from the context of harlotry, the physical body must be meant, and the statement asserts that the body has nothing to do with sin. Some versions read, "Every other sin" (so ESV, NAB, NEB, REB, RSV) or "All other sins" (NJB), but the Greek text has simply *pan hamartēma,* and no variant reading adds *allo,* "other."

This puzzling statement has been subject to many varying interpretations (Allo [*1 Cor*, 148] counted almost thirty of them; cf. Dautzenberg, *Studien*, 142–47), and a very common interpretation is comparative: "other sins do not leave anything like the same filthy stain on our bodies as fornication does" (Calvin, quoted by Barrett, *1 Cor*, 150–51; similarly Robertson-Plummer, *1 Cor*, 128; see further Gundry, *Sōma*, 71–75).

Perhaps the best way to understand it is as yet another Corinthian slogan, as Murphy-O'Connor has argued ("Corinthian Slogans"; similarly Collins, Hays, Horsley; Romaniuk, "Exégèse," 201–2; Miguens, "Christ's 'Members,' " 39; Radcliffe, " 'Glorify God,' " 310). The slogan would mean that "the physical body is morally irrelevant, for sin takes place on an entirely different level of one's being" (Murphy-O'Connor, 393). Paul, however, answers that sinning Christians have put their "members slavishly at the disposal of impurity and iniquity" (Rom 6:19; cf. Rom 12:1–2), and they may not invoke such a slogan. This Paul explains in the next clause.

but the fornicator sins against his own body. This is Paul's reaction to such a slogan. He is formulating a criticism of it and prescinds from what he wrote in vv. 9–10 about fornicators, the greedy and idolaters, whose sins prevent them from inheriting the kingdom of God. Greed and idolatry might be "outside the body," but they are not a concern to Paul now. Fornication, however, is committed against the body of the individual who engages in it, because *to idion sōma*, "his (or her) own body," is meant to be the means of "personal self-comunication." "The immoral person perverts precisely that faculty within himself that is meant to be the instrument of the most intimate bodily communication between persons" (Byrne, "Sinning," 613). The Christian who thus sins ruins his own status before God, as Paul prescinds from the effect such a sin would have on the prostitute. In saying "his own body," Paul may be echoing a notion found in LXX Sir 23:17, which reads:

anthrōpos pornos en sōmati sarkos autou ou mē pausētai heōs an ekkausē pyr; anthrōpō pornō pas artos hēdys, ou mē kopasē heōs an teleutēsē,

a man who commits fornication in the body of his flesh will not cease until fire burns (him) up; to a fornicator all bread is sweet, he will not cease until he dies."

See also LXX Prov 20:2 (*hamartanei eis tēn heautou psychēn*, "sins against his own soul"); Sir 10:29; 19:2–3 (cf. Fisk, "*Porneuein*").

Sōma here cannot be "perhaps the body of Christ" (*pace* Soards, *1 Cor*, 132), because there is no hint in this text of the ecclesiastical sense of *sōma*. It denotes rather the physical human body that is "in touch with the outside world of persons, powers, and events" (Byrne, "Sinning," 610 [following Käsemann]).

19. *Or do you not realize that your body is the temple of the Holy Spirit, which is within you and which you have from God?* In 3:16, Paul called the Christian community of Corinth "the temple of God" and said that "the Spirit of God" dwelt in it, but now he teaches something very similar about the individual Christian and

his or her body. Thus Paul affirms not only the corporate, but also the individual sense of the indwelling Spirit of God, without seeking to explain which one is speculatively prior to the other. See Rom 8:9–11, where he also says that "the Spirit of God dwells in you," and makes a number of other assertions about the relation of the individual Christian to Christ and the Spirit (see *Romans*, 480–81, 490–91). Individual Christians have the Spirit, because they have been "washed" (6:11), and this is another reason why they cannot enter into a union with a harlot. Although Paul usually writes *pneuma hagion*, he now emphasizes the sanctity of the Spirit by putting *hagion* first. Philo also calls the human soul a house of God (*De somniis* 1.23 §149): *Spoudaze oun, ō psychē, theou oikos genesthai hieron hagion*, "Be zealous, O soul, to become a house of God, a holy temple."

and that you are not your own. This concluding clause gives Paul's answer to the question about freedom implied in v. 12 above. In effect, Paul is contrasting the indic. and the impv. as he says, You are a Christian; so live as a Christian, for "you belong to Christ" (3:23): you as an individual Christian do not belong to yourself, but to Christ Jesus, whom you reckon to be your *kyrios*.

20. *For you have been bought at a price.* This is the reason why Christians are not their own and may not misuse their bodies. Paul refers to the death of Jesus Christ and views that shedding of his blood as a price paid for the redemption of his followers, the onerous burden that Christ Jesus bore for humanity. Yet he never explains further the meaning of the "price," either its amount or to whom it has been paid. It fits in, however, with his idea of redemption as an effect of the Christ-event (recall 1:30), i.e., that Christians have been ransomed or bought back by Christ from bondage to sin and now belong to a new *kyrios* (see *PAHT* §PT75). Cf. Gal 3:13; 4:5, where Paul has employed *exagorazō*, the compound of *agorazō* used here, to express the same idea; these verbs differ considerably from the usual Greek word used for the sale or manumission of slaves in the contemporary world (see Lyonnet, "L'emploi," 85–89; Spicq, *TLNT*, 1:26–28). Cf. 1 Pet 1:18–19; Rev 5:9. The Vg speaks of it as *pretio magno*, "great price." Paul will repeat this idea in 7:23.

So glorify God with your body. Or "in your body." The impv. is plur., as is the poss. adj. "your." So Paul is recommending to the Christian community of Corinth a corporate honoring of God. *Sōma*, however, is sing., and in light of the foregoing context it suggests that all Corinthian Christians should see to it that God is honored in the individual conduct of their bodily lives. Rather than use the physical "body" for fornication, they should use it to honor and praise God. This is the only time that Paul exhorts Christians to glorify God in this way, and it serves to show that even the human body can enter such service of God. Yet Paul wrote about himself to the Philippians, "According to my eager expectation and hope, I shall not be put to shame in any way, but with all boldness, both now and always, Christ will be magnified in my body, whether through life or through death" (Phil 1:20).

Some MSS (C³, D², K, L, P, Ψ, 1739ᵐᵍ) add at the end of the verse: *kai en tō pneumati hymōn, hatina estin tou theou*, "and with your spirit, which are of God." This is an added gloss, unrelated to the argument of the paragraph, which speaks of the sanctity only of the body, with no mention of the human spirit (see Metzger, *TCGNT*, 488). It is also ungrammatical, because the neut. plur. rel. pron. has no antecedent.

BIBLIOGRAPHY

Baldanza, G., "L'uso della metafora sponsale in 1 Cor 6,12–20: Riflessi sull'ecclesiologia," *RivB* 46 (1998) 317–40.

Bartling, W. J., "Sexuality, Marriage, and Divorce in 1 Corinthians 6:12–7:16: A Practical Exercise in Hermeneutics," *CTM* 39 (1968) 355–66.

Bof, G., "Il *sōma* quale principio della sessualità in Paolo," *BeO* 19 (1977) 69–76.

Bowald, B., and J. Halter, " 'Preist Gott mit eurem Leib!' (1 Kor 6,20): Leiblichkeit aus biblisch-ethischer Perspektive," *Diakonia* 33 (2002) 235–41.

Burkill, T. A., "Two into One: The Notion of Carnal Union in Mark 10,8; 1 Kor 6,16; Eph 5,31," ZNW 62 (1971) 115–20.

Butting, K., "Pauline Variations on Genesis 2.24: Speaking of the Body of Christ in the Context of the Discussion of Lifestyles," *JSNT* 79 (2000) 79–90.

Byrne, B., "Eschatologies of Resurrection and Destruction: The Ethical Significance of Paul's Dispute with the Corinthians," *DRev* 104 (1986) 288–98.

——, "Sinning against One's Own Body: Paul's Understanding of the Sexual Relationship in 1 Corinthians 6:18," *CBQ* 45 (1983) 608–16.

Claudel, G., "1 Kor 6,12–7, 40 neu gelesen," *TTZ* 94 (1985) 20–36.

Crofts, M., "Some Considerations in Translating 'Body' in 1 Corinthians," *Notes* 119 (1987) 40–49.

D'Agostino, M., "Un Paolo stoico o un Epitetto paolino? Ripensare gli slogan in 1Cor 6,12–20," *RivB* 52 (2004) 41–75.

Dautzenberg, G., *Studien zur paulinischen Theologie*, 142–68.

Derrett, J. D. M., "Right and Wrong Sticking (1 Cor 6,18)?" *EstBíb* 55 (1997) 89–106.

Dodd, B. J., "Paul's Paradigmatic 'I' and 1 Corinthians 6:12," *JSNT* 59 (1995) 39–58.

Fauconnet, J.-J., "La morale sexuelle chez Saint Paul: Analyse et commentaire de 1 Co 6, 12 à 7, 40," *BLE* 93 (1992) 359–78.

Fisk, B. N., "*Porneuein* as Body Violation: The Unique Nature of Sexual Sin in 1 Corinthians 6.18," *NTS* 42 (1996) 540–58.

Fuchs, E., "Die Herrschaft Christi: Zur Auslegung von 1 Kor 6,12–20," *Neues Testament und christliche Existenz: Festschrift fur Herbert Braun* . . . (ed. H.-D. Betz and L. Schottroff; Tübingen: Mohr [Siebeck], 1973) 183–93.

Gravrock, M., "Why Won't Paul Just Say No? Purity and Sex in 1 Corinthians 6," *WW* 16 (1996) 444–55.

Gruber, M., " 'Verherrlicht Gott in eurem Leib' (1 Kor 6,20): Zu einer Theologie und Spiritualität des Leibes bei Paulus und im Neuen Testament," *TGeg* 44 (2001) 264–73.

Jensen, J., "Does *porneia* Mean Fornication? A Critique of Bruce Malina," *NovT* 20/3 (1978) 161–84.

Kempthorne, R., "Incest and the Body of Christ: A Study of I Corinthians vi. 12–20," *NTS* 14 (1967–68) 568–74.

Kirchhoff, R., *Die Sünde gegen den eigenen Leib: Studien zu porne und porneia in 1 Kor 6,12–20 und dem sozio-kulturellen Kontext der paulinischen Adressaten* (SUNT 18; Göttingen: Vandenhoeck & Ruprecht, 1994).

Klein, G. L., "Hos 3:1–3—Background to 1 Cor 6:19b–20?" *CTR* 3 (1988–89) 373–75.

Lowrie, W., " 'Glorify God in Your Body,' " *TTod* 10 (1953–54) 492–500.

Lyonnet, S., "L'emploi paulinien de *exagorazein* au sens de 'redimere,' est-il attesté dans la littérature grecque?" *Bib* 42 (1961) 85–89.

Malina, B., "Does *porneia* Mean Fornication?" *NovT* 14 (1972) 10–17.

Maurer, C., "Ehe und Unzucht nach 1. Korinther 6,12–7,7," *WD* 6 (1959) 159–69.

Miguens, M., "Christ's 'Members' and Sex (1 Cor 6, 12–20)," *Thomist* 39 (1975) 24–48.

Miller, J. I., "A Fresh Look at I Corinthians 6. 16f.," *NTS* 27 (1980–81) 125–27.

Murphy-O'Connor, J., "Corinthian Slogans in 1 Cor 6:12–20," *CBQ* 40 (1978) 391–96.

Nejsum, P., "The Apologetic Tendency in the Interpretation of Paul's Sexual Ethics," *ST* 48 (1994) 48–62.

O'Rourke, J. J., "Does the New Testament Condemn Sexual Intercourse outside Marriage?" *TS* 37 (1976) 478–79.

Porter, S. E., "How Should *kollōmenos* in 1 Cor 6,16.17 Be Translated?" *ETL* 67 (1991) 105–6.

Radcliffe, T., " 'Glorify God in Your Bodies': 1 Corinthians 6,12–20 as a Sexual Ethic," *NBf* 67 (1986) 306–14.

Robinson, J. A. T., *The Body: A Study in Pauline Theology* (London: SCM, 1966).

Romaniuk, K., "Exégèse du Nouveau Testament et ponctuation," *NovT* 23 (1981) 195–209, esp. 199–205.

Rosner, B. S., "A Possible Quotation of Test. Reuben 5: 5 in 1 Corinthians 6:18a," *JTS* 43 (1992) 123–27.

———, "Temple Prostitution in 1 Corinthians 6:12–20," *NovT* 40 (1998) 336–51.

Schnelle, U., "1 Kor 6:14—eine nachpaulinische Glosse," *NovT* 25 (1983) 217–19.

Son, S. A., "Implications of Paul's 'One Flesh' Concept for His Understanding of the Nature of Man," *BBR* 11 (2001) 107–22.

Yamauchi, E., "Cultic Prostitution: A Case Study in Cultural Diffusion," *Orient and Occident: Essays Presented to Cyrus H. Gordon* . . . (ed. H. A. Hoffner, Jr.; Kevelaer, Germany: Butzon & Bercker; Neukirchen-Vluyn: Neukirchener-V., 1973) 213–22.

Yoon, D., "The Economy of God in First Corinthians 6:17," *Affirmation & Critique* 4/4 (1999) 40–45.

Ziesler, J. A., "*Sōma* in the Septuagint," *NovT* 25 (1983) 133–45.

III. Answers to Queries About Moral and Liturgical Problems (7:1–14:40)

◆

A. MARRIAGE AND CELIBACY IN THE PASSING WORLD (7:1–40)

12   a. *Marriage Is Good,*
Celibacy Is Good: Their Obligations
and Place (7:1–9)

7:1 Now for the matters about which you wrote: It is good for a man not to touch a woman. ²Yet because of instances of fornication, each man should have his own wife, and each woman her own husband. ³The husband should fulfill his conjugal duty to his wife, and likewise the wife to her husband. ⁴The wife does not have authority over her own body, but rather her husband does; likewise a husband does not have authority over his own body, but rather his wife does. ⁵Do not deprive one another, except perhaps by mutual consent for a time, to be free for prayer; but then be together again, so that Satan may not tempt you because of your lack of self-control. ⁶I say this as a concession, not as a command. ⁷I wish that all were as I myself am, but each one has a particular gift from God, one of one kind and one of another. ⁸Now to the unmarried and to widows I say: it is good for them to remain as I am, ⁹but if they are not exercising self-control, they should marry; for it is better to marry than to burn.

COMMENT

Paul now turns to topics treated in a letter that has been sent to him by Corinthian Christians. No one knows how he received such a missive. It might have been brought to him by "some of Chloe's people" (1:11) or, more likely, by the messengers mentioned in 16:17, Stephanas, Fortunatus, and Achaicus. It seems to have been occasioned by Paul's previous letter mentioned in 5:9, in which he counseled Corinthian Christians "not to associate with sexually immoral people."

That undoubtedly raised questions in the minds of some Corinthian Christians about various topics, such as, "Is sexual intercourse to be allowed at all?" "Is it right for a man to touch his wife?" Paul now answers such queries in an ad hoc fashion, and his discussion should not be taken as a formal treatise on marriage or virginity. The order of topics may be following that of the queries posed to him in the letter. One need only look at vv. 6, 10, 12, 17, 25, 26, 35, 40 to see how Paul is developing a set of regulations concerning marriage and virginity, as Richardson ("I Say, not the Lord") has pointed out, even if one hesitates to label them "early Christian Halakah."

A fortiori, what Paul now writes about these topics does not cope with findings of modern psychology or sociology bearing on marriage, celibacy, or human sexuality. Hence it is misguided to subject this chapter to a psychoanalytical study, such as Eickhoff has done, who catalogues Paul's "false" presupposition[s], "erroneous" misunderstanding of woman as "a conscious temptress for man," or "delusion[s]" in various areas, and even ends with "a little speculation about Paul's understanding of his own sex drive" ("A Psychoanalytical Study," 36). This turns out to be an analysis of a man who lived about 2000 years ago, and limited to passages in 1 Corinthians (the only Pauline writing cited!). To many other writers, this chapter is a misguided treatise on marriage and virginity, as they read it with preconceptions often derived from modern attitudes or even from other passages in the Pauline corpus. They at times fail to discern adequately what Paul is actually saying. Without agreeing with all the details in his article, I find myself in basic agreement with the "reassessment" of this chapter proposed by Moiser. Although marriage and virginity (or celibacy) are the main topics in this chapter, it deals with a number of other issues that are often overlooked: the widowed, virgin daughters, slaves, freedmen, and children.

The first topic that Paul takes up is marriage. This topic is related to the issues of sexual morality treated in chaps. 5 and 6, and v. 2 will echo what Paul has been discussing in 6:12–20. In those chapters, sexuality was partly a matter of an open and free way of living ("for me all things are permissible"), and Paul had to deal with adulterous incest and fornication or harlotry in such a context. Now the topic has a different perspective, reflecting a more restricted view of Christian life. In the first section (vv. 1–9), Paul deals with some aspects of marriage, and only incidentally with virginity or celibacy. His views are not dominated by idealism, but by a positive realistic view of such states of life, which per se have nothing to do with sexual immorality of any sort.

Paul begins with a general statement: "It is good for a man not to touch a woman." Unfortunately, he does not explain that statement further, simply taking it for granted that he will be understood. Some versions and many commentators think that Paul is quoting a saying from the letter that has been sent to him, asking whether he would approve of such an idea, i.e., that abstention from marriage or abstention from intercourse within marriage would be the answer to sexual immorality. It may even have been a slogan that some Corinthians were espousing, and that others were querying. Whether it is a Corinthian slogan or not, Paul enunciates it at the very beginning of his discussion in this chapter and gives the impression that he is per se in favor of the idea that it expresses, although some interpreters claim that he is rejecting the Corinthian saying (e.g., Phipps, "Is Paul's Attitude"). Certainly Paul realizes the problem that such a view so stated can cause in human life, and so he proceeds to qualify it in v. 2, in which he comes out strongly in favor of monogamous marriage. Qualifications or exceptions run throughout this chapter: in vv. 5, 9, 11a, 21, 28, 36, 39; in some cases they are expressed as a present general condition (vv. 11a, 28, 39), in others as a simple condition (vv. 9, 21, 36).

Having advocated monogamous marriage, Paul enunciates another principle, stressing the mutual obligation that married persons have to their spouses in intercourse (7:3–4). In marriage, the husband has the right to intercourse with his wife, and she with him; both are equal in this regard, and neither can deprive the other of that right, and neither can act as though he or she owned his or her own body. In this regard, having expressed the principle, Paul again adds a qualification: "Do not deprive one another," except perhaps by mutual consent, for a time, and for a good reason (e.g., prayer). This Paul acknowledges by way of concession. Thus in vv. 1–4 Paul affirms not only monogamous marriage, but also the equality of spouses in that union. He does this without invoking the formula he will use in Gal 3:28: "neither Jew nor Greek, neither slave nor free, neither male nor female"; or what he will imply in vv. 32–34, when he enlarges his view of Christian marriage and the spouses' mutual concern for each other, even beyond the matter of intercourse that is mentioned in vv. 3–4.

The first statement that Paul quoted or enunciated in v. 1b, however, is given further development when he says, "I wish that all were as I myself am" (7:7a); now he counsels the unmarried and widow(er)s "to remain as I am" (7:8). Again he qualifies his principle by adding a fundamental conviction: God calls human beings to diverse modes of life, "Each one has a particular gift from God" (7:7bc); some are called to marriage, and some to virginity.

In this pericope, one notes three reasons for what Paul has been saying about marriage, each of them negative: (a) "because of instances of fornication" (7:2); (b) "that Satan may not tempt you because of your lack of self-control" (7:5e); (c) "it is better to marry than to burn" (7:9c). Such negative reasons are undoubtedly evoked by what he realizes is the problem in the Corinthian community, but it does not follow that Paul "evaluates marriage as a thing of less value than 'not touching a woman' (v. 1); indeed, he regards it as an unavoidable evil" (Bultmann, *TNT*, 1:202). That is to exaggerate the negative assertions. What has to be noted in the course of this lengthy chapter, however, is the otherwise positive form of the statements that Paul makes. He makes use of the comparative *kreitton/ kreisson*, "better," only in the restricted remarks of vv. 9 and 38; so he is not saying that celibacy or virginity is a better calling than marriage, as the teaching of this chapter is often paraphrased or encapsulated. For otherwise he employs *kalon*, "good," especially when he sets forth his principles (vv. 1, 8, 26 bis). His statements are consequently measured and should be judged accordingly (see further Léon-Dufour, "Mariage et continence," 324–25; Bartling, "Sexuality, Marriage," 361–62); for a view that interprets *kalon* in a comparative sense, see Zeller, "Der Vorrang."

Paul's thoughts on human marriage are colored somewhat by the tradition of his Jewish background, in which marriage was seen to be the object of the first imperative laid on human beings in the OT, "Increase and multiply" (Gen 1:28), for marriage was considered a divine institution (Gen 2:24). Cf. also Exod 20:14, 17b; Lev 18:20; Qoh 9:9; Ps 128:3. Josephus summarized Jewish teaching on it thus:

> The law [of Moses] recognizes only the natural sexual intercourse with a wife, and that if one intends to procreate children. . . . It orders (us), in marrying, not to be influenced by dowry, nor to take a woman by force, nor to win her by craftiness or deceit, but to woo her from him who is authorized to give her away. . . . The husband must have intercourse with this (wife) alone, and it is impious to assault her who belongs to another man. (Ag. Ap. 2.24 §§199–201)

Paul, however, says nothing in this chapter (or elsewhere) about the procreation of children as the intention of marriage, as mentioned by Josephus. See also Philo, De spec. leg. 3.6 §§32–36, who interprets Lev 18:19–22. Certain elements of Paul's teaching on marriage and celibacy find parallels in ideas also current in the Greek world of his time, especially in the writings of Stoics and Cynics. By and large, Stoic teachers maintained that people who respected the gods would consider it a moral duty to marry and have children, because that fostered the city-state. An example is C. Musonius Rufus, Fragm. XIII^A, which reads:

biou kai geneseōs paidōn	The main point of marriage is
koinōnian kephalaion einai gamou.	a sharing of life and procreation of children.
ton gar gamounta, ephē,	For, he used to say, the husband
kai tēn gamoumenēn epi toutō synienai chrē	and his spouse must come together,
hekateron thaterō, hōsth' hama	one with the other in such wise that they
men allēlois bioun,	live with each other together,
hama de <paido>poieisthai,	procreate [children] together,
kai koina de hēgeisthai panta	and hold all things in common,
kai mēden idion, mēd' auto to sōma,	and nothing as one's own, not even the body itself.

Such a view of human life differed from that of the Cynics, who often maintained that marriage distracted one from the pursuit of a really simple life of independence, renunciation of possessions and social entanglements. There are, however, other elements that distance Paul from Musonius's views on marriage and the gift of celibacy, and Musonius maintained that erotic desire was justified only when indulged in for procreation (see Ward, "Musonius and Paul").

As for Paul's advocacy of virginity, that is usually judged to be something new on the Jewish scene. The only clear instance of nonmarriage in the OT is the prophet Jeremiah, to whom the word of the Lord came instructing him not to take a wife in view of the doom facing the country at that time (Jer 16:1–4). Later on, some Essene Jews in Judea practiced celibacy (Pliny the Elder, Nat. Hist. 5.15.73). Josephus even records that they did not marry because they held marriage in "contempt" (*J.W.* 2.8.2 §120); but cf. 2.8.13 §§160–61, where he knows of some Essenes who did marry. Cf. the account in Philo, *Hypothetica* 11.14 §380, and also that about the related Therapeutae in Egypt, who avoided marriage. Josephus also mentions Bannus (*Life* 2 §11), who lived as a hermit in the desert. The NT says nothing about John the Baptist or Jesus of Nazareth marrying. Isolated instances of celibacy are also known in the much later rabbinic tradition, e.g., Simeon ben Azzai (Tomson, *Paul and the Jewish Law*, 106 n. 60; cf. van der Horst, "Celibacy in Early Judaism").

In the Greek world of Paul's day, there were likewise instances of what has been misnamed sacral celibacy: Plutarch (*De Iside et Osiride* 2 §§351f–352a) tells of service in the Temple of Isis requiring abstention from food and sexual intercourse. In the first century, Apollonius of Tyana was a noted celibate Neopythagorean wandering sage (Philostratus, *Vita Apollonii* 1.13 *ad finem*). See further Deming, *Paul*.

In this first section (7:1–9), Paul is confronting the Corinthian situation, as v. 1 makes clear, but nowhere in this text does one find traces of Gnostic tenets or ideas of contemporary mystery religions, sometimes said to be reflected in various verses of chap. 7. Similarly, the evidence that Corinthian Christians were advocating ascetic ideas based on words of Jesus preserved in "Q" passages of the Synoptic tradition (Balch, "Backgrounds of I Cor. VII," 356–57) is highly tenuous and speculative, despite the occasional, coincidental occurrence of similar verbs, as Schrage ("Zur Frontstellung," 227) has rightly shown. The same has to be said about alleged archaeological evidence of "sacral celibacy" within marriage, *pace* Oster ("Use, Misuse," 62). The views about marriage and virginity that are found in chap. 7 are those that Paul has developed in light of problems in the church of Roman Corinth with which he has had to cope, but they are relativized by his basic service of Jesus Christ and what was inaugurated by him (see Adinolfi, "Il matrimonio").

NOTES

7:1. *Now for the matters about which you wrote.* Corinthian Christians were seeking advice from the founder of their community, who is now far removed from them. The prep. phrase *peri de* will recur in 7:25; 8:1; 12:1; 16:1, 12. There is no guarantee that its further instances will refer to the same letter sent by the Corinthians; it may simply introduce a new topic (M. Mitchell, "Concerning *peri de*"). For the omission of the rel. pron. *ha*, "which," see BDF §294.4. Some MSS (A, D, F, G, Ψ, Koine text-tradition) add *moi*, "to me," which is lacking in the best MSS (P⁴⁶, ℵ, B, C, 33, 81, 1739).

It is good for a man not to touch a woman. The statement employs *kalon*, "good," as in vv. 8, 26; 9:15; Rom 14:21; Gal 4:18. *Pace* Weiss (*1 Cor*, 170), Conzelmann (*1 Cor*, 115), Caragounis (" 'Fornication,' " 546), it should not be translated, "it is better"; that introduces a comparative not expressed in Paul's Greek text, a comparative that has often led to the tendentious reading of this chapter mentioned in the COMMENT above. *Kalon* has often been understood as a reflection of LXX Gen 2:18, *ou kalon einai ton anthrōpon monon*, "It is not good for the man to be alone." That is also perhaps the reason why the statement is formulated from the viewpoint of the man, in addition to the prevailing emphasis in the culture of Paul's day. In using *kalon*, Paul is not justifying his position by invoking a divine command; he is formulating the thesis abstractly, in a philosophical way: "it is good," perhaps even morally good (as BDAG, 505, takes it) or ethically good.

The statement may reflect a debate among Christians of Corinth; if it does, it might have been a slogan in use among them and could have been set in quotation marks (as in NRSV, NAB, REB, ESV; for a list of interpreters who so understand these words, see Phipps, "Is Paul's Attitude," 131 n. 16). In this instance, however, it is far from certain that it is a slogan, because it might also be a Pauline answer to a question posed in the letter that he has received (as argued by Gramaglia, "Le fonti," 483–501; Yarbrough, *Not Like*, 93); cf. RSV, NJB, NEB. As Barrett notes, "Even if Paul did not himself coin the sentence he quotes it without immediate indication of disapproval, and yet goes on not merely to sanction marriage but to disapprove of abstinence within marriage" (*1 Cor*, 154). Whatever its origin, Paul puts it first, agreeing with it, and so it serves as a principle for what he is going to say about marriage. As such, it presupposes that Christians are free and capable of following such a norm as he is introducing for the guidance of a man and a woman in their dealings with each other in such a union.

Paul writes *kalon anthrōpō gynaikos mē haptesthai*, with no article before either noun. Although *anthrōpos* means "human being," the contrast with *gynē*, "woman," shows that he understands it as "a male human being," as in Gal 5:3 and often in the LXX. Hence it should not be translated in v. 1b, ". . . not to touch his wife," *pace* Winter (*After Paul Left*, 225; Baumert, *Woman and Man*, 30, 33). Moreover, no limitation of the statement is implied, such as "(on occasion)" (ibid., 30). Eventually, Paul comes to the question of abstinence in marriage in v. 5, but the principle stated now is generic, and it is not expressed as a command (with an impv.). Hence, questionable indeed are such versions as "not to marry" (NIV; see Fee, "1 Corinthians 7:1"), or "to remain unmarried" (Goodspeed), because they introduce a specific meaning not in the Greek text; even worse is the rendering, "to have nothing to do with women" (NEB). In v. 2 Paul will use *gynē* and *anēr* in the sense of "wife" and "husband," but that is because he is speaking of them in a marital union.

Paul uses the mid. voice of *haptō*, "touch," in the sense of sexual contact, as the verb is used in LXX Gen 20:4, 6; Ruth 2:9; Prov 6:29; also Plato, *Leg*. 8.840a; Aristotle, *Pol*. 7.14.12 (1335b); Josephus, *Ant*. 1.8.1 §163. As Fee has shown, the phrase *haptesthai gynaikos* is "a euphemism for sexual intercourse" ("1 Corinthians 7:1," 307–8). To make it mean "to marry" upsets the balance that Paul otherwise has in the chapter, which is merely introduced by v. 1, between marriage and celibacy. For he is using a phrase that builds on what he has been saying in 6:12–20 and is important for 7:2, where he clearly comes out in favor of marriage.

Ever since Paul wrote it, the saying has been regarded as an ascetic ideal, sometimes paraphrased with philosophical, ideological, and even gnostic nuances

that he himself would never have recognized. For it as an ascetic principle, see
Tertullian, *De Monogamia* 3.2; CCLat 2.1231; Jerome, *Adv. Iovinianum* 1.7; PL
23.229; Augustine, *Confess.* 2.2.3; CSEL 33.31; *De Nuptiis et Concupiscientia*
1.16.18; CSEL 42.230–31. See Deming, *Paul,* 110–15.

2. *Yet because of instances of fornication, each man should have his own wife,
and each woman her own husband.* Lit. "because of fornications." The acc. plur.
porneias is used, as also in Matt 15:19; Mark 7:21 (distinguished from "adultery"),
to denote individual acts of fornication that can happen among human beings.
Many think that *porneia* is employed here in a more generic sense, "sexual immorality" (see NOTES on 5:1, 9); that is possible, but the version in JB is surely
awry ("since sex is always a danger"). In any case, this verse qualifies the principle
expressed in v. 1b and adapts it to Paul's view of monogamous marriage, even if it
does not express a positive reason for marriage. The motivation is expressed only
negatively as the avoidance of acts of *porneia,* and this is stated as the mutual obligation of both man and woman. Generic exclusion of fornication from human
conduct was already set forth in 6:16, 18; now the exclusion is expressed explicitly
as a reason for marriage. See also 1 Thess 4:3, *apechesthai hymas apo tēs porneias,*
"to keep yourselves from fornication."

For the idiom *echein gynaika/andra,* "have a wife/husband" = "be married," see
NOTE on 5:1; it is not the same as *gamein,* "marry," i.e., enter into marriage. The
3d pers. sing. impv. *echetō* formulates a command (Lindemann, *1 Cor,* 158); and
the modifiers *heautou,* "his own," and *idion,* "her own," stress the exclusivity of
the marital bond (= no other partner). What Paul says here and in v. 3 shows how
he conceived husband and wife to be on a par, how marriage provides the only
place for the legitimate expression of sexuality, and how different it was from the
prevailing standards in Roman society, where fidelity was expected of the woman,
but extramarital relations were presumed for the man (see Peterman, "Marriage").

At the heart of Paul's thinking about the marital union lies Gen 2:18–24, and
especially v. 24, which was quoted by him in 6:16 as an argument against fornication (see NOTE there), even though it is not cited here. Cf. 1 Thess 4:3–8; also
Test. Levi 9.9–10; Collins, "The Unity."

3. *The husband should fulfill his conjugal duty to his wife, and likewise the wife
to her husband.* Lit. "to the woman let the man render . . . , and the woman to the
man," in chiastic arrangement. The 3d pers. sing. pres. impv. *apodidotō,* "let him/
her render," expresses the abiding mutual obligation (*opheilēn*) that husband and
wife have in the marital union. The husband's body is not his own once he enters
marriage, and the wife's body is not her own either. Although this verse explains
the mutual obligation of husband and wife in marriage, it says nothing about the
purpose of that obligation. Paul prescinds from the Jewish emphasis on the procreation of children (see Josephus, *Ag. Ap.* 2.24 §199 [quoted above]). Instead of
opheilēn, MSS K, L, and the Koine-text tradition soften the meaning in reading
opheilomenēn eunoian, "the goodwill owed (to her)" (Metzger, *TCGNT,* 488).

The Greek language uses *anēr* for a "male human being" or "man" as well as for
"husband," and *gynē* for a "female human being" or "woman" as well as for

"wife." In v. 1 the translation "man" and "woman" was preferred because of the generic principle there enunciated. However, in v. 2 the same words are rendered "husband" and "wife," because that verse speaks of monogamous marriage, an aspect of which Paul now discusses.

Paul's comment and what he says further in vv. 4–5 have been occasioned by problems about intercourse and abstinence from it, which apparently caused quarreling (and perhaps even attempts at divorce) among Corinthian Christian spouses. Having quoted vv. 3–5, Tomson remarks, "Here Paul moves along the lines of the Tannaic halakha" (*Paul and the Jewish Law,* 107). That Paul is reflecting some Palestinian Jewish tradition about the mutual obligation of spouses is correct, but that he is somehow echoing later Tannaitic tradition is another matter, because that is not attested earlier than the third century A.D.

4. *The wife does not have authority over her own body, but rather her husband does; likewise a husband does not have authority over his own body, but rather his wife does.* The mutuality of obligation is pressed further and expressed in parallel statements so as to become a curb to the freedom of persons who have entered the marital union. The *opheilē,* "duty, obligation" or what is owed to one's consort, is more important than the *exousia,* "right, freedom of choice, authority," of the individual spouse. Precedence was given to the husband in v. 3, but now it is given equally to the wife. Thus Paul insists that "husband and wife have equal conjugal obligations and equal sexual rights" (Schüssler Fiorenza, *In Memory,* 224). Verses 3–4 imply that there were instances in Corinth of Christian spouses not agreeing on abstention from marital intercourse or asserting one's rights over one's body. Paul, however, emphasizes the value of Christian marriage, in which the physical body (*sōma*) of the husband or wife is meant for marital intercourse with the spouse, as his Jewish heritage based on Gen 2:24 recognized. It thus seeks to eliminate all selfishness from this aspect of marital life. What Paul teaches in v. 4 finds parallels in some Greek writers: Plutarch, *Moralia* 139c; Musonius Rufus, *Frg.* 9.5, 7.

By *sōma* Paul does not mean "the whole, indivisible body-spirit human being in its stance over against God, people, and the world," *pace* Bruns ("Die Frau," 193; similarly Padgett "Feminism," 126). Nor is Paul engaged in polemics against "gnosticizing tendencies in Corinth" (Bruns, "Die Frau," 182 n. 13), which are scarcely "universally recognized"; there is hardly a hint in this text of its *sarx/pneuma* dualism (ibid., 186). What should be noted is that in vv. 32–34, where Paul contrasts the unmarried with the married (man and woman), he at least implies other mutual concerns of one spouse for the other as part of marriage that go beyond that of intercourse. Moreover, what he says both here in v. 4 and later in vv. 32–34 has nothing to do with the formula he will use in Gal 3:28.

5. *Do not deprive one another, except perhaps by mutual consent for a time.* Lit. "do not cheat one another," the negative impv. *mē apostereite* echoes what Paul said in 6:7–8 about cheating. Paul recognizes, however, the possibility of individual preferences of married spouses, and so he qualifies his command; he stresses that even abstention from marital intercourse must be temporary and governed by

"mutual consent," lest a spouse feel cheated and lest it become an end in itself. That is why he uses *pros kairon*, "for a limited time" (BDAG, 497), as in 1 Thess 2:17; LXX Wis 4:4; Josephus, *J.W.* 6.3.2 §190. The phrase does not mean "on suitable occasions," *pace* Scarpat ("Nisi forte"), as Prete ("Il significato") has shown; it means "for a short time." This advice undoubtedly was sparked by a question that the Corinthian Christians had asked in their letter. Perhaps the query was motivated by OT passages that speak of abstention from intercourse with a woman on certain occasions, such as 1 Sam 21:4–6; Lev 15:18; Exod 19:15, as Lietzmann (*1 Cor*, 30) has suggested; cf. Deming, *Paul*, 122–26. What Paul is speaking about is clearly not a "practice of celibacy when it confronts a spouse's conjugal rights," *pace* Poirier and Frankovic, "Celibacy and Charism," 2. Celibacy denotes a state of living unmarried, or of not having a spouse, or of living as a virgin; the practice of it does not encounter a spouse's conjugal rights.

to be free for prayer. Lit. "that you (plur.) may have time for prayer." This is to be understood as an example of a legitimate reason for such temporary abstinence from intercourse within marriage. Cf. *Test. Naphtali* 8.8, "There is a time for intercourse with a wife, and a time to abstain for the purpose of his prayer." This was also recognized in the later Jewish tradition, as was abstention in order to study the Torah (see Str-B 3.371–72). Recall also Tob 8:4–8, where Tobiah summons his bride Sarah to get out of bed in order to pray that the Lord grant them mercy. But beware of Jerome's translation in the Vg, where Tobiah and Sarah are said to abstain from intercourse for three nights in order to pray. An instance of such prayer might be that for the city, recommended in Jer 29:7. Some MSS (ℵ², Koine text-tradition) read *tē nēsteiā kai tē proseuchē*, "for fasting and prayer," undoubtedly a copyist's correction influenced by Mark 9:29.

but then be together again. The Greek phrase *epi to auto*, "together," is used euphemistically for marital intercourse (BDAG, 363). Some MSS (P⁴⁶, Ψ, Koine text-tradition) read *synerchēsthe*, "(that) you come together" (influenced by 11:20?) instead of the better-attested *ēte*, "(that) you be." Schrage (*1 Cor*, 2:69) prefers to read *synerchēsthe*.

so that Satan may not tempt you because of your lack of self-control. Lit. "because of your self-indulgence, incontinence," but *akrasia* was often used in antiquity as a synonym of *akrateia*, "without self-control" (LSJ, 54), which would give Satan scope for his testing. On Satan, see NOTE on 5:5. Paul speaks of the archenemy of humanity as seeking to seduce married couples, when he means that they themselves might succumb to a lack of self-control. Recall the role of Satan in Job 1:12a–c, which, however, lacks any mention of temptation; cf. 1 Thess 3:5, where he is called "the tempter." In 1QS 3:24, the one who causes the Sons of Light to stumble is the "Angel of Darkness."

6. *I say this as a concession, not as a command.* Lit. "by way of concession," i.e., to meet you halfway (BDAG, 950), "This" refers to the abstention of v. 5, as Kremer (*1 Cor*, 132) rightly notes; it is meant to bolster the "except" of that verse (Barrett, *1 Cor*, 157); similarly Kistemaker, *1 Cor*, 214; Schrage, *1 Cor*, 71–72 (also "Zur Frontstellung," 232); Lindemann, *1 Cor*, 160. Some commentators, however, claim that "this" refers to either v. 2 or to the whole of vv. 2–5, i.e., that

Paul is not really bidding Corinthian Christians to marry, but in light of the problems of *porneia*, he is only conceding that they may marry (Lietzmann, *1 Cor*, 30; Conzelmann, *1 Cor*, 118; Merklein, *1 Cor*, 2:110–11; Robertson-Plummer, *1 Cor*, 135). That, however, is far from clear, because the imperatives in vv. 2–3 do not express merely a concession being made by Paul. Indeed, they come closer to *epitagē*, "command," as Schrage notes. Cf. 2 Cor 8:8, where Paul similarly formulates a strong suggestion that he says is not a command. In the next verse, Paul will go beyond this mere concession. In using the 1st pers. sing. (*legō*), Paul is introducing his personal authority behind the concession that he is making (see Gooch, "Authority and Justification," 65).

B. Winter ("1 Corinthians 7:6–7," and *After Paul*, 233–40) relates *touto*, "this," to what is to come, appealing to 1:12; 7:26, 35; 15:50; Rom 6:6; Gal 3:17, where Paul writes *legō/nomizō/ ginōskō de touto . . . hoti/hina . . .* , and *touto* introduces a following object clause. So the concession of v. 6 would refer not to anything in vv. 2–5, but to v. 7: "And this I am saying . . . by way of concession and not of command, [that] I wish rather . . ."(*After Paul*, 234). That, however, is a last-ditch solution; Winter has to put brackets around "that" in his translation and speak of "an implied 'that' " (ibid.). True, at times *touto* introduces a coming *hoti/hina* clause (BDF §289.3), but then that conj. is not lacking in the sentence. Here, however, *touto* does not so function; it is pointing to something previously mentioned (BDF §290.1), i.e., what he conceded in v. 5.

7. *I wish that all were as I myself am.* Lit. "I desire all human beings to be even as myself," i.e., unmarried or celibate—or at least capable to resist sensual allurements, "which make it possible for him to live without marriage" (Barrett, *1 Cor*, 158). Paul's words express an attainable wish and explain why what he is saying is not by way of a command (v. 6); the reason for his words will come in v. 8. The verb *thelō* is used similarly in 7:32; 10:20, 27; 11:3; 14:5.

but each one has a particular gift from God, one of one kind and one of another. Cf. Rom 12:6, where Paul likewise speaks of gifts (*charismata*) that differ according to the grace (*charin*) given to individual Christians. Hence marriage or non-marriage is not just a matter of individual preference, but a divine gift to the individual person. In this context, both states of life are regarded as a "particular gift (*idion charisma*) from God." Conzelmann states that marriage is not "here described as a charisma" (*1 Cor*, 118); but that is what the text clearly says. Instead of adversative *de*, many MSS (ℵ², B, D², Ψ,1739, 1881 and the Koine text-tradition) have *gar*, "for," which expresses the reason for v. 6a.

Celibacy or virginity as a gift involves *enkrateia*, "self-control," which in Gal 5:23 is listed specifically among the fruits of the Spirit; it is the opposite of *akrasia*, "lack of self-control" (v. 5). There is, however, more to the celibate state of life than merely *enkrateia*, as will emerge in vv. 25–35 below. Paul uses no term like "command" or "counsel" but speaks of both marriage and celibacy as gifts of God, hence as an invitation or call.

What Paul says in v. 7bc makes it clear that he does not regard marriage as a "necessary evil" (*vielfach notwendigwerdendes Übel*, Lietzmann, *1 Cor*, 29) and can recognize in it "nothing good," but at most a basic *adiaphoron* or indifferent matter (ibid.). *Pace* Lindemann (*1 Cor,* 161), *idion . . . charisma* does not mean merely "Christian life generally," in which asceticism or the lack of it plays no role. It may be precisely the opposite of that view, if that "gift" involves a call to celibate life.

8. *Now to the unmarried and to widows I say: it is good for them to remain as I am.* The RSV, ESV render this verse, "to remain single as I do"; similarly NRSV, NIV: "remain unmarried as I am." Although that might be a legitimate interpretation of Paul's words, "single" or "unmarried" is not found in the Greek text. The REB has "stay as they are," which is a gratuitous change of the text. Barrett (*1 Cor,* 161) has "remain as they are, as I do myself," which reads more into the text than is there.

Paul is concluding his discussion of the principles that should govern marriage as he mentions two groups of Christians who are not married: the *agamoi,* "unmarried," and *chērai,* "widows" (or widowers). To these he recommends that they should remain as he is, which may be a further application of what he said in the statement with which he began in v. 1. Again he uses *kalon,* as there; it is a philosophical recommendation, a follow-up of his use of *thelō* in v. 7, and not a command. As Senft (*1 Cor,* 91) notes, "Paul says again to this group what he has already said in vv. 1 and 7a," recalling with Bachmann that *legō* is emphatic, "I declare." It is wrong to interpret *kalon* as "preferable," as do some interpreters. Paul states it as the choice that he has made and recommends it as a good thing; and the reasons for it he sets out in vv. 26, 28, 32–35 below.

The adj. *agamos,* "unmarried," occurs in the NT only in this chapter (vv. 8, 11, 32, 34). In v. 11 it denotes a woman separated in divorce; in v. 32, a single man, contrasted with *ho gamēsas,* "married man"; and in v. 34, a single woman, who is also called *hē parthenos,* "virgin" (in some MSS; see NOTE there). Here in v. 8, it occurs along with "widows" in a paragraph where Paul's main concern is marriage. Does that mean that *agamos* means "no longer married"? Arens thinks so ("Was St. Paul Married," 1189; similarly Murphy-O'Connor, *Paul: A Critical Life,* 64–65). That, however, is far from clear, because it loads the *alpha*-privative of the adj. with unexpected freight. Moreover, 1 Cor 9:5 ("Do we not have the right to bring along a Christian wife, as do the rest of the apostles?") means that, in giving up that right, Paul was *agamos* in the sense of 7:32, i.e., that he was *parthenos* and that that is what he meant when he wished that "all were as" he himself was (7:7a). *Pace* Arens (ibid.), that does not necessarily "suggest that Paul was in principle opposed to marriage," because v. 7b states his genuine conviction.

Was Paul a widower? Jeremias ("War Paulus Witwer?") once argued that Paul, prior to his Christian call, was such, because, as an ordained Jewish *ḥākām* with ability to make legal decisions (see Acts 9:1–2), he would have had to be married and 40 years old according to rabbinic tradition. That thesis, however, is not without its anachronistic problems, and it has met with little favor (see Fascher, "Zur Witwerschaft"; Oepke, "Probleme," 406–10). The same understanding of this verse, however, has been advocated by Phipps ("Is Paul's Attitude," 128); and Menoud ("Mariage et célibat," 23 n. 1), who conjectures that Paul "lived, ever since his conversion, separated from his wife (*agamos*), who remained faithful to the Jewish law," a view questioned by Wili, "Privilegium Paulinum." For Fee (*1 Cor*, 287–88), *agamoi* = "widowers." (For what it is worth, Eusebius quotes Clement of Alexandria who maintained that Paul did "not hesitate in one of his letters to address his wife whom he did not take about with him in order to facilitate his mission" [*HE* 3.30.1]. Clement refers to Phil 4:3, where Paul addresses someone as *se, gnēsie syzyge*, taking it to mean "you, dear wife" [*Strom.* 3.53.1; GCS 52.220]; cf. Origen, *Comm. in Rom.* 1.1; PL 14.839; RSV has rather "true yokefellow"; ESV, "true companion"; NRSV, "my loyal companion"; NAB, "my true yokemate.")

9. *but if they are not exercising self-control, they should marry.* I.e., "marriage is a necessity if one cannot live the asexual life demanded by freedom from the marriage bond" (Schüssler Fiorenza, *In Memory*, 223). The verb in the protasis of this qualification is the pres. *ouk enkrateuontai*, which expresses the actual lack of "sexual continence" (BDAG, 275 [with neg. *ou* instead of *mē* for emphasis in a simple condition, as in Rom 8:9c]); so understood also by Lindemann, *1 Cor*, 163. Cf. the meaning of the same verb in 9:25. It is often translated, "if they cannot exercise self-control" (RSV; similarly NIV, ESV, Conzelmann, Soards, Robertson-Plummer, Kremer), but the verb does not say "cannot," and Paul did not write *ei de ou dynantai enkrateuesthai*. He is saying that, if unmarried persons or widow(er)s are falling into the same problem of *porneia* as the persons mentioned in v. 2, then let them get married. Paul is reckoning with a factual situation (the lack of the same *enkrateia*), and so he concludes his general remarks about married life. At any rate, he is not speaking of individuals endowed with celibacy as a gift of God (v. 7).

for it is better to marry than to burn. Or "than to be burned." Now one meets the first instance of the comparative *kreitton*, "better," in this chapter, and it does not occur in a comparison of marriage and celibacy. The infin. *pyrousthai* is being used, but in what sense? When "cannot" is used in the protasis, then it is understood as mid. voice and in a metaphorical sense, "burn with sexual desire" (BDAG, 899), which is the sense frequently presented in this apodosis (so Conzelmann, invoking Lang, *TDNT*, 6:948–51; Barrett, *1 Cor*, 161; Fee, *1 Cor*, 289; Kremer, *1 Cor*, 133; Lindemann, *1 Cor*, 163). In support of such a meaning, one often appeals to 2 Cor 11:29 (burn with emotion [indignation]); and extrabiblically to the late poems associated with the name of Anacreon (*Erōs, sy d' eutheōs me pyrōson. ei de mē, sy kata phlogos takēsēi*, "O Love, set me immediately aflame; if not, you yourself will melt in flames" (*Anacreontea* 11.14–16).

However, Barré has argued that *pyroun*, though used in the LXX with the meaning "burn" with emotion (Sir 23:17; 2 Macc 4:38; 10:35; 3 Macc 4:2), is not used there *absolutely*, but always with modifiers expressing the emotion (*thymois* or *stenagmois*). Moreover, he cites other NT occurrences of the verb (Eph 6:16; 2 Pet 3:12; Rev 1:15; 3:18) and the cog. noun *pyrōsis* (1 Pet 4:12; Rev 19:8, 18), all of which are found in contexts of eschatological judgment. Since in this chapter Paul discusses various marital and nonmarital states in light of an imminent parousia (7:17–35), Barré argues that "to burn" means "to be burned in the fires of judgment or Gehenna" ("To Marry," 200; so too Russell, "That Embarrassing Verse"; Bruce, *1 Cor*, 68 ["may mean 'to burn with passion', but might possibly mean 'to burn in Gehenna' because of falling into fornication (in thought if not in action)"]; Witherington, *Women*, 31: "Barré's view cannot be ruled out"). A similar interpretation has been proposed by Binni ("1 Cor 7,9"), who claims that Paul is using a "midrash," which exploits the similarity of Hebrew words reflected in this verse: 'ēš, "fire," and 'îš, "man," and 'iššāh, "woman"; an intriguing suggestion, but unfortunately there is no evidence of a rabbinic midrash in the Greek text of this verse.

Nevertheless, as Cambier notes, one has to put Paul's statement "in its historical and sociological context. . . . [It] is not a Pauline judgment about marriage! It is an occasional remark addressed to Christians of a community of a precise date: let them, such Christians, not make a pretense of living a celibate life to which they have not been called!" ("Doctrine paulinienne," 21).

BIBLIOGRAPHY

Adinolfi, M., "Il matrimonio nella libertà dell'etica escatologica di 1 Cor. 7," *Anton* 51 (1976) 133–69.

———, "Motivi parenetici del matrimonio e del celibato in 1 Cor. 7," *RivB* 26 (1978) 71–91.

Arens, E., "Was St. Paul Married?" *TBT* 66 (1973) 1188–91.

Baltensweiler, H., *Die Ehe im Neuen Testament: Exegetische Untersuchungen über Ehe, Ehelosigkeit und Ehescheidung* (ATANT 52; Zurich: Zwingli-V., 1967).

Barré, M. L., "To Marry or to Burn: *Pyrousthai* in 1 Cor 7:9," *CBQ* 36 (1974) 193–202.

Baumert, N., *Ehelosigkeit und Ehe im Herrn: Eine Neuinterpretation von 1 Kor 7* (FzB 47; Würzburg: Echter-V., 1984).

———, *Woman and Man in Paul: Overcoming a Misunderstanding* (Collegeville, MN: Liturgical, 1996) 30–49.

Binni, W., "1Cor 7,9: un 'midrash' paolino," *RivB* 52 (2004) 87–95.

Bouwman, C., "Paulus en het celibaat," *Bijdr* 37 (1976) 379–90.

Bruns, B., " 'Die Frau hat über ihren Leib nicht die Verfügungsgewalt, sondern der Mann . . .": Zur Herkunft und Bedeutung der Formulierung in 1 Kor 7,4," *MTZ* 33 (1982) 177–94.

Cambier, J.-M., "Doctrine paulinienne du mariage chrétien: Étude critique de 1 Co 7 et d'Ep 5, 21–33 et essai de leur traduction actuelle," *ÉgT* 10 (1979) 13–59.

Caragounis, C. C., " 'Fornication' and 'Concession'?: Interpreting 1 Cor 7,1–7," *The Corinthian Correspondence* (BETL 125; ed. R. Bieringer) 543–59.

Cartlidge, D. R., "1 Corinthians 7 as a Foundation for a Christian Sex Ethic," *JR* 55 (1975) 220–34.

Collins, R. F., "The Unity of Paul's Paraenesis in 1 Thess 4.3–8, 1 Cor 7.1–7, a Significant Parallel," *NTS* 29 (1983) 420–29.

Delling, G., *Paulus' Stellung zu Frau und Ehe* (BWANT 56; Stuttgart: Kohlhammer, 1931).

Deming, W., *Paul on Marriage and Celibacy: The Hellenistic Background of 1 Corinthians 7* (SNTSMS 83; Cambridge: Cambridge University Press, 1995; 2d ed.; Grand Rapids: Eerdmans, 2004).

Eickhoff, A. R., "A Psychoanalytical Study of St. Paul's Theology of Sex," *Pastoral Psychology* 18/173 (1967) 35–42.

Ellis, J. E., "Controlled Burn: The Romantic Note in 1 Corinthians 7," *PRSt* 29 (2002) 89–98.

Fascher, E., "Zur Witwerschaft des Paulus und der Auslegung von I Cor 7," *ZNW* 28 (1929) 62–69.

Fee, G. D., "1 Corinthians 7:1 in the *NIV*," *JETS* 23 (1980) 307–14.

Fischer, J. A., "1 Cor. 7:8–24: Marriage and Divorce," *BR* 23 (1978) 26–36.

Garland, D. E., "The Christian's Posture toward Marriage and Celibacy: 1 Corinthians 7," *RevExp* 80 (1983) 351–62.

Glaser, J. W., "Commands—Counsels: A Pauline Teaching?" *TS* 31 (1970) 275–87.

Gooch, P. W., "Authority and Justification in Theological Ethics: A Study in 1 Corinthians 7," *JRE* 11 (1983) 62–74.

Gordon, J. D., *Sister or Wife? 1 Corinthians and Cultural Anthropology* (JSNTSup 149; Sheffield: Sheffield Academic, 1997).

Gramaglia, P. A., "Le fonti del linguaggio paolino in *1 Cor*. 7, 35 e 7, 1," *Aug* 28 (1988) 461–501.

Gundry-Volf, J. M., "Controlling the Bodies: A Theological Profile of the Corinthian Sexual Ascetics (1 Cor 7)," *The Corinthian Correspondence* (BETL 125; ed. R. Bieringer), 519–41.

Horst, P. W. van der, "Celibacy in Early Judaism," *RB* 109 (2002) 390–402.

Jeremias, J., "War Paulus Witwer?" *ZNW* 25 (1926) 310–12.

———, "Nochmals: War Paulus Witwer?" *ZNW* 28 (1929) 321–23.

Kleinschmidt, F., *Ehefragen im Neuen Testament: Ehe, Ehelosigkeit, Ehescheidung, Verheiratung, Verwitweter und Geschiedener im Neuen Testament* (Arbeiten zur Religion und Geschichte des Urchristentums 7; Frankfurt am M.: P. Lang, 1998).

Léon-Dufour, X., "Mariage et continence selon S. Paul," *À la rencontre de Dieu: Mémorial Albert Gelin* (Le Puy: Editions X. Mappus, 1961) 319–29.

MacArthur, J., *Guidelines for Singleness and Marriage* (Chicago, IL: Moody, 1986).

Matura, T., "Le célibat dans le Nouveau Testament d'après l'exégèse récente," *NRT* 97 (1975) 481–500, 593–604.

Menoud, P.-H., "Mariage et célibat selon saint Paul," *RTP* 1 (1951) 21–34.

Mitchell, M. M., "Concerning *peri de* in 1 Corinthians," *NovT* 31 (1989) 229–56.

Moiser, J., "A Reassessment of Paul's View of Marriage with Reference to 1 Cor. 7," *JSNT* 18 (1983) 103–22.

Niederwimmer, K., *Askese und Mysterium: Über Ehe, Ehescheidung und Eheversicht in den Anfängen des christlichen Glaubens* (FRLANT 113; Göttingen: Vandenhoeck & Ruprecht, 1975).

Oepke, A., "Probleme der vorchristlichen Zeit des Paulus," *TSK* 105 (1933) 387–424, esp. 406–10.

Oster, R. E., Jr., "Use, Misuse and Neglect of Archaeological Evidence in Some Modern Works on 1 Corinthians (1 Cor 7,1–5; 8,10; 11,2–16; 12,14–26)," *ZNW* 83 (1992) 52–73.

Peterman, W., "Marriage and Sexual Fidelity in the Papyri, Plutarch and Paul," *TynBul* 50 (1999) 163–72.

Phipps, W. E., "Is Paul's Attitude toward Sexual Relations Contained in 1 Cor 7. 1?," *NTS* 28 (1982) 125–31.

Poirier, J. C., and J. Frankovic, "Celibacy and Charism in 1 Cor 7:5–7," *HTR* 89 (1996) 1–18.

Prete, B., *Matrimonio e continenza nel cristianesimo delle origini: Studio su 1 Cor. 7,1–40* (Studi biblici 49; Brescia: Paideia, 1979).

———, "Il significato della formula *pros kairon* (Vg: *ad tempus*) in 1 Cor 7,5," *RivB* 49 (2001) 417–37.

Richardson, P., " 'I Say, not the Lord': Personal Opinion, Apostolic Authority and the Development of Early Christian Halakah," *TynBul* 31 (1980) 65–86.

Russell, K. C., "That Embarrassing Verse in First Corinthians!" *TBT* 18 (1980) 338–41.

Scarpat, G., "*Nisi forte ex consensu ad tempus*: A proposito di *pros kairon* di 1Cor 7,5," *RivB* 48 (2000) 151–66.

Schrage, W., "Zur Frontstellung der paulinischen Ehebewertung in 1 Kor 7,1–7," *ZNW* 67 (1976) 214–34.

Ward, R. B., "Musonius and Paul on Marriage," *NTS* 36 (1990) 281–89.

Wili, H.-U., "Das Privilegium Paulinum (1 Kor 7, 15f)—Pauli eigene Lebenserinnerung? (Rechtshistorische Anmerkungen zu einer neueren Hypothese)," *BZ* 22 (1978) 100–108.

Winter, B. W., "1 Corinthians 7:6–7: A Caveat and a Framework for 'the Sayings' in 7:8–24," *TynBul* 48 (1997) 57–65.

Yarbrough, O. L., *Not Like the Gentiles: Marriage Rules in the Letters of Paul* (SBLDS 80; Atlanta: Scholars, 1985) 89–122.

Zeller, D., "Der Vorrang der Ehelosigkeiten in 1 Kor 7," *ZNW* 96 (2005) 61–77.

13 b. *The Lord's Command: No Divorce (7:10–11)*

7:10 To the married, however, I give this command, not I but the Lord: that a wife should not be separated from her husband; 11 but if indeed she is separated, she must either remain unmarried or be reconciled to her husband; and that a husband should not divorce his wife.

COMMENT

Paul's discussion moves on to another topic about marriage. Whereas he has counseled the unmarried and widows to remain unmarried (7:8), his advice now to married Christians is that they remain married. In v. 5, he conceded that spouses could abstain from intercourse within marriage, but now he prohibits their breaking up their marital union. In v. 6, Paul made a distinction between what he considered a concession and a command, as he passed on his own preference for consideration by Corinthian Christians. Now he passes on a command about divorce, which comes not from himself, but from the Lord.

In this matter, Paul is tributary to an early Christian tradition. Although his formulation of the prohibition of divorce is not an exact reproduction of Jesus' words, it is the earliest extant form of a reminiscence of them. The prohibition stemming from Jesus of Nazareth is diversely attested elsewhere in the NT: Mark 10:2–12, esp. vv. 9, 11 (where what was once addressed by God to Jews of old is extended by Jesus to all human beings); Luke 16:18; Matt 5:31–32; 19:3–9, esp. v. 6. In light of this inherited teaching, it seems strange that Paul would have to reiterate it for Corinthians, stressing it in such wise that it almost sounds like new teaching. Yet something in the Corinthian Christian community has given rise to a discussion of marriage and divorce, to which Paul now reacts.

The prohibition of divorce, as formulated by Paul, is absolute, with no exceptions envisaged, as it appears also in Mark 10:9–12 and Luke 16:18. The form of the prohibition preserved in the Matthean Gospel, however, envisages an exception: in 5:31–32, *parektos logou porneias*, "except in the matter of illicit marital union"; in 19:6–9, *mē epi porneia*, "except for illicit marital union" (for the specific meaning of *porneia* in the Matthean Gospel and the reason for the exceptions there, see Fitzmyer, "Matthean Divorce Texts"). *Pace* Olender ("Paul's Source"), allusions in the Pauline text to the divorce tradition as it is preserved in Matt 19:3–12 are overdrawn and practically nonexistent. If Paul knew about the exceptions mentioned in the later Matthean texts, which in itself is highly unlikely, he must have considered them inapplicable to the Corinthian situation (see Laney, "Paul and the Permanence," 285).

The prohibition of divorce, coming from Jesus, differs from the Palestinian Jewish custom of permitting divorce (based mainly on Deut 24:1–4, where Mosaic legislation allowed a man to give his wife a "writ of divorce"), of which Paul was certainly aware. For him, however, neither husband nor wife is to be separated or divorced from the other. If a woman is divorced, she is to remain unmarried or be reconciled. Thus, Paul envisages no further marriage for the woman after such a separation. Moreover, he adds explicitly, the husband is not to divorce his wife (v. 11c). According to Schüssler Fiorenza, "despite the explicit instruction of the Lord, wives—who are mentioned first and with more elaboration in 7:10f—still have the possibility of freeing themselves from the bondage of patriarchal marriage, in order to live a marriage-free life. If they have done so, however, they must remain in this marriage-free state. They are allowed to return to their husbands, but they may not marry someone else" (*In Memory*, 222). Nowhere in the text, however, is there any basis for what is called "the bondage of patriarchal marriage," and the instruction of the Lord applies equally to the Christian woman and the Christian man; neither of them is to be divorced from the other.

The prohibition in v. 10, expressed by the aor. pass. infin. (*mē chōristhēnai*, "not to be separated"), is formulated at first from the woman's position: she is not to be divorced from her husband. That formulation reflects the Palestinian Jewish view of marriage according to Mosaic law, which Paul sums up in Rom 7:2–3: "A married woman is bound by law to her husband while he is alive. But if the husband dies, she is released from the law regarding her husband. Accordingly, she will be called an adulteress if she gives herself to another man, while her husband is still alive. But if her husband dies, she is free of that law and does not become an adulteress if she gives herself to another man." See also v. 39a below, "A wife is bound to her husband as long as he lives."

Underlying this understanding of marriage is the OT view of the wife as the chattel or possession of the husband. Sarah, who was taken from Abraham by Abimelech, king of Gerar, is described as *wĕhî' bĕ'ūlat ba'al,* "for she is a man's wife" (RSV), but lit. "for she is lorded over [or owned] by a master/owner" (Gen 20:3; cf. Deut 22:22). The "married man" was *ba'al 'iššāh,* "master/owner of a woman" (Exod 21:3, 22; cf. 2 Sam 11:26b; Prov 12:4a; Deut 21:13de). For this reason many OT passages assert the husband's rights and authority: Exod 20:17b; 21:22; Deut 5:21; 22:22; Num 30:6–8,10–14; Sir 25:26 (cf. de Vaux, *AI,* 26). Hence the wife could commit adultery against her husband, and another man lying with her would do the same (Lev 20:10), i.e., violate the rights of her husband.

Moreover, in Palestinian Judaism the wife could not divorce her husband, whereas he could divorce her (Deut 24:1–4; cf. Jer 3:1). The "writ of divorce" (*sēpher kĕrîtût,* Jer 3:8; Isa 50:1 [LXX: *biblion apostasiou*]), written by the husband, was given to the woman, often with a clause explicitly permitting her to give herself to another man or go wherever she pleased. See the Murabba'at Aramaic papyrus (§19, dated A.D. 111? [DJD, 2:104–9]), called *spr trwkyn wgṭ šbqyn,* "writ of repudiation and bill of divorce," authored by Joseph bar Naqsan and issued to Miryam bĕrat Yehonatan (see Fitzmyer, "Divorce among First-Century Palestinian Jews"). Thus divorce was tolerated in ancient Palestinian Judaism (Deut 24:1–4), even though voices also spoke against it: Mal 2:14, 16; Prov 2:17; Sir 7:19, 26, and the Essenes of Qumran (see below).

At times it has been claimed that ancient Jewish women could divorce their husbands, i.e., initiate proceedings against them. Brooten ("Konnten Frauen"; "Zur Debatte"), misusing alleged evidence gathered by Bammel ("Markus 10,11f"), claimed that they could do so in ancient Palestine. Her thesis, however, has been contested seriously (see Schweizer, "Scheidungsrecht," 294–97; Tomson, *Paul and the Jewish Law,* 109 n.78; Weder, "Perspektive"; Fitzmyer, "So-Called Aramaic Divorce Text"). Obviously, some women in ancient Judea were what Jeremiah called a "faithless wife" (3:20, *bāgĕdāh 'iššāh*), who even tried to divorce their husbands. Josephus tells of the most famous case, that of Salome, the sister of Herod the Great, who had quarreled with her husband Costobarus and "immediately sent him a document, dissolving the marriage" (*grammateion, apolymenē ton gamon*). Josephus, however, adds immediately that that was not according to Jewish laws (*ou kata tous Ioudaiōn nomous*): "For a man among us it is possible to do this, but not even a divorced woman may marry again on her own initiative unless her former husband consents" (*Ant.* 15.7.10 §259); see other instances in Josephus, *Ant.* 18.5.4 §136 (Herodias); *Ant.* 20.7.2 §§142–43 (Drusilla); *Ant.* 4.8.23 §253; cf. Philo, *De spec. leg.* 3.5 §§30–31 (comment on Deut 24:4). For Josephus's own divorces, see *Life* 75 §§414–15, 426.

What Josephus says differs little from the later rabbinic regulation recorded in *m. Yebamoth* 14:1: "A woman is put away with her consent or without it, but a husband can put away his wife only with his own consent" (ed. H. Danby, 240). See further *m. Gittin* 9:1–3, 8, 10; *m. Ketuboth* 7:9–10; *m. Kiddushin* 1:1; cf. Schubert, "Ehescheidung." Care must be used, however, in citing the later rabbinic regulations, because it is far from clear that such regulations were already in vogue in pre-70 A.D. Palestinian Judaism, *pace* Lövestam ("Divorce"), who naively cites not only the Mishnah, but also the sixth-century *Babylonian* Talmud and the still later *Midrash Rabbah*.

Divorce initiated by a woman was envisaged as a possibility in the fifth-century Jewish military colony at Elephantine in Egypt; a number of Aramaic marriage contracts from that place provide for it explicitly: "Should Miptaḥiah rise up in an assembly tomorrow [or] some other [da]y and say, 'I divorce [lit. I hate] my husband Eshor,' the divorce-fee is on her head" (*AP* 15:22–23; see *WA*, 243–71; *AP* 9:8–11; *BMAP* 2:9; 7:25). That possibility, however, is almost certainly owing to the special circumstances of Jews living in Egypt, and no evidence from contemporary or later Palestinian Judaism supports anything of the kind, not even Mur 20 i 6 (wrongly restored by Milik in DJD, 2:113; see Fitzmyer, "So-Called Aramaic Divorce Text").

In fact, Qumran literature records that some Palestinian Jews (Essenes) opposed divorce. In the Temple Scroll (11QTemple[a] [11Q19] 57:17–19) one reads: "And he shall not take in addition to her another wife, for she alone shall be with him all the days of her life; and if she dies, he shall take for himself another (wife) from his father's house, from his clan." This is part of the statutes for the king and the army, which is a paraphrase of Deut 17:17a ("He [the king] shall not multiply wives for himself lest his heart turn away" [RSV]). The first clause of the sectarian text (11Q19) precludes polygamy, but the reason added in the second clause makes it clear that the king is not to divorce his wife. This prohibition casts light on CD 4:12b–5:14a (the first instance of *zĕnût* proscribed there); see further Yadin, *Temple Scroll*, 1:355–57, whose interpretation I am following; cf. Fitzmyer, "Matthean Divorce Texts," 91–99; Tomson, *Paul and the Jewish Law*, 111; Schubert, "Ehescheidung," 27.

By way of contrast to the normal Palestinian Jewish practice in this matter, divorce was possible in the Greco-Roman world either by common agreement of the spouses, or at the instigation of either the husband or the wife. See Seneca, *De beneficiis* 3.16.2; cf. Delling, "Ehescheidung" (for Assyrian, Egyptian, Greek, and Roman practice); Erdmann, *Die Ehe*, 386–403; Harrison, *The Law of Athens*, 39–44. Greek writers who mention divorce are: Diodorus Siculus (*Hist.* 12.18.1), who notes the woman's right to divorce [*apolyein*] her husband; Plutarch, *Pericles* 24.5 §165d; Isaeus, *Or.* 2.8–9; 3.78; Demosthenes, *Or.* 30.4, 15, 17–18, 26; 41.4; Herodotus, *Hist.* 6.63. Roman writers are: Cicero, *Philipp.* 2.28.69; *De Orat.* 3.40; *Pro Cluen.* 5.14; Plautus, *Miles Glor.* 4.4.3 §1167.

Three further things should be noted about the Pauline formulation. First, the prohibition is attributed to "the Lord." Thus Paul invests the prohibition with the authority of *ho Kyrios*, meaning not only that the teaching does not originate with himself, in contrast to 7:12, 25, but also that, even though it stems from the earthly Jesus, it now bears the authority of the risen Christ. "It is a supratemporal command" (Conzelmann, *1 Cor*, 120). Second, Paul passes on the prohibition in indirect discourse, whereas the pronouncement in the Synoptics is presented as a dominical saying in direct discourse: "What God has joined together, let no human being put asunder," and "Anyone who divorces his wife and marries another woman commits adultery." This explains also the shift from Paul giving a command to the Lord giving it; Paul does not quote the dominical saying, but paraphrases it in his own words. Third, the Greek text of N-A^{27} sets v. 11a–b in dashes, and the RSV translates the words in parentheses: "but if she does [separate], let her remain single or else be reconciled to her husband." This reflects the view of some interpreters (e.g., Baltensweiler [*Ehe*, 187], Kremer, Lindemann), who regard the words so marked off as a Pauline insertion into the charge that stems from Jesus, which would be identified only with vv. 10c and 11c. In fact, J. Weiss (*1 Cor*, 178–79) considers them to be probably an interpolation. The insertion is said to be an explication of the charge about divorce itself in terms of a possible subsequent marriage with another person. Since other forms of Jesus' prohibition of divorce in the NT, however, refer at times to a subsequent marriage (Mark 10:11a; Matt 19:9b; Luke 16:18), it is far from certain that it is a Pauline insertion, even though it is a Pauline formulation; it could represent a development in the pre-Pauline tradition beyond that which stems from Jesus himself. My translation has done away with the dashes and parentheses, because vv. 10c and 11 (in its entirety) are Paul's rephrasing of the dominical saying.

Murphy-O'Connor thinks that the insertion refers to "a specific incident at Corinth," which is envisaged in Paul's statements in vv. 3–5 above, i.e., a case of Corinthian spouses quarreling over intercourse and abstention from it (see NOTE on v. 3), and quarreling so intensely that the ascetic husband had already decided to divorce his wife because of it. Paul's answer would be to counsel against such divorce and recommend reconciliation. This leads Murphy-O'Connor to maintain that the dominical logion of v. 10c "does not control Paul's thought in 7:1–11," but is "an afterthought" added to this specific instance "because of its pastoral utility." "Paul considered Jesus' prohibition of divorce, not as a binding precept, but as a significant directive whose relevance to a particular situation had to be evaluated by the pastor responsible for the community" ("Divorced Woman," 606; followed by Omanson, "Some Comments"). That v. 10c is an afterthought and not a binding precept is highly speculative and ultimately to be rejected. Rather, the prohibition of divorce that Paul passes on has been occasioned by a Corinthian Christian woman either refusing sexual relations with her husband or perhaps even trying to seek her own divorce, because Paul formulates the prohibition first apropos of the wife (Fee, *1 Cor*, 290). Others think that the question of a possible divorce has arisen in Roman Corinth because some Christian spouses there were already abstaining from intercourse for ascetic reasons and were minded to separate completely to achieve better asceticism (so Hurd, *Origin*, 167; Barrett, *1 Cor*, 162).

In a culture in which divorce has become the norm, this text has become a bone of contention. Some find Paul and Jesus too harsh and try to find ways around the plain sense of the text. Others . . . make divorce the worst of all sins in the church. Neither of these seems an appropriate response. . . . there is little question that both Paul and Jesus disallowed divorce between two believers, especially when it served as grounds for remarriage. (Fee, *1 Cor*, 296)

For Paul, the reason for disallowing divorce is the unitive character of marriage and the mutual giving of the persons of the spouses, yes even of their bodies (vv. 3–4), in the spirit of Christian love, which "does not seek its own interests" (13:5b).

NOTES

7:10. *To the married, however, I give this command.* Paul uses *parangellō,* "I enjoin, give orders, command," as again in 11:17; 1 Thess 4:11, which differs from a "concession" (*syngnōmē*), but would not differ from *epitagē* (see 7:6 above). This would be an example of what Paul called in 4:17c "my ways in Christ [Jesus]," which he taught in every church.

not I but the Lord. Thus Paul not only corrects himself, but knowingly cites Jesus' prohibition of divorce and passes it on in indirect discourse to married believers in an absolute, unqualified form, as coming from the risen Christ. Cf. 14:37, "a commandment of the Lord."

that a wife should not be separated from her husband. Or "not be divorced." As formulated, the prohibition of divorce is stated universally, with no specification of its being intended only for Christians (contrast vv. 12–15, where "brother" or "sister" appears). The verb is the aor. pass. infin., *mē chōristhēnai,* which depends on a verb implicit in the preceding clause: the Lord commands that. . . . For the passive meaning, see BDAG (1095), "*be separated,* of divorce."

Some MSS (A, D, F, G, 1505, 1881) read rather the pres. infin., *chōrizesthai,* an insignificant variant, if it is understood as pass.; but if taken as middle, it could tolerate the meaning, "separate herself," which may be a copyist's correction to prepare for vv. 13c and 15. Other MSS (P[46], 614) have the 3d pers. sing. pres. impv., *mē chōrizesthō,* "let her not be separated," or "let her not separate herself," which eliminates the need to understand the implicit verb of command for the infin., but which is almost certainly a copyist's correction in light of Mark 10:9 or of 1 Cor 7:15. Moreover, it creates an anomaly, because the infin. *aphienai* (v. 11c) is read in the second part and has no similar variant; that argues for the correctness of the aor. pass. infin.

The RSV, NRSV, ESV, NAB, however, translate the aor. pass. infin. as intransitive act., "should not separate"; similarly Baltensweiler, *Ehe,* 187; Baumert, *Woman and Man,* 50; Collins, *1 Cor,* 262; Fee, *1 Cor,* 293; Garland, *1 Cor,* 280–81; Kremer, *1 Cor,* 137–38; Lövestam, "Divorce," 62; Neirynck, "The Sayings," 161; Pesch, *Freie Treue,* 60; Schrage, *1 Cor,* 2:89, 99 (*sich . . . nicht scheiden soll*); Senft, *1 Cor,* 90, 92 (*ne se sépare pas*). Thus the aor. pass. infin. is taken as parallel to the act. infin. *aphienai,* said of the husband (v. 11c). This understanding of the aor. pass. infin. was proposed by Lietzmann (*1 Cor,* 31), who asserts that it "must have (this) meaning." The aor. pass. of *chōrizō* is translated as "departed, went away" in such texts as Acts 18:1; 1 Chr 12:9; 2 Macc 5:21; 12:12; 1 Esdr 5:39; Neh 9:2, but the nuance is not always clear, and some of these instances can just as easily be rendered as real passive forms. See also Polybius, *Hist.* 3.94.9; Heraclitus, *De incred.* 8.

If the act. intransitive were a correct translation, it would mean that Jesus' prohibition of divorce had already been recast in pre-Pauline tradition, adapting it
to a non-Palestinian setting, viz., the Greco-Roman world, in which a woman
could divorce her husband, as Lietzmann recognized. (This recasting has happened, indeed, in the second part of the prohibitive saying of Jesus preserved in
Mark 10:12: "If she divorces her husband and marries another, she commits adultery," where the evangelist explicitly has extended Jesus' prohibition to the Gentile world for which his Gospel was being written. Lindemann [*1 Cor*, 164] goes so
far as to think that Paul shared this view—but that is scarcely expressed in his
Greek text.)

It is, however, far from certain that the Pauline formulation should be taken as
act., "should not separate." I once succumbed to this mode of translation, because
of the common way Paul's words have often been rendered (*PAHT* §PT147), but
I now revert to the translation that I had proposed earlier (*TAG*, 81), that *mē
chōristhēnai* is to be taken as passive, as NJB, Warren ("Did Moses," 49), and Orr-
Walther have understood it (*1 Cor*, 211 [with no discussion of the problem]). *Pace*
Fee (*1 Cor*, 293 n. 14), a point has to be made of the passive, since there is no justification for taking an *aor. pass. infin.* as equivalent to an intransitive act. form
such as *aphienai* (his reference to *koimaō* is not a valid parallel, since it means
"lull, put to sleep" [LSJ, 967]); or as a form that can have "a middle sense" (Garland, *1 Cor*, 281; Thiselton, *1 Cor*, 520). It is to be understood as passive, just as is
katallagētō in v. 11, "be reconciled."

Moreover, because Paul's formulation of the prohibition, even though
couched in indirect discourse, is the earliest form that we have inherited, the passive interpretation of it agrees better with the Palestinian Jewish context in which
Jesus would have uttered it. (See the formulation in Luke 16:18, which is the most
primitive form among the Synoptics; cf. *Luke*, 1120.) Murphy-O'Connor, who
has acknowledged the passive force of *chōristhēnai*, says that "in Paul the passive is
sometimes used with the connotation 'to allow oneself to be' (e.g., 1 Cor 6:7; Rom
12:2)," with a note referring to BDF §314 ("Divorced Woman," 602). The two
Pauline passages he cites, however, have pres. mid.-pass. forms, and they should
be taken as mid. (not pass.), which is likewise true of most of the instances in BDF
§314. None of them shows that an *aor. pass. infin.* can be taken in any other sense
than passive: hence, not "that she should not allow herself to be divorced," but
"that she should not be divorced (at all)." The verse, therefore, says nothing about
a wife's "willing acceptance."

In this verse Paul uses *chōrizō*, the verb that commonly means "divorce" in
Classical and Hellenistic Greek writers (e.g., Isaeus, *Or.* 8.36; Euripides, *Frg.*
1063.13; Polybius, *Hist.* 31.26.6), as well as in Greek marriage contracts (MM,
696; P. Rylands, 2.154:25 [LCL *Select Papyri*, 1.14–15]; Preisigke-Kiessling,
Wörterbuch, 2. 767). It also appears in Jesus' words in Mark 10:9 and Matt 19:6,
mē chōrizetō. It may not be "a technical expression for 'divorce,' " as some writers
have maintained (e.g., Fischer, "1 Cor. 7:8–24," 27), but it certainly was employed in ancient Greek to designate what is commonly called divorce, i.e., the
sending away of a spouse, thereby dissolving the marital union. *Pace* Borchert

("1 Corinthians 7:15," 128), there is no real distinction between Malachi's use of *šallaḥ*, "sending away" (2:16) and Jeremiah's use of *kĕrîtût*, "dismissal, divorce" (3:8), even though they may express different aspects of the separation. They occur together in the classic MT passage about divorce, LXX Deut 24:1 (see also Baltensweiler, *Ehe*, 45: *chōrizō* as "Terminus technicus für die Ehescheidung").

11. *but if indeed she is separated, she must either remain unmarried or be reconciled to her husband.* Lit. "let her remain . . . let her be reconciled"—both verbs in the apodosis are 3d pers. sing. impvs. Paul is qualifying his command of v. 10c and is simply reckoning with a hypothetical situation in a generic way. The RSV translates the aor. pass. subjunct. *chōristhē* as an act. intransitive, "but if she does" (i.e., separate), which is, again, equally questionable.

Is Paul recommending one or two options to the separated woman: remain unmarried *or* be reconciled to her believing husband, or remain unmarried *and* be reconciled? Schrage (*1 Cor*, 2:102) takes it the first way; but Collins (*1 Cor*, 262, 269–70), the second way. The Greek text itself supports the former: two alternatives (remain unmarried or be reconciled), but not a third way (marriage to another man; see Laney, "Paul and the Permanence," 285). According to the Synoptic Gospels, that would be adultery (Mark 10:11; Luke 16:18), which Paul does not mention.

Is Paul addressing a specific existing situation (perhaps that of some Corinthian Christian woman who has been divorced)? Hardly, for he formulates the matter as a hypothetical case that could happen, either in a present general or future more vivid condition (BDF §373.3). Cf. 7:28, *ean de kai gamēsēs*, "if indeed you do marry." In such a condition, the *aor. pass. subjunctive* cannot refer to a past event, "un fait déjà posé, connu" (*pace* Allo, *1 Cor*, 163; Dungan, *Sayings*, 89; Conzelmann, *1 Cor*, 120). Similarly, Murphy-O'Connor ("Divorced Woman," 603), who cites BDF §373 to the effect that the subjunctive can be used in conditions "referring to something that was impending in past time"; but he fails to notice that BDF gives no example of an aor. pass. that supports such an interpretation. See also Collins, *Divorce*, 15; Fee, *1 Cor*, 294–95; Garland, *1 Cor*, 283; Lindemann, *1 Cor*, 164, who argue similarly; also Pearson in his review of Dungan's book ("Jesus' Teachings," 350).

Paul asserts a general prohibition of another marriage after divorce, such as was actually possible according to Deut 24:2. He is not contemplating a future exception to the dominical command but is addressing a hypothetical situation: the possible divorce of a Christian woman, which should not happen, but which may happen (understanding a situation similar to what Mark 10:12bc is coping with). Similarly, Garland *1 Cor*, 283; Baumert, *Ehelosigkeit* 66. It does not mean that "Paul *permits the divorce if it has taken place*: 'let her remain unmarried' " (Dungan, *Sayings*, 92 [his italics]). Paul is simply reckoning with a possible future situation and forbidding further marriage, even if he does not introduce the term "adultery." The prohibition of further marriage is intended to support reconciliation. Paul may envisage the case of impossible reconciliation, when he says that she should remain unmarried.

and that a husband should not divorce his wife. Lit. "and a husband (is) not to divorce (his) wife." Paul restates the same prohibition as in v.10c, but now from the standpoint of the man, using *mē aphienai*, pres. infin. of *aphiēmi*, also governed by the verb of command implicit in v. 10ab. *Aphiēmi* was likewise commonly employed for divorce in Greek writers of the Classical and Hellenistic periods (e.g., Herodotus, *Hist.* 5.39; Euripides, *Androm.* 973; Plutarch, *Pomp.* 44; possibly Josephus, *Ant.* 15.7.10 §259 [doubtful reading]). Elliott ("Paul's Teaching," 223–25) tries to distinguish between *aphiēmi* and *chōrizein*, understanding the former to mean legal divorce and the latter mere separation: so Paul would permit separation, but not divorce; similarly Witherington, *Women*, 31–32. That distinction, however, is untenable, since both words are well attested in the sense of separation meaning divorce, and Paul does not show any awareness of the modern distinction of "separation" and "divorce" (see Hays, *1 Cor*, 120). The whole point in vv. 10–11 is that Christians must not divorce.

BIBLIOGRAPHY

Bammel, E., "Markus 10,11f. und das jüdische Eherecht," *ZNW* 61 (1970) 95–101.

Bonsirven, J., *Le divorce dans le Nouveau Testament* (Paris/Tourni: Desclée, 1948) 50–60.

Borchert, G. L., "1 Corinthians 7:15 and the Church's Historic Misunderstanding of Divorce and Remarriage," *RevExp* 96 (1999) 125–29.

Brooten, B., "Konnten Frauen im alten Judentum die Scheidung betreiben? Überlegungen zu Mk 10, 11–12 und 1 Kor 7, 10–11," *EvT* 42 (1982) 65–80.

——, "Zur Debatte über das Scheidungsrecht der jüdischen Frau," *EvT* 43 (1983) 466–78.

Catchpole, D. R., "The Synoptic Divorce Material as a Traditio-Historical Problem," *BJRL* 57 (1974–75) 92–127, esp. 103–10.

Collins, R. F., *Divorce in the New Testament* (GNS 38; Collegeville, MN: Liturgical Press, 1992) 9–39.

Delling, G., "Ehescheidung," *RAC* 4 (1959) 709–13.

Elliott, J. K., "Paul's Teaching on Marriage in First Corinthians: Some Problems Reconsidered," *NTS* 19 (1972–73) 219–25.

Erdmann, W., *Die Ehe im alten Griechenland* (Münchener Beiträge zur Papyrusforschung und antiken Rechtsgeschichte 20; Munich: Beck, 1934; repr. New York: Arno, 1979).

Fitzmyer, J. A., "Divorce among First-Century Palestinian Jews," *H. L. Ginsberg Volume* (ErIsr 14; Jerusalem: Israel Exploration Society, 1978) 103*–110*.

——, "The Matthean Divorce Texts and Some New Palestinian Evidence," *TS* 37 (1976) 197–226; repr. *TAG*, 79–111.

——, "The So-Called Aramaic Divorce Text from Wadi Seiyal," *Frank Moore Cross Volume* (ErIsr 26; Jerusalem: Israel Exploration Society, 1999) 16*–21*. (Unedited proof)

Garuti, P., "*Scripsit vobis praeceptum istud*: Gesù, il ripudio e la scrittura fallace," *Angelicum* 82 (2005) 335–54.

Harrison, A. R. W., *The Law of Athens: The Family and Property* (Oxford: Clarendon, 1968).

Instone Brewer, D., "Deuteronomy 24:1–4 and the Origin of the Jewish Divorce Certificate," *JJS* 49 (1998) 230–43.

Laney, J. C., "Paul and the Permanence of Marriage in 1 Corinthians 7," *JETS* 25 (1982) 283–94.

Lindemann, A., "Die Funktion der Herrenworte in der ethischen Argumentation des Paulus im Ersten Korintherbrief," *The Four Gospels 1992: Festschrift Frans Neirynck* (BETL 100; 3 vols.; ed. F. van Segbroeck et al.; Louvain: Leuven University/Peeters, 1992), 1:677–88.

Lövestam, E., "Divorce and Marriage in the New Testament," *JLA* 4 (1981) 47–65.

Murphy-O'Connor, J., "The Divorced Woman in 1 Cor 7:10–11," *JBL* 100 (1981) 601–6.

Neirynck, F., "The Sayings of Jesus in 1 Corinthians," *The Corinthian Correspondence* (BETL 125; ed. R. Bieringer), 141–76, esp. 158–76.

Olender, R. G., "Paul's Source for 1 Corinthians 6:10–7:11," *FM* 18/3 (2001) 60–73.

Omanson, R. L., "Some Comments about Style and Meaning: 1 Corinthians 9.15 and 7.10," *BT* 34 (1983) 135–39.

Pearson, B. A., "Jesus' Teachings as Regulations in the Early Church," *Int* 26 (1972) 348–51.

Pesch, R., *Freie Treue: Die Christen und die Ehescheidung* (Freiburg im B.: Herder, 1971) 60–67.

Schubert, K., "Ehescheidung im Judentum zur Zeit Jesu," *TQ* 151 (1971) 23–27.

Schweizer, E., "Scheidungsrecht der jüdischen Frau? Weibliche Jünger Jesu?" *EvT* 42 (1982) 294–300.

Theobald, M., "Jesu Wort von der Ehescheidung: *Gesetz oder Evangelium?*" *TQ* 175 (1995) 109–24.

Vawter, B., "Divorce and the New Testament," *CBQ* 39 (1977) 528–42.

Warren, A., "Did Moses Permit Divorce? Modal *wĕqāṭal* as Key to New Testament Readings of Deuteronomy 24:1–4," *TynBul* 49 (1998) 39–56.

Weder, H., "Perspektive der Frauen?" *EvT* 43 (1983) 175–78.

Witherington, B., *Women in the Earliest Churches* (SNTSMS 59; Cambridge: University of Cambridge Press, 1988) 26–41.

Yadin, Y., *The Temple Scroll* (3 vols. + brochure; Jerusalem: Israel Exploration Society, 1983).

Zimmermann, M., and R. Zimmermann, "Zitation, Kontradiktion oder Applikation? Die Jesuslogien in 1 Kor 7,10f. und 9,14: Traditionsgeschichtliche Verankerung und paulinische Interpretation," *ZNW* 87 (1996) 83–100.

14   c. *Paul's Advice: Peaceful Mixed Marriage, but Pauline Concession (7:12–16)*

7:12 To the rest I say, I and not the Lord: if any brother has a wife who is an unbeliever and she agrees to live with him, he should not divorce her; 13 and if any woman has a husband who is not a believer and he agrees to live with her, she should not divorce her husband. 14 For the unbelieving husband has been made holy through his wife, and the unbelieving wife has been made holy through the brother. Otherwise your children would be unclean, but as it is they are holy. 15 If the unbelieving partner separates, however, let him do so. The brother or sister is not bound in such cases. But God has called you in peace. [16]For all you know, wife, you might save your husband; or for all you know, husband, you might save your wife.

COMMENT

So far Paul has written about both the marriage and the single status of Corinthians who have become converts to Christianity; now he continues his comments, taking up the issue of mixed marriage, the union of a believing Christian with one who is not, and the consequent problems that might arise from such a union. He realizes that some Corinthians had married before their conversion and so would now have a pagan husband or wife. He says nothing to discourage such a union or bring it to an end. What Paul now writes, he clearly distinguishes from the command of the Lord that he discussed in vv. 10–11, implying that he is unaware of any similar dominical command concerning such a marital union. So it is a matter of Paul's advice and pastoral counsel for a situation, which differ from the prohibition of divorce for Christians.

Some commentators (e.g., Menoud, "Mariage et célibat"; Bouwman, "Paulus en het celibaat") think that Paul is describing in these verses his own personal experience, the separation from his wife caused by his conversion to Christianity. However, this is highly unlikely in view of what he writes in vv. 7–8 and 9:5 and what we otherwise know of his life, as Wili ("Das Privilegium Paulinum") has shown.

If an unbeliever can live in peace with a Christian, Paul is all in favor of such a marital union, because he realizes that the Christian spouse brings holiness to the unbeliever and to the children who are born of such a union. If, however, the unbelieving spouse cannot continue to live peacefully in such a union, Paul is willing to concede separation, i.e., divorce. In his view, the Christian spouse is not bound in such a case, because "God has called you in peace," i.e., to live in peace; and thus he indirectly ascribes to God the advice that he is passing on about putting asunder a marital union (see Bartling, "Sexuality, Marriage," 366). Such peace, however, involves something more, because in Paul's view a peaceful union is ordered as a means of the salvation for husband and wife.

In effect, two questions are discussed in this pericope: (1) May Christians and non-Christians live together in a marital union, or should such a union be broken up? Or, to put the question in light of what Paul taught in chap. 6 about fornication, "Can a 'member of Christ' have sexual intercourse with someone who does not belong to the body of Christ?" (Schüssler Fiorenza, *In Memory*, 222). (2) If the non-Christian spouse obtains a divorce, is the Christian bound to remain unmarried in light of v. 11 above, i.e., is the Christian still bound by the union already entered into? Paul answers the questions by making a distinction, but in reality he gives one answer to both questions: peace is the goal of married life. This consideration is implied in his first answer and is stated explicitly in the second. So his concession gives an authoritative interpretation to the dominical prohibition of divorce.

Three aspects of marriage should be noted in this pericope. First, it implies that a marital union brings holiness to the spouses. Even though Paul in this pericope is speaking of mixed marriages, he would scarcely deny that effect to the peaceful marriage of Christian spouses as well. Second, the same extension of his argument would be valid for the children born of two Christian spouses, who are also "holy." Third, Paul sees the husband and wife as the possible source of salvation to each other. Unfortunately, he never explains further this aspect of marriage, and one is left to speculate about his intended meaning.

In effect, Paul has modified in v. 15 the prohibition of divorce, which stems from Jesus, and in this he is like the evangelist of the First Gospel, who added the exceptive phrases mentioned above. Yet even though these modifications do not come from Jesus of Nazareth himself, they are found in the inspired writings of the NT. Together these two instances raise a crucial question today, which I once formulated: "If Matthew under inspiration could have been moved to add an exceptive phrase to the saying of Jesus about divorce that he found in an absolute form in either his Marcan source or in 'Q,' or if Paul likewise under inspiration could introduce into his writing an exception on his own authority, then why cannot the Spirit-guided institutional church of a later generation make a similar exception in view of problems confronting Christian married life of its day or so-called broken marriages (not really envisaged in the NT)—as it has done in some situations?" (TAG, 100). For an evangelical reaction to this question, see Stein, " 'Is It Lawful,' " 121 n. 18.

The problems that Paul discusses in these verses are related to those discussed by patristic writers of the following centuries of the early church, and MacDonald ("Early Christian Women") has shown that for the most part they concerned mixed marriages of pagan husbands with Christian wives.

NOTES

7:12. *To the rest I say, I and not the Lord.* Although the phrase *hoi loipoi*, "the rest," could refer to all other Christians in Corinth (e.g., the *agamoi* of v. 8), it has to be understood as "others," because the second part of the verse immediately restricts it to Christians married to non-Christians, i.e., to people in mixed marriages. Paul gives his advice in an authoritative manner, even though it is not a counsel derived from Jesus Christ. Cf. the Pauline use of *hoi loipoi* for predominantly pagan groups in 1 Thess 4:13; 5:6; Phil 1:13; cf. Eph 3:2.

if any brother has a wife who is an unbeliever and she agrees to live with him, he should not divorce her. Lit. "let him not divorce her." *Mē aphietō* is another form of the infin. used in v. 11c. For "to have a wife," meaning to live in continuous union with a woman, see NOTE on 7:2. The concord in which the two spouses live is a sign of the good will that is needed for such peaceful cohabitation. The verb *syneudokei*, meaning "joins in approval" (of such a union) and expresses the active willingness of the wife to share married life with a Christian husband. Paul uses again *adelphos* for a believing Christian, as in 1:1 (see NOTE there), and by contrast he employs *apistos*, "unbelieving," of the wife, which denotes that she is a pagan, as in 6:6 (see NOTE there), i.e., one who does not live in Christian faith.

Pace Tomson (*Paul*, 118), Paul is not talking about anything like "informal marriage," an option given in Hellenistic law; such an interpretation reads unrelated notions into Paul's words. Only modern eisegesis finds *apistos* to include those baptized in infancy as "Christians only in name and who do not have any true faith" (Byron, "Brother or Sister," 519), a distinction of which Paul scarcely dreams; similarly for the view of Christian that *apistos* means "unfaithful," and not "unbeliever" ("1 Corinthians 7:10–16"). What Paul is saying here is that a Christian spouse is not to seek divorce, even if married to an unbeliever; see also v. 27a, 39a.

13. *and if any woman has a husband who is not a believer and he agrees to live with her, she should not divorce her husband.* Lit. "let her not divorce (her) husband." So Paul expresses the equality of spouses in the marital union, but strangely enough, he simply employs *gynē*, "woman," when he might have used *adelphē*, "sister" (= female Christian) to make the parallel perfect; his formulation otherwise repeats words of the preceding verse. The situation, however, is expressed now in terms of Greco-Roman customs, according to which a woman could divorce her husband. In writing to Christians of Roman Corinth about this matter, Paul no longer limits his perspective to his Jewish background, and the impossibility of a woman divorcing her husband, as was the case in vv. 10–11. Some MSS (A, B, D², Ψ, 33, 1739, 1881) read *hētis*, the fem. rel. pron., "who," at the beginning of the verse, instead of *ei tis*, "if any," which is read by the best MSS. Mss Ψ, 1881, and the Koine text-tradition read rather *auton*, "him," instead of "her husband," a copyist's correction to make a parallel with the end of v. 12

14. *For the unbelieving husband has been made holy through his wife, and the unbelieving wife has been made holy through the brother.* I.e., when the Christian spouse has decided to maintain the marital union despite problems that might arise. Paul writes *en tē gynaiki* and *en tō adelphō*, which many versions render as "through," but BDAG (329 §9a) takes *en* in a causal sense, "on account of"; Garland (*1 Cor*, 287) understands it in a locative sense. Some MSS (ℵ², D², and the Koine text-tradition) read rather at the end, *andri*, "the husband"; and MS 629 has *andri tō pistō*, "the believing husband," as MSS D, F, G, 629 add *tē pistē*, "the believing," to "wife," earlier in the verse.

Of both the unbelieving husband and wife, Paul uses the verb *hēgiastai*, the perf. pass. of *hagiazō*, "set something aside for a cultic purpose, consecrate, make holy," as in LXX Exod 29:37, 43–44, with the implication that this consecration is produced by God (divine passive); cf. 6:11. The perf. tense would express the condition resulting from such consecration. In the following clause it is seen that "holy" is contrasted with "unclean." Perhaps some Christians of Roman Corinth feared that a mixed marriage would make the Christian spouse (and perhaps the community itself) "unclean." Paul is not suggesting that the believer should try to convert the unbelieving spouse, but rather that such a marriage is legitimate in God's sight and that the unbelieving husband somehow shares "in God's covenanted people through her" (Collins, *1 Cor*, 271; similarly, Martens, "First Corinthians 7:14"). How? By marriage itself (Orr-Walther, *1 Cor*, 212); through baptism of the Christian (Collins, *1 Cor*, 266).

It is not easy to explain the concept of holiness of which Paul speaks here. For many commentators, he is using *hagiazō* and the adj. *hagios* in a unique way (Barrett, *1 Cor*, 164; Allo, *1 Cor*, 166; Kümmel in Lietzmann, *1 Cor*, 176–77), which differs from the status of holiness that comes from faith of a believing Christian, because the unbeliever lacks that. It would denote rather an extrinsic holiness through contact with the conduct and love of a person who is holy, i.e., a Christian regarded as *hēgiasmenos/ē*, "consecrated," as Israelites of old (Deut 33:3; 4 Macc 17:19). Moreover, because of 6:11 ("you have been washed, you have been sanctified"), Robertson-Plummer even say that *hēgiastai* refers to "the baptismal consecration . . . in which the unbelieving husband shares through union with a Christian wife" (*1 Cor*, 141–42). Others maintain that, just as in Israel females belonged to the covenant not through circumcision, demanded of males, but through a "contagious holiness" derived from the male head of the household; so children born to a Christian parent were considered holy by contagion (Walther, "Übergreifende Heiligkeit"; similarly Daube, "Pauline Contributions," 240: "In Judaism, it is invariably the woman who is consecrated to spouse by the man. . . . His [Paul's] extension of consecration [to the woman] is totally untraditional"). Cf. Schüssler Fiorenza, *In Memory*, 222–23. This seems the best explanation.

Murphy-O'Connor argues, however, that Paul uses the *hagios*-terms, in two different ways: (1) to denote "holiness" as a characteristic of those baptized into Christ, who are called "saints" (1 Cor 1:2; 6:11) and are separated from the profane and sinful world (Rom 6:22); and (2) to denote "holiness" as a pattern of behavior, as in 1 Cor 7:34 (predicated of the unmarried woman or virgin); 1 Thess 4:1–7 (the ethical conduct of *adelphoi*, who walk with and please God); Rom 6:19–22; 12:1–2 (holiness realized through a continuous effort of fidelity). "Those who in virtue of a divine call have been separated from the 'world' are expected to exhibit a pattern of behaviour that is the antithesis of their former conduct" ("Works," 355). The latter sense of holiness is found in 7:14, where the pagan spouse, agreeing to live with a Christian, thus brings his or her behavior in line with both the Creator's intention in marriage (Gen 2:24) and the Lord's directive prohibiting divorce (7:10–11). In this regard, the pagan's behavior is identical with that of the Christian, and predication of holiness in this sense is justified, despite the difference that the believer's internal attitude is involved in an explicit commitment to Christ, whereas the pagan's internal attitude for maintaining marriage may be quite different. There is an external identity in the holiness of conduct. This may explain why Paul can continue with the sentiment expressed in the following sentence. In any case, the Christian in such a mixed marriage is quite different from the one who has intercourse with a harlot (6:15–16; 7:1b), and God's sanctifying power is stronger than the disbelief of the spouse (recall Lev 21:8: "I, the Lord, who sanctify you, am holy"). Cf. *1 Clem.* 46.2: "Cling to the saints, because those who so cling will be made holy."

Otherwise your children would be unclean, but as it is they are holy. Paul introduces another reason, as he addresses Corinthian Christians directly, as he did above in v. 5. The reason, now introduced by "otherwise," seems to mean that, if the reason given in v. 14a does not convince, this one has to be considered. The phrase, "your (plur.) children," might seem at first to refer to all children of Corinthian Christians, including those of believing spouses. Best ("1 Corinthians 7:14," 159) so understands it, noting that *tekna*, "children," could be both young and adult (as in Titus 1:6; 1 Tim 3:4–5; Col 3:20–21); similarly Senft (*1 Cor*, 93–94). In the present context, however, the presumption is that children mentioned are unbelievers and not baptized. As such, they might be regarded as *akatharta*, "unclean," understood in a Jewish ethical sense as contaminated by paganism or polytheism and defiled by such contact (as in Isa 52:1d; Amos 7:17e), and not merely in a ritual sense. Yet born of a mixed marriage, where a spiritual peace reigns, the status of such children would be affected by the behavior of their peaceful parents. So the children too share their parents' holiness, because they are remotely part of the Christian community, even though their mother or father might not be a believer. Thus they "now" (*nyn de*) benefit also from the spiritual milieu in which they live and grow up, because God's sanctifying power is greater than any unbelief. They are *hagia*, because they share somehow in the consecration expressed by *hegiastai* of v. 14b.

Sometimes commentators have tried to interpret *akatharta* as "illegitimate," or "of doubtful stock" (Ford, "Hast," 77), but there is no evidence for that meaning of the adj. Nor is there evidence in the text that Paul is thinking of the children as "holy," because they have been baptized.

15. *If the unbelieving partner separates, however, let him do so.* Lit. "separates himself, let him be separated." In this qualification of what he said in v. 12, Paul concedes full divorce in the case of an unbeliever who deserts his Christian spouse or gives her a writ of divorce so as to separate from her. This case is different from that of vv. 12–14, and it bears a certain similarity to the Jewish divorce of foreign (pagan) wives (Ezra 10:3, 19). Although Paul uses the same verb *chōrizō*, as in vv. 10–11, it is no longer the aor. pass. infin. or subjunct. as there, but the pres. mid. indic., followed by the pres. mid.-pass. 3d sing. impv. Hence a married Christian person is freed from the marital bond, not by divorce (vv. 10–11), not by adultery, but by desertion of the unbelieving spouse (v. 15).

The brother or sister is not bound in such cases. Lit. "has not been enslaved" or "is not held in a state of slavery" to such a deserting spouse. There is no conj. introducing v. 15b, and that raises a question about the relation of v. 15b to v. 15a and v. 15c. Although the verb *douloō*, "enslave," occurs here and the notion of slavery appears in vv. 17–24, v. 15b may seem to introduce "what follows rather than concludes what precedes" (Deming, *Paul*, 150). However, v. 16 is related rather closely to vv. 12–15a; so v. 15b is best taken with what precedes. It may seem strange that Paul would associate marriage to slavery, but that association is found in Philo, who, in telling of Essenes who did not take wives, ascribes to them the idea that one who is bound to a wife and children "has passed from freedom into slavery" (*ant' eleutherou doulos*, *Hypothetica* 11.17).

Paul uses the perf. pass. verb *dedoulōtai*, which technically expresses the condition of a slave (*doulos*), who would be contrasted with one who is free (*eleutheros* [see Rom 7:3]). So he concedes the freedom and right to remarriage for the Christian (see NOTE on 1:1 for *adelphos* = Christian) after such a divorce, as Conzelmann (*1 Cor*, 123), Héring (*1 Cor*, 153) acknowledge. A similar situation was contemplated for a divorced wife in Judaism, as Deut 24:2 makes clear; for later rabbinic legislation, see *m. Gittin* 9:3. Likewise in the Greco-Roman world (Delling, "Ehescheidung," 709–13). However, Fee claims that Paul means only that the Christian spouse "is not bound to maintain the marriage if the pagan partner opts out," and that remarriage "is not an issue at all. . . . [o]ne is bound to a marriage until death breaks the bond (7:39)" (*1 Cor*, 302–3; similarly, Olender, "Pauline Privilege"). Lindemann (*1 Cor*, 166) rightly comments that the statement *ou dedoulōtai* would make no sense, if it meant that the Christian spouse after the separation of the unbeliever were still bound. For Paul it all depends on who the person is from whom the desire of separation proceeds. In v. 11a, he says *menetō* and *katallagētō* because the spouses are Christian, but in v. 15a the unbeliever is the active agent of divorce, to whom Paul says *chorizesthō*, without adding *menetō* or *katallagētō*. Hence *ou dedoulōtai*. In vv. 12–16, Paul says nothing against a further marriage (differently from Mark 10:11–12).

But God has called you in peace. Or "into peace," if the prep. *en* is understood as interchangeable with *eis* (see BDF §206.1; *IBNTG*, 79). At first sight, this seems to give the reason for Paul's concession: peace should be the characteristic of a Christian life. Such a divorce would lead to peace.

The problem is to decide whether this sentence is to be taken with what precedes or what follows. Since it uses *de*, "but," it seems to have an adversative sense introducing a restriction to what precedes, i.e., to the concession admitted in v. 15a. In that case, the clause would then introduce what follows in v. 16. Some argue that if it were intended to explain what precedes, one would have expected *gar*, "for," instead of *de*, "but."

At any rate, "peace" seems to mean harmony in personal relationships, but then one wonders how this would be descriptive of divorced spouses, for whom reconciliation seems out of the question. Paul, however, seems to mean that a Christian spouse divorced by such an unbeliever is still one "called" by God to live in some sense "in peace" (cf. Rom 12:18; 14:19). Therefore the one "called" to Christianity should be able to enjoy such peace in the new condition in which he or she now exists, after the unbelieving spouse has gone off. Conzelmann (*1 Cor*, 124) rightly notes, "Paul is not thinking of remarriage (after reconciliation); the peace in question is valid independently of the behavior of the pagan partner."

Some MSS (P⁴⁶, ℵ², B, D, F, G, Ψ, 33, 1739, 1881, and the Koine text-tradition) read rather *hēmas*, "us," which would give the sentence an even wider extension and create even more of a problem.

In the later tradition and practice of the Roman Catholic Church, this Pauline verse is normally seen as the basis of what came to be called the "Pauline Privilege" (see DH §§768–69, 777–79), viz., a partner of a heathen marriage can contract a new marriage on becoming a Christian, if the other (non-Christian) partner wanted to separate or put obstacles in the way of the Christian's faith or conduct. That is a development in Canon Law that goes beyond the limits of the case envisaged by Paul (see further Prete, *Matrimonio*, 156–60; Giavini, "I Cor. 7," 259).

16. *For all you know, wife, you might save your husband; or for all you know, husband, you might save your wife.* Lit. "you will save . . . , you will save. . . ." This verse, with its double rhetorical formulation is meant to conclude the section, in which Paul has been discussing mixed marriages, but in reality the sentiment expressed in it could be applied to marriage in general and probably should not be limited only to mixed marital unions. Paul is trying to get spouses in all marital unions to reflect on the ultimate good that they can do to and for each other.

The Greek text begins, *tí gar oidas, gynai, ei* . . . , which has often been translated as a double rhetorical question: "For how do you know, wife, whether you will save . . . ?" (RSV, NAB, NIV). The sense of the question would be expressing a doubt: You cannot be sure that by continuing to live with such an unbeliever you might convert or save him or her.

In the late nineteenth century, however, J. B. Lightfoot called attention to the meaning of the idiom, *tí oidas/oiden ei*, which does not emphasize a doubt, but expresses a hope. He cited the LXX usage in 2 Sam 12:22 (*tís oiden ei eleēsei me ho kyrios kai zēsetai to paidarion*, "Who knows, perhaps the Lord will take pity on me, and the lad will live"); Esth 4:14; Jon 3:9; Joel 2:14, and concluded that "the whole sentence expresses a hope" and that "this saving of the husband (or wife) is worth any temporal inconvenience" (*Notes on Epistles*, 227). This interpretation has been furthered by Jeremias ("Die missionarische Aufgabe"), who understands the expression to mean "perhaps," and has added references to extrabiblical Greek writers: Epictetus, *Diss.* 2.20.30; 2.22.31; 2.25.2; *Joseph and Aseneth* 54.12–13; Ps.-Philo, *LAB* 9.6; 25.7; 30.4; 39.3 (*quis scit si*); cf. Homer, *Odys.* 3.216; Sophocles, *Antig.* 521; Plato, *Gorg.* 492e); see also Burchard, "*Ei* nach"; "Fussnoten," 170–71. For Jeremias, the sense of the verse would be: Do not break up your marriage with an unbelieving partner willing to remain with you; perhaps you will be his (or her) salvation. Paul's thought, then, would be similar to 1 Pet 3:1b–2, where the author similarly exhorts wives in a mixed marriage. That sense, however, would make this verse refer to the peaceful mixed marriage of vv. 12–14; it hardly refers to the situation of v. 15. One must remain skeptical, however, about Jeremias's characterization of marriage as a missionary endeavor.

It seems preferable to follow J. B. Lightfoot and then extend it to all marriages, not just to the different kinds of mixed marriage treated in vv. 12–15, because the verse, with its generic address of "wife" and "husband" not only unifies Paul's advice about mixed marriages, but hints at the broader salvific aspect of Christian marriage too. A translation similar to that given in the lemma is found in the NRSV, NEB, REB. Such an understanding of this verse was known also to Tertullian (*Ad Uxorem* 2.2.3); Theodoret (*In. Ep. ad Cor. I* 7.16; PG 82.277); Augustine (*De Adulter. Coniugiis* 1.13) and some other patristic writers. Kubo ("I Corinthians vii. 16"), however, maintains that many of the alleged parallels in the LXX and extrabiblical texts are uncertain and that the tone of 7:16 is also one of uncertainty; he prefers the pessimistic translation of the RSV, but his skepticism is not fully convincing.

BIBLIOGRAPHY

Best, E., "1 Corinthians 7: 14 and Children in the Church," *IBS* 12 (1990) 158–66.

Blinzler, J., "Zur Auslegung von 1 Kor 7,14," *Neutestamentliche Aufsätze: Festschrift für Prof. Josef Schmid* . . . (Regensburg: Pustet, 1963) 23–41.

Burchard, C., "*Ei* nach einem Ausdruck des Wissens oder Nichtwissens Joh 9,25, Act 19,2, I Cor 1,16; 7,16," *ZNW* 52 (1961) 73–82.

——, "Fussnoten zum neutestamentlichen Griechisch," *ZNW* 61 (1970) 157–71.

Byron, B., "The Brother or Sister Is Not Bound: Another Look at the New Testament Teaching on the Indissolubility of Marriage," *NBf* 52 (1971) 514–21.

Christian, E., "1 Corinthians 7:10–16: Divorce of the Unbeliever or Reconciliation with the Unfaithful," *JATS* 10 (1999) 41–62.

Daube, D., "Pauline Contributions to a Pluralistic Culture: Re-Creation and Beyond," *Jesus and Man's Hope* (2 vols.; ed. D. G. Miller and D. Y. Hadidian; Pittsburgh, PA: Pittsburgh Theological Seminary, 1970–71), 2. 223–45.

Delling, G., " 'Nun aber sind sie heilig,' " and "Zur Exegese von 1. Kor. 7,14," and *Gott und die Götter: Festgabe für Erich Fascher* . . . (Berlin: Evangelische Verlagsanstalt, [1958]) 84–93; repr. *Studien zum Neuen Testament und zum hellenistischen Judentum* (Göttingen: Vandenhoeck & Ruprecht, 1970) 257–69, 281–87.

Ford, J. M., " 'Hast Thou Tithed Thy Meal?' and 'Is Thy Child Kosher?' (1 Cor. x. 27 ff. and 1 Cor. vii. 14)," *JTS* 17 (1966) 71–79.

Giavini, G., "I Cor. 7: Nuove ricerche: Matrimoni misti e 'Privilegio Paolina,' " *ScCatt* 108 (1980) 255–63.

Harrington, W. J., "The New Testament and Divorce," *ITQ* 39 (1972) 178–87.

Jeremias, J., "Die missionarische Aufgabe in der Mischehe (I Cor 7,16)," *Neutestamentliche Studien für Rudolf Bultmann* . . . (BZNW 21; ed. W. Eltester; Berlin: Töpelmann, 1954; 2d ed., 1957) 255–60.

Kubo, S., "I Corinthians vii. 16: Optimistic or Pessimistic?" *NTS* 24 (1978) 539–44.

Lightfoot, J. B., *Notes on Epistles of St Paul from Unpublished Commentaries* (London: Macmillan, 1904)

MacDonald, M. Y., "Early Christian Women Married to Unbelievers," *SR* 19 (1990) 221–34.

Martens, M. P., "First Corinthians 7:14: 'Sanctified' by the Believing Spouse," *Notes* 10/3 (1996) 31–35.

Moynihan Gillihan, Y., "Jewish Laws on Illicit Marriage, the Defilement of Offspring, and the Holiness of the Temple: A New Halakic Interpretation of 1 Corinthians 7:14," *JBL* 121 (2002) 711–44.

Murphy-O'Connor, J., "Works without Faith in I Cor., vii, 14," *RB* 84 (1977) 349–61.

Olender, R. G., "The Pauline Privilege: Inference or Exegesis?" *FM* 16/1 (1998) 94–117.

Stein, R. H., " 'Is It Lawful for a Man to Divorce His Wife?'" *JETS* 22 (1979) 115–21.

Walther, G., "Übergreifende Heiligkeit und Kindertaufe im Neuen Testament," *EvT* 25 (1965) 668–74.

15   d. *Basic Principle:*
Remain in the Status in Which You
Were Called (7:17–24)

7:17 Nevertheless, each one should lead the life that the Lord has assigned, as God has called each of you. So I order in all the churches. 18 Was anyone called when he was circumcised? He should not try to undo his circumcision. Was anyone called when he was uncircumcised? He should not be circumcised. 19 Circumcision means nothing, and uncircumcision means nothing; but obeying God's commandments is what counts 20 Each one should remain in the state in which he was called. 21 Were you a slave when you were called? Do not worry about it, but if indeed you can gain your freedom, take advantage rather of it. 22 For the one who was a slave when called by the Lord is the Lord's freedman; so too the one who was free when called is Christ's slave. 23 You were bought at a price; do not become slaves to human beings. 24 Brothers, each one should remain before God in the state in which he was called.

COMMENT

In continuing his comments on the problems that have beset the Corinthian Christians in the matters of sex and marriage, Paul now introduces a fundamental principle that should govern all their thinking and conduct. What Paul enunciates in this pericope is immediately occasioned by his discussion of marriage and celibacy in 7:1–9, marriage and divorce in 7:10–11, and mixed marriages in 7:12–16. These problems are specific, and Paul handles them as applications of the general principle now to be discussed in vv. 17–24 (see Fischer, "1 Cor. 7:8–24"). His discussion reverts in effect to the qualification that he enunciated in 7:7b, that "each one has a particular gift from God." That gift is treated now in diatribe-like style.

Christians are to consider well the status to which God has called them, remain in it, and not try to change it. This is fundamental to the Christian vocation: Lead the life the Lord has assigned to you (7:17, 24). This is what Paul has insisted on in all the communities that he has founded and evangelized. One's ethnic, social, or legal status in life is of little importance. Whether one has come from a Jewish or Gentile background makes no difference; whether one is a slave or a free person is immaterial. One can be a Jewish Christian or a Gentile Christian; one can be a Christian slave or a Christian free person. The all-important aspect of life is to recognize that one is a Christian, which means that one stands before God in a proper relationship of service and obedience to His commandments in the conduct of life, as taught by Jesus of Nazareth. Concern to change one's social or worldly status, e.g., by marriage or divorce, could distract from the fundamental obligation of every called Christian. The believer is thus challenged to remain married or unmarried, circumcised or uncircumcised, slave or free, or as Paul phrased it in the so-called baptismal formula of Gal 3:26–28, "For in Christ Jesus you are all sons of God through faith; for as many of you were baptized into Christ have put on Christ. There is neither Jew nor Greek, there is neither slave nor free, there is neither male nor female; for you are all one in Christ Jesus." See also 1 Cor 12:13.

Some commentators consider these verses (17–24) to be a digression because the topics treated in vv. 1–16 and 25–40 are not mentioned (so Senft, *1 Cor*, 95 ["excursus"]; Lindemann, *1 Cor*, 168 ["reichende *digressio*"]; Kistemaker, *1 Cor*, 229). These verses, however, present a theological reflection that is fundamental to the rest, and it is best to recognize them as formulating a principle on which the other more specific topics are based, for the verses in this pericope have been carefully formulated. Verse 17 has a double subordinate clause, both introduced by *hōs*, "as," and a double instruction, both introduced by *houtōs*, "so," with the command expressed first as an impv. (lit. "let him walk") and then with the verb of command ("I order"). Two examples are given: about circumcision/uncircumcision (vv. 18–19); then about slavery/freedom (vv. 21–23). There is also a double repetition (vv. 20, 24) of the principle of v. 17.

As important as these verses are to the discussion about marriage, etc. in chap. 7, one has to ask why Paul singles out these two examples of social status in this context. The first may come from Paul's own background as a Jewish Christian and his call to become "the apostle of the Gentiles" (Rom 11:13). The second example may be derived from the sexual availability of slaves in the ancient world where they were owned often for *porneia*; as such, when they were converted to Christianity, certain problems arose, as Glancy ("Obstacles") has shown. In the second of the examples, Paul touches, as it were in passing, on a question that has more aspects than can be handled in a commentary such as this, viz., the matter of slavery. To appreciate the aspect of it presented in this paragraph, one must realize that Paul reckons with the institution of slavery, which was fully accepted in the Greco-Roman world in which he lived and worked, i.e., the legal ownership and manumission of slaves. This differed considerably from the modern political problem of the emancipation of slaves or the abolition of slavery. A manumitted slave became a freed person (Greek *apeleutheros*, Latin *libertus*), who normally lived in a certain relationship to the former master, now usually called a patron (Greek *prostatēs*, Latin *patronus*). In time, perhaps after a generation or so, such freed persons' status or relationship disappeared or was forgotten, and their descendants were no longer so regarded (which may even have been the situation from which Paul himself came, given his Jewish background; nevertheless in Acts 22:27, Paul boasts, "I was born a Roman citizen"). The possibility of manumission often colored the life, conduct, and obedience of a slave, and for many it became a goal. Now Paul considers the question of the manumission of a slave who has become a Christian. Although the status of the Christian slave is mentioned, it is not the major thrust of his discussion in this pericope, because it acts only as an example along with others. For another Pauline reaction to slavery, one should read his letter to Philemon about the slave Onesimus. Even though the sentiment expressed in this passage echoes in part the baptismal formula of Gal 3:26–28, quoted above, Paul significantly omits one of the pairs, "neither male nor female," revealing the status that it occupied in his thinking.

Paul's main stress is that the Christian belongs to the Lord, whether one be a freed person or a slave, because "you were bought at a price" (7:23a), repeating a notion already expressed in 6:20, and meaning by the death and resurrection of Jesus Christ, who is now the slave's *kyrios*, "master/Lord."

NOTES

7:17. *Nevertheless, each one should lead the life that the Lord has assigned, as God has called each of you.* Lit. "but, as the Lord has allotted to each one, as God has called each one, so let him walk." The repetition of "each" is important, because Paul wants the Corinthians to realize the divine concern for the individual in the call that God has made. God's gracious call to Christianity comes to individuals as they are. This call explains in fact what Paul meant by *idion charisma*, "particular gift," of v. 7 above. Greek MSS vary considerably between *ho kyrios* and *ho theos*; see *apparatus criticus*. In any case, *ho kyrios* here equals *ho theos*. The sentence begins with *ei mē*, "but, nevertheless," as in Gal 1:19, in the adversative, non-exceptive sense (see BDF §§376; 448.8; BDAG, 278 §6i; Harder, "Miszelle").

The verb *kalein* denotes not merely a "call" to salvation or to Christianity, as in 1:9 (see NOTE there; also Gal 1:15; Rom 8:30; 9:24), but a call to it in a certain ethnic, legal, or social status, reiterated in vv. 20 and 24; with the same verb in vv. 18, 21–22. Paul's principle presupposes what he has already said in 1:9; 7:7b, 15c. Again he uses *peripatein*, "walk," for the conduct of human life; see NOTE on 3:3.

So I order in all the churches. I.e., founded by Paul. Some MSS (D*, F, G) read rather *didaskō*, "I teach," a reading that may be influenced by 4:17. Cf. 11:34; 16:1; 2 Cor 8:1; see NOTE on 1:2 and INTRODUCTION pp. 81–82.

18. *Was anyone called when he was circumcised? He should not try to undo his circumcision.* Lit. "let him not pull (the foreskin) over," the mid. voice of *epispaō* in this sense is found only here. It would refer to what some Palestinian Jews had tried to do, when games played in the nude were introduced along with the Hellenistic gymnasium in Jerusalem in the secularizing reign of Antiochus IV Epiphanes, as recorded in 1 Macc 1:15 (*epoiēsan heautois akrobystias*, "they made for themselves foreskins"); that is also noted in Josephus, *Ant.* 12.5.1 §241.

Paul's first example of a social status that is inconsequential to the Christian vocation is taken from the mixed community of Jewish and Gentile Christians in Roman Corinth. He uses an example from his own Jewish background to show that it makes no difference that one comes to Christianity from Judaism. There is no need to deny that ethnic background. One's physical condition has no bearing on the grace of vocation; to try to alter that condition would be a misunderstanding of God's election.

Was anyone called when he was uncircumcised? He should not be circumcised. This is the counterpart of v. 18a. The Gentile converted to Christianity has no need of circumcision, as Paul recognized in the case of Titus (Gal 2:3). His reason is stated in the following verse. (On the Lucan account of the circumcision of Timothy, see NOTE on 4:17; cf. *Acts*, 573–76.)

19. *Circumcision means nothing, and uncircumcision means nothing.* I.e., as far as the Christian vocation is concerned. As a Jew, Paul would have thought otherwise, for he knew that God commanded Abraham and his descendants, "Every male among you shall be circumcised" (Gen 17:10c; cf. Josephus, *Ant.* 1.10.5 §192; 1.12.2 §214). Now Paul repeats in effect what he had written to the Galatians, "If you receive circumcision, Christ will be of no advantage to you" (Gal 5:2; cf. 5:6; 6:15). As Schüssler Fiorenza has put it, "The religious/biological sign of initiation to Jewish religion is no longer of any relevance to Christianity" (*In Memory*, 221).

but obeying God's commandments is what counts. Paul's formulation is elliptical; one has to supply: "is something" (i.e., the opposite of "nothing"). The *tērēsis entolōn*, which echoes Sir 32:23, is demanded of the individual Christian no matter what his or her ethnic background or social status might be. Paul is referring to other "commandments" than that of circumcision ordered in Gen 17:9–13. "Keeping the commandments" was a technical expression (Matt 19:17; 1 Tim 6:14) for the Jew, but Paul's stance (stated in Gal 5:2, 6; 6:15) was confirmed in the "council" of Jerusalem (Gal 2:1–10; cf. Acts 15:5–12). For him, the Christian is a "new creation" (Gal 6:15), guided by *hypakoē pisteōs*, "the commitment of faith" (Rom 1:5; 16:26), and all that that entails. Although some commandments of the Mosaic law have become obsolete, others continue to be valid, even for Christians; see Thielman, "Coherence."

20. *Each one should remain in the state in which he was called.* Lit. "in the call in which each was called, in that let him (or her) remain." So Paul repeats in effect the principle enunciated in v. 17. The noun *klēsis* might be understood as the call to Christianity (as in Phil 3:14; cf. Eph 4:1; 2 Tim 1:9), which is also the sense in which the verb *kalein* is used in the subordinate clause of this verse. The noun has to be understood, however, in a broader sense to include the "status" or "condition" of being a Jew or a Gentile, slave or free, in which the call to Christianity has come to the individual involved, as in 1:26. See Lietzmann, *1 Cor*, 32; Lindemann, *1 Cor*, 171; cf. especially Schmidt, *TDNT*, 3: 491–92 n. 1. Note how the matter is formulated in 7:24.

21. *Were you a slave when you were called? Do not worry about it.* Lit. "as a slave you were called; let it not be a concern to you." The first part of this problematic verse gives the same answer as that of vv. 18–19, and the two following parts are more or less parenthetical, because they provide a second example drawn from social status that is of little ultimate consequence for the called Christian. They counsel slaves with comforting words in a manner that has little relevance to the rest of the paragraph, advising them to appreciate better their call to freedom precisely as Christians. The first clause (v. 21a) may be a question (as translated here), or an elliptical protasis of a conditional sentence, to which v. 21b is the apodosis; it gives then the same answer as vv. 18–19. Then follows v. 21c, which acts as a qualification. A slave could be a good Christian, as Paul recognizes in the Letter to Philemon. He seeks now only to bring slaves to a better understanding of their social condition.

Doulos, "slave," used here and in vv. 22–23 and 12:13, denoted in ancient culture and in Greek and Roman law an "animated tool" (*empsychon organon,* Aristotle, *Nicom. Ethics* 8.11.6 §1161b). As such, the slave had no rights: *nullum ius habet* (*Digest* 4.5.1) and no obligation (to serve anyone but the master) (*Digest* 50.17.22). The slave had, however, certain advantages at times, and these made some of them prefer to remain in slavery.

but even if you can gain your freedom, take advantage rather of it. I.e., if you can be manumitted in a legal procedure. This is a qualification of what has been said in v. 21ab, but it is expressed in a difficult shortened sentence that is ambiguous. The protasis is introduced by adversative and conditional conjs., *all' ei kai,* "but even if," and the apodosis contains an enigmatic comparative adv. *mallon* and an aor. impv., *chrēsai,* lit. "use more" or "use rather," which has no object expressed. So make use of what? The relation of this clause to v. 21ab as well as to what follows in vv. 22–23 is not easy to explain. Since v. 22 forms a logical sequel to v. 21ab, v. 21c seems to be parenthetic (so interpreted by Thrall, *Greek Particles,* 78–82; Lindemann, *1 Cor,* 172–73) and may address a situation different from v. 21ab.

Four different interpretations have been given to the last two words (*mallon chrēsai*) of the apodosis:

(1) Some would take them as they stand, without an object understood (as in Epictetus, *Diss.* 2.21.20; *P.Oxy.* 16.1865.4; cf. Dodd, "Notes from Papyri," and to mean, "be all the more useful," i.e., work all the harder; or even though a freed person, be as industrious as a slave (BDAG, 1087).

(2) Bartchy (*First-Century Slavery,* 183) would understand the indirect obj. of *chrēsai* to be the dat. *tē klēsei* (understood from v. 20): "But if, indeed, you become manumitted, by all means [as a freedman] live according to [God's calling]." This interpretation finds support in the sense of the verb *chraomai* as used by Josephus, *Ant.* 11.6.12 §281; 13.9.1 §257; 14.7.2 §116 ("living according to the laws" [of the Jews]). This meaning, however, is subtle and not easily suited to the context, because the verb basically means "to make use of, employ" (see Fee, *1 Cor,* 316).

(3) Some would understand a dat., *douleiā,* "make better use of (your) slavery," i.e., make better use of your present condition (e.g., RSV, note, NRSV, NAB, SBJ, *1 Cor,* 40; *Peshitta;* John Chrysostom [*Hom. in I Cor.* 19.4; PG 16.156], Theodoret [*Interpr. Ep. I Cor.* 7.21; PG 82.280], and most older commentators; among moderns, Bellen, Benanti, Conzelmann, Corcoran, Kremer, Lietzmann, Schlier). This understanding is said to accord better with Paul's instruction in v. 20b, *en tautē menetō,* "in that let him remain"; and with v. 21a (cf. 12:13; Gal 3:28). It is considered strange, however, because one would expect the pres. impv., not the aor. *chrēsai.*

(4) Others would understand a dat., *eleutheriā,* "take advantage rather of (such) freedom," i.e., make the most of the opportunity to be freed (so RSV, REB; Erasmus, Luther [*Comm. on 1 Cor.* 7: LW 28.42–43], Calvin, T. de Bèze; among moderns, Braxton, Callahan, Dawes, Deming, Fee, Godet, Goudge, Harrill, J. B. Lightfoot, Lindemann, Robertson-Plummer, Schrage, Schüssler Fiorenza, Trummer). This best suits the parenthetic character of v. 21b, the initial adversa-

tive conj. *alla*, and the aor. impv. *chrēsai*, and it finds support in 7:23b. It also is an example of a pattern of argument attested in other ancient writers, where one finds a statement of fact (or a rhetorical question), followed by an imperative, and then a different recommendation: 21a, 21b, 21c; Paul himself argues similarly in vv. 18–19, 27. Some interpreters even invoke the principle of 7:15 in favor of this view (Kremer), but rightly so? See further Bartchy, *First-Century Slavery*; Harrill, *Manumission*; Lindemann, *1 Cor*, 172–73.

22. *For the one who was a slave when called by the Lord is the Lord's freedman.* Lit. "the slave called in the Lord is the Lord's freedman," in chiastic formulation. In this verse, Paul is contrasting the Christian status of a slave (*doulos*) and that of a freed person (*apeleutheros*). His explanation directly explains v. 21ab, but also has a bearing on v. 21c. In the Greco-Roman world of Paul's time, a slave who was manumitted became *apeleutheros* or *libertus* and entered a new relationship with his former *kyrios*, who became his *patronus*. So Paul draws an analogy: a slave called to Christianity may be a slave of the earthly master but achieves the status of *apeleutheros*, "freed person," as far as the Lord is concerned, because he is liberated from "the powers of darkness, the slaveholders of this age" (BDAG, 101). As a slave, he should continue to serve his earthly master, but with a renewed Christian motivation. Cf. 1 Pet 5:10, "the God of all grace, who has called you in Christ"; also John 8:36.

so too the one who was free when called is Christ's slave. The one who enjoys "free" social and political status, however, in responding to the Christian call, becomes *doulos Christou*, a designation that Paul often uses of himself (Rom 1:1; Gal 1:10; Phil 1:1; cf. Eph 6:6), as did other early Christians (Jas 1:1; 2 Pet 1:1; Jude 1). The reason for this designation is the allegiance denoted thereby to the lordship of the risen Christ, recognized as *Kyrios* (see NOTE on 1:2 and INTRODUCTION pp. 72–73). Cf. Phlm 16, where the pair *doulos* and *kyrios*, "slave" and "master, lord," are found together.

23. *You were bought at a price.* In this context of slavery, Paul repeats what he had enunciated earlier in 6:20. There it was a question of avoiding the immorality of fornication, and it was quoted to recall to Corinthian Christians that their bodies were temples of the Holy Spirit and that they did not belong to themselves (i.e., they were not free to do with their bodies whatever they pleased). Now he employs the saying to explain why they are slaves of Christ, bought for the service of the Kyrios, because "you belong to Christ" (3:23). In this way, both slaves and freeborn are equal in the Christian community.

do not become slaves to human beings, i.e., to the mentality of pagans of Roman Corinth, among whom you live. As Christians, their bondage is to the risen Christ, who should be the master (*kyrios*) of their lives, and in no sense should they become indentured to other human beings. If one asks about those who were already slaves in the Greco-Roman system before the call to Christianity, the fourth way of understanding v. 21cd provides the sense in which Paul's words now are to be understood.

24. *Brothers, each one should remain before God in the state in which he was called.* Lit. "each one in what one was called, brothers, let him remain in that be-

fore God." This cumbersome conclusion repeats in effect the fundamental principle enunciated in v. 17 above, and reiterated in v. 20, but now without the problematic *klēsis*.

BIBLIOGRAPHY

Bartchy, S. S., *Mallon Chrēsai: First-Century Slavery and the Interpretation of 1 Corinthians 7:21* (SBLDS 11; Missoula: University of Montana Press, 1973; repr. Atlanta: Scholars, 1985).

Bellen, H., "*Mallon chrēsai* (1 Cor. 7,21): Verzicht auf Freilassung als asketische Leistung?" *JAC* 6 (1963) 177–80.

Benanti, O., " 'Se anche puoi divenire libero . . .' (1 Cor 7,21)," *RBR* 16/1–2 (1981) 125–29.

Blaschke, A., *Beschneidung: Zeugnisse der Bibel und verwandter Texte* (TANZ 28; Tübingen/Basel: Francke, 1998).

Braxton, B. R., *The Tyranny of Resolution: I Corinthians 7:17–24* (SBLDS 181; Atlanta: Society of Biblical Literature, 2000).

Callahan, A., "A Note on I Corinthians 7:21," *JITC* 17/1–2 (1989–90) 110–14.

Corcoran, G., "Slavery in the New Testament I," *MilS* 5 (1980) 1–40; "II," *Mils* 6 (1980) 62–83.

Dawes, G. W., " 'But If You Can Gain Your Freedom' (1 Corinthians 7:17–24)," *CBQ* 52 (1990) 681–97.

Deming, W., "A Diatribe Pattern in 1 Cor. 7:21–22: A New Perspective on Paul's Directions to Slaves," *NovT* 37 (1995) 130–37.

Dodd, C. H., "Notes from Papyri," *JTS* 26 (1924–25) 77–78.

Gayer, R., *Die Stellung des Sklaven in den paulinischen Gemeinden und bei Paulus: Zugleich ein sozialgeschichtlich vergleichender Beitrag zur Wertung des Sklaven in der Antike* (Europäische Hochschulschriften 23/78; Bern: H. Lang, 1976).

Glancy, J. A., "Obstacles to Slaves' Participation in the Corinthian Church," *JBL* 117 (1998) 481–501.

Harder, G., "Miszelle zu 1. Kor. 7, 17," *TLZ* 79 (1954) 367–72.

Harrill, J. A., *The Manumission of Slaves in Early Christianity* (HUT 32; Tübingen: Mohr [Siebeck], 1995) 62–128.

———, "Paul and Slavery: The Problem of 1 Corinthians 7:21," *BR* 39 (1994) 5–28.

———, "Slavery and Society at Corinth," *TBT* 35 (1997) 287–93.

Horn, F. W., "Der Verzicht auf die Beschneidung im frühen Christentum," *NTS* 42 (1996) 479–505.

Jones, F. S., *"Freiheit" in den Briefen des Apostles Paulus: Eine historische, exegetische und religionsgeschichtliche Studie* (GTA 34; Göttingen: Vandenhoeck & Ruprecht. 1987) 27–69.

Martin, D. B., *Slavery as Salvation: The Metaphor of Slavery in Pauline Christianity* (New Haven: Yale University Press, 1990).

Neuhäusler, E., "Ruf Gottes und Stand des Christen: Bemerkungen zu 1 Kor 7," *BZ* 3 (1959) 43–60.

Schulz, S., *Gott ist kein Sklavenhalter: Die Geschichte einer verspäteten Revolution* (Zurich: Flamberg-V.; Hamburg: Furche-V., 1972).

Spicq, C., "Le vocabulaire de l'esclavage dans le Nouveau Testament," *RB* 85 (1978) 201–26.

Steinmann, A., *Paulus und die Sklaven zu Korinth: 1 Kor. 7,21 aufs neue untersucht* (Braunsberg: Grimme, 1911).

——, "Zur Geschichte der Auslegung von 1 Kor 7,21," *TRev* 16 (1917) 340–48.

Tabet, M., "La situazione ordinaria di vita come 'chiamata' in 1 Cor 7,17–24," *RivB* 53 (2005) 277–312.

Thielman, F., "The Coherence of Paul's View of the Law: The Evidence of First Corinthians," *NTS* 38 (1992) 235–53.

Trummer, P., "Die Chance der Freiheit: Zur Interpretation des *mallon chrēsai* in 1 Kor 7, 21," *Bib* 56 (1975) 344–68.

Vollenweider, S., *Freiheit als neue Schöpfung: Eine Untersuchung zur Eleutheria bei Paulus und seiner Umwelt* (FRLANT 147; Göttingen: Vandenhoeck & Ruprecht, 1989).

Winter, B. W., *Seek the Welfare of the City: Early Christians as Benefactors and Citizens* (Carlisle, UK: Paternoster; Grand Rapids: Eerdmans, 1994) 145–64.

16   e. *Advantage of Virginity* (7:25–35)

[7:25] Now concerning virgins, I do not have a command from the Lord, but I give my opinion as one who by the Lord's mercy is trustworthy. [26] I think, therefore, that, in view of the impending crisis, it is good for a person to remain as he is. [27] Are you bound to a wife? Do not seek release. Are you without a wife? Do not look for one. [28] But if indeed you do marry, you would not sin; and if a virgin marries, she would not sin. Yet such people will face troubles in earthly life, and I would spare you that. [29] What I mean, brothers, is that time is running out. From now on let even those who have wives live as though they had none; [30] those who mourn as though they did not; those who are happy as though they were not; those who buy as though they had no possessions; [31] and those who deal with the world as though they had no use of it. For the shape of this world is passing away. [32] I want you to be free of concern. The unmarried man is concerned about the Lord's affairs, how he may please the Lord. [33] But a married man is concerned about the affairs of this world, how he may please his wife; [34] and he is divided. An unmarried woman or virgin is concerned about the Lord's affairs, that she may be holy in both body and spirit; but the married woman is concerned about the affairs of this world, how she may please her husband. [35] I am saying this for your own good, not to lay a restriction on you, but for the sake of good order and devotion to the Lord without distraction.

COMMENT

Paul returns to the specific topics such as he had been discussing before he took up in the preceding pericope (vv. 17–24), the fundamental norm or principle that he is applying to the questions of marriage and celibacy: not changing the kind of life to which Christians have been called. He will repeat the principle in v. 26b. In

7:8, he has given some counsel to the "unmarried and widows," and he now turns to further issues concerning *hoi agamoi*, "the unmarried," dealing with a specific group of them, *parthenoi*, "virgins," those who have not yet been married. (In v. 11 Paul used *agamos* to denote a married woman who had been divorced: she was to remain unmarried, i.e., was not to seek another spouse.)

Although *parthenos* is understood from vv. 28 and 34 to mean a girl of marriageable age, not yet engaged or joined in a marital union, some of Paul's remarks in vv. 25–35 are at times applicable also to celibate males. Commentators since the time of Theodore of Mopsuestia have often understood Paul's advice in this part of chap. 7 to mean *parthenos* in this broader sense, because he addresses a husband in v. 27a, a bachelor in v. 27c, and speaks about an "unmarried man" in v. 32, who is contrasted with a "married man" in v. 33.

Although Paul begins this discussion with *peri de*, which echoes that of 7:1a, there is no certainty that the topic of "virgins" was one about which Corinthian Christians had inquired in their letter to him; but it could have been. Because they were inquiring about the role of sex in their lives (7:1b–2), he may well be answering now a related query, the role of virginity in Christian life.

In this matter, Paul has no dominical saying derived from Jesus of Nazareth to pass on (in contrast to v. 10) and gives only his counsel about virginity as a trustworthy opinion, which is based on three reasons. First, it is colored by his view of "the shape of this world" (7:31), which involves an "impending crisis" (7:26a), because "time is running out" (7:29). With that eschatological conviction in mind, Paul applies the principle enunciated in vv. 17, 20, and 24 to the state of marriage and virginity in general: "It is good for a person to remain as he is" (7:26b). This application he further explains in vv. 27–28ab.

Second, another reason for his opinion, likewise motivated by the shape of this world, "I want you to be free of concern" (7:32; cf. 7:28cd). This reason leads him to advise the nonuse of marriage, mourning, happiness, possessions, and even of "this world" (7:30–31). Concern about such matters could preoccupy one, for whom service of the Lord should be more important.

Third, his real motivation for virginal life is concern "for the Lord's affairs," how one may "please the Lord" (7:32), i.e., a "devotion to the Lord without distraction" (7:35).

"The whole discussion of marriage in this chapter is influenced by Paul's eschatological awareness in addition to his pastoral concern" (Bruce, *1 Cor*, 74). For Paul, virginity is not only "good" (*kalon*, 7:8, 26), "a gift from God" (7:7), but also something that he prefers (7:7a, 28f, 32a, 38b). His opinion stands in contrast to the view of virginity expressed in the OT, especially that of Jephthah's daughter who mourns her passing from this life as a mere virgin (Judg 11:37–40), or that bemoans the fallen virgin Israel (Amos 5:2; Joel 1:8), and the virgin daughter Judah (Lam 1:15). Although Paul cites no saying of Jesus in favor of virginity, the saying recorded in Matt 19:12cd, about those who have made themselves eunuchs for the kingdom of heaven, was new, and it may have begun already to inform Christian thinking even prior to Paul. Recall also what was said by the eunuch in Isa 56:3b–5b about his being "a dry tree," but to whom God promises "an everlasting name." In any case, Paul clearly sees the unmarried man or woman differently from the married, when it is a question of dedication to "the affairs of the Lord" (7:32–34): of the latter he says, "he is divided" (7:34a). Even if one reads these Pauline verses as disqualifying "married people theologically as less engaged missionaries," it cannot be said that "his theology was wrong," *pace* Schüssler Fiorenza (*In Memory*, 226). His theology has withstood and will withstand all such advocacy interpretation.

What Paul says about marriage and virginity in this passage sounds at times like views advocated by some Stoic writers in the Greco-Roman world; in an earlier COMMENT (on 7:1–9) notice has already been taken of such views, and further details will be given in the NOTES that follow. Finally, one should guard against interpreting Paul's words in this passage as giving advice and counsel to a group of ascetic virgins in Corinth, who were exercising some sort of spiritual leadership in the Corinthian church, *pace* Cha ("Ascetic Virgin"). There is Pauline counsel here for "virgins," and ultimately in the pericope that follows for a specific "virgin," but that this means he was addressing a problem created by a group of persons under some kind of vow in ascetic life is simply not evident in the text.

NOTES

25. *Now concerning virgins.* Paul begins a new topic with the introductory *peri de*, "virgins," which has not yet been treated in vv. 1–24. The noun *parthenos* denoted in antiquity a girl *apeiros andros*, "without experience of a man" (Menander, *Sicyonius* 372–73); *hē mē ekdedomenē andri*, "who has not been given to a man' (LXX Lev 21:3); cf. LXX Judg 21:12; Delling, *TDNT*, 5:826–37). Elsewhere in the NT it denotes (14 times) a chaste marriageable girl (except Rev 14:4, where it is figurative: *parthenoi*, those who have not defiled themselves with idolatry). Its fem. gender is clear in vv. 34, 36–38, and probably also in v. 28, where the fem. article is missing in some MSS (B, F, G). Here, however, *parthenoi* has to be understood as masc. as well as fem., because v. 26 extends its connotation to *anthrōpos*, "human being," and v. 32 applies it to masc. *ho agamos*. For this reason, the RSV, REB render it "the unmarried." The translation "betrothed" (ESV, Hurley, "To Marry," 16; Elliott, "Paul's Teaching") is tendentious and wrong; and *parthenoi*, as "widow(er)s married only once" (Ford, "Levirate Marriage," 362) is bizarre. The noun occurs elsewhere in the Pauline corpus only in 2 Cor 11:2 (in a figurative sense; see *EDNT*, 3:40).

I do not have a command from the Lord, but I give my opinion as one who by the Lord's mercy is trustworthy. Lit. "pitied enough to be trustworthy," an epexegetical infin. (*IBNTG*, 127). Contrast 7:10, and compare 2 Cor 8:8–10, where the same contrast of *epitagē* and *gnōmē* is noted about another matter. Even though he expresses an opinion, Paul knows that his ministry is graced by divine mercy (see 2 Cor 4:1), and so he claims that he can be trusted; cf. 1 Thess 2:4., where Paul similarly mentions God's approval that he enjoys and the gospel with which he has been entrusted. Greek *gnōmē* actually means more than the modern English "opinion," bearing even the nuance of "judgment," as in 7:40; often it means "purpose," "decision," "counsel," and even "maxim," as in the rhetorical tradition of ethical teaching among ancient Greeks and Romans (see Ramsaran, "More than an Opinion," who argues that its use is a mark of Paul's argumentative craft to convince Corinthian Christians of his trustworthy view of the matter). It is far from clear that, in so expressing himself, it is merely "Paul the theologian speaking in his own name," and not giving "an *apostolic* judgment" (*pace* Guillemette, "Is Celibacy Better?" 15).

26. *I think, therefore, that, in view of the impending crisis, it is good for a person to remain as he is.* Lit. "I think therefore this to be good because of the impending need, that it is good for a human being to be in this way," where the infin. *to houtōs einai* (preceded by the neut. anaphoric article *to*) means "as one is" (BDF §399.1). The Greek of this verse is cumbersome.

Paul gives a reason for repeating the principle enunciated in vv. 17, 20, and 24: "in view of the impending crisis." *Anankē* can denote "necessity, pressure" of any kind (Matt 18:7; Rom 13:5), but at times in apocalyptic writings it refers to a coming crisis or distress (e.g., the final days of a siege or persecution: Luke 21:23; 2 Cor 6:4; Josephus, *J.W.* 5.13.7 §571). The perf. ptc. *enestēkōs* can mean either "happening now, present" (3:22; Rom 8:38; Gal 1:4; Heb 9:9; 3 Macc 1:16; BDAG, 337) or "threatening, being imminent" (1 Macc 12:44; LXX 1 Kgs 12:24x; Isocrates, *Or.* 5.2; Polybius, *Hist.* 3.97.1; cf. BDAG, 337).

What is the "impending crisis"? Is it restricted to "troubles in earthly life" (*en sarki*, 7:28c)? So SBJ, *1 Cor*, 41. "Famine, grain shortages" (Winter, *After Paul*, 6, 224)—a meaning that hardly suits the present context!—Or is it related to "the shape of this world" that "is passing away" (7:31b)? It does not seem to be the former, because the climax of vv. 25–31, expressed in v. 31, implies that "impending crisis" has an eschatological nuance. As Baasland rightly notes, it denotes here "etwa endzeitliche Drangsal" (hardship of the last days) and differs from its meaning in 7:37 ("sexual impulse") or in 9:16 ("[divine] compulsion"). It resembles its use in LXX Zeph 1:15, *hēmera thlipseōs kai anankēs*, "a day of distress and anguish" ("*Anankē* bei Paulus," 358, 365). Conzelmann (*1 Cor*, 132) also recognizes that this phrase "at last affords the long-awaited eschatological grounding"; similarly Bellinato, "O pensamento." This motivation for celibacy finds a parallel in the life of the prophet Jeremiah, who was warned by Yahweh "not to take a wife" in view of the doom coming upon the land in the Babylonian Captivity (Jer 16:2–4).

27. *Are you bound to a wife? Do not seek release.* I.e., separation from her. Paul's counsel echoes, in effect, vv. 10–11 (about no divorce), but now it is because of the "impending crisis" (*anankē*). The perf. tense in *dedesai* expresses the condition of the marital bond that began in the past and continues to exist. Rom 7:2 (*hē gar hypandros gynē tō zōnti andri dedetai nomō*, "thus a married woman is bound by law to her husband as long as he is alive") shows that Paul is speaking about a husband and wife, and not merely about an engaged couple, as J. K. Elliott maintains ("Paul's Teaching"); cf. BDAG, 222. Paul recommends that such a union continue, even in view of the impending crisis, because of the principle of v. 20: "each should remain in the state in which he was called." However, Paul considers first a husband in this and the following alternative, which widens the mean-

ing of virginity so that it is not restricted only to females; see also v. 32b (*ho agamos*). Paul's style here is noteworthy: the resolution of a periodic sentence into disconnected components (see BDF §§464, 494).

Are you without a wife? Do not look for one. The perf. *lelysai* might seem to mean, "have you been loosed from a wife," i.e., by death or divorce. The NEB understands it of one whose marriage has "been dissolved." In view of the preceding question, however, it must mean, "Have you been free of any bond to a wife?" BDAG notes that "a previous state of being 'bound' need not be assumed" (607). So Paul's words would be directed to bachelors as well as widowers, because they are simply echoing his fundamental principle stated above. The initial verb *lelysai* picks up on the last word of the preceding sentence, another disconnected component, *lysin*, "release." In saying this, Paul is not speaking against marriage as such.

28. *But if you marry, you would not sin.* Since Paul states only his opinion and gives advice, the person concerned must take responsibility and decide. If one makes a different decision and adopts a different form of life, Paul hastens to add that that is not sinful. The conditional sentence is strange, because the protasis expresses a present general condition (*ean* with the subjunct. *gamēsēs* [which could also be taken as future more vivid, as does Conzelmann]), but the apodosis uses *ouk hēmartes*, which has been called a proleptic aor. (ZBG §257) or a futuristic aor. (BDF §333.2); hence the translation given in the lemma.

The best reading of the verb in the protasis is *gamēsēs*, but some MSS (K, L) use the more correct, classical aor. subjunc. *gēmēs*; and others (D, F, G) read rather *labēs gynaika*, "take a wife," a reading probably influenced by v. 29b.

and if a virgin marries, she would not sin. Another example singles out *hē parthenos*, "the virgin," with fem. art., which relates this instance to the topic begun in v. 25, even though the fem. art. is lacking in MSS B, F, G (because of haplography). The article (*hē*) is generic (BDF §252). Again the conditional sentence has the same strange mixture of tenses.

Yet such people will face troubles in earthly life. Lit. "trouble in the flesh," where *thlipsis* is not "synonymous with *anankē*" of v. 26 (*pace* Conzelmann, *1 Cor*, 132), because, although the verb is fut., the "trouble" will not be caused only by an outward circumstance, persecution or the "shape of this world." *Thlipsis* will afflict the flesh of human beings (cf. 2 Cor 2:4; 12:7), where "in the flesh" does not denote merely sexual enticements (as in 7:2, 9), but connotes also the troubling and worrisome lives that many people lead in this world, with a spouse and children.

and I would spare you that. Lit. "and I am sparing you that." Having made a concession (v. 28ab) in light of his fundamental principle, Paul stresses a consideration still expressed in eschatological terms, as the next verse makes clear. He prefers to spare Corinthian Christians the agony of deciding what is better for themselves, their spouses, and their children.

29. *What I mean, brothers, is that time is running out.* Lit. "this I declare (*phēmi*, cf. 15:50), the critical time has been limited/shortened," where the perf. pass. ptc. of *systellō*, "draw together, shorten," is used without any indication of the agent by which it has been done. Paul is emphasizing that one should not regard the pres-

ent age, in which the Corinthian Christian community is living, as everlasting. In the apocalyptic passage of Mark 13:20, a shortening of days is ascribed to "the Lord," and that has given rise to a similar understanding of this Pauline expression, especially if it is related to Paul's reference to the Parousia itself, "the day of our Lord Jesus Christ" (1:8). "Time" is not the translation of *chronos*, which measures the passing of hours and days, but *kairos*, "critical time," the same as what Paul calls in Rom 3:26 *ho nyn kairos*, "the present time," i.e., the eschatological now (see *Romans*, 343–44, 353), marked by God's intervention and guidance through the salvific Christ-event. Paul adds a different aspect to this "time," viz., its curtailment, as he seeks to intensify in vv. 29–31 the eschatological motivation of his treatment of marriage and virginity for Christians, "upon whom the ends of the ages have met" (10:11). Cf. Rom 13:1. He wants to express freedom to engage in life in this world as if one were not in it, and so he takes an apocalyptic view of the world.

From now on let even those who have wives live as though they had none. Or "therefore," because it is difficult to say whether the adv. phrase *to loipon* is being used in a temporal sense (Cavallin) or in an inferential sense (BDAG, 602–3). The temporal sense may be preferred because of the general future or eschatological thrust of Paul's argument in this part of chap. 7.

In saying this, Paul is not uttering a deprecating judgment against marriage, even though he recognizes that married men become absorbed in family affairs and problems; he is not recommending that they abandon their responsibilities to spouses and children, but rather wants them to learn to live as if they no longer had wives and children. For the thrust of his argument is: because of the impending crisis it is not good to marry; for if one were to marry, one would be assuming obligations that the crisis will make it impossible to fulfill. Cf. the saying of the Lucan Jesus (Luke 14:26), about a disciple who is expected to hate father, mother, wife, children, and even his own life.

Paul uses *hōs mē*, "as though not," five times, not necessarily in dependence on Stoic argumentation, even though his formulation may resemble Stoic antitheses (Conzelmann, *1 Cor*, 133), but on a tradition inspired by the words of Jesus in the Sermon on the Mount (Matt 6:19–34), who urged his followers not to store up treasures on earth, but in heaven. To such a tradition, Paul gives a clearer eschatological cast. The five instances juxtapose "five examples of 'worldly' involvement—including marriage—and five corresponding, suggested ideal modes of behavior" (Wimbush, *Paul the Worldly Ascetic*, 28). Wimbush compares the imperatives in 6 Ezra 16:40–44, and eventually concludes rightly that Paul's relativizing argument "(*hōs mē = amerimnos*) *is used not for debunking, but for accepting involvement in, the structures of the world, with the proviso that concern for 'the things of the Lord' take priority*" (ibid., 96 [his italics]).

For a striking example of similar Cynic antitheses, see Diogenes of Sinope, preserved in Diogenes Laertius, *Vitae* 6.29 (cf. Penna "San Paolo"; also Schrage, "Die Stellung"). What in Stoic thinking was an aloof reaction to the world of human existence has now been cast in terms of another world dominated by the Christ-event, with a destiny that is different. Christians may live in the world, but

Paul calls them to consider a lifestyle that is detached from it so that they may devote themselves to the Lord's affairs.

30. *those who mourn as though they did not; those who are happy as though they were not; those who buy as though they had no possessions.* Three further examples of people affected by the impending crisis are mourners, rejoicers, and buyers. In each case, what is crucial in these aspects of human life takes on a Judeo-Christian dimension that is eschatologically different. Cf. Luke 6:16–21, 25b; Rom 12:15. The dialectic tension in these instances is not merely between the present and the future, but between Christians and the world in which they find themselves. The four antitheses expressed in vv. 30–31 have been compared with similar antitheses in Stoic diatribe, but they should rather be compared with 4 Ezra 16:42–45, and more closely even with those expressed by Paul in 4:10–13a.

31. *and those who deal with this world as though they had no use of it.* Lit. "and those using the world." The fourth and last example is comprehensive, summing up the others. In other words, Christians should live in this world as it has been transformed by the Christ-event, as though they were not ruled and dominated by deceptive demands of this world. "Those who are called by God to remain in the world (vv. 17–24) are exhorted rather to live 'as though not exploiting the world' " (Doughty, "Presence and Future," 71–72). Cf. Rom 12:2, where Paul urges his addressees not to conform themselves to this present world (*mē schēmatizesthe tō aiōni toulō*).

For the shape of this world is passing away. The pres. tense of *paragei* in this statement explains the comprehensive antithesis just expressed: the outward appearance of the present mode of earthly life is going out of existence, because it is to be transformed as a result of the Christ-event. So Paul views the age in which he was living as he adds this to what he has already said about it in vv. 26 and 29. *Paragei*, "is passing away," is a form of the verb used in LXX Ps 144:4, "The days of a human being are like a passing shadow." The phrase *to schēma tou kosmou*, however, is known in Greek literature, found (with a different connotation) in Eurpides, *Bacchae* 832; Philostratus, *Vita Apoll.* 8.7 §312, and lacking an eschatological connotation.

32. *I want you to be free of concern.* This statement could refer to what Paul has already written in v. 28cd, but it more directly refers to what is coming in the following verses, because the adj. *amerimnous*, "without concern," is echoed in the verb in the following sentence, *merimnā*. Paul is expressing his pastoral care by providing guidance to the celibate male, and is undoubtedly using a notion often associated with marriage in Stoic writings, *merimna*, "anxiety, worry, care" (BDAG, 632), along with *perispasmos*, "distraction, preoccupation." See Hierocles, *Peri gamou* 22.24, excerpted in Stobaeus, *Anthologium* (ed. O. Hense, 4.504); also Balch, "1 Cor 7:32–35."

The unmarried man is concerned about the Lord's affairs, how he may please the Lord. Paul understands that *ho agamos* is spared worry about a wife and children and other related concerns so that he can concentrate on "the Lord's affairs" (*ta tou kyriou*). Paul makes this assertion about an unmarried man in the context of an exhortation in favor of virginity. What he thus asserts is intended as a recommendation to consider the appropriateness of "pleasing the Lord" in a celibate way of life. "To please the Lord" is a consideration found elsewhere in Pauline writings, when the Apostle seeks to motivate human conduct (1 Thess 4:1; 2:4, 15; Rom 8:8; 2 Cor 5:9). Some of the other passages speak of pleasing "God," whence the variant *theō* for this verse in MSS F, G, and Latin versions. *Pace* Guillemette ("Is Celibacy Better," 18), Jerome did not "wrongly" translate, when he wrote *quomodo placeat Deo*; he translated what he read in such MSS.

What are *ta tou kyriou*, "the Lord's affairs"? Even though Paul adds immediately, "How he may please the Lord" and such a clause can be found elsewhere in his writings, it does not help much in determining the connotation of "the Lord's affairs." One might think of prayer, presence in cultic or church assemblies, charitable works, even preaching, but are such items sufficient motivation for an unmarried life? Perhaps what Paul says in 9:19–23 about his own dedication gives a hint about what is meant here by "the Lord's affairs." It is gratuitous eisegesis to introduce the explanation of working "full time" for the affairs of the Lord, meaning thereby "the spread of the Gospel on foreign soil or even simply the founding of Churches" (Guillemette, ibid., 21). Wimbush rightly sees that Paul is speaking rather about a form of asceticism or "ascetic behavior (or renunciation in general) and self-understanding" (*Paul the Worldly Ascetic*, 7).

33. *But a married man is concerned about the affairs of this world, how he may please his wife.* This is simply the opposite formulation of v. 32b, with *ta tou kosmou* replacing *ta tou kyriou*, and *tē gynaiki* replacing *tō kyriō*.

34. *and he is divided.* Lit. "and he has been divided," the verb, being perf. pass. *memeristai* expresses the conclusion of v. 33. This is the reading in the earliest Alexandrian and Western MSS (P[15, 46], ℵ, A, B, D*, P, 33, 1739). Some MSS (Dc, F, G, K, L, Ψ, 614), however, omit the first *kai*, and so *memeristai* would be taken with the following sentence (in MS 1241 it is followed by *de*), and its subj. would be *hē gynē hē agamos*, "the unmarried woman." This reading, however, is not favored by text critics today (Metzger, *TCGNT*, 490).

As the text stands, Paul is saying that the attention of a married man is divided as he seeks to please both his wife and the Lord. Even though Paul may be agreeing with Stoic thought to some extent in this regard about concern and distraction, he does have a nuance that is not found in Stoic writers, the concern for the things of the risen Christ as well as an eschatological perspective in which he casts his discussion of unmarried life.

An unmarried woman or virgin is concerned about the Lord's affairs, that she may be holy in both body and spirit. Lit. "and the unmarried woman and the virgin" (with a sing. verb), which is the preferred reading today, but it is not universally attested; some MSS (P[46], ℵ, A, 33) have the adj. *agamos* with both *gynē* and *parthenos*, so that *hē gynē hē agamos* could refer to a widow and *hē parthenos hē agamos* to a virgin (see Metzger, *TCGNT*, 490). Guenther ("One Woman or Two"), however, has shown that Paul is speaking here of only one woman, "the unmarried and chaste woman."

The first part of this sentence parallels that about the unmarried man in v. 32b. Paul thus treats the virgin equally with the unmarried man. The second part of the sentence adds a new consideration, "that she may be holy in both body and spirit," i.e., that her dedication to the Lord and ascetic withdrawal from worldly concerns may be expressed in all that she is. In writing "body and spirit" (see NOTE on 2:4), which are terms not used in opposition here, but in a sense of wholeness, Paul is referring to the unmarried woman's entire person; such a woman is holy not only in her inward being, but also in her physical virginal body.

MacDonald ("Women Holy") argues that Paul was extending to ordinary Corinthian Christian women, who were striving to be holy in remaining unmarried, the hope of a new kind of freedom in the social world of Roman Corinth. Paul's remarks are cautious, because he realizes that celibacy for them might not always remain possible. Even though Paul has spoken first about "the unmarried man" (v. 32), "the impulse for celibacy came mainly from women, since the celibate efforts of these traditionally subordinate members of the community would most likely require the blessing of males if the community was to continue as a mixed group" (ibid., 172). Paul's comments then instill a sense of eschatological reservation into such concerns, as he warns Corinthian Christians of a concern that could engulf both ways of life and be distracting. Cf. 1 Thess 5:23; 1 Cor 5:3 (used in contrast).

but the married woman is concerned about the affairs of this world, how she may please her husband. This is the exact counterpart of the married man in v. 33.

35. *I am saying this for your own good.* Lit. "for what is advantageous to you (plur.)," i.e., for the benefit of the Corinthian church, and not for any benefit to Paul himself.

not to lay a restriction on you. Lit. "not to throw a noose (*brochon*) about you." Paul utilizes a term known to the Cynic philosopher Diogenes of Sinope, who taught that for the conduct of life one needs "reason or a halter" (*dein logon ē brochon*), i.e., self-control or suicide (quoted in Diogenes Laertius, *Vitae* 6.24). Paul, however, does not seek to curtail the freedom of Corinthian Christians or deprive them of it, but rather to order their outlook properly and lead them to a better role in the service of the Lord and the community. See 2 Cor 4:5.

but for the sake of good order and devotion to the Lord without distraction. Three qualities sum up Paul's counsel to the Corinthians about virginity; they are expressed in two substantivized adj. and an adv. His advice about virginity seeks *to euschēmon*, "that which is seen to contribute to propriety and good order," or what Greek society would advocate for public decorum (see Epictetus, *Diss.* 4.1.163; 4.12.6); *to euparedron*, "that which sits well in attendance upon" (the Lord), like wisdom attending God's throne (Wis 9:4); and *aperispastōs*, "without distraction." The last quality is the most important, for Paul's whole discussion about virginity has been building up to this significant adv., with which the verse emphatically ends. In using this adv., Paul may have been borrowing an idea from current Stoic philosophy; see Epictetus, *Diss.* 3.22.69: *mē pot' aperispaston einai dei ton Kynikon holon pros tē diakoniā tou theou*, "whether the Cynic should (not) be undistracted, wholly (devoted) to the service of God." This would have entailed abstention from marriage and other mundane obligations (BDAG, 101). See further Epictetus, *Diss.* 1.29.59; 2.21.22; also Balch, "1 Cor 7:32–35"; Fredrickson, "No Noose," 421–23.

BIBLIOGRAPHY

Baasland, E., "*Anankē* bei Paulus im Lichte eines stoischen Paradoxes," *Geschichte—Tradition—Reflexion: Festschrift für Martin Hengel* . . . (3 vols.; ed. H. Cancik et al.; Tübingen: Mohr [Siebeck], 1996), 3:357–85.

Balch, D. L., "1 Cor 7:32–35 and Stoic Debates about Marriage, Anxiety, and Distraction," *JBL* 102 (1983) 429–39.

Bellinato, G., "O pensamento de São Paulo acerca de celibato na Primeira Carta aos Coríntios (Cor 5 [*sic*, read 7], 25–35)," *RCB* 13 (1976) 90–98.

Botman, H. R., and D. J. Smit, "1 Corinthians 7:29–31: 'To Live . . . as if It Were not!" *JTSA* 65 (1988) 73–79.

Bound, J. F., "Who Are the 'Virgins' Discussed in 1 Corinthians 7:25–38?" *EvJ* 2 (1984) 3–15.

Cavallin, A., "*(to) loipon*: Eine bedeutungsgeschichtliche Untersuchung," *Eranos* 39 (1941) 129–44.

Cha, J.-S., "The Ascetic Virgin in 1 Corinthians 7:25–38," *AJT* 12 (1998) 89–117.

Chmiel, J., "Die Interpretation des paulinischen *hōs mē* im 1 Kor 7,29–31," *Analecta Cracoviensia* 18 (1986) 197–204.

Coppens, J., "L'Appel paulinien à la virginité," *ETL* 50 (1974) 272–78.

Doughty, D. J., "The Presence and Future of Salvation in Corinth," *ZNW* 66 (1975) 61–90.

Elliott, J. K. "Paul's Teaching on Marriage in I. Corinthians: Some Problems Considered," *NTS* 19 (1972–73) 219–25.

Fischer, J. A., "Paul on Virginity," *TBT* 72 (1974) 1633–38.

Ford, J. M., "Levirate Marriage in St Paul (1 Cor. vii)," *NTS* 10 (1963–64) 361–65.

———, "St Paul the Philogamist (I Cor. vii in Early Patristic Exegesis)," *NTS* 11 (1964–65) 326–48.

Fredrickson, D. E., "No Noose Is Good News: Leadership as a Theological Problem in the Corinthian Correspondence," *WW* 16 (1996) 420–26.

Genton, P., "1 Corinthiens 7/25–40: Notes exégétiques," *ETR* 67 (1992) 249–53.

González Ruiz, J. M., "¿Un celibato apostólico? (1 Cor 7, 25–38)," *XVII Semana bíblica española (24–28 Sept. 1956)* (Madrid: Consejo Superior de Investigaciones Científicas, 1958) 273–91.

Guenther, A. R., "One Woman or Two? 1 Corinthians 7:34," *BBR* 12 (2002) 33–45.

Guillemette, N., "Is Celibacy Better?" *Landas* (Manila) 10 (1996) 3–38.

Gundry-Volf, J. M., "Celibate Pneumatics and Social Power: On the Motivations for Sexual Asceticism in Corinth," *USQR* 48/3–4 (1994) 105–26.

Hierzenberger, G., *Weltbewertung bei Paulus nach 1 Kor 7,29–31: Eine exegetisch-kerygmatische Studie* (Düsseldorf: Patmos, 1967).

Hurley, R., "To Marry or Not to Marry: The Interpretation of 1 Cor 7:36–38," *EstBíb* 58 (2000) 7–31.

Kuck, D. W., "The Freedom of Being in the World 'As if Not' (1 Cor 7:29–31)," *CurTM* 28 (2001) 585–93.

Legrand, L., "The Prophetical Meaning of Celibacy," *Scripture* 12 (1960) 97–105; 13 (1961) 12–20.

Léon-Dufour, X., "Du bon usage de ce monde: 1 Co 7, 29–31," *AsSeign* 34 (1973) 26–31.

MacDonald, M. Y., "Women Holy in Body and Spirit: The Social Setting of 1 Corinthians 7," *NTS* 36 (1990) 161–81.

Navarro Puerto, M., "La *parthenos*: Un futuro significativo en el aquí y ahora de la comunidad (1 Cor 7,25–38)," *EstBíb* 49 (1991) 353–87.

Niederwimmer, K., "Zur Analyse der asketischen Motivation in 1 Kor 7," *TLZ* 99 (1974)
    241–48.
Penna, R., "San Paolo (1 Cor 7,29b–31a) e Diogene il Cinico," *Bib* 58 (1977) 237–45.
Pilch, J. J., "Who Is a Virgin?" *TBT* 40 (2002) 248–52.
Ramsaran, R. A., "More Than an Opinion: Paul's Rhetorical Maxim in First Corinthians
    7:25–26," *CBQ* 57 (1995) 531–41.
Schrage, W., "Die Stellung zur Welt bei Paulus, Epiktet und in der Apokalyptik: Ein
    Beitrag zu 1 Kor 7,29–31," *ZTK* 61 (1964) 125–54.
Vögtle, A., *Das Neue Testament und die Zukunft des Kosmos* (Düsseldorf: Patmos, 1970)
    80–92.
Wimbush, V. L., *Paul the Worldly Ascetic: Response to the World and Self-Understanding
    according to 1 Corinthians 7* (Macon: Mercer University Press, 1987).

17   f. *Marriage of a Virgin*
in Certain Conditions (7:36–38)

[7:36] If someone thinks that he is behaving improperly toward his virgin, and if she
(or he) is at a critical stage, and so it has to be, let him do as he wishes. He is committing no sin; let them get married. [37] But the one who stands firm in his mind,
who is under no compulsion and has control of his own will, and has made up
his mind to keep his virgin (unmarried) will be doing well. [38] So then both the
one who marries his virgin does well, and the one who does not marry her will do
better.

COMMENT

Although these three verses are related to the foregoing passage (vv. 25–35), they
are more concerned with marriage than with virginity. In v. 34, Paul spoke of "an
unmarried woman or virgin," but now he takes up two special cases of marriage,
one the marriage of a virgin in a special situation (vv. 36–38), and the other that of
a widow (vv. 39–40). In both cases it is a question of a possible change in marital
status, and Paul's advice is diverse.

In the first instance, treated in this pericope, the issue concerns *parthenos*, but
what Paul says about her is far from clear. Three main interpretations of this difficult passage have been proposed, and none of them is without its problems.

First, the difficulty begins with *tis*, "someone," who is clearly a man because of
the masc. poss. pron. *autou*, "his virgin," but what is meant by *parthenos*? A long-
standing meaning has been "virgin daughter," as the word is used at times in some
Greek writers (Sophocles, *Oed. Tyr.* 1462; Apollonius Rhodius, *Argonautica* 3.86;
Diodorus Siculus, *Bibl. Hist.* 16.55.3; 20.84.3; Josephus, *Ant.* 1.11.5 §205); cf. the
Vg: *super virgine sua. Tis* would then refer to her father, who in ancient society
had the authority (*patria potestas* in the Roman concept of the family [= *exousia*,
v. 37]) and the duty of giving his daughter away in marriage to a suitor. The com-

pound adj. *hyperakmos* (v. 36) would be understood as fem. and mean that she is "past the bloom of youth," or *superadulta*. This interpretation is often supported by reference to Sir 42:9, where a father worries about his daughter, whether she be married, or unmarried past her prime (*mēpote parakmasē*), or unfaithful in marriage. At first sight, this meaning of *tis* seems to be called for by the verb *gamizō*, "give in marriage" (v. 38). However, *parthenos*, meaning "daughter," encounters serious difficulty with the verb *gameitōsan*, "let them get married" (v. 36). Who is meant by the 3d pers. plur. verb? It hardly seems to be, "Let the father and his daughter marry." Further objections against this interpretation are: Why would Paul use *tis* and *tēn parthenon autou* to refer to a father and his daughter, when he could have used the specific words, *patēr* and *thygatēr*; and nothing in the preceding ten verses prepares for such a relationship.

To get around such objections, a variant of this interpretation is proposed sometimes, which understands the verses to refer to a guardian (*tutor*) and his ward (*pupilla*) or adopted daughter; or even to a master and his slave, to whom he had promised virginal status (Schiwietz, O'Rourke, Klauck) . In such a case, the improper behavior might be the guardian's or master's desire to marry her or perhaps his reluctance to allow the girl to marry and his desire to keep her to be an old maid. The crucial verses, then, are translated:

> If someone thinks that he is behaving improperly toward his virgin (daughter/ward/slave), if she is past the bloom of youth, and so it has to be, let him do as he wishes. He is committing no sin; let them get married. . . . So then both the one who gives his virgin in marriage does right, and the one who does not give her in marriage will do better.

This interpretation has been proposed by many commentators (with varying nuances): John Chrysostom (*De virginitate* 78; PG 48.590), Theodoret (*In ep. I ad Cor.* 7.36; PG 82.284), Epiphanius, Ambrose, Augustine; Luther (*7. Kap. Cor.* [1523] 36; WAusg. 12.140), Calvin (*1 Ep. Cor.* 7.36; ed. Pringle, 39.264–65), Bengel; Allo, Bachmann, Edwards, Godet, Grosheide, Heinrici, Huby, Jacono, Kuss, J. B. Lightfoot, Morris, Robertson-Plummer, Sickenberger, Spicq; also the KJV, JB. Of the three interpretations, this long-standing one has the least to be said for it today (see Schrenk, *TDNT*, 3:60).

Second, *parthenos* is understood rather of a "betrothed virgin," one to whom *tis* has been engaged, or his fiancée. This is explained sometimes by recalling the difference in Jewish marriage between betrothal (*'ērûsîn*) and actual taking in marriage (*nîśû'în*) and imagining some reason to postpone the latter. The betrothal was a formal engagement to marry, which made the woman committed to the prospective husband so much so that any intercourse with another man would have made her an adulteress. A similar engagement was known also in the Roman world. In this case, *hyperakmos* is understood usually as masc. and refers to the fiancé's strong passions (although the NIV still understands it as "if she is getting along in years"). Such an understanding of *parthenos* makes the verb *gameitōsan*, "let them marry" (v. 36), easier to understand, but it creates a problem for *gamizōn*

(v. 38), if one tries to take it in its usual sense. It is further problematic in making Paul's comment on such a man's decision to marry his fiancée seem strange, "He is committing no sin" (v. 36e), because Paul has already addressed this issue (v. 9). Another objection against this interpretation comes from the lack of other instances of *parthenos* meaning "betrothed" without some specifying adj. (e.g., *emnēsteumenē*, as in Luke 1:27). In any case, Paul would be counseling the engaged man either to marry or, better, to put off the marriage and let her remain as betrothed. The crucial verses, then, are translated:

> If someone thinks that he is behaving improperly toward his (betrothed) virgin, if he is at his sexual peak, and so it has to be, let him do as he wishes. He is committing no sin; let them get married. . . . So then both the one who marries his betrothed does right, and the one who does not marry her will do better.

This interpretation was first proposed in 1874 by W. C. van Manen and is used (with varying nuances) by Barrett, Belkin, Bruce, Chadwick, Collins, Conzelmann (?), Deming, Fee, Garland, Horsley, Hurley, Kistemaker, Kruse, Kümmel, Leal, Lindemann, Marinelli, Merklein, Schrage, Senft, Thiselton, and others; see also RSV, NAB, NRSV, ESV, REB, NIV, NJB.

Third, a different situation has been envisaged: that of a Christian "virgin" committed to preserving her virginity who has taken up ascetic cohabitation with a unmarried man who would respect her resolve. This has been called a "spiritual marriage," in which intercourse was not practiced by such ascetic partners. Such a union was unknown in Judaism, and this would be the earliest attestation of it among Christian men and women. It may be hinted at also in the Shepherd of Hermas, *Sim.* 9.11.1–9. The improper behavior would in this case be the man's inability to control his sexual desire and his indulgence in unwanted advances. Paul's counsel advises such individuals about further conduct in such a union. The crucial verses, then, are translated:

> If someone thinks that he is behaving improperly toward his (spiritual) virgin, if he is at his sexual peak, and so it has to be, let him do as he wishes. He is committing no sin; let them get married. . . . So then both the one who marries his virgin does right, and the one who does not marry her will do better.

This interpretation is sometimes said to have been first proposed in 1892 by C. Weissäcker, and it has been extended by Grafe and Achelis, who related it to the third-century practice of *virgines subintroductae* (inducted virgins) in some forms of monastic life. It is still proposed (with varying nuances) by Beck, Conzelmann (?), Delling, Héring, Hurd, Kruse, Lietzmann, Moffatt, Murphy-O'Connor, Niederwimmer, Peters, Seboldt, and others, especially in the last hundred years (Peters, "Spiritual Marriage"); NEB. In this interpretation, the verb *gameitōsan*, "let them get married," becomes otiose, because they are already married. It is a matter of debate, moreover, whether there actually were in Roman Corinth such ascetic virgins as part of the Christian community; there is no evidence for them. How would the idea of a spiritual marriage be reconciled with what Paul has written about the physical relationship of Christian marriage in vv. 1–5? (Garland, *1 Cor*, 339). One should hesitate to read into Paul's words all the later problems of ecclesiastical discipline about *virgines subintroductae* or *parthenoi syneisaktai* (see Oepke, "Irrwege"; Deming, *Paul on Marriage*, 40–47).

In this pericope, Paul undoubtedly is addressing either those who have not yet been married or, more likely, have not yet indulged in marital intercourse. Realist that he is, he recommends marriage, when "it has to be" (v. 36c), which is an application of what he has already said in v. 9, even though he himself prefers that the virgin be kept as she is, i.e., unmarried, so that she may be "concerned about the Lord's affairs" and may be "holy in both body and spirit" (v. 34).

NOTES

7:36. *If someone thinks that he is not behaving properly toward his virgin.* The clause is introduced by *de*, "but," and the infin. *aschēmonein*, "behave improperly," stands in contrast to *to euschēmon*, "(contributing to) good order," of v. 35. The impropriety is not specified, but would have to be judged from the context, which could be social, legal, or moral. It will vary here depending on the sense given to "his virgin," as explained above, and on the meaning given to the adj. in the following clause. *Pace* Bound ("Who Are the 'Virgins'"), *tēn parthenon autou* cannot mean the man's own "virginity," because *parthenos* is a concrete noun, not the abs. *parthenia* or *partheneia*. This meaning was used also by certain patristic writers (see Allo, *1 Cor*, 185, who recognizes it for what it is, a subterfuge).

and if she (or he) is at a critical stage. Lit. "if he (she) is *hyperakmos*." The compound adj. *hyperakmos* (= *hyper*, "beyond" [as in 2 Cor 1:8] + *akmē*, "highest point, peak") is of common gender, either masc. or fem.; so one cannot tell from it how the subject of the verb "is" should be understood, whether "he" or "she." Moreover, the adj. has been understood often either in a temporal sense, "beyond the bloom of youth" (Diodorus Siculus, *Bibl. Hist.* 32.11.1, using *akmē* of a marriageable woman's highest age); or in an intensive sense, "oversexed," or "straining at one's sexual peak" (Diodorus Siculus, *Bibl. Hist.* 36.2.3, which uses the cog. verb *akmazō* of a man's *erōs*, "love"). The first of these meanings is contested at times (see Winter, "Puberty or Passion"), and the second even more so (O'Rourke, "Hypotheses," 292; Allo, *1 Cor*, 192). In any case, the adj. certainly means more than that the girl has reached puberty and is "fully developed," as Ford would have it ("Levirate Marriage," 364), regardless of the later rabbinic usage to which she refers.

The different ways of understanding *tis* and the adj. *hyperakmos* have been listed in the COMMENT above, along with the choices of various versions. The NAB paraphrases the clause and disregards the gender of the adj., leaving it undecided, "if a critical moment has come."

and so it has to be. The subj. of the verb *opheilei* is unclear; it does not seem to be either *parthenos* or *tis*; so it is often taken as impersonal, referring to the situation described so far as inevitably leading to marital union, or perhaps referring to external social pressure in the culture in which the person was living (see Chadwick, " 'All Things,' " 267).

let him do as he wishes. Or possibly "let her do as she wishes." Although it is impossible to tell who the subject is, more than likely it refers to the man (*tis*). In either case, it expresses the complete freedom that the subject has. Interpreters who take *parthenos* to be "virgin daughter" understand this clause as an expression of *patria potestas*, the father's authority and power to give his daughter away in marriage. If it is a spiritual marriage, it could refer to either spouse, but again the man is the more likely subject.

He is committing no sin. Or possibly, "she is committing no sin." Paul repeats what he has already said in v. 28, making sure that no one misunderstands him in this matter, that marriage in itself, and even in such a situation, is not sinful.

let them get married. Lit. "let them marry." This is the problematic 3d pers. plur. verb (*gameitōsan*) that causes difficulty for the traditional interpretation (father or guardian of a virgin daughter or ward); see COMMENT above. To obviate the difficulty, some MSS of the western text-tradition (D*, F, G, 1505) read the sing. impv. *gameitō*, "let him get married," which does not really help, because the text still would not indicate who the man is. Robertson-Plummer translate the verb, "Let the daughter and her suitor marry" (*1 Cor*, 159; similarly Kugelman, "1 Cor. 7:36–38," 65); O'Rourke ("Hypotheses," 298): "her future partner"; but "suitor" or "partner" is supplied from their argument and read into the Greek text, which has no such term. In the spiritual-marriage interpretation, this word would have to mean, "let them consummate the marriage by intercourse," which it does not really mean (Fee, *1 Cor*, 352). The verb is best understood when either the second or third interpretation mentioned in the COMMENT is used.

37. *But the one who stands firm in his mind, who is under no compulsion and has control of his own will.* Paul states in three ways the freedom of conviction of the man (masc. *hos, autou, echōn*) in such a marital situation. This insistence on the freedom of decision suits better the man in an engagement or a spiritual marriage than it does a father or a guardian. *Anankē* is now used in the sense of "sexual impulse"; see NOTE on 7:26, but *thelēma*, "will," is rarely so employed, because elsewhere in Pauline writings it denotes God's will; in extrabiblical writings it sometimes has a sexual connotation (desire). That, however, would suit more the engaged man than a father. For the anacoluthon here, see BDF §478.3.

and has made up his mind to keep his virgin (unmarried) will be doing well. Lit. "has decided this in his own heart, to keep his own virgin," i.e., not to follow his sexual desire but to keep her as she is (as a virgin). The opinion Paul expresses now agrees with what he said in vv. 7–8 above. For a parallel use of *tērein* in regard to marriage, see Achilles Tatius, *Clitophon et Leucippe* 8.18.2 (*parthenon gar tēn korēn mechri toutou tetērēka*, "I have kept the girl a virgin up to now"). *Pace* Ford ("Levirate Marriage," 364), *tērein* in this context does not mean to "support financially."

38. *So then both the one who marries his virgin does well, and the one who does not marry her will do better.* In both clauses Paul writes *kai ho gamizōn*, the pres.

ptc. of the verb that normally means "give (a woman) in marriage," as in Mark 12:25; Matt 24:38; Luke 17:27.

The second-century grammarian, Apollonius Dyscolus, explained the difference between *gameō* and *gamizō* respectively as *gamou metalambanō*, "I take in marriage," and *gamou tini metadidōmi*, "I give to someone in marriage" (*De syntaxi* 3.31 [p. 280, 11]). This meaning makes some commentators insist that Paul is speaking about a father (or guardian) and his daughter (or ward); e.g., Robertson-Plummer.

Lietzmann (*1 Cor*, 35–36), however, noted that such a grammatical rule of Apollonius has many known exceptions (e.g., *hystereō/hysterizō*; *komeō/komizō*; *ginōskō/gnōrizō*) and that Hellenistic Greek has many verbs ending in -*izō* without a causative meaning. So he concluded that one should render *gamizō* here as *gamon poiein*, "make a marriage" (= *gameō*, "marry"). His opinion has been widely followed (see BDF §101; MM, 121; BDAG, 188), even though no one has been able to document such a meaning of *gamizo* apart from this occurrence.

A number of commentators fail even to note the problem that this difference of verbs makes: Collins, *1 Cor*, 302–3; Soards, *1 Cor*, 164. Hurley, in dependence on Pötscher, suggests that *gamizōn* can also mean "celebrate the wedding," but then he translates the first instance (v. 38a) as "he who marries his betrothed," but the second as "he who does not celebrate the wedding" ("To Marry," 31). That is puzzling, to say the least.

Paul may be expressing his preference for the preservation of a spiritual marriage among Corinthian Christians, or may be advising an engaged couple. In either case, his preference (v. 38b) is not a statement of a principle, but it is given as a solution to an isolated troubling case; it certainly contributed to the development of attitudes about marriage and celibacy in the course of the history of the Christian church.

BIBLIOGRAPHY

Achelis, H., *Virgines subintroductae: Ein Beitrag zum vii. Kapitel des I. Korintherbriefs* (Leipzig: Hinrichs, 1902).

Bauer, J. B., "Was las Tertullian 1 Kor 7,39?" ZNW 77 (1986) 284–87.

Beck, W. F., "Brief Studies: 1 Cor 7:36–38," CTM 25 (1954) 370–72.

Belkin, S., "The Problem of Paul's Background: III. Marrying One's Virgin," JBL 54 (1935) 49–52.

Chadwick, H., " 'All Things to All Men' (I Cor. ix. 22)," NTS 1 (1954–55) 261–75.

Collins, J. J., "Bulletin of the New Testament: The Pauline Epistles," TS 17 (1956) 531–48, esp. 541–42.

Derrett, J. D. M., "The Disposal of Virgins," in his *Studies in the New Testament: Volume One, Glimpses of the Legal and Social Presuppositions of the Authors* (Leiden: Brill, 1977) 184–92.

Ford, J. M., "The Rabbinic Background of St. Paul's Use of *hyperakmos* (1 Cor. vii 36)," JJS 17 (1966) 89–91.

Kruse, H., "Matrimonia 'Josephina' apud Corinthios?" VDom 26 (1948) 344–50.

Kümmel, W. G., "Verlobung und Heirat bei Paulus (I. Cor 7,36–38), *Neutestamentliche*

Studien für Rudolf Bultmann . . . (BZNW 21; ed. W. Eltester; Berlin: Töpelmann, 1954) 275–95; repr. in his *Heilsgeschehen und Geschichte: Gesammelte Aufsätze 1933–1964* (Marburg: Elwert, 1965) 310–27.

Kugelman, R., "1 Cor. 7:36–38," *CBQ* 10 (1948) 63–71.

Leal, J., "Super virgine sua (1 Cor 7,37)," *VDom* 35 (1957) 97–102.

Marinelli, D., "De virginibus in 1 Cor 7,36–38," *SBFLA* 4 (1953–54) 184–218.

O'Rourke, J. J., "Hypotheses Regarding 1 Corinthians 7,36–38," *CBQ* 20 (1958) 292–98.

Peters, G., "Spiritual Marriage in Early Christianity: 1 Cor 7:25–38 in Modern Exegesis and the Earliest Church," *TrinJ* 23 (2002) 211–24.

Pötscher, W., "Die Wortbedeutung von *gamizein* (1 Kor 7,38)," *Würzburger Jahrbuch für Altertum* 5 (1979) 99–103.

Richard, L.-A., "Sur I Corinthiens (vii, 36–38): Cas de conscience d'un père chrétien ou 'mariage ascétique'? Un essai d'interprétation," *Mémorial J. Chaine* (Lyons: Facultés Catholiques, 1950) 309–20.

Schiwietz, S., "Eine neue Auslegung von I Kor. 7, 36–38," *TGl* 19 (1927) 1–15.

Seboldt, R. H. A., "Spiritual Marriage in the Early Church: A Suggested Interpretation of 1 Cor. 7:36–38," *CTM* 30 (1959) 103–19, 176–89.

Winter, B. W., "Puberty or Passion? The Referent of *hyperakmos* in 1 Corinthians 7:36," *TynBul* 49 (1998) 71–89.

18   g. *Marriage of a Widow*
(7:39–40)

[7:39] A wife is bound to her husband as long as he lives; but if her husband dies, she is free to be married to whomever she wishes, but only in the Lord. [40] In my judgment, she is more blessed if she remains as she is—and I think that I too have God's Spirit.

COMMENT

By an association of ideas, Paul now turns to a second case of a possible change in marital status, viz., that of a Christian widow. The topic has already been introduced in 7:8–9 above.

NOTES

7:39. *A wife is bound to her husband as long as he lives.* This notion of marriage is presupposed in what Paul wrote in v. 10 above; it is formulated from the standpoint of Jewish tradition. See the regulation in 11QTemple[a] (11Q19) 57:18: "She alone shall be with him all the days of her life" (recall the COMMENT on 7:10–11 above). Cf. Rom 7:2, where Paul speaks of *hypandros gynē*, "a married woman," and adds *nomō* (a reference to the Mosaic law), which is added also here in some MSS (א[2], D, F, G, Ψ). This reading caused Tertullian to forbid a second marriage even to Christian widows (see Bauer, "Was las"). Ms K and the Bohairic version add to the main clause *gamō*, "in marriage."

but if her husband dies. Lit. "is put to sleep," aor. pass. subjunctive in a pres. general condition (see NOTE on 7:10). This euphemism for death is common in Greek literature (e.g., Homer, *Il.* 11.241; Sophocles, *Electra* 509; in LXX Gen 47:30; Deut 31:16; 1 Kgs 11:43; in funerary epitaphs [*New Docs* 3:93]), and it is used elsewhere by Paul (11:30; 15:6, 18, 20, 51; 1 Thess 4:14–15). Some MSS (A, 0278) read rather *apothanē*, "dies."

she is free to be married to whomever she wishes. In v. 8, Paul expressed his opinion that a widow should not marry; now he asserts her freedom to do so, obviously from the standpoint of Jewish tradition, which would also be true of the Greco-Roman world. Her situation is similar to that of the woman in Deut 21:14, *eleuthera de estin*, "she is free."

but only in the Lord. This nuance is new, in that Paul prefers that she marry a Christian, which is a counsel against entering into a mixed marriage. Paul is undoubtedly extending a Jewish notion, expressed in such OT endogamic regulations as Deut 7:3; Ezra 9:2; 11QTemple[a] (11Q19) 57:19 ("from his father's house and from his family"), to the Christians of Corinth. Cf. the stipulation in an Aramaic Jewish writ of divorce of A.D. 111, which allows the divorced woman "to go off and become the wife of any Jewish man that she wishes" (Mur 19:6–7; DJD 2:105).

40. *In my judgment, she is more blessed if she remains as she is,* i.e., as a widow. So Paul returns to the preference expressed in v. 8, which is now called *gnōmē*, "opinion, way of thinking," and recalls what he said in v. 25. It thus differs from *parangellō*, "give command," of v. 10 and *epitagē*, "command," of v. 25 (see NOTE there). Cf. 2 Cor 8:10, where Paul speaks similarly of his "opinion"; and also the advice about young widows in 1 Tim 5:14. The widow will be *makariōtera*, the comparative of the word usually used for beatitudes (cf. Rom 14:22); hence "more blessed," in the sight of God, and not merely in her own eyes or those of other human beings.

and I think that I too have God's Spirit. I.e., what it takes to make Paul *hikanos*, "competent," as a minister of the new covenant and preacher of God's gospel; see 2 Cor 3:5–6. Paul thus supports his *gnōmē* against those who in the Corinthian community were claiming apparently the Spirit's inspiration for their own views (see NOTE on 2:4). Mss P[15] and 33 read rather *Christou*, "Christ's Spirit," an insigificant variant.

B. FREEDOM AND THE EATING
OF MEAT SACRIFICED TO IDOLS
(8:1–11:1)

19   a. *Idol Meat and the Role of*
          Knowledge and Love in Christian
          Fellowship (8:1–13)

8:1 Now for meat sacrificed to idols: we realize that "we all possess knowledge." Knowledge puffs up, but love builds up. 2 If anyone imagines that he knows something, he does not yet know it as he ought to. 3 But if one loves God, one is known by him. 4 So about the eating of meat sacrificed to idols: we know that "an idol is nothing at all in this world" and that "there is no God but one." 5 For even if there are so-called gods either in heaven or on earth — indeed, there are many "gods" and many "lords" —

6 yet for us there is one God, the Father,
from whom come all things and toward whom we tend;
and there is one Lord, Jesus Christ,
through whom all things come and through whom we are destined.

7 But all do not possess this knowledge. Some because of their habitual association up to this time with idols eat such meat as sacrificed to idols, and their conscience, being weak, is defiled. 8 Yet food will not bring us before God. We are neither worse off if we do not eat, nor better off if we do. 9 Only see to it that this very right of yours does not become a stumbling block for the weak. 10 For if someone sees you, with your knowledge, reclining at table in an idol's temple, will not his conscience, weak as it is, be emboldened to eat meat sacrificed to idols? 11 So because of your knowledge this weak person, a brother for whom Christ died, is brought to destruction. 12 When you sin in this way against your brothers and strike at their conscience, weak as it is, you are sinning against Christ. 13 Therefore, if food causes my brother to fall, I shall never eat meat again, so that I may not cause my brother to fall.

COMMENT

Paul now moves on to another topic, once again introduced by *peri de*, a topic that has caused trouble in the Christian community of Roman Corinth, about which he has learned in some way. There is no certainty that it was mentioned in the letter sent to him (7:1). There are, however, in this pericope a number of sayings that seem to reflect ideas that were being bandied about in the community, and Paul may be quoting them (vv. 1b, 4b) in order to comment on their pertinence to the topic at hand, viz., the eating in temple banquets of meat that has been sacrificed to idols. The topic of chap. 8 is linked to what follows up to 11:1, and indirectly with the eating of other food and the Lord's Supper in 10:14–22 and 11:17–34; this must be noted even though there are other topics that intrude into the discussion at times, some with abrupt transitions.

As with topics treated in earlier chapters, Paul sees the immediate problem of eating meat that has been sacrificed to idols against a larger background and with implications that some of the Corinthian Christians do not realize. This accounts for the manner in which he treats the topic, when he contrasts knowledge and love and introduces the question of sinning against fellow Christians, or even sinning against Christ himself in the eating of such food. Moreover, he relates the whole issue to a basic affirmation of Christian faith in vv. 5–6.

Paul begins his discussion of the topic with the eating of meat sacrificed to idols in a temple of a pagan god and how Christians should regard such a practice. In Roman Corinth, the cult of Greek, Roman, and other foreign gods was ubiquitous; it probably did not differ much from that of ancient Athens described by Luke in Acts 17:16, 22–23b. A glance at the plan of the excavated forum of Roman Corinth (fig. 2) detects the numerous temples and shrines in it dedicated to various gods that non-Christian Corinthians reverenced. Civic and social life in such a city would have meant an obligation to join in festivals, celebrations, and public ceremonies on occasions when religion and politics were not clearly demarcated; there were also many guilds of tradesmen and other voluntary associations in which specific gods were honored with banquets and sacrificial meals. Feasts in honor of various deities were celebrated regularly in numerous temples, when food (cereals, cheese, honey) were offered and animals (goats, cows, bulls, horses) were sacrificed to them, according to the manuals of the *pontifices*. The meat of animals so slaughtered, when not fully consumed in sacrifice, was often eaten by the offerers and attending temple servants. The latter sold at times the surplus meat on markets (see Ogilvie, *Romans and Their Gods*, 41–52, on the Roman mode of sacrifice; Scullard, *Festivals*, 22–27; Casabona, *Récherches*, 28–38).

For Jewish Christians in Corinth, such deities and the sacrifices made to them would have meant little or nothing, because they would have been guided by their own monotheistic tradition, which inveighed against foreign gods and was formulated in such OT passages as Deut 32:15–18 ("They provoked Him to jealousy with strange gods; with abominable practices they stirred Him to wrath"); Ps 106:34–39. Philo warned fellow Jews, who were inclined to join others in contributions (*symbolai*) and club subscriptions (*eranoi*), as he commented on Exod 23:2 about "following many to do evil" (*De inebrietate* 7 §§25–26).

For non-Jewish Corinthians converted to Christianity, however, banquets in Greek and Roman temples would have become a problem, because of their former habits of partaking in such banquets and the popular pressure of such customs. In this pericope, Paul recognizes the force of habit (8:7b) and the effect that the customary dining in temple ceremonies would create for some Corinthian Christians. Can Christians take part in such sacred meals offered to those gods and before their idols? Paul's reaction to this problem seems to be double. On the one hand, in vv. 1–6 he formulates a principle about idol meat: for Christians who love God, an idol is nothing at all, i.e., has no reality; so per se idol-meat would be inconsequential. On the other hand, however, in vv. 7–13 he realizes that the eating of meat sacrificed to idols in temple banquets could scandalize fellow Christians, especially those with weak consciences.

Three further pericopes will follow that are related to what Paul begins here. The first is a digression on his example as an apostle, sparked by what he will say in 8:13, in which he discusses his apostolic authority and his consequent right to receive support from the community that he has been serving, but also his restraint in the use of that right (9:1–27). The second pericope is again double, in which Paul reacts to the danger of idolatry in the Corinthian practice (10:1–22). Finally Paul adds his advice about eating at home meat bought in pagan markets or that which is to be consumed by one who is a guest invited to dine in a house of a Corinthian who is not a Christian (10:23–11:1).

Three interpretations of these chapters (8–10) are currently given.

1. Some commentators maintain that, though Paul agrees with those who possess knowledge (about the nonentity of idols and its implications), he encourages them to be sensitive of their fellow Christians who have a weak conscience about idol meat. So Barrett ("Things Sacrificed").
2. Others claim that Paul intends to persuade those who have knowledge to abstain completely from idol meats precisely because it has been associated so much with idolatry. So Cheung, Fee, Witherington.
3. Still others think that Paul seeks to persuade those who possess knowledge to adopt his policy of not using their very "right" to consume such idol meat even in temple banquets. So Still. The last mode of interpretation seems to be the best.

Even though these issues seem secondary to us many centuries later, they represent problems that can affect Christians of any age: e.g., the relation of the Christian community to the surrounding secular culture, the strained relations between individuals or groups within the community, and the problem of the relation of abstract knowledge to the pursuit of love or charity in the conduct of Christian life.

In this first pericope, Paul, who has at times already written about idolatry (1 Thess 1:9–10; Gal 4:8–9; 5:20), turns now to comment on eating food possibly related to it. *Pace* Garland (*1 Cor*, 353–54), there is no evidence that Paul has already "discussed this issue with the Corinthians," and none that Paul has taken up a new policy on idol meat "adopted by the apostolic council, which conflicted with his earlier instructions." Even though the same word *eidōlothyta*, "idol meats," also occurs in Acts 15:29, there is no indication in 8:1–10 or 10:19 of this letter, where the word appears, that the issue is the same as in Acts (see further below). In vv. 1–6, Paul agrees partly with the thinking of those Corinthian Christians who "possess knowledge": nothing is wrong with such idol meat per se; so they have a right to eat it. In vv. 7–13, however, Paul introduces a restriction about eating it, which comes not from the meat itself, but from the context in which it is eaten (in a temple banquet honoring a pagan god) and from one's concern for other individual fellow Christians, some of whose consciences may be weak in this regard. Hence one has to be guided, not only by knowledge, but also by love and concern, and indirectly by Paul's own example (as he argues in the end).

In developing his thoughts about this problem, Paul mentions certain basic ideas that Christians should be expected to know, but might overlook: (1) that an idol has no reality in this world (8:4b); (2) that there is no God but one (8:4c); (3) that the fundamental Christian confession is, One God and one Lord of all (8:6); (4) that food will not bring us closer to God (8:8a); and (5) that a fellow Christian, no matter how weak in conscience, is one for whom Christ has died (8:11).

The topic of chap. 8 and of 10:1–11:1, the eating of idol meat in different contexts, may seem to be related to Rom 14:1–15:13, part of a letter that Paul still has to compose. Some commentators assume that the problem of those "weak" in conscience in 1 Corinthians 8 is the same as that in Romans, because in both letters there is a common idea that what one eats may affect others. That, however, is a superficial way of discussing the matter, because there are notable differences in the two contexts:

1. In Romans, the contrast is between the "weak" (*asthenēs* or *adynatos*) and the "strong" (*dynatos*). Some commentators on 1 Corinthians also speak of the "strong," as if they were a group of Christians in Roman Corinth who differed from the weak group (e.g., Murphy-O'Connor, *St. Paul's Corinth*, 190; "Freedom," 545; Mitchell, *Paul*, 126 [she even identifies the "weak" and the "strong" as "factions within the community"]). Paul, however, never uses the expression, "the strong," in these chapters, and nothing indicates that either the weak or the strong were groups or factions. In this passage, Paul does speak of some individual Corinthians as *astheneis*, "weak," (8:9, 11) or of those whose conscience is "weak" (8:7, 10, 12; again 9:22); but they stand in contrast to those who "possess knowledge" (8:1b, 7, 10).

2. The kind of food is different. In 1 Corinthians, the problem is *eidōlothyta*, "meat sacrificed to idols" (8:1, 4, 7, 10; 10:19) or *hierothyton* (10:28), whereas in Romans the "weak" eat only vegetables (14:2) and the others "eat meat or drink wine" (14:21), and they are at length called "the strong" (15:1); the issue there is related to Jewish dietary regulations, whereas here the matter is pagan food. Paul fully agrees with the "strong" in Romans, when he declares "all things are indeed clean" (14:20), i.e., all foods can be eaten. In 1 Corinthians, however, he agrees only partly with those who "possess knowledge" that one can eat meat that has been sacrificed to idols, because "an idol is nothing at all in this world" (6:4); but one cannot eat it precisely "as sacrificed to idols" (6:7).

3. In 1 Corinthians, Paul speaks about a weak person's "conscience" (*syneidēsis*) being defiled, whereas that term, although it appears in Rom 2:15; 9:1; 13:5, is never used in the discussion about food in 14:1–15:13. There *pistis* occurs instead, which many translate as "faith," but which I prefer to render as "conviction" (see *Romans*, 686–700).

4. What Paul says in Romans is undoubtedly a more mature reflection on the problem of eating certain kinds of food, but it is understood there from the viewpoint of the Christian gospel and its implications. Here in 1 Corinthians, the issue is discussed from the more practical viewpoint of knowledge, love, conscience, and freedom.

The difference between the two types of Corinthian Christian individuals has been explained by Theissen (*Social Setting*, 121–43) as a clash between two socioeconomic groups, the indigent "weak" and the affluent "strong." The weak, as members of the lower strata of Corinthian society, would seldom have eaten meat in their everyday lives and when they did, it would have been as part of pagan religious celebrations, whence would have come their hesitations. The strong, however, were the prosperous group accustomed to eating meat, and they would have developed no negative reactions. Whether one can thus explain the difference between the weak and those possessing knowledge in this context is problematic. It has more recently been shown that, although meat was more expensive than such staples as cereals and vegetables, it was eaten more regularly by the nonprosperous in the Roman world than Theissen allows. Ancient writers have been cited in abundance to show how often meat was consumed (see Meggitt, "Meat Consumption"). Hence, one should be careful not to explain the contrast between the weak and those possessing knowledge in these Pauline chapters solely in terms of socioeconomic factors. It is important to note that, as Brunt has put it,

Paul treats the question [of idol meat] by changing the focus to the issue of Christian love rather than simply giving 'the answer' to the question, and in doing so he presents an example of principled, ethical thinking where love and respect for others transcend the rightness or wrongness of the act itself. The bottom line of Paul's treatment of the issue is not the eating or not eating of food offered to idols, but the love which should govern relationships where food offered to idols is concerned." ("Rejected, Ignored," 115)

Although the question in 8:1–13 has to do with *eidōlothyta*, "meats sacrificed to idols," Paul's treatment of it has nothing to do with the Jerusalem decision of Acts 15:13–29, *pace* T. W. Manson, "Corinthian Correspondence," 200–201; Hurd, *Origin*, 259–62; Barrett, "Things Sacrificed," 149–51; Garland, *1 Cor*, 353, 357.

That decision made in Jerusalem was sent by James and others in the form of a letter to the local churches of Antioch, Syria, and Cilicia. The letter uses the same term *eidōlothyta* in v. 29 as one of the four things that are to be avoided by Gentile Christians of those churches who are living in close proximity with Jewish Christians (food contaminated by idols, illicit marital unions, meat of strangled animals, and blood). As far as one can reconstruct the situation today, Paul knew nothing of that Jerusalem decision. Moreover, it had nothing to do with the other decision made at the "Council" (Acts 15:3–12), which settled in the negative the issue of circumcision and obligation to observe the Mosaic law for Gentile Christians. That "conciliar" decision corresponds to what Paul wrote about in Gal 2:1–10. There were two different Jerusalem decisions: one made by the "Council" (Acts 15:3–12), and the other made by James and others for the local churches of Antioch, Syria, and Cilicia (Acts 15:22–29). The latter Jerusalem decision was sent by James and other Jerusalem authorities, and it is often wrongly called "the Apostolic Decree" by many interpreters, who consider it to be a decision of the "Council." That is because they fail to recognize that Luke has joined the two Jerusalem decisions into one story and thereby gives the impression that the so-called Apostolic Decree was issued at the "Council" itself. Yet even in the Lucan story of Acts, Paul, who was present at the "Council" and refers to it in Gal 2:1–10, only learns about that second decision several years later from James himself, when he returns to Jerusalem at the end of his third missionary journey in Acts 21:25. Moreover, the eating of blood and of meat improperly slaughtered is wholly absent from this Corinthian passage, as is also *porneia* in the sense in which it is used in Acts. So the Corinthian question of the eating of idol meat while reclining at table in an idol's temple has to be interpreted in and for itself, without any reference to the abstract problem of Acts 15:22–29 (see further *Acts*, 538–69; cf. J. Weiss, *History of Primitive Christianity*, 1.260–61). Moreover, the later treatment of *eidōlothyta* by Luke in Acts 15 shows "no awareness of Paul's approach," despite Luke's interest in Paul's ministry (see Brunt, "Rejected, Ignored," 120). Hence, it is wrong to try to interpret these three chapters of 1 Corinthians in light of the Lucan story about a Jerusalem decree involving *eidōlothyta*, despite the use of the same term in Acts 15:29. There is no evidence that Paul had taught the Corinthians one thing about idol meat and that he had to change it in view of an alleged "new policy on idol food" (Garland, *1 Cor*, 353). The "conciliar" decision (Acts 15:3–12) and the letter sent by James and others (Acts 15:22–29) may have happened prior to Paul's writing of this letter to Corinthian Christians, but the Lucan account of those two Jerusalem decisions was not composed until several decades later, and that Lucan account shows no awareness of the problem that Paul is facing in this episode (see INTRODUCTION pp. 50–51).

Moreover, the issue of *eidōlothyta* in 1 Corinthians has nothing to do with the use of the word in Rev 2:14, 20, where it also occurs, along with *phagein*, "eat," and *porneusai*, "fornicate," despite the superficial pairing of such words. The referents there are rather Balaam and his influence at Peor (Num 31:16) and the Jezebel story (LXX 1 Kgs 16:31; 18:19). Even though Revelation was composed several decades after 1 Corinthians, the issue of *eidōlothyta* treated there shows no dependence on this Pauline letter. Similarly for the prohibition of eating *eidōlothyton* in *Did.* 6.3, which may repeat general NT teaching about it, but it scarcely echoes the nuanced Pauline treatment of the matter in this passage, especially because of the reason given there, *latreia gar esti theōn nekrōn*, "for it is the worship of dead gods."

Furthermore, it is sheer speculation to suggest that the question of eating idol meat in a pagan temple at Corinth was raised by the Cephas faction. Such a consideration would relate this question to the issue of the rivalries in chaps. 1–4, but there is no evidence in 1 Corinthians, even indirect, that connects these two matters, *pace* Barrett ("Things Sacrificed," 150).

This pericope is important, however, not only because of Paul's treatment of idol meat, knowledge, conscience, and love, but also because of the fundamental affirmation of Christian faith that it also contains about one God and one Lord in v. 6. Three questions are normally asked about this affirmation: Is Paul citing an already existent formula? What literary form is involved in it? What intellectual background does it reflect?

To the first question, some commentators regard the affirmation as a citation of a preexistent formula, because its formulation is somewhat different from Paul's usual mode of expression: "The phrasing has not been chosen by Paul ad hoc. The content is not 'Pauline'; and it reaches far beyond the context" (Conzelmann, *1 Cor*, 144 n. 38). The phrase *heis theos ho patēr* does not appear elsewhere in the Pauline corpus, and the relation of Christ to *ta panta* as one of mediation is expressed only here. So it seems most likely that Paul is borrowing a pre-Pauline formula.

Apropos of the second question, Murphy-O'Connor ("I Cor., viii, 6," 254–59) has shown that the formula is not a confession, but an acclamation, a spontaneous reaction of wonder at the power experienced by adherents of a deity (recall that of Acts 19:28, 34: "Great is Artemis of the Ephesians"). He agrees with Kerst ("1 Kor 8,6") that it is most likely a baptismal acclamation, and it would be acclaiming "the salvific action of God in Christ," which is derived from some pre-Pauline liturgical usage.

Third, the background of the acclamation is double, because the first part echoes the OT monotheistic affirmation of "one God" (Deut 5:7; 6:4), and the second part echoes the primitive Christian kerygma (cf. 1 Cor 12:3; Rom 10:9). Conzelmann (*1 Cor*, 144 n. 38) has analyzed it as "a formal framework into which the detailed, in itself independent, Christological exposition was inserted." That does not say much, however, about the double set of prep. phrases. Others have related them to various Greek philosophical formulas. Ever since the studies of Norden (*Agnostos Theos*, 240–50), Peterson (*Heis Theos*, 253–56), and Dupont (*Gnosis*, 335–41), many interpreters have related the acclamation to Greek Stoic cosmological formulas that speak of *panta*, "all things" or *to pan*, "the All" (= the universe), with parallel prep. phrases. These are said to have influenced Paul here and also in 1 Cor 11:12; Rom 11:36; Col 1:16–20. The Pauline acclamation is not simply the same as the pantheistic formula, *hen to pan kai di' autou to pan kai eis auto to pan* ("All is one, and through it [comes] all; and for it the all exists," *Alchim. Gr.* 133 [Norden, *Agnostos Theos*, 249]), even though it may come close to the Stoic doxology found in second-century Marcus Aurelius, *Medit.* 4.23: *ō physis, ek sou panta, en soi panta, eis se panta*, "O Nature, from you are all things, in you are all, toward you are all" (said of the World [as a Stoic deity]). However, the double set of phrases is not fully accounted for, because different sorts of causality are expressed in them. More recently Horsley ("The Background") has called attention to formulas derived from earlier Greek philosophical writings, Platonic and Aristotelian, which were used of the *archai*, "(primal) causes," and were taken over by Philo of Alexandria (*Quaestiones in Genesim* 1.58 or *De Cherubim* 35 §§125–27). They explain better the background of the Pauline double acclamation with its diverse prep. phrases expressing different causalities.

Murphy-O'Connor, however, has questioned this cosmological interpretation of v. 6 in this chapter. He rightly notes that Rom 11:36 may be similar to the Stoic parallels, because there Paul's prep. phrases all refer to the same subject: *ex autou kai di' autou kai eis auton ta panta*. This, however, is not true of 1 Cor 8:6, where there is a twice-repeated shift from *ta panta* to *hēmeis*, and the four prep. phrases (*ex hou, di' hou, di' autou, eis auton*) do not refer to the same subject. Hence there are no precise parallels for this Pauline formulation, which both Norden and Dupont themselves had to admit. Moreover, Murphy-O'Connor has rightly argued that no convincing evidence has been brought forth to show that Paul's formulation has "a purely cosmological meaning" ("I Cor., viii, 6," 262). Some Pauline passages may be evocative of Stoic parallels (Rom 11:36; 1 Cor 11:12; Col 1:16–20; Eph 4:6), but he queries whether *ta panta* in them really "means 'das All,' " and whether, even in Rom 11:36, Paul is "thinking in cosmic terms" (ibid., 263). Elsewhere in Pauline letters *ta panta* is referred to God in a soteriological sense (1 Cor 2:10–13; 12:4–6; 2 Cor 4:14–15; 5:18; Rom 8:28, 31–32), and in light of this usage the soteriological sense of v. 4 must be stressed. The acclamation, therefore, expresses a movement and a direction, which can be paraphrased: "From God come all things which enable us to return to him. All these things are given through Christ and in him we go to the Father" (ibid., 265). That is what has to be emphasized in the interpretation of this chapter. This Pauline passage is remarkably relevant now.

> In countries with a religiously mixed population, Christians are constantly confronted with analogous situations which involve questions of religious collaboration, integration, syncretism, apartheid and social obligations toward non-Christians concerning some form of cultic involvement. On a broader scale, whatever the cultural background may be, every Christian community has to deal with basic ethical problems comparable to those raised by the conflict in Corinth. Paul's nuanced reaction and masterly solution appears to be of lasting relevance." (Delobel, "Coherence and Relevance," 190)

Paul shows that

> acting on the basis of mere propositional knowledge about God is insufficient. Believers must understand fully the broad sweep of theological implications and let their conduct be leavened with love. Presuming to possess knowledge gives one a false sense of superiority and security. Fee . . . states, "The abuse of others in the name of 'knowledge' indicates a total misunderstanding of the nature of Christian ethics, which springs not from knowledge but from love." Love deflates the vanity and arrogance that knowledge feeds and disarms it so that it is not used to hurt others. (Garland, *1 Cor*, 391–92)

NOTES

8:1. *Now for meat sacrificed to idols.* Lit. "but concerning things (cultically) sacrificed to an idol." The compound Greek noun *eidōlothyton* is rare and usually is said to be derived from Jewish usage (Büchsel, *TDNT* 2:373; Songer, "Problems,"

364), with a derogatory connotation, because it is a combination of *eidōlon*, "idol" (a noun that often occurs in the LXX) and the substantivized Greek verbal adj., *thyton*, "something offered by burning." Christian writers imitate the Jewish usage (Acts 15:29; 21:25; Rev 2:14, 20; *Did.* 6.3). Usually Greek speakers would say *hierothyton*, "something sacred offered/sacrificed (to a deity)," which appears in 10:28, where a Greek is being quoted. However, *eidōlothyton* occurs in earlier(?) Jewish Greek writings only in 4 Macc 5:2 (dated A.D. 35–118) and perhaps in *Or. Sibyll.* 2.96 (if that passage is not influenced by Acts 15). Afterwards, it is abundantly attested in patristic writings (Witherington, "Not so Idle Thoughts," but his distinction between *eidōlothyton* as an animal sacrificed before an idol and eaten in its presence and *hierothyton* as meat coming from an idol's temple and eaten elsewhere is not certainly correct). From v. 7b, one learns that the problem in vv. 1–13 is not the meat in itself, but the "eating" of it by converts while "reclining at table in an idol's temple" (v. 10), i.e., eating it precisely as sacrificed to a pagan god (*hōs eidōlothyton*), as Fee rightly insists ("*Eidōlothyta* Once Again"). Before he takes up that aspect, however, Paul discusses idol meat and its relation to Christian faith and more generally to abstract knowledge and love among Christians.

Portions of sacrificial meat were burned on altars of a Greek or Roman god (Aristotle, *Oeconomica* 1349b 13; Plutarch, *Quaest. conviv.* 8.8.3 §729c), as the deity's portion, but other portions were either consumed in the temple by those offering sacrifice (thus honoring the god), or sold later on the market (*makellon*, 10:25); the problem of such meat in markets will preoccupy Paul in chap. 10.

we realize that "we all possess knowledge." I.e., about such matters as eating *eidōlothyta*. Again Paul, making use of diatribe-like style, quotes a Corinthian slogan and agrees with it in principle, even if he qualifies it in the following comment (vv. 1c–3b). The slogan sounds like an aphorism, and it may be just another way of saying what was in another slogan, "For me all things are permissible" (6:12). Undoubtedly it was being bandied about by individual Christians with a robust conscience, by those "possessing knowledge." "All" means not all human beings, but all individuals who utter such a slogan. Why their stance is described in terms of "knowledge" will emerge in v. 4, where its connotation has to do with a philosophical estimate of idols. *Pace* Fee (*1 Cor*, 366 n. 34) and Garland (*1 Cor*, 368), "knowledge" here is hardly "a gift of the Spirit" or an "illumination that comes from the Spirit," because, if it were, Paul would not say about it what appears in his next comment. The idiom *gnōsin echein*, "have or possess knowledge," is found in the LXX (Hos 4:6; 2 Macc 6:30). Needless to say, this mention of *gnōsis* has nothing to do with Gnosticism, which should not be introduced into the understanding of what Paul says or presupposes here.

As Paul introduces his own critical comment, he says *oidamen*, "we realize," identifying himself with Corinthian Christians to whom he is writing, perhaps even borrowing the first plural from the slogan quoted. He himself uses *oidamen* elsewhere at times (8:4; 2 Cor 5:1; Rom 2:2; 3:19; 7:14; 8:22, 28); but some commentators prefer to read here *oida men*, "I realize," with the contrasting particle *men*, noting that MS P⁴⁶ reads the corresponding *de* in the following sentence. To accept that reading, however, would be to destroy the important parallel between 8:1b and 8:4, where the first plur. *oidamen* occurs again, after Paul's critical comment in 8:2–3.

Knowledge puffs up, but love builds up. So Paul qualifies the Corinthian slogan; in v. 7 he will comment further on it. Knowledge, he knows, is important, when it is right, but it can lead to arrogance, and he has already used the verb *physioō*, "puff up," in 4:6, 18, 19; 5:2 to indicate other ways in which Corinthian Christians were acting arrogantly (in asserting allegiance to a favorite preacher; in tolerating incest in their midst). Now he applies it to a more abstract matter, *gnōsis*, "knowledge," which can puff up without filling. As Greeks, with a noble heritage in their philosophical tradition in which "knowledge" was esteemed, such Christians may have been defending their stance by appealing to that heritage. Paul, however, proposes another consideration, viz., the edifying or upbuilding character of *agapē*, "love," which must be the measure of all Christian conduct and freedom. This factor has already been mentioned in 4:21 (in an entirely different context), and to it he will return in 13:1–13, esp. 13:4. Such "love" must be shown to all, especially to "a brother for whom Christ died" (v. 11), weak though he may be.

Although Paul recognizes a certain kind of "knowledge" to be among the *pneumatika* bestowed by the Spirit (12:8), he will express his reservations even about such an endowment in his treatment of love in 13:2, 8. The reason for his reservation is set forth now: its possible tendency to arrogance, along with its inability to do what love can do, i.e., to "build up" (as in 3:10–17; 10:23; 14:4, 17), or have a salutary effect on the community as a whole; cf. 1 Thess 5:11. For the proper Christian relationship of love to knowledge, see Phil 1:9–10, where Paul prays that his addressees' love may increase ever more and more in knowledge and every kind of perception. What Paul says now about knowledge and love is echoed in the third-century Coptic *Gospel of Philip* 110a: " 'Knowledge' of the truth lifts up . . . , 'but love builds up' " (see Schneemelcher, *NTApocr*, 1:202).

2. *If anyone imagines that he knows something, he does not yet know it as he ought to.* Paul introduces two parallel simple conditional sentences in vv. 2–3 to explain what he said in v. 1cd (BDF §372.2). The first one stresses that one should not be too confident about what one claims to know, because proper knowledge has its conditions. But what does Paul mean by "something" (omitted, by homoeoteleuton, in the oldest Greek MS, P⁴⁶), and what does he imply by the "not yet"? Since the latter adv. is scarcely an allusion to the afterlife, it may refer to better or more profound wisdom "in this age" (3:18). The "something" is a topic only partly understood now; but if one had real knowledge of it, one would perhaps be less confident. Eventually, however, that "something" turns out to be God, as the following verse suggests, supported by v. 6 (so Conzelmann, *1 Cor*, 141 n. 16). *Kathōs dei*, "as one ought to," suggests that genuine knowledge is something relative; cf. Rom 8:26; 12:3. One can understand something to a degree, but not fully comprehend it without an affectionate awareness that should accompany it. Hence real Christian knowledge cannot be content with the mere acquisition of information about a thing, even about God (or gods). For that kind of knowledge depends on God's knowing of the human person: God's initiative, accepted in

faith, results in knowledge of Him, and above all in love of Him, as the next verse makes clear. As a result, love becomes more important than knowledge.

3. *But if anyone loves God, that one is known by him.* This second condition expresses the important alternative, as it introduces "love" and its object, which is no longer a vague "something," but "God," as in Deut 6:5; 10:12; 11:1, 13, 22; Josh 22:5; Ps 18:1; 31:22. Although its apodosis (*houtos egnōstai hyp' autou,* "that one is known by him") might seem at first sight to be ambiguous, because the masc. prons., *houtos* or *autou* could refer either to *tis,* "anyone," or to *theon,* "God," Paul's words echo an OT sentiment: "The Lord knows those who are his" (LXX Num 16:5 [even quoted in 2 Tim 2:19]). See also Ps 139:1; Deut 34:10. Paul thus continues to explain the role of love that he mentioned in v. 1, because without love real knowledge cannot exist. Knowledge and love are related, but each in a different way. The love of God that a Christian may have has already been mentioned in 2:9 (see NOTE there *ad finem*) and will reappear in Rom 8:28 (a problematic verse transmitted in diverse forms; see *Romans,* 523–24). Such a love is very different from the knowledge one has of things in this world. In fact, it springs from the fact that such a lover has already been known by no one other than God. Implied is the love that God has for such a known one and the way that it has been manifested by divine election. Paul will return to this proper form of knowledge and love in 13:12. Cf. Gal 4:9, where Paul speaks of reciprocal knowledge; also 1 John 4:19, where it is a matter of reciprocal love. Paul is using this idea of the love of God, which he has inherited from his Jewish background, to offset any merely abstract knowledge of God (*ginōskein theon*), and this is important for his entire discussion in chaps. 8–10 (see Wischmeyer, *"Theon agapan"*). Thus Paul relates "knowledge" about meat sacrificed to idols to what a Christian should really know and realize about how related love can build up. Such knowledge will provide the proper perspective to judge idols, as v. 4 will show.

The oldest MS of 1 Corinthians (P[46]) lacks both *ton theon* and *hyp' autou,* and the latter phrase is absent also in MSS ℵ*, 33, resulting in the strange reading, "if anyone loves, that one is known," declared by Fee to be "the Pauline original or else the work of an editorial genius" (*1 Cor,* 367). See, however, Metzger, *TCGNT,* 490–91 for a better assessment of the reading: a correction probably introduced as a parallel to v. 2 by a scribe who expected Paul was going to say, "If anyone loves God, this man truly knows him," but the surprising turn of expression is characteristically Pauline (Gal 4:9; cf. also 1 Cor 13:12).

4. *So about eating meat sacrificed to idols: we know that "an idol is nothing at all in this world" and that "there is no God but one."* Again Paul quotes two sayings being used as slogans by the Corinthian Christians who "possess knowledge." It is difficult to express in English the parallelism of the two verbless Greek sayings: "(there is) no idol in the world" (*or* "an idol in the world [is] nothing") and "(there is) no God but one." Emphasis falls on the nonexistence of the idol (i.e., no divine being really exists in the idol, 1 Thess 1:9) and on the uniqueness of God. An idol was supposed to be an image of a Canaanite, Greek, Roman, or Egyptian god; so if such gods really do not exist, their idols are meaningless entities (see Giblin, "Three Monotheistic," 529–32). Hence food offered to them cannot be contaminated or affected by them (see 10:19). Christians in Roman Corinth "possessing

knowledge" (8:10) were exercising their right and freedom with such slogans, even sharing in temple banquets, because their outlook was untroubled by such nonentities as unreal idols.

The first saying reflects the OT prohibition of idols: Lev 19:4 ("you shall not follow after idols"); 26:1 (called in Hebrew 'ĕlîlîm, "nonentities," but in the LXX eidōla); Deut 32:21; Jer 8:19c; 10:8 (called in Hebrew hăbālîm, lit. "vapors, breaths," but in the LXX eidōla or mataia, "vanities"); Ps 115:4–8; LXX 1 Chr 16:26, "All the gods of the nations are idols, but our God has made the heavens." Sometimes Jewish teaching equated idols with "demons" (daimonia, Deut 32:17; Ps 106:36–37). The etymology of the Hebrew word for idol ('ĕlîl) is uncertain, but it is often explained as "worthless" or "nonentity" (TDOT, 1:285). If the latter meaning were correct, those who "possess knowledge" might have been using the basic sense of the term in calling it "nothing at all." This term became frequent for "idols" in the later rabbinic tradition (see Str-B, 3:53–60), naively used by some commentators as if it might have some relevance for interpreting first-century Greek texts (e.g., Garland, 1 Cor, 372, quoting the sixth-century Babylonian Talmud, 'Abod. Zar. 55a).

The second slogan echoes the famous commandment or Šĕma' of ancient Israel, Deut 6:4, "Hear, O Israel: Yahweh is our God, Yahweh alone" (MT: Yhwh 'eḥād). This becomes in the LXX: akoue, Israēl, kyrios ho theos hēmōn kyrios heis estin, "Hear, O Israel, the Lord is our God, the Lord alone." So the oneness of the God of Israel was emphasized, and Paul repeats it in his own formulation (see also LXX Deut 4:35, 39; Isa 44:6, 8; 45:5).

5. For even if there are so-called gods either in heaven or on earth—indeed there are many "gods" and many "lords." Lit. ". . . , as there are (indeed). . . ." Paul makes a concession for the sake of his argument, admitting that he is aware of the belief of Canaanites, Egyptians, Greeks, Romans, and others in many "gods" (e.g., El, Elyan, Baal; Horus, Isis, Osiris; Zeus, Apollo, Athena, Aphrodite, Poseidon, Dionysus, Ares, Artemis; Jupiter, Mars, Juno, Minerva, Roma) and their respect for many "heroes" called kyrioi (apotheosized humans such as Heracles, Asclepius, various Roman emperors, who were accorded the title divus), as well as of the sacrifices offered in honor of such beings. He is recalling this fact to all Corinthians, but especially to the individual Christians who "possess knowledge" and who have been asserting their right and freedom to eat idol meat. Although idols are nonentities, many people subjectively consider them to be really existent, and Pausanias (Descr. Graec. 1–5) lists the gods worshipped by Corinthians in the second century of the Christian era.

Theos, "god," and thea, "goddess," were titles given in the contemporary Greco-Roman world to awesome transcendent beings believed to exercise control over human life and affairs and to bestow benefits on human beings (see Acts 7:40, 43; 12:22; 19:37; 28:6; 2 Thess 2:4). In the Greek world, polytheism or the belief in many gods (in a hierarchical system, with Zeus as the "father of men and gods" (patēr andrōn te theōn te, Homer, Iliad 15.47), was typical in the Greco-Roman period. See Betz, EDNT, 140–42; Kleinknecht, TDNT, 65–79 (on the Greek concept of deity); Anderson, IDB, 2:407–17 (on names of gods).

Kyrios, "lord," occurs absolutely as a Greek title for both gods and human rulers in the ancient world of the eastern Mediterranean area, being attested from at least the beginning of the first century B.C. in texts from Egypt, Syria, and Asia Minor (see Fauth, "Kyrios," *Der kleine Pauly*, 3:413–17; Fitzmyer, "Semitic Background," 135 n. 26).

The words *eiper einai*, "even if there are," express a simple, real condition (BDF §372), which is not contrary to fact, and to it corresponds the clause, *hōsper einai*, lit. "as there are (indeed)," which means that the verb in each case has to be understood in the same sense. Although it might seem that Paul is thus affirming the existence of such beings, it is really his way of expressing his awareness of a belief in their alleged existence and of worship of them, or perhaps his awareness of the reality of idols that depict them. It is probably the latter, because elsewhere he speaks more negatively, e.g., in Gal 4:8, "You were enslaved to gods that by nature do not exist" (*tois physei mē ousin theois*).

The phrase "either in heaven or on earth" expresses only a lack of interest in detail, as in 3:22; it is not an attempt to universalize or to admit that some gods are active in an upperworld and others in the underworld, or even to reckon with deified Roman rulers. Lindemann (*1 Cor*, 191) understands both v. 5 and v. 6 to be an anacoluthon.

6. *yet for us there is one God, the Father, from whom come all things and toward whom we tend.* This verse begins with *all' hēmin*, "but for us," an adversative conj. that seems to begin Paul's reaction, although Hofius ("Einer ist Gott," 99–101) would understand vv. 4–6 as a quotation from the letter of the Corinthians. In this context, *hēmin* does not mean "for us human beings," but "for us Christians" (a so-called ethical dative, BDF §192: *dativus commodi*), who are thus set over against heathen contemporaries.

Paul now gives a summary of traditional Christian belief in one God, which restates the monotheism inherited from Judaism and stands over against the polytheism expressed in v. 5. As Conzelmann has put it, "The gods *become* gods by being believed in, and faith in the *one* God and the *one* Lord creates freedom no longer to recognize these powers" (*1 Cor*, 145). The uniqueness of God is repeated in Rom 3:29–30, the God not only of Jews, but of Gentiles too. Faith in the "one God" means belief in His sameness toward all human beings (see Demke, " 'Ein Gott' ").

In the first statement, *heis theos*, "one God," echoes the OT tradition (LXX Deut 6:4, quoted above; see also LXX Deut 32:39; Isa 43:10–11; 44:6; 45:6); but it is modified in two ways. First, *heis theos* is explained as *ho patēr*, which has to be taken as the distinctively Christian epithet for God. God is now understood as the origin or source from which come all things (11:12), as well as the blessings that Christians enjoy; and He is likewise the goal of Christian existence. The two prep. phrases express God's efficient and final causality in Pauline soteriology: *ex hou*, "from whom," and *eis auton*, "toward Him" (see Rom 11:36a).

For Paul's own use of *patēr* as a title for God, see 1:3; 15:24; 2 Cor 1:2, 3; 11:31; Rom 1:7; 6:4; 8:15; 15:6; etc. In the OT, God is acknowledged as Father of corporate Israel: "Has not one God created us? Is there not one Father of all of us?" (LXX Mal 2:10; cf. Isa 63:16; 64:8; Deut 32:6; Jer 3:19; 31:9; Ps 103:13; *TDNT*, 5:973–74). In saying "one God," Paul means not only an indivisible or discretely unique being, but also "one" in contrast to the "many" gods just mentioned, something like Eph 4:6, *heis theos kai patēr pantōn*, "one God and father of all."

Although many commentators speak of Paul's cosmic perspective, expressed in both clauses by *ta panta*, "all things," which is supposed to echo Stoic philosophical usage, the Pauline (or better, the pre-Pauline) formulation found here differs considerably from such usage (see COMMENT above).

Second, the first statement is joined by the parallel statement about "one Lord," with two further explicative prep. phrases. The whole complex is a double nominal sentence, which needs no verbs in Greek, but which has to be rendered with verbs in English, and the peculiar sense of the prep. phrases has to be filled out (see Sagnard, "A propos"). The bountiful activity is initiated by the Father, but it is mediated by the Lord, as the following clause makes clear.

and there is one Lord, Jesus Christ, through whom all things come and through whom we are destined. Lit. "through whom all things and we through him," an ellipsis with two pregnant prep. phrases, *di' hou* and *di' autou*. Just as *ho patēr* was used as the Christian epithet for *theos*, so now *Iēsous Christos* is given as the name of the specifically Christian *kyrios*. He is further understood not only as the mediator through whom (*di' hou*) all things come to be, but also as the means through whom (*di'autou*) Christians attain the goal of their existence, that toward which Christians are tending or are destined (viz., the *eis auton* of v. 6b). The two prep. phrases express instrumental causality with reference to origin and goal.

Although Murphy-O'Connnor (*NJBC*, 806) says, "There is no allusion to the preexistence of Christ," Lindemann rightly speaks of the *kyrios* here as "the preexistent mediator of creation" in his explanation of the first phrase (*1 Cor*, 193); similarly Collins (*1 Cor*, 320); Conzelmann (*1 Cor*, 145); Fee (*1 Cor*, 375–76); Héring (*1 Cor*, 66); Kremer (*1 Cor*, 175); Merklein (*1 Cor*, 2:190); Robertson-Plummer (*1 Cor*, 168); J. Weiss (*1 Cor*, 225). What was asserted as the role of personified Wisdom in creation in the OT (Prov 8:22, 27, 30; Wis 9:1–2; cf. Jer 10:12) or of God's word (Ps 33:9; Sir 42:15) is now predicated of Christ himself (cf. John 1:3; Col 1:15–16). The second phrase, however, goes beyond that, as it hints at Christ's soteriological role on behalf of Christians, viz., his mediatorial role in their destiny as well or in the goal of the "new creation."

Although this Pauline acclamation is being made over against the polytheism of the Greco-Roman world, in which Corinthian Christians were living, the distinction that Paul makes between *heis theos* and *heis kyrios* (note the parallel anarthrous use of *heis*) sets him over against his own Jewish background. This is clear when one compares this acclamation with Deut 10:17, which reads:

ho gar kyrios ho theos hymōn,	For the Lord (is) your God;
houtos theos tōn theōn kai kyrios tōn kyriōn,	he is God of gods and Lord of lords,
ho theos ho megas kai ischyros kai ho phoberos,	a great, mighty, and awesome God.

A binitarian pattern of Christianity is likewise expressed here; it is the origin of the worship of Christ, who is reverenced along with the God of Judaism (see Hurtado, "Origins"). For a likely explanation of the development of this pre-Pauline acclamation, see Langkammer ("Literarische und theologische Einzelstücke"), who ascribes to Paul himself its soteriological nuances.

7. *But all do not possess this knowledge.* Lit. "but (this) knowledge is not in all (people)." Although the explanation given in vv. 4bc–6 refers immediately to the knowledge of those designated by the "we know" of v. 4, it indirectly includes the "all" who "possess knowledge" (v. 1) about the eating of meat sacrificed to idols; thus it has corrected the slogan quoted in v. 1b. Having laid down the monotheistic and Christological basis of his argument in vv. 4bc–6, Paul now returns to the problem of v. 1b and qualifies it still further, denying that "all possess knowledge." At first he continues in the 3d pers. plur., which he had been using in the foregoing verses.

For there are among Corinthian Christians some individuals who "do not possess" such knowledge, because they are still influenced by their former ways of thinking about gods and food associated with sacrifices to them. They regard the eating of such food as the consuming of it in honor of a pagan god. These individuals cannot "bring themselves to believe that these gods, who formerly seemed so real, were in fact nothing" (Dawes, "The Danger," 89).

Some because of their habitual association up to this time with idols eat such meat as sacrificed to idols, and their conscience, being weak, is defiled. Paul recognizes the force of habit (what people had been doing before conversion) and realizes that some of them have not yet fully adjusted their outlook to their new situation, i.e., to the monotheism of Christianity and the reverence of the risen Christ. The danger they face is that, if they "eat such meat as sacrificed to idols" (*hōs eidōlothyton*), their conscience is defiled. This is the major problem that Paul discusses, as Fee rightly recognizes ("*Eidolōthyta* Once Again"), *pace* Fisk ("Eating"). In using "weak," Paul may be adopting a term employed by the knowledgeable Corinthian Christians who were referring to confrères as such (Collins, *1 Cor*, 326), or he himself may be constructing hypothetically a title for such individuals (Hurd, *Origin*, 125). He predicates that name of them in vv. 9, 11, but here he applies it to their "conscience." That into which the weak are being led is the "sin of idolatry, which is so forcefully condemned in chap. 10. In particular, the behavior of those 'having knowledge' is leading the 'weak' into the mistaken judgment that they may take part in cultic meals in pagan temples. Because the 'weak' lack a clear conviction regarding the nonexistence of pagan gods, this action is for them an act of idolatry" (ibid., 98). Since Paul says "up to this time," he is not speaking of Jewish Christians, but is alluding to the pagan past of other Corinthian Christians.

The best reading is *synētheia*, "habit, habitual association," but some MSS (ℵ², D, G, 88, 614) have *syneidēsei*, "conscience," a copyist's error or, more likely, assimilation to that word in the next clause.

Although Paul spoke of himself in 4:4 with the cog. verb, *ouden . . . emautō synoida*, "I am not conscious of anything," he now uses the noun *syneidēsis* for the first time (see also 8:10, 12; 10:25, 27, 28, 29 bis; 2 Cor 1:12; 4:2; 5:11; Rom 2:15; 9:1; 13:5). In fact, this is its earliest occurrence in the NT, and some say that Paul first introduced the notion into Christian writings (*EDNT*, 3:301). In the Greek language, *syneidēsis* first appeared in the sense of "consciousness, awareness of information about something" (Chrysippus, quoted in Diogenes Laertius, *Vitae* 7.85: "every animal has consciousness of its makeup"; cf. LXX Qoh 10:20). In time it was applied to the awareness one has of deeds about to be done or already done, especially in regard to their good or bad character. As such, it is a quality of the "mind" that acts as a moral arbiter or internal judge of what is right or wrong, as a guide for coming moral action, but also as a judge of one's past actions or of those of others. Indeed, some Pauline instances of *nous*, "mind," function in the same way (Rom 7:23, 25). *Syneidēsis* has no counterpart in the Hebrew OT or in QL; it is a Greek notion derived from contemporary popular philosophy. It enters the Jewish tradition via the LXX (Qoh 10:20 [as a translation of Hebrew *madda'*, "knowledge"]); is found in deuterocanonical Wis 17:10; and perhaps in Sir 42:18. In LXX Job 27:6 one finds the cog. verb, *synoida emautō*, "I am conscious of. " That *syneidēsis* in the moral sense is derived from Stoicism is hardly correct, as is sometimes held; so Pierce has shown (*Conscience*, 13–20).

What is important to realize in the Pauline use of the term, however, is the influence of what *Tôrāh*, "law," meant for a Jew, for this colors somewhat the Greek notion, as Thrall has rightly noted ("Pauline Use"). See further *PAHT*, §PT144; *Romans*, 128; Gooch, "Conscience"; Dawes, "The Danger," 93–97.

The conscience of the weak is defiled (*molynetai*), because, in eating *eidōlothyta* precisely, "as sacrificed to idols," that person's conscience is stained by an idolatrous act. However, the person who "possesses knowledge" (that an idol is nothing) does not regard meat eaten in a pagan temple in that way, "as sacrificed to idols." Paul makes no effort here to correct or strengthen the weak persons; instead he seeks only to have others respect such fellow Christians; in 10:14–22, he will again address the problem, from a slightly different perspective.

8. *Yet food will not bring us before God.* The shift from the 3d pers. plur., used in v. 7 and the foregoing verses, to the 1st pers. plur. is undoubtedly a sign that this whole verse might well be a saying that those who "possess knowledge" in the Corinthian community were actually using (Grosheide, *1 Cor*, 194; Murphy-O'Connor, "Food," 293). It reads like a protest from them and may be another way of phrasing the slogan about food in 6:13. God, who is said there to do away with both food and stomach, may now be thought of as a judge, because the verb *parastēsei* can have the nuance of "bringing" a matter "before" a judge, as in 2 Cor 4:14; cf. Rom 14:10. The forensic nuance is not certain, and perhaps it means only "to bring close to God" (BDAG, 778). "The men of knowledge deny that they are in any danger of incurring the wrath of God, and in order to drive this point home offer a concrete criterion" (Murphy-O'Connor, "Food," 297), which follows in the rest of the verse. Although Paul makes the saying his own, he does not say that one has to eat idol meat to prove that one is free; he leaves it open, to eat or not to eat. Some MSS (‭א‬², D, Ψ, 1881 and the Koine text-tradition), however, read the pres. verb *paristēsi* (and F, G have *synistēsi*, "brings together"), which might be an attempt to line up v. 8a with v. 8bc, where the verbs are in the present tense.

We are neither worse off if we do not eat, nor better off if we do. Lit. "neither, if we do not eat, are we left deficient, nor, if we do eat, do we have abundance," i.e., left with a deficiency or an abundance of divine approval. *Pace* Collins (*1 Cor*, 321, 325), the main verbs do not mean "be inferior," "be superior"; they express a lack or an abundance.

The reading translated in the lemma is that of MSS P⁴⁶, A*, B, 33*, 1739, etc., whereas MSS D, F, G, and many patristic citations invert the verbs, putting the positive first, "neither, if we eat, do we have an abundance, nor, if we do not eat, are we left deficient." A third reading is given by MSS A², 17, which transposes the negative *mē* from the second to the first clause (in the second reading above), "neither, if we do not eat, do we have an abundance, nor, if we eat, are we left deficient." Zuntz (*The Text*, 161–62) prefers the second reading; Murphy-O'Connor ("Food," 295), the third reading ("it is precisely what one would have expected the Corinthian men of knowledge to have said"); but the majority of commentators adopt the first reading (many of whom do not discuss the text-critical problem). Lindemann (*1 Cor*, 196) argues against the third reading and rightly defends the first. Paul is drawing a conclusion from the explanation already given in vv. 4–6, according to which the eating of *eidōlothyta* is per se indifferent; but the quoted saying speaks only of "food" (*brōma*), not of *eidōlothyta*; and of "eating" in general, not *hōs eidōlothyton* (v. 7).

Murphy-O'Connor ("Food," 298) considers the "abundance" to be a reference to spiritual gifts, which are neither increased nor decreased as one abstains or partakes, because the verb *perisseuō* is invariably used by Paul "in reference to spiritual goods of the New Age." Similarly Garland, *1 Cor*, 385. This meaning is not impossible, but it is far from certain; and Paul's real concern is something different, as the following verse reveals.

9. *Only see to it that this very right of yours does not become a stumbling block for the weak.* Shifting to the 2d pers. plur., Paul addresses his imperative to imaginary individuals among the Corinthian Christians who "possess knowledge." Even though he agrees basically with their thinking, he refuses to go along with their conclusion and their conduct, because he is concerned about the influence their thinking may have on fellow Christians. The "right" (*exousia*) of such knowledgeable Christians to freedom of judgment about such food and consequent consumption of it cannot be the ultimate criterion of Christian conduct, especially if it may become *proskomma*, "a stumbling block," for a weak fellow Christian. The contrast is between a "right" and a "stumbling block." In Rom 14:13, Paul uses *proskomma ē skandalon*, "a stumbling block or an obstacle," in a very similar way.

B. Winter (*After Paul Left*, 5) illustrates the "right," of which Paul speaks, with that of those who enjoyed Corinthian (i.e., Roman) citizenship and could attend the civic dinners that the president of the Isthmian Games regularly hosted in the temple of Poseidon at nearby Isthmia (see Gebhard, "Isthmian Games"). Converts to Christianity with weak consciences would have been uncertain and hesitant about partaking in such dinners, whereas those for whom an idol was "nothing," would have exploited such a "right." Even if those who possess knowledge have the right to eat at such dinners, Paul in this pericope is not relating their consumption of such food to idolatry and demons, as he will later (10:1–22). He does not say here that the act in which the right is exercised "inherently defiles the knower. The only warning deals with the effect on the weaker brother" (Still, "Paul's Aims," 335). In view of this, Paul is building up his argument for the nonuse of the right that those who possess knowledge actually have.

10. *For if someone sees you, with your knowledge, reclining at table in an idol's temple.* Lit. "you (sing.) possessing knowledge." Paul now gives a specific example, switching to the 2d pers. sing., as he speaks of an individual who possesses knowledge. Reference is being made to banquets that Corinthians held, not necessarily in the main part of a temple, but in side rooms often constructed with *triclinia* (three-sided, U-shaped benches on which diners reclined while eating). Murphy-O'Connor has called attention to the Corinthian temple Asclepieion, which had been constructed originally in the fourth century B.C., damaged when the city was sacked in 146, and restored in part by the colonists in 44 B.C. It seems to have had three dining rooms built on the east side of a courtyard. In each one there were couches around the walls that could accommodate eleven persons, in front of which there were seven smaller tables, and in the center an area for cooking. The dining rooms were part of the temple, but they accommodated private parties or banquets (*St. Paul's Corinth*, 186–90). Ancient invitations to such temple banquets are extant (*New Docs*, 1:5 §1b ; cf. P. Oxy. 111:52; 1,100:2 [to sup at the couch of the lord Serapis in the Serapeum]).

Some Corinthian Christian, possessing the knowledge (*gnōsis*) described in vv. 4–6, would partake of such food without staining his or her conscience; but such dining could have repercussions, if such an individual were seen by "weak" Christians consuming it in *eidōleion*, in a "place of worship with a cult image" (BDAG, 280). The implication would be that such an individual was honoring the god worshiped there. *Eidōleion* is found in the LXX (Dan 1:2; 1 Esdr 2:7; Bel 10; 1 Macc 1:47; 10:83) and extrabiblically only in Jewish writings (*Test. Job* 5.2). The verb *katakeimai* is the technical term for "reclining at table," see Mark 14:3; Luke 5:29; 7:37. Paul's argument here means that someone seen dining in an "idol's temple" is consuming the meat precisely "as sacrificed to idols" (v. 7); that is why the conscience of the weak person is defiled. It is impossible to say whether, when Paul speaks of "seeing," he refers to a real instance of such observation or is merely constructing a hypothetical case.

will not his conscience, weak as it is, be emboldened to eat meat sacrificed to idols? Lit. "be built up," i.e., persons with a weak conscience would be encouraged to the extent that they too might eat such meat precisely as offered to a pagan god (v. 7). Such upbuilding or encouragement is said in irony (Conzelmann, *1 Cor*, 149: "with grim irony"; Héring, *1 Cor*, 68), because the example given by those who have knowledge is no edification at all. For those so "edified," to take part in such meals would be "an act of idolatry" (Dawes, "The Danger," 96). So Paul answers in these vv. 7–13 those who possess knowledge about idols and food offered to them, but he is indirectly urging such people to the nonuse of the right they have to do so.

11. *So because of your knowledge this weak person, a brother for whom Christ died, is brought to destruction.* Lit. "for destroyed is the weak one by your knowl-

edge . . . ," with the main verb (*apollytai*) placed at the head of the sentence for emphasis. Using the conj. *gar*, "for," Paul joins his concluding remarks not only to the concrete instance of v. 10, but also to his exhortation of v. 9. He now invokes tradition when he says, "for whom Christ died," as he will again in Rom 14:15, "Let not the food you eat bring ruin to such a one for whom Christ died"; cf. 14:20, "Do not demolish the work of God for the sake of food" (see *Romans*, 694–98). For the tradition, see 15:3; 1 Thess 5:10; Rom 5:6, 8. Paul's concern is not just for the weak conscience (v. 7), but for *ho asthenōn*, "the weak person," who happens to be *adelphos*, "a fellow Christian." He or she really is not being "built up" by the other Christian's knowledge, which no longer merely "puffs up" (v. 1), but has become destructive (of the weak person's salvation, as the verb often connotes [1:18; 10:10; 15:18; Rom 14:15; 2 Cor 2:15]). The "weak person" is being led through "knowledge" to ruin, the opposite of the effect of Christ's death.

12. *When you sin in this way against your brothers and strike at their conscience, weak as it is, you are sinning against Christ.* Paul returns to the 2d pers. plur., as in his exhortation of v. 9, for he seeks to get all the Corinthian Christians to reflect on the example just given and the implications of it. His emphasis falls both on the adv. *houtōs*, "in this way," and on "Christ," at the end of the sentence. Again he uses *hamartanein eis*, "sin against," as in 6:18 (with a different object, "one's own body"); the idiom occurs elsewhere in the NT (Luke 15:18, 21; 17:4; Acts 25:8), imitating a usage of the LXX (Gen 20:6, 9; Exod 10:16; 1 Kgs 15:18). To "strike at their conscience" means that such activity would mislead "weak persons," who would be led to believe that they too could indulge in an act which for them would be idolatrous. Paul judges that such activity constitutes a "sin" against a fellow Christian, and even against Christ himself, because he died for such a confrère. Recall the Lucan story of Paul's experience of the risen Christ on the road to Damascus in Acts 9:4–5: " I am Jesus, whom you are persecuting." Murphy-O'Connor would understand "Christ" here as designating "the community" of Corinthian Christians, as in 6:15; 12:12 (*NJBC*, 806). That may be valid for 12:12, but it is far from certain here because of the personal "Christ" in v. 11. BDF §442.9 understands *kai* before the ptc. *typtontes* as explicative, "even striking . . . ," which is possible, but not certain.

13. *Therefore, if food causes my brother to fall into sin, I shall never eat meat again, so that I may not cause my brother to fall.* Paul finally formulates his conclusion about the eating of idol meat in terms of what he personally would do, and so he avoids commanding others to do the same. Indirectly he is commending himself as an example of Christian conduct (cf. 4:16; and the end of this discussion in 11:1). Paul recognizes that he too has the same "right" (*exousia*, v. 9) as those who possess knowledge, but he is willing to relinquish it. He thereby teaches concern and love for fellow Christians as something far more important than right thinking or abstract knowledge about *eidōlothyta*. He also speaks in hyperbole of *kreas*, "meat," meaning every kind of meat, because he wants to stress the seriousness of the issue and the responsibility that individuals with knowledge have toward those who are weak. In such a way, love will truly build up (8:1d). In both subordinate clauses, Paul uses the verb *skandalizō*, "cause to stumble, cause to

sin," which is related to the "stumbling-block" (*proskomma*) of v. 9. The possessive pron. *mou* is missing twice in MSS (D²), F, G, and in MSS a, b of the VL, which gives an even broader extension to Paul's resolve.

BIBLIOGRAPHY (See Bibliography on 8:1–11:1)

Barrett, C. K., "Things Sacrificed to Idols," *NTS* 11 (1964–65) 138–53.

Brunt, J., "Rejected, Ignored, or Misunderstoood? The Fate of Paul's Approach to the Problem of Food Offered to Idols in Early Christianity," *NTS* 31 (1985) 113–24.

Cancrini, A., *Syneidesis: Il tema semantico della "conscientia" nella Grecia antica* (Lessico intellettuale europeo 6; Rome: Edizioni dell'Ateneo, 1970).

Casabona, J., *Récherches sur le vocabulaire des sacrifices en Grec des origines à la fin de l'époque classique* (Gap: Éditions Ophrys, 1966).

Coune, M., "Le problème des idololythes et l'éducation de la syneidêsis," *RSR* 51 (1963) 497–534.

Davis, J. A., "The Interaction between Individual Ethical Conscience and Community Ethical Consciousness in 1 Corinthians," *HBT* 10/2 (1988) 1–18.

Dawes, G. W., "The Danger of Idolatry: First Corinthians 8:7–13," *CBQ* 58 (1996) 82–98.

Delobel, J., "Coherence and Relevance of 1 Cor 8–10," *The Corinthian Correspondence* (BETL 125; ed. R. Bieringer), 177–90.

Demke, C., " 'Ein Gott und viele Herren': Die Verkündigung des einen Gottes in den Briefen des Paulus," *EvT* 36 (1976) 473–84.

Denaux, A., "Theology and Christology in 1 Cor 8,4–6: A Contextual-Redactional Reading," *The Corinthian Correspondence* (BETL 125; ed. R. Bieringer), 593–606.

Dupont, J., *Syneidèsis aux origines de la notion chrétienne de conscience morale* (Studia Hellenistica 5; Louvain: Bibliotheca Universitatis, 1948) 119–53.

Eckstein, H.-J., *Der Begriff Syneidesis bei Paulus: Eine neutestamentlich-exegetische Untersuchung zum 'Gewissensbegriff'* (WUNT 2/10; Tübingen: Mohr [Siebeck], 1983).

Fee, G. D., "*Eidōlothyta* Once Again: An Interpretation of 1 Corinthians 8–10," *Bib* 61 (1980) 172–97.

Feuillet, A., "La profession de foi monothéiste de 1 Cor. VIII, 4–6," *SBFLA* 13 (1962–63) 7–32.

Fisk, B. N., "Eating Meat Offered to Idols: Corinthian Behavior and Pauline Response in 1Corinthians 8–10 (A Response to Gordon Fee)," *TrinJ* 10 (1989) 49–70.

Gebhard, E. R., "The Isthmian Games and the Sanctuary of Poseidon in the Early Empire," *The Corinthia in the Roman Period* (JRASup 8; ed. T. E. Gregory; Ann Arbor: University of Michigan Press, 1994) 78–94.

Giblin, C. H., "Three Montheistic Texts in Paul," *CBQ* 37 (1975) 527–47.

Gooch, P. W., " 'Conscience' in 1 Corinthians 8 and 10," *NTS* 33 (1987) 244–54.

Grässer, E., " 'Ein einziger ist Gott" (Röm 3,30): Zum christologischen Gottesverständnis bei Paulus," *"Ich will euer Gott werden": Beispiele biblischen Redens von Gott* (SBS 100; Stuttgart: Katholisches Bibelwerk, 1981) 177–205.

Heil, C., *Die Ablehnung der Speisegebote durch Paulus: Zur Frage nach der Stellung des Apostels zum Gesetz* (Weinheim: Beltz Athenäum, 1994) 177–235.

Hofius, O., " 'Einer ist Gott—Einer ist Herr': Erwägungen zu Struktur und Aussage des Bekenntnisses 1.Kor 8,6," *Eschatologie und Schöpfung: Festschrift für Erik Grässer . . .* (BZNW 89; ed. M. Evang et al.; Berlin: de Gruyter, 1997) 95–108.

Horsley, R. A., "The Background of the Confessional Formula in 1 Kor 8,6," *ZNW* 69 (1978) 130–35.

——, "Gnosis in Corinth: I Corinthians 8. 1–6," *NTS* 27 (1980–81) 32–51.

Hurtado, L. W., "The Origins of the Worship of Christ," *Themelios* 19/2 (1994) 4–8.

Kerst, R., "1 Kor 8,6 — ein vorpaulinisches Taufbekenntnis?" *ZNW* 66 (1975) 130–39.

Langkammer, H., "Literarische und theologische Einzelstücke in I Kor. viii. 6," *NTS* 17 (1970–71) 193–97.

Manson, T. W., "The Corinthian Correspondence," *Studies in the Gospels and Epistles* (ed. M. A. Black; Manchester: Manchester University Press; Philadelphia: Westminster, 1962) 190–209.

Marmorstein, A., *The Old Rabbinic Doctrine of God* (Jews' College Publications 10 and 14; Oxford: Oxford University Press; London: H. Milford, 1927, 1937).

Meggitt, J. J., "Meat Consumption and Social Conflict in Corinth," *JTS* 45 (1994) 137–41.

Murphy-O'Connor, J., "I Cor., viii, 6: Cosmology or Soteriology?" *RB* 85 (1978) 253–67.

——, "Food and Spiritual Gifts in 1 Cor 8:8," *CBQ* 41 (1979) 292–98.

——, "Freedom or the Ghetto (*I Cor.*, viii, 1–13; x, 23–xi, 1)," *RB* 85 (1978) 543–74; repr. in *Freedom and Love* (ed. L. de Lorenzi; Rome: St. Paul's Abbey, 1981), 7–38.

Norden, E., *Agnostos Theos: Untersuchungen zur Formengeschichte religiöser Rede* (Stuttgart: Teubner, 1912; repr. Darmstadt: Wissenschaftliche Buchgesellschaft, 1971).

Ogilvie, R. M., *The Romans and Their Gods in the Age of Augustus* (Ancient Culture and Society; New York: Norton, 1969).

Peterson, E., *Heis Theos: Epigraphische, formgeschichtliche und religionsgeschichtliche Untersuchungen* (FRLANT 41; Göttingen: Vandenhoeck & Ruprecht, 1926).

Pierce, C. A., *Conscience in the New Testament* (SBT 15; London: SCM, 1955) 60–65.

Sagnard, F. M. M., "A propos de I Cor., viii, 6," *ETL* 26 (1950) 54–58.

Scullard, H. H., *Festivals and Ceremonies of the Roman Republic* (London: Thames and Hudson; Ithaca: Cornell University Press, 1981).

Smit, J. F. M., "1 Cor 8,1–6: A Rhetorical *Partitio*: A Contribution to the Coherence of 1 Cor 8,1–11,1," *The Corinthian Correspondence* (BETL 125; ed. R. Bieringer) 577–91.

Songer, H. S., "Problems Arising from the Worship of Idols: 1 Corinthians 8:1–11:1," *RevExp* 80 (1983) 363–75.

Still, E. C., "The Meaning and Uses of *eidōlothyton* in First Century Non-Pauline Literature and 1 Cor 8:1–11:1: Toward Resolution of the Debate," *TrinJ* 23 (2002) 225–34.

Thrall, M. E., "The Pauline Use of *syneidēsis*," *NTS* 14 (1967–68) 118–25.

Vogel, M. H., "Monotheism," *Encyclopaedia Judaica* (16 vols.; Jerusalem: Keter, 1971), 12:260–63.

Weiss, J., *The History of Primitive Christainity* (2 vols.; New York: Wilson-Erickson, 1937).

Wischmeyer, O., "*Theon agapan* bei Paulus: Eine traditionsgeschichtliche Miszelle," *ZNW* 78 (1987) 141–44.

Witherington, B., III, "Not so Idle Thoughts about *eidolothutōn*," *TynBul* 44 (1993) 237–54.

——, "Why Not Idol Meat? Is It What You Eat or Where You Eat It?" *BRev* 10/3 (1994) 38–43, 54–55.

BIBLIOGRAPHY ON 8:1–11:1

Batelaan, L., *De kerk van Korinthe en wij: De actualiteit van Paulus' eerste brief aan Korinthiërs (1 Kor. 8–11:1)* (Franeker: Wever, 1971).

Bouttier, M., "1 Co 8–10 considéré du point de vue de son unité," *Freedom and Love* (ed. L. de Lorenzi; Rome: St. Paul's Abbey, 1981), 205–25.

Cheung, A. T., *Idol Food in Corinth: Jewish Background and Pauline Legacy* (JSNTSup 176; Sheffield: Sheffield Academic, 1999).

Cooper, E. J., "Man's Basic Freedom and Freedom of Conscience in the Bible: Reflections on 1 Corinthians 8–10," *ITQ* 42 (1975) 272–83.

Ehrhardt, A., "Social Problems in the Early Church," *The Framework of the New Testament Stories* (Manchester: Manchester University, 1964) 275–312.

Fotopoulos, J., "Arguments Concerning Food Offered to Idols: Corinthian Quotations and Pauline Refutations in a Rhetorical *Partitio* (1 Corinthians 8.1–9)," *CBQ* 67 (2005) 611–31.

——, *Food Offered to Idols in Roman Corinth: A Social-Rhetorical Reconsideration of 1 Corinthians 8:1–11:1* (WUNT 2/151; Tübingen: Mohr Siebeck, 2003).

Galiazzo, D., "Gli idolòliti," *RBR* 9/2 (1974) 5–32.

Gardner, P. D., *The Gifts of God and the Authentication of a Christian: An Exegetical Study of 1 Corinthians 8–11:1* (Lanham, MD: University Press of America, 1994).

Garland, D. E., "The Dispute over Food Sacrificed to Idols (1 Cor 8:–11:1)," *PRSt* 30 (2003) 173–97.

Geyser, A. S., "Paul, the Apostolic Decree and the Liberals in Corinth," *Studia Paulina in Honorem Johannis de Zwaan septuagenarii* (ed. J. N. Sevenster and W. C. van Unnik; Haarlem: Bohn, 1953) 129–38.

Gooch, P. D., *Dangerous Food: 1 Corinthians 8–10 in Its Context* (Studies in Christianity and Judaism 5; Waterloo, Ont.: Wilfrid Laurier University, 1993).

Harding, M., "Church and Gentile Cults at Corinth," *GTJ* 10 (1989) 203–23.

Horrell, D., "Theological Principle or Christological Praxis? Pauline Ethics in 1 Corinthians 8.1–11.1," *JSNT* 67 (1997) 83–114.

Horsley, R. A., "Consciousness and Freedom among the Corinthians: I Corinthians 8–10," *CBQ* 40 (1978) 574–89.

Kloha, J., "Idols, Eating and Rights (1 Cor. 8:1–11:1): Faithful and Loving Witness in a Pluralistic Culture," *ConcJ* 30 (2004) 173–202.

Lambrecht, J., "Universalism in 1 Cor 8:1–11:1," *Collected Studies* (AnBib 147), 63–70.

Meeks, W. A., "The Polyphonic Ethics of the Apostle Paul," *Annual of the Society of Christian Ethics* (1988) 17–29.

Moreno García, A., and R. Saez Gonzalvez, "El problema de los idolotitos en 1 Co 8–11 como humus de los banquetes judeo-cristianos," *EstBíb* 59 (2001) 47–77.

Newton, D., *Deity and Diet: The Dilemma of Sacrificial Food at Corinth* (JSNTSup 169; Sheffield: Sheffield Academic, 1998).

Oropeza, B. J., "Laying to Rest the Midrash: Paul's Message on Meat Sacrificed to Idols in Light of the Deuteronomic Tradition," *Bib* 79 (1998) 57–68.

Probst, H., *Paulus und der Brief: Die Rhetorik des antiken Briefes als Form der paulinischen Korintherkorrespondenz (1 Kor 8–10)* (WUNT 2/45; Tübingen: Mohr [Siebeck], 1991).

Serna, E. de la, "¿'Ver-juzgar-actuar' in San Pablo?" *RevistB* 52 (1990) 85–98.

Smit, J. F. M., *"About the Idol Offerings": Rhetoric, Social Context and Theology of Paul's Discourse in First Corinthians 8:1–11:1* (CBET 27; Louvain: Peeters, 2000).

——, "The Rhetorical Disposition of First Corinthians 8:7–9:27," *CBQ* 59 (1997) 476–91.

Söding, T., "Starke und Schwache: Der Götzenopferstreit in 1 Kor 8–10 als Paradigma paulinischer Ethik," *ZNW* 85 (1994) 69–92.

Still, E. C., "Paul's Aims Regarding *eidōlothyta*: A New Proposal for Interpreting 1 Corinthians 8:1–11:1," *NovT* 44 (2002) 333–43.

Virgulin, S., "Gli idololiti in 1 Cor 8,1–11,1a," *ED* 39 (1986) 307–20.

Willis, W. L., *Idol Meat in Corinth: The Pauline Argument in 1 Corinthians 8 and 10* (SBLDS 68; Chico, CA: Scholars, 1985).

Winter, B. W., "Theological and Ethical Responses to Religious Pluralism — 1 Corinthians 8–10," *TynBul* 41 (1990) 209–26.

20

b. *Freedom and Restraint of an Apostle (9:1–27)*

9:1 Am I not free? Am I not an apostle? Have I not seen Jesus our Lord? Are you not the product of my work in the Lord? 2 If to others I am not an apostle, surely I am to you. For you are the seal of my apostolate in the Lord. 3 This is the defense I make before those who would pass judgment on me. 4 Do we not have the right to eat and drink? 5 Do we not have the right to bring along a Christian wife, as do the rest of the apostles, and the Lord's brothers, and Cephas? 6 Or is it only I and Barnabas who do not have the right not to work? 7 Who serves as a soldier at his own expense? Who plants a vineyard and does not eat of its fruit? Who shepherds a flock and does not drink of its milk? 8 Am I saying this merely from a human point of view, or does not the law also say the same thing? 9 For it stands written in the law of Moses, "*You shall not muzzle the ox while it is threshing.*" Is God concerned about oxen? 10 Or does he really speak for our sake? For it was written for our sake, because the plowman ought to plow in hope, and the thresher (thresh) in hope of receiving a share. 11 If we have sown spiritual seed among you, is it too much that we should reap a material harvest from you? 12 If others share this rightful claim on you, should not we all the more so? Yet we have not used this right. Rather, we put up with everything so as not to put an obstacle in the way of the gospel of Christ. 13 Do you not realize that those who are engaged in temple service eat [what] belongs to the temple, and those who minister at the altar share in what is offered on the altar? 14 In the same way the Lord too has ordered those who preach the gospel to get their living from the gospel. 15 I, however, have used none of these things. Nor do I write this that it may be done so in my case. I would rather die than have someone deprive me of my boast. 16 If I preach the gospel, there is no reason for me to boast. For compulsion lies upon me! Woe to me if I do not preach it! 17 If I do so willingly, I have a recompense; but if I do so unwillingly, I have been entrusted with a stewardship. 18 What then is my recompense? That, when I preach, I may offer the gospel free of charge so as not to make full use of my right in preaching the gospel. 19 For though I am free and belong to no one, I have made myself a slave to all so that I may win over as many as possible. 20 To Jews I became like a Jew to win over Jews; to those under the law I became like one under the law — though I myself am not under the law — that I might win over those under the law. 21 To those without the law I became like one without the law — though I am not without God's law, being under the law of Christ — that I might win over those without the law. 22 To the weak I became weak, that I might win over the weak. I have become all things to all people that I might save at least some. [23] I do it all for the sake of the gospel, so that I may have a share in it. [24] Do you not realize that all runners in the stadium run in the race, but only one wins the prize? Run, then, so as to win. [25] Every athlete exercises self-control in every way; they do it to win a perishable crown, but we an imperishable one. [26] I at least do not run aimlessly; I do not box as if I were beating the air. [27] Rather, I pommel my body and subjugate it, lest in preaching to others I myself might be disqualified.

COMMENT

Paul has finished his immediate comments on one aspect of the problem of meat sacrificed to idols, a topic to which he will return in chap. 10, to treat it from different perspectives. In the meantime, he takes up an issue important to him, even though it constitutes a digression in the arguments that he is addressing to the Corinthian Christians on idol meat. It is not introduced by *peri de*, as were the topics in 7:1, 25; 8:1, but it has to do with both the liberty and the right that Paul has as an apostle, and only indirectly with those who "possess knowledge," but eventually with the situation of every Christian.

This topic may have emerged because of the slogan in 6:12, "For me all things are permissible," a slogan on which Paul will comment again in 10:23, since it formulates an attitude about freedom. Some Corinthian Christians might well wonder whether there is any sense in which the slogan might apply even to Paul. This topic has also been involved more directly in the stance of some Corinthian individuals in 8:7–12 about the eating of idol meat in temples of pagan gods. Even though Paul basically has agreed with them about the nonentity of idols and the right that those who "possess knowledge" to partake of such food there, he invoked another principle and expressed his own personal concern for fellow Christians, especially those with a weak conscience. Some of his readers might be surprised by his generic conclusion in 8:13, where he willingly accepts a restriction of his personal apostolic right and liberty. This now has occasioned the digression on Paul's authority and his willingness to give up his right, about which one reads in this chapter.

Paul also seems to be responding to opposition to him in Roman Corinth among some who have queried his use of the title "apostle," as he does in 1:1; 4:9 of this letter. They seem to have found it difficult to allow that he was on the same level as the Jerusalem apostles (cf. 15:5–8). He has also proposed himself as someone to imitate (4:16) and will do so again in 11:1. The arguments that he sets out in this chapter about his apostolic role continue that idea, as Schrage has rightly recognized in calling Paul's discussion an *exemplum* (*1 Cor*, 2:280). That was the implicit point of what Paul asserted about resolving to eat no meat in 8:13, and it will be also in the first verses of this chapter. Moreover, the rivalries of which he spoke in chaps. 1–4 reveal that some of the opposition to him may have been centered in different house-churches in Corinth, other than that of Stephanas (1:16; 16:15; see Betz-Mitchell, "Corinthians," 1:1141; Klauck, *Hausgemeinde*, 20–40).

Perhaps, too, because Paul did not exploit the right of an apostle to be supported by the community, some were concluding that he was not really an apostle. In any case, Paul in this chapter gives not only a defense of himself as *apostolos* (v. 3), but also proposes himself as someone with an apostolic "right" (*exousia*, vv. 4–6, 12), who has chosen not to exploit it. The freedom that he thus enjoys has a connection with the "right" that he acknowledged in 8:9, but it is not quite the same, because it now has to do with his personal liberty as an apostle, which he claims but chooses to exercise with restraint (9:12cd, 15, 23). This digression, then, tells us much about Paul himself and how he views his apostolic role in his evangelistic endeavors.

In the first section (9:1–18), Paul explains why he has conducted himself among the Corinthian Christians as he has and presents reasons for his apostolic authority and the rights that flow from that status supported by Scripture and the command of the Lord; but he carefully explains why he has chosen freely to renounce such rights. In the second section (9:19–23), he presents himself as a model for the Corinthian community: through faith he is free and subject to no one, but in love he is a slave, who has freely become all things to all people in the hope of saving some of them. In the last section (9:24–27), he exhorts the Corinthian Christians to share his self-discipline as he freely seeks to attain his goal and to imitate his nonuse of his right.

For some interpreters, vv. 24–27 at the end of this section create a special problem, because they do not seem to help the argument that Paul has been presenting up to v. 23, and some see them as more closely related to the discussion in 10:1–22 (J. Weiss, Schmithals, *Gnosticism*, 93–95; Sumney, "The Place," 331–32). These verses, however, are transitional and serve to bring Paul's argument back to the topics that he will treat in chap. 10. Even though Paul in vv. 24–27 focuses on disciplined living, he is still presenting himself as an example of one who gives up a right for the good of the community. That is why he ends his remarks with: "Lest in preaching to others I myself might be disqualified" (v. 27). Sumney rightly argues that Paul's argument in 9:19–23 parallels 8:9–13 and spells out the possible consequences of the participation of those who "possess knowledge" in pagan temple meals for both themselves and the "weak." That parallel, however, does not undo the exemplary character of Paul's disciplined life and what it should mean to the community of Corinthians who may be debating about him. What Paul says in vv. 24–27 shows that he is concerned about his own salvation, but it shows much more, because it presents him as an example and model for others, especially in light of the examples that he is going to draw from Israel's ancestors in 10:1–5. That is why these verses are transitional, but also part of the unit that makes up chap. 9 (see further Pfitzner, *Paul and the Agon Motif*, 83–87; Hays, *1 Cor*, 155).

Above all to be noted in this chapter is the diatribe-like style of argumentation and the abundant use of rhetorical questions (19 of them), which make up the way Paul marshals his argumentative discussion. The questions appear at seven places in the course of this digression, sometimes in groups to make a particular point, sometimes more or less alone in support of a certain consideration:

1. Four simple rhetorical questions appear in v. 1, using the 1st pers. sing. in some way; they are followed by three statements (likewise in the 1st pers. sing. in vv. 2–3). Together they constitute Paul's defense as an apostle.
2. Eight (or seven, with the last one double) questions are formulated in vv. 4–8, with three expressed in the 1st pers. plur. (vv. 4–5, and implicitly v. 6). This group seeks to establish Paul's apostolic rights (to eat and drink, to have a wife-companion, not to have to do other kinds of work), and it ends with a quotation of Scripture.
3. Two rhetorical questions are posed concerning God's concern about support for evangelists (vv. 9c, 10a).
4. Two further questions form the apodosis of conditions posed in the 1st pers. plur. (vv. 11b, 12b), which either contrast a material harvest and spiritual seed sown or contrast Paul and other evangelists; they are followed by two statements, giving Paul's first conclusion (v. 12cd).
5. A compound rhetorical question appears in v. 13a–b, comparing Paul with temple servants, which is followed by a command of the Lord about the gospel preacher's recompense (v. 14).
6. A further rhetorical question occurs in v. 18a, explaining Paul's view of his recompense in this whole matter.
7. The final rhetorical question (v. 24a) introduces a metaphorical argument drawn from athletic contests and the discipline they demand, which Paul introduces to explain his own self-restraint in preaching the gospel. Here he introduces a more generic consideration and even formulates an imperative about such discipline (v. 24b).

In this complex series of rhetorical questions, three crucial statements set forth Paul's fundamental attitude: v. 12cd, "Yet we have not used this right"; v. 15a, "I, however, have used none of these rights"; and v. 23, "All this I do for the sake of the gospel, so that I may have a share in it." The basis of his explanation is found in vv. 16–22: his obligation to preach the gospel to all alike, Jew or Greek; and it all ends with the metaphorical exposé of self-restraint needed in athletic contests (vv. 24–27).

What Paul says in vv. 19–23 about his freedom and making himself "all things to all people" has at times been seen as inconsistent with the way he reacted to Peter in the so-called Antioch incident (Gal 2:11–14). Is it inconsistency, or only apparently so? See Carson, "Pauline Inconsistency"; Richardson, "Pauline Inconsistency."

NOTES

9:1. *Am I not free? Am I not an apostle?* Paul begins this digression with four rhetorical questions, each one introduced by a form of *ou*, which implies an affirmative answer. He speaks in the 1st pers. sing., continuing his statement of 8:13, and asks about his personal liberty, using again the adj. *eleutheros* already employed of others (7:22, 39). His questions imply that Corinthian Christians should know well his freedom and his apostolic authority, but may be overlooking them. He enjoys, moreover, not just a generic Christian freedom, but rather an apostolic freedom, having opened this letter to the Corinthians with the self-identification, *apostolos Christou Iēsou* (see NOTE on 1:1). Now he uses that status as the basis of his personal liberty and will reiterate it in a different way in v. 19. In MSS D, F, G, Ψ, and the Koine text-tradition, the first two questions appear in the opposite order.

Have I not seen Jesus our Lord? This is Paul's essential reason for insisting on his apostolic calling and status, again something that the Corinthian Christians should know. He has been a witness of the risen Christ, as he will assert again in 15:8: *ōphthē kamoi,* "he appeared to me." In Gal 1:16, he wrote, God "was pleased to reveal his Son to me, in order that I might preach him among the Gentiles." So Paul often recalled his call and the divine commission to act as an authoritative emissary; cf. 2 Cor 11:5; 12:11–12; Rom 11:13.

In Acts 1:22, Luke uses the same idea as one of his qualifications for membership in the Twelve, but phrases it abstractly: one had to be "a witness to his resurrection," to which Luke adds two other qualifications: he had to be "a man" (*anēr*) and "one of those who have been part of our company all the while the Lord Jesus moved in and out among us." According to the Lucan criteria, Paul could not have been numbered among the Twelve (see *Acts,* 226), and in fact is never so presented in the NT. Yet even Luke recorded that Paul had seen the Lord (Acts 9:17 [*ophtheis*], 27 [*eiden*]; 22:14 [*idein*]). For the relatively rare Pauline expression, "Jesus our Lord" (without "Christ"), see 5:4; Rom 4:24; 16:20.

Are you not the product of my work in the Lord? Lit. "my work" or "my workmanship" (RSV). The fourth rhetorical question flows directly from the second one. *Ergon* expresses what the "Apostle" has achieved among the Christians of Roman Corinth as a commissioned emissary of the risen Lord, which they should know. Indirectly, he is referring to himself as the founder of the Corinthian church (recall 3:6a, 10b; 4:15b). The "proclamation" that he has made in the midst of that congregation came "with a demonstration of the Spirit and with power" (2:4); that is his gifted "work."

2. *If to others I am not an apostle, surely I am to you.* Paul adds two related statements to his four rhetorical questions. He, who had to do battle to be recognized as *apostolos* in the early church, vehemently insists on this status, as he does in Gal 1:1; and in different terms in 2 Cor 3:1b–2, when he will ask whether he needs a letter of recommendation for acceptance among Corinthian Christians. They should be the last people to question his claim to apostleship. Who the "others" are who might question his claim to be an apostle is a matter for speculation, because Paul has not identified them. Other Christian communities do exist, with which Paul has had nothing to do. The "others," however, seem to be among the rival groups of chaps. 1–4 or members of some such local church. There is no evidence that Paul is referring to Cephas as one who questions his right to be called an apostle, *pace* Vielhauer ("Paul and the Cephas Party").

For you are the seal of my apostolate in the Lord. This is Paul's stately affirmation as he makes use of a technical term for ancient authentication, *sphragis,* "seal, signet(-ring)," a means of certifying ownership or verifying validity or empowerment. The Christians of Roman Corinth are themselves the authentic proof that Paul has carried out among them his authorized mission as an "apostle."

3. *This is the defense I make before those who would pass judgment on me.* Those "passing judgment" directly refers to the "others" of v. 2, whoever they may be; indirectly they may include those who have sided with other preachers, for their preferred allegiance would imply passing judgment on Paul. He now urges them to check his authentication. The pron. *hautē*, "this," although occupying the last place in the Greek sentence, refers to what Paul has just said in vv. 1–2, as in 7:20 (BDR §290.3; Robertson-Plummer, *1 Cor*, 179; Schrage, *1 Cor*, 2:281). That is all that he is going to say in defense of his apostolic authority (see Nickel, "Parenthetical Apologia").

Paul makes use of two forensic terms in this verse, *apologia*, "defense," as he speaks on his own behalf (compare its use in Acts 25:16; 2 Tim 4:16), and *anakrinō*, "conduct a judicial hearing or examination," as he mentions those who pass judgment (cf. Luke 23:14; Acts 24:8).

4. *Do we not have the right to eat and drink?* Now Paul introduces a new series of rhetorical questions in vv. 4–8, this time seven of them, and the last one is double (the first two, introduced by *mē ouk*, expect an affirmative answer, BDF §427.2). As a truly valid and authentic "apostle," he enjoys *exousia*, "a right," which flows from that status; it is a right that he claims but that he may give up freely. He sets it forth in detail in the following questions. The first concerns his freedom to eat and drink as he pleases, a right that he has willingly restricted already in 8:13. Now he reasserts his fundamental and apostolic right in this matter as the background for that restriction. As formulated now in generic terms, it hardly concerns only idol meat, the problem that gave rise to Paul's argument in 8:7–12 and the eventual expression of a restriction of it in 8:13. There it concerns "meat" in general (*kreas*), and not just idol meat (*eidōlothyton*). However, it also means his "right" (as founder and evangelizer) to eat and drink at the Corinthian community's expense, as the following context makes clear.

5. *Do we not have a right to bring along a Christian wife?* Or "a woman who is a believer?" (*adelphēn gynaika*, lit. "a sister (as) a wife/woman"). *Adelphē*, "sister," means not a female sibling, but a female fellow Christian (see NOTE on 1:1; cf. 7:15; Rom 16:1; Phlm 2). The infin. *periagein* refers to having a woman as a companion on his missionary journeys (e.g., to care for one's material needs). If *gynaika* is to be understood as "wife," then Paul is asserting a right of which he is actually not making use (recall 7:7a, 8, where he speaks of himself in the 1st pers. sing. as unmarried). The 1st pers. plur. now could be editorial, meaning himself, or it could refer to Barnabas and himself, as in v. 6. Examples of such husband-wife pairs would be Prisca and Aquila (Rom 16:3) and Andronicus and Junia (Rom 16:7 [see *Romans*, 737–38]; cf. Klauck, *Hausgemeinde*, 30, 59). Mss F, G and a, b of the VL omit *adelphēn* and read instead only the plur. *gynaikas*, "wives," which Bauer ("Uxores") claims is the original reading; moreover he maintains that *gynaika periagein* means simply "to have a wife," and not "to take a wife about

with one," but Diogenes Laertius (*Vitae* 6.97) uses a cog. verb (*symperiēei*, "went about with") in his account about the Cynic philosopher Crates who took his like-minded wife on his philosophical excursions (BDAG, 798). So the usual transla-tion, "bring/take along," is to be preferred.

Clement of Alexandria had a different understanding of the words *adelphēn gy-naika*: "They [the Apostles], in conformity with their ministry, concentrated with-out distraction on preaching, and took their women as sisters, not as wives, to be their fellow-ministers for house-wives, through whom the teaching about the Lord penetrated into the women's quarters without scandal" (*Stromateis* 3.6.53.3; GCS 15.220 [cf. FC 85.289]). Similarly, Augustine, *De opere monachorum* 4; CSEL 41.538–39; FC 16.338. That is a possible meaning, but it seems to read more into the matter than the Greek text expresses.

More is almost certainly implied in Paul's question than that apostles had the right to marry, which would have been taken for granted then. From vv. 6–8, where apostles and missionaries have the right to maintenance from the church or community evangelized, it seems to be implied in the question that Paul now asks whether the Christian wife who accompanies an apostle would be entitled to the same support? So Lietzmann (*1 Cor*, 40) argued, basing his argument not only on the conj. *ē*, "or," (which introduces v. 6, and Paul's emphasis given to the sub-ject, "only I and Barnabas"), but also on the interpretation of John Chrysostom and Theodoret: "at the expense of the community." Similarly Conzelmann, Robertson-Plummer, Kremer, Lindemann.

as do the rest of the apostles. Who the *hoi loipoi apostoloi* are in this case is not easy to say. They are distinguished clearly from "the Lord's brothers" (see the next phrase). Since Cephas is to be mentioned, the adj. "other" may mean apostles dif-ferent from Paul, Barnabas, and Cephas (the first two mentioned are called *apos-toloi* in Acts 14:4, 14 [a problematic text; see *Acts*, 526]). Certainly the phrase does not mean missionaries in general, because the "apostles" were a definite group in the primitive church, which initially shaped its structure, but which eventually gave way to others (see *Acts*, 220–21). Although Luke restricted the meaning of *apostoloi* to the Twelve (see Luke 6:13, "he chose twelve of them, whom he named apostles"; also his account of the reconstitution of the Twelve, Acts 1:15–26), there is no evidence that Paul shared that view. In 1 Cor 15:5–7, he dis-tinguishes "the Twelve" from "all the apostles" (who are, hence, a larger group). Together with the Twelve, he and Barnabas would number fourteen, which might even grow to sixteen, if Andronicus and Junia (Rom 16:7) are considered "apostles," as some commentators have maintained since patristic times (another problematic text; see *Romans*, 737–38). See also 2 Cor 8:23, where unnamed *apostoloi* are mentioned. Who, then, is meant by *hoi loipoi apostoloi*? No one can say for sure.

The testimony of Papias, recorded in Eusebius, *HE* 3.39.9, about the marital status of "Philip the Apostle" (and his daughters) is a classic confusion of "Philip the evangelist," known from Acts 6:5; 8:5–13, 26–40; 21:8–9, with one of the Twelve having the same name (Acts 1:13), about whom nothing is known, apart from what is recounted in John 12:21–22.

and the Lord's brothers. This phrase is equally problematic. In Gal 1:19, Paul speaks of James of Jerusalem as *ton adelphon tou kyriou*, "the Lord's brother." Possibly he is now referring to this James. Was James of Jerusalem an apostle? It depends on how *ei mē* in Gal 1:19 is understood: It can be exceptive, meaning, "I saw none of the other apostles [apart from Cephas] except James. . . ." (so translated in KJV, NKJV, RSV, NRSV, ESV, NEB, REB). That would make this James an apostle (contrary to 1 Cor 15:5–7, where he is distinguished from the Twelve and "all the apostles"). Or *ei mē* can be adversative, the equivalent of *alla*, "but" (as it is used in Gal 1:7; 2:16 [*ean mē*]; Matt 5:13; 12:4; 17:8; Mark 4:22; 9:8 [see app. crit. *alla*]; Luke 2:46; 4:26, 27), and would mean, "I saw none of the other apostles, but only James, the Lord's brother" (as it is rendered in NIV, NAB; cf. ZBG §470; Moulton, *Grammar*, 2:468; 3:330). Then he would not be an apostle. If James of Jerusalem were an apostle, then he would be part of the preceding group, "the apostles," and the problem would be compounded: Who, then, would be "the Lord's brothers"?

A further question is: How is one to understand *adelphoi*, "brothers"? Certainly, it does not mean fellow Christians, as often in this letter (see NOTE on 1:1), but rather is to be understood as in Acts 1:14c. In Classical and Hellenistic Greek, the normal meaning of *adelphos* is "blood brother," i.e., a male child born of the same mother. This is the sense that Meier finds here ("Brothers and Sisters").

In the LXX, however, *adelphos* translates Hebrew *'āḥ*, even when it is used in the broader sense of "kinsman, relative" (e.g., Gen 13:8; 14:16; 24:48; 29:12, 15; 31:23, 32; Lev 10:4; 1 Chr 9:6; 23:22; Tob 5:13–14; 7:2 [in MS S, whereas MSS A, B read *anepsiō*, "cousin"]; see BDAG, 18). The wider sense is also attested for Aramaic *'ăḥā'* (see WA, 221; Grelot, "Noms de parenté"). In Greek papyri from Egypt, *adelphos* sometimes has this broader meaning (see Tscherikower, "Jewish Religious Influence," 32–33 [and p. 36: said to occur also in *Adler Pap. Gebelen* 7.6]); but *adelphos* is found also in other metaphorical senses (for officials, friends, business partners; see Arzt-Grabner, " 'Brothers' and 'Sisters' "). In which sense is *adelphos* to be understood here, "blood brother" or "relative"? (In any case, *adelphos* in the broader sense is not to be translated "cousin," since Greek has a specific word for that relationship, either *adelphidous* or *anepsios* [the latter appears in Col 4:10]).

The reason why "the Lord's brothers" is problematic is because of Mark 6:3, "Is not this the craftsman, the son of Mary, and brother of James, Joses, Judas, and Simon, and are not his sisters here with us?" when that Marcan verse is considered along with Mark 15:40, 47; 16:1, where two of the four *adelphoi* are mentioned again. In the latter passages, "Mary, the mother of James the younger and Joses" can scarcely be a circumlocution used by the evangelist to designate the mother of the person crucified on Golgotha, before whose cross she is standing. Hence *adelphos* in Mark 6:3, where the four are mentioned, must be understood in the broader sense, "kinsman, relative." This is why some interpreters hesitate to understand *adelphos* as "blood brother" in this passage (see Chapman, "Brethren," 417). "In any case they were persons whose close relationship to the Lord gave them distinction in the primitive Church: what they did constituted a precedent"

(Robertson-Plummer, *1 Cor*, 182). See Eusebius, *HE* 2.1.2; 2.23.1; 7.19.1 (on their succession to the bishopric of Jerusalem). Cf. Blinzler, *Brüder*, 18–23, 45, 92, 123; Bienert, "Relatives of Jesus."

and Cephas? For his marital status, see Mark 1:30, where his mother-in-law (*penthera Simōnos*) is mentioned. Although Cephas would be part of the "apostles" mentioned earlier in the verse, he is singled out and mentioned last simply because of his importance in the early church and because his influence was already invoked in Corinth (1:12 [see NOTE there]; 3:22). Here Paul is saying that Cephas was accompanied on his ministry by his wife, whose name is unknown (see Klauck, *Hausgemeinde*, 30, 59). To see Cephas as the head of the opposition to Paul in Corinth goes beyond the evidence provided in this letter.

6. *Or is it only I and Barnabas who do not have the right not to work?* I.e., not to enjoy support from the community they have evangelized. Because *monos* is singular and refers only to the following *egō*, "I," Paul must have added "Barnabas" as an afterthought, presupposing that the Corinthians would know of instances where the two of them did not have such support. Paul uses the infin. *ergazesthai*, "work," which from 4:12 clearly means "to toil, work with one's hands," a form of labor that was not commonly done by one who was a teacher. It is not easy to explain the "right" (*exousia*) of which Paul speaks here, because one cannot tell whether he is thinking of support from the Corinthians for the evangelization of Corinth or for some other missionary endeavor, such as he mentions in Phil 4:15–18. In any case, he will be mentioning soon his giving up of such a right to support.

Barnabas is mentioned for the first and only time in this letter. Presumably, he was known to the Corinthians; otherwise Paul would not be mentioning him. No one knows how the Corinthians would have come to know about him. He is mentioned by Paul in Gal 2:1, 9, 13, a letter that theoretically could have come to the knowledge of Corinthian Christians, but it is not otherwise known to have reached them. This reference to Barnabas was written from Ephesus toward the end of Paul's third missionary journey, and the way Paul refers to him implies that they are still good friends.

From Acts 4:36 one learns that his name was Joseph and that he was called Barnabas by the apostles (with a strange Lucan explanation of its meaning [see *Acts*, 320–21]). Thereafter in the Lucan account of Paul's missionary journeys, Barnabas is a companion and coworker of Paul (9:27; 11:22, 30; 12:25), especially during the first mission (13:1, 2, 7, 43, 46, 50; 14:12, 14, 20), at the "Council" (15:2, 12), and in Antioch (11:15–26; 15:22, 25, 35). When Paul decides after the "Council" to set out on the second mission, there is a break between them over the conduct of John Mark (15:36–39), after which one hears no more about Barnabas, until he appears in Eusebius, *HE* 1.12.1; 2.1.4 (where he is said to have been one of the Seventy disciples sent out by Jesus); 2.3.3; 2.8.2; 7.25.15 (as a coworker of Paul). The *Ep. Barn.* is listed by Eusebius among the nongenuine (i.e., noncanonical) writings of the NT (*HE* 3.35.4; but cf. 6.14.1).

7. *Who serves as a soldier at his own expense?* Or "with his own rations?" The Greek word *opsōnion* originally referred to cooked rations given to soldiers, but in

time it came to connote the money given for the purchase of such rations (see Caragounis, "*Opsōnion*"). The implied answer to Paul's question is: "No one." Having cited the example of the rights of other Christian missionaries in the early church, Paul now turns to commonsense analogies. This rhetorical question is the first of series of three similarly formulated commonsense arguments in support of Paul's contention expressed in the question of v. 6 and implied in that of vv. 4–5. The Christian apostle is compared with a soldier serving his country in time of war, who does not have to provide for his own rations, meals, or means of livelihood, but has a right to such sustenance from the country's government. Cf. 2 Tim 2:4–6; and contrast 2 Thess 3:6–12.

Who plants a vineyard and does not eat of its fruit? Paul's second comparison of the apostle with a vintner echoes Deut 20:6, "What man is there that has planted a vineyard and has not enjoyed its fruit?" Cf. Prov 27:18. Even the vintner has a right to the fruit of the vine.

Who shepherds a flock and does not drink of its milk? Lit. "of the milk of the flock," Paul's third comparison of the apostle with a shepherd, who has a right to drink the milk of the flock that he tends. The threesome, soldier, vintner, and shepherd, though drawn from different social levels and with differing modes of recompense, produces the convincing argument that Paul seeks to make.

8. *Am I saying this merely from a human point of view, or does not the law also say the same thing?* This double rhetorical question shifts the argument from the common-sense level to a legal and biblical one. Paul introduces the two questions with *mē*, expecting a negative answer in the first and a positive answer in the second, which also has *ou* (BDF §427.2). In order to stress the ordinary way of viewing things, he uses again *kata anthrōpon* (lit. "according to a human being"), as in 3:3 (see NOTE there). By way of contrast, he cites *ho nomos*, "the law" (as in 14:34; Gal 4:21), which is clarified in the next verse as the Mosaic law. The same mode of reference is found in Josephus, *J.W.* 7.5.7 §162.

9. *For it stands written.* See NOTE on 1:19.

in the law of Moses. This is the only occurrence of this phrase in Pauline writings; cf. Luke 2:22; 24:44; John 7:23; Acts 13:38; 15:5; 28:23; Heb 10:28. It imitates LXX Josh 9:2, *katha gegraptai en tō nomō Mōysē*, "As it has been written in the law of Moses," and its sense is based on LXX Deut 31:9, *egrapsen Mōysēs ta rēmata tou nomou toutou eis biblion*, "Moses wrote the words of this law in a book." Paul will refer to this law in 14:21 (without mentioning Moses) and in 14:34 (without "Moses" or an explicit introductory formula); both here and in 9:20–22 it is used only in a generic way (see Hollander, "Meaning of the Term"). Cf. 15:56.

This law was also known among writers in the Greco-Roman world: e.g., Diodorus Siculus (*Bibl. hist.* 1.94.2) records that Moses gave laws to the Jews from a god called *Iaō* (an ancient Greek way of writing *Yāhû*, an alternative form of *Yahweh* used as the theophoric element of many Hebrew masc. names; the Greek form *Iaō* is also found in 4QLXXLev[b] 20–21:4 [DJD 9.174]).

"You shall not muzzle the ox while it is threshing." Paul cites Deut 25:4, which in the LXX reads, *ou phimōseis boun aloōnta*, "you shall not muzzle a threshing

ox," with which some MSS of this passage agree verbatim (P[46], א, A, B[2], C, D[1], Ψ, 33, 1881), whereas others (B*, D*, F, G, 1739) substitute a nonliterary verb, *kēmōseis*, with the same meaning (read by N-A[27], as *lectio difficilior* and avoiding assimilation to the LXX). So the Mosaic law prescribed that the farmer should not prevent an ox from enjoying the benefits of its threshing work. Jewish interpreters extended the provision: Josephus alludes to the same text (*Ant.* 4.8.21 §233), when he explains Deut 24:19, about harvesters leaving sheaves for sojourners, the fatherless, and widows and about having regard for the support of other human beings. At least since the time of Calvin, commentators have mentioned that Deut 24:14–15 (about not depriving the poor and needy, the hired hand, or the sojourner of his daily wage) would have been a more apt OT text to suit Paul's argument. That consideration, however, makes Paul's use of Deut 25:4 all the more intriguing, for this same OT text is cited also in 1 Tim 5:18 (see Smit, "You Shall Not").

In its original pentateuchal context, the saying seems isolated, because the preceding verses (Deut 25:1–3) deal with the restricted number of stripes that one may inflict in the corporal punishment on an offender, and the following vv. 5–10 with the obligation of levirate marriage. The whole is preceded by a variety of humanitarian and cultic regulations (23:15–24:22). In such a context, it becomes apparent that, though the words of v. 4 historically concerned the treatment of the threshing ox, they are addressed to the human being who sets the animal to work; it is merely a part of instructions for the people of Israel. The implication of the quotation is that it is more important for the apostle to derive some benefit from his work of evangelization.

Commentators have debated how Paul is using this quotation. Some think that he is interpreting Deuteronomy in a figurative sense (without further specification): so Grosheide, *1 Cor*, 205; Schrage, *1 Cor*, 2.299; Soards, *1 Cor*, 189. Others in an allegorical sense: so Arndt, "Meaning"; Hanson, *Living Utterances*, 136; Jeremias, "Paulus als Hillelit," 88–89; Kremer, *1 Cor*, 187; Lee, "Studies," 123; Lohse, "Kümmert," 314; Longenecker, *Biblical Exegesis*, 126. Instone Brewer ("1 Corinthians 9.9–11"), however, claims that Paul uses a "literal interpretation of the plain meaning of the [OT] text"; but his explanation depends not so much on the OT text of the saying as on far-fetched rabbinic interpretations dating from centuries later than Paul, which can scarcely pass for contemporary exegesis or a "literal" meaning. Some interpreters have tried to insist that Paul is giving a literal theological exegesis of Deut 25:4: so Kaiser, "Current Crisis," 13–14. This would be close to the meaning that I perceive here, but it is problematic, because, when one uses literal, it must have the historical sense expressed by the author, whereas Paul, in asking the following questions, is adding a sense, which is no longer literal (see the excursus in Lindemann, *1 Cor*, 204–5).

Is God concerned about oxen? Paul's first rhetorical question is introduced again by *mē*, which expects a negative answer. *Pace* Lee ("Studies," 123), it cannot mean a cautious deprecatory assertion like *haud scio an*, "I do not know whether . . ."; that would require *mē* with the subjunctive (Goodwin, *Moods and Tenses*, 92–93). Because of his Jewish background, Paul would know that his He-

brew Scriptures depicted God concerned for animals (e.g., Ps 104:14, 21, 27); yet
in this context he also gives to the prohibition of Deut 25:4 an added connotation,
a *sensus plenior* (fuller sense): "If God cares for animals he cares more for human
beings" (Murphy-O'Connor, *NJBC*, 807). If the threshing ox may feed on the
grain on which it works, then the apostle may find his needs provided for from
his preaching of the gospel. Paul's question sounds like the statement of Philo,
"The law is not concerned with irrational beings, but with those that have mind
and reason" (*De spec. leg.* 1.48 §260; see also *De virtutibus* 27 §145; *De somniis*
16 §§93–94). Whereas Philo's outlook led to his allegorical mode of interpreting
Scripture, Paul's mentality merely gives a fuller meaning to an OT statement,
which is seen in his second rhetorical question, "Or does he really speak for our
sake?" For Paul is not only actualizing the literal meaning of the OT verse, but
his quotation of it expresses its *sensus plenior* (which must be understood in the
strict theological sense in which that phrase was originally coined [see Brown, *The
Sensus Plenior*, 92], and restricted only to those OT texts that are so extended in
Scripture itself or in its theological, dogmatic outgrowth [see *Romans*, 409]). So
understood, it is clear that not every verse of Scripture has a *sensus plenior*. In any
case, there is no need to invoke here a figurative or allegorical understanding of
Deut 25:4, which is being used in a sense other than literal.

Lohse ("Kümmert") has called attention to a similar Stoic teaching preserved
in Cicero, *De natura deorum* 2.133, which says that the vast system of the universe
(the ebb and flow of rivers, alternation of night and day, etc.) has been mar-
velously administered by divine intelligence "not for the sake of animals" (*bes-
tiarum*) or "for dumb and irrational beings" (*mutorum et nihil intelligentium
causa*), but "that the world and all the things that it contains were made for the
sake of gods and human beings" (*deorum et hominum causa factum esse mundum
quaeque in eo sint omnia*).

10. *Or does he really speak for our sake?* I.e., for us Christians. Paul's further
question uses *pantōs*, "by all means, certainly" (BDAG, 755) and the 1st pers.
plur., as he did in 8:6. It is, in part, an actualization or rereading of an OT passage,
in a way that is not completely heterogeneous to the OT sense. Others (Conzelmann, *1 Cor*, 155) take the 1st pers. plur. as meaning "men in general."

For it was written for our sake. The prep. phrase occupies the first place in the
Greek of this clause, thus giving an emphatic yes to the preceding question, for
gar (not translated here) introduces the reason for the quoting of Deut 25:4 and
conveys that "yes" (BDF §452.2). See further actualizing statements of Paul in
10:11, "were written down as a warning for us"; Rom 4:23–24, "were written not
only for his [Abraham's] sake, but for ours too"; 15:4. What was written of old,
even in the OT, often has lasting pertinence for Christian life, and Paul quotes the
OT as an integral part of his rhetorical argument (see Collins, " 'It Was Indeed
Written' ").

*because the plowman ought to plow in hope, and the thresher (thresh) in hope of
receiving a share.* The meaning and function of this double subordinate clause are
problematic because of the meaning of the introductory conj. *hoti*, the elliptical
form of the second half, and its transmitted text.

Some commentators (Collins, Conzelmann, Lindemann, Senft, J. Weiss) understand *hoti* to mean "that" and take it as introducing a quotation from some unknown apocryphal writing. N-A[27] even cites the following words in italic Greek, as if they were a quotation, but with the marginal note *unde?* (whence?). However, "to take *egraphē* as referring to what follows, and introducing another quotation, is a most improbable construction: there is no such Scripture" (Robertson-Plummer, *1 Cor*, 185). Some commentators, however, try to explain the words as a citation of Sir 6:19, "Approach her as the plowman and sower, and await her good fruits." That may have some similarity, but it is scarcely the source of Paul's words. *Hoti*, however, is understood better in a causal sense, "because," since it then introduces the following words as an elaboration of the meaning of Deut 25:4, in which Paul extends the analogy of the threshing ox to other types of farming (so Barrett, *1 Cor*, 206; Fee, *1 Cor*, 398, 408; Garland, *1 Cor*, 411; Kistemaker, *1 Cor*, 293; Lietzmann, *1 Cor*, 41). For both the plowman at the start of the season and the thresher at its end expectantly await the results of the harvest. The "hope" of the two of them is natural, and Paul extends such a hope analogously in the next verse.

The text of the last phrase is not uniformly transmitted. In MSS P[46], ℵ*, (A), B, C, P 33, 69, it is read as *ep' elpidi tou metechein* (translated in the lemma), where the infin. *aloan*, "to thresh," has to be understood after the subject of the second clause, *ho aloōn*, "the thresher," as the parallel to the infin. "to plow" in the first part. Copyists, who failed to notice that understood infin., changed the words to *tēs elpidos autou metechein*, "to share in his hope" (MSS D*, F, G, 181, 197, 1836). Subsequent copyists combined the readings: *tēs elpidos autou metechein ep' elpidi* (MSS ℵ[c], D[b, c], K, L, Ψ, 88, 326; see Metzger, *TCGNT*, 492). So one has to follow the text of N-A[27] but disregard the italic Greek.

11. *If we have sown spiritual seed among you, is it too much that we should reap a material harvest from you?* Lit. "if we sowed spiritual things in you, is it a great (thing) if we reap fleshy things of you?" So Paul concludes this part of his discussion. The 1st pers. plur. is at least editorial, as in vv. 4, 5 above, but it could also refer to Barnabas and himself. Once again Paul contrasts *pneumatika* and *sarkika*; cf. 3:1, and esp. Rom 15:27, where he uses the contrast of the same terms in speaking about the contributions of the Gentile Christians of Macedonia and Achaia for the poor of the Jerusalem community. Now in Roman Corinth he has sown the seed that has led to spiritual benefits for the Christians there, but what material things he might have gained from them, yet never took, were trivial in comparison.

12. *If others share this rightful claim on you, should not we all the more so?* The "others" were such preachers as Apollos (1:12; 3:4, 22), Cephas (1:12; 3:22), or even Timothy (4:17), whom the Corinthian Christians may have supported materially when they worked among them, but none of them is identified by Paul, who is thinking again implicitly of his role as founder of the Corinthian community.

Yet we have not used this right. Rather, we put up with everything so as not to put an obstacle in the way of the gospel of Christ. Lit. "so as not to produce any hindrance to the gospel of Christ." Paul finally adds a statement to the long series of rhetorical questions that began in v. 4. He asserts boldly that he has not used any of the rights for which he was arguing and hints at what he said about working with his own hands in 4:12. In 2 Cor 11:7–9, he goes even further, insisting that he preached God's gospel to the Corinthians *dōrean*, "for nothing," because his needs were taken care of by fellow Christians of Macedonia (cf. 12:13; 1 Thess 2:9). Instead, his concern has always been for "the gospel of Christ," undoubtedly an obj. gen., the good news that he has been preaching about Christ.

13. *Do you not realize that.* See NOTE on 3:16.

those who are engaged in temple service eat [what] belongs to the temple, and those who minister at the altar share in what is offered on the altar? In vv. 13–18, Paul's argument moves into another dimension, even though it resembles what he has been saying in vv. 7–12. It is no longer a comparison of himself with soldiers, vintners, or shepherds, but now with temple ministers, lit., "those officiating at sacred rites" (*ta hiera*) and "those posted alongside the altar of sacrifice" (*paredreuontes tō thysiastēriō*). One is reminded of the OT regulations about portions of sacrifices reserved for priests in the tent of meeting and later in the Jerusalem Temple (Num 18:8–20), and also of tithes for the Levites (Num 18:21–24); cf. Deut 18:1–5. There were similar regulations for ministers who served in Greek and Roman temples so that the predominantly Gentile Christians of Corinth would readily have understood Paul's argument, no matter which custom he had in mind. Given what Paul writes in 10:20 about pagan services, it is not likely that he is thinking so much of Greek or Roman ministers. He is citing the instance of those engaged in temple service merely for the sake of comparison in order to make a point in his argument about entitlements and rights of apostles.

14. *In the same way the Lord too has ordered those who preach the gospel to get their living from the gospel.* Lit. "to live from the gospel." In beginning with *houtōs kai*, "in the same way," Paul introduces a further argument drawn from authority. He is aware of a saying of Jesus of Nazareth, recorded in the Synoptic Gospels as addressed to disciples sent out during his earthly ministry, "Stay at that one house, eating and drinking what they have, for the laborer deserves his pay." Paul's use of *misthos* in vv. 17–18 echoes the form of the saying in the missionary discourse of the Lucan Gospel (Luke 10:7) more closely than that in the Matthean (Matt 10:10b), which has *trophē* instead of *misthos*. There are other echoes of the Synoptic tradition here (see Murphy-O'Connor, "What Paul Knew," 39; Neirynck, "Paul and the Sayings," 304–6). How Paul would have learned about that saying of Jesus is difficult to say; it may have been part of what he learned from "those who were apostles before me" (Gal 1:17), or even from Cephas, with whom he stayed for "fifteen days" on a visit to Jerusalem (Gal 1:18). The saying turns up again in 1 Tim 5:18; and *Did.* 13.1 echoes the Matthean form in its paraphrase applied to a prophet (see Harvey, " 'The Workman' "). For the OT background of the saying, see Num 18:31; 2 Chr 15:7.

Paul, however, formulates the saying in indirect discourse as a command of "the Lord" (*ho kyrios dietaxen*), as he did the saying about divorce in 7:10; now he applies such a saying to the preaching of "the gospel," his favorite way of summing up the Christian message (see NOTES on 1:17 and 4:15). Cf. Gal 6:6; 1 Tim 5:18c;

Did. 13.1 for various ways the saying of Jesus has been transmitted (see Harvey, " 'The Workman' ").

According to Murphy-O'Connor, "The arguments in vv. 7, 8, and 13 gave Paul a privilege that he was free to waive, but the dominical directive imposed an obligation. The fact that he did not obey indicates that for him even commands of the Lord were not binding precepts" (*NJBC,* 807; cf. "What Paul," 40). By "commands," Murphy-O'Connor means not only 9:14, but also 7:10 (about divorce); similarly Dungan, *Sayings,* 20. The two instances, however, are not the same. The "command" in 9:14, even though expressed as *dietaxen,* "has ordered," is Paul's own formulation of an instruction that was meant to give missionaries a benefit, which they could exploit or not; it laid an obligation not on them, but on the community that they evangelized. According to Fee, "Jesus' word itself is not a 'command' but a proverb" (*1 Cor,* 413); the reason for so regarding it can be seen in 1 Tim 5:18 and *Did.* 13.1. Horrell maintains that the object of *dietaxen* is "the missionaries" (" 'The Lord Commanded,' " 595), which is perhaps correct, but the verb is still Paul's formulation of the command, or his way of establishing the right that he had for support from the preaching of the gospel. Paul could consider something to be a command of the Lord and still judge that he himself did not have to take advantage of a "right" that such a command accorded him (see further Neirynck, "The Sayings," 174–76; Schrage, *1 Cor,* 2:310). That Paul's renunciation of his right to support from the community is the basis for "the Corinthians' subsequent anger against Paul" is sheer speculation, 2 Cor 11:7–12; 12:13–18 notwithstanding, because it is far from certain that those verses of that letter refer to the situation Paul is discussing here. Moreover, the later use of *parangellō* in Mark 6:6; Matt 10:5, which formulates a command given to the apostles, is irrelevant to this discussion in 1 Corinthians. For Paul's use of "the Lord," when citing a saying of Jesus, see NOTE on 7:10.

15. *I, however, have used none of these things.* Lit. "not one of these things" (*oudeni toutōn*), but the antecedent of this neut. expression is not clear. It is regularly taken to mean "right(s)" (so the RSV, NRSV, ESV, NAB, NIV). In this paragraph, however, "right" is *exousia,* a fem. noun (vv. 4–6, 12, 18 [usually sing.]). In using the neut. plur. *toutōn,* Paul is probably referring to the various things mentioned in the preceding verses that support such a "right," as he repeats in stronger form what he said in v. 12c and even begins the repetition with the emphatic *egō de,* no longer using the editorial "we." Others have used these rights, but not he. Indirectly he is proposing himself as an example (see 11:1). The perf. tense in *kechrēmai* stresses the ongoing nature of Paul's refusal to exploit the rights that his status as an apostle gives to him. There is not even a hint that he has refused to exploit them to the benefit of others; he speaks solely about himself.

Nor do I write this that it may be done so in my case. Paul seeks no provision for himself; see v. 18c below. He again uses the epistolary aor., as in 5:11, because he is not saying this to draw his nonuse of support to the attention of the Corinthian Christians so that they may think of supporting him in the future.

I would rather die than have someone deprive me of my boast. Lit. "for it is good for me to die rather than (that) no one will empty my boast," reading with the best MSS (P⁴⁶, ℵ*, B, D*, 33, 1739), *kalon gar moi mallon apothanein ē to kauchēma* *mou oudeis kenōsei.* There is, however, no guarantee that the verse has been correctly transmitted (Metzger, *TCGNT*, 492). Perhaps Paul deliberately has changed the sentence in midstream (anacoluthon noted in BDF §393.2; cf. Lietzmann, *1 Cor*, 43). Other mss (ℵᶜ, C, Dᵇ, K, P, Ψ, etc.) read *hina tis*, "in order that someone," instead of *oudeis*, "no one," thus correcting the anomalous text. The translation in the lemma carries enough sense in the present context, whatever the true reading might be. Just as he relinquished his right to "eat meat" (8:13), so now he "insists that he will continue his actual practice of not using his right to material support from the Corinthians" (Still, "Paul's Aims," 339).

16. *If I preach the gospel, there is no reason for me to boast.* Lit. "there is for me no boast." The following statement explains why Paul makes this disclaimer. Some mss (ℵ*, D*, F, G) strangely read *charis*, "grace," instead of *kauchēma*, "boast."

For compulsion lies upon me! Woe to me if I do not preach it! There can be no boasting in what one has to do, and Paul *must* preach the gospel. This "compulsion" (*anankē*) is not merely a psychological condition; it expresses a compulsion exercised on Paul from outside.

> "*Ananke* lies upon me" is said of destiny which lays hold on a man, not of feelings which animate us, nor of an obligation which we have to satisfy. The recollection of the Damascus experience, however, does serve as an illustration; yet it will not do as a canon of interpretation, because Paul is not looking back on what happened in the past and on its effects, but speaking of his service in the present. In the last resort, it is not just any situation which is calling the apostle to the work, nor is it an emergency. His commission, and the compulsion arising out of it, originate with his Lord. . . . the voices of Old Testament prophets have not infrequently been recognized as the closest parallels to our Pauline passage; in them, similarly, the commission to preach is described an an ineluctable destiny and the prophet even haggles with God about his fate. If the Old Testament "Woe is me" stands as an antithesis to the Pauline "*Ananke* lies upon me," this acts as a reminder that "Woe," both in the Old and New Testaments, can signify a personification of the divine curse and eschatological wrath, in the power of which God executes his judgments. (Käsemann, "Pauline Version," 229)

Paul's words about this need to preach the gospel echo those of Jeremiah and his need to proclaim God's word (Jer 1:6–7; 20:9); also Amos's words (3:8). *Anankē* denotes here "the power of the divine will which radically and successfully challenges man and makes its servant its instrument." As a converted Jew, Paul cannot be speaking, "like the Greek with his *anankē* or the Roman with his *fatum,* of an impersonal force of blind ill-omen or chance. He may indeed be making use of the Greek concept, but only in order to delineate the character of the divine power as sovereign, inexorable and ineluctable" (ibid., 230). Yet that does not mean that Paul must preach the gospel *gratis,* even though that is what he has been doing, and therein lies his "boast."

In the second exclamation, Paul uses an OT imprecatory formula, *ouai moi,* "woe to me," which is found verbatim with the 1st pers. sing. pron. only in Tob 10:5 (MS S), but abundantly elsewhere with other persons (e.g., LXX Hos 9:12 [*ouai autois* = Hebrew *'ôy lāhem*]). Cf. the related formulas, *oimmoi egō*, LXX Jer 15:10; and Hebrew *'ôy lî*, Isa 6:5, which becomes in the LXX, *ō talas egō*, "O wretch that I am."

17. *If I do so willingly, I have a recompense.* Paul makes use of a financial term, *misthos*, "remuneration for work done." That remuneration is neither an echatological recompense nor the material support of the Corinthian community, but rather the satisfaction of doing what he is expected to do. At least that seems to be the meaning of the first part of this verse, which along with the following part of the verse has always been a *crux interpretum*.

but if I do so unwillingly, I have been entrusted with a stewardship. I.e., what I have in such a case is a stewardship with which I have been entrusted—something that I am expected to carry out with fidelity. Paul's sentiment seems to be like that of Luke 17:10, "So you too should say, when you have done all that is commanded you, 'We are unprofitable servants; we have only done what we were supposed to do.' "

18. *What then is my recompense? That, when I preach, I may offer the gospel free of charge so as not to make full use of my right in preaching the gospel.* This verse is the logical conclusion of the second alternative of v. 17. It means that Paul is identifying his "recompense" (*misthos*) with his "boast" (*kauchēma*, v. 15). He must preach the gospel; that is the "stewardship" (*oikonomia*) with which he has been entrusted; but he is under no obligation to preach it "free of charge" (*adapanon*), as he has been doing (cf. 2 Cor 11:7). In so acting, he has a reason for his "boast," and this is his "recompense." This brings to an end the first section of Paul's discussion in this chapter.

19. *For though I am free and belong to no one, I have made myself a slave to all so that I may win over as many as possible.* Lit. "being free of all, to all have I enslaved myself that I might gain the more." As Paul returns to the first topic, freedom, announced in 9:1, he enunciates a principle that lies under all that he has been saying so far in this chapter. In this section (vv. 19–23), he explains further his motivation for the right that he has freely renounced in vv. 15–18.

Paul is scarcely referring to his freedom as a Roman citizen, which he never mentions in any of his letters, but rather to a more basic freedom, the independence from all other human beings as a Christian apostle. And yet, there is the paradox, because he has indentured himself to the service of others to win over as many of them as possible to the Christian gospel and to Christ Jesus. This is a global statement using "all," as it introduces three specific groups that Paul will mention whom he has sought to "win over" to Christ, which in v. 22b will be interpreted as salvation (*sōsō*). As Bornkamm has rightly noted, "Paul could not modify the gospel itself according to the particular characteristics of his hearers. The whole of his concern is to make clear that the changeless gospel, which lies upon him as his *anankē* (9:16), empowers him to be free to change his stance" ("Missionary Stance," 196). The changeless gospel accosts its hearers in their historical situation, and Paul does not seek to change that (1 Cor 7:17–24). So he accommodates himself to the situation of his different hearers.

Daube ("*Kerdainō* as a Missionary Term") has contested the "missionary" sense of the verb, insisting rather that its use with a pers. obj. in the sense of "gaining, winning over" someone for the kingdom is rather an idea borrowed from various Hebrew verbs used in rabbinic literature such as *kānas*, "gather," or *qānāh*, "acquire." Yet he gives no example of such verbs being translated by *kerdainō*; and his whole argument merely shows that sages of the later rabbinic tradition had similar ideas. On the contrary, BDAG (541) clearly admits the sense of *kerdainō* meaning "gain" someone for the Reign of God. "To win over" means to "bring them closer to Christ's way" (see Neller, "1 Corinthians 9:19–23").

In vv. 19–23, Paul's argument becomes a parallel to what he asserted in 8:9–13, and it provides a justification for what he maintained in those verses. A chiasmus exists in the Greek text that can be seen in a literal English version: "free of all — to all have I enslaved myself." It is, however, problematic in that *pantōn* and *pasin* may be either masc. or neut.; I have taken them as masc. because later on in the sentence *pleionas*, "the more," is masc. plur., and the examples in the coming verses are persons.

20. *To Jews I became like a Jew to win over Jews.* Paul speaks of his conduct as a Christian apostle of Jewish background who has sought to win over some of his former coreligionists to the gospel, the first of the three specific groups. He is referring to either Jewish Christians or Judaizers who would consider themselves to be under the law. Because, however, he was born a Jew, it is strange that he now says, "I became like a Jew." He undoubtedly means that he not only lived with them and dealt with them socially, but deliberately followed Jewish practices dictated by the Mosaic law, even though it is not easy to explain specifically what these might have been from any of his writings. That he evangelized Jews in various situations is implied by 2 Cor 11:24, where he speaks of having "received at the hands of Jews the forty lashes less one," where *hypo Ioudaiōn* suggests that he so suffered as a Christian, but he never tells us for what reasons he experienced such synagogue floggings. See *m. Makkoth* 3.1–8 for many reasons for such flogging in the later rabbinic tradition. In any case, the following clause explains the sense in which the Christian Paul now means his becoming "like a Jew."

In Acts, however, Luke depicts the converted Paul so observing Jewish practices (having Timothy circumcised [16:1–3]; cutting his hair at Cenchreae [because of a Nazirite vow, 18:18]; purifying himself in the Jerusalem Temple [21:23–26]), although Bornkamm is one of several interpreters willing to speak out "against the reliability of the report" of Timothy's circumcision ("Missionary Stance," 203). Paul himself recognized at times the privileged situation of his former coreligionists in God's salvific plan (Rom 1:16; 2:9: "the Jew first but also the Greek"), which explains why he is depicted often by Luke going first to the Jewish synagogue on his arrival in a new town to begin his evangelization of it (13:5, 14, 46; 14:1; 17:1, 10, 17; 18:4).

to those under the law I became like one under the law. This clause is best understood as a mere parallel to the first clause in this verse, even though there is no similar parallel expressed in vv. 21–22; Paul adds it in view of what he will assert in the coming clause. On "the law," see NOTE on 9:8. "Those under the law" is a designation for Jews in Gal 4:5, and the opposite, "those not under the law," denotes

Christians in Gal 5:18; Rom 6:14–15. Consequently, Paul, in adding this clause to the first one where Jews are explicitly mentioned is scarcely distinguishing Torah-faithful Jews from judaizing Christians, *pace* Lindemann (*1 Cor*, 212), Gal 4:21 notwithstanding. How Paul became "like one under the law" creates the same problem as "like a Jew" in the first clause (see above).

though I myself am not under the law. This important qualification finds an explanation in Gal 2:15–16, where Paul speaks of himself and Cephas, "We ourselves, who are Jews by birth and not Gentile sinners, know that a human being is not justified by works of the law, but through faith in Jesus Christ." That is why he can now phrase his relation to the law as he does here; to be justified Paul feels no obligation to observe the Mosaic law and all its precepts.

This clause, however, is missing in MSS D^2, (L), Ψ, 1881, and the Koine texttradition, but found in MSS ℵ, A, B, C, D*, F, G, P, 33, 104, 365, 1175, 1505, 1739. Despite its being read in these important copies, Tomson regards it as "added later . . . in view of the development of anti-Judaism" (*Paul*, 277), but offers no evidence of such development. Note the Lucan formulation of the matter in Acts 13:38–39, the only place in the Lucan writings where Paul is depicted preaching justification, but where it is interpreted as "the forgiveness of sins," a Lucan effect of the Christ-event (see *Acts*, 518–19).

that I might win over those under the law. In Rom 11:13–14, Paul similarly asserts, "I make much of this ministry of mine in the hope that I may stir up my own people [lit. my own flesh] to jealousy and save some of them."

21. *To those without the law I became like one without the law.* I.e., like Gentiles, or "Greeks" (1:22), with no obligation to observe the Mosaic law, the second of the three specific groups. Paul himself was not "lawless" or an antinomian with disdain for all legal regulations, as the next clause will make clear, but he became like those who were "law-less." This statement merely formulates his conviction as *ethnōn apostolos*, "apostle of the Gentiles" (Rom 11:13), a conviction explained in Gal 2:19–20: "Through the law I died to the law, that I might live for God. I have been crucified with Christ. It is no longer I who live, but Christ who lives in me."

It is not easy to capture the rhetoric of this verse and express its equivalence in English, because four times Paul uses words that are compounds of *nomos*, "law," which refers in this passage to the Mosaic law. He begins by referring to Gentiles as people who are *anomoi*, "law-less," i.e., "without the (Mosaic) law," and identifies himself also as *anomos* in the same sense; but then he denies that he is *anomos*, "lawless," i.e., one who spurns all law in the sight of God, because he is *ennomos Christou*, "in/under the law of Christ," a law different from that of Moses.

though I am not without God's law, being under the law of Christ. Whereas Paul once lived as one under "God's law," as it was given to Israel by Moses, he now sees himself legally bound in some sense to Christ. In Gal 6:2, he speaks of fulfilling "the law of Christ," in a context where it means bearing the burdens of one another (a matter of fraternal correction). Dodd once sought to explain *ennomos Christou* as "a code of precepts to which a Christian . . . is obliged to conform," because Gal 6:2 "is embedded in a series of moral injunctions forming part of what is called the 'ethical section' of the epistle" ("*Ennomos Christou*," 138). In the same article, Dodd tried to relate to this phrase other references to "commands" of the Lord in 1 Cor 7:10, 25; 9:14. Yet even if one has to reckon with such commands in this letter, it is quite another thing to speak of *ennomos Christou* as connoting a "code," similar to that of Moses. Nowhere in Pauline writings is "the law of Christ" further explained; yet it is hardly meant as a new legal code, even if it is meant to be something that replaces the code of old. No better is the explanation of Tomson that Paul "positively . . . is Law-respecting 'under the aspect of Christ': he does not observe the Law as an aim in itself and standing alone but as one among various members of Christ's body" (*Paul*, 280). That is hardly correct.

The sense of *ennomos Christou* has to be sought in what Paul has written about Christ and faith in him that he regards as the response to "God's gospel" (Rom 1:1). In Gal 5:6, Paul speaks of Christian faith "working itself out through love," and in Rom 13:8–10 he explains how love works in Christian life: "the one who loves another has fulfilled the law. . . . Love does no wrong to a neighbor, for love is the fulfillment of the law." There, although "law" refers again to the Mosaic law (quoted in 13:9), it can be seen that Christian love, which springs from faith, and to which Paul will devote chap. 13, constitutes "the law of Christ," "the law of the Spirit of life in Christ Jesus" (Rom 8:2), or "the law of faith" (Rom 3:27), which is the "principle" of faith. So it is not to be understood as a legal code; nor is it the Mosaic law respected by Paul "under the aspect of Christ," but it is only "law" in a wholly analogous sense. It is the way Christ exercises his lordship over those who are called to him (see Winger, "Law of Christ").

that I might win over those without the law. I.e., to win over Gentiles to Christ Jesus. The same purpose clause expresses Paul's goal again, even though the form is no longer *kerdēsō*, as in vv. 19, 20be, but *kerdanō*, a variant form of the aor. subjunctive (BDAG, 541). The latter is read in mss ℵ*, A, B, C, F, G, P, but mss P⁴⁶, ℵ², D, Ψ have *kerdēsō*, a copyist's harmonization with vv. 19, 20, 22.

22. *To the weak I became weak, that I might win over the weak.* The "weak" (*astheneis*) are the third specific group that Paul has sought to win over. For many commentators, Paul thus returns to the topic of chap. 8 and refers to those "weak" in conscience about idol meat (8:7–13); but it might perhaps be understood in a broader sense, as he will use the term in Rom 14:1; 15:1 For Barrett (*1 Cor*, 215), they are "Christians not yet fully emancipated from legalism"; similarly (with differing nuances) for Conzelmann (*1 Cor*, 161); Hays (*1 Cor*, 155); Kremer (*1 Cor*, 195); Robertson-Plummer (*1 Cor*, 192); Soards (*1 Cor*, 193). For others, the "weak" are the sociologically insecure, as in 1:27b (so Fee, *1 Cor*, 431). In such interpretations, the "weak" are considered Christians, and the meaning of *kerdainō* has then to have a nuance slightly different from vv. 19, 20, 21 (Barrett; Grosheide, *1 Cor*, 214). That, however, becomes even more problematic. For Lietzmann (*1 Cor*, 43), they are "Halbchristen" (half-Christians), a term that needs further explanation. Others understand the "weak" as non-Christians (Jews or Gentiles), as are the other groups in vv. 19–21, people whom Paul sought to win over to Christ as converts. The "weak," then, would be like those mentioned

in Rom 5:6, "While we were still helpless (*ontōn hēmōn asthenōn eti*), Christ died . . . for the godless," i.e., those powerless to achieve salvation for themselves (Black, "A Note"; Garland, *1 Cor*, 433–34; somewhat similarly, J. Weiss, *1 Cor*, 245; Schrage, *1 Cor*, 2:345–46: "timid and superstitious non-Christians"). This seems to be a better interpretation, for there is no certainty that the "weak" people now mentioned are to be found only in Corinth; they could be found elsewhere. They are mentioned last in the list of three groups, because "weak" is the climactic and comprehensive term summing up the situation of the other two groups (Jews and Gentiles); so Hays, *1 Cor*, 154. It is perhaps better to leave the weak further undetermined, whether they be Christians or not, because Paul's argument applies to "all."

When Paul says, "I became weak," there is no conj. *hōs*, "as, like," as in *hōs Ioudaios* (v. 20) or *hōs anomos* (v. 21), even though it is read here in some MSS (‭א²‬, C, D, F, G, Ψ, and the Koine text-tradition), which is recognized as a copyist's harmonization. Nor is there an explanatory clause, as in vv. 20d, 21b. In saying that he "became weak," Paul is giving up his right to be "strong," and it might even mean that Paul is abasing himself socially as he identifies himself with those mentioned (1:27b) or, more likely, even considering himself theologically one of the godless in order to win the different groups over to Christ.

I have become all things to all people that I might save at least some. Or "that by all means I might save some," because the adv. *pantōs* can express either the lowest possible estimate or a strong assumption (BDAG, 755). Whereas Paul had used the aor. *egenomēn* in vv. 20, 22a, he now employs he perf. *gegona*, "I have become," to stress the lasting effect of his condition (Lindemann, *1 Cor*, 213). So Paul formulates his fundamental principle in evangelization, whether those he would win over be weak or knowing, Jew or Greek, slave or free. This statement, using *pasin, panta, pantōs*, shows that the groups are merely examples by which Paul illustrates his principle. Implied is his love and concern for the salvation of "all," no matter what their social or ethnic condition or religious conviction may be. Cf. 10:33, which fills out what Paul says here; see also Rom 11:14. The "some" stands in contrast to the "as many as possible" (*tous pleionas*, lit., "the more," v. 19).

23. *I do it all for the sake of the gospel, so that I may have a share in it.* Lit. "so that I may become a sharer in it," i.e., a participant in its benefits. Two points are asserted here: The preaching of the gospel and its progress have constituted a goal in Paul's life, as 1:17 and 1 Thess 2:2 also make clear, for he regarded it as something very precious to him, and likewise the treasuring of a share that he was able to have in its blessings, especially the salvation that it promises. In using *synkoinōnos*, Paul could also mean a share that he might have in the ministry of spreading the gospel (BDAG, 952; cf. Hooker, "Partner"). He "who loves can and must renounce his rights, however well-founded they may be, if he is to go on really loving and serving effectively. Once that is clear, the fundamental problem of our passage can be formulated thus: 'How can the man who experiences the compulsion of the Gospel as that of his destiny at the same time be, and remain, the man who loves?' " (Käsemann, "Pauline Version," 233). So Paul draws the second section of this chapter to an end, to which he now adds a transitional exhortation.

24. *Do you not realize that.* Again Paul makes use of a rhetorical question as an introduction, as in v. 13 above, where a different illustration was brought in; see NOTE on 3:16.

all runners in the stadium run in the race, but only one wins the prize? Run, then, so as to win. So Paul introduces another consideration of the way his freedom has been restricted; it is drawn from the discipline needed in athletic contests. The verb *trechō,* "run," is taken from foot racing in a stadium, and *brabeion* has its primary sense of "prize, award" (in an athletic contest). The second-century writer, Lucian of Samosata, composed a dialogue on athletics in which he records a similar account of contests: Many are the contestants, who undergo hardships in the chance that they might win, "but only one of all of them, the victor" gets the prize (*Anacharsis* 13). Paul makes use of this comparison because of the second point he made in v. 23, his sharing in the blessings of the gospel. He must be careful to respect the demands of the gospel in his own life, just as the runner must in a race. Cf. Phil 3:14; 2 Tim 4:7. Although the goal concerns Paul personally, he formulates it generically and even includes an impv., as if he were coaching prospective runners.

The discipline of which Paul speaks may be drawn from what he undoubtedly knew of the Isthmian Games, which were celebrated every other year at Isthmia, in honor of the sea god Poseidon and the youth god Palaimon, under the auspices of the neighboring city of Corinth (see Broneer, "Apostle Paul," 7–12). There were also the well-known Olympic Games, from which philosophers in the Greco-Roman world, especially of the Stoic and Cynic traditions, derived metaphors for expressing their ethical teaching (see Pfitzner, *Paul and the Agon Motif,* 28–35; Schwankl, " 'Lauft' ").

25. *Every athlete exercises self-control in every way.* Although Paul used the verb *enkrateuomai* in 7:9 in a context of sexual continence, he now uses it in a more generic sense of self-control, such as would be demanded by athletic contests. A generic sense of *enkrateia* is found likewise in Philo, when he speaks of the Therapeutae and their cultivation of it as "the foundation of life" (*De vita contemplativa* 4 §34). Cf. 2 Pet 1:6.

they do it to win a perishable crown, but we an imperishable one. The victory crown (*stephanos*) at the Isthmian Games was a wreath made of either pine needles (*stephanos ek pityos,* Lucian, *Anarchasis* 9–10) or wild celery; and in the first century A.D., most likely of the latter (so Broneer, "Apostle Paul," 16–17; cf. Papathomas, "Das agonistische Motiv," 225–33). Lucian tells of what competitors endure to get possession "of an apple and an olive-branch" (*Anacharsis* 13). Whatever runners in such games may contend for, Paul's goal is entirely different, a crown that does not wither. The "we" may again be editorial, or refer to Paul and Barnabas as examples of runners, or to Christians in general, with whom Paul would identify himself. *Martyrdom of Polycarp* (19.2) speaks of Polycarp as a martyr who won *ton tēs aphtharsias stephanon,* "the crown of immortality."

26. *I at least do not run aimlessly; I do not box as if I were beating the air.* Lit. "I at least run as not without purpose, I so box, as one not beating air." So Paul applies the metaphor to himself in the contest in which he is engaged, as he preaches the gospel. He is serious about what he is doing and does not spare him-

self in the effort needed in his evangelization. Paul shifts the image of himself from a runner in a race to an another kindred strenuous athlete, that of a boxer in a ring, as he employs the verb *pykteuō*, "box," i.e., strike "with the fist" (*pyx* [adv.]). The boxing may not involve another boxer, as the next verse suggests.

27. *Rather, I pommel my body and subjugate it, lest in preaching to others I myself might be disqualified.* Lit. "I strike under the eye" (*hypōpiazō*), which actually means to give (someone) a black eye, but here it has "my body" as its object, a strange combination; and it is followed by an equally strange verb with the same object, "I lead (my body) into slavery" (*doulagōgō*). Despite the images that the two verbs convey, Paul is employing contemporary vivid athletic images that express the self-restraint and discipline necessary to achieve a goal, and these he applies to his apostolic task (see Papathomas, "Das agonistische Motiv," 240–41, who shows that Paul's use of such terminology conforms well with the athletic contests of his day and the motivation that inspired them). Paul's purpose is expressed in the last clause, *mē pōs . . . autos adokimos genōmai*, "lest I myself might become (one) not standing the test," i.e., not having achieved the goal, to which his preaching would have been summoning others. Paul's disciplined life in the service of the gospel is meant to be an example for Corinthian Christians in their pursuit of life. Cf. his use of athletic imagery and the goal of life in Phil 3:12–16 (see Metzner, "Paulus und der Wettkampf").

BIBLIOGRAPHY (See also Bibliography on 8:1–11:1, pp. 350–52)

Adler, E. N., et al. (eds.), *The Adler Papyri: The Greek Texts* . . . (London: Oxford University Press/H. Milford, 1939; repr. Milan: Cisalpino-Galliardica, 1974) 21–23.
Arndt, W., "The Meaning of 1 Cor. 9,9.10," *CTM* 3 (1932) 329–35.
Arzt-Grabner, P., " 'Brothers' and 'Sisters' in Documentary Papyri and in Early Christianity," *RivB* 50 (2002) 185–204.
Barton, S. C., "All Things to All People": Paul and the Law in the Light of 1 Corinthians 9.19–23," in *Paul and the Mosaic Law* (WUNT 89; ed. J. D. G. Dunn; Tübingen: Mohr [Siebeck], 1996) 271–85.
Bauer, J. B., "Uxores circumducere (1 Kor 9,5)," *BZ* 3 (1959) 94–102.
Bienert, W. A., "The Relatives of Jesus," in Schneemelcher, *NTApocr*, 1:470–88.
Black, D. A., "A Note on 'the Weak' in 1 Corinthians 9,22," *Bib* 64 (1983) 240–42.
Blinzler, J., *Die Brüder und Schwestern Jesu* (SBS 21; Stuttgart: Katholisches Bibelwerk, 1967).
Bornkamm, G., "The Missionary Stance of Paul in I Corinthians 9 and in Acts," *Studies in Luke-Acts: Essays Presented in Honor of Paul Schubert* (ed. L. E. Keck and J. L. Martyn; Nashville, TN: Abingdon, 1966) 194–207.
Broneer, O., "The Apostle Paul and the Isthmian Games," *BA* 25 (1962) 1–31.
Brown, R. E., *The Sensus Plenior of Sacred Scripture* (Baltimore: St. Mary's University Press, 1955).
Caragounis, C. C., "*Opsōnion*: A Reconsideration of Its Meaning," *NovT* 16 (1974) 35–57.
Carson, D. A., "Pauline Inconsistency: Reflections on I Corinthians 9.19–23 and Galatians 2.11–14," *Churchman* 100 (1986) 6–45.
Chapman, J., "The Brethren of the Lord," *JTS* 7 (1905–6) 412–34.

Collins, R. F., " 'It Was Indeed Written for Our Sake' (1 Cor 9,10): Paul's Use of Scripture in the First Letter to the Corinthians," *SNTU* A20 (1995) 151–70.

Craffert, P. F., " 'Seeing' a Body into Being: Reflections on Scholarly Interpretations of the Nature and Reality of Jesus' Resurrected Body," *R&T* 9 (2002) 89–107.

Daube, D., "*Kerdainō* as a Missionary Term," *HTR* 40 (1947) 109–20.

Dautzenberg, G., "Der Verzicht auf das apostolische Unterhaltsrecht: Eine exegetische Untersuchung zu 1 Kor 9," *Bib* 50 (1969) 212–32.

Didier, G., "Le salaire du désintéressement (*I Cor.* ix, 14–27)," *RSR* 43 (1955) 228–51.

Dodd, C. H., "*Ennomos Christou,*" *More New Testament Studies* (Manchester, UK: Manchester University Press, 1968) 134–48.

Garrison, R., "Paul's Use of the Athlete Metaphor in 1 Corinthians 9," *SR* 22 (1993) 209–17.

Grelot, P., "Les noms de parenté dans le livre de *Tobie,*" *RevQ* 17 (1996) 327–37.

Hall, B., "All Things to All People: A Study of 1 Corinthians 9:19–23," *The Conversation Continues: Studies in Paul and John in Honor of J. Louis Martyn* (ed. R. T. Fortna and B. R. Gaventa; Nashville: Abingdon, 1990) 137–57.

Hanson, A. T., *The Living Utterances of God: The New Testament Exegesis of the Old* (London: Darton, Longman and Todd, 1983).

Harvey, A. E., " 'The Workman Is Worthy of His Hire': Fortunes of a Proverb in the Early Church," *NovT* 24 (1982) 209–21.

Hollander, H. W., "The Meaning of the Term 'Law' (*Nomos*) in 1 Corinthians," *NovT* 40 (1998) 117–35.

Hooker, M. D., "A Partner in the Gospel: Paul's Understanding of Ministry," *EpRev* 25/1 (1998) 70–78.

Horrell, D., " 'The Lord Commanded . . . but I Have not Used . . .': Exegetical and Hermeneutical Reflections on 1 Cor 9.14–15," *NTS* 43 (1997) 587–603.

Instone Brewer, D., "1 Corinthians 9.9–11: A Literal Interpretation of 'Do not Muzzle the Ox,' " *NTS* 38 (1992) 554–65.

Jeremias, J., "Paulus als Hillelit," *Neotestamentica et semitica: Studies in Honour of Matthew Black* (ed. E. E. Ellis and M. Wilcox; Edinburgh: Clark, 1969) 88–94.

Joubert, S., "1 Corinthians 9:24–27: An Agonistic Competition?" *Neotestamentica* 35 (2001) 57–68.

Kaiser, W. C., Jr., "The Current Crisis in Exegesis and the Apostolic Use of Deuteronomy 25:4 in 1 Corinthians 9:8–10," *JETS* 21 (1978) 3–18.

Käsemann, E., "A Pauline Version of the 'Amor Fati,' " *New Testament Questions*, 217–35.

Klauck, H.-J., *Hausgemeinde und Hauskirche im frühen Christentum* (SBS 103; Stuttgart: Katholisches Bibelwerk, 1981).

Kreuzer, S., "Der Zwang des Boten—Beobachtungen zu Lk 14,23 und 1 Kor 9,16," *ZNW* 76 (1985) 123–28.

Lee, G. M., "Studies in Texts: 1 Corinthians 9: 9–10," *Theology* 71 (1968) 122–23.

Lohse, E., " 'Kümmert sich Gott etwa um die Ochsen?' Zu 1 Kor 9,9," *ZNW* 88 (1997) 314–15.

Meier, J. P., "The Brothers and Sisters of Jesus in Ecumenical Perspective," *CBQ* 54 (1992) 1–28.

Metzner, R., "Paulus und der Wettkampf: Die Rolle des Sports in Leben und Verkündigung des Apostels (1 Kor 9.24–7; Phil 3.12–16)," *NTS* 46 (2000) 565–83.

Murphy-O'Connor, J., "What Paul Knew of Jesus," *ScrB* 12 (1981–82) 35–40.

Nasuti, H. P., "The Woes of the Prophets and the Rights of the Apostle: The Internal Dynamics of 1 Corinthians 9," *CBQ* 50 (1988) 246–64.

Neirynck, F., "Paul and the Sayings of Jesus," *L'Apôtre Paul* (BETL 73; ed. A. Vanhoye), 265–321.

Neller, K. V., "1 Corinthians 9:19–23: A Model for Those Who Seek to Win Souls," *ResQ* 29 (1987) 129–42.

Nickel, K., "A Parenthetical Apologia: 1 Corinthians 9: 1–3," *CurTM* 1 (1974) 68–70.

Papathomas, A., "Das agonistische Motiv 1 Kor 9.24ff. im Spiegel zeitgenössischer dokumentarischer Quellen," *NTS* 43 (1997) 223–41.

Pfitzner, V. C., *Paul and the Agon Motif: Traditional Athletic Imagery in the Pauline Literature* (NovTSup 16; Leiden: Brill, 1967).

Pratscher, W., "Der Verzicht des Paulus auf finanziellen Unterhalt durch seine Gemeinden: Ein Aspekt seiner Missionsweise," *NTS* 25 (1978–79) 284–98.

Richardson, P., "Pauline Inconsistency: I Corinthians 9: 19–23 and Galatians 2: 11–14," *NTS* 26 (1979–80) 347–62.

——, and P. W. Gooch, "Accommodation Ethics," *TynBul* 29 (1978) 89–142.

Schwankl, O., " 'Lauft so, dass ihr gewinnt': Zur Wettkampfmetaphorik in 1 Kor 9," *BZ* 41 (1997) 174–91.

Smit, J. F. M., " 'You Shall not Muzzle a Threshing Ox': Paul's Use of the Law of Moses in 1 Cor 9,8–12," *EstBíb* 58 (2000) 239–63.

Sumney, J. L., "The Place of 1 Corinthians 9:24–27 in Paul's Argument," *JBL* 119 (2000) 329–33.

Theissen, G., "Legitimation und Lebensunterhalt: Ein Beitrag zur Soziologie urchristlicher Missionare," *NTS* 21 (1974–75) 192–221.

Theobald, M., " 'Allen bin ich alles geworden . . .' (1 Kor 9, 22b): Paulus und das Problem der Inkulturation des Glaubens," *TQ* 176 (1996) 1–6.

Thielman, F., "The Coherence of Paul's View of the Law: The Evidence of First Corinthians," *NTS* 38 (1992) 235–53.

Tscherikower, V., and F. M. Heichelheim, "Jewish Religious Influence in the Adler Papyri?" *HTR* 35 (1942) 25–44.

Willis, W., "An Apostolic Apologia? The Form and Function of 1 Corinthians 9," *JSNT* 24 (1985) 33–48.

Winger, M., "The Law of Christ," *NTS* 46 (2000) 537–46.

21   c. *Israel's Example Warns*
Christians Not to Partake of Pagan
Temple Meals (10:1–22)

10:1 I do not want you to be unaware, brothers, that all our ancestors were under the cloud and that all passed through the sea. 2 All of them were baptized into Moses in the cloud and in the sea. 3 All ate the same spiritual food, 4 and all drank the same spiritual drink, for they used to drink of a spiritual rock that followed them, and the rock was Christ. 5 Nevertheless, God was not pleased with most of them, for they were laid low in the wilderness. 6 Now in view of these things they have become archetypes for us, so that we may not crave for evil even as they did. 7 Do not become idolaters as some of them did, as it stands written: *"The people sat down to eat and drink, and they got up to revel."* [8]We should not indulge in fornication, as some of them did; and twenty-three thousand of them fell in a single day. [9]We should not put Christ to the test, as some of them did; and were destroyed by serpents. [10]Do not grumble, as some of them did, and were destroyed by the Destroyer. [11]These things were happening to them prefiguratively and were written down as a warning for us, upon whom the ends of the ages have met. [12]Consequently, whoever thinks that he is standing firm should see to it that he does not fall. [13]No trial has overtaken you but what is human. God is trustworthy, and he will not allow you to be tried beyond what you can bear; but with the trial he will provide also a way out, so that you may be able to endure it. [14]Therefore, my dear friends, flee from idolatry. [15]I am speaking as to wise people; judge for yourselves what I am saying. [16]Is not the cup of blessing that we bless a participation in the blood of Christ? Is not the bread that we break a participation in the body of Christ? [17]Because there is one loaf, we, though many, are one body, for we all partake of the one loaf. [18]Consider the people of Israel. Are not those who eat the sacrifices participants in the altar? [19]What then am I saying? That meat sacrificed to idols is something? Or that an idol is something? [20]Rather, what they sacrifice [they sacrifice] to demons and not to God, and I do not want you to become partners of the demons. [21]You cannot drink the cup of the Lord and the cup of demons as well; you cannot partake of the table of the Lord and the table of demons. [22]Or are we stirring the Lord to jealousy? Are we stronger than he?

COMMENT

Paul has finished his digression about his status as an apostle and its consequent freedom and rights, but also about his example as one who exercises self-restraint in exploiting such rights on behalf of preaching the gospel to others. Now he returns to the question of idol meat, in order to discuss other aspects of it. *Eidōlothyton,* "meat sacrificed to idols," was used in 8:1, 4, 7, 10; it turns up in this section only in 10:19. Although Paul mentioned *eidōlolatrēs,* "idolater," in 5:10, 11; 6:9, he will refer to that kind of person again in 10:7 and will formulate a generic warning, "flee from idolatry" in 10:14, echoing his admonition about flight from fornication (6:18). Now one sees that the eating of idol meat has assumed a broader perspective; it is no longer simply a problem for those whose conscience is "weak" (8:7), but one related to idolatry, which a Christian must shun. Verses 1–22 form a unit, because v. 1a calls attention to the topic to be discussed now, and its conclusion is set forth in v. 21, to which the rhetorical questions of v. 22 resound.

The desert experience of Israel of old presented monitory examples and teaches Christians not only how they should deal with idol meat (vv. 1–14), but also how they should think about their participation in the Lord's Supper (vv. 15–22), which is not unrelated. Paul discusses that experience from this double perspective. He treats it under four headings:

1. Beginning with "our ancestors," he cites five privileges of "all" the Israelites who wandered in the desert after their deliverance from Egyptian bondage: how God accompanied them in a cloud, rescued them from the pursuing

Egyptians at the Reed Sea, guided them through Moses, supplied them with food, and gave them water to drink (vv. 1–4).

2. Paul then recounts five incidents that tell how God became displeased at the rebellious conduct of "most/some of them": their covetous craving for evil, their adoration and idolatrous feasting in the Golden Calf episode, their fornication with Moabite women, their testing the Lord, and their grumbling against Him (see Perrot, "Les exemples"). Because of all this, God laid them low in the desert and destroyed them (vv. 5–10).

3. In all that happened to them, they became premonitory archetypes for us Christians, who live in a new age, when God does not try us beyond what we can bear. Consequently, we must flee from all idolatry (vv. 11–14).

4. Furthermore, as Christians, who share in the body and blood of Christ at the Table of the Lord, we cannot share also in the table of demons, thus provoking the Lord to anger (vv. 15–22). Note the contrast between *pantes*, "all," in vv. 1–4 and *pleiones/tines autōn*, "most/some of them," in vv. 5–10, each occurring five times.

The major problem in this pericope is the way it is to be related to the rest of Paul's discussion of the problem of idol meat. In chap. 8, he adopted a double, rather lenient view of the matter, agreeing basically with those who "possess knowledge" that an idol was a nonentity in this world (vv. 1–6), but insisting on a restriction to their basic freedom derived from such knowledge for the sake of the "weak" (vv. 7–13); and in the case that he will discuss in 10:23–31 he will again return to such a point of view. Now, however, Paul's attitude is much more absolute: "flee from idolatry" (v. 14), because "you cannot partake of the table of the Lord and the table of demons" (v. 21). That is addressed to all Corinthian Christians, both the weak and those who possess knowledge. Other minor problems are found in the reference to baptism in v. 2, the meaning of "spiritual" in vv. 3–4, the reference to Christ as the following rock (v. 4), the testing of Christ ([if the reading is correct] v. 9), and the hortatory applications in the whole passage. Moreover, the references to the Lord's Supper (vv. 16–21) are all indirect, as Porter ("Interpretaton," 34) has called them, because they are brought in not as a discussion of the Eucharist as such, but only to advance Paul's argument against idolatry.

If one prescinds from the minor issues, is Paul making use of a Jewish composition—something like Psalm 78, esp. vv. 12–22? There may be a similarity, but nothing allows one to conclude that Paul is borrowing an already existing composition. Some commentators try to distinguish different literary genres in the passage: a midrash in vv. 1–5 (J. Weiss, Borgen, Lindemann, Martelet); a previously composed brief homily in vv. 1–13 or 14, or even vv. 1–22 (Meeks, Senft, Collier [with differing nuances and analyses]); or "a piece of teaching that was already established before the composing of the epistle" (Conzelmann, *1 Cor*, 165). Cope even regards it as a section that does not belong here, being a later editor's interpolation "intended to bring Paul into line with the widely held views of subsequent Christianity" ("First Corinthians 8–10," 115). Such attempts are interesting, but useless in the long run, since they carry little conviction, mainly because of the multiple variety of analyses proposed. Paul is not constructing a detailed exegesis of the OT passages he mentions; they are rather instances cited to address a Corinthian problem and supply premonitory instances to support his admonitions.

The first part of this pericope is heavily dependent on passages in Numbers (alluding to 11:4, 34–35; 14:20–35; 21:4–9; 25:1–9 esp. in its LXX form), even apart from Exod 32:6, which is explicitly quoted in v. 7. The extent to which it uses Jewish traditions attested only later in rabbinic writings is a debatable issue (v. 4). In any case, Paul's use of the OT is neither midrashic nor pesher-like, *pace* McEwen, "Paul's Use"; those literary genres have a definite form, which is well known, but which is not in evidence here.

The interpretation of this passage has been bedeviled by a number of issues, often hermeneutical, that have little to do with Paul's message. The first of these issues concerns the extent of the passage: is the unit to be found in vv. 1–13 or vv. 1–22? Many commentators recognize that 10:23–11:1 is closely related to the argument of 8:1–13, because Paul's discussion of the eating of idol meat follows similar lines, but that in 10:1–22 he proposes an entirely different and basic consideration. Yet the discussion of it does not stop at 10:13, even though one may be inclined to regard vv. 1–13 as a homily (with *pantes* in five parallel clauses and with "some" in five negative statements) and an *inclusio* in vv. 6, 11 (so Meeks, " 'And Rose up' "). In fact, however, vv. 14–22 contain Paul's main argument, to which vv. 1–13 are merely building up. Hence, *pace* Allo, Barrett, Bruce, Collins, Conzelmann, Fee, Garland, Grosheide, Héring, Horsley, Kistemaker, Kremer, Kugelman, Merklein, Murphy-O'Connor, Robertson-Plummer, Senft, Schrage, Soards, Thiselton, it is not right to treat vv. 1–13 separately from vv. 14–22. In vv. 1–13, Paul does criticize a Corinthian practice using examples drawn from "our ancestors," and that criticism is different from the one he draws from the Lord's Supper in vv. 16–21; but it is only in the latter part (vv. 14–22) that Paul makes his main point, in vv. 14, 20–21. So Hays, Lietzmann, Lindemann, Smit, J. Weiss, M. Willis rightly interpret vv. 1–22 as a unit.

Second, in this passage Paul refers in various ways to baptism, the Lord's Supper, and "Christ" (v. 4c), uses "spiritual" three times (of food, drink, and rock), and adopts the terms *typoi* (v. 6) and *typikōs* (v. 11), which show that he is discussing what happened to "our ancestors" not only from a historical perspective, but is actualizing those instances as premonitions for Christians of Roman Corinth. As a result, many commentators on this passage introduce terms such as "sacraments," "sacramentalism," or maintain that what Paul was counteracting in Corinth was a form of "hypersacramentalism." Such terms, however, are misleading, because, even though what Paul calls baptism and the Lord's Supper indeed became sacraments in the later Christian dogmatic tradition, he himself never refers to them as such, and the problems in Corinth, as described in this letter, give no evidence of any form of sacramentalism. For this reason, to cite but one example, it is awry when Conzelmann (*1 Cor*, 165) asks, "Does he [Paul] think that the process recounted in the Old Testament [v. 2: the baptism of all into Moses] was really a sacrament?" Conzelmann later qualifies his phraseology when he speaks of the "spiritual" food, drink, and rock of vv. 3–4 as "not of a real Old Testament sacrament, but of prefiguration" (ibid., 166); similarly Lindemann, *1 Cor*, 219, 223. It is awry because one should not refer to OT rites as sacraments.

Third, Paul's use of *typoi* (v. 6) encourages some commentators to indulge in typological interpretation, a mode of interpretation that was born of later conceptions, and is sometimes strange to what Paul is saying in this passage.

Lastly, some of the OT passages to which Paul refers in this passage underwent further development in later Jewish interpretation of the rabbinic tradition, and some commentators bring in such later Jewish interpretation to explain Paul's words. Thus Barrett thinks that Paul coins the phrase about baptism "into Moses," not only because God delivered his people from Egyptian bondage through Moses, "but also because of the Jewish belief that the 'latter Redeemer' [the Messiah] would be as the 'former Redeemer' [Moses]" (*1 Cor*, 221). See also Garland, who quotes the text to which Barrett alludes, *Eccles. Rab.* 1.9, in full. The trouble is the dating of such late Jewish traditions, because "the text . . . may have originated in the eighth century in Palestine" (Strack-Stemberger, *ITM*, 345).

In any case, the pericope is very important, not only because it deals with what should be the Christians' attitude to idolatry, but also because it reveals how important the reverent celebration of the Lord's Supper is for the life of the Christian community at any time and for the common ethical conduct of life in that community. One has to recognize the importance of "one loaf" and "one body" for its unity in Christ.

NOTES

10:1. *I do not want you to be unaware, brothers.* Paul indulges in litotes in this introductory formula, and he will use it again in 12:1; 2 Cor 1:8 (1st pers. plur.); Rom 1:13; 11:25; 1 Thess 4:13 (1st pers. plur.). It introduces something that he considers important and wishes to make explicit. At times he substitutes for it the positive verb, *gnōrizō*, "make known," as in 12:3; 15:1; Gal 1:11; 2 Cor 8:1; cf. 11:3, "I want you to realize." On "brothers," see NOTE on 1:1. The translation in the lemma has omitted the introductory conj. *gar*, "for," which shows that the discussion now beginning is meant to give the basis for the preceding exhortation with which chap. 9 ended. The discussion will continue until 11:1.

that all our ancestors were under the cloud. In vv. 1–4, Paul writes of the privileged experiences of those whom he calls "our ancestors" (*hoi pateres hēmōn*), i.e., the desert generation of Israelites, as *hoi pateres* is used again in Heb 1:1; 8:9; *1 Clem.* 30.7; 60.4 In mentioning them as "our" ancestors, Paul speaks as one of Jewish birth, but he is including the predominantly Gentile Christian community of Roman Corinth in "our," because Christians are for him in a new sense "the Israel of God" (Gal 6:16). In Phil 3:3, he even thinks of Christians as "the circumcision, those who worship by the Spirit of God and boast in Christ Jesus." Cf. the use of *hoi pateres* in Rom 9:5; 11:28; Acts 3:13, 25, where the sense of this title is restricted to "the patriarchs," just as the sing. *patēr* is used of Abraham in

Rom 4:1, 16. *Pace* Barrett (*1 Cor*, 220), there is no evidence that Paul has derived the term from "an existing Exodus midrash." Paul is simply assuming that the Christians of Corinth are familiar with the OT episodes to which he alludes. His emphasis falls on "all," used twice in this verse and repeated in vv. 2, 3, 4, but then restricted in vv. 5, 7, 8. In this first verse Paul alludes to two of the desert experiences of Israel of old, their being led by God by a cloud and their passing through the Reed Sea.

In saying "under the cloud," Paul alludes to LXX Exod 13:21–22, which reads:

ho de theos ēgeito autōn, hēmeras men en stylō nephelēs dēixai autois tēn hodon ouk exelipen ho stylos tēs nephelēs hēmeras . . . enantion pantos tou laou,

God led them, during the day in a pillar of cloud to show them the way . . . and the pillar of cloud did not depart during the day from the presence of all the people.

Cf. Ps 105:39: "He spread a cloud for a covering." It refers to the deliverance of Israel fleeing from Egypt and wandering in the desert toward the Reed Sea: "Whenever the cloud went up from over the tent, the people of Israel thereupon set out; in the place where the cloud stood still, they encamped" (Num 9:17; used in 4Q365 31a–c:5; see also Exod 40:38; Wis 19:7). That is why Paul says they were "under" the cloud, which otherwise accompanies them. In the later rabbinic tradition, one reads that the Hebrews were covered by the cloud, undoubtedly in dependence on Ps 105:39; see Str-B, 3:405–6. Nothing in this part of the verse suggests that Paul is already alluding to baptism, *pace* Conzelmann, *1 Cor*, 165; or even to Jewish proselyte baptism, *pace* Kümmel in Lietzmann, *1 Cor*, 180; Jeremias, "Paulus als Hillelit," 90.

and that all passed through the sea. Paul alludes further to the crossing of the Reed Sea by the Israelites in LXX Exod 14:22, *eisēlthon hoi huioi Israēl eis meson tēs thalassēs kata to xēron*, "the Israelites entered into the midst of the sea on dry ground." Cf. Ps 78:13: "He divided the sea and made them pass through it, and caused the waters to stand like a heap."

2. *All of them were baptized into Moses in the cloud and in the sea.* In this verse, Paul interprets the desert experience of the ancient Israelites by likening it to the salvific baptismal experience of Christians. As Christians are saved by being "baptized into Christ Jesus" (Rom 6:3; cf. Gal 3:27), so Israel of old was related salvifically to Moses by the cloud and the sea; he brought them to deliverance and safety.

Cf. 1 Pet 3:20–21, where baptism is compared with an OT event, viz., Noah's ark, in which eight persons "were saved through water." One might have expected Paul to argue similarly, i.e., the other way round; but for him Christian "baptism" is clearly the prime analogate in his comparison. In Exodus, the "cloud" is the privileged sign of God's salvific presence to the Israelites wandering in the desert with Moses, as it guides them on their way to the Promised Land; and the "sea" recalls how God delivers them from pursuing Egyptians, as Moses leads them across the Reed Sea. Their relation to him is, therefore, special (see Exod 14:31); but nothing in the OT expresses that relation in terms of "baptism." It is Paul who formulates the baptism "into Moses," in imitation of the expression he will use about Christian baptism in Rom 6:3. He means only that the Israelites had in Moses someone analogous to Christ, into whom Christians are baptized. Moses is associated with *hoi pateres*, which is being used in the generic sense, "ancestors, forebears." They are related to Moses through the cloud and the sea, just as Christians are related to Christ through baptism. Moses appears elsewhere as a figure foreshadowing Jesus Christ (Rom 10:5; 2 Cor 3:7–15). Some MSS (P⁴⁶ᶜ, B, 1739, 1881, and Koine text-tradition) read the aor. mid. *ebaptisanto*, "they got themselves plunged/baptized for Moses" (BDAG, 165), thereby stressing the voluntary act that affirms dependence on his leadership.

3. *All ate the same spiritual food.* Paul now alludes to the privileged feeding of the Israelites, for God told Moses, "Say to them: 'In the evening twilight you will eat meat (Hebrew *bāśār*; LXX *krea*), and in the morning you will have your fill of bread, so that you will recognize that I am Yahweh, your God' " (Exod 16:12). Thus the Israelites were fed with quail (Hebrew *śĕlāw*; LXX *ortygomētra*, Exod 16:13; cf. Num 11:31; Ps 78:27 ['*ôph kānāph*, "winged fowl"]; 105:40a; Wis 16:2b; 19:12; Josephus, *Ant.* 3.1.5 §25 [*ortygōn plēthos*]), and with "bread from heaven" (*leḥem min haššāmayim*, LXX: *artous ek tou ouranou*), which was rained down upon them in the desert (Exod 16:4). Eventually, the bread came to be called "manna" (Aramaic *mannā*', derived from the Hebrew question that the Israelites asked when they first saw it, *mān hû*', "what is it?" Exod 16:14–15, 31, 35; Deut 8:3). In Ps 78:24–25, it becomes "the bread of angels" (LXX); Wis 16:20, "food of angels." In Neh 9:20, manna is associated with God's gift of his "good Spirit." Josephus refers to it as "sent down from heaven to them, food for forty years" (*Ant.* 3.1.6 §32; cf. Exod 16:35). The adj. *auto*, "same," is not read in P⁴⁶.

The food is called "spiritual" by Paul, mainly because it was given to them by God in a wondrous way to sustain their natural lives, and it symbolized His presence among them through the gift of His Spirit (Neh 9:20). It may also be "spiritual," because Paul sees it prefiguring the eucharistic bread, which probably also explains why it is said to be the "same" food for "all," as he prepares for the *koinōnia* that he will introduce in v. 16.

4. *and all drank the same spiritual drink.* Paul alludes to the privileged water that Moses provided for the Israelites to drink, when he at God's command struck the rock at Horeb (Exod 17:6) or at Kadesh (Num 20:7–11); cf. Ps 78:15. Again, it is called the "same spiritual," mainly because it was God-given, but perhaps also because it is prefiguring the sharing of the eucharistic drink (v. 16).

for they used to drink of a spiritual rock that followed them. Or "accompanied them." Exod 17:6 says nothing about such a rock at Horeb; nor does Deut 8:15, "water from the flinty rock"; or Isa 48:21; Neh 9:15; Ps 105:41; 114:8. Paul seems to be alluding to a passage in Numbers 20, which recounts the march of the Israelites through Moabite territory. When they arrive at Ar, its chief city (Num 21:15), a poetic fragment, often called the "Song of the Well" (Num 21:16–18), narrates how water was wondrously supplied to them. Verse 16 begins, *ûmiššām bĕʾ ērāh hîʾ bĕʾ ēr*, "and (they journeyed) from there [from Ar] to Beʾer, that is (the)

Well"; and the text continues, "of which the Lord said to Moses, 'Gather the people, and I shall give them water' " (a reference to the story of Moses supplying the Israelites with water at Kadesh, Num 20:7–11). Again, the rock is called "spiritual," because it is God-given.

From these poetic verses there eventually developed in Jewish tradition the idea of the rock itself, which supplied the water, "accompanying" the wandering Israelites, just as the cloud, quail, and the manna did. The earliest attestation of this tradition about the accompanying rock, after this Pauline reference, is found in Pseudo-Philo, *LAB* 10.7: *Populum autem suum deduxit in heremum quadraginta annis . . . et puteum aqu[a]e consequentis eduxit eis,* "For forty years he led his people in the desert . . . and provided for them a well of following water" (usually dated A.D. 70–100); also 11:15; 20:3 (see *OTP*, 2:317, 319, 329). For the still later targumic (*Tg. Onqelos* Num 21:16–20) and rabbinic development (*Tos. Sukkah* 3.11), in which the rock (or well) is described as peripatetic, see Str-B, 3:406–8; also Cullmann, *TDNT*, 6:97; Enns, The 'Moveable Well' "; but cf. Driver, "Notes," 15–18; Ellis, "A Note"; Schmitt, "Petra autem."

Pace Bandstra ("Interpretation," 12–13), the more or less contemporary interpretation (*Quod deterius* 31 §§115–18; *Leg. alleg.* 2.21 §86) that Philo gives about the "rock" in the wilderness has interesting allegorical meanings, but they have nothing to do with the Jewish legend that Paul uses here.

and the rock was Christ. Although this is a parenthetical remark, Paul thinks that Christ was actually the accompanying rock, conceived of as the source of water that saved the Israelites in their desert wanderings. Paul thus applies to Christ an appellation often given to Yahweh as the helper or aide of Israel, called in Hebrew *ṣûr*, "Rock" (Deut 32:4, 15, 18, 30, 31 [MT; LXX: *ho theos*]; 2 Sam 22:3 [LXX: *petra mou*]). He now makes it refer to the rock of Horeb (Exod 17:6) or of Kadesh (Num 20:8), from which the Israelites were given the water.

Cf. the way Wis 11:4 speaks of those who journeyed through the wilderness and called upon Wisdom, who supplied them with wisdom, which is called "water from flinty rock" (*edothē autois ek petras akrotomou hydōr* [see Deut 8:15]), an aspect that Philo exploits in *Leg. alleg.* 2.21 §86. Cullmann rightly notes, "Later Judaism does not interpret the rock of Ex. 17 and Nu. 20 Messianically" (*TDNT* 6:97), but Kreitzer ("1 Corinthians 10:4," 112–17) naively thinks that he can find evidence in Jewish legends for "a Pre-existent Messiah," misinterpreting Philo, *Leg. alleg.* 2.21; Wis 11:1–4; and (3d-cent.) *Tg. Onqelos* of Exod 17:5–7.

Paul uses the impf. *ēn*, "was," which implies that he is thinking of the preexistent Christ as that rock (so Conzelmann, *1 Cor*, 166–67; Robertson-Plummer, *1 Cor*, 201–2; Bandstra, "Interpretation," 14; et al.; but cf. Garland, *1 Cor*, 458). The impf. stands in contrast to Gal 3:16, where Christ is (*estin*) the "offspring" of Abraham in a parallel predication. Conzelmann (*1 Cor*, 167 n. 26) cites a similar interpretation of an OT text in QL: "The well is the law" (CD 6:4 [an interpretation of the same OT passage, Num 21:18!]), which is likewise pres. tense. See also 1QS 8:7, "It [the community] is the tested wall/rampart"; CD 20:3 (= 9:3). Recall the allegorical use of *estin* in Acts 4:11, "This is the stone"; Gal 4:24–25. There was already a hint at the preexistence of Christ in 8:6d; cf. 2 Cor 8:9

(*eptōcheusen*); Gal 4:4; Rom 1:3; 8:3; Phil 2:5 (see *Romans*, 484–85). Unfortunately, Paul does not develop further the nature of the relationship of Christ to the rock, or its connection to what he said of him in 8:6. He implies, however, that Christ in some way was already a salvific force for the Israelites of old.

5. *Nevertheless, God was not pleased with most of them, for they were laid low in the wilderness.* Having recounted the four privileges accorded to "all our ancestors," Paul now tells of the catastrophe that "most of them" (*hoi pleiones*) encountered as a result of their rebellious reaction to God's aid during the exodus. Paul uses the neg. of *eudokein en* to express God's displeasure, as in LXX Jer 2:19; 14:10, 12; Ps 151:5; Sir 34:19. Conzelmann (*1 Cor*, 167) rightly says that *eudokein* does not express "an emotion on God's part"; but when he goes on to say that it rather "means his election, or, to put it otherwise, negates his rejection," that is almost certainly wrong. Paul is saying that God rejected "most of them," whom he laid low in the desert. The verb *katestrōthēsan*, "were laid low, killed," is a divine passive.

Paul is alluding to an OT passage such as Num 14:16, 29–32, where the Israelites made a foolhardy attack on Canaan, and the Lord laid them low in the desert. When Moses prayed for the rest of the Israelites, he was told that only Caleb, Joshua, and "little ones" would enter the Promised Land. In LXX Num 14:16, the act. voice of the same verb and the prep. phrase occur, *katestrōsen autous en tē erēmō*, "(the Lord) laid them low in the wilderness," i.e., the foolhardy Israelites, whom Paul calls *hoi pleiones*. Cf. Heb 3:17, which also alludes to Num 14:29–32. See Ps 78:31 (LXX MSB, S: *pleiosin*); Sir 45:19.

Mitchell (*Paul*, 138–39), however, claims that the event referred to in v. 5 "is clearly Num 11:33, where God 'struck a very great plague against the people' " for craving after the food they had eaten in Egypt. That reference, however, is unlikely, given the verbal similarity of v. 5 to Num 14:16, which many commentators have recognized (e.g., Robertson-Plummer, Conzelmann, Lindemann), and despite the fact that v. 6 ends with *kathōs kakeinoi epethymēsan*, "as they too craved." That may indeed echo the craving in Num 11:4 (*epethymēsan epithymian*, "they craved exceedingly [lit., "they craved a craving"]), or 11:13, to which Mitchell refers; but it cannot invalidate the verbal allusion to Num 14:16. Moreover, her reference to Josephus, *Ant.* 3.13.1 §295 and his use of *stasiazein*, "to rebel," apropos of Num 11:4, as related to "factionalism" is simply far-fetched.

6. *Now in view of these things they have become archetypes for us.* The pron. *tauta* is not to be taken as the subj. of the verb, as is often done, but rather as an adv. acc., as Baumert has rightly shown ("*Eis to*," 13); and the subject of the 3d pers. plur. verb is "most of them," i.e., most of "our ancestors," immediately before (v. 5).

Greek *typos* means a "mark made by a blow" (*typtein*, "strike"); "impression, stamp, engraved mark." It was often used to mean "copy, image, replica," and from this meaning it developed into "archetype, pattern, model" (LSJ, 1835), and even "example" (1 Thess 1:7; Phil 3:17). In this verse, Paul calls "the ancestors" *typoi hēmin*, "archetypes for us." They are prototypes who should influence Christian conduct in a monitory way (see v. 11), so that our mode of life might not be governed similarly by craving instead of pure and blameless conduct before the Day of the Lord (cf. Phil 1:10). Because Paul uses *typoi*, we can understand the foreshadowing connotations of other terms already used in this section, such as "baptized" (v. 2), "spiritual food" (v. 3), "spiritual drink" (v. 4a), and "the rock was Christ" (v. 4c).

From Paul's use of *typos*, there develops in Christian tradition the technical notion of an OT "type," to which corresponds a NT "antitype" (cf. Rom 5:14) — or what has been called "typology," a loaded term with many connotations, not all of which would be found this early in the NT itself (see Goppelt, *Typos*; Brown, *NJBC*, art. 71 §§45–48).

so that we may not crave for evil even as they did. Lit. "so that we may not be cravers of evil things, as they too craved." This subordinate clause is introduced by *eis to* with the acc. subj. of the infin. According to BDF §402.2, it denotes "purpose or result," but Baumert (*"Eis to"*) has shown that it expresses only result, whereas *eis to* with an infin. (without the acc. subj.) expresses purpose. Paul then is trying to forestall a consequence that is destructive.

Paul's use of *epithymētas*, "cravers," and of the verb *epethymēsan* alludes to the LXX Num 11:4, 34–35; Ps 78:29–30; 106:14, which mentions the craving (*epithymia*) of the wandering Israelites after the food (meat, fish, cucumbers, melons, leeks, onions, and garlic) that they had eaten in Egypt. The food in itself would not have been evil, but the craving for it became evil in the situation in which the Israelites found themselves, having been freed from Egyptian bondage and led into the desert by God's chosen leaders, Moses and Aaron. The craving was a form of complaint against God and His providence for them. When Philo (*De spec. leg.* 4.24 §§126–29) comments on the craving (*epithymia*) of Num 11:31–34, he cites gluttony (*gastrimargia*), greed (*akratōr*), and self-indulgence (*kathēdypathein*) as examples of it.

7. *Do not become idolaters, as some of them did.* Paul warns the Corinthians about the danger of idol worship as he switches now from the 1st pers. plur. of v. 6 to the 2d pers. plur. impv. It is a concluding exhortation that he derives from the account of the craving of Israelite ancestors. Craving for food might lead to craving for idol meat, and so he now introduces idolatry as a specific danger, against the background of which his further remarks about "our ancestors" will be made.

Paul now alludes to Exod 32:1–6, where the Israelites during the forty-day absence of Moses on the mountain rebelled against him and begged Aaron to fashion for them "gods who shall go before us." Aaron consented and took their gold rings to fashion them into a molten calf. Then he proclaimed a feast on the morrow, when the people rose early to adore it and feast before it. This was the classic incident in the Exodus from Egypt when the grumbling Israelites became idolaters. Their grumbling and craving had led even to such idolatry. To emphasize the seriousness of such craving Paul quotes *the* OT verse about idolatry, which is the only explicit OT quotation in this passage.

as it stands written. See NOTE on 1:19.

"The people sat down to eat and drink, and they got up to revel." This is an exact quotation of LXX Exod 32:6. The idolatrous worship of the Israelites took the

form not only of a banquet, in which Israel ate (probably quail and manna) and drank water (from the rock), but also of a sport or dance, in which they reveled before the golden calf that they were worshipping. Recall Ps 106:19, "They made a calf in Horeb and worshipped a molten image." Ironically, the same verb (*paizō*) is used of David and the house of Israel making merry "before the Lord" in 2 Sam 6:5, as they feast before the ark of the covenant (6:17–19). In Exod 32:19, Moses is said to see "the calf and the dancing" (*ton moschon kai tous chorous*); so the reveling is interpreted as "dancing" (BDAG, 1087). That it has an erotic or sexual overtone is far from certain, even though *paizō* is said to have that sense in Gen 26:8 (*TDNT*, 5:629), a passage that is wholly unrelated to this one. Paul cites the passage from Exodus 32 because he realizes that Christians would not worship idols explicitly, but they might be moved to join in festivities that their heathen neighbors held in honor of gods. "What evil desires had led the fathers so to desecrate the manna? After receiving food and drink, had they felt secure (v. 12), superior, immune to rejection, expectant of an easier lot, and therefore inclined by dancing 'to put the Lord to the test'?" (Minear, "Paul's Teaching," 87).

8. *We should not indulge in fornication, as some of them did; and twenty-three thousand of them fell in a single day.* Lit. "and let us not fornicate." Paul now shifts to the 1st pers. plur., as he alludes to another OT incident of idolatry, that at Shittim, where Israelites are said to have played the harlot with daughters of Moab, who invited them to the sacrifices of their gods, "and the people ate, and bowed down to their gods" (Num 25:1–2). As a result, God's anger burned against Israel, and Num 25:9 records that 24,000 Israelites died by plague. Thus an association of idolatry and fornication is made in vv. 7–8; but Paul does not say explicitly what Wis 14:12 does, "The idea of making idols was the origin of fornication."

The number Paul uses (23,000), however, differs from Num 25:9 (MT and LXX). Possibly he is alluding to the OT incident from memory (so Barrett, *1 Cor*, 225; Lietzmann, *1 Cor*, 47; Robertson-Plummer, *1 Cor*, 205); or he may be influenced by yet another incident recorded in Num 26:62, where the number of dead Israelites is given as 23,000, "every male from a month old and upward" (so Collins, *1 Cor*, 371; Kremer, *1 Cor*, 206). Even though the Greek text of Paul's second clause in this verse resembles Exod 32:28 ("there fell of the people on that day about three thousand men"), the number used there almost certainly has had nothing to do with Paul's 23,000, *pace* Koet, "Old Testament Background," 611–12.

9. *We should not put Christ to the test, as some of them did.* Lit. "and let us not test Christ." The reading *Christon* is the *lectio difficilior* (MSS P⁴⁶, D, E, F, G, K, L, Ψ, 1739, 1881, the Koine text-tradition, and many patristic quotations [see Osburn, "The Text," 201–2]), but other MSS (ℵ, B, C, P, 33, 104, 326, 365) and some patristic quotations read *kyrion*, "Lord"; and a few (A, 2, 61*, 81, 254) have *theon*, "God." The two latter readings are undoubtedly a correction of copyists who could not see how Israelite ancestors would have tried to put Christ to the proof (Metzger, *TCGNT*, 494). However, most older commentators preferred to read *kyrion* and to understand it as in the LXX, meaning Yahweh.

Paul is referring to Israel's frequent trying of the Lord's patience during its desert wanderings, such as is recorded in Exod 16:2–3; 17:2–3, 7; 32:1–4; Num 14:22; 21:4–9; Deut 6:16; Ps 78:18 (LXX has the same verb, *exepeirasan*). Paul's exhortation (*mēde ekpeirazōmen*, "let us not test") addressed to the Corinthians remains generic, but it connotes conduct related to idol meat and fornication, two topics that he has already discussed and related to Christ (8:11–12; 6:15). As in 10:4, Paul is again linking christologically the desert experience of Israel to that of Corinthian Christians; as Corinthians are putting Christ to the test by their conduct, so "our ancestors" of old did to God. Some typology is involved. As in 1 Thess 4:6, Paul is warning his addressees that "the Lord is an avenger" (*ekdikos kyrios*), and so they should not try his patience.

and they were destroyed by serpents. Lit. "they perished." Paul is alluding to Num 21:5–6, where the Lord sent fiery serpents among the Israelites because they spoke up against him and Moses, even though the OT text there does not speak of testing.

10. *Do not grumble, as some of them did.* Lit. "as some of them grumbled." This exhortation becomes even more generic, as Paul switches from the 1st pers. plur. hortatory remark to a 2d pers. plur. impv. Grumbling was a form of rebellious discontent for which the Israelites during their wanderings were well known (LXX Exod 16:2, 7–9, 12; Num 11:1; 14:2, 27, 29, 36; 16:11–35; 17:6), expressed by the same noun or verb, *gongysmos* or *(dia)gongyzō*. It was another form of putting God to the test, because it stemmed from the precarious form of their existence and their lack of trust in Moses and God. Cf. Ps 106:13–15, 25–26, 28

and were destroyed by the Destroyer. Paul may be alluding to Exod 12:23, where the firstborn of Egypt were slain by a "Destroyer" sent by God against all the houses, the lintels and doorposts of which were not marked with the blood of the Passover lamb. Paul's word *olothreutēs*, "Destroyer," is found only in Christian writings. It is derived from the pres. ptc., *ton olethreuonta*, "the destroying one," used of the angelic agent of divine punishment in that Exodus passage (*TDNT*, 5:169–70). Paul is applying it to a much broader context, the general grumbling of the Israelites of old, some of whom perished indeed because of their grumbling (Num 16:11–35; 17:6–15), but the specific agent of their perdition was not called a "Destroyer," and the ptc. *(ex)olethreuōn* also occurs elsewhere in LXX 1 Chr 21:12, 15; Wis 18:25. On the difference of spelling (NT *olothreuō*, but LXX and Classical Greek *olethreuō*), see BDF §32.1 (remote vocalic assimilation).

11. *These things were happening to them prefiguratively and were written down as a warning for us.* With this summary, Paul concludes his exhortation drawn from the conduct of Israelite ancestors. He writes *typikōs*, using an adv. form of the noun *typoi* (v. 6), which sums up the exhortation of that verse. What happened to those of "our ancestors" has to serve as a warning to Christians of every age, but Paul sees it as especially applicable to the Christians of his day, as the next clause reveals.

upon whom the ends of the ages have met. This clause is meant to designate the time in which the Corinthian Christians find themselves, but its meaning is problematic. Some commentators insist that *telos* means "end" and translate the clause, "upon whom the end of the ages has come," taking the plur. *telē* as sing., as in Aelius Aristides 44.17K. So it would refer to "the end of a unity" (Barrett, *1 Cor,* 227–28; Bruce, *1 Cor,* 93; Conzelmann, *1 Cor,* 164, 168; BDAG, 32–33; Garland, *1 Cor,* 465; Lietzmann, *1 Cor,* 47 [referring to Heb 9:26 as parallel]; Lindemann, *1 Cor,* 222), but that rendering gives a rare meaning to the plur. *telē* and does not explain the plur. *aiōnōn* adequately.

Others, however, insist that the verb *katantaō* cannot mean simply "come." It denotes rather "arrive at, reach, come opposite to, meet" (J. Weiss, *1 Cor,* 254; similarly Hēring, *1 Cor,* 80–81), as in 14:36; Phil 3:11; Eph 4:13. This rendering would understand "the ages" (*aiōnes*) as two, the first of which has come to completion, and the second, just begun: the contemporary generation of early Christians are those for whom the two ages have "come opposite" each other or "met" in their lifetimes. One age has reached its *telos,* and the other has just begun (in the coming of Jesus of Nazareth). There is nothing in the present context to suggest that Paul is thinking in terms of "les temps messianiques" (SBJ, *1 Cor,* 48). J. Weiss's interpretation seems preferable, because Paul, with his Jewish background, would have been acquainted with the apocalyptic division of time or history into such periods (*4 Ezra* 6:7–10; *1 Enoch* 91.12–17; *T. Levi* 14.1; 1QpHab 7:1–9; see further *PAHT,* §PT42).

A third meaning has been suggested by Bogle, that *telos* is used in the sense of a "sacred rite," as in Plato, *Rep.* 560e ("the soul of someone initiated with grand rites" [*teloumenou psychēn megaloisi telesi*]). Hence Paul's text would mean, ". . . for us, who are the heirs of the Mysteries of the ages," i.e., those "to whom the eternal mysteries have come down." That, however, is a far-fetched suggestion that scarcely suits the context.

No matter which interpretation of "ends" is preferred, Paul's implication is that such events about "our ancestors" have been recorded in the OT for the instruction of Christians, to admonish them in every age about God's reaction to human complaints, rebellion, testing, and probing.

12. *Consequently, whoever thinks that he is standing firm should see to it that he does not fall.* Lit. "let him who believes he is standing see to it lest he fall." So Paul begins to formulate the climax of his hortatory discussion based on the monitory prototypes of "our ancestors" (10:1–4). He again uses the 3d pers. sing. impv. in the apodosis of a condition; cf. 3:18; 8:2. He is warning against self-deception, in a maxim-like utterance. "Standing" is a Pauline way of expressing Christian existence based on faith, the response to the gospel; see 7:37; 15:1; 2 Cor 1:24; Rom 11:20; Gal 5:1. "Does not fall" echoes the "fall" of the ancestors mentioned in v. 8. Paul is urging that Corinthian Christians, especially those who "possess knowledge" (8:1,10) or who confidently utter the slogan of 6:12, see to it that they do not suffer the same fate as such ancestors.

13. *No trial has overtaken you but what is human.* Paul assures the Corinthian community that it is not yet facing a probing or testing that comes from God. If there is some distress or trial, it stems only from a human source that may be of little consequence and may have to be tolerated. It may be trying those who possess knowledge. There is no hint here of *tentatio daemoniaca* and 10:20–21 is not yet in view.

God is trustworthy. See NOTE on 1:9, and cf. 2 Cor 1:18; 1 Thess 5:24.

and he will not allow you to be tried beyond what you can bear. Lit. "and God is faithful, who will not allow you. . . . " The connecting particle *de* in this case is not adversative, but asseverative, because God is trustworthy. Each instance will show that He is such indeed, even to the end, but He may permit Christians to be confronted with a trial that is suited to their ability.

but with the trial he will provide also a way out, so that you may be able to endure it. It is not clear whether this verse is to be understood generically of every trial that a Christian may face, or *the* eschatological trial involving one's salvation? The noun *ekbasis,* "way out," certainly could mean the latter, the eschatological trial, but Christians may also rely on God for the *ekbasis* of lesser struggles throughout the course of life. In this context, Paul seems to be thinking primarily of trials involving idol meat or seduction to idolatry.

14. *Therefore, my dear friends, flee from idolatry.* This is Paul's basic exhortation about idol meat, repeating what he said in v. 7a, but now in a more abstract way. He thereby implies that no matter what good one does in life, the Christian must flee from the worship of false gods and serve only "the one God, the Father, . . . and the one Lord, Jesus Christ" (8:6). The reason for that will be given in the relation of dumb idols to demons in vv. 20–21. Cf. 1 John 5:21, "Children, keep yourselves from idols." The connection of this verse to what immediately precedes is not the most logical, but the introductory conj. *dioper,* "therefore," is really connecting the following verses (15–22) with vv. 1–13; cf. 8:13. Israel's involvement with idolatry and fornication led to its downfall, despite its attempts to follow the teaching of Moses.

Paul addresses the Corinthians as *agapētoi mou,* "my beloved," expressing his genuine affection for Corinthian Christians, as he will again in 15:58; cf. Phil 2:12; 4:1. The impv. *pheugete,* "flee," echoes his admonition about fornication in 6:18.

15. *I am speaking as to wise people; judge for yourselves what I am saying.* This verse is a generic introduction to what Paul now proposes, a perspective on idolatry that he derives from Christian celebration of the Lord's Supper (vv. 16–17) and from Jewish participation in the Temple sacrifices (v. 18). He wants those Corinthians, who "possess knowledge" and who think that they can freely take part in pagan temple banquets, to reflect with him on the relation of eating such idol meat to their dining at the table of the Lord. Their social conduct has an objective dimension that they, wise people though they are, have not been considering. In reality, that dimension is a matter of Christian faith. Paul begins his discussion with a reference to himself, as he did in 1:12; 6:5; 7:6, 8. In speaking to the addressees as *phronimoi,* "wise, sensible," Paul is not being ironic, but he is flattering them into recognizing the correctness of his counsel.

16. *Is not the cup of blessing that we bless a participation in the blood of Christ?* Or "a communion with" (RSV marginal note). I.e., do not we Christians share in the life-blood of the crucified Christ, when we partake together of the contents of the cup in the liturgical celebration of his death (11:26)? In drinking from that cup, the believing Christian partakes of Christ's blood and shares in the benefits

of his death, the shedding of that blood. Paul's question is intended to recall to Corinthian Christians what they should know but may be overlooking. He thus makes the Christian celebration of the Lord's Supper a criterion for judging other meals, especially those involving idol meat.

"The cup of blessing" is an expression apparently derived from the Jewish Passover meal (*kôs šel běrākāh* [Str-B 4/2:630]), but it is being applied by Paul to the eucharistic cup (and its contents) in the Christian celebration of the Lord's Supper. In his account of the institution of that Supper, Paul will refer to "the cup after the supper" (11:25 [see NOTE there]), which may be the same. There, however, Paul does not cite a liturgical formula with the verb *eulogein*, "bless," nor does Luke in his similar narrative (22:20); and both Mark 14:23 and Matt 26:27 have the verb *eucharistein*, "give thanks" (cf. Luke 22:17). Whether there was much difference in Hebrew or Aramaic between "blessing" and "giving thanks" is a minor debatable issue. The phrase does not mean that the cup brings a blessing; it is rather the cup over which one pronounces a blessing, as the rel. clauses indicate (cf. Mark 8:7). It is disputed whether the name, "cup of blessing," is to be given to the third cup (*birkat hammāzôn*), as is commonly suggested, or to the fourth cup at the Passover meal (*birkat haššîr*, so Cohn-Sherbok), or to the second cup (Sigal), as they are identified in the later Mishnaic tractate *Pesaḥim* 10:1–7.

What the cup of blessing brings in the Lord's Supper is *koinōnia*, "communal participation" or "sharing" in the blood of Jesus Christ. This means that Christians who partake of the Lord's Supper are "united with the Lord in intimacy undreamed of by the OT worshipper who (through the priest) poured the blood on the altar, or, at best, was sprinkled with it" (Siegman, "Blood of Christ," 20). Since the association of "life" with "blood" is made clear in Lev 17:11, "the life-principle of the flesh is in the blood" (*nepheš habbāśār baddām*; in the LXX: *hē gar psychē pasēs sarkos haima autou estin*, "for the life-principle of all flesh in its blood"), the participation means a communal sharing in the life-blood of Christ. Cf. also Lev 17:14; *EDNT*, 1:37–39. In speaking of such a participation, Paul is invoking a primitive Christian tradition, which will emerge more clearly in chap. 11. On "participation," see NOTE on 1:9; cf. Panikulam, *Koinōnia*, 17–30; also Sebothoma, "Koinonia in 1 Cor. 10.6"; William-Tinajero, "Christian Unity."

Is not the bread that we break a participation in the body of Christ? Or "a communion with" (RSV marginal note). Breaking bread was a common expression for taking a meal (Mark 8:6, 19), but it became in time a stereotyped expression for sharing in the Christian Eucharist as a whole (see NOTE on 11:24). Now, however, Paul uses it as an expression parallel to "the cup of blessing that we bless." As that cup was a participation in or commmunion with the blood of Christ, so the bread is a participation in or communion with the body of Christ. *Koinōnia*, however, also implies a common sharing with one another in this body and blood of Christ, as v. 17 makes clear. The KJV translated *koinōnia* as "communion," and this rendering provided English-speaking Christians with the biblical basis for the term, "Holy Communion," for what is normally called today the Eucharist.

Artos would normally denote ordinary bread, but it was used also for unleavened bread, such as would be eaten at a Passover meal (see NOTE on 11:23). Instead of the nom. *ho artos* as the subject of *estin*, followed by the rel. pron. in the acc. case, Paul uses *ton arton*, the acc., which has been attracted to the case of the rel. pron., by inverse attraction (BDF §295).

To sōma tou Christou is used in three different senses in Pauline writings: (1) literally, of the historical body of Christ crucified (Rom 7:4); (2) analogously, of the ecclesiastical body of Christ (1 Cor 12:27 [with *ekklēsia* mentioned explicitly in 12:28]; cf. Eph 4:12); and (3) liturgically of the eucharistic body of Christ (1 Cor 10:16; 11:27). The phrase also occurs in Col 2:17, but in an entirely different sense, juxtaposed there to *skia*, "shadow." Lindemann (*1 Cor*, 224) notes the different word order in this part of v. 16, where the verb *estin* stands at the end of the sentence and establishes a stronger connection of *koinōnia* to *sōma*. It also helps one to understand better the corporate sense of the ecclesiastical meaning of the phrase (see Sklba, "Body of Christ").

Although this verse teaches some important effects of the Lord's Supper, which will have to be recalled when 11:23–25 is interpreted, the participation now mentioned is meant to provide the background for Paul's argument against Christians taking part in meals in pagan temples and consuming meat sacrificed to idols. In reality, however, what he says here about participation in the cup and bread expresses "the consequence of Paul's understanding of the words of institution. In it he draws a parallel between Christian participation in the Eucharist (10:16–17) and the participation of Jews (10:18) and pagans (10:19–20) in their ritual meals. It is often assumed that Paul is arguing from the implications of such rituals to the meaning of the Eucharist, but the very structure of the text makes it much more probable that the reverse is true" (Murphy-O'Connor, "Eucharist and Community," 58).

The fact that it mentions the cup before the bread has been related to other ancient testimonies about the Eucharist with the order cup-bread (*Did.* 9.1–2; the questionable short text of Luke 22:15–20; and a Papias quotation preserved in Irenaeus, *Adv. Haer* 5.33.3–4; see McGowan, "First Regarding the Cup"). Nothing much can be made of this fact.

17. *Because there is one loaf, we, though many, are one body, for we all partake of the one loaf.* Lit. "because (there is) one bread, we the many are one body." Conzelmann (*1 Cor*, 170), however, translates, "For we are one body, one bread, many as we are," but that is not what Paul has written, because we are not "one bread." The "one bread," of which we partake makes us "one"; it unifies us. Though Christians are many and diverse, they are united in union with Christ through sharing in the one bread. This is the climax of Paul's argument. There is "a shift in meaning here from the body of Christ crucified for Christians to that body which they form. But as this makes the one person of Christ, crucified and risen, given for all, shared by all, to be that which constitutes the unity of the many members of the community, it is very difficult to regard the idea of the Church as the Body of the risen Christ as prior to, or independent of, that of Christians sharing in the death of Christ" (Wedderburn, "Body of Christ," 76). We recognize the "one body" in the one loaf that we break and the purpose of Jesus' death, which is to summon all those who share in consuming that one loaf to unity in and with Christ (see Prout, " 'One Loaf' ").

The effect of *koinōnia* in the one eucharistic body of Christ is that "we share" (*metechomen*) with one another in that one loaf, which brings about a unity of all Christians with the risen Lord, in "one body," which now takes on the further nuance of the ecclesiastical body, or what Mitchell calls "the cultic unity" (*Paul*, 142). Bread is a form of food for life, and so our common sharing in the oneness of that sustenance brings about a union of all Christians in and through the life of Christ himself. The phrase, *hen sōma*, expresses the unity of the ecclesiastical body without the mention of Christ, as in 12:13; Rom 12:5; cf. Col 3:15; Eph 2:16; 4:4; and even without the adj. *hen*, in Col 1:18, 24; Eph 1:23; 5:23, 30. A few MSS (D, F, G) add *kai tou henos potēriou*, "and of the one cup," but that is a copyist's harmonization.

18. *Consider the people of Israel.* Lit. "look at Israel according to the flesh," the ethnic or historical-empirical Israel of old, which Paul will distinguish in Rom 9:6 from those who are truly "Israel," the people of God in the OT (see *Romans*, 559–60). Now Paul contrasts old Israel with Christians, whom he has called "the Israel of God" (Gal 6:16). For the same use of *kata sarka*, see Rom 4:1 (said of Abraham as forefather) and Gal 4:23.

Are not those who eat of the sacrifices participants in the altar? I.e., partners, sharers in the altar. Another rhetorical question compares Christian partakers of the Lord's Supper with Israel of old. When the Israelites offered their sacrifices and partook of them (Deut 12:6–7; 14:26; Lev 3:1–17; 7:11–36; 10:12–15; 1 Sam 9:12–13), they in effect identified themselves with what was offered on the altar of sacrifice and with the Lord, on whose altar the sacrifice was offered (see de Vaux, *Studies*, 32: "the victim is immolated . . . it is shared between God, the priest, and the offerer"; Kremer, *1 Cor*, 213; Collins, *1 Cor*, 380; Soards, *1 Cor*, 210). Paul's question formulates the matter in the abstract, but one will look in vain for such an abstract formulation in the OT itself. What Paul says here about *koinōnoi tou thysiastēriou*, "participants of the altar," reflects his Jewish background, and that kind of thinking is still further developed in the later rabbinic tradition, which even speaks of the altar acquiring "the right to the flesh of the offering" (*m. Zebahim* 12.2; *m. Menahoth* 6.2).

Some commentators (e.g., Garland, *1 Cor*, 478; Kistemaker, *1 Cor*, 346; Schrage, *1 Cor*, 2.443; Thiselton, *1 Cor*, 771), however, would refer this Israelite practice, not to sacrifices in the Jerusalem Temple, but rather to the altar (*thysiastērion*) erected before the golden calf (Exod 32:5), as in 10:7–8. Such an interpretation is possible; but Paul's words are not so limited, being more generic in their formulation, and the view that he enunciates would be applicable even to sacrifices offered by Gentiles to heathen gods.

In any case, Paul is arguing primarily from the function of the altar in the cult of Israel and the relation of worshippers who offered sacrifices at it. What he says is predicated by implication of the table of the Lord in the Christian cult (see Brunner, "Bedeutung des Altars").

19. *What then am I saying?* This question refers, not to v. 18 alone (*pace* Schrage), but to the verb ("I am saying") that Paul used in v. 15, when he began his discussion about the worship of idols (v. 14).

That meat sacrificed to idols is something? Paul's further rhetorical question (*hoti eidōlothyton ti estin;*) returns finally to the topic of 8:1, 4, 10. With it he is forestalling an objection. Even though this and the following rhetorical question are not introduced by *mē*, his questions expect a negative answer. He means that *eidōlothyton* is only a piece of meat, really unchanged in being offered to a temple's idol.

Or that an idol is something? The idol is no more, in reality, than the wood, metal, or stone out of which it has been made; it might be an image of a god, but does such a god really exist? That question takes care of the objective situation, but what about the subjective conviction of the person who so sacrifices? Paul's answer to that aspect comes in the next verse, which stresses the demonic reality of such eating.

20. *Rather what they sacrifice [they sacrifice] to demons and not to God.* Some MSS (P^{46vid}, ℵ, A, C, P, Ψ, 33^{vid}, 81, 104, 1739, etc.) read *ha thyousin ta ethnē*, "what the Gentiles sacrifice." That subject of this clause has usually been considered an ancient gloss introduced into the text in these MSS lest the 3d pers. plur. verb be understood to refer to the Israelites of v. 18 (see Metzger, *TCGNT*, 494). The reading is also problematic, because a neut. plur. subject usually takes a sing. verb in Greek.

Paul is alluding to LXX Deut 32:17a, *ethysan daimoniois kai ou theō, theois hois ouk eidēsan*, "they [rebellious Israelites] sacrificed to demons [Canaanite deities] and not to God, to gods whom they knew not." The last words in Paul's statement, *kai ou theō*, however, do not mean "and to a non-god," as some commentators render them, following the unfortunate RSV translation of Deut 32:17a (Fee, *1 Cor*, 472 n. 47; Robertson-Plummer, *1 Cor*, 216). Paul implicitly applies the words, however, to heathen Corinthians and the meats offered in sacrifice to their gods. Moreover, he implies that Christians of Corinth, who "possess knowledge" that allows them freely to associate with heathen Corinthians and to eat idol meat, were forgetting the connection of such meat to the subjective conviction of idolaters, who were indeed sacrificing to such demons. Cf. LXX Ps 106:28.

In Classical Greek texts, *daimonion* is a substantivized neut. of the adj. *daimonios*, a shortened expression for *pneuma daimonion*, "demonic spirit." The adj. denotes something "coming from heaven, heaven-sent," and its neut. often means a transcendent incorporeal being of divine character. *Daimonion* can even mean "Divine Power" or "Divinity" (Herodotus, *Hist.* 5.87), and often an "inferior divine being" (Plato, *Sympos.* 202e: *pan to daimonion metaxy esti theou te kai thnētou*, "every *daimonion* is between a god and a mortal") or even the "genius" or "deity" that inspired Socrates (Xenophon, *Memor.* 1.1.2). In time, it came to denote a "spirit," either good or evil, and then especially an "evil spirit, demon" (*TDNT*, 2:8–10); and so it is used often in the LXX (Deut 32:17; Tob 3:8; Ps 91:6). In this last sense, Paul uses the word here.

and I do not want you to become partners of the demons. I.e., those who share in a worship service of such gods (in reality, demons). Whereas Paul uses no art. with "demons" in v. 20a, he now inserts one before "demons" in v. 20b, meaning those in Corinth. Cf. this last statement with what Paul said in 8:4–5 about the reality of idols. Now he is not warning the Corinthian Christians about becoming partners of idols (which have no reality), but rather partners with idolaters and so with the demons in whose honor they consume the idol meat.

21. *You cannot drink the cup of the Lord and the cup of demons as well.* Paul concludes his argument about the idolatry involved in eating idol meat, first with two parallel neg. statements. If Christians understand what participation in the Lord's Supper really means, then sharing a cup in honor of pagan gods is out of the question. The two cannot go together. Paul employs "drink the cup of" as in LXX Isa 51:17; Ezek 23:31–33. So Paul sharply states the dilemma and continues it in the following parallel sentence. Paul again uses *Kyrios* as a Christological title; see NOTE on 1:2.

you cannot partake of the table of the Lord and the table of demons. The phrase *trapeza kyriou*, "table of the Lord," is found in LXX Mal 1:7, 12, where the post-exilic prophet inveighs against priests in Judah who offered polluted food on the altar and thus despised the name of the Lord (Yahweh). Paul adopts it and applies it to the Christian celebration of the "Lord's Supper" (11:20), alluding to what he said in v. 16 above. Imitation of the LXX phrase may explain the omission of the art. before all four gens. in this verse (but see DBF §259.3). He then extends the meaning of *trapeza* even to the altar of pagan gods, as in LXX Isa 65:11: *hetoimazontes tō daimoni trapezan*, "setting a table for a demon." That his extension is not gratuitous is shown by an ancient Greek dinner invitation, the text of which invites someone to "dine in the Serapeion at the *klinē* (reclining dinner-couch) of the Lord Serapis tomorrow" (P. Oxy. 110, lines 1–3; *New Docs,* 1:5). The Serapeion was a structure dedicated to the god Serapis.

22. *Or are we stirring the Lord to jealousy?* Paul adds to his conclusion a further consideration, which he formulates in the 1st pers. plur., making himself one with his addressees. He sees the issue once again as involving something more than the mere consumption of idol meat in a pagan temple. Idolatrous conduct on the part of Israelites of old once provoked Yahweh to anger, and Paul's further comment alludes to such anger recorded, for instance, in the Song of Moses in Deut 32:21, "They have stirred me to jealousy with what is not a god (*ep' ou theō*); they have provoked me with their idols." See also Exod 32:5, the OT passage that Paul cited in 10:7. In alluding to the Song of Moses, Paul stresses that God's anger cannot be braved with impunity. Cf. Exod 20:4–5; 34:14; Josh 24:19–20; Ps 78:58. Paul makes a different use of Deut 32:21 in Rom 10:19, where it is a question of stirring Israel to jealousy of the Gentiles who are accepting the gospel (see *Romans,* 599–600).

Are we stronger than he? Paul's final rhetorical question on this topic is introduced by *mē*, expecting a neg. answer, and amounts to a comment that is puzzling in its present context, especially since he formulates it again in the 1st pers. plur. One wonders what the comparison of the strength of believers with God' strength has to do with idolatry. Some commentators think that Paul is implying that God is stronger than the so-called strong (those who "possess knowledge") in the Co-rinthian community, who care not about the "weak." That implication, however, would be ironic, but it is problematic because in this letter Paul has nowhere designated a group in Corinth as "the strong."

Paul may rather be thinking of such OT passages as Qoh 6:10b, "It is known what a human being is, and that he cannot dispute with one stronger than he"; or even Job 9:32; 37:23; Isa 45:9. None of these passages, however, says anything about divine jealousy or idolatry. Since in v. 7 Paul has cited Exod 32:6 in a reference to the episode about the Golden Calf and in the rest of that passage in Exod 32 there is mention of God's wrath burning against the people whom he brought from Egypt "with great power and mighty hand" (32:11), perhaps one need look no further for the OT background to v. 22b. This suggestion builds on what Rosner (" 'Stronger than He' ") has written, who complicates the matter, however, with elaborate anachronistic quotations from later targumic traditions about God's strength.

BIBLIOGRAPHY (See also Bibliography on 8:1–11:1, pp. 350–52)

Aalen, S., "Das Abendmahl als Opfermahl im Neuen Testament," *NovT* 6 (1963) 128–52.

Adamo, D. T., "The Lord's Supper in I Corinthians 10:14–22, 11:17–34," *AfrTJ* 18 (1989) 36–48.

Baarda, T., "I Corinthe 10,1–13: Een schets," *GTT* 76 (1976) 1–14.

Bandstra, A. J., "Interpretation in 1 Corinthians 10:1–11," *CTJ* 6 (1971) 5–21.

Baumert, N., "*Eis to* mit Infinitiv," *FilolNT* 11 (1998) 7–24.

———, "*Koinōnia tou haimatos tou Christou* (1 Kor 10,14–22)," *The Corinthian Correspondence* (BETL 125; ed. R. Bieringer), 617–22.

Bogle, M. M., "*Ta telē tōn aiōnōn*, 1 Corinthians x.11: A Suggestion," *ExpTim* 67 (1955–56) 246–47.

Borgen, P., "Nattverdtradisjonen i 1. Kor. 10 og 11 som evangelietradisjon," *SEA* 51–52 (1986–87) 32–39.

Broer, I., " 'Darum: Wer da meint zu stehen, der sehe zu, dass er nicht falle': 1 Kor 10, 12f im Kontext von 1 Kor 10, 1–13," *Neues Testament und Ethik: Für Rudolf Schnackenburg* (ed. H. Merklein; Freiburg im B.: Herder, 1989) 299–325.

Bruni, G., "Eucaristia nella prima lettera ai Corinti (10, 1–18; 11, 17–34)," *RBR* 12/3 (1977) 35–55.

Brunner, P., "Die Bedeutung des Altars für den Gottesdienst [sic] der christlichen Kirche," *KD* 20 (1974) 218–24.

Cohn-Sherbok, D., "A Jewish Note on *to potērion tēs eulogias*," *NTS* 27 (1980–81) 704–9.

Collier, G. D., " 'That We Might not Crave Evil': The Structure and Argument of 1 Corinthians 10.1–13," *JSNT* 55 (1994) 55–75.

Cope, L., "First Corinthians 8–10: Continuity or Contradiction?" *ATRSup* 11 (1990) 114–23.

Driver, S. R., "Notes on Three Passages in St. Paul's Epistles," *Expos* 3/9 (1889) 15–23.

Dschulnigg, P., "Überlegungen zum Hintergrund der Mahlformel in JosAn: Ein Versuch," *ZNW* 80 (1989) 272–75.

Ellis, E. E., "A Note on First Corinthians 10:4," *JBL* 76 (1957) 53–56.

Enns, P. E., "The 'Moveable Well' in 1 Cor 10:4: An Extrabiblical Tradition in an Apostolic Text," *BBR* 6 (1996) 23–38.

Goppelt, L., *Typos: The Typological Interpretation of the Old Testament in the New* (Grand Rapids: Eerdmans, 1982) 145–46.

Hahn, F., "Teilhabe am Heil und Gefahr des Abfalls: Eine Auslegung von 1 Ko 10,

1–22," *Freedom and Love: The Guide for Christian Life* (ed. L. de Lorenzi, 1981), 149–71.

Inostra-Lanas, J. C., *Moisés e Israel en el desierto: El midrás paulino de 1 Cor 10,1–13* (Plenitudo temporis 6; Salamanca: Universidad Pontificia, 2000).

Jeske, R. L., "The Rock Was Christ: The Ecclesiology of 1 Corinthians 10," *Kirche: Festschrift für Günther Bornkamm* . . . (ed. D. Lührmann and G. Strecker; Tübingen: Mohr [Siebeck], 1980) 245–56.

Jourdan, G. V., "*Koinōnia* in I Corinthians 10:16," *JBL* 67 (1948) 111–24.

Klauck, H.-J., " 'Leib Christi' — Das Mahl des Herrn in 1 Kor 10–12," *BK* 57 (2002) 15–21.

Koester, C. R., "Promise and Warning: The Lord's Supper in 1 Corinthians," *WW* 17 (1997) 45–53.

Koet, B. J., "The Old Testament Background to 1 Cor 10,7–8," *The Corinthian Correspondence* (BETL 125; ed. R. Bieringer), 607–15.

Kreitzer, L., "1 Corinthians 10:4 and Philo's Flinty Rock," *CV* 35 (1993) 109–26.

Malina, B. J., *The Palestinian Manna Tradition* (AGSU 7; Leiden: Brill, 1968) 94–99.

Martelet, G., "Sacrements, figures et exhortation en 1 Cor X, 1–11," *RSR* 44 (1956) 323–59, 515–59.

McEwen, A., "Paul's Use of the Old Testament in 1 Corinthians 10:1–4," *VR* 47 (1986) 3–10.

McGowan, A., " 'First Regarding the Cup . . .': Papias and the Diversity of Early Eucharistic Practice," *JTS* 46 (1995) 551–55.

Meeks, W.A., " 'And Rose up to Play': Midrash and Paraenesis in 1 Corinthians 10:1–22," *JSNT* 16 (1982) 64–78.

Minear, P. S., "Paul's Teaching on the Eucharist in First Corinthians," *Worship* 44 (1970) 83–92.

Minto, A. L., "1 Corinthians 10:1–13: Paul's Interpretation of Exodus and the Divine Pedagogy," *Fides Quaerens Intellectum* 2 (2002–3) 181–226.

Murphy-O'Connor, J., "Eucharist and Community in First Corinthians," *Worship* 50 (1976) 370–85; 51(1977) 56–69.

Oropeza, B. J., "Apostasy in the Wilderness: Paul's Message to the Corinthians in a State of Eschatological Liminality," *JSNT* 75 (1999) 69–86.

Osburn, C. D., "The Text of 1 Corinthians 10: 9," *New Testament Textual Criticism: Its Significance for Exegesis: Essays in Honour of Bruce M. Metzger* (ed. E. J. Epp and G. D. Fee; Oxford: Clarendon, 1981) 201–12.

Perrot, C., "Les exemples du désert (1 Co. 10.6–11)," *NTS* 29 (1983) 437–52.

Porter, C. L., "An Interpretation of Paul's Lord's Supper Texts: 1 Corinthians 10:14–22 and 11:17–34," *Encounter* 50 (1989) 29–45.

Prout, E., " 'One Loaf . . . One Body,' " *ResQ* 25 (1982) 78–81.

Rosner, B. S., " 'Stronger than He?' The Strength of 1 Corinthians 10:22b," *TynBul* 43 (1992) 171–79.

Schmitt, J., " 'Petra autem erat Christus' (I Cor., x, 4b)," *Maison Dieu* 29 (1952) 18–31.

Schüssler Fiorenza, E., "Tablesharing and the Celebration of the Eucharist," *Concilium* 152 (1982) 3–12.

Sebothoma, W., "Koinonia in 1 Cor. 10:16: Its Significance for Liturgy and Sacrament," *Questions Liturgiques* 70 (1989) 243–50.

——, "Koinonia in 1 Corinthians 10:16," *Neotestamentica* 24 (1990) 63–69.

Siegman, E. F., "The Blood of Christ in St. Paul's Soteriology," *Proceedings of the Second Precious Blood Study Week August 2–4 1960* (Rensselaer, IN: St. Joseph's College Press, 1962) 11–35.

Sigal, P., "Another Note to 1 Corinthians 10.16," *NTS* 29 (1983) 134–39.

Sklba, R. J., "Body of Christ," *TBT* 40 (2002) 219–23.

Smit, J., " 'Do not Be Idolaters': Paul's Rhetoric in First Corinthians 10:1–22," *NovT* 39 (1997) 40–53.

Söding, T., "Eucharistie und Mysterien: Urchristliche Herrenmahlstheologie und antike Mysterienreligiösität im Spiegel von 1Kor 10," *BK* 45 (1990) 140–45.

Vaux, R. de, *Studies in Old Testament Sacrifice* (Cardiff: University of Wales Press, 1964).

Wedderburn, A. J. M., "The Body of Christ and Related Concepts in 1 Corinthians," *SJT* 24 (1971) 74–96.

William-Tinajero, L. M., "Christian Unity: The Communal Participation in Christ's Body and Blood," *One in Christ* 40/2 (2005) 46–61.

22   *d. Dictates of Conscience about Market and Idol Meat (10:23–11:1)*

[10:23] "All things are permissible," but not all are beneficial. "All things are permissible," but not all edify. [24] No one should seek his own advantage, but that of his neighbor. [25] Eat whatever is sold in the meat market, without raising a question in conscience. [26] *"For the earth and its fullness are the Lord's."* [27] If some unbeliever invites you (to dinner) and you want to go, eat whatever is put before you without raising a question in conscience. [28] But if someone says to you, "This is sacrificial meat," do not eat it for the sake of the one who informed you and for the sake of conscience. [29] I mean, not your conscience, but the other's. For why should my freedom be determined by someone else's conscience? [30] If I partake with thanks (to God), why am I reviled for what I give thanks? [31] So whether you eat or drink or whatever you do, do all for the glory of God. [32] Avoid giving offense, whether to Jews or Greeks or the church of God, [33] even as I try to please everyone in every way, not seeking my own good but that of the many that they may be saved. [11:1] Be imitators of me, as I am of Christ.

COMMENT

Paul returns more directly to what he had been saying in 8:1–13, esp. 8:7–13, before his digression in chap. 9 and his discussion of the consumption of idol meat from the double perspective of idolatry and participation in the Lord's table (10:1–22). This passage is not directly connected with the topic of the preceding pericope, but it is not unrelated. It has to do with food bought in a market or served to one as a guest in a private home. Paul begins it with the double repetition of the Corinthian slogan, "All things are permissible," already commented on in 6:12. His first comment is the same, but the second immediately recasts it on a wider scale, the building up of the community.

The connection of this passage with 8:1–13 is seen in the use again of the same vocabulary, such as "edify," "conscience," and "offense," and of Paul's argument about concern for others in the community. The situation with which Paul deals, however, is no longer that of a banquet "in an idol's temple" (8:10), but the eating at home of meat bought in a marketplace (10:23–26) or a meal of a guest invited to a private dinner (10:27–31). Apparently, Paul himself had eaten such meat, because he speaks of being "reviled" for what he gives thanks (10:29). In the course of his discussion, however, Paul again takes up the question of the conscience of a "weak" Christian, even though the person is not so named in this pericope (10:28–29). He stresses rather the edification of the community as a whole (10:23; recall 8:1, 10), while counseling Corinthians not to scruple about eating at home meat bought in a market or consuming meat at a dinner to which one is invited by an unbelieving friend. In such a private setting, however, Paul introduces an important exception about meat declared to be *hierothyton*, which brings in the matter of conscience in a new way. In all things, one should be concerned not to give offense, either to Jew, Gentile, or Christian; rather "do all for the glory of God" (10:31b). "Be imitators of me, as I am of Christ" (11:1).

The RSV sets vv. 28–29a in parentheses, which makes v. 29b function as a comment on v. 24 and on the conscience mentioned in v. 27; the parentheses have been abandoned in NRSV and ESV, but the problem of those verses remains.

After a brief introduction, the pericope contains a series of seven imperatives and three explanatory comments, one of which is an OT quotation. The seven imperatives: Let no one seek his own advantage (v. 24); eat what is sold in the market (v. 25); eat what is put before you as a guest (v. 27); do not eat meat declared sacrificial (v. 28); do all for the glory of God (v. 31); avoid giving offense to anyone (v. 32); and be imitators of me, as I am of Christ (11:1). The OT reason is set forth in v. 26; and other reasons in vv. 29–30 and 33.

The argument proceeds in chiastic form, as Fee (*1 Cor*, 478) has shown:

A (23–24) Criterion: the good of others
  B (25–27) Personal freedom with regard to meat
    C (28–29a) Criterion illustrated: Freedom curtailed for sake of others
  B' (29b–30) Personal freedom defended
A' (31–33f) Criterion generalized: that all may be saved

Such a form reveals that vv. 32–33 are scarcely meant to be Paul's "manifesto," introducing what he will set forth in 11:1–16, *pace* Rigato ("Una rilettura").

NOTES

10:23. *"All things are permissible," but not all are beneficial. "All things are permissible," but not all edify.* As in 6:12, the slogan is quoted twice, and in each case Paul adds a restrictive comment, but "for me" is omitted, save in some MSS ($\aleph^2$, C^3, H, Ψ, and the Koine text-tradition), where copyists have secondarily introduced it. Paul's first comment echoes Sir 37:28a, "Not everything is good for everyone." Paul's second comment differs in introducing a broader, ecclesiological consideration, viz., the building up of the Corinthian Christian community, whereas in 6:12 it concerned an individual's conscience being dominated unduly. By putting the two comments together, Paul means that the only really "beneficial" thing is that which edifies or builds up the community. Cf. Rom 14:19.

24. *No one should seek his own advantage, but that of his neighbor.* Lit. "let no one seek what is his own," a 3d pers. sing. impv., the first of the seven impvs.; but the subject and verb of the second clause have to be supplied, "let each one seek." So Paul returns to the topic of 8:1–13, and the proverb-like statement shows that he is not speaking of individual edification in v. 23, but that of the community. His comment is a sapiential aphorism and resembles what he says elsewhere (Rom 15:2–3; Phil 2:4–5), when he refers to the example of Christ. The "neighbor" is expressed in Greek simply as "the other," and may have the connotation of one "with whom I instinctively disagree" (Barrett, *1 Cor,* 240).

25. *Eat whatever is sold in the meat market.* Paul's second impv. is clear: no one should scruple over the meat that is commonly sold in the markets of the Corinthian forum. It is *adiaphoron,* an "indifferent" matter of no consequence.

The Greek word *makellon* is known from an inscription of Epidaurus (ca. 400 B.C.), meaning "enclosure" (*Inscriptiones Graecae . . . Vol. IV ed. minor* [Berlin: de Gruyter, 1929] §102:296, 298). It is debated whether it is related to Latin *macellum,* which means "meat market" (Plautus, *Amphitryon* 1012; Terence, *Eunuchus* 255; Cicero, *De div.* 2.27 §59). A later Greek masc. noun, *makellos,* also meaning "meat market," is known from Aesop, *Vitae* G 51 P* (*ho makellos,* where pork can be bought); Plutarch, *Quaest. Rom.* ⁵⁴§277d–e; cf. Dio Cassius, *Rom. Hist.* 62.18.3 (Nero dedicated *tēn agoran tōn opsōn, to makellon ōnomasmenon*). Remains of a *makellon* seem to have been found in the excavations of Corinth, and a fragmentary Latin inscription with MACELLV[ ] has turned up (West, *Corinth* 8/2 §124). Other *makella* are known from Pompeii, Rome, and Gerasa, which shed some light on that at Corinth (see Cadbury, "The Macellum"; Gill, "The Meat-Market"; Koch, " 'Alles' ").

It is far from clear that "very little other meat [other than that 'coming from pagan temples'] was available" in a city like Corinth, *pace* Schneider, *TDNT,* 4:372. Meat offered in sacrifice to pagan gods did appear at times in *makella,* which were often found close to temples, but there is no reason to say that it alone and no other meat or food was available there (such as fish, olives, cheese, vegetables—see the list of ancient foods in Plato, *Resp.* 372c; or the expensive meats [lamb, beef, veal, fish, pork], about which Euclio complains in Plautus, *Aulularia* 373–75). There is no way of knowing how much food bought in the *makellon* would have a connection with idols (cf. Cadbury, "The Macellum," 141; Barrett, "Things Sacrificed," 144–47; esp. Koch, " 'Alles' ").

without raising a question in conscience. Lit. "examining nothing in conscience." That seems to mean that more than idol meat would be available in the usual *makellon.* Such questioning about the source of the meat, however, is precisely what a Jew would do. According to the third-century *Mishnah,* a Jew could buy meat in a common market only when the animal had not been slaughtered by a non-Jewish butcher, had not been associated with a pagan cult, and was not *ṭĕrêpāh* (having a fatal, organic disease); see *m. Ḥullin* 1:1; *m. Abodah Zarah* 2:3; 5:5 cf. Str-B, 3:420. Hence "Paul is nowhere more un-Jewish than in this *mēden anakrinontes*. His whole life as a Pharisee had been essentially one of *anakrisis*, not least into foods" (Barrett, "Things Sacrificed," 146). The *Vita Aesopi* 51 (W-text) mentions that idol meat in the market was at times distinguished from ordinary meat, and Pliny the Elder (*Ep.* 10.96.10) speaks of the availability of sacrificed meat for the purchaser (see Isenberg, "Sale"). Commentators sometimes ask how many Corinthian Christians would have been rich enough to buy meat from a *makellon* regularly. That question, however, does not concern Paul, but see Meggitt, "Meat Consumption." (The prohibition of eating *eidōlothyta* in Acts 15:29 is wholly unrelated to what Paul says here; see COMMENT on 8:1–13.)

26. *"For the earth and its fullness are the Lord's."* As the basis for what he has just said in v, 25, Paul quotes the LXX of Ps 24:1, adding only the introductory *gar*. Cf. Ps 50:12; 89:12. The words later became part of a standard Jewish blessing of food; see Lohse, "Zu I Cor." As Paul cites them in this context, they supply the reason for his second imperative, meaning that even meat which has been offered to an idol, which is now being sold indiscriminately in a market, still belongs to God and is part of his gifts to human beings. For another way of phrasing the matter, see Rom 14:14. Here *kyrios* is used of God, as in the Christian MSS of the LXX itself, and not of the risen Christ, *pace* Murphy-O'Connor ("Freedom," 557–58), who thinks that "God" is the source of the distinction of clean and unclean foods and hence the freedom the Christian now has comes from Christ; but see Acts 10:15. From a different point of view, the same idea is affirmed in 1 Tim 4:4; Mark 7:1–8, 19 (esp. 19b).

27. *If some unbeliever invites you (to dinner) and you want to go, eat whatever is put before you without raising a question in conscience.* Paul's third impv. supplies the logical conclusion from what Paul has been saying in vv. 25–26: the freedom of Christians to dine privately with unbelievers in their houses, without scruples. The pron. "you" is 2d pers. plur.; so Paul is addressing the Corinthian community, or at least several members of it, and not necessarily only those "possessing knowledge," even though the inviting host is *tis tōn apistōn*, "some individual among the unbelievers." Many Corinthian Christians would have had nonbelieving friends who might tender an invitation to dine in their houses, and such dining would not have been a participation in "the table of demons" for such Christians (v. 21), because the setting of the meal is different, a private home, and not an idol's temple, as in 8:10. The intermediate clause, "and you want to go," expresses not a reluctant desire, but rather the proper freedom of desiring to accept the invitation. Paul repeats the concluding clause of v. 25, which thus joins this case to the foregoing in vv. 25–26. Nothing should arouse the Christian conscience in such acceptance.

As an illustration of an ancient invitation to dinner, some commentators (e.g., Lindemann, *1 Cor*, 232) cite that found in *P. Oxy.* 1.110 (see NOTE on 8:10), but that is an invitation not to dine in a private home, but *en tō Sarapeiō*, "in the temple of (the god) Sarapis." It is, then, irrelevant here. Furthermore, an allusion to Exod 34:15, which has some similarity of wording, is sometimes said to be found here, but that too is irrelevant, because that passage has to do with sacrifices to foreign gods.

28. *But if someone says to you, "This is sacrificial meat," do not eat it for the sake of the one who informed you.* In this verse and v. 29a, Paul's fourth impv. is uttered in the context of a private meal, and not that of 8:10, "reclining at table in an idol's temple," to which what Paul has written in 10:21–22 would rather apply. He parenthetically introduces a hypothetical case that is the opposite of v. 27, and the meat is now called *hierothyton*, "something offered or sacrificed to a deity," as a non-Jewish Greek-speaking person might put it (see NOTE on 8:1). (*Hierothyton* is the reading in the best MSS, but MSS C, D, F, G, Ψ, 33 have *eidōlothyton*, a copyist's harmonization of the term with what is found in other verses of these chapters.)

The problem now is to decide who "someone" might be in this private setting. First, it is hardly the host himself, *pace* Witherington (*Conflict*, 227), because *tis* (v. 28) is a subject different from that in v. 27 (= the host). Second, although the words quoted might seem like the remark of a Corinthian nonbelieving dinner-guest (so Lietzmann, *1 Cor*, 51; Garland, *1 Cor*, 496; N. Watson, *1 Cor*, 108), such a person is scarcely the informant meant by the rest of the verse; how would he know about it? Third, it could be a Greek-speaking Christian fellow guest at the dinner, one convinced that the meat is *hieron*, "sacred." Collins (*1 Cor*, 384), however, understands him to be a slave serving the dinner, "who speaks out of concern for the Christian," who would have been like the "weak" of 8:10 and 9:22 (even though that term does not appear in this chapter). He or she might still use the older noun, *hierothyton*, out of habit and would be an object of Paul's concern, as he refers to "the one who informed you." The difficulty is that nothing in the text reveals the motivation of the remark (scruples?, attempt to embarrass or test?), and so there is no way of being sure.

and for the sake of conscience. I.e., once again the conscience is involved, whereas it was not mentioned in the cases of vv. 25, 27, where the food was an adiaphoron. This situation, then, differs too from that of vv. 19–20, where Paul spoke of the objective reality of idols and of the meat sacrificed to them as to demons. Now it is a matter of subjective judgment, how that meat is being judged by a conscience as *hieron*, "sacred." For that reason, Paul says, "Do not eat it," a neg. plur. impv., addressed to the Corinthian community.

29. *I mean, not your conscience, but the other's.* Lit. "I mean not one's own conscience, but that of the other (person)," i.e., the conscience of the fellow guest or the slave who is the informant. Paul's words are vague, but he most likely refers to a fellow Christian, not an unbeliever. A pagan's conscience presumably would not be offended by a Christian eating *hierothyton*. Mss F, G read *apistou*, which makes the "other" an unbeliever (also Latin versions, VL, Vg). "Christian freedom must be exercised with the conscience of others in mind" (Watson, "1 Corinthians 10:23–11:1," 315).

For why should my freedom be determined by someone else's conscience? After the parenthesis of vv. 28–29a, Paul himself now comments further on what he said about conscience in v. 27, continuing in the 1st pers. sing., as in v. 29a, and understanding the conj. *gar*, "for," as the link with v. 27. In the context of the private meal served even by an unbeliever, there is no reason for the Christian guest not to eat what is served him or her, for there is no reason to question it "in conscience." Moreover, v. 30 follows logically on this. In v. 31, Paul resumes the 2d pers. plur. impv. He introduces this question in v. 29b with *hinatí* (in many MSS written as two words), which stands for *hina tí genētai*, "for what reason does it happen (that)?" (BDF §12.3; §299.4), hence, "to what end, why?" In effect, the question agrees with the position of those who possess knowledge in chap. 8 and asserts the freedom of the individual conscience.

The second part of this verse and the next verse have been much debated, being notoriously difficult to interpret. For instance, (1) for Lietzmann (*1 Cor*, 52), they are an expostulation of the so-called strong Christian, in diatribe-like style, but they are not directly answered; Paul continues in his own way with 10:31–11:1. But how does one know that the verses are a diatribe-like expostulation? There is no dialogue in the text. (2) Tomson (*Paul*, 213–16) claims that *syneidēsis* should be understood as "intention," analogous to the rabbinic use of Hebrew *da'at*, and hence Paul's words would mean, "the pagan's intention toward idolatry prohibits the Christian's eating." But that interpretation hardly corresponds to Paul's usual use of *syneidēsis*. (3) The best solution is to take vv. 29b–30 as commentary on v. 27 (so RSV; Bruce, *1 Cor*, 100–101; Hays, *1 Cor*, 177–78; Garland, *1 Cor*, 499).

30. *If I partake with thanks (to God), why am I reviled for what I give thanks?* I.e., when a Christian says grace before a meal (perhaps silently when invited by a unbelieving host), how can he or she thank God for something that is evil or wrong, and so he or she would have to be faulted for consumption of such food? Paul will not allow "someone else's conscience" to be a judge of him or restrict his freedom or rights, even though he might restrain that freedom himself, as he has already done in 8:13. This stance provides the basis for what he will assert in vv. 31–32. Cf. Rom 14:6b; also 1 Tim 4:3–4.

31. *So whether you eat or drink or whatever you do, do all for the glory of God.* This is Paul's fifth impv., which states the principle governing his discussion in the latter part of this chapter, as he shifts from the 1st pers. sing. used in vv. 29b–30 to the 2d pers. plur. All human activity should be carried out "for the glory of God," i.e., as a form of praise of God, and not motivated by food laws or the satisfaction of one's natural appetite, or even by the assertion of one's personal liberty (Bruce, *1 Cor*, 101).

Paul repeats this motivation for human conduct, which is derived from his Jewish doxological background, again in 2 Cor 1:20; 4:15; Rom 15:7; Phil 1:11; 2:11; cf. Rom 11:36; *pace* Lindemann (*1 Cor*, 234), not Rom 1:23; 3:23, where the same phrase is used, but not in doxological fashion. The Jewish usage (*likbôd 'Ēl*) is found in 1Q19 13:1; 1QS 10:9; or as *likbôd 'ĕlōhê ṣĕbā'[ôt]* in 1QSb 4:25; cf. 1QH 16(old 8):5; 18(old 10):12; 1QM 4:6, 8; cf. 1 Esdr 9:8; 4 Macc 1:12 ("giving glory").

32. *Avoid giving offense, whether to Jews or Greeks or the church of God.* Lit. "become those not causing (others) to stumble," with *aproskoptoi* used as in Sir 32:21; Phil 1:10. This sixth impv. is only a simple application of the principle just

stated in v. 31. Paul does not specify what the offense might be. Three groups of humanity (Jews, Gentiles, and Christians) are singled out, the first two of which are "outsiders" (5:12), described by the pair, "Jews or Greeks," a combination that appears elsewhere (1:22, 24; 12:13; Gal 3:28; Rom 1:16; 2:9–10 [collective sing.]). Paul would want God's church to be attractive to both of them as outsiders; cf. 1 Thess 4:12 (see *Romans*, 250–51). As Lindemann (*1 Cor*, 234) notes, this is the earliest instance in Christian literature of "the church of God" recorded as an entity set over against Jews and Greeks in human history. On "church of God," see NOTE on 1:2.

33. *even as I try to please everyone in every way, not seeking my own good but that of the many that they may be saved.* The verb *areskō* has many nuances, and Paul scarcely means that he is merely currying favor (cf. 1 Thess 2:4; Gal 1:10); he seems rather to be using it as it occurs in Greek public documents that honor individual citizens for having pleased the populace by their public service (see Demosthenes, *Ep.* 3.27). Paul has been seeking to render service to everyone without deference, either to himself or any other individual. The goal in his entire ministerial activity is the salvation of all, of which he has already spoken in 1:18, 21; 9:22. The contrast between "everyone" (*pasin*) and "the many" (*tōn pollōn*) is not to be pressed, because the latter is often used as a literary circumlocution for "all" (cf. Rom 5:15, 19; 2 Cor 2:17; BDAG, 848; *Romans*, 419).

11:1. *Be imitators of me, as I am of Christ.* Paul's final impv. repeats what he said in 4:16 (see NOTE there), as he urges Corinthian Christians to follow his example, now in his unstinting service of all. He has already proposed himself implicitly as a model in the matter of not eating meat in 8:13; now he repeats that even on a broader scale. The subordinate clause that he adds to his imperative finds its explanation in what Timothy would explain to them in 4:17, "my ways in Christ [Jesus]." It also eliminates any suggestion of pride or arrogance on Paul's part, because he acknowledges that he himself is an imitator. Cf. Phil 3:17; 1 Thess 1:6.

BIBLIOGRAPHY (See also Bibliography on 8:1–13, pp. 349–50)

Cadbury, H. J., "The Macellum of Corinth," *JBL* 53 (1934) 134–41.
Gill, D. W. J., "The Meat-Market at Corinth (1 Corinthians 10:25)," *TynBul* 43 (1992) 389–93.
Isenberg, M., "The Sale of Sacrificial Meat," *CP* 70 (1975) 271–73.
Koch, D.-A., " 'Alles, was *en makellō* verkauft wird, esst . . .': Die *macella* von Pompeji, Gerasa und Korinth und ihre Bedeutung für die Auslegung von 1 Kor 10,25," *ZNW* 90 (1999) 194–219 (+ plates I–IV).
———, " 'Seid unanstössig für Juden und für Griechen und für die Gemeinde Gottes' (1 Kor 10,32): Christliche Identität im *makellon* in Korinth und bei Privateinladungen," *Paulus, Apostel Jesu Christi: Festschrift für Günter Klein* . . . (ed. M. Trowitzsch; Tübingen: Mohr Siebeck, 1998) 35–54.
Lohse, E., "Zu 1 Cor. 10, 26.31," *ZNW* 47 (1956) 277–80; repr. *Die Einheit des Neuen Testaments: Exegetische Studien zur Theologie des Neuen Testaments* (Göttingen: Vandenhoeck & Ruprecht, 1973) 245–48.

Paige, T., "Stoicism, *Eleutheria*, and Community at Corinth," *Worship, Theology and Ministry in the Early Church: Essays in Honor of Ralph P. Martin* (JSNTSup 87; ed. M. J. Wilkins and T. Paige; Sheffield: Sheffield Academic, 1992) 180–93.

Rigato, M.-L., "Una rilettura di 1 Cor 10,32–33 + 11,1–16," *RivB* 53 (2005) 31–70.

Smit, J. F. M., "The Function of First Corinthians 10,23–30: A Rhetorical Anticipation," *Bib* 78 (1997) 377–88.

Vollenweider, S., *Freiheit als neue Schöpfung*, 220–32.

Waele, F. J. de, "The Roman Market North of the Temple at Corinth," *AJA* 34 (1930) 432–54, esp. 453–54.

Watson, D. F., "1 Corinthians 10:23–11:1 in the Light of Greco-Roman Rhetoric: The Role of Rhetorical Questions," *JBL* 108 (1989) 301–18.

C. PROBLEMS ABOUT SACRED ASSEMBLIES (11:2–34)

23　　a. *Women Worshipping with Uncovered Heads (11:2–16)*

[11:2] I praise you because you have been mindful of me in everything and are holding to the traditions, just as I passed them on to you. [3] But I want you to realize that Christ is the head of every man, man is the head of woman, and God is the head of Christ. [4] Every man who prays or prophesies with covered head brings disgrace upon his head; [5] and every woman who prays or prophesies with uncovered head brings disgrace upon her head, for that is one and the same thing as her shaved head. [6] For if a woman does not cover her head, she should have her hair cut off; but if it is disgraceful for a woman to have her hair cut off or to be shaved, then she should cover her head. [7] A man ought not cover his head, since he is the image and glory of God; but a woman is the glory of man. [8] For man did not come from woman; but woman from man. [9] Nor was man created for woman, but woman for man. [10] For this reason a woman ought to have authority over her head, because of the angels. [11] In the Lord, however, neither is woman independent of man, nor man of woman. [12] For just as woman came from man, so man is born of woman; but everything comes from God. [13] Judge for yourselves: Is it proper for a woman to pray to God with uncovered head? [14] Does not nature itself teach you that if a man wears his hair long, it is degrading for him; [15] but if a woman wears her hair long, it is her glory? For her hair has been given [to her] for a covering. [16] If anyone is inclined to be argumentative (about this), we have no such custom, nor do the churches of God.

COMMENT

Paul now moves on to another topic, which has nothing to do with meat sacrificed to idols but with the conduct of Christians in their cultic assemblies. This is the third set of problems (the two passages in chap. 11) that he has been discussing in this part of his letter. Nothing indicates with certainty that such problems were mentioned in the letter sent to Paul (7:1), but they may have been. He takes up these matters, having somehow learned about them, and finds fault with such Corinthian Christian conduct. His discussion has to do with sacred assemblies, in which Christians gather to pray and prophesy, and to celebrate the Lord's Supper (11:2–23). It deals at first (vv. 2–16) with an aspect of worship that is in itself trivial, but in which he once again finds considerations of greater import. This is not surprising, because by now in this letter one has learned how Paul often judges matters against a greater theological background than what at first appears.

The surface issue now is: May a Christian woman take part in a liturgical service with uncovered head? It is not easy to state just what was going on in the Corinthian community, with which Paul finds fault. It is often thought that Greek women were accustomed to wear a veil in public and often even at home, if they were married, but at times removed it in heathen religious assemblies, and that such a custom was being imitated by Christian women in Roman Corinth in their cultic gatherings (e.g., Allo, *1 Cor*, 258). Whether that is the practice or not to which Paul is reacting, he is seeking to counteract what he considers an abuse among Christian Corinthian women. His reaction is complicated, because his reasons for it involve the way he understands the role of man and woman in their relation to Christ and God.

There are many analyses of this pericope, which do not always agree in detail; so it is necessary at the outset to clear the air about some of the details. First, the problem that Paul is addressing is that of Christian women praying or prophesying with uncovered heads; this emerges from vv. 5–6, 10, 13, 15. In the course of his discussion, Paul compares the woman with a man. Although some recent commentators have understood the topic to be "Men and Women in Prayer and Proclamation" (Lindemann, *1 Cor*, 237) or "the manner in which women and men should wear their hair praying and prophesying" (Schüssler Fiorenza, *In Memory*, 227; similarly Barrett, Fee, Kistemaker, Thiselton), it has normally been seen as a discussion about women and the covering of their heads in worship (and still is among many modern commentators: Bruce, Conzelmann, Delobel, Garland, Grosheide, Kremer, Lietzmann, D. B. Martin, Perriman, Robertson-Plummer, Schrage, Senft, J. Weiss). The problem is not that Corinthian men were praying or prophesying with covered heads, even though Paul's rhetorical comparison leads him to formulate it so in order to make his point by contrast. It is important not to confuse such rhetoric with the substance of his argument. Hence, *pace* Winter (*After Paul*, 121), this passage continues, indeed, to be "about 'the veiling of women.' " Of the fifteen verses in this pericope, two are neutral (vv. 2, 16); two deal with *anēr*, "man" (vv. 4, 14); but five with *gynē*, "woman" (vv. 5, 6, 10, 13, 15); and six mention both *anēr* and *gynē* (vv. 3, 7, 8, 9, 11, 12 [where apart from the last two the rest express the relationship of woman, the main subject, to man]). From such data one gets the impression that Paul is indeed concerned with the head-covering of women in this pericope, and it "does not deal with the men" (Padgett, "Feminism," 127). Similarly Garland, *1 Cor*, 506–8; Lindemann, *1 Cor*, 247.

Second, the problem is about a woman wearing a head-covering or her failure to do so (v. 5, *akatakalyptō tē kephalē* ["with uncovered head"]; v. 6, *katakalyptesthō* ["let her cover herself"]; v. 13); it is not a way of dressing her hair or a specific hairdo, despite some of Paul's comparisons that refer to shorn hair (v. 6), shaved head (v. 6), or long hair (vv. 14, 15), *pace* Isaksson (*Marriage*, 165–68); Murphy-O'Connor (*CBQ* 50:268–69); Schüssler Fiorenza (*In Memory*, 227). It has nothing to do with "disheveled hair" or "flowing and unbound hair" (ibid.), or with "a bare-faced woman" (Robertson-Plummer), or with the oriental face covering of some Islamic cultures. It concerns the use of something like a head veil, a *mantilla*, but could have been part of a garment drawn up over the head (see Motta, "The Question").

Third, it is wholly gratuitous to introduce into the interpretation of this pericope a consideration of male homosexual styles of wearing hair. Paul speaks of the degrading case of a man wearing long hair (v. 14). This has been explained by Murphy-O'Connor ("Sex," 485–87; *CBQ* 50:268) and some others, by referring to Philo's negative description of pederasts and their mode of braiding and adorning the hair of their heads (*De spec. leg.* 3.7 §37). Philo does not use the verb *komaō*, which Paul has in vv. 14–15, and none of the verbs that he does use appears in this Pauline passage. To introduce such a consideration into the interpretation of this passage is simply an unnecessary distraction from its many real problems (see Martin, *Corinthian Body*, 296 n. 19).

Fourth, some interpreters (e.g., Holmyard, Bachmann), recalling Paul's later comment that "women should remain silent in the churches" (14:34), have tried to interpret the praying and prophesying of women in this pericope as having nothing to do with church assemblies. Paul almost certainly has this kind of cultic gathering in mind, because v. 16 ends by saying that the practice which has appeared in the Corinthian community is not what is done in "the churches of God," i.e., in other Christian cultic assemblies. The problem has indeed arisen precisely in the Corinthian church's liturgical gathering.

Fifth, this passage has to do with community worship, but it is not related to the problems of chaps. 12–14, even though chap. 14 deals also with community gatherings and a woman's role is an issue toward the end of it (14:34–35). Schüssler Fiorenza argues that in chaps. 11–14 Paul's main argument concerns "indecency and right order, values which are not specifically Christian" (*In Memory*, 227). What she says about the argument from order is correct for chap. 14, but it has little relevance here in chap. 11, where the matter concerns a Christian woman praying or prophesying in public with uncovered head and the disgrace that that implies.

Sixth, Paul is dealing with a specific problem about the activity of Corinthian women in the community's cultic assembly, not with general questions such as the "eschatological woman," the inferiority of women, women's ministry, the role of women in the church, or even about the ordination of women. When this passage is read with such questions in mind, there is the tendency to read more into the text than what Paul has expressed. True, some of Paul's statements have at times a broad connotation, because he has curtailed his mode of speech or even generalized a formulation. When one prescinds from the immediate context in which such speech or formulation occurs, however, there is danger of raising issues foreign to the context. (For an example of how a Pauline generalization can create exegetical problems, when the context is not kept in mind, see Rom 4:2 [about Abraham's "deeds"]; cf. *Romans*, 361, 372–73.)

In the course of his intricate comments on the conduct of such Corinthian Christian women, Paul sets forth with some rhetoric and a surprising sobriety of tone five reasons why a woman should not pray or prophesy in a cultic assembly with uncovered head:

1. Biblically, the order of creation found in the Genesis story reveals that woman has been created "for man," to be his companion and helper; hence as "the glory of man," she should cover her head (vv. 7–12).
2. Theologically, the ordered headship of God, Christ, man, and woman calls for it (v. 3).
3. Sociologically, convention, based on "nature" itself, considers a woman's uncovered head in such a situation as shameful and a disgrace (vv. 6, 13–15).
4. As a matter of ecclesiastical discipline, "the churches of God" have no such custom as uncovered heads of women at prayer in a cultic assembly (v. 16).
5. "Because of the angels" (v. 10).

In the long run, Paul himself is aware that his arguments in this matter are not going to convince everyone; hence his protasis in v. 16, "If anyone is inclined to be argumentative (about this)," as he invokes church discipline to end the discussion. Paul's argument is complicated, but it is not "notoriously obscure," as Hays would have us believe (*1 Cor*, 183), or "far from being intelligible even today" (Schüssler Fiorenza, *In Memory*, 219). Padgett, who has called Schüssler Fiorenza's interpretation of this passage "an exciting one" and "an interesting interpretation," finally admits that "it has all the marks of being read into the text on the basis of parallel movements in Hellenistic religions, rather than arising from the text" ("Feminism," 126–27).

Some interpreters (Walker, Cope, Trompf, Mount) have even argued that these verses (or at least vv. 3–16) are interpolated and have not been composed by Paul, and that v. 17 is a logical sequel to v. 2. That view of this passage, however, has not gone without strong criticism (see Murphy-O'Connor, "The Non-Pauline Character" and "Interpolations," 87–90). It is too easy a way to get rid of a complicated passage in Pauline writings. Ellis (*NTS* 32:493), however, considers vv. 3–16 to be a Pauline composition, but introduced secondarily by him into the already-composed letter.

To appreciate Paul's discussion in this pericope, one should note the flow of his argument:

v. 3:	Programmatic statement: Paul's basic theological principle.
vv. 4–6:	His thesis set forth: the difference between the heads of man and woman in public prayer (a rhetorical contrast).
vv. 7–9:	His explanatory argument that asserts the relation of woman to man.
v. 10:	Concluding statement: the woman's obligation to have authority over her head (with an added reason, "because of the angels").
vv. 11–12:	His qualifying counterargument "in the Lord," corresponding to vv. 7–9.
vv. 13–15:	Social-propriety argument: referring again to the topic of vv. 4–6, now in terms of "nature."
v. 16:	Admonition based on church discipline.

In verses 5b–6 and 13b, Paul in no way asserts that "recreated woman has an authority equal to that of the man (vv. 10–12)," *pace* Murphy-O'Connor, "Sex," 498. That is to read a distracting issue into the text, which says nothing about it.

NOTES

11:2. *I praise you because you have been mindful of me in everything and are holding to the traditions, just as I passed them on to you.* In this introductory verse, Paul begins with *captatio benevolentiae*, a conciliatory note, which joins well his counsel in v. 1 to be imitators of him, but which he will modify in the next passage; cf. vv. 17 and 22 with this verse. He begins with "praise," because, although he cannot approve of the Corinthian practice that he will now discuss, he admits that Corinthian Christians in general have been adhering to traditions that he has already taught them (B. W. Winter, *After Paul*, 3). Hurd (*Origins*, 67) relates what Paul says about "traditions" in this verse to the letter of 7:1; his words may even be an indirect quotation of what the Corinthians wrote. Theoretically, this is possible, but it may be only initial conciliatory rhetoric designed "to placate them so that they will be receptive to critical advice" (Mitchell, *Paul*, 260). The "traditions" are unspecified, but they must have some connection with the topic to be discussed in vv. 3–16, and are so regarded by Meier ("On the Veiling"). Cf. 2 Thess 2:15; 3:6. Ellis identifies the "traditions" mentioned here (and in 14:34–35) as "principles of a domestic code on the relationship of husband and wife which . . . had been adapted from Jewish antecedents and was probably in use within the Pauline and Petrine missions from the beginning" ("Traditions," 492); that sounds plausible, but this passage deals with more than the relationship of husband and wife.

Although Paul has used the verb *paradidōmi*, "hand over" (someone, 5:5) and will so use it in 11:23b; 13:3; 15:24; Rom 1:24, 26, 28; 4:25; 6:17; 8:32, he now employs it (with the cog. noun, *paradosis*) in the technical sense of "transmitting" or "passing on" a tradition; in this sense, it will occur again in 11:23a; 15:3; also in 1 Thess 2:13; 4:1; Gal 1:9, 12; Phil 4:9. For the use of such Greek terms about Jewish traditions, see Mark 7:3–4; Acts 6:14; Josephus, *Ant.* 13.10.6 §297 (Pharisaic rules); also *Ant.* 19.1.5 §31 (passing on a Roman *sēmeion*, "password"). Cf. the corresponding later rabbinic use of *qibbēl min*, "receive from," and *māsar lĕ-*, "pass on to" (*m. Aboth* 1.1; *pace* Jeremias [*Eucharistic Words*, 104], Mishnaic terminology is not "pre-Pauline"). In QL the verb *māsar* occurs in this sense only in CD 3:3, where Abraham is said to "pass on" God's commandments (*miṣwōt ʾĒl*) to Isaac and Jacob. Cf. Wis 14:15, where Greek *paredōken* is used of a pagan grief-stricken father who fashioned an image of his dead child and "passed on" secret rites and initiations in his idolatry. The Greek terms *paradidonai* and *paralambanein* were also used similarly in the Greek world, at least since Plato (see Klauck, "Presence," 61).

3. *But I want you to realize that.* Again Paul uses this introductory clause for an important statement; see NOTE on 3:16. Cf. 10:1; 12:1; Rom 1:13; Col 2:1.

Christ is the head of every man, man is the head of woman, and God is the head of Christ. This is the fundamental theological principle that will govern Paul's discussion in this pericope, a principle of headship or preeminence that prevails in the Christian community—a three-part enunciation that he asserts but does not further explain.

"Of every man Christ is the head": Paul's word order is noteworthy, for *pantos andros* stands in first place, "of every male of the human family" (Robertson-Plummer, *1 Cor*, 229), not *pantos anthrōpou*, "of every human being." The art. *ho* before *Christos* is omitted in some MSS (B*, D*, F, G), but read in many others (P⁴⁶, ℵ, A, Bᶜ, C, D², Ψ, 33, 1739), as it is before *Christou* at the end of the verse. It would make little difference to understand the term as "the Messiah" rather than as Jesus' second name; in either case, he is the Son sent by the Father so that we might be adopted as sons (Gal 4:4; cf. Rom 8:32; 1 Thess 1:10). The sense of the verse is clear: As God is preeminent over Christ, so Christ is preeminent over every man, and man is preeminent over woman. The meaning of the last clause echoes what is explicit in God's words to the woman in Gen 3:16e ("He shall rule over you"). The whole verse is but another way of affirming what Paul has already asserted in 3:23, "You belong to Christ, and Christ to God." This principle so enunciated shows that Paul is indeed propounding a hierarchy; and the third element of it is part of it, and not just an affirmation of gender differences or of functions between partners, *pace* Fiddes, " 'Woman's Head.' " Despite the contention of some commentators, there is no need to invoke here an *eikōn*-series (series of images) rooted in Hellenistic-Jewish cosmological speculation, as Delobel rightly notes ("1 Cor 11:2–16," 377). Cf. Col 2:10; Eph 1:22; 4:15.

The crucial term is *kephalē*, and its meaning is controverted:

(1) Basically, it denotes the physical, anatomical "head" of a human being or animal; it is used in this sense of the human head in vv. 4a, 5a, 7, 10; 12:21 (letters indicating which occurrence is meant when there is more than one instance in a given verse). This meaning agrees with thousands of instances of the word in Greek literature.

(2) Metaphorically, *kephalē* stands at times for the whole person, especially in an apostrophe or salutation, *philē kephalē*, "Dear Head" (Homer, *Iliad* 8.281); this may be its meaning in v. 4b, 5b.

(3) Again metaphorically, *kephalē* is said to mean "source" in a few instances: Herodotus, *Hist.* 4.91 (*kephalai*, "sources" of a river [along with *pēgai*, "springs"]; *Orphic Frag.* 21A (Zeus possibly as "source" or "beginning" of all things); Philo, *De cong. erud. causa* 12 §61 (Esau as *kephalē* of a clan, progenitor); *De praem. et poen.* 20 §215; Artemidorus Daldianus, *Oneirocriticon* 1.2; 1.35; 3.66 (= father, source or cause of life). There is no instance of it meaning the "source" of individual persons.

(4) Again metaphorically, *kephalē* is also used as "head," meaning "controlling agent," "ruler," or "leader," as in "head" of a department or "headmaster." For instance, Plato (*Timaeus* 44d) calls the physical head "the most divine [part] and governor of everything within us." This metaphorical sense is found often in the LXX: e.g., Judg 11:11; 2 Sam 22:44: Ps 18:43; Isa 7:8–9; Jer 38:7; Deut 28:13, 44; Isa 9:13–14; 19:15 (in the last four instances contrasted with figurative *oura*, "tail"); Philo, *De spec. leg.* 3.33 §184; Josephus, *J.W.* 4.4.3 §261 (Jerusalem as "head" of whole nation); Plutarch, *Cicero* 14.4–6 (head of the republic = leader); Libanius, *Or.* 20.3. Traditionally, it has been understood in this sense here: Paul would be asserting the "superior rank" (BDAG, 542) of God, Christ, and man (*anēr*) in v. 3, and perhaps in vv. 4b, 5b. Paul would be using this sense in his theological principle because it bears on what individuals do with the anatomical head in worship.

See further Grudem, "Does *kephalē*" (an examination of 2,336 instances in Greek literature); "Meaning . . . Response"; "Meaning of *kephalē*"; *Evangelical Feminism*, 590–97; Fitzmyer, "*Kephalē* in 1 Corinthians 11.3," *TAG*, 341–48; Cotterell and Turner, *Linguistics*, 145. For perfunctory criticism of such examples, see Perriman, "The Head" (not always cogent); Cervin, "Does *kephalē* Mean " 'Source' "; Fee, *1 Cor*, 502 n. 42; Fiddes, " 'Woman's Head.' "

It is sometimes said that the metaphorical meaning "head," denoting a human being of preeminence or superior rank, did not exist in ancient Greek prior to the Byzantine or patristic period, and that neither LSJ, nor MM, nor the lexica of Preisigke or Chantraine have listed any instances of *kephalē* in this sense (Schlier, *TDNT*, 3:674; Murphy-O'Connor, "Sex," 491–92). It is found, however, in the recent BDAG (542: "being of high status," "*head*". . . to denote superior rank), with no mention of the meaning "source." Also in Louw and Nida, *Greek-English Lexicon of the New Testament Based on Semantic Domains* (New York: United Bible Societies, 1988) §87.51; and in the dictionaries of F. Passow (*Handwörterbuch der griechischen Sprache* [2 vols.; Leipzig: Vogel, 1831], 1. 1270: *Hauptperson*) and H. van Herwerden (*Lexicon graecum suppletorium et dialecticum* [2 vols.; Leiden: Sijthoff, 1910] 797: *dux*). Hence it is clear that, when Paul as a Hellenistic Jewish Christian writer used *kephalē*, he could have meant by it "preeminent person" or even "a person having authority over" others. See further Grudem, *Evangelical Feminism*, 587–90 (esp. the letter of P. Glare, the editor of the *Supplement* to LSJ, to Grudem about the "not very satisfactory" entry on *kephalē* in LSJ).

The metaphorical meaning, "source," however, has been preferred by Barrett, Baumert, Bruce, Cervin, Colpe, Delobel, Fee, Kroeger, Mickelsen, Scroggs, Murphy-O'Connor ("G[ree]k *kephalē* never connotes authority or superiority . . . ; 'source' (LSJ 945) is the only appropriate meaning here, *the source of every person's new being is Christ*" [*NJBC*, 808 (his emphasis; note his translation of *pantos andros*!); also *CBQ* 42:491–94]). Thus Paul would only be stating the relation of woman, man, and Christ to their origin or source. It is not explained, however, in what sense Christ can be said to be the "origin" or "source" of *anēr* to suit this context. Moreover, to say that in this passage "Christ is seen as a sort of 'second Adam' " (Baumert, *Woman*, 185) is exegetically unsound, even apart from "second Adam" being a patristic, non-Pauline formulation (cf. 15:45, "last Adam"!). Even if he were such, what would that mean in this context? However, this figurative meaning, "source," has also been contested seriously (Cotterell and Turner, *Linguistics*, 145; Grudem, "Meaning of *kephalē*"; Perriman, "The Head," 616); and it is questionable whether it suits the Pauline context any better than the traditional figurative sense. Schlier (*TDNT*, 3:679) tried to combine the two figurative meanings: "*kephalē* implies one who stands over another in the sense of being the ground of his being." But what does that mean? Lindemann (*1 Cor*, 240) rejects both "authority over" and "source" and claims that the word means only that one person precedes another, that *kephalē* means only "that which is preeminent," so that the person receives honor or glory. Having said that, Lindemann concludes that the verse formulates "eine durchgehende Hierarchie (Gott-Christus-Mann-Frau [a thorough hierarchy, God-Christ-man-woman])." If, however, such a "hierarchy" is found here, it cannot imply only preeminence. Similarly Garland (*1 Cor*, 516), who follows Perriman and prefers the meaning, "that which is most prominent, . . . preeminent." For criticism of the meaning "preeminence," see Grudem, "The Meaning," 37–39. In any case, this verse formulates the theological grounding for the rest of Paul's argument in the following verses.

Finally, one should compare the related, but slightly different concept in Eph 5:23: *anēr estin kephalē tēs gynaikos, hōs kai ho Christos kephalē tēs ekklēsias*, "the husband is the head of the wife, just as Christ is the head of the church." There the translation of *anēr* and *gynē* as "husband" and "wife" is correct, as the context shows.

4. *Every man who prays or prophesies with covered head brings disgrace upon his head.* Lit. ". . . prophesies having (something) down from (the) head disgraces his head." *Pace* Garland (*1 Cor*, 511, 517), the English language will not tolerate the literal translation, "having down from the head." The phrase *kata kephalēs echōn* is usually understood as meaning a veil or cover hanging from the head (BDAG, 511; BDF §225.2; *IBNTG*, 60), as in LXX Esth 6:12 (*lypou-menos kata kephalēs*, "mourning with head covered"; cf. Plutarch, *Mor.* 200f: *kata tēs kephalēs echōn to himation*, "having a cloak (hanging) from the head; also Plutarch, *Caesar* 739cd; *Brutus* 991f; *Cicero* 885c. In Josephus, the passages usually cited (see Oster, "When Men," 486 n. 6) use the words, but apply them to someone else's head. *Pace* Schrage (*1 Cor*, 2.505–6); Lindemann (*1 Cor*, 240), that the phrase

means the same thing as a man wearing long hair, mentioned in v. 14, is far from certain. If Paul intended to speak of such a male hairstyle, he would have expressed it here as clearly as he does in v. 14, as Fee rightly recognizes (1 Cor, 506).

Nor is there any hint that this clause refers to "male homosexuals" wearing long hair (so Murphy-O'Connor, NJBC, 809). The translation of kata kephalēs echōn as "makes motions with his head" (Baumert, Woman, 184) is simply far-fetched. The expression tēn kephalēn kataischynein is also found in Josephus, Ant. 20.4.2 §89, but in a different sense, "to befoul the head" (with ashes, while fasting and praying).

That Roman statues have been found depicting men capite velato ("with veiled head," i.e., with part of their toga drawn over their heads) while praying or offering a libation to gods is clear (see Gill, "The Importance"; Oster, "When Men," 496–502). There is even such a statue said to be of Augustus from the first-century Julian Basilica in the Corinthian forum; another of Nero (see Johnson, Corinth 9: Sculpture, 70–72 §134). They portray the emperors as Roman magistrates, combining their religious, civil, and legal roles as head of the empire. It is further argued that the "socially elite" of Corinth adopted this practice and that "Christians who were not among the elite also chose to follow this custom when they undertook to pray or prophesy" (B. W. Winter, After Paul, 122–23). The evidence for such a custom is far from clear, and even though there is abundant evidence of such men covering their heads in Roman worship, it has little to do with what Paul is talking about in this passage. Is one to understand this verse as an expression of Paul's criticism ("brings disgrace upon his head") or condemnation of a Roman official custom or religious practice? Hardly. What is the connection between such a Roman practice and the alleged use of head coverings of Corinthian Christian men? Nothing emerges.

The context of prayer and prophecy that are mentioned is the Christian cultic or church assembly; hence "prays" means praying aloud to God, possibly even as a leader of the gathering in a house-church. "Prophecy" has to be understood as it will be used in 13:9; 14:1, 3, 22, 24, 31, 39, of a form of delivering God's word to the assembly by Spirit-inspired preaching based on Scripture (see Perrot, "Prophètes"). Pace Hooker ("Authority," 414), praying to God or prophesying does not mean that one is "obedient to God alone." Such exclusivity is not even implied.

In the context that Paul envisages, the "disgrace" stems from the man's concealing his status as the "image and glory of God," as it will be expressed in v. 7. The words, "disgraces his head," could mean "disgraces himself," if sense 2 above of kephalē were to be understood, meaning the whole person (see above; cf. Schlier, TDNT, 3:674; Murphy-O'Connor, "Sex," 485); but preferably it means that he disgraces Christ, "the head of every man," as in v. 3, from whom he would be concealing himself (SBJ, Cor, 50; Fee, 1 Cor, 506; Schrage, 1 Cor, 2:505). It is eisegetical to read into the meaning of this verse "the clear association of this practice with pagan devotion, pulling the toga over the physical head in Christian worship would shame the spiritual head of the man, Christ" (Garland, 1 Cor, 517).

Is Paul referring to an actual practice among Corinthian male Christians? Or is his example merely a rhetorical and hypothetical counterpart to the problem that he is really discussing, viz., Corinthian Christian women praying or prophesying with heads uncovered? The latter is the better explanation, because of vv. 5–6, the thrust of vv. 7 and 10, and esp. because of v. 13. Similarly Fee, *1 Cor*, 505 ("a hypothetical situation for the man"); Robertson-Plummer, *1 Cor*, 229; Garland, *1 Cor*, 517.

5. *and every woman who prays or prophesies with uncovered head brings disgrace upon her head.* This is the concluding counterpart of v. 4, for which that verse was a rhetorical preparation, and with all the same exegetical problems. "Her head" could mean "the man" of v. 3, but in light of what follows in vv. 5b–6c, it probably means her own physical head, and not both "heads," because the noun is singular.

Two things, however, are important in this verse: (1) Paul speaks of *akataka-lyptō tē kephalē*, "the uncovered head," of the woman as the counterpart of *kata kephalēs echōn* of the man in v. 4, which shows that the latter phrase cannot mean merely the man's wearing of long hair as in v. 14, but rather the covered head of a male (BDF §225.2); (2) Paul recognizes that Christian women did partake actively in such public prayer and prophecy in a church assembly. This new status of women is not the problem, even if it differs from the custom with which Paul as a Jew would have been acquainted, as Hooker has rightly argued ("Authority," 416). It seems rather that Paul has learned that some Christian married women in Corinth were praying or prophesying in such a cultic assembly without the customary head covering. Such a woman would bring disgrace to her husband because she seems to consider herself on the same level as he.

Is Paul's assertion restricted to "married women"? Greek *gynē* can mean either "woman" (14:34–35) or "wife" (7:16). The former sense is almost certainly meant in 11:3c. Here in v. 5 it might have the latter sense, as some commentators understand it (e.g., B. W. Winter, *After Paul*, 127), because of the mention of the head covering, which was characteristic of married women outside their homes in Roman culture. The phrase *pasa de gynē*, "every woman," however, seems to express a wider extension: a woman of indeterminate marriage status. As Williams has put it, "The veil is a symbol of a woman's shame, worn in public to mark her off as a private person intent on guarding her purity and so maintaining the honour of her husband or father" ("Lifting the Veil," 57–58).

Some commentators have argued that the modal dat. *akatakalyptō tē kephalē* does not mean "with uncovered head" and has nothing to do with a veil or cover, but means rather "loosed hair" itself as a "covering" of the head (Murphy-O'Connor, "Sex," 488; similarly Lindemann, *1 Cor*, 241; Hays, *1 Cor*, 185–86; Schüssler Fiorenza, *In Memory*, 227: "with flowing and unbound hair"; de Mingo, "Saint Paul," 14; Khiok-khng, "Differentiation," 12).

Some of these commentators even argue that *akatakalyptos* in LXX Lev 13:45 is used of the head of a leper and translate the Hebrew, as does the RSV, "Let the hair of his head hang loose." However, the Hebrew pass. ptc. in the clause, *rō'šô yihyeh pārûă'*, means, "Let his head be unbound," in the sense, "let him not wear a turban" (see BDB, 828). That, however, does not mean that the LXX adj.

akatakalyptos has the same semantic connotation as the Hebrew ptc. The Greek clearly means, "let his head be uncovered" (*hē kephalē autou akatakalyptos*), and it says nothing about the state of the leper's hair itself, whether groomed and kempt or disheveled and loosed, the RSV and Hurley ("Did Paul," 198–99) notwithstanding. Cf. the description of a woman in prayer coming with an offering of barley meal *akatakalyptō tē kephalē*, "with uncovered head" (Philo, *De spec. leg.* 3.10 §60). Finally, the last word in v. 6, a 3d pers. sing. pres. mid. impv., *katakalyptesthō*, lit. "let her cover herself," clinches the matter. All of this means that Paul is talking about a veil or some kind of head covering distinct from the woman's hair itself. Garland (*1 Cor*, 519) rightly insists, "Paul's mention of hair in 11:14–15 and shaved heads in this passage . . . is only by way of illustration. It serves to bolster his argument about head covering and is not the central problem."

for that is one and the same thing as her shaved head. Or possibly "as a shaved woman," since no noun is expressed in the Greek, and the fem. ptc. *exyrēmenē*, "shaved," can modify either *kephalē* or *gynē* (understood). One would not have expected this added reason for the disgrace, that the uncovered head of a woman differed not from a female shaved head, which Paul considers not only offensive, but also shameful. This added reason, based on conventional thinking, is expressed with hyperbole and is important for what follows in Paul's argument. *Pace* Lindemann (*1 Cor*, 241), this comparison does not settle the matter that it has to do with *Haartracht* (hairdo) and not head covering or veil. It is also going too far to say that "the removal of their hair symbolizes the shameful uncovering of their genitals that has transpired in some socially unacceptable transgression," as D. B. Martin would have it (*Corinthian Body*, 243). Such symbolism is eisegetical; it is scarcely to be found in Paul's text.

6. *For if a woman does not cover her head, she should have her hair cut off.* Lit. "does not cover herself, let her have her hair cut off," since *keirasthō* is 3d pers. sing. aor. mid. impv. with the causative sense, "let her have herself shorn" (BDF §317; BDAG, 538). So judges Paul with a touch of sarcasm. Offensive as this statement may seem today, it is clear that Paul meant what he wrote here.

but if it is disgraceful for a woman to have her hair cut off or to be shaved, then she should cover her head. Lit. "let her cover herself." The subj. of the protasis is actually a substantivized double infin., *to keirasthai* (aor. mid.) *ē xyrasthai* (either pres. mid. of *xyraō* [strange combination] or aor. mid. of *xyrō* [BDF §101]), which is almost impossible to translate exactly. Paul means that the woman should go the full way, not just being shorn (as in v. 6a), but even being shaved. That expresses the extent of her disgrace. He is appealing to social convention, which normally would regard the shorn or shaved female head as shameful, and which he will eventually relate to nature itself (v. 14). For the shaved female head as a disgrace, see Aristophanes, *Thesm.* 837; *T. Job* 23:7; 24:7–10. The verb in the apodosis, *katakalyptesthō* (3d pers. sing. pres. mid. impv.), can only mean, "let her cover herself," i.e., put a covering on her head of hair (cf. the same verb with *tēn kephalēn* in v. 7).

7. *A man ought not cover his head, since he is the image and glory of God.* This

verse and the two following formulate Paul's explanation about why a man has · preeminence over a woman. A negative obligation is expressed by *ouk opheilei katakalyptesthai*, lit. "he must not cover himself (as to the head)," which will find its positive correspondent obligation in v. 10 below, used of the woman; cf. *ouk opheilomen* (Acts 17:29). The complementary infin. does not mean "bind up his head," *pace* Murphy-O'Connor (*NJBC*, 809). Cf. Josephus, *Ant.* 7.10.5 §254: *katakalypsamenou de tou basileōs kai stenontos*, "While the king with covered head was moaning" (for his son, a reference to 2 Sam 1:5[6]).

"Image and glory of God" is a description developed by Paul from LXX Gen 1:26, where God in deciding to create human beings says:

poiēsōmen anthrōpon kat' eikona hēmeteran kai kath' homoiōsin,

let us make a human being according to our image and likeness.

See also Gen 1:27; cf. 5:1. Because of what he has written in v. 3 above, Paul now modifies that allusion, applying it to *anēr* and thus restricting it to a male human being, and using *doxa*, "glory, splendor" instead of *homoiōsis*, "likeness." Cf. Wis 2:23; Sir 17:3b. Paul does not exploit the idea of "image," but is interested rather in *doxa*, "glory, honor," because that offsets the idea of disgrace or shame that dominates his discussion in vv. 4–6. This status of *anēr* is especially true when he would be praying or prophesying, when he may not disguise the fact that, as a creature, he gives God glory (see further Feuillet, "L'Homme 'gloire de Dieu,' " who rightly insists that *doxa* does not mean "reflection" [as Lietzmann, *1 Cor*, 52 has it], but rather "glory" given to another, as Gen 2:18–25 suggests [also in "La dignité"]; cf. Jervell, *Imago Dei*, 292–312). Cf. the different way in which Paul uses "image" and "glory" of Christ in 2 Cor 4:4; and the different treatment of the "image" of Gen 1:26 in Philo, *Leg. alleg.* 1.12 §§31–33.

but a woman is the glory of man. In Gen 1:26–27 the woman was included in the creation of *anthrōpos* (= Hebrew *'ādām*, "human being"), but Paul avoids that inclusion in order to express the difference of the sexes: what *anēr* is with respect to God, that "woman" is with respect to "man"; each gives glory to the higher being. Such glory does not imply submission, subjection (*hypotagē*), or obedience (*hypakoē*), terms that Paul does not use in this context. Again, in line with what he asserted in v. 3, he regards the woman as *doxa andros*, "glory of man," because of what he will say in v. 9. Instead of alluding merely to Gen 1:16–27, Paul is rather giving abstract formulation to what is taught in Gen 2:18, 21–24, where "woman" is formed from "man." As an equal creature, she too is an image of God, but Paul passes over that idea of "image" and now makes her "the glory of man." She is a person in whom a man can take pride (see Feuillet, "L'homme 'gloire de Dieu' "). This assertion thus becomes part of the basis for Paul's concluding *dia touto*, "for this reason," in v. 10. Cf. the OT way of putting the relation of woman to man in LXX Prov 11:16, *gynē eucharistos egeirei andri doxan*, "a gracious wife brings glory to her husband" (see Jaubert, "Le voile").

8. *For man did not come from woman; but woman from man.* Lit. "man is not from woman." In this and the following parenthetical verse, Paul is arguing from

the order in the second creation account (Gen 2:7), where "the man" (*hā'ādām, ton anthrōpon*) is fashioned first, then the woman in vv. 20–23 ('*iššāh, gynaika*), and esp. 2:23: *ek tou andros autēs elēmphthē autē*, "she was taken from her man." He may also be aware of what his own Jewish tradition derived from such a passage, viz., the subordination of the wife to the husband, as Josephus records it, *Ag.Ap.* 2.24 §201: "God has given authority [*to kratos*] to the man"; but Paul does not repeat that idea and will modify it in v. 11 below. His argument about the relation of woman to man from the order of creation does not contradict the so-called baptismal formula of Gal 3:28, when that verse is rightly understood (see Röhser, "Mann und Frau").

Gal 3:28 reads, "There is neither Jew nor Greek, there is neither slave nor free, there is neither male nor female (*ouk eni arsen kai thēly*), for you are all one in Christ Jesus (*pantes gar hymeis heis este en Christō Iēsou*)." In vv. 27–29, Paul argues that such differences as exist in this earthly life (ethnic, social, sexual) may have to continue to distinguish Christians, but they do not upset the unity that Christians enjoy "in Christ Jesus." In the immediately preceding context, Paul argued that human beings were subjected to a "custodian" (*paidagōgos*), i.e., the law, but now faith has come and liberated those who have faith in Christ Jesus; and so they are no longer so subjugated, but despite all their ethnic, social, and sexual differences they are all incorporated into Christ ("all one in Christ") and so are "Abraham's offspring, heirs according to the promise" (v. 29). Because the promise is eschatological, Christians do not yet have full possession of it.

9. *Nor was man created for woman, but woman for man.* Lit. "for the sake of woman . . . for the sake of man," as Paul paraphrases the Genesis account (see *IBNTG*, 55; BDF §222). In this, the second part of his parenthetical statement, Paul alludes to Gen 2:18, 20, where the woman is said to have been created *lô 'ēzer kĕnegdô*; in the LXX, *autō boēthon kat' auton*, "(as) a helper fit for him."

10. *For this reason a woman ought to have authority over her head.* Paul draws a conclusion from the theological and biblical arguments that precede about the maintenance of order and the relation of woman to man (respectively, vv. 3–7 and the parenthetical remarks in vv. 8–9), beginning it with a resumptive *dia touto*, "for this reason." In using *opheilei*, he formulates the woman's positive obligation ("moral duty," *TDNT*, 2:574), which corresponds to the negative obligation of the man in v. 7.

The meaning of *exousia*, lit. "authority, state of control over something," is much debated. Although the Vg translated it literally as *potestatem*, many ancient versions and patristic comments rendered it by Greek *kalymma*, "veil," as a variant reading (still present in the *app. crit.* of N-A²⁷), whence the RSV rendering, "veil." This is a reading, however, that is found in no Greek MS (Metzger, *TCGNT*, 495). Older commentators often tried to explain *exousia* as a mistranslation of some Aramaic word (either *šlṭ'*, said to mean "veil," which was confused with *šlṭ*, "power" [A. Jirku] or *šlṭwnyh*, same explanation [G. Kittel]; or *ḥûmrā'*, meaning "power" or "veil" [G. Schwarz]; cf. *TDNT*, 2:574). Although I once followed Kittel's explanation (*ESBNT*, 194), I recognize today that that meaning of Greek *exousia* would scarcely have been understood by Paul's Corinthian readers.

Today, one finds two main interpretative translations:

(1) "Sign/symbol of authority" (NRSV, NAB, JB, ESV, NEB, REB, *Einheit-sübersetzung*, French Bishops' *La Bible*), by which is meant a "symbol of her authority over her head," but sometimes a "symbol of the authority . . . of the woman's husband, to whom she is subordinate," but then it would say nothing about an unmarried woman (Hooker, "Authority," 414).

(2) "Symbol/sign of subjection" (Theodoret, Theophylact, Goodspeed, SBJ), or "sign of dependence" (*Sacra Bibbia* [UTET, Rizzoli]; French *TOB*). The latter meaning of subjection atttributes to the noun a pass. sense that is unusual, because, although McGinn says that the idiom *exousian echein* "occurs only once in the Greek NT, here in 1 Cor 11" (*"exousian echein,"* 97), it is actually found 29 times in the NT, and in all the other instances it has an act. meaning, "have the right to control something or do something" (see Hall, "Problem of Authority"). This is why the preponderance of modern versions uses the first sense, which gives better expression to the woman's obligation. When understood together with v. 11, "in the Lord," it can even mean a sign of power from the risen Christ and of the dignity to which she has been raised (see Feuillet, "Signe de puissance").

However, the genuine force of *exousia* is best brought out by the simple translation, "a woman ought to have authority over her head," in the sense that, in covering it, she actively exercises control over it, "so as not to expose it to indignity." "If she unveils it, every one has control over it and can gaze at her so as to put her out of countenance" (Robertson-Plummer, *1 Cor*, 232; similarly Hall, "Problem of Authority," 41–42; Garland, *1 Cor*, 525). The head covering is a sign of the power received from the Lord (v. 11) and of the dignity she has to worship and praise God in the presence of the angels, as the Greek prep. phrase that follows in this verse suggests.

Murphy-O'Connor (*NJBC*, 809) would rather explain the words thus: "Paul takes it for granted that women play a leadership role in the community (v 5). She enjoys this authority precisely as a woman, and so must stress her sex by her hairdo." That is a paraphrastic explanation, however, which reads far too much into Paul's words. The same has to be said for the interpretation of Christian ("Prophets"), who maintains that the woman covers her head to show that she speaks as a prophetess, as God's messenger, and not on her own authority. Likewise eisegetical is the idea that the prophetic woman's authority *epi tēs kephalēs* means authority, even "ecclesial authority," over her head, who is "*ho anēr*, 'the man' (v. 3)" (McGinn, *"exousian echein,"* 97), because that goes against all that Paul has been asserting since v. 4.

because of the angels. This prep. phrase gives yet another reason for Paul's conclusion, in addition to that introduced by *dia touto*, but it is highly enigmatic. At least seven interpretations have been proposed for the phrase, *dia tous angelous*:

(1) "Because of the bishops" (or "presbyters"), understanding *angelous* as "angels of the churches," as in Rev 2:1, 8, 12. (Ephraem, Ambrosiaster, Pelagius, Primasius of Hadrumetum, Bornhäuser, Rose); but such an explanation scarcely suits this context.

(2) "Human messengers," because attempts to explain them as heavenly beings

yields no satisfactory explanation (Murphy-O'Connor, *CBQ* 50:271 n. 19; but elsewhere he explains, "in order not to scandalize envoys from other churches. Same usage in Gal 4:14" [*NJBC*, 809]; similarly Winandy, "Un curieux *casus pendens*"; Padgett, "Paul on Women," 81); or inquisitive "messengers" sent as spies by Roman authorities fearful lest the cultic assemblies of Corinthian Christians might have seditious intent, to whom an unveiled woman in such an assembly might seem like a promiscuous Roman wife (Winter, *After Paul*, 133–38). Again, this meaning hardly suits the context (so Garland, *1 Cor*, 526), not to mention that *angelos* is never so used elsewhere by Paul (see Luke 9:52; 7:24; Jas 2:25).

(3) "In imitation of the angels," as in Isa 6:2, where seraphim, as subordinate beings, cover feet and loins in the presence of the Lord (Meyer, Roesch, Mezzacassa, Lösch); a meaning that might suit the context, but is very subtle.

(4) "By way of the angels," meaning the angels who appeared at the time of Christ's resurrection (Matt 28:2, 5; Mark 16:5; Luke 24:4, 23; John 20:12), through which woman shares in the new creation (Rigato). This meaning has no connection whatsoever with the context.

(5) "Because of (the work of) the angels," i.e., woman was formed from man by the creative act of angels, as vv. 7–9 suggest (BeDuhn). An unlikely interpretation.

(6) "Because of the (fallen) angels," i.e., the "sons of God" of Gen 6:2. This interpretation is traced back to Tertullian, *De virginibus velandis* 7.2 (CCLat 2.1216); *Adv. Marcionem* 5.8.2 (CCLat 1.685) and still is given by many modern commentators, who at times understand *exousia* as "veil" in the sense of a "magic power or charm" to frighten away such beings, or a sign of modesty to conceal the woman's seductive charms from the angels (so with varying nuances: Bousset, Corrington, Dibelius, Ellul, Jervell, Lietzmann, D. B. Martin, Meier, Weber, J. Weiss; *EDNT*, 1:15; cf. *T. Reuben* 5.1, 5–6); but nowhere else in the NT does *angelos* ever have such a negative meaning, which, moreover, is irrelevant to this context of Christian prayer.

(7) "Because of the (good) angels," who are considered assisting at gatherings of public worship, as in Ps 138:1 (LXX: *enantion angelōn psalō soi*, "before angels shall I sing your praise"); cf. Tob 12:12; Rev 8:3, where an angel functions as a mediator of the prayers of holy people (so Theodoret, Brun, Collins, Delobel, Garland, Hays, Moffatt, Schrage, *1 Cor*, 2:517; also Murphy-O'Connor, "Sex," 497). These angels are explained further at times as cosmic guardians of the order of the world (SBJ, *Cor*, 51; Str-B, 3:437–39); or even as those addressed, when God said in Gen 1:26, "Let *us* make a human being" (as Philo held, *De opificio mundi* 24 §75, even though he never calls them *angeloi*, but rather God's *synergoi*). "The angels" here have nothing to do with the mediation of prophecy, Rev 22:7–10 notwithstanding. That they give the woman the "power" to prophesy is simply far-fetched, *pace* Schüssler Fiorenza (*In Memory*, 228); nor is there any indication that women letting their hair down in the presence of the angels would be "cultically unclean persons" (ibid.), because there is "absolutely no indication that Paul is speaking about uncleanness here" (Padgett, "Feminism," 127). Nor is there any indication in the text that the angels are the mediators, not just of prophecy, but of prophetic authority, as McGinn would have us believe ("*Exousian echein*," 100; her only reference is to Schüssler Fiorenza).

The seventh sense is the one to be preferred in this passage, for the woman must have authority over her head and cover it, not only because she is in the presence of men, but because she is praying in the presence of God and His angels. In their presence she must not expose "the glory of man" (11:7). If she were to pray or prophesy with uncovered head, she would be exposing herself, the glory of man, and so would not be glorifying God (modifying slightly Hooker, "Authority," 414–15). A woman, now sharing in public worship, contrary to Jewish practice, has authority from God (or Christ) to do so; with the glory of man covered, she gives God glory, as does the man with uncovered head (see Hall, "A Problem").

A further consideration, however, can be added in support of the seventh interpretation, derived from QL that speaks of "holy angels" being present at gatherings of the Essene community, to whose sight persons with bodily defects were not to be exposed. Thus:

> Nor shall anyone afflicted with any form of human uncleanness be admitted into the assembly of these (people, *bqhl 'lh*); nor shall anyone who becomes afflicted in this way be allowed to retain his place in the midst of the congregation: no one afflicted with a bodily defect, injured in feet or hands, or who is lame, blind, deaf or dumb, or who has a visible blemish in his flesh . . . , for holy angels are in their [congre]gation. (1QSa 2:3–9)

Similarly in 1QM 7:4–6: "No lame, blind, or paralyzed man, or one with a permanent blemish in his flesh . . . for holy angels accompany their armies"; 4QM[a] 1–3:10; CD 15:15–17; 4QD[b] 17 i 6–8. The background for this regulation may be found in the rules for Aaronid priests in Lev 21:17–23 (which, however, does not mention angels). That tenet of Essene belief goes beyond the OT data. In any case, it is similar to what Paul says in 11:10, for he has been speaking of a sacred assembly in which people pray and prophesy, and he thinks that a woman doing this should have her head covered "because of the angels," i.e., so that they would not have to gaze upon what he calls *aischron*, "something disgraceful" (v. 6), the uncovered head, which is for him the equivalent of a shorn or shaved female head, which would be like a defect for the Essenes (see Fitzmyer, "A Feature"; Cadbury, "Qumran Parallel"; cf. Schelkle, *Gemeinde von Qumran*, 82). I continue to prefer this explanation, even though D. B. Martin thinks that he has evidence for "prophylactic veils" on women in antiquity that were intended to protect them from "the angelic phallus"! (*Corinthian Body*, 245; cf. 299 n. 66).

11. *In the Lord, however, neither is woman independent of man, nor man of woman.* Lit. "neither is woman without man nor man without woman," and the prep. *chōris* is ambiguous, because it can mean either that "neither (is) woman (anything) apart fr. man" (BDAG, 1095), or that "neither is woman otherwise than man" (see LSJ, 2016). Kürzinger ("Frau und Mann") prefers the latter, translating *chōris* as "different from," and appealing to the use of this prep. in LXX Gen 26:1 ("a famine different from the earlier famine").

Having set forth the reasons for his position about a woman praying or prophesying with head covered, Paul now introduces a qualification about the relation of woman to man in Christ Jesus. Although the biblical argument from Genesis, which Paul has used thus far and which would agree with his Jewish tradition, sets up a definite relationship of woman to man, a further Christian consideration now limits it, for "in the Lord," i.e., in the sight of the risen Christ (see NOTE on 1:3), there can be no separation or independence of woman from man, or man from woman (*oute gynē chōris andros oute anēr chōris gynaikos*). Paul introduces the qualification with the conj. particle *plēn*, "however," to conclude his discussion and stress what is essential (BDF §449.2). It also serves to limit Paul's words to their context, the use of a head covering by a woman in public worship.

12. *For just as woman came from man, so man is born of woman; but everything comes from God.* Lit., "just as the woman (is) from (*ek*) the man, so too the man (is) through (*dia*) the woman." The first clause (*ek tou andros*) alludes again to the creation of woman in Gen 2:21–23, mentioned in v. 8b, and the second (*dia tēs gynaikos*) expresses a well-known fact. The third clause, however, affirms not only that both man and woman have "come from God," but everything (the whole universe) likewise does. Paul's argument thus moves from a Christological consideration (v. 11) to a *theo*-logical one, to the Creator-God. *Panta*, "all (things)," is being used, not in a Stoic cosmological sense, but as in the OT (Gen 2:3; Neh 9:6; Ps 8:7; 104:24; Isa 40:26; 44:24; cf. Ps 24:1–2; 89:12); see Murphy-O'Connor, *RB* 85 (1978) 263; W. J. Webb, "Balancing." (The parentheses that surround vv. 11–12 in the RSV, intended apparently to mitigate what Paul had said in vv. 8–10, have been removed in the NRSV and ESV.)

13. *Judge for yourselves: Is it proper for a woman to pray to God with uncovered head?* As he calls on Corinthian Christians to reflect on the matter, Paul begins the conclusion of his argument, an appeal with two rhetorical questions, which returns his discussion to that of vv. 4–6 above. The first question formulates an argument from propriety, partly governed by social convention (with human judgment invoked), and partly by a further consideration of what he has been saying. For he does not speak of a woman simply praying in a sacred assembly, as in v. 5 above, but now of her prayer addressed "to God." Is this the kind of situation in which a woman should assert her equality with man and uncover her head? Paul expects the Corinthians to say no.

14. *Does not nature itself teach you that if a man wears his hair long, it is degrading for him?* Lit. ". . . that a man, if he wears his hair long, it is degrading for him?" For the anacoluthon in the Greek sentence, see BDF §466.1. Paul's second rhetorical question, expecting the answer yes (introduced by *oude*), appeals to *physis*, "nature," by which he means only "the regular or established order of things" (BDAG, 1070). He also personifies it as a teacher of human beings, but "it simply represents the general order of nature and its only task is to remind us of what is seemly and becoming" (Koester, *TDNT*, 9:272). The order, however, stems more from convention than from "nature," as moderns normally understand the word (see Wischmeyer, "*Physis* und *ktisis*").

Komaō, "wear the hair long," denotes something quite different from wearing a beard, by which "nature" has indeed distinguished men and women (Epictetus, *Disc.* 1.16.9–10). If Paul means only custom or usual practice, he may be appealing to Roman custom, where short-cropped male hair was usual, but Greek custom was not so uniform or well established. In any case, in support of what he has just said, he is appealing from a consideration of social propriety, now joining to it a consideration of *atimia*, "dishonor, disrespect, disgrace" which is the opposite of *doxa*, "glory, honor, splendor," in human society. That Paul thinks that long hair for a man "is a sign of homosexuality" (Murphy-O'Connor, *NJBC*, 809) is highly questionable, as Lietzmann (*1 Cor*, 55) recognized long ago.

15. *but if a woman wears her hair long, it is her glory?* This is the counterpart of v. 14, and it corresponds more to convention, for *doxa* now has the connotation of favorable reputation (BDAG, 257). Paul likewise says this in contrast to the "disgrace" of the uncovered or shaven female head mentioned in vv. 5b–6.

For her hair has been given [to her] for a covering. Lit. "has been given [to her] instead of a wrap-around mantle" (*anti peribolaiou*). The word *autē*, "to her," is omitted in some MSS (P⁴⁶, D, F, G, Ψ, and the Koine text-tradition). The perf. pass. *dedotai* indicates a permanent endowment by God, for it a divine pass. (ZBG §236). The woman's long hair is a gift of God for a definite purpose, i.e., for her glory; and yet Paul wants her to cover this "wrap-around mantle" whenever she prays to God in public. For ancient evidence of "Greco-Roman customs" of female hairdos, see Thompson, "Hairstyles," 112; cf. Gill, "The Importance." That the hair of a woman in this passage "is part of the female genitalia" and that modern interpreters "confuse a testicle (*peribolaion*) with a head covering" (T. W. Martin, "Paul's Argument," 84) is completely far-fetched.

16. *If anyone is inclined to be argumentative (about this), we have no such custom, nor do the churches of God.* Paul is aware that his complicated arguments about this problem may not be convincing to everyone. So, in effect, he appeals to Christian church discipline or custom (or what would later be called canon law); and Schüssler Fiorenza rightly calls it "an authoritarian appeal" (*In Memory*, 229). On "church of God," see NOTE on 1:2.

BIBLIOGRAPHY

Adinolfi, M., "Il velo della donna e la rilettura paolina di 1 Cor. 11,2–16," *RivB* 23 (1975) 147–73.

Arichea, D. C., Jr., "The Covering on a Woman's Head: Translation and Theology in 1 Corinthians 11.2–16," *BT* 55 (2004) 460–69.

Baumert, N., *Antifeminismus bei Paulus: Einzelstudien* (FzB 68; Würzburg: Echter-V., 1992) 53–108, esp. 56–65.

Bedale, S., "The Meaning of *kephalē* in the Pauline Epistles," *JTS* 5 (1954) 211–15.

BeDuhn, J. D., " 'Because of the Angels': Unveiling Paul's Anthropology in 1 Corinthians 11," *JBL* 118 (1999) 295–320.

Bilezikian, G., *Beyond Sex Roles* (2d ed.; Grand Rapids: Baker, 1990) 215–52.

Blattenberger, D. E., III, *Rethinking 1 Corinthians 11:2–16 through Archaeological and Moral-Rhetorical Analysis* (Lewiston, NY: Mellen, 1997).

Bornhäuser, D., " 'Um der Engel willen': 1 Kor. 11,10," *NKZ* 41 (1930) 475–88.

Bouwman, G., " 'Het hoofd van de man is de vrouw': Een retorische analyse van 1 Kor. 11,2–16," *TvT* 21 (1981) 28–36.

Brown, S., "The Dialectic of Relationship: Paul and the Veiling of Women in 1 Corinthians 11:2–16," *Salesianum* 67 (2005) 457–77.

Brun, L., " 'Um der Engel willen' 1 Kor 11,10," *ZNW* 14 (1913) 298–308.

Cadbury, H. J., "A Qumran Parallel to Paul," *HTR* 51 (1958) 1–2.

Cervin, R. S., "Does *kephalē* Mean 'Source' or 'Authority Over' in Greek Literature? A Rebuttal," *TrinJ* 10 (1989) 85–112.

Christian, E., "Prophets under God's Authority: Headcoverings in 1 Corinthians 11:1–16," *JATS* 10 (1999) 291–95.

Cope, L., "1 Cor 11:2–16: One Step Further," *JBL* 97 (1978) 435–36.

Corrington, G. P., "The 'Headless Woman': Paul and the Language of the Body in 1 Cor 11:2–16," *PRSt* 18 (1991) 223–31.

Cotterell, P., and M. Turner, *Linguistics and Biblical Interpretation* (London: SPCK, 1989) 141–45.

Delobel, J., "1 Cor 11:2–16: Toward a Coherent Explanation," *L'Apôtre Paul* (BETL 73; ed. A. Vanhoye), 369–89.

Ellis, E. E., "Traditions in 1 Corinthians," *NTS* 32 (1986) 481–502.

Ellul, D., " 'Sois belle et tais-toi!' Est-ce vraiment ce que Paul a dit? A propos de I Co 11,2–16," *Foi et vie* 88/5 (1989) 49–58.

Engberg-Pedersen, T., "1 Corinthians 11:16 and the Character of Pauline Exhortation," *JBL* 110 (1991) 679–89.

Feuillet, A., "La dignité et le rôle de la femme d'après quelques textes pauliniens: Comparaison avec l'Ancien Testament," *NTS* 21 (1975) 157–91.

———, "L'Homme 'gloire de Dieu' et la femme 'gloire de l'homme' (*I Cor.*, xi, 7b)," *RB* 81 (1974) 161–82.

———, "Le signe de puissance sur la tête de la femme: 1 Co 11, 10," *NRT* 95 (1973) 945–54.

Fiddes, P. S., " 'Woman's Head Is Man': A Doctrinal Reflection upon a Pauline Text," *Baptist Quarterly* (London) 31 (1985–86) 370–83.

Fitzmyer, J. A., "Another Look at *Kephalē* in 1 Corinthians 11. 3," *NTS* 35 (1989) 503–11; repr. in *According to Paul: Studies in the Theology of the Apostle* (New York: Paulist, 1993) 80–88.

———, "A Feature of Qumrân Angelology and the Angels of I Cor. xi. 10," *NTS* 4 (1957–58) 48–58; repr. with postscript (1966) in *Paul and Qumran* (ed. J. Murphy-O'Connor; London: Chapman, 1968) 31–47; and in *ESBNT* (1971), 187–204.

———, "*Kephalē* in I Corinthians 11:3," *Int* 47 (1993) 52–59; repr. *TAG* (2d ed., 1998), 341–48.

Gielen, M., "Beten und Prophezeien mit unverhüllten Kopf? Die Kontroverse zwischen Paulus und der korinthischen Gemeinde um die Wahrung der Geschlechtsrollensymbolik in 1 Kor 11,2–16," *ZNW* 90 (1999) 220–49.

———, " 'Gehört es sich, dass eine Frau unverhüllt zu Gott betet?' Der Streit um Kopfdeckung oder Frisur in 1 Kor 11,2–16," *BK* 57 (2002) 134–38.

Gill, D. W. J., "The Importance of Roman Portraiture for Head-Coverings in 1 Corinthians 11:2–16," *TynBul* 41 (1990) 245–60.

Greig, J. C. G., "Women's Hats—1 Corinthians xi.1–16," *ExpTim* 69 (1957–58) 156–57.

Grudem, W., "Does *kephalē* ('Head') Mean 'Source' or 'Authority over' in Greek Literature? A Survey of 2,336 Examples," *TrinJ* 6 (1985) 38–59.

———, "The Meaning of *Kephalē* ('Head'): A Response to Recent Studies," *TrinJ* 11 (1990) 3–72.

———, "The Meaning of *Kephalē* ('Head'): An Evaluation of New Evidence, Real and Alleged," *JETS* 44 (2001) 25–65.

Hall, D. R., "A Problem of Authority," *ExpTim* 102 (1990–91) 39–42.

Hasler, V., "Die Gleichstellung der Gattin: Situationskritische Reflexionen zu I Kor 112–16," *TZ* 50 (1994) 189–200.

Holmyard, H. R., III, "Does 1 Corinthians 11:2–16 Refer to Women Praying and Prophesying in Church?" *BSac* 154 (1997) 461–72.

Hooker, M. D., "Authority on Her Head: An Examination of I Cor. xi. 10," *NTS* 10 (1963–64) 410–16; repr. in *From Adam to Christ: Essays on Paul* (Cambridge: Cambridge University Press, 1990) 113–20.

House, H. W., "A Biblical View of Women in the Ministry. Part 2 (of 5 Parts): Should a Woman Prophesy or Preach before Men?," *BSac*145 (1988) 141–61.

Hurley, J. B., "Did Paul Require Veils or the Silence of Women? A Consideration of I Cor. 11:2–16 and I Cor. 14:33b-36," *WTJ* 35 (1972–73) 190–220.

Ince, G., "Judge for Yourselves: Teasing out Some Knots in 1 Corinthians 11:2–16," *ABR* 48 (2000) 59–71.

Isaksson, A., *Marriage and Ministry in the New Temple: A Study with Special Reference to Mt. 19.13–12* [sic] *and 1 Cor. 11.3–16* (Acta seminarii neotestamentici upsaliensis 24; Lund: Gleerup, 1965) 155–85.

Jaubert, A., "Le voile des femmes (I Cor. xi. 2–16)," *NTS* 18 (1971–72) 419–30.

Jervis, L. A., " 'But I Want You to Know . . .': Paul's Midrashic Intertextual Response to the Corinthian Worshipers (1 Cor 11:2–16)," *JBL* 112 (1993) 231–46.

Jirku, A., "Die 'Macht' auf dem Haupte (1 Kor. 11,10)," *NKZ* 32 (1921) 710–11.

Kähler, E., *Die Frau in den paulinischen Briefen unter besonderer Berücksichtigung des Begriffes der Unterordnung* (Zurich: Gotthelf-V., 1960).

Khiok-khng, Y., "Differentiation and Mutuality of Male-Female Relations in 1 Corinthians 11:2–16," *BR* 43 (1998) 7–21.

Kittel, G., "Die 'Macht' auf dem Haupte (1 Cor xi.10)," in *Rabbinica: Paulus im Talmud, Die 'Macht' auf dem Haupte, Runde Zahlen* (Arbeiten zur Vorgeschichte des Christentums I/3; Leipzig: Hinrichs, 1920) 17–31.

Klauck, H.-J., "Presence in the Lord's Supper: 1 Corinthians 11:23–26 in the Context of Hellenistic Religious History," *One Loaf, One Cup* (ed. B. F. Meyer), 57–74.

Kroeger, C. C., "The Classical Concept of *Head* as 'Source,' " *Equal to Serve* (ed. G. Gaebelein Hull; Grand Rapids: Baker Books, 1998) 267–83 (Appendix III).

———, "Head," *Dictionary of Paul and His Letters* (ed. G. F. Hawthorne et al.; Downers Grove, IL: InterVarsity, 1993) 375–77.

Küchler, M., *Schweigen, Schmuck und Schleier* (NTOA 1; Freiburg in der Schweiz: Universitätsverlag; Göttingen: Vandenhoeck & Ruprecht, 1986) 73–112.

Kürzinger, J., "Frau und Mann nach 1 Kor 11,11f.," *BZ* 22 (1978) 270–75.

Larsen, I., "1 Corinthians 11.10 Revisited," *BT* 48 (1997) 345–50.

Liefeld, W. L., "Women, Submission and Ministry in 1 Corinthians," *Women, Authority and the Bible* (Downers Grove, IL: InterVarsity, 1986), 134–60, esp. 136–48.

Lösch, S., "Christliche Frauen in Corinth: Ein neuer Lösungsversuch," *TQ* 127 (1947) 216–61.

Lowery, D. K., "The Head Covering and the Lord's Supper in 1 Corinthians 11:2–34," *BSac* 143 (1986) 155–63.

Martin, D. B., *The Corinthian Body* (New Haven: Yale University Press, 1995).

Martin, T. W., "Paul's Argument from Nature for the Veil in 1 Corinthians 11:13–15: A Testicle instead of a Head Covering," *JBL* 123 (2004) 75–84.

Martin, W. J., "I Corinthians 11:2–16: An Interpretation," *Apostolic History and the Gospel: Biblical and Historical Essays Presented to F. F. Bruce* . . . (ed. W. W. Gasque and R. P. Martin; Exeter, UK: Paternoster; Grand Rapids: Eerdmans, 1970) 231–41.

McGinn, S. E., "*Exousian echein epi tēs kephalēs:* 1 Cor 11:10 and the Ecclesial Authority of Women," *Listening* 31/2 (1996) 91–104.

Meier, J. P., "On the Veiling of Hermeneutics (1 Cor 11:2–16)," *CBQ* 40 (1978) 212–26.

Mickelsen, B., and A. Mickelsen, "What Does *Kephalē* Mean in the New Testament?" *Women, Authority and the Bible* (Downers Grove, IL: InterVarsity, 1986) 97–110.

Mingo, A. de, "Saint Paul and Women," *TD* 51 (2004) 9–18.

Motta, Q., "The Question of the Unveiled Woman (1 Co. xi. 2–16)," *ExpTim* 44 (1932–33) 139–41.

Mount, S., "1 Corinthians 11:3–16: Spirit Possession and Authority in a Non-Pauline Interpolation," *JBL* 124 (2005) 313–40.

Murphy-O'Connor, J., "1 Corinthians 11:2–16 Once Again," *CBQ* 50 (1988) 265–74.

——, "The Non-Pauline Character of 1 Corinthians 11:2–16?" *JBL* 95 (1976) 615–21.

——, "Sex and Logic in 1 Corinthians 11:2–16," *CBQ* 42 (1980) 482–500.

Oster, R., "When Men Wore Veils to Worship: The Historical Context of 1 Corinthians 11. 4," *NTS* 34 (1988) 481–505.

Padgett, A., "Feminism in First Corinthians: A Dialogue with Elisabeth Schüssler Fiorenza," *EvQ* 58 (1956) 121–32.

——, "Paul on Women in the Church: The Contradictions of Coiffure in 1 Corinthians 11.2–16," *JSNT* 20 (1984) 69–86.

——, "The Significance of *anti* in 1 Corinthians 11:15," *TynBul* 45 (1994) 181–87.

Payne, P. B., "Response," *Women, Authority and the Bible* (Downers Grove, IL: InterVarsity, 1986), 118–32.

Pérez Gordo, A., "¿Es el velo en *1 Co 11,2–16* símbolo de libertad o de sumisión?" *Burgense* 29 (1988) 337–66.

Perriman, A. C., "The Head of a Woman: The Meaning of *kephalē* in 1 Cor. 11:3," *JTS* 45 (1994) 602–22.

Perrot, C., "Prophètes et prophétisme dans le Nouveau Testament," *LumVie* 22/115 (1973) 25–39.

Rigato, M.-L., "A quali angeli allude Paolo nella Prima Lettera ai Corinzi (11,10)?" *RivB* 41 (1993) 305–13.

Roesch, K., " 'Um der Engel willen' (1 Kor. 11,10)," *TGl* 24 (1932) 363–65.

Röhser, G., "Mann und Frau in Christus. Eine Verhältnisbestimmung von Gal 3,28 und 1 Kor 11,2–16," *SNTU* A22 (1997) 57–78.

Rose, P., "Power on the Head," *ExpTim* 23 (1911–12) 183–84.

Rossetti, C. L., " '*Vir caput mulieris*' (1Cor 11,3–Ef 5,22)? Indagine teologica sul senso di una metafora circa il rapporto uomo-donna (prima parte)," *Anthropotes* 19 (2003) 145–83.

Sandt, H. van de, "I Kor. 11,2–16 als een retorische eenheid," *Bijdr* 49 (1988) 410–25.

Schelkle, K. H., " 'Denn wie das Weib aus dem Mann ist, so auch der Mann aus dem Weib' (1 Kor 11,12): Zur Gleichberechtigung der Frau im Neuen Testament," *Diakonia* 15 (1984) 85–90.

——, *Die Gemeinde von Qumran und die Kirche des Neuen Testaments* (Düsseldorf: Patmos, 1960).

Schirrmacher, T., *Paulus im Kampf gegen den Schleier: Eine alternative Auslegung von 1. Korinther 11,2–16* (Biblica et symbiotica 4; Bonn: Verlag für Kultur und Wissenschaft, 1993).

Schwarz, G., "*Exousian echein epi tēs kephalēs?* (1. Korinther 11,10)," *ZNW* 70 (1979) 249.

Scroggs, R., "Paul and the Eschatological Woman," *JAAR* 40 (1972) 283–303.

——, "Paul and the Eschatological Woman Revisited," *JAAR* 42 (1974) 532–37.

Shoemaker, T. P., "Unveiling of Equality: 1 Corinthians 11:2–16," *BTB* 17 (1987) 60–63.

Smith, D. C., "Paul and the Non-Eschatological Woman," *Ohio Journal of Religious Studies* 4 (1976) 11–18.

Spicq, C., "Encore la 'puissance sur la tête' (I Cor. xi.10)," *RB* 48 (1939) 557–62.

Thompson, C. L., "Hairstyles, Head-Coverings, and St. Paul: Portraits from Roman Corinth," *BA* 51 (1988) 99–115.

Trompf, G. W., "On Attitudes toward Women in Paul and Paulinist Literature: 1 Corinthians 11:3–16 and Its Context," *CBQ* 42 (1980) 196–215.

Tucker, R. A., "Response," *Women, Authority and the Bible* (Downers Grove, IL: InterVarsity, 1986), 111–17.

Walker, W. O., "1 Corinthians 11:2–16 and Paul's Views Regarding Women," *JBL* 94 (1975) 94–110.

———, *Interpolations in the Pauline Letters*, 91–126.

———, "The Vocabulary of 1 Corinthians 11.3–16: Pauline or Non-Pauline?" *JSNT* 35 (1989) 75–88.

Waltke, B. K., "1 Corinthinas 11:2–16: An Interpretation," *BSac* 135 (1978) 45–57.

Watson, F., "The Authority of the Voice: A Theological Reading of 1 Cor 11.2–16," *NTS* 46 (2000) 520–36.

Webb, W. J., "Balancing Paul's Original-Creation and Pro-Creation Arguments: 1 Corinthians 11:11–12 in Light of Modern Embryology," *WTJ* 66 (2004) 275–89.

Weber, W., "Die paulinische Vorschrift über die Kopfbedeckung der Christen," *ZWT* 46 (1903) 487–99.

Weeks, N., "Of Silence and Head Covering," *WTJ* 35 (1972–73) 21–27.

Williams, R., "Lifting the Veil: A Social-Science Interpretation of 1 Corinthans 11:2–16," *Consensus* 23/1 (1997) 53–60.

Wilson, K. T., "Should Women Wear Headcoverings?" *BSac* 148 (1991) 442–62.

Winandy, J., "Un curieux *casus pendens*: 1 Corinthiens 11.10 et son interprétation," *NTS* 38 (1992) 621–29.

Wischmeyer, O., "*Physis* und *ktisis* bei Paulus: Die paulinische Rede von Schöpfung und Natur," *ZTK* 93 (1996) 352–75.

24   b. *Abuses at the Celebration of the Lord's Supper and Its Meaning (11:17–34)*

[11:17] In giving the following instructions, I do not praise (you), because you hold your meetings not to your advantage, but to your disadvantage. [18] First of all, I hear that, when you meet as a church, there are divisions among you, and in part I believe it. [19] No doubt there have to be factions among you, so that the tried and true among you may be recognized. [20] Although you hold your meetings in one place, it is not to eat the Lord's supper. [21] For as you eat, each one goes ahead with his own meal, and one goes hungry, while another gets drunk. [22] Do you not have houses to eat and drink in? Are you not showing contempt for the church of God and making those who have nothing feel ashamed? What am I to say to you?

Should I praise you? In this I offer no praise. ²³ For I received from the Lord what I passed on to you, that the Lord Jesus, on the night he was handed over took bread, ²⁴ and having given thanks, broke it, and said, "This is my body, which is for you. Do this in remembrance of me." ²⁵ In the same way, the cup too, after the supper, saying, "This cup is the new covenant in my blood. Do this, whenever you drink it, in remembrance of me." ²⁶ For as often as you eat this bread and drink the cup, you proclaim the Lord's death until he comes. ²⁷ Consequently, whoever eats the bread or drinks the cup of the Lord unworthily will have to answer for the body and blood of the Lord. ²⁸ One should take stock of himself and so eat of the bread and drink of the cup. ²⁹ For anyone who eats and drinks without acknowledging the body eats and drinks judgment upon himself. ³⁰ For this reason many among you are weak and infirm, and a number are dying. ³¹ But if we were to evaluate ourselves correctly, we would not be subject to judgment. ³² Since we are being judged by [the] Lord, we are being chastened, that we may not be condemned along with the world. ³³ Consequently, my brothers, when you meet together to eat, await the arrival of one another. ³⁴ If anyone gets hungry, he should eat at home, that you may not meet together only to be condemned. As for the other matters I shall give directives when I come.

COMMENT

Paul now turns to a more serious problem in the Christian assemblies of Roman Corinth, which has to do with their gathering for a common meal and the celebration of the Lord's Supper. Again, we do not know how Paul has learned about this problem, but he mentions that he has heard reports about "divisions" in their meetings (v. 18), and it is clearly of greater importance to him than the trivial issue treated in the preceding passage. He will now insist that there can be no real celebration of the Lord's Supper as long as their liturgical assemblies are marred by unworthy conduct that is divisive and factious and not marked by the same concern "for others" that Jesus manifested at the Last Supper.

This pericope has five parts:

1. 11:17–22, a description of the social conduct of Corinthian Christians for which Paul has no praise. Although they come together for a common purpose, their behavior is divisive, ill suits the celebration of the Lord's Supper, and shows contempt for God's church.
2. 11:23–25, the tradition about the institution of the Lord's Supper.
3. 11:26–28, Paul's interpretation of the meaning of the memento directive: reception of the Supper must be worthy.
4. 11:29–32, Paul's verdict on the prevailing situation and its relation to "judgment."
5. 11:33–34, Paul's concluding directives about "meeting together."

In contrast to v. 2 above, Paul makes it clear that he has no praise for the Corinthians (vv. 17, 22d–e), because, when they come together as "church" to take a common meal, they neglect the meaning of the Lord's Supper.

Their neglect has been described differently by various commentators:

1. J. Weiss considered vv. 18–34 to have been composed for a context entirely different from the one in which they are now found, because the *schismata* are not really explained.

2. Some (e.g., Lietzmann, *Mass*, 207–8) thought that Corinthian Christians had abandoned the idea of receiving the Lord's body and regarded the blessed bread as ordinary food; their comon meal was no longer a commemorative celebration of the Last Supper related to the death of the Lord, but rather a continuation of table fellowship with the earthly Jesus, celebrated with joy over his resurrection and in expectation of his Parousia.

3. Schmithals (*Gnosticism in Corinth*, 250–56) believed that the Corinthian Christians whom Paul was criticizing were Gnostic *pneumatics* who were "opposing the sacrament of the body and blood of Christ. . . . For them a cultic meal at the center of which stands the crucified, sarkical Jesus is inconceivable. If they participate in the Supper, this is done from the outset not in order to observe the *kyriakon deipnon* but to eat a profane meal" (254). Their attitude toward the Lord's Supper is "no different in principle from that toward the sacrifices to the idols. For them neither meal had any cultic meaning, since the 'accursed' Jesus was just as much a 'Nothing' as were the gods of the heathen" (255). Such *pneumatics* espoused a radical, but spiritualized Christology, divorced from any relation to Jesus "according to the flesh," and their private profane meal stands in opposition to the common Lord's Supper.

4. Chrupcała ("Chi mangia") thinks that the divisions arose because the well-to-do at Corinth ate a secular meal separate from the common eucharistic banquet, and that Paul was insisting that the Eucharist has to involve all believers; those who preferred the secular meal were unworthy of the Eucharist.

5. Bornkamm ("Lord's Supper"), along with many other commentators who find the preceding explanations inadequate, explains the situation as one in which the conduct of Corinthian Christians during the meal taken before the celebration of the Lord's Supper makes it impossible for them to participate worthily and properly in the body and blood of Christ (10:16). The Christians of Corinth always regarded the celebration of the Lord's Supper as a sacred meal, but they have been celebrating it as a service in which the breaking of bread and the distribution of the cup are separated from each other by a regular full meal, in which they eat together what each has contributed according to his or her means, as is suggested by Mark 14:22 ("As they were eating, he took bread . . ."; *cf. Did.* 10.1). The problem is that the meal has become one that, although they come together to dine in common, each one shapes it according to his or her likes and enjoyment, and they fail to share with one another, as "each one goes ahead with his own meal" (11:20–21) and does not wait for another (11:33). Thus the celebration of the Lord's Supper has become an occasion for social discrimination and divisive conduct. In doing this, they are eating the bread and drinking the cup of the Lord "unworthily" (v. 27). Such conduct only "shows contempt for the church of God" (v. 22). That is why Paul advises that they "await the arrival of one another" (v. 33) or eat at home, if they are hungry (v. 34). He is trying to correct a practice that he considers out of accord with what the Lord's Supper was meant to recall,

viz., Christ's sacrifice for others. Bornkamm's analysis is basically correct, even if one differs with him over some details (see also Hofius, "Herrenmahl"; Schottroff, "Holiness and Justice"). One difference has been suggested by others (e.g., by Klauck, *1 Cor*, 81; Lang, *1 Cor*, 148–49): the breaking of eucharistic bread and the drinking of the eucharistic cup had already been joined together in a ritual and situated at the end of what was meant to be the common meal.

Paul's criticism of the way that Corinthian Christians have been celebrating the Lord's Supper with discriminatory practices has been explained further by appeals to the archaeological evidence from the excavations of ancient Corinth. Murphy-O'Connor (*St. Paul's Corinth*, 178) considers the excavated villa at Anaploga as a typical house having a large room that he calls a *triclinium* (a dining room with three couches in front of its walls in the shape of a U), which opens onto an *atrium*. Because not all the congregants would fit into the *triclinium*, the host would invite to it his closest friends among them, and the rest could take places in the *atrium*, where conditions were greatly inferior, or in the nearby peristyle court. Hence the house space would have partly contributed to the problem of discrimination, especially if the congregants did not all arrive at the same time; and socially lower-class people might also be so relegated. This explanation has also been proposed by Lampe ("Das korinthische Herrenmahl," 20), Collins (*1 Cor*, 418–19), Hays (*1 Cor*, 196), Garland (*1 Cor*, 536). Further study, however, of the archaeological evidence has called this explanation into question, because there is no evidence that the large room called *triclinium* was actually used for such a purpose (banquet), and the issue of social strata of Corinthian Christians is likewise a controverted question, which no one can really answer today (see Horrell, "Domestic Space," 354–55, 357–59; also his *Social Ethos*, 91–101). He writes:

> Despite the major and long established excavations at Corinth, very little is known about the character of many of the residential areas of Roman Corinth, since excavations have been largely concentrated around the forum area, on the sanctuaries of Demeter and Kore and of Asclepius, on a small number of selected villas, and on other significant structures in and outside the city. ("Domestic Space," 360)

Buildings to the east of the Theatre have been excavated since 1980s, but none of them offers evidence that "Christians ever met in any" of them, "any more than in the villa at Anaploga" (ibid., 365). Moreover, "there is as yet no direct archaeological evidence for Christianity at Corinth until around and after the fourth century" (ibid., 365–66). Hence, "it means confessing that we are — and are likely to remain — unable to ascertain any architectural explanation for the Corinthian *schismata*" (ibid., 369).

As a result of Paul's critical remarks in vv. 22 and 34, the consumption of the ordinary food and drink came to be separated in church tradition from the celebration of the Lord Supper. Eventually it was called *Agapē*, sometimes translated as "Love-Feast" (Ignatius, *Smyrn.* 8.2: *agapēn poiein*; cf. Jude 12; and the variant reading *agapais* in some MSS of 2 Pet 2:13). It is, however, a matter of debate among commentators on this Pauline passage as to how clearly one can distinguish in it details belonging to the *kyriakon deipnon* and to others as part of a meal separate from the Eucharist. Toward the end of the first century, the *Didache* (9.1, 5) uses the noun *eucharistia* clearly as the name for the rite of drinking the cup and breaking the bread. Moreover, *ca.* 110 Pliny the Younger, in his letter to the emperor Trajan about Christians, speaks of them thus:

> *soliti stato die ante lucem convenire, carmenque Christo quasi deo dicere secum invicem, quibus peractis morem sibi discedendi fuisse rursusque coeundi ad capiendum cibum promiscuum tamen et innoxium,*

> (they are) accustomed to assemble before dawn on a fixed day and chant alternately a hymn to Christ as to a god when that is finished, they have the habit of departing and gathering together again to partake of ordinary, harmless food. (*Ep.* 10.96.7)

This double meeting that Pliny reports is usually thought to be a reference first to the Eucharist and then to the Agape. By the time of Cyprian (died A.D. 258), there was a clear distinction between the Eucharist, celebrated with fasting in the morning, and the Agape, taken in the evening (see further Keating, *The Agapé*).

In any case, we may presume that Corinthian Christians gathered together at the house of a well-to-do Christian (e.g., at the house of Gaius, who is mentioned in Rom 16:23), perhaps on "the first day of every week" (1 Cor 16:2) and brought food with them to be shared with others, before they "broke bread" and "blessed the cup" at the end of the meal, thus celebrating the Lord's Supper with prayers, hymns, and the reading of Scripture. The order of these elements of their assembly is a matter of debate, whether one views it as a bread rite, then full meal, and a cup rite, or otherwise. In any case, Paul's account of such an assembly cites the misdemeanors that occurred, and his verdict is that such Corinthians were not really celebrating the "Lord's Supper."

This pericope, however, is important, because, in vv. 23b–25, it contains the earliest account of the institution of the Eucharist. Paul has given us no indication of the source from which he has derived the account (a cultic aetiology) that he passes on. One has to relate his verses to the accounts in the Synoptic Gospels: Mark 14:22–24; Matt 26:26–28; and Luke 22:17–20. In each case, liturgical forms of the early Christian tradition about the Lord's Supper are being quoted. Even though one is dealing with a tradition that is traced back ultimately to Jesus of Nazareth, the differences in the various forms reveal that cultic or liturgical formulas are being cited, and that none of them can be regarded as *ipsissima verba Iesu*. There is some similarity in the Pauline and Lucan forms of the tradition (the only ones that contain the memento directive), and another similarity in the Marcan and Matthean forms, which differ a bit from those of Paul and Luke. It is sometimes thought that the Marcan and Matthean forms reflect a liturgical tradition inherited from Jerusalem, whereas the Pauline and Lucan forms reflect that of Antioch; but there is no certainty about such origins. The Notes below will list the differences when they are important. In any case, the Pauline form is the earliest attested, and it thus rivals the earliest of the Synoptic accounts, i.e., Mark 14:22–24.

There has been considerable discussion about the Last Supper and the nature of it. First of all, there is debate about its historicity. Did Jesus of Nazareth celebrate a final meal with his apostles on the night he was arrested? According to Crossan, Jesus did not have a supper as a distinctive meal "known beforehand, designated specifically, or ritually programmed" (*Historical Jesus*, 361). So the Pauline and Synoptic accounts of Jesus' words and gestures would be a creation of the early church ("a cult legend") to celebrate the saving death of Jesus. However, in favor of the historical Last Supper, one can cite the following reasons:

1. Its multiple attestation: in Paul, in the interrelated Synoptic Gospels, and in the independent Johannine Gospel, chap. 13 (which, although it lacks an account of the institution of the Eucharist, attests the gathering of Jesus and his apostles for the Supper).

2. The criterion of coherence: for the Last Supper fits in with the series of other meals taken by Jesus with his followers, for which he was at times criticized (Matt 11:19), but which he saw in a different sense as an extension of his salvific mission to sinful or outcast fellow Israelites.

3. If these considerations support the historicity of the Supper as a whole, they also can be applied to Jesus' words and gestures in general; there are differences in the wording of Jesus' sayings over the bread and the cup, which are owing to the individual evangelist's literary reworking of inherited material, but they are minor, noncontradictory, and do not affect the substance of the sayings.

4. Paul introduces Jesus' words by appealing to an existing tradition, which he has already passed on the Christians of Roman Corinth, when he first evangelized them; and the lack of a perfect parallelism in the words over the cup with those over the bread argues in favor of a tradition being quoted as received.

5. John 6:51 ("the bread which I shall give . . . is my flesh") and 6:54–55 ("he who eats my flesh and drinks my blood has eternal life . . . , for my flesh is truly food, and my blood truly drink") in its own literary way independently echoes the tradition that Paul passes on now.

6. Perhaps the biggest problem about the historicity of the Last Supper is Jesus' invitation to his Jewish disciples to drink his blood (in light of the prohibition of eating blood in Lev 7:26–27; 17:10, 12, 14; see Cahill, "Drinking Blood").

In general, see further Meier, "The Eucharist"; Fuller, "Double Origin"; Reumann, "The Last"; Brawley, "Table Fellowship."

Second, is the Last Supper an imitation of Hellenistic cult meals, or adopted from "the gnostic myth of an Archetypal Man" (Käsemann, "Pauline Doctrine," 109, 117), or developed from Jewish meals (a *qiddûš* meal, with a special blessing to "sanctify" it, eaten at the beginning of a Sabbath; a *ḥăbûrah* meal, one shared by a "company" of friends [religious Jews]; an Essene meal [K. G. Kuhn, "Lord's Supper"; 1QS 6:1–6; 1QSa (1Q28a) 2:17–21; also H. W. Kuhn, "Qumran Meal"]; Josephus, *J.W.* 2.8.5 §§12–31; Flusser, "The Last Supper and the Essenes"). Jeremias (*Eucharistic Words of Jesus*, 26–36) has discussed the pros and cons of such proposals and shown most convincingly that the background of the Last Supper or Eucharist is to be found in the Jewish Passover meal (ibid., 41–88). Jesus would not only have celebrated the Passover meal with his apostles, but reinterpreted elements of it so that they became the Christian Eucharist (see *Luke*, 1389–95). Much of Jeremias's explanation is used in the interpretation of verses that follows. See Bahr, "Seder of Passover," who comes to the same conclusion as Jeremias, but who uses anachronistically much rabbinical evidence that has little pertinence to the first century A.D.; also Thiselton, *1 Cor*, 871–74, who concludes that "a Passover frame is presupposed" for the interpretation of Jesus' Last Supper and "the Lord's Supper (and its tradition)"; Routledge, "Passover and Last Supper." For arguments, not always convincing, against identifying the Last Supper as a Passover meal, see Bornkamm, "Lord's Supper," 132–34.

Fuller ("Double Origin," 66–69) notes that, even if one cannot be certain about this background of the Last Supper and its relation to the Jewish Passover meal, B. Lohse (*Das Passafest*) has shown that Christians at a very early date celebrated Passover in a specifically Christian way by fasting in reparation for the crucifixion of Jesus at the season of Passover, and then feasting with both Agape and Eucharist. Such an observance of Passover in this Christian sense supplies, then, the best explanation for many of the details in the NT accounts of the institution of the Eucharist. *Pace* Pesch ("Last Supper," 68), "all characteristics which are bound to and conditioned by the situation of the paschal meal" do not disappear in the Pauline account; clearly some are still there.

This Pauline passage is important as the earliest attestation of the way Jesus instituted the Eucharist, depicting his words and gestures over the bread and cup of wine as he reinterprets some of the Passover elements anew. His words and deeds have symbolic meaning, as they prefigure his coming death and imitate symbolic acts of prophets of old. In Jeremiah 19, the prophet is told by God to buy a potter's earthen flask and break it in the sight of the elders and senior priests of Jerusalem, saying, "So shall I break this people and this city, as one breaks a potter's vessel" (19:11). See also the symbolic actions of the prophet Ezekiel (4:1–3; 5:1–5); cf. the action of Agabus in Acts 21:21. With such prophetic symbolic action, Jesus is depicted dining with his apostles at the Last Supper, as he celebrates it *hyper hymōn*, "for you," thus stressing its vicarious character (see Dupont, " 'Ceci est mon corps,' " 1033–36).

This passage and the Synoptic accounts of the eucharstic institution often give rise to a further question about how Jesus of Nazareth viewed his coming death, especially in light of what he said and did at the Last Supper. Certain elements in this Pauline account may hint at an answer to such a question, but one must remember that it is, in the long run, a formulation composed some time after the event and dependent on a liturgical tradition. Even though it is the earliest account we have, it is not a stenographic or cinematic report of Jesus dining with his apostles on the night he was handed over. The full answer to that question would depend on more than this Pauline account (cf. Pesch, "The Last Supper").

Finally, noteworthy in this early Pauline record is the absence of any indication of who was to be the presider at the celebration of the Eucharist that Jesus directs his followers to repeat. The question is often asked today: Who presided at the early church's liturgy? In this passage, the "you" whom Paul addresses (vv. 17–22) is plural, denoting the group that meets "as a church" (v. 18), and the individuality that he criticizes is indefinite (*hekastos*, "each one," v. 21). Similarly in vv. 23–26, the "you" is again plural, meaning the congregation. So nothing can be deduced from these verses about a eucharistic minister, even if Paul elsewhere is aware of someone presiding over early congregational assemblies: *proïstamenos*, "someone standing at the head" (1 Thess 5:12; cf. Rom 12:8 [see *Romans*, 649]). Unfortunately, nothing is said there about the nature of such presiding or whether it is envisaged as a eucharistic assembly. Cf. 1 Tim 5:17; Justin Martyr, *Apology I* 65,67 (*proestos*).

NOTES

11:17. *In giving the following instructions, I do not praise (you).* Lit. "in commanding this," which refers to what follows. Indirectly Paul alludes to the conciliatory statement (v. 2) with which he began chap. 11, now qualifying it with a reprimand (v. 20 gives its substance), as he will again in v. 22. To be noted is the rhetorical *inclusio* with v. 22, "In this I offer no praise." Some MSS (A, C, and many minuscules) read rather *parangellō ouk epainōn*, "in not praising, I command," which alters the emphasis.

because you hold your meetings not to your advantage, but to your disadvantage. Lit. "you come together," explained in v. 18. The rest of the sentence is an understatement in light of Paul's further remarks in vv. 18b–22b. His text says nothing about when, where, or how often such Corinthian Christians were coming together. Cf. Acts 20:7, "On the first day of the week, when we gathered to break bread. . . ."

18. *First of all, I hear that, when you meet as a church, there are divisions among you.* Lit. ". . . meet in assembly" (or "in church"). Paul begins with *prōton men*, "first of all," with no follow-up, as he does again in Rom 3:20; but he continues rather in v. 20 with *oun*, "therefore." Again he writes *akouō*, "I hear," as in 5:1, referring to some report that has come to him. In combining *synerchesthai* with *en ekklēsiā*, Paul makes use of a well-known Greek expression for the gathering of an assembly of the body politic, but he now means it in a Christian sense, i.e., as "in church," or as members gathering in cultic assembly to celebrate the Lord's Supper. He speaks with irony, as he notes that there is no real unity of assembly because of their *schismata*, "divisions." Cf. the same generic use of *ekklēsia* in 14:4, 5, 19, 28, 35. The setting for such a cultic coming-together was undoubtedly a house-church (cf. 16:19; Rom 16:5), since at this early period *ekklēsia* was not yet used in the sense of a separate building called "a church" (see Murphy-O'Connor, *St. Paul's Corinth*, 178–85). In using "church" in this context of the Eucharist, Paul is stressing the ecclesial significance of the Lord's Supper, a significance that he already implied in common participation in the blood and the body of Christ in 10:16–17 (see Stuhlmacher, "Das neutestamentliche Zeugnis").

Although Paul uses the same word *schismata* as in 1:10, the dissensions within the Corinthian church are now of a different kind; there they were created by preacher allegiance, here it is a matter of bad manners of individuals (or perhaps of separate social groups) who fail to share food in a common meal (see v. 34b). Some commentators, however, do relate the present problem to the same factions as in 1:10 (e.g., Lietzmann, *1 Cor*, 55; Lindemann, *1 Cor*, 250). At any rate, Paul means that, though their gathering together was supposed to be a sign of unity, their mode of gathering only highlights their inequality and lack of unity.

and in part I believe it. Paul is shrewd enough to admit that he does not believe all that he has heard about Corinthian Christians.

19. *No doubt there have to be factions among you, so that the tried and true among you may be recognized.* Paul joins this comment to the preceding verse with *gar*, introducing an explanation. What Paul called *schismata* in v. 18, he now calls *haireseis*, with little intended difference in meaning between them. (He is not using either word in the later sense of schism and heresy.) He believes that splits of this sort are almost inevitable, even in the Christian community that he has founded, but he hopes that because of them those who are "genuinely" Christian (*dokimoi*) will come to be known; for those who conduct themselves in a truly Christian manner will stand apart. In any case, Paul does not want the Corinthian community to suffer from such discriminatory strife.

Is Paul speaking as someone "resigned," or perhaps "with irony"? (so Lietzmann, Collins, Garland). The force of *dei*, "it is necessary," however, is not clear. Some think that the necessity of such factions is rather "divine, eschatological" (Kümmel, followed by Barrett, *1 Cor*, 262; Murphy-O'Connor, *NJBC*, 809; Dupont, "L'Église," 690–91; Fee, *1 Cor*, 538). Justin Martyr (*Dial. Tryph.* 35.3) went so far as to associate these divisions with sayings of Jesus about false prophets recorded in Matt 7:15; 24:11, 24. Recall also the warning of Paul in his farewell speech at Miletus (Acts 20:29–30).

In vv. 28–32 below, Paul will return to such inevitable divisions and factions when he speaks of judgment, to which he could be alluding here; cf. 2 Cor 5:10. The divisions, however, may just as well stem from local social conditions, seating arrangements at dinners, or the kind of food served, etc. (see Martial, *Epigr.* 3.60; Younger Pliny, *Ep.* 2.6; Juvenal, *Sat.* 5.162). It seems preferable to say that Paul is indicating ironically the reason for his dismay at the dissensions and why he cannot praise the Corinthian Christians. Thiselton (*1 Cor*, 858), however, would take the saying, "there have to be factions," as an utterance of the Corinthians themselves; see further Campbell, "Does Paul Acquiesce."

20. *Although you hold your meetings in one place.* Lit. "you coming together in one place," the ptc. can be understood either concessively (as in the lemma) or temporally, "when you. . . ." (*IBNTG*, 102). The prep. phrase *epi to auto* may connote not only the gathering of Christians in one locality, as in 14:23, but also their assembling there for one purpose. The latter connotation would make the "divisions" and "factions" even more detrimental to the union for which they have assembled. For other instances of the same phrase, see Acts 1:15; 2:1, 44. The implied purpose of their assembly is to share a meal together and to celebrate the

Lord's Supper; this implication leads to Paul's strict censure, stated in the following main clause. Because Paul uses a form of the same verb (*synerchomenōn*) employed in v. 17 (*synerchesthe*), that means that he is referring to the same problem of their assembly; there is no need to think of some other abuse.

it is not to eat the Lord's supper. I.e., you may have come together for a meal, but you cannot call it the supper of "the Lord," because your divisive and factious conduct negates that meal's unitive purpose. "If the Lord's Supper is not rightly celebrated, then it is not celebrated at all" (Hofius, "Lord's Supper," 78). Their conduct Paul describes and criticizes in the next verse.

The anarthrous *kyriakon deipnon*, "the Lord's supper," is a technical term that denotes the meal eaten by Christians who commemorate that taken by Jesus with his apostles before he died, the so-called Last Supper, at which he instituted the Eucharist. This is the only place in the NT where this term occurs, but *kyriakos* appears also in Rev 1:10, "the Lord's day," i.e., Sunday. In the contemporary Greek world, *kyriakos* meant "belonging to an owner" (*kyrios*) and often had the connotation of "imperial," when used for the treasury, services, and finances of the Roman emperor (who was often called *Kyrios*); see Deissmann, *LAE*, 361–62; *Bible Studies* (Edinburgh: Clark, 1901) 217–18; *TDNT*, 3:1095–96. The adj. was adopted by early Christians and given the connotation that *Kyrios* normally has in the NT (see NOTE on 1:3). Paul has already spoken of Christians drinking "the cup of the Lord" and partaking of "the table of the Lord" (10:21), depicting the risen Christ as the host who welcomes those "baptized in his name" (1:13; cf. Rev 3:20 [see Grelot, "Repas seigneurial," 205–6]). The common noun, *deipnon*, was used for the main daily meal, usually taken in the evening; see Luke 14:12 (cf. *Luke*, 1047). It could also denote a festal meal or banquet (Luke 14:16, 24).

21. *For as you eat, each one goes ahead with his own meal, and one goes hungry, while another gets drunk.* Lit. "for in eating, each goes on ahead to take one's own supper " (BDAG, 872). Paul puts the pron. *hekastos*, "each one," at the head of the verse in order to emphasize the individuality. The phrase *to idion deipnon*, "one's own supper," stands in contrast to *kyriakon deipnon*. It is not the Lord, but the (selfish) individual who determines the consumption of food and drink. In using *hekastos*, Paul is repeating an accusation that he made in 1:12 about a different topic, for once again it is selfish behavior that is at fault, and the use of *idion*, "one's own," intensifies it. The pron. will reappear in 14:26. The phrase *en tō phagein*, "in eating," refers to what was intended to be a common meal, but is not.

Prolambanei means "takes in advance of" (others [see Mark 14:8]), i.e., not together with others. Instead of eating in a common group and sharing the food, each partakes of what he or she has brought and does not "wait for one another" (11:33). The further description of one such diner who goes ahead as "hungry" and another as "drunk" stands in contrast to "those who have nothing" (v. 22).

Speculation reigns among interpreters who try to figure out the precise defect to which Paul refers (see Fee, *1 Cor*, 540; Garland, *1 Cor*, 534; Theissen, *Social Setting*, 147–50). Some maintain that *prolambanei* does not mean "take in advance," but merely "consume" or "devour." Such meanings, however, are questionable, especially in this context with v. 33, despite numerous attempts so to understand it (see Conzelmann, *1 Cor*, 195 n. 22; Garland, *1 Cor*, 540–41; Hofius, "Lord's Supper," 91; Surburg, "The Situation"). In any case, real table fellowship is lost through the inequality expressed (recall Paul's analogous description of Corinthian Christians in 1:26); and individual selfishness causes further social divisions and factions, neglect of the poor, those whom Paul calls "have-nots" (v. 22). Cf. the description of the rich and poor in Jas 2:2–6.

22. *Do you not have houses to eat and drink in?* With emphasis Paul asks his first rhetorical question in this passage, implying that Corinthian addressees should separate eating and drinking for ordinary purposes (e.g., to satisfy hunger [see v. 34]) from the common celebration of the Lord's Supper. He introduces his question with *mē*, expecting a neg. answer to the question, which, however, has a further neg. *ouk*, as in 9:4, 5, 6 (see BDF §427.2). His fuller answer to such divisive conduct is given only in vv. 33–34. Those verses, along with this one, eventually led to the separation of the celebration of the Lord's Supper from the taking of a common ordinary meal, which came to be called Agape.

Are you not showing contempt for the church of God and making those who have nothing feel ashamed? Lit. "making those-not-having feel ashamed," usually taken to mean the "have-nots," but sometimes the substantivized ptc. *tous mē echontas* is understood with the obj. *oikias* (from v. 22a), "those not having houses"; so Barrett, *1 Cor*, 263 (as a possible alternative). Paul, then, asks, Is not your conduct, when each one eats for himself or herself, whether much or little, expressing disrespect for the congregation assembled to worship God? Worse still, are not some of you, who are well off, making those who have nothing feel ashamed? Here finally Paul expresses the basis for the fault of the "divisions" and "factions" of vv. 18–19. Although he does not use those "possessing knowledge," as in the question of idol meat, the situation is analogous: a limited number of individual Christians is again at fault, even though Paul's initial comments are addressed to all church members, even those "who have nothing." On "church of God," see NOTE on 1:2. This phrase, as used here, assumes a nuance of gravity that such Corinthian Christians are neglecting.

What am I to say to you? Should I praise you? In this I offer no praise. So, with rhetorical *inclusio*, Paul concludes the first part of his discussion, as he again qualifies what he said in 11:2 and repeats more strongly what he wrote in 11:17.

Paul proceeds from his rebuke of the Corinthian Christians directly to a quotation of the early tradition about the institution of the Eucharist, joining it only by the vague connective *gar* and an emphatic *egō*. The tradition is cited, not "only by way of illustration" (*pace* Garland, *1 Cor*, 545), but as the basis for his further comments on Corinthian Christian practice. It is an important step in his argument, because that practice has in effect been neglecting the real meaning of the eucharistic celebration and its concern "for others."

23. *For I received from the Lord what I passed on to you.* The technical language of tradition, *paralambanō*, "receive," and *paradidōmi*, "hand on, pass on," reappears, as it will again in 15:3 (see NOTE on 11:2). Paul appeals to tradition in his argumentation, to a tradition that has already taken shape in the first generation of the church after Christ's exaltation and before he joined it. It is a traditional for-

mula that he has not only received himself, but has already passed on (*ho kai paredōka*) to Corinthian Christians when he evangelized that Roman colony.

As in 7:10, an early tradition, derived ultimately from Jesus of Nazareth and now quoted by Paul, is traced by him to "the Lord," not in the sense that he has had a direct communication from the risen Christ about this supper, but that what he has received as tradition he now vests with the authority of the risen Christ, the one who was given up to death but is now the Exalted One (Bornkamm, "Lord's Supper," 131). In introducing this statement with *egō*, Paul not only stresses his own reception of the tradition, but contrasts himself with *hymin*, "you," the Corinthians to whom he recalls what he has already taught them. See 1 Thess 2:13.

that the Lord Jesus, on the night he was handed over, took bread. Lit. "on the night on which he was handed over," i.e., Paul again uses *paradidomi*, but this time in the same sense as in 5:5, and absolutely. *Paredideto*, as impf. pass., could refer to the arrest of Jesus following the activity of Judas Iscariot, well known from the passion narratives of the Gospels (Matt 26:15 [*paradōsō*]; Mark 14:10, 21 [*paradidotai*]; Luke 22:4, 21; John 13:2), to which Paul is scarcely referring, because he never seems to refer to him elsewhere or to what he did. It could be understood rather as either a divine pass. (handed over by God [Coleman, "Translation"]) or a mid., "he [Jesus] was handing himself over."

This expression along with the verbs that follow are derived from an early liturgical tradition, which not only has retained the chronological reference, "on the night he was handed over" (cf. Mark 14:30: *tautē tē nykti*, which also adds, "while they were eating" [the Passover meal], 14:22), but has also invested the words with a soteriological nuance, and probably even with an echo of the Servant Song of LXX Isa 53:6 (*paredōken*), 12 (*paredothē*). Recall Rom 4:25; 8:32; Gal 2:20. ". . . they are intended to remind the Corinthians of that grave earnestness of the meal which they have tended to neglect" (Jeremias, *Eucharistic Words*, 74 n. 4). The emphatic naming of "the Lord Jesus" stresses that he, whose action is about to be described, is the same one whose presence will be experienced in the sharing of his "cup" and his "table" (10:21), or the "Lord's supper" (11:20).

"Took bread" (*elaben arton*) is the same expression as that in Mark 14:22; Matt 26:26; Luke 22:19 (ptc. *labōn*). It is the first of four formulaic verbs in the eucharistic tradition. Although Wellhausen ("Arton") once argued that *artos* referred to "leavened bread" and concluded that, therefore, the Last Supper could not have been a Passover meal (also Finegan, *Überlieferung*, 62), that interpretation was duly questioned by Beer (*Pesachim*, 96) and others. That *artos* can mean "unleavened bread" is seen from LXX Exod 29:2, where *artous azymous* translates Hebrew *leḥem maṣṣôt*; cf. Lev 2:4; 8:26; Num 6:19; Philo, *De spec. leg.* 2.28 §158; Josephus, *Ant.* 3.6.6 §142 (the bread of the Presence in the Temple is called *artous dōdeka azymous*, "12 unleavened loaves"); 3.10.7 §255; Jeremias, *Eucharistic Words*, 62–65. Mss of the Western textual tradition (D*, F. G) read *ton arton*, "the bread," which is hardly original.

24. *and having given thanks.* Paul writes *eucharistēsas*, as does Luke 22:19, whereas Mark and Matthew have rather *eulogēsas*, "having blessed" or "having

given praise." (In the LXX *eulogein* regularly translates Hebrew *brk*, "bless," and only rarely the hiphil of *ydy* [e.g., Isa 12:1 (MSS B, 5); 38:19], "thank"; this at least shows the related meaning of *eulogēsas* and *eucharistēsas*.) The thanks is given to God, as in LXX Jdt 8:25; 2 Macc 1:11; 10:7; Philo, *De spec. leg.* 2.33 §204; 3.1 §6; Josephus, *Ant.* 1.10.5 §193. From the use of the ptc. *eucharistēsas* in Paul and Luke comes the common name "Eucharist" for the Christian rite, which carries out the directive enshrined in vv. 24c, 25c. The "thanksgiving" connotes God's blessing on what is broken. Whereas it is often considered to be a term derived from a Hellenistic Jewish Christian community, one should recall its likely Palestinian background as well, for one finds *'ôdĕkāh 'ădônāy kî*, "I thank you, O Lord, that...," abundantly in the Qumran *Thanksgiving Psalms* (Robinson, "Die Hodajot-Formel," 194-235; Audet, "Esquisse historique"). For a later Christian thanksgiving formula, see *Did.* 9.3-4.

broke it, and said. I.e., the loaf is not cut, but divided in pieces in order to be shared or distributed. The verb *klaō* occurs in the NT only in the context of breaking bread at a meal (Luke 24:20; Acts 2:46; 27:35; Mark 8:6, 19; 14:22; Matt 14:19; 15:36; 26:26; cf. LXX Jer 16:7; Lam 4:4), and "to break bread" was an ordinary way of saying "to eat a meal." From it Luke derives his special eucharistic term, "the breaking of the bread" (24:35; Acts 2:42; 20:7, 11; cf. *Did.* 9.2-3). Despite what is claimed at times, "the breaking of bread" was not the earliest title for the celebration of the Lord's Supper, antedating "Eucharist." It is a Lucan term for it. Moreover, Mark 8:6 shows that the two actions of giving thanks and breaking bread were joined even in a non-Eucharistic meal.

The breaking of bread, however, scarcely is being used in a metaphorical sense for the "breaking"of Jesus' body (in his passion or death); that is too subtle and hardly required in the understanding of this action (see Bornkamm, "Lord's Supper," 139), although Winnett ("Breaking") has so seen it.

This is my body. The sentence *touto mou estin to sōma* is basically the same in Mark 14:22 and the other Synoptic Gospels, except for the word order (here *mou* precedes the verb and the noun to which it refers, whereas it usually follows *sōma* [in P[46] it precedes the noun]). The placing of the pers. pron. before the noun may be a Pauline modification of the traditional wording (so Schürmann). In some MSS (C[3], Ψ, the Koine text-tradition) and some ancient versions, Jesus' words begin with "Take, eat," which are derived secondarily from Matt 26:26 (see Metzger, *TCGNT*, 496).

What is striking is the neut. dem. pron. *touto*, "this," when one would have expected the masc. *houtos* or even *houtos ho artos*, "this bread." The bread, however, is that over which Jesus has given thanks, but the gender of the pron. is attracted to that of neut. *sōma*, "body." Jesus' implicit distributive gesture, however, may bring it about that the pron. *touto* actually refers to Jesus' action of giving the bread as his body. In v. 25b, the same pron. is used with "cup," *touto to potērion*.

In the ancient Passover seder, the *paterfamilias* recited an Aramaic formula that explained the unleavened bread with a reference to Exod 13:6-8 and Deut 26:5-11: *ha' laḥma' dĕ'onyā' dî 'ăkalû 'ăbāhātanû bĕ'ar'a' dĕmiṣrayim*, "This is the bread of affliction (= Hebrew *leḥem ʿōnî*), which our ancestors ate in the land of Egypt" (see *m. Pesaḥim* 10:4–5; Jeremias, *Eucharistic Words*, 54). Jesus, however, while imitating that formula, interprets the bread of the new Passover (recall 5:7) by identifying it with his own body. He gives his followers not only bread to eat, but a crucial part of himself, the part of himself that will suffer, "the body of Christ" (Rom 7:4). The noun *sōma* has to be linked to *haima* in v. 25; the two taken together are correlative terms and are not to be understood independently of each other.

In the OT, Hebrew *bāśār*, "flesh," often denoted "body" (Ezek 11:19; 36:26; Ps 63:2; Job 4:15); but because in the LXX *sōma* translates a variety of Hebrew words and quite often Hebrew *bāśār* (Lev 15:13, 16, 19; 16:1, 24, 26, 28), "body and blood" was a literary variant of "flesh and blood," a way of speaking of the transient character of a mortal human being (Sir 14:18; 17:31 [*sarx kai haima*]; cf. Matt 16:17; Gal 1:16; 1 Cor 15:50); the words can also denote the components of an animal to be slaughtered or sacrificed (Lev 17:11, 14; Jeremias, *Eucharistic Words*, 221–22).

Some interpreters, however, have tried to understand Greek *sōma* here not as "body," but as "self" (so Léon-Dufour, "Prenez," 225), a sense said to be found elsewhere in the NT (1 Cor 9:27; 13:3; Rom 12:1; Phil 1:20), as well as in Classical and Hellenistic Greek (Aeschines, *Or.* 2.58; Xenophon, *Anab.* 1.9.12; Appian, *Rom. Hist.* 11.7.41). So too BDAG, 984; Bultmann, *TNT*, 1:192, 195. In none of these alleged instances, however, is the meaning "self" unambiguously the only meaning; in fact, in some of them the meaning of physical living body is clearly preferable (see Gundry, *Sōma*, 12–13, 36–37, and esp. 25).

In rabbinic, medieval, and modern Hebrew, the word for "body" is *gûph* or *gûphāh* (fem.), which occurs only in ancient Hebrew in 1 Chr 10:12 and means a "corpse." It seems that influence from Greek philosophical thinking aided the semantic development of it from "corpse" to "body" (in a living sense), but there is no evidence that that development was already afoot in Jesus' day. Paul's emphasis on the physical, living "body" elsewhere in this letter (chaps. 6, 15) makes it wise to retain that sense here too, and certainly not in the gnostic sense that Käsemann ("Doctrine," 129–30) seeks to import.

From a philological point of view, it is impossible to tell whether the verb *estin* is to be understood as "is really," "is identical with" (as the verb "to be" is used in Luke 3:22; 4:34; 6:5; Matt 3:17; 10:2; 13:55; 14:2) or "is symbolically," "is analogously" (as in John 10:7–11; 11:25; 15:1; Gal 4:24). That Jesus' words and gestures were symbolic is clear; but the question is whether the symbolism excludes all realism or whether they might be both symbolic and realistic. (If Jesus of Nazareth were using Aramaic, or even Hebrew, at the Last Supper, no verb would have been used, since the juxtaposition of the subject and predicate in a nominal sentence suffices in these languages to express the pres. tense of the verb "to be": *dēn biśrî*, "this is my flesh." One could add the 3d pers. pron. as the copula, without changing the meaning: *dēn biśrî hûʾ* (see Jeremias, *Eucharistic Words*, 233; "Zur Exegese," 60). Jeremias insists that the words over the bread do not mean, "My person means for you so much as eating and drinking," as some have sought to understand them. For in a Semitic nominal sentence the subject always stands first, as in *hā' lahmā' dĕ'onyā'* (see above; ibid.). In later Syriac, the Aramaic word *pagrā'*, "body," emerges: *hānaw pagry*, "this is my body.")

The Pauline interpretive vv. 26–29, however, when joined with the idea of *koinōnia*, "participation," in the body and blood of Christ (10:16), became the basis for the early Christian understanding of the Greek verb *estin* in the realistic sense. By sharing in the action that constitutes the *anamnēsis* of the Lord's Supper, his followers become participants in the new covenant that the giving of his body and blood connotes (v. 25). What Paul thus teaches in this passage as a whole is likewise affirmed in a different way in John 6:53–56. "Whatever objections may be raised against the term 'Real Presence', it expresses exactly what Paul wanted to say" (Käsemann, "Doctrine," 128; similarly Bornkamm, "Lord's Supper," 139).

That realistic sense was not questioned until the Middle Ages (by Ratramnus of Corbie, 9th century, and Berengar of Tours, 11th century [*ODCC*, 190–91, 1367]), but eventually was reaffirmed in church tradition by many theologians, popes, and especially the Council of Trent (DH 1636, 1651), in its effort to curb the solely symbolic interpretation of some Reformers, especially Zwingli (*ODCC*, 1784).

which is for you. Lit. "that for you," i.e., (my body is) for you (plur.), who participate in this meal. The prep. phrase, *to hyper hymōn*, is not found in the Marcan or Matthean form of the tradition (which has rather *hyper/peri pollōn*, "for many," as part of the words over the cup). Luke 22:19 has a form with an added ptc., *to hyper hymōn didomenon*, "that being given for you," with which one should compare the reading in some MSS of 1 Cor 11:24: *to hyper hymōn thryptomenon* (D); *to hyper hymōn klōmenon* (ℵ[c], C[3], D[b,c], G, K, P, Ψ, 81, 614, 1739[mg]), both meaning, "that being broken for you" (see Metzger, *TCGNT*, 496). The addition of such ptcs. makes clear that "given" or "broken" is to be understood in a sacrificial sense (see *Luke*, 2.1400); and it will be accomplished on the cross of the crucified Jesus, about whom Paul wrote earlier (1:18, 23; 2:2); in Rom 7:4 he will refer to the historical body and call it "the body of Christ." That sense is implied also in the reference to the "covenant" in v. 25 and to Jesus' "death" in v. 26, not to mention the implication of 10:21–22. The prep. phrase alone in the Pauline formulation (without "given" or "broken") may possibly mean no more than "which is (food) for you," because, if one eats it, one finds life in a new sense. The use of the prep. phrase (with an introductory article *to*) is usually judged as not coming from a Semitic tradition and is often regarded as a Pauline modification (see Jeremias, *Eucharistic Words*, 104, 167; Käsemann, "Doctrine," 129). But Hofius (*"To sōma to hyper hymōn"*) has shown that it has a parallel in Lev 5:8 (*to peri tēs hamartias proteron*, "the first one for the sin offering") and Deut 28:23 (*ho ouranos ho hyper kephalēs sou chalkous kai hē gē hē hypokatō sou sidēra*, "the heavens over your head [shall be] brass, and earth under you [shall be] iron"). So he queries the Greek-speaking origin of the Pauline phrase.

To what does the art. *to* refer in the prep. phrase? It could be *touto* (= forward-looking dem. pron. "this," i.e., this broken piece of bread [BDF §290.3–4]). Or it may be *mou to sōma*, "my body." The first is not impossible, but the more obvious referent is "my body," because the dem. pron. is already neut. to agree with the predicate *sōma*, and not with the masc. *artos* (BDF §132.1). It hardly refers to the action of breaking, as Betz ("Gemeinschaft," 411) would have it.

In any case, the vicarious connotation of the prep. phrase is clear: this is the intention of the word reinterpreting the Passover bread of old; it also implies a soteriological aspect of Jesus' handing over his body in death *for others*. The vicarious sense of the prep. *hyper* can be found in 1 Cor 15:3, 29; 2 Cor 5:14; Rom 5:6; 8:32. See also Sir 29:15; 2 Macc 7:9; 8:21; Josephus, *Ant.* 13.1.1 §6 (*apothnēskein hyper autōn*, "to die for them"); *J.W.* 2.10.5 §201 (*hyper tosoutōn hetoimōs epidōsō tēn emauton psychēn*, "for the sake of so many I shall readily give my life"). Above, I admitted that the verb *paredideto* might echo Isa 53:6, 12, as other commentators have often suggested, but it is going too far to say that *to hyper hymōn* "reflects the 'for you' of Isa 53:12," *pace* Thiselton (*1 Cor*, 877), because that phrase does not occur in either the MT or the LXX of v. 12, which says only *autos hamartias pollōn anēnenken kai dia hamartias autōn paredothē*, "He took away the sins of many and was handed over for their sins." The words, "which is for you," are meant to draw those who partake of the Lord's Supper into the saving self-sacrifice of Jesus, whose death is implied, but will be introduced explicitly in v. 26.

Do this in remembrance of me. Or even more lit., "Keep doing this. . . ," i.e., keep performing the same action over bread as I am doing, and do it in memory of me or as my memorial. This memento directive is found in neither the Marcan nor the Matthean parallel, but appears verbatim in Luke 22:19d; in a slightly different form, it is repeated in v. 25c. Since it does not occur in the Marcan and Matthean parallels, it may represent a secondary feature in the early tradition; but because both Luke and Paul have it, without any evidence of a Lucan borrowing from Paul, it must mean that they both have inherited the memento directive from an earlier liturgical tradition. Possibly it was *not* part of the tradition at first, when the celebration was actually carrying out its rubric-like direction. In time, the rubric became part of the formula to be recited, and so it was inherited by Paul and Luke (see Benoit, "Accounts," 82–83), but B. Smith ("More Original Form," 184–86) includes it twice in his reconstruction.

The phrase *eis tēn emēn anamnēsin*, "in remembrance of me," is a modification of an OT phrase; see Lev 24:7 (*eis anamnēsin*, "for a remembrance," used for the frankincense and salt put on the Bread of the Presence); Ps 38:1; 70:1; Wis 16:6 (see Jones, "Anamnēsis in the LXX"; Betz, "Gemeinschaft," 411). The modification is the added *emēn*, "my" or "of me," i.e., a remembrance of Jesus and his actions at the Last Supper, but also " 'in remembrance of' the crucified one, who gave up his body for his own" (Hofius, "Lord's Supper," 103). The purpose of the *anamnēsis* directive is not a reminder for God, but for human beings.

The directive, *touto poieite*, as *anamnēsis*, is not to be understood as a borrowing from Hellenistic memorial feasts commemorating dead persons, as older commentators once wanted to interpret it (e.g., Lietzmann, *1 Cor*, 58, 93 [§§5–7], 186); nor even from Palestinian Jewish prayer formulas, ". . . that God may remember me," i.e., the Messiah (*pace* Jeremias, *Eucharistic Words*, 252 [see Millard, "Covenant," 245–46; Kosmala, "Das tut"; but cf. Capes, "Lord's Table," who tries to support Jeremias]); nor from various instances of "remembering" God's wondrous redemptive deeds in such passages as Neh 9:17 (LXX 2 Esdr 19:17); Ps 77:12; 78:42; *Test. Job* 14.3 (*pace* Kilpatrick, "L'Eucharistie," 197–98). Nor is *anamnēsis* to be understood to mean "proclamation" (Kilpatrick, *The Eucharist in Bible*, 14–16). It is rather a reinterpretation of the *anamnēsis* that the Passover meal itself was intended to be: "That you may remember the day of your departure from the land of Egypt all the days of your life" (Deut 16:3d; cf. Exod 12:14: "This day will be for you a memorial" [*lĕzikkārôn*; LXX: *mnēmosynon*]; 13:3; *Jub.* 49:7). So Käsemann ("Pauline Doctrine," 120) has rightly understood it. As Jesus has substituted himself for the Passover lamb (recall 5:7), so the memento of him is to replace the *anamnēsis* of Passover itself. Further implications of this will appear in v. 26: "The remembrance of the past is thought of as becoming actual in the present" (Klauck, "Lord's Supper," 383). It is not merely a recollection of Jesus and what he did at the Last Supper, but a representing of him and a *reenactment of his acts* at the Last Supper for the conscious awareness of the Christians of Roman Corinth, "une réalité actuelle et présente" (Dahl). Arnesen ("Myth") and Clancy ("Old Testament Roots") argue against the notion of representing, but their argument is scarcely convincing; see Childs, *Memory*, 74–75. Paul is concerned to affirm the cultic nature of the eating of this bread and the drinking of this cup (v. 26), which have been consecrated by the Lord's words. They are thus recalled in order to give the participants a share through faith in what God has promised will be implemented through the saving death of Jesus and to invite them to emulate his offering of himself on behalf of others in their treatment of other Christians who share the Lord's Supper with them. The memento directive is not for the meal as a whole, but for the two acts of eating bread and drinking from the cup in particular (Bornkamm, "Lord's Supper," 140–41 [modified]). As Fuller has noted, " 'me' stands for Jesus in his whole redemptive significance: it is the eschatological redemptive event that is recalled in its dynamic power" ("Double Origin," 68; see also Klauck, "Presence," 72–74).

The later rabbinic tradition also regarded the Passover celebration as a feast of remembrance par excellence: "In every generation a man must so regard himself as if he came forth himself out of Egypt, for it is written, *And thou shalt tell thy son in that day saying, It is because of that which the Lord did for me when I came forth from Egypt*" (Exod 13:8). Later Christian tradition understood the memento directive in still another way, in terms of the Sacrament of Orders (see Thomas Aquinas, *Summa theologica*, Suppl. 37, 5 ad 2; the Council of Trent, sess. XXII [DH §§1740, 1752]).

25. *In the same way, the cup too, after the supper, saying*. I.e., "the cup of blessing" (10:16), the cup over which a blessing is pronounced. Luke 22:20a has the same words in a slightly different order: *kai to potērion hōsautōs meta to deipnēsai*, where the adv. *hōsautōs*, "likewise, too," separates the word for "cup" from the prep. phrase. The "cup" referred originally to one of the various cups of wine drunk at the Passover meal, but it is not possible today to say for certain to which one it might refer, except that it followed the consumption of the Passover lamb. It is often thought to have been the third cup (but see Bahr, "Seder of Passover,"

201; also the debate mentioned in NOTE on 10:16). In its present context, however, "the cup too, after the supper," means after the eating of the distributed eucharistic bread. Whether these words tell us anything about the order of the elements of the Corinthian meal and its Eucharist is a matter of much debate today, but it is really a question of little significance.

There is also some debate among commentators about the understanding of Paul's phrase *hōsautōs kai to potērion meta to deipnēsai*, "in the same way, the cup too after the supper." Is the final prep. phrase to be understood in a temporal, adv. sense, or is it to be taken in an adj. sense modifying "the cup"? The different word order in Luke 22:20a, where the adv. *hōsautōs* separates the prep. phrase from the noun, has already been mentioned. Pesch (*Abendmahl*, 44) and Stuhlmacher ("Das neutestamentliche Zeugnis," 14) understand the Pauline phrase in the adj. sense, "the cup after the supper," i.e., the third cup (at the end of the Passover meal). However, Hofius maintains that this understanding of the words is philologically "impossible," because "the article would have necessarily had to stand before the prepositional phrase: *to poterion to [!] meta to deipnesai*," and he cites BDR §§269.2; 272, and others who agree with him ("Lord's Supper," 81–82). Yet even BDR §272.3–4 gives occurrences of the adj. sense of a prep. phrase without such an article; in addition to the Pauline instances cited there (Rom 6:4; 10:1; 1 Cor 10:18; 2 Cor 9:13) one can further cite Rom 1:3 (*huiou theou en dynamei*); 10:6; Gal 3:11; 1 Cor 2:7. Hofius further maintains that "no reference of any kind to the Passover meal is in evidence" and that "the Pauline tradition gives us a description of Jesus' Last Supper that exhibits the typical elements of a Jewish meal" ("Lord's Supper," 83). Most of the rabbinic support that he invokes, however, comes from texts dating long after the Pauline period. Hofius concludes that the Lord's Supper *paradosis* used by Paul, especially *meta to deipnēsai*, speaks of a meal between the bread rite and the cup rite (ibid., 88). Perhaps, but even Hofius relates the memento directive to "statements about Passover" (ibid., 104).

"This cup is the new covenant in my blood." I.e., the new covenant is concluded or ratified with my blood (or by means of my blood). Luke 22:20b has the same formula, but without the verb *estin*, which appears here. Both the Pauline and the Lucan formulas identify the cup (and its contents) with the new covenant, whereas Mark 14:24 identifies the cup (and its contents) with the blood itself: "This is my blood of the covenant, which is poured out for many"—a form which lacks the word *potērion*, "cup," and (in the best Greek MSS) also the adj. *kainēs*, "new." It is almost impossible to say which of the two forms of the saying over the cup, Marcan or Pauline, is more original; Jeremias, Bultmann, and others think that the Marcan form is (see Wagner, "Der Bedeutungswandel," 539–40). The Marcan formula is closer to Exod 24:8 (*idou to haima tēs diathēkēs*), but not even it has the addition found in Matt 26:28, "for the forgiveness of sins." The Pauline prep. phrase *en tō emō haimati*, "in my blood," expresses the mode in which the covenant is ratified. *Pace* Pesch ("Last Supper," 70), this phrase hardly "presupposes the idea of expiation (Is 53:12)," because the alleged allusion in it to the Fourth Isaian Servant Song is far-fetched.

The Marcan formula, *to haima mou tēs diathēkēs*, though clear enough in Greek, becomes problematic, when one tries to retrovert it into Aramaic, because a suffixal form (*děmî*, "my blood") is not usually followed by a gen. expression (see Jeremias, *Eucharistic Words*, 193–94). There are, however, examples of such a construction in later Aramaic, such as Syriac; see Emerton, "The Aramaic"; "*To haima*"; but cf. Casey, "Original Aramaic Form" (*dmy dnh, dqym' hw', mt'šd 'l śg'yn* — highly unlikely.). This problem, however, does not affect the Pauline formulation.

"The new covenant" refers to a pact understood as already known. It is, in fact, an allusion to Jer 31:31–34 (LXX 38:31–34), the promise made by Yahweh of a pact that he would make with "the house of Israel and the house of Judah," not like that "made with their fathers. . . . I will put my law within them, and I will write it upon their hearts, and I will be their God, and they shall be my people." The phrase, "new covenant," was adopted also by the Essenes of Qumran among pre-Christian Jews of Judea to describe their community (CD 6:19; 1QpHab 2:4–6). Wagner ("Der Bedeutungswandel," 541–43) makes much of the absence of any mention of blood in the Jeremiah passage, maintaining that it was used to form the old covenant that was transgressible and was indeed transgressed, whereas "blood" would be incompatible with the "new covenant," of which Jeremiah spoke. Hence the concept of "new covenant" has undergone a change of meaning, when Jesus uses it in this Pauline formulation as a means of ratifying the new covenant that is now established. Moreover, Wagner thinks that the Pauline form of Jesus' words, especially *touto to potērion hē kainē diathēkē estin* is the more primitive form of the saying, older than the Marcan (with this Smith ["More Original Form," 182] would agree, adding the phrase, *en tō haimati mou*). Wagner's view may have some validity, but Jesus' words over the cup, in either the Marcan or Pauline form, are not without allusion to Exod 24:8. The promise of an eschatological new covenant now finds implementation and fulfillment in words of Jesus uttered over the cup, as he refers to the blood that he will shed in his death on the cross as the means by which the new pact is established now between God and His people. Cf. Heb 9:20; 10:16–18. This "new covenant" reflects the "old covenant" (2 Cor 3:14), the pact made by Yahweh with the people of Israel on the mountain (Sinai), when Moses took the blood of twelve sacrificed oxen and sprinkled it, half on the people and half on the twelve stones of the altar in token of the pact: *idou to haima tēs diathēkēs hēs dietheto kyrios pros hymas*, "Look, the blood of the covenant which the Lord has made with you!" (Exod 24:8). In this new form, the covenant is established "in my blood," i.e., the shedding of Jesus' own blood now functions in the *thysia sōtēriou*, "sacrifice of salvation" (LXX Exod 24:5). The Pauline formula may be less obviously an allusion to Exod 24:8 than the Marcan, but the mention of both *diathēkē* and *haima* make the allusion clear nonetheless. Those who partake of the cup become the new covenant community. For the figurative use of "cup," recall Ps 116:13 (*kôs yěšû'ôt*, "cup of salvation").

Käsemann ("Doctrine," 120) translates *diathēkē* as "decree" or "ordinance," and explains it as that by which Christ has established the new divine order of the kingdom as a present reality (ibid., 128). Such a meaning suits an extrabiblical meaning of the word *diathēkē*. One must recall, however, that *diathēkē* regularly translates Hebrew *běrît*, "covenant," in the LXX, i.e., the pact that God made with Israel. That pact was thought to be different from the parity treaty of old, which would have been called in Greek *synthēkē*, "a pact between equals." Rather the "covenant" was closer in form and stipulations to the ancient suzerainty treaty, a pact between an overlord and a vassal, for Yahweh and Israel resembled more the overlord and vassal. That is why *diathēkē* was used in the LXX, a word which in the Hellenistic world eventually also meant "last will," "testament," as in Gal 3:15, i.e., a legal means of disposing of property (usually with promissory obligation; see BDAG, 228). From that double nuance comes the meaning of *diathēkē* as both "covenant" and "testament" (see Karrer, "Der Kelch des neuen Bundes").

Still another connotation of "blood" in the OT has to be considered, since Jesus' words over the cup imply, as did those over the bread, that his "life" is involved. According to Lev 17:14, "the life (*nepheš*) of all flesh is its blood" (see NOTE on 10:16).

Do this, whenever you drink it, in remembrance of me. This is a repetition of v. 24d, now applied to the drinking of the cup, as often as one partakes of it. More than likely, Paul is responsible for the repetition of the memento directive in this verse, and the sense in which he understands it is expressed in v. 26. Although this Pauline formula expresses no vicarious purpose for Christ's blood, such as one finds in Luke 22:20c, "which is poured out for you," the directive to repeat what Christ has done preserves the meaning of the death of Jesus and proclaims its redemptive significance (so Käsemann, "Doctrine," 121; who, however, goes too far when he claims that this is "an obligatory formula of sacred Law").

26. *For as often as you eat this bread and drink the cup, you proclaim the Lord's death.* In this and the two following verses, introduced by *gar*, "for," which shows that they are no longer part of the *paradosis* that he has been passing on (*pace* Garland, *1 Cor*, 535; D. Smith, *From Symposium*, 188), Paul gives his interpretation of the Lord's Supper. Since Jesus is being spoken about in the 3d pers. sing. ("the Lord's death"), it is clearly not part of the inherited tradition. The first clause is a Pauline comment on the memento directive and the frequency implied in the last form of it in the subordinate clause of v. 25. The active sharing of the bread and cup (recall 10:16) is a way not only of expressing one's belief in the presence of Christ in the Eucharist and of commemorating the Last Supper, but also of announcing to others what the death of Jesus has achieved for all Christian believers. The act of sharing is not only memory and recollection, but above all proclamation, based on the Passover event of old, "For Christ, our Passover lamb, has been sacrificed" (5:7). *Pace* Kilpatrick (*The Eucharist in the Bible*, 14–16), this double aspect of the Eucharist, remembrance and proclamation, is not to be neglected (see Garlatti, "La eucaristía"). Even if *anamnēsis* itself does not mean "proclamation," the verb *katangello*, which in extrabiblical texts often denotes the proclamation of events in sacred festivals (*TDNT*, 1:70), now associates such an announcement with the recollection of this significant and salvific event. As Pfitzner remarks, "There is no worship without remembering, and there is no

liturgical remembering without proclamatory narrative" ("Proclaiming," 16). In Gal 2:20, Paul explains, "I have been crucified with Christ; it is no longer I who live, but Christ who lives in me; and the life that I now live in the flesh I live by faith in the Son of God who loved me and gave himself for me." Cf. 2 Cor 4:10–11. The proclamation "has the character of a confession of praise, directed to God, to whose revelation it responds, but simultaneously directed to the world, to whom the saving death of Christ and his present rule are solemnly announced" (Bornkamm, "Lord's Supper," 141). Note the 2d pers. plur. verbs, *esthiete . . . pinete . . . katangellete*, which stress the involvement of the entire community, viz., of all who share in the Lord's Supper. It is for this reason that Christians gather in unison to celebrate the Supper, and thus proclaim its enduring effects; it is also the response of the church to God, because it is the Supper of the community, and not merely of individuals. That corporate share can be good and salvific, but it can also be disastrous, as the following verses make clear. Mss P⁴⁶, ℵ², C¹, D¹, Ψ, 1739 and Koine text-tradition read *touto* after *potērion*, "this cup."

until he comes. The sharing in the Lord's Supper not only looks back with *anamnēsis* to the death of Jesus on Calvary and proclaims it at present, but it also looks forward to his eschatological "coming," to the Parousia of the risen and exalted Christ (of which Paul will speak again, praying in Aramaic, *Marana tha* [16:22]). In *Did.* 10:6, these words precede mention of *eucharistein* (possibly a reference to the use of them in a eucharistic celebration). Recall earlier Pauline references to the "Day" of the Lord (1:8; 5:5). In 12:13, Paul will speak of Christians as united in the meantime in the ecclesiastical "body of Christ" and "given one Spirit to drink." In that Spirit they are to proclaim the effects of the death of Christ until he arrives in glory. Jeremias (*Eucharistic Words*, 253) has pointed out that *achri hou elthē* with a prospective subjunctive is not a mere temporal expression, but has the connotation of a final or purpose clause (BDF §383.2) so that it means "until (the goal is reached, that) he comes." This interpretation has been supported by Hofius ("Bis dass er kommt"), who calls attention to the same force of Hebrew ʿ*ad* in Isa 62:1, 6–7; Job 14:14; Ps 123:2. Cf. the phrase for messianic expectation in QL: ʿ*ad bôʾ* (1QS 9:11; 4Q252 5:3) or ʿ*ad ʿămôd* (CD 12:23; 20:1).

27. *Consequently, whoever eats the bread or drinks the cup of the Lord unworthily will have to answer for the body and blood of the Lord.* Lit. "will be caught in (obligation to) the body and blood," and the fut. *enochos estai* is to be understood eschatologically. The unworthy reception of the Eucharist is regarded by Paul as a serious matter, and he formulates it with a threat of judgment. Such unworthy recipients will be held responsible for the death of the Lord. In the present context of his criticism of the way Corinthian Christians have been joining their celebration of the Eucharist with other undignified modes of common dining, his words are aimed directly at the Corinthian misdemeanors, as are also his comments in vv. 28–29. Having used the 2d pers. plur. in v. 26, Paul now expresses the matter in a more generalized fashion, using the 3d pers. sing. ("Whoever eats," *hos an esthiē*) and undoubtedly intends to make his view of unworthy reception apply to any mode of such reception. Bread and cup, body and blood of the Lord

correspond to each other in an unmistakable way, and their implication should not be missed; they have become for Paul the real "spiritual food" and "spiritual drink" of 10:3–4. His words thus affirm the real presence of the Lord in the eucharistic food and drink, as he will again in v. 29.

28. *One should take stock of himself and so eat of the bread and drink of the cup.* Lit. "let a human being examine himself," i.e., let each one scrutinize whether he rightly understands what remembrance of the Lord, his Supper, and his death actually mean and whether one is disposed to proclaim them by such eucharistic reception. Self-examination and acknowledgement of one's status are to precede participation in the Supper. "Therefore any worshipper is behaving himself inappropriately at the Eucharist who does not reckon with the self-manifestation of the Lord and therefore who is not in fact celebrating the *kyriakon deipnon*" (Käsemann, "Doctrine," 123). This counsel is meant specifically for the Corinthian Christians who are being summoned to reckon with the selflessness of Jesus at the Last Supper and to cope with their questionable conduct; but, as elsewhere at times, Paul generalizes in writing *anthrōpos* here and "the one eating and drinking" in the next verse so that his words take on a meaning for all time. Hence "to eat the Lord's Supper worthily, one must recognize that all Christians, rich and poor, are joined together in Christ, share equally in his blessings, and should be treated worthily" (Garland, *1 Cor*, 551), but they have to "take stock" of themselves and so eat of the bread and drink of the cup.

29. *For anyone who eats and drinks without acknowledging the body eats and drinks judgment upon himself.* Lit. "the one eating and drinking and not discerning the body," i.e., not recognizing how "the body" is now different. Some MSS (ℵ², C³, D, F, G, Ψ, 1881) add the adv. *anaxios*, "unworthily," but that is a secondary addition derived from v. 27. Similarly, most of the same MSS add *kyriou* after "the body," which is again unnecessary. In mentioning only "the body" and not "the blood" as well, Paul is merely simplifying his mode of speech; body and blood are meant. What, however, is meant by "acknowledging the body"? Different answers have been given: (1) acknowledging the body of the Lord in the bread, i.e., distinguishing it from ordinary bread or profane food (so many medieval interpreters; among moderns, J. Weiss, *1 Cor*, 291; Allo, *1 Cor*, 253; Lietzmann, *1 Cor*, 59); this meaning, however, seems to be foreign to the present context; (2) acknowledging the body of Christ in the church, as in 10:16–17; 12:27–28, i.e., the Lord's presence among his people (e.g., Kümmel in Lietzmann, 186; Bruce, *1 Cor*, 115; Kremer, *1 Cor*, 253; Fee, *1 Cor*, 553–54; Collins, *1 Cor*, 439; Bornkamm, "Lord's Supper," 149; Käsemann, "Doctrine," 130); this meaning, however, seems to strain the sense of the ptc. *diakrinōn*, especially with *to sōma* as its obj.; (3) in light of vv. 24 and 27, acknowledging the body would mean taking stock of oneself in order to eat the bread and drink of the cup worthily as "the body and blood of the Lord" (v. 27; e.g., Barrett, *1 Cor*, 274–75; Kamp, "With Due Honor"; Schrage, *1 Cor*, 3.52; Thiselton, *1 Cor*, 893). The last mentioned seems to be preferable in this context.

The "judgment" (*krima*), of which Paul speaks, is somewhat explained in the verses that follow (30–34c), as he employs various forms of the cog. verb *krinō*, "judge," with different nuances, and it is not easy to capture them exactly in an English translation. Note the sequence of *krima,* "judgment," *mē diakrinōn,* "not acknowledging" (v. 29); *diekrinomen,* "we were to evaluate," *ekrinometha,* "we would be subject to judgment" (v. 31); *krinomenoi,* "being judged." *katakrithōmen,* "we may be condemned" (v. 32); *eis krima,* "to judgment" (v. 34c). Paul means that the participant in the Lord's Supper exposes himself or herself to judgment, not only in the sense that all human beings must appear before the divine tribunal (Rom 2:5–6; 14:10c; 2 Cor 5:10), but in the special sense called for in v. 27. Hence the proper scrutiny of "the body" would demand of Corinthian Christians a change in the way they treat others in their coming together to celebrate the Lord's Supper.

30. *For this reason many among you are weak and infirm, and a number are dying.* Lit. "are being lulled to sleep," used euphemistically for death, as in 7:39. This statement is meant as an illustration of the "judgment" mentioned in v. 29. Paul is alluding to the experience of Corinthian Christians, some of whom have been afflicted with sickness and death. How he has come to know about this situation is not indicated. The "weak" are hardly the same as those "weak" in conscience of 8:10, because the second adj., "infirm," makes it clear that they are physically weak; and that is supported by the following words about the dying. Hence these terms are scarcely to be understood only in a spiritual sense, as "weak in faith," "spiritually ill," or "spiritually asleep," as Schneider ("Glaubensmängel") has tried to take them; see Robertson-Plummer, *1 Cor,* 253. The spiritual food and drink of the Eucharist may have become for them like poison (*pharmakon thanatou,* Lietzmann, *1 Cor,* 59). Recall 10:5, where Paul argued similarly about an OT crisis, and also 10:12, "Whoever thinks that he is standing firm should see to it that he does not fall." In the history of the exegesis of 1 Corinthians, this verse has not had many interpreters.

Paul's comment may be made from his Jewish background, which sometimes related sickness to divine punishment for sinful conduct and transgressions (reflected in Exod 4:11; Deut 32:39; Sir 27:27–29; 38:9–10; 2 Macc 4:38; 9:5–6; also in Mark 2:1–12; John 9:2; cf. Str-B, 1:495–96; 2:193–97, for the later rabbinic tradition). In any case, Paul does not mean that the worthy reception of the Eucharist protects from sickness or death; nor does he regard the breaking of bread as *pharmakon athanasias,* "the medicine of immortality," the antidote of not dying, as did Ignatius of Antioch (*Eph.* 20.2). He may have the Corinthian church as a whole in mind, for it is sick, and the unworthy reception of the Eucharist allows such destructive forces to afflict it.

31. *But if we were to evaluate ourselves correctly, we would not be subject to judgment.* Lit. "we would not be judged," i.e., not be in a state of being judged. In this contrary-to-fact condition (BDF §360.4), which Paul introduces with adversative *de,* he identifies himself with his addressees, using the 1st pers. plur.; thus he softens the tone of his admonition: If Christians were in the habit of scrutinizing themselves and their actions rightly in reference to the bread and cup of the Lord in which they would share, they would not find themselves "being judged" or suffering such things as weakness, illness, and death.

32. *Since we are being judged by [the] Lord, we are being chastened, that we may not be condemned along with the world.* Afflictions such as sickness and death may reveal to us the Lord's judgment, but they really have a medicinal and educative purpose, that we may not share in the long run in any eschatological condemnatory judgment. Cf. Prov 3:12. *Katakrithōmen* is a compound form of *krinō* that always implies guilt; cf. Rom 2:1. The noun *kosmos*, "world," carries the negative connotation of the world of human beings who oppose God, as in 1:27–28; 6:2; 2 Cor 1:12; 5:19; Rom 3:6; cf. 1 Pet 4:17. The way that Paul has spoken of judgment in vv. 27–32 helps one to understand properly the eschatological meaning of the Lord's Supper, "until he comes."

33. *Consequently, my brothers, when you meet together to eat, await the arrival of one another.* After his general remarks in vv. 31–32, Paul returns in this and the following verse to the topic of the divisive situation in the Corinthian community described above in vv. 18–22. With the ptc. *synerchomenoi*, "in coming together," which echoes *synerchesthe* of v. 17 above, he explains how their meetings should be conducted in the house-churches of Roman Corinth. If they are going to meet in order to share a common meal and at that gathering celebrate the Lord's Supper, they should do it in an orderly fashion, awaiting the arrival of all members. See 16:11 for the same sense of *ekdechomai*, "wait for." Then they would be "acknowledging the body" of the Lord with proper deference. So Paul seeks to reintroduce the proper sense of fellowship and sharing that should characterize their gatherings. This would prevent the greedy from "going ahead" with their own meals (*prolambanein*), as in v. 21. *Pace* Fee, Paul is not "urging the wealthy to demonstrate normal Christian hospitality" (*1 Cor*, 568); he is addressing his counsel to all (*allēlous*), no matter what their social status may be or the reason for not arriving at the same time.

34. *If anyone gets hungry, he should eat at home.* If hunger really becomes a problem, there is another way of handling it, apart from eating at the common gathering ahead of others. Consumption at home would eliminate solitary or private eating in a common setting. The prep. phrase *en oikō*, "at home," stands in contrast to that of v. 18, *en ekklēsiā*, "in a church gathering."

that you may not meet together only to be condemned. Lit. "that you may not come together for judgment," with the noun *krima* bearing the nuance of "condemnation" (= *katakrima*, the cog. noun of the last verbal form *katakrithōmen* in v. 32). The gathering together in common by Christians should not be the cause or even the occasion of negative judgment.

As for the other matters I shall give directives when I come. "One may guess for ever, and without result, as to what things the Apostle was going to set in order" (Robertson-Plummer, *1 Cor*, 255). Recall 4:19 and 7:17c.

BIBLIOGRAPHY (See also Bibliography on 10:1–22, pp. 395–97)

Aitken, E. B., "Ta drōmena kai ta legomena: The Eucharistic Memory of Jesus' Words in First Corinthians," *HTR* 90 (1997) 359–70.

Alappatt, V., "Pauline Perspective on 'the Lord's Supper,'" *BiBh* 26 (2000) 62–81.

Arnesen, A., "The Myth of Anamnesis," *Theology* 105 (2002) 436–43.

Audet, J.-P., "Literary Forms and Contents of a Normal *Eucharistia* in the First Century," *SE I* (TU 73; Berlin: Akademie-V., 1959) 643–62; (and in a considerably revised form) "Esquisse historique du genre littéraire de la 'bénédiction' juive et de l'Eucharistie' chrétienne," *RB* 65 (1958) 371–99.

Bahr, G. J., "The Seder of Passover and the Eucharistic Words," *NovT* 12 (1970) 181–202.

Beer, G., *Die Mischna II/3: Pesachim* (Giessen: Töpelmann, 1912).

Benoit, P., "The Accounts of the Institution and What They Imply," *The Eucharist in the New Testament: A Symposium* (ed. J. Delorme; Baltimore: Helicon, 1964) 71–101.

Betz, H. D., "Gemeinschaft des Glaubens und Herrenmahl: Überlegungen zu 1Kor 11,17–34," *ZTK* 98 (2001) 401–21.

Blue, B. B., "The House Church at Corinth and the Last Supper: Famine, Food Supply, and the *Present Distress*," *CTR* 5 (1990–91) 221–39.

Boismard, M.-E., "The Eucharist According to Saint Paul," *The Eucharist in the New Testament* (ed. J. Delorme; Baltimore: Helicon, 1964), 125–39.

Bonsirven, J., " 'Hoc est corpus meum': Recherches sur l'original araméen," *Bib* 29 (1948) 205–19.

Bornkamm, G., "The Lord's Supper and Church in Paul," *Early Christian Experience*, 123–60.

Brawley, R. L., "Table Fellowship: Bane and Blessing for the Historical Jesus," *PRSt* 22 (1995) 13–31.

Brown, D., "The Breaking of the Bread," *Theology* 75 (1972) 477–82.

Burkill, T. A., "The Last Supper," *Numen* 3 (1956) 161–77.

Cahill, M. J., "Drinking Blood at a Kosher Eucharist? The Sound of Scholarly Silence," *BTB* 32 (2002) 168–81.

Campbell, R. A., "Does Paul Acquiesce in Divisions at the Lord's Supper?" *NovT* 33 (1991) 61–70.

Capes, D. B., "The Lord's Table: Divine or Human Remembrance?' *PRSt* 30 (2003) 199–209.

Casey, M., "The Original Aramaic Form of Jesus' Interpretation of the Cup," *JTS* 41 (1990) 1–12.

Chenderlin, F., "Do This as My Memorial": The Semantic and Conceptual Background and Value of *Anamnesis in 1 Corinthians 11:24–25* (AnBib 99; Rome: Biblical Institute, 1982).

Childs, B. S., *Memory and Tradition in Israel* (SBT 37; London: SCM, 1962).

Chrupcała, L. D., "Chi mangia indegnamente il corpo del Signore (1 Cor 11,27)," *SBFLA* 46 (1996) 53–86.

———, " 'Fate questo in memoria di me' (Lc 22,19b; 1 Cor 11,24–25): Ma fare che cosa esattamente? Storia, teologia e prassi a confronto," *SBFLA* 53 (2003) 123–56.

Clancy, R. A. D., "The Old Testament Roots of Remembrance in the Lord's Supper," *ConcJ* 19 (1993) 35–50.

Coleman, P., "The Translation of *paredidoto* in 1 Co 11[23]," *ExpTim* 87 (1975–76) 375.

Cremer, F. G., "Der 'Heilstod' Jesu im paulinischen Verständnis von Taufe und Eucharistie: Eine Zusammenschau von Röm 6,3f und 1 Kor 11,26," *BZ* 14 (1970) 227–39.

Crossan, J. D., *The Historical Jesus: The Life of a Mediterranean Jewish Peasant* (San Francisco: Harper, 1991).

Dahl, N. A., "Anamnesis," *ST* 1 (1947) 69–95.

Das, A. A., "1 Corinthians 11:17–34 Revisited," *CTQ* 62 (1998) 187–208.

Dupont, J., " 'Ceci est mon corps,' 'Ceci est mon sang,' " *NRT* 80 (1958) 1025–41.

———, "L'Église à l'épreuve de ses divisions (*1 Co*, 11, 18–19)," *Paul de Tarse: Apôtre de notre temps* (ed. L. de Lorenzi), 687–96.

Emerton, J., "The Aramaic Underlying *to haima mou tēs diathēkēs* in Mk. xiv. 24," *JTS* 6 (1955) 238–40.

———, "*To haima mou tēs diathēkēs*: The Evidence of the Syriac Versions," *JTS* 13 (1962) 111–17.

Engberg-Pedersen, T., "Proclaiming the Lord's Death: 1 Corinthians 11:17–34 and the Forms of Paul's Theological Argument," *Pauline Theology, Volume II: 1 & 2 Corinthians* (ed. D. M. Hay), 103–32.

Finegan, J., *Die Überlieferung der Leidens- und Auferstehungsgeschichte Jesu* (BZNW 15; Giessen: Töpelmann, 1934).

Flusser, D., "The Last Supper and the Essenes," *Imanuel* 2 (1973) 23–27.

Fuller, R. H., "The Double Origin of the Eucharist," *BR* 8 (1963) 60–72.

Garlatti, G. J., "La eucaristía como memoria y proclamación de la muerte del Señor (Aspectos de la celebración de la cena del Señor según San Pablo)," *RevistB* 46/4 (1984) 321–41; 47/1–2 (1985) 1–25.

Garuti, P., "*Postquam coenatum est* . . . Due percorsi socratici nella cristologia paolino-lucana: La *Cena del Signore* (Lc 22,14.20; 1 Cor 11,23.25)," *Angelicum* 80 (2003) 663–87.

Gaventa, B. R., " 'You Proclaim the Lord's Death': 1 Corinthians 11:26 and Paul's Understanding of Worship," *RevExp* 80 (1983) 377–87.

Gentry, L., "Beyond Remembering: Proclaiming the Death in the Supper," *ResQ* 41 (1999) 241–43.

Goguel, M., "La relation du dernier repas de Jésus dans I Cor., 11, et la tradition historique chez l'apôtre Paul," *RHPR* 10 (1930) 61–89.

Gregg, D. W. A., "Hebraic Antecedents to the Eucharistic *Anamnesis* Formula," *TynBul* 30 (1979) 165–68.

Grelot, P., "L'Institution du 'Repas du Seigneur': Pour une lecture des textes parallèles," *EV* 106/34–36 (1996) 474–79.

———, "Le repas seigneurial (*1 Co* 11, 20)," *La Pâque du Christ, mystère de salut: Mélanges offerts au P. F.-X. Durrwell* . . . (LD 112; Paris: Cerf, 1982) 203–36.

Hahn, F., "Herrengedächtnis und Herrenmahl bei Paulus," *LJ* 32 (1982) 166–77.

———, "Das Herrenmahl bei Paulus," *Paulus, Apostel Jesu Christi: Festschrift für Günter Klein* (ed. M. Trowitzsch; Tübingen: Mohr Siebeck, 1998) 23–33.

Henderson, S. W., " 'If Anyone Hungers . . . ': An Integrated Reading of 1 Cor 11.17–34," *NTS* 48 (2002) 195–208.

Hofius, O., " 'Bis dass er kommt' I. Kor. XI. 26," *NTS* 14 (1967–68) 439–41; repr. *Paulusstudien I*, 241–43.

———, "Herrenmahl und Herrenmahlsparadosis: Erwägungen zu 1 Kor 11,23b–25," *ZTK* 85 (1988) 371–408; repr. *Paulusstudien I*, 203–40.

———, "The Lord's Supper and the Lord's Supper Tradition: Reflections on 1 Corinthians 11:23b–25." *One Loaf, One Cup* (ed. B. F. Meyer), 75–115.

———, "*To soma to hyper hymon* 1 Kor 11,24," *ZNW* 80 (1989) 80–88.

Horrell, D. G., "Domestic Space and Christian Meetings at Corinth: Imaging New Contexts and the Buildings East of the Theatre," *NTS* 50 (2004) 349–69.

———, "The Lord's Supper at Corinth and in the Church Today," *Theology* 98 (1995) 196–202.

———, *The Social Ethos of the Corinthian Correspondence* (Edinburgh: Clark, 1996).

Huser, T., "Les récits de l'institution de la Cène: Dissemblances et traditions," *Hokhma* 21 (1982) 28–50.

Jeremias, J., "The Last Supper," *JTS* 50 (1949) 1–10.

———, " 'This Is My Body . . . ,' " *ExpTim* 83 (1971–72) 196–203.

———, "Zur Exegese der Abendmahlsworte Jesu," *EvT* 7 (1947–48) 60–63.

Jones, D., "*Anamnēsis* in the LXX and the Interpretation of 1 Cor. xi. 25," *JTS* 6 (1955) 183–91.

Kamp, C. H., "With Due Honor to the Lord's Body: An Exegetical Study on I Cor 11:29," *RefR* 10/3 (1957) 38–42.

Karrer, M., "Der Kelch des neuen Bundes: Erwägungen zum Verständnis des Herrenmahls nach 1 Kor 11,23b–25," *BZ* 34 (1990) 198–221.

Käsemann, E., "The Pauline Doctrine of the Lord's Supper," *Essays*, 108–35.

Keating, J. F., *The Agapé and the Eucharist in the Early Church: Studies in the History of the Christian Love-Feasts* (London: Methuen, 1901).

Kertelge, K., "Die soteriologischen Aussagen in der urchristlichen Abendmahlsüberlieferung und ihre Bedeutung zum geschichtlichen Jesus," *TTZ* 81 (1972) 193–202.

Kilpatrick, G. D., "L'Eucharistie dans le Nouveau Testament," *RTP* 14 (1964) 193–204.

———, *The Eucharist in Bible and Liturgy: The Moorhouse Lectures 1975* (Cambridge: Cambridge University Press, 1983).

Klauck, H.-J., *Herrenmahl und hellenistischer Kult: Eine religionsgeschichtliche Untersuchung zum ersten Korintherbrief* (NTAbh n.s. 15; Münster in W.: Aschendorff, 1982).

———, "Lord's Supper," *ABD*, 4:362–72.

Kobayashi, N., "The Meaning of Jesus' Death in the 'Last Supper' Traditions," *TJT* 8 (1992) 95–105.

Koester, C. R., "Promise and Warning: The Lord's Supper in 1 Corinthians," *WW* 17 (1997) 45–53.

Kosmala, H., " 'Das tut zu meinem Gedächtnis,' " *NovT* 4 (1960) 81–94.

Kremer, J., "Eucharistie und Abendmahl: Überprüfung einer Neuinterpretation an 1 Kor 11, 17–34," *StZ* 220 (2002) 767–80.

———, " 'Herrenspeise'—nicht 'Herrenmahl': Zur Bedeutung von *kyriakon deipnon phagein* (1 Kor 11,20)," *Schrift und Tradition: Festschrift für Josef Ernst* . . . (ed. K. Backhaus und F. G. Untergassmair; Paderborn: Schöningh, 1996) 227–42.

Kuhn, H.-W., "The Qumran Meal and the Lord's Supper in Paul in the Context of the Graeco-Roman World," *Paul, Luke and the Graeco-Roman World: Essays in Honour of Alexander J. M. Wedderburn* (JSNTSup 217; ed. A. Christophersen et al.; Sheffield: Sheffield Academic, 2002) 221–48.

Kuhn, K. G., "The Lord's Supper and the Communal Meal at Qumran," *The Scrolls and the New Testament* (ed. K. Stendahl; New York: Harper & Bros., 1957) 65–93, 259–65.

Lampe, P., "The Corinthian Eucharistic Dinner Party: Exegesis of a Cultural Context (*1 Cor. 11: 17–34*)," *Affirmation* 4/2 (1991) 1–15.

———, "The Eucharist: Identifying with Christ on the Cross," *Int* 48 (1994) 36–49.

———, "Das korinthische Herrenmahl im Schnittpunkt hellenistisch-römischer Mahlpraxis und paulinischer Theologia Crucis (1 Kor 11,17–34)," *ZNW* 82 (1991) 183–213.

Léon-Dufour, X., " 'Prenez! Ceci est mon corps,' " *NRT* 104 (1982) 223–40.

Lietzmann, H., *Mass and Lord's Supper: A Study in the History of the Liturgy* (Leiden: Brill, 1953); repr. with Intro. and Further Inquiry by R. D. Richardson (1979).

Lohse, B., *Das Passafest der Quartadecimaner* (BFCT 2/54; Gütersloh: Bertelsmann, 1953).

Luke, K., " 'The Night in Which He Was Delivered up' (1 Cor 11:23)," *BiBh* 10 (1984) 261–79.

Luz, U., "Das Herrenmahl im Neuen Testament," *BK* 57 (2002) 2–8.

Maccoby, H., "Paul and the Eucharist," *NTS* 37 (1991) 247–67.

Marxsen, W., *The Lord's Supper as a Christological Problem* (Facet Books 25; Philadelphia: Fortress, 1970).

McGowan, A. B., " 'Is There a Liturgical Text in This Gospel?': The Institution Narratives and Their Early Interpretive Communities," *JBL* 118 (1999) 73–87.

Meding, W. von, "1 Korinther 11,26: Vom geschichtlichen Grund des Abendmahls," *EvT* 35 (1975) 544–52.

Meier, J. P., "The Eucharist at the Last Supper: Did It Happen?" *TD* 42 (1995) 335–51.

Merklein, H., "Erwägungen zur Überlieferungsgeschichte der neutestamentlichen Abendmahlstraditionen," *BZ* 21 (1977) 88–101, 235–44; repr. *Studien zu Jesus und Paulus* (WUNT 43; Tübingen: Mohr [Siebeck], 1987) 157–80.

Millard, A. R., "Covenant and Communion in First Corinthians," *Apostolic History and the Gospel: Biblical and Historical Essays Presented to F. F. Bruce* . . . (ed. W. W. Gasque and R. P. Martin; Exeter, UK: Paternoster, 1970) 242–48.

Murphy-O'Connor, J., "House Churches and the Eucharist," *TBT* 22 (1984) 32–38.

Neuenzeit, P., *Das Herrenmahl: Studien zur paulinischen Eucharistieauffassung* (SANT 1; Munich: Kösel, 1960).

Nicholson, G. C., "Houses for Hospitality: 1 Cor 11:17–34," *Colloquium* 19/1 (1986) 1–6.

Passakos, D. C., "Eucharist in First Corinthians: A Sociological Study," *RB* 104 (1997) 192–210.

Paulsen, H., "Schisma und Häresie: Untersuchungen zu 1 Kor 11,18. 19," *ZTK* 79 (1982) 180–211.

Perrot, C., " 'C'est pourquoi il y a parmi vous beaucoup de malades' (1 Co 11, 30)," *Supplément* 170 (1989) 45–53.

Pesch, R., *Das Abendmahl und Jesu Todesverständnis* (QD 80; Freiburg im B.: Herder, 1978).

——, "The Last Supper and Jesus' Understanding of His Death," *BiBh* 3 (1977) 58–75.

Petuchowski, J. J., " 'Do This in Remembrance of Me' (1 Cor 11.24)," *JBL* 76 (1957) 293–98.

Pfitzner, V. C., "Proclaiming the Name: Cultic Narrative and Eucharistic Proclamation in First Corinthians," *LTJ* 25 (1991) 15–25.

Reumann, J., "The Last and the Lord's Supper," *Lutheran Theological Seminary Bulletin* 62 (1982) 17–39.

Robinson, J. M., "Die Hodajot-Formel in Gebet und Hymnus des Frühchristentums," *Apophoreta: Festschrift für Ernst Haenchen* . . . (BZNW 30; Berlin: Töpelmann, 1964) 194–235.

Ródenas, A., " 'Eso no es comer la cena del Señor' (1 Cor. 11, 20b)," *Salm* 22 (1975) 555–61.

Routledge, R., "Passover and Last Supper," *TynBull* 53 (2002) 203–21.

Ruckstuhl, E., "Neue und alte Überlegungen zu den Abendmahlsworten Jesu," *SNTU* 5 (1980) 79–106.

Sánchez Caro, J. M., " 'Probet autem seipsum homo' (1 Cor 11, 28): Influjo de la praxis penitencial eclesiástica en la interpretación de un texto bíblico," *Salm* 32/3 (1985) 293–334.

Schneider, S., "Glaubensmängel in Korinth: Eine neue Deutung der 'Schwachen, Kranken, Schlafenden' in 1 Kor 11,30," *FilolNT* 9 (1996) 3–19.

Schottroff, L., "Holiness and Justice: Exegetical Comments on 1 Corinthians 11.17–34," *JSNT* 79 (2000) 51–60.

Schürmann, H., "Das apostolische Interesse am eucharistischen Kelch," *MTZ* 4 (1953) 223–31.

———, "Jesus' Words in the Light of His Actions at the Last Supper," *Concilium* 10/4 (1968) 61–67.

Smith, B. D., "The More Original Form of the Words of Institution," *ZNW* 83 (1992) 166–86.

Smith, D. E., *From Symposium to Eucharist: The Banquet in the Early Christian World* (Minneapolis: Fortress, 2003) 173–217.

Stuhlmacher, P., "Das neutestamentliche Zeugnis vom Herrenmahl," *ZTK* 84 (1987) 1–35.

Stürmer, K., "Das Abendmahl bei Paulus," *EvT* 7 (1947–48) 50–59.

Surburg, M. P., "The Situation at the Corinthian Lord's Supper in Light of 1 Corinthians 11:21: A Reconsideration," *ConcJ* 32 (2006) 17–37

———, "Structural and Lexical Features of 1 Corinthians 11:27–32," *ConcJ* 26 (2000) 200–217.

Theissen, G., *The Social Setting of Pauline Christianity*, (Philadelphia: Fortress, 1982) 145–74.

Theobald, M., " 'Tut dies zu meinem Gedächtnis!' Die Eucharistie in der frühen Kirche," *Orientierung* 69 (2005) 76–80.

Traets, C., "Les paroles sur la coupe pendant la prière eucharistique: Trois considérations bibliques et liturgico-pastorales," *Questions Liturgiques* 77 (1996) 135–51, 213–28.

Wagner, V., "Der Bedeutungswandel von *běrît ḥădāšāh* bei der Ausgestaltung der Abendmahlsworte," *EvT* 35 (1975) 538–44.

Wellhausen, J., "*Arton eklasen*, Mc 14,22," *ZNW* 17 (1906) 182.

Winnett, A. R., "The Breaking of the Bread: Does It Symbolize the Passion?" *ExpTim* 88 (1976–77) 181–82.

Winter, B. W., "The Lord's Supper at Corinth: An Alternative Reconstruction," *RTR* 37 (1978) 73–82.

D. PROBLEMS CAUSED BY CHARISMATICS IN THE BODY OF CHRIST (12:1–14:40)

25   a. *Discernment of Spirits (12:1–3)*

12:1 Now, brothers, I do not want you to be uninformed about spiritual gifts. 2 You realize that, when you were pagans, you were attracted and carried away again and again to dumb idols. ³Therefore, I make known to you that no one who is speaking by the Spirit of God says, "Accursed is Jesus"; and no one can say, "Jesus is Lord," save by the Holy Spirit.

COMMENT

Paul now takes up yet another problem that was affecting life in the Christian community of Roman Corinth. In this case, it is no longer a question of conduct in sacred assemblies but has to do rather with the way Christians have been making use of spiritual endowments they have diversely received, with a certain competitiveness that does not always conduce to the good of the community, which will eventually be identified as "Christ" and "the Body of Christ." This topic of spiritual endowments is lengthy and complicated, and in one way or another it will occupy the next three chapters of this letter (12:4–14:40). Some commentators have even suggested that *pneumatika* is a title that should be given to chaps. 12–16 (Smalley, "Spiritual Gifts," 431); that, however, is debatable, but it certainly applies to chaps. 12–14. As will emerge in due course, Paul is reacting against some Corinthian Christians who are vaunting one gift over another (especially speaking in tongues as the main gift of the Spirit), and in order to counteract that, he is seeking to put all *pneumatika*, "spiritual things," especially the endowments of the Spirit, in a proper perspective.

Once again, it is not easy to say how Paul has learned about this problem, but he will discuss it at length and give his views on this important matter that confronts the Corinthian community. He introduces the topic with *peri de*, as he did in 7:1, 25; 8:1; as in the latter two instances, there is no certainty that this issue was mentioned in the letter to which he began his reply in 7:1, although some commentators still interpret the phrase in that way. In any case, the topic that Paul now takes up has nothing to do with "the other matters" that he promised to handle (11:34), when he came to Corinth the next time.

In this section of the letter, Paul discusses what constitutes the shape of the Christian church. He has used the word *ekklēsia* a number of times already (1:2; 4:17; 6:4; 7:17; 10:32; 11:16, 18, 22), and it now appears before chap. 14 only once (12:28), but the topic of these chapters says much about the relation of members of the church to one another, and above all about it as a Spirit-guided, organized body. He begins by stressing the animating guidance of the Spirit in the confessing body of believers who make it up and who should be utilizing their manifold gifts for the good order of the church and not for anarchic disorder.

Apparently, some Corinthian Christians have been maintaining that certain gifts of the Spirit were better than others, were striving for so-called higher gifts, and even claiming that speaking in tongues was a sign for unbelievers, and that prophecy was meant for believers. They were also querying the role of women in the church. In response, Paul shows that the gifts of the Spirit are varied but that each is meant to contribute to the common good, but he insists that love must be the indispensable motivation of all of them, that intelligible speech is needed for common worship and evangelization, and that Christian worship demands the building up of all members in the community, male and female alike. So Paul argues in these three chapters, 12 through 14 (see further Talbert, "Paul's Understanding").

In the first passage, 12:1-3, Paul sets forth his fundamental thesis about the role of the Spirit; it is not an initial digression, when rightly understood, because it contrasts what Paul makes known about that Spirit with what Corinthian Christians have been ignoring or failing to recognize. The three verses are united by an epistemological theme, which must be rightly understood. They are followed in vv. 4-11 by a sober discussion of the various gifts that come from the one Spirit. Thereafter, in chap. 12, Paul teaches that the many gifted members all form one body, "the body of Christ," which is the church.

The first topic is *pneumatika*, "spiritual things," those aspects or factors of Christian community life that stem from the influence of the Spirit (*pneuma*). The first aspect concerns something very fundamental: How does one judge whether the Spirit's influence is behind certain practices in Corinth, either the cursing of Jesus or the acknowledgment of his lordship? For one cannot make the basic Christian profession of faith, save with the grace of the Spirit. Paul thus gives a negative and a positive way of discerning who is speaking with that Spirit, or who is a real Christian.

"Accursed is Jesus" seems to have been a slogan that some people in Roman Corinth were using and that Paul has learned about. Some commentators, however, prefer to think that Paul himself has coined that saying as a literary device that stands in contrast to the fundamental Christian confession, "Jesus is Lord" (Maly, de Broglie, Conzelmann, Bassler, Fee, Hays, Holtz). This view, however, is rather unlikely, even if it is not easy to say just who might have been using such a slogan. The context seems to demand that this negative utterance would stem either from some Christians or from some pagan Corinthians.

Could it have been used by Jewish opponents of Christianity, as some commentators have maintained (Cullmann, Derrett, Garland, Moffatt, Schlatter, Talbert)? Their main reason is that *anathema* as a curse formula comes from "only Jewish usage" (Schmithals, *Gnosticism*, 125 [following many others: Behm, *TDNT*, 1:354; Lietzmann, Kümmel]). Paul mentions *ethnē* in v. 2 as a description of the former status of Corinthian Christians to whom he is writing, and that is a typically Jewish term for Gentiles (see Derrett, "Cursing Jesus," for many attempts to explain the phrase as a slogan).

Schmithals is convinced that they were Gnostic Christians, who "confess 'Christ,' whom Paul proclaims as the Son of God. But that this Christ is born *ek gynaikos* (Gal. 4:4), that he is thus *ho Iēsous*—this they deny, and in ecstasy they express this denial in the harsh words *anathema Iēsous*" (*Gnosticism*, 127). The main argument for such an interpretation of this passage is derived from Origen, *Contra Celsum* 6.28 (GCS 3.98), which tells about Ophite Gnostics who would "not admit anyone into their meeting, unless he has first pronounced curses against Jesus" (*ean mē aras thētai kata tou Iēsou* [Chadwick, *Origen*, 344]). See also Origen, *Catena* frg. 47: *ei mē anathematisē ton Iēsoun*, "unless he (first) curses Jesus" (Jenkins, "Origen," 30). Similarly Brox ("*Anathema*"), who cites also Irenaeus, *Adv. Haer.* 1.24.4. This interpretation, however, is contested by Pearson ("Did the Gnostics"; *The Pneumatikos-Psychikos Terminology,* 47–50); cf. Conzelmann, *1 Cor,* 205 n. 10. Moreover, it is far from clear that any Gnostics existed in Roman Corinth in the first century, and "the contrast between the heavenly Christ and the earthly Jesus is only attested in much later sources, among Christian Gnostics who were familiar with Paul's letters" (van Unnik, "Jesus," 114).

However, Pliny the Younger, in writing to the emperor Trajan (ca. A.D. 110), tells how he ordered people in his province (Bithynia in Asia Minor) to revile Christ: . . . *praeterea male dicerent Christo, quorum nihil cogi posse dicuntur qui sunt re vera Christiani,* "that they should moreover revile Christ; none of which things those who are truly Christian, it is said, can be induced to do"; . . . *et Christo male dixerunt,* "and they reviled Christ" (*Ep.* 10.96.5–6). Perhaps Paul already knew of similar attempts to revile Christ in Roman Corinth.

Recently, B. W. Winter has made a plea for the interpretation of these verses of 1 Corinthians in light of curse practices of the ancient world, especially of curse tablets discovered in many places of the eastern Mediterranean area and even at Corinth. He cites isolated words from a so-called Corinthian curse tablet "against Karpime Babbia, *Erme chthonie ta megala,*" which he says means " 'Hermes of the Underworld [grant] a curse.' " Hence "it would not be unreasonable to render *anathema Iēsous* as 'Jesus [grants or gives] a curse' " (*After Paul Left,* 175–76). The full text of the inscription is not supplied so that one cannot judge the accuracy of this translation or interpretation; and as Garland has noted, "In none of the inscriptions cited does the word *anathema* occur" (*1 Cor,* 569).

In the long run, the Gnostic anathema, the reviling of Christ mentioned by Pliny, and the curse tablets of the ancient Greek world provide only a generic background for the Pauline phrase, but none of them really helps in the interpretation of the Pauline formula.

In this passage, Paul is instructing Corinthian Christians. He wants them to realize what they have been ignoring or failing to recognize: what comes from the inspiration of God's Spirit and what attraction to dumb idols should mean in their lives. To acknowledge that "Jesus is Lord" is not only to repeat the basic Christian affirmation but to recognize what that has to mean in one's life and conduct, when one lives under such inspiration and for the good of the whole body, of which they are merely members. In order to achieve his purpose, Paul cites an ancient cursing practice to illustrate how one should learn to discern the spirits behind certain customs. Is one being led by God's Spirit or by dumb idols?

NOTES

12:1. *Now, brothers, I do not want you to be uninformed about spiritual gifts.* Lit. "but concerning spiritual things, I do not want you to be ignorant." For *peri de,* see NOTE on 7:1. Paul begins his teaching about "spiritual things" (*tōn pneumatikōn*) with the formulaic introduction to an important topic (*ou thelō hymas agnoein*), which he has already used in 10:1 (see NOTE there). He now softens the use of it by calling the Corinthians *adelphoi*, "fellow-Christians" (see NOTE on 1:1), but he is insisting on their failure to recognize what is at stake; he criticizes their lack of knowledge and their defective understanding.

Since *tōn pneumatikōn* is gen. plur., it could be understood as neut., as in 9:11; 10:3-4; 14:1b, "spiritual things," or as masc., "spiritual persons," as in 2:15; 3:1; 14:37. Seeing that it is introducing chapters dealing with "gifts" (*charismata*, 12:4) and that 14:1 has the neuter, commentators generally understand it here as neut.; hence the translation in the lemma. Some, however, prefer to take it as masc. (J. Weiss, *1 Cor*, 294; Bruce, *1 Cor*, 116; Schmithals, *Gnosticism*, 171-72; Garland, *1 Cor*, 561-64; Ekem, "Spiritual Gifts").

The *pneumatika* come from the Spirit and are meant for the good of the Christian community as a whole. *Pace* Käsemann ("Ministry," 66), it is far from certain that Paul is "taking up and using a technical term of Hellenism" or adopting the terminology of what he calls "the enthusiasts at Corinth." That the word *pneumatika* has been used by Pre-Socratic and other Greek writers is admitted (BDAG, 837), but whether it is used by them in the specific or technical sense meant here is the problem. Moreover, *pneumatika* are not simply to be equated with *charismata*, as do many interpreters (e.g., Kremer, *1 Cor*, 258), using the latter term that is proper in Rom 12:6, but *tōn pneumatikōn* embraces not only *charismata* but also other specific endowments of the Spirit (see vv. 4-6 below).

2. *You realize that, when you were pagans, you were attracted and carried away again and again to dumb idols.* Lit. "you know that, when you were nations." The noun *ethnē* is employed in a specific Jewish sense, for that part of humanity that does not worship the God of Israel, as in LXX Deut 18:9; 2 Kgs 17:8; Wis 14:11; 15:15; Lett Jer 6:4; Rom 3:29; 9:24; 11:13; 15:10 (= LXX Deut 32:43). Paul reacts first to Corinthian Christians of pagan background, as he recalls their former heathen status, just as he addressed other Gentile Christians in 1 Thess 1:9; 4:5; Gal 4:8. It is, however, too much to say, as does Hays (*1 Cor*, 209), that "Gentile Corinthian Christians have now been made part of Israel. . . . become grafted into Israel (cf. Rom. 11:17-24)." That is how Paul will put the matter in Romans, but it does not suit this context.

In contrast to their former status of ignorance, which Paul mentioned in v. 1, he now says (without a connecting particle), *Oidate*, "you know," "you realize." Verse 2 is thus a comment on *agnoein* of v. 1, and in v. 3 he will continue this theme of knowledge, *gnōrizō hymin*, "I make known to you." This link in these three verses is important, because it emphasizes that a Christian too is led to such a confession through knowledge coming from the guiding Spirit.

The syntax of the subordinate clause introduced by *hoti*, "that," is difficult. The fact that *hoti* is followed immediately by the temporal conj. *hote*, "when," is not the problem. The latter introduces a further subordinate clause, "when you were pagans," but its verb *ēte* has to be understood again with the final word in the verse, the ptc. *apagomenoi*, "(you were) being led/carried away (to dumb idols)" in ignorance, which is the verb of the *hoti* clause. That verb is modified further by another subordinate clause, *hōs an ēgesthe*, lit. "as you were attracted/led," where the impf. with *an* is not easily explained. BDF §367 and ZBG §358 explain it as a

substitute for the Classical Greek use of the opt. "for iteration"; hence the translation in the lemma, "were attracted and carried away again and again." Some MSS
(B², F, Gᶜ, 1241) read rather *hōs anēgesthe*, "as you were led up." The verb *apagō*
means "lead away," often by force (Mark 14:44; 15:16); but here it connotes rather
"being led astray" (BDAG, 95). Unfortunately, Paul does not say by whom or by
what, apart from the idols that he calls "dumb," which characteristic such Corinthian Christians did not recognize in their ignorance.

It is often thought that Paul is alluding to orgiastic rites of some pagan cults, in
which participants in a trance were thought to be "led away" or "attracted," i.e.,
possessed by preternatural beings. For instance, the second-century Greek writer,
Lucian of Samosata, depicts Paris, of Homer's *Iliad*, speaking of the power of
love and saying to his comrade at Troy, the commander Protesilaus, "You know
that it is not our choosing, but some powerful being (*daimōn tis*) leads us wherever
it wills, and it is impossible to oppose it" (*Mortuorum dialogi* 27.1 §411). So the
"leading astray" has been interpreted by many commentators, who emphasize
the subordinate clause, "when you were pagans," and neglect the Jewish background of Paul's criticism of idols now said to be "dumb" (Barrett, *1 Cor*, 278–79;
Conzelmann, *1 Cor*, 205; Collins, *1 Cor*, 447; Bassler, "1 Cor 12:3," 417; Kremer,
1 Cor, 258).

"Dumb idols," however, is an echo of Jewish teaching; see Ps 115:5 (LXX
113:12); Hab 2:18–19 (*eidōla kōpha*); 1 Kgs 18:26–29; Bar 6:7; 3 Macc 4:16. Such
"idols" have revealed nothing, since they do not speak, and so cannot contribute
anything that might be considered *pneumatika*. Instead of *aphōna*, "speech-less,
dumb," some MSS (F, G) read *amorpha*, "shape-less, misformed."

This characterization of pagan idols, however, reveals that Paul is not inveighing so much against the ecstatic state of former pagans as he is against their "uninformed" ignorance about the relation of "spiritual things" to the Spirit of God,
which he is trying to correct (without engaging in polemic) by the use of the
knowledge theme that unites these three verses. Paul would be saying that such
former pagans had been led astray unconsciously and unwittingly by their misin-
formation to the worship of idols. Maly ("1 Kor 12,1–3") thinks that there is an ab-
breviated allusion here to the idol worship of Deut 28:36–37. This is why Paul
seeks in v. 3 and later in 12:4–14:40 to set the Corinthians straight and get them to
realize that the basic confession of a Christian is inspired by the Spirit. Once this
is realized, then Corinthian Christians will understand how to assess properly the
variety of gifts that comes from the same Spirit. So basically Méhat ("L'Enseignement"), following in part de Broglie ("Le texte fondamental"), Cornely, and some
medieval interpreters. Similarly, Bassler, ("1 Cor 12:3," 417): "the relationship
between v 2 and v 3 is viewed as one of analogy, not contrast." Paul is appealing to
Corinthian experience, as he tries to instruct them. Vos ("Das Rätsel") would
have us believe that the "riddle" of these three verses is best explained by their
rhetorical function, but that is a forced explanation of what is scarcely there. The
unity of these verses is to be found in their concentration on knowledge and realization, and this is what Paul is stressing: he is "making known" (v. 3) what they
have been "uninformed" about (v. 1).

3. *Therefore, I make known to you that no one who is speaking by the Spirit of God says, "Accursed is Jesus."* Lit. "Jesus (is) anathema," i.e., a curse, which is parallel to the declaration or confession, "Jesus (is) Lord." Paul begins his explanation with *dio*, "therefore," and emphasizes that he is correcting their ignorance, as he cites first a negative, then a positive example of how one discerns the working of the Holy Spirit. He has already spoken of "the Spirit of God" (2:10–11, 14; 7:40 [see NOTE on 2:4]), "the Spirit coming from God" (2:12), "the Spirit of God (that) dwells in you" (3:16), and "the Spirit of our God" (6:11). To this Spirit, now understood as the presence of God in the community (see 12:11), Paul here explicitly refers. He stresses that no one influenced by that Spirit could ever utter anything against Jesus of Nazareth. Paul uses *gnōrizō hymin*, "I make known to you," as in Gal 1:11; 2 Cor 8:1; he will again introduce his discussion with it in 1 Cor 15:1.

"Accursed is Jesus" (*anathema Iēsous*) is a Corinthian slogan, uttered by enemies of the Christian gospel and of the movement that sought to propagate it, even though some prefer to understand it as a literary device fashioned by Paul himself as the opposite of *Kyrios Iēsous* (see the COMMENT above). So also Bassler, who adds that Paul "is drawing on his own personal biography to support his argument" ("1 Cor 12:3," 418), i.e., that Paul as a Jew would have cursed Jesus. Some other commentators relate the slogan to the curse of Deut 21:22–23 ("cursed be everyone who has been hanged on a tree"), as it is applied in Gal 3:13 to Christ crucified, even though the LXX uses *epikataratos*, "cursed," rather than *anathema* (so Lindemann, *1Cor*, 265; Kremer, *1 Cor*, 259; van Unnik, "Jesus," 120–21). The slogan, then, would be that of unbelieving Corinthian Jews who regarded the crucifixion of Jesus as an instance that fell under that Deuteronomic curse.

Because in the second part of this verse *Kyrios Iēsous* is almost universally understood as a declaration, "Jesus is Lord," its counterpart *anathema Iēsous* must also be so understood: hence "Accursed is Jesus" or "Jesus is accursed!" (ESV). It is not to be taken as a wish, "Jesus be cursed!" (RSV), or "Let Jesus be cursed!" (NRSV), even though Paul uses *anathema* as a wish in Rom 9:3; Gal 1:8–9; and 1 Cor 16:22. The declarative form of the slogan is what is meant.

The phrase *anathema Iēsous* combines the name of Jesus of Nazareth with a common imprecation or curse formula, *anathema*. Originally, this Greek word denoted a "votive offering *set up* in a temple" (from *ana + tithēmi*; cf. Luke 21:5 [*v. l.*]; 2 Macc 2:13; Philo, *De Mos.* 1.45 §253). Such dedicated objects came in time to be regarded as taboo, i.e., removed from ordinary use or contact (especially among Jews, under OT influence), and the word connoted a "cursed object." Its earliest occurrence is found in the LXX, where it often renders Hebrew *ḥērem*, "something banned, devoted to destruction": *estai hē polis anathema*, "the city will be a curse" (Josh 6:17); *to onoma tou topou ekeinou Anathema*, "the name of that place 'Curse' " (Num 21:3); its older form, *anathēma*, is found in Deut 7:26; Jdt 16:19; cf. also LXX Lev 27:28–29; Deut 13:13–18. It also occurs in secular Greek curse tablets from Megara (*IG*, 3 §2; cf. MM, 33), and that means that it had spread from its Jewish origin.

and no one can say, "Jesus is Lord," save by the Holy Spirit. I.e., no one can utter the fundamental and traditional Christian confession of faith unless graced by God's Spirit. Thus Paul is reminding the Corinthian Christians that all of them have acknowledged the risen Christ when they turned to him in faith.

Paul's argument makes use of a traditional acclamation and repeats the same idea in a different way in Rom 10:9. This affirmation is enshrined also at the end of the famous pre-Pauline hymn to Christ in Phil 2:11 (see Fitzmyer, "Aramaic Background"). It not only extols the name *Kyrios*, which Paul frequently uses for the risen Christ, but it gives poetic utterance to the basic confession and proclamation of what has already shaped the Christian church, "Jesus is Lord." In that hymn, the church acknowledges that Jesus precisely as the risen Christ is worthy of the same adoration that Isa 45:23 accords to Yahweh (see *EDNT*, 2:328–31). It has often been regarded as derived from a baptismal liturgy (so Bassler, "1 Cor 12:3," 416; Kramer, *Christ, Lord, Son of God*, 65–70; Collins, *1 Cor*, 446). Moreover, as Pearson has noted (*The Pneumatikos-Psychikos Terminology*, 48), Paul makes no distinction here between *Christos* and *Iēsous*: "It is not a matter of variant confessions or variant christologies."

The difference is that no one can make that Christian confession "save by the Holy Spirit," i.e., the faith required to utter it comes only from God's grace, bestowed by His Spirit. See also Rom 8:9; Eph 2:8; 1 John 4:2–3. Paul's mode of argumentation in these three verses is paralleled elsewhere: 1 Thess 4:13–15; 1 Cor 8:1–4; 15:1–4 (see Méhat, "L'Enseignement," 405–8). Holtz ("Kennzeichen") would insist that the only one who can say "Jesus is Lord" is the Christian whose life is faithful to the Lord in obedience; but that is pressing beyond what Paul says in these verses. The manifestation of the Spirit in a Christian's life is not only a matter of confessing, but why that is so, Paul continues to explain in the following passage.

BIBLIOGRAPHY (See also Bibliography on 12:1–14:39)

Bassler, J. M., "1 Cor 12:3—Curse and Confession in Context," *JBL* 101 (1982) 415–18.
Broglie, G. de, "Le texte fondamental de Saint Paul contre la foi naturelle (*I Cor.*, xii,3)," *RSR* 39 (1951) 253–66.
Brox, N., "*Anathema Iēsous* (1 Kor 12,3)," *BZ* 12 (1968) 103–11.
Caddeo, S., "L'opera dello Spirito," *RBR* 8/4 (1973) 59–89.
Chadwick, H., *Origen: Contra Celsum Translated with an Introduction and Notes* (Cambridge: Cambridge University Press, 1953).
Derrett, J. D. M., "Cursing Jesus (I Cor. xii. 3): The Jews as Religious 'Persecutors,' " *NTS* 21 (1974–75) 544–54.
Fitzmyer, J. A., "The Aramaic Background of Philippians 2:6–11," *CBQ* 50 (1988) 470–83; repr. in *According to Paul* (New York: Paulist, 1993) 89–105, 149–51.
———, "Kyrios," *EDNT*, 2:328–31.
Holtz, T., "Das Kennzeichen des Geistes (1 Kor. xii. 1–3)," *NTS* 18 (1971–72) 365–76.
Jenkins, C., "Origen on I Corinthians," *JTS* 9 (1907–8) 231–47, 353–72, 500–514; 10 (1908–9) 29–51.
Kramer, W. R., *Christ, Lord, Son of God*, 65–66, 167–68.

Maly, K., "1 Kor 12, 1–3, eine Regel zur Unterscheidung der Geister?" *BZ* 10 (1966) 82–95.
Méhat, A., "L'Enseignement sur 'les choses de l'Esprit' (1 Corinthiens 12, 1–3)," *RHPR* 63 (1983) 395–415.
Paige, T., "1 Corinthians 12.2: A Pagan *Pompe?*" *JSNT* 44 (1991) 57–65.
Pearson, B. A., "Did the Gnostics Curse Jesus?" *JBL* 86 (1967) 301–5.
Scroggs, R., "The Exaltation of the Spirit by Some Early Christians," *JBL* 84 (1965) 359–73, esp. 365–68.
Silberman, L. H., "Anent the Use of Rabbinic Material," *NTS* 24 (1977–78) 415–17.
Unnik, W. C. van, "Jesus: Anathema or Kyrios (1 Cor. 12: 3)," *Christ and Spirit in the New Testament: In Honour of Charles Francis Digby Moule* (ed. B. Lindars and S. S. Smalley; Cambridge: Cambridge University Press, 1973) 113–26.
Vos, J. S., "Das Rätsel von 1 Kor 12:1–3," *NovT* 35 (1993) 251–69.

BIBLIOGRAPHY ON 12:1–14:39

Baker, D. L., "The Interpretation of 1 Corinthians 12–14," *EvQ* 46 (1974) 224–34.
Bittlinger, A., *Gifts and Graces: A Commentary on I Corinthians 12–14* (London: Hodder and Stoughton, 1967).
Brockhaus, U., *Charisma und Amt: Die paulinische Charismenlehre auf dem Hintergrund der frühchristlichen Gemeindefunktionen* (Wuppertal: Brockhaus, 1972).
Campenhausen, H. von, *Kirchliches Amt und geistliche Vollmacht in den ersten drei Jahrhunderten* (BHT 14; Tübingen: Mohr [Siebeck], 1953) 32–65.
Carson, D. A., *Showing the Spirit: A Theological Exposition of 1 Corinthians 12–14* (Grand Rapids: Baker, 1987).
Dominy, B., "Paul and Spiritual Gifts: Reflections on I Corinthians 12–14," *SwJT* 26/1 (1983–84) 49–68.
Dunn, J. D. G., *Jesus and the Spirit: A Study of the Religious and Charismatic Experience of Jesus and the First Christians as Reflected in the New Testament* (London: SCM, 1975).
Dupont, J., "Dimension du problème des charismes dans 1 Co 12–14," *Charisma und Agape* (ed. L. de Lorenzi), 7–21.
Ekem, J. D., " 'Spiritual Gifts' or 'Spiritual Persons'? 1 Corinthians 12:1a Revisited," *Neotestamentica* 38 (2004) 54–74.
Ellis, E. E., *Prophecy and Hermeneutic in Early Christianity: New Testament Essays* (WUNT 18; Tübingen: Mohr [Siebeck], 1978) 23–44.
Fee, G. D., "Tongues—Least of the Gifts? Some Exegetical Observations on 1 Corinthians 12–14," *Pneuma* 2 (1980) 2–14.
Fraikin, D., " 'Charismes et ministères' à la lumière de *1 Co* 12–14," *ÉgT* 9 (1978) 455–63.
Frid, B., "Structure and Argumentation in 1 Cor 12," *SEA* 60 (1995) 95–113.
Heckel, U., "Paulus und die Charismatiker: Zur theologischen Einordnung der Geistesgaben in 1Kor 12–14," *TBei* 23 (1992) 117–38.
Jackson, T. A., "Concerning Spiritual Gifts: A Study of I Corinthians 12," *FM* 7/1 (1989) 61–69.
Lampe, P., "The Corinthian Worship Services in Corinth and the Corinthian Enthusiasm (*1 Cor. 12–14*)," *Affirmation* 4/2 (1991) 17–25.
MacGorman, J. W., "Glossolalic Error and Its Correction: 1 Corinthians 12–14," *RevExp* 80 (1983) 389–400.

Martin, D. B., "Tongues of Angels and Other Status Indicators," *JAAR* 59 (1991) 547–89.

Martin, R. P., *The Spirit and the Congregation: Studies in 1 Corinthians 12–15* (Grand Rapids: Eerdmans, 1984).

McEleney, N. J., "Gifts Serving Christ's Body," *TBT* 33 (1995) 134–37.

Mills, W. E., "Early Ecstatic Utterances and Glossolalia," *PRSt* 24 (1997) 29–40.

Osborn, E., "Spirit and Charisma," *Colloquium* 7/1 (1974) 30–41.

Patrick, J., "Insights from Cicero on Paul's Reasoning in 1 Corinthians 12–14: Love Sandwich or Five Course Meal?" *TynBul* 55 (2004) 43–64.

Perrot, C., "Charisme et institution chez Saint Paul," *RSR* 71 (1983) 81–92.

Pesce, M., "L'Apostolo di fronte alla crescita pneumatica dei Corinti (1Cor 12–14): Tentativo di un'analisi storica della funzione apostolica," *Cristianesimo nella Storia* 3 (1982) 1–39.

Robinson, D. W. B., "Charismata versus Pneumatika: Paul's Method of Discussion," *RTR* 31 (1972) 49–55.

Röhser, G., "Übernatürliche Gaben? Zur aktuellen Diskussion um die paulinische Charismen-Lehre," *TZ* 52 (1996) 243–65.

Rowe, A. J., "1 Corinthians 12–14: The Use of a Text for Christian Worship," *EvQ* 77 (2005) 119–28.

Schatzmann, S. S., *A Pauline Theology of Charismata* (Peabody, MA: Hendrckson, 1987).

———, "Purpose and Function of Gifts in 1 Corinthians," *SwJT* 45 (2002) 53–68.

Scippa, V., "I carismi per la vitalità della chiesa: Studio esegetico su 1Cor 12–14; Rm 12, 6–8; Ef 4, 11–13; 1 Pt 4, 10–11," *Asprenas* 38 (1991) 5–25.

Seyer, H. D., *The Stewardship of Spiritual Gifts: A Study of First Corinthians, Chapters Twelve, Thirteen, and Fourteen and the Charismatic Movement* (Madison: FAS, 1974).

Shepherd, W. D., *The Corinthian Church and the Gifts of the Holy Spirit* (Houston: Armstrong, 1996).

Smalley, S. S., "Spiritual Gifts and I Corinthians 12–16," *JBL* 87 (1968) 427–33.

Talbert, C. H., "Paul's Understanding of the Holy Spirit: The Evidence of 1 Corinthians 12–14," *PRSt* 11/4 (1984) 95–108.

Thomas, R. L., *Understanding Spiritual Gifts: A Verse-by-Verse Study of 1 Corinthians 12–14* (Chicago: Moody, 1978; 2d ed.; Grand Rapids: Kregel, 1999).

Trummer, P., "Charismatischer Gottesdienst: Liturgische Impulse aus 1 Kor 12 und 14," *BLit* 54/3 (1981) 173–78.

26   b. *The Variety of the Gifts and the One Spirit (12:4–11)*

12:4There are different sorts of gifts, but the same Spirit; 5there are different sorts of service, but the same Lord; 6there are different sorts of work, but the same God, who produces all of them in everyone. 7To each individual is given the manifestation of the Spirit for some good. 8To one is given through the Spirit the utterance of wisdom; to another, the utterance of knowledge through the same Spirit; 9to another, faith by the same Spirit, and to another, gifts of healing by that one

Spirit; [10] to another, the working of mighty deeds; to another, prophecy; to another, discernment of spirits; to another, kinds of tongues; to another, the interpretation of tongues. [11] But one and the same Spirit produces all these, bestowing them individually on each one as it wills.

COMMENT

Paul continues his discussion of *ta pneumatika* recognized to be at work in the Corinthian community. He has just given a negative and positive way of recognizing the genuine influence of the Spirit, but now he realizes how diverse the manifestations of the Spirit can be and wants Corinthian Christians to acknowledge their real source and unique character so that the diversity of gifts may not become detrimental to the unity of the community. As Käsemann has seen it, "This is Paul's way of putting an end to the confusion" in Corinth, for he is stressing that "*Pneuma* is the power of the Transcendent and therefore the community which received this *Pneuma* is, according to I Cor. 2.9ff., the place of the presence of the heavenly reality in our world. . . . *Pneuma* is for Paul . . . the power of the Resurrection because it is the power of the Risen One" ("Ministry," 67–68). The diversity of the Spirit's endowments, however, must serve the common "good" (*pros to sympheron*, v. 7).

When Paul lists the *pneumatika*, in addition to *charismata*, "gifts," *diakoniai*, "services," and *energēmata*, "works" (vv. 4–6), he mentions nine more of them: utterance of wisdom, utterance of knowledge, faith, healing, miracle working, prophecy, discernment of spirits, speaking in tongues, and interpretation of such speech (vv. 8–10). This list of *pneumatika* (12:4–10) is similar to other lists in the Pauline corpus: 12:28–30; Rom 12:6–8; cf. Eph 4:11. In general, no two lists agree in content, and the order of the endowments is not the same; hence no significance can be attributed to the order. In this list (12:4–10), in particular, the order is of little significance, except that tongues and their interpretation are at the bottom of it, as they will be again in 12:28–30. Some commentators note the introductory prons. in the dat., *hō*, "to one" (v. 8a), *allō*, "to another" (vv. 8b, 9b, 10abce), and *heterō*, "to (still) another" (vv. 9a, 10d), and try to use the last two as signs setting off the last two classes, but no clear division is thus achieved, and the diversity of attempts to classify them shows the futility of it.

The way in which the *pneumatika* are expressed in the Greek text, sometimes by names of persons so endowed, sometimes as abstract abilities or actions, is strange and difficult to render accurately in English; so the reader is forewarned about differences in modern translations of the lists. All are gifts of the Spirit freely endowed, but not all involve dramatic action or emotional experience. Three significant endowments, however, "apostles," "prophets," and "teachers" are numbered explicitly (see below; cf. Nardoni, "The Concept").

"Kinds of tongues" (12:10) was a phenomenon in the early church that is not easy to understand. Because it is absent from the lists in Romans and Ephesians and because Paul puts it and the interpretation of it at the end of two of his lists of *pneumatika* in this chapter and devotes a considerable amount of space to them in

14:1–33, he clearly had many difficulties with this phenomenon in the Corinthian community, even though he recognized it as a gift of the Spirit. Indeed, it is undoubtedly the main reason why he takes up the whole question of *pneumatika* at this point in his letter (see Mitchell, *Paul*, 270).

Noteworthy in this pericope is the way Paul describes the different *pneumatika*, either as *charismata*, "gifts," *diakoniai*, "services," or *enērgēmata*, "works," and the way he ascribes them, whatever their diversity, to the Spirit, the Lord, and God (= the Father). This triadic source of *ta pneumatika* is thus an important Pauline contribution to the doctrine of the Trinity, to be formulated fully in the patristic period. Nowhere, however, in his letters does Paul have a clear notion of the Spirit as a person. Cf. 2 Cor 13:13(14) for another Pauline contribution to that developing doctrine.

In recent decades one has heard often about "charismatics" among Christians of various denominations and their emphasis on speaking in tongues and other phenomena as manifestations of intense religious experience ascribed to the Spirit. Yet, as R. E. Brown asks, "Are charismatics today experiencing what is described in I Cor 12?" (*Introduction*, 532).

NOTES

12:4. *There are different sorts of gifts, but the same Spirit.* Lit. "diverse allotments (*diaireseis* [this noun occurs only here in the NT]) of gifts," i.e., a different disposition, assignment of them. Though they come from the one Spirit, they are allotted differently; though from one source, they are diverse in kind.

Paul has already used *charisma* in the sense of a "favor bestowed" or "gift" in 1:7 and 7:7 (sexual continence). Here and in v. 31 he employs the plur. generically to denote nonmaterial endowments coming from "the same Spirit," i.e., the one just mentioned in 12:3, which enables all Christians, Jewish and Gentile alike, to acknowledge the risen Christ as "Lord." In vv. 9, 28, 30, the plur. appears again, but with a specific modifier, *charismata iamatōn*, thus denoting a special kind of charism. For other ways in which Paul uses the noun *charisma*, see Rom 1:11; 5:15–16; 6:23; 11:29; 2 Cor 1:11; in none of these passages does it have the specific nuance it has in vv. 9, 28, 30 of this passage. Moreover, in Rom 12:6, Paul plays on the similarity of *charisma* to *charis*, "grace," words which are etymologically only remotely related, in order to stress how *charismata* denote specific participations of individual Christians in God's grace; in fact, some of the individual endowments mentioned there as *charismata* are callled here generically *pneumatika* (see *Romans*, 646–47). Furthermore, the word *charisma* is never used for a gift that one human being gives to another, but always denotes a divine gift (Rom 11:29; 1 Cor 7:7; 12:28). Here *charismata* are specific forms of *pneumatika*, distinct from those to be mentioned in vv. 5–6.

5. *there are different sorts of service, but the same Lord.* Paul sets *diakoniai* apart from *charismata*, even though *diakoniai* are also forms of *pneumatika*.. The *diakonia*, "service" or "ministry," that a Christian is equipped to perform within the community, comes from the one *Kyrios*, viz., the risen Christ, acknowledged in

the confession of 12:3, and to continue his work. The *diakonia* denotes not a service to the community, but a service rendered within it to God. Cf. Rom 12:7, where Paul speaks of community service as *diakonia*. In 1 Cor 3:5, *diakonos* was used of a special minister (Apollos or Paul); in 16:15, *diakonia* will describe the ministry of Stephanas and his household; in 2 Cor 4:1; 5:18; 6:3 it designates Paul's own ministry. The word, however, does not yet have the special connotation (deacon) that it may have in Phil 1:1 and will acquire still later in 1 Tim 3:8, 12; Ignatius, *Ephes.* 2.1; *Smyrn.* 8.1 (see J. N. Collins, *Diakonia*, 232–33).

Hence, *pace* Käsemann, *diakoniai* are not "interchangeable with the charismata" ("Ministry," 65; 69 [mistakenly related to *klēsis*, "calling"]; 71 [mistakenly related to "household codes"]). If they were interchangeable, why does Paul separate them (employing *diaireseis* three times), ascribe them to different sources, and in each case use *to auto* or *ho autos*? Nor do the *charismata* related to God's call of Israel in Rom 11:29 have anything to do with *diakoniai* or other gifts accorded to Christians in this context. Moreover, those mentioned in 1 Cor 7:7 can only be cited here with a great manipulation of context. The list of ministries or "different charismata" that Käsemann gives (ibid., 69) is simply overdrawn (see J. N. Collins, "Ministry"; Vanhoye, *I Carismi*, 29, 54).

6. *there are different sorts of work, but the same God, who produces all of them in everyone.* Lit. "the one producing all. . . ." *Energēma*, which occurs only here and in v. 10 in the NT, denotes a "work" or "task" different from the *diakoniai* of v. 5, but something that one performs to promote the good of the community, as do the other forms of *pneumatika*. An example of such *energēmata* is given in v. 10, "the working of mighty deeds," and perhaps others in v. 28 (*antilēmpseis, kybernēseis,* "assistants, administrators").

Such "works" are produced in Christians by *Theos*, "God," meaning "the Father," as often in the NT (e.g., 2 Cor 3:3; 5:18; 13:12; Rom 5:11). Note how the expression *ho autos theos*, "the same God," which follows upon *to auto pneuma* (v. 4), and *ho autos kyrios* (v. 5), links the three sources of the different *pneumatika* triadically.

Even though the last clause in the verse modifies only "God," it could just as easily have been added at the end of vv. 4 and 5 as well. The verb *energein*, "work in," "produce," is found elsewhere of God's activity (Gal 2:8; 3:5; Phil 2:13). Paul is not trying to explain the differences among *charismata, diakoniai,* and *energēmata*, but asserting rather the uniqueness of the triadic divine source of such spiritual realities in the Christian community, as diverse as they may be.

7. *To each individual is given the manifestation of the Spirit for some good.* The diverse *pneumatika* listed in vv. 4–6 are now summed up as "the manifestation of the Spirit," and their purpose is expressed as *pros to sympheron*, lit. "in accordance with what is advantageous" (BDF §239.8), i.e., to the community (*sympheron* being the substantivized neut. pres. ptc. of *sympherō*). Paul's contrasting emphasis falls on the first and last words, "to each" and "for the good" (of all in the community, as the context makes clear, and not merely for the good of the individual to whom the endowment is allotted). "Each" denotes not only diversity, but also individuality, for Paul thinks indeed that "every last person in the community" is so

endowed, *pace* Fee (*1 Cor*, 389); that is what *ekastō* at the head of the verse means. Paul is implying that no one in the community has a monopoly on the Spirit, to the neglect of others; the Spirit works in all, but in different ways.

The noun *phanerōsis*, "manifestation," is important, for Paul is not speaking only of the internal gifts of the Spirit but of the external signs of the presence and activity of the Spirit within the community. The "manifestation" is not different from the "fruit" of the Spirit (Gal 5:22). *Phanerōsis* occurs also in 2 Cor 4:2 with an obj. gen., "manifestation of the truth," and so the question is: Is the gen. *pneumatos* to be taken here as obj., i.e., that the gift manifests the Spirit (to others in the community); or as subj., i.e., what the Spirit manifests in the gift given? Either sense would suit the context. In the following verses (8–10), Paul will spell out in detail a list of further manifestations.

8. *To one is given through the Spirit the utterance of wisdom.* This verse further explains v. 7, in that it repeats the same verb (*didotai*) and now illustrates "each individual" as "one" and "another." The phrase *logos sophias*, "an utterance of wisdom," would mean the power to communicate profound Christian truths to others, because Paul is not speaking merely of the internal gift, but the way it is manifested. It is probably the wisdom of which Paul spoke in 2:6–13 (God's wisdom hidden in a mystery). Smalley ("Spiritual Gifts," 428) relates this endowment specifically to the "apostles" of 12:28–29, but there is no reason so to restrict it. For an attempt to line up the individual manifestations in vv. 8–10, 28–29 in parallel columns, see Garland, *1 Cor*, 580; the attempt reveals more the diversity than the similarity of them and that Paul was scarcely trying to construct such a parallel.

to another, the utterance of knowledge through the same Spirit. How the communication of *gnōsis* now mentioned by Paul differs from that of *sophia* of the first clause is not easy to say, especially since both have their source in the Spirit. Wisdom has already been explained as related to the hidden designs of God (2:6–13), whereas knowledge may mean such elementary truths as knowing that "an idol is nothing at all in this world" (6:4). In 13:2, *gnōsis* will reappear in a list between "prophecy" and "mysteries," on the one hand, and "the faith to move mountains," on the other; and again in 14:6 between "revelation" and "prophecy and instruction." Although Paul sometimes speaks negatively of *gnōsis* (8:1, 7, 10, 11; 13:8), he also speaks positively of it (1:5; 2 Cor 2:14; 4:6; 6:6; 8:7; 10:5; 11:6). So it seems to connote some basic awareness given to Christians, perhaps analogous to the occult knowledge said to be associated with mystery religions in the ancient world of Paul's time.

9. *to another, faith by the same Spirit.* Since this *pistis* denotes a special kind of *pneumatika* given only to some individuals, it cannot have the normal Pauline sense of response to the gospel (as in Rom 10:8, "the word of faith that we preach"; 10:9–10, 17), as Lindemann (*1 Cor*, 267) prefers to interpret it, maintaining that Paul does not distinguish levels of faith. Rather it is "the faith to move mountains" (1 Cor 13:2; cf. Matt 17:20; 21:21; BDAG, 820; Kremer, *1 Cor*, 264; Garland, *1 Cor*, 581), or perhaps "a faith especially effective in sustaining others" (Brown, *Introduction*, 531 n. 59).

to another, gifts of healing by that one Spirit. I.e., *charismata*, "gifts" resulting in different kinds of cures (*iamata*), as in vv. 28, 30 below. Early Christians are depicted praying in Acts 4:30 for power to do so, where the related noun *iasis*, "ability to cure," occurs. See Acts 3:1–10; 5:15, for accounts of such healings. Instead of *heni pneumati*, "by (that) one Spirit," some MSS (ℵ, C³, D, F, G) read *autō*, "the same," but that is a copyist's harmonization with v. 9a.

10. *to another, the working of mighty deeds.* Lit. "workings of powers," i.e., miracles undoubtedly different from healings of v. 9b; see vv. 28–29 below (without *energēmata*). Some MSS (P⁴⁶, D, F, G) read rather *energeia dynameōs*, "working of power." The word *dynamis*, "power, might," especially in the plur. (*dynameis*), is often used in the NT for the wondrous deeds or miracles of Jesus recounted in the Gospels (Mark 6:2; Matt 7:22; 11:20, 21, 23; 13:54, 58; Luke 10:13; 19:37); cf. Acts 2:22; 10:38. For such deeds within the Christian community, see 1 Thess 1:5; Gal 3:5; 2 Cor 12:12; Acts 19:11.

to another, prophecy. I.e., dynamic, effective, and hortatory preaching of the gospel as a gift of the Spirit (see NOTE on 11:4). It is listed again in vv. 28–29 below, but as "prophets," and as the first of the *charismata* in Rom 12:6; cf. 1 Cor 13:2, 8. The Christian sense of this word has to be set over against the use of *prophēteia* and *prophētēs* in the contemporary Greek world, where *prophēteia* denoted the "gift of interpreting the will of the gods," or "an oracular response," often given in a trance or ecstasy. Lucian even calls it *diēs phrenos estin aporrōx*, "a portion broken off of the divine mind" (*Alex.* 40, 60; LSJ, 1539). The prophet, (Gk. *ho prophētēs*) was the agent who did so (but cf. *TDNT*, 6:784, for the dates when these Greek words are attested [*prophēteia* only in 2d cent. A.D.]). Such a Greek usage may have influenced the Christian understanding of the term, but it has to be related also to that of the LXX, and especially to the OT meaning of "prophecy," which per se has nothing to do with predicting the future (even though that might be involved on occasion). It was considered a gift of the Spirit (e.g., Ezek 2:2–3), but also as something that was dying out in Israel (see Ps 74:9; Dan 3:38; 1 Macc 9:27). Now it is understood as reappearing among Christians in a new form.

Prophēteia is a combination of prep. *pro*, " in front of, in place of," and *phēmi*, "speak," an utterance made for God; *prophētēs*, "one who speaks for someone else," i.e., a spokesperson or mouthpiece of God. The OT sense is seen in Exod 4:10–16: Moses, having been told by God to go to speak to the Hebrews in Egypt, protests that he is slow of speech and not eloquent enough. Moses is told to take his brother Aaron with him; "you shall speak to him and put the words in his mouth, and I will be with your mouth and his mouth. . . . He shall speak for you to the people; he shall be a mouth for you, and you shall be to him as God." Cf. Jer 1:9; 2 Sam 12:25; but NT prophecy has none of the trance or ecstasy sometimes associated with prophecy in the OT (e.g., Num 11:25–29; 1 Sam 10:6, 10–11). Hence the Christian sense of the word "prophecy" has to be understood as a Spirit-inspired dynamic and effective preaching of the Scriptures and the gospel, as Paul makes clear below, in 14:1, 3–6, 24, 29, 31 (see Aune, *Prophecy*, 256–58; Grudem, *Gift of Prophecy*).

to another, discernment of spirits. Lit. "discernings of spirits," i.e., various abilities to evaluate and distinguish the origin of diverse promptings in life (now named *pneumata*), whether they come from God, or Satan, or other human beings. The phrase, *diakriseis pneumatōn*, occurs only here in the Greek Bible, and such *pneumata* must not be confused with *pneumatika* (v. 1), which have already been presented as the gifts of the Holy Spirit. These *pneumata* are derived at times from the "human spirit" (2:11; cf. related expressions in 2:11–16; 14:29, also 1 Thess 5:19–22; 1 John 4:1, which speak differently of the same activity). Later, *Did.* 11.7–10 speaks of such discernment applied to prophets:

> [7] Do not test or evaluate every prophet who speaks with spirit (*en pneumati*), 'for every sin will be forgiven, but not this one' [Matt 12:31]. [8] Yet not everyone who speaks with spirit is a prophet, unless he has the ways (*tropous*) of the Lord. From their ways, then, the false prophet and the (real) prophet will be known. [9] No prophet who orders a meal (*horizōn trapezan*) with spirit will eat of it; otherwise he is a false prophet. [10] Every prophet who teaches the truth, if he does not do what he teaches, is a false prophet.

See further Therrien, *Discernement.* The discernment, however, should not be limited to prophets, because there is no indication in the text that Paul so intended such a gift (*pace* Martucci "*Diakriseis*"). The attempt made by Dautzenberg ("Zum religionsgeschichtlichen Hintergrund") to interpret *diakriseis pneumatōn* as "interpretations of the revelations of the Spirit" is far from correct, because *diakrisis* does not mean "interpretation," but rather "distinguishing, differentiation" (BDAG, 231), e.g., of good and evil. It is a term for evaluation, as Grudem ("A Response") has shown.

to another, kinds of tongues. Whereas Paul used *hō men gar*, "to one," followed by several instances of *allō de*, "to another," in vv. 8–10abc, he now switches to asyndetic *heterō*, to express "to (still) another" (v. 10d), as he introduces this endowment of the Spirit.

The phrase, *genē glōssōn*, "kinds of tongues" or "kinds of language," occurs again only in v. 28. By *glōssa* Paul does not mean the anatomical "tongue" of a human being, the organ for eating and talking, but he uses it figuratively of "speech, language." Theoretically, *genē glōssōn* could denote different foreign languages spoken by human beings (*xenologia*), but, in referring it to *pneumatikon*, someone who speaks in such "tongues," Paul means vocal utterances of unusual nature not understood by others, as it becomes clear in chap. 14. Sometimes he calls them simply *glōssai*, "tongues" (12:10e, 30; 13:1, 8; 14:5a, 5c, 6, 18, 22, 23, 39 [often with the verb *laleō*, "speak"]), sometimes in the sing. *glōssa*, "tongue" (14:2, 4, 9, 13, 14, 19, 26, 27 [often with *laleō*]). Since no article precedes the noun, an idiomatic usage is being employed.

Part of the problem in understanding the idiom is its origin. Is the expression *glōssais lalein*, "speak in tongues," ever used before Paul? Some commentators think that it was "a common Semitic idiom" (Engelbrecht, " 'To Speak,' " 295). Reference is made to Isa 28:11, a verse that Paul quotes in 14:21, "By people speaking strange tongues and by lips of foreigners will I speak to this people." In its LXX form it has *dia glōssēs heteras . . . lalousin,* "through another (*or* different) tongue . . . they will speak"; similarly Isa 19:18, which also uses the words of speaking a foreign language. In five other passages of the LXX, *glōssa* and *lalein* occur together (Jer 9:4; Job 33:2; Pss 37:30; 39:4; 109:2), but they are all instances of the anatomical "tongue" uttering something (justice, truth, lies), nothing unintelligible. In QL, moreover, a phrase of Isa 28:11 is applied figuratively to the Seekers after Smooth Things who speak "with uncircumcised lip and an alien tongue" to mislead "the men of truth," i.e., the members of the comunity (1QH[a] 10[old 2]:18–19; similarly 12[old 4]:16). There are, then, in earlier Jewish writings metaphorical instances of "tongue" and "to speak" combined. Engelbrecht also cites later rabbinic examples from the Mishnah and the targums (ibid., 300–302), but none of them has the meaning used in chaps. 12 and 14 of this letter (see also Harrisville, "Speaking in Tongues").

A phenomenon related to such speaking in tongues is described later in Acts 2:4–11; 10:45–46; 19:6. There the nature of the phenomenon is complicated by Luke's description of the effect of the Spirit on Pentecost: "They began to speak in *other* tongues" (2:4), which for most commentators means *xenologia,* "speaking in foreign tongues," a miraculous phenomenon that suits the first Christian pentecostal situation (recall the many nations listed in Acts 2:6–11; cf. *Acts,* 239). Elsewhere in Acts, however, Luke describes speaking in tongues (10:45–46; 19:6) in a way similar to what Paul mentions in 1 Corinthians 12 and 14. Apart from these Pauline and Lucan passages, the phenomenon is not known elsewhere in the NT, although some interpreters try to understand "new tongues" (in the late, longer ending of the Marcan Gospel, 16:17) in this way.

From the words Paul uses in 12:30 (*glōssais lalousin*) is formed the commonly used modern term, "glossolalia," which appears nowhere in Pauline writings or in any patristic writer; it is not found in standard Greek dictionaries (LSJ, Lampe, Sophocles, Bailly). The closest form one can find is *glōssologia,* a noun used by the fifth-century rhetorician, Procopius of Gaza (*Prov.* 10:31; PG 87.1321D), meaning "chatter."

In general, patristic interpreters understood Pauline *genē glōssōn* as xenologia (as in Acts 2:4), or at times as "angelic tongues" (as in 1 Cor 13:1); see Parmentier, "Zungenreden." The latter term is also used by some modern commentators to explain *genē glōssōn* (D. B. Martin, "Tongues"; Dunn, *Jesus and the Spirit,* 243–44), but no one can say what that means, because no one knows whether angels have tongues. In 13:1 Paul uses "angelic tongues" in irony, and so it is better avoided in the discussion of Paul's phrase here.

From these NT passages come the two main ways in which the phrase *genē glōssōn* is understood today: (1) as utterances made outside the normal patterns of intelligible speech (BDAG, 201–2), sometimes translated as "ecstatic utterance" (NEB), "various ecstatic utterances" (Goodspeed), or "the strange speech of persons in religious ecstasy" (BDAG, 201); and (2) as foreign, unintelligible human utterances. These two ways are formulated differently by various commentators; for a useful survey, see Cartledge, "Nature and Function."

A reason for espousing the first explanation is given by Conzelmann, who maintains:

> The designation glōssai, 'tongues,' tells us nothing about the phenomenon. If we would explain it, then we must set out from comparable material in the history of religion, above all from the Greek motif of the inspiring pneuma, which is expressed in Mantic sources, and is bound up more particularly with Delphi. The deity speaks out of the inspired man's mouth; he himself does not know what he is saying. In Delphi the priests interpret the Pythia's babblings (1 Cor, 234).

Conzelmann further cites Heraclitus, Frag. 92:

> Sibylla de mainomenō stomati agelasta kai akallōpista kai amyrista phthengomenē chiliōn etōn exikneitai tē phōnē dia ton theon,

> The Sibyl with raving mouth uttering her unlaughing, unadorned, unincensed words reaches out over a thousand years with her voice, through the (inspiration of the) god.

It is, however, a matter of no little debate, whether Paul means anything like the "ecstatic utterance" of the contemporary Greco-Roman world, even if it is so understood in NEB and by Harrisville, "Speaking"; Tuland, "Confusion," 209.

Other interpreters insist rather on the second meaning, "the miraculously given ability to speak a human language foreign to the speaker" (Gundry, " 'Ecstatic' "); similarly Davies, Greene, and Engelbrecht, who notes, "While examples of ecstatic speech are common [in Greek literature outside the NT], the expression 'to speak in a tongue' is essentially unknown in pre-Christian Greek apart from the passages in the Septuagint mentioned above" (" 'To Speak,' "296). That has to be recalled in light of what Conzelmann has written above. From the way Paul speaks of this phenomenon in the rest of this chap. and in chap. 14, however, it seems best to recognize it as some form of noncommunicative utterance or incoherent babbling.

The trouble with these explanations is that they describe, on the one hand, the psychological state of the speaker, and, on the other, the speech product (foreign language), which is a problematic mixture, like comparing apples and oranges (see Poythress, "The Nature"). Whatever the meaning of the phrase, Paul recognizes the phenomenon as a spiritual gift to individuals in the Christian community (12:10, 30), as an endowment or manifestation of the Spirit (12:7, 11). He will have more to say about it in chap. 14, and his treatment of it in this letter shows how little he esteems it, as he has to deal with this specific Corinthian phenomenon. In v. 30, Paul asks whether pantes glōssais lalousin, "all speak in tongues," which implies that all do not, but which also gives meaning to the phrase used here: some do so talk. His further treatment of this phenomenon is found in 13:1; 14:2–33, 39, and in 13:8c he even predicts that it "will come to an end." Significantly, he makes no mention of it among the *charismata* he lists in Rom 12:6–8, and it does not appear in Eph 4:11.

For various analyses of the modern phenomenon of glossolalia, see Fabbro, "Prospettive"; Goodman, *Speaking in Tongues*; Hoekema, *What about Tongue-Speaking?*; Kildahl, *Psychology*; Landes and Koop, "Sociolinguistic Exploration"; E. D. Mills, *Speaking*; Samarin, *Tongues of Men and Angels*. That the modern phenomenon has anything to do with what Paul is talking about is a question not easily answered, especially in light of what he says in 13:8c.

to another, the interpretation of tongues. This endowment is related to the preceding one and implies that what is spoken in tongues can be put into articulate speech. Such articulation would be required, when speaking in tongues occurs in a community assembly; it may even be a special kind of discernment. Since the tongue utterance is presumably intelligible to the speaker, and to him or her alone, someone else endowed with this related gift would have to be on hand to articulate whatever pertinence the mysterious utterance might have for the community (see Thiselton, "Interpretation"). It might even be given to the speakers themselves, but then what guarantee would there be of the objective reality of either endowment, the "tongues" or the "interpretation"?

11. *But one and the same Spirit produces all these, bestowing them individually on each one as it wills.* "All these" (*panta de tauta*) stands in emphatic position at the head of the sentence, summing up the endowments that Paul has set forth in vv. 4–10. What was said above about "God" (v. 6b) is repeated about God's Spirit, now said to be "one and the same," a combination of the two modifiers used in v. 9. Paul's stress is on "all these" gifts in order to show that such characteristics that individual Christians possess are not personal achievements, but endowments derived solely from a divine source (Spirit, Lord, or Father) and destined for the good (12:7) of the whole community, which Paul will now proceed to explain in greater detail.

BIBLIOGRAPHY (See Bibliography on 12:1–14:39, pp. 461–62)

Best, E., "The Interpretation of Tongues," *SJT* 28 (1975) 45–62.

———, "Prophets and Preachers," *SJT* 12 (1959) 129–50.

Buonaiuti, E., "I carismi," *Ricerche religiose* 4 (1928) 259–61.

Callan, T., "Prophecy and Ecstasy in Greco-Roman Religion and in 1 Corinthians," *NovT* 27 (1985) 125–40.

Cartledge, M. J., "The Nature and Function of New Testament Glossolalia," *EvQ* 72 (2000) 135–50.

Collins, J. N., *Diakonia: Re-interpreting the Ancient Sources* (Oxford/New York: Oxford University Press, 1990).

———, "Ministry as a Distinct Category among Charismata (1 Corinthians 12:4–7)," *Neotestamentica* 27 (1993) 79–91.

Cothenet, E., "Prophétisme dans le Nouveau Testament," *DBSup*, 8:1222–1337.

Currie, S. D., " 'Speaking in Tongues': Early Evidence Outside the New Testament Bearing on 'Glōssais Lalein,' " *Int* 19 (1965) 274–94.

Dautzenberg, G., *Urchristliche Prophetie: Ihre Erforschung, ihre Voraussetzungen im Judentum und ihre Struktur im ersten Korintherbrief* (BWANT 104; Stuttgart: Kohlhammer, 1975).

———, "Zum religionsgeschichtlichen Hintergrund der *diakrisis pneumatōn* (1 Kor 12,10)," *BZ* 15 (1971) 93–104.

Davies, J. G., "Pentecost and Glossolalia," *JTS* 3 (1952) 228–31.

Doldán, F. L., "Consideraciones bíblicas sobre los carismas," *RevistB* 64 (2002) 61–67.

Engelbrecht, E. A., " 'To Speak in a Tongue': The Old Testament and Early Rabbinic Background of a Pauline Expression," *ConcJ* 22 (1996) 295–302.

Esler, P. F., "Glossolalia and the Admission of Gentiles into the Early Christian Community," *BTB* 22 (1992) 136–42.

Fabbro, F., "Prospettive d'interpretazione della glossolalia paolina sotto il profilo della neurolinguistica," *RivB* 46 (1998) 157–78.

Fascher, E., *Prophētēs: Eine sprach- und religionsgeschichtliche Untersuchung* (Giessen: Töpelmann, 1927) 184–86.

Forbes, C., "Early Christian Inspired Speech and Hellenistic Popular Religion," *NovT* 28 (1986) 257–70.

———, *Prophecy and Inspired Speech in Early Christianity and Its Hellenistic Environment* (WUNT 2/75; Tübingen: Mohr [Siebeck], 1995; repr. Peabody, MA: Hendrickson, 1997).

Gillespie, T. W., *The First Theologians: A Study in Early Christian Prophecy* (Grand Rapids: Eerdmans, 1995) 97–164.

Goodman, F. D., "Phonetic Analysis of Glossolalia in Four Cultural Settings," *JSSR* 8 (1969) 227–39.

———, *Speaking in Tongues: A Cross-Cultural Study of Glossolalia* (Chicago: University of Chicago Press, 1972).

Greene, D., "The Gift of Tongues," *BSac* 22 (1865) 99–126.

Grudem, W. A., *The Gift of Prophecy in 1 Corinthians* (Washington, DC: University Press of America, 1982).

———, "A Response to Gerhard Dautzenberg on 1 Cor. 12,10," *BZ* 22 (1978) 253–70.

Gundry, R. H., " 'Ecstatic Utterance' (N.E.B.)?" *JTS* 17 (1966) 299–307.

Harrisville, R. A., "Speaking in Tongues: A Lexicographical Study," *CBQ* 38 (1976) 35–48.

Hill, D., *New Testament Prophecy* (Atlanta: John Knox, 1979) 118–40.

Hoekema, A. A., *What about Tongue-Speaking?* (Grand Rapids: Eerdmans, 1966).

House, H. W., "Tongues and the Mystery Religions of Corinth," *BSac* 140 (1983) 134–50.

Johnson, L. T., "Glossolalia and the Embarrassments of Experience," *PSB* 18 (1997) 113–34.

Käsemann, E., "Ministry and Community in the New Testament," *Essays*, 63–94.

Kildahl, J. P., *The Psychology of Speaking in Tongues* (New York: Harper & Row, 1972).

Knudsen, R. E., "Speaking in Tongues," *Foundations* 9 (1966) 43–57.

Landes, J., and T. J. Koop, "A Sociolinguistic Exploration of Glossolalia," *University of Michigan Papers in Linguistics* 1/4 (1975) 1–21.

Losada, D., "Dones, ministerios y amor en la Primera Carta a los Corintios," *RevistB* 37 (1975) 335–40.

MacArthur, J., *Speaking in Tongues* (Chicago: Moody, 1988).

Martucci, J., "*Diakriseis pneumatōn* (1 Co 12,10)," *ÉgT* 9 (1978) 465–71.

Mills, E. D. (ed.), *Speaking in Tongues: A Guide to Research on Glossolalia* (Grand Rapids: Eerdmans, 1986).

Mills, W. E., "Early Ecstatic Utterances and Glossolalia," *PRSt* 24 (1997) 29–40.

Müller, U. B., *Prophetie und Predigt im Neuen Testament: Formgeschichtliche Untersuchungen zur urchristlichen Prophetie* (SNT 10; Gütersloh: Mohn, 1975).

Nardoni, E., "The Concept of Charism in Paul," *CBQ* 55 (1993) 68–80.

Parmentier, M., "Das Zungenreden bei den Kirchenvätern," *Bijdr* 55 (1994) 376–98.

Poythress, V. S., "The Nature of Corinthian Glossolalia: Possible Options," *WTJ* 40 (1977–78) 130–35.

Samarin, W. J, "Glossolalia as Learned Behavior," *CJT* 15 (1969) 60–64.

——, *Tongues of Men and Angels: The Religious Language of Pentecostalism* (New York: Macmillan, 1972).

Scippa, V., *La glossolalia nel Nuovo Testamento: Ricerca esegetica secondo il metodo storicocritico e analitico-strutturale* (Naples: M. D'Auria, 1982).

Sullivan, F. A., "Speaking in Tongues," *LumVit* 31 (1976) 145–70.

Therrien, G., *Le discernement dans les écrits pauliniens* (EtBib; Paris: Gabalda, 1973).

Thiselton, A. C., "The 'Interpretation' of Tongues: A New Suggestion in the Light of Greek Usage in Philo and Josephus," *JTS* 30 (1979) 15–36.

Tugwell, S., "The Gift of Tongues in the New Testament," *ExpTim* 84 (1972–73) 137–40.

Tuland, C. G., "The Confusion about Tongues," *Christianity Today* 13 (1968–69) 207–9.

Turner, M., *The Holy Spirit and Spiritual Gifts in the New Testament Church and Today* (rev. ed.; Peabody, MA: Hendrickson, 1998).

Unger, M. F., *New Testament Teaching on Tongues* (Grand Rapids: Kregel, 1972).

Vanhoye, A., *I carismi nel Nuovo Testamento* (Rome: Biblical Institute, 1986) 32–105.

Williams, K., "Life in the Spirit and the Gifts of the Spirit," *Doctrine and Life* 28 (1978) 68–76.

27   c. *The Many Members* *of the One Body (12:12–31)*

[12:12]For as the body is a unit and has many members, and all the members of the body, though many, form one body, so too it is with Christ. [13]For by one Spirit we were all baptized, in fact, into one body, whether Jews or Greeks, slaves or free, and we were all given one Spirit to drink. [14]Indeed, the body does not consist of one member, but of many. [15]If the foot says, "Because I am not a hand, I do not belong to the body," it would not for that reason belong any less to the body. [16]And if the ear says, "Because I am not an eye, I do not belong to the body," it would not for that reason belong any less to the body. [17]If the whole body were an eye, where would hearing be? If the whole body were hearing, where would the sense of smell be? [18]Now as it is, God has arranged the members in the body, each one of them, just as he wanted them. [19]If they were all one member, where would the body be? [20]As it is, there are many members, but one body. [21]So the eye cannot say to the hand, "I have no need of you"; or again, the head to the feet, "I have no need of you." [22]Rather, the members of the body that seem to be weaker are all the more necessary; [23]and those parts of the body that we consider less honorable we surround with greater honor; and our unpresentable parts are treated with greater propriety, [24]whereas our presentable parts have no need of this. Indeed, God has so blended the body, giving greater honor to a part that lacks it, [25]so that there may be no discord in the body, but that the members have the same concern for each other. [26]If, indeed, one member suffers, all suffer with it; if [one] member is honored, all the members rejoice with it. [27]Now you are the body of Christ, and individually members of it; [28]and in the church God has appointed some to be, first of all, apostles; second, prophets; third, teachers; then, workers of mighty deeds, then those with gifts of healing, assistants, administrators, speakers of kinds of tongues. [29]Are all apostles? Are all prophets? Are all teachers? Do all work mighty deeds? [30]Do all have gifts of healing? Do all speak in tongues? Do all interpret? [31]But are you striving for the greater gifts? Now I shall show you a still more excellent way.

COMMENT

Having set forth his understanding of the variety of *pneumatika* and their unique divine source, Paul proceeds to another aspect of the phenomena that their diversity creates in the Christian community. He passes, in effect, from the many to the one, and from a discussion of *pneuma*, "Spirit" (vv. 7–9, 11) to that of *sōma*, "body" (vv. 12–20, 22–25, 27), and likens the multiplicity of those who have "manifestations" (12:7) of the Spirit to that of "members" in the one human body. He identifies the members of the community, first, as "Christ" (12:12), then as the "body of Christ" (12:27), and eventually as "the church" (12:28). As such, the many members of the Christian community must use all their diverse manifestations of the Spirit "to the good" (12:7) of the whole, because Christ is the unifying principle of the church. Just as the human body unifies the plurality of its members, so Christ unifies the diversity of endowed Christians. As Soards rightly notes, "in Christ unity dominates diversity and makes diversity genuinely meaningful and constructive" (*1 Cor*, 263), so that no one can vaunt his or her individual endowment over that of others at the expense of such unity. Because such vaunting was at work in the Corinthian church, Paul seeks to correct it. His correction still has to be recalled even when modern charismatics vaunt their experiences in what should be the one body of Christ.

Paul's argument proceeds in stages. First, in vv. 12–14 he describes the relation of many members to one body (note the *inclusio* in *sōma* and *polla* in vv. 12 and 14 [disregard the paragraphing in N-A[27]]); v. 13 is parenthetic, as it joins with the topic of vv. 4–11 and extends it to ethnic and social groups. Second, in vv. 15–26 Paul describes in detail how multiple and diverse members are related to and serve the one human body formed by God's design. Third, in v. 27 Paul shifts to the 2d pers. plur. to apply his teaching about Christians forming "the body of Christ." Fourth, Paul identifies that body as the church and explains how various endowed members play roles in it in vv. 28–30. Finally, he concludes with a question and a statement in v. 31, which is transitional to chap. 13.

The main isssue in this pericope is the ecclesiastical sense of the "body of Christ," which now appears. Absent from earlier Pauline letters (1 Thessalonians,

Galatians, and even Philippians), it now emerges, in a letter in which Paul has been coping with various divisive phenomena in the Corinthian community (rivalries owing to allegiance to preachers, divisive problems in liturgical gatherings, and diverse vaunting of individual spiritual gifts). This idea of the church as the body of Christ only gradually dawned on Paul as he sought to cope with problems in the Christian communities that he had founded. It was almost certainly not an insight that he had at the time of his call on the road to Damascus. In the Lucan account of that event, when he was accosted by the risen Christ, he asked, "Who are you, sir?" He heard the answer, "I am Jesus whom you are persecuting" (Acts 9:5), but that answer cannot be so interpreted that he immediately became aware of the church as the body of Christ. The church as the body of Christ is not an element in Lucan theology (see *Acts*, 425). Rather, it took time for this important idea in Pauline theology to surface. Now by means of the "body of Christ," Paul seeks to instill in Corinthian Christians a sense of their corporate identity—of the unity of all of them in Christ, different though they are individually. Paul uses the same distinction of the one body and many members in Rom 12:4–5, but does not relate them there to the church, as he does here.

The background or origin of this figurative use of *sōma* in such a phrase is disputed. At least four explanations have been given for it:

1. A development of the OT idea of the corporate personality. "Basic to the phrase 'the Body of Christ' is Christ as a corporate personality, and he is this to the Church as a whole, and not to each of the individual congregations separately" (Best, *One Body*, 104).

2. A development from the use of terracotta votive offerings (hands, feet, arms, legs, breasts, etc.). These were found in the Asclepieion, a temple just inside the north wall of the city of Corinth near the Lerna Spring (see fig. 1, p. 23), which represented the healed parts of a human body that the god Asclepius was believed to have cured. They are said to have reminded Paul of society as wounded humanity and would have inspired his discussion of *sōma* in this passage (Hill, "The Temple"; Murphy-O'Connor, *St. Paul's Corinth*, 190–91; *NJBC*, 810; Garner, "The Temple").

3. A borrowing of the idea of the *Urmensch*, or "primal man," from the Gnostic myth of the Redeemer. He with the Gnostics among human beings form "his *soma* a cosmic entity" (Bultmann, *TNT*, 1:299, cf. 106; Schmithals, *Office of Apostle*, 201–4). On this notion, see Wedderburn, "Body of Christ," 80–86.

4. A borrowing of the idea of the state or civil society conceived of as the "body politic" from ancient Greek philosophy. This notion is found as early as Aristotle (*Polit.* 5.2.7 §1302b, 35–36), and it became a tenet of Stoic philosophy: Dionysius of Halicarnassus, *Rom. Ant.* 3.11.5; Dio Chrysostom, *Disc.* 34.20; Philo, *De spec. leg.* 3.23 §131 (*hina pasa hēlikia kai panta merē tou ethnous hōs henos sōmatos eis mian kai tēn autēn harmozētai koinōnian*, "so that every age and all parts of the nation may be united into one and the same fellowship as of one body"; Plutarch, *Coriolanus* 6.3–4; *Moralia* 426a ("Is there not here a single body [*hen sōma*] composed of disparate bodies, such as an assembly [*ekklēsia*] or an army or a chorus, each one of which happens to have a faculty of living, thinking, and learn-

ing . . . ?"); *Philopoemen* 8.3 (1.360c); Sextus Empiricus, *Adv. Mathematicos* 9.78). The idea is implied in Epictetus, *Diss.* 2.5.24–27; 2.10.3–4, and it also appears as *corpus* in Latin writers influenced by Stoics (Cicero, *Or. Philip.* 8.5.15; *De Officiis* 3.5.21–22; Seneca, *Ep. mor.* 95.52). The figure would thus express the moral unity of citizens or soldiers cooperating to achieve a common goal (of justice, peace, prosperity, and well-being for all).

Also to be noted is the famous parabolic fable of Menenius Agrippa, "The Belly and the Limbs," preserved in Livy, *Ab urbe condita* 2.32.9–12, which likewise compares the state to a human body, as it exhorts the ordinary people (*plebs*) to end rebellion and support the leaders (*patres*). This fable, comparing *polis* and *sōma*, is used also in Dionysius Halicarnassus, *Ant. Rom.* 6.86.1–3 (cf. 6.83.2); Xenophon, *Mem.* 2.3.18; Plutarch, *Coriolanus* 6.2–4 (see also Nestle, "Die Fabel").

Of these different explanations, the fourth is the most likely, as Mitchell (*Paul*, 268–29) rightly notes. Paul would then have taken over this Greek philosophical notion and given it his own distinctive Christian nuance, the church as "the body of Christ." Cf. Wedderburn, "Body of Christ."

Two further aspects of this figurative usage of *sōma* should be noted. First, of itself it expresses at most a moral unity of individual Christians in the body (as in Rom 12:4–8). If more is to be associated with "the body of Christ," one has to bring in further considerations, such as the implications of 1 Cor 6:15–17, which in its reference to the sexual union of "bodies" in fornication would express more than merely a moral union with Christ; or 10:16–17, which expresses the participation of all Christians who share in the one eucharistic bread and cup as a "participation in the body of Christ." And yet, Christians are not physically united with Christ as are the yolk and albumen of an egg. So it is not easy to describe specifically the nature of this union of Christians and Christ. Second, because Paul has already spoken of Christ as "the head" (11:3) and now speaks of his "body," one should not yet conclude that he has already developed the idea of Christ as the head of the church. That will come in the Deutero-Pauline letters (Colossians and Ephesians), where the themes of head, body, and church are are all brought together in the cosmic view of Christ (Col 1:18, 24; Eph 1:23; see further *PAHT* §PT122–27). Later on, Eusebius will even speak of "the body of Christians" (*to sōma tōn Christianōn, HE* 10.5.10–12).

NOTES

12:12. *For as the body is a unit and has many members, and all the members of the body, though many, form one body.* Lit. "as the body is one." Paul plays with the distinction, well known in earlier Greek philosophy, of "the One and the Many" (see Sprague, "Parmenides, Plato"). In the following verses he will give examples of the "many" different members in the "one" body. In saying that they "form one body," he is using *sōma* in a figurative sense (see COMMENT above); by it he is recalling the organic unity of the body and connoting its relation to a human being as a corporeal unit. This is offered as an explanation of the diversity of endowments mentioned in vv. 8–10, which has already been attributed to the one Spirit in v. 11. Some MSS ($\aleph^2$, D, Ψ, and the Koine text-tradition) add *tou henos* after *sōmatos*, "of the one body," which may be a scribal attempt at harmonization. Philo, who notes that "nature" delights in the number seven, counts seven members of the human body: head, neck, breast, hands, belly, abdomen, feet (*Leg. alleg.* 1.4 §§8, 12).

so too it is with Christ. Lit. "so also Christ (*or* the Christ)." This might seem like an elliptical statement, but note the comparison, *kathaper . . . to sōma . . . houtōs kai ho Christos*, "as . . . the body, . . . so also the Christ"; and contrast the form of the comparison made in Rom 12:4–5: "For just as we have many members in one body and all of the members do not have the same function, so we, though many, are one body in Christ and individually members of one another."

This remarkable identification of Christians with Christ makes use of the name *Christos* as a way to speak of what will be explained further in v. 27 as the "body of Christ." Allo (*1 Cor*, 328) regarded this occurrence of *Christos* in its collective sense as unique; see also Wolff, *1 Cor*, 2. 107; Kremer, *1 Cor*, 270; but recall 1:13: "Is Christ divided?" "The community is 'Christ' insofar as it is the sphere where the saving power of the Spirit is at work" (Murphy-O'Connor, "Christ and Ministry," 126).

> The unity of Christ, as of the human body, is his [Paul's] starting point. He then proceeds to show that the body cannot in fact consist only of 'one member', but must be 'many' (v. 14). The point of the verses that follow (15–21) is *not* that the different members must be united among themselves (the question of schism does not enter until v. 25, and then it is quite incidental to the passage), but precisely that there must be more than one member if there is to be a body at all. (Robinson, *The Body*, 59)

It clearly does not mean only, "So it is also, where Christ is," as some commentators have understood it (e.g., Schlier, *Christus und die Kirche*, 40–41). Paul is repeating, in effect, what he already said in 6:15, "Do you not realize that your bodies are members of Christ?"

13. *For by one Spirit we were all baptized, in fact, into one body.* Or "in one Spirit," since the force of the prep. *en* is not clear, whether it is to be understood as instrumental or local (BDF §§195, 219–20). The statement, introduced by explanatory *kai gar*, "for in fact" (BDF §452.3), is made to say why all Christians constitute "Christ" in a somatic sense. Through the "one Spirit" (already mentioned in 12:9, 11) all Christians have been plunged into or immersed in "one body," i.e., into Christ. As Paul asked in 1:13 whether Corinthians had been "baptized" in his name (see NOTE there), he now uses the same formula to express union with Christ; cf. also his formulation about the Israelites and Moses in 10:2. Even though he adds the mention of the Spirit, it is highly unlikely that Paul is referring to anything different from the well-known early Christian tradition about baptism by water and its effects (see Rom 6:3–4; 1 Cor 1:13–17, and esp. 6:11, "you have been washed"). He is making use of such traditional teaching to ad-

vance his argument about the one body of believers that baptism in one Spirit brings about despite the remarkable variety of the members and their endowments. This verse is one of the fundamental Pauline texts that teach the incorporation of baptized believers into Christ (see further *PAHT* §PT116–27). For the understanding of this verse as water baptism, see Bultmann, *TNT*, 1:138; Beasley-Murray, *Baptism*, 167–71; Schnackenburg, *Baptism*, 83. It is baffling to read that "one is hard pressed to find an equation between baptism and the reception of the Spirit in Paul's letters" (Fee, *1 Cor*, 604), when that is exactly what this verse is affirming (see Bultmann, *TNT*, 1:333).

It has, moreover, little to do with what is often called in modern times "baptism in the Holy Spirit" by modern Pentecostalists (see Harrington, "Baptism in the Holy Spirit," 43–44). Indeed, the following clause, which speaks of "drinking" the Spirit, implies that the baptism of which Paul speaks is one of water. There is no "early Christian tradition" for a baptism in the Spirit as distinct from water baptism (*pace* Garland, *1 Cor*, 591; Cottle, " 'All Were Baptized,' " 76). That is certainly not Pauline teaching, which is clearly a development of the OT teaching of Ezek 36:25–27, where "clean water . . . a new heart . . . and a new spirit" are promised; cf. Joel 2:28 (pouring out of God's Spirit). That the verb *baptizō* is used at times in the NT in a figurative or analogous sense is admitted (e.g., Mark 10:38; Luke 12:50), but this usage is not predicated of Christians and is not found so in Pauline writings.

whether Jews or Greeks, slaves or free. These phrases emphasize the meaning of "we . . . all" in the main statement. For all believers, no matter what their diverse religious, ethnic, social, or economic background may be, share one and the same union with the risen Christ through baptism "in the one Spirit" and thus belong to the "one body." For the first pair, see NOTE on 1:23; cf. 10:32. The two pairs occur also among the three mentioned in Gal 3:28, but speculation runs wild when commentators try to determine why Paul omits here the third one, "male or female," even though there is no reason why he should mention it. See, however, Schüssler Fiorenza, *In Memory*, 218. For the Pauline assertion has nothing to do with equality or with the relation of what she calls "patriarchal marriage" to the constitution of the "new community in Christ" (ibid., 211). The affirmation in Gal 3:28 means only that the "ethnic, social, and gender distinctions conventionally made in society are irrelevant for determining who is 'in Christ' as a result of baptism and confession of Jesus as Christ and Lord" (Elliott, "Jesus Movement," 180).

Lietzmann (*1 Cor*, 63) finds Paul's use of these phrases "disruptive," because, though the use of them in Gal 3:28 aims at unity, the emphasis here is on diversity. They are not disruptive, however, because they give a concrete illustration of the unity that should dominate the diversity that they seek to express (so Lindemann, *1 Cor*, 272).

and we were all given one Spirit to drink. Lit. "we were all caused to drink one Spirit," for the acc. with a pass. verb, see BDF §159.1. Paul repeats *hen pneuma*, "one Spirit," in the sense that it is the cause of the unity. The "drinking" of the Spirit has been diversely explained: either as another figurative reference to baptism (already mentioned in the first part of the verse), or as the drinking of the eucharistic cup (so Augustine, Luther, Calvin, Schlatter, Wendland, Conzelmann; see 1 Cor 10:4). The latter is less likely because nowhere in the NT or early patristic writers is the Spirit ever said to be bestowed through the Eucharist. Cuming (*"Epotisthēmen"*) calls attention to the meaning of *potizō,* "to water," as when one waters a plant or a garden (already used in 3:6, "Apollos watered"), which was given by Chrysostom, who rejected the allusion to the Eucharist (*Hom. in Ep. 1 ad Cor.* 30.2; PG 61.251); it would then be a reference to baptism "administered by affusion": "we all had the one holy Spirit poured over us." Cf. Rom 5:5. Rogers (*"Epotisthēmen* Again"), however, insists rightly on the meaning of *potizō* as "cause to drink" the "one Spirit," in which the Christian has not only been immersed, but which is "within" the Christian (6:19). Thus the second clause is merely a literary parallel to the first, that affirms the same thing about water baptism. "Baptism as the rite of initiation into the Christian society was at once the means of entry into the one Body and into Christ: the baptized were made members of the Christ, they were all one man in Christ" (Robinson, " 'In the Name,' " 199). All Christians endowed with diverse gifts of the Spirit have been joined "into one body" and thus enjoy the same intimate union with Christ, as in Gal 3:27–28. *Pace* Hanimann ("Nous avons"), the two clauses of this verse do not describe a double rite of Christian initiation, baptism in the name of Jesus (as in Acts 8:12–17; 19:1–6), and imposition of hands conferring the Spirit. That is not only a misreading of Acts (on these passages, see *Acts,* 406, 643–44), but a foisting on the Pauline text concerns of later systematic theology (about the sacrament of Confirmation).

14. *Indeed, the body does not consist of one member, but of many.* Paul now begins an unusual and elaborate illlustration of the diversity of the many members that constitute the one body, as he repeats the "one" and the "many" of v. 12. It lasts through v. 24, and many of the verses need little comment. The differentiation of the parts of the body is what is essential to the illustration; in vv. 14–20 the necessity of diversity is stressed.

15. *If the foot says, "Because I am not a hand, I do not belong to the body," it would not for that reason belong any less to the body.* In this instance, and also in the following comparisons (vv. 16, 21), Paul resorts to a *reductio ad absurdum* as he personifies an inferior part of the body and makes it grumble against a more important part. The phrase *ou para touto,* "not for that," expresses causality; it is also found in 4 Macc 10:19. Since the apodosis begins with *ou* and continues with the neg. *ouk estin,* N-A[27] and some commentators (i.e., Kremer) take the verse as a question, "Would it for that reason . . . ," as in v. 17. In that case, however, one would expect an initial *mē,* which would anticipate a negative answer. So others (RSV, Robertson-Plummer, Conzelmann, Lindemann, BDAG, 758; BDF §§236.5, 431.1) take the double negative as an emphatic affirmative statement, "It would *not.* . . ."

16. *And if the ear says, "Because I am not an eye, I do not belong to the body," it would not for that reason belong any less to the body.* As in v. 15, now the ear is personified.

17. *If the whole body were an eye, where would hearing be? If the whole body were hearing, where would the sense of smell be?* With questions Paul emphasizes the important differences of various members of the body. Each member has its own function, and so it cannot look down on that of another or covet the function of another. Sprague ("Parmenides, Plato," 212) calls attention to the same kind of argument about different virtues in Plato, *Meno* 73D–74a.

18. *Now as it is, God has arranged the members in the body, each one of them, just as he wanted them.* See 15:38, where Paul repeats this idea. God has made the human body to be a unit, despite the diversity of members, which are not all uniform in structure or function. This Pauline comment about God's design interrupts the comparative illustration, which continues in the next verse.

19. *If they were all one member, where would the body be?* I.e., would it still be a body? This verse, even though it resumes the thinking of v. 17, is actually the counterpart of v. 14 above. Some MSS (B, F, G, 33) omit *ta panta*, "all"; then "it" (= body) must be understood from v. 18: "if it were one member."

20. *As it is, there are many members, but one body.* This statement repeats in its own way what Paul affirmed in v. 12a, and it is also analogous to v. 18. The succinctness of its expression, *polla men melē, hen de sōma*, suggests that Paul is quoting a proverb, which is formulated like the Greek philosophical problem of "the One and the Many."

21. *So the eye cannot say to the hand, "I have no need of you"; or again, the head to the feet, "I have no need of you."* The comparison now continues with connective *de* (BDF §462.1), and the more important organs of the body are personified and mentioned first, but despite their importance they are not self-sufficient or independent; they do depend on organs that might seem less important. So Paul emphasizes the interdependence of members of the body. The "eye" was already used in vv. 16–17, and "hand" and feet" in v. 15, but the "head" is new. Note the similar comparison of head and feet as parts of the body in *1 Clem.* 37.5. "Eye" and "head" are metaphors for leaders in the community, whereas "hand" and "feet" stand for laborers and slaves, and they all need each other.

22. *Rather, the members of the body that seem to be weaker are all the more necessary.* The apparently "weaker" members are, in fact, the more valuable parts of the body, and even indispensable, such as the eyes. Paul now introduces a triple comparison that involves the "weaker" (*asthenestera*), "less honorable" (*atimotera*), and "unpresentable" (*aschēmona*) members of the human body, using three alpha-privative adjs. (one of positive degree, and two of comparative degree). In making such a comparison, Paul metaphorically reflects the status of various Corinthian Christians. The "weaker" may echo those in Roman Corinth to whom he has already referred (in 8:9–10; 9:22; 11:30), but not necessarily so. In any case, "this comment does not follow strictly from verse 21" (Hays, *1 Cor*, 215).

23. *and those parts of the body that we consider less honorable we surround with greater honor.* Lit. "we drape around with. . . ." Paul plays with negative and positive uses of *timē*, "honor," contrasting it with an alpha-privative related adj., *atimotera*, "less honorable." He is probably thinking of arms and legs that are usually covered and sometimes adorned. It is not easy to say to whom Paul might be re-

ferring in the Corinthian community by this or the following metaphorical use of body parts. Cf. LXX Esth 1:20, where the same verb, *peritithēmi*, occurs along with the noun, *timē*, "honor," but in an entirely different sense (about wives who are to accord honor to their husbands, as a result of a royal edict).

and our unpresentable parts are treated with greater propriety. Paul alludes to the elaborate use of clothing to cover the *partes minus honestae*, i.e., the private parts. Important as they are to human life, they are protected from public exposure.

24. *whereas our presentable parts have no need of this.* I.e., members of the body that need neither covering nor adornment; they are called *ta euschēmona* (lit. "elegant in figure or shape," and so appropriate for display), and they stand in contrast to the three classes of organs just mentioned.

Indeed, God has so blended the body, giving greater honor to a part that lacks it. As in v. 18, Paul again speaks of God's design in creating the human body, as he now alludes to the natural instinct that human beings have to cover certain parts of the male and female body. That instinct stems from the way God has designed the human body, balancing its parts so that human beings develop a sense of propriety and care for the proper order of all of them.

25. *so that there may be no discord in the body, but that the members have the same concern for each other.* Significantly, Paul again uses *schisma*, "discord" (recall 1:19; 11:18), in this conclusion that he draws from the illustrative comparison that he has been making since v. 12. As there can be no discord between parts of the human body, whether weak, "less honorable," and "unpresentable" or strong, of "greater honor," and "presentable," there may be no discord in the body of the Christian community, where concern for one another and due respect should reign supreme. "Concern" is expressed by *merimnaō*, the verb that Paul used in 7:32–34, but it now explains why there can be no "discord" in the body, which " 'is' the working together of the parts" (Conzelmann, *1 Cor*, 214). Cf. also Rom 12:5. In the second clause, the subject *ta melē* is a neut. plur., which should have a sing. verb, but Paul uses the plur. *merimnōsin*, because "the argument requires that the members be thought of as many and separate" (Robertson-Plummer, *1 Cor*, 276).

26. *If, indeed, one member suffers, all suffer with it; if [one] member is honored, all the members rejoice with it.* This verse further illustrates Paul's conclusion, as it explains the mutual and reciprocal nature of the "concern" of v. 25: not only must Christian sympathy reign in the community, but also corporate rejoicing, for they share with one another such experiences. Cf. Rom 12:15.

27. *Now you are the body of Christ, and individually members of it.* Lit. "You are Christ's body, and members (of it) in part" (*ek merous*). Paul returns to what he said in v. 12c above, thus explaining his identification of Corinthian Christians with Christ. Again he uses *sōma Christou*, this time anarthrously, which in this context must mean, "the body of Christ." It is intended analogically in the ecclesiastical sense (see NOTE on 10:16), as is clear from v. 28. When this assertion is understood together with what Paul affirmed in 10:16 about the bread that we break being "a participation in the body of Christ" and with the tradition quoted

in 11:24, "This is my body, which is for you," it is clear that the ecclesiastical sense of "the body of Christ" has grown out of the sense of the crucified body of Christ, who is now the risen Lord, as Wedderburn rightly argues: "If Christians are united with Christ's crucified body they are similarly united with his risen body. It is one Christ, crucified and risen, with whom we are united" ("Body of Christ," 80).

The phrase *ek merous* (lit. "from a part") stresses the individuality of Christians as parts of the body (BDF §212: "[each] for his part"); but it has at times been understood also in another sense, viz., that Corinthian Christians were not the whole church, but part of the universal church (so John Chrysostom, Bengel). The Vg strangely reads the second clause as: *et membra de membro*, "and members from a member."

28. *and in the church God has appointed some to be, first of all, apostles.* Lit. "and whom God has put in the church, first, as apostles," for the anacoluthon (with v. 27), see BDF §442.9. The close association of *ekklēsia* with *sōma Christou* (12:27) is to be noted. In Rom 12:4–5, where one finds a similar teaching about individual Christians as members of the body of Christ, there is no mention of *ekklēsia* (see PAHT §PT122–27, 133–37).

Paul gives specific examples to explain the phrase *melē ek merous*, "individually members of it," of v. 27 and lists again individual *pneumatika* (12:1) that God has granted to the church, some of them *charismata*, some *diakoniai*, and some *energēmata* (12:4–6). The first three are singled out by being numbered and designated by the titles of persons who are officeholders. The numbering undoubtedly is meant to indicate an order of importance, as many commentators understand it, but it could be simply an indication of historical time when such functions emerged in the church. In either case, what is all-important is God's appointment: those who are apostles in the Christian community have not chosen this task for themselves.

The first place is assigned to *apostoloi*, "commissioned emissaries," witnesses of the risen Christ, a title already known from 1:1 (see NOTE there); 4:9; 9:1, 2, 5; see further 12:29; 15:7, 9. Cf. Eph 4:11–12, where they similarly head the list of roles "given" by the ascended Christ "for the work of ministry, for the building up of the body of Christ." The "apostles" are not, however, to be restricted in the Lucan sense to the Twelve (Luke 6:13; Acts 1:13, 21–22, 26); for they would have included Paul and Barnabas (Acts 14:4, 14 [on this problematic occurrence, see *Acts*, 526]), possibly Andronicus and Junia (Rom 16:7 [see *Romans* 737–39]), possibly "James, the brother of the Lord" (Gal 1:19 [see NJBC, art. 47 §16, but also the NOTE on 9:5 above]), and unnamed individuals (1 Cor 9:5; 15:7; 2 Cor 8:23). In this passage the apostolic role is to be understood as a form of *diakonia*, "ministry" or "service" (12:5), as are the next two (so Kremer, *1 Cor*, 262).

second, prophets. The second form of ministry is assigned to *prophētai*, "prophets," the dynamic and effective Spirit-guided preachers of the gospel (see NOTE on 12:10). They head the list in Rom 12:6, where they are mentioned as a form of *charismata*; they occupy the second place too in the list of Eph 4:11, but the first place in the Antiochene church (Acts 13:1). More will be heard about such Christians in 14:3–4, 22–24, 29, 32, 37, or about those who might so classify themselves. Paul understands them as a class distinct from apostles and teachers. Apostles and prophets are also mentioned together in Eph 2:20; 3:5; Rev 18:20 (*hagioi, apostoloi, prophētai*); *Did.* 11.3–6, 7–12 (see further Greeven, "Propheten," 3–15).

third teachers. The third form of ministry is assigned to *didaskaloi,* "teachers," who instruct and pass on the *didachē tōn apostolōn,* "the teaching of the apostles" (Acts 2:42). They likewise appear in Rom 12:7 and Eph 4:11, but in the fifth place. In *Did.* 11:1, however, they precede the apostles and prophets, but they were not listed above in vv. 4–11. Barnabas, Simeon called Niger, Lucius of Cyrene, Manaen, and Saul [Paul] are mentioned among "prophets and teachers" in the church of Antioch (Acts 13:1). Note also the threesome in 1 Tim 2:7, where the author calls himself *kēryx, apostolos, didaskalos,* "herald, apostle, and teacher"; cf. 2 Tim 1:11 (see Greeven, "Propheten," 16–31).

The singling out of these three officeholders and the numbering of them imply that Paul understands some endowments to be more significant than others because of their role in the founding and governance of the church, and this impression will be supported by Paul's treatment of prophecy and speaking in tongues in chap. 14. The difference of the three roles, however, is part of the diversity that Paul sees in the church, but that diversity should not be used to undermine the unity of the one body.

then, workers of mighty deeds. Lit. "then mighty deeds." Whereas the first three ministries were designated by the titles of officeholders and by numbers, the last five are listed simply as ministries by abstract nouns, without any indication of their order or importance; they seem to be a group of less significance. The first of these is given as *dynameis,* but in v. 10 above the gift was called *energēmata dynameōn,* "the workings of mighty deeds" (see NOTE there), and a form of the first word is added in the translation of the lemma here. This would be a role in the church that falls not under *diakoniai,* but *energēmata,* "works" (12:6). Cf. 3:5, where the ptc. *energōn dynameis* is used of God himself.

then those with gifts of healing. The same phrase was used in 12:9, *charismata iamatōn,* clearly a reference to individuals with a specific *charisma* of curing, as in 12:4.

assistants. Lit. "helps, helpful deeds," probably meaning individuals who manage things or who devote themselves to charitable aid. The term *antilēmpsis* occurs nowhere else in the NT, but see LXX Ps 22:20; Sir 11:12; 2 Macc 8:19; 3 Macc 5:50. The related verb, however, *antilambanesthai,* "to help," is found in Acts 20:35. It is probably to be understood as an *energēma.* This noun and the two following are added asyndetically to the list.

administrators. Lit. "administrations, acts of guidance," probably another *energēma,* which is that of leadership and guidance in the church, because *kybernēsis* denotes the task of a pilot of a ship (*kybernētēs,* Acts 27:11; Rev 18:17); perhaps like *proïstamenos,* "leader," of Rom 12:8. The abstract noun is found only here in the NT, but see LXX Prov 1:5; 11:14; 24:6, where it means "wise guidance" (RSV). A gifted church administrator is not the sort of person one would consider today among the *pneumatikoi,* but Paul does see his or her role as Spirit endowed (see Roberts, "Seers").

speakers of kinds of tongues. Lit. "kinds of tongues," the same abstract phrase, *genē glōssōn*, appears in v.10 above. Again it is mentioned at the end of the list, because it is the main difficulty that these endowments of the Spirit have been creating in the church of Roman Corinth, as will be seen in chap. 14.

29–30. *Are all apostles? Are all prophets? Are all teachers? Do all work mighty deeds? 30. Do all have gifts of healing? Do all speak in tongues? Do all interpret?* In these two verses Paul merely asks seven rhetorical questions using the same terms as in v. 28 and adding "the interpretation of tongues," mentioned at the end of 12:10. His questions expect the answer "no" (*mē*) and stress the diversity of roles that members of the body of Christ have; no one individual has all these roles, just as no role is played by everyone. Hence, diversity is needed for the good of the unity of the whole church. Again, speaking in tongues and the interpretation of it are at end of the list. One should compare Paul's mode of argument here with a similar one, using different titles drawn from military service, in *1 Clem.* 37.3–4.

31. *But are you striving for the greater gifts?* I.e., *charismata* that are superior (and not merely for such as speaking in tongues, as will emerge in chap. 14). So Paul with irony queries Corinthian Christians as he realizes that some of them covet important spiritual roles in the community. Although he does not specify, he may be referring to the three numbered in v. 28 or at least to prophecy, with which he will compare speaking in tongues in chap. 14, but only after he has finished saying what has to be said about all the listed *pneumatika* in their relation to *agapē* in chap. 13. The irony is seen in that they are striving for what is in reality a gift of the Spirit. Robertson-Plummer (*1 Cor*, 282), who take the verb *zēloute* as an impv., think that Paul is urging Corinthian Christians to strive "by prayer and habitual preparation" to obtain them; similarly Barrett (*1 Cor*, 296). How can one reconcile such striving with the emphasis on the gift character of these endowments? If Paul's words are understood as an ironic question, however, they would be merely a buildup to v. 31b and to his climax in chap. 13, which seems to be a preferable way to understand them. Such a translation makes the next statement (12:31b) an even more telling corrective.

The form *zēloute*, usually understood as an impv. (as in 14:1, 39), could also be understood as an indic. in a statement, "You are striving for (what you think are) the greater gifts" (cf. 14:12; see Iber, "Zum Verständnis"; Louw, "The Function"). Some MSS (D, F, G, Ψ, and the Koine text-tradition) read rather *kreittona*, "the better" (gifts), an insignificant variant reading.

Now I shall show you a still more excellent way. Lit. "I am showing," a pres. with fut. connotation (BDF §323). This is Paul's introduction to chap. 13. N-A[27] reads *kai eti kath' hyperbolēn hodon hymin deiknymi*, lit. "and I am still showing you a way to an extraordinary degree." Mss P[46], D*, (F, G) read *ei ti*, instead of the adv. *eti*, "still," and Debrunner would translate it: "if (there is) something in an extraordinary way, then I show you a way" ("Über einige Lesarten," 37). That is still somewhat problematic in this context.

Paul employs the prep. phrase *kath' hyperbolēn* also in Gal 1:13; 2 Cor 1:8; 4:17; Rom 7:13 but in an adv. sense to mark the surpassing quality of something. Here, however, it seems rather to function as an adj., because as an adv. it would ill suit the verb *deiknymi*. *Pace* van Unnik ("Meaning," 157), it cannot be taken as modifying *zēloute*, be zealous "even to the highest degree," because it is too far separated from that verb. Barth (*Resurrection*, 79) comes closer to the sense intended, when he speaks of "a way incomparable of its kind that leads more directly to the goal than all other ways," because the phrase "acquires a certain significance only when to the comparative contained in *kath' hyperbolēn* we supply *tōn charismatōn*, 'than the gifts' " (Conzelmann, *1 Cor*, 216). What follows in chap. 13 will help the understanding of how the diverse endowments of the Spirit set forth in vv. 4–11 can find a "way" that goes beyond them and thus serves the "one body" of the Christian church, "the body of Christ," in a surpassing way.

Paul uses *hodos*, "way," in a figurative sense of a "teaching"; it resembles a usage found often in contemporary philosophical schools of the Greco-Roman world (see *TDNT*, 5:43–47), but also in the LXX (Judg 2:22 [*tēn hodon kyriou*]; Ps 1:6; 37:34; Prov 28:23); cf. *Did.* 1.1; *Ep. Barn.* 18.1; 19.1.

BIBLIOGRAPHY (See also Bibliography on 12:1–14:39, pp. 461–62)

Baker, J. P., *Baptized in One Spirit: The Meaning of 1 Corinthians 12:13* (London: Fountain Trust, 1967).

Beasley-Murray, G. R., *Baptism in the New Testament* (London: Macmillan, 1962).

Best, E., *One Body in Christ: A Study in the Relationship of the Church to Christ in the Epistles of the Apostle Paul* (London: SPCK, 1955).

Bouttier, M., "*Complexio oppositorum*: Sur les formules I Cor. xii. 13: Gal. iii. 26–28; Col. iii. 10, 11," *NTS* 23 (1976–77) 1–19.

Budillon, J., "La première épître aux Corinthiens et la controverse sur les ministères," *Istina* 16 (1971) 471–88.

Cottle, R. E., " 'All Were Baptized,' " *JETS* 17 (1974) 75–80.

Cuming, G. J., "*Epotisthēmen* (I Corinthians 12. 13)," *NTS* 27 (1980–81) 283–85.

Daines, B., "Paul's Use of the Analogy of the Body of Christ—With Special Reference to 1 Corinthians 12," *EvQ* 50 (1978) 71–78.

Debrunner, A., "Über einige Learten der Chester Beatty Papyri des Neuen Testaments," *ConNeot* 11 (1947) 33–49.

Elliott, J. H., "The Jesus Movement Was not Egalitarian but Family-Oriented," *BibInt* 11 (2003) 173–210

Farrell, T., "We All Ate from the Same Soul," *Notes* 10/1 (1996) 20–26.

Garner, G. G., "The Temple of Asklepius at Corinth and Paul's Teaching," *BurH* 18/4 (1982) 52–58.

Greeven, H., "Propheten, Lehrer, Vorsteher bei Paulus," *ZNW* 44 (1952–53) 1–43.

Hainz, J., *Ekklesia* (BU 9; Regensburg: Pustet, 1972) 48–103.

Hanimann, J., " 'Nous avons été abreuvés d'un seul Esprit': Note sur *1 Co 12, 13b*," *NRT* 94 (1972) 400–405.

Harrington, D. J., "Baptism in the Holy Spirit: A Review Article," *CS* 11 (1972) 31–44.

Havet, J., "Christ collectif ou Christ individuel en I Cor., xii, 12?" *ETL* 23 (1947) 499–520.

Hill, A. E., "The Temple of Asclepius: An Alternative Source for Paul's Body Theology?" *JBL* 99 (1980) 437–39.

Iber, G., "Zum Verständnis von I Cor 12,31," *ZNW* 54 (1963) 43–52.

Käsemann, E., *Leib und Leib Christi: Eine Untersuchung zur paulinischen Begrifflichkeit* (BHT 9; Tübingen: Mohr [Siebeck], 1933).

———, *Perspectives on Paul* (Philadelphia: Fortress, 1971) 102–21.

Kilpatrick, G. D., "A Parallel to the New Testament Use of *sōma*," *JTS* n.s. 13 (1962) 117.

Knox, W. L., "Parallels to the N. T. Use of *sōma*," *JTS* 39 (1938) 243–46.

Lindemann, A., "Die Kirche als Leib: Beobachtungen zur 'demokratischen' Ekklesiologie bei Paulus," *ZTK* 92 (1995) 140–65; repr. in his *Paulus, Apostel und Lehrer der Kirche: Studien zu Paulus und zum frühen Paulusverständnis* (Tübingen: Mohr Siebeck, 1999) 132–57.

Louw, J. P., "The Function of Discourse in a Sociosemiotic Theory of Translation Illustrated by the Translation of *zēloute* in 1 Corinthians 12.31," *BT* 39 (1988) 329–35.

Macías, B., "1 Cor 12,13: Una conjetura renacentista . . . *kai pantes eis hen pneuma epotisthēmen*," *FilolNT* 7 (1994) 209–14.

Manson, T. W., "A Parallel to a N. T. Use of *sōma*," *JTS* 37 (1936) 385.

Merklein, H., "Entstehung und Gehalt des paulinischen Leib-Christi-Gedankens," *Studien zu Jesus und Paulus* (WUNT 43; Tübingen: Mohr [Siebeck], 1987) 319–44.

Meuzelaar, J. J., *Der Leib des Messias: Eine exegetische Studie über den Gedanken vom Leib Christi in den Paulusbriefen* (Assem: Van Gorcum, 1961) 20–40, 143, 169.

Nestle, W., "Die Fabel des Menenius Agrippa," *Klio* 21 (1927) 350–60.

Park, H.-W., *Die Kirche als "Leib Christi" bei Paulus* (TVG Monographien und Studienbücher 378; Giessen/Basel: Brunnen, 1992).

Perlewitz, M. F., "The Unity of the Body of Christ," *TBT* 18 (1980) 394–98.

Riesenfeld, H., "La voie de charité: Note sur I Cor. xii, 31," *ST* 1 (1948) 146–57.

Roberts, P., "Seers or Overseers?" *ExpTim* 108 (1996–97) 301–5.

Robinson, J. A., " 'In the Name,' " *JTS* 7 (1905–6) 186–202.

Rogers, E. R., "*Epotisthēmen* Again," *NTS* 29 (1983) 139–42.

Schlier, H., *Christus und die Kirche im Epheserbrief* (Tübingen: Mohr [Siebeck], 1930).

Schnackenburg, R., *Baptism in the Thought of St. Paul: A Study in Pauline Theology* (Oxford: Blackwell; New York: Herder and Herder, 1964).

Smit, J. F. M., "Two Puzzles: 1 Corinthians 12.31 and 13.3: A Rhetorical Solution," *NTS* 39 (1993) 246–64.

Söding, T., " 'Ihr aber seid der Leib Christi' (1 Kor 12,27): Exegetische Beobachtungen an einem zentralen Motiv paulinischer Ekklesiologie," *Catholica* 45 (1991) 135–62; repr. in *Das Wort vom Kreuz: Studien zur paulinischen Theologie* (WUNT 93; Tübingen: Mohr [Siebeck], 1997) 272–99.

Sorg, T., "Viele Glieder—ein Leib: Bibelarbeit über 1. Korinther 12.12–27," *TBei* 13 (1984) 193–200.

Sprague, R. K., "Parmenides, Plato, and I Corinthians 12," *JBL* 86 (1967) 211–13.

Unnik, W. C. van, "The Meaning of 1 Corinthians 12:31," *NovT* 35 (1993) 142–59.

Wedderburn, A. J. M., "The Body of Christ and Related Concepts in 1 Corinthians," *SJT* 24 (1971) 74–96.

Zimmermann, A. F., *Die urchristlichen Lehrer: Studien zum Tradentenkreis der didaskaloi im frühen Urchristentum* (WUNT 2/12; Tübingen: Mohr [Siebeck], 1984) 92–113.

28   d. *The More Excellent Way:*
          Hymn to Love (13:1–13)

¹³ˀ¹ If I speak with human and angelic tongues, but do not have love, I am only resounding brass or a clanging cymbal. ²If I have the gift of prophecy and comprehend all mysteries and all knowledge, and if I have all the faith to move mountains, but do not have love, I am nothing. ³If I dole out all I own and hand over my body in order to boast, but do not have love, I gain nothing. ⁴[Love] is patient; love is kind. Love is not jealous; [love] does not brag; it is not arrogant. ⁵It is not rude; it does not seek its own interest; it does not become irritated; it does not reckon with wrongs. ⁶It does not delight in wrongdoing, but rejoices with the truth. ⁷It puts up with all things, believes all things, hopes for all things, endures all things. ⁸Love never fails. If there are prophecies, they will be brought to naught; if tongues, they will come to an end; if knowledge, it will be brought to naught. ⁹For we know in part, and we prophesy in part, ¹⁰but when what is perfect comes, the partial will be brought to naught. ¹¹When I was a child, I spoke as a child, I thought as a child, I reasoned as a child. When I became a man, I did away with childish things. ¹²For at present we see by reflection, as in a mirror, but then face to face; at present I know only in part, but then I shall know fully, even as I have been fully known. ¹³And now faith, hope, love remain, these three; but the greatest of these is love.

COMMENT

In this passage Paul explains what he meant by "a still more excellent way" in 12:31, and he devotes to it a discussion of *agapē*, "love," which in this chapter will be presented as the highest and unsurpassed gift of God. Whether or not this passage should be called a hymn, ode, or psalm, as it has been known for a very long time, is a matter of considerable debate today, mainly because it is lacking in meter. Those who have spoken against it as a hymn are mainly J. Weiss, von Harnack, Fridrichsen, and Spicq (see Sanders, "First Corinthians 13," 159), and they have influenced many other interpreters. It is rather a descriptive, didactic, and hortatory passage composed with no little rhetoric, and differs considerably from the style of the rest of the letter, as well from other NT passages that are usually considered hymnic: Phil 2:6–11; Col 1:15–20. It has no liturgical traces, no parallelism, and contains no mention of Christ (*pace* Johansson ["1 Cor. xiii"], his historical person is not meant by *agapē*), and even lacks all explicit reference to God. Many interpreters, however, continue to entitle it as a hymn or psalm (e.g., R. E. Brown, Johansson ["a hymn to Christ"], Lietzmann, Robertson-Plummer), and I have retained the title so often used, even though I recognize it as structured prose, scarcely poetical or lyrical, yet marked with rhetorical and balanced pairs, antithesis, chiasmus, hyperbole, and anaphora. It is a rhetorical encomium of love, intended as an exhortation for Corinthian Christians (see Sigountos, "The

Genre"). It is "an important instruction on the basic reality of Christian morality" (Spicq, *Agape*, 2:141).

Literary parallels in Greek and Hellenistic Jewish writings to this extended treatment of love are several. The most important parallel is found in Wis 7:22–23, with its 21 (3 × 7) characteristics of *sophia*, "wisdom," and the subsequent development of it in 7:24–8:1. Of less significance are the parallels in Plato, *Symposium* 197c–e (qualities of *erōs*, "love"); Maximus of Tyre, *Diss.* 20.2 (*erōs*); *1 Esdras* 4:34–40 (*alētheia*, "truth"); Sophocles, *Antigone* 332–75 (*anthrōpos*).

This passage is often seen as problematic because it seems to interrupt Paul's discussion of *pneumatika*, "spiritual gifts," begun in chap. 12 and continued in chap. 14. It is somewhat like chap. 9 in its relation to chaps. 8 and 10. In this case, it is not so much a digression, being more related to what has preceded in chap. 12, but it still reads like a small independent or self-contained treatise; and if 12:31b and 14:1a were disregarded, 14:1bc would be a good sequel to 12:31a. Consequently, some commentators think of chap. 13 as out of place: J. Weiss (*1 Cor*, 311) considered the original place for this "fully self-contained unit" to be after chap. 8; others that it was composed for another occasion and purpose and then inserted here (Schenk, Héring); and still others that it is a non-Pauline interpolation (Titus, Walker). The majority of interpreters, however, reckon with it as a genuinely Pauline composition, even though they often regard it as a rhetorical *digressio* (so Corley, "Pauline Authorship"; Collins, *1 Cor*, 471; Garland, *1 Cor*, 605; Robertson-Plummer, *1 Cor*, 285). A number of recent studies has been devoted specifically to the rhetoric of the chapter (M. M. Mitchell, Standaert, Smit), but they actually contribute little to the real understanding of it (see Lambrecht, "Most Eminent," 83–87). I hesitate to label the passage a digression or an insertion, because, as I see it, it is the *climax* to what Paul has been teaching in chap. 12 about the *pneumatika* and the diverse kinds of them, whether *charismata, diakoniai*, or *energēmata*, even though there is no longer any mention of the Spirit in the verses of this chapter. Love is different from those endowments of the Spirit, surpassing all of them as the greatest gift of God. In their own way and somewhat abstractly, these verses sum up what Paul has been saying elsewhere in this letter about the characteristics of Christian life when lived in Christ. Just as "God's foolishness is wiser than human wisdom" (1:25), so love is greater than all other spiritual endowments (see further Cuvillier, "Entre théologie de la croix").

The teaching in this passage has often been discussed. The main treatises on *agapē* have been written by Nygren (*Agape and Eros*), Spicq (*Agape*), Warnach (*Agape*), and Söding (*Das Liebesgebot* and *Die Trias*).

Paul's encomium of love falls into three sections, which can be distinguished by their different rhetorical forms: (1) vv. 1–3, the need to have love, without which all other gifts (tongues, prophecy, wisdom, knowledge, faith to move mountains, and service of others) are worthless (expressed in three conditions with anaphoric *ean* and the repeated secondary condition clause, "if I do not have love"); (2) vv. 4–8a, sixteen Greek verbs that express characteristics of love, seven positive and nine negative; and (3) vv. 8b–12, the lasting character and superiority of love (formulated as three conditions with anaphoric *eite*, three temporal clauses with anaphoric *hote*, and two concluding antithetic temporal statements involving *arti*, "now," and *tote*, "then"). The conclusion is stated in v. 13, summing up the lasting nature of love and employing *meizōn*, "greatest," which echoes *meizona* of 12:31. Paul's discussion of love is meant to exhort Christians of Corinth to consider their behavior in light of it, because it must be the basis of all their social interaction (Mitchell, *Paul*, 274). Most commentators consider vv. 4–7 to be the second section, but I prefer to follow Focant, who includes the sixteenth verb (v. 8a) with the 15 that precede, as does also Lacan ("Les trois").

Thus in its present context, chap.13, while acting as a comment on the endowments of the Spirit in chap. 12, discusses the basic element of Christian experience and on a level far higher than that of chaps. 12 or 14. *Agapē* is something in that experience that transcends the endowments coming from the Spirit, and so it is the highest of divine gifts. It cannot simply be considered a human virtue, and it is in no sense the product of human effort or achievement.

Four words were used for "love" in ancient Greek literature: *erōs, philia, agapē,* and *storgē,* with their cog. verbs, *eraō* or *eraomai, phileō, agapaō,* and *stergō. Erōs,* the most commonly used, meant love or desire generically as attracted by the goodness of the object, and specifically connoted the proper conjugal passion of a man and woman. *Erōs* was personified as the god of love (*Anacreon,* 65). In Greek philosophical texts, *erōs* was thought to motivate also the search for perfect truth and beauty in the world in their various degrees and manifestations. In the LXX, *erōs* occurs only twice (Prov 7:18; 30:16 [passages difficult to understand]). In the NT, however, neither *erōs* nor its verb *eraō* or *eraomai* ever occur. *Philia* meant "love, friendship," especially that of equals, comrades, and members of a family; it is found only in Jas 4:4 ("friendship with the world"). Paul uses its cog. verb, *phileō,* only in 1 Cor 16:22, in a formula that he may be borrowing; this verb is found otherwise 28 times in the NT (Matthew, Luke, Titus, James, and especially in John [of Jesus and his disciples]). *Agapē* was a rare word in extrabiblical Greek, often regarded as a shortened form of *agapēsis,* which occurs in Aristotle's writings (e.g., *Metaphysica* 980a 22). *Agapē* emerges first in the LXX, where it is used 18 times, often to translate Hebrew *'ahăbāh* in the sense of sexual love (Cant 2:5–7; 8:6–7), but also of the love of God (Wis 3:9); from there it spreads to other Greek Jewish writings. In secular Greek writings it appears for the first time in the first century A.D. (Spicq, *TLNT,* 1:18). The NT preference for *agapē* and its verb *agapaō* is undoubtedly owing to influence of the LXX, whether it expresses love of human beings or of God (MM, 1–2; *EDNT,* 1:8–12; 3:425–26; *TDOT,* 1:99–118; *TDNT,* 1:38–44; *TLNT,* 1:8–22). It can mean the "love" of husband and wife and express erotic passion, but in time, especially in Hellenistic Jewish and Christian writings, it acquired a more general, ethical connotation: a spontaneous inward affection of one person for another that manifests itself in an outgoing concern for the other and impels one to self-giving. *Storgē* was hardly ever used for sexual love, but it did express the love of parents for children, and vice versa. Neither it nor its cog. verb is ever found in the NT; in the LXX, it occurs in 3 Macc 5:32; 4 Macc 14:13, 14, 17. For the relation of two of the verbs, *phileō* and *agapaō,* see Aristotle, *Rhetoric* 1.11.17 §1371a; cf. Xenophon, *Memor.* 2.7.9, 12. Söding ("Das Wortfeld") has shown that the NT usage is closely related to the LXX usage, but also has some relation to extrabiblical religious and philosophical writings (see also Wischmeyer, "Vorkommen").

In the Judeo-Christian tradition, however, the supreme object of love would be God (Deut 6:4–5; Mark 12:29–30), who is also said to love his people (Deut 33:3; 7:8, 13; Hos 3:1; 11:1, 8–9; 14:5; Isa 43:4). For Paul the process of love thus begins in God, whose love "has been poured into our hearts through the Holy Spirit that has been given to us" (Rom 5:5), and this through Christ Jesus, who loved us when we were still sinners (Rom 5:8; 8:31–39; 2 Cor 13:11, 13; 1 Thess 1:4). According to Gal 5:6, love is the way true Christian faith "works itself out," because it is "a fruit of the Spirit" (Gal 5:22). This is why Paul can maintain that "the one who loves another has fulfilled the law . . . , for love is the fulfillment of the law" (Rom 13:8–10). Although most of these qualities of "love" are found in other Pauline writings, they fill in his description beyond what he says about it here, where he uses the noun *agapē* nine times in thirteen verses. In vv. 4–8a, Paul even personifies *agapē*, as he does truth in v. 6b, and such personification raises the question whether *agapē* does not ultimately tell us about God giving himself in this gift, even though Paul mentions neither God nor Christ in this passage. Nonetheless, *agapē* remains the supreme quality of Christian existence. Justified and sanctified by Christ, Christians become the channel of passing on his love to others, when they allow their love to vitalize the endowments that they have received from the Spirit. Cf. the Johannine way of putting the same topic: John 3:16; 1 John 3:1; 4:7–12.

That *agapē* is regarded by Paul as another *charisma* (Lietzmann, *1 Cor*, 64–65) is hardly correct, as Bornkamm ("More Excellent," 190 n. 18) has rightly seen, since 14:1 separates it from *pneumatika*. Still more questionable is Käsemann's contention that *agapē* in this passage is to be interpreted as a gnostic eon and the spiritual gifts as " 'parts' of the eon," which would return to the whole at the eschaton (*Leib*, 173–74).

The asyndetic formula, "faith, hope, love," with which the passage comes to an end (13:13), is unique even in Pauline writing, but it is scarcely his creation here, because he has already used the threesome elsewhere in varied formulations (1 Thess 1:3; 5:8; Gal 5:5–6). J. Weiss thought that it was an inherited early Christian formula (*1 Cor*, 320), but there is no evidence of it before Paul's use. After Paul, the threesome frequently occurs: Col 1:4–5; Eph 4:2–5; 1 Pet 1:3–8; Heb 6:10–12; *Ep.Barn.* 1.4; 11.8; Polycarp, *Phil.* 3.2–3 (see W. Weiss, "Glaube — Liebe — Hoffnung").

Lietzmann (*1 Cor*, 67) and others, following Reitzenstein, cite a formula found in the writings of the philosopher Porphyry of Tyre (A.D. 232–305), who in his *Ep. ad Marcellam* 24 mentions:

tessara stoicheia malista kekratynthō peri theou: pistis, alētheia, erōs, elpis. pisteusai gar dei, hoti monē sōtēria hē pros ton theon epistrophē, kai pisteusanta hōs eni malista spoudasai talēthē gnōnai peri autou, kai gnonta erasthēnai tou gnōsthentos, erasthenta de elpisin agathais trephein tēn psychēn dia biou. . . . stoicheia men oun tauta kai tosauta kekratynthō.

four first principles especially have been maintained about God: faith, truth, love, hope. For one must believe that one's only salvation is in turning to God, and that the believer must make every effort possible to know the truth about him; and that the one who knows must be enamored of the One known, and the one who loves must nourish his soul during life with good hopes. . . . Let, then, these our principles be maintained. (ed. Nauck, 289)

From such evidence it is argued that Corinthians would have had a similar foursome, *pistis, gnōsis* (instead of *alētheia*), *agapē* (instead of *erōs*), and *elpis*, and that Paul would have stricken *gnōsis*, in order to fashion his threesome. A similar explanation was given by Bultmann, who even characterized *gnōsis* as Gnostic (*TDNT*, 1:710). Such an explanation, however, is problematic, because, though the parallel is interesting, there is no evidence of its use among contemporary Corinthian Christians—apart from such speculation. Paul has already used the threesome elsewhere (see above); and the late date of Porphyry's four-element formula complicates the argument. Since this passage is not written in a polemical tone, why would Paul want to eliminate "knowledge" from such a formula when he has already mentioned it as a gift of the Spirit in 12:8 (Kümmel in Lietzmann, *1 Cor,* 189)? The threesome seems to be employed as the counterpart of prophecy, tongues, and knowledge of 13:8; they will "end" or "be brought to nothing," but "faith, hope, love remain."

The reader should beware of the eisegetical interpretation of this chapter given by K. Barth, *Resurrection,* 71–88. Chapter 13 is hardly the "direct prelude to the theme of which chapter 15 will treat" (ibid., 72). The theme of chap. 13 is quite different from that of chap. 15, despite the eschatological character that one may find in both of them. This chapter forms, rather, the climax of Paul's discussion of *pneumatika* in chap. 12, giving a preeminent place to *agapē,* "love," after which he returns in chap. 14 to two *pneumatika* to put them in a proper perspective (see further Bultmann, "Karl Barth," 78–80).

If for Kugelman this chapter is "one of the most sublime passages of the entire Bible" (*JBC* art. 51 §78), it is for Stuart, "Paul at his most manipulative" because "its message is that it is only through Paul that the Corinthians can experience the love of God in Christ because only Paul, no other Christian teacher, possesses that love. In short, love is Paul" ("Love Is . . . Paul," 265)! Hardly; see C. J. Waters, " 'Love is . . . Paul'—A Response."

NOTES

13:1. *If I speak with human and angelic tongues.* I.e., with all tongues that possibly can be imagined, even with hyperbole. This is the first of the three conditional statements, in two of which the two-part protasis (positive and negative) alludes to one or other of the spiritual endowments mentioned in chap. 12; the second is even double or triple. The emphatic first position is given to tongues, which is the next-to-last-mentioned in the preceding lists of *pneumatika* (12:10, 28–29) and the least important among them—undoubtedly the one that was creating most of the trouble at Corinth. There is no reason to restrict "human tongues" to foreign languages, *pace* I. J. Martin, because Paul is trying to say that even if he were the most eloquent of human beings in any language or even the best-endowed speaker in tongues, he would be nothing without love. On "angels," see NOTE on 4:9.

What is meant by "angelic tongues" is not easy to say. A similar expression is found in *T. Job* 48.3, *aphenxato de tē angelikē dialektō*, "She [Hemera] chanted in the angelic language" (ed. S. Brock, 56). Later rabbinic tradition among Jews considered Hebrew, *lĕšôn haqqōdeš*, "language of the sanctuary," to be angelic speech (Str-B, 3:449). Sometimes it is thought that Paul is alluding to what he heard in his vision and will call *arrēta rhēmata*, "things that no human can express" (2 Cor 12:4), but angels are not mentioned there, and there is no reason to think that the *rhēmata* were uttered by such beings.

Paul is simply indulging in rhetorical hyperbole, and using a bit of irony, as he joins contrary terms to express the totality of those who use speech. *Pace* Garland (*1 Cor*, 611), it is not "misleading" to say that Paul is using hyperbole. No one knows what angelic language is, or even whether angels have tongues; and it is far from certain that Paul considers angelic tongues as "the very epitome of the gift of tongues" (*EDNT*, 1:14), or even "the language of worship" (Spicq, *Agape*, 145). Even if some Corinthian Christians were so referring to their endowment, Paul considers such a language useless.

The "I" in these first statements, and in vv. 11–12, is to be understood as rhetorical, as in Wis 7:8–10; Sir 51:13–22 (so J. Weiss, *1 Cor*, 311; Lindemann, *1 Cor*, 282; Wischmeyer, *Der höchste Weg*, 90–91; Mitchell, *Paul*, 58), meaning "*homo religiosus Christianus*" (Bornkamm, "More Excellent," 181). Far less likely is the autobiographical meaning: that the seven things mentioned in vv. 1–3 are anchored in Paul's own "apostolic behavior" (Holladay, "Apostolic Paradigm," 89; Lambrecht, "Most Eminent," 87). 14:18 might seem to support the latter interpretation, but see NOTE there for the sense of that problematic verse.

but I do not have love. I.e., if I lack this most crucial characteristic of Christian life, expressed thus in the alternative protasis of the first three conditions. Love's worth is seen in the contrast it forms to the seven hypothetical gifts or acts with which it is compared. The expression "to have love," which recurs in 2 Cor 2:4; Phil 2:2; cf. John 5:42; 13:35; 15:13, denotes not just the possession of love, but the *exercise of it* toward other human beings or God. Earlier occurrences of this notion are found in 2:9; 8:1, 3, where it refers to love of God.

I am only resounding brass or a clanging cymbal. In the apodosis, *gegona*, lit. "I have become," is a perf. that is the equivalent of a pres. tense, because the three clauses are present general conditions (*ean* + subjunct., and pres. indic. [*eimi*, v. 2; *ōpheloumai*, v. 3]).

The phrase *chalkos ēchōn* has often been translated as "a resounding/noisy gong" (e.g., RSV, NEB, NIV, Goodspeed), but it is far from certain that *chalkos*, "copper" (or "brass, bronze," when alloyed with tin) is referring to another musical instrument parallel to *kymbalon*. Vitruvius (*De architectura* 5.3.8) tells of *organa in aeneis lamminis aut corneis echeis* [= *ēcheiois*] *ad cordarum sonitum claritatem* ("devices with bronze plates or horn [as] sounding boards [he uses the Greek word] for the clear sound of string instruments"), employed in theaters for acoustical purposes (see also 5.5.1, 7–8). This seems to be the object to which Paul alludes (see Harris, " 'Sounding Brass' "; Klein, "Noisy Gong"). It would have been a well-understood comparison in Corinth, which was famous for its manufacture of bronze vessels, especially that used for acoustical purposes (see Murphy-O'Connor, "Corinthian Bronze," who is a bit skeptical of Vitruvius's testimony). Cf. Herodotus, *Hist.* 4.200. Plato (*Prot.* 329a) compares the bombast of Sophist orators to a bronze that echoes long after it is struck.

Kymbalon, usually plur., denotes metal basins that are struck against each other to make a shrill sound, as in LXX 1 Sam 18:6; 1 Chr 13:8; 15:16, 19; Ps 150:5; they were often employed in the liturgy of the Temple. With it Paul uses the neut. ptc. *alalazon*, which describes an inarticulate sound, often heard in wailing (see Mark 5:38).

The two phrases, resounding brass and clanging cymbal, describe the empty (meaningless) speech of someone speaking in tongues without love: sound perhaps, but only reverberations of an empty mind having no effect on the Christian community and its common endeavor. Note the similarity of argument in vv. 1–3 to that of Matt 23:16–22, where Jesus criticizes blind guides who swear by the Temple, its gold, and its altar. Paul is not rejecting outright such speaking in tongues, prophecy, or knowledge, but only maintaining that such would-be religious actions carried out without love become worthless and meaningless. T. K. Sanders ("New Approach," 617) understands *ē* as "rather than" and translates, "I am a dinging piece of bronze rather than a joyfully sounding cymbal." That, however, is not what the Greek text means, because the ptc. *alalazon* is related to *alala*, an "outcry," associated with wailing and mourning (BDAG, 41; cf. Thiselton, *1 Cor*, 1039).

2. *If I have the gift of prophecy and comprehend all mysteries and all knowledge.* Lit. "if I have prophecy and . . . ," which recalls the *pneumatikon* of 12:10, 28–29, Spirit-inspired dynamic and effective preaching based on Scripture, and not the gift of foretelling the future, as it has sometimes been interpretred. The comprehension of "all mysteries" may allude to Paul's discussion of wisdom and its relation to the hidden counsels of God, the "heavenly secrets" of 2:1 (see NOTE there); 2:7; 4:1; the word occurs again in 14:2; 15:51 (J. Weiss [*1 Cor*, 314] thinks Paul is referring to the last mentioned or to Rom 11:25). Cf. 4QEnGiants[a] (4Q203) 9:3: *dî kôl razayyāʾ yād[ēăʿ ʾantāh]*, "for [you k]now all mysteries." *Gnōsis*, "knowledge," is neither that commended by Paul (1:5) nor that with which he found fault (2:1–6; 8:1), but rather that listed among the *pneumatika* (12:8). Now Paul degrades it, considering it worthless without love (see Bultmann, *TDNT*, 1:710, but ignore what he calls Paul's "opposition to Gnosticism"). Lindemann (*1 Cor*, 283) notes that "all knowledge" is a phrase used of God in 1QH[a] 19(old 11):8 (*kwl dʿh*); see also 1QS 11:18; 4QInstruction[d] (4Q418) 69 ii 11. Chiasmus is found in *ta mystēria panta kai pasan tēn gnōsin*, "mysteries all and all knowledge."

and if I have all the faith to move mountains. Lit. "so as to move mountains," a result clause. An allusion to 12:9 (see NOTE there), where it was simply called *pistis*, without the clarifying modifiers used here. They remind one of the words of Jesus recorded later in Mark 11:22–23; Matt 17:20; 21:21.

but do not have love, I am nothing. "Spiritually a cipher" (Robertson-Plummer).

In other words, all such *pneumatika* amount to zero without the animating force of love, which Paul is going to describe in detail in vv. 4–8a.

3. *If I dole out all I own and hand over my body.* Lit. " if I give away all bit by bit to feed others." Another double condition parallels the construction of v. 2 and expresses self-denying situations that go beyond *pneumatika* and might still occur without love. The first example may be an allusion to the God-appointed *pneumatikon* called *antilēmpseis*, "assistants" (12:28), those who serve the physical needs of others, perhaps the poor in the community. The extreme of such assistance is expressed by giving away *panta ta hyparchonta mou*, "all that belongs to me," and not just that which I do not need. Possibly this is an allusion to the words of Jesus recorded in Luke 12:33 ("Sell your belongings and give them away as alms") cf. Matt 19:21. Even such an extreme divesting of self would mean nothing without love. For other uses of *psōmizō*, "feed" (someone), see Rom 12:20; LXX Deut 32:13; *1 Clem.* 55.2.

The second example goes even further and expresses a climax, "handing over" my body (*paradō*, as in 5:5 [see NOTE there]) and not just my possessions, which means to give up one's life for the sake of others, or possibly to go into slavery in place of someone else, i.e., some sort of ultimate self-sacrifice for the sake of another.

in order to boast. I.e., as Paul himself has done in 9:15–16, if this reading is correct. The best MSS (P⁴⁶, ℵ, A, B, 048, 33) read subjunct. *kauchēsōmai*, "that I may boast," preferred by N-A²⁷, NAB, NRSV, Benoit, Giesen, Héring, Petzer, et al.

Other MSS (C, D, F, G, L, 81) have the fut. indic. *kauthēsomai*, and a few (Ψ, 1739ᶜ) have its more correct aor. subjunct. form *kauthēsōmai*, both meaning "that I may be burned." Such a reading suits better the second part of the protasis, because it supplies a concrete form of the way one might give up one's life by fire (as Shadrach, Meshach, and Abednego were willing to do in Dan 3:95 [Theodotion]), and it brings the comparison to a suitable climax. However, it is not the *lectio difficilior*, and both forms of the verb *kaiō*, "burn," look like a copyist's correction to make sense of a difficult reading, since boasting is harder to explain, because it sounds too much like self-glorification. Sometimes, however, Paul regards boasting as apostolically justified, as in 2 Cor 8:24; Phil 2:16; 1 Thess 2:19 (see Metzger, *TCGNT*, 497–98). Many versions and commentators, however, continue to read "that I may be burned" (RSV, NKJV, NIV, REB, ESV; Barrett, Conzelmann, Fee, Garland, Kremer, Lietzmann, Lindemann, Robertson-Plummer, Senft), considering the clause as parallel to the result clause of v. 2, "so as to move mountains." The reading is much debated: Benoit, "Codex," 74; Caragounis, " 'To Boast' "; Elliott, "In Favour"; Kieffer, "Afin que"; Petzer, "Contextual Evidence"; Riesenfeld, "Vorbildliches Martyrium"; J. F. Smit, "Two Puzzles," 255–63.

but do not have love, I gain nothing. Notice the progression in the apodoses of the first three verses: "I produce nothing of value" (v. 1); "I am of no value" (v. 2); "I gain nothing of any value" (v. 3), i.e., gain nothing eschatologically, as *ōpheleō* means in Mark 8:36. In other words, human achievements and even spiritual gifts prove to be worthless, if they have not been vitalized by love, which is the sine qua non of Christian life.

4. *Love is patient; love is kind.* With this verse Paul begins the second section of his presentation (vv. 4–8a), in which he personifies love "as a thinking and choosing being which inspires the behavior of the faithful in many different fields" (Spicq, *Agape*, 150). He lists its sixteen characteristics by the use of the same number of verbs. The symmetry of his short sentences allows the character of love to emerge. Paul shows that love is not a mere feeling, but it evokes a mode of action.

Patience and kindness are the first of seven pairs of characteristics. They are expressed positively, as will be the last two pairs introduced by the fourfold *panta*, "all things." Before the last two, a single positive statement is also introduced (v. 6b). The characteristics express the opposite of all that a human being in his or her native condition may stand for, because Christian love transcends that condition. The opposite of such characteristics would undoubtedly describe the conduct of many Corinthian Christians to whom Paul is writing. The first pair is chiastically arranged, but depending on how one punctuates the verse, one can take the second *hē agapē* either with the verb that precedes (as in the lemma, which respects the chiasmus), or with the verb that follows (as in the RSV, Lietzmann).

The first positive characteristic expresses a passive response to others: being slow to lose tolerance of others; the second expresses an active response: looking for a way to be constructive. Paul uses the pres. tense of two verbs, the compound *makrothymeō*, "be long-suffering, remain tranquil while waiting" (cf. the exhortation in 1 Thess 5:14), and *chrēsteuomai*, "be kind," a verb found only here in the Greek Scriptures (cf. *1 Clem.* 13.2); it expresses a generous welcome that one accords another. Cf. 2 Cor 6:6; Gal 5:22. "Kindness" is to be distinguished from "endurance," the last of the characteristics in v. 7d.

[Love] is not jealous; it does not brag. I.e., it is not intolerant of rivalry or unfaithfulness, and it does not engage in self-glorification. At the beginning of this first pair of negative characteristics, *agapē* is repeated in most Greek MSS. In some (B, 33), however, it is omitted; hence the square brackets (Metzger, *TCGNT*, 498–99). The verbs in this pair are *zēloō*, which often means in a positive sense, "strive, exert oneself earnestly" (12:31; 14:1, 39), but it also has a negative sense, intended here, "envy, be jealous about" (the achievements or status of someone else [Acts 7:9; 17:5]), and the rare *perpereuomai*, "be vainglorious," or anxious to impress others. This pair would suit the Corinthian problem of rivalry (3:3); cf. Jas 3:14; 4:2. (N-A[27] wrongly puts a comma before bracketed *hē agapē*, meaning that it is the subj. of the following verb; that it is indeed, but then *ou zēloi* "hangs in the air" [Lindemann, *1 Cor*, 287]. The comma should be omitted.)

it is not arrogant. Lit. "it does not puff itself up," which says practically the same thing as the preceding characteristic, because it means "being conceited," or cherishing inflated ideas of one's own importance. Paul has used the verb *physioō* several times already in this letter (4:6, 18, 19; 5:2; 8:1), and now he offers an antidote for it. The other part of this pair is expressed at the beginning of the next verse; the verse numbering has not respected the pairs.

5. *It is not rude.* Lit. "does not behave discourteously," i.e., it has good manners; this second verb (*aschēmonein*) of the second negative pair occurred in a sexual context at 7:36 (being indecent), but here it has a more generic nuance of lacking

in propriety. It is actually the active (negative) sense of a verb that can also mean "suffer shame" or "incur disgrace" (LXX Deut 25:3; Ezek 16:7, 22, 29). Ms P[46] strangely reads *ouk euschēmonei*, "does not behave with decorum," obviously a scribal error caused by distraction (Metzger, *TCGNT*, 499), but preferred by Debrunner, Kümmel in Lietzmann, *1 Cor*, 189.

it does not seek its own interest. Lit. "the things of itself," i.e., what is to its own advantage. This first item of the third negative pair asserts fully the essence of Christian love: disinterestedness. A form of the expression *ta heautēs*, "the things of itself," was already met in 10:24; cf. Phil 2:21. It criticizes selfishness or preoccupation with self, and it may even castigate the mentality behind the trivial lawsuits of chap. 6. The implication is that love seeks rather the common good of the community. Some MSS (P[46c], B) read rather *to mē ta heautēs*, "what is not its own," i.e., what does not belong to it, a notion that is quite different from the selfishness implied in the reading translated in the lemma.

it does not become irritated. Or "it does not let itself be exasperated," i.e., provoked (to anger or impatience)," which is related to *makrothymei* of v. 4. The verb *paroxynō* is used of Paul in Athens irritated by the sight of many idols (Acts 17:16). In the LXX it regularly expresses how God was "provoked" by the rebellion and grumbling of the Israelites in the desert (Num 14:11; 16:30; Deut 9:7–8, 19).

It does not reckon with wrongs. Lit. "it takes no note of evil," i.e., it cherishes no resentment over an injury received. Or possibly *ou logizetai to kakon* means, "It does not plot evil," for this characteristic may echo LXX Zech 8:17, "nor should anyone of you plot evil against his neighbor" (*tēn kakian tou plēsion autou mē logizesthe*). This is the first verb of the fourth pair of negative characteristics; its counterpart is found at the beginning of the next verse. Cf. 2 Cor 2:5–11 (Paul's own example).

6. *It does not delight in wrongdoing.* I.e., love takes no pleasure in seeing wrong or injustice (*adikia*) done to someone else; it does not share the joy of those who offend or gloat over evil they have done. This is further explained in the following positive characteristic.

but rejoices with the truth. Truth is here personified, as love has been since v. 4. What is meant by *alētheia* is not that which is known about God (Rom 1:18) or the "truth of the gospel" (Gal 2:5, 14), but truth in a more philosophical sense, probably the quality that reckons carefully with reality and is meant to guide all human life, as in 2 Cor 13:8; Gal 4:16. When it prevails, then love can rejoice with it.

7. *It puts up with all things, believes all things.* This is the sixth pair, a positive expression with *panta* twice, which will be followed by yet another pair that also has *panta* twice. The first verbs are *stegō*, "keep confidential," i.e., be silent about what is displeasing in another person (cf. 9:12; Sir 8:17), or makes allowance because it has no limit to its endurance; and *pisteuō*, "believe, consider worthy of trust." In this context (following *stegō*), the verb *pisteuō* must mean trusting bona fide and accepting another's word rather than suspecting it unduly; it gives a favorable interpretation to what it hears. The opposite of it is found in 1 Thess 3:1, 5 ("when we could bear with it no longer").

hopes for all things, endures all things. So runs the final pair of positive characteristics of love. The verbs are *elpizō*, "hope (for)," and *hypomenō*, "remain (behind), hold out, endure," i.e., Christian love knows no hopeless causes and no fading of its hopes, because it does not despair of the future. Moreover, it holds fast as it tolerates all things in its trust of the neighbor and is not crushed by coldness. See Rom 8:24b; 12:12.

8. *Love never fails.* Lit. "never falls," i.e., falls to pieces, collapses (BDAG, 815), or proves to be ineffective, no matter what happens to all the other characteristics. It stands when all else falls. The words *oudepote piptei* do not mean "never ends" (RSV, NRSV, ESV) or "never comes to an end" (NEB); that nuance is still to be expressed in v. 13. Paul repeats *agapē* again, as he lists its sixteenth characteristic, and uses an emphatic adv. *oudepote*, which occurs only here in his writings.

This statement leads up to the third part of his discussion (vv. 8b–12), which now begins, as he stresses the abiding and superior quality of love and compares it with *pneumatika*, "spiritual things," which are "for this world only" (Robertson-Plummer, *1 Cor*, 295). *Agapē* here opens a rhetorical *inclusio* with v. 13, the next time the word appears, and it is the word with which his whole discussion ends.

If there are prophecies, they will be brought to naught. This and the two following statements are introduced by the depreciatory conj. *eite*, which continues Pauline skepticism about the endowments that was already mentioned in vv. 1–2. What he will say about such speech phenomena as prophecy and tongues in chap. 14 explains why he uses *eite* here. In contrast to never-failing love, they will come to an end. The plur. of *prophēteia* seems to mean different kinds of prophetic talents. Earlier in the letter, "prophecy" was seen to mean Spirit-inspired dynamic and effective preaching based on Scripture (12:10); now one learns that even such an endowment will cease and pass away (BDAG, 525). That Paul is serious about this cessation of prophecy can be seen from the skepticism he has already expressed about it in 1 Thess 5:19–22. The same verb (*katargeō*) is used again of knowledge at the end of this verse; its fut. tense has an eschatological nuance that will become clearer in the coming verses. What Plutarch similarly says "About the Obsolescence of Oracles" may be comparable, but there is a difference between Christian prophecy and the divination of the Delphic Oracles (see Green, " 'As for Prophecies' ").

if tongues, they will come to an end. Lit. "will cease" (*pausontai*, which specifies clearly the eschatological sense of the other verb being used, *katargeō*, "bring to naught"). Paul alludes to *genē glōssōn* of 12:10, 28–29. *if knowledge, it will be brought to naught.* This is an allusion to *gnōsis* in 12:8b, which despite its importance in human life, and even more so as *pneumatikon*, an endowment of the Spirit, it too will have its limits. What is known will have little pertinence in the *eschaton*.

9. *For we know in part, and we prophesy in part.* In this and the following verse, Paul shifts to the generic 1st pers. plur., as he discusses the partial and ephemeral character of *gnōsis* and *prophēteia*. The phrase *ek merous*, lit. "from a part," i.e., partially, is placed emphatically at the head of each clause and is meant differently from its use in 12:27. No matter what the endowment, it supplies only a bit of the reality to be known or preached, understood either quantitatively (fragmen-

tary knowledge) or qualitatively (indistinct or fuzzy concepts); (see McElhanon, "1 Corinthians 13:8–12").

10. *but when what is perfect comes, the partial will be brought to naught.* Again the same verb (*katargeō*) is used of "the partial." Set in contrast to *ek merous* is *to teleion*, "the perfect" or "the complete," a term that conveys the idea of the highest standard, expressed by the substantivized neut. of the adj., which has already been used in 2:6 for the "mature" Christian.

To what "the perfect" refers is much debated. It is scarcely related to the completion of the NT canon, as some have tried to take it; such an extraneous meaning is foreign to this context. *To teleion* has been understood as Christian maturity, as in 2:6 (so ancient Montanists, Mani; among modern interpreters, Salvoni, "Quando sarà venuto"). It seems, however, to express rather some sort of goal; it has undoubtedly something to do with the *eschaton* or what Paul calls "the Day of the Lord" (1:8; 3:13; 5:5) or with the *telos*, "end" (of the present era), as in 15:24. So it has been interpreted by many patristic writers (see Shogren, "How Did?"); and among moderns by Bruce, Godet, Robertson-Plummer. When it "comes" (eschatologically), tongues, knowledge, and prophecy, no matter how useful such endowments may be at present, will cease to be, because Paul sees no continuity between the partial and the complete. He maintains that "the partial" will be brought to naught because it is transitory and incomplete (see Martens, "First Corinthians 13:10").

11. *When I was a child, I spoke as a child, I thought as a child, I reasoned as a child.* Paul again shifts to the 1st pers. sing., as in vv. 1–3. He adopts the first singular expression as a rhetorical device to drive home the universal thrust of what he has been saying about love. The singular shifts to the plural in v. 12. In comparison with love, all speech, thought, and reasoning are only of infantile dimension. Paul uses *nēpios* in its basic sense, and not in the sense of the "immature" Christian of 3:1 (see NOTE there). As *nēpios* means *in-fans*, i.e., speech-less, so are all such attempts at communication, which remain uncommunicative, because the speech, thoughts, and reasoning of a child are governed by the wishes and dreams of tiny childhood.

When I became a man, I did away with childish things. Lit. "I brought to naught the things of a child." Paul uses the perf. of the same verb as in vv. 8, 10. Infancy and adulthood are set in contrast, as continuity is denied between them. The term contrasted with "child" is *anēr*, which in this case means not simply a male human being, but a male adult close to the age of 50. (Pseudo-)Hippocrates, whose work, *Peri Hebdomadōn*, is quoted by Philo (*De opificio mundi* 36 §105), gives the seven stages of human life as *paidion, pais, meirakion, neaniskos, anēr, presbytēs, gerōn*, "little boy, boy, lad, young man, man, elderly man, old man," and Philo explains them. So *anēr* would be someone about 49 years of age (see *Philemon*, 105). Cf. Epictetus, *Encheiridion* 51.1. A saying somewhat similar to Paul's, but not identical, is found in Xenophon, *Cyrop.* 8.7.6, who distinguishes his boyhood, youth, mature manhood, and old age.

12. *For at present we see by reflection, as in a mirror.* Lit. "we gaze with the help of a mirror in riddle form (*or* in an indirect image)," i.e., we see not the thing itself,

but only an image or reflection of it, as in a mirror. Unfortunately, Paul uses no obj. with the verb *blepomen* and does not say what we see, because he is more interested in the mode of seeing than its object.

Having contrasted in v. 11 the past (childhood) with the present (adult manhood), Paul further contrasts the present (*arti*) with what is to come (*tote*). He thus introduces a new consideration, involving sight or vision, as he will again in 2 Cor 4:18; Rom 8:24c–25, but now he formulates it with apocalyptic dress (Rev 22:8). His contrast is between the way we now see reality, and the way we shall see it, when *to teleion* comes.

The phrase *en aignimati* is problematic, because *ainigma* means "riddle, puzzling saying," and it is not clear how it can be said of vision or of what is seen. The RSV, NRSV, and ESV translate it "dimly"; the NAB, "indistinctly"; the REB, "puzzling reflections only." Because the following phrase expresses clarity of vision, this phrase seems intended to say the opposite of such clarity; hence "dimly" or "indirectly" seen. Its meaning is helped by *ainigma* used in LXX Num 12:8, where God is said to speak to Moses, "mouth to mouth, plainly, and not in riddles" (*stoma kata stoma lalēsō autō, en eidei kai ou di' ainigmatōn*), where *ainigmata* stands in contrast to *eidos*, "form, appearance," which enables one to see that *ainigma* here can be used as the opposite of clarity (see Robertson-Plummer, *1 Cor*, 298). Cf. LXX Deut 28:37. Senft (*1 Cor*, 171) claims, however, that "the mirror is a symbol of clarity," and finds fault with commentators who speak of the "bad quality" of ancient mirrors, the images of which were said to be "blurred and distorted" (Spicq, *Agape*, 160). Senft is right in his criticism, because there were many good mirrors; but the quality of the mirror is not the issue; it is rather that in a mirror, whether good or poor, one sees only a reflection or image of the thing, not the thing itself. Hence my translation, "by reflection."

The mention of a "mirror" has led many commentators to seek parallels to Paul's use, but not many of them are really pertinent. Some (e.g., Hoffmann, "Pauli Hymnus"; Perry) think that the mention of the mirror is an allusion to the Platonic allegory of the cave (*Rep.* 7.1–3 §§514–18). That, however, is somewhat far-fetched, because there is not a hint of Platonism in the text, and Plato speaks of shadows and images, but not of a mirror. The same has to be said about an allusion in the text to what has been called katoptromancy, i.e., the use of mirrors for divination, which enabled a person to foresee the future and transform oneself (Achelis, "Katoptromantie"; Héring, *1 Cor*, 120). Or the mention of a mirror in the *Odes of Solomon* 13: "The Lord is our mirror. Open (your) eyes and see them in him, and learn the manner of your face" (*OTP*, 2:747).

One passage in Plutarch, however, might have some pertinence, since it uses both *ainigma*, "riddle," and *esoptron*, "mirror," and in a sense not far removed from Paul's meaning. It speaks of the worship of animals among the Egyptians, and Plutarch says that "in considering the problem of the Divine" (*ainigma tou theiou*), one should honor animals "not in themselves, but through them honor the Divine, since they are by their nature rather clear mirrors (*hōs enargesterōn esoptrōn*)" (*De Iside et Osiride* 76 §382a–b; see Gill, "Through a Glass"; Hugedé, *Métaphore du miroir*, 128, 145).

Moreover, because wisdom is said to be "a spotless mirror (*esoptron akēlidōton*) of God's activity" (Wis 7:26), some commentators (e.g., Lindemann, *1 Cor*, 291) think that Paul is referring to our present indirect knowledge of God, with which he is comparing what he expresses in the next phrase. This is a plausible suggestion, and one can compare Philo's similar use of "mirror" (*katoptron*) for God's activity in the world (*De decalogo* 21 §105). In this context, it enables one to supply an object for Paul's verb *blepomen*.

Paul again shifts to the 1st pers. plur., making it likely that the sing. in v. 11 was meant rhetorically, not personally (Kritzer, "Zum Wechsel").

but then face to face. I.e., when "what is perfect" will have come. The phrase *prosōpon pros prosōpon* is derived from LXX Gen 32:31, where Jacob is said so to have seen God; cf. Deut 34:10 (Moses knew God *prosōpon kata prosōpon*); 5:4. This phrase, which is borrowed from such OT passages and with which *blepomen* is understood, further suggests that Paul is thinking of God as the obj. of the verb, even though no object is expressed.

at present I know only in part, but then I shall know fully. This is again a rhetorical 1st pers. sing. formulation of a self-evident truth, that what is known now about God is only partial; but it will be different when "what is perfect comes." The contrast between *arti*, "now," and *tote*, "then," is the same as in v. 12a, but it now becomes apparent that the contrast is not merely temporal, but also qualitative. The fut. compound verb *epignōsomai* is likewise important, because, although the compound often means no more than the simple *ginōskō* (*TDNT*, 1:703), it does have at times the connotation, "know fully, deeply" (Luke 24:16, 31; Acts 12:14; Rom 1:32; 2 Cor 6:9; cf. BDAG, 369 [1a, 3]), as is true also of the cog. noun, *epignōsis* (Rom 3:20). Senft (*1 Cor*, 171) calls it "la connaissance parfaite." Moreover, the next clause explains that this knowledge, which the "I" shall have, is intimately related to "being known," as Lindemann rightly stresses (*1 Cor*, 292).

Some commentators would restrict this fuller knowledge to "this present life," with "no reference to the beatific vision" (Murphy-O'Connor, *NJBC*, 810; Miguens, "1 Cor 13:8–13," 87; Standaert, 140). Admittedly, Paul is not using a term like "beatific vision," but it is far from clear that he is affirming something only about this present life. Much depends here on the meaning given to v. 13.

even as I have been fully known. Paul now employs the pass. of the compound verb *epiginōskō*, which was used in the preceding clause; it is a divine passive (ZBG §236). This knowing and being known have sometimes been said to be derived from Hellenistic Mystery Religions, in which such knowledge is said to lead to being deified. It is, however, characteristically Pauline, in that for him being known by God precedes all other knowledge (see 8:2–3; Gal 4:9; Rom 8:28–30; cf. 2 Tim 2:19), as he builds on various OT expressions about God's prior knowledge and election of His agents (see Gen 18:19; Exod 33:12; Jer 1:5; Hos 13:5; Amos 3:2). Once again, the "I" is not Paul alone, but the Christian who "is known" by God and is chosen by His prevenient grace (Bornkamm, "More Excellent," 186). "Our knowledge of God will be a function of God's knowledge of us" (Spicq, *Agape*, 166), just as Paul has already said in 8:3, "If anyone loves God, that one is known by him." When the "then" comes, "I shall have complete knowledge, even as God has complete knowledge of me" (ibid.).

13. *And now faith, hope, love remain, these three.* So Paul draws his description of love to a close, with a verse that has many problems, not the least of which is the connection of the threesome to what has immediately preceded in vv. 10–12 and the addition of faith and hope to a discussion that has involved so far only love. It is a formula that is meant to terminate the discussion of love and its relation to the *pneumatika*, but it introduces a further discussion of two of them; and its wording raises a number of questions.

One thing is clear, however; *pistis* is not the same as that in v. 2, "faith to move mountains"; rather it now denotes the full sense of saving and justifying "faith," the response to the Christian gospel, as in other Pauline passages (Rom 10:6–10: belief in the death and resurrection of Christ Jesus), and especially in those in which the triad further occurs (1 Thess 1:3; 5:8; Gal 5:5–6; cf. Col 1:4–5). Note also the linking of love to faith in 1 Cor 16:13–14; 1 Thess 3:6; Phlm 5. The triad, however, is meant to replace the threesome of tongues, prophecy, and knowledge of vv. 1–2 and 8.

The first difficulty is the meaning of the adv. *nyni*, "now." It is scarcely to be understood as the equivalent of the temporal adv. *arti* (v. 12a), which was contrasted with *tote*, "then," another adv. of time. It is rather expressing a logical conclusion, as in Rom 7:17: "but now," i.e., as the situation is (BDAG, 682). Cf. also 1 Cor 12:18; 15:20; 2 Cor 8:11, 12.

Because vv. 8b–12b already refer to the eschaton, faith, hope, and love are understood sometimes as remaining forever. In this interpretation, the verb *menei* has a future nuance, as in 3:14; 2 Cor 3:11, and is taken as equivalent to *oudepote piptei*, "never fails" (v. 8). Moreover, *agapē*, which opened a rhetorical *inclusio* there, closes it in this verse. In both cases, the affirmation is eschatological, "remains forever," i.e., "enduring not only in this age but also in the age to come" (Barrett, *1 Cor*, 308; similarly Johansson, "I Cor. xiii"; Kistemaker, *1 Cor*, 470–71; Lindemann, *1 Cor*, 293; Neirynck, "De grote drie"; Schrage, *1 Cor*, 3:318–19).

Such an eschatological understanding of v. 13, however, encounters a difficulty, when it is compared with 2 Cor 5:7, "For we walk by faith, not by sight," and Rom 8:24bc, "A hope that is seen is no hope at all. Who hopes for what he sees?" These two Pauline passages speak of faith and hope in this life, and they make it difficult to think of them as remaining or lasting forever in an eschatological sense, i.e., into "the age to come" (see Lacan, "Les trois").

Others maintain that Paul is thinking rather of two stages in a Christian's earthly experience. In 2:6–3:4 Paul has already spoken of these stages, using the vocabulary, *nēpios* and *teleios*, of an "immature" and "mature" Christian, or referring to the "fleshy" and "spiritual" aspects of the earthly Christian life. Now he has contrasted *ek merous* and *to teleion* in vv. 10 and 12, and the *arti* and the *tote* in v. 12 would refer to these two stages of such earthly life. (So Miguens, "1 Cor 13:8–13"; Murphy-O'Connor, *NJBC*, 811; Hays, *1 Cor*, 230–31; Fee, *1 Cor*, 650).

This interpretation encounters a difficulty when one asks what is meant by seeing "face to face" (13:12). It may be an allusion to the difference of Moses' experience of God from that of other prophets (Num 12:6–8), but is it merely a literary allusion and nothing more? Moreover, if the spiritual gifts of prophecy, tongues, and knowledge are to pass away (v. 8), when *to teleion* comes, and "love never fails" (vv. 8–10), something must perdure. Again, the verbs *blepomen*, "we gaze," and *ginōskō*, "I know," have no obj. expressed; but God is almost certainly implied, because the last clause in v. 12, "even as I have been fully known," must refer to God's knowledge of "me." Any other maturity in Christian life becomes almost meaningless in this context, as Carson notes: "*any* preparousia maturity simply trivializes the language of verse 12" (*Showing the Spirit*, 71).

One has, then, to steer a course between these two modes of understanding this part of v. 13. Faith, hope, and love remain in this life for the Christian, even if all other *pneumatika* pass away. They are essential to Christian life, "these three"; they are implied in v. 7 above. Then one must listen to what Paul says in the last clause of this verse.

The verb *menei* is sing., despite the plur. subject, perhaps agreeing with the neut. plur. appositive, *ta tria tauta* (BDF §133). In MS P[46] and some patristic writers (e.g., Clement, Augustine), there is a different word order, where the appositive becomes the subj., which then rightly calls for the sing.: *menei ta tria tauta, pistis, elpis, agapē*; but that may be a scribal correction. It is better to retain the order in N-A[27], and then one should distinguish the "remaining" that the verb denotes: the triad "remains" in this life, from the crucifixion to the parousia of Christ (1:7–8), but love also "remains" beyond it, because of its superior quality explained in the next clause.

but the greatest of these is love. Lit. "the greater of these is love," a good example of the disappearance of a distinction between the comparative and superlative degrees of an adj. in Hellenistic Greek (BDF §244.1; ZBG §148). However, R. P. Martin ("Suggested Exegesis") would retain the comparative degree and translate, ". . . greater than these (three) is the love [of God]." That may be good theology, but Paul did not write what is now in the square brackets, and the foregoing context, dealing with human love, demands that human love be included in *hē agapē*, the predicate of this clause, at least in some way.

Love is superior to the other two, faith and hope, not only because it plays the supreme role in Christian earthly life, but especially because it perdures even into "the age to come." Of the three, it is eschatological, has eternal value, and is the reason why the Christian will "know fully" and be "fully known," i.e., by God.

In Paul's view of earthly Christian life, however, "by faith we walk" (2 Cor 5:7): in this earthly life "faith remains," as that by which we conduct ourselves. "Love," however, is also that through which faith "works itself out" (Gal 5:6) in this earthly life. It is, then, the supreme way of Christian life: "Love does no wrong to a neighbor, for love is the fulfillment of the law" (Rom 13:10; see further *Romans*, 679). In this sense, then, love also "remains" in this life. Moreover, "hope remains" in this life, but in this life only (Rom 8:24–25). *Pace* Bultmann, it is not a "confidence which, directed away from the world to God, waits patiently for God's gift, and when it is received does not rest in possession but in the assurance that God will maintain what He has given" (*TDNT*, 2:532). Such "confidence" and "assurance," however, are marks of human faith, not of hope. In Rom 8:22–25, Paul characterizes human hope and relates it to the expectation of all creation; and in v. 7 above he even says, "Love hopes for all things, endures all things," i.e., in this life. "Faith and hope will pass away and be replaced by sight and fulfillment. Only eschatological love will remain for ever and will never end" (Lambrecht, "Most Eminent," 102). When that for which the Christian hopes is reached, then only love will still perdure, even in "the age to come": *menei eis ton aiōna tōn aiōnōn* (to borrow a saying about God's righteousness from LXX Ps 112:9). That will be true both of the Christian's love of God and of God's prior love of the Christian. As a result, one can agree with Spicq that "it is not in the heaven that St. Paul has just described that faith, hope, and charity 'endure,' but in Corinth under the circumstances of everyday Christian life. Charisms are only an accessory and even exceptional element in this life. The essential element is charity, but charity is not alone" (*Agape*, 169). In other words, Paul is emphasizing the role of the triad for Corinthian Christian life, but love or charity "will continue to exist in the next world where it will guarantee the definitive vision and communion with God. Its excellence is primarily eschatological" (ibid., 170). "Love" is also the greatest because with it the Christian shares in what is unique to God, who has neither faith nor hope, whereas what God does is love, and without it he would not be God (see Morton, "Gifts in the Context of Love").

Other ways of considering it are sometimes added, but they can be questioned. Thus, whereas faith and hope are the virtues of humans or creatures, love is divine (Robertson-Plummer, *1 Cor*, 300). That is partly true, because love must characterize human earthly life too.

In this way, then, Paul relates love to the overemphasis on *pneumatika* among Corinthian Christians. These gifts have value, indeed, for earthly life, but love is the essential characteristic of Christian life not only in this age, but also in the age to come. It is the "greatest," because it is the mark not only of eternity, but of the present as well.

BIBLIOGRAPHY (See also Bibliography on 12:1–14:39, pp. 461–62)

Achelis, H., "Katoptromantie bei Paulus," *Theologische Festschrift für G. Nathanael Bonwetsch* . . . (Leipzig: Deichert, 1918) 56–63.

Balducelli, R., *Il concetto teologico di carità attraverso le maggiori interpretazioni patristiche e medievali di I ad Cor. XIII* (Studies in Sacred Theology 2/48; Washington: Catholic University of America Press, 1951).

Barr, A., "Love in the Church: A Study of First Corinthians 13," *SJT* 3 (1950) 416–25.

Barth, K., *The Resurrection of the Dead*, 71–88.

Bassett, S. E., "1 Cor. 13,12: *blepomen gar arti di' esoptrou en ainigmati*," *JBL* 47 (1928) 232–36.

Behm, J., "Das Bildwort vom Spiegel 1 Korinther 13, 12," *Reinhold Seeberg Festschrift* (2 vols.; Leipzig: Deichert, 1929), 1:315–42.

Blaiklock, E. M., *The Way of Excellence: A New Translation and Study of 1 Corinthians 13 and Romans 12* (London: Pickering & Inglis, 1968).

Blair, H. J., "First Corinthians 13 and the Disunity at Corinth," *TTE* 14/1 (1983) 69–77.

Bornkamm, G., "The More Excellent Way: I Corinthians 13," *Early Christian Experience*, 180–93.

Brennan, J., "The Exegesis of 1 Cor. 13," *ITQ* 21 (1954) 270–78.

Brock, S. P., *Testamentum Iobi* (Leiden: Brill, 1967).

Bultmann, R., "Karl Barth, *The Resurrection of the Dead*," *Faith and Understanding I* (tr. L. P. Smith; New York: Harper & Row, 1969) 66–94.

Bunch, T. G., *Love: A Comprehensive Exposition of 1 Corinthians 13* (Washington, DC: Review and Herald, 1952).

Caragounis, C. C., " 'To Boast' or 'To Be Burned'? The Crux of 1 Cor 13:3," *SEA* 60 (1995) 115–27.

Corley, J., "The Pauline Authorship of 1 Corinthians 13," *CBQ* 66 (2004) 256–74.

Cuvillier, E., "Entre théologie de la Croix et éthique de l'excès: Une lecture de 1 Corinthiens 13," *ETR* 75 (2000) 349–62.

Danker, F. W., "The Mirror Metaphor in 1 Cor. 13:12 and 2 Cor. 3:18," *CTM* 31 (1960) 428–29.

Dreyfus, F., "Maintenant la foi, l'espérance et la charité demeurent toutes les trois (1 Cor 13,13)," *SPCIC*, 1. 403–12.

Drummond, R. J., "The Greatest of These Is What?" *EvQ* 23 (1951) 5–7.

Elliott, J. K., "In Favour of *kauthēsomai* at I Corinthians 13,3," *ZNW* 62 (1971) 297–98.

Flood, E., "Christian Love: Some Pauline Reflections," *CR* 69 (1984) 233–37.

Focant, C., "1 Corinthiens: Analyse rhétorique et analyse de structures," *The Corinthian Correspondence* (BETL 125; ed. R. Bieringer), 199–245.

Gerhardsson, B., "1 Kor 13: Zur Frage von Paulus' rabbinischen Hintergrund," *Donum gentilicium: New Testament Studies in Honour of David Daube* (ed. E. Bammel et al.; Oxford: Clarendon, 1978) 185–209. Cf. *SEA* 39 (1974) 121–44.

Giesen, H., "Apostolische Aktivität ohne Liebe? Zum Verständnis von 1 Kor 13,3b," *TGeg* 27 (1984) 104–11.

Gill, D. H., "Through a Glass Darkly: A Note on 1 Corinthians 13,12," *CBQ* 25 (1963) 427–29.

Green, G. L., " 'As for Prophecies, They Will Come to an End': 2 Peter, Paul and Plutarch on 'The Obsolescence of Oracles,' " *JSNT* 82 (2001) 107–22.

Greenlee, J. H., " 'Love' in the New Testament," *Notes* 14/1 (2000) 49–53.

Grossouw, W., "L'Espérance dans le Nouveau Testament," *RB* 61 (1954) 508–32, esp. 516–18.

Harbsmeier, G., *Das Hohelied der Liebe: Eine Auslegung des Kapitels 1. Korinther 13* (BibS[N] 3; Neukirchen: Buchhandlung des Erziehungsverein, 1952).

Harnack, A. von, "Das Hohe Lied des Apostels Paulus von der Liebe (I. Kor. 13) und seine religionsgeschichtliche Bedeutung," *SPAW* 7 (1911) 132–63.

Harris, W., "Echoing Bronze," *Journal of the Acoustical Society of America* 70 (1981) 1184–85.

——, " 'Sounding Brass' and Hellenistic Technology: Ancient Acoustical Device Clarifies Paul's Well-Known Metaphor," *BARev* 8/1 (1982) 38–41.

Hayes, D. A., *The Heights of Christian Love: A Study of First Corinthians Thirteen* (New York/Cincinnati: Abingdon,1926).

Hocking, D., *Chapter 13* (Eugene, OR: Harvest House Publishers, 1992).

Hoffmann, E., "Pauli Hymnus auf die Liebe," *Deutsche Vierteljahrschrift für Literaturwissenschaft und Geistesgeschichte* 4 (1926) 58–73.

——, "Zu 1 Cor. 13 und Col. 3,14," *ConNeot* 3 (1938) 28–31.

Bibliography 13:1–13 505

Holladay, C. R., "1 Corinthians 13: Paul as Apostolic Paradigm," *Greeks, Romans, and Christians: Essays in Honor of Abraham J. Malherbe* (ed. D. L. Balch et al.; Minneapolis: Fortress, 1990) 80–98.

Houghton, M. J., "A Reexamination of 1 Corinthians 13:8–13," *BSac* 153 (1996) 344–56.

Hugedé, N., *La métaphore du miroir dans les épîtres de saint Paul aux Corinthiens* (Bibliothèque théologique; Neuchâtel: Delachaux et Niestlé, 1957) 139–84.

Hunter, A. M., "Faith, Hope, Love—A Primitive Christian Triad," *ExpTim* 49 (1937–38) 428–29.

Johansson, N., "I Cor. xiii and I Cor. xiv," *NTS* 10 (1963–64) 383–92.

Käsemann, E., "Love Which Rejoices in Truth," *Religion and the Humanizing of Man* (ed. J. M. Robinson; Waterloo, Ont.: Council on the Study of Religion, 1972) 55–65.

———, "Unterwegs zum Bleibenden: 1 Korinther 13," *Kirchliche Konflikte I* (Göttingen: Vandenhoeck & Ruprecht, 1982) 104–15.

Kahlefeld, H., "Die Rede von der Liebe (1 Kor 13)," *Kleine Schriften: Aufsätze aus den Jahren 1959 bis 1979* (Frankfurt am Main: Josef Knecht, 1984) 190–96.

Kieffer, R., " 'Afin que je sois brûlé' ou bien 'afin que j'en tire orgueil'? (I Cor. xiii. 3)," *NTS* 22 (1975–76) 95–97.

———, *Le primat de l'amour: Commentaire épistémologique de 1 Corinthiens 13* (LD 85; Paris: Cerf, 1975).

Klein, W. W., "Noisy Gong or Acoustic Vase? A Note on 1 Corinthians 13.1," *NTS* 32 (1986) 286–89.

Kritzer, R. E., "Zum Wechsel vom Simplex und Kompositum in 1 Kor 13,12," *BN* 124 (2005) 103–4.

Lacan, M.-F., "Les trois qui demeurent: *I Cor.* 13, 13," *RSR* 46 (1958) 321–43.

Lambrecht, J., "The Most Eminent Way: A Study of 1 Corinthians 13," *Pauline Studies* (BETL 115), 79–107.

Lehmann, E., and A. Fridrichsen, "1 Kor., 13: Eine christlich-stoische Diatribe," *TSK* 24 (1922) 55–95.

Lund, N. W., "The Literary Structure of Paul's Hymn to Love," *JBL* 50 (1931) 266–76.

Martens, M. P., "First Corinthians 13:10: 'When That Which is Perfect Comes,' " *Notes* 10/3 (1996) 36–40.

Martin, I. J., III, "I Corinthians 13 Interpreted by Its Context," *JBR* 18 (1950) 101–5.

Martin, R. P., "A Suggested Exegesis of 1 Corinthians 13:13," *ExpTim* 82 (1970–71) 119–20.

Marxsen, W., "Das 'Bleiben' in 1. Kor 13,13," *Neues Testament und Geschichte: Historisches Geschehen und Deutung im Neuen Testament: Oscar Cullmann* . . . (ed. H. Baltensweiler und B. Reicke; Zurich: Theologischer-V., 1972) 223–29.

McElhanon, K. A., "1 Corinthians 13:8–12: Neglected Meanings of *ek merous* and *to teleion*," *Notes* 11/1 (1997) 43–53.

Mell, U., "Die Entstehungsgeschichte der Trias 'Glaube Hoffnung Liebe' (1.Kor 13,13)," *Das Urchristentum in seiner literarischen Geschichte: Festschrift für Jürgen Becker* . . . (BZNW 100; ed. U. Mell and U. B. Müler; Berlin: de Gruyter, 1999) 197–226.

Michaelis, W., "*Hē agapē oudepote piptei*," *Paulos—Hellas—Oikumene (An Ecumenical Symposium)* (Athens: Student Christian Association of Greece, 1951) 135–40.

Miguens, E., "1 Cor 13:8–13 Reconsidered," *CBQ* 37 (1975) 76–97.

Montgomery Hitchcock, F. R., "The Structure of St. Paul's Hymn of Love," *ExpTim* 34 (1922–23) 488–92.

Morton, R., "Gifts in the Context of Love: Reflections on 1 Corinthians 13," *ATJ* 31 (1999) 11–24.

Murphy-O'Connor, J., "Corinthian Bronze," *RB* 90 (1983) 80–93.

——, "St Paul on Love," *P&P* 15 (2001) 129–33.

Neirynck, F., "De grote drie: Bij een nieuwe vertaling van I Cor., xiii,13," *ETL* 39 (1963) 595–615.

Nygren, A., *Agape and Eros* (rev. ed.; London: SPCK, 1982) 105–45.

O'Brien, J., "Sophocles' Ode on Man and Paul's Hymn on Love: A Comparative Study," *CJ* 71 (1975–76) 138–51.

Pedersen, S., "Agape—der eschatologische Hauptbegriff bei Paulus," *Die paulinische Literatur und Theologie: The Pauline Literature and Theology: Anlässlich der 50. jährigen Grundungs-Feier der Universität von Aarhus* (ed. S. Pedersen; Århus: Aros; Göttingen: Vandenhoeck & Ruprecht, 1980) 159–86.

Perry, A. S., "1 Corinthians xiii.12a: *blepomen gar arti di' esoptrou en ainigmati*," *ExpTim* 58 (1946–47) 279.

Petzer, J. H., "Contextual Evidence in Favour of *kauchēsōmai* in 1 Corinthians 13. 3," *NTS* 35 (1989) 229–53.

Philonenko, M., "Rhétorique paulinienne et terminologie qoumrânienne," *RHPR* 84 (2004) 149–61.

Portier-Young, A., "Tongues and Cymbals: Contextualizing 1 Corinthians 13:1," *BTB* 35 (2005) 99–105.

Rad, G. von, "Die Vorgeschichte der Gattung von 1. Kor. 13,4–7," *Geschichte und Altes Testament: Festschrift für Albrecht Alt* (BHT 16; Tübingen: Mohr [Siebeck], 1953) 153–68; repr. *Gesammelte Studien zum Alten Testament* (Munich: Kaiser, 1971) 281–96.

Reitzenstein, R., *Historia monachorum und Historia Lausiaca: Eine Studie zur Geschichte des Mönchtums und der frühchristlichen Begriffe Gnostiker und Pneumatiker* (FRLANT 24; Göttingen: Vandenhoeck & Ruprecht, 1916) 238–55.

Riesenfeld, H., "Etude bibliographique sur la notion biblique d'*agapē*, surtout dans I Cor. 13," *ConNeot* 5 (1941) 1–27.

——, "Note bibliographique sur I Cor. xiii," *Nuntius sodalicii neotestamentici upsaliensis* 6 (1952) 47–48.

——, "Note sur 1 Cor. 13," *ConNeot* 10 (1946) 1–3.

——, "Note supplémentaire sur I Cor. xiii," *ConNeot* 12 (1948) 50–53.

——, "Vorbildliches Martyrium: Zur Frage der Lesarten in 1 Kor 13,3," *Donum gentilicium . . .* (ed. E. Bammel et al.; Oxford: Clarendon, 1978) 210–14.

Salvoni, F., "Quando sarà venuto ciò che è perfetto l'imperfetto scomparirà (*1 Cor* 13,10)," *RBR* 12/1 (1977) 7–31.

Sanders, J. T., "First Corinthians 13: Its Interpretation since the First World War," *Int* 20 (1966) 159–87.

Sanders, T. K., "A New Approach to 1 Corinthians 13. 1," *NTS* 36 (1990) 614–18.

Schindele, M. P., " 'Denn unser Erkennen ist Stückwerk' (I Kor 13,8)," *ErbA* 48 (1972) 220–22.

Schlier, H., "Über die Liebe: 1 Korinther 13," *Die Zeit der Kirche: Exegetische Aufsätze und Vorträge* (5th ed.; Freiburg im B.: Herder, 1972) 186–93.

Schrage, W., "Was bleibt und was fällt: Zur Eschatologie in 1 Kor 13,8–13," *Paulus, Apostel Jesu Christi: Festschrift für Günter Klein . . .* (ed. M. Trowitzsch; Tübingen: Mohr Siebeck, 1998) 97–107.

Seaford, R., "1 Corinthians xiii. 12," *JTS* 35 (1984) 117–20.

Shogren, G. S., "How Did They Suppose 'the Perfect' Would Come? 1 Corinthians 13.8–12 in Patristic Exegesis," *Journal of Pentecostal Theology* 15 (1999) 99–121.

Sigountos, J. G., "The Genre of 1 Corinthians 13," *NTS* 40 (1994) 246–60.

Smedes, L. B., *Love within Limits: A Realist's View of 1 Corinthians 13* (Grand Rapids: Eerdmans, 1978).

Smit, J. F. M., "The Genre of 1 Corinthians 13 in the Light of Classical Rhetoric," *NovT* 33 (1991) 193–216.

Söding, T., "Gottesliebe bei Paulus," *TGl* 79 (1989) 219–42.

———, *Das Liebesgebot bei Paulus: Die Mahnung zur Agape im Rahmen der paulinischen Ethik* (NTAbh 26; Münster in W.: Aschendorff, 1995).

———, *Die Trias Glaube, Hoffnung, Liebe bei Paulus: Eine exegetische Studie* (SBS 150; Stuttgart: Katholisches Bibelwerk, 1992).

———, "Das Wortfeld der Liebe im paganen und biblischen Griechisch," *ETL* 68 (1992) 284–320.

Spicq, C., *Agape in the New Testament* (3 vols.; St. Louis: Herder, 1963–66), 2. 138–72.

———, "L'*agapē* de I Cor., xiii: Un exemple de contribution de la sémantique à l'exégèse néo-testamentaire," *ETL* 31 (1955) 357–70.

Standaert, B., "1 Corinthiens 13," *Charisma und Agape* (ed. I. de Lorenzi), 127–39, 139–47.

Stuart, E., "Love is . . . Paul," *ExpTim* 102 (1990–91) 264–66.

Thomas, R. L., " 'Tongues . . . Will Cease,' " *JETS* 17 (1974) 81–89.

Titus, E. L., "Did Paul Write I Corinthians 13?" *JBR* 27 (1959) 299–302.

Walker, W. O., Jr., "Is First Corinthians 13 a Non-Pauline Interpolation?" *CBQ* 60 (1998) 484–99; repr. in *Interpolations in the Pauline Letters* (JSNTSup 213; Sheffield: Sheffield Academic, 2001) 147–65.

Warnach, V., *Agape: Die Liebe als Grundmotiv der neutestamentlichen Theologie* (Düsseldorf: Patmos, 1951).

Waters, C. J., " 'Love is . . . Paul'—A Response," *ExpTim* 103 (1991–92) 75.

Weiss, W., "Glaube–Liebe–Hoffnung: Zu der Trias bei Paulus," *ZNW* 84 (1993) 196–217.

White, R. F., "Richard Gaffin and Wayne Grudem on 1 Cor 13:10: A Comparison of Cessationist and Noncessationist Argumentation," *JETS* 35 (1992) 173–81.

Wischmeyer, O., *Der höchste Weg: Das 13. Kapitel des 1. Korintherbriefes* (SNT 13; Gütersloh: Mohn, 1981).

———, "Traditionsgeschichtliche Untersuchung der paulinischen Aussagen über die Liebe (*agapē*)," *ZNW* 74 (1983) 222–36.

———, "Vorkommen und Bedeutung von Agape in der ausserchristlichen Antike," *ZNW* 69 (1978) 212–38.

Wong, E., "1 Corinthians 13:7 and Christian Hope," *LS* 17 (1992) 232–42.

29   e. *The Value of Certain Spiritual Gifts: Prophecy and Tongues (14:1–25)*

14:1 Pursue love, and strive earnestly for spiritual gifts, especially that you may prophesy. 2 For one who speaks in a tongue speaks not to human beings, but to God, since no one comprehends, and he utters mysteries in spirit. 3 The one who

prophesies, however, speaks to human beings for their edification, encouragement, and consolation. [4]The one who speaks in a tongue edifies himself, but the
one who prophesies edifies the church. [5]I should like everyone of you to speak in
tongues, but even more so to prophesy. One who prophesies is greater than one
who speaks in tongues, unless he interprets, so that the church may be edified.
[6]Now, brothers, if I come to you speaking in tongues, what good will I be to you, if
I do not speak to you with some revelation or knowledge or prophecy or instruction? [7]Similarly, if inanimate things that make sounds, such as a flute or a harp, do
not emit their tones distinctly, how will what is being played with flute or harp be
recognized? [8]In fact, if a trumpet gives an unclear sound, who will get ready for
battle? [9]So with you too. Unless you utter intelligible speech with your tongue,
how will the utterance be comprehended? For you will be speaking into the
breeze. [10]For there are perhaps many different kinds of languages in the world,
and none without meaning. [11]If then I do not understand the meaning of a utterance, I shall be a foreigner to the one who speaks, and the speaker a foreigner to
me. [12]So too with you. Since you strive earnestly for spirits, seek to abound in
them for the edification of the church. [13]For this reason, the one who speaks in a
tongue should pray that he may interpret (what he says). [14][For] if I pray in a
tongue, my spirit is praying, but my mind is unproductive. [15]So what is to be
done? I shall pray with my spirit, but I shall also pray with my mind; I shall sing
with my spirit, but I shall also sing with my mind. [16]Otherwise, if you bless [with]
your spirit, how shall one who holds the place of an outsider say "Amen" to your
thanksgiving, when he does not know what you are saying? [17]You are giving
thanks well enough, but the other person is not edified. [18]I thank God that I speak
in tongues more than all of you! [19]But in church I prefer to speak five words with
my mind, so as to instruct others, than ten thousand words in a tongue. [20]Brothers,
stop being childish in your thinking; rather be infants in regard to wickedness, but
in thinking be mature. [21]It stands written in the law:

"By people speaking strange tongues and by lips of foreigners
      will I speak to this people,
   but even so they will not listen to me," says the Lord.

[22]Consequently, tongues are meant to be a sign not for believers, but for unbelievers; prophecy, however, is not for unbelievers, but for believers. [23]If then the
whole church meets in one place and everyone speaks in tongues and outsiders or
unbelievers come in, will they not say that you are out of your mind? [24]But if
everyone prophesies and some unbeliever or outsider comes in, he will be convinced by all and called to account by all: [25]the secrets of his heart will be laid
bare, and so, falling down, he will worship God and declare, "God is truly in your
midst."

COMMENT

Paul returns to the discussion of *pneumatika*, begun in chap. 12, where he related
them to the body of Christ or the church. Now after his climactic treatment of
love in chap. 13, which is more valuable in Christian life than any such spiritual
gift, he treats in particular two of the *pneumatika*, speaking in tongues and proph-

ecy, and their relation to each other, especially when the Christian community gathers in a worship service. As is evident from this passage, he thinks more highly of the latter than he does of the former, even if he never forbids speaking in tongues, but recognizes it as a gift of the Spirit and does not speak of it as a "problem," as Stendahl notes ("Glossolalia," 110). That phenomenon seems to have been the major reason why he broached the topic of spiritual gifts in general in this letter to the Christians of Roman Corinth. In chap. 12, Paul listed twelve kinds of *pneumatika*, and the bottom of the list was reserved for speaking in tongues and the interpretation of such utterance. Some Corinthians seem to have given it an undue importance so that it even affected their social intercourse; apparently it was vaunted as a sign that they were Spirit guided, and so they have created some tension in the community. Of this Paul does not approve, because it does not contribute in an intelligent way to the building up of the body of Christ, whereas he grants that "prophecy," i.e., the Spirit-inspired dynamic preaching of the gospel could be such an intelligible mode. The main reason for this judgment is that prophecy can profit both believers and unbelievers, whereas speaking in tongues does not, being merely a way to emphasize individualism, at best a "sign for unbelievers."

Did Paul himself speak in tongues? One way of reading this passage, especially v. 18, would lead one to answer that question affirmatively, and that way is commonly proposed by many commentators, who then wrestle with what some have called the "contradiction" or "unexpected shift" that Paul writes in the following verses; but that way usually misses the irony with which he speaks in certain verses.

One can distinguish six sections in this passage: (1) 14:1–5, the contrast of speaking in tongues and prophecy and their respective value for edification; (2) 14:6–11, three didactic arguments about intelligibility and the dubious merits of tongues speaking, drawn from Paul's ministry, the sounds of musical instruments, and human foreign languages; (3) 14:12–13, Paul's first conclusion; (4) 14:14–17, the speaking in tongues and its neglect of the mind in public worship; (5) 14:18–21, Paul's ironic use of tongues and Scripture; (6) 14:22–25, Paul's conclusion: tongues and prophecy as signs and the effects that they usually have.

NOTES

14:1. *Pursue love, and strive earnestly for spiritual gifts, especially that you may prophesy.* Lit. "spiritual things" (neut. *pneumatika*). The first two clauses of this verse are transitional, summing up both chaps. 13 and 12. Paul has just finished his discussion of love, stating that it was the greatest quality of Christian life. So not surprisingly, in returning to the topic of *pneumatika*, he counsels, first of all, the pursuit of love. Although the verb *diōkō* normally means "pursue" in the sense of chasing after or pressing on (toward a goal, as in Phil 2:14), it is often used in a figurative sense of striving for, aspiring to, as in Rom 9:30–31; 12:13; 14:19. So it is meant here.

The second clause directly echoes 12:31, as the verb *zēloute* is repeated in its positive sense (cf. 2 Cor 11:2; Phil 3:6), and less directly 12:1, where *pneumatika* were first mentioned in this part of the letter. In the third clause, introduced by *mallon de* ("rather" [BDAG, 614]), Paul corrects himself and expresses his preference among the *pneumatika* that he will treat in this chapter, viz., prophecy (on which see NOTES on 11:4 and 12:10); in 12:28 it is numbered in the second place as "prophets" (after "apostles"), and probably was meant to be understood among the "greater gifts" of 12:31. In 1 Thess 5:20, Paul says, "Do not despise prophecy," because as Spirit-inspired preaching, it builds up the Christian community. How different it is from some OT instances of "prophecy"; cf. Num 11:24–29; 1 Sam 10:5–6, where it resembles the glossolalia that Paul is criticizing (see Callan, "Prophecy and Ecstasy").

2. *For one who speaks in a tongue speaks not to human beings, but to God.* The Greek words, *ho lalōn glōssē*, lit. "the one speaking with a tongue," are ambiguous—how else would one speak? See Jas 3:5a. Given the context of these chapters, esp. 12:10, 28, however, the words have become a technical term (see NOTE on *genē glōssōn* at 12:10) and refer to what has come to be called glossolalia (see *TDNT*, 1:722–26; cf. *ABD*, 6:596–600 for its possible relation to similar phenomena in the Greco-Roman world [where it is never referred to as "speaking in tongues"]). Such speech, which Paul admits can be "interpreted" or put into articulate human speech (see vv. 5, 13), is not only addressed to God, being Spirit inspired, but now is said to be intelligible only to God. Whoever so speaks, speaks to no human being, and consoles only himself or herself. Having admitted this to be speech addressed only to God, Paul becomes more pejorative in his judgment, for in v. 9d he says that such a person speaks "into the breeze."

The phenomenon cannot mean speaking in foreign tongues, *pace* Bellshaw, "Confusion," Zerhusen, "Problem Tongues." That is undoubtedly the meaning of *lalein heterais glōssais* in Acts 2:4 (see *Acts*, 239), but, as elsewhere in Acts, it denotes here rather some sort of utterance beyond the patterns of normal human speech (see NOTE on 12:10). Such an utterance may be audible to other human beings, but it is addressed only to God. Paul makes this concession about God being addressed thereby, because he realizes that the phenomenon is one of the Spirit's manifestations, but he so treats this phenomenon because he is seeking to counteract the undue emphasis being given to it among Corinthian Christians.

It is not right to relate this phenomenon to what Paul speaks about in Rom 8:26–27, as does Stendahl ("Glossolalia," 110–11). There Paul uses *stenagmois alalētois*, "with ineffable sighs" (or "with sighs too deep for words," RSV), but that is his description of the way that the Spirit "intercedes for us," as it "comes to the aid of our weakness." Nothing in that text of Romans suggests that the Spirit produces in human beings such utterances, and that passage in Romans has nothing to do with such *pneumatika* as Paul is discussing here.

since no one comprehends. Lit. "no one hears," i.e., hears with understanding, as the verb is employed also in Gal 4:21, and often in the Gospels (e.g., Mark 4:9, 23; 7:15; Luke 8:8). No other human being in the worship service grasps the meaning of what is being uttered.

and he utters mysteries in spirit. Here *mysteria* means what transcends normal human understanding (BDAG, 662b; Lindemann, *1 Cor*, 297). Even if "mysteries" were taken to mean some sort of "revealed truths," such an utterance of them fails to pass them on to others, because "no one hears" the utterance with comprehension.

However, some commentators try to understand *mysteria* together with *pneumati*, as uttering "secret truths [of God] in the Spirit," which the speaker alone shares with God (Vg: *Spiritu autem loquitur*), but which others, even those who are Christians, do not understand (BDAG, 662a; see RSV, Hays, *1 Cor*, 235). It is, however, far from certain that the dat. *pneumati* refers to the Holy Spirit in this case. *Pneuma* has been used of the human spirit in 2:11; 4:21; 5:3–4; 7:34, and will so appear in vv. 14–15, 32 below; 2 Cor 2:13; it is better so understood here, as in NAB, meaning that the speaker speaks to his or her own spirit. The speaker utters something transcendent, which his spirit may possibly grasp, but which his own *nous*, "mind," does not comprehend (note the distinction of terms in v. 15). Mss F, G and some Latin versions read the nom. *pneuma*, which would rather mean "the spirit utters mysteries." Whose "spirit"? Metzger (*TCGNT*, 499) has no comment on this variant reading, which is hardly an improvement.

3. *The one who prophesies, however, speaks to human beings for their edification, encouragement, and consolation.* Lit. "addresses edification . . . to . . . ," for the verb *lalei* is being used with three abs. nouns as direct objs. Paul is not referring to a group of Corinthian prophets, but the ptc., *ho prophēteōn*, refers to an isolated instance when prophecy occurs in that community. The noun *oikodomē* is being employed differently from its occurrence in 3:9, now in the more usual metaphorical sense of "edification," i.e., the qualitative building-up of the Christian community (as in 8:1; 10:23; 14:4, 5, 12, 26; 2 Cor 5:1; 10:8; 12:19; 13:10; Rom 14:19; 15:2; 1 Thess 5:11). Note the important contrast: speaking in tongues is addressed to God, but prophecy to human beings. It is striking that the motivation for such utterance is no longer love (as one might have expected after chap. 13), but edification, encouragement (as in Rom 15:4–5), and consolation. Fee (*1 Cor*, 660) thinks that by prophecy Paul does not mean "a prepared sermon, but the spontaneous word given to God's people," but such a limitation of NT "prophecy" is far from clear—a "modern" distinction, which is recognized as such by Lindemann (*1 Cor*, 299).

4. *The one who speaks in a tongue edifies himself, but the one who prophesies edifies the church.* So Paul sharpens the contrast between these two *pneumatika*. Even though one speaks with a Spirit-inspired tongue, which "no one (else) comprehends" (v. 2), one thereby edifies only oneself; and therein lies the difficulty, for it promotes excessive individualism. Paul's remark is derogatory, *pace* Garland (*1 Cor*, 634), who tries vainly to see in such speech some "benefit," if "only to the individual." Paul's preference is clearly for the use of the *pneumatikon* that builds up the particular church, now called *ekklēsia* (even without the art., as if it were a proper noun or its name, BDR §254.6). Mss F, G add *theou*, "of God."

5. *I should like everyone of you to speak in tongues, but even more so to prophesy.* What Paul admits about the gift of the Spirit in the first clause is conditioned by what he says in the second, which is again introduced by the corrective *mallon de*

(BDF §392), thus closing a rhetorical *inclusio* opened in 14:1. Paul never denies the source of such speech, and that is the reason for the respect that the first clause expresses. It is a concession, because Paul's preference is given due utterance in the second clause, since it is one of the "greater gifts" of 12:31. The syntax is strange: in the first clause Paul uses *thelō*, "I wish," with a complementary infin., but in the second clause he shifts to *hina* with the subjunct., which is the usual mode of expressing purpose. It is a way of repeating what he already wrote in v. 1. He thus ends with an expressed wish that corresponds to his real estimate of these *pneumatika*. The comparison of this Pauline judgment with the OT episode of Moses and the prophets, Eldad and Medad, in Num 11:26–30 by some commentators (Kistemaker, *1 Cor*, 481; Thiselton, *1 Cor*, 1097) is simply far-fetched. As already indicated, that episode involves a different kind of "prophecy," and it has nothing to do with speaking in tongues — or with Paul's wish.

One who prophesies is greater than one who speaks in tongues. Again Paul states his relative esteem for these *pneumatika*, and in the coming verses (6–12) he insists on the inferiority of speaking in tongues.

unless he interprets, so that the church may be edified. Or possibly, "unless someone (different from the speaker) interprets," i.e., puts into articulate words what was uttered; see v. 13, but also v. 27 (and NOTE there; cf. Thiselton, " 'Interpretation' "). Some MSS (0243, 1505, 1739, 1881) read *diermēneuei tis*, thus adding "someone"; there are other readings of less importance for this verse, which has not been transmitted uniformly. Thus Paul concedes that "interpretation" is the only way that speaking in tongues might build up the Christian community. He has already listed the "interpretation of tongues" as a *pneumatikon* (12:10, 30) and is now referring to that gift, but he makes no mention here of the Spirit as its source. What he says does not contradict 12:30, where Paul recognized that not all have the gift of interpretation. He did not specify there who was endowed with it; nor has he said that one person could have only one gift, either speaking or interpreting. He is merely stressing the need of the articulation of the utterance of the tongue speaker, if there is to be any benefit from it for the church. The clause is introduced by *ektos ei mē*, which is pleonastic: "except, unless" (see BDF §376); it thus qualifies the first clause, which has asserted the greater value of prophecy when it comes to building up the church. It expresses a condition that must be fulfilled before speaking in tongues can achieve the same effect as prophecy, and Paul never intimates that the interpreted utterance so succeeds.

6. *Now, brothers, if I come to you speaking in tongues, what good will I be to you, if I do not speak to you with some revelation or knowledge or prophecy or instruction?* This humorous statement has to be compared with what Paul said in 2:1–2 as the way he first evangelized Corinthians. With the logical *nyni de, adelphoi,* this verse introduces the first of three didactic arguments (vv. 6–11), in which Paul proposes analogies about the relative merits of speaking in tongues and prophecy, the theme already announced in v. 5: unless speech communicates intelligibly, it accomplishes nothing.

Paul's first analogical comparison refers to his own ministry, but the "I" is really rhetorical, as in 13:1–3, 11, 12b; he could have said, "If someone comes. . . ."

Since "no one comprehends" what is spoken in tongues (14:2), Paul realizes that even he, with all his God-given apostolic authority and guidance, would be useless to the Christians of Corinth, if he were to speak in tongues.

Human utterance used in evangelization should take one of the four forms of sacred communication: *apokalypsis*, "revelation," or the disclosure of some heavenly or divine truth, as in 14:26; Gal 2:2; *gnōsis*, "knowledge," or a human explanation of the same, possibly Spirit guided, as in 12:8; *prophēteia*, "prophecy," or the utterance of a spokesperson for God, again possibly Spirit guided, as in 12:10, 28; 14:22; or *didachē*, "instruction," or a mode of teaching, which is now mentioned for the first time in this letter and is found elsewhere in Pauline writings only in Rom 6:17; 16:17. It is, however, the abstract noun related to the "teachers" of 12:28, the third of the numbered roles given to the church, and in effect one of the *pneumatika*.

7. *Similarly, if inanimate things that make sounds, such as a flute or a harp, do not emit their tones distinctly, how will what is being played with flute or harp be recognized?* Lit. "do not make a distinction in their tones." This is Paul's second analogical argument (vv. 7–8), drawn from lifeless musical instruments. If their sounds cannot be heard properly and distinctly, they are kakophonous and convey no melody that a human being can appreciate. So it is with speaking in tongues. If lifeless musical instruments must have clarity of tone and distinctness to achieve their purpose, so must human speech.

Paul mentions two different well-known musical instruments: *aulos*, "flute," which occurs only here in the NT (see LXX 1 Sam 10:5); and *kithara*, "harp, lyre," which appears in Rev 5:8; 14:2 (see LXX Gen 31:27); the two are mentioned together in Philo, *Leg. alleg.* 2.18 §75. The former is a wind instrument, whereas the latter a stringed instrument, and the sounds they emit are quite different. The verse begins with the adv. *homōs*, which normally is adversative, meaning "nevertheless," but Paul now uses it rather in its older comparative meaning, "equally, likewise," as in Gal 3:15; *Ps.-Clem. Hom.* 3.15.3; 19.23.1. Cf. Homer, *Od*.11.565; BDF §450.2; BDAG, 710 (see Jeremias, "*Homōs*"; Keydell, "*Homōs*").

8. *In fact, if a trumpet gives an unclear sound, who will get ready for battle?* A further example makes use of another musical instrument, the military trumpet or bugle and its distinctive sound as a signal for attack, halt, or retreat in a battle (see Exod 19:13; Num 10:9; 2 Sam 2:28; Zeph 1:16). The rhetorical question expects the answer, "No one."

9. *So with you too. Unless you utter intelligible speech with your tongue, how will the utterance be comprehended?* Lit. "through the tongue, i.e., the physical organ of speech (on *dia* and the article before *glōssēs*, see NOTE on 12:10). Paul applies examples of musical instruments to human speech used by Corinthian Christians. Unless speech passes on something intelligible, it does not achieve its purpose, and the utterance is incomprehensible. Here *glōssa* is stressed by the emphatic position of the phrase, preceding the introductory conj. of the clause. The neg. of *eusēmon logon*, "intelligible, recognizable speech," could be illustrated by someone speaking a foreign language that is not understood by those present, but more than likely it refers to an inarticulate succession of words that

give the impression of language, but are unintelligible to the hearers. Having used the rhetorical "I" in v. 6, Paul now shifts to the 2d pers. plur. "you" (in the same rhetorical sense). Cf. Rom 6:11; 2 Cor 10:7c, for the same phrase (*houtōs kai hymeis*) in applying an argument to Paul's addressees.

For you will be speaking into the breeze. Lit. "into the air," i.e., to the winds. Whereas, in v. 2 above, Paul admitted that someone speaking in tongues would be speaking "to God," as in prayer, he now maintains that the one uttering incomprehensible sounds would not be speaking "for God," as in prophecy, but speaking only to "the breeze" or "the air."

10. *For there are perhaps many different kinds of languages in the world, and none without meaning.* Lit. "so many, if it might be, are the kinds of voices . . . and not one is voiceless (*aphōnon*)." Mss ℵ², D², Ψ, and the Koine text-tradition add *autōn*, "(not one) of them." Paul's third analogical argument (vv. 10–11) is drawn from the many different sounds that the human tongue was meant to make, as he refers to the diverse foreign "languages" that were spoken in his day. He calls them *phōnai*, as in LXX 2 Macc 7:8, 21, 27; 4 Macc 12:7; 16:15, to distinguish them from *glōssai*, which he has been using for glosslalia. None of them was without meaning to those who spoke them, even if they were incomprehensible to others present. There may be an allusion to Gen 11:1, which (before the Tower of Babel) mentions *phōnē mia*, "one voice." The phrase *genē phōnōn* is modeled on *genē glōssōn* of 12:10. The final adj. is *aphōnon*, a combination of alpha privative and the root *phōn-*, "sound heard or pronounced to convey an idea or emotion"; hence "incapable of conveying meaning."

The clause, *ei tychoi*, "if it might be, if it should turn out that way," is a stock expression for "perhaps," meant to restrict the adj. *tosauta*, "so many" (with the potential opt., inherited from Classical Greek; BDF §385.2; BDAG, 1019).

11. *If then I do not understand the meaning of an utterance, I shall be a foreigner to the one who speaks, and the speaker a foreigner to me.* Lit. "I shall be a barbarian . . . , and the speaker a barbarian in me," i.e., in my estimation. Paul applies the third analogical argument to the rhetorical "I" again, making an illustrative comparison. He uses *dynamin tēs phōnēs*, "force of the sound," in the sense of its "meaning" or "the capacity to convey thought" (BDAG, 263).

Barbaros originally referred to a non-Greek-speaking person. The adj. was formed onomatopoetically from a reduplicated *bar*, which to ancient Greeks imitated the unintelligible sounds of the speech of foreigners; they even likened them to the twittering of birds (Herodotus, *Hist.* 2.57). The Roman poet Ovid recorded a thought similar to that of Paul: *Barbarus hic ego sum, quia non intelligor ulli*, "Here I am a barbarian, because I am not understood by anyone" (*Tristia* 5.10.37). Cf. Rom 1:14; Col 3:11. In the periods of Classical and Hellenistic Greek, the adj. often connoted peoples less cultured, among whom were included the noted enemies, Persians and Egyptians; and in the Roman period, the Gauls, Germans, and Spaniards (see Windisch, *TDNT*, 1:547; Balz, *EDNT*, 1:197–98), but that is not the sense in which Paul is using the word. For him it means that he would be a speaker of a foreign language that would not be understood; but it also implies that he would be like an outsider to the community, in which he should be recognized as *adelphos*, and that is why speaking in tongues is detrimental to the unity of the community. Just as differences of language make people into foreigners, so unintelligible utterances create barriers to comprehension and foment disunity.

12. *So too with you. Since you strive earnestly for spirits, seek to abound in them for the edification of the church.* Lit. "since you are strivers for spirits." Paul's first conclusion (vv. 12–13) applies his three-part analogical argument to Corinthian Christians. He uses a strange description of them, *zēlōtai pneumatōn,* "strivers for spirits," which NRSV, NIV render as "eager for spiritual gifts," and RSV, ESV as "manifestations of the Spirit," but NAB has "spirits," as in the lemma. *Pneumatikōn* is read instead in a few MSS (P, 1175), but they are not important ones. The verb of the subordinate clause (*zēloute*) alludes to that in 12:31 and 14:1, and so Paul does not criticize the Corinthians' pursuit of such gifts, but he recommends to them a proper motive for such pursuit and striving: that they abound in them for the building up of the Christian community. The expression is still puzzling; how can they "seek to abound" in what is a gift? It is clear that Paul is trying to inculcate a proper reason for the use that Corinthian Christians would make of the abundance of spiritual gifts received.

13. *For this reason, the one who speaks in a tongue should pray that he may interpret (what he says).* Lit. "wherefore, let the one speaking in a tongue pray that he may interpret." Or possibly, "that someone may interpret." The subj. of the subordinate verb is the same as that of the main verb, but many commentators think that an indef. subject should be supplied (as in v. 27). Paul's immediate intention is to recommend that the gift of speaking in tongues always be accompanied by the gift of making such an utterance articulate (12:10e), i.e., so that a human mind or intelligence is somehow involved. Otherwise it has no value for the good of the community. As a gift, "interpretation" is something for which one may pray. The number of times that Paul repeats the need for interpretation, however, gives the impression that it does not happen very often and that "tongues" remain deficient.

14. *[For] if I pray in a tongue, my spirit is praying, but my mind is unproductive.* Lit. "is fruitless." Paul now introduces in vv. 14–17 a series of arguments from a different viewpoint against speaking in tongues. This series is connected to the preceding by the mention of prayer in vv. 13–14. Again, Paul speaks with the rhetorical "I."

In his reaction to the phenomenon of tongues, Paul's arguments now appeal to the mind (*nous*), which is the God-given intellect that human beings have by which they think and judge rationally about things perceived or experienced (Rom 7:23; 12:2): "a function of the man who is in posssession of his senses . . . the understanding which produces clear thoughts in intelligible words" (*TDNT,* 4:959). The distinction that Paul makes between *to pneuma mou* and *ho nous mou* is not easily understood at first. Fee (*1 Cor,* 670) only confuses matters by interpreting "my spirit" as "my S/spirit," because Paul's phrase would then imply that the Holy Spirit could be "mine" in some way, as even Barrett had to admit eventually was problematic (*1 Cor,* 320). Although Collins (*1 Cor,* 501) rightly insists that Paul "pleads that the spirit and the mind work together," it is far from certain that for Paul "the spirit is the faculty by which one is in communion with the deity. The mind is an organ of thought that allows for ordinary communication among human beings" (ibid., 502). If that were true, how could Paul say in the next verse that he will "pray" and "sing with my mind" (presumably to God)? By *pneuma*, Paul cannot mean "the superior part of his soul," *pace* Dupont ("Le problème," 5; similarly Collins, *1 Cor*, 501), because Paul's contrast of *pneuma* and *nous* implies that the *nous* is superior to *pneuma*, which is rather the inward immaterial faculty of a human being that wills and reacts emotionally to things about them and that is open to the influence of the divine Spirit; it thus differs from the *nous* that makes rational judgments about such things and enables a human being to communicate consciously with God (in prayer and song). Note the role that is ascribed to its cog. verb *noeō* in Rom 1:20, where God's "invisible qualities, his eternal power and divinity, are perceived by reflection" (*nooumena kathoratai*), a function of the *nous*. Sometimes *nous* may be in conflict with *pneuma*, which because of its emotional nature may blind the mind and interfere with its rational conduct. The one "who speaks with tongues retains his *nous* even though it is seized by the *pneuma*" (Behm, *TDNT*, 4:959 n. 37). Paul clearly considers the *nous* more important, even if he concedes that such speaking in tongues might be a form of prayer, a means of communing with one's Maker. He speaks of it as prayer, because in v. 2 he admitted it was a form of speaking "to God." It is not easy to say what form of prayer such a tongue utterance might be, whether adoration, praise, thanksgiving, or supplication, because it may be nothing more than a mode of speaking "into the breeze" (v. 9). In any case, during such utterances the "mind is unproductive," not reaping a spiritual benefit for the speaker or building up the community: there is no "edification of the church" (v. 12). The ideal prayer to God is that uttered by all human faculties working together. Again, Fee ("Toward a Pauline Theology") only confuses the matter by maintaining that what Paul means here by speaking in tongues corresponds to his cryptic reference to praying in the Spirit (Rom 8:26–27). The "ineffable sighs" of Rom 8:26 are not human sighs, but those of the Spirit, which is the source of all genuine Christian prayer, whether uttered by charismatics or eggheads; those sighs have nothing to do with glossolalia (see further *Romans*, 518–19).

15. *So what is to be done? I shall pray with my spirit, but I shall also pray with my mind.* I.e., without speaking in tongues. Paul begins with an elliptical question, *tí oun estin*, "What then is (the upshot)?" As in 14:26; Rom 3:9; 6:15, it introduces his concluding reaction to the phenomenon he has been discussing; in this case, to the fruitlessness of speaking in tongues. To "pray with my spirit" might be a way of praying in tongues, but it cannot be restricted to that mode, because the human spirit can commune emotionally with God in other ways. Paul thus admits that such praying with one's spirit has some value, but praying with one's mind is far better and more important, because it makes use of the most important God-given faculty that a human being possesses. The fut. tense is meant logically, as in a conclusion that expresses the summation of his argument.

I shall sing with my spirit, but I shall also sing with my mind. I.e., sing psalms to

God, in such wise that I shall build up the community. Paul again uses the fut. tense, this time of the verb *psalō*, often found in the Greek Psalter (Ps 7:17; 9:2; 138:1). Such singing is but another example that bolsters up his argument; joined with prayer it reflects both Jewish and early Christian worship services (*ABD*, 3:350–51). Cf. Rom 15:9; Eph 5:19.

16. *Otherwise, if you bless [with] your spirit.* I.e., if you do praise or thank God only with a nonrational part of you, i.e., as you might pray in an utterance of tongues, now said to be *[en] pneumati*, "[with] (your) spirit." Mss P⁴⁶, ℵ*, A, F, G omit the prep. *en*, probably in imitation of v. 15. Paul concedes this to provide a basis for what he has just written in vv. 14–15. He also switches from the rhetorical "I" to the 2d sing., also to be taken rhetorically. Once again, *pneumati* has to be understood as the human "spirit," not the Holy "Spirit," *pace* Fee, *1 Cor*, 671.

how shall one who holds the place of an outsider say "Amen" to your thanksgiving, when he does not know what you are saying? Paul's argument involving the *nous* takes a new turn. Using a rhetorical question, he makes it clear that no one apart from the speaker will "know" or "understand" what is being said in tongues, and so no one else will be able to join in with the utterance of the "spirit" and say "Amen" to it, least of all the uninitiated. The Christian assembly will not pray but rather grow silent.

The phrase, *ho anaplērōn ton topon tou idiōtou*, "who fills up the place of the unskilled/uninstructed," is problematic. It seems to mean someone without any experience or acquaintance of the gift of speaking in tongues. The meaning of *idiōtēs* is hardly to be restricted to *apistoi*, "unbelievers" (v. 22), even though in v. 23 *idiōtai* are listed along with "unbelievers," for the word could easily refer to Christians unacquainted with such an arcane and irrational phenomenon (*EDNT*, 2:172–73). BDAG (468) takes it to mean "prospects for membership" in the Christian community, who would be "relatively outsiders." Whatever the sense of the term, they might be inclined to say "Amen" in community prayer. To what *ton topon*, "the place," refers is also debatable. It scarcely refers to a room in a house-church, where Christians are gathered with some who speak in tongues, and where some outsiders may have been welcomed. It seems to be used rather in a generic sense, "place, position."

Adding "Amen" to a prayer of praise or a doxology is a good Jewish custom attested in the OT (LXX Neh 5:13; 8:6; 1 Chr 16:36) and in QL (1QS 1:20; 2:10, 18 [frequently doubled after blessings and curses]). It was adopted in the Christian liturgy and is attested elsewhere in Pauline writings (Gal 1:5; Rom 1:25; 9:5; 11:36; 15:33; 16:24, 27).

The noun *eucharistia* does not mean Eucharist here, but simply "thanksgiving," a form of prayer that Paul does not distinguish from "blessing" (v. 16a), because of his Semitic background (in Hebrew the hiphil conj. of *ydy* can mean "praise" or "thank"). The cog. verb, *eucharisteō*, appears in 1:4, 14; 14:17, 18.

17. *You are giving thanks well enough, but the other person is not edified.* I.e., because he or she does not understand your irrational and unintelligible utterance, and there is no building up of the community. Paul uses the 2d sing. pers. pron., *sy*, in the emphatic first position in the sentence; once again, it is rhetorical "you"

and stands in contrast to the rhetorical "I" of vv. 11, 14–15. The "you" is the tongue speaker, and the "other person" is the "outsider" of v. 16. The verb *eucharisteis*, "you are giving thanks," is in parallel with *eulogēs*, "you are blessing," of v. 16a. In using *kalōs*, "well (enough)," Paul begins his irony (see Robertson-Plummer, *1 Cor*, 314: "perhaps a touch of irony"), which will continue in the following verses, despite the reluctance of commentators to recognize it here (Fee, *1 Cor*, 674 n. 48; Garland, *1 Cor*, 642).

18. *I thank God that I speak in tongues more than all of you!* Verses 18–19 form a remark that Paul introduces about himself, before he addresses the Corinthians directly in v. 20 and quotes Scripture to them in v. 21. With the introductory verb *eucharistō*, Paul now uses the personal "I," not the rhetorical "I" of vv. 6, 11, 14–15. The two clauses of this verse are asyndetic and paratactic (BDF §471.1, 415); the "that" has been added in the translation, as in RSV, NAB, NRSV, ESV. Cf. Vg: *Gratias ago Deo quod omnium vestrum lingua loquor.*

At first sight, it might look as though Paul "has held back one important bit of information" about himself, which he now discloses "for rhetorical impact," as he says that he enjoys the spiritual gift of speaking in tongues more frequently or more intensely than all the Corinthians (Hays, *1 Cor*, 237). So seriously are these words of Paul understood by most commentators: Allo, *1 Cor*, 364; Barrett, *1 Cor*, 321; Beare, "Speaking," 244; Chadwick, "All Things," 269; Collins, *1 Cor*, 503; Conzelmann, *1 Cor*, 239; Dupont, "Le problème," 6; Fee, *1 Cor*, 675; Garland, *1 Cor*, 642; Grosheide, *1 Cor*, 327–28; Héring, *1 Cor*, 127; Horsley, *1 Cor*, 185; Hurd, *Origin*, 185–88; Kistemaker, *1 Cor*, 496; Kremer, *1 Cor*, 304; Lindemann, *1 Cor*, 306; Robertson-Plummer, *1 Cor*, 314; Schrage, *1 Cor*, 3. 403; Senft, *1 Cor*, 178; Soards, *1 Cor*, 288; Stendahl, "Glossolalia," 113; Sweet, "A Sign," *passim*; Thiselton, *1 Cor*, 1117; J. Weiss, *1 Cor*, 331.

Such an alleged endowment has a "doubtful relation to the experience" that Paul describes in 2 Cor 12:3–4, when he heard "things that cannot be uttered," as Bruce well notes, who also says that "if he claims the gift here, it is to depreciate it immediately" (*1 Cor*, 132). Yet that is to fail to appreciate that, as Paul's argument develops in the next few verses, his words in this verse continue the irony begun in v. 17. It will continue in v. 21, as he quotes the OT in the same way and applies that to himself. The ironic sense of "I thank God" is matched by Paul's use of the same expression in 1:14, where he shows the absurdity of people siding with him as a preacher who baptized some of them. Hence, it is stretching a point to say that Paul is merely seeking common ground here with the Corinthians whom he is trying to correct and that he considers speaking in tongues to be "a wonderful and treasured gift, part of the complete spectrum of Christian experience" (Stendahl, "Glossolalia," 113).

19. *But in church I prefer to speak five words with my mind, so as to instruct others, than ten thousand words in a tongue.* I.e., in a Christian liturgical gathering, five words uttered with rational intelligibility will have more hortatory and didactic effect than thousands of twitterings in tongues. To "instruct others" means to play the role of a "teacher" in the church, a *pneumatikon* that Paul has listed among the "greater gifts" of the Spirit (12:31; cf. 12:28; 14:6 [end]).

This verse carefully formulates the reason for the foregoing ironic statement. "Five" is meant as an example, a typical amount, "several," as in Luke 12:6; 14:19, whereas "ten thousand" is the usual rhetorical exaggeration for innumerable amounts. The contrast of five and ten thousand is deliberately grotesque and suits the irony of the foregoing statement.

For the ellipsis of the adv. *mallon* with the verb *thelō*, see BDF §§245.3, 480.4. There is no reason to restrict the "others," who would be instructed, to the unbelieving spouses mentioned in 7:12–16; they are more likely the "outsiders" of v. 16 above or the "unbelievers" of vv. 22–24 below.

20. *Brothers, stop being childish in your thinking; rather be infants in regard to wickedness, but in thinking be mature.* As Paul addresses the Corinthian Christians directly, this verse introduces an OT passage that deals with those who speak in other tongues. It is the beginning of his concluding remarks after the arguments that he has been presenting in vv. 14–17. His remarks also allude to what he has said in 13:11 about speaking, thinking, and reasoning as a child (see also 3:1–3). Notice the antithetic parallelism in: (a) *mē paidia ginesthe*, (b) *tais phresin* : : (b') *tais de phresin*, (a') *teleioi ginesthe*, (a) "stop being childish," (b) "in thinking" : : (b') "but in thinking," (a') "be infants."

In speaking of "thinking," Paul uses the plur. of *phrēn*, "thought," which is roughly the equivalent of *nous*, "mind." He recommends childlike guilelessness if it is a question of doing or plotting evil, but he wants Corinthians to develop the intelligent maturity that their status as adult Christians demands, as he once again predicates of them the adj. *teleioi* (see NOTE on 2:6). Said in this context, the contrast means that they should grow up and realize that speaking in tongues is a very immature way of Christian prayer or conduct. Paul, however, realizes that he may not convince intellectually all of the Corinthian tongue speakers and that he might just as well be "speaking in tongues" to them. That is why he now proceeds to quote Scripture, especially a passage from Isaiah about tongues.

21. *It stands written in the law:* This introductory formula is added asyndetically (see NOTES on 1:19 and 9:9). Although Paul is about to quote words of the prophet Isaiah, he introduces them as "the law," using *nomos*, not in the specific sense of the law of Moses or the Pentateuch, but as a generic term for the Hebrews Scriptures or the OT, as he does in Rom 3:19a, 31b (see *Romans*, 131–32; cf. Hollander, "The Meaning of the Term" [see NOTE on 9:8]). See John 10:34; 12:34; 15:25.

"By people speaking strange tongues and by lips of foreigners / will I speak to this people, / but even so they will not listen to me," says the Lord. Paul quotes a form of Isa 28:11, 12d, which uses some of the words of Isaiah, but which differs considerably from the wording and sense of both the LXX and the MT; and to it he himself appends, "says the Lord."

In the Book of Isaiah, the words are part of the threatening oracles uttered against Ephraim and Judah, especially against the scoffing rulers in Jerusalem, who have been rejecting the words of Yahweh's prophet (see the almost unintelligible context of Isa 28:10). Isa 28:11 is a rewriting of Deut 28:49, and in the Hebrew original, the Isaian text runs, "For by (invaders of) stammering lips and alien tongue he [the Lord] will speak to this people, / to whom he has said, 'This is rest; cause the weary to rest; this is the place of repose.' But they were unwilling to listen." Hence the people of Ephraim and Judah would have to listen unwillingly to Yahweh's words through invaders speaking in Assyrian. This, however, becomes in the LXX:

dia phaulismon cheileōn dia glōssēs heteras, hoti lalēsousin tō laō toutō, legontes autō, Touto to anapauma tō peinōnti kai touto to syntrimma, kai ouk ēthelēsan akouein,

With contempt of lips, with another tongue, for they will speak to this people, saying to it, "This is the rest for the hungry, and this is the affliction"; and they were unwilling to listen.

Paul takes over some of the words and applies them to God, whom his formulation depicts addressing the Corinthian Christians. His form of the quotation preserves a few words from the beginning of v. 11 and from the last clause of v. 12 in Isaiah, as he applies them to speaking in tongues as glossolalia. Noteworthy is the change to the first person ("I," meaning God) and also Paul's addition of "says the Lord," which makes God utter this statement through the prophet to the Corinthians. He omits the prophet's message about "rest" and makes the unintelligible speech of the invaders the object of what they refuse to listen to. Although *glōssēs heteras* in the LXX of Isaiah refers to a foreign language that is not understood, Paul applies it to the incomprehensible speaking in tongues in his technical sense.

Has Paul so reworded the Isaian text himself, or is he quoting a different Greek translation, or perhaps a way that the words of Isaiah were being used in early-church polemical circles? Sweet ("A Sign," 244) thinks it is an instance of the last-mentioned possibility, and Origen attributed the Pauline quotation to a Greek version of Isaiah by Aquila (*Philocalia* 9), but no one can really say. More than likely it is an instance of Paul's free use of the words of Isaiah, or less likely a quotation from memory, which is not verbatim.

Above in v. 2, Paul maintained that "speaking in tongues" is not understood because it is unintelligible ("no one comprehends"); now the words of Isaiah say that it is because "this people" is unwilling to listen to those who so speak to them. The reason for the difference is that Paul's ironic use of the words of Isaiah continues the latter idea in the following verse, because he is writing to those who are unwilling to listen to him. Thus, with no little irony Paul is making the words of Isaiah refer to himself. In preaching to the Corinthians, he might just as well be speaking in tongues or even in a foreign language for all the good it does with "this people." This, then, explains why he said above in irony that he speaks in tongues more than all of the Corinthians (v. 18). It is, however, too much to say with Hays that "Paul's argument here is somewhat garbled" (*1 Cor*, 140), because he has missed the irony of the statement.

22. *Consequently, tongues are meant to be a sign not for believers, but for unbe-*

lievers. Paul now draws his conclusion, introduced by *hōste*, not so much from the words of Isaiah, as from all his foregoing arguments. His concluding thesis now is: "Speaking in tongues" is meant to be a "sign," just as "prophecy" is. It is Paul himself who introduces *sēmeion*, "sign," for it is a word not used in the quotation from Isaiah, in order to relate such speaking in tongues and prophecy to believers and unbelievers. (It is like *eis sēmeion* in Deut 6:8; 11:18; Josh 4:6 [prep. *eis* with the accus. and the verb "to be" as a substitute for a predicate nom., possibly a Semitism (BDF §145.1)]).

Many commentators relate this sign function of tongue speaking and prophecy to the Isaian passage, as if "prophecy" were just as much a sign as "speaking in tongues." Isaiah's words, however, are applicable only to the latter, not to the former, because they do not mention prophecy. Paul may be valiantly trying to find some good in the irrational and childish phenomenon, but it is something which believers realize that it is not meant to be a *sēmeion*, "sign," for them.

prophecy, however, is not for unbelievers, but for believers. The clause is elliptical; one has to supply "is a sign" in this second part. Jeremias ("Chiasmus," 147) notes the chiastic arrangement of this verse:

> *hōste hai glōssai eis sēmeion eisin*
>> *ou tois pisteuousin alla tois apistois*
> *hē de prophēteia*
>> *ou tois apistois alla tois pisteuousin.*

Again, Paul finds advantage only in one of these two spiritual gifts, seeing Spirit-inspired dynamic preaching of the gospel as a positive "sign" having its effect on those who become "believers," i.e., those who accept what is so preached. This preference is not a conclusion from the quoted words of Isaiah, but simply a repetition of what Paul has already said in vv. 1–5. The "sign" for unbelievers is "speaking in tongues," which is further explained in v. 23; and what is meant is that "unbelievers will be confirmed in their unbelief" (Sweet, "A Sign," 244). Gladstone ("Sign Language") would paraphrase this verse thus: "Therefore tongues are a sign, not resulting in believers, but in unbelievers. But prophecy [is a sign], not resulting in unbelievers, but resulting in believers." It should also be noted here that Paul speaks only of "tongues" as such a "sign," and he does not distinguish interpreted tongues from uninterpreted tongues. As he sees it, the troublesome phenomenon is "tongues," pure and simple.

23. *If then the whole church meets in one place and everyone speaks in tongues and outsiders or unbelievers come in, will they not say that you are out of your mind?* Lit. "that you are crazy?" Paul uses the strong verb *mainomai*, "be crazy, rave," which often denoted in antiquity that someone was possessed by a *daimōn* (Herodotus, *Hist.* 4.79; John 10:20). With two hypothetical examples, Paul stresses that the Corinthian Christians, who are making so much of such tongue utterances, should understand that they are giving a "sign" (v. 22) to unbelievers or outsiders. Hence such people might deride them as maniacs or equate them with devotees of the mystery religions of Cybele-Demeter or Dionysus, or the Bacchic

rite, who were known for ecstatic forms of worship (see "Cybele" and "Dionysus," OCD, 303–4, 352–53, 716–17). They would never think of becoming Christians. On "in one place," see NOTE on 11:20.

24. *But if everyone prophesies and some unbeliever or outsider comes in, he will be convinced by all and called to account by all.* This is a hypothetical example parallel to v. 23. The "sign" given by Spirit-inspired preaching will have a three-stage effect on the unbeliever or uninstructed person: conviction, scrutiny, and exposure of his or her heart. Paul's rhetoric leads him to speak of "everyone" prophesying, because that is a formulation parallel to what he wrote in v. 23, "everyone speaking in tongues."

25. *the secrets of his heart will be laid bare, and so, falling down, he will worship God, and declare.* Lit. "falling on his face." The corresponding reactions of the unbeliever or uninstructed person, who is convinced by the Spirit-inspired preaching, are conversion, submission, and adoration. Recall 4:5, where Paul speaks of the Lord exposing the hidden "motives of our hearts." Cf. 2 Cor 4:2; Rom 2:16. The "heart" is understood as the part of a human being involved in faith (Rom 10:9–10: "If you profess with your lips that 'Jesus is Lord,' and believe in your heart that God has raised him from the dead, you will be saved"). Falling on one's face is a LXX expression for homage; see Gen 17:3; Ruth 2:10. When the Christian community assembled for worship gives such a sign through the gift of prophecy, it becomes an important factor in the missionary endeavor of the church (see Rebell, "Gemeinde als Missionsfaktor").

"*God is truly in your midst.*" Paul formulates the convert's declaration by quoting a clause from Isa 45:14, which in the LXX runs, *en soi ho theos estin*, but he changes the sing. pron. of the LXX to the plur. In the context of Isaiah, the words record what the nations (Egypt, Ethiopia, and Seba, which would bring their tribute to Israel), would finally admit about Israel and its God (Isa 43:3). Cf. 1 Kgs 18:39; Zech 8:23; Dan 2:46–47. Paul quotes them without an introductory formula in order to stress the good "sign" that prophecy could be, and he says nothing comparable about the *pneumatikon*, the use of which he is reluctant to see continue in practice among the Christians of Roman Corinth.

BIBLIOGRAPHY (See also Bibliography on 12:1–14:39, pp. 461–62)

Aker, B. C., "The Gift of Tongues in 1 Corinthians 14:1–5," *Paraclete* 29/1 (1995) 13–21.
Alvarez de Linera, A., "El glosólalo y su intérprete," *EstBíb* 9 (1950) 193–208.
Beare, F. W., "Speaking with Tongues: A Critical Survey of the New Testament Evidence," *JBL* 83 (1964) 229–46.
Bellshaw, W. G., "The Confusion of Tongues," *BSac* 120 (1963) 145–53.
Chester, S. J., "Divine Madness? Speaking in Tongues in 1 Corinthians 14.23," *JSNT* 27 (2005) 417–46.
Dupont, J., "Le problème des langues dans l'église de Corinthe (*I Cor. XIV*)," *Proche-Orient Chrétien* 12 (1962) 1–12.
Fee, G. D., "Toward a Pauline Theology of Glossolalia," *Crux* 31 (1995) 22–23, 26–31.
Gillespie, T. W., "A Pattern of Prophetic Speech in First Corinthians," *JBL* 97 (1978) 74–95.

Gladstone, R. J., "Sign Language in the Assembly: How Are Tongues a Sign to the Unbeliever in 1 Cor 14:20–25?" *Asian Journal of Pentecostal Studies* 2 (1999) 177–93.

Grudem, W., "1 Corinthians 14.20–25: Prophecy and Tongues as Signs of God's Attitude," *WTJ* 41 (1979) 381–96.

Hartman, L., "1 Co 14,1–25: Argument and Some Problems," *Charisma und Agape (1 Ko 12–14)* (ed. L. de Lorenzi), 149–69, 170–99; repr. in *Text-Centered New Testament Studies: Text-Theoretical Essays on Early Jewish and Early Christian Literature* (WUNT 102; ed. D. Hellholm; Tübingen: Mohr Siebeck, 1997) 211–33.

Hodges, Z. C., "The Purpose of Tongues," *BSac* 120 (1963) 226–33.

Hoekema, A. A., *What about Tongue-Speaking?* (Grand Rapids: Eerdmans, 1966).

Jeremias, J., "*Homōs* (I Cor 14,7; Gal 3,15)," *ZNW* 52 (1961) 127–28.

Johanson, B. C., "Tongues, a Sign for Unbelievers? A Structural and Exegetical Study of I Corinthians xiv. 20–25," *NTS* 25 (1978–79) 180–203.

Johnson, L. T., "Norms for True and False Prophecy in First Corinthians," *AmBenR* 22 (1971) 29–45.

Keydell, R., "*Homōs*," *ZNW* 54 (1963) 145–46.

Klauck, H.-J., "Mit Engelzungen? Vom Charisma der verständlichen Rede in 1 Kor 14," *ZTK* 97 (2000) 276–99.

Kuss, O., "Enthusiasmus und Realismus bei Paulus," *Auslegung und Verkündigung I* (Regensburg: Pustet, 1963) 260–70.

Martin, I. J., "Glossolalia in the Apostolic Church," *JBL* 63 (1944) 123–30.

Rebell, W., "Gemeinde als Missionsfaktor im Urchristentum: I Kor 14,24f, als Schlüsselsituation," *TZ* 44 (1988) 117–34.

Roberts, P., "A Sign—Christian or Pagan?" *ExpTim* 90 (1978–79) 199–203.

Robertson, O. P., "Tongues: Sign of Covenantal Curse and Blessing," *WTJ* 38 (1975) 43–53.

Salzmann, J. C., *Lehren und Ermahnen: Zur Geschichte des christlichen Wortgottesdienstes in den drei ersten Jahrhunderten* (WUNT 2/59; Tübingen: Mohr [Siebeck], 1994) 50–77.

Sandnes, K. O., "Prophecy—A Sign for Believers (1 Cor 14,20–25)," *Bib* 77 (1996) 1–15.

Saucy, R., "An Open but Cautious View," *Are Miraculous Gifts for Today? Four Views* (ed. R. B. Gaffin and W. A. Grudem; Grand Rapids: Zondervan, 1996) 97–148.

Schweizer, E., "The Service of Worship: An Exposition of I Corinthians 14," *Int* 13 (1959) 400–408.

Smit, J. F. M., "Tongues and Prophecy: Deciphering 1 Cor 14,22," *Bib* 75 (1994) 175–90.

Stendahl, K., "Glossolalia—The NT Evidence," *Paul among Jews and Gentiles and Other Essays* (Philadelphia: Fortress,1976; London: SCM, 1977) 109–24.

Sweet, J. P. M., "A Sign for Unbelievers: Paul's Attitude to Glossolalia," *NTS* 13 (1966–67) 240–57.

Williams, C. G., "Glossolalia as a Religious Phenomenon: 'Tongues' at Corinth and Pentecost," *Religion* 5 (1975) 16–32.

Zerhusen, B., "The Problem Tongues in 1 Cor 14: A Reexamination," *BTB* 27 (1997) 139–52.

30

f. *Order in the Use of Gifts (14:26–33)*

14:26 So what is to be done, brothers? When you come to a meeting, everyone has a psalm, an instruction, a revelation, a tongue, or an interpretation. All these things should be for edification. 27 If someone speaks in a tongue, it should be two, or at most three, but each in turn, and someone should give an interpretation. 28 But if there is no interpreter, the speaker should keep silent in church and speak only to himself and to God. 29 Two or three prophets should speak, and the rest should evaluate (what is said). 30 If something is revealed to another person sitting there, the first speaker should become silent. 31 For you are all able to prophesy one by one, in order that all may learn and all be encouraged. 32 Indeed, spirits of prophets are subject to the control of prophets. 33 For God is not a God of disorder, but of peace, as in all the churches of the saints.

COMMENT

Paul ends the lengthy discussion of spiritual gifts given to individuals in the Corinthian church by insisting on due order in the use of such gifts so that peace and harmony may be preserved in the community. He begins by describing an imaginary church gathering at which individuals, led by the creative activity of the Spirit, arrive with five different gifts: with a psalm, an instruction, a revelation, an utterance in tongues, and an interpretation of such utterance. They are to be used only for the edification of the congregation as a whole. In commenting on the use of individual gifts, Paul begins with the lowest and most troublesome in his list, with speaking in tongues; for those who so speak, he gives directives. Then come directives for prophets, and then for those who have the gift of revelation, which is strange, because Paul has not mentioned *apokalypsis*, "revelation," among the *pneumatika* earlier. In fact, he now implicitly adds three further *pneumatika* to the twelve presented in 12:4–10. Paul treats the three of them in ascending order, beginning with speaking in tongues at the bottom. Strikingly, he says nothing about the Eucharist or about who would preside over their gatherings, which seem to lack all structure. For this reason he is moved to call for good order, even in Spirit-led assemblies, lest spontaneity give way to disorder and chaos.

NOTES

14:26. *So what is to be done, brothers?* Lit. "what, then, is it?" i.e., what does it mean or what is the upshot of this discussion. Paul repeats the question asked in v. 15 above and begins his concluding discussion with *oun*, "so, then, therefore." He again addresses the Corinthian Christians as "brothers," as in vv. 6, 20; see NOTE on 1:1.

When you come to a meeting. Lit. "when you come together," i.e., in a liturgical or cultic gathering. Paul makes use of the same verb that he has in 11:17, 18, 20, 33, 34, when dealing with abuses related to the Lord's Supper; see also 14:23.

everyone has a psalm, an instruction, a revelation, a tongue, or an interpretation. Paul describes an imaginary prayer gathering, citing examples of the spiritual gifts that individual Corinthian Christians might bring to it: one comes to sing a hymn of praise (as in the OT Psalter), another to teach some Christian truth, another to pass on some further understanding of God's self-communication (recall v. 6), another to speak in tongues, and still another with the gift to recast such an utterance in articulate sounds. Such abundant diversity of *pneumatika* could create disorder in their gathering, and Paul is anxious to have them conduct themselves with due order.

All these things should be for edification. I.e., for the building up and harmony of the community; "edification," not love, is the primary motivation. Paul formulates a comunity rule (*panta pros oikodomēn genesthō*), as he recommends again the same idea as in 14:3–5, 12, 17 (cf. 10:23). The conclusion of this discussion is found in 14:40, when Paul says, "All things should be done properly and in due order," with *panta . . . genesthō*, "all things . . . be done" (forming a rhetorical *inclusio*).

27. *If someone speaks in a tongue, it should be two, or at most three, but each in turn.* Lit. "two, or at most three, at a time (i.e., in any given meeting) and according to a part" (see BDAG, 57, 512). The protasis of this conditional sentence is clear, but the first part of apodosis is elliptical (*kata dyo ē to pleiston treis, kai ana meros* (lit., "by two or at most three, and in part"), with no verb expressed; and the second part is introduced by the second *kai*, and has a 3d sing. pres. impv., "let one interpret" (see next NOTE). Having mentioned five different spiritual gifts, Paul begins with a regulation about the one that has been causing most of the trouble. He does not forbid it outright, but his all-important regulation is introduced: orderliness. The utterance may go on, but only under certain conditions: one at a time, and in awaiting one's turn. Two equally important regulations are stated in the next clause and verse.

and someone should give an interpretation. I.e., in order that the minds of all present at that time may comprehend what communication is being made to the common gathering. The pron. *heis* makes it clear that someone other than the speaker is to "interpret" the utterance, i.e., put it in articulate speech; contrast vv. 5, 13, where the speaker may be the one who is expected to interpret. As Lindemann (*1 Cor*, 313) points out, Paul treats the interpretation of tongues as a gift distinct from tongues (12:10), and so the likelihood is that the interpreter is usually different from the speaker.

28. *But if there is no interpreter, the speaker should keep silent in church and speak only to himself and to God.* I.e., because no one in the congregation will understand the utterance being made. Paul softens his directive by adding the last phrase, "and to God," as a sort of afterthought. The basis for the addition has already been expressed in v. 2. Paul is speaking clearly and dismisses uninterpreted tongue utterances.

The syntax in this verse is complicated. The verb, *sigatō*, "let him be silent," follows immediately on the protasis, so that it might seem that the "interpreter" is the subj. of that impv. What Paul means is clear: the subj. of the 3d sing. impv., the one speaking in tongues, has to be supplied according to the context (= *tis* in v. 27). What is said in vv. 27–28 reveals that Paul would gladly do away with speaking in tongues, but he knows that he cannot (see v. 39).

29. *Two or three prophets should speak.* The same limited number should be applied even to those whom the Spirit moves to preach dynamically, especially for the sake of good order and the building up of the Christian community.

and the rest should evaluate (what is said). Lit. "let the others pass judgment on," what is being said by such Christian prophets (see NOTES on 12:10, 28; 11:4). Even those who exercise the ministry of *prophēteia* are subject to the scrutiny of others in the Christian community; cf. 14:16. The *alloi*, "rest," theoretically could mean other such prophets, but they are not the only members of the community who have the gift of "the discernment of spirits" (12:10); hence "others" with this gift would be among those who can evaluate carefully prophetic preaching (see 1 Thess 5:20–21).

30. *If something is revealed to another person sitting there.* The verb *apokalyphthē* is another instance of the divine passive (ZBG §236), meaning "revealed by God" (as in Rom 1:17; cf. Phil 3:15). Such a gift of God's Spirit would be clearly more important even than the inspired preaching of the Christian prophet or speaker in tongues who may already be at the podium. *Pace* Witherington (*Women*, 93), it is far from clear that this verse refers to "prophecy," because this verse does not state "prophecy is the utterance of a revelation that comes to a person spontaneously." This verse deals with *apokalypsis*, "revelation," a different gift, even though it has not been mentioned in the list of *pneumatika* in chap. 12 (see COMMENT above).

the first speaker should become silent. Lit. "let the first become silent," i.e., the speaker who is number one at the moment, whether speaking in prophecy or in tongues. Again Paul uses the 3d pers. sing. impv. *sigatō*, as in v. 28, "let him become silent," so that order, not commotion, may reign. Paul's regulation for the Christian community thus resembles what the Qumran *Manual of Discipline* regulated for the good order of sessions of its assembly (1QS 6:10–13): that no one should talk during the discourse of his confrère, or before one who ranked ahead of him, or without the consent of the Many.

31. *For you are all able to prophesy one by one, in order that all may learn and all be encouraged.* I.e., if you make room, one for the other. The result of such Spirit-inspired preaching will be that all will learn and will be exhorted mutually (*parakalōntai*). The prep. phrase *kath' hena*, "one by one," qualifies *pantes*, meaning "all" those who receive a *pneumatikon*, if and when they receive it. It does not mean that Paul is encouraging all Corinthians "to try their hands at prophesying," *pace* Hays (*1 Cor*, 243). Because prophecy is one of the endowents of the Spirit, "all" may be possible recipients of such a gift, but it does not depend on their individual endeavors.

32. *Indeed, spirits of prophets are subject to the control of prophets.* In this proverb-like statement (see Robertson-Plummer, *1 Cor*, 323), Paul gives the basis

for his remarks in vv. 29–31 and recognizes the difference between Christian prophets whose spirits enable them to speak in the name of God, and pagan sibyls or pythonesses, whose oracles were beyond all their control and whose utterances went on and on. In this way of understanding this difficult verse, the gen. plur. *prophētōn* refers to the same group of gifted Christian persons as *prophētais*.

Some commentators seek to distinguish the persons meant, as did Origen who considered all Christians present to be prophets (see *JTS* 10:41). In this sense, Paul's counsel about not quenching the Spirit or despising prophecy, but testing everything might be in order (1 Thess 5:19–21). It is, however, difficult to understand how *pneumata prophētōn*, "spirits of prophets," should then be understood. That phrase is found also in Rev 22:16 too, but in an entirely different sense, which does not help here.

33. *For God is not a God of disorder, but of peace.* So Paul expresses the fundamental reason for the order that he has been advocating since v. 27. It is not a limiting comment on v. 32 alone, as the comma used in N-A²⁷ might suggest. God himself, who is the source of the inspired preaching, is also on the side of good order and peace in the Christian community, especially at its liturgical or cultic gatherings. They cannot be dominated by *akatastasia*, "disorder," or "opposition to established authority" (BDAG, 35), a term used of civil strife or pandemonium, but now applied to "the specific manifestation of Corinthian partisanship and divisiveness in the worship of the community" (Mitchell, *Paul*, 173).

as in all the churches of the saints. I.e., in all assemblies of God's dedicated people, i.e., Christians. Paul now uses *ekklēsia* in the sense of a congregational meeting of Christians for worship or liturgy, as in 1:2 (see NOTE there); 4:17; 7:17; 11:16, designating, perhaps specifically, those meetings held in so-called house-churches, as in 16:19. The phrase, "churches of the saints," is unusual, since it is found nowhere else in the Pauline writings, or even in the NT or writings of the Apostolic Fathers. That is a factor that makes some commentators relate v. 33b to v. 34, especially those who think that vv. 34–35/36 are a non-Pauline interpolation.

It is, then, a matter of debate just where this clause belongs. N-A²⁷, many versions (RSV, NRSV, ESV, NIV, REB, Goodspeed), and many commentators (Allo, Bruce, Collins, Conzelmann, Garland, Grosheide, Kistemaker, Kremer, Lindemann, Soards, Thistleton) make it the introduction to vv. 34–35. That, however, then makes *en tais ekklēsiais*, "in the churches" (v. 34), a redundancy that does not sit well in this context. According to Clarke, it is "an ugly sentence" (" 'As in All the Churches,' " 145). Attaching it to the end of the first part of v. 33, as I have done, is better (as do also Barrett, Clarke, Fee, Hays, Murphy-O'Connor ["Interpolations," 90], Robertson-Plummer, Schrage; also KJV, NKJV); but the connection is still not perfect, even if what is done in all such churches is a sign of order and not disorder. The clause seems to be echoing what Paul has said in 4:17; 7:17; and especially 11:16, about customs or characteristics of other churches, even though it has no verb such as "teach" or "command." Order and peace, however, would characterize other "churches," where God's dedicated people are found, and where God is found to be a God of peace. If, however, one were to take

v. 33a ("for God is not a God of disorder, but of peace") as a parenthetic statement, then the "as" clause would modify either v. 32 or vv. 26–32, as Clarke recommends (" 'As in All the Churches,' " 146).

BIBLIOGRAPHY (See also Bibliography on 12:1–14:39, pp. 461–62)

Bryce, D. W., " 'As in All the Churches of the Saints': A Text-Critical Study of 1 Corinthians 14:34–35," *LTJ* 31 (1997) 31–39.

Clarke, G., " 'As in All the Churches of the Saints' (1 Corinthians 14.33)," *BT* 52/1 (2001) 144–47.

Dautzenberg, G., "Tradition, paulinische Bearbeitung und Redaktion in 1 Kor 14, 26–40," *Tradition und Gegenwart: Ernst Schering* . . . (Theologie und Wirklichkeit 5; ed. B. Jendorff and G. Schmalenberg; Bern: H. Lang; Frankfurt am M.: P. Lang, 1974) 17–29.

Dunn, J. D. G., "The Responsible Congregation (1 Co 14,26–40)," *Charisma und Agape* (ed. L. de Lorenzi), 201–36, 236–69.

Richardson, W., "Liturgical Order and Glossolalia in 1 Corinthians 14. 26c–33a," *NTS* 32 (1986) 144–53.

Wiefel, W., "Erwägungen zur soziologischen Hermeneutik urchristlicher Gottesdienstformen," *Kairos* 14 (1972) 36–51.

Witherington, B., III, *Women in the Earliest Churches* (SNTSMS 59; Cambridge: Cambridge University Press, 1988) 90–104.

31   g. *Women Speaking in Cultic Assemblies (14:34–36)*

[14:34] "Women should remain silent in the churches. For they are not allowed to speak, but should be subordinate, even as the law says. [35] If they want to learn something, they should ask their own husbands at home. For it is disgraceful for a woman to speak in church." [36] What, did the word of God originate with you? Or are you the only ones it has reached?

COMMENT

Paul now moves to a very specific case of conduct in sacred assemblies. It may seem to be only loosely related to the speaking in tongues and prophecy that he has been discussing in the preceding pericopes, but it has to do with speaking and the good order of the assembled congregation, in which "all these things should be done for edification" (14:26). There is also a connection of these verses to the mention of "silence" in vv. 28, 30, and to "learning" in v. 31. Now it is a question of women speaking in church or in the cultic assembly, and whether that is a sign of "disorder" (v. 33a). Per se it has nothing to do with *glōssais lalein*, "speaking in tongues," because now *lalein* alone is the issue, although Eriksson ("Women

Tongue Speakers") has tried so to interpret this passage, as he differs with Wire, who would see it as a case of their "prophesying" to each other (*Corinthian Women Prophets*, 157). These three verses seem to be a self-contained unit, but because they deal with women speaking in cultic gatherings, they have only a general connection with what precedes and follows.

This practice in the Corinthian church may be an imitation of the part that women took in some of the contemporary pagan cultic gatherings in honor of Dionysus, Demeter, Aphrodite Acraea (see Oepke, *TDNT*, 1:786).

These verses are, however, the subject of much controversy because of several difficulties that one encounters in this passage:

1. The verses interrupt the discussion about speaking in tongues and prophesying, to which Paul returns in vv. 37–40.

2. The prohibition of women speaking in church seems to counter what Paul has already admitted in 11:5, where he spoke of a "woman who prays or prophesies" (in a common worship service), even though he criticized one who did so "with uncovered head." Perhaps too it runs counter to the "all" used of prophecy in 14:31.

3. The allusion to "the law" in v. 34 is a most unusual way of arguing for Paul.

4. In v. 36, although "you" (*hymōn, hymas*) could be either masc. or fem., in the second question it is modified by a masc. adj., *monous*, "alone," which raises a question about who is meant by "you."

5. Some MSS of the Western text-tradition (D, E, F, G, 88*), some forms of the Vetus Itala (d, g), and some patristic or medieval writers (Ambrosiaster, Sedulius Scotus) read vv. 34–35 after what is now 14:40 (the text-critical problems are discussed fully by Miller, Niccum, Odell-Scott, Payne, Ross, and Wire).

6. This prohibition of women speaking in church is similar to 1 Tim 2:11–12 ("Let a woman learn in silence with all submissiveness. I allow no woman to teach or to have authority over men; she is to keep silent"). That form of the prohibition is even more generic, because there is no mention of "church" or a cultic setting, but it uses some of the same vocabulary as the Corinthian passage; see also 1 Pet 3:1–5; *1 Clem.* 1.3; 21.6–7.

7. The nature of v. 36, which is sometimes separated from vv. 34–35 and sometimes related to them, is just as problematic as v. 33b (does it belong to v. 33a, or does it introduce vv. 34–35/36)?

Because of such difficulties, there are five main ways in which this passage has been interpreted:

1. Verses 34–36 are regarded as a genuine Pauline composition, transmitted somewhere in all Greek MSS of 1 Corinthians, in which the Apostle reacts negatively to the practice of some Corinthian Christian women who have been pressing for equality and speaking out in sacred assemblies; he would be trying to save the women from disgracing themselves. In this attitude, he would be assuming a position quite different from what he has written in Gal 3:28, because his concern now is to insure the inner stability and order of this church. So (with varying nuances: whether the words are intended as a universal directive or merely as a corrective of a specific practice; or general chatter; or questions coming from those

not leading public prayer) Baumert, Blum, Bruce, Holladay, Kremer, M. M. Mitchell, Orr-Walther, Schüssler Fiorenza, Soards, Thrall, Witherington.

2. Verses 34–35 (33b–36) are Pauline but stem from a letter different from that in which chap. 11 would have appeared, so that v. 37 follows logically on v. 33a. Then there would be no real contradiction between chap. 11 and chap. 14. So (with varying nuances among those who consider the letter to be compiled from a number of Pauline writings) Klauck, Wolff, Schmithals. The problem that this explanation faces is to explain how conditions in Corinth would have developed so much in the period between such writings that makes Paul judge now that he has to write so radically.

3. Verses 34–35 (33b–36) are said to be a post-Pauline interpolation, stemming from the same milieu that produced 1 Tim 2:11–21, with even some of the same vocabulary. It would, then, be "a reflection of the bourgeois consolidation of the church, roughly on the level of the Pastoral Epistles; it binds itself to the general custom" (Conzelmann, 1 Cor, 246), or even would be "the prohibition of a male chauvinist" (Murphy-O'Connor, "Interpolations," 94); some think that it reflects a practice of Christian circles in Rome toward the end of the first century. So the majority of commentators today (with varying nuances): Aalen, Barrett (with hesitation), Bousset, Cleary, Cope, Delling, Fee, Fitzer, Fuller, Hays, Keck, Lindemann, Munro, Payne, Roetzel, Schrage, Schweizer, Scllin, G. F. Snyder, Trompf, Walker, J. Weiss, Zuntz; note too the parentheses in NRSV. This explanation is problematic because little is ever said about why the interpolation was introduced into this letter, and why precisely at this point.

4. Verses 34–35 (33–36) are not a post-Pauline interpolation, but a parenesis added by Paul in a marginal note at 14:33a, which he considered appropriate to his concern about proper order in the Christian community; this note was eventually drawn into the text, either after v. 33 or v. 40. So Ellis, Barton. See the criticism of this view by Barrett (1 Cor, 332).

5. Verses 34–35 are considered to be a quotation of what some Corinthian Christian men have been maintaining against women who have been speaking out in cultic assemblies. It has come to Paul's attention, just as did the slogans quoted earlier in the letter (6:12, 13; 8:1, 4, 5; 10:23). Paul's reaction to the statement quoted is expressed in v. 36, which is introduced by the disjunctive particle *ē*, "or," used here twice with two rhetorical questions (as also in 11:22b), along with the masc. *monous* modifying *hymas*, referring to such Corinthian men. So (with differing nuances) Bilezikian, Flanagan, Gourgues, Kaiser, Snyder, Odell-Scott, Talbert.

In this case, the three verses were written by Paul, but vv. 34–35 are the quotation of a view that is not his. His reaction is expressed in v. 36, vague though it is, and its implication would be egalitarian and would contradict neither 11:5 nor Gal 3:28. Even though this last interpretation may not fully satisfy either the understanding of v. 36 or its connection with what precedes, it is better than the other interpretations, *pace* Hays (1 Cor, 248), Garland (1 Cor, 667); and it rightly severs the close connection of v. 36 to vv. 34–35, as even Murphy-O'Connor ("Interpolations," 90, 92) has recognized.

No matter what interpretation of these verses one adopts, one has to recognize the contentious character of them. Unfortunately, that character has been exploited in all sorts of modern feminist movements. Perhaps one could agree somewhat with Baumert:

> In any case Paul is not here intending to set limits to a basic movement for emancipation, but rather to take the position that currently *certain* women, on the basis of their newfound freedom, have gone too far—and this is even perceived by other women. He is thus not anticipating a universal protest by women, but, as with 11:16, from "some contentious people" (men and women). Here, however, they should first subordinate themselves to the community assembly. This implies a subordination to the men only indirectly; and it applies also to unmarried women and to widows. (*Woman and Man*, 197–98)

Lest too much be made of these controversial Pauline verses, it is well to repeat the comment of Calvin (cited by Barrett, *1 Cor*, 333): "The discerning reader should come to the decision, that the things which Paul is dealing with here, are indifferent, neither good nor bad; and that they are forbidden because they work against seemliness and edification."

NOTES

14:34. *Women should remain silent in the churches.* Lit. "let women be silent in the cultic assemblies," i.e., in the various house-churches of Corinth. Paul quotes the saying of some Corinthian men who undoubtedly might allow the women to join audibly in "Amen" to a prayer, as in the thanksgiving of 14:16, but would exclude them from any form of active public speaking in churches (now in the plur., in contrast to the sing. "church" used so far in this chapter [vv. 4–5, 12, 19, 23, 28]); the prep. phrase echoes 11:16c. Some MSS (D, F, G, K, L) add *hymōn*, "your (wives)," which is otherwise omitted in the best MSS. In either case, one should note the difference from 11:5, where the sing. *gynē* is found, whereas here it is plur. *hai gynaikes*. The silence is general and absolute, and not merely while someone else is speaking (v. 30), as Kremer (*1 Cor*, 312) would have it; nor does it refer to something specific (like idle gossip).

For they are not allowed to speak. Lit. "it is not permitted to them." A form of the same verb *epitrepō*, "permit, allow," is found in the parallel passage of 1 Tim 2:12.

but should be subordinate. Lit. "let them subordinate themselves" (3d plur. pres. mid. impv.), but some MSS (D, F, G, Ψ, 0243, 1739, 1881, and the Koine text-tradition) read rather the pres. mid. infin. *hypotassesthai*, which would be dependent on the main verb, i.e., "(are allowed) to subordinate themselves"; for the resulting zeugma, see BDF §419.2. The cog. noun *hypotagē*, "submissiveness," is found in 1 Tim 2:11. The conj. *alla* introduces, not a contrast, but an additional consideration in an emphatic way (BDF §448.6).

even as the law says. Paul writes *ho nomos*, which is an explicit reference to the Mosaic law, as in 9:8 (see NOTE there), 9, 20–22; 14:21; cf. Rom 3:19; 7:7. There is not even a hint that Paul is thinking of Roman law. This clause refers, however, not to any specific pentateuchal or OT regulation about women speaking in cultic assemblies, but is meant to explain the immediately preceding clause about a woman's subordination to her husband, because LXX Gen 3:16 states, *autos sou kyrieusei*, "he shall rule over you." Josephus undoubtedly echoes a common Jewish interpretation of this passage of Genesis: *gynē cheirōn, phēsin, andros eis hapanta*, "woman, it [the Law] says, is inferior to man in all things," and *theos gar andri to kratos edōken*, "for God has given authority to the man" (*Ag.Ap.* 2.1.24 §201).

What connection that legal view of a wife's relation to her husband has to do with her keeping silent in cultic gatherings is not clear, except that it is invoking a Jewish custom, apparently derived from it as a sort of "unwritten law," forbidding women to come to the lectern in the synagogue (Str-B, 3:467). The Corinthian men would be echoing perhaps a custom derived from Jewish tradition, which they think of as "the law." It is not correct, however, to translate *ho nomos* simply as "the Jewish *tradition* decrees," as does Baumert (*Woman and Man*, 197 [his italics]), because that would relativize the law itself.

35. *If they want to learn something, they should ask their own husbands at home.* Or "they should ask their own men in (the) house," because the conjugal setting is not obvious, and "the phrase is appropriate not only for wives, since daughters, widows, and women slaves are just as subordinate to the man of the house" (Wire, *Corinthian Women Prophets*, 156). They might want to learn something about what has been revealed or taught or announced in prophecy (14:26). Although asking for a clarification would hardly be a sign of self-assertion or even of a lack of submissiveness, some Corinthian men would apparently not permit even such a question in church, even in a house-church. Even though unmarried women or those married to unbelievers are not considered, there is little reason to think that the prohibition is addressed only to wives.

For it is disgraceful for a woman to speak in church. Or "to talk in the assembly." This clause formulates the reason for the prohibition advocated by the Corinthian men in a very generic statement. Paul himself has already made a similar derogatory judgment of the woman who would pray or prophesy in a public worship service with an uncovered head, regarded there as the equivalent of a shorn or shaved head (11:6). Cf. Eph 5:12; Titus 1:11.

The disgrace would be seen not only from the viewpoint of Jewish custom or tradition, but from what ancient society, in which the woman lived, would normally think about her behavior. That judgment would be conditioned by contemporary mores and culture, well illustrated by the negative criticism of the public activity of women in Juvenal's satire, "On the Ways of Women," *Sat.* 6.434–56; in Plutarch, *Coniugalia praecepta* 31 §142d; or Aristophanes' comedy, *Ecclesiazusae*, in which the women of Athens take over the city's *ekklēsia*, "(civil) assembly," from the vacillating male members and adopt a form of socialism with common ownership of property and abolition of marriage (see further Barrett, *1 Cor*, 331; Garland, *1 Cor*, 668).

Sometimes it is said that the verb *lalein* is being used in the old classical sense of "chatter" and that the criticism concerns "an outburst of feminine loquacity," but Barrett (*1 Cor.*, 332) has shown that Paul, who employs the verb often, never uses it in that sense. A questionable loaded sense is likewise given to *lalein* by Baumert, who renders it, "speak her mind in public" (*Woman and Man*, 197 [even italicized in his translation of the passage]). Because vv. 1–33 have been dealing with various forms of Spirit-inspired speaking, Blum thinks that the prohibition of speaking concerns "all Spirit-granted speaking of women in community assemblies" ("Das Amt," 151). That seems, however, to restrict the meaning too much. Would Paul have regarded *proseuchesthai* and *prophēteuein* (11:5) as a form of "speaking" (*lalein*)? This is where the inconsistency between chaps. 11 and 14 is usually seen.

36. *What, did the word of God originate with you?* Lit. "Or, has . . . come forth from you?" This verse, with its double-rhetorical question, formulates Paul's reaction to the attitude of Corinthian Christian men quoted in the two preceding verses. Paul's phrase, *ho logos tou theou*, may be derived from LXX Jer 1:2, but he is using it in the sense of the "gospel," the Christian message, as in 1 Thess 2:13; 2 Cor 2:17; 4:2; Rom 9:6. In the LXX the more common phrase is *logos kyriou*, "the word of the Lord," a communication from Yahweh. Paul wants the Corinthian Christian men to realize that neither the gospel nor its implications for life have had a starting-point among them, and so they are in no way a law unto themselves. This interpretation of v. 36 seeks to give full force to the introductory ptc. *ē*, "or," which Paul often writes when introducing rhetorical questions (e.g., 1:13; 6:2, 9, 19; 9:6; 11:22). Along with the RSV, I have translated it as "What!" in the lemma above. It marks an alternative, as it introduces the two questions that express Paul's impatience with the attitude of such Corinthian men expressed in vv. 34–35.

Some commentators, however, have understood *ho logos tou theou* as meaning a communication from the God "of peace" (v. 33), with which verse they have always seen this verse linked (e.g., Barrett, *1 Cor*, 333). That, however, might suit the otherwise usual understanding of v. 36 as related to vv. 34–35. Murphy-O'Connor ("Interpolations," 92) would take v. 36 as a conclusion to vv. 26–33, but those verses need no such conclusion (see Odell-Scott, "In Defense," 101), and v. 36 is ill-suited as a comment on v. 33a–b. Moreover, there is no likelihood that "v. 36 should be seen as a typical Pauline outburst that had been building up for a while in reaction to all the abuses he had been dealing with in 1 Corinthians 11–14," *pace* Witherington (*Women*, 98–99). Why should that "outburst" come just here? It clearly is directed only against what has been quoted in vv. 34–35.

Or are you the only ones it has reached? Lit. "or has it reached you alone" (*hymas monous* [masc.]). Christian men of Roman Corinth were not the only ones evangelized, and so some respect must be had for Christians in other communities and their customs. The masc. form of the pron. must not be missed, and it is inadequate to translate them simply as "you people only" (Wire, *Corinthian Women Prophets*, 157).

BIBLIOGRAPHY

Aalen, S., "A Rabbinic Formula in 1 Cor 14,34," *SE II* (TU 87; Berlin: Akademie-V., 1964) 513–25.

Adinolfi, M., "Il silenzio della donna in 1 Cor. 14, 33b–36," *BeO* 17 (1975) 121–28.

Allison, R. W., "Let Women Be Silent in the Churches (1 Cor. 14.33b–36): What Did Paul Really Say, and What Did It Mean?" *JSNT* 32 (1988) 27–60.

Alonso Díaz, J., "Restricción en algunos textos paulinos de las reivindicaciones de la mujer en la Iglesia," *EstEcl* 50 (1975) 77–93.

Arichea, D. C., "The Silence of Women in the Church: Theology and Translation in 1 Corinthians 14.33b–36," *BT* 46 (1995) 101–12.

Barton, S. C., "Paul's Sense of Place: An Anthropological Approach to Community Formation in Corinth," *NTS* 32 (1986) 225–46, esp. 229–34.

Baumert, N., *Woman and Man in Paul* (Collegeville, MN: Liturgical, 1996) 195–98.

Blum, G. G., "Das Amt der Frau im Neuen Testament," *NovT* 7 (1964–65) 142–61.

Crüsemann, M., "Irredeemably Hostile to Women: Anti-Jewish Elements in the Exegesis of the Dispute about Women's Right to Speak (1 Cor. 14.34–35)," *JSNT* 79 (2000) 19–36.

Dautzenberg, G., "Zur Stellung der Frauen in den paulinischen Gemeinden," *Studien zur paulinischen Theologie und zur frühchristlichen Rezeption des Alten Testaments* (Giessener Schriften zur Theologie und Religionspädagogik 13; Giessen: Selbstverlag des Fachbereichs, 1999) 223–57, esp. 231–42.

Ellis, E. E., "The Silenced Wives of Corinth (1 Cor. 14: 34–5)," *New Testament Textual Criticism: Its Significance for Exegesis: Essays in Honour of Bruce M. Metzger* (ed. E. J. Epp and G. D. Fee; Oxford: Clarendon, 1981) 213–20.

Eriksson, A., " 'Women Tongue Speakers, Be Silent': A Reconstruction through Paul's Rhetoric," *BibInt* 6 (1998) 80–104.

Fitzer, G., "*Das Weib schweige in der Gemeinde*": Über den unpaulinischen Charakter der *mulier-taceat-Verse in 1. Korinther 14* (Theologische Existenz heute 110; Munich: Kaiser, 1963).

Flanagan, N. M., and E. H. Snyder, "Did Paul Put Down Women in 1 Cor 14: 34–36?" *BTB* 11 (1981) 10–12.

Gourgues, M., "¿Quién es misógino: Pablo o algunos Corintios?" *Anámnesis* 12 (2002) 17–24.

Hasitschka, M., " 'Die Frauen in den Gemeinden sollen schweigen': 1 Kor 14,33b–36— Anweisung des Paulus zur rechten Ordnung im Gottesdienst," *SNTU* A22 (1997) 47–56.

House, H. W., "The Speaking of Women and the Prohibition of the Law," *BSac* 145 (1988) 301–18.

Hufeisen, B. (ed.), "*Das Weib soll schweigen . . .*" (1. Kor. 14,34): *Beiträge zur linguistischen Frauenforschung* (Kassler Arbeiten zur Sprache und Literatur 19; Frankfurt am M.: P. Lang, 1993).

Isaak, J. M., "Hearing God's Word in the Silence: A Canonical Approach to 1 Corinthians 14. 34–35," *Direction* 24/2 (1995) 55–64.

Jervis, L. A., "1 Corinthians 14.34–36: A Reconsideration of Paul's Limitation of the Free Speech of Some Corinthian Women," *JSNT* 58 (1995) 51–74.

Klauck, H.-J., "Vom Reden und Schweigen der Frauen in der Urkirche," *Gemeinde, Amt, Sakrament: Neutestamentliche Perspektiven* (Würzburg: Echter-V., 1989) 232–45.

Kleinig, J. W., "Scripture and the Exclusion of Women from the Pastorate (I)," *LTJ* 29 (1995) 74–81.

Kontzi-Meresse, N., "Le silence des femmes dans l'assemblée: Reflexion autour de 1 Corinthiens 14,34–35," *ETR* 80 (2005) 273–78.

Küchler, M., *Schweigen, Schmuck und Schleier: Drei neutestamentliche Vorschriften zur Verdrängung der Frauen auf dem Hintergrund einer frauenfeindlichen Exegese des Alten Testaments im antiken Judentum* (NTOA 1; Göttingen: Vandenhoeck & Ruprecht; Freiburg in der S.: Universitätsverlag, 1986) 54–63.

Lockwood, P. F., "Does 1 Corinthians 14: 34–35 Exclude Women from the Pastoral Office?" *LTJ* 30 (1996) 30–38.

Longstaff, T. R. W., "The Ordination of Women: A Biblical Perspective," *ATR* 57 (1975) 316–27.

Maier, W. A., "An Exegetical Study of 1 Corinthians 14.33b–38," *CTQ* 55 (1991) 81–104.

Miller, J. E., "Some Observations on the Text-Critical Function of the Umlauts in Vaticanus, with Special Attention to 1 Corinthians 14.34–35," *JSNT* 26 (2003–4) 217–36.

Munro, W., "Women, Text and the Canon: The Strange Case of 1 Corinthians 14:33–35," *BTB* 18 (1988) 26–31.

Nadeau, D. J., "Le problème des femmes en 1 Co 14/33b–35," *ETR* 69 (1994) 63–65.

Niccum, C., "The Voice of the Manuscripts on the Silence of Women: The External Evidence for 1 Cor 14.34–5," *NTS* 43 (1997) 242–55.

Odell-Scott, D. W., "Editorial Dilemma: The Interpolation of 1 Cor 14:34–35 in the Western Manuscripts of D, G and 88," *BTB* 30 (2000) 68–74.

———, "In Defense of an Egalitarian Interpretation of 1 Cor 14:34–36: A Reply to Murphy-O'Connor's Critique," *BTB* 17 (1987) 100–103.

———, "Let the Women Speak in Church: An Egalitarian Interpretation of 1 Cor 14:33b–36," *BTB* 13 (1983) 90–93.

Paige, T., "The Social Matrix of Women's Speech at Corinth: The Context and Meaning of the Command to Silence in 1 Corinthians 14:33b–36," *BBR* 12 (2002) 217–42.

Payne, P. B., "Fuldensis, Sigla for Variants in Vaticanus, and 1 Cor 14.34–5," *NTS* 41 (1995) 240–62.

———, "Ms. 88 as Evidence for a Text without 1 Cor 14.34–5," *NTS* 44 (1998) 152–58.

Petzer, J. H., "Reconsidering the Silent Women of Corinth—A Note on 1 Corinthians 14:34–35," *Theologia Evangelica* 26 (1993) 132–38.

Ross, J. M., "Floating Words: Their Significance for Textual Criticism," *NTS* 38 (1992) 153–56.

Rowe, A., "Silence and the Christian Women of Corinth: An Examination of 1 Corinthians 14:33b–36," *CV* 33 (1990) 41–84.

Schulz, R. R., "Another Look at the Text of 1 Corinthians 14:33–35," *LTJ* 32 (1998) 128–31.

Schüssler-Fiorenza, E., *In Memory of Her* (New York: Crossroad, 1984) 226–33.

Stichele, C. Vander, "Is Silence Golden? Paul and Women's Speech in Corinth," *LS* 20 (1995) 241–53.

Ukachukwu Manus, C., "The Subordination of the Women in the Church: 1 Co 14: 33b–36 Reconsidered," *Revue Africaine de Théologie* 8 (1984) 183–95.

32   h. *Due Order in*
            All Things (14:37–40)

³⁷ If anyone considers himself a prophet or a spiritual person, he should know well that what I am writing to you is a commandment of the Lord. ³⁸ If anyone disregards it, he is disregarded. ³⁹ Consequently, [my] brothers, strive earnestly to prophesy, and do not forbid speaking in tongues. ⁴⁰ But all things should be done properly and in due order.

COMMENT

Paul now concludes his discussion of the conduct of Corinthian Christians endowed with *pneumatika* in cultic assemblies. He draws a general conclusion from all that he has been saying about prophecy and speaking in tongues, the two *pneumatika* that he has been treating in this chapter. These verses, however, can also be taken as a general conclusion to the whole topic of *pneumatika*, which began at 12:1. Paul invokes a "commandment of the Lord" (v. 37), which echoes "the word of God" of v. 36, and which cannot be disregarded. Moreover, all things are to be done "properly and in due order" for the sake of building up the church. Paul does not forbid speaking in tongues in a church gathering; nor does he deny that it may come from the Spirit; but he does not think very highly of it, and that is why he has put it at the bottom of his list of *pneumatika*. If it comes to a preference between speaking in tongues or prophecy, he would prefer the latter, but he restricts the use of that too, for the same reason.

NOTES

14:37. *If anyone considers himself a prophet or a spiritual person, he should know well that what I am writing to you is a commandment of the Lord.* Paul's argument now resembles his concluding statement in 11:16, which also began with the same introductory words, *ei tis dokei*, "if anyone thinks," and expresses an authoritative conclusion (cf. 3:18; 8:2; Gal 6:3; Phil 3:4). He invokes *kyriou entolē*, "a commandment of the Lord," in order to offset the influence of someone who might consider himself or herself a spokesperson for God (*prophētēs*) or a mature Christian (*pneumatikos*, as in 2:15, "subject to no one's scrutiny"). Cf. Paul's formulation in 7:10, but also 7:12, 25. It is far from clear that *pneumatikos* refers to a separate group in Corinth, the so-called pneumatics (*pace* Conzelmann, *1 Cor*, 246, who even calls them "ecstatics"). If it did so refer, why is it sing.? Käsemann regards these Pauline decisions as pronouncements of the Apostle made under the sanction of divine law (*New Testament Questions*, 74). Some MSS (D², Ψ, and the Koine text-tradition) read rather the plur. *kyriou eisin entolai*, "are commandments of the Lord."

It is a matter of debate whether *kyrios* refers to God, last mentioned in v. 36, with whose name *entolē* usually occurs (so Wolff, *1 Cor*, 347), or to the risen Christ (Schrage, *1 Cor*, 3:460; Lindemann, *1 Cor*, 322). It is preferably to be understood as the latter, because that is the more common meaning of *kyrios* in the Pauline writings, apart from his LXX quotations. Unfortunately, no one has been able to specify what the commandment would be in the early Christian tradition, in either case, whether it refers merely to vv. 34–35, or to the whole matter of *pneumatika*, which seems more likely given the mention of "prophet" and "spiritual person" in the same sentence. See further C. Stettler, "The 'Command of the Lord.' "

The verse stresses indirectly Paul's authority; as an apostle, he cannot pass on a commandment of the Lord without being ignored. He is referring to all that he has said since v. 26 about edification or the building up of the church. Zuntz (*Text of the Epistles*, 139–40), however, maintains that *kyriou entolē* is not a Pauline term.

38. *If anyone disregards it, he is disregarded.* I.e., by God or by "the Lord," another instance of the divine passive (ZBG §236), and of a sentence of holy law (Käsemann, *New Testament Questions*, 68–69). Cf. Paul's similar statement in 3:17, "If anyone destroys God's temple, God will destroy him." *Ius talionis*, "the right of retaliation," is again involved, and Paul is proclaiming it. The implication is that a person who disregards such a commandment is not really part of the community. In the Greek text, the verb in the protasis, *agnoei*, has no obj. expressed, but it most probably is "the commandment of the Lord," i.e., what Paul has just said about the risen Christ as the ultimate critic of the conduct of Corinthian Christians. However, one could understand "the Lord" as the obj., which would make an equally telling criticism.

Some important MSS (P⁴⁶, B², K, Ψ, 81, 614) read rather 3d pers. sing. impv. *agnoeitō*, "let him [the Lord] disregard (him)," in the apodosis. The alternation, however, of act. and pass. forms of the same verb is found elsewhere in Paul's style (see 8:2–3); hence the preference in N-A²⁷ for the pass. *agnoeitai* (see Metzger, *TCGNT*, 500). This verb is the same as that with which Paul began his discussion of *pneumatika* in 12:1, where it is used, however, in a different sense, "be ignorant, uninformed."

39. *Consequently, [my] brothers, strive earnestly to prophesy, and do not forbid speaking in tongues.* So Paul benevolently concludes his criticism, beginning with *hōste*, "consequently," and again addressing the Corinthian Christians as "brothers" (recall vv. 6, 20, 26). After all his negative comments about the disorder that speaking in tongues can cause, he does not forbid it, even though he once again expresses his preference for prophecy, as in 14:1.

[T]he main purpose of Paul is to discourage the practice of speaking with tongues among Christians. He does not suggest that it is an evil; for him, it is in its own way a manifestation of the Spirit; but he certainly directs his readers to seek other manifestations, and especially to seek gifts that will be helpful to the church at large. The "prophecy" of which he speaks, which he sets far above the "speaking with tongues," is likewise an utterance prompted by the Holy Spirit;

but it is intelligible, it brings penitence to the hearer, and convinces him that God is present (v. 24 f.). Paul will not ask that speaking with tongues be forbidden (v. 39), but he certainly seeks to direct the energies of Christians into other channels and insists that there are other ways of serving God in the power of his Spirit, which will be of far more benefit to the church. . . .

It is perhaps sufficient to note that it [speaking with tongues] is not regarded by any NT writer as a normal or invariable accompaniment of the life in grace, and there is no justification in the classical documents of the Christian faith for holding it to be a necessary element in the fullest spiritual development of the individual Christian or in the corporate life of the church. (Beare, "Speaking," 244)

The two infins. *prophēteuein* and *lalein glōssais* not only form a rhetorical *inclusio* with 14:1–2, but are fitted with the neut. article *to* as substantive objs. (BDF §399.1) of the impv. *zēloute*, which also closes the *inclusio* begun in 14:1. Important MSS omit the poss. pron. *mou* in the apostrophe (P⁴⁶, B², D*, F, G, Ψ, 0243, 33, 1739, 1881); hence the square brackets. On the order of the Greek words and the inclusion of the prep. *en* before *glōssais*, see P⁴⁶, which in this case supports the reading of Western MSS (D*, F, G), see Zuntz, *Text of the Epistles*, 29–31.

40. *But all things should be done properly and in due order.* Lit. "let all be in fitting fashion and according to order." Cf. 16:14. Harmony and order should reign in any assembly of God's people, "so that you may command the respect of outsiders" (1 Thess 4:12a). Recall the rhetorical *inclusio* of v. 26, with *panta . . . ginesthō*, "let all things be done." So Paul ends his exhortation about *pneumatika* in the Corinthian church.

BIBLIOGRAPHY (See also Bibliography on 12:1–14:39, pp. 461–62)

Stettler, C., "The 'Command of the Lord' in 1 Cor 14,37—A Saying of Jesus?" *Bib* 87 (2006) 42–51.

IV. INSTRUCTION ABOUT THE KERYGMA, GOSPEL, AND RESURRECTION OF THE DEAD (15:1–58)

33   A. THE PREACHED GOSPEL AND KERYGMA ABOUT THE RISEN CHRIST (15:1–11)

15:1 I make known to you, brothers, the gospel that I preached to you, which you received, and on which you have taken your stand; 2 by it you are also being saved, if you hold fast to the word I preached to you. Otherwise you have believed in vain. 3 For I passed on to you as of prime importance what I also received: that Christ died for our sins according to the Scriptures; 4 that he was buried; that he was raised on the third day according to the Scriptures; 5 and that he appeared to Cephas. Then to the Twelve. 6 Thereafter he appeared at one time to more than five hundred brothers, most of whom are still alive, though some have fallen asleep. 7 Thereafter he appeared to James, and then to all the apostles. 8 Last of all, as to one untimely born, he appeared to me. 9 For I am the least of the apostles, and not fit to be called an apostle, because I persecuted the church of God. 10 But by the grace of God I am what I am, and his grace in me has not been without effect; rather, I worked harder than all of them—not I, but the grace of God [that is] with me. 11 So whether it was I or they, in this way we preach, and in this way you came to believe.

COMMENT

Paul has now finished giving his answers to various questions that the Christians of Corinth had sent to him in the letter mentioned in 7:1 and also his reactions to various problems that he has learned about in the Corinthian church. These questions and problems have occupied him since chap. 7, and more than a good half of this letter has been devoted to them. He takes up now a new topic, and he will deal with it in this lengthy chap. 15. Once again Paul has somehow learned about a problem in the Corinthian community, that "some" Christians there were saying that "there is no resurrection of the dead" (15:12b). In a sense, this is the most serious problem that he addresses in this letter, and the instruction that he will give about this eschatological topic is the most important in the whole letter. As he has done in the case of other problems, he relates this one to a broader issue, which is basic to the topic, viz., its relation to the fundamental Christian belief, its kerygma and the gospel. With that he begins, almost without a formal transition, apart from the emphatic verb *gnōrizō*, "I make known to you." In effect, he is repeating what he has already proclaimed to them when he first evangelized Corinth.

The somewhat abrupt beginning of this new topic has made some commentators query the pertinence of chap. 15 to the rest of the letter. Schmithals (*Gnosticism*, 91–92) maintains that chap. 15 "breaks the connection of 16:1 (*peri tēs logeias* ["concerning the collection"]) with the statements *peri tōn pneumatikōn* in chaps. 12–14"; chap. 15 belongs to what he calls Letter A, because "15:1 follows well after 11:34." Others, however, rightly insist on the place of chap.15 in the letter as a whole, and this not only because of the importance of the topic relative to the others treated earlier, but also because of the eschatological thrust of the teaching found here. K. Barth has stressed this aspect of chap. 15, noting that, although other topics have been rather loosely strung together, there is a unity in the letter that is now perceived in this chapter, which is dominated by Paul's eschatological teaching about the resurrection of the dead (*Resurrection*, 96–100; cf. Schrage, *1 Cor*, 4:8). For there have been eschatological considerations in some earlier discussions (e.g., 1:7–8; 3:12–15; 4:5; 5:5; 6:14; 7:29–31; 11:26c; 13:13), which now find their climax here. It is, however, a matter of no little debate, whether Paul's treatment of love in chap. 13 is so intimately related to the discussion of the resurrection of the dead, as Barth has proposed (love as the manifestation of the Ultimate), and whether the topic is obscured here by apocalyptic trappings. However, Price ("Apocryphal Apparitions") would have us believe that vv. 3–11 are an interpolation made by an "early catholic" scribe, because they constitute a major problem for Pauline authorship in that in Gal 1:1, 11–12 Paul assserts that his gospel was not of human origin.

Paul's discussion of the resurrection of the dead is a well-defined treatise in this chapter, and it falls into four major parts:

1. A preparatory introduction about the gospel, which he has already preached to Corinthians, and its content: the basic kerygma about the death and resurrection of Christ (15:1–11).
2. Belief in the coming resurrection of the dead as rooted in Christ's resurrection (15:12–34).
3. How the resurrection of the dead will take place (15:35–49).
4. The resurrection as victory over death through Christ (15:50–58).

Subdivisions of parts 2 and 3 will be indicated below.

In the introductory verses 1–11, Paul's argument is kerygmatic, i.e., based on the common preaching of the early church. He recalls to the Corinthian Christians the salvific value of the gospel that has already been preached to them, by himself as the founder of the church in that city (3:10; 4:15), but also by other evangelists whom he has mentioned earlier (1:12). Now he insists on that traditional good news of salvation, for which they must have due respect. Paul is not trying to convince the Corinthian Christians of the reality of Christ's resurrection, which some of them are inclined to disregard; he offers no proof of this truth, but makes use of it in his argument as an event that has already been proclaimed by the church's preaching.

Paul merely repeats the basic Christian *kērygma*, "proclamation," which eventually developed into the gospel tradition and gave us the four canonical Gospels (see Schwankl, "Auf der Suche"). In vv. 3b–5a, he passes on a formula, a fragment of that primitive tradition that he himself has received (Dodd, *Apostolic Preaching*, 9–11; Dibelius, *From Tradition*, 18–19; Baird, "What Is"). As he will argue, the resurrection of the dead is based on the resurrection of Christ that that kerygmatic tradition proclaims. In citing the kerygma, Paul is conscious of a genuine continuity between his own preaching and the primitive proclamation of the Jerusalem community concerning the major events that gave life to the Christian church (Delling, "Die bleibende Bedeutsamkeit").

The pre-Pauline proclamation is evident in its stereotyped formulation: four clauses, each introduced by *hoti*, "that." It announces the death of Christ for our sins, his burial, his resurrection, and his appearance to Cephas. It can be set forth as follows:

(a) *hoti Christos apethanen*   that Christ died for our sins
         hyper tōn hamartiōn hēmōn
         kata tas graphas   according to the Scriptures
      (a') *kai hoti etaphē*   that he was buried
(b) *kai hoti egēgertai tē hēmerā tē tritē*   that he was raised on the third day
         kata tas graphas   according to the Scriptures
      (b') *kai hoti ōphthē Kēphā.*   that he appeared to Cephas.

The two main parallel affirmations are (a) "Christ died" and (b) "he was raised." Each is modified by a prep. phrase, "for our sins" and "on the third day," and each has the addition, "according to the Scriptures." Each affirmation is concluded further with a short parallel assertion (a') "he was buried" and (b') "he appeared to Cephas." The words *kai hoti* may be Pauline additions to emphasize the individual items, as Murphy-O'Connor has argued ("Tradition," 583–84); and he is also correct in insisting that *Kēphā* belongs with *ōphthē* as part of the original formula (against Bammel, "Herkunft," 402); similarly Pratscher, *Herrenbruder Jakobus*, 30.

After that kerygmatic fragment, the terminology changes, with the names of other persons to whom the risen Christ also appeared, being introduced by *eita*, "then," *epeita*, "thereafter" (twice), *eita*, and *eschaton de*, "and last of all." (The medieval verse division does not respect the Greek style.) To the fragment of the kerygma quoted in vv. 3b–5a, Paul has added part of a list of early witnesses of the risen Christ in vv. 5b–7. The appearance to James and the apostles is a parallel to Cephas and the Twelve, and it undoubtedly comes from an equally early pre-Pauline tradition, but was not necessarily part of the primitive kerygma itself (Bartsch, "Argumentation"), although some writers so consider it (e.g., Allen, "Lost Kerygma"). Winter ("I Corinthians xv 3b–7") makes the suggestion that Paul has contracted v. 7, which originally read: *eita tois apostolois kai pasin tois adelphois*, "then to the apostles and all the brothers." But not likely. That the parallel statement about James and the apostles is a testimony from a rival group in the early church, as von Harnack once claimed, is far from certain; "the list does not contain a polemical note" (Conzelmann, *1 Cor*, 252). "It is clear that the enumeration is meant as a historical, chronological one" (Conzelmann, "On the Analysis," 23; see further Mussner, "Zur stilistischen und semantischen Struktur"; Pratscher, *Herrenbruder Jakobus*, 41–43).

It is a matter of debate whether the Greek text in these verses is a translation of a Semitic original from an Aramaic-speaking community (Jerusalem?) or a borrowing from a mixed Jewish-Gentile Hellenistic church (Antioch?). Jeremias (*Eucharistic Words*, 101–5) cited six items that he maintained were not Pauline formulations and hence derived from a Semitic original: (1) *hyper tōn hamartiōn hēmōn*, "for our sins"; (2) *kata tas graphas*, "according to the Scriptures"; (3) the perf. verb *egēgertai*, "was raised"; (4) postpositive ordinal number *tritē*, "third"; (5) the verb *ōphthē*, "appeared"; and (6) *hoi dōdeka*, "the Twelve," a term not otherwise used by Paul. He also cited at least seven Semitic features in these verses. Others, however, have not been so sure about its original formulation in a Semitic language, even though they are willing to trace the verses to a Palestinian origin, especially since there is no known Semitic equivalent of *kata tas graphas*. Moreover, the verb *ōphthē* occurs in many theophanies in the LXX (e.g., Gen 12:7; 17:1; 18:1; Exod 3:2–3), and *tē hēmerā tē tritē* is found in LXX Hos 6:2 (see Conzelmann, "On the Analysis"; Klappert, "Zur Frage"; and esp. van Cangh, " 'Mort pour nos péchés' "). One should also be wary about the Aramaic or Semitic evidence that Jeremias uses; much of it comes from periods far later than the first Christian century (and the same goes for forms mentioned by Conzelmann and use of the Targum of Isaiah by Klappert). Moreover, it is far from certain that what Jeremias derives from the Mishnah "is . . . pre-Pauline" (*Eucharistic Words*, 104). Even if the formula is rooted in a Palestinian tradition, as is quite likely, this Greek form of it could well have taken shape in a Hellenistic Christian community (see also Güttgemanns, "*Christos*"; Webber, "A Note").

The mention of the risen Christ's appearance to Paul (v. 8) once again elicits a defense of his apostolate (15:9–10), as he recalls his role as a persecutor and God's gracious call that turned him into a Christian apostle. His apostolate apparently has been under attack again in Corinth, but he now maintains that he has worked hard among Corinthian Christians, even if he has not solved all the problems that have emerged among them. This is, then, a renewed development of Paul's struggle to be recognized as *apostolos* (see NOTE on 9:1). Even if he now emphasizes that he is the "last" and the "least" of the apostles, he implies that he is on equal footing with Cephas and the Twelve, who have just been mentioned. He has just cited the traditional gospel and regards the interpretation of it as part of his apostolic authority (see further von der Osten-Sacken, "Die Apologie"). (One must guard against using the three Lucan criteria for membership in the Twelve [Acts 1:21–22; cf. *Acts*, 226] as the basis for judging who an apostle is. Paul's struggle for recognition as an apostle was in part owing to the use of such criteria, especially that of having been a witness of the ministry of the earthly Jesus.)

Finally, Paul ends this passage with the assertion (15:11) that Corinthian Christians came to belief in the risen Christ through the preaching of the same gospel (15:1), whether it was done by him or by other commissioned emissaries. Thus he provides the basis for his coming argument about the resurrection of the dead and for the refutation of the view to be expressed in v. 12b. Since Jesus was indeed raised from the dead, Christians too may expect to share in such a revival after death.

Because Paul cites a bit of the early Christian kerygma about the risen Christ, this passage is usually regarded as preserving the oldest record of the Christian belief in the resurrection of Jesus of Nazareth. Along with 1 Thess 1:10 and Rom 4:25; 6:3–4, which echo the same pre-Pauline kerygma, it is older than any of the reports in the four Gospels, and for that reason is highly esteemed (see Kremer, *Das älteste Zeugnis*; Lehmann, *Auferweckt*; Lichtenstein, "Die älteste christliche Glaubensformel").

A further issue about Paul's argument is whether he was making belief in the resurrection of Christ credible as an objective historical event, which both K. Barth and Bultmann have questioned (Bultmann: ". . . the resurrection [of Christ], of course, simply cannot be a visible fact in the realm of human history" [*TNT*, 1:295; also 305]). In contrast to their position, many interpreters maintain that Paul is insisting indeed in these verses on the "reality" of Christ's resurrection (so rightly Lambrecht, "Line of Thought," 124; Schrage, *1 Cor*, 4:72). The answer to that question is complicated, however, because Paul's argument is based on the kerygma and the gospel, which were intended to evoke an affirmation of Christian faith, precisely that which Paul notes at the end of v. 11, "in this way you came to believe." His argument in vv. 1–11 stresses that Christ's resurrection has been the essence or core of the preached gospel. If there is any hesitation about that, one need only look at the protasis of v. 12, *ei de Christos kēryssetai*: "If, then, Christ is preached. . . . " For this reason I hesitate to agree with Lambrecht that "in verses 1–11 Paul emphasizes the facticity of Christ's resurrection" (*Collected Studies*, 89). The move from the preaching of Christ's resurrection (vv. 1–12) to the factual character of it comes in vv. 14, 17, where it is expressed in a negative protasis.

Barrett has called attention to the keryma's passive formulation, Christ "was raised" (*egēgertai*), i.e., by God (a divine passive; but note the act. formulation in v. 15; 6:14), which is

an affirmation about God which historical evidence as such cannot demonstrate (or, for that matter, disprove). Yet it is not unrelated to history, for the affirmation began to be made at a particular point in time, which can be dated by historical means, and it was motivated by occurrences which can be described in historical terms. These occurrences Paul goes on to list in outline. . . .

[They] cannot prove more than that, after the crucifixion, certain persons believed that they had seen Jesus again; they cannot prove the Christian doctrine of the resurrection, since this involves a statement about the action of God incapable alike of observation and demonstration. . . . [Paul] includes them [the names] as part of the primitive testimony which he begins to quote at verse 3b" (1 Cor, 341).

Although one has to reckon with this aspect of the kerygma, Fuller, following Niebuhr, rightly queries the application of modern historical methodology to the resurrection of Christ and the imposition of "alien categories on Biblical thought," because the biblical sense of history, especially *Heilsgeschichte*, distinguishes empirical or observable occurrence and revelatory faith-event ("The Resurrection of Jesus Christ," 9–10). Moreover, as Conzelmann has put it, "Paul does not have to prove the resurrection [of Christ] to Corinthian Christians because they do not doubt it" ("On the Analysis," 23). What "some"of them have been denying is the consequences of it, what flows from it about their own destiny.

NOTES

15:1. *I make known to you, brothers.* See 12:3, where Paul employed the same verb to emphasize the importance of his assertion about speaking with God's Spirit. In using it now along with *euangelion*, Paul is politely chiding the Corinthians about what they have already heard from his original evangelization of Corinth and is coaxing them to renewed awareness. Cf. the use of the same verb in 2 Cor 8:1; Gal 1:11. Radl ("Der Sinn") rightly insists on the meaning of the verb, "I make known to you," and criticizes the interpreters who understand it as "I would remind you" (e.g., Ruef, 1 Cor, 157; Allo, 1 Cor, 389); he also argues that *gnōrizō* introduces not just the gospel, but the whole of vv. 1–11.

the gospel that I preached to you. Paul recalls what he said in 4:15, where he noted that he became the father of the Corinthian community through the gospel (see NOTE there for the implications of *euangelion* as the special word for the Christian "good news"). Recall too the emphasis that Paul put on the "gospel" in 9:12–23; cf. 1:17; 1 Thess 2:13; Gal 1:11.

which you received, and on which you have taken your stand. In adding the first rel. clause, which looks to the past, Paul is stressing that God's gospel has, indeed, been the essence of the Christian tradition (see NOTE on 11:23). Cf. Gal 1:9, for a similar stress on the transmitted gospel, which tolerates no rival. The second rel. clause stresses the present condition of Corinthian Christians, as also in Phil 4:9. The perf. *hestēkate* expresses a past action the effect of which continues into the present, meaning that they have been living according to that gospel and have not abandoned it. Cf. 2 Cor 1:24; Rom 5:2; 11:20.

2. *by it you are also being saved.* I.e., you are already in the process of salvation, which is not yet complete; recall 1:18, 21. The gospel is not merely something proclaimed in the past, but it also has present soteriological importance. The third rel. clause looks to the future, as Paul links to the gospel "salvation," which is an

effect of the Christ-event that still has to come to its full implementation (see *PAHT* §PT71).

if you hold fast to the word I preached to you. Lit. ". . . to what word (*tíni logō*) I preached (it) to you," i.e., with what formulation of words I preached that gospel. The continuing of the Corinthian Christians to be among *hoi sōzomenoi*, "those who are being saved" (1:18), is thus doubly conditional: first, they must adhere firmly to the preached gospel. Instead of *ei katechete*, "if you hold fast," some MSS (D*, F, G) and copies of the VL (a, b, t) and the Vg read *opheilete katechein*, "you ought to hold fast."

The syntax of this clause is a bit complicated. I have taken *tíni logō* as practically the equivalent of *hō logō*, as another clause modifying *euangelion*, as do the rels., *ho, ho kai, en hō*, and *di' hou* earlier (so Kümmel in Lietzmann, *1 Cor*, 191; Lindemann, *1 Cor*, 327; cf. BDR §298.8; BDF §478). Others understand *tíni logō* as it is used in Acts 10:29, "for what reason," "why": "why I preached (it) to you, if you hold fast (to it)" (so Kremer, *1 Cor*, 321). Lietzmann (*1 Cor*, 76) also understands it thus, but begins a new (interrogative) sentence with it: "With what sort of formulation did I preach (it) to you?" See Conzelmann (*1 Cor*, 248 n. 4) for other less likely modes of understanding the clause and its syntax. *Pace* Garland (*1 Cor*, 682), *tíni logō* does not refer to the "content" of the gospel; nor to its "substance" (Thiselton, *1 Cor*, 1185); it denotes form and means "what form of words," as Barrett (*1 Cor*, 336) rightly notes; see also Croy, "A Note."

Otherwise you have believed in vain. Or possibly, "unless you have . . . ," as in 14:5. The second condition: the credence they have put in the gospel as "good news" may have been needless, not well considered. Paul is implying that at least some Corinthian Christians are confused and may not have been clinging to the gospel as it was preached to them, but that they must remedy that situation, if it is really so. So he seriously, and not with "irony" (*pace* Fee, *1 Cor*, 721), introduces the importance of the preached gospel and its formulation, on which he is going to build his argument. The verb *episteusate* will be repeated at the very end of v. 11, thus forming a rhetorical *inclusio*, indicating that vv. 1–11 are a literary unit.

3. *For I passed on to you as of prime importance what I also received.* Paul intends this as an explanation of *tíni logō* of v. 2. In explaining it, he again makes use of the technical Greek terms for tradition, *paradidonai* and *paralambanein* (see NOTES on 11:2, 23). To that vocabulary he adds the prep. phrase *en prōtois*, lit. "among (the) first (things)," hence those "of prime importance." The adj. "first," is not to be taken in a temporal sense, but in a qualitative sense, as Kremer rightly insists ("Vor allem"). This invocation of tradition is thus very significant for his whole argument in this long chapter, and that is why he invokes it at the outset. In chap. 11, Paul traced the tradition he mentioned there to "the Lord," but does not do so here. In Gal 1:1, 11–12, Paul insisted that the gospel he was preaching was not a human fabrication or coming from human beings, but that it came to him *di'apokalypseōs Iēsou Christou*, "through a revelation of Jesus Christ." This insistence does not contradict what he now asserts about his dependence on tradition, because in Galatians he is referring not to the formulation, but to the content of the gospel as a whole. In using *tíni logō*, he insists on the very formulation, which

he has inherited from tradition; failure to note this distinction has made Price ("Apocryphal Apparitions") claim that vv. 3–11 are an interpolation. For a different explanation of the statements in Galatians 1 and here, see Sanders, "Paul's 'Autobiographical' Statements."

that Christ died for our sins according to the Scriptures. This is the first element in the inherited form of the primitive Christian kerygma, which is repeated in a slightly different formulation in 1 Pet 3:18. It begins with a statement affirming Christ's death, as in 1 Thess 4:14, and continues with an expression of the vicarious character of that death *hyper tōn hamartiōn hēmōn,* "on behalf of our sins." This phrase occurs only here and in Gal 1:4a. It expresses, however, an early Christian conviction differently formulated in 1 Thess 5:10; Rom 4:25a; 5:6, 8; 2 Cor 5:15; cf. Heb 1:12; 1 John 4:10 (see Breytenbach, "Christus starb für uns"; de Saeger, " 'Für unsere Sünden"). In 2 Cor 5:21, Paul writes about the real meaning of that death: "On behalf of our sins he [God] made him [Christ] to be sin who knew no sin, so that we might become the uprightness of God" (see *Romans,* 258). So the kerygma affirms the salvific effect of Jesus' death; Paul himself will link to it an affirmation of Christ's resurrection in Rom 4:25: "who was handed over (to death) for our trespasses and raised for our justification," for in his thinking the death and resurrection of Christ are intimately linked as the means of human salvation and justification. *Christos* is used without an art., hence as Jesus' second name, as in vv. 12–14, 16–20, 23a, as Güttgemanns has argued in great detail against Jeremias's contention that it was a title ("*Christos* in 1. Kor. 15, 3b").

With the prep. phrase *kata tas graphas,* "according to the Scriptures," the formula makes use of a standard Greek phrase for referring to the Hebrew Scriptures (LXX 1 Chr 15:15; 2 Chr 30:5), with the plur. *hai graphai* designating the whole OT (cf. Rom 1:2; 15:4), the sacred writings entrusted to Israel of old (cf. Rom 3:2; also Mark 12:24; 14:49; Matt 21:24; Luke 24:27, 32). This phrase is added in order to call attention to Christ's death as something that has happened in God's plan for the salvation of humanity; the same is true of its addition in v. 4b.

The phrase is problematic, because the kerygmatic fragment does not indicate where Christ's death for our sins would be found in the OT. Commentators generally understand it as an implicit reference to the fourth Servant Song of Isaiah, especially LXX Isa 53:5 (*dia tas hamartias hēmōn*), 6, 8–9, 12, mainly because of 1 Pet 2:22–25 (see Lindemann, *1 Cor,* 330). It is idle to try to trace the reference to either the Hebrew original or a late targumic version of the Servant Song (*pace* Pastor-Ramos, "Murió"), because pre-Christian Judaism never applied that Servant Song to the expiatory death of martyrs or righteous persons, not to mention a suffering Messiah (see van Cangh, " 'Mort pour nos péchés"). However, Jeremias maintained that Jesus of Nazareth himself spoke of his death in terms of this Servant Song (*New Testament Theology,* 287–88); he is followed by Fee, *1 Cor,* 724; Garland, *1 Cor,* 685. That may be, but what is the evidence for it?

4. *that he was buried.* The second element of the kerygma thus stresses the reality of Jesus' death. Faith in the resurrection and the proclamation of it are set forth in the context of Jesus' death, which cannot be neglected, and his burial (recall Rom 6:4, where Paul again mentions the latter; cf. Col 2:12). The gospel tradition

records his burial in each of the four passion narratives (Mark 15:46; Matt 27:60; Luke 23:53; John 19:42); see also Acts 13:29. Lindemann (*1 Cor*, 331) calls attention to the LXX formulation, *apethanen . . . kai etaphē*, "died and was buried," in Gen 35:19; Deut 10:6; Judg 8:32, which is echoed in these verses; also Judg 12:7, 10, 15. Cf. Luke 16:22.

There is no mention of the empty tomb in this kerygmatic fragment, and its absence has often been used to question the Gospel accounts of it or to maintain that it was an item that was only added to the primitive preaching at a later date. What is usually overlooked, however, is the stereotyped four-part formulation of the tradition cited here (set forth in the COMMENT above), which presents the essentials of death, burial, resurrection, and appearance in a well-established enumerative mode of expression, but not with all the details (see Mussner, "Zur stilistischen," 408–9). It presumes that Christ's risen body (unmentioned) was no longer where it was laid in burial (see Mánek, "The Apostle Paul," 280; Foulkes, "Some Aspects"; Sider, "St. Paul's Understanding," 140; Moule, "St Paul and Dualism," 122 n. 1).

that he was raised on the third day according to the Scriptures. The third element of the kerygmatic fragment preserves the primitive affirmation of the resurrection of Christ, using the perf. pass. verb *egēgertai*, "he has been raised," i.e., by God the Father, as in 15:14, 16–17, 20. The aor. pass. forms *ēgerthē, egertheis* are the more usual Pauline formulation (Rom 4:25; 6:4, 9), as well as act. forms that express the Father's efficient causality of the event (1 Thess 1:10; 1 Cor 6:14 [*ho de theos kai ton kyrion ēgeiren*, "God has raised up the Lord"]; Gal 1:1; Rom 8:11 [*egeirantos*]; 2 Cor 4:14; Rom 4:24; cf. also Acts 10:40); the perf. (ptc.) is found in 2 Tim 2:8. The perf. " 'sets forth with the utmost possible emphasis the abiding results of the event', although the definite mark of time (*tē hēmerā tē tritē*) makes it very difficult to find an idiomatic English translation which will do it justice" (*IBNTG*, 15; cf. ZBG §278). The verb *egēgertai* does not denote merely resuscitation (as in the case of Lazarus, who was restored to physical life on earth in John 12:1), but rather implies exaltation (Phil 2:9: *kai ho theos auton hyperypsōsen*, "and God exalted him" [where there is no mention of the resurrection]; cf., however, Acts 2:32–33; 5:30–31, where both aspects of the Father's activity are mentioned [*egeiren . . . hypsōsen*, "raised . . . exalted"]), i.e., to the glorious presence of the Father, whence Christ appeared to his witnesses. Hence, *pace* Kattackal ("Christ Is Risen," 150), the translation of the NRSV, "has been raised," is not wrong.

Moreover, nothing is said in the kerygmatic fragment itself about the nature of Christ's resurrection, whether or not it involved *sōma*, "body" (or any cog. term); nor is there any mention of *ek nekrōn*, "from the dead." These details, however, will emerge in Paul's developing interpretation of the kerygma in the following verses.

The ancient kerygma also affirms that Christ was raised "on the third day" and "according to the Scriptures." Each prep. phrase, however, calls for explanation. "On the third day" (*tē hēmerā tē tritē*) is a traditional phrase, which often occurs elsewhere (Matt 16:21; 17:23; 20:19; Luke 9:22; 18:33; 24:7, 46; Acts 10:40), and which counts both ends, i.e., the day of Jesus' death and burial, an intervening day (Sabbath, Mark 16:1), and "the first day of the week" (Mark 16:2), which is the day of the discovery of the empty tomb. No NT text describes Jesus' resurrection itself as a perceptible event, such as Luke does for Christ's ascension (Luke 24:50–51; Acts 1:9–11); or as the apocryphal *Gospel of Peter* (35–42) does for his resurrection (Schneemelcher, *NTApocr.*, 1:224–25). Not even Matt 28:2–3, which tells of an earthquake and the angel of the Lord opening the tomb, says anything descriptive of the resurrection itself.

Just when the "resurrection" of Jesus took place is problematic. The resurrection narratives in all four Gospels tell only of the discovery of the empty tomb on what would be "the third day," whereas in the Lucan Gospel the already crucified Jesus on the day before the Sabbath promises the penitent thief, "Today (*sēmeron*) you will be with me in Paradise" (23:43), i.e., in the glorious presence of God, his Father (23:46). That too explains why the risen Christ asks the two disciples on the road to Emmaus, "Was it not necessary (past tense, imperf. *edei*) for the Messiah to suffer these things and so enter into his glory?" (Luke 24:26). The risen Christ asks that question on the evening of the very day of the discovery of the empty tomb. Thus his passage to glory (i.e., to the glorious presence of his Father), or to "Paradise," is already spoken of in the past tense. Wright, who has rightly assessed the "conclusions" that a historian should draw from the empty tomb and the convincing appearances of Jesus bodily alive, and their bearing on Christian origins, continues to speak, nevertheless, of "a three-day gap" ("Jesus' Resurrection," 627). Yet the problem in this kerygmatic affirmation still remains, and it will bear on the explanation to be given of Jesus' resurrection below (see COMMENT on vv. 20–28).

Given the ancient way of counting both ends of a time span, it was easy for early Christians (at least from Tertullian [*Adv. Marcionem* 4.43.1; CCLat 1.661] on) to see Christ's resurrection as a fulfillment of Hos 6:2, "After two days he will revive us; on the third day he will raise us up, that we may live before him." The prophet's words in their original context expressed the hope that in a short time God would restore the fortunes of Israel, after repentance for its involvement in the cult of Baal. Hence this use of "on the third day" would have a literary reminiscence of the prophet's words, which are now applied to the resurrection of Christ in such an interpretation (Dupont, "Ressuscité," 746–48; McArthur, " 'On the third Day' "; McCasland, "Scripture Basis"; but cf. Bacon, " 'Raised' ").

This possible allusion to Hos 6:2 may be the reason why "according to the Scriptures" is used in this part of the kerygmatic fragment. The same Greek phrase, *hē hēmera hē tritē*, however, can be found elsewhere in the LXX (Exod 19:11, 16; 2 Kgs 20:5), and so one should not press any specific OT text too much to explain the kerygmatic "according to the Scriptures." Grosheide (*1 Cor*, 350) thinks the reference is to Jonah 2:1 (recall Matt 12:40); Christensen ("And That He Rose") thinks that it is rather to Gen 1:11–13, when the tree of life was planted on the third day of creation; similarly Watt. However, Metzger has called attention to an analogous set of phrases in 1 Macc 7:16–17, where *en hēmerā miā*, "on one day," is followed by another *kata ton logon, hon egrapsen auton*, "according to the word, which he wrote," which introduces a quotation of Ps 79:2–3, a quotation that has only little connection with the topic, to which it is supposed to be related ("Suggestion," 121). All of which makes it likely that one should not press the connection between the two prep. phrases in this verse too much. There is, moreover, another expression, *meta treis hēmeras*, "after three days," which has been used for Jesus' resurrection in other NT accounts (Matt 27:63; Mark 8:31; 9:31; 10:34). Perhaps only the first part of the clause is to be understood as foreshadowed in the OT (Metzger, ibid.).

5. *and that he appeared to Cephas*. Lit. "and that he was seen to Cephas." The fourth element of the kerygmatic fragment mentions Christ's appearance to Cephas, thus preserving an ancient recollection, which Luke also records independently in his Gospel (24:34, *ontōs ēgerthē ho kyrios kai ōphthē Simōni*, "the Lord has truly been raised and has appeared to Simon"). This independent attestation makes it almost certain that *ōphthē kēpha* was the real ending of the primitive kerygma, which has sometimes been questioned. The mention of Cephas takes for granted that he is well known. Apart from Gal 2:7–8, it is the name Paul normally uses for Simon Peter (see NOTE on 1:12; cf. 3:22; 9:5). Cf. the later (independent?) narrative of the risen Christ's appearance to Peter in John 21:7. Cephas is mentioned first because of the prominence that he already enjoyed among the followers of Jesus; cf. John 21:15–18. As used here, it is a pre-Pauline Peter formula. *Pace* Conzelmann ("On the Analysis," 22), this appearance to Cephas did not make "him the foundation" of the church and leader of the Twelve; it was the other way round: he appeared to Cephas because he was already the leader.

The strange use of the aor. pass. of the Greek verb *horaō*, "see," as a way of saying "he appeared" is a Hebraism preserved in the LXX (e.g., Gen 12:7; 17:1; 18:1; 26:2, 24; 31:13; 35:9; 48:3; Exod 3:2; 6:3; 16:10; Lev 9:23; Num 14:10; 16:19; 17:7; 20:6; Judg 13:3; 1 Kgs 3:5 [usually translating Hebrew *wayyērā'*, niphal impf.]). When translated into Greek as *ōphthē*, the aor. pass. took on an intransitive meaning, "appeared." Philo (*De Abrahamo* 17 §80) explains the form: (God) "revealed his nature to the extent that the beholder was capable of seeing. So it is said, not that the Sage saw God, but that 'God was seen by the Sage' (*ho theos ōphthē tō sophō*). For it would be impossible for anyone by himself to perceive the truly existent Being, if He did not reveal and manifest Himself." The early Christian tradition about the risen Christ's appearances, then, imitated this Hebraic usage. If it were originally expressed in Aramaic, it would have been *'ithāzî*, "he was seen" (= "he appeared"), for this form is now attested in 1QapGen 12:3; 21:8; 22:27; 4QEn^c 1 vi 13. The semitized Greek verb is used of Elijah's appearance in Mark 9:4; cf. Acts 13:31 (BDF §313); contrast the Hellenistic verb *ephanē*, "he appeared" (Mark 16:9; see Pelletier, "Les apparitions"). On the Septuagintal usage of the verb, its significance as a marker of epochs of salvation, and the similar function that it can play in the NT, see Bartsch, "Inhalt und Funktion." For a modern attempt, however, to demythologize the appearance to Cephas, see Michaelis, *TDNT*, 5:538–39.

then to the Twelve. Although many commentators relate this phrase to the fragment of the kerygma that Paul has just quoted in vv. 3b–5a, it almost certainly was not part of it. As the others still to be named, it is introduced by the adv. *eita*, "then," and the change of style relates it to what follows, despite the medieval verse division and numbering, which has often led interpreters to relate this appearance to the preceding one about Cephas.

Paul now adds a list of persons (vv. 5b–7), to whom the risen Christ appeared beyond Cephas. "The Twelve" is part of a pre-Pauline list of witnesses (see Dodd, "Appearances," 27–30; Bammel, "Herkunft," 402–8; Glombitza, "Gnade," 285), because this is the only place in the Pauline letters where *hoi dōdeka* occurs. Paul never refers to them as such, even though this was already the stereotyped title in the early church for the original group of disciples that Jesus chose as his closest collaborators (Mark 3:14–19; Matt 10:1–4). Only Luke among the evangelists specifies that the Twelve were called "apostles" by Jesus himself: "whom he named apostles" (Luke 6:13). For Luke, "the apostles" were "the Twelve," and "the Twelve" were "the apostles" (see NOTE on 1:1). That this title has anything to do with the mention of "twelve men" or "twelve chiefs (of the priests)" in QL (e.g., 1QS 8:1; 4Q259 2:9; 1QM 2:1–2; 4Q494 1:44) is far from certain, *pace* Flusser ("Qumran und die Zwölf"). After all, "twelve" was a cherished number in ancient Israel, because of its association with the sons of Jacob and the twelve tribes, even echoed in Rev 21:12.

In reflecting this primitive kerygma, Mark 16:14; Matt 28:16 more accurately record that the risen Christ appeared *tois hendeka*, "to the Eleven," because Judas Iscariot would not have been with the rest (cf. Luke 24:36). Some MSS, chiefly of the Western text-tradition (D*, F, G, 330, 464*) and some ancient versions (VL, Vg) in fact read here *hendeka*, "Eleven" (see Metzger, TCGNT, 500). Cf. Acts 1:26. This list of official witnesses knows nothing about the demise of Judas (see Acts, 217–20).

6. *Thereafter he appeared at one time to more than five hundred brothers.* This appearance is not recorded elsewhere in the NT, and it has nothing to do with Pentecost (Acts 2), despite claims that it does (e.g., Craig-Short, *1 Cor*; Gilmour, "The Christophany"; see Lohse, TDNT, 6:51 n. 51; especially Sleeper, "Pentecost and Resurrection"). The event of Pentecost was not a Christophany, but an outpouring of the Spirit. No one knows whether the 500 refers to a group in Jerusalem or in Galilee (so Bishop, "Risen Christ," alluding to Matt 28:16–20). Murphy-O'Connor, following a suggestion of Wilckens (*Missionsreden*, 74), has argued plausibly that all of v. 6 has been added to the list by Paul himself, because his "purpose was apologetic" ("Tradition," 585–86); he wanted to "underline the objectivity of the experience" and "to show that the resurrection could be verified" (ibid., 589). Hence, one has to rule out a purely internal experience of these recipients of the appearance (for a wholly different, far-fetched explanation, see Kearney, "He Appeared"). On "brothers," see NOTE on 1:1; the word occurs with *hoi pleiones* also in Phil 1:14. The traditional verb *ōphthē* is repeated here and in vv. 7–8.

most of whom are still alive, though some have fallen asleep. Lit. "have been put to sleep," i.e., have died (see NOTES on 7:10, 39). Cf. 1 Thess 4:13–15. This would be Paul's "note of regret," the second clause of which is tautological. Where does the emphasis lie, on their death, or on the fact that some are still alive? Probably the latter, because the implication is that they could still provide the testimony themselves, although Bartsch ("Argumentation") finds the emphasis to be on those who have died, because that would be an argument against the denial of their resurrection.

7. *Thereafter he appeared to James.* This is James of Jerusalem (Acts 12:17; 15:13; 21:18), who also is presumed to be well known. This appearance to James stands in obvious parallelism to that of Cephas in v. 5a. The appearance to James is also recorded in *Gospel of the Hebrews* §7 (see Jerome, *De viris inlustribus* 2; cf. Schneemelcher, *NTApocr.*, 1:178).

"James" is neither of those so named in the lists of the Twelve apostles (Mark 3:16, 18; Matt 10:2, 3; Luke 6:14, 15; Acts 1:13), despite the way Gal 1:19 is often translated, "I saw none of the other apostles except James" (KJV, NKJV, RSV, NRSV, ESV), which would mean that the James Paul encountered in Jerusalem on his first visit there after his conversion was an apostle, but that translation is highly questionable (see NOTE on 9:5). In Gal 1:19, James of Jerusalem is described as "the Lord's brother," which is undoubtedly the reason for the separate mention of him in this official list of those to whom the risen Christ appeared. In later history, he is called the first "bishop" of Jerusalem (Eusebius, *HE* 2.23.1).

"James" is the common English translation of Greek *Iakōbos*, "Jacob," but it is an unfortunate transcription of the Greek name and hardly corresponds to the OT *Ya'ăqôb* (Gen 25:26). "James" was the result of the transliteration of the Greek name into Latin *Jacobus*, which, by the dissimilation of bilabial *b* into bilabial *m*, became *Jacomus*. This form then became Italian *Giacomo*, Old French *Gemmes*, Spanish *Jaime*, and English *James*.

and then to all the apostles. I.e., apart from me (Paul). The implication is that "the apostles" were more numerous than the Twelve already mentioned in v. 5b (see NOTE on 1:1); so this phrase is commonly understood by interpreters. Others than the Twelve are given this title in the NT: Paul and Barnabas (Acts 14:4, 14 [problematic appellation; see *Acts*, 526]); possibly Andronicus and Junia (Rom 16:7 [see *Romans*, 737–40]); an unnamed person (2 Cor 8:23). In 1 Cor 9:5; 12:28; Gal 1:17, 19, the plural *apostoloi* appears without any specification of their number. Murphy-O'Connor ("Tradition," 587–88) has argued plausibly that the postpositive position of *pasin*, "all" (after *tois apostolois*) is a Pauline addition to the traditional phrase because of what he is going to say about himself in v. 8. It stresses the contrast. However, Pratscher (*Herrenbruder Jakobus*, 36) considers *apostoloi pantes* to be pre-Pauline.

8. *Last of all, as to one untimely born, he appeared to me.* Lit. "as it were, to a miscarriage he appeared also to me," with the crucial words *ōphthē kamoi* in emphatic position at the end. "Last of all" follows on "then" (v. 5b), "thereafter" (v. 6a, 7a), and "then" (v. 7b). This is another of Paul's additions to the list of witnesses of the risen Christ that he has been citing since v. 5b. Paul is appealing to his own experience of having seen the risen Christ as a means of affirming the resurrection of Christ, but also perhaps as a way of legitimating his apostolic authority, as he has already done in 9:1–2, and indirectly in Gal 1:12, 15, when he appealed to the event on the road to Damascus. That was directly a defense of his gospel, but also of his call as an apostle.

Some commentators think that in using *ektrōma*, "miscarriage," Paul is quoting a term that some of his opponents used of him (e.g., J. Weiss, *1 Cor*, 350–51). Mitchell ("Reexamining") believes that the usual translation of *ektrōma* as "untimely born" is inadequate; she thinks that it should rather be "the abortion," i.e., one who has been cast aside [from the apostles] and rejected in the same way as an aborted fetus (ibid., 484). That may be, but there is no way of being sure about it.

Paul uses three derogatory terms of himself: "last of all," "untimely born," and "least of the apostles," and it has been debated whether "untimely born" is to be related to the first term (because he was not a witness of Jesus' earthly ministry) or to the third term (because he persecuted God's church), or whether it is to be understood independently of them. In any case, Paul is most likely using *ektrōma* in a figurative sense, as in the LXX (Num 12:12; Job 3:16; Qoh 6:3), meaning by it someone in the condition of death to whom grace has nevertheless been shown. Still more important is how Paul at the beginning of the verse explains his status as the "last" of those to whom the risen Christ appeared, not that he is "the final apostle" (*pace* Jones, "1 Corinthians 15:8"). He makes no distinction between the risen Christ's appearance to him (after Pentecost) and the appearances to others between the day of the discovery of the empty tomb and the Ascension. He is not trying to say that there were no further appearances of the risen Christ after him, but is only explaining the sense of the gen. "of all," as he puts himself at the bottom of the list, even though he claims to be an "apostle" of equal rank. It is best understood as an expression of humility, as in Ignatius, *Rom.* 9.2: "because I am not worthy, being the last of them, and a miscarriage"(so Spicq, *TLNT*, 1465; cf. Boman, "Paulus"; Fridrichsen, "Paulus"; Bjorck, "Nochmals"; Schneider, *TDNT*, 2:465–67; Hollander and van der Hout, "Apostle Paul," 229–32).

Paul made a similar assertion about his apostolic rank and its basis in 9:1. This testimony is important, because Paul is the only NT writer who maintains that he personally has had a vision of the risen Christ. (Compare the testimony of the author of 2 Peter about having seen the transfiguration of Jesus during his earthly ministry [2 Pet 1:16–18], and John the seer's vision of the heavenly Christ with apocalyptic trappings in Rev 1:12–20 — an entirely different literary genre.) Nevertheless, Paul is putting himself on the same level as Cephas and James (vv. 5a, 7a), two of those whom he called "pillars" of the church in Gal 2:9, even though he is last of all. For Paul's own description of his encounter with the risen Christ, see Gal 1:15–16: "He [God], who set me apart from my mother's womb and called me through his grace, was pleased to reveal his Son to me that I might preach him among the Gentiles." Nickelsburg explains: "He was an *ektrōma* with respect to the purpose for which he was appointed from the womb. In spite of this, God revealed the risen Christ to him and made him what he was intended to be from the womb" ("An *Ektrōma*," 204). Cf. Acts 9:3–6; 22:6–8; 26:14–18 for the Lucan descriptions of that encounter.

9. *For I am the least of the apostles, and not fit to be called an apostle.* Paul begins with the affirmation that he is "the least" among the apostles, because he was the last to be added to that group and because he is less than the rest for reasons set forth in the next clause. Paul intends this self-evaluation from the standpoint of Christ, not from that of those who refused to regard him as an apostle. He is not

trying to defend his apostolic role, but is seeking rather to get Corinthian Christians to realize the value of the gospel that he has preached to them. Cf. 4:3; and also Eph 3:8, "the least of all the saints"; and 1 Tim 1:15.

because I persecuted the church of God. Paul speaks of his persecution of Christians in Gal 1:13; Phil 3:6, and Luke has recorded it in Acts 8:3; 9:1, 4, 21; retold in Acts 22:4, 7, 19; 26:10–11, 14. On "church of God," see NOTE on 1:2.

10. *But by the grace of God I am what I am.* I.e., a Christian apostle, who has been called by the risen Christ and has labored for the Lord. So Paul speaks proudly of the influence of divine grace in his life, yet with modesty.

and his grace in me has not been without effect. Or "in vain." Lit. "did not prove to be empty," i.e., worthless. This reflects again Paul's struggle to be recognized as an apostle in parts of the early church. He purposely ascribes to God's grace his call to be an authorized emissary of Christ Jesus. Cf. 2 Cor 6:1; 1 Thess 2:1.

rather, I worked harder than all of them. Either "than all of them together" or "than any one of all of them." Cf. 2 Cor 11:5, 23–27 for details of that labor. Paul is using some of the words of the second Servant Song of Isa 49:4, where the servant complains that he has "worked in vain" (*kenōs ekopiasa*). Thus Paul explains why God's grace has not been without effect in his career, not that he is better than others because of the harder work he has done, but that the grace enabled him to do harder work.

not I, but the grace of God [that is] with me. Significantly, Paul corrects himself as he denies human achievement and asserts the priority of divine grace in his ministry. Yet he does not say "that is within me," writing rather [*hē*] *syn emoi*, and not [*hē*] *en emoi*, or even *hē eis eme* (as in P[46], syr[hmg]), as he affirms his cooperation with divine grace. Paul is not afraid of synergism, as he duly acknowledges how God has been accompanying his work and guiding his evangelization. Verses 9–10 are not only apologetic, but also a digression leading up to v. 11 and the rest of the argument, on which Paul will build his refutation of the opinion to be cited in v. 12b.

11. *So whether it was I or they, in this way we preach.* I.e., with the assistance of God's grace, all commissioned emissaries have been preaching the same gospel (mentioned in 15:1) about the resurrection of the *dead* Jesus of Nazareth and the impact that his death and resurrection have had on humanity. No matter what the status was of those who evangelized Corinth, whether Paul himself or any of the others, the same gospel was proclaimed. Who are meant by *ekeinoi*, "they"? In the immediate context it probably refers to "all of them" of v. 10, i.e., the "apostles" of v. 9; but Paul could be referring again to Apollos and Cephas, because the Corinthians would have been familiar with them and possibly other apostolic preachers and teachers.

and in this way you came to believe. Paul uses the ingressive aor. *episteusate* (*IBNTG*, 10–11), i.e., through the instrumentality of such preaching of the gospel you became Christians in your response to it. Hence, you Corinthians cannot neglect this common basis of your Christian faith. Recall also 3:5. So Paul is establishing the basis of the argument that he is about to develop concerning the resurrection of the dead. His emphasis lies on faith, which is the way a human being

accepts the resurrection of Jesus Christ announced in that gospel preached by
Paul in conjunction with the others.

BIBLIOGRAPHY

Allen, E. L., "The Lost Kerygma," NTS 3 (1956–57) 349–53.

Bacon, B. W., " 'Raised the Third Day,' " Expos 8/26 (1923) 426–41.

Baird, W., "What Is the Kerygma? A Study of 1 Cor. 15:3–8 and Gal 1:11–17," JBL 76 (1957) 181–91.

Bammel, E., "Herkunft und Funktion der Traditionselemente in 1. Kor. 15, 1–11," TZ 11 (1955) 401–19.

Bartolomé Lafuente, J. J., " 'Soy lo que soy por gracia de Dios' (1 Cor 15,10): La experiencia de la gracia como clave para la comprensión de Pablo," EstBíb 57 (1999) 125–46.

Bartsch, H.-W., "Die Argumentation des Paulus in I Cor 15,3–11," ZNW 55 (1964) 261–74.

——, "Inhalt und Funktion des urchristlichen Osterglaubens," NTS 26 (1979–80) 180–96.

Berlendis, A., "Risurrezione di Gesù in Paolo (1 Cor 15,1–8)," RBR 8/4 (1973) 19–58.

Biser, E., "Die älteste Ostergeschichte: Zur Jesusmystik des Apostels Paulus," GL 55 (1982) 139–48.

Bishop, E. F. F., "The Risen Christ and the Five Hundred Brethren (1 Cor 15,6)," CBQ 18 (1956) 341–44.

Bjorck, G., "Nochmals Paulus abortivus," ConNeot 3 (1938) 3–8.

Boman, T., "Paulus abortivus (1. Kor. 15,8)," ST 18 (1964) 46–50.

Breytenbach, C., " 'Christus starb für uns': Zur Tradition und paulinischen Rezeption der sogenannten 'Sterbeformeln,' " NTS 49 (2003) 447–75.

Cangh, J.-M. van, " 'Mort pour nos péchés selon les Écritures' (1 Co 15,3b): Une référence à Isaïe 53?" RTL 1 (1970) 191–99.

Cerfaux, L., "Die Tradition bei Paulus," Catholica 9 (1952–53) 94–104.

Chamblin, K., "Revelation and Tradition in the Pauline Euangelion," WTJ 48 (1986) 1–16.

Charlot, J. P., The Construction of the Formula in 1 Corinthians 15,3–5 (Munich: [No publisher], 1968).

Christensen, J., " 'And That He Rose on the Third Day according to the Scriptures,' " SJOT 4 (1990) 101–13.

Conzelmann, H., "On the Analysis of the Confessional Formula in I Corinthians 15:3–5," Int 20 (1966) 15–25.

Croy, N. C., "A Note on 1 Corinthians 15,1–2," BT 55 (2004) 243–46.

Delling, G., "Die bleibende Bedeutsamkeit der Verkündigung des Anfangs im Urchristentum," TLZ 95 (1970) 801–9.

De Saeger, L., " 'Für unsere Sünden': 1 Kor 15,3b und Gal 1,4a im exegetischen Vergleich," ETL 77 (2001) 169–91.

Dibelius, M., From Tradition to Gospel (New York: Scribner's Sons, n.d. [1934?]; repr. Cambridge: James Clarke, 1971).

Dochhorn, J., "Auferstehung am dritten Tag? Eine problematische Parallele zu Hos 6,2," ZAH 11 (1998) 200–204.

Dodd, C. H., The Apostolic Preaching and Its Developments (London: Hodder & Stoughton, 1951).

——, "The Appearances of the Risen Christ: An Essay in Form-Criticism of the Gospels,"

Studies in the Gospels: Essays in Memory of R. H. Lightfoot (ed. D. E. Nineham; Oxford: Blackwell, 1957) 9–35.

Dupont, J., "Ressuscité 'le troisième jour,' " *Bib* 40 (1959) 742–61; repr. *Studia biblica et orientalia* (AnBib 11/2; Rome: Biblical Institute, 1959) 174–93.

Fergusson, D., "Barth's *Resurrection of the Dead*: Further Reflections," *SJT* 56 (2003) 65–72.

Flusser, D., "Qumran und die Zwölf," *Initiation* (Studies in the History of Religions: NumenSup 10; ed. C. J. Bleeker; Leiden: Brill, 1965) 134–46.

Foulkes, F., "Some Aspects of St. Paul's Treatment of the Resurrection of Christ in 1 Corinthians XV," *ABR* 16 (1968) 15–30.

Fridrichsen, A., "Paulus abortivus: Zu 1 Kor. 15,8," *Symbolae philologicae O. A. Danielsson octogenario dicatae* (Uppsala: Lundequistska Bokhandeln, 1932) 78–85; repr. *Exegetical Writings: A Selection* (WUNT 76; Tübingen: Mohr [Siebeck], 1994) 211–16.

Fuller, R. H., "The Resurrection of Jesus Christ," *BR* 4 (1960) 8–24.

Gilmour, S. M., "The Christophany to More than Five Hundred Brethren," *JBL* 80 (1961) 248–52.

Glombitza, O., "Gnade—Das entscheidende Wort: Erwägungen zu 1. Kor. xv 1–11, eine exegetische Studie," *NovT* 2 (1957) 281–90.

Grieb, A. K., "Last Things First: Karl Barth's Theological Exegesis of 1 Corinthians in *The Resurrection of the Dead*," *SJT* 56 (2003) 49–64.

Güttgemanns, E., "*Christos* in 1. Kor. 15, 3b—Titel oder Eigenname?" *EvT* 28 (1968) 533–54.

Hollander, H. W., and G. E. van der Hout, "The Apostle Paul Calling Himself an Abortion: 1 Cor. 15:8 within the Context of 1 Cor. 15:8–10," *NovT* 38 (1996) 224–36.

Jeremias, J., *Eucharistic Words* (London: SCM; Philadelphia: Fortress, 1966) 101–5.

——, *New Testament Theology* (London: SCM, 1971) 287–88.

——, "Nochmals artikelloses *Christos* in I Cor 14,3," *ZNW* 60 (1969) 214–19.

Jones, P. R., "1 Corinthians 15:8: Paul the Last Apostle," *TynBul* 36 (1985) 3–34.

Kattackal, J., "Christ Is Risen or Christ Is Raised?" *BiBh* 27 (2001) 147–54.

Kearney, P. J., "He Appeared to 500 Brothers (I Cor. xv 6)," *NovT* 22 (1980) 264–84.

Klappert, B., "Zur Frage des semitischen oder griechischen Urtextes von I. Kor. xv. 3–5," *NTS* 13 (1966–67) 168–73.

Kloppenborg, J., "An Analysis of the Pre-Pauline Formula 1 Cor 15:3b–5 in Light of Some Recent Literature," *CBQ* 40 (1978) 351–67.

Kramer, W., *Christ, Lord, Son of God*, (SBT 50; London: SCM, 1966) 19–21.

Kremer, J., *Das älteste Zeugnis von der Auferstehung Christi: Eine bibeltheologische Studie zur Aussage und Bedeutung von 1 Kor 15,1–11* (SBS 17; Stuttgart: Katholisches Bibelwerk, 1966; 3d ed., 1970).

——, "Das leere Grab—ein Zeichen: Zur Relevanz der historisch-kritischen Exegese für die kirchliche Verkündigung," *TPQ* 149 (2001) 136–45.

——, " 'Vor allem habe ich euch überliefert . . .': Bibeltheologische Erwägungen zum unverkürzten Verkünden von Gottes Wort," *Die Freude an Gott—unsere Kraft: Festschrift für Otto Bernhard Knoch* . . . (ed. J. J. Degenhardt; Stuttgart: Katholisches Bibelwerk, 1991) 176–82.

Lambrecht, J., "Line of Thought in 1 Cor 15,1–11," *Pauline Studies* (BETL 115), 109–24.

——, "Three Brief Notes on 1 Corinthians 15," *Collected Studies* (AnBib 147), 71–85.

Lehmann, K., *Auferweckt am dritten Tag nach der Schrift: Früheste Christologie, Bekenntnisbildung und Schriftauslegung im Lichte von 1 Kor 15,3–5* (QD 38; Freiburg im B.: Herder, 1968).

Lichtenstein, E., "Die älteste christliche Glaubensformel," *ZKG* 63 (1950–51) 1–74.

Lindars, B., *New Testament Apologetic: The Doctrinal Significance of the Old Testament Quotations* (London: SCM, 1961) 59–72.

Lindemann, A., "Paulus als Zeuge der Auferstehung Jesu Christi," *Paulus Apostel Jesu Christi: Festschrift für Günter Klein* . . . (ed. M. Trowitzsch; Tübingen: Mohr Siebeck, 1998) 55–64.

Mánek, J., "The Apostle Paul and the Empty Tomb," *NovT* 2 (1957) 276–80.

McArthur, H. K., " 'On the Third Day,' " *NTS* 18 (1971–72) 81–86.

McCasland, S. V., "The Scripture Basis of 'On the Third Day,' " *JBL* 48 (1929) 124–37.

Metzger, B. M., "A Suggestion Concerning the Meaning of 1 Cor. xv. 4b," *JTS* 8 (1957) 118–23.

Mitchell, M. W., "Reexamining the 'Aborted Apostle': An Exploration of Paul's Self-Description in 1 Corinthians 15.8," *JSNT* 25 (2002–3) 469–85.

Moule, C. F. D., "St Paul and Dualism: The Pauline Conception of Resurrection," *NTS* 12 (1965–66) 106–23.

Munck, J., "Paulus tamquam abortivus (1 Cor. 15:8)," *New Testament Essays: Studies in Memory of Thomas Walter Manson 1893–1958* (ed. A. J. B. Higgins; Manchester, UK: Manchester University Press, 1959) 180–93.   ·

Murphy-O'Connor, J., "Tradition and Redaction in 1 Cor 15:3–7," *CBQ* 43 (1981) 582–89.

Mussner, F., "Zur stilistischen und semantischen Struktur der Formel von 1 Kor 15,3–5," *Die Kirche des Anfangs: Festschrift für Heinz Schürmann* . . . (ed. R. Schnackenburg et al.; Leipzig: St. Benno, 1977) 405–16.

Nickelsburg, G. W. E., "An *ektrōma*, Though Appointed from the Womb: Paul's Apostolic Self-Description in 1 Corinthians 15 and Galatians 1," *HTR* 79 (1986) 198–205.

Osten-Sacken, P. von der, "Die Apologie des paulinischen Apostolats in 1 Kor 15,1–11," *ZNW* 64 (1973) 245–62.

Pastor-Ramos, F., " 'Murió por nuestros pecados' (1 Cor 15,3; Gal 1,4): Observaciones sobre el origen de esta fórmula en Is 53," *EstEcl* 61 (1986) 385–93.

Patterson, S. J., "Why Did Christians Say: 'God Raised Jesus from the Dead'? 1 Cor 15 and the Origins of the Resurrection Tradition," *Forum* 10 (1994) 135–60.

Pelletier, A., "Les apparitions du Ressuscité en termes de la Septante," *Bib* 51 (1970) 76–79.

Plevnik, J., "Paul's Appeals to His Damascus Experience and 1 Cor. 15:5–7: Are They Legitimations?" *TorJT* 4 (1988) 101–11.

Pratscher, W., *Der Herrenbruder Jakobus und die Jakobustradition* (FRLANT 139; Göttingen: Vandenhoeck & Ruprecht, 1987) 29–48.

Price, R. M., "Apocryphal Apparitions: 1 Corinthians 15:3–11 as a Post-Pauline Interpolation," *JHC* 2/2 (1995) 69–99.

Radl, W., "Der Sinn von *gnōrizō* in 1 Kor 15,1," *BZ* 28 (1984) 243–45.

Richter, H.-F., *Auferstehung und Wirklichkeit: Eine exegetische, hermeneutische und ontologische Untersuchung zu I. Korinther 15,1/11* (Berlin: Verlag Lebendiges Wort, 1969).

Sabugal, S., "La manifestación del resucitado a Pablo: 1 Cor 15,8–11," *Revista augustiniana de espiritualidad* 16 (1975) 87–101.

Saint-Arnaud, G.-R., "La grâce du 'troisième jour,' " *RevScRel* 75 (2001) 338–64.

Sanders, J. T., "Paul's 'Autobiographical' Statements in Galatians 1–2," *JBL* 85 (1966) 335–43, esp. 337–38.

Schaefer, M., "Paulus, 'Fehlgeburt' oder 'unvernünftiges Kind'? Ein Interpretationsvorschlag zu 1Kor 15,8," *ZNW* 85 (1994) 207–17.

Schenk, W., "Textlinguistische Aspekte der Strukturanalyse, dargestellt am Beispiel von 1 Kor xv. 1–11," *NTS* 23 (1976–77) 469–77.

Schütz, J. H., "Apostolic Authority and the Control of Tradition: I Cor. xv," *NTS* 15 (1968–69) 439–57.

Schwankl, O., "Auf der Suche nach dem Anfang des Evangeliums: Von 1 Kor 15,3–5 zum Johannes-Prolog," *BZ* 40 (1996) 39–60.

Schweizer, E., "Two New Testament Creeds Compared: I Corinthians 15.3–5 and I Timothy 3.16," *Current Issues in New Testament Interpretation: Essays in Honor of Otto A. Piper* (ed. W. Klassen and G. F. Snyder; New York: Harper, 1962) 166–78.

Seeberg, A., *Der Katechismus der Urchristenheit* (Theologische Bücherei 26; Leipzig: Deichert, 1903; repr. Munich: Kaiser, 1966) 45–58.

Sider, R. J., "St. Paul's Understanding of the Nature and Significance of the Resurrection in I Corinthians xv 1–19," *NovT* 19 (1977) 124–41.

Sisti, A., "La risurrezione di Cristo nella catechesi apostolica (1 Cor. 15,1–11)," *ED* 28 (1975) 187–203.

Sleeper, C. F., "Pentecost and Resurrection," *JBL* 84 (1965) 389–99.

Smit-Sibinga, J., "1 Cor. 15:8/9 and Other Divisions in 1 Cor. 15:1–11," *NovT* 39 (1997) 54–59.

Tatum, W. B., "The Resurrection & Historical Evidence: Wolfhart Pannenberg on 1 Corinthians 15," *Forum* 10 (1994) 249–54.

Tomson, P. J., "La première épître aux Corinthiens comme document de la tradition apostolique de Halakha," *The Corinthian Correspondence* (BETL 125; ed. R. Bieringer), 459–70.

Vögtle, A., "Wie kam es zur Artikulierung des Osterglaubens?" *BLeb* 14 (1973) 231–44; 15 (1974) 16–37, 102–20, 174–93.

Watt, R. J. G., "On the Third Day," *ExpTim* 88 (1976–77) 276.

Webber, R. C., "A Note on 1 Corinthians 15: 3–5," *JETS* 26 (1983) 265–69.

Wilckens, U., *Die Missionsreden der Apostelgeschichte* (WMANT 5; Neukirchen: Neukirchener-V., 1974).

Winter, P., "1 Corinthians xv 3b–7," *NovT* 2 (1957–58) 142–50.

Wright, N. T., "Jesus' Resurrection and Christian Origins," *Greg* 83 (2002) 615–35.

B. BELIEF IN THE RESURRECTION OF THE DEAD ROOTED IN CHRIST'S RESURRECTION (15:12–34)

34   a. *If Christ Has Not Been Raised (15:12–19)*

15:12 If, then, Christ is preached as raised from the dead, how can some of you say that there is no resurrection of the dead? 13 If there is no resurrection of the dead, then neither has Christ been raised. [14] If Christ has not been raised, then our preaching has [also] been useless, and useless has been your faith. [15] Then we have been found to be false witnesses about God, because we testified of God that he raised Christ, when he did not raise him, if indeed the dead are not raised. [16] For if the dead are not raised, neither has Christ been raised. [17] Yet if Christ has not been raised, your faith is worthless, and you are still in your sins; [18] and those who have fallen asleep have perished in Christ. [19] If only for this life we have hoped in Christ, then we are of all human beings the most to be pitied.

COMMENT

Having related the resurrection of Christ to the Christian gospel and the fundamental affirmation of apostolic preaching, Paul now turns to the denial of the resurrection of the dead, as he once again quotes a Corinthian statement. Differently from the way he sought to have Corinthian Christians handle the case of a man living with his father's wife in 5:1–5, where he counseled them to "hand this man over to Satan," he now prefers to argue philosophically with the Corinthians about this matter. So he tries to show that the view that "some" Corinthian Christians have been advocating (v. 12) is illogical, baseless, and a contradiction of the most crucial Christian belief. Just how the "some" are related to other Corinthian Christians whom Paul has been criticizing in this letter is difficult to say. There is no certainty that they are different from those who were responsible for the preacher rivalries of chap. 1 or those who were creating division at the celebration of the Lord's Supper in chap. 11. In any case, Paul's arguments are directed to all the Corinthian Christians. He is not trying to establish for pagans either the fact or the possibility of the resurrection of the dead. He is arguing with Christians and seeks to demonstrate to them that belief in the resurrection of Christ, which he assumes they still hold, and the conduct of a life lived in Christian faith inevitably imply a belief in the resurrection of the dead. In effect, his mode is *argumentum ad hominem*.

Paul introduces his argument with a conditional sentence (v. 12), which is followed by two others (vv. 13–14), from which he draws his first conclusion (v. 15), "We have been found to be false witnesses about God." Then follows another pair of conditional sentences (vv. 16–17), parallel to vv. 13–14, which enables him to conclude that, if such skeptics are right, then "those who have fallen asleep have perished in Christ" (v. 18); and his conclusion stands in v. 19, that Christians "of all human beings are the most to be pitied" (v. 19). Note how vv. 16–17 follow even the mode of argumentation of vv. 13–14: If not A, then not B; if not B, then C + D; then the conclusion.

Paul's *ad hoc* philosophical argument makes four points: if the Corinthian skeptics are right, then (1) Christ has not been raised from the dead (vv. 13, 16); (2) Paul's preaching has been useless, and he has borne false witness to God (vv. 14b, 15); (3) the faith of Corinthian Christians is worthless, and they are still in their sins (vv. 14c, 17bc); and (4) Christians who have died are simply lost (v. 18).

There has been no little debate, especially among German commentators, about the logic of Paul's argument. Bucher presents the argument thus: (1) If there is no resurrection of the dead, then Christ too has not been raised (vv. 13–19). (2) But Christ indeed has been raised (v. 20). (3) Therefore there is a resurrection of the dead. So it is claimed that Paul's argumentation is quite logical. It is, however, not an ideal Aristotelian syllogism, and it has even been called Stoic-Megarian logic ("Die logische Argumentation"; see also his "Auferstehung Christi": the resurrection of Christ is the basis for the resurrection of the dead). Bachmann ("Zur Gendankenführung"), however, finds Bucher's argumentation faulty, because he concludes to a general resurrection of the dead in the future, whereas Paul has shown only that Christ is the instance that proves that some do return from the realm of the dead, but that is not what will happen generally in the future for everyone, but is what has already happened. See also his "Rezeption" (a particular resurrection, not a general resurrection of all the deceased); and "Zum 'argumentum resurrectionis' " (anastasis nekrōn does not refer to the general resurrection, but only to a possibility of resurrection). Bucher ("Nochmals zur Beweisführung"), however, adamantly defends Paul's logic. Even if it is judged faulty by the norm of Aristotelian logic, Bucher has caught what Paul is trying to say (see also Stenger, "Beobachtungen"; Vos, "Die Logik," who agrees with Bucher, but concludes only to a possibility of the resurrection of others than Christ, which Lambrecht ["Just a Possibility?"] questions; Zimmer, "Das argumentum resurrectionis").

A further issue, however, concerns the way one is to understand the denial of the resurrection of which Paul speaks in the apodosis of v. 12. The answer is complicated and has to be given on the basis of what appears in chap. 15 of this letter, by a sort of mirror reading, and from this chapter alone (without trying to use 2 Corinthians 5, which may seem to be related but is actually a different problem). Denial of the resurrection of the dead would mean that "some" Corinthian Christians were maintaining something about the afterlife. In general, the answers given to that question by modern interpreters fall into three categories, as Sellin (Der Streit, 17) and Tuckett ("The Corinthians," 251–61) have shown.

1. A Denial of Postmortem Existence, which would mean that some Corinthian Christians considered death to be the end of everything, as did the Athenians mentioned in Acts 17:32, and as did either Epicurean skeptics (OCD, 23–24) or Sadducean Jews (Acts 23:8); or according to some interpreters, only those alive at the parousia would live in the new age, whereas those who died before it were simply lost (Schweizer, Schlatter, Spörlein, Vos, "Argumentation"). This explanation is sometimes proposed as a view that Paul mistakenly attributes to the Corinthians (Bultmann, TNT, 1:169; Schmithals, Gnosticism, 156). It encounters the difficulty that v. 29 or vv. 29–32 speak of Corinthians being baptized for the dead, which implies something quite different from such an extreme denial (see Hurd, Origin, 197; cf. Hoffmann, Die Toten, 245–46).

2. Denial of the Bodily Nature of the Resurrection, which would mean either a belief in immortality of the soul (psychē), a disembodied soul, as did many Greeks before and during Paul's day, e.g., Socrates in Plato, Phaedo 66e–70a (Bachmann, Garland, Hays, Horsley, Lietzmann, T. W. Manson, Murphy-

O'Connor, Robertson-Plummer, Ross, Sider), or a belief in some sort of bodiless existence as *pneumatikoi*, with a divine indwelling "Spirit" (de Boer, Fee, Pearson, Schrage, Sellin, Wedderburn,). Hence the question asked in v. 35b, "With what kind of a body will they come?" becomes important. This is probably the best explanation of the denial, even though Conzelmann strangely thinks that Paul's argument "is not in harmony with this interpretation. He does not emphasize the bodily character of the resurrection" (*1 Cor*, 261–62). Then what is the point of vv. 36–49, where "the body" is certainly envisaged in some form?

3. *Denial of the Futurity of the Resurrection*, which would mean that some Corinthian Christians were claiming that the resurrection has already taken place in some sense, as 1 Cor 4:8 seems to refer to a realized eschatology. This would be a conviction or knowledge (*gnōsis*) that the parousia already took place at Christ's resurrection and that they were already sharing at present through baptism and faith in the risen life of Christ (cf. Col 2:12–13; 3:1), in a manner somewhat similar to what Hymenaeus and Philetus are said to have held in 2 Tim 2:18, "That the resurrection is past already"; cf. the later *Treatise on the Resurrection* 49.15: "Already you have the resurrection" (Barrett, G. Barth, Bartsch, Godet, Heinrici, Héring, Käsemann, Kistemaker, Kümmel, Lindemann, Plank, Schmithals, Schniewind, Schütz, von Soden, Thiselton, Tuckett, Wedderburn, Wilson). This explanation of the denial encounters the problem, Why would Paul object to such a denial by asking, "How can some of you say that there is no resurrection of the dead"? He is not countering those who say that the resurrection is "past already," but that there is none at all. The whole thrust of vv. 13–19 seems to be against this interpretation, because Paul argues that to deny the resurrection of the dead is to deny that Christ died and was raised from the dead. Moreover, such an interpretation fails to reckon with the physical nature of death; how could the "resurrection" be experienced this side of death? (see Hurd, *Origin*, 285–86).

How is Paul's answer to the question of the resurrection of the dead to be related to what he has written already in 6:14, "By his power God raised up the Lord, and he will also raise us up"? In others words, Paul has already affirmed in this letter not only Christ's resurrection, but also the destiny of Christians, who are to share in his risen life. Here in chap. 15, one sees that he not only affirms them both again, but now in a polemical context, and with stress on the bodily character of the existence of Christians in that destiny. For a Gnostic reading of this passage, see Pagels, "Mystery of the Resurrection."

A further minor problem is created by v. 20, which is considered by N-A[27] to be the beginning of the next pericope, but which some commentators (e.g., Lietzmann, *1 Cor*, 79) take as the concluding verse of this passage. It is a transitional verse, but it is better taken with the following pericope (as in N-A[27], RSV).

Lastly, it should be recalled that resurrection of the dead is a belief that emerges in Judaism only in the late pre-Christian centuries. Normally, one cites Dan 12:2 as the sole clear mention of it, "Many of those who sleep in the dust of the earth shall awake, some to everlasting life, and some to shame and everlasting contempt." Earlier passages, such as Isa 26:19; Ps 49:15; Hos 6:1–3; 13:14; Ezek 37:1–14, seem to mention it, but none of them is clear, for at times it seems to be used figuratively of the restoration of Israel in some blessed future (see Schmitz, "Grammar"). Earlier views of postmortem existence are grim (Ps 88:11–13; Isa 14:9–11), but what one finds in deuterocanonical 2 Macc 7:9, 14, 22–23, 29; 12:43; 14:46 changes the picture of the afterlife, because there one finds belief in the resurrection of martyrs, especially in 2 Macc 7:14, where one of the tortured brothers chooses "to die at the hands of men and to cherish the hope that God gives of being raised again by him"; cf. 7:36. Mention of the eschatological resurrection recurs in other late Jewish writings, such as *1 Enoch* 51:1; *Syr. Apoc. Baruch* 50:2–3; 51:1–3; *Test. Benj.* 19:8–10; *Test. Job* 4:9.

In the Book of Wisdom, however, one finds rather *athanasia*, "immortality," as the reward of the suffering righteous person. This is rather a notion borrowed from the Greek world about the afterlife (3:4; 4:1; 8:13, 17; 15:3). In the first Christian century, Palestinian Jews were divided over the issue, with Pharisees and Essenes affirming the resurrection and Sadducees denying it, because it is not taught in the Law of Moses (i.e., the Pentateuch); see Acts 23:6–8; Josephus, *Ant.* 18.1.3 §14; 18.1.4 §16; *J.W.* 2.8.14 §§163–65. How much relevance this Jewish belief would have for the Corinthian problem is hard to say, because the Corinthian denial of the resurrection of the dead undoubtedly emerged from a different, most likely Greco-Roman, background.

That background, however, was quite different from the age-old belief in Egypt about the afterlife, which involved the cult of Osiris, the god of the Underworld, in which people thought that after death they would, like Osiris, enjoy everlasting life. This belief explains the elaborate burial customs of the Egyptians, their tombs and pyramids, their practice of funerary gifts, and the mummification of their dead. They recognized the distinction of soul and body, and believed that at death the soul went to heavenly realms (a place in the sky among the stars), and the body to the earth, but terrestrial life was lived in a consciousness of death and an elaborate preparation for dying in order to join Osiris and to dwell in the house of eternity (see Morenz, *Egyptian Religion*, 183–213; Bostock, "Osiris," 267–69). The cults of Isis and Osiris were widely known in the Greek world of the eastern Mediterranean in Paul's day, but it is highly questionable whether any of the ideas of Egyptian afterlife affected Paul's thinking. Bostock goes too far when he suggests that Paul adopted "motifs and concepts from Egyptian thought" ("Osiris," 271), because the change from an animated body to a spiritual body (15:44) is clearly predicated in Greek, not Egyptian terms.

NOTES

15:12. *If, then, Christ is preached as raised from the dead.* Lit. "if Christ is preached, that he has been raised from the dead," i.e., the fact that "Christ has been raised" is the essence of the Christian gospel, and the kerygma continues to proclaim it, as in v. 4b. To two words derived from the kerygma, *Christos* and *egēgertai*, Paul now adds *ek nekrōn*, "from the dead," which makes explicit the meaning of the verb; see the occurrence of this phrase in 1 Thess 1:10; Gal 1:1; Rom 4:24; 8:11; 10:9 (cf. Kramer, *Christ, Lord*, 19–26). In vv. 14, 17, Paul will reformulate the protasis of the condition in terms of the *fact* of Christ's resurrection; he begins here by stressing the *preaching* of it. The phrase *ek nekrōn* lacks the art., when it denotes the dead in general (as in vv. 12bis, 13, 15, 16, 20, 21, 29b, 32).

how can some of you say that there is no resurrection of the dead? Lit. "how do some among you say . . . ?" So Paul expresses his surprise and indignation, as he confronts the skepticism of some Christians of Corinth. It is impossible to say how many "some" might mean, or whether they are related to any of the rivalries reported earlier in the letter, or how influential they might have been in spreading their ideas.

Paul's question, however, raises one for the interpreter: When Paul first preached the gospel to Corinthians about the resurrection of Christ "from the dead" and his appearances to many, did he also preach about the "resurrection of the dead"? Or is he announcing this truth to them for the first time, now that some Christians to whom the risen Christ appeared "have fallen asleep"? (v. 6). Have their deaths before the parousia occasioned the problem that Paul is confronting? It might be another instance of what he had to handle in 1 Thess 4:13–17. So Wilson ("The Corinthians," 102–3) would have us believe. Such an interpretation is not impossible, but one would expect that, because Paul had already encountered the problem of Christians dying before the parousia in Thessalonica, he would have related the afterlife of Corinthians to that of the risen Christ at the time of his initial evangelization of Corinth.

Anastasis nekrōn, "resurrection of the dead," would have been familiar to Greek-speaking Jews, since the notion appears in Palestinian Judaism of the second century B.C.: "Many of those sleeping in the dust of the earth will wake up [LXX: *anastēsontai*; Theodotion: *egerthēsontai*], some to life eternal, some to shame and eternal contempt" (Dan 12:2). In 2 Macc 7:14 one finds both the verb *anastēsesthai* and the noun *anastasis*; cf. 12:43. Hence there is no need to appeal to Egyptian religion as the background of what Paul is trying to teach Corinthian Christians, *pace* Bostock ("Osiris"). What is the evidence that the Egyptians spoke of "resurrection" in the afterlife? Does the word or the idea even occur in the *Pyramid Texts, Coffin Texts,* or *The Book of the Dead?*

In a place like Corinth, however, where Greek and Roman philosophy reigned, resurrection would have been scoffed at, as did the sneering Athenians, when Paul mentioned it in his address at the Areopagus (Acts 17:32). In the Greek world of a half-millennium earlier, the tragedian Aeschylus put on the lips of Apollo the assertion, "When the dust has soaked up the blood of a man, once he has died, there is no resurrection" (*outis est' anastasis, Eumenides* 647–48; cf. *Agamemnon* 1360). Similar statements can be found also in Herodotus, *Hist.* 3.62; Homer, *Iliad* 24.551; Sophocles, *Electra* 137–42. Yet even in that world there was the legend of Alcestis, who was willing to die for her husband and whose good deed was rewarded by the gods, who granted *ex Hādou aneinai palin tēn psychēn*, "to let loose again her soul from Hades" (Plato, *Symposium* 179c; cf. *OCD,* 36). *Anastasis nekrōn* may be a quoted Corinthian phrase, to which Paul replies, using the verb *egeirō,* "I raise," from his Jewish background.

Among early Christians, however, belief in the resurrection of the dead often prevailed, and the phrase was current in varying forms: Rom 1:4; Matt 22:31; Luke 20:35; Acts 4:2; 24:21; 26:23; Heb 6:2 (*EDNT*, 1:90–91). For various ways of understanding the Corinthian denial, see the COMMENT above.

13. *If there is no resurrection of the dead, then neither has Christ been raised.* Paul's philosophical argument now begins, as he tries to reduce the denial *ad absurdum*: If there is no "resurrection of the dead," then Christ's resurrection is unthinkable, indeed impossible! Paul uses a simple condition (*ei* + pres. indic., *ouk estin*) to express logical reasoning (BDF §372.2). Yet he implies that, if Christ has been raised (as indeed the kerygma proclaims), then dead people too can awaken from the sleep of death. So Corinthian skeptics cannot deny one without denying the other—indeed, without denying a basic Christian belief.

14. *If Christ has not been raised, then our preaching has [also] been useless, and useless has been your faith.* Another simple condition has two consequences, expressed in the double apodosis. The adj. *kenos* was used in v. 10, when Paul asserted that divine grace was not "without effect" in his life. Now he applies the same idea not only to apostolic preaching of the gospel about the risen Christ, but also to the response of Christian faith made to that preaching, putting the adj. in the emphatic first place in each apodosis. If Christ has not actually been raised, then both the preaching and faith are "unproductive, void, empty, or useless," i.e., "devoid of any spiritual value" (Garland, *1 Cor*, 701). For further uses of the adj. *kenos*, see 1 Thess 2:1; 3:5; Gal 2:2; Phil 2:16; 2 Cor 6:1.

The "faith" is the same as that mentioned in v. 11c. A number of MSS (B, D*, 0243, 0270*, 6, 33, 81, 1739, 1881) read *hēmōn*, "our," at the end, instead of "your" faith. That reading would make Paul include his own "faith" in the risen Christ, which resulted from the appearance to him on the road to Damascus and which was far from useless, in that because of it he became "the apostle of the Gentiles" (Rom 11:13). The first *kai*, "also," is missing in some MSS (P[46], ℵ[2], B, Ψ, 0243, etc.); hence the square brackets.

Whereas in v. 12 Paul argued from the preaching of Christ's resurrection, he now moves to a further consideration, viz., the fact of Christ's resurrection, from which his argument will continue (as he repeats the negative protasis and then asserts the fact again in v. 20).

15. *Then we have been found to be false witnesses about God.* Lit. "we are found to be false witnesses of God," an obj. gen., explained in the following clause. This is Paul's first conclusion. By "we," Paul means himself and the "they" of v. 11, the other commissioned emissaries who preach the gospel. Though they speak in God's name, they would all be known to have announced what is untrue.

because we testified of God that he raised Christ, when he did not raise him, if indeed the dead are not raised. I.e., we have foisted upon you and all those whom we have evangelized a hoax of no little proportion. Paul again ascribes to God the efficient causality of Christ's resurrection, as in 6:14; Rom 4:24; 8:11, etc. That would be the untruth that they have been proclaiming. Even though most of Paul's argument about the resurrection of the dead depends on the resurrection of Christ, he has not forgotten the role that God the Father has played in the resurrection, and of this role he and others have been witnesses (see Wargnies, "Témoins de Dieu").

16. *For if the dead are not raised, neither has Christ been raised.* This verse parallels the argument of v. 13, as it begins the second pair of conditions. The apodosis is identical in each verse, but the protasis now has the concrete verb, *ouk egeirontai*, whereas that of v. 13 used the abs. noun, *anastasis nekrōn*.

17. *Yet if Christ has not been raised, your faith is worthless.* I.e., futile, fruitless (*mataia*), another way of saying "without effect" (v. 14), unable to secure salvation or forgiveness, because all that Paul thought that he had achieved has really failed, and he can no longer bring any advantage to those who have believed. Recall v. 2c above.

and you are still in your sins. I.e., because you have not found the "justification" that was the result of Christ's resurrection. See Rom 4:25, "Who was handed over (to death) for our trespasses and raised for our justification," a verse that is not be understood as though Paul meant that human trespasses were removed by Christ's death and that human justification was achieved by his resurrection; they are so formulated in a literary parallelism in which both effects are to be ascribed to both the death *and* the resurrection (see *Romans*, 389). Now he implies clearly that the removal of human sins is indeed an effect of Christ's resurrection (see Stanley, *Christ's Resurrection*, 120–22, 171–73).

18. *and those who have fallen asleep have perished in Christ.* Lit. "those who have been lulled to sleep" (see NOTES on 7:10, 39), i.e., those who have died believing in Christ, and the effects of the Christ-event are lost (*apōlonto*) in nothingness, just as he is. They too have suffered the same fate. This is the conclusion that Paul derives from vv. 16–17, and it corresponds to that in v. 15. Instead of being justified Christians whom God has "glorified" (Rom 8:30), "their end is destruction" (*apōleia*, Phil 3:19). The faith that they put in Christ's gospel (see v. 2 above) has not saved them. "Those who have fallen asleep" are at least those mentioned in v. 6b above (see NOTE there).

Many versions and commentators take the prep. phrase, *en Christō*, as modifying the ptc. *hoi koimēthentes* (lit., "those having been lulled to sleep"), but as Lindemann (*1 Cor*, 340) notes, Paul has not written *hoi en Christō koimēthentes* (lit., "those having been lulled to sleep in Christ"), comparing 7:22; 2 Cor 3:14; 12:19. Moreover, he points out that Paul is not speaking about dying in Christ, as in 1 Thess 4:16, because that would be a delusion, if v. 17 were true. Similarly, Barrett (*1 Cor*, 349) remarks, following Lietzmann (*1 Cor*, 79), "*those who have fallen asleep in Christ* is already an impossible expression, since if Christ was not raised from the dead there is no one in Christ; if being in Christ is a real possibility, those who have fallen asleep (cf. xv. 6) in him will be no more finally dead than he is."

19. *If only for this life we have hoped in Christ, then we are of all human beings the most to be pitied.* Or perhaps "if only in this life we have been those who hope in Christ, . .," because Paul uses the periphrastic perf. ptc. with the verb "to be" (*elpikotes esmen*, see BDF §352), either as a mere substitute for the perf. indic. (*ēlpikamen*), or he intends the ptc. as a substantive (which is less likely, since it is without an article).

The adv. *monon*, "only," is problematic, since it is the last Greek word in the protasis. It has been understood in four ways:

1. With *ēlpikotes esmen*, "we only hoped," but Paul never uses the noun *elpis* or the verb *elpizō* elsewhere in such a negative sense (13:7, 13; 1 Thess 4:13; Rom 4:18; 5:5; 8:24–25).
2. With *en Christō*, "only in Christ," which is too restrictive theologically.
3. With the initial prepositional phrase, *en tē zōē tautē*, "only in this life," as in the lemma (and NIV); this seems to suit best the rest of the sentence, despite the distant word order.
4. With the whole protasis (so Barrett, *1 Cor*, 349–50: "—that and nothing more—"; similarly Garland, *1 Cor*, 703). Again, the comparative is used in the sense of the superlative (see NOTE on 13:13).

Paul seems to be saying that, if our hope in Christ is limited only to what we may share with him in this life, with no prospect of a share in his glorious and resurrected life, then we are to be pitied indeed, because all is lost. Cf. the similar sentiment expressed in *Syr. Apoc. Bar.* 21.13: "If there were this life only, which belongs to all human beings, nothing could be more bitter than this," uttered in a context of a place reserved for the end of sinners and the righteous.

Paul was aware that many non-Christians of his day entertained a vague hope in some form of future life in Elysium or the Isles of the Blessed (see *OCD*, 23), but he knew from his faith what a share in the glorious life of the risen Christ would be for his fellow Christians.

BIBLIOGRAPHY

Bachmann, M., "1 Kor 15,12f.: 'Resurrection of the Dead' (= Christians)?" *ZNW* 92 (2001) 295–99.

——, "Noch einmal: 1 Kor 15, 12ff und Logik," *LB* 59 (1987) 100–104.

——, "Rezeption von 1. Kor. 15 (V. 12ff.) unter logischem und unter philologischem Aspekt," *LB* 51 (1982) 79–103.

——, "Zum 'argumentum resurrectionis' von 1 Kor 15,12ff nach Christoph Zimmer, Augustin und Paulus," *LB* 67 (1992) 29–39.

——, "Zur Gedankenführung in 1 Kor. 15, 12ff," *TZ* 34 (1978) 265–76.

Barth, G., "Zur Frage nach der in 1 Korinther 15 bekämpften Auferstehungsleugnung," *ZNW* 83 (1992) 187–201.

Binder, H., "Zum geschichtlichen Hintergrund von I Kor 15,12," *TZ* 46 (1990) 193–201.

Boer, M. C. de, *The Defeat of Death: Apocalyptic Eschatology in 1 Corinthians 15 and Romans 5* (JSNTSup 22; Sheffield: Sheffield Academic, 1988) 93–114.

Bostock, D. G., "Osiris and the Resurrection of Christ," *ExpTim* 112 (2000–2001) 265–71.

Bucher, T. G., "Allgemeine Überlegungen zur Logik im Zusammenhang mit 1 Kor 15, 12–20," *LB* 53 (1983) 70–98.

——, "Auferstehung Christi und Auferstehung der Toten," *MTZ* 27 (1976) 1–32.

——, "Die logische Argumentation in 1. Korinther 15,12–20," *Bib* 55 (1974) 465–86.

——, "Nochmals zur Beweisführung in 1. Korinther 15, 12–20," *TZ* 36 (1980) 129–52.

Crüsemann, F., "Schrift und Auferstehung: Beobachtungen zur Wahrnehmung des auferstandenen Jesus bei Lukas und Paulus und zum Verhältnis der Testamente," *Kirche und Israel* 17 (2002) 150–62.

Dahl, M. E., *The Resurrection of the Body: A Study of I Corinthians 15* (SBT 36; London: SCM, 1962).

Doohan, L., " 'If Christ Has Not Been Raised, Your Faith Is Futile and You Are Still in Your Sins' (1 Cor 15:17)," *ScrC* 33 (2003) 250–55.

Fezer, K., *Totenauferstehung: Ein Bibelkurs über 1 Korinther 15* (Stuttgart: Calwer-V., 1934).

Frick, P. L., *The Resurrection and Paul's Argument: A Study of First Corinthians Fifteenth Chapter* (Cincinnati: Jennings and Graham; New York: Eaton and Mains, 1912).

Hasler, V., "Credo und Auferstehung in Korinth: Erwägungen zu I Kor 15," *TZ* 40 (1984) 12–33.

Hoffmann, P., *Die Toten in Christus: Eine religionsgeschichtliche und exegetische Untersuchung zur paulinischen Eschatologie* (NTAbh n.s. 2; Münster in W.: Aschendorff, 1966) 245–46.

Horsley, R. A., " 'How Can Some of You Say That There Is No Resurrection of the Dead?' Spiritual Elitism in Corinth," *NovT* 20 (1978) 203–31.

Janssen, C., "Bodily Resurrection (1 Cor. 15)? The Discussion of the Resurrection in Karl Barth, Rudolf Bultmann, Dorothee Sölle and Contemporary Feminist Theology," *JSNT* 79 (2000) 61–78.

Kremer, J., "Das leere Grab — ein Zeichen: Zur Relevanz der historisch-kritischen Exegese für die kirchliche Verkündigung," *TPQ* 149 (2001) 135–45.

Lambrecht, J., "Just a Possibility? A Reply to Johan S. Vos on 1 Cor 15,12–20," *ZNW* 91 (2000) 143–45; repr. *Collected Studies* (AnBib 147), 87–90.

Lindemann, A., "Paulus und die korinthische Eschatologie: Zur These von einer 'Entwicklung' im paulinischen Denken," *NTS* 37 (1991) 373–99, esp. 381–84.

Morenz, S., *Egyptian Religion* (Ithaca: Cornell Univeristy Press, 1973).

Pagels, E. H., " 'The Mystery of the Resurrection': A Gnostic Reading of 1 Corinthians 15," *JBL* 93 (1974) 276–88.

Ross, J. M., "Does 1 Corinthians Hold Water?" *IBS* 11 (1989) 69–72.

Rusche, H., "Die Leugner der Auferstehung von den Toten in der korinthischen Gemeinde," *MTZ* 10 (1959) 149–51.

Schmitz, P. C., "The Grammar of the Resurrection in Isaiah 26:19c," *JBL* 122 (2003) 145–49.

Schniewind, J., "Die Leugner der Auferstehung in Korinth," *Nachgelassene Reden und Aufsätze* (ed. E. Kähler; Berlin: Töpelmann, 1952) 110–39.

Sellin, G., *Der Streit um die Auferstehung der Toten: Eine religionsgeschichtliche und exegetische Untersuchung von 1 Korinther 15* (FRLANT 138; Göttingen: Vandenhoeck & Ruprecht, 1986).

Spörlein, B., *Die Leugnung der Auferstehung: Eine historisch-kritische Untersuchung zu I Kor 15* (Münchener Universitäts-Schriften 7; Regensburg: Pustet, 1971).

Stanley, D. M., *Christ's Resurrection in Pauline Soteriology* (AnBib 13; Rome: Biblical Institute, 1961) 94–127.

Stenger, W., "Beobachtungen zur Argumentationsstruktur von 1 Kor 15," *LB* 45 (1979) 71–128.

Trevijano Etcheverria, R., "Los que dicen que no hay resurrección (1 Cor 15, 12)," *Salm* 33 (1986) 275–302.

Tuckett, C. M., "The Corinthians Who Say 'There Is No Resurrection of the Dead' (1 Cor 15,12)," *The Corinthian Correspondence* (BETL 125; ed. R. Bieringer), 247–75.

Vos, J. S., "Argumentation und Situation in 1Kor. 15," *NovT* 41 (1999) 313–33.

———, "Die Logik des Paulus in 1 Kor 15,12–20," *ZNW* 90 (1999) 78–97.

Wargnies, P., "Témoins de Dieu qui relève les morts: Un regard sur *1 Co 15*, 1–19," *NRT* 121 (1999) 353–71.

Wedderburn, A. J. M., *Baptism and Resurrection: Studies in Pauline Theology against Its Graeco-Roman Background* (WUNT 44; Tübingen: Mohr [Siebeck], 1987) 6–37.

———, "The Problem of the Denial of the Resurrection in I Corinthians xv," *NovT* 23 (1981) 229–41.

Wilson, J. H., "The Corinthians Who Say There Is No Resurrection of the Dead," *ZNW* 59 (1968) 90–107.

Zimmer, C., "Das argumentum resurrectionis 1Kor 15, 12–20," *LB* 65 (1991) 25–36.

35   b. *Christ Has Been Raised as the Firstfruits! (15:20–28)*

15:20 Now, then, Christ has been raised from the dead as the firstfruits of those who have fallen asleep. 21 For since death came through a human being, so the resurrection of the dead comes also through a human being. 22 For just as in Adam all die, so too in Christ all will be brought to life; 23 but each one in turn: Christ the firstfruits, then at his coming, those who belong to Christ. 24 Then will come the end, when he hands over the kingdom to God the Father, after having destroyed every dominion, authority, and power. 25 For he must reign until *he has put* all *enemies under his feet.* 26 The last enemy to be destroyed is death; 27 *for he has put all things in subjection under his feet.* When it says that "all things" have been subjected, it clearly means, apart from him who subjected all things to him. 28 When all things are subjected to him, then the Son himself will [also] be made subject to him who subjected all things to him, so that God may be all in all.

COMMENT

Having sought to present a logical argument against the denial of the resurrection of the dead (especially in vv. 13 and 16), Paul now repeats again the kerygma that "Christ has been raised," and indeed "from the dead," to which he now further adds "as the firstfruits of those who have fallen asleep," because denial of the future resurrection of the dead is implicitly a denial of Christ's resurrection and a contradiction of apostolic preaching. In order to present his full argument to the Corinthian denial, he finds it necessary to reformulate belief in the resurrection of Christ himself. This he does from two perspectives: from an Adam-Christ typology (vv. 21–23), and then from an apocalyptic consideration of Christ's relation to God the Father at "the end" (vv. 24–28). According to G. Barth ("Erwägungen"), vv. 20–28 are not an apocalyptic excursus, but a theological argument that makes them the peak of this chapter. That they are a theological argument is admissible, but the last five verses certainly have apocalyptic trappings, which are not found in

vv. 21–23. Hence Paul's theological argument in this paragraph is both typological (vv. 21–23) and apocalyptic (vv. 24–28).

Paul's creative reaction to the Corinthian denial is influenced partly by his Jewish background, especially when he relates Jesus' own death and resurrection to the eschatological resurrection of the dead. He understands the resurrection of Jesus to be like that of the Maccabean martyrs (see the COMMENT on vv. 12–19); after death he is "raised" to the glorious presence of the Father, "exalted," as he puts it in Phil 2:9. As such, he is "the firstfruits of those who have fallen asleep" (15:20), i.e., the beginning of the eschatological resurrection of the dead. Holleman ("Jesus' Resurrection," 656) finds an inconsistency in Paul's teaching, because in 1 Thess 4:13–18 Paul expects the resurrection of the dead to take place on earth. That may be, for 4:16 says that "the Lord himself will descend from heaven . . . and the dead will rise first"; but it does not stop there, because the apocalyptic description ends with the affirmation of Christian destiny, "and so we shall always be with the Lord," i.e., in the Father's glorious presence. That is hardly an inconsistency with what is asserted here in 1 Corinthians 15.

Paul's contention is presented in five points:

1. "Christ has been raised from the dead as the firstfruits of those who have fallen asleep" (v. 20; cf. v. 23).
2. A "human being" was responsible for death among humans, but a "human being" is also responsible for the coming resurrection of the dead (v. 21).
3. As Adam brought death to those related to him, so Christ brings life for those who belong to him.
4. As the risen Lord, Christ has to "reign" as long as human history continues (v. 25), until the time of his "coming" (v. 23), when having done away with all enemies, including death itself, he will hand over sovereignty to God the Father, who has subjected all things to him as "the Son" (v. 28).
5. The goal of all this will be "so that God may be all in all." Thus Paul acknowledges God as the final cause of all that exists.

In all of this, Paul is affirming not only the certainty of Christ's resurrection, but also Christ's resurrection as the guarantee of the futurity and certainty of the resurrection of the dead (zōopoiēthēsontai, "will be brought to life," v. 22), "each one in turn" (v. 23), once death, "the last enemy," has been destroyed (v. 26). "The stress thus appears to be quite as much on the futurity of the final defeat of death as on its certainty" (Tuckett, "The Corinthians," 264).

This passage ends with five important verses (24–28), which explain the "turn" and the "end," and then assert the soteriological role of Christ, who not only exercises regal dominion over cosmic forces but will also bring them to an end, including death itself. When he has thus subdued them, he will hand over dominion to the Father, and, as Son, he himself will be subjected to the Father, in order that God may be God over all. These verses may seem like a digression, because they make no mention of human beings, even of "those who belong to Christ," or of the topic of the resurrection of the dead; and yet their importance to what Paul has been arguing for in the preceding vv. 12–19 is especially great: the role of the risen Christ over death, which afflicts all human beings. Moreover, what is the relation of Christ to God, who "raised Christ" (v. 15)? Those who deny the resurrection of the dead (v. 12b) are denying, in effect, the power of God over death and God's role in all things. The reign of Christ is, in fact, an all-important stage of salvation history, the goal of which is God all in all (see Dykstra, "I Corinthians 15:20–28"). These verses also prepare for what Paul will discuss in vv. 29–57, and in vv. 51–55 the apocalyptic description will turn to human beings.

Schmithals ("Pre-Pauline Tradition") regards chap. 15 and 16:13–24 as part of a letter that Paul once wrote to Corinthian Christians and that vv. 20–28 are an older creedal instruction. Verses 24b, 25, 28 are said to be part of a pre-Pauline tradition. It may be that some tradition is being used here, but the whole explanation depends on Schmithals's questionable theory of the composition of this letter as a whole.

NOTES

15:20. *Now, then, Christ has been raised from the dead as the firstfruits of those who have fallen asleep.* Paul introduces this section of his argument with *nyni de*, lit. "but now," which is to be understood in a logical sense, as in 12:18 and most likely in 13:13 (cf. Rom 3:21; 6:22; 7:6). He again uses the phraseology of the kerygma (v. 4b), as modified in v. 12, "Christ has been raised from the dead," to which he now adds, *aparchē tōn kekoimēmenōn*, "firstfruits of those who have fallen asleep" (for the euphemism of death, see NOTES on 7:10, 39). The risen Christ is the model and guarantee of the resurrection of dead Christians.

The noun *aparchē* denoted originally the "firstfruits" of the harvest, the flawless first part of food, vegetables or fruit, which, when offered to God, was considered dedicated and holy and betokened the consecration of the whole harvest, which could then be put to the use of Israel (see Exod 22:28; 23:19; 34:26; Lev 23:9–14; Num 15:18–21; Deut 18:4; cf. *TLNT*, 1:145–52). The term, "firstfruits," is sometimes applied to converts to Christianity (16:15; Rom 16:5). On occasion, it was used, however, also in the sense of "earnest money," or "guarantee" of what was still to come, like *arrabōn* (2 Cor 1:22; 5:5 [see *TDNT*, 1:486; *EDNT*, 1:116–17]). Thus, Christ was not only the "first" to be raised from the dead, but likewise the "pledge" or "guarantee" of the resurrection of all the Christian dead. See Rom 8:29.

21. *For since death came through a human being, so the resurrection of the dead comes also through a human being.* In two verbless clauses, Paul alludes to the account in Gen 3:17–19, which tells how it came about that *anthrōpos* experiences death. There Adam is punished by God for listening to his wife and eating the forbidden fruit: "On the day you eat of it, you shall surely die" (2:17); "You are dust, and unto dust you shall return" (3:19). Cf. Rom 5:12 ("Sin entered the world through one man, and through sin death, and so death spread to all human beings"), 18. Now Paul fashions the counterpart of that allusion, stressing not sin (as in Romans 5), but death: through another human being, one from Nazareth,

comes *anastasis nekrōn*, "the resurrection of the dead." Christ is referred to as *anthrōpos*, as in 1 Tim 2:5 (*anthrōpos Christos Iēsous*). The mediating idea is *di' anthrōpou*, "through a human being." Even though there is no verb in either clause, the implied causality of Adam's act for universal human death is clear. From that flows likewise the corresponding implied causality of the resurrection of the dead "through" another "human being."

22. *For just as in Adam all die.* What was just enunciated by an abstraction is now repeated in a concrete form, as Paul interprets *'ādām* of Gen 3:17 as the name of the first human being, the historical Adam, whom he knows only from the written account in the Pentateuch. He regards "all" humanity as somehow incorporated in him and thus sharing in his condemnation to death. Paul employs the Greek phrase *en tō Adam*, "in Adam," which differs drastically from the Greek prepositional phrase *eph' hō* (Rom 5:12), which means "with the result that" (see *Romans*, 413–17). The VL and Vg wrongly translated *eph' hō* into Latin as *in quo*, "in whom," and on this translation so much of the Western Church's theology of Original Sin was built: that all sinned in Adam. In other words, the statement here in 1 Corinthians differs from Rom 5:12 in ascribing to Adam only the death of all humanity that descended from him, whereas in Romans Paul ascribes the sin of all humanity as well as the death. Adam is understood thus as a corporate personality.

According to Conzelmann (*1 Cor*, 268), "the designation of Adam and of Christ as *anthrōpos*, 'man,' presupposes the idea of the 'primal man,' and likewise the view of the Fall as the cause of death. But now, already in v. 21 we have indications of a modification of the mythical schema." Nevertheless, Conzelmann is reluctant to relate what he calls "the Fall" to "Gen 3." Such an interpretation, however, reads into Paul's text ideas born of an ideology wholly alien to it. For Paul asserts that "in Adam all die," and that is clearly an allusion to Genesis 2–3. Moreover, there is no need to refer *anthrōpos* to the myth of the "primal man" (*Urmensch*), since there is no evidence that Paul ever thinks in terms of it. Likewise, "the Fall" is a late Christian term, derived from the patristic period (esp. from Augustine's theory of helping or elevating grace [*De peccatorum meritis et remissione* 2.17.26]; cf. ODCC, 597–98).

so too in Christ all will be brought to life. Lit. "all will be made alive," i.e., all human beings will have the possibility of sharing in the new life that comes *en tō Christō*. Paul now affirms the futurity of the resurrection, as he will again in v. 52 (*egerthēsontai*). The phrase *en tō Christō* could be understood in a instrumental sense, "through Christ," but given the parallelism in the verse to *en tō Adam*, it is better taken in the corresponding incorporative sense. Through faith and baptism a human being is incorporated into Christ and thus finds life "in Christ" (see *PAHT* §PT117, 121). The fut. verb *zōopoiēthēsontai*, "will be made alive," is a divine passive (ZBG §236), meaning that God will make human beings share in the risen life of the Lord. As Adam led humanity to death, so Christ, because he has shared humanity, will lead all human beings (who accept him) to resurrection. Cf. Rom 4:17; 8:11.

23. *but each one in turn.* Lit. "each in his own group" (or "division"), since the

word *tagma* is a technical military term for "detachment, troop." What Paul means by it is explained in the rest of the verse. Verses 23–28 clarify how those to be resurrected "will be made alive" (the fut. pass. verb of v. 22b). "If the military image predominates, it pictures Christ as the leader (captain; Heb. 2:10) rising first, then his sleeping army rising when the last trumpet sounds (1 Cor. 15:52)" (Garland, *1 Cor*, 708).

Christ the firstfruits, then at his coming, those who belong to Christ. As *aparchē*, Christ, by being the first to be raised from the dead, leads the way to risen life, for "those who belong to him." The phrase, *hoi tou Christou*, lit. "those of Christ," makes clear Paul's perspective; he is speaking only of Christians, despite the "all" in v. 22. That pron. now takes on the meaning, "all who belong to Christ," as it is expressed also in Gal 5:24. What God has done for Christ, he will likewise do for those who belong to Christ. For a rare apocalyptic description of such an event, see 1 Thess 4:16–17.

Their turn will come *en tē parousiā autou*, "at his coming," to which Paul has already alluded in 1:7, 8; 5:5. Now, however, he uses *parousia*, which lit. means "presence" (as in 16:17; Phil 2:12; 2 Cor 10:10), but often was used in biblical and extrabiblical Greek to mean "arrival, coming" (= the first stage of presence, as in 2 Cor 7:6–7; Phil 1:26). Eventually, it became the technical term for what Paul has already called "the revelation (*apokalypsis*) of our Lord Jesus Christ" (1:7), because of its use in 1 Thess 2:19; 3:13; 4:15; 5:23; cf. 2 Thess 2:1. The resurrection of Christian dead will take place at the parousia of Christ (1 Thess 4:16–17).

24. *Then will come the end.* Lit. "then (will be) the end," with *estai* understood (BDAG, 998); *to telos* is used, as in 1:8, to denote that which will be described in v. 28 below, the "final consummation." This verbless phrase (*eita to telos*) is the immediate sequel and counterpart of "each one in turn" (v. 23), but as Robertson-Plummer note (*1 Cor*, 354), it may also "balance *aparchē*" of v. 23. The noun *to telos* has been understood in three ways: (1) as an adv. acc., "finally"; (2) as a noun, "the rest"; and (3) as a noun, "the end, final consummation." Because it is followed by two explanatory temporal clauses, introduced by *hotan*, "when," that shows that *telos* must be understood in a temporal sense. It denotes, then, the end of human history, and perhaps what God has envisaged as the goal of that history (Schrage, *1 Cor*, 4:169). Cf. Matt 24:14, *kai tote hēxei to telos*, "and then the end will come."

It is difficult, however, to determine whether Paul is using the adv. *eita*, "then," as a logical particle, identifying "the end" with the "coming" (*parousia*) of the Lord itself, or as a temporal particle, meaning that an interval sets in after that "coming" before the "end" (so Bruce, *1 Cor*, 147; Lietzmann, *1 Cor*, 80; Lindemann, "Parusie Christi"; Turner, "Interim"; Wallis, "The Problem"). In either case, *telos* denotes the time when the risen Christ's reign comes to an end (v. 28). Implied is the sequence that the resurrection of the dead must follow thereon. The best interpretation is that the kingdom is Christ's present cosmic lordship exercised from heaven, which began when he as "firstfruits" was raised from the dead. So the destruction of death, the resurrection of all believers, and the parousia of Christ constitute the "end" (see Hill, "Paul's Understanding").

Because of the ambiguous *eita*, some commentators introduce the question of a terrestrial interim reign of Christ, joining to this verse a reference to the "thousand years" of the reign of the risen Christ in Rev 20:5–6. One should beware, however, of importing such an idea into this Pauline text, which, even though it obviously has an apocalyptic thrust, says nothing about a millennarian earthly reign of Christ; nor does 1 Thess 4:13–18, when that passage is rightly understood. Hence it better to take *eita*, "then," as a logical particle.

Another meaning, however, has been given to *to telos* by some commentators who understand it as "the rest," i.e., the third *tagma* (after the two implied in v. 23 above). The first *tagma* would be Christ, the *aparchē*; the second, "those who belong to Christ"; and the third, dead unbelievers, pagan and Jewish (which would explain also the "all" of v. 22); cf. Rev 20:5 (*hoi loipoi*). So argues Lietzmann (*1 Cor*, 80), followed by J. Weiss (*1 Cor*, 358), Oepke (*TDNT*, 1:371), and Leal (" 'Deinde finis' "), who maintains that *telos* can mean that. Such a meaning of *telos*, however, is as yet unattested elsewhere, as Héring ("Saint Paul, " 304–6) and others have shown (Kümmel in Lietzmann, *1 Cor*, 193; Delling, *TDNT*, 8:358). Nor does Paul ever say anything about the resurrection of unbelievers (Grosheide, *1 Cor*, 365). Furthermore, it is not right to take *to telos* in the sense of an adv. acc., "then, finally," as G. Barth proposes, because it is not a Pauline usage (Senft, *1 Cor*, 198).

when he hands over the kingdom to God the Father. Lit. "to God and Father," which has to be understood as hendiadys, as in 2 Cor 1:3, *ho theos kai patēr tou kyriou hēmōn Iēsou Christou*, "God and Father of our Lord Jesus Christ"; cf. 11:31; Rom 15:6. "The kingdom of God" has already appeared in 4:20; 6:9, 10, but then as a stereotyped phrase. Now, however, "kingdom" alone is used, and it characterizes the reign of Christ up until "the end," denoting the sovereignty that belongs to the God of heaven, a notion perhaps inherited from Dan 2:44. The implication is that such sovereignty has been entrusted to the Son (15:28), whose rule continues until "the end."

after having destroyed every dominion, authority, and power. Lit. "when he destroys," the clause is introduced by *hotan*, "when" (with subjunctive *katargēsē*, the same verb as that in 1:28; 2:6; 6:13; 13:8, 10, 11), and it is actually parallel to that in the preceding clause; but it must precede it in time.

The threesome, *archē, exousia, dynamis*, are abstract terms for some sort of governing entities, probably supraterrestrial or even mythological, two of which are mentioned in Rom 8:38 along with *angeloi*, "angels." Because of that association, these abstract terms are often interpreted as different types, ranks, or orders of angels (cf. Eph 1:21; 3:10; 6:12; Col 1:16 [see *Romans*, 535]), although some commentators have preferred to understand them as "imperial political institutions with superhuman power" (Horsley, *1 Cor*, 205). Per se, the terms could be understood as either good or bad, but in this context they are to be "destroyed," because they belong to the category of "enemies" (15:25), along with "the last enemy" (15:26) of humanity. Their destruction denotes the elimination of all opposition to the Son's sovereignty. When he at last reigns supreme, then he will turn over the kingdom to the Father. That meaning assumes that the subj. of *katargēsē* is the same as that of *paradidō*, viz., Christ. Heil ("Theologische Interpretation"), however, insists that the subj. of all verbs in this passage from v. 24c to v. 28c is *ho theos* expressed in v. 28c.

25. *For he must reign until he has put all enemies under his feet.* Paul continues his explanation, that Christ "must reign," using the apocalyptic impersonal *dei* to express a necessity that Scripture imposes (cf. 2 Cor 5:10), as he alludes to Ps 110:1. In the LXX, it reads, *kathou ek dexiōn mou, heōs an thō tous echthrous sou hypopodion tōn podōn sou*, "sit at my right hand, until I make your enemies a footstool for your feet." Paul adapts the royal psalm, in which God promises victory to a Davidic king at his coronation, making Christ's reign replace his "sitting at the right hand," and changing the person of the verb from "I" to "he" (meaning God the Father), the first "your" to "all," and the second "your" to "his" (meaning Christ's). Lambrecht ("Paul's Christological Use," 507) thinks that the "he" and "his" refer both to Christ. In either case, Paul applies the words of the psalm to the risen Christ, who is understood to be ruling at present as a king. Note the apocalyptic use of the infin. *basileuein*, "reign," as in Rev 11:15. (Such a function of Christ is reflected also in the words of the angel Gabriel to Mary in the Lucan infancy narrative: "He will be king over the house of Jacob forever," Luke 1:33.) So Paul envisages the risen Christ necessarily reigning as king as of his resurrection, while God (or he) brings it about that all his cosmic adversaries are subdued. *Pace* Hays (*1 Cor*, 265, who follows Witherington), Christ's reign here is not being presented "as a frontal challenge to the ideology of imperial Rome." Nothing in the text supports such a reference (see rather Borman, "Psalm 110"; Tilly, "Psalm 110").

Paul does not introduce formally his use of Psalm 110 and seems to presuppose that his Corinthian readers would recognize the OT allusion, because Ps 110:1 was often used by early Christians in reference to Christ's resurrection (see Acts 2:33–35; Rom 8:34; Mark 12:36; 14:62; Luke 20:42–44; 22:69; Col 3:1; Heb 1:13). Paul may be merely alluding to this psalm because he is using a Christological tradition in which Ps 110:1 and Ps 8:7 together had already been applied to Christ's resurrection. Note esp. Eph 1:20–23, where Ps 110:1 is used again in conjunction with *archē, exousia, dynamis*, and *kyriotēs*, "dominion, authority, power, and lordship," in a way very similar to v. 24 here (see de Boer, "Paul's Use").

26. *The last enemy to be destroyed is death.* Lit. "(as) the last enemy, death is destroyed." *Thanatos* is personified, as in Rom 5:14, 17; 6:9 (cf. Hos 13:14c; Jer 9:21; Sir 14:12), but, as an "enemy," it too will be done away with, as a sign that the resurrection life will prevail. It is "the last enemy," because its destruction is related to "the end" (v. 24), as the use of the pres. pass. of the same verb (*katargeitai*) reveals, which is also a divine passive (ZBG §236), because God will destroy death. Thus the dominion of death that began with Adam (v. 22) comes to an end, and "all will be brought to life" in Christ.

27. *for he has put all things in subjection under his feet.* Paul adds an explanatory clause, as he shows how God the Father has subjected (aor. *hypetaxen*) "all things" in the world to the risen Christ, and not to Death, even though personified *thanatos* is the last masc. noun mentioned in the preceding clause, to which gen.

autou might be thought to refer. The reason for this lack of clarity is that Paul is quoting and adapting Ps 8:7, again without an introductory formula.

Psalm 8 is a hymn celebrating God's glory manifest in creation and the dignity of human beings to whom all creation has been made subject, an echo of Gen 1:26, 28. In the LXX, v. 7 reads, *panta hypetaxas hypokatō tōn podōn autou,* "You have subjected all things under his [the son of man's] feet." Paul slightly modifies the quotation, while preserving its sense. Even in the LXX, "all things" (*panta*) occupies the emphatic first place, which suits Paul's purpose as he adapts the words to the risen Christ; *pace* Garland (*1 Cor,* 713), not to "to the Messiah." "All things" would include death, so that these allusions to the Psalms show that Christ will indeed be made to conquer death itself and make the resurrection possible. Psalm 8:7 is likewise associated with Ps 110:1 in Eph 1:20–22, a context in which similar cosmic governing entities are also mentioned. Cf. Heb 1:13–2:8 (see Wallis, "Use of Psalms 8 and 110," but beware of his millennarian interpretation). Paul's text possibly means Christ by both "he" and "his," but the more important idea is the subjection of "all" to him, whether it be God or Christ who subjects. For Heil and de Boer, "God" is the subject, but for Lambrecht, it is "Christ."

When it says that "all things" have been subjected, it clearly means, apart from him who subjected all things to him. I.e., apart from God the Father. Strictly speaking, the subj. of *eipē* in the subordinate clause should be the same as the subj. of *hypetaxen* at the beginning of the verse, "when God says . . . ," whereas the following neut. *dēlon hoti* has to be taken as "it clearly means that. . . ." Commentators, however, debate the possible subj. of *eipē:* "It can be God, the biblical text, or even Christ" (Kremer, *1 Cor,* 345); it is "Scripture" (Collins, *1 Cor,* 554; Conzelmann, *1 Cor,* 274; Fee, *1 Cor,* 758; Garland, *1 Cor,* 713); it is "God" (Heinrici, *1 Cor,* 472; Heil). It is scarcely to be taken as God, because Paul nowhere else ever speaks of God speaking in this way, when an OT passage is quoted or alluded to. Actually, the verb is used impersonally, as *phēsin* is in 6:16; see also *tí legei,* "What does it say?" (Rom 10:8; cf. Gal 3:16; 2 Cor 6:2). That is followed logically by the neut. *dēlon hoti.* "it (is) clear that. . . ."

28. *When all things are subjected to him, then the Son himself will [also] be made subject to him who subjected all things to him.* Recall 1:9, where Paul speaks of Christians called by God "into companionship with his Son, Jesus Christ our Lord." Now he affirms the role that Christ presently plays in human history, as an agent exercising God's sovereignty, as long as it lasts. Once "all things are subjected to him," i.e., once all his enemies are subdued, human history comes to an end (15:24). Then as Son, Christ "will be made subject" (*hypotagēsetai*), i.e., will hand over all authority ("the kingdom") to the Father, "who has put all things under his feet" (v. 27), because Christ's regnal and salvific role will be at an end. Richards ("*Hypotagēsetai*") would rather translate the verb as mid., "the Son will also subject himself." Can the fut. pass. tolerate a middle meaning? Zerwick (*GAGNT,* 2:529) thinks it can; also BDF §76.1. This verse, introduced by *hotan* (as in vv. 24b,c, 27b), is again related to "the end" (v. 24a). Some important MSS (B, D*, F, G, 0243, 33, 1739) omit *kai,* "also," modifying "the Son himself"; hence the square brackets.

This is the only place in the Pauline corpus where the apostle uses the absolute expression, "the Son," of the risen Christ, and thus it is as close as Paul ever comes to an assertion of the intrinsic relationship of the Son to the Father. Implicitly it is playing on the mutual relation of "son" and "father" that every human being instinctively knows; but it is also one of the NT springboards for the relation of two persons of the Trinity in later Christian theology. These verses also played a role in the later theological problem of Subordinationism (see *ODCC*, 1552–53).

so that God may be all in all. Paul ends these five verses (24–28) with a purpose clause that affirms that God (the Father, 15:24) will be the goal or final cause of everything. In "the end," God will reign supreme over "all things" (neut. [*ta*] *panta*), for all will be subordinate to him. The dat. pl. *pasin* is likewise neut., comprehending both persons and things. All will be ordered by God to himself directly, with no further need of mediation, not even of the "kingdom" or the "reign" of Christ (vv. 24, 25). "This is to be understood in terms of Rom. [11:36] . . . 'soteriologically, not metaphysically'. . . . It is not the absorption of Christ and mankind, with consequent loss of distinct being, into God; but rather the unchallenged reign of God alone, in his pure goodness" (Barrett, *1 Cor*, 361). Hence anyone who would deny the resurrection of the dead would, in effect, be denying God's power over the dead and his reign over everything.

In Col 3:11 and Eph 1:23 the phrase *ta panta en pasin* is predicated of Christ, but in an entirely different sense (related to the church).

BIBLIOGRAPHY

Allo, B., "Saint Paul et la 'double résurrection' corporelle," *RB* 41 (1932) 188–209.
Barrett, C. K., *From First Adam to Last: A Study in Pauline Theology* (New York: Scribner, 1962).
Barth, G., "Erwägungen zu 1. Korinther 15, 20–28," *EvT* 30 (1970) 515–27.
Boer, M. C. de, "Paul's Use of a Resurrection Tradition in 1 Cor 15:20–28," *The Corinthian Correspondence* (BETL 125; ed. R. Bieringer), 639–51.
Borman, L., "Psalm 110 im Dialog mit dem Neuen Testament," *Heiligkeit und Herrschaft: Intertextuelle Studien zu Heiligkeitsvorstellungen und zu Psalm 110* (Biblisch-Theologische Studien 55; ed. D. Sänger; Neukirchen-Vluyn: Neukirchener-V., 2003) 171–205.
Brandenburger, E., *Adam und Christus: Exegetisch-religionsgeschichtliche Untersuchung zu Röm. 5,12–21 (1. Kor. 15)* (WMANT 7; Neukirchen-Vluyn: Neukirchener-V., 1962).
Caird, G. B., *Principalities and Powers: A Study in Pauline Theology* (Oxford: Clarendon, 1956).
Carr, W., *Angels and Principalities: The Background, Meaning, and Development of the Pauline Phrase hai archai kai hai exousiai* (SNTSMS 42; Cambridge: Cambridge University Press, 1981).
Craig, W. L., *Assessing the New Testament Evidence for the Historicity of the Resurrection of Jesus* (Lewiston: Mellen, 1989).
Douty, N. F., *Death Vanquished: First Corinthians Fifteen* (Grand Rapids: Zondervan, 1939).

Dykstra, W., "I Corinthians 15:20–28, an Essential Part of Paul's Argument against Those Who Deny the Resurrection," *CTJ* 4 (1969) 195–211.

Eriksson, A., "Elaboration of Argument in 1 Cor 15:20–34," *SEA* 64 (1999) 101–14.

Fredrickson, D., "God, Christ, and All Things in 1 Corinthians 15:28," *WW* 18 (1998) 254–63.

García, J. M., "Acontecimientos después de la venida gloriosa (1 Cor 15,23–28)," *EstBíb* 58 (2000) 527–59.

Gielen, M., "Universale Totenauferweckung und universales Heil? 1 Kor 15,20–28 im Kontext paulinischer Theologie," *BZ* 47 (2003) 86–104.

Goguel, M., *La foi à la résurrection de Jésus dans le christianisme primitif: Étude d'histoire et de psychologie religieuses* (Bibliothèque de l'École des Hautes Études, Sciences religieuses 47; Paris: Leroux, 1933).

Heil, U., "Theo-logische Interpretation von 1 Kor 15,23–28," *ZNW* 84 (1993) 27–35.

Héring, J., "Saint Paul, a-t-il enseigné deux résurrections?" *RHPR* 12 (1932) 300–320.

Hill, C. E., "Paul's Understanding of Christ's Kingdom in I Corinthians 15:20–28," *NovT* 30 (1988) 297–320.

Holleman, J., "Jesus' Resurrection as the Beginning of the Eschatological Resurrection (1 Cor 15,20)," *The Corinthian Correspondence* (BETL 125; ed. R. Bieringer), 653–60.

Jansen, J. F., "I Cor. 15. 24–28 and the Future of Jesus Christ," *SJT* 40 (1987) 543–70.

Johnson, A., "Firstfruits and Death's Defeat: Metaphor in Paul's Rhetorical Strategy in 1 Cor 15:20–28," *WW* 16 (1996) 456–64.

Lambrecht, J., "Paul's Christological Use of Scripture in 1 Cor 15.20–28," *Pauline Studies* (BETL 115), 125–49.

———, "Structure and Line of Thought in 1 Cor. 15,23–28," (BETL 115), 151–60.

Leal, J., " 'Deinde finis' (1 Cor. 15,24a)," *VDom* 37 (1959) 225–31.

Lewis, S. M., *"So That God May Be All in All": The Apocalyptic Message of 1 Corinthians 15,12–34* (Tesi Gregoriana, ser. teol. 42; Rome: Universitas Gregoriana, 1998).

Lindemann, A., "Die Auferstehung der Toten: Adam und Christus nach 1. Kor 15," *Eschatologie und Schöpfung: Festschrift für Erich Grässer* (BZNW 89; ed. M. Ewang et al.; Berlin: de Gruyter, 1997) 155–67.

———, "Parusie Christi und Herrschaft Gottes: Zur Exegese von 1Kor 15,23–28," *WD* 19 (1987) 87–107.

Lüdemann, G., *The Resurrection of Jesus: History, Experience, Theology* (London: SCM, 1994) 33–109.

Marxsen, W., *Jesus and Easter: Did God Raise the Historical Jesus from the Dead?* (Nashville: Abingdon, 1990).

———, *The Resurrection of Jesus of Nazareth* (Philadelphia: Fortress; London: SCM, 1970).

Morissette, R., "La citation du Psaume viii, 7b dans I Corinthiens xv,27a," *ScEs* 24 (1972) 313–42.

Nadeau, M.-T., "Qu'adviendra-t-il de la souveraineté du Christ à la fin des temps?" *ScEs* 55 (2003) 61–74.

Oberdorfer, B., " 'Was sucht ihr den Lebendigen bei den Toten?' Überlegungen zur Realität der Auferstehung in Auseinandersetzung mit Gerd Lüdemann," *KD* 46 (2000) 225–40.

Richards, W. L., "*Hypotagēsetai* in 1 Corinthians 15:28b," *AUSS* 38 (2000) 203–6.

Schendel, E., *Herrschaft und Unterwerfung Christi: 1 Korinther 15,24–28 in Exegese und Theologie der Väter bis zum Ausgang des 4. Jahrhunderts* (BGBE 12; Tübingen: Mohr [Siebeck], 1971).

Schmithals, W., "The Pre-Pauline Tradition in 1 Corinthians 15:20–28," *PRSt* 20 (1993) 357–80.

Schrage, W., "Das messianische Zwischenreich bei Paulus," *Eschatologie und Schöpfung* (BZNW 89; ed. M. Ewang; Berlin: de Gruyter, 1997), 343–54.

Templeton, D. A., "Paul the Parasite: Notes on the Imagery of 1 Corinthians 15:20–28," *HeyJ* 26 (1985) 1–4.

Tilly, M., "Psalm 110 zwischen hebräischen Bibel und Neuen Testament," *Heiligkeit und Herrschaft 110* (Biblisch-Theologische Studien 55; ed. D. Sänger; Neukirchen-Vluyn: Neukirchener-V., 2003), 146–70.

Turner, S., "The Interim, Earthly Messianic Kingdom in Paul," *JSNT* 25 (2002–03) 323–42.

Vidal, S., *La resurrección de Jesús en las cartas de Pablo: Análisis de las tradiciones* (Biblioteca de Estudios Bíblicos 50; Salamanca: Sígueme, 1982).

Wallis, W. B., "The Problem of an Intermediate Kingdom in I Corinthians 15:20–28," *JETS* 18 (1975) 229–42.

——, "The Use of Psalms 8 and 110 in I Corinthians 15:25–27 and in Hebrews 1 and 2," *JETS* 15 (1972) 25–29.

Wilcke, H.-A., *Das Problem eines messianischen Zwischenreiches bei Paulus* (ATANT 51; Zurich: Zwingli-V., 1967) 56–108.

36   c. Ad hominem *Arguments for the Resurrection of the Dead (15:29–34)*

15:29 Otherwise what will people do who undergo baptism on behalf of the dead? If the dead are not raised at all, why then are people baptized on their behalf? 30 As for us, why do we endanger ourselves at every hour? 31 Day after day I face death — as surely as is the boast over you, [brothers], that I have in Christ Jesus our Lord. 32 If, humanly speaking, I fought with wild beasts at Ephesus, what did I gain? If the dead are not raised, *"Let us eat and drink, for tomorrow we die."* 33 Do not be led astray. "Bad company corrupts good habits." 34 Become sober as you ought, and sin no more. For some have no knowledge of God, and I say this to your shame.

COMMENT

Paul passes on abruptly to another stage in his argument against the Corinthian Christian skeptics. Having reaffirmed, like a prophet of old, the resurrection of Christ as the firstfruits from the dead in vv. 20–28, he returns to a continuation of his logical arguments presented in vv. 12–19 above. Paul now argues from experience, first from what he has learned and then from his personal troubles. He begins abruptly by referring to a practice of Corinthian Christians that he has heard about, the reception of baptism on behalf of the dead. Using diatribe-like style, Paul asks his imaginary Corinthian interlocutor three questions, the first two about that Corinthian practice, and the third about the implication of no resurrection of the dead for his own ministry and his personal experience, when he once came close to death. He concludes further, If the dead are not raised, why not follow Isaiah's advice (Isa 22:13) and make the most out of life? Yet all of these considerations have further implications, for they entail Corinthian misconduct and even ignorance of God. So run Paul's ad hominem arguments in this stage of his reaction to the denial of the resurrection of the dead.

The major problem in this passage is the interpretation of *hoi baptizomenoi hyper tōn nekrōn*, "those who undergo baptism on behalf of the dead," or "in place of the dead" in v. 29. The Corinthian practice to which Paul is alluding is mentioned only here, and not with sufficient clarity to understand precisely what the nature of the practice was. Consequently, the number of explanations of vv. 29–30 that have been proposed are legion (see English, "Mediated"; Foschini, "Those Who Are Baptized"; Rissi, *Die Taufe für die Toten*). DeMaris has done well to situate the problem in what is known from archaeology and ancient anthropology about concern for the dead and the passage from life to death among contemporary Greeks and Romans, especially at Isthmia and in Corinthia as the centers where the cults of Palaimon and Demeter developed ("Corinthian Religion"). Such a concern about the afterlife and the underworld among Corinthians might explain why Christians who lived there developed their own practice of showing concern for the dead, whatever explanation is found best suited for "baptism on behalf of the dead" (see also DeMaris, "Demeter in Roman Corinth"; "Funerals and Baptisms"). Recall too Paul's discussion of baptism related to burial in Rom 6:3–4. Marmorstein also relates to this passage the episode in 2 Macc 12:39–45, where Judas Maccabee provides an expiatory sacrifice in Jerusalem for those slain "inasmuch as he had the resurrection of the dead in view" ("Paulus und die Rabbinen," 278).

The most commonly proposed explanations of the Corinthian practice are the following six, but each is proposed often with varying nuances by different interpreters:

1. Living Christians underwent vicarious or proxy baptism, i.e., water baptism in the Christian rite on behalf of persons (e.g., relatives) who had died without being baptized, so that those persons might be saved or gain access to the kingdom of God. This explanation understands the words *baptizomenoi, hyper* ("on behalf of" or "in place of"), and *tōn nekrōn* simply in their normal sense. Paul would be mentioning this practice to show its discrepancy with the denial of the resurrection. This is the only attested instance of such a practice in NT times, and for that reason the correctness of the interpretation is often questioned, to say nothing of its superstitious character, and a practice that is hard to integrate into the theology of baptism found elsewhere in Pauline writings.

However, some writers of the patristic period knew of it as a practice among heretics: e.g., Tertullian, *De resur. mortuorum* 48.11: *uicarium baptisma* (CCLat 2.989); *Adv. Marcionem* 5.10.1–2 (as practiced by Marcionites; CCLat 1.692); Epiphanius, *Panarion* 28.6.4 (practice of followers of Cerinthus; GCS 25.318); John Chrysostom, *Hom. in Ep. 1 ad Cor.* 40.1 (PG 61.347). A form of it is in vogue among Mormons (Church of Latter Day Saints of Jesus Christ).

This explanation is used by the majority of interpreters today: e.g., Barrett, K.

Barth, Beasley-Murray, Collins, Conzelmann, DeMaris, Downey, Edwards, Fee, Hays, Horsley, Hurd, Lietzmann, Orr-Walther, Rissi, Schrage, Senft, Taylor, Tuckett, Wedderburn, J. Weiss, Wolff.

2. Christians were being baptized for (their) "dead or dying bodies," "for those about to die," "for those in deadly peril" in order to obtain the resurrection. So many Greek patristic writers, esp. Chrysostom, *Hom in Ep. 1 ad Cor.* 40.2 (PG 61.349); Tertullian, Erasmus; among modern interpreters, Garland, A. R. Krauss, R. P. Martin, Oliver, Talbert, Thompson. Somewhat similarly: "for the sake of their dying bodies," because *hyper tōn nekrōn* refers not to masc. *hoi nekroi* but to neut. *ta nekra (sōmata)*, i.e., in view of their own approaching death. So O'Neill, Campbell.

3. Baptism was accepted "for the sake of the dead" or "because of the dead," i.e., baptism accepted by a person who was previously well disposed to Christianity and has been influenced by a Christian who advocated his or her conversion but has died; so those baptized become Christians because of the dead believer's influence in order to be united with him or her at the resurrection. So Findlay, Howard, Jeremias, Raeder, Reaume, Robertson-Plummer, Schnackenburg, Thiselton.

4. Christian water baptism was done with a variety of nuances:

a. "on account of the dead," i.e., for Paul and his fellow apostles, because the larger context of the verse speaks of Paul as an apostle who continually faces deadly danger (vv. 30–31). So White. In similar fashion, Heawood would take "the dead" to mean Christ.

b. "Over (the graves of) the dead." So M. Luther; Grosheide.

c. "For those dead in sin." So Hofmann.

5. Baptism was understood figuratively: martyrdom, or baptism not of water, but of blood, something like that of which Jesus speaks in Luke 12:50 or Mark 10:38, a "baptism" that faces him (= death). In that case, *hyper tōn nekrōn* would mean "to be baptized, not as one is by water baptism in order to enter the church of the living, but to enter that of the dead . . . by a communion with the dead" (Godet, *1 Cor*, 2. 386).

6. An entirely different explanation has been given by Murphy-O'Connor: *hoi baptizomenoi* does not refer to baptism at all in "a sacramental sense," as elsewhere in Pauline writings, but is to be understood in the Hellenistic Greek sense of *baptizō*, "immerse, go under, perish," as in drowning (see Mark 10:38; Luke 12:50, as Godet noted; cf. *TDNT*, 1:529–46, esp. 530). This meaning is claimed to suit better the context of 15:29, being related not only to the preceding passage, which ends with the service of "the Son," but also to the labor and struggles of Paul in God's service (vv. 30–32a). *Tōn nekrōn* is understood metaphorically, as referring to those who are "dead" to spiritual truths, whereas *nekroi* in the second question, modified by the immediately preceding adv. *holōs*, would mean "those who are really dead." The first question in v. 29 would not be Paul's query, but a slogan, "a contemptuous gibe addressed to Paul and his co-workers" by *pneu-*

matikoi at Corinth who deny the resurrection, as they comment on his (and their) labors among the dead *psychikoi* who do not understand what he has been trying to preach. The second question is Paul's own reformulation of the gibe. Murphy-O'Connor's translation of v. 29: "Why are they destroying themselves on account of those dead (to higher spiritual truths)? If those who are really dead are not raised, why are they being destroyed on their account?" His explanation of the situation: The "spirit-people" at Corinth—those who denied the resurrection [v. 12, alluding to *pneumatikoi* of 2:6–16]—had mocked Paul for the effort he expended on those whom they considered merely "soul-people" [*psychikoi* of 2:6–16, dead to true Wisdom]. "By radicalizing the gibe in the second question, Paul draws attention to the implications of such effort. He would not be working himself to death, were he not absolutely convinced that the dead would be raised" (*NJBC*, 813; see also his " 'Baptized for the Dead' ").

Problem: Can the verb *baptizō* really tolerate the meaning "destroy"? Why should *hoi baptizomenoi* be plural if it is part of a Corinthian slogan referring to Paul? To invoke "co-workers" is gratuitous; there is nothing in the text to suggest it.

Although Kistemaker (*1 Cor*, 558) assumes "that Paul vigorously denounced such actions," many commentators note that, whatever the practice meant, Paul does not approve of it or criticize it. Rather he makes use of it only to score a point in his argument, to show that Corinthian practice itself argues that the dead indeed can be raised (e.g., Oepke, *TDNT*, 1:542; Schrage, *1 Cor*, 239–40; Senft, *1 Cor*, 202). If there were no resurrection of the dead, then such baptism would be meaningless (see English, "Mediated").

NOTES

15:29. *Otherwise what will people do who undergo baptism on behalf of the dead?* Lit. "since (then) what will they do, those being baptized [*or* those having themselves baptized] . . . ?" Paul begins with two rhetorical questions. The conj. *epei* is being used elliptically, "since in that case," as in 5:10; 7:14; 14:16; Rom 3:6; 11:6, 22 (BDAG, 360). One has to understand a protasis: "If there is no resurrection of the dead" (15:12b). The fut. *tí poiēsousin* asks a generic logical question: what is the sense or value of their action? What will they achieve by it? Compare the similar questions about pointless further activity in LXX Jer 4:30; Hos 9:5; 1 Cor 15:32b.

Hoi baptizomenoi (preferably pass.) normally refers to the Christian rite of initiatory washing with water instituted after Jesus' death (Matt 28:19), by which a person is incorporated into the one body of Christian believers (Rom 6:3b; 1 Cor 12:13; see NOTE on 1:14); it identified the one baptized with the death of Christ and implied a renunciation of sin; its purpose was "the forgiveness of sins" (Acts 2:38). Figurative or other meanings, however, have been given in this instance to the ptc. because of the following prep. phrase (see COMMENT above). The explanation of vicarious or proxy baptism remains the most plausible, even though its meaning is not fully clear.

The prep. phrase *hyper tōn nekrōn* is difficult to interpret. The phrase can mean, "in place of the dead," i.e., proxy baptism for friends or relatives who had died unbaptized (BDAG, 1031). This explanation of the problematic phrase is probably the best, but one cannot rule out completely other meanings, e.g., a causal sense (White, "Baptized on Account of the Dead" [even though the rest of his explanation that "the dead" are the "apostles" is far-fetched]; see also Patrick, "Living Rewards"). Equally far-fetched is the interpretation sometimes suggested that one should simply punctuate the verse differently, by putting a question mark after *baptizomenoi*, a full stop after *egeirontai*, and another question mark after *hyper autōn*: "Otherwise what will people do who undergo baptism? (Something) for the dead (bodies), if the dead are not raised at all. Why then are people baptized for them?" (see Badcock, "Baptism"; Thompson, "I Corinthians 15,29"). That translation is hardly comprehensible.

If the dead are not raised at all, why then are people baptized on their behalf? This further question repeats the sense of the former, but it contains the adv. *holōs*, which queries any form of denial of the resurrection. The adv., however, stands immediately before substantivized *nekroi*, but it is understood by many commentators to modify the neg. verb *ouk egeirontai*, as in the lemma, but its position has been taken by others as a sign that such a translation is wrong (see O'Neill, "1 Corinthians 15²⁹"; Murphy-O'Connor [see COMMENT above]). In 5:1; 6:7 *holōs* is set immediately before the word it modifies; also in Josephus, *J.W.* 4.6.1 §364; 5.5.5 §219; *Ant.* 2.16.3 §344.

30. *As for us, why do we endanger ourselves at every hour?* In this third question, Paul turns to the implication that the denial of the resurrection of the dead would have for himself or other Christians like him. If Paul is using the editorial "we," then it would refer to his personal ministry, as described in 2 Cor 11:23–27; but he could also be including other Christians who have also been living their lives in expectation of a future resurrection. The denial of it would make not only Paul's life and ministry absurd, but even the life and conduct of all Christians, who do not undergo such vicarious baptism for the dead, but who incur risk simply by being Christians.

31. *Day after day I face death—as surely as is the boast over you, [brothers], that I have in Christ Jesus our Lord.* Paul now switches to the 1st pers. sing., in order to underline the jeopardy in which his own ministry has been putting him, i.e., perils that come to him from without, such as he mentions in 2 Cor 1:8–10; 11:23d, 28: afflictions that he experienced in Asia, the province of which Ephesus is the capital, from which he writes this letter to the Christians of Roman Corinth.

To such an admission, Paul adds an oath, introduced by the Classical Greek asseverative particle *nē*, which is found only here in the NT, but occasionally in the LXX (Gen 42:15, 16) and which governs the accus. (BDF §149). He thereby assures Corinthian Christians that they are his pride, when his relation to Christ and to them is considered, because they are the fruit of his evangelization among them (see Deer, "Whose Pride"). The poss. adj. in *tēn hymeteran kauchēsin* has to be understood as the equivalent of an obj. gen., "my boast over you" (BDF §285.1), as Murphy-O'Connor has rightly argued ("Interpolations," 93), against

MacDonald's suggestion to take *hēn echō en Christō Iēsou tō kyriō hēmōn* as an interpolation ("Conjectural Emendation," 270–72). In many MSS (P⁴⁶, D, F, G, Ψ, 075, 0243, 1739, 1881, and the Koine text-tradition) *adelphoi* is omitted, but it appears in many equally important (ℵ, A, B, K, P, 33, 81, 104, 365, 1175, etc.) and is expected in such an asseveration (see Metzger, *TCGNT*, 501). MacDonald would have us believe that the final rel. clause of the verse is a scribal addition added to harmonize this text with 2 Tim 4:17, where "Paul" boasts of being rescued "from the lion's mouth."

32. *If, humanly speaking, I fought with wild beasts at Ephesus, what did I gain?* Lit. "what to me the gain?" It is not easy to say whether this is a past simple condition, because the apodosis is expressed elliptically (without a verb). It could also be taken as a contrary-to-fact condition, with the particle *an* missing in the ellipse (see BDF §360.1), "if I had fought with wild beasts, what would I have gained?" Its force, then, would not be as strong in Paul's argument; so it is better taken as a past factual statement, even though one cannot determine today to what Paul is alluding. He uses *kata anthrōpon* again (see 3:3; 9:8; cf. Gal 1:11; 3:15; Rom 3:5), in emphatic position, to stress the hypothetical consideration he is proposing: why should he as a human being have faced such danger, if there were not the motivation that the resurrection of the dead promises?

Strikingly, Paul says this in a letter that he is writing to Corinthian Christians from the city of Ephesus itself (16:8), where this event is said to have happened. So it refers to an experience he had in this city prior to the writing of this letter. His argument is that he has not undergone all of this just for a trifling goal in this life, but because of his own belief in the resurrection of the dead.

He uses the verb *thēriomacheō*, "fight with wild beasts," but in what sense, literal or figurative, as he refers to some harrowing opposition that faced him in Ephesus? He alludes to it again in 2 Cor 1:8–10, where he admits that he despaired of life itself, but the details of which he does not recount (not even in 2 Cor 6:5 or 11:23–29). As a result, commentators are divided. Some insist on the literal sense (J. Weiss, Bowen), but the majority of interpreters take it in a figurative sense: e.g., Coffin "The Meaning," 175 ("contending with beasts in human form" [cf. *kata* in Eph 4:24; Phil 3:2]). Osborne ("Paul," 229–30) cites a parallel in QL, where 1QpHab 12:4–5 comments on the "beasts" of Hab 2:17 and explains them as "the simple folk of Judah, those who observe the Law." It thus gives a similar figurative meaning of "people" to *hbhmwt*, "the beasts," of Habakkuk. Malherbe ("The Beasts") cites many similar instances of figurative usage in the moralistic literature of the Greeks, especially the Cynic-Stoic tradition. Cf. Ignatius, *Rom.* 5.1, where the figurative meaning is clear.

The riot at Ephesus, described by Luke in Acts 19:21–41, may have had something to do with the experience of which Paul speaks here, but that description does not involve so much danger for Paul as his words now imply. So the account in Acts could refer to some other experience. A number of NT interpreters think that some of the Pauline captivity letters (Phil 1:7, 14, 17; Phlm 1) may have been composed during an Ephesian imprisonment of Paul, and they appeal to this passage and that in 2 Corinthians 1 as referring to it.

If the dead are not raised, "Let us eat and drink, for tomorrow we die." This is the crucial philosophical argument for Paul, no matter how the denial of the Corinthian skeptics was formulated. If it at least implies that the dead will not be raised, then one should forget about an afterlife. The only logical conclusion is that formulated centuries before by the prophet Isaiah (22:13b). In the LXX it runs, *phagōmen kai piōmen, aurion gar apothnēskomen,* which Paul quotes verbatim and which translates well the Hebrew infins. absol. of the MT. In the oracle of Isaiah, however, the words were part of a warning to Jerusalem about coming destruction, to which the inhabitants were reluctant to give credence, a reaction that would rebound against them. Paul cites the words and accommodates them to stress the consequences of a negligent dismissal of the future resurrection of the dead. No article is used with *nekroi,* "(the) dead," because the concept, not the collectivity, is being discussed (BDF §254.2).

For similar sayings, see Luke 12:19; Isa 56:12; Wis 2:5–6; *Anthol. Graec.* 11.56.1–2 (*pine kai euphrainou, tí gar aurion ē tí to mellon, oudeis gnōskei,* "Drink and enjoy yourself! What tomorrow and the future [will bring] no one knows").

33. *Do not be led astray.* Paul repeats advice that he gave in 6:9b, even though the context is quite different; it also appeared in Gal 6:7. Cf. Jas 1:16; Luke 21:8. He realizes that the skepticism of some Corinthian Christians about the resurrection of the dead might be entailing other inadmissible attitudes or conduct. So he ends his logical argumentation with generic hortatory remarks. Compare 3:18.

"Bad company corrupts good habits." Paul adds a popular proverb, which was apparently first coined by Menander (342–290 B.C.) in *Thais,* frg. 218 (LCL, *Menander,* 1.356: *phtheirousin ēthē chrēsth' homiliai kakai*). In the proverb, the noun *homiliai* is used in its basic meaning, "associations, social groupings": hence *homiliai kakai,* "bad associations." From that sense it developed also the meaning of "conversations," viz., that in which a group or association usually engages. Paul adds this proverb, drawn from the Greek culture in which Christians of Roman Corinth lived, in order to warn them to be careful about the influence of that culture on their mode of life, and especially about their thinking (see also Philostratus, *Vitae Sophistarum* 501, for a similar view, but not in proverbial form [Lee, "Philostratus"]).

34. *Become sober as you ought, and sin no more.* Lit. "become sober uprightly." The first aor. impv. may counsel care in drinking, such as v. 32c might inspire; but it obviously assumes a wider figurative sense in such a generic exhortation: "come to a sober and right mind" (NRSV), in which it is followed by a pres. impv. about not continuing to live in sin. Cf. Eph 4:26. Kent ("A Fresh Look") rightly interprets this as a Pauline plea for holiness to counteract Corinthian ignorance and neglect of God; he is insisting on moral and doctrinal purity.

For some have no knowledge of God. Paul again speaks of "some," as he did in v. 12b, when he introduced the topic of the denial of the future resurrection of the dead. Perhaps he is implying that these same Corinthians have no proper sense of God. He uses the phrase *agnōsia theou* (lit. "ignorance of God"), which appears in the opening verse of the famous passage on pagan idolatry in Wisdom 13, a passage to which Paul alludes in Rom 1:18–32. Cf. 1 Thess 4:5; 1 Pet 2:15; esp. Acts

26:8, "Why is it considered so unbelievable among you that God should raise the dead?" This Lucan formulation expresses well the sense of Paul's criticism.

and I say this to your shame. Paul repeats a sentiment that he expressed earlier (6:5), now in a matter of greater shame because it is related to a fundamental knowledge of God and his power (see Rom 1:20, "his eternal power and divinity," which those without the gospel fail to recognize).

BIBLIOGRAPHY

Badcock, F. J., "Baptism for the Dead," *ExpTim* 54 (1942–43) 330.

Bowen, C. R., " 'I Fought with Beasts at Ephesus,' " *JBL* 42 (1923) 59–68.

Bruce, F. F., "Baptism for the Dead," *ExpTim* 55 (1943–44) 110–11.

Campbell, R. A., "Baptism and Resurrection (1 Cor 15:29)," *ABR* 47 (1999) 43–52.

Coffin, C. P., "The Meaning of 1 Cor. 15:32," *JBL* 43 (1924) 172–76.

Deer, D. S., "Whose Pride/Rejoicing/Glory(ing) in I Corinthians 15.31?" *BT* 38/1 (1987) 126–28.

DeMaris, R. E., "Corinthian Religion and Baptism for the Dead (1 Corinthians 15:29): Insights from Archaeology and Anthropology," *JBL* 114 (1995) 661–82.

———, "Demeter in Roman Corinth: Local Development in a Mediterranean Religion," *Numen* 42 (1995) 105–17, esp. 114.

———, "Funerals and Baptisms, Ordinary and Otherwise: Ritual Criticism and Corinthian Rites," *BTB* 29 (1999) 23–34.

Downey, J., "1 Cor 15:29 and the Theology of Baptism," *ED* 38 (1985) 23–35.

English, A. C., "Mediated, Mediation, Unmediated: 1 Corinthians 15:29: the History of Interpretation and the Current State of Biblical Studies," *RevExp* 99 (2002) 419–28.

Foschini, B. M., " 'Those Who Are Baptized for the Dead, I Cor 15:29: An Exegetical Historical Dissertation," *CBQ* 12 (1950) 260–76, 379–88; 13 (1951) 46–78, 172–98, 276–83; repr. as book with same title (Worcester, MA: Heffernan, 1951).

Heawood, P. J., "Baptism for the Dead," *ExpTim* 55 (1943–44) 278.

Kent, H. A., Jr., "A Fresh Look at 1 Corinthians 15:34: An Appeal for Evangelism or a Call to Purity?" *GTJ* 4/1 (1983) 3–14.

Kuss, O., "Zur Frage einer vorpaulinischen Todestaufe," *MTZ* 4 (1953) 1–17.

Lee, G. M., "Philostratus and St. Paul," *ZNW* 62 (1971) 121.

MacDonald, D. R., "A Conjectural Emendation of 1 Cor 15:31–32: Or the Case of the Misplaced Lion Fight," *HTR* 73 (1980) 265–76.

Malherbe, A. J., "The Beasts at Ephesus," *JBL* 87 (1968) 71–80.

Marmorstein, A., "Paulus und die Rabbinen," *ZNW* 30 (1931) 271–85, esp. 277–85.

Martin, H. V., "Baptism for the Dead," *ExpTim* 54 (1942–43) 192–93.

Murphy-O'Connor, J., " 'Baptized for the Dead' (I Cor., XV, 29): A Corinthian Slogan?" *RB* 88 (1981) 532–43.

Oliver, A. B., "Why Are They Baptized for the Dead? A Study of I Cor. 15:29," *RevExp* 34 (1937) 48–53.

O'Neill, J. C., "1 Corinthians 15,29," *ExpTim* 91 (1979–80) 310–11.

Osborne, R. E., "Paul and the Wild Beasts," *JBL* 85 (1966) 225–30.

Patrick, J. E., "Living Rewards for Dead Apostles: 'Baptised for the Dead' in 1 Corinthians 15.29," *NTS* 52 (2006) 71–85.

Preisker, H., "Die Vikariatstaufe I Cor 15,29—ein eschatologischer, nicht sakramentaler Brauch," *ZNW* 23 (1924) 298–304.

Raeder, M., "Vikariatstaufe in I Cor 15,29?" ZNW 46 (1955) 258–61.

Reaume, J. D., "Another Look at 1 Corinthians 15:29, 'Baptized for the Dead,' " *BSac* 152 (1995) 457–75.

Reitzenstein, R., *Die Vorgeschichte der christlichen Taufe* (Leipzig/Berlin: Teubner, 1929) 43–44.

Rissi, M., *Die Taufe für die Toten: Ein Beitrag zur paulinischen Tauflehre* (ATANT 42; Zurich: Zwingli-V., 1962).

Salvoni, F., "Il battesimo per i morti," *RBR* 8/4 (1973) 7–17.

Taylor, N. H., "Baptism for the Dead (1 Cor 15:29)," *Neotestamentica* 36 (2002) 111–20.

Thompson, K. C., "I Corinthians 15,29 and Baptism for the Dead," *SE II* (TU 87: Berlin: Akademie-V., 1964) 647–59.

Thomson, J. R., "Baptism for the Dead," *ExpTim* 55 (1943–44) 54.

White, J. R., " 'Baptized on Account of the Dead': The Meaning of 1 Corinthians 15:29 in Its Context," *JBL* 116 (1997) 487–99.

C. HOW WILL THE RESURRECTION OF THE DEAD TAKE PLACE? (15:35–49)

37   a. *Analogies of Seeds, Bodies, and Splendor (15:35–41)*

[15:35] But someone will say, "How are the dead raised? With what kind of a body will they come?" [36] Fool! What you sow is not brought to life unless it dies. [37] And what you sow is not the body that will come to be, but a bare kernel, perhaps of wheat or of something else. [38] God gives it a body as he has chosen, and to each kind of seed its own body. [39] For all flesh is not the same; there is one kind for human beings, another for animals, another for birds, and another for fish. [40] There are both heavenly bodies and earthly bodies; the splendor of the heavenly bodies is one thing; that of the earthly is another. [41] There is one splendor for the sun, another for the moon, and still another for the stars. For star differs from star in splendor.

COMMENT

Paul now comes to the crucial questions in the matter of the denial of the resurrection of the dead. Up to this point in chap. 15, he has not mentioned "body," and it appears here for the first time. To appreciate the flow of the argument in this chapter, it is important to recall that in vv. 1–11, where Paul quoted the preached gospel and used the kerygmatic fragment in vv. 3b–5a, the crucial words were *Christos . . . egēgertai*, "Christ was raised." In that first pericope there was no mention of either "from the dead" or "body." Then in v. 12, when he took up the issue of the denial of the resurrection of the dead, he spoke of Christ having been raised *ek nekrōn,* "from the dead," because he argued to deny the resurrection of the dead would be to deny Christ's resurrection from the dead. That was his first addition to the kerygmatic proclamation. In vv. 12–19 and again in vv. 29–34, his argument about the denial was conducted mostly on logical premises and with ad hominem arguments. In vv. 20–28, however, he reaffirmed the kerygmatic proclamation about the resurrection of Christ, but with a further addition: *Christos egēgertai ek nekrōn aparchē tōn kekoimēmenōn,* "Christ has been raised from the dead as the firstfruits of those who have fallen asleep." Yet, not even in that typological and apocalyptic discussion, where "as the firstfruits of those who have fallen asleep" has been added, is there any mention of a bodily resurrection. Now in v. 35, *sōma* is introduced, and the issue of bodily resurrection is thus broached.

Whereas in v. 12 Paul began the argument for the fact of the resurrection, now in v. 36 he begins the argument about the mode of the resurrection of the dead. The style of Paul's argumentation changes, as he introduces an imaginary interlocutor in the diatribe-like style that he is employing. The two questions, with which he begins in v. 35, may have been posed by the Corinthians who had come to him (Stephanas, Fortunatus, Achaicus of 16:17), or, more likely they are simply part of Paul's diatribe-like rhetorical style (questions such as his imaginary interlocutor might ask). In handling the two questions that are thus posed, he treats the second question first in vv. 36–49, and then the first question in vv. 50–57. *Pace* Garland (*1 Cor,* 727) and Usami ("How Are," 474), and others, Jeremias does not err in arguing that Paul deals with two questions, even if one disagrees with Jeremias's alleged chiastic structure; the two questions are indeed related, but they do not "ask the same thing." So too judge Sider ("Pauline Conception"); Soards (*1 Cor,* 342).

In vv. 36–41, Paul argues analogically about "the kind of body." He employs three analogies: comparing the body with seeds, different (earthly and heavenly) bodies, and the difference of their splendor. In using such analogies, Paul has given up the ad hominem arguments of vv. 29–34. The analogies do not prove the resurrection of the dead, but they provide the first step of a plausible mode of understanding it, and they are drawn from ordinary everyday experience.

Morissette, following others, has found interesting parallels to this passage in various rabbinic writings that discuss the resurrection of the dead (e.g., *b. Sanhedrin* 90b; *Midrash Qoh.* 1.10 [27b]; *Pirqe de-R. Eliezer* 33 [17c]), and speaks of Paul "touching up the rabbinic matter with essential elements of christology" ("La condition," 211; cf. 224–27). Not only are the parallels far-fetched, but they are drawn from writings that date from the sixth, eighth, and eighth/ninth Christian centuries; it is hardly likely that Paul is touching up what he undoubtedly did not know. This has been duly recognized also by Asher ("*Speiretai,*" 107). Nor is it likely that "this Jewish way of arguing is surely very old and can be traced back to the time of the NT," *pace* Usami (" 'How Are,' " 476). Where does one find the evidence of it in NT times?

NOTES

15:35. *But someone will say, "How are the dead raised? With what kind of a body will they come?"* Lit. "do they come," the verb is pres. The conj. *alla*, "but," marks the beginning of a new form of argument, and the fut. *erei*, "will say," a Koine Greek substitute for the Classical potential opt., formulates a likely objection (BDF §385.1). The "someone" might be one of the "some" of v. 12b. The interrogative adv. *pōs*, "how," introduces the first question and stands in contrast to the affirmative conj. *hoti* of v. 12 above, which introduced arguments for the fact of the resurrection of the dead. Now the first question asks about its mode. The second question, which introduces the term *sōma*, bolsters the first, seeking with irony, or perhaps satire, an explanation about the kind of a body that will be involved. Here Paul uses for "the dead" the arthrous form *hoi nekroi*, by which he means deceased Christians, as in vv. 42, 52; this differs from the anarthrous form used earlier for the dead in general (see NOTE on 15:12).

The simple verb *erchontai* can be understood as meaning either "come back" or "come on the scene." See *Syr. Apoc. Baruch* 49.2–3 for a similar question about the body in a Jewish writing (usually dated A.D. 101–5): "In what form will those live in your day, and what will they look like thereafter? Will they then take up their present form. . . ?" An answer, different from Paul's, is given to that question.

On *sōma*, see NOTE on 6:14. It is here that the famous explanation of "body" as "self" or as "a being who has a relationship to himself," either appropriate or perverted, given by Bultmann (*TNT*, 1:195), breaks down. In fact, he even goes so far as to say that Paul's use of *sōma* in this passage shows that his "capacity for abstract thinking is not a developed one." For Paul "does not distinguish terminologically between *soma* in the basic sense of that which characterizes human existence and *soma* as the phenomenon of the material body" (ibid., 198). Therefore,

> he connects the idea of somatic existence in the eschatological consummation with a mythological teaching on the resurrection (I Cor. 15). In it *soma* must appear somehow or other as a thing of material substance, or as the 'form' of such a thing. And since the substance of the resurrection-body cannot be flesh and blood' (I Cor. 15:50), the unfortunate consequence is that *pneuma* must be conceived as a substance of which that *soma* consists (ibid.).

In other words, Bultmann's explanation of *sōma* again proves to be inadequate, as Gundry has argued (*Soma*, 164–69); cf. Usami (" 'How Are,' " 471–72). This is especially so, because the second question is formulated as a Corinthian would ask it, coming from a Greco-Roman world, where the dichotomy of body and soul would be a common way of thinking. Moreover, Paul's answer in vv. 37–41 is given with *sōma* understood as what Bultmann disparagingly calls "form" above. The same disagreement has to be expressed about the meaning of *sōma* given by Morissette, "L'Expression *sōma*."

36. *Fool! What you sow is not brought to life unless it dies.* This is the beginning of Paul's answer to the second question of v. 35 about the body, and it will con-

tinue until v. 49. In order to answer the ironic question, he begins vehemently with an expletive, *aphrōn*, "Fool!" and with the pron. *sy*, "you" (sing.), placed emphatically outside the rel. clause, which follows (BDF §475.1), and in which it really belongs, as if to say, "You fool!" (Perhaps too it is added in contrast to God in v. 38 [so Asher, Usami].) It is intended to call attention to what one should already know from experience or from the simple observation of nature. In using the expletive, Paul rhetorically puts the skeptic in his place, even before he has offered any reasons for what he is maintaining. The expletive echoes OT sayings such as Ps 14:1 ("the fool says in his heart, 'There is no God' "), and Paul himself uses the term of those who have failed to recognize and honor God in Rom 1:21–22.

Paul now adds the first of three analogies that he will develop in this passage. Asher ("*Speiretai*," 107–8) claims that this verse is not an analogy of "the resurrection of the dead," but rather an illustration of "the creative power of God." That it indeed illustrates that power has to be admitted, but it is still an analogy of the resurrection of the dead, because Paul says "what you sow is not brought to life unless it *dies*." Older commentators may have stressed too much the comparison of sowing with burial, or even with predeath existence, and neglected the aspect that Asher argues for, viz., the creative power of God; but even admitting that, one has to realize that it is still an analogy of the resurrection of the dead. Paul stresses that death must precede resurrection, because the Corinthian denial involves *anastasis nekrōn*.

The explanation is given with an ancient understanding of what happens in the biological process when a seed becomes a plant or tree (recall Mark 4:27c, about the sower who knows not how the seed grows). The life of the seed does not end; otherwise it could not pass on its life. A seed, however, must cease to be seed in order to become a new living organism; in that sense, it "dies." An acorn must dissolve and cease to be an acorn, before the oak "is brought to life" (*zōopoieitai*, a divine passive) from it. This Paul explains in the next verse.

37. *And what you sow is not the body that will come to be, but a bare kernel, perhaps of wheat or of something else.* As in 14:10, Paul writes *ei tychoi*, idiomatically meaning "perhaps" (see NOTE there; cf. BDF §385.2). The adj. *gymnon*, "bare," may suit better the human being to whom the seed is compared, but one must remember that before farmers sow grains, they often have to strip them of a natural covering, the sheath that grew about the grain and protected it from the elements, so that its bare kernel might more easily dissolve and become the new organism. Yet not even the bare kernel (the acorn) is identical with the organism to come (the oak); there has to be some kind of change or transformation despite the sameness or continuity of life that persists. Both here and in the following verse, Paul uses *sōma* of plants or trees, and the earthly human body is compared to a "bare kernel," all of which are kinds of matter, despite their form. Usami rightly notes that Paul uses no term that even hints at "the separation of a 'pneuma' or an 'immortal soul' from a decomposing body" (" 'How Are,' " 481).

Compare the ancient way Jesus puts it in the later Johannine Gospel 12:24: "Unless a grain of wheat falls into the earth and dies, it remains alone; but if it dies, it bears much fruit"; and the fuller description given in *1 Clem.* 24.5, which speaks too of the "bare" kernel. Note the different usage of "bare" and "robed" body in the eighth-century rabbinic text, *Pirqe de Rabbi Eliezer* 33 (17c).

38. *God gives it a body as he has chosen, and to each kind of seed its own body.* It is God, not the kernel sowed or the farmer who sows it, who supplies the form of the new organism, its "body" (*sōma*). For the creator God has determined what sort of body should come from each seed in the generation of life. Paul is indirectly alluding to the creation account of Gen 1:11–12: ". . . fruit trees bearing fruit, in which is their seed, each according to its kind." No matter how many seeds there are or how often they may resemble each other, each one in ceasing to be a seed becomes a definite "body" of its own species. The identity or continuity between the seed sowed and "the body that will come to be" (*to sōma to genēsomenon*) comes from the determination of the Creator. Note the tenses of the verbs describing God's activity: "gives" and continues to give (pres. *didōsin*), as he "has chosen," i.e., has determined in creation (aor. *ethelēsen*, as in 12:18, contrasted with the pres. of the Spirit's activity in 12:11). Cf. Pss 115:3b (= LXX 113:11c); 135:6 (LXX 134:6), psalms that laud God's power.

39. *For all flesh is not the same.* Paul now introduces another analogy and brings into the discussion yet another term that will be important in his discussion, and especially in the history of the interpretation of his arguments: *sarx*, "flesh," which now appears in a neutral, not dualistic, sense (Schrage, 1 Cor, 289), as in LXX Gen 7:21 (*pasa sarx*). What he says about it now, that *sarx* is not all the same, will also prove to be true of *sōma*, "body," and of *doxa*, "splendor, glory, radiance." The vv. 39–41c are formulated very carefully to bring out nine things that are contrasted: *allē men . . . allē de* (three times), *hetera men . . . hetera de*, *allē . . . kai allē . . . kai allē*, all without a verb (BDF §127.5). The otherness or differences likewise come from God's creative determination.

there is one kind for human beings, another for animals, another for birds, and another for fish. In the terrestrial realm, Paul chooses examples of the diversity of flesh, and they are given in a descending order of intricacy, which reverses the order of creation in the account of the Priestly Document, Gen 1:20–27. (The order in the Yahwist Document of Gen 2:7, 19–23 is different: man, animals, birds, woman.)

40. *There are both heavenly bodies and earthly bodies.* Just as there is an otherness or diversity of *sarx* in the terrestrial realm, as v. 39b illustrates, so there is a diversity of *sōmata*, heavenly and earthly, when the terrestrial and celestial realms are compared. What Paul means by earthly bodies is clear (of humans [v. 35], of plants [vv. 37–38]), but what he might have meant by the heavenly bodies (*sōmata epourania*), is perhaps less so, as the history of exegesis, especially in the patristic and medieval periods, shows. However, "Paul is appealing to the Corinthians' experience of nature, to the things which they see day by day" (Robertson-Plummer, *1 Cor*, 371), and, as the next verse explains, he is thinking about stars and planets. In this sense, the word *sōma* appears in Ps.-Aristotle, *De mundo* 2.2 §391b (*sōmata theia*); Maximus of Tyre, *Dialexeis* 21.8b (*di' ouranou kai tōn en autō sōmatōn*, "through the heaven and the bodies in it"). In Jewish literature, stars were often considered to be animate (*1 Enoch* 18.13–16; 21.3–6; Philo, *De plant.* 3 §12 [*zōa*

noera]). As God gave different bodies to plants, animals, etc. (v. 38), so too he has given differences to heavenly bodies.

the splendor of the heavenly bodies is one thing; that of the earthly is another. The point of Paul's third comparison is the relative *doxa*, "splendor, glory, radiance," of the different kinds of bodies, whether terrestrial or celestial, and the word *doxa* is employed in its normal, nonmetaphorical, sense. The difference in splendor is again owing to God's creative determination.

41. *There is one splendor for the sun, another for the moon, and still another for the stars. For star differs from star in splendor.* Paul makes this observation not only from experience, but also as an appeal to common knowledge: the diverse beauty of the heavenly bodies, their light and their heat, is known to all. See Sir 43:1–10 for a detailed description of them, which even calls them *horama doxēs*, "a spectacle of splendor." Paul's point is that God, who created bodies of such known and recognized diverse splendor, has also made human bodies of present and future existence, which may be quite diverse and beyond our present comprehension. He thereby implies that the risen human body will be quite different from the known earthly body, i.e., not just a reanimated corpse. Finally in v. 41d, Paul introduces a verb (*diapherei*, "differs"), after the verbless contrasts of vv. 39–41c.

BIBLIOGRAPHY

Ahern, B. M., "The Risen Christ in the Light of Pauline Doctrine on the Risen Christian (1 Cor 15:35–57)," *Resurrexit: Actes du Symposium International sur la Resurrection de Jésus* (ed. E. Dhanis; Vatican City: Editrice Vaticana, 1974) 423–35.

Altermath, F., *Du corps psychique au corps spirituel: Interprétation de 1 Cor. 15, 35–49 par les auteurs chrétiens des quatre premiers siècles* (BGBE 18; Tübingen: Mohr [Siebeck], 1977).

Bonneau, N., "The Logic of Paul's Argument on the Resurrection Body in 1 Cor 15:35–44a," *ScEs* 45 (1993) 79–92.

Burchard, C., "1 Korinther 15,39–41," *ZNW* 75 (1984) 233–58.

Carrez, M., "With What Body Do the Dead Rise Again?" *Concilium* 60 (1970) 92–102.

Dunn, J. D. G., "How Are the Dead Raised? With What Body Do They Come? Reflections on 1 Corinthians 15," *SwJT* 45 (2002) 4–18.

Lys, D., "L'Arrière-plan et les connotations vétérotestamentaires de *sarx* et de *sōma* (Étude préliminaire)," *VT* 36 (1986) 163–204.

Matand Bulembat, J.-B., *Noyau et enjeu de l'eschatologie paulinienne: De l'apocalyptique juive et de l'eschatologie hellénistique dans quelques argumentations de l'Apôtre Paul: Etude rhétorico-exégétique de 1 Co 15,35–38; 2 Co 5,1–10 et Rm 8,18–30* (BZNW 84; Berlin/New York: de Gruyter, 1997).

Morissette, R., "La condition de ressuscité, 1 Corinthiens 15, 35–49: Structure littéraire de la péricope," *Bib* 53 (1972) 208–28.

——, "L'Expression *soma* en 1 Co 15 et dans la littérature paulinienne," *RSPT* 56 (1972) 223–39.

Padgett, A. G., "The Body in Resurrection: Science and Scripture on the 'Spiritual Body' (1 Cor 15:35–38)," *WW* 22 (2002) 155–63.

Riesenfeld, H., "Paul's 'Grain of Wheat' Analogy and the Argument of 1 Corinthians 15,"
    The Gospel Tradition (Philadelphia, PA: Fortress, 1970) 171–86.

Sider, R. J., "The Pauline Conception of the Resurrection Body in I Corinthians xv.
    35–54," *NTS* 21 (1974–75) 428–39.

Teani, M., "L'argomentazione paolina in *1 Cor* 15,35–49," *RdT* 41 (2000) 537–50.

Toloni, G., "*Sōma/gᵉwiyyâ* (Na 3, 3b) alla luce delle versioni antiche," *AION* 56 (1996)
    1–13.

Usami, K., " 'How Are the Dead Raised?' (1 Cor 15, 35–58)," *Bib* 57 (1976) 468–93.

Vincent, J.-M., " 'Avec quel corps les morts reviennent-ils?': L'usage des écritures dans 1
    Corinthiens 15,36–45," *Foi et vie* 100/2 (2001) 63–70.

Ziesler, J. A., "*Sōma* in the Septuagint," *NovT* 25 (1983) 133–45.

38   b. *Application of the Analogies (15:42–49)*

15:42 So too it is at the resurrection of the dead. What is sown is perishable; what is raised is imperishable. 43 It is sown in dishonor; it is raised in splendor. It is sown in weakness; it is raised in power. 44 An animated body is sown, a spiritual body is raised. If there is an animated body, there is also a spiritual body. 45 Thus it also stands written: *The* first *man*, Adam, *became a living being*; the last Adam, a life-giving Spirit. 46 But the spiritual was not first; rather, the animated was, and thereafter the spiritual. 47 The first man was from the earth, earthly; the second man, from heaven. 48 As was the earthly one, so too are all the earthly; and as is the heavenly one, so too are all the heavenly. 49 Just as we have borne the image of the earthly one, so too shall we bear the image of the heavenly one.

COMMENT

Having drawn various analogies about the diversity of seeds and bodies in vv. 36–41, Paul now proceeds to apply the implications of such instruction to the resurrection of deceased Christians and to give an apocalyptic answer to the second question of v. 35, "With what kind of a body will they come?" His definitive answer is given in v. 44a of this pericope, "a spiritual body is raised," and in v. 44b he argues *a minori ad maius*. It is, however, presented in a fuller form as he mentions three further qualities of that body: imperishable, robed in splendor, and powerful. Thus, in a series of parallel couplets (vv. 42b–44a), four qualities of the risen body are presented as the opposite of four qualities of the earthly human body. Four antitheses are expressed by the divine passive verbs, *speiretai* — *egeiretai*: whereas the present human body is perishable, without honor, weak, and animated (*psychikon*), the human body of the resurrection will be imperishable, radiant, powerful, and spiritual (*pneumatikon*).

To that description, Paul, in quoting Scripture (Gen 2:7), adds a comparison of the creation of the first man, Adam, with "the last Adam," or the Adam of the eschaton, the risen Christ, and then of them as the "earthly" man and the "heavenly" man (vv. 45–49). "The resurrection, like the original creation of Adam, is a creative act of God" (Asher, "*Speiretai*," 105). Moreover, the eschatological aspect is introduced in vv. 44b–49, because *sōma psychikon* and *sōma pneumatikon* contrast not only times (*prōtos* and *eschatos*), but also the terrestrial and the celestial.

Is Paul's comparison of Adam and Christ worked out in terms of Philo's interpretation of the creation of two types of human beings, one "earthly" (*gēinos*), the other "heavenly" (*ouranios* or *noētos, asōmatos, aphthartos*), according to the two accounts of creation in Genesis chaps. 1 and 2? See Philo, *Legum allegoriae* 1.12 §§31–32; *De opificio mundi* 46–47 §§134–38; *Quaest. in Gen.* 1.4. There are certain similarities, at times the same or very similar wording (Adam as *ho prōtos anthrōpos ho gēgenēs*), but there is no way of being certain that Paul is actually using or alluding to such Philonic teaching, because the vast majority of the vocabulary is quite different. Hultgren ("The Origin," 344–57) has shown that Paul is not reversing Philo or combating Hellenistic Jewish anthropology, but is deriving his two Adams simply from his interpretation of Gen 2:7.

The same has to be said about Paul's reference to Adam and the role of Adam in the *Apocalypse of Moses* (part of *The Life of Adam and Eve* [see AOT, 147–67]). There the emphasis is on the sin of Adam and its effect on all who are descended from him, even though God promises (§28.4) to raise him up, grant him to eat of the Tree of Life, and let him become "immortal for evermore." That there is some similarity with Paul's treatment of "the first man, Adam" is clear, but the parallel with "the last Adam" is completely overdrawn. Hence one cannot say with Sharpe that "in the *Apoc. Mos.* the sinful Adam and the exalted Adam function theologically in a manner similar to the function of the First Adam and the Second Adam used by St. Paul to contrast Christ the redeemer with Adam the sinner" ("The Second Adam," 35). The "exalted Adam" is hard to find and is not said to be "life-giving"!

Again, one should beware of the exaggerated interpretation of vv. 45–46 given by Davies, who tried to show that later rabbinic teaching already had the idea of all humanity united in Adam, supposedly based on *m. Sanh.* 4.5 (cf. Black, "The Pauline Doctrine of the Second Adam"). Even Hultgren's attempt to derive Paul's "two Adams" doctrine from Palestinian Judaism founders because his evidence is taken from late rabbinic writings such as: (1) the midrash on Gen 2:7 in *Gen. Rab.* 14.2–5; (2) the midrash on Gen 1:26 in *Gen. Rab.* 8.1; (3) *Midrash Teh.* on Ps 139:5–6. Hultgren acknowledges the "quite late" date of these writings, and says that it "is impossible to prove that Paul knew any such exegesis" ("The Origin," 363); yet he blithely maintains that "these rabbinic parallels provide the closest intellectual framework for Paul's doctrine of the two Adams" (ibid., 366). However, these would-be parallels are just that, parallels to Paul's discussion here, but there is simply no evidence of any real contact or of Pauline dependence on them. The sooner they are forgotten, the better the interpretation may become.

Widmann, who earlier argued that 1 Cor 2:6–16, was an interpolated paragraph, regards vv. 44b–48 likewise as an interpolation ("1 Kor 2,6–16," 47–48). He notes the break in the argument that is found in v. 44 between part a and part b (see the paragraphing in JB amd NAB). As in chap. 2, where the quotation in v. 9 comes from an apocryphal writing, he claims that the quotation in v. 45 is similar. Moreover, the contrast expressed in v. 48, called "gnostic," is said to be contradicted in v. 49. However, Murphy-O'Connor ("Interpolations," 94) has rightly disposed of this interpretation, mainly because the quotation in v. 45 is simply a reworking of the LXX of Gen 2:7 and not derived from an apocryphal writing, and the alleged contradiction between vv. 48 and 49 comes merely from Widmann's mistranslation of the text.

The most important item in this Pauline passage is the notion of the "spiritual body." Just what is meant by that phrase has been discussed over the centuries, ever since Paul first formulated it. In the patristic period the discussion was devoted to the resurrection of the *flesh* (with Jerome and Augustine), about which Paul says nothing, even though the word "flesh" appears in v. 39 above. Yet that idea dominated the discussion throughout the medieval period as well, as the creeds and church documents up until the Second Council of Lyons (A.D. 1274) reveal (DH §§2, 5, 10–30, 36, 41, 60, 63, 190, 540, 574, 684, 797, 854), even if on occasion the original idea appeared as *resurrectio mortuorum*. The four qualities of the risen body of which Paul spoke (vv. 42–44a) became the four *dotes*, "gifts" or "qualities," which dominated the discussion and church teaching thereafter.

In modern times a break with the traditional categories came with Bultmann in his effort to demythologize the NT. His break was to abandon the patristic and medieval notion of the four qualities (*dotes*) of the risen body and to speak of *sōma pneumatikon* as a "Spirit-ruled *soma*." Bultmann's starting-point: For Paul, the human self was not characterized by the Greek philosophical dichotomy of *sōma* and *psychē*, "body" and "soul." Rather *sōma* denoted for him the human being as visible, tangible. One does not have a body, but one is *sōma*, a way of saying "self" (Phil 1:20; Rom 6:12–13). Sometimes Paul uses *sarx* as the equivalent of *sōma* (1 Cor 6:16, quoting Gen 2:24; 2 Cor 4:10–11), but more frequently "flesh" denotes the human being as material, earthbound, and weak, the human creature left to itself (1 Cor 1:29). Hence Paul would be speaking of "a life *kata sarka* (according to the flesh) but never of a life *kata sōma* (according to the body)" (*TNT*, 1:201). Consequently, at the resurrection the *sōma* would not be reconstituted flesh, but it would be transformed so that it would no longer be dominated by *sarx*, but ruled by the Spirit. So the resurrection of the dead means the appearance of "a Spirit-ruled *sōma*."

Bultmann's interpretation of the risen body met with both positive and negative criticism. Those who followed him (sometimes with slightly differing nuances) were M. Dahl, *The Resurrection of the Body*, 94 (the "body-spiritual," or "a personality completely controlled and informed by the creative Spirit of God and therefore beyond corruption"); Barrett, *1 Cor*, 372–73 (a "new body, animated by the Spirit of God, with which the same man will be clothed and equipped in the age to come"); Murphy-O'Connor, *NJBC*, 813 ("the human body as adapted by the Spirit of God for a completely different mode of existence"); Collins, *1 Cor*, 567 (an "inspirited body," or a body as "human insofar as he or she is energized by

the Spirit of the living God [*pneuma*]"); Conzelmann, *1 Cor*, 283 ("not simply a
body consisting of *pneuma*, but one determined by *pneuma*").

J. A. T. Robinson (*The Body*) rejected the idea of any future physical resurrection, insisting rather that the resurrection of the body starts at baptism, when a
Christian becomes "one Spirit" (i.e., one spiritual body) with the Lord (1 Cor
6:17). Its ultimate destiny, by incorporation into the Body of Christ, is transformation from being a natural body to become a *sōma pneumatikon* (1 Cor 15:44). The
completion of this transformation must wait upon the day of the Parousia. Somewhat similarly, Ross ("Hold Water").

Conservative reaction to Bultmann's interpretation was inevitable, and interpreters such as Grosheide insisted on the notion of a fleshy resurrection, a resurrection of the body that is altered: "One and the same body is sown in one quality
and raised in another, but all the same it remains the same body" (*1 Cor*, 384–85).
Similarly, Schep: "The resurrection body will consist of glorified flesh" (*The Nature*, 184). Likewise Gundry, *Soma in Biblical Theology*, 165–66: Insisting that
sōma means a physical body, not person, he described *sōma pneumatikon* as "not
a bodily form with spirit as its substance," but "a physical body renovated by the
Spirit of God and therefore suited to a heavenly immortality."

Finally, Hays recognized the oxymoron that Paul actually uses: "spiritual body"
does not mean a body determined by the Spirit (*1 Cor*, 272); it is rather a body
"free from decay and weakness that we know in the present life" (270); a "paradoxical expression" that "confounds human finite understanding," but then he
proceeds to define it! Similarly, Perkins: a contradiction in terms. Rahner: "language of paradox" (*Man in the Church*, 214). This is the only explanation of the
term that is really admissible: an oxymoron (so Horsley, *1 Cor*, 311).

NOTES

15:42. *So too it is at the resurrection of the dead.* After the analogies of vv. 36–41,
Paul begins to apply what he has been citing as illustrations to the resurrection of
the Christian dead (*tōn nekrōn*, see NOTE on v. 35) in this verse and the following
ones up to v. 49.

What is sown is perishable; what is raised is imperishable. Lit. "It [the body] is
sown in corruption; it is raised in incorruptibility." The verb *speiretai*, "it is sown,"
which rhymes with *egeiretai*, introduces each of the coming four couplets in
vv. 42b–44a, as it picks up the analogy of vv. 36–37; the subj. of the verb is *sōma*,
clearly expressed, if only in the last couplet (v. 44a). *Pace* Garland (*1 Cor*, 732),
the subject is not "one of the dead."

The earthly human body is said to be "sown," and often that image is said to
resemble burial. "It is in corruption before it reaches the grave" (Robertson-
Plummer, *1 Cor*, 372), and thus it is subject to decomposition and decay
(*phthora*). So the metaphor is understood by many commentators: J. Weiss, *1 Cor*,
371; Grosheide, *1 Cor*, 383–84; Kistemaker, *1 Cor*, 573; Kremer, *1 Cor*, 356; Orr-
Walther, *1 Cor*, 343. Others, however, think that by "sowing" Paul means rather
"mortal life itself," which precedes the "harvest of resurrection life" (Bruce, *1 Cor*,
152; similarly Fee, *1 Cor*, 784; Conzelmann, *1 Cor*, 283).

However, Asher ("*Speiretai,*" 102) considers both of these explanations of "sowing" to be inadequate and argues rather that Paul is contrasting "human origins" with resurrection and is using the verb *speiretai* "as an anthropogenic metaphor describing the creation of the first human being, Adam." He interprets the two verbs *speiretai* and *egeiretai* as divine passives, and so the first verb would refer to the creation of Adam (and humanity). He further illustrates this metaphoric meaning of "sowing" with many instances from the Greco-Roman world, which was predominantly an agriculturally dependent society with many beliefs and practices that understood humanity having its origin from the earth's soil (e.g., the Athenian festival of Thesmophoria; the Theban myth of Cadmus's sowing the teeth of the dragon of Ares, from which sprang the *Spartoi* ["sowed men"]; myths recorded in Platonic writings [esp. *Timaeus* 42d; *Politicus* 272d–e]). He also shows how that metaphor was used by Philo: *espeiren ho theos en tō gēgenei phronēsin te kai aretēn,* "God sowed in the earthborn one understanding and virtue" (*Leg. alleg.* 1.26 §79; cf. *De opif. mundi* 13 §43). Although these instances show that there was indeed such an anthropogenic metaphor of sowing, it is impossible to show that Paul actually meant his use of *speiretai* in this sense, even if it is a plausible explanation.

In any case, the human body "dies," as does a seed (v. 36), but that is not the end of it. It "is raised," and that means that it "is brought to life," as is the seed (v. 36), by God (divine passive, ZBG §236). The first quality of the risen body, however, is expressed as an abstraction, *aphtharsia,* "imperishability, incorruptibility." In this and the two following verses, Paul employs the rhetorical device of antithetic parallelism (with pass. verbs), which concisely makes the point that he considers important (see BDF §§489–90). From v. 42b to v. 44a, Paul has eight pass. verbs, four pairs (*speiretai—egeiretai*), in contrast to the act. verbs used in vv. 37–41; but they correspond to the *zōopoieitai* of v. 36. Cf. Rom 8:21; Gal 6:8. Paul is speaking of physical corruptibility, dishonor, and weakness, but not of moral, as some commentators would have us believe in these contrasts (see Sider, "Pauline Conception," 433). Since the subject remains the same in vv. 42b–44, some bodily continuity is being suggested in the process of transformation.

43. *It is sown in dishonor; it is raised in splendor.* Whereas the earthly human body is subject to *atimia,* "dishonor," the second quality of the risen body is *doxa,* "splendor, glory, radiance." See NOTE on 2:7. The human body, thus sown, "has lost all rights of citizenship (*atimia*), and, excepting decent burial, all rights of humanity" (Robertson-Plummer, *1 Cor,* 372). Recall how Paul contrasts "decay" (*phthora*) with "splendor, glory" (*doxa*) in Rom 8:21, a slightly different consideration. Cf. also Rom 9:21; Phil 3:21.

It is sown in weakness; it is raised in power. Whereas the earthly human body is powerless, subject to frailty and weakness (astheneia), the third quality of the risen body is *dynamis,* "power." It thus shares in the power given by the Creator. The same contrast is found in 2 Cor 12:9; 13:4.

44. *An animated body is sown, a spiritual body is raised.* This is the climactic fourth couplet. Now the earthly human body is called *psychikon,* "animated," i.e., having an *anima* (= Greek *psychē,* "soul, life principle"), which the Vg renders as *corpus animale.* The adj. *psychikos* has already been used in 2:14 to describe a

human being not particularly attuned to the work of the Holy Spirit, someone different from *pneumatikos*, one who is open to the Spirit's influence (2:13, 15; 3:1). In the last-mentioned instance (3:1), *pneumatikos* is contrasted with *sarkinos*, which seems to mean the same type of person as *psychikos* (2:14), but one dominated by the cravings of *sarx*, "flesh," which is suited more to the Christian who has made no progress in the spiritual life (not an unbeliever, who has only an animated body). Such a meaning of *psychikos* has some relation to *sōma psychikon* here, because it is contrasted with *sōma pneumatikon*, but the connotation is now slightly different. Being derived from the noun *psychē*, which is the vital or animating principle of ordinary earthly life, *psychikon* means an "animated" (body). Paul would have written *sōma sarkikon*, "body of flesh," if he wanted to stress that dualistic fleshy aspect of the body; but he has written *sōma psychikon*, "animated body," because of what he is going to say about Adam as *psychē zōsa* in v. 45. Note too that, whereas the difference in vv. 42–43 was expressed by one term of the contrast being fitted with *alpha* privative: *aphtharsia / phora; atimia / doxa; astheneia / dynamis*; the contrast now is *psychikon / pneumatikon*, neither of which has the *alpha* privative. The spiritual body will be to the animated body what the plant is to the seed, and there would be a certain continuity (Clavier, "Brèves remarques," 347).

The real problem, however, is the meaning of *sōma pneumatikon*, which seems to attribute to *sōma* a meaning that is diametrically opposed to "body." The basic meaning of *pneuma* is "breathing, blowing, air in movement," hence "wind" (BDAG, 832); see Exod 15:10; John 3:8a. From that it came to mean "breath" or "(life-)spirit," i.e., that which gives life or animates the body of a human being or animal: *to pneuma tou stomatos autou*, "the breath of his mouth" (2 Thess 2:8). See further LXX Job 8:2; Judg 15:19 (*epestrepsen to pneuma autou en autō, kai anepsyxen*, "and his spirit returned to him, and he revived"); Gen 6:17 (*pasa sarx en hē estin pneuma zōēs*, "all flesh in which is the breath of life"); Qoh 3:21; 1 Sam 30:12; Matt 27:50 (*kraxas phōnē megalē apēken to pneuma*, "crying out in a loud voice, he gave up [his] spirit"); John 19:30. *Pneumatikos* is the adj. expressing the same idea. In other words, then, *pneuma / pneumatikon* normally means all that *sōma* is not. In effect, as Paul employs oxymoron to formulate his answer, the phrase is a rhetorical device that links contradictory terms in a unit to produce an expression of tension; "a juxtaposition of words apparently contradictory of each other" (Smyth, *Greek Grammar*, §3035; cf. Krentz, "Sense of Senseless Oxymora," 583–84; see COMMENT above for a summary of ways in which the phrase has been interpreted).

If there is an animated body, there is also a spiritual body. This follows logically if one admits that there is such a pair as *psychikon / pneumatikon*, which, as we have shown above, has been used already by Paul. Paul argues *a minori ad maius*, as he gives his answer to the second question of v. 35. As a result of the contrast, "spiritual body" must mean a human body as transformed by God through Christ for a new mode of existence, under the influence of *Pneuma*, "Holy Spirit." Yet that is a description of extrinsic influence on *sōma*, and it really tells us nothing about a "spiritual body" *in se*; hence the oxymoron remains.

One must remember that Paul has had no personal experience of such a "body," and in attempting an apocalyptic description of it, he is content to express it by oxymoron. It is easier to say what Paul did not mean than to say what he meant: not a resuscitated body of flesh; not the earthly body simply endowed with new *dotes*, "qualities." All such formulations are in vain. One should learn to live with the oxymoron. As Lindemann has noted, *sōma pneumatikon* expresses what is "sehr 'unkörperlich' " ("very 'unbodylike,' " *1 Cor*, 360).

45. *Thus it also stands written.* See Note on 1:31. Paul now invokes the OT to bolster up his discussion and confirm his understanding of the risen body, especially the difference between *psychikon* and *pneumatikon*. The quotation is neither "midrashic" nor "targumic," *pace* Usami (" 'How Are,' " 477); that is a misuse of terms that have a distinct meaning.

The first man, Adam, became a living being. Paul quotes Gen 2:7, which in the LXX reads, *egeneto ho anthrōpos eis psychēn zōsan*, lit. "the human became a living soul (= being)," to which he adds two words, *prōtos*, "first" (man), because the adj. is masc., and the name, *Adam*. The Hebrew of the MT has *wayĕhî hā'ādām lĕnepheš ḥayyāh*, to which the LXX corresponds exactly, translating *hā'ādām* as *ho anthrōpos*, as did Aquila too, whereas Symmachus and Theodotion translated it as *ho Adam*, "Adam became . . . " (see Wevers, *Notes*, 25 n. 20). Mss B, K, 326, 365 of 1 Corinthians omit *anthrōpos*, "man," but it is read by the best Greek texts.

In the Greek form that he is using, Paul includes the name, Adam, thus historicizing *hā'ādām*, even as he does in Rom 5:12, 14 (see *Romans*, 407–10). In the creation account, *hā'ādām* is said to have become a "life-endowed being," when God's breath vitalized a body formed from the soil of the earth. He thus became the "first" *'ādām*, "human being," or the head of the human race. There is not even a hint here that Adam is being considered "as a sinner," *pace* Sider ("Pauline Conception," 434); he is simply the first human being created. What interests Paul most in this verse from Genesis is not the word *anthrōpos*, but the phrase *psychē zōsa*, lit. "living soul," i.e., life-endowed being, because it associates Adam, the first human being, with the realm of *psychē*, to which the adj. *psychikos* is related. Thus Adam's body was *psychikon*, "animated," i.e., the kind that is sown (v. 44a). Contrast the way Greek Wis 16:11 reformulates the creation of Adam: *ton empneusanta autō psychēn energousan kai emphysēsanta pneuma zōtikon*, the one "who inspired in him an active soul and breathed into him a living spirit" (RSV), which associates *pneuma* with creation and is thus quite different from the thinking of Paul in this passage.

the last Adam, a life-giving Spirit. I.e., Christ, who has already been contrasted with Adam in v. 22, is now recognized as the Adam of the eschaton, "the last Adam," who through his resurrection has become *pneuma zōopoioun*, lit. "a life-making Spirit." (The oldest ms of 1 Corinthians, P[46] omits *Adam*.) Paul adds this clause (v. 45c) to contrast it with v. 45b. In this way, what was asserted in vv. 21–22 is now more fully explained. Christ belongs to the realm of *pneuma*, to which the adj. *pneumatikos* is related. Thus his risen body became *pneumatikon*, "spiritual," i.e., like that of human beings to be raised (v. 44b). He is also the last Adam, because there will be no other head of the human race in any sense after him.

Moreover, he passes on a higher form of life, not one related to *psychē*, but to *pneuma*. In his antithetic comparison, Paul likewise stresses that, as Adam was the first being to enjoy earthly human life, which as *sōma psychikon* came to all others through him, so Christ, the "last Adam," is the source of risen life in glory, which as *sōma pneumatikon* comes to all who belong to him (recall v. 22b: *zōopoiēthēsontai*, "will be brought to life"). They are those who become members of his body through faith and baptism (12:13) and through participation in his body and blood (10:16–17). The contrast between *psychē* and *pneuma* thus bolsters his distinction between *sōma psychikon* and *sōma pneumatikon*. In v. 23 above, Paul called Christ *aparchē tō kekoimēmenōn*, "firstfruits of those who have fallen asleep," but now Christ is also *pneuma zōopoioun*, "a life-giving spirit," and in Rom 8:29–30 Paul will speak of Christ as *prōtotokon en pollois adelphois . . . toutous kai edoxasen*, "the firstborn among many brothers . . . these he also glorified."

When Paul admits that the risen Christ becomes *pneuma*, he alludes to what he teaches elsewhere: in 2 Cor 3:17, "Now the Lord is the Spirit"; and Rom 1:4, "established as the Son of God with power by a spirit of holiness as of his resurrection from the dead," where *kata pneuma hagiosynēs* stands in contrast to *kata sarka*, and describes something that is intrinsic to the risen Christ (see *Romans*, 233–37); 14:9 (ibid., 691). These are Pauline passages where it is difficult to distinguish the risen Christ from the Spirit; see further *PAHT* §PT61. In any case, it is clear that the Spirit is somehow involved in the coming resurrection of the dead, as far as Paul is concerned, and as is evident from what Paul will write in Rom 8:9–13, as a follow-up of what he writes here (see further Brodeur, *Holy Spirit's Agency*).

Some interpreters try to find literary sources for Paul's use of the "last Adam," ascribing it to gnostic or proto-gnostic speculation (Schmithals, Jervell) or even to Jewish rabbinic thinking (Davies, Usami). Yet even Usami has to admit that "Jewish texts which contain a 'second' or 'last' Adam cannot be found" ("How Are," 484). The phrase is a Pauline creation, an extrapolation from the biblical text that he has just quoted.

46. *But the spiritual was not first; rather, the animated was, and thereafter the spiritual.* Paul generalizes, because *to pneumatikon* is not restricted to *sōma*, and the lower comes before the more important. Paul may be asserting this to counteract a viewpoint of some Corinthian Christians; in any case, he is still thinking in terms of *psychē zōsa* of v. 45b. The priority is explained in the following verse.

47. *The first man was from the earth, earthly.* This verbless double nominal sentence contrasts Adam and Christ further. Adam is said to be "from the earth," because God formed him from ʿ*āphār*, "dry topsoil," in MT Gen 2:7, and the LXX translates it as *choun apo tēs gēs*, "soil from the earth," and so he is *choïkos*, "dusty, earthly." Paul thus alludes to the Genesis account. — For an attempt to relate Paul's teaching about Adam to the Gnostic myth of the *Urmensch*, "primal man," see Conzelmann, *1 Cor*, 284–86; it is highly far-fetched, as Lindemann also recognizes (*1 Cor*, 362: "wenig wahrscheinlich" ["hardly probable"]).

the second man, from heaven. By contrast, Christ is now called *ho deuteros anthrōpos*, and from this phrase patristic writers developed the title for him, "the second Adam," a phrase that Paul never employs. For Paul, Adam is the "type" (*typos*, as in Rom 5:14c), Christ is the "antitype" (*antitypos*), not the other way round, as Conzelmann would have it (*1 Cor*, 284).

Christ as the man "from heaven" stands in contrast to "the first man from earth." By "heaven" Paul means the realm where God and the risen Christ dwell and are active (Rom 1:18; 10:6; cf. Col 4:1; Eph 6:9). It may be an allusion to Christ's coming parousia, as in 1 Thess 4:16 (not to his incarnation, as in John 3:31, 13; see *TDNT*, 9:478); elsewhere Paul speaks of Christ as from heaven (Rom 10:6). By putting it that way, Paul is simply rephrasing his pneumatic status, because in "heaven" the risen Christ shares the glory of his Father and has a body of glory.

The second clause of this verse has been variously transmitted in different MSS, as Lindemann notes, "for dogmatic reasons" (*1 Cor*, 361): ℵ², A, D¹, Ψ, 075, 1739 ᵐᵍ and the Koine text-tradition have *anthrōpos ho kyrios*, "the (second) man, the Lord"; P⁴⁶ has *anthrōpos pneumatikos*, "the spiritual man"; but the best MSS (ℵ*, B, C, D*, F, G, 0243, 6, 33, 1175, 1739) read it as in the lemma. The Latin text of F, G even adds the equivalent of *ho ouranios*, *homo de caelo caelestis*, thus creating a better parallel to the first clause, but that is clearly secondary. For a different application of "earthly" and "heavenly" to the newly created human, see Philo, *Leg. alleg.* 1.12 §31.

48. *As was the earthly one, so too are all the earthly.* I.e., as was Adam, so are all human beings descended from him, who are still on earth. In two parallel verbless sentences, Paul expresses an effect of the corporate personality of Adam, already noted in v. 22, and then the difference for Christ. The descendants of Adam belong to the realm of *to psychikon*, because they bear all the traits inherited from him who was their head. Made of the earth's soil, to soil they will return (Gen 3:19).

and as is the heavenly one, so too are all the heavenly. The reason for this has already been expressed by Paul in 6:14, "By his power God raised up the Lord, and he will also raise us up," to share in the same risen life of the Lord in glory. Again the corporate personality of the risen Christ is implied. Cf. Rom 8:29 ("Those whom he foreknew, he also predestined to be conformed to the image of his Son that he might be the firstborn of many brothers"); 2 Cor 3:18; Phil 3:20–21; 1 Thess 4:16.

49. *Just as we have borne the image of the earthly one, so too shall we bear the image of the heavenly one.* I.e., just as all Christians have the same sort of body and condition as Adam had (*psychikon*), so after this earthly experience they will have the same sort of body and condition as the heavenly risen Christ (*pneumatikon*). In a sense, this verse is parallel to v. 44b above, in that it is drawing a logical conclusion from what Paul has been arguing.

In using the 1st pers. plur. in both clauses of this verse, Paul is stressing the identity of the person involved. He is imitating a motif already expressed in Gen 5:3, where it is recounted that at the age of 130 Adam, who had been formed by God "in His image" (*kath' eikona hēmeteran*, 1:26), became the father of Seth "in his own image" (*kata tēn eikona autou*). See further Gen 9:6c and 1:27; cf. 2 Cor 3:18.

The antithetic comparison carries over to Christians who "will bear" (fut. indic. *phoresomen*) the image of the "last Adam," the "heavenly one." However, many MSS (P⁴⁶, ℵ, A, C, D, F, G,Ψ, 075, 0243, 33, 1739 and the Koine text-tradition) read the cohortative subj. *phoresōmen*, "let us bear the image . . . ," but N-A²⁷ prefers to follow the inferior reading because the context demands an indic., not a hortatory form (see Metzger, *TCGNT*, 502). Sider, however, prefers the hortatory form as "the older reading" ("Pauline Conception," 434); similarly Fee (*1 Cor*, 795): the Corinthians "are being urged to conform to the life of the 'man of heaven' as those who now share his character and behavior."

BIBLIOGRAPHY

Abernathy, D., "Christ as Life-giving Spirit in 1 Corinthians 15:45," *IBS* 24 (2002) 2–13.

Asher, J. R., *Polarity and Change in 1 Corinthians 15: A Study of Metaphysics, Rhetoric and Resurrection* (HUT 42; Tübingen: Mohr Siebeck, 2000).

———, "*Speiretai*: Paul's Anthropogenic Metaphor in 1 Corinthians 15:42–44," *JBL* 120 (2001) 101–22.

Audet, L. "Avec quel corps les justes ressuscitent-ils? Analyse de 1 Corinthiens 15:44," *SR* 1 (1971) 165–77.

Black, M., "The Pauline Doctrine of the Second Adam," *SJT* 7 (1954) 170–79.

Brodeur, S., *The Holy Spirit's Agency in the Resurrection of the Dead: An Exegetico-Theological Study of 1 Corinthians 15,44b–49 and Romans 8,9–13* (GTS 14; Rome: Università Gregoriana, 1996).

Clavier, H., "Brèves remarques sur la notion de *sōma pneumatikon*," *The Background of the New Testament and Its Eschatology: In Honour of Charles Harold Dodd* (ed. W. D. Davies and D. Daube; Cambridge: Cambridge University Press, 1956) 342–62.

Davies, J. G., "Factors Leading to the Emergence of Belief in the Resurrection of the Flesh," *JTS* 23 (1972) 448–55.

Dunn, J. D. G., "1 Corinthians 15: 45 — Last Adam, Life-giving Spirit," *Christ and Spirit in the New Testament: Studies in Honour of Charles Francis Digby Moule* (ed. B. Lindars and S. S. Smalley; Cambridge: Cambridge University Press, 1973) 127–41.

Graham, E. A., " 'The Heavenly Man': A Survey of the Documentary Evidence," *CQR* 113 (1932) 224–39.

Hultgren, S., "The Origin of Paul's Doctrine of the Two Adams in 1 Corinthians 15.45–49," *JSNT* 25 (2002–3) 343–70.

Hunt, A. R., *The Inspired Body: Paul, the Corinthians, and Divine Inspiration* (Macon: Mercer University Press, 1996).

Jucci, E., "Terreno, psichico, pneumatico nel capitolo 15 della Prima Epistola ai Corinzi," *Henoch* 5 (1983) 323–41.

Kennedy, H. A. A., "St. Paul and the Conception of the 'Heavenly Man,'" *Expos* 8/7 (1914) 97–110.

Knox, W. L., "Origen's Conception of the Resurrection Body," *JTS* 39 (1938) 247–48.

Krentz, E., "The Sense of Senseless Oxymora," *CTM* 28 (2001) 577–84.

Morissette, R., "L'Antithèse entre le 'psychique' et le 'pneumatique' en I Corinthiens, xv, 44 à 46," *RevScRel* 46 (1972) 97–143.

O'Donoghue, N. D., "The Awakening of the Dead," *ITQ* 56 (1990) 49–59.

Painchaud, L., "Le sommaire anthropogonique de *l'Ecrit sans Titre* (NH II, 117:27–118:2) à la lumière de *1 Co* 14:45–47," *VC* 44 (1990) 382–93.

Pamment, M., "Raised a Spiritual Body: Bodily Resurrection according to Paul," *NBf* 66 (1985) 372–88.

Reyero, S., " *'Estin kai (sōma) pneumatikon,'* 1 Cr 15,44b," *Studium* 15 (1975) 151–87.

Robinson, J. A. T., *The Body: A Study in Pauline Theology* (SBT 5; London: SCM, 1952) 79–83.

Schep, J. A., *The Nature of the Resurrected Body: A Study of the Biblical Data* (Grand Rapids: Eerdmans, 1964).

Schmisek, B. J., *The Spiritual Body: Paul's Use of* sōma pneumatikon *in 1 Corinthians 15:44* (diss.; Washington, DC: Catholic University of America, 2002).

Schneider, B. V., "The Corporate Meaning and Background of 1 Cor 15,45b," *CBQ* 29 (1967) 450–67.

Scroggs, R., *The Last Adam: A Study in Pauline Anthropology* (Philadelphia: Fortress, 1966) 82–112.

Sharpe, J. L., III, "The Second Adam in the Apocalypse of Moses," *CBQ* 35 (1973) 35–46.

Stegmann, B. A., *Christ, the "Man from Heaven": A Study of 1 Cor. 15,45–47 in the Light of the Anthropology of Philo Judaeus* (Catholic University of America, New Testament Studies 6; Washington, DC: Catholic University of America, 1927).

Stemberger, G., *Der Leib der Auferstehung: Studien zur Anthropologie und Eschatologie des palästinischen Judentums im neutestamentlichen Zeitalter (ca. 170 v. Cr.[sic]—100 n. Chr.)* (AnBib 56; Rome: Biblical Institute, 1972).

Wedderburn, A. J. M., "Philo's 'Heavenly Man,' " *NovT* 15 (1973) 301–26.

39   D. THE RESURRECTION AS VICTORY OVER DEATH THROUGH CHRIST (15:50–58)

[15:50] Now, what I mean, brothers, is that flesh and blood cannot inherit the kingdom of God; nor does the perishable inherit imperishability. [51] Look, I am telling you a mystery: we shall not all fall asleep, but we shall all be changed, [52] in an instant, in the twinkling of an eye, at the last trumpet. For the trumpet will sound, and the dead will be raised imperishable, and we shall all be changed. [53] For what is perishable must don imperishability; and what is mortal, immortality. [54] When what is perishable dons imperishability and what is mortal dons immortality, then the saying that stands written will come true:

"*Death has been swallowed up in victory.*
[55]*Where, O death, is your victory?*
Where, O death, is your sting?"

[56] The sting of death is sin, and the power of sin is the law. [57] But thanks be to God! He grants us the victory through our Lord Jesus Christ. [58] Consequently, my dear

brothers, be steadfast, unshaken, devoting yourselves at all times to the work of the Lord, knowing that in the Lord your toil is not in vain.

COMMENT

Paul now draws his discussion of the resurrection of the dead to a close. What he now says in vv. 50–58 is closely related to what he has just established in vv. 35–49, even though he is, in effect, answering the first question posed in v. 35, "How are the dead raised?" Some commentators, such as Garland and those whom he follows, see too great a division in this distinction of the two questions of v. 35, which is not intended at all. Paul's basic answer to the first question is supplied now in vv. 52, 51b, and 57b: "In an instant . . . we shall all be changed," and God "grants us the victory [over death] through our Lord Jesus Christ."

Since Paul, as he writes this letter, has had no personal experience of that victory, he adopts an apocalyptic mode to describe it. With stage props, such as are known in apocalyptic writings, he attempts to describe the future resurrection of those who die in Christ.

It is a matter of debate among commentators whether v. 50 is the conclusion of the preceding pericope (vv. 42–49), where Paul has applied the analogies of seeds, bodies, and splendor to human beings, or the beginning of this discussion (vv. 50–58). N-A^{27}, NAB, NIV, NEB, REB, NRSV, ESV take v. 50 with vv. 51–58, whereas the RSV reads it with the preceding pericope. In any case, v. 50 is clearly transitional. One can distinguish two main sections in this passage, vv. 50–53, where Paul sets forth the proper theological understanding of the event of the resurrection in light of his discussion in vv. 35–49, and vv. 54–57, where he presents the transformation of the dead in light of certain OT prophetic utterances. Whether one should call vv. 54–57 a "midrash," as does Morissette, may be debated, because those verses hardly meet the normal understanding of that Jewish literary form (see R. Bloch, *DBSup*, 5:1263–81; "Midrash," in *Approaches to Ancient Judaism* [ed. Green] 29–50). Finally, in v. 58 the Apostle Paul concludes his remarks on the problem of the resurrection of the dead.

It is also a matter of no little debate how vv. 50–57 are to be related to 2 Cor 5:1–5. Some commentators find a development in Paul's thinking between the two letters: here he seems to think that he will survive until the parousia, whereas in 2 Corinthians his experience makes him think that his own death is imminent (so Benoit, Bruce, Dodd). Others view the two passages as affirming the same consistent view of the resurrection of the dead at the parousia (so Dupont; see further Gillman, "Thematic Comparison"). Be that as it may, it is an issue about which the interpreter of 2 Corinthians has to be more concerned.

NOTES

15:50. *Now, what I mean, brothers, is that flesh and blood cannot inherit the kingdom of God.* Lit. "Look, this I declare (*phēmi*)." Paul introduces this new development in his argument with the same formula that he used in 7:29, as he seeks to draw attention to this important stage of his argument. It serves as a transition from vv. 43–49 to this new consideration.

Inheritance of the kingdom of God was already mentioned in 6:9–10 (see NOTE on 6:9). In the present context, it is another way of speaking about the risen life of Christians, and the resurrection of the dead, as the following clause makes clear. In other words, human beings, being mortal and left to themselves, cannot bring about the resurrection of the dead. Paul's reply to the first question of v. 35 ("How are the dead raised?) begins with a negation: human beings cannot raise themselves. "Our present bodies . . . are abolutely unfitted for the Kingdom: there must be a transformation" (Robertson-Plummer, *1 Cor*, 376). Therefore, earthly bodies, as such, have no power to bring about the eschatological state of the Christian.

The pair *sarx kai haima* is an expression derived from Jewish tradition (LXX Sir 14:18; 17:31; Philo, *Quis div. rer. heres* 12 §57) and is found again in Gal 1:16; Matt 16:17; and in the later rabbinic tradition (*b. Sanhedrin* 91a; *b. Berakoth* 28b, etc.). Note the sing. verb, which reveals the unit that it is, but which copyists in some MSS have changed to the plur. (A, C, D, Ψ, 075, 0243, 33, 1739). In inverse order, the phrase appears in Eph 6:12; Heb 2:14. It is a literary way of speaking of mortal humanity, in contrast to God and other transcendent beings, and especially in its frailty or weakness (inability to cope with what is needed). *Pace* Sider ("Pauline Conception," 437), it does not mean a human being "*qua* transitory, frail sinner," since the last characteristic is never intimated in any of the texts. As "flesh and blood," the physical body cannot become a risen or spiritual body on its own; it will be transformed only by God who has raised Christ. The phrase is used normally only of living human beings, and so the resurrected body cannot be merely "flesh and blood" (see Morissette, "La chair").

nor does the perishable inherit imperishability. Because flesh and blood are doomed to dissolution, they do not have within them the wherewithal to withstand such decomposition (*hē phthora*) or the potential to overcome it. The word strictly means "dissolution, decomposition," but it can also denote "the state of being perishable" or "that which is perishable" (BDAG, 1055). This clause is merely explanatory, as it formulates a synonymous parallel to what flesh and blood cannot do; it is not an antithetic parallel, or what Jeremias (" 'Flesh and Blood,' " 152) calls "synthetic" parallelism. "The perishable" is the animated body that has to die, because death is the transition between the two states of such life; and this is true of all human beings with such a body.

51. *Look, I am telling you a mystery.* Paul is passing on to Corinthian Christians a divine truth hidden from them until now (see NOTE on *mystērion*, 2:1), and he introduces it with *idou* (actually the sing. aor. mid. impv. of *eidon*, fitted with the accent of a particle), often used in the LXX to translate Hebrew *hinnēh*, "behold" (e.g., Gen 48:2). Cf. Paul's use of *mystērion* in Rom 11:25, where he passes on a truth about the future salvation of Israel; also Rom 16:25; and its use in the LXX in apocalyptic writings such as Dan 2:28–29 bis. By way of contrast, when Paul speaks about the same topic in 1 Thess 4:15–17, he affirms it there as "a word of the Lord." Here he passes on the "mystery" about the risen body and provides

the biblical basis for the creedal affirmation, *anastasin nekrōn kai zōēn tou mellontos aiōnos* or *resurrectionem mortuorum et vitam venturi saeculi* (Nicene-Constantinopolitan Creed, DH §150), "the resurrection of the dead and the life of the world to come."

we shall not all fall asleep, but we shall all be changed. The coming transformation of all Christians, whether they die before or are still alive at the parousia of the risen Lord, is assured. This truth is the mystery made known to Paul, who is now passing it on. Cf. 1 Thess 4:15–17, which has a certain parallel affirmation, even if it differently asserts the resurrection of the dead and the parousia as "the word of the Lord." It says nothing, however, about transformation, and it has a different *Sitz im Leben* (see Delobel, "The Fate"; Löhr, "1 Thess 4,15–17"). What Paul now affirms is not a quotation, but rather his own formulation, couched in the 1st pers. plur., to include himself. The verb *allagēsometha* is a divine passive (see ZBG §236), "we will be changed," by God, who is understood as the agent of the transformation; or perhaps the risen Christ is, as in Phil 3:21 (see Gillman, "Transformation," 322–23).

It is a matter of debate whether Paul in this passage is looking forward to the parousia of Christ. Barrett thinks that he believed that the parousia would happen in his own generation (*1 Cor*, 381). Perriman, however, maintains that Paul is not thinking of the parousia here at all ("Paul and the Parousia"). Be that as it may, Paul is paraphrasing what he has already written in 6:14, "God raised up the Lord, and he will raise us up too by his power." In Phil 3:20–21, Paul ascribes the change to Christ: "We await a Savior, the Lord Jesus Christ, who will transform our lowly body to be like his glorious body, by the power that enables him to subject all things to himself." The emphasis is on the transformation, as Paul expects the change to remedy the deficiency of v. 50: "a state of (continued) sleep is rejected for all believers," whereas "transformation is promised for all believers" (Perriman, "Paul and the Parousia," 515), and "all" means both living and dead Christians (recall 1 Thess 4:16c–17).

Again, the euphemism of falling asleep is employed; see NOTES on 7:10, 39. In this verse Paul expresses in positive fashion what was implicit in the negative answer of v. 50. For a Jewish parallel stating a similar transformation, see *Syr. Apoc. Bar.* 51.10.

The reading of v. 51, *ou koimēthēsometha, pantes de allagēsometha*, "we shall not fall asleep, but we shall all be changed," is found in MSS B, Dc, K, P, Ψ, 81, 614, and in many ancient versions, and it is used in almost all critical editions of the Greek NT today. After the death of Paul, however, and that of the Corinthian addressees (and well before the parousia), this reading was seen to be problematic, and the neg. *ou* was transferred by copyists to the second clause: "We shall all fall asleep, but we shall not all be changed" (in MSS ℵ, A*, 0243, C, 33, 1739). A conflated reading, with *ou* in both clauses, is found in MSS P⁴⁶, Aᶜ, and was read by Origen.

A more radical change, however, is found in MS D*, in VL, Vg, and read by Marcion and Tertullian, which changes *koimēthēsontai*, "we shall fall asleep," to *anastēsometha, ou*, "we shall arise, but we shall not all be changed" (see

Metzger, *TCGNT*, 502). This last reading, because it was used in the Vg (*omnes quidem resurgemus, sed non omnes immutabimur*), dominated much of the Latin theological tradition of the Western Church for centuries (see further Brandhuber, "Die sekundären Lesarten"; Jones, "Vulgate Text"; Oppenheim, "I Kor. 15,51"; Romeo, "Omnes quidem resurgemus"; Saake, "Kodikologisch"; Vaccari, "Il testo").

52. *in an instant, in the twinkling of an eye, at the last trumpet.* Three further apocalyptic stage props are adopted by Paul to describe the resurrection of the dead. The first two phrases occur only here, and nowhere else in the NT or LXX. *Atomos* is actually an adj., "indivisible," but it is substantivized and denotes an indivisible moment of time. The noun *ripē* actually means "a throwing," the swing or force by which something is thrust forward; used of an eye, it means its "rapid movement," hence "twinkling." Mss P⁴⁶, D*, F, G, 0243, 6, 1739 read rather *ropē*, which has the same meaning.

The "trumpet" as an apocalyptic trapping is found in Zech 9:14; Isa 27:13; Joel 2:15; 2 Esdras 6:23; Rev 8:2, 6, 13; 11:15 (seven of them); 1 Thess 4:16; Matt 24:31; *Protevangelium Jacobi* 8.3 (*salpinx kyriou*); *Or. Sibyll.* 4.174 (*OTP*, 1:388); 1QM 7:13–14 (description of the eschatological war between the sons of light and the sons of darkness). It is often a trapping that accompanies a theophany, as in Exod 19:13, 16, 19; Zech 9:14. Because its sound will be heard at "the end" (v. 24), it is called the "last."

For the trumpet will sound, and the dead will be raised imperishable, and we shall all be changed. Paul makes himself and the Corinthian Christians whom he is addressing the subjects of the remarkable transformation that is to take place at the parousia of the risen Lord, but he has no idea when it will take place. He speaks of *hoi nekroi*, "the dead," without any limit or restriction, and says of them, *egerthēsontai aphthartoi*, "will be raised imperishable," using the same verb as that employed for Christ in the kerygma of v. 4 and subsequently in vv. 12–17; and the implication is that the raising and the change will be produced by God. On *aphthartoi*, see v. 42c. Some MSS (A, D, F, G, P) read *anastēsontai*, "will rise," instead of *egerthēsontai*, "will be raised," a reading undoubtedly influenced by 1 Thess 4:16b.

53. *For what is perishable must don imperishability, and what is mortal, immortality.* Lit. "this perishable thing must put on itself . . . , and this mortal thing. . . ." The substantivized neut. adj. refers to *sōma*, and the dem. adj. *touto*, used four times here, undoubtedly refers to Paul's own body, which he expects will undergo change and don imperishability and immortality, involving continuity and discontinuity. Even though he mentions in the second clause *athanasia*, "immortality," it almost certainly has to be understood in a generic sense of "not dying," because it expresses the opposite of *to thnēton*, "the mortal," and the whole argument in this chapter has been about the OT concept of bodily resurrection (recall Dan 12:2), and not the Greek philosophical idea of "immortality" and its implied dichotomy of "body" and "soul" in the Greek, esp. Platonic, sense. For the idea of "donning, putting on" in the afterlife, see 2 Cor 5:2, 4, which is a passage similar to this one, but with a different thrust (see Gillman, "Thematic Comparison").

Paul uses the aor. mid. infin., *endysasthai*, "put on itself," in the sense of undergoing a transformation, making it depend on the impersonal verb *dei*, "it is necessary," which apocalyptically expresses the inevitable result of divine action.

54. *When what is perishable dons imperishability and what is mortal dons immortality, then the saying that stands written will come true.* Lit. "when this perishable thing . . . this mortal thing." The first clause, in effect, repeats v. 53, as a preparation for the coming Scripture quotation. A shorter form of it is preserved in some MSS (P⁴⁶, ℵ*, 088, 0121a, 0243, 1739*): *hotan de to thnēton touto endysētai tēn athanasian*, "When that which is mortal dons immortality" (see Metzger, *TCGNT*, 502). Here Paul speaks of two elements of discontinuity (imperishability and immortality), not of three, *pace* Sider ("Pauline Conception," 438); "freedom from sin" is not mentioned at all.

Noteworthy is the formula used to introduce the coming OT quotations, *tote genēsetai ho logos ho gegrammenos*, which has its Hebrew counterpart in CD 7:10–11, *bbw' hdbr 'šr ktwb bdbry yš'yh*, "when the saying will come (true) which was written in the words of Isaiah"; see also CD 19:7 (cf. *ESBNT*, 13, 46–47).

Death has been swallowed up in victory. Or "by victory." Paul quotes at first a form of Isa 25:8, which in the MT reads, *billaʿ hammāwet lāneṣaḥ*, "He [the Lord] will swallow up death forever" [*or* "completely"]. The words are taken from the so-called Isaiah Apocalypse (24:1–27:13), and they speak of the consummation of God's work on earth, His eschatological judgment, victory, and banquet for his people. The LXX, however, reads: *katepien ho thanatos ischysas*, "Death having become strong has swallowed up [the people?]," which makes little sense in its context. Paul's form of the saying preserves the sense of the MT, even if it casts them in the pass. voice and renders the last word, *lāneṣaḥ*, "forever," as *eis nikos*, "in victory," a possible translation of the prep. phrase also attested in Aquila and Theodotion (see Morissette, "Un midrash," 169; cf. Harrelson, "Death and Victory," 152–55; Rahlfs, "Über Theodotion-Lesarten," 183–84). What is important for Paul is that the "last enemy" (15:26) proleptically has been destroyed; "victory" over death has been achieved. Moreover, the passive is divine (ZBG §236), in that God has conquered death. (Some MSS [P⁴⁶, B] read here and in v. 55 *neikos* instead of *nikos*; it does not mean "strife," however, for it is merely an itacistic spelling of *nikos*.)

55. *Where, O death, is your victory? / Where, O death, is your sting?* Paul's second quotation of Scripture is a form of Hos 13:14, which in the MT reads:

'ĕhî dĕbārêkā māwet,	I shall be your plagues, Death;
'ĕhî qŏṭābĕkā šĕ'ôl,	I shall be your destruction, Sheol!

Hosea's words mean that the Lord will punish Israel and Ephraim with the destruction of death and the underworld. The LXX retains the sense of the Hebrew but renders the words differently,

pou hē dikē sou, thanate;	Where is your penalty, Death?
pou to kentron sou, hadē;	Where is your sting, Hades?"

Paul uses the LXX form but repeats *nikos* from his form of Isa 25:8 to replace *dikē*, "penalty," thus radically changing the sense of Hosea's words in the first of the clauses quoted. He uses the words in an entirely different meaning, not only changing a key word, but wresting the sayings from their original context to serve his own purpose. For him, death has now lost its fearsome control over humanity. Human beings may still die, but their mortality is but a transit to a better life. The noun *kentron*, "goad," is found in LXX Prov 26:3, used in a different sense; here it denotes the "prickly sting" that the goad should produce, but no longer can, because Hades has lost its power (see Harrelson, "Death and Victory," 155–57).

56. *The sting of death is sin, and the power of sin is the law.* The sting that death has lost, according to the Scripture that Paul has quoted, suggests to him a further development. This bit of Pauline theology is awkward in this context, and some commentators think that the verse is either an interpolated gloss (Heinrici) or else a genuine Pauline comment, secondarily added later (J. Weiss, *1 Cor*, 380). Lindemann (*1 Cor*, 371) notes that v. 57 follows better on v. 55 than it would on v. 56; but "there are no solid reasons to justify the many attempts to strike out this verse as a later gloss" (*TDNT*, 3:667; see also Horn, "1 Korinther 15,56").

In any case, Paul does not explain further the meaning of these statements and expects that the Corinthians will understand what he means by them. They have to be understood in light of what Paul has written elsewhere about the relation of the law to sin and death, especially in his letter to the Romans, where he will personify them as three actors on the stage of human history, which began with Adam in Eden. Sin entered the world of human beings through Adam, and Death through Sin (Rom 5:12), and they still dominate the lives of humans. Sin, moreover, has power over them because of the law, for not only "through the law comes the real knowledge of Sin" (Rom 3:20), because it unmasks Sin's character as a violation of God's will (Rom 7:7, 13), but the prescriptions of the law, if they are not observed, produce transgressions of it (Gal 3:19). So the law—good, just, and holy though it is in itself (Rom 7:12)—indirectly promotes the reign of Sin (Rom 4:15), because of which "all die" (1 Cor 15:22). What Paul says in this verse explains what he presupposed in vv. 20–28 above (see Söding, "Die Kraft"; cf. Hollander and Holleman, "Relationship"; Horn, "Ein exegetischer Stachel"; Vlachos, "Law, Sin, and Death").

57. *But thanks be to God! He grants us the victory through our Lord Jesus Christ.* Paul praises and expresses his thanks to God and invites all Christians to do the same with him, when they realize the continuing victory over sin and death that comes through the Lord, the risen Christ. It is not a prize that Christians themselves have won in their struggles of this life, but a "victory" that God has enabled them to enjoy and share with their fellow believers. Cf. Rom 7:25, where Paul gives thanks to God through Christ in a very similar way; cf. 2 Cor 2:14; 8:16; 9:15 (see Banks, "Romans 7:25a"). He gives thanks for the "victory," because this is the second major affirmation about the resurrection of the dead in this pericope; for the first, see v. 52, "In an instant . . . we shall be changed." With this affirmation, Paul concludes his arguments about the resurrection of the dead.

58. *Consequently, my dear brothers, be steadfast, unshaken, devoting yourselves*

at all times to the work of the Lord. Paul's final exhortation of the Corinthian Christians is generic, as he urges them to steadfast devotion to the service of the Lord. This means ridding themselves of all skepticism about the resurrection of the dead and renewing a dedication to the gospel as it has been preached to them. To his usual term of address, Paul adds *agapētoi,* "beloved (brothers)," as in Phil 4:1 (cf. 1 Cor 4:14).

The phrase *to ergon tou kyriou,* "the work of the Lord," will appear again in 16:10 as a way of expressing the evangelical ministry, in which both Paul and Timothy are engaged. Cf. Phil 3:30, where Epaphroditus's ministry is character-ized as "the work of Christ." In each case, the subj. gen. expresses the one who has assigned the task to Paul, Timothy, or Epaphroditus. Here the phrase has a broader comprehension, denoting all that Corinthian Christians do in their ser-vice of the Lord, and the gen. is rather objective. Such service is more important than all disputatious denials of the resurrection of the dead or queries about its na-ture; that is why Paul recommends it to them.

knowing that in the Lord your toil is not in vain. If there were no resurrection of the dead, their labor in serving the Lord might well be in vain, but Paul ends by as-suring them otherwise, alluding to 15:14. For their "toil," being done "in the Lord," has saved it from being without effect in their lives and future existence (see PAHT §PT121). His words echo those of the Book of Isaiah, who consoled Israel in light of God's promise to create a new heaven and a new earth (65:23). Cf. 1 Thess 3:5; 2 Chr 15:7.

BIBLIOGRAPHY

Banks, R., "Romans 7.25a: An Eschatological Thanksgiving?" *ABR* 26 (1978) 34–42.

Brandhuber, P., "Die sekundären Lesarten bei 1 Kor. 15, 51: Ihre Verbreitung und Entste-hung," *Bib* 18 (1937) 303–33, 418–38.

Delobel, J., "The Fate of the Dead according to 1 Thes 4 and 1 Cor 15," *The Thessalonian Correspondence* (BETL 87; ed. R. F. Collins; Louvain: Peeters/Leuven University, 1990) 340–47.

García Pérez, J. M., "1 Co 15,56: ¿una polémica contra la ley judía?" *EstBíb* 60 (2002) 405–14.

Gewalt, D., "1 Thess 4, 15–17; 1 Kor 15, 51 und Mk 9, 1 – Zur Abgrenzung eines 'Herren-wortes,' " *LB* 51 (1982) 105–13.

Gillman, J., "A Thematic Comparison: 1 Cor 15:50–57 and 2 Cor 5:1–5," *JBL* 107 (1988) 439–54.

——, "Transformation in 1 Cor 15, 50–53," *ETL* 58 (1982) 309–33.

Green, W. S. (ed.), *Approaches to Ancient Judaism* (Missoula: Scholars, 1978).

Harrelson, W. J., "Death and Victory in 1 Corinthians 15:51–57: The Transformation of a Prophetic Theme," *Faith and History: Essays in Honor of Paul W. Meyer* (ed. J. T. Carroll et al.; Atlanta: Scholars, 1990) 149–59.

Hollander, H. W., and J. Holleman, "The Relationship of Sin, Death, and the Law in 1 Cor 15:56," *NovT* 35 (1993) 270–91.

Horn, F. W., "1 Korinther 15,56 – ein exegetischer Stachel," *ZNW* 82 (1991) 88–105.

Jeremias, J., " 'Flesh and Blood Cannot Inherit the Kingdom of God' (I Cor. xv. 50)," *NTS*

2 (1955–56) 151–59; repr. in *Abba* (Göttingen: Vandenhoeck & Ruprecht, 1966) 298–307.

Jones, A., "The Vulgate Text of I Cor. xv, 51 and the Greek Text," *Scripture* 2 (1947) 45–48.

Löhr, G., "1 Thess 4:15–17: Das 'Herrenwort,'" *ZNW* 71 (1980) 269–73.

Luedemann, G., "The Hope of the Early Paul: From the Foundation-Preaching at Thessalonika to 1 Cor. 15:51–57," *PRSt* 7 (1980) 195–201.

Merklein, H., "Der theologe als Prophet: Zur Funktion prophetischen Redens im theologischen Diskurs des Paulus," *NTS* 38 (1992) 402–29.

Morissette, R., " 'La chair et le sang ne peuvent hériter du règne de Dieu' (*I Cor.*, *xv*, 50)," *ScEs* 26 (1974) 39–67.

———, "Un midrash sur la mort (I Cor., xv, 54c à 57)," *RB* 79 (1972) 161–88.

Olson, M. J., *Irenaeus, the Valentinian Gnostics, and the Kingdom of God (A.H. Book V): The Debate about 1 Corinthians 15:50* (Lewiston, NY: Mellen, 1992).

Oppenheim, P., "1 Kor. 15, 51: Eine kritische Untersuchung zu Text und Auffassung bei den Vätern," *TQ* 112 (1931) 92–135.

Perriman, A. C., "Paul and the Parousia: 1 Corinthians 15. 50–57 and 2 Corinthians 5. 1–5," *NTS* 35 (1989) 512–21.

Rahlfs, A., "Über Theodotion-Lesarten im Neuen Testament und Aquila-Lesarten bei Justin," *ZNW* 20 (1921) 182–99, esp. 183–84.

Romeo, A., " 'Omnes quidem resurgemus' seu 'Omnes quidem nequaquam dormiemus' (I Cor. 15, 51)," *VDom* 14 (1934) 142–48, 250–55, 267–75, 313–20, 328–36, 375–78.

Saake, H., "Die kodikologisch problematische Nachstellung der Negation (Beobachtungen zu 1 Kor 15,51)," *ZNW* 63 (1972) 277–79.

Sebastian, K. M., "The Victory over Death," *Jeevadhara* 9 (1979) 128–38.

Söding, T., " 'Die Kraft der Sünde ist das Gesetz' (1 Kor 15,56): Anmerkungen zum Hintergrund und zur Pointe einer gesetzeskritischen Sentenz des Apostels Paulus," *ZNW* 83 (1992) 74–84; repr. *Das Wort vom Kreuz: Studien zur paulinischen Theologie* (WUNT 93; Tübingen: Mohr [Siebeck], 1997) 93–103.

Swete, H. B., "The Resurrection of the Flesh," *JTS* 18 (1916–17) 135–41.

Vaccari, A., "Il testo 1 Cor. 15,51," *Bib* 13 (1932) 73–76.

Vlachos, C. A., "Law, Sin, and Death: An Edenic Triad? An Examination with Reference to 1 Corinthians 15:56," *JETS* 47 (2004) 277–98.

Wevers, J. W., *Notes on the Greek Text of Genesis* (SBLSCS 35; Atlanta: Scholars, 1993).

ADDITIONAL BIBLIOGRAPHY ON RESURRECTION (15:1–58)

Biser, E., *Paulus, der letzte Zeuge der Auferstehung: Antworten für heute* (Schlüssel zur Bibel; Regensburg: Pustet, 1981).

Boer, M. C. de, *The Defeat of Death: Apocalyptic Eschatology in 1 Corinthians 15 and Romans 5* (JSNTSup 22; Sheffield: Sheffield Academic, 1988).

Boers, H. W., "Apocalyptic Eschatology in I Corinthians: An Essay in Contemporary Interpretation," *Int* 21 (1967) 50–65.

Borchert, G. L., "The Resurrection: 1 Corinthians 15," *RevExp* 80 (1983) 401–15.

Bynum, C. W., *The Resurrection of the Body in Western Christianity, 200–1336* (Lectures on the History of Religions Sponsored by the American Council of Learned Societies 15; New York: Columbia University Press, 1995).

Candlish, R. S., *Studies in First Corinthians 15: Life in a Risen Savior* (Grand Rapids: Kregel Publications, 1989).

Cavallin, H. C. C., *Life after Death: Paul's Argument for the Resurrection of the Dead in I Cor 15* (ConBNT 7; Lund: Gleerup, 1974).

Cullmann, O., *Immortality of the Soul or Resurrection of the Dead?* (London: Epworth, 1958).

Flood, E., "Paul on the Resurrection," *CR* 69 (1984) 140–44.

Frutiger, S., "La mort, et puis . . . avant?: 1 Corinthiens 15," *ETR* 55 (1980) 199–229.

Greshake, G., and J. Kremer, *Resurrectio mortuorum: Zum theologischen Verständnis der leiblichen Auferstehung* (Darmstadt: Wissenschaftliche Buchgesellschaft, 1986).

Harris, M. J., "Resurrection and Immortality in the Pauline Corpus," *Life in the Face of Death: The Resurrection Message of the New Testament* (ed. R. N. Longenecker; Grand Rapids: Eerdmans, 1998) 147–70.

Holleman, J., *Resurrection and Parousia: A Traditio-Historical Study of Paul's Eschatology in 1 Corinthians 15* (NovTSup 84; Leiden: Brill, 1996).

Kwiran, M., *The Resurrection of the Dead: Exegesis of 1 Cor. 15 in German Protestant Theology from F. C. Baur to W. Künneth* (Basel: F. Reinhardt, 1972).

Mason, J. P., *The Resurrection according to Paul* (Lewiston, NY: Mellen, 1993).

Moiser, J., "1 Corinthians 15," *IBS* 14 (1992) 10–30.

Mussner, F., " 'Schichten' in der paulinischen Theologie dargetan an 1 Kor 15," *BZ* 9 (1965) 59–70.

Pagels, E. H., " 'The Mystery of the Resurrection'. A Gnostic Reading of 1 Corinthians 15," *JBL* 93 (1974) 276–88.

Plank, K. A., "Resurrection Theology: The Corinthian Controversy Reexamined," *PRSt* 8 (1981) 41–54.

Porter, S. E., M. A. Hayes, and D. Tombs (eds.), *Resurrection* (JSNTSup 186; Sheffield: Sheffield Academic, 1999).

Rahner, K., *Man in the Church* (Theological Investigations 2; Baltimore: Helicon, 1963).

Ross, J. M., "Does 1 Corinthians 15 Hold Water?" *IBS* 11 (1989) 69–72.

Scaer, D. P., "Luther's Concept of the Resurrection in His Commentary on I Corinthians 15," *CTQ* 47 (1983) 209–24.

Sloan, R., "Resurrection in I Corinthians," *SwJT* 26/1 (1983) 69–91.

Trummer, P., *Anastasis: Beitrag zur Auslegung und Auslegungsgeschichte von I Kor. 15 in der griechischen Kirche bis Theodoret* (Dissertationen der Universität Graz 1; Vienna: Notring, 1970).

Verburg, W., *Endzeit und Entschlafene: Syntaktisch-sigmatische, semantische und pragmatische Analyse von 1 Kor 15* (FzB 78; Würzburg: Echter-V., 1996).

Vorster, J. N., "Resurrection Faith in 1 Corinthians 15," *Neotestamentica* 23 (1989) 287–307.

Wagner, G., "If Christians Refuse to Act, then Christ Is Not Risen: Once More 1 Corinthians 15," *IBS* 6 (1984) 27–39.

Watson, D., "Paul's Rhetorical Strategy in 1 Corinthians 15," *Rhetoric and the New Testament: Essays from the 1992 Heidelberg Conference* (JSNTSup 90; ed. S. E. Porter and T. H. Olbricht; Sheffield: Sheffield Academic, 1993) 231–49.

V. CONCLUSION (16:1–24)

◆

40   A. COLLECTION FOR GOD'S DEDICATED PEOPLE (16:1–4)

16:1 Now for the collection for God's dedicated people: As I ordered the churches of Galatia, so you too should do. 2 On the first day of every week, each one of you should lay something aside and store it up, in keeping with your income, so that there will be no collections at the time when I come. 3 When I arrive, I shall send those whom you accredit with letters to carry your gift to Jerusalem. 4 If it will be fitting for me to go too, they will go along with me.

COMMENT

Paul has brought his discussion of the problem of the resurrection of the dead to an end, as well as the other various problems that have been brought to his attention either by reports or the letter that the Corinthian Christians sent him (7:1). As he now brings this letter to a close, he turns to another topic, which once again is introduced by *peri de*. In this case, those words may very well introduce a topic that was inquired about in the letter that Paul received from the Christians of Corinth, because it is likely that he had already said something about the collection, to which he now refers, in the (lost) letter mentioned in 5:9 above. The few verses that he devotes to the collection for the poor among the Christians of "Jerusalem" (16:3) give merely a few concrete instructions about how one is to take it up and send it on. If Paul were making this request for the first time, he would undoubtedly be giving more of a background for his request than he now supplies in vv. 2–4. One need only read what he has written already about his eagerness to remember the poor in Gal 2:10, and will write about aid for God's dedicated people in Jerusalem that he will mention in his letter to the Romans (15:25–27, 31) to see how he treats it when he suggests it to a congregation that he writes to for the first time. Later he will devote a more detailed and anxious appeal to the Corinthians for the poor of Jerusalem in 2 Corinthians 8 and 9 (where the difference of approach in those chapters argues for an origin of those chapters in different contexts, a problem that marks that conflated letter).

The collection itself was the result of a decision that Paul mentions was made at the Jerusalem "Council" (Gal 2:10): "They would have us remember the poor," which Paul said that he was eager to do. From Rom 15:26 one learns that it came to be thought of as "some contribution (*koinōnia*) for the poor of the saints in Jerusalem." There Paul mentions both Macedonia and Achaia as having kindly decided to share in that effort, as he exhorts the Christians of Rome to consider helping too. His main argument there is that "if Gentiles have come to share in the spiritual blessings of Jerusalem Christians, they ought to be of service to them in material things" (Rom 15:27). So Paul undoubtedly sought to make the Gentile Christians of such places as Macedonia and Achaia aware of the solidarity that they had with Christians of the mother church of Jerusalem and Judea. In writing to the Corinthians about the collection now, he is speaking to Christians who actually live in Achaia. So the reference in his letter to the Romans to "Achaia" would suppose as its background that about which he now writes. Lindemann (*1 Cor*, 374), following others, sees this topic as a concrete follow-up on 15:58, "your toil," so that it makes a good sequel to the end of the discussion in that chapter.

In Acts, the only time that the collection is mentioned is when Paul defends himself before the governor Felix. There he says that "after an absence of several years, I had come to bring alms to the people of my race and to make my offerings" (Acts 24:17). Luke has clearly not emphasized the importance of the collection to the same extent as did Paul himself. The "alms" were meant actually for converted Jews (Rom 15:26), but there is no indication in any of Paul's letters that he would have excluded "people of my race" from sharing in the help that he was bringing (as Rom 15:31 might imply, where he mentions his anxiety about the welcome that he would encounter there from "unbelievers in Judea"). Luke has simply understood the collection that Paul was bringing to Jerusalem as another instance in his story of alms for Israel (Luke 7:5; Acts 10:2), as Berger has well explained the historical context of the Pauline collection ("Almosen für Israel"). As in Israel of old, "almsgiving" was understood as a form of righteousness (*ṣĕdāqāh*) and as an expression of belonging to God's people, so too the collection that Paul was urging Corinthian Christians to take up would be a sign of their unity and solidarity with the dedicated people of the mother church of Judea, where the good news of the gospel was preached for the first time.

NOTES

16:1. *Now for the collection for God's dedicated people.* Lit. "Now concerning the collection for the saints" (see NOTE on 1:2; cf. 6:1–2); with *peri de* Paul announces a new topic (see NOTE on 7:1). The *hagioi*, "saints," are mentioned in the context of the collection also in 2 Cor 8:4; 9:1, 12; Rom 15:25–26, 31. In v. 3, he specifies that they are those in Jerusalem, as he does also in Romans (see Keck, " 'Poor among the Saints' "). Paul uses here and in v. 2 *logeia*, "collection," a word that is not often found in Greek literary texts, but appears in business documents on papyri and in inscriptions for a "collection of money" or "tax" (*TDNT*, 4:282–83;

MM, 377); it occurs also in texts mentioning collections for sacred purposes. Since Paul uses it only here, the term may have appeared in the Corinthians' letter to Paul (7:1), whence he has picked it up from their questions about it.

In 2 Cor 8:4; 9:13; Rom 15:26, the word for "collection" is rather *koinōnia*, "sharing, contribution," and in 2 Cor 9:1, 12, 13, it is *diakonia*, "service," since a collection could be understood as a form of service. That may be the sense in v. 15 below. Despite what some commentators have said about the meaning of *logeia*, it does not mean a "tax" imposed by the Jerusalem church on Gentile Christian communities. Paul clearly speaks of the collection as a voluntary contribution made by the churches of Achaia to help the poor of the mother church. Nothing in the text makes it sound like the Temple tax levied annually on Jews everywhere.

The background for the collection, however, may very well have been the Jewish custom of almsgiving for Israel, the donations given by sympathizers and new converts to Judaism, whose "righteous deeds" connoted in time "alms" (for Israel) and were understood not only as a means of expiating sins (Sir 3:30; Tob 4:7–11), but of manifesting unity and solidarity with God's people. Paul would have been well acquainted with such a custom and was seeking to instill its counterpart in Gentile Christians, whom he wanted to relate to the Jewish Christians of the mother church.

As I ordered the churches of Galatia, so you too should do. Lit. "as I gave instructions to," with the same verb that occurred in 9:14. The phrase, "churches of Galatia," occurs in the prescript of the letter to the Galatians (1:2), where the plur. *ekklēsiai* denotes particular churches of the area of Northern Galatia. Paul recommends to Corinthian Christians the example of those churches, as he did for Thessalonians, when he counseled them to imitate the churches of Judea (1 Thess 2:14), albeit in another manner of imitation.

According to the account in Acts, Paul would have first evangelized Galatian territory on his second missionary journey (16:6) and passed through that area again at the beginning of the third journey on his way to Ephesus (18:23). Shortly after his arrival in Ephesus, he wrote his letter to the Galatian churches, and Gal 4:13 implies that a second visit to Galatia has already taken place. While there, on that second visit, he must have "ordered" the Galatians to consider taking up a contribution for the "poor" of Jerusalem, as he now admits here. He mentioned such "poor" in Gal 2:10, but there is actually no further instruction or order to the Galatians about the collection in that letter itself. Now, however, Paul repeats the counsel to the Corinthians that he says he gave the Galatians, along with some specific instructions how they are to do it (see Wedderburn, "Paul's Collection," 96–97).

Galatia was the area where the ancient *Galatai* settled after their invasion of the lower Danube area and Macedonia and their defeat by the Aetolians in 278 B.C. Having then crossed the Hellespont after that defeat, they settled between the Sangarius and Halys Rivers, in the three towns of Ancyra, Pessinus, and Tavium. The Galatai were eventually subdued by the Romans about 189 B.C., and during the Mithridatic Wars they remained loyal to Rome. As a result, their territory was gradually expanded. About 40 B.C., some areas of Pisidia, Phrygia, Lycaonia, and

Isauria became part of Galatia. When its last king, Amyntas, willed his land to Rome, it was incorporated into the Roman province of *Galatia*, which covered more than the early Galatian country of northern Asia Minor. Paul wrote his letter to the churches of North Galatia from Ephesus ca. A.D. 54 (see further *NJBC*, 780–81).

2. *On the first day of every week.* Or "every Sunday" (BDAG, 910). Lit. "on every (day) one of the week." For the use of a cardinal numeral instead of an ordinal in such dating, see Mark 16:2; Acts 20:7. The best MSS read the sing. *sabbatou*, whereas others (ℵ², 075, 0121, 0243, 1739) have the more usual plur. (*sabbatōn*) of the Greek word, which actually means "sabbath" or "seventh day," but which came to be used in both the sing. and the plur. for a "period of seven days" or "week."

The "seventh day" as a day of rest was not a Greek or Roman custom; the Greeks normally used three ten-day cycles in a month, and the Romans and Etruscans had an eight-day cycle, with seven work days and a market day (*nundinae*). The seven-day cycle actually dates back to Mesopotamian, especially Babylonian practice, but Josephus claimed that in his day there was not "a city (*polis*) of the Greeks or any barbarian, not even a single nation (*ethnos*), where our custom of not working on the seventh day has not been imported" (*Ag.Ap.* 2.39 §282; see *New Docs*, 9:113–18). At any rate, early Christians followed the Jewish practice and recognized at first the seventh day as the sabbath (*sabbaton*), which was followed by the "first (day) of the week" (*mia sabbatōn*, lit. "[day] one of the week," Mark 16:2; Matt 28:1; or *prōtē sabbatōn*, "first [day] of the week," Mark 16:9). Toward the end of the first century A.D., Christians began to speak of the first day of the week as *hē kyriakē hēmerā*, "the Lord's day" (Rev 1:10; cf. *Did.* 14.1), thus honoring it as the day when they recalled his resurrection.

Sunday is singled out for the collection by Paul probably because of the liturgical assembly on that day, which would remind the Corinthian Christians of periodically laying aside something for the poor, perhaps too as a way of honoring the Lord on that day (see Llewelyn, "Use of Sunday"; but also Young's "Response"). Paul, however, does not say anything about the Corinthians coming together on the first day of the week, not using *synerchomenōn hymōn*, as in 11:18. Cf. Acts 20:7: "On the first day of the week, when we gathered to break bread."

each one of you should lay something aside and store it up, in keeping with your income. Lit. "let each one of you put (aside) for himself, storing up whatever one gains." The phrase *par' heautō*, "for himself," is problematic, appearing with the distributive pron. *hekastos* and the verb *tithétō*; it probably is meant to stress the individual contribution; but sometimes it has been understood as "at home" (Buck, "Collection," 2; cf. Xenophon, *Memor.* 3.13.3); and in Josephus, *Ant.* 9.4.4 §68, it even occurs alongside *oikade*, "in his own house." Nothing is said, however, where the collection of what is stored up should take place.

The verb *euodoō* means "go along a good road," and in the NT it is used only in the pass. voice in a figurative sense, "prosper, succeed in business, gain." Paul instructs individual Corinthian Christians ("each one of you") to put something aside regularly so that an amount can accumulate and become a fitting gift for the poor of Jerusalem. The last clause in Paul's instruction ("in keeping with your income") shows that he was aware of the diversity of economic status among the Christians of Roman Corinth.

so that there will be no collections at the time when I come. Paul does not want the collection to be taken up at the last minute, and he is seeking to avoid having to spend time going about begging or pressuring Corinthian Christians personally. They are to give freely what they can and want to, and he implies that none of it will be coming to him. His own ministry is concerned with more important things than seeing to the collection on his arrival in Corinth; recall the statement about his priorities in 9:15.

3. *When I arrive, I shall send those whom you accredit with letters to carry your gift to Jerusalem.* Lit. "your (sign of) favor, benefaction," a rare use of *charis*, which is found again in 2 Cor 8:4, 6–7, 19. Paul speaks of his coming visit to Corinth, which he will explain more in vv. 5–9. He will then expect the Christians to choose individual trustworthy members of their church to be emissaries who will carry letters of recommendation along with the gift to the Christians of Jerusalem, and he promises to write for them such commendatory letters. Collins ("Reflections," 41) suggests that Paul uses the plur. *epistolōn*, "letters," because "each member of the delegation should be accompanied by a letter of recommendation," even though the plur. of *epistolē* was often used in ancient Greek for a single missive (BDAG, 381). The choice of such emissaries is to be made, however, with scrutiny: *hous ean dokimasēte*, "whomever you consider qualified."

Their destination is *Ierousalēm*; this is the only time the site of the mother church is mentioned in this letter. Cf. Rom 15:19, 25, 26, 31. It was the royal city of the Davidic dynasty, where the Temple, Israel's place of worship, was duly located; there alone was it to sacrifice to Yahweh. To it Jews of the diaspora sent gifts for sacred purposes (Philo, *Leg. ad Gaium* 23 §§156, 312–13, 315). It became also the matrix of Christianity, because there the Christ-event took place. For Paul it was likewise the place where he met those who were "apostles before me" (Gal 1:17a), where he learned from Cephas (Gal 1:18), and where his gospel met with apostolic approval (Gal 2:2). Here and in Romans he writes *Ierousalēm*, whereas in Gal 1:17–19 and 2:1 he spells the name *Hierosolyma*, using the form commonly found in extrabiblical Greek writers. It originally was a neut. plur. form, but eventually was treated as fem. sing. (see Matt 2:3; 3:5), undoubtedly because that was the gender of the more Semitic form *Ierousalēm* (see Gal 4:25–26; Acts 5:28; LXX).

4. *If it will be fitting for me to go too, they will go along with me.* Lit. "also worthy of me to travel." Paul uses the gen. of the articular infin. with the adj. *axion* (see BDF §400.3). At this time, he has not yet decided that he will carry the collection for the poor to Jerusalem. By the time that he writes Romans just a few months later, the decision will have been made, as Rom 15:25–26 makes clear. Nothing is said about the conditions under which it would become *axion*, "fitting, worthy, proper," for Paul to travel to Jerusalem. Robertson-Plummer (*1 Cor*, 387) speculate that the reason why Paul is expressing this doubt is that the Corinthians were "niggardly, or at least somewhat backward in giving." That might be, but Garland

(*1 Cor*, 756) also speculates that that attitude would "rankle the Corinthians." Who can say?

BIBLIOGRAPHY

Allo, E.-B., "La portée de la collecte pour Jérusalem dans les plans de Saint Paul," *RB* 45 (1936) 529–37.
Bassler, J. M., *God & Mammon: Asking for Money in the New Testament* (Nashville: Abingdon, 1991) 89–101.
Beckheuer, B., *Paulus und Jerusalem: Kollekte und Mission im theologischen Denken des Heidenapostels* (Europäische Hochschulschriften 23/611; Frankfurt am M./New York: P. Lang, 1997).
Berger, K., "Almosen für Israel: Zum historischen Kontext der paulinischen Kollekte," *NTS* 23 (1976–77) 180–204.
Buck, C. H., Jr., "The Collection for the Saints," *HTR* 43 (1950) 1–29.
Cerfaux, L., " 'Les Saints' de Jérusalem," *ETL* 2 (1925) 510–29; repr. in *Recueil Lucien Cerfaux* (3 vols.; Gembloux: Duculot, 1954–62), 2:389–413.
Collins, R. F., "Reflections on 1 Corinthians as a Hellenistic Letter," *The Corinthian Correspondence* (BETL 125; ed. R. Bieringer), 39–61.
Eckert, J., "Die Kollekte des Paulus für Jerusalem," *Kontinuität und Einheit: Für Franz Mussner* (ed. P.-G. Müller and W. Stenger; Freiburg im B.: Herder, 1981) 65–80.
Georgi, D., *Remembering the Poor: The History of Paul's Collection for Jerusalem* (Nashville: Abingdon, 1992).
Keck, L. E., " 'The Poor among the Saints' in Jewish Christianity and Qumran," *ZNW* 57 (1966) 54–78.
——, "The Poor among the Saints in the New Testament," *ZNW* 56 (1965) 100–129.
Llewelyn, S. R., "The Use of Sunday for Meetings of Believers in the New Testament," *NovT* 43 (2001) 205–23.
Nickle, K. F., *The Collection: A Study in Paul's Strategy* (SBT 48; London: SCM: Naperville, IL: Allenson, 1966).
Verbrugge, V. D., *Paul's Style of Church Leadership Illustrated by His Instructions to the Corinthians on the Collection: To Command or Not to Command* (San Francisco: Mellen Research University Press, 1992) 25–94.
Wedderburn, A. J. M., "Paul's Collection: Chronology and History," *NTS* 48 (2002) 95–110.
Young, N. H., " 'The Use of Sunday for Meetings of Believers in the New Testament': A Response," *NovT* 45 (2003) 111–22.

41   B. PAUL'S TRAVEL PLANS (16:5–9)

16:5 I shall come to you, after I pass through Macedonia; for I shall be going through Macedonia. 6 Perhaps I shall stay or even spend the winter with you so that you may send me on my way, wherever I shall be going. ⁷For I do not want to see you now only in passing. I hope to spend some time with you, if the Lord permits. ⁸But I shall stay on in Ephesus until Pentecost. ⁹A great door for effective work has opened to me, but there are many opponents.

COMMENT

Having instructed the Corinthian Christians about the way a collection is to be taken up for the poor of Jerusalem, Paul proceeds to inform them of his plans for traveling so that he will be able to be with them soon in Corinth. He has already told them that he was coming (4:19; 11:34; cf. 14:6) and even hinted at it in v. 3 of the preceding paragraph. Now he explains what route he will take before he arrives. The mention of Macedonia means that he will be traveling to Corinth mostly over land, across the Hellespont, and then through northern Greece, before descending toward Athens and Corinth. He writes that he will probably even spend the winter with them, but he intends to stay on in Ephesus, from which this letter comes, until Pentecost. Hence he is compoing this letter to the Corinthians in the spring of the year A.D. 57 (see INTRODUCTION pp. 43, 48).

Paul elsewhere speaks of his travel plans toward the end of letters: 2 Cor 12:14–13:1; Rom 15:22–32; Phlm 22. In them he does not merely reveal his route(s), but states his desire to be with the addressees. With this letter, he is expressing his epistolary presence (*parousia*) to the Christians of Roman Corinth, but in mentioning his travel plans he makes clear his desire to be with them personally .

Paul speaks of the opportunity of evangelization that he still has in Ephesus, but also of the opposition that continues to face him there; yet he gives no hint as to who the "many opponents" might be. Recall what he said in 15:32 about fighting with "wild beasts" in this city.

NOTES

16:5. *I shall come to you, after I pass through Macedonia; for I shall be going through Macedonia.* Lit. "when I am going through," a second aor. subjunct. in a future temporal clause. In 4:19 Paul promised that he would come to the Corinthians "very soon, if the Lord wills"; but now we see how that promise takes a more definite shape. Paul does not plan to sail from Ephesus to Corinth, as the account in Acts 18:18–19 indicates might have been a possibility; rather he will travel overland at least as far as Troas, whence he would take a ship to Neapolis, near Philippi. His plan to pass through Macedonia is recorded also in Acts 19:21, "Paul made up his mind to travel through Macedonia and Achaia again and then go on to Jerusalem"; cf. Acts 20:2. That Lucan account joins Achaia, where Corinth is, to Macedonia so that it agrees with what Paul writes here. The pres. *dierchomai* has future connotation (BDF §323.1).

That Paul at some point in his missionary career worked in Macedonia is clear from Phil 4:15, where he speaks graciously to the Philippians for the aid he received from them, "at the beginning of (his) evangelization, when I came from Macedonia." Suggs would have us believe that *en archē tou euangeliou,* "at the beginning of the evangelization," means that "Paul's initial activity was among the Macedonians" ("Concerning the Date"), i.e., that Paul began his missionary endeavors among Gentiles of Macedonia. However, that interpretation of Phil 4:15 is far from certain. For Paul in an earlier letter has already hinted that his activity of evangelization had begun in "the regions of Syria and Cilicia," when he was still not known by sight to the churches in Judea, who had heard about him, that "he who once persecuted us is now preaching the faith he once tried to destroy" (Gal 1:21–23). Hence in Phil 4:15 Paul means "at the beginning of (his) evangelization" of Philippi, after a period of work in northern Greece or Macedonia.

Makedonia was the region in mountainous northern Greece, bordering on Illyria and the Nestos River; it stretched from the Aegean Sea to the Adriatic. Through it ran the Via Egnatia, a famous ancient road from Neapolis to Dyrrachium. The towns of Neapolis, Philippi, Thessalonica, and Berea, which Paul had evangelized, were part of the Roman province of Macedonia at this time.

Macedonia had been founded as a political area in the seventh century B.C. by kings residing at Edessa and Pella. Under Philip II (359–336 B.C.), it became the leading power in Greece. In 293 B.C. the Antigonids gained control, and their last king, Perseus, was defeated in 168 by the Romans. Then Macedonia was divided into four regions. In 148 B.C. it became a Roman province, and from A.D. 15–44 was governed by an imperial legate resident in Moesia; later it was made a senatorial province. Roman colonies were established in Dyrrhachium, Pella, and Philippi (see Davies, "The Macedonian Scene"; Edson, "Macedonia," 125–36; Lemerle, *Philippes et la Macédoine,* 1:7–68).

6. *Perhaps I shall stay or even spend the winter with you so that you may send me on my way, wherever I shall be going.* Lit. "but with you perhaps I shall stay," with the prep. phrase (*pros hymas* [BDAG, 875: "at, by, near," which is different from the meaning in v. 5]) put in the emphatic first position. Paul thus stresses that the Corinthian community is more important to him than Macedonia; that is because of the prominence of Roman Corinth as a town in Greece at that time. Winter was not the time for extensive travel, especially if it involved taking a ship at any point, because of what the Romans called *mare clausum,* "the closed Sea," when Mediterranean storms made travel by ship unmanageable (roughly October to March). As it eventually turns out, Paul did spend the winter of A.D. 57–58 in Corinth ("three months," Acts 20:3), whence he wrote the Epistle to the Romans (see *Romans,* 85–87). In Rom 15:24, Paul again expresses his expectation that that community will speed him on his way, in that case to Spain; but here he leaves his destination undetermined. As it turns out, he will go from Corinth to Jerusalem with the collection, before going from Jerusalem to Rome (as a prisoner).

The word *tychon* is the neut. accus. aor. ptc. of *tynchanō,* "happen, experience," used as an adv., "perhaps"; lit. it would mean something like "(if) it turns out that way" (BDF §424). It is found only here in the NT, apart from two instances in MS D of Luke 20:13 and Acts 12:15; but it was used often by Classical

Greek writers (Xenophon, *Anab.* 6.1.20; Ps.-Plato, *Alcib.* 2.140a, 150c; see LSJ, 1833).

7. *For I do not want to see you now only in passing.* The reason why Paul says this may be found in 11:34, where he promised to "give directives" about "other matters" when he would arrive in Corinth. His sojourn in Corinth will be of longer duration than that of his "passing" through Macedonia.

I hope to spend some time with you, if the Lord permits. Note the same sort of declaration in 4:19, with a similar condition; cf. Heb 6:3; Acts 18:21; Jas 4:15. Paul is stressing that all his future plans are dependent on God's will for him. In 2 Cor 1:15–17, Paul tells of a change of plans. Cf. Rom 1:10; 15:32, where Paul speaks similarly of God's will. A similar mode of expression is found at times in secular Greek writings: Ps.-Plato, *Alcib.* 1.135d; Josephus, *Ant.* 20.12.1 §267 (*kan to theion epitrepē*, "if the Deity allows").

8. *But I shall stay on in Ephesus until Pentecost.* I.e., in the city from which Paul writes this letter, which has been the center of his evangelization during his third missionary journey, recounted in Acts 18:23–20:38.

Ephesos was then the seat of the governor of the Roman province of Asia. In Paul's day, it was an Aegean seaport near the mouth of the Cayster River. At that time the river was navigable up to the city, which lay about 5 km to the east, but which during the course of the centuries since has silted up, so that Efes today no longer seems to be a seaport town. It was a city where Jews had been granted Ephesian citizenship (Josephus, *Ant.* 12.3.2 §§125–26). For many Greek inscriptions dating from the Ephesus at this period, see Levinskaya, "Asia Minor," 137–52, esp. 143–48.

Whether Paul refers to "Pentecost" as a Jewish feast only, or as a Christian feast is difficult to say, since it is not known just when Christians began to celebrate Pentecost as a liturgical feast (*TDNT*, 6:52). More than likely, he means it in the Jewish sense; in any case, Paul is planning to leave Ephesus and to travel in the late Spring of that year.

Hē Pentēkostē was the "fiftieth day" from the morrow of Sabbath of Passover (Lev 23:15–16), the Feast of New Grain (Wheat); cf. Exod 23:16; 34:22; Deut 16:9–12. In Tob 2:1 it is known as "Pentecost, our feast, the festival of the Seven Weeks" (4QTob[a] ar [4Q196] 2:11: *ḥag šabûʿayyāʾ*, "Feast of Weeks"); cf. Greek Tob 2:1; 2 Macc 12:32. It was the first Jewish feast to be celebrated after Passover.

When Josephus speaks of Pentecost, he says, *hē pentēkostē hēn Hebraioi asartha kalousi*, "the fiftieth (day), which Jews call Asartha" (*Ant.* 3.10.6 §252). This name can only be Aramaic *ʿaṣartāʾ*, related to Hebrew *ʿăṣeret*, "solemn assembly." It means that first-century Palestinian Jews were celebrating Pentecost as "the Feast of Assembly," which accounts for the sojourn of many Jews from the diaspora in Jerusalem at the time of Peter's Jerusalem address to "all the house of Israel" (Acts 2:36) on the "day of Pentecost" (Acts 2:1). For the possibility of more than one Pentecost among some Palestinian Jews, see the mention of three feasts of 50 days in the Qumran Temple Scroll, 11QTemple[a] 18:10–13 (new grain); 19:11–14 (new wine); 21:12–16 (new oil); cf. *Acts,* 234–35.

The story of the first Christian Pentecost is recounted by Luke in Acts 2:1–41.

620 COMMENTARY AND NOTES

There the emphasis falls not so much on the gift of the Spirit ("the promise of the Father") and its effect on the disciples in their Spirit baptism as on the first opportunity that they had to bear official testimony to the risen Christ and proclaim him to "the whole house of Israel." That proclamation took places on the first great feast after the Passover, on which Jesus of Nazareth was crucified. Pentecost was also celebrated as a feast of the renewal of the covenant that God had made with Israel (perhaps alluded to in 2 Chr 15:10–12; 1QS 1:8–2: 18; and clearly in *Jubilees* 6). The significance, then, of this famous feast of postexilic Judaism assured it to become a Christian feast as well, but one does not know when the liturgical celebration of it among early Christians began (see Marshall, "Significance of Pentecost").

9. *A great door for effective work has opened to me.* Lit. "a door has opened for me, great and effective." This explains Paul's decision to continue on in Ephesus for a while. In 2 Cor 2:12, Paul will express almost the same opportunity about Troas, another town in Asia Minor north of Ephesus. Cf. Acts 14:27, where Luke recounts the return of Paul and Barnabas to Antioch after the first missionary journey and tells how Paul spoke of God opening "the door of faith to the Gentiles." That is more or less the sense of the image used by Paul in this verse; cf. Col 4:3.

but there are many opponents. I.e., many who are standing in Paul's way as he tries to bring the gospel to people in that provincial capital. In admitting this, Paul is explaining further why he feels called to continue his work of evangelization in Ephesus, before returning to the Christians of Roman Corinth. Among the opponents may be the "wild beasts" of 15:32, if that expression is to be understood figuratively (see NOTE there).

Recall too the Lucan account of the riot of the Ephesian silversmiths in Acts 19:23–41. Even though it is described at first as "no small disturbance concerning the Way," it is eventually directed against Paul, who not only in Ephesus, but in all Asia, "has convinced and led astray a great number of people," telling them that "handmade gods are no gods at all" (19:26). In Phil 3:18 Paul also speaks of "many" who do not appreciate his evangelization. For the way Paul's plans develop, after he has written these verses, see 2 Cor 1:15; 2:12; 12:18. At first, while still in Ephesos, he rewords what he has written here, then proceeds to Troas, hoping to find Titus there, and then goes still farther into Macedonia, where he eventually finds Titus, who was returning to him.

BIBLIOGRAPHY

Davies, P. E., "The Macedonian Scene of Paul's Journeys," BA 26 (1963) 91–106.
Edson, C., "Macedonia," *Harvard Studies in Classical Philology* 51 (Cambridge: Harvard University Press, 1940) 125–36.
Koester, H. (ed.), *Ephesos, Metropolis of Asia: An Interdisciplinary Approach to Its Archaeology, Religion, and Culture* (Harvard Theological Studies 41; Valley Forge: Trinity Press International, 1995).
Lemerle, P., *Philippes et la Macédoine orientale à l'époque chrétienne et byzantine* (Bibliothèque des Écoles Françaises d'Athènes et de Rome 158; 2 vols.; Paris: de Boccard, 1945).

Levinskaya, I., "Asia Minor," *The Book of Acts in Its Diaspora Setting* (Book of Acts in Its First Century Setting 5; Grand Rapids: Eerdmans, 1996) 137–52.

Marshall, I. H., "The Significance of Pentecost," *SJT* 30 (1977) 347–69.

McDonald, W. A., "Archaeology and St. Paul's Journeys in Greek Lands," *BA* 3/2 (1940) 8–24.

Potin, J., *La fête juive de la Pentecôte* (2 vols.; LD 65; Paris: Cerf, 1971).

Suggs, M. J., "Concerning the Date of Paul's Macedonian Ministry," *NovT* 4 (1960) 60–68.

42   C. COMMENDATION OF TIMOTHY AND APOLLOS (16:10–12)

16:10 If Timothy comes, see that he has nothing to fear in your company; for he is doing the work of the Lord, just as I am. 11 No one, then, should disdain him. Send him on his way in peace, so that he may come to me, for I am awaiting him with the brothers. 12 As for our brother Apollos, I strongly urged him to come to you with the brothers; but it was not at all his will to come now. He will come when he has the opportunity.

COMMENT

Paul continues his concluding remarks by commending to the Christians of Corinth one of his fellow workers, Timothy, about whom he seems to have some concern, and he also informs them about the preacher Apollos. The Corinthians seemingly wanted to have the latter come to them again, and perhaps had even inquired about his return in the letter that they had sent to Paul (7:1).

In vv. 10–11, Paul adopts the style of *epistolē systatikē*, "letter of recommendation," even if its brevity prevents it from being considered a real instance of such a letter; see Rom 16:1–2, where Paul similarly recommends Phoebe, a minister of the church of Cenchreae. In these verses, Paul expresses his appreciation of Timothy and commends him to proper treatment by the Christians of Corinth.

NOTES

16:10. *If Timothy comes, see that he has nothing to fear in your company.* Lit. "that he may be without fear among you." Timothy has already been mentioned in 4:17, where Paul said that he was sending him on to Corinth (see NOTE there); so his "if" really means "when." In Acts 19:22, Luke records that Paul "sent off two of his assistants, Timothy and Erastus, into Macedonia," but that Paul himself "stayed on for a while in Ephesus." That accords with what Paul writes here, even if there is no mention of Erastus. Now, however, he is anxious that Timothy be made to feel at home among the Christians of Roman Corinth and encounter no undue or negative reactions in his dealings with them, especially because he is Paul's fellow worker (*synergos*, 1 Thess 3:2; Rom 16:21). This implies that Timothy is not the bearer of this letter to the Corinthian Christians and that this letter is expected to arrive in Corinth before Timothy does. Paul writes *blepete hina*, "see that," the same expression that he used in a negation in 8:9. Surprisingly, Paul recommends that Timothy should not have to fear any danger in Corinth.

for he is doing the work of the Lord, just as I am. The phrase *to ergon kyriou* has already been met in 15:58 (see NOTE there); now it is a designation of the activity in which both Timothy and Paul are engaged. Paul implies that Timothy should receive as much attention from the Corinthians as he himself would because of this common ministry on behalf of the gospel and the spread of the Christian church, especially among Gentiles.

11. *No one, then, should disdain him.* I.e., treat him as of no account because of his youth (see 1 Tim 4:12) or his timidity (2 Tim 1:7), a characterization that may not be meant for Timothy himself, but for the reader (see Hutson, "Was Timothy Timid?").

Send him on his way in peace. I.e., let him know that he enjoys your good will. *Eirēnē*, "peace," has already appeared in 1:3 (see NOTE there); 7:15; 14:33. Paul employs an OT motif about traveling "in peace" (1 Sam 20:42; 2 Kgs 5:19) and urges his addressees to expedite Timothy's further journey, because Paul is awaiting his arrival.

so that he may come to me, for I am awaiting him with the brothers. There is no indication about who "the brothers" might be. Acts 19:22 tells of Erastus being sent with Timothy to Macedonia, but who else could be meant is not clear. The prep. phrase, "with the brothers," could modify either "him" or the subj. of the verb, "I." More than likely, it is the fellow Christians who are accompanying Timothy who are meant. Cf. 2 Cor 8:18, 22 (is the unnamed "brother" Timothy?).

12. *As for our brother Apollos, I strongly urged him to come to you with the brothers.* Lit. "Concerning Apollos, (our) brother, I urged him much." Paul begins this verse with *peri de* (see NOTE on 7:1), marking a new topic, as Paul passes from the mention of Timothy to Apollos. The latter has been mentioned earlier: 1:12 (see NOTE there); 3:4–6, 22; 4:6, where he is spoken of as a preacher rivaling Paul and exercising a considerable ministry. The Lucan story of Apollos's journeys is found in Acts 18:24–19:1a. The commendation of Apollos that Paul's words imply stands in contrast to some of the remarks used about him earlier. It is clear that, even if Paul has not approved of preacher rivalries (chaps. 1–4), he felt no specific animosity toward Apollos, whom he now calls *adelphos*, "brother," and the latter's failure to come back to Corinth has nothing to do with Paul. Some MSS (‫א‬*, D*, F, G, and the Vg) read after the initial prep. phrase *dēlō hymin hoti*, "I make clear to you that" I strongly urged . . . , which merely emphasizes Paul's statement. Once again, who "the brothers" are is left unexplained. It seems likely that Paul mentions Apollos's delay in coming to Corinth because in their letter the Corinthian Christians had asked about him.

but it was not at all his will to come now. Lit. "it was not at all the will . . . ," there being no indication in the Greek as to whose will is meant; but it must be Apollos's will, since there is no reason to think that God's will is implied, although some commentators have understood it that way (J. Weiss, *1 Cor*, 385; Kümmel in Lietzmann, *1 Cor*, 196; *TDNT*, 3:59; Barrett, *1 Cor*, 391; Bruce, *1 Cor*, 160; Héring, *1 Cor*, 153). Lindemann (*1 Cor*, 382) rightly regards that as improbable; similarly Allo (*1 Cor*, 462); Robertson-Plummer (*1 Cor*, 392); Fee (*1 Cor*, 824); Kremer (*1 Cor*, 373). The text seems to suggest that Apollo was judging that the moment was not yet propitious for him to return; perhaps he was judging that way because he too was aware of the preacher rivalries and did not approve of them any more than Paul did, especially since they in effect pitted him against Paul.

He will come when he has the opportunity. I.e., when he finds the *kairos,* the proper time. It may indeed imply that Apollos is reluctant to return to Corinth so long as there is an Apollos group active there (see Robertson-Plummer, *1 Cor*, 393).

BIBLIOGRAPHY

Alexander, J. P., "The Character of Timothy," *ExpTim* 25 (1913–14) 277–85.
Hertling, L., "1 Kor 16,15 und 1 Clem 42," *Bib* 20 (1939) 276–83.
Hutson, C. R., "Was Timothy Timid? On the Rhetoric of Fearlessness (1 Corinthians 16:10–11) and Cowardice (2 Timothy 1:7)." *BR* 42 (1997) 58–73.

43   D. CONCLUDING EXHORTATION (16:13–18)

[16:13] Be on your guard. Stand fast in the faith; be courageous; be strong. [14] Let all your deeds be done in love. [15] You know that the household of Stephanas is the firstfruits of Achaia, and that they have devoted themselves to the service of God's dedicated people — so I urge you, brothers, [16] be submissive to such people and to every fellow worker and laborer (among them). [17] I was happy at the arrival of Stephanas, Fortunatus, and Achaicus, because they have made up for what was lacking from you. [18] They have refreshed my spirit as well as yours. So give recognition to such people.

COMMENT

Having given his instructions about the coming of Timothy and the news about Apollos's delay, Paul now adds general hortatory words to his concluding remarks. The transition to this paragraph is abrupt, and the paragraph mixes both exhortation (vv. 13–14, 15c–16, 18b) and information about Corinthians who have come to Paul in Ephesus (vv. 15ab, 17–18a). The caution expressed in vv. 13–14 has certainly nothing to do with Apollos; it has to be understood in a generic way, because Paul is using apocalyptic expressions in v. 13. Paul's counsel continues even after that until v. 18b is reached.

NOTES

16:13. *Be on your guard.* Lit. "be watchful" or "stay awake," an apocalyptic command also in the eschatological discourse of Mark 13:35, 37; cf. Mark 14:38; Rev 3:2–3. Paul's counsel is one of general alertness needed in the conduct of Christian life, which becomes a bit more specific in the following remarks, as Paul warns Corinthian Christians against threats to their faith.

Stand fast in the faith. I.e., in one's fundamental commitment to the gospel. The best comment on this advice is found in Phil 1:27, "Conduct yourselves in a manner worthy of the gospel so that, whether I come and see you or am absent, I may hear reports about you, that you are standing fast in one spirit, with one mind striving side by side for the faith of the gospel." Cf. Gal 5:1; Phil 4:1; 1 Thess 3:8; Rom 11:20. Here Paul speaks of "faith," the response to the preached gospel, not to "traditions that are the foundation of the community and that Paul passed on to them," *pace* Garland (*1 Cor*, 766).

be courageous; be strong. Lit. "act like a man; be mighty." The combination of the impvs. of *andrizomai* and *krataioō* imitates a combination of verbs found in LXX 2 Sam 10:12; Ps 27:14; 31:25 (= MT *ḥāzaq wĕ'ămaṣ*), intended to recommend a courageous and valiant stance or mode of action. See also LXX Deut 31:6, 7, 23; Josh 1:6, 7 (with a different second verb having the same meaning, *ischyein*). Cf. Eph 6:10.

14. *Let all your deeds be done in love.* What Paul urged in chap. 13 about the place of "love" in Christian life is now repeated in this short hortatory counsel at the end of his letter.

15. *You know that the household of Stephanas is the firstfruits of Achaia.* The Greek text of v. 15 is anomalous, for it begins with *parakalō de hymas, adelphoi,* "but I urge you, brothers," after which comes what is quoted in the lemma. Words like those used at the beginning of v. 15, however, are needed to introduce the subordinate *hina* clause, with which v. 16 begins, which is a strange anacoluthon. Following many other modern commentators, I have moved the introductory words *parakalō . . .* to the end of v. 15 so that they can lead up to v. 16. If one does not move the introductory words, one has to reckon with a parenthetic remark in the rest of v. 15 (see BDF §465).

In 1:16 Paul admitted that he had baptized Stephanas and his household; now we learn that they are *aparchē tēs Achaïas,* "the firstfruits of Achaia" (see NOTE on 15:20, *aparchē*), i.e., the first converts to Christianity in the Roman province of Achaia. The same description is given of Epaenetus (Rom 16:5), except that there it is for the province of "Asia" (which name strangely appears here instead of "Achaia" in MS P[46], a copyist's egregious error!). In Acts 17:34, Luke tells of a few Athenians, who had listened to Paul's discourse at the Areopagus and who "joined him and became believers; among these were Dionysius, a member of the Areopagus, and a woman named Damaris." That would have happened before Paul came from Athens to Corinth; so they too would have been among *aparchē tēs Achaïas*, in the Lucan story of Paul in Achaia, but Paul makes no mention of those Athenians. Some MSS (ℵ², D, 104, 629, 1175, 1241, 2464) add "and Fortunatus," whereas F, G add "and Fortunatus and Achaicus," scribal harmonizations with v. 17.

Achaïa would have been the most important part of Greece in Paul's day. It included the central part of the country (Aetolia, Acarnania, part of Epirus, Thessaly, and the Cyclades Islands) as well as the northern part of the Peloponnesus (from Elis to Megara). It was the center of political life especially from 280 to 146 B.C., when it was dominated by the Romans on the defeat of the Aegean League and the fall of Corinth to L. Mummius (see Pausanias, *Descr. Graec.* 7.16.7–10). Eventually, under Roman domination Augustus made it an independent senatorial province in 27 B.C. (Strabo, *Geogr.* 17.3.25), with a proconsul of pretorian rank residing in Corinth.

and that they have devoted themselves to the service of God's dedicated people. Lit. "to the service of the saints." The meaning of the phrase *eis diakonian tois hagiois* is debated. It could denote simply some generic service for the "saints" who were in need of it (so BDAG, 230); or it could mean some kind of specific aid or financial support for the saints (= the poor of Jerusalem), because *diakonia* is used in the financial sense in Acts 6:1; 11:29; 12:25. In this case, Stephanas and his household may have taken it upon themselves to render financial support to the "saints," presumably of Jerusalem. Although the sense of *diakonia* escapes us, Paul says that the Corinthian Christians would understand what he meant (*oidate*, "you know"). Lietzmann (*1 Cor*, 89) finds in the mention of *diakonia* "the roots of the office of *diakonoi* ["deacons"], which even in Rom 16:1 is known in Corinth's port of Cenchreae; cf. Phil 1:1." That may be reading too much into a noncommittal Pauline text, but *1 Clem.* 42.4 also speaks of the apostles having "appointed their first converts (*tas aparchas autōn*) . . . as bishops and deacons (*episkopous kai diakonous*) of future believers," thus using two of the words (*aparchē* and *diakon-*) that Paul uses here (see Hertling, "1 Kor 16, 15").

so I urge you, brothers. See NOTE at the beginning of v. 15.

16. *be submissive to such people and to every fellow worker and laborer (among them).* Lit. "that you too be submissive," a subordinate clause introduced by *hina*. Paul thus urges Corinthian Christians to be submissive to the leadership of Fortunatus and others who labor with him on their account, because they are exemplary Christians.

17. *I was happy at the arrival of Stephanas, Fortunatus, and Achaicus.* Stephanas has been known since 1:16 (see NOTE there); 16:15. Fortunatus and Achaicus are otherwise unknown Corinthian Christians, but a person with the Latin name, *Fortunatus*, is mentioned in *1 Clem.* 65, who may be the same person. The name *Achaikos* is a grecized form of a Latin name, *Achaicus*, meaning "somebody from Achaia" or "related to Achaia," and it implies that he, though a native of Achaia, may have been living elsewhere, where he was given this name. Meeks (*First Urban*, 56) regards him as a freedman colonist who came to Corinth from Italy.

Paul speaks of the *parousia* of these three Corinthians, using this noun in its basic sense of "presence," or perhaps better "arrival," i.e., the first stage of their presence; contrast the use of it in 15:23, where it is already the technical term denoting the second coming of the Lord (see NOTE there). What caused Paul's happiness is explained in the following clause.

because they have made up for what was lacking from you. Lit. "filled up your deficiency," i.e., my lack of you (or lack of information about you). Paul mentions his deprivation, but these three men have compensated for the absence of the Corinthian community. Instead of the poss. adj. *hymeteron,* some MSS (P⁴⁶, ℵ, A, Ψ, 075, and the Koine text-tradition) read rather the poss. pron. *hymōn,* which does not change the meaning much, being an obj. gen.

18. *They have refreshed my spirit as well as yours.* Lit. "have caused my spirit to rest." The three Corinthians refreshed Paul's spirit by supplying much information about what was going on in the community that Paul had founded not many years before; it is not said anywhere in this letter that the three of them brought to Paul the letter mentioned in 7:1, but they may have done so. Paul uses *pneuma* in the sense of his own human spirit, almost as the equivalent of his "self," as in Phil 4:23; Gal 6:18; Phlm 25 (see also NOTE on 2:11). How the three of them refreshed Paul's spirit is clear enough, but not so clear is how they refreshed the "spirit" of the Corinthians. Perhaps it means that the Corinthian community sent the three men as delegates to inquire of Paul his opinion concerning various problems that had arisen, and that this delegation of the three was already a source of consolation or refreshment for the community.

So give recognition to such people. At the end of v. 16 Paul counseled the Corinthians to be submissive to such "fellow workers and laborers"; now he adds his counsel that they acknowledge the contribution that these people have made to the community as a whole.

BIBLIOGRAPHY

See p. 623.

44   E. GREETINGS AND FINAL FAREWELL (16:19–24)

16:19 The churches of Asia send you greetings. Aquila and Prisca, together with the church at their house, send you many greetings in the Lord. 20 All the brothers greet you. Greet one another with a holy kiss. 21 I, Paul, write this greeting in my own hand. 22 If anyone does not love the Lord, let him be accursed! *Marana tha!* 23 The grace of our Lord Jesus be with you! 24 My love be with all of you in Christ Jesus!

COMMENT

Paul finally arrives at the end of his long letter to the Christians of Roman Corinth and, as usual, ends with a customary epilogue. He sends the community greetings from the churches of the province of Asia; from Aquila, Prisca, and the church that meets in their house; and from all the Christians that are with him. He himself sends the holy kiss greeting and pens it in his own handwriting, which means that he has dictated this letter to a scribe, who wrote it out for him. At the very end he adds a final (eschatological) curse and blessing, the latter in a triple formulation, the first of which is in Aramaic, *marana tha!*, "Our Lord, come!"

NOTES

16:19. *The churches of Asia send you greetings.* The word *ekklēsia* is again used in the plur., denoting particular communities in diverse locales of the province, as in 7:17; 11:16; 14:33, 34; 16:1. Because Paul is writing this letter to the Christians of Roman Corinth from Ephesus, the capital of the Roman province of Asia, he includes the churches of the province in the greetings that he is sending, probably to make the Corinthian Christians aware of their solidarity with another great body of Christians. Where the churches might be located is anyone's guess: Colossae, Hierapolis, Laodicea (Col 1:2; 2:1; 4:13); possibly the six other churches of Rev 1:11 (Smyrna, Pergamum, Thyatira, Sardis, Philadelphia, Laodicea). Verse 19 is missing in MS A, probably because of homoeoarcton (vv. 19 and 20 both begin with *aspazontai*).

Asia was the western Roman *provincia* in Asia Minor, which had been formed in 133 B.C., when the last king of Pergamum bequeathed his realm to the Romans. Alexander the Great had conquered the area in 334 B.C., and after his death the territory came under Seleucid control, until the kings of Pergamum succeeded in wresting it from the latter's domination. In time the province embraced areas of Mysia, Aeolis, Ionia, Lydia, Phrygia, and Caria, i.e., the Anatolian peninsula from Propontis in the north to the Mediterranean in the south. From the time of Augustus it was a senatorial province, governed by proconsuls, who usually resided in Ephesus (see further Chapot, *La province romaine*; Trebilco, "Asia," 291–362).

Aquila and Prisca, together with the church at their house, send you many greetings in the Lord. Lit. "greet you much in the Lord," with the sing. verb denoting the pair (but MSS B, F, G, 075, 0121, 0243, 33, 1729 read the plur. *aspazontai*). This married couple were collaborators of Paul at various stages of his second and third missionary journeys: "fellow workers of mine in Christ Jesus," who "risked their necks for me" (Rom 16:3–4). They are well known to the Corinthian community, as this greeting makes clear, because they once resided in Corinth, where Paul first made their acquaintance (Acts 18:2–3; see further Müller, "Priska und Aquila").

Akylas is a grecized form of the Latin cognomen *Áquila* (meaning "eagle"); cf. Cicero, *Philip. Or.* 11.6.14. Here it is the name of a Jewish tradesman, who appears in Rom 16:3–5a; Acts 18:2, 18, 22 (MS 614), 26; 2 Tim 4:19. In Acts he is described as *Pontikos tō genei*, "a man of Pontus by race/nation," originally a diaspora Jew from Pontus in Asia Minor on the Black Sea, who had shortly before arrived in Corinth from Italy along with his wife, who in Acts is called by the diminutive name *Priskilla*, "Priscilla" (18:2, 18, 26 [read here in some of MSS: A, C, D, F, G, K, L, P, Ψ]), whereas *Priska* is the form used in the Pauline corpus (read by P⁴⁶, ℵ, B, M, 33, 226). *Priska* is a grecized form of a fem. Latin adj. *prisca*, meaning "primitive, ancient." See further D. A. Kurek-Chomycz, "Is There."

Paul met Prisca and Aquila in Corinth, when he first arrived there. Shortly before, they had come to Corinth from Italy because "Claudius had ordered all Jews to leave Rome" (see INTRODUCTION pp. 37–40; cf. *Acts*, 619–25). Paul not only lodged with them, but plied the same trade as they, "for they were tent makers by trade" (Acts 18:3). They accompanied Paul when he left the Corinthian Christians toward the end of his second missionary journey and sailed to Syria with him (Acts 18:18). When they landed at Ephesus, Paul left Priscilla and Aquila there, as he continued on his journey to Caesarea Maritima, Jerusalem, and Antioch in Syria (thus ending his second journey, Acts 18:19–22). This explains why greetings from them are being sent from Ephesus to the Corinthian church in the conclusion of this letter. Were they already Christians when Paul first encountered them in Corinth? Probably, because Paul has already identified Stephanas and his household as the "firstfruits of Achaia" (v. 15), which he would not have been able to say, if he had been instrumental in the conversion of Prisca and Aquila.

"The church at their house" (*hē kat' oikon autōn ekklēsia*) is mentioned again in Rom 16:5. The phrase, *hē kat' oikon*, is ambiguous; it could mean either "according to (their) household," i.e., the church made up of members of the household of Aquila and Prisca; or it could refer to their material "house," in which they and other local Christians met regularly for worship, i.e., a house-church. The latter sense is more likely, and it is to be located probably in Ephesus itself. For the expression *hē kat' oikon ekklēsia*, see Phlm 2; Col 4:15; Ps.-Clem. *Recognitions* 10.71 (GCS 51.371). These, then, are the earliest references to groups of Christians meeting together for worship in individual houses. Undoubtedly in bigger towns there would have been more than one such church. Christians would have so met after they had broken away from the Jerusalem Temple and local synagogues in order to conduct their own prayer services and liturgies by themselves. The house-church was one of the factors in early Christianity that aided the spread of the gospel and contributed to the growth of the church, its structure, and its life. The mention of such house-churches also implies the centrality of the home in early Christian life. The household (*familia*) was the unit, and sometimes was even converted as a whole (Acts 16:33). There is evidence of such *domus ecclesiae* in later times at Rome (see further *Romans*, 736; Branick, *House Church*, 58–61; Filson, "Significance"; Gielen, "Zur Interpretation"; Klauck, *Hausgemeinde*; Vogler, "Die Bedeutung").

20. *All the brothers greet you.* I.e., all the Christians of Ephesus.

Greet one another with a holy kiss. Paul often ends a letter with a command to kiss one another (1 Thess 5:26; 2 Cor 13:12; Rom 16:16; cf. 1 Pet 5:14: "kiss of

love"). In speaking of a "holy kiss," Paul is safeguarding it from any erotic connotation. He may be using in this epistolary context what was perhaps a liturgical gesture at the celebration of the Lord's Supper; so the gesture is known later on
(Justin, *Apology* 1.65.2). "The admonitions to kiss one another serve to stress the
liberty to express without inhibition to all people of whatever background, rank or
gender, the ardour of *agapē* in any context. The 'holy kiss' is a public declaration
of the affirmation of faith: 'In Christ there is neither male nor female, Jew nor
Greek, slave nor free' (Gal 3.29)" (Klassen, "Sacred Kiss," 135). It was a concrete
manifestation of the unity and fellowship of Christians, no matter what their
social status might be. Cuming ("Service-Endings") argues that this clause, used
in the close proximity of v. 23, echoes the ending of an early church prayer service, which was nonsacramental, noneucharistic, at which the epistle was read.
Perhaps. In time it became known as "the kiss of peace," gathering the latter connotation from "the God of peace" (Rom 16:19; see further Benko, "The Kiss";
Ellington, "Kissing"; Hofmann, *Philema hagion*, 8–10; Perella, *Kiss Sacred and
Profane*, 12–18; J. A. T. Robinson, "Earliest Christian Liturgical Sequence").

21. *I, Paul, write this greeting in my own hand.* Lit. "the greeting in my hand, of
Paul," which is elliptical and verbless. Cf. Gal 6:11, where Paul makes a similar
statement at the end of a dictated letter, as he calls attention to the coarse, large
letters with which he writes in contrast to the trained scribe's skilled handwriting.
By writing in his own hand, Paul is, in effect, authenticating the letter, as it were,
"signing" it, for he even includes his name in the gen. case. Cf. Phlm 19; imitated
in Col 4:18; 2 Thess 3:17 (see Nijenhuis, "Greeting").

22. *If anyone does not love the Lord, let him be accursed.* Lit. "let him be anathema" (*or* "a curse"); on which see NOTE on 12:3. In this statement, Paul does not
use the verb *agapaō*, but rather *phileō*, "have affection for," which appears
nowhere else in his uncontested writings and may, then, reveal that he is employing a stereotyped formula (see the COMMENT on 13:1–13 for the different words
for love in Greek). Its meaning is: Whoever does not love the Lord, rejects him
and does not belong to him (see Spicq, "Comment"). No indication is given
about who *tis*, "anyone," might be.

In any case, this anathema is a strange ending to a Pauline letter, especially because it occurs in the midst of other greetings and benedictions. It may, however,
be occasioned by Paul's realization of the opposition to him that still exists in Corinth and perhaps will even be exaggerated because of what he writes in this letter.
In contrast to this curse, he concludes the letter with three blessings. Recall Gal
1:8–9, where a similar curse is leveled against anyone, even an angel from heaven,
who would preach a gospel different from that preached by Paul. Cf. Acts 23:14.

Marana tha! This is the first blessing that Paul invokes on the Corinthian community. He prays in Aramaic and asks thereby that the risen Christ make his presence felt among the Corinthians soon. In praying in Aramaic, Paul is in effect
following early Christian tradition and its recollection that Jesus of Nazareth himself prayed in Aramaic (Mark 14:36; cf. Gal 4:6; Rom 8:15). Once again he alludes to the parousia of the Lord, as he did in 4:5; 5:5; 11:26; 15:23.

The blessing that Paul utters in Aramaic finds its Greek counterpart at the end of the Book of Revelation (22:20): *Amēn, erchou kyrie Iēsou*, "Amen. Come, Lord Jesus!" It also appears as part of a final blessing of the eucharistic liturgy recorded in *Did.* 10.5–6: *ei tis hagios estin, erchesthō. ei tis ouk esti, metanoeitō. Maranatha. Amēn*, "If anyone is holy, let him/her come. If anyone is not, let him/her repent. Our Lord, come! Amen."

As the saying is preserved in Greek majuscule MSS of this letter, it is written in *scriptio continua* as one word, **MAPANAΘA** (see N. Schmidt, "*Maranatha*"). It has been debated for decades how one should divide the letters, whether *māran* '*ăthā*' or *mārānā*' *thā*', and how to interpret the second element, whether as a ptc. ('*āthē*, "is coming"), a perf. ('*ăthā*', "has come"), or an impv. ('*ăthā*' or *thā*', "come!"). Because the word with a suffix for "our Lord" has turned up recently in a contemporary Aramaic text from Qumran as *mārānā*', the first question about the division of the letters is now settled in the way that Halévy years ago understood it ("Découvertes," 9), and not in the way Rüger ("Zum Problem") would have it. In 4QEnoch[b] (4Q202) 1 iii 14 (= *1 Enoch* 9:4), one finds *['nth hw'] mrn' rb' [hw]*' (= *mārānā*' *rabbā*'), "[you are] our great Lord." This form of the 1st pers. plur. suffix (*-nā*') occurs also in Ezra 5:12; Dan 3:17; in Elephantine texts, *AP* 81:110, 115, and elsewhere in Palestinian Aramaic (1QapGen 19:12, 13; 21:5; 11QtgJob 26:5). Hence the Greek form *maranatha* is most likely an elision of Aramaic *mārānā*' '*ăthā*', "our Lord, come!" Theoretically, Greek *tha* could also represent an apocopated Aramaic impv. *thā*' (i.e., one that has lost the initial *aleph* with its reduced vowel); but such an impv. is found only in later Aramaic, esp. Syriac. So it is better explained as an elision of two words, one ending with a long *ā*' and the following beginning with '*ă*-. This imperatival form thus would agree with the Greek form preserved in Rev 22:20, and so it would put an end to the speculation about Greek *tha* representing an Aramaic pres. ptc. or a perf. indic., as many Greek patristic writers and the Syriac tradition interpreted it (see further Fitzmyer, "New Testament Kyrios").

Because *marana tha* follows upon the imprecation *ētō anathema* and because it was not rightly understood, it was considered for centuries to be an invocation reinforcing and supporting the preceding imprecation. Such an understanding is found even in Canon 75 of the Fourth Council of Toledo (A.D. 633): *qui contra vestram* [sic, read *nostram*] *definitionem praesumpserit, anathema, maranatha (hoc est) perditio in adventum Domini sit & cum Iuda Ischariot partem habeat . . . ,* "Whoever presumes (to speak) against our definition, let him be anathema, maranatha (that is) perdition at the coming of the Lord, and let him rank with Judas Iscariot. . . ." * In modern times, such an interpretation of *maranatha* has been advocated by Peterson, Bornkamm, Kuhn, Moule. The last mentioned notes that the phrase is preceded by a curse or ban formula also in *Did.* 10.5–6 and in Rev 22:20. Such an interpretation, however, stems almost certainly from a later period, when the original sense of *marana tha* was lost, and it was thought to be a

---

*J. D. Mansi, *Sacrorum conciliorum nova et amplissima collectio, Tomus decimus* (Firenze: Zatta, 1764) 639.

foreign curse (a sort of abracadabra), supporting the immediately preceding *ētō anathema*. That even accounts for the misspelling of the word in a fourth- or fifth-century Greek inscription, *maranathan* (*CIG*, 4. 9303).

Another problem with the word is whether the coming of the Lord is linked to the Eucharist. This link is made in the *Did.* 10.5–6, at least as it is usually interpreted. There is no certainty, however, that Paul is thinking of the coming of the eucharistic Lord. Some modern commentators even resort to the maledictory interpretation of the word in order to avoid this eucharistic link.

Finally, even when writing a Greek letter to the Christians of Roman Corinth, Paul concludes with an untranslated Aramaic blessing, using a fixed formula well known in the early Christian communities, even as *abba* was, although unlike the latter it is not accompanied by a Greek translation, *abba, ho patēr*, "Abba, Father" (Mark 14:36, repeated by Paul in Gal 4:6; Rom 8:15). The formulas stem from the mother church in Judea and were utilized even in Gentile Christian communities, where Aramaic was never used as *lingua franca*.

23. *The grace of our Lord Jesus be with you!* The second blessing is Paul's usual concluding form, which occurs also in 1 Thess 5:28; Rom 16:20; cf. 2 Thess 3:18. Paul prays that the risen Lord's favor (*charis*) will be shown to the Corinthian community; as in 2 Cor 8:9; 12:9. In 2 Cor 13:13 the formula becomes triadic. Mss $\aleph^2$, A, C, D, F, G, Ψ, 075, 0121, 0243, 1739, etc. add *Christou*.

24. *My love be with all of you in Christ Jesus!* The third blessing is an expression of Paul's own affection (*hē agapē mou*) for the Corinthian community despite all the troubles he has been having with it. This is the only place in the Pauline corpus that Paul speaks of his love for the addressees. Recall 4:14–15, 21. Cf. 2 Cor 12:14. Many MSS ($\aleph$, A, C, D, Ψ, 075, 1739[c], and the Koine text-tradition) add *Amēn*.

A *subscriptio* is found in many manuscripts; the main ones are *pros Korinthious a'* (found in MSS $\aleph$, A, B*, C, [D*, F, G, Ψ], 33, 81); but in B1, P one finds *pros Korinthious a' egraphē apo Ephesou* (see 16:8); but D[2], 075, 1739 have *pros Korinthious a' egraphē apo Philippōn dia Stephanou kai Phortounatou kai Achaïkou kai Timotheou*, "First (letter) to the Corinthians was written from Philippi by Stephanus, Fortunatus, and Achaicus and Timothy"!

BIBLIOGRAPHY

Bahr, G., "Paul and Letter Writing in the Fifth [sic, read First] Century," *CBQ* 28 (1966) 465–77.

——, "The Subscriptions in the Pauline Letters," *JBL* 87 (1968) 27–41.

Banks, R. R., *Paul's Idea of Community* (rev. ed.; Peabody, MA: Hendrickson, 1994).

Benko, S., "The Kiss," *Pagan Rome and the Early Christians* (Bloomington: Indiana University Press; London: Batsford, 1984) 79–102.

Branick, V., *The House Church in the Writings of Paul* (ZSNT; Wilmington: Glazier, 1989).

Button, B., and F. J. van Rensburg, "The 'House Churches' in Corinth," *Neotestamentica* 37 (2003) 1–28.

Chapot, V., *La province romaine proconsulaire d'Asie* (Paris: Bouillon, 1904).

Cuming, G. J., "Service-Endings in the Epistles," *NTS* 22 (1975–76) 110–13.

Ellington, J., "Kissing in the Bible: Form and Meaning," *BT* 41 (1990) 409–16.

Filson, F. V., "The Significance of the Early House Churches," *JBL* 58 (1939) 105–12.

Gielen, M., "Zur Interpretation der paulinischen Formel *hē kat' oikon ekklēsia*," *ZNW* 77 (1986) 109–25.

Gnilka, J., "Die neutestamentliche Hausgemeinde," *Freude am Gottesdienst: Aspekte ursprünglicher Liturgie* (ed. J. Schreiner; Stuttgart: Katholisches Bibelwerk, 1983) 229–42.

Harrison, J., "Paul's House Churches and the Cultic Associations," *RTR* 58 (1999) 31–47.

Hofmann, K.-M., *Philema hagion* (BFCT 2/38; Gütersloh: Bertelsmann, 1938).

Klassen, W., "The Sacred Kiss in the New Testament: An Example of Social Boundary Lines," *NTS* 39 (1993) 122–35.

Klauck, H.-J., *Hausgemeinde und Hauskirche im frühen Christentum* (SBS 103; Stuttgart: Katholisches Bibelwerk, 1981).

Kurek-Chomycz, D. A., "Is There an 'Anti-Priscan' Tendency in the Manuscripts? Some Textual Problems with Prisca and Aquila," *JBL* 125 (2006) 107–28.

Müller, C. G., "Priska und Aquila: Der Weg eines Ehepaares und die paulinische Mission," *MTZ* 54 (2003) 195–210.

Nijenhuis, J., "This Greeting in My Own Hand—Paul," *TBT* 19 (1981) 255–58.

Perella, N. J., *The Kiss Sacred and Profane: An Interpretative History of Kiss Symbolism and Related Religio-Erotic Themes* (Berkeley: University of California Press, 1969).

Richards, E. R., *The Secretary in the Letters of Paul* (WUNT 2/42; Tübingen: Mohr [Siebeck], 1991).

Schumacher, R., "Aquila und Priscilla," *TGl* 12 (1920) 86–99.

Spicq, C., "Comment comprendre *philein* dans I Cor. xvi.22?" *NovT* 1 (1956) 200–204.

Thraede, K., "Ursprünge und Formen des 'Heiligen Kusses' im frühen Christentum," *JAC* 11–12 (1968–69) 124–80.

Trebilco, P., "Asia," *The Book of Acts in Its Graeco-Roman Setting* (Book of Acts in Its First Century Setting 2; Grand Rapids: Eerdmans, 1994) 291–362.

Vogler, W., "Die Bedeutung der urchristlichen Hausgemeinde für die Ausbreitung des Evangeliums," *TLZ* 107 (1982) 785–94.

Weima, J. A. D., *Neglected Endings: The Significance of the Pauline Letter Endings* (JSNTSup 101; Sheffield, UK: Sheffield Academic, 1994).

BIBLIOGRAPHY ON *MARANATHA*

Adam, A., "Erwägungen zur Herkunft der Didache," *ZKG* 68 (1957) 1–47, esp. 6 n. 14.

Albright, W. F., and C. S. Mann, "Two Texts in I Corinthians," *NTS* 16 (1969–70) 271–76.

Bickell, G., "Die neuentdeckte 'Lehre der Apostel' und die Liturgie," *ZKT* 8 (1884) 400–412, esp. 403 n. 3.

Black, M., "The Maranatha Invocation and Jude 14, 15 (*1 Enoch* 1:9)," *Christ and Spirit in the New Testament: In Honour of Charles Francis Digby Moule* (ed. B. Lindars and S. S. Smalley; Cambridge: Cambridge University Press, 1973) 189–96.

Bornkamm, G., "The Anathema in the Early Christian Lord's Supper Liturgy," *Early Christian Experience*, 169–76, 178–79.

Deissmann, A., *Die Urgeschichte des Christentums im Lichte der Sprachforschung* (Tübingen: Mohr [Siebeck], 1910) 25–29.

Dunphy, W., "Maranatha: Development in Early Christology," *ITQ* 37 (1970) 294–308.

Emerton, J. A., "*Maranatha* and *Ephphata*," *JTS* 18 (1967) 427–31.

Field, F., *Notes on the Translation of the New Testament: Being the Otium norvicense (pars tertia)* (Cambridge: Cambridge University Press, 1899) 180.

Fitzmyer, J. A., "New Testament Kyrios and Maranatha and Their Aramaic Background," *TAG,* 218–35, esp. 223–29 (with older bibliography).

Halévy, J., "Découvertes épigraphiques en Arabie," *REJ* 9 (1884) 1–20.

Harris, J. R., *The Teaching of the Apostles (Didachē tōn apostolōn) Newly Edited, with Facsimile, Text and a Commentary* . . . (Baltimore: Johns Hopkins University Press; London: Clay and Sons, 1887), pl. VII, fol. 79a, line 12.

Heitmüller, W., "Zum Problem Paulus und Jesus," *ZNW* 13 (1912) 320–37, esp. 333–34.

Hommel, E., "Maran atha," *ZNW* 15 (1914) 317–22.

Horner, G., "A New Papyrus Fragment of the *Didaché* in Coptic," *JTS* 25 (1923–24) 225–31.

Klein, G., "Maranatha," *RGG* 4 (1960) 732–33.

Kuhn, K. G., "*Maranatha,*" *TDNT,* 4:466–72.

Langevin, P.-E., *Jésus Seigneur et l'eschatologie: Exégèse de textes prépauliniens* (Studia 21; Bruges/Paris: Desclée de Brouwer, 1967) 168–208.

Leclerq, H., "Maranatha," *DACL* 10/2 (1932) 1729–30.

Luke, K., "Maranatha (1 Cor 13:22 [sic, read 16:22])," *BiBh* 10 (1984) 54–73.

Moule, C. F. D., "A Reconsideration of the Context of *Maranatha* (1 Cor 16.22)," *NTS* 6 (1959–60) 307–10.

Nöldeke, T., Review of E. Kautzsch, *Grammatik des Biblisch-Aramäischen,* GGA 1884/2, 1014–23, esp. 1023.

Peterson, E., *Heis Theos: Epigraphische, formgeschichtliche und religionsgeschichtliche Untersuchungen* (FRLANT 41; Göttingen: Vandenhoeck & Ruprecht, 1926) 130–31.

Robinson, J. A. T., "Traces of a Liturgical Sequence in 1 Cor. 16$^{20-24}$," *JTS* 4 (1953) 38–41; repr. as "The Earliest Christian Liturgical Sequence?" in *Twelve New Testament Studies* (SBT 34; London: SCM, 1962) 154–57.

Rüger, H. P., "Zum Problem der Sprache Jesu," *ZNW* 59 (1968) 113–22, esp. 120–21.

Salguero, J., "Maranatha," *CB* 26 (1969) 73–80.

Schmidt, C., "Das koptische Didache-Fragment des British Museum," *ZNW* 24 (1925) 81–99, esp. 98.

Schmidt, N., "*Maranatha,* I Cor. xvi.22," *JBL* 13 (1894) 50–60; 15 (1896) 44 n. 14.

Schulz, S., "Maranatha und Kyrios Jesus," *ZNW* 53 (1962) 125–44.

INDEX OF COMMENTATORS AND
MODERN AUTHORS

◆

Authors mentioned in COMMENTS and NOTES normally are not listed here, but rather those in the GENERAL BIBLIOGRAPHY, and in the bibliographies at the end of INTRODUCTION sections and at the end of pericopes.

Simon, W. G. H., 107
Sisti, A., 247, 557
Sklba, R. J., 397
Sleeper, C. F., 557
Slingerland, D., 39, 47
Sloan, R., 610
Smalley, S. S., 461, 462, 600, 632
Smallwood, E. M., 38, 47
Smedes, L. B., 507
Smit, D. J., 55, 321
Smit, J. F. M., 150, 247, 350, 351, 376,
    397, 404, 486, 507, 523
Smith, B. D., 453
Smith, D. C., 425
Smith, D. E., 36, 453
Smith, L. P., 504
Smit-Sibinga, J., 557
Smyth, H. W., 66, 68
Snyder, E. H., 534
Snyder, G. F., 107, 557
Soards, M. L., 107, 124, 189, 260
Söding, T., 93, 150, 167, 190, 351, 397,
    486, 507, 609
Somerville, R., 107
Son, S. A., 272
Songer, H. S., 350
Sontheimer, W., 29
Sorg, T., 486
Souter, A., 98
South, J. T., 115, 247
Sparks, H. F. D., xv, 190
Spawforth, A. J. S., 33, 36
Spencer, W. D., 227
Spicq, C., xxiii, 107, 227, 311, 425, 507,
    632
Spilly, A. P., 125, 129
Spittler, R. P., 115
Spörlein, B., 566
Sprague, R. K., 486
Staab, K., 97
Stam, C. R., 107
Standaert, B., 507
Stanley, A. P., 107
Stanley, C. D., 115
Stanley, D. M., 227, 566
Stauffer, E., 205
Stedman, R. C., 115
Steen, C. C. van den, 99
Stegmann, B. A., 601
Stein, A., 260

Stein, R. H., 304
Steinmann, A., 312
Stemberger, G., xix, 601
Stendahl, K., 451, 523
Stenger, W., 566, 616
Sterling, G. E., 190
Stettler, C., 538
Steward-Sykes, A., 53
Steyn, G. J., 127, 129, 260
Stichele, C. Vander, 535
Still, E. C., 227, 350, 351
Stowers, S. K., 67, 68
Strack, H. L., xix, xxii,
Strecker, G., 260, 396
Strobel, A., 107
Strugnell, J., 227
Strüder, C. W., 149
Stuart, E., 507
Stuhlmacher, P., 190, 453
Stürmer, K., 453
Suggs, M. J., 621
Sullivan, F. A., 473
Summers, R., 117
Sumney, J. L., 376
Surburg, M. P., 453
Surgy, P. de, 107
Swartz, S. M., 117
Sweet, J. P. M., 523
Swete, H. B., 609

Tabet, M., 312
Tajra, H. W., 39, 47
Talbert, C. H., 107, 462
Tatum, W. B., 557
Taylor, N. H., 585
Teani, M., 591
Templeton, D. A., 577
Temporini, H., xv, 93
Terry, R. B., 118
Testuz, M., 47
Theis, J., 115
Theissen, G., 115, 118, 376, 453
Theobald, M., 296, 376, 453
Therrien, G., 473
Thielman, F., 312, 376
Thiselton, A. C., 107, 118, 247, 473
Thomas, R. L., 462, 507
Thompson, C. L., 425
Thompson, F. H., 29
Thompson, K. C., 585

INDEX OF SUBJECTS

◆

Body
Of Christ, 77, 83, 146, 269, 390–91,
427, 438–39, 446–47, 455, 474–77,
481, 508
Human, 85–86, 239, 262, 265–67,
269–70, 280, 319–20, 438, 479,
585–91, 595
Politic, 475
Spiritual, 561, 593–94, 596
Bondage, Egyptian, 377, 380
Boxing, 374
Brass, 492
Breaking bread, 429, 437
Brother *(adelphos)*, 243, 248, 253, 298,
300, 359, 622
Burial, 541, 546, 594

Caesar, Julius, 22, 25
Calf, Golden, 378, 385, 395
Catamite, 255
Celibacy, 88, 273–87, 315, 320, 327
Cenchreae, 21–22, 28, 33, 126, 621
Cephas, 74, 136–37, 143–45, 191–92, 197,
208, 210, 212, 221, 335, 358, 360,
364, 541–42, 549
Change, 604–5
Charismatic(s), 453
Chiasmus, 66, 265, 398
Child(ren), 297–98, 300, 498
Chloe, 136, 141, 193, 273
Christ, 72, 77, 343, 383, 386, 403, 477
Blood of, 389–90, 427, 442
Body of, 77, 83, 146, 269, 390–91, 427,
438–39, 446–47, 455, 474–76, 481,
508
Christ Jesus, 72, 75
Crucified, 70–71, 153, 159–60, 172
Members of, 266, 474
Risen, 74, 230, 290, 310, 319, 436,
539–57
Terrestrial reign of, 572
Christ-Event, 318
Effects of the, 76–77, 545
Christology, 71–77. 343–44
Church, 298, 327, 432, 454, 474, 476,
482, 508, 511, 515, 518, 521, 525,
627–28
Discipline, 84
Ekklēsia, 81–82

Of God, 81, 125, 402, 407, 421, 435,
553
Of the saints, 85, 527
Teaching about, 81–85
Circumcision, 305, 307–8
Claudius, emperor, 25, 37–39
Cloud, pillar of, 377–78, 381
Collection for the poor, 611–16
Colonia Laus Iulia Corinthiensis, 25
Command, 282, 292
Of the Lord, 292, 297, 314, 354, 366,
536
Of God, 308
Concession, 281–82, 296
Concubine, 234
Conscience, 87, 333, 344–45, 348,
397–404
Corinth, 21–29, 125, 617
Christians of, 31–32
Church of, 37–47
Evangelization of, 37–38, 40,
191–92
Excavations of, 27, 428
Gulf of, 21, 23, 126
Map(s) of, 23, 26
Old, 22–24
People of, 30–36
Roman, 25–28, 31–35
Corinthia, 21–22, 578
Corinthians, First, 49–53
Bibliography, General, 95–118
Composition, 43, 48–50
Date, 48
Dictation, 50, 64
Form, 54–59
Language and style, 64–68
Occasion, 51
Outline, 57–58
Purpose, 52
Teaching, 69–93
Text, 60–63
Corinthians, Second, 43–44, 49
Corinthians, Third, 44–45
Corporate personality, 475
Court, pagan, 247–72
Covenant, 439, 442
Creation, new, 235
Order of, 416
Crisis, impending, 315